P9-CJP-672

A Companion to Japanese History

BLACKWELL COMPANIONS TO WORLD HISTORY

This series provides sophisticated and authoritative overviews of the scholarship that has shaped our current understanding of the past. Each volume comprises between twenty-five and forty concise essays written by individual scholars within their area of specialization. The aim of each contribution is to synthesize the current state of scholarship from a variety of historical perspectives and to provide a statement on where the field is heading. The essays are written in a clear, provocative, and lively manner, designed for an international audience of scholars, students and general readers. The Blackwell Companions to World History is a cornerstone of Blackwell's overarching Companions to History series covering British, American, and European History.

Published

A Companion to the History of the Middle East
Edited by Youssef M. Choueiri

A Companion to Japanese History
Edited by William M. Tsutsui

BLACKWELL COMPANIONS TO HISTORY

Published

A Companion to Western Historical Thought
Edited by Lloyd Kramer and Sarah Maza

A Companion to Gender History
Edited by Teresa A. Meade and Merry E. Wiesner-Hanks

BLACKWELL COMPANIONS TO BRITISH HISTORY

Published

A Companion to Roman Britain
Edited by Malcolm Todd

A Companion to Eighteenth-Century Britain
Edited by H. T. Dickinson

A Companion to Britain in the Later Middle Ages
Edited by S. H. Rigby

A Companion to Nineteenth-Century Britain
Edited by Chris Williams

A Companion to Tudor Britain
Edited by Robert Tittler and Norman Jones

A Companion to Early Twentieth-Century Britain
Edited by Chris Wrigley

A Companion to Stuart Britain
Edited by Barry Coward

A Companion to Contemporary Britain
Edited by Paul Addison and Harriet Jones

BLACKWELL COMPANIONS TO EUROPEAN HISTORY

Published

A Companion to Europe 1900–1945
Edited by Gordon Martel

A Companion to the Worlds of the Renaissance
Edited by Guido Ruggiero

A Companion to Nineteenth-Century Europe
Edited by Stefan Berger

A Companion to the Reformation World
Edited by R. Po-chia Hsia

BLACKWELL COMPANIONS TO AMERICAN HISTORY

Published

A Companion to the American Revolution
Edited by Jack P. Greene and J. R. Pole

A Companion to 20th-Century America
Edited by Stephen J. Whitfield

A Companion to 19th-Century America
Edited by William L. Barney

A Companion to the American West
Edited by William Deverell

A Companion to the American South
Edited by John B. Boles

A Companion to American Foreign Relations
Edited by Robert D. Schulzinger

A Companion to American Indian History
Edited by Philip J. Deloria and Neal Salisbury

A Companion to the Civil War and Reconstruction
Edited by Lacy K. Ford

A Companion to American Women's History
Edited by Nancy A. Hewitt

A Companion to American Technology
Edited by Carroll Pursell

A Companion to Post-1945 America
Edited by Jean-Christophe Agnew and Roy Rosenzweig

A Companion to African-American History
Edited by Alton Hornsby

A Companion to the Vietnam War
Edited by Marilyn B. Young and Robert Buzzanco

A Companion to American Immigration
Edited by Reed Ueda

A Companion to Colonial America
Edited by Daniel Vickers

A COMPANION TO JAPANESE HISTORY

Edited by

William M. Tsutsui

Blackwell
Publishing

© 2007 by Blackwell Publishing Ltd

BLACKWELL PUBLISHING
350 Main Street, Malden, MA 02148–5020, USA
9600 Garsington Road, Oxford OX4 2DQ, UK
550 Swanston Street, Carlton, Victoria 3053, Australia

The right of William M. Tsutsui to be identified as the Author of the Editorial Material in this Work has been asserted in accordance with the UK Copyright, Designs, and Patents Act 1988.

First published 2007 by Blackwell Publishing Ltd

2   2008

Library of Congress Cataloging-in-Publication Data

A companion to Japanese history / edited by William M. Tsutsui.
p. cm. — (Blackwell companions to world history)
Includes bibliographical references and index.
ISBN: 978-1-4051-1690-9 (hardback : alk. paper)
1. Japan—History. I. Tsutsui, William M. II. Series.

DS835.C65 2006
952—dc22

2006006918

A catalogue record for this title is available from the British Library.

Set in 10/12pt Galliard
by SPi Publisher Services, Pondicherry, India
Printed and bound in Singapore
by COS Printers Pte Ltd

The publisher's policy is to use permanent paper from mills that operate a sustainable forestry policy, and which has been manufactured from pulp processed using acid-free and elementary chlorine-free practices. Furthermore, the publisher ensures that the text paper and cover board used have met acceptable environmental accreditation standards.

For further information on
Blackwell Publishing, visit our website:
www.blackwellpublishing.com

Contents

Maps

Notes on Contributors

E. Taylor Atkins, Associate Professor of History at Northern Illinois University, is the author of *Blue Nippon: Authenticating Jazz in Japan* (2001), winner of the John Whitney Hall Prize of the Association for Asian Studies, and the editor of *Jazz Planet* (2003). He is currently preparing a book entitled *Primitive Selves: Korean Folk Performance in the Japanese Gaze*.

Philip C. Brown teaches Japanese history at the Ohio State University. He is the author of many studies on domain and state formation in early modern Japan, including *Central Authority and Local Autonomy in the Formation of Early Modern Japan: The Case of Kaga Domain* (1993). His current research concerns village and state responses to the risks of flooding and landslides in early modern and modern Japan.

Leo Ching is the author of *Becoming "Japanese": Colonial Taiwan and the Politics of Identity Formation* (2001). He is currently working on a book on anti-Japanism in Asia. He teaches at Duke University.

Ray Christensen is Associate Professor and Chair of the Department of Political Science at Brigham Young University. A specialist in Japanese politics, comparative politics, international law, and electoral systems, he is the author of *Ending the LDP Hegemony: Party Cooperation in Japan* (2000).

Frederick R. Dickinson is Associate Professor of Japanese History at the University of Pennsylvania. He is the author of *War and National Reinvention: Japan in the Great War, 1914–1919* (1999) and numerous articles on the politics and culture of Japanese diplomacy in the early twentieth century.

Kevin M. Doak holds the Nippon Foundation Endowed Chair in Japanese Studies and is the Chairman of the Department of East Asian Languages and Cultures at Georgetown University. He has published widely on Japanese nationalism, ethnicity, literature, and philosophy. His most recent book is *A History of Nationalism in Japan: Placing the People* (2006).

Steven Ericson is an Associate Professor of History at Dartmouth College. He specializes in Japanese government–business relations and industrial and financial policy during the Meiji period. He is the author of *The Sound of the Whistle: Railroads and the State in Meiji Japan* (1996).

W. Miles Fletcher III is Professor of History at the University of North Carolina at Chapel Hill. He has served as Chair of the Curriculum in Asian Studies and is currently Associate Chair of the Department of History. He has published two books, *The Search for a New Order: Intellectuals and Fascism in Prewar Japan* (1982) and *The Japanese Business*

Community and National Trade Policy, 1920–1942 (1989), as well as a number of articles on topics pertaining to modern Japanese economic and business history. His current project focuses on Japan's industrialization, state–business relations, and the Japanese cotton textile industry.

Bai Gao is Professor of Sociology at Duke University. He is the author of Economic Ideology and Japanese Industrial Policy: Developmentalism from 1931 to 1965 (1997), which received the Hiromi Arisawa Memorial Award of the Association of American University Presses, and Japan's Economic Dilemma: The Institutional Origins of Prosperity and Stagnation (2001).

Andrew Edmund Goble is Associate Professor of Premodern Japanese History and of Religious Studies at the University of Oregon, and was Head of the Department of Religious Studies from 1999 to 2005. His current research is in the field of medieval Japanese medical history, and his most recent article (in Monumenta Nipponica, Autumn 2005) was on the topic of medieval wound medicine. His other research interests and publications have covered intellectual history, Buddhism and society, and social and political history.

Sally A. Hastings is Associate Professor of History and Chair of the Asian Studies Program at Purdue University and editor of the U.S.–Japan Women's Journal. Her publications include Neighborhood and Nation in Tokyo, 1905–1937 (1995) and several book chapters and articles on modern Japanese women. She is now finishing a book on the first generation of women legislators in Japan, 1946–74.

Glenn D. Hook is Professor of Japanese Studies and Director of the Graduate School of East Asian Studies at the University of Sheffield. His research interests are in Japan's international relations. His recent publications include Militarization and Demilitarization in Contemporary Japan (1996), Japan's Contested Constitution: Documents and Analysis (coauthor, 2001), and Japan's

International Relations: Politics, Economics and Security (coauthor, 2005).

Mark J. Hudson is an Associate Professor at the Institute of History and Anthropology, University of Tsukuba. His research interests include hunter-gatherers, world systems theory, and bioarchaeology. He is the author of Ruins of Identity: Ethnogenesis in the Japanese Islands (1999), which was awarded the John Whitney Hall Prize of the Association for Asian Studies.

James L. Huffman is H. Orth Hirt Professor of History at Wittenberg University. A former newspaper reporter, he has written widely on the political impact of Japan's early press. His works include Creating a Public: People and Press in Meiji Japan (1997), A Yankee in Meiji Japan: The Crusading Journalist Edward H. House (2003), and Modern Japan: A History in Documents (2004).

G. Cameron Hurst III is Professor of Japanese and Korean Studies, Director of the Center for East Asian Studies, and Chair of the Department of East Asian Languages and Civilizations at the University of Pennsylvania. His primary research and teaching interests lie in premodern Japanese history and Korean studies. He is the author of Insei: Abdicated Sovereigns in the Politics of Late Heian Japan, 1086–1185 (1976), The Armed Martial Arts of Japan (1998), and coauthor with Stephen Addiss of Samurai Painters (1983), among other publications.

Mark Jones is an Assistant Professor of History at Central Connecticut State University. He is completing a book entitled Children as Treasures: The Middle Classes and Childhood in Early Twentieth-Century Japan.

J. Victor Koschmann is Professor of Modern Japanese History in the Department of History at Cornell University. He has written Revolution and Subjectivity in Postwar Japan (1996) and coedited (with Yamanouchi Yasushi and Narita Ryūichi) Total War and "Modernization" (1998).

Stephen S. Large, Reader in Modern Japanese History at the University of Cambridge, was educated at Harvard and the University of Michigan. His books include *The Rise of Labor in Japan: The Yūaikai, 1912–1919* (1972), *Organized Workers and Socialist Politics in Interwar Japan* (1981), *Emperor Hirohito and Shōwa Japan: A Political Biography* (1992), and *Emperors of the Rising Sun: Three Biographies* (1997); he also edited *Shōwa Japan: Political, Economic and Social History, 1926–1989*, 4 vols. (1998). His current research is on nationalist extremism in twentieth-century Japan.

Michael Lewis is Professor of History and Director of the Asian Studies Center at Michigan State University. His scholarly work focuses on the social history of state formation in modern Japan, particularly the social, political, economic, cultural, and environmental transformations, integrative and disintegrative, that made for a strong Japanese state and weak civil society. He is the author of *Rioters and Citizens: Mass Protest in Imperial Japan* (1990) and *Becoming Apart: National Power and Local Politics in Toyama, 1868–1945* (2000).

Lawrence E. Marceau is currently Senior Lecturer in Japanese at the University of Auckland, New Zealand. A specialist in Japanese literature in the early modern period, his research interests include the relationship between literary thought and production, the relationship between language and image, gender issues, literary reactions to stimuli from continental Asia, alternative literary genres, and the history of woodblock printing and publishing. He is the author of *Takebe Ayatari: A Bunjin Bohemian in Early Modern Japan* (2004), coauthor of *The Floating World of Ukiyo-e: Shadows, Dreams, and Substance* (2001), and, most recently, contributor to the *Hotei Encyclopedia of Japanese Woodblock Prints* (2006).

Y. Tak Matsusaka is Associate Professor of History at Wellesley College. He is the author of *The Making of Japanese Manchuria, 1904–1932* (2001) and is currently working on a study of popular nationalism and the politics of armament in Meiji and Taishō Japan.

Gavan McCormack is a Professor in the Research School of Pacific and Asian Studies, Australian National University. His recent books include *The Emptiness of Japanese Affluence* (2nd rev. edn., 2001); the jointly edited volume *Multicultural Japan: Palaeolithic to Postmodern* (1996); *Japan's Contested Constitution: Documents and Analysis* (with Glenn Hook, 2001); and *Ogasawara shotō: Ajia Taiheiyō kara mita kankyō bunka* (The Ogasawara Islands: Asia-Pacific Perspectives on the Environment, coedited with Guo Nanyan, 2005).

Mark Metzler is an Assistant Professor of Japanese history at the University of Texas at Austin. His book *Lever of Empire: The International Gold Standard and the Crisis of Liberalism in Prewar Japan* (2006) explores Japan's place in the failure of international economic stabilization after World War I. He is now doing research on the success of stabilization after World War II.

Ian Neary taught in the Departments of Politics at Huddersfield, Newcastle, and Essex Universities before taking up an appointment in the Nissan Institute, Oxford University in 2004. He has published on human rights issues, including the *buraku* problem, and on industrial policy, especially the pharmaceutical industry. He is presently completing a critical biography of Matsumoto Jiichirō.

Peter Nosco is Professor and Head of the Department of Asian Studies at the University of British Columbia. A specialist in the intellectual and social history of early modern Japan, he is the author of *Remembering Paradise: Nativism and Nostalgia in Eighteenth-Century Japan* (1990) and the editor of *Confucianism and Tokugawa Culture* (1984). His current work examines underground religious movements, voluntary associations, and issues related to the globalization of ethics.

Edward E. Pratt is Associate Professor of History and Dean of Undergraduate Studies at the College of William and Mary. He is the author of *Japan's Protoindustrial Elite: The Economic Foundations of the Gōnō* (1999).

Eric C. Rath is an Associate Professor of Premodern Japan in the History Department at the University of Kansas. His research interests are medieval and early modern cultural history including the performing arts, foodways, and urban agriculture. His book *The Ethos of Noh: Actors and Their Art* was published in 2004.

Wesley Sasaki-Uemura is an Associate Professor in the History Department at the University of Utah, specializing in modern Japan. He has written *Organizing the Spontaneous: Citizen Protest in Postwar Japan* (2001) and "Competing Publics: Citizen Groups, the Mass Media and the State in the 1960s" in the journal *Positions* (Spring 2002).

Elise K. Tipton is Associate Professor of Japanese Studies and Chair of Japanese and Korean Studies at the University of Sydney, Australia. She is the author of *The Japanese Police State: The Tokkō in Interwar Japan* (1991), editor of *Society and the State in Interwar Japan* (1997), and coeditor with John Clark of *Being Modern in Japan: Culture and Society from the 1910s to the 1930s* (2000). Her most recent book is *Modern Japan: A Social and Political History* (2002). Her research continues to focus on the relationship between society and the state during the interwar years.

Hitomi Tonomura is a member of the Department of History and the Women's Studies Program at the University of Michigan. She is the author of *Community and Commerce in Late Medieval Japan: The Corporate Villages of Tokuchin-ho* (1992) and an editor of *Women and Class in Japanese History* (1999). She has written numerous articles on women and gender, including "Black Hair and Red Trousers: Gendering the Flesh in Medieval Japan" in *American Historical Review* (Feb. 1994), winner of the 1995 Art-

icle Prize of the Berkshire Conference on Women Historians; and "Women and Inheritance in Japan's Early Warrior Society" in *Comparative Studies in Society and History* (July 1990).

William M. Tsutsui is Professor of History at the University of Kansas. A specialist in the business, economic, and cultural history of twentieth-century Japan, he is the author of *Banking Policy in Japan: American Efforts at Reform during the Occupation* (1988), *Manufacturing Ideology: Scientific Management in Twentieth-Century Japan* (1998), and *Godzilla on My Mind: Fifty Years of the King of Monsters* (2004). He is the editor of *Banking in Japan*, 3 vols. (1999) and, with Michiko Ito, *In Godzilla's Footsteps: Japanese Pop Culture Icons on the Global Stage* (2006). He has received the Newcomen Society Award for Excellence in Business History Research and Writing, the John Whitney Hall Prize of the Association for Asian Studies, and the William Rockhill Nelson Award for Literary Excellence. He is currently conducting research on the enviromental history of modern Japan and the globalization of Japanese popular culture since World War II.

Charles Weathers is a Professor in the Graduate School of Economics, Osaka City University, specializing in Japanese industrial relations and political economy. His research interests include wage-setting and women and non-regular workers. His publications include "In Search of Strategic Partners: Japan's Campaign for Equal Opportunity" in *Social Science Japan Journal* (Apr. 2005), "The Decentralization of Japan's Wage Setting System in Comparative Perspective" in *Industrial Relations Journal* (June 2003), and a coedited volume, *Nihon seisansei undō no genten* (Wellsprings of the Productivity Movement in Japan, 2004).

Introduction

William M. Tsutsui

Although Japan has a long and rich history, Western efforts to comprehend, chronicle, and analyze that history are a relatively recent development. The first attempts by Europeans and Americans to explore Japanese history after the "opening" of the nation in the 1850s were the uncoordinated efforts of gentlemen amateurs, non-professionals once described by John Whitney Hall as a "coterie of interested foreign residents of Tokyo."[1] With the exception of Sir George Sansom, whose 1931 survey *Japan: A Short Cultural History* may have been the most important English-language work in the field prior to World War II, "the bulk of Western work on Japanese history was derivative or episodic in nature," "primarily diplomatic or antiquarian in orientation."[2] In the United States and Britain, the academic study of Japan was slow to develop before the war: American colleges and universities, for instance, offered a total of only twenty-one courses dealing with Japan (covering topics from religion to art to literature) in 1930 and, even a decade later, only a handful of institutions provided instruction in Japanese language and history.[3] World War II, however, catalyzed a significant international expansion of scholarly attention to Japan; as the "natural result of the popular boom of interest in Japan stimulated by the war and its aftermath and by the increased opportunities which Westerners had to come in contact with the Japanese people,"[4] the professional practice of Japanese history developed steadily. In the 1950s and 1960s, monographic works in English on Japan's past began to appear in considerable numbers for the first time and, by 1970, one survey counted 408 Japan specialists (in all fields) in the United States. This growth only accelerated in the 1980s and 1990s, reflecting both Japan's ascent to economic "great power" status and the diffusion of area studies in American universities. By 1995, a Japan Foundation report counted over 1,500 Japanese studies experts on faculties in the United States and the proliferation of scholarly books, articles, edited collections, and translations proceeded apace, with even selective bibliographies of English-language sources in Japanese history running to many hundreds of pages.[5] Although as recently ago as the 1960s, a researcher could comfortably stay abreast of all publications on Japan in English, by the 1980s one could realistically aspire only to maintain familiarity with the literature in one's specific discipline and, by the turn of the new millennium, the pace of scholarly productivity had risen to the point that even keeping up with the output in some subfields (like modern social history) was becoming a challenge.

For most of the twentieth century, at least up through the 1960s, the mainstream of historical scholarship in Japan was resolutely (and often crabbedly) Marxian in orientation. Obsessed with teasing the pathologies from a Japanese past seemingly replete with oppression, militarism, and inequity, historians in Japan, "weighed down by the memory of the war and the pessimistic assessment of their Marxist methodology, continued to focus on Japan's backwardness, on the persistence of feudal hangovers, and on an essentially negative assessment of Japan's modern experience."[6] Such an approach never proved terribly appealing in North America or Britain, although the eclectic Marxian scholarship of the mid-century Canadian historian E. H. Norman, resuscitated in the 1970s by John Dower, was an important exception.[7] Instead, rejecting Marxian lamentation, the first generations of postwar Western – and particularly American – historians of Japan embraced the more optimistic perspective of "modernization theory" to structure their narratives. These scholars figured "the rise of modern Japan" as an edifying success story, an almost textbook case of the inevitable triumph of rationality, democracy, and capitalism, a trajectory interrupted in the Japanese example only by a "temporary" and "aberrant" prewar turn to authoritarianism and expansionism. The history written in this vein substituted a modernizing teleology – "a steadily upward course toward a more open and democratic society"[8] – for a Marxian one, as "modernization theory represented an anti-Marxist and highly ethnocentric theoretical model, in which it was presumed that all non-communist countries would and should become increasingly similar to the advanced nations of Europe and the United States as they 'modernized' along capitalist lines."[9] Thus, the assumed endpoint of Japan's historic "upward course" was becoming "just like us," tracing a step-by-step process of convergence toward the modern ideal of all-American economic, political, and social freedom.

For the better part of four decades after World War II, modernization theory was unquestionably the orthodoxy of American historical studies of Japan. Historians working in this paradigm produced an extensive and valuable literature; as Martin Collcutt has noted, "This institutional, predominantly 'top-down' view was important in establishing a basic framework of postwar scholarship, in deepening our understanding of the ... political and social structure, and in defining much of the research terrain and terms of debate."[10] But discontent with the modernization approach began brewing in the 1970s, first among left-leaning scholars who were not satisfied with the unexamined narrative of success, harmony, and "progress" delineated by postwar historians. A younger generation questioned the received wisdom of unproblematized "common sense" history and the notion that modernization theory was somehow less rigid, less political, and "less value laden" than other models of historical analysis.[11] Modernization historiography was criticized as "paternalistic condescension" born of postwar Western "hubris,"[12] and increasing numbers of skeptical scholars found themselves unable to reconcile celebratory accounts of "the rise of modern Japan" with clear evidence for pervasive conflict, frequent protest, a diversity of social experiences, and substantial divergence from an "American" path of development throughout Japanese history.

Although modernization theory continues to cast a long shadow over the study of Japanese history in the West, and especially in the United States, the historical literature in English has become much more diverse in terms of approach, subject matter, and audience since the 1980s. Interdisciplinary cross-pollination, debates in critical theory, and methodological developments have had a significant impact on recent research in the field. Indeed, the scholarship on Japan has participated in all of the major trends in historiography over the past twenty-five years, from the "new" cultural history, to the "linguistic turn" and postmodernism, to rational choice theory, to the current surge of interest in transnational history and the study of race and ethnicity. Many observers (and practitioners) have seen this diversification as "constructive and illuminating,"[13] deepening our understanding through an appreciation of the complexity and particularity of the Japanese experience, bringing much needed richness, dynamism, and intellectual vitality to the field. Others, however, have found recent developments "undermining and inimical."[14] Traditionalists have bemoaned the new scholarship for the frequent opacity of its theory-heavy idiom, the alleged superficiality of its empirical research, and its ever greater specialization, with "broad studies on the general features of [Japanese] society ... replaced or obscured by deeper but narrower studies."[15]

With the increasing diversity of the study of Japanese history has come (perhaps inevitably) a certain fragmentation, the apparent manifestation of what John Whittier Treat has called a "centrifugally disintegrating profession," what Mary Elizabeth Berry described as a "collapse of paradigmatic analysis," and what John Whitney Hall once self-righteously decried as "a morass of relativity."[16] Despite such handwringing, Helen Hardacre has made the compelling argument that fragmentation and the loss of the ideological and methodological consensus actually reflects the maturation of Japanese history as a scholarly field in the West: "Japanese studies' increasing specialization within the disciplines in United States universities is a mark of its increasing sophistication and acceptance, even as specialization and professionalization make it unlikely that a single perspective could emerge to capture the attention of the whole field again."[17] And, in fact, just about the only thing that is certain among the ongoing debates in Japanese history is that "no over-arching, unifying perspective [has yet] arisen to replace the modernization framework," or soon seems likely to.[18] As John Dower nicely summarized it,

What, in conclusion, can we say about the overall impression of Japan that emerges from the recent English-language scholarly literature? We can say, perhaps, that we have gained immeasurably in detail but lost any real sense of organizing principle; that we no longer have a clear conception of the structures of power, but rather are confronted by a world of fragmentation and multiple causality; and that greater emphasis is now placed on the ways in which Japan diverges from so-called Western patterns of thought and behavior than on its convergence. ... No one, however, can any longer point to a dominant paradigm governing Western perceptions of Japan.[19]

But, for all the dynamism, creativity, and intellectual variety apparent among historians of Japan today, Japanese history cannot honestly be judged a "paradigm generating" field, a theoretically or methodologically innovative part of the larger discipline of history. Andrew Gordon has rightly noted that some individual works in Japanese studies have exerted wider disciplinary influence (notably Chalmers Johnson's *MITI and the Japanese Miracle* and its model of the "developmental state")[20] and, at the turn of the twenty-first century, two exceptional works of Japanese history did win back-to-back Pulitzer Prizes and attract wide readerships in the profession and among the general public.[21] Yet the field has the longstanding reputation of being derivative rather than innovative, the fault perhaps of the fact that, for much of the postwar period, Japan was steadfastly judged by scholars to be the exception not the rule, an exotic outlying case divorced from the mainstreams of world history. Generations of Japan experts embraced this view as well, holding up Japanese history as so distinctive (what Andrew Gordon called "uniquely unique")[22] as to be essentially incommensurable with the histories of Europe, the United States, or the rest of the world. As Helen Hardacre explained it,

> In examinations of modernization around the globe, Japan specialists could enjoy the role of "spoiler" in theoretical discussions, usually able to show that "Japan doesn't fit." From the standpoint of the disciplines, Japan was an interesting, odd "case," the source of endless puzzles, but rarely was it recognized as providing conceptual or theoretical innovation in its own right.[23]

Only relatively recently have Western scholars begun actively to conceive of Japan as part of the greater flow of world history, as a site for exploring global phenomena like modernization, imperialism, and environmental change, rather than as an inscrutable enigma, an eternal latecomer, or a culturally exceptional odd nation out. If this trend continues, and if the field remains as lively and contentious as it has over the past quarter-century, then Japanese history may yet prove a trend-setting "paradigm generator" for the discipline.

Over the years, several notable projects have provided "state of the field" surveys of Japanese history as written in the United States and Western Europe.[24] Prior to the 1960s, such syntheses were largely unnecessary due to the small volume of English-language scholarship available. Between 1960 and 1968, however, a series of six international symposia on "the problems of modernization in Japan" was organized by a group of prominent researchers (led by the historian John Whitney Hall) and funded by the Ford Foundation. Six volumes of essays from the meetings, which aspired to being "both representative of current scholarship on Japan and comprehensive in their coverage of one of the most fascinating stories of national development in recent history,"[25] were published by Princeton University Press. These collections, which covered only the Tokugawa period onwards and which included an eclectic blend of work from the social sciences and the humanities, "set the debate in Japanese studies through the 1960s and early 1970s."[26] Landmarks in the application of modernization theory to Japanese history and contemporary affairs, the volumes defined the postwar Western orthodoxy of historical scholarship on Japan.

In 1970, planning began on *The Cambridge History of Japan*, an immense six-volume series which aimed "to put before the English-reading audience as complete a record of Japanese history as possible."[27] Published between 1988 and 1999, the Cambridge History volumes were anachronisms from the moment they appeared, "caught in a time warp," as John Dower described them.[28] Resolutely chronological in organization, conservative in thematic coverage (with an emphasis on tried-and-true categories of political, economic, and social history), and only slightly adventurous in terms of periodization (devoting separate volumes to the nineteenth century and the twentieth century, rather than utilizing the standard chronological watersheds of 1868 and 1945), *The Cambridge History of Japan* was a monumental compendium of traditional historiographical concerns. Very much an intellectual and methodological descendant of the earlier Princeton University Press series (and, not coincidentally, also co-organized by John Whitney Hall), the Cambridge History was squarely in the hoary modernization paradigm and excluded mention of most of the critical new approaches to Japanese history that were already transforming the contours of the field by the 1980s.

Helen Hardacre's 1998 edited collection, *The Postwar Developments of Japanese Studies in the United States*, is the latest attempt to survey the English-language historiography on Japan. A short and selective overview, Hardacre's volume – the product of the twenty-fifth anniversary symposium at the Reischauer Institute of Japanese Studies at Harvard University – is an uneasy mixture of challenging essays on the leading edge of scholarship and more conservative pieces (running the gamut from tame to downright reactionary) that decry the intellectual diversification of the field over the past quarter-century. Such fractured perspectives may reflect the decline which H. D. Harootunian and Masao Miyoshi detect in "state of the field" overviews in the recent past:

> Humanities scholars over the past several decades have shown a marked loss of interest in the general survey and bibliography of studies in a given field. Once an obligatory reference for all scholars, young or old, such listing and ranking of antecedent scholarly achievements are not infrequently attempted, and seldom respected in most branches of the humanities. The bibliography is after all the mapping and chronology of a discourse. It is difficult to compile at a moment like ours where the required central authority for evaluation has largely vanished from the arena of scholarship. This difficulty may reflect the general skepticism regarding authority, or the recent cultural turn toward poststructuralism, or the simple acceptance of diversity and fracture within disciplinary practice. . . . And yet a total absence of attempts to sort out, interrelate, and map out ideas and analyses could result in a loss of critical scholarship, coherent reference, and articulate knowledge.[29]

This *Companion to Japanese History* aims to meet just this need for "critical scholarship, coherent reference, and articulate knowledge." It provides a concise summary of the current state of English-language scholarship in the field, balancing coverage of "traditional" themes and approaches with an attentiveness to current trends and emerging perspectives. Reflecting the profoundly interdisciplinary nature of the humanities and the social sciences at the start of the new millennium, the authors of the thirty chapters presented here include not just historians but anthropologists, literature specialists, political scientists, and sociologists as well. These scholars have brought to this collection not only great expertise in the various aspects of Japan's historical experience, but also a diverse and representative range of contemporary theoretical and methodological approaches. What's more, highlighting the global diffusion (and institutionalization) of the study of Japanese history, the contributors to this volume are as varied geographically as they are intellectually, with scholars currently working in the United States, Great Britain, Australia, Japan, Canada, and New Zealand all represented here.

Approximately two-thirds of this *Companion to Japanese History* is devoted to a chronological survey, while the remaining one-third examines thematic issues that cut across the established chronological boundaries. In keeping with the current interests of scholars, students, and general readers in the West (and reflecting the relative volume of historical research published in English), Japan's modern history receives somewhat more attention than its premodern history in the chronological sections here.[30] It should also be noted that the periodization used to structure this volume is entirely conventional. This choice should not be taken as an unreflective endorsement of the tried-and-true chronological divisions of Japanese history; scholars have long debated (and will continue to contest) the specifics and standards of periodization, the utility of politically freighted terms like "medieval" and "early modern," and questions of continuity and change across supposed historical watersheds like 1868 and 1945. But since the periodization of Japanese history widely accepted since World War II has very much come to shape the literature in the field (as well as the research specializations of scholars within it), it has been adopted for the basic framework of the chronological survey here.

Part I covers Japanese history prior to 1600, with chapters on Japan's earliest history (from ethnic origins and the findings of archaeology through the Nara period), the Heian period, and medieval Japan. Part II examines early modern Japan from the unification of the sixteenth century through the Tokugawa shogunate. Individual chapters focus on political, social and economic, intellectual, and cultural developments. Part III treats the period from the Meiji Restoration of 1868 through the end of World War II, with seven chapters devoted both to broad areas of change (political development, social and economic trends, intellectual and cultural history, and international relations) and to specific subperiods and topics (the Restoration and the early Meiji period, the Japanese empire, and the so-called Fifteen-Year War). Part IV synthesizes the scholarship on postwar Japan, drawing on social science research as well as the growing historical literature on the period. Separate chapters address the Allied occupation, politics, economic transformations, society and culture, and Japan's place in the postwar world system.

The eleven chapters in Part V focus on thematic concerns and alternative histories, with a particular emphasis on approaches and issues which have emerged over the past quarter-century and will shape the future development of scholarship in the field. These chapters are carefully defined in topical focus but sweeping in chronological breadth, allowing the authors to explore long-term patterns of continuity, rupture, evolution, and innovation. The thematic chapters also foreground the new scholarly concerns, conceptual categories, and methodological innovations that have reshaped the writing of Japanese history since the decline of the modernization theory orthodoxy in the 1980s. Thus, themes often ignored in sources like *The Cambridge History of Japan* – women, sexuality, and gender; popular culture; regional and local history; individual, class, and national identity; Japan's place in Asia; environmental history – are developed here at length and in depth. The themes addressed, while broadly representative of established and emerging directions in the field, are inevitably incomplete and selective. Even in a book of this length, not all deserving areas of historical inquiry could be considered fully: coverage of military, urban, and educational history, to name but a few, might easily have been added to the thematic chapters had space permitted; the histories of Japanese religion and of high culture (literature, the visual arts, architecture) are subjects so rich and well studied as to be worthy of their own "state of the field" survey volumes. As Peter Duus once pithily put it, "time is short, history long, and such truncation inevitable."[31]

In fact, just as this volume cannot aspire to thematic comprehesiveness, it likewise cannot for a moment pretend to be encyclopedic in its coverage of the facts, figures, debates, and discourses of the full sweep of Japanese history and historiography. Readers might find some areas here less well developed than may be expected (such as the political history of the Yamato and Nara periods, or the workings of "Taishō democracy") and some familiar historical landmarks, heroes, and legends (the stories of the "three unifiers," the making of the Manchurian Incident, the writing of the 1946 constitution) either casually mentioned or missed altogether. One of the editors of *The Cambridge History of Japan* captured the dilemma – and the unavoidable compromise – nicely in stating that "it seemed wiser to plan the volume as a discursive guide to ... Japan than as a complete Baedeker with each site and vista along the way properly noted and catalogued."[32] But, that caveat aside, one will find in this *Companion to Japanese History* not only a broad, rich, and up-to-date survey of the English-language literature, but also discussions of most of the "great debates" in Japanese history (from the roots of the Meiji Restoration to the question of Japanese "fascism"), concise introductions to topics of heightening scholarly interest (from the origins of the Japanese people to the culture of Japanese colonialism), remarkable insights on unexpected subjects (from the politics of dam-building to the rise of volunteerism in the 1990s), and some well-informed (and occasionally provocative) speculation on the direction of future scholarship in the field.

Needless to say, just as the Princeton University Press series on the modernization of Japan seems a relic of the 1960s and a cold war mindset, and *The Cambridge History of Japan* a monument to a conservative orthodoxy already well in decline by the 1980s, so this *Companion to Japanese History* will one day (hopefully some decades down the road) be seen as an intellectual artifact of a specific time and place, a memento of the turn of the twenty-first century in a diverse and fragmented scholarly landscape. Such an observation should not diminish the value of this volume (or similar efforts at survey and synthesis) so much as affirm the constantly changing nature of historical inquiry and the continuing vitality of the study of Japanese history in the English-speaking world. This volume is, in the end, but a snapshot of a historiographical discourse in endless flux, growth, and creative contestation.

A Note on Japanese Names

Throughout this volume, Japanese names are rendered in accordance with Japanese custom, the family name preceding the given name. The names of Japanese authors of English-language works are cited with the given name first. As is standard practice, macrons have been omitted in well-known Japanese place names (Tōkyō, Ōsaka, Kyōto, Kōbe).

NOTES

The editor wishes to thank Tessa Harvey and Angela Cohen, who were models of good humor, tact, and patience through the long gestation of this collection. The contributors were uniformly generous, gracious, and thoroughly professional. Financial support for the writing of this introduction was provided by the General Research Fund of the University of Kansas. Sheree Willis supplied Pinyin transliterations of Chinese names and terms. Marjorie Swann, as always, was there for advice on grammar, help with the proofreading, and endless support and encouragement.

1 Hall, *Japanese History*, p. 4.
2 Ibid., p. 5.
3 Janssens and Gordon, "A Short History of the Joint Committee on Japanese Studies," p. 2.
4 John W. Hall, "Foreword," in Jansen, ed., *Changing Japanese Attitudes toward Modernization*, p. v.
5 On the number of Japanese studies scholars in the United States, see Patricia Steinhoff, "Japanese Studies in the United States: The 1990s and Beyond," in *Japan in the World, the World in Japan*, p. 222. Important bibliographies include Dower, with George, *Japanese History and Culture from Ancient to Modern Times*, and Wray, *Japan's Economy*.
6 F. G. Notehelfer, "Modern Japan," in Norton, ed., *The American Historical Association's Guide to Historical Literature*, p. 380.
7 Dower, ed., *Origins of the Modern Japanese State*.
8 Notehelfer, "Modern Japan," p. 380.
9 John Dower, "Sizing Up (and Breaking Down) Japan," in Hardacre, ed., *The Postwar Development of Japanese Studies in the United States*, p. 6.
10 Martin Collcutt, "Premodern Japan," in Norton, ed., *The American Historical Association's Guide to Historical Literature*, p. 357.
11 Notehelfer, "Modern Japan," p. 380. Marius Jansen noted in 1989 that modernization "represented an effort to avoid politics and to substitute one generalization for others, in the hope that it would prove more objective and more inclusive" (Jansen, "Introduction," in Jansen, ed., *The Cambridge History of Japan*, vol. 5, *The Nineteenth Century*, p. 43).
12 Dower, "Sizing Up (and Breaking Down) Japan," pp. 6–7.
13 Helen Hardacre, "Introduction," in Hardacre, ed., *The Postwar Developments of Japanese Studies in the United States*, p. xii.
14 Ibid.
15 Collcutt, "Premodern Japan," p. 360.
16 Treat and Berry, quoted in Dower, "Sizing Up (and Breaking Down) Japan," p. 21; John W. Hall, "Changing Conceptions of the Modernization of Japan," in Jansen, ed., *Changing Japanese Attitudes toward Modernization*, p. 15.
17 Hardacre, "Introduction," p. xiii.
18 Ibid.
19 Dower, "Sizing Up (and Breaking Down) Japan," p. 32.
20 Andrew Gordon, "Taking Japanese Studies Seriously," in Hardacre, ed., *The Postwar Developments of Japanese Studies in the United States*, pp. 392–400.
21 Dower's *Embracing Defeat: Japan in the Wake of World War II* was awarded the 2000 Pulitzer Prize for General Non-Fiction. Bix's *Hirohito and the Making of Modern Japan* won the following year in the same category.
22 Gordon, *A Modern History of Japan*, p. xiii.

23 Hardacre, "Introduction," p. x. Even in 1977, John Whitney Hall observed that "Since World War II Japanese specialists have, as private scholars, crashed the elite levels of higher education, but we have yet to establish the value of the subjects we control to the basic concerns of the disciplines we find ourselves [in]" (quoted in Janssens and Gordon, "A Short History of the Joint Committee on Japanese Studies," p. 8).

24 Several works in English have surveyed research on Japan in other parts of the world; see, for example, King, *The Development of Japanese Studies in Southeast Asia*, and Kilby, *Russian Studies of Japan*. Useful works on the writing of Japan's history by Japanese scholars include Mehl, *History and the State in Nineteenth-Century Japan*; Hoston, *Marxism and the Crisis of Development in Prewar Japan*; Brownlee, *Japanese Historians and the National Myths, 1600–1945*; Brownlee, ed., *History in the Service of the Japanese Nation*. The tradition of writing monumental multi-author, multi-volume overviews of Japanese history is well established in Japan; representative collections include *Iwanami kōza, Nihon rekishi*, 26 vols. (Tokyo: Iwanami Shoten, 1975–7), and *Iwanami kōza, Nihon tsūshi*, 21 vols., 4 suppl. (Tokyo: Iwanami Shoten, 1993–6).

25 Hall, "Foreword," p. vii.

26 Janssens and Gordon, "A Short History of the Joint Committee on Japanese Studies," p. 3. The six volumes in the series were: Jansen, ed., *Changing Japanese Attitudes toward Modernization* (1965); Lockwood, ed., *The State and Economic Enterprise in Japan* (1965); Dore, ed., *Aspects of Social Change in Modern Japan* (1967); Ward, ed., *Political Development in Modern Japan* (1968); Morley, ed., *Dilemmas of Growth in Prewar Japan* (1971); Shively, ed., *Tradition and Modernization in Japanese Culture* (1971).

27 John Hall, Marius Jansen, Madoka Kanai, and Denis Twitchett, "General Editors' Preface," in Duus, ed., *The Cambridge History of Japan*, vol. 6, *The Twentieth Century*, p. vii.

28 Dower, "Sizing Up (and Breaking Down) Japan," p. 21. The six volumes were Brown, ed., *The Cambridge History of Japan*, vol. 1, *Ancient Japan* (1993); Shively and McCullough, eds., The *Cambridge History of Japan*, vol. 2, *Heian Japan* (1999); Yamamura, ed., *The Cambridge History of Japan*, vol. 3, *Medieval Japan* (1990); Hall, ed., *The Cambridge History of Japan*, vol. 4, *Early Modern Japan* (1991); Jansen, ed., *The Cambridge History of Japan*, vol. 5, *The Nineteenth Century* (1989); and Duus, ed., *The Cambridge History of Japan*, vol. 6, *The Twentieth Century* (1988).

29 H. D. Harootunian and Masao Miyoshi, "Introduction: The 'Afterlife' of Area Studies," in Miyoshi and Harootunian, eds., *Learning Places*, pp. 8–9.

30 For an interesting discussion of the rationale for this focus on the more recent past, see Totman, *A History of Japan*, pp. 6–8.

31 Peter Duus, "Preface to Volume 6," in Duus, ed., *The Cambridge History of Japan*, vol. 6, *The Twentieth Century*, p. xviii.

32 Ibid., p. xvii.

BIBLIOGRAPHY

Bix, Herbert. *Hirohito and the Making of Modern Japan*. New York: HarperCollins, 2000.

Brown, Delmer M., ed. *The Cambridge History of Japan*, vol. 1, *Ancient Japan*. Cambridge: Cambridge University Press, 1993.

Brownlee, John. *Japanese Historians and the National Myths, 1600–1945*. Vancouver: UBC Press, 1997.

Brownlee, John., ed. *History in the Service of the Japanese Nation*. Toronto: University of Toronto–York University Joint Centre on Modern East Asia, 1983.

Dore, R. P., ed. *Aspects of Social Change in Modern Japan*. Princeton: Princeton University Press, 1967.

Dower, John. *Embracing Defeat: Japan in the Wake of World War II*. New York: Norton 1999.

Dower, John, ed. *Origins of the Modern Japanese State: Selected Writings of E. H. Norman*. New York: Pantheon, 1975.

Dower, John, with George, Timothy. *Japanese History and Culture from Ancient to Modern Times: Seven Basic Bibliographies*, 2nd edn. Princeton: Markus Wiener, 1995.

Duus, Peter, ed. *The Cambridge History of Japan*, vol. 6, *The Twentieth Century*. Cambridge: Cambridge University Press, 1988.

Gordon, Andrew. *A Modern History of Japan: From Tokugawa Times to the Present*. New York: Oxford University Press, 2003.

Hall, John W. *Japanese History: New Dimensions of Approach and Understanding*, 2nd edn. Washington DC: Service Center for Teachers of History, publication no. 24, 1966.

Hall, John W., ed. *The Cambridge History of Japan*, vol. 4, *Early Modern Japan*. Cambridge: Cambridge University Press, 1991.

Hardacre, Helen, ed. *The Postwar Developments of Japanese Studies in the United States*. Leiden: Brill, 1998.

Hoston, Germaine. *Marxism and the Crisis of Development in Prewar Japan*. Princeton: Princeton University Press, 1986.

Jansen, Marius, ed. *Changing Japanese Attitudes toward Modernization*. Princeton: Princeton University Press, 1965.

Jansen, Marius, ed. *The Cambridge History of Japan*, vol. 5, *The Nineteenth Century*. Cambridge: Cambridge University Press, 1989.

Janssens, Rudolph, and Gordon, Andrew. "A Short History of the Joint Committee on Japanese Studies," available online at <http://www.ssrc.org/programs/publications_editors/publications/jcjs.pdf> accessed Mar. 1, 2006.

Japan in the World, the World in Japan. Ann Arbor: University of Michigan Center for Japanese Studies, 2001.

Kilby, E. Stuart. *Russian Studies of Japan*. London: Macmillan, 1981.

King, Frank. *The Development of Japanese Studies in Southeast Asia*. Hong Kong: Centre of Asian Studies, University of Hong Kong, 1969.

Lockwood, William, ed. *The State and Economic Enterprise in Japan*. Princeton: Princeton University Press, 1965.

Mehl, Margaret. *History and the State in Nineteenth-Century Japan*. Basingstoke, UK: Macmillan, 1998.

Miyoshi, Masao, and Harootunian, H. D., eds. *Learning Places: The Afterlives of Area Studies*. Durham, NC: Duke University Press, 2002.

Morley, James, ed. *Dilemmas of Growth in Prewar Japan*. Princeton: Princeton University Press, 1971.

Norton, Mary Beth, ed. *The American Historical Association's Guide to Historical Literature*, 3rd edn. New York: Oxford University Press, 1995.

Shively, Donald, ed. *Tradition and Modernization in Japanese Culture*. Princeton: Princeton University Press, 1971.

Shively, Donald, and McCullough, William, eds. *The Cambridge History of Japan*, vol. 2, *Heian Japan*. Cambridge: Cambridge University Press, 1999.

Totman, Conrad. *A History of Japan*. Oxford: Blackwell, 2000.

Ward, Robert, ed. *Political Development in Modern Japan*. Princeton: Princeton University Press, 1968.

Wray, William. *Japan's Economy: A Bibliography of Its Past and Present*. New York: Marcus Wiener, 1989.

Yamamura, Kozo, ed. *The Cambridge History of Japan*, vol. 3, *Medieval Japan*. Cambridge: Cambridge University Press, 1990.

PART I

Japan before 1600

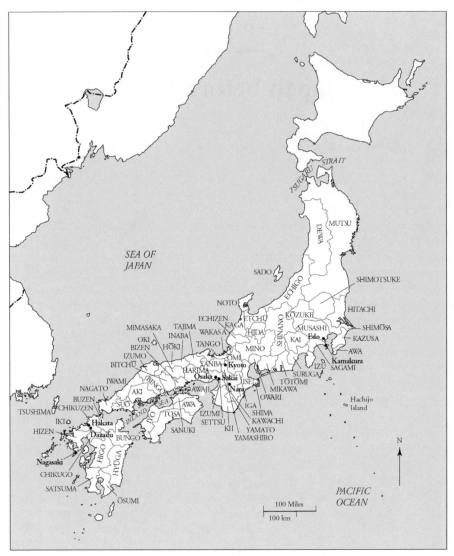

Map 1 The Traditional provinces of Japan

CHAPTER ONE

Japanese Beginnings

Mark J. Hudson

Japan has one of the oldest and most active traditions of archaeological research in the world. This chapter uses evidence from archaeology and related fields to provide a thematic overview of the history of the Japanese islands from the first human settlement through to the Nara period of the eighth century AD. It must be stressed that given the frantic pace of archaeological excavation in Japan today, many of the conclusions presented here may soon be changed by new discoveries. The aim of this chapter, therefore, is to summarize the main themes and areas of debate in ancient Japan rather than to attempt an exhaustive discussion of specific aspects of the archaeological record.

Periodization

The Paleolithic period starts with the first human occupation of Japan, which was perhaps as late as 35,000 years ago. The Paleolithic was followed by the Jōmon period, which most archaeologists begin with the first appearance of pottery around 16,500 years ago. The Jōmon is usually divided into six subphases termed Incipient, Initial, Early, Middle, Late, and Final; a seventh phase, the Epi-Jōmon, is found only in Hokkaidō. Considering the very long duration of the Jōmon period and the ecological diversity of the Japanese archipelago, it is not surprising that there is great cultural variation within the Jōmon tradition. Rather than a single "Jōmon culture" it is more appropriate to speak of plural Jōmon *cultures*, but specialists continue to debate how we should classify the Jōmon phenomenon. Jōmon populations from Kyūshū expanded south into the Ryūkyūs from about 7,000 years ago, developing there into a quite different culture that is termed "Early Shellmound" by Okinawan archaeologists. Jōmon sites are found as far north as Rebun Island, but Sakhalin appears to have been outside the area of regular Jōmon settlement.

The arrival of full-scale agriculture in Japan around 400 BC marks the beginning of the Yayoi period.[1] The following Kofun period then commences with the construction of large, keyhole-shaped burial mounds around AD 300 – or perhaps half a century earlier if one assumes that the "great mound ... more than a hundred paces in diameter" in which, according to the *Wei zhi*, Queen Himiko was buried shortly after 247 was a keyhole-shaped tomb.[2] Although large tomb mounds were no longer built by the late seventh century, archaeologically the Kofun period is usually continued through to the beginning of the Nara period (710–94), thus overlapping with the Asuka era (552–710). The Yayoi and Kofun cultures did not spread to the Ryūkyūs or Hokkaidō. In the central and northern Ryūkyūs, a poorly understood Late Shellmound phase began about 300 BC and continued until the beginning of the Gusuku period in the twelfth century.[3] In Hokkaidō, the Epi-Jōmon (c.100 BC–AD 650) was followed by the Satsumon (c.650–1200) and Ainu periods (c.1200–1868). The coastlines of northern and eastern Hokkaidō also saw an incursion by the people of the Okhotsk culture (c.550–1200).[4]

History of Research

Archaeology and anthropology were introduced into Japan from Europe and North America in the late nineteenth century, but both of these fields built upon native traditions of historical inquiry.[5] In the Tokugawa period, both "national learning" (*kokugaku*) and Neo-Confucian scholars developed a strong interest in the earliest history of Japan. Despite differences in philosophical outlook – which mainly revolved around the influence of China on ancient Japan – both schools relied primarily on the semi-mythological texts of the eighth century, the *Kojiki* and *Nihon Shoki*. It was not until after American biologist Edward Morse (1838–1925) dug at Ōmori in Tokyo in 1877 that a concept of an archaeological record outside written texts gradually began to develop in Japan.

Japanese archaeology developed in the European tradition of "archaeology as history" rather than in the American tradition of "archaeology as anthropology." Archaeology in Japan can also be classified as "national archaeology," which is defined by Bruce Trigger as a "culture-historical approach, with [an] emphasis on the prehistory of specific peoples."[6] In the postwar era, Japan has developed one of the most active traditions of archaeological research anywhere in the world. After the defeat of fascism in 1945, archaeology came to be seen as a way of reconstructing the history of ordinary Japanese people rather than that of the emperor and aristocracy. Economic growth associated with the so-called "Construction State" also led to a phenomenal increase in salvage archaeology from the 1960s. The amount of archaeological information that has been recovered from Japan over the past forty years is unparalleled – but so also is the ensuing destruction of archaeological resources.[7]

Humans and the Environment

Changes in the physical, chemical, and biological environment form the background to the human settlement and history of Japan. Japan is a rugged, mountainous land with significant climatic and biotic diversity from north to south. Although for much of its earlier geological history the Japanese landmass was not an island chain, Japan is now a series of islands that form the eastern edge of north Eurasia.[8] Land bridges with Korea developed at least twice during the Middle Pleistocene but there was no such land bridge in the Late Pleistocene, even at the coldest stage of the last glacial maximum (LGM) about 18,000 years ago. The main islands of Honshū, Kyūshū, and Shikoku were connected in the Late Pleistocene, with the Inland Sea forming a large plain. Hokkaidō was separated from Honshū by the Tsugaru Strait, though connected in the north to Sakhalin and the Asian mainland. The current form of the Japanese archipelago began to take shape after 15,000 years ago.[9]

During the LGM, mean annual temperatures were 7–8°C colder than present and the vegetation of Japan was very different to that of today.[10] Tundra and shrub tundra was found across much of Hokkaidō and a boreal coniferous forest extended through northern Honshū into the highlands of western Japan. Temperate conifers and mixed broadleaf trees were distributed in coastal areas of the Kantō and in western Japan. Warm broadleaf evergreen forest was found only in a refugium at the southernmost tip of Kyūshū.

Climatic warming after the LGM was followed by a sudden return to very cold conditions during the Younger Dryas, a global climatic stage that is dated to about 13,000 to 11,600 years ago on Greenland ice core data. The precise effects of the Younger Dryas in East Asia remain poorly understood, but it has been argued that the rapid changes in stone tools and other cultural traits in the Incipient Jōmon are due to this stage of climatic instability.[11] Following the Younger Dryas, the climate gradually became warmer, reaching a peak in the "Holocene Optimum" around 7,000–6,000 years ago when sea levels were some two to six meters higher than present.

In addition to climatic change, the prehistory of Japan cannot be considered without reference to the frequent earthquakes and volcanic eruptions that affected the archipelago. The two largest volcanic eruptions in Japanese prehistory were those of the Aira and Kikai calderas, both in southern Kyūshū and dated to about 22,000 and 7,300 years ago, respectively. The Kikai eruption and associated earthquakes and tsunami was probably so devastating that Kyūshū was abandoned by Jōmon populations for several centuries.[12]

Population History

The earliest human fossils from Japan belong to a juvenile from Yamashita-chō Cave, Okinawa dating to about 32,000 years ago and the question of who was the first human to settle the archipelago remains controversial.[13] The first Paleolithic site in Japan was dug in 1949 at Iwajuku, Gunma prefecture. Later research has identified some 5,000 Paleolithic sites in Japan but all secure dates are later than 35,000 years ago. A series of proposed Early Paleolithic sites dug in the 1960s and 1970s remains controversial.[14] Other work centered on Miyagi prefecture in the late 1970s to late 1990s reported a number of Early Paleolithic localities dating back as early as 600,000 years ago, but all of these sites were later found to have been faked by amateur archaeologist Fujimura Shin'ichi.[15]

Southeast Asia and southern China were settled by *Homo erectus* from soon after two million years ago. In north China, the famous "Peking Man" site of Zhoukoudian near Beijing dates to after 460,000 years ago, but *Homo erectus* tools dated earlier than 730,000 years have been found in the Nihewan Basin in Hebei.[16] *Homo erectus* adapted to many different environments in Asia and it is not clear why Japan was apparently not settled prior to the appearance of modern humans. However, the sudden expansion of sites in Japan after 35,0000 years ago is consistent with the worldwide trend toward the occupation of new, previously uninhabited environments after the appearance of *Homo sapiens.*

At the end of the Pleistocene, it is likely that new groups reached Japan bringing microblades and other technologies. With so few human skeletal remains dating to the Paleolithic and the first half of the Jōmon, however, it is unclear to what extent the peoples of the Jōmon tradition derived from Paleolithic ancestors in Japan or else represented a new population influx at the Paleolithic–Jōmon transition. Much clearer evidence for immigration comes in the Yayoi period when continental migrants brought farming into the Japanese islands. A range of biological data has been used to argue that the modern Japanese derive primarily from these Yayoi era immigrants and their descendants, though some admixture with native Jōmon populations certainly occurred in many areas.[17] This Yayoi immigration model does not necessarily require a huge number of initial migrants: if population growth was high amongst the Yayoi farmers then their numbers would have rapidly increased at the expense of Jōmon hunter-gatherers.[18] Archaeological evidence suggests the source of these agricultural immigrants was the Korean peninsula, but the scarcity of skeletal remains from this period in Korea has precluded extensive comparisons of human biological remains.

It seems most likely that the agricultural immigrants of the Yayoi period also brought the Japanese language from the Korean peninsula. In the past, Japanese was often seen as forming part of an Altaic language family, but recently many linguists have come to see the structural similarities between the "Altaic" languages as due to areal diffusion.[19] Certainly, the archaeological record offers no support for the speculative models of Altaic expansions proposed by some linguists.[20] Most linguists and archaeologists also continue to be highly skeptical about proposed links between Japanese and the Austronesian and Austroasiatic families of Southeast Asia.[21] Japonic – the Japanese language family that contains Japanese, Ryūkyūan, and their various historical dialects – appears to be related most closely to Old Koguryo and thus its roots can be initially placed on the Korean peninsula; attempts to determine the earlier roots of Japonic at present remain controversial.[22]

As noted, Jōmon populations from Kyūshū expanded south into the Ryūkyūs as far as Okinawa Island. However, the southern Ryūkyūs (Miyako to Yonaguni) were not settled from Japan at this stage. The prehistory of these Sakishima Islands is characterized by an early ceramic Shimotabaru phase that probably began in the second millennium BC. This was followed, after an apparent hiatus, by an aceramic culture with shell adzes that perhaps began in the late first millennium BC.[23] The precise origin of both of these cultures is unknown but is possibly to be found in the Philippines or neighboring areas of island Southeast Asia. After 1300, the Sakishima Islands were gradually incorporated into the Chūzan kingdom of Okinawa Island.[24]

From the early days of Japanese anthropology it had been assumed that the Ainu of Hokkaidō and the Okinawans of the Ryūkyū Islands derive primarily from Jōmon ancestors rather than the mainland Yayoi Japanese.[25] Work over the last decade or so, however, has shown that the modern Okinawans are biologically much closer to the Japanese than to the Ainu or prehistoric Jōmon people.[26] These recent results suggest significant gene flow into the Ryūkyūs from Japan by at least the Gusuku period, although there is little archaeological evidence for such immigration and the historical context of this population movement remains unclear. The Ryūkyūan languages are closely related to Japanese and must have replaced earlier languages in the Okinawan Islands. Although proto-Ryūkyūan must have split from the Nara dialects before the eighth century, recent research suggests its spread into Okinawa may have been rather later, perhaps around AD 900.[27] A deeper understanding of the population history of the Ryūkyū Islands will be an important focus of research over the next decade or so.

In the north, research continues to affirm close biological similarities between the historic Ainu and Jōmon populations. Here, however, the situation is complicated by linguistic and archaeological evidence that suggests the Ainu may be derived from Jōmon populations of the Tōhoku region rather than Hokkaidō. Based on ancient borrowings from Japanese and the low dialect diversity of Ainu, linguist Juha Janhunen has proposed that the Ainu language spread from northern Honshū into Hokkaidō in the Satsumon period (c.650–1200).[28] Archaeologically, the large differences between the cultures of the Epi-Jōmon and Satsumon periods certainly can be seen to support population influx from the Tōhoku into Hokkaidō in the seventh century AD. This is also an area on which further research is warranted. Although the Ainu nation today may oppose any suggestion that their ancestors arrived in Hokkaidō as recently as the seventh century, this Tōhoku origin model does not contradict the long, indigenous history of the Ainu in Japan.

Technology

As elsewhere, stone tools are the main archaeological evidence for the Paleolithic period in Japan. The reduction of risk in obtaining food and other resources appears to be one of the main determinants of stone tool variability.[29] The early stages of the Late Paleolithic in Japan are marked by "knife-shaped tools" made on parallel-sided blades.[30] Knife-shaped tools appear to have been used for a variety of purposes and are characterized by relatively few task-specialized shapes.[31] A more specialist tool type of the Late Paleolithic is an edge-ground axe that may have been used for woodworking.[32] The last stage of the Paleolithic in Japan is characterized by microblabes – small stone tools that were hafted to organic armatures to make composite spears and other weapons. In Japan, microblades appear first at the Kashiwadai 1 site in Hokkaidō at about 20,000 years ago; sites in the rest of the archipelago follow several thousand years later. Analysis of the technology of Japanese microblades has suggested that Late Pleistocene hunters in northern Japan operated under more environmental constraints and risks than those in the south of the country.[33]

Recent calibrated radiocarbon dates place the earliest pottery in Japan, at the Ōdai Yamamoto I site in Aomori prefecture, at about 16,500 years ago.[34] This pottery is the oldest from anywhere in the world but similar final Pleistocene dates have been reported for pottery from China and the Amur Basin and it is not yet clear if Jōmon ceramics developed in isolation or as part of a wider East Asian ceramic technology. Ceramic vessels provided a convenient method of cooking large quantities of ecologically low-ranked foods such as plants and shellfish, as well as a means of food storage in a seasonal, temperate environment.

Although some non-sedentary foragers are known to have used pottery, the large quantity of ceramics found in many Jōmon sites suggests a relatively high level of sedentism in that tradition – though few, if any, Jōmon groups were fully sedentary.[35] The semi-subterranean pit house was the basic dwelling of the Jōmon period but ethnographic parallels suggest these buildings would have only been used in the winter months. A raised-floor structure is also commonly found at Jōmon sites; these are usually interpreted as store-houses. Most Jōmon sites are small clusters of a few pit buildings but many very large sites are also known, especially from the Early and Middle phases. Sannai Maruyama in Aomori, the largest Jōmon site discovered so far, has produced over 600 pit buildings, but it is not clear how many of these were occupied simultaneously.[36]

There is no evidence for the use of coastal resources in Paleolithic Japan, although any Late Pleistocene coastal sites would have been flooded by later rises in sea level. That Paleolithic people had the ability to cross water is clear from finds of obsidian from Kozushima Island which was brought to the Kantō region as early as 30,000 years ago.[37] The discovery of over a hundred dugout canoes from Jōmon sites suggests that these vessels were the main method of water transportation. That the Jōmon people were not confined to rivers and coasts, however, is shown by Early Jōmon remains from Hachijō Island, some 200 kilometers from Honshū. Jōmon fishing was conducted with hooks and harpoons, both of which first appear in the Initial phase. The use of nets is assumed from probable net-sinkers and an actual fish weir was found in a Late Jōmon context at Shindanai, Iwate prefecture.[38]

Various new technologies, including lacquerware, basketry, and textiles, were adopted over the long history of the Jōmon period.[39] Many of these technologies served to increase the productive efficiency of the Jōmon economy, but this does not mean that the Jōmon economy as a whole was gradually evolving toward a radically different socioeconomic system. Jōmon society remained "conservative" in many respects; despite knowledge of rice and other crops there seems to have been no attempt by Jōmon populations to adopt full-scale farming. This "conservatism" ended dramatically in the Yayoi period when new technologies of food production enabled a qualitative expansion of the economy. The introduction of metals into Japan in the Yayoi also had profound effects on technology and production, as well as on the reproduction of political power. Bronze working was widespread in China by the early second millennium BC but was slow to spread to the Japanese archipelago. Iron, in contrast, spread almost immediately and the introduction of iron tools on the continent from the fifth century BC has been suggested as an important causal factor in the diffusion of farming to Japan.[40]

In Japan, iron was mainly used for agricultural and other tools whereas ritual artifacts were mainly made of bronze. Some casting of bronze and iron began in Japan by about 100 BC, but the raw materials for both metals were initially intro-duced from Korea and China. In the Yayoi, bronze weapons and bells evolved from practical tools to ornate, ceremonial artifacts. In northern Kyūshū, bronze weapons are found as grave goods in elite burials at sites such as Yoshinogari, but elsewhere weapons and bells are usually discovered as hoards buried away from settlements. At Kojindani in Shimane prefecture, six bells, sixteen spearheads, and 358 swords were found on an isolated hillside. Such hoards are often interpreted as resulting from community-based agricultural rituals.

The Kofun period saw a massive "technology transfer" from the Korean peninsula to the Japanese islands that included ironworking, agricultural technology, wheel-thrown stoneware, architectural techniques, and technologies of administration.[41] Several scholars have argued that the uneven diffusion of this technology hampered agricultural growth in many regions.[42] At first, the Yamato state tried to monopolize new technologies, which could be an important source of political power.[43] The increasing need for the Nara state to be based on non-staple wealth finance, however, led to the spread of various technologies to the provinces and resulted in geographically uneven but extensive economic growth across Japan.[44]

Subsistence and Economy

Traditional Japanese civilization was based on agriculture, but Japan also has one of the longest histories of hunter-gatherer societies in East Asia. In the main islands, farming was introduced in the Yayoi period, but in the Ryūkyūs hunter-gathering continued until at least the eighth century and in Hokkaidō until the late nineteenth century.

Few faunal remains are available from Paleolithic sites in Japan and discussions of Paleolithic subsistence rely more on informed guesswork than actual data. Plant foods would have been limited in the dense boreal forests of the late glacial maximum (LGM).[45] The hunting of large animals is suggested by remains of *Palaeoloxodon naumanni* (Naumann's elephant) and *Sinomegaceros yabei* (Yabe's giant deer) at the Lake Nojiri and Hanaizumi sites, but some recent research has concluded that large migratory mammals were rare in Pleistocene Japan.[46] The early adoption of pottery in Japan in turn suggests that plant foods quickly became a very important resource once the climate began to warm up after the LGM. Pleistocene megafauna became extinct in Japan between 15,000 and 10,000 years ago, leaving the medium- and small-sized mammals found in the archipelago today.

Humans could have attempted to adapt to the difficult conditions in Late Pleistocene Japan by increased storage, evidenced archaeologically by sedentism, mass capture and preservation techniques, and the exchange of prestige items as "social storage."[47] Little evidence of these adaptations is to be found in Paleolithic Japan, however. Sedentism and storage did not become important until the Jōmon. Pit-traps for hunting are known from almost 30,000 years ago at the Hatsunegahara A site in Shizuoka Prefecture, but they did not become widespread until the Initial Jōmon phase.[48]

The Jōmon diet included a broad range of plant, animal, and marine foods. Remains of salmon bones from the Maeda Kochi site in Tokyo show that this fish was exploited from as early as the Incipient phase. Shell middens are known from the Initial phase and more than 3,000 Jōmon shell middens have been identified. These middens have produced a variety of shellfish as well as the remains of sea mammals and inshore and offshore fish. Deer and wild boar were the main terrestrial animal species exploited. The domesticated dog is present from the Initial phase and was probably used in hunting. Nuts, roots, and berries are thought to have been the main wild plant foods exploited by Jōmon peoples. There is also increasing evidence that a number of plants were cultivated. These plants include hemp (*Cannabis sativa*), perilla (Japanese *shiso/egoma*), burdock (*Arctium lappa*), bottle gourd (*Lagenaria siceraria*), barnyard millet (*Echinochloa utilis*), adzuki and mung beans (*Vigna angularis* and *V. radiatus*), and the lacquer tree (*Rhus vernicifera*).[49] Rice, barley, and broomcorn and foxtail millet were also present in some Jōmon sites by the end of that period.[50] The yam *Dioscorea japonica* has been proposed as an important resource in the Middle Jōmon of central Honshū but direct evidence is lacking. Disturbance of forests around Jōmon villages probably encouraged the growth of chestnut and walnut trees.[51] DNA analysis of chestnuts (*Castanea crenata*) from Jōmon sites has shown that some samples have a low genetic diversity, which suggests management practices by Jōmon populations, particularly at Sannai Maruyama.[52]

These plant cultivation and management practices had little influence on the overall organization of Jōmon society. In contrast, the full-scale farming of the Yayoi period marked a very different intensive and expansionary economic system. In addition to the traditional emphasis on cultivation and domestication, archaeologists have recently stressed the *social* aspects of farming as a threshold involving the creation of artificial agro-ecosystems.[53] When possessing a nutritionally complementary range of domesticated plants and animals, agriculture can be seen as a social system that is *expansionary, exploitative*, and based on principles of social *exclusion*. In Japan, this agricultural system was initially associated with immigration from the Korean peninsula. Population growth amongst early Yayoi farmers then led to the rapid expansion of Yayoi culture as far as northern Honshū.

The expansion of Yayoi culture is known from the excavation of over 100 rice paddy field sites dating to that period. Without doubt rice was an important crop during the Yayoi but barley, millet, and other cultivated and wild plants were also consumed in large quantities. Domesticated pigs and, more rarely, chickens are known from Yayoi contexts but it is not clear how important these animals were as food sources. The hunting of deer and wild boar certainly continued through the Yayoi and Kofun periods, as did river and ocean fishing. After the introduction of Buddhism into Japan in the late sixth century, it is often argued that religious prohibitions meant that fish and shellfish became the main sources of animal protein. Archaeological evidence, however, has clearly shown that a range of mammals continued to be utilized for food and other resources through to the Tokugawa period.[54]

Sociopolitical Change

Anthropologists have long been interested in how the small-scale societies characteristic of hunter-gatherers developed into stratified, organizationally complex chiefdoms and states. The rise of class divisions and the state has been a major topic of research for Japanese archaeologists since World War II; research on the evolution of Paleolithic and Jōmon societies has, in contrast, been slower to develop. In Japan, the study of Paleolithic society has largely been approached through work on settlement patterns. Possible remains of tents have been found at Kashiwadai 1 in Hokkaidō dating to about 20,000 years ago but, from the fact that dwellings and hearths are rare in the knife-shaped tool cultures of Honshū south, Inada Takashi has argued that society at that time was rather unstable, with nuclear families usually not forming independent residential units.[55] The view that, amongst hunter-gatherers, nuclear families had not yet separated out from band-wide households goes back to

Engels and is part of a broader debate on the social organization of foragers.[56] Archaeologically, however, such arguments from the *absence* of preserved features are difficult.

A landmark volume on hunter-gatherers published in 1968 made two basic assumptions about foragers, that "(1) they live in small groups and (2) they move around a lot."[57] Archaeological research in the 1970s and 1980s, however, soon demonstrated that many prehistoric hunter-gatherers lived in quite sedentary villages with large populations. Within this research, the Japanese evidence figured prominently in a 1981 book called *Affluent Foragers,* but following this publication only a few archaeologists retained an interest in the comparative study of Jōmon hunter-gatherers.[58] The Jōmon is perhaps the most materially affluent hunter-gatherer culture known through archaeology. It is presently unclear, though, whether that material affluence was matched by the type of complex social organization known ethnographically for some hunter-gathering societies where social differentiation was hereditary and leaders controlled non-kin labor.[59]

A great variety of ritual artifacts is known from the Jōmon, including clay figurines and masks, phallic stone rods, and highly ornate lacquer and ceramic vessels. Stone and wooden circles are also present; the two stones circles at Ōyu in Akita Prefecture have diameters of 45 and 40 meters.[60] The prominence of these artifacts and sites has led to the Jōmon being widely interpreted as a "magico-ritual" society within Japanese archaeology.[61] Other influential studies of Jōmon social organization have focused on settlement duality and reconstructions of postmarital residence.[62]

Although written records are unknown in Japan itself until the eighth century, Chinese dynastic histories make some mention of the land of the "Wa," who are thought to be the Yayoi Japanese. The *Wei zhi,* compiled in 280, contains a short description of the economy and society of the Wa people and of the diplomatic relations between the Wei and the Wa polity of Yamatai and its Queen Himiko. The location of Yamatai is unclear from the text; northern Kyūshū and the Kinai region have been suggested as the two main possible locations. The *Wei zhi* suggests Yamatai controlled most of western Japan in the third century, but the archaeological record does not support such a degree of political unification until much later.

Archaeologists have proposed the existence of several chiefdom-type polities in western Japan in the Yayoi. These were regional polities based on a large, central settlement with populations of perhaps several thousand people. Such polities may correspond to the "countries" (Chinese *guo*) described in the *Wei zhi* but their political control did not extend beyond their particular basin or river valley. The site of Yoshinogari in Saga Prefecture was probably the center of one of these chiefdoms: defensive ditches with watchtowers enclose an area of 25 hectares; the rulers of this settlement lived in a central residential precinct and were buried in a 40 by 26 meter mound. Many Yayoi chiefdoms in western Japan were engaged in conflicts with neighboring groups to gain access to water and other resources and to extend their power. Such conflicts are mentioned in the *Wei zhi* and are evidenced archaeologically by defended settlements, the widespread presence of weapons, and discoveries of human skeletons with war-related injuries. Over 150 Yayoi period skeletons are known with embedded arrowheads, cut marks, or decapitated skulls. Through warfare, trade and alliance-building, the chiefdoms of the Kinai region had considerably extended their power by the third century AD. By around AD 250, the mound burials of the Yayoi had developed into the huge standardized keyhole-shaped tombs of the Kofun period; in the fourth century these Kofun tombs quickly spread around the Inland Sea and beyond.

An archaic state is a large-scale society structured on a hierarchy of class rather than kinship and which has extensive powers in warfare and administrative control. Archaeologically, archaic states can be identified by royal palaces, temples and priestly residences, royal tombs, a settlement hierarchy with at least four levels (cities, towns, and large and small villages), and evidence of a bureaucracy.[63] In Japan, although royal tombs can be said to make their appearance with the keyhole-shaped mounds of the late third century AD, the other features only appear in the seventh to eighth centuries. The territorial state of the Nara period marks the emergence of a fully fledged archaic state organized on Chinese models of government known in Japanese as the *ritsuryō* system.[64]

The ritual hierarchy of the keyhole tombs gives the impression of a centralized society, but administrative power in the Kofun period seems to have been diffuse and *heterarchical*, that is having different, non-hierarchical functions within the same system. Several archaeologists have explained Kofun society through the concept of a chiefly alliance or confederacy.[65] Critics of the chiefly alliance theories have discussed the ways in which the strongest polity of the Kinai region attempted to increase its power through trade, tribute, and technology.[66] Control over access to iron and trade with the Asian continent appear to have been major factors in the growth of class stratification in Japan. Archaeologically, this is evidenced by changes at the end of the Yayoi period.[67] In the Middle Yayoi, power was negotiated through bronze bells and weapons that served as "inalienable goods" that were not widely exchanged or circulated but were used in ceremonies of authentication and commemoration.[68] From the end of the Middle Yayoi, however, these bronzes began to be deposited in hoards and the growing trade in iron fueled a "prestige goods" economy using Chinese mirrors and other objects.[69] Complex societies can be financed by "staple finance" or "wealth finance": the former involves obligatory payments of agricultural surplus by commoners whereas the latter is the use of special objects (prestige goods or money) as "political currencies."[70] The basic tension in premodern Japanese history between these two forms of state finance dates back to the Yayoi period when the economic basis of wet-rice farming was both expanded and contested by prestige goods such as bronze mirrors. When the state was strong it could control access to wealth finance in Japan by supporting the local production of previously imported goods or by controlling the means of transportation or trade routes.[71] The Kofun period shift to locally produced stone imitations of shell bracelets previously made on tropical shells imported from the Ryūkyūs is a good example of the former, and the *sakoku* trade restrictions of the Tokugawa attest to the enormous importance of wealth finance in the medieval era in Japan.

In recent years historians have produced a number of sophisticated analyses of the nature of state power in Japan, especially in the Tokugawa period.[72] Much less comparable work has been conducted by anthropologists on the archaic state in the archipelago. Given the many outward continuities in premodern Japanese politics (most prominently the emperor) there is a tendency to overemphasize the stability of the state in Japanese history. Like many other archaic states, however, the state in Japan appears to have been inherently unstable and went through clear "peaks and valleys" of consolidation and weakness. Although anthropological research on the state in Japan has so far emphasized state formation, anthropological theory holds considerable potential for understanding the operation and structure of states, as well as their origins.[73]

Conclusions

This chapter has presented some brief glimpses into the kaleidoscope of anthropological and archaeological research on ancient Japan. One American archaeologist has recently written that, "To say that Japan is the most thoroughly understood prehistoric area in the world does not begin to present the detailed information that is available on ancient life in Japan. Japanese archaeologists have established an incredibly active research tradition and exposed a record of prehistoric events in the Japanese archipelago that is simply amazing."[74] This archaeological record is increasingly being incorporated into the Japanese literature on the history of Japan, but in the West, historians have been much slower to use the results of archaeological research.[75] Western archaeologists working on Japan have, in turn, largely been interested in anthropological rather than historical questions. Although this chapter has covered only the periods up to the eighth century, archaeological evidence continues right through to the Tokugawa and Meiji periods – or in some cases even later, as with the work on World War II sites in Okinawa. The different traditions of the "two cultures" of history and anthropological archaeology continue to make dialog difficult, but the challenge and adventure of Japanese archaeology in the early twenty-first century is to use the wealth of archaeological evidence from Japan to contribute to anthropological theory in general whilst, at the same time, using archaeology to further our understanding of Japanese history.

NOTES

1   Recent radiocarbon dates from the National Museum of Japanese History place the beginning of the Yayoi period at about 1000 BC. The researchers involved in this work have published a book (Harunari and Imamura, *Yayoi jidai no jitsunendai*) but their results have not yet appeared in a refereed journal and debate over these dates look set to continue for some time.
2   The *Wei zhi* is a late third-century Chinese dynastic history which represents the first historical description of Japan. For an English translation of the section on Japan, see Tsunoda and Goodrich, *Japan in the Chinese Dynastic Histories*.
3   For details of the Ryūkyū sequence, see Pearson, "The Place of Okinawa in Japanese Historical Identity."
4   For the later prehistory of Hokkaidō, see Imamura, *Prehistoric Japan*, pp. 199–204, and Hudson, *Ruins of Identity*, pp. 206–32.
5   Bleed, "Almost Archaeology."
6   Trigger, *A History of Archaeological Thought*, p. 174.
7   On postwar Japanese archaeology, see Pearson, "The Nature of Japanese Archaeology," and Mizoguchi, "The Reproduction of Archaeological Discourse."
8   On the early geological history of Japan, see Barnes, "Origins of the Japanese Islands."

9   This environmental research is summarized by Keally, "Environment and the Distribution of Sites in the Japanese Palaeolithic," p. 25.

10 For climate reconstructions, see Tsukada, "Vegetation in Prehistoric Japan," and Yasuda, *Prehistoric Environment in Japan.*

11 Teshigawara, *Jōmon bunka*, pp. 52–7.

12 Machida, "The Impact of the Kikai Eruptions on Prehistoric Japan."

13 Matsu'ura, "A Chronological Review of Pleistocene Human Remains from the Japanese Archipelago," p. 186.

14 Ikawa-Smith, ed., *Early Paleolithic in South and East Asia.*

15 Japanese Archaeological Association, ed., *Zen, chūki kyūsekki mondai no kensho*; Hudson, "For the People, By the People."

16 See the summary by Olsen, "China's Earliest Inhabitants."

17 This question of Yayoi immigration has a long history of research which is summarized by Hudson, *Ruins of Identity.* The basic model supported by many Japanese anthropologists is described in Hanihara, "Dual Structure Model for the Population History of the Japanese."

18 Nakahashi and Iizuka, "Anthropological Study of the Transition from the Jōmon to the Yayoi"; and Aoki and Tuljapurkar, "Hanihara's Conundrum Revisited."

19 For a theoretical discussion of areal contact, see Dixon, *The Rise and Fall of Languages*, esp. p. 32 on Altaic.

20 Hudson, *Ruins of Identity*, pp. 86–7.

21 On Austronesian, see Hudson, "Japanese and Austronesian."

22 For an up-to-date collection of papers on this question, see Osada and Vovin, eds., *Perspectives on the Origins of the Japanese Language.*

23 The precise chronology of both of these cultures is uncertain. See Ohama, *Yaeyama no kōkogaku.*

24 Pearson, "Excavations at Sumiya and Other Sakishima Sites."

25 See Hanihara, "Dual Structure Model for the Population History of the Japanese."

26 Dodo et al., "Ainu and Ryūkyūan Cranial Nonmetric Variation"; Hatta et al., "HLA Genes and Haplotypes Suggest Recent Gene Flow to the Okinawa Islands"; and Pietrusewsky, "A Multivariate Craniometric Study of the Inhabitants of the Ryūkyū Islands."

27 Serafim, "When and from Where did the Japonic Language Enter the Ryūkyūs?"

28 Janhunen, "A Framework for the Study of Japanese Language Origins," p. 481.

29 Torrence, "Hunter-Gatherer Technology."

30 For more details on Late Paleolithic tool types, see Keally, "Environment and the Distribution of Sites in the Japanese Palaeolithic."

31 Sato, *Nihon kyūsekki bunka no kōzō to shinka*, p. 295.

32 Ikawa-Smith, ed., "Late Pleistocene and Early Holocene Technologies," p. 204.

33 Bleed, "Cheap, Regular, and Reliable," p. 101.

34 Habu, *Ancient Jōmon of Japan*, pp. 28–30.

35 For pottery use by non-sedentary groups, see Rice, "On the Origins of Pottery," p. 29.

36 For the settlement archaeology of Sannai Maruyama, see Habu, *Ancient Jōmon of Japan*, pp. 108–32.

37 Keally, "Environment and the Distribution of Sites in the Japanese Palaeolithic," p. 24.

38 For a summary of fishing technology, see Imamura, *Prehistoric Japan*, pp. 73–7.

39 On these Jōmon technologies, see Habu, *Ancient Jōmon of Japan*, pp. 214–21.

40 Imamura, *Prehistoric Japan*, pp. 217–18.

41 This transfer of technology is discussed by Farris, *Sacred Texts and Buried Treasures*, pp. 68–105.

42   See Terasawa, "Commentary on the Productive Capacity of Early Japanese Rice Farm-
     ing," and Farris, *Population, Disease, and Land in Early Japan, 645–900.*
43   On irrigation technology, see Wakasa, "Water Rights, Water Rituals, Chiefly Compounds,
     and *Haniwa.*"
44   For an archaeological study of this process, see Uno, *Ritsuryō shakai no kōkogakuteki
     kenkyū.* The concept of wealth finance is discussed in the section on "Sociopolitical
     Change."
45   Keally, "Environment and the Distribution of Sites in the Japanese Palaeolithic,"
     pp. 26–7.
46   See discussion in Mizoguchi, *An Archaeological History of Japan,* p. 61.
47   Rowley-Conwy and Zvelebil, "Saving It for Later."
48   For a discussion of Jōmon pit-traps, see Imamura, *Prehistoric Japan,* pp. 79–88.
49   Crawford, "Prehistoric Plant Domestication in East Asia."
50   These finds are summarized by Hudson, *Ruins of Identity,* pp. 106–15.
51   Nishida, "The Emergence of Food Production in Neolithic Japan."
52   Sato et al., "Evidence for Jōmon Plant Cultivation Based on DNA Analysis of Chestnut
     Remains."
53   For a theoretical discussion of this issue, see Spriggs, "Early Agriculture and What Went
     Before in Island Melanesia."
54   See, for example, Uchiyama, "San'ei-cho and Meat-eating in Buddhist Edo."
55   Inada, "Subsistence and the Beginnings of Settled Life in Japan," p. 21.
56   For a summary of this debate, see Ingold, "On the Social Relations of the Hunter-
     Gatherer Band," p. 401.
57   Lee and DeVore, "Problems in the Study of Hunters and Gatherers," p. 11.
58   Koyama and Thomas, eds., *Affluent Foragers.*
59   This definition of complex hunter-gatherers follows Arnold, "The Archaeology of Com-
     plex Hunter-Gatherers," p. 78.
60   For an overview of this material, see Habu, *Ancient Jōmon of Japan,* ch. 5.
61   This view has recently been criticized by Kosugi, "Jōmon bunka ni sensō wa sonzai shita
     no ka?"
62   These studies are summarized by Habu, *Ancient Jōmon of Japan,* pp. 138–41.
63   Flannery, "The Ground Plans of Archaic States."
64   For introductory accounts of the Nara state, see Brown, ed., *The Cambridge History of
     Japan,* vol. 1, and Tsuboi and Tanaka, *The Historic City of Nara.*
65   Kondo, *Zenpokoenfun no jidai.*
66   Tsude, "The Kofun Period and State Formation."
67   Fukunaga, "Social Changes from the Yayoi to the Kofun Periods."
68   For a recent archaeological discussion of "inalienable goods," see Mills, "The Establish-
     ment and Defeat of Hierarchy."
69   Tsude, "The Kofun Period and State Formation," pp. 81–2.
70   Earle, *How Chiefs Come to Power,* pp. 70–4.
71   Ibid., p. 73.
72   See Roberts, *Mercantilism in a Japanese Domain,* and Walker, *The Conquest of Ainu
     Lands,* pp. 17–47.
73   See, for example, Marcus's discussion of "The Peaks and Valleys of Ancient States."
74   Bleed, "Cheap, Regular, and Reliable," p. 95.
75   Notable exceptions include Farris, *Sacred Texts and Buried Treasures,* and Piggott, *The
     Emergence of Japanese Kingship.* European archaeologists are also often more comfortable
     with combining archaeological and historical data, as for example with Seyock, *Auf den
     Spuren der Ostbarbaren.*

BIBLIOGRAPHY

Aoki, Kenichi, and Tuljapurkar, Shripad. "Hanihara's Conundrum Revisited: Theoretical Estimates of the Immigration into Japan during the 1000 Year Period from 300 BC to AD 700." *Anthropological Science* 108 (2000): 305–19.

Arnold, Jeanne E. "The Archaeology of Complex Hunter-Gatherers." *Journal of Archaeological Method and Theory* 3 (1996): 77–126.

Barnes, Gina L. "Origins of the Japanese Islands: The New 'Big Picture'." *Japan Review* 15 (2003): 3–50.

Bleed, Peter. "Almost Archaeology: Early Archaeological Interest in Japan." In Richard J. Pearson, Gina L. Barnes, and K. L. Hutterer, eds., *Windows on the Japanese Past: Studies in Archaeology and Prehistory.* Ann Arbor: Center for Japanese Studies, University of Michigan, 1986.

Bleed, Peter. "Cheap, Regular, and Reliable: Implications of Design Variation in Late Pleistocene Japanese Microblade Technology." In R. G. Elston and S. L. Kuhn, eds., *Thinking Small: Global Perspectives on Microlithization.* Archeological Papers of the American Anthropological Association 12. Arlington, Va.: American Anthropological Association, 2002.

Brown, Delmer M., ed. *The Cambridge History of Japan*, vol. 1, *Ancient Japan.* Cambridge: Cambridge University Press, 1993.

Crawford, Gary W. "Prehistoric Plant Domestication in East Asia." In C. W. Cowan and P. J. Watson, eds., *The Origins of Agriculture: An International Perspective.* Washington DC: Smithsonian Institution Press, 1992.

Dixon, Robert M. W. *The Rise and Fall of Languages.* Cambridge: Cambridge University Press, 1997.

Dodo Yukio, Doi Naomi, and Kondo Osamu. "Ainu and Ryūkyūan Cranial Nonmetric Variation: Evidence which Disputes the Ainu–Ryūkyū Common Origin Theory." *Anthropological Science* 106 (1998): 99–120.

Earle, Timothy. *How Chiefs Come to Power: The Political Economy in Prehistory.* Cambridge: Cambridge University Press, 1997.

Farris, William Wayne. *Population, Disease, and Land in Early Japan, 645–900.* Cambridge, Mass.: Council on East Asian Studies, Harvard University, 1985.

Farris, William Wayne. *Sacred Texts and Buried Treasures: Issues in the Historical Archaeology of Ancient Japan.* Honolulu: University of Hawai'i Press, 1998.

Flannery, K. V. "The Ground Plans of Archaic States." In G. M. Feinman and J. Marcus, eds., *Archaic States.* Santa Fe, NM: School of American Research Press, 1998.

Fukunaga, S. "Social Changes from the Yayoi to the Kofun Periods." In *Cultural Diversity and the Archaeology of the 21st Century*, ed. Society of Archaeological Studies. Okayama: Kōkogaku Kenkyūkai, 2004.

Habu, Junko. *Ancient Jōmon of Japan.* Cambridge: Cambridge University Press, 2004.

Hanihara, K. "Dual Structure Model for the Population History of the Japanese." *Japan Review* 2 (1991): 1–33.

Harunari Hideji and Imamura Mineo, eds. *Yayoi jidai no jitsunendai: tanso 14 nendai o megutte.* Tokyo: Gakuseisha, 2004.

Hatta, Y., et al. "HLA Genes and Haplotypes Suggest Recent Gene Flow to the Okinawa Islands." *Human Biology* 71 (1999): 353–65.

Hudson, M. J. "Japanese and Austronesian: An Archeological Perspective on the Proposed Linguistic Links." In K. Omoto, ed., *Interdisciplinary Perspectives on the Origins of the Japanese.* Kyoto: International Research Center for Japanese Studies, 1999.

Hudson, Mark J. *Ruins of Identity: Ethnogenesis in the Japanese Islands.* Honolulu: University of Hawai'i Press, 1999.

Hudson, Mark J. "For the People, By the People: Postwar Japanese Archaeology and the Early Paleolithic Hoax." *Anthropological Science* 113:2 (Aug. 2005): 131–9.

Ikawa-Smith, Fumiko. "Late Pleistocene and Early Holocene Technologies." In R. J. Pearson, G. L. Barnes, and K. L. Hutterer, eds., *Windows on the Japanese Past: Studies in Archaeology and Prehistory.* Ann Arbor: Center for Japanese Studies, University of Michigan, 1986.

Ikawa-Smith, Fumiko, ed. *Early Paleolithic in South and East Asia.* The Hague: Mouton, 1978.

Imamura, Keiji. *Prehistoric Japan: New Perspectives on Insular East Asia.* Honolulu: University of Hawai'i Press, 1996.

Inada, Takashi. "Subsistence and the Beginnings of Settled Life in Japan." In *Cultural Diversity and the Archaeology of the 21st Century,* ed. Society of Archaeological Studies. Okayama: Kōkogaku Kenkyūkai, 2004.

Ingold, Tim. "On the Social Relations of the Hunter-Gatherer Band." In R. B. Lee and R. Daly, eds., *The Cambridge Encyclopedia of Hunters and Gatherers.* Cambridge: Cambridge University Press, 1999.

Janhunen, Juha. "A Framework for the Study of Japanese Language Origins." In T. Osada and A. Vovin, eds., *Perspectives on the Origins of the Japanese Language.* Kyoto: International Research Center for Japanese Studies, 2003.

Japanese Archaeological Association, ed. *Zen, chūki kyūsekki mondai no kensho.* Tokyo: Nihon Kōkogaku Kyōkai, 2003.

Keally, C. T. "Environment and the Distribution of Sites in the Japanese Palaeolithic: Environmental Zones and Cultural Areas." *Bulletin of the Indo-Pacific Prehistory Association* 10 (1991): 23–39.

Kondō Yoshirō. *Zenpokoenfun no jidai.* Tokyo: Iwanami, 1983.

Kosugi, Y. "Jōmon bunka ni sensō wa sonzai shita no ka?" In *Bunka no tayōsei to hikaku kōkogaku,* ed. Society of Archaeological Studies. Okayama: Kōkogaku Kenkyūkai, 2004.

Koyama Shūzō and Thomas, D. H., eds. *Affluent Foragers: Pacific Coasts East and West.* Osaka: National Museum of Ethnology, 1981.

Lee, R. B., and DeVore, I. "Problems in the Study of Hunters and Gatherers." In R. B. Lee and I. DeVore, eds., *Man the Hunter.* Chicago: Aldine, 1968.

Machida, H. "The Impact of the Kikai Eruptions on Prehistoric Japan." In M. J. Hudson, ed., *Interdisciplinary Study on the Origins of Japanese Peoples and Cultures.* Kyoto: International Research Center for Japanese Studies, 2000.

Marcus, Joyce. "The Peaks and Valleys of Ancient States: An Extension of the Dynamic Model." In G. M. Feinman and J. Marcus, eds., *Archaic States.* Santa Fe, NM: School of American Research Press, 1998.

Matsu'ura, S. "A Chronological Review of Pleistocene Human Remains from the Japanese Archipelago." In K. Omoto, ed., *Interdisciplinary Perspectives on the Origins of the Japanese.* Kyoto: International Research Center for Japanese Studies, 1999.

Mills, B. J. "The Establishment and Defeat of Hierarchy: Inalienable Possessions and the History of Collective Prestige Structures in the Pueblo Southwest." *American Anthropologist* 106 (2004): 238–51.

Mizoguchi, Koji. "The Reproduction of Archaeological Discourse: The Case of Japan." *Journal of European Archaeology* 5 (1997): 149–65.

Mizoguchi, Koji. *An Archaeological History of Japan, 30,000 B.C. to A.D. 700.* Philadelphia: University of Pennsylvania Press, 2002.

Nakahashi, T., and Iizuka, M. "Anthropological Study of the Transition from the Jōmon to the Yayoi Periods in Northern Kyūshū Using Morphological and Paleodemographic Features." *Anthropological Science,* Jap. ser. 106 (1998): 31–53.

Nishida, Masaki. "The Emergence of Food Production in Neolithic Japan." *Journal of Anthropological Archaeology* 2 (1983): 305–22.

Ōhama Eikan. *Yaeyama no kōkogaku*. Ishigaki: Sakishima Bunka Kenkyūjo, 1999.

Olsen, John W. "China's Earliest Inhabitants." *Journal of East Asian Archaeology* 2 (2000): 1–7.

Osada Toshiki and Vovin, Alexander, eds. *Perspectives on the Origins of the Japanese Language*. Kyoto: International Research Center for Japanese Studies, 2003.

Pearson, Richard J. "The Nature of Japanese Archaeology." *Asian Perspectives* 31 (1992): 115–27.

Pearson, Richard J. "The Place of Okinawa in Japanese Historical Identity." In Donald Denoon, Mark J. Hudson, Gavan McCormack, and Tessa Morris-Suzuki, eds., *Multicultural Japan: Palaeolithic to Postmodern*. Cambridge: Cambridge University Press, 1996; rev. edn., 2001.

Pearson, Richard J. "Excavations at Sumiya and Other Sakishima Sites: Variations in Okinawan Leadership around AD 1500." *Bulletin of the Indo-Pacific Prehistory Association* 23 (2003): 95–111.

Pietrusewsky, Michael. "A Multivariate Craniometric Study of the Inhabitants of the Ryūkyū Islands and Comparisons with Cranial Series from Japan, Asia, and the Pacific." *Anthropological Science* 107 (1999): 255–81.

Piggott, Joan R. *The Emergence of Japanese Kingship*. Stanford, Calif.: Stanford University Press, 1997.

Rice, P. M. "On the Origins of Pottery." *Journal of Archaeological Method and Theory* 6 (1999): 1–54.

Roberts, Luke. *Mercantilism in a Japanese Domain: The Merchant Origins of Economic Nationalism in 18th-Century Tosa*. Cambridge: Cambridge University Press, 1998.

Rowley-Conwy, P., and Zvelebil, M. "Saving It for Later: Storage by Prehistoric Hunter-Gatherers in Europe." In P. Halstead and J. O'Shea, eds., *Bad Year Economics: Cultural Responses to Risk and Uncertainty*. Cambridge: Cambridge University Press, 1989.

Sato, Hiroyuki. *Nihon kyūsekki bunka no kōzō to shinka*. Tokyo: Kashiwa Shobō, 1992.

Sato, Y., Yamanaka, S., and Takahashi, M. "Evidence for Jōmon Plant Cultivation Based on DNA Analysis of Chestnut Remains." In J. Habu, J. M. Savelle, S. Koyama, and H. Hongo, eds., *Hunter-Gatherers of the North Pacific Rim*. Osaka: National Museum of Ethnology, 2003.

Serafim, Leon A. "When and from Where Did the Japonic Language Enter the Ryūkyūs?" In T. Osada and A. Vovin, eds., *Perspectives on the Origins of the Japanese Language*. Kyoto: International Research Center for Japanese Studies, 2003.

Seyock, Barbara. *Auf den Spuren der Ostbarbaren: Zur Archäologie protohistorischer Kuturen in Südkorea und Westjapan*. Münster: LIT Verlag, 2004.

Spriggs, M. "Early Agriculture and What Went Before in Island Melanesia: Continuity or Intrusion?" In D. R. Harris, ed., *The Origins and Spread of Agriculture and Pastoralism in Eurasia*. London: UCL Press, 1996.

Terasawa Kaoru. "Commentary on the Productive Capacity of Early Japanese Rice Farming." In Yasuda Yoshinori, ed., *The Origins of Pottery and Agriculture*. New Delhi: Lustre Press, 2002.

Teshigawara Akira. *Jōmon bunka*. Tokyo: Shin Nihon, 1998.

Torrence, R. "Hunter-Gatherer Technology: Macro- and Microscale Approaches." In C. Panter-Brick, R. H. Layton, and P. Rowley-Conwy, eds., *Hunter-Gatherers: An Interdisciplinary Perspective*. Cambridge: Cambridge University Press, 2001.

Trigger, Bruce G. *A History of Archaeological Thought*. Cambridge: Cambridge University Press, 1989.

Tsuboi Kiyotari and Tanaka Migaku. *The Historic City of Nara: An Archaeological Approach*. Paris and Tokyo: UNESCO and Centre for East Asian Cultural Studies, 1991.

Tsude, H. "The Kofun Period and State Formation." *Acta Asiatica* 63 (1992): 64–86.

Tsukada, M. "Vegetation in Prehistoric Japan: The Last 20,000 Years." In R. J. Pearson, G. L. Barnes, and K. L. Hutterer, eds., *Windows on the Japanese Past: Studies in Archaeology and Prehistory.* Ann Arbor: Center for Japanese Studies, University of Michigan, 1986.

Tsunoda, Ryusaku, and Goodrich, L. Carrington. *Japan in the Chinese Dynastic Histories.* South Pasadena, Calif.: P. D. and Ione Perkins, 1951.

Uchiyama, J. "San'ei-cho and Meat-eating in Buddhist Edo." *Japanese Journal of Religious Studies* 19 (1992): 299–303.

Uno Takao. *Ritsuryō shakai no kōkogakuteki kenkyū.* Toyama: Kashiwa Shobō, 1991.

Wakasa, T. "Water Rights, Water Rituals, Chiefly Compounds, and *Haniwa*: Ritual and Regional Development in the Kofun Period." In *Cultural Diversity and the Archaeology of the 21st Century*, ed. Society of Archaeological Studies. Okayama: Kōkogaku Kenkyūkai, 2004.

Walker, Brett L. *The Conquest of Ainu Lands: Ecology and Culture in Japanese Expansion, 1590–1800.* Berkeley: University of California Press, 2001.

Yasuda Yoshinori. *Prehistoric Environment in Japan: Palynological Approach.* Sendai: Institute of Geography, Tōhoku University, 1978.

FURTHER READING

The best introduction to the archaeology is Gina L. Barnes, *China, Korea and Japan: The Rise of Civilization in East Asia* (London: Thames and Hudson, 1993), which brilliantly integrates ancient Japan into the regional context. Keiji Imamura, *Prehistoric Japan: New Perspectives on Insular East Asia* (Honolulu: University of Hawai'i Press, 1996) provides a more detailed account of Japanese archaeology. An up-to-date analysis of the Jōmon can be found in Junko Habu, *Ancient Jōmon of Japan* (Cambridge: Cambridge University Press, 2004). Mark Hudson, *Ruins of Identity: Ethnogenesis in the Japanese Islands* (Honolulu: University of Hawai'i Press, 1999) contains an extensive discussion and bibliography on research relating to the origins of Japanese peoples. William Wayne Farris, *Sacred Texts and Buried Treasures: Issues in the Historical Archaeology of Ancient Japan* (Honolulu: University of Hawai'i Press, 1998) discusses aspects of the historical archaeology of the Yayoi to Nara periods. Volume 1 of *The Cambridge History of Japan* (Cambridge: Cambridge University Press, 1993) remains an essential overview of the documentary history of ancient Japan. The major texts of the Nara period are available in English translation as *Kojiki*, translated by Donald Philippi (Tokyo: University of Tokyo Press, 1968) and *Nihongi: Chronicles of Japan from the Earliest Times to* AD *697*, translated by W. G. Aston (Rutland, Vt.: Charles E. Tuttle, 1972).

CHAPTER TWO

The Heian Period

G. Cameron Hurst III

Heian is Japan's classical age, when court power was at its zenith and aristocratic culture flourished. Understandably, it has long been assiduously studied by historians. The Heian period is the longest of the accepted divisions of Japanese history, covering almost exactly 400 years. Its dates seem obvious: "The Heian period opened in 794 with the building of a new capital, Heian-kyō, later known as Kyoto. ... The Heian period closed in 1185 when the struggle for hegemony among the warrior families resulted in the victory of Minamoto no Yoritomo and most political initiatives devolved into his hands at his headquarters at Kamakura."[1] Although the establishment of a new capital would seem irrefutable evidence of the start of a new "period," some argue that the move of the capital from Nara to Nagaoka in 784 better marks the beginning of the era. Indeed, some even consider the accession of Emperor Kammu in 781 a better starting date. Heian gives way to the next period, the Kamakura era, at the end of the twelfth century and the conclusion of the Gempei War. The end dates are even more contested and include (1) 1180 and Taira no Kiyomori's forced move of the capital to Fukuhara; (2) 1183 and the flight of the Taira from the capital; (3) 1185, the end of the war and Retired Emperor Go-Shirakawa's confirmation of Minamoto no Yoritomo's right to appoint *shugo* and *jitō*, or (4) 1192 and Yoritomo's appointment as shōgun. The most conventional date, as indicated in *The Cambridge History of Japan*, is 1185.

The Heian period obviously takes its name from the fact that the capital was located there, although of course that situation did not technically change for the rest of premodern Japanese history, even if the center of *power* may have shifted. But the subsequent period is marked off by the assumption of greater political power by the newly risen warrior class, whose political center was established by Yoritomo in Kamakura. Thus the Heian period is essentially a political division reflecting an era in which power was exercised from the capital at Heian. In distinction to the subsequent eras of warrior power, it is seen as an age dominated by a small cluster of aristocrats who ruled under the aegis of the emperor by mastery of the civil rather than the military arts. Thus, the term "Heian" (the characters mean "peace" and "tranquility") suggests cultural considerations as well as political, namely literature, art, Chinese learning, and Buddhist thought. Indeed, for contemporary Japanese the most vivid reminders of their Heian period are likely Murasaki Shikibu's literary classic *Genji monogatari* (*The Tale of Genji*) and the cultural splendor of the early eleventh century.

Historical Limitations

The study of Heian history is limited by the amount of surviving materials and their focus. There is an almost inevitable problem that the focus is on the politics and culture of the capital and its immediate environs (the five home provinces or *gokinai*) rather than the provinces. Partly that has to do with the survival of historical materials. It is virtually axiomatic that the closer we come to the present era, the greater the availability of printed materials for the study of history. Thus the Heian period is definitely resource-rich compared to the Nara period, yet it is woefully bereft of documents compared, for example, to the Kamakura.

Court-sponsored official histories came to an end with the death of Emperor Kōkō in 887, and later private histories were much abbreviated in coverage and focused more upon the activities of the inner court. Thanks to the heroic efforts of the late Takeuchi Rizō, however, all the surviving diplomatics (*komonjo*) of the period are collected into the *Heian ibun*. For the first 300 years of the period, until the inauguration of Shirakawa's rule as abdicated emperor, there are only 1,250 such documents. (Yet we know that the *ritsuryō* state generated a mountain of paperwork. It is estimated that in the tenth century, for example, central government scribes produced more than 350 million characters per year! This figure is impressive, even though it does not even include "numerous documents issued by provincial and district offices and villages, Buddhist institutions, personal writings, or correspondence.")[2] Thereafter surviving documents increase in number, but the collected Kamakura period sources (*Kamakura ibun*) far outnumber Heian documents, although the period covers only a century and a half. Fortunately, these few Heian documents can be supplemented by a number of surviving diaries of courtiers, primarily members of the Fujiwara clan such as Michinaga and Sanesuke and at least two emperors; but while these are often quite detailed in nature, their scope is limited to say the least, concerned largely with the details of court life in the capital. Thus, the period is not easily recreated from the surviving materials.

A good example, to be discussed at greater length below, is the early tenth century when the strenuous efforts of Emperor Kammu to reinvigorate the *ritsuryō* institutions were abandoned for a series of reforms of local control that more realistically addressed the complex mix of public and private land holdings in the countryside. While the outlines of the changes have become clear over the past few decades, detailed sources on the actual political decision-making process are rare indeed.

By comparison, there is a rather large collection of literary outpourings from the Heian period in various genres, so that, compared to the work of historians of Heian politics and society, literature specialists have considerable materials to rely upon. This has tended to skew writings on the Heian period towards the cultural aspects of the society, especially outside of Japan. In English, for example, there is a decided lack of materials on the history of the Heian period, despite its length and recognized importance in Japanese history. Only in 1999 did Cambridge University Press publish volume 2 (*Heian Japan*) of its *Cambridge History of Japan*, despite the fact that the authors had been working on it for at least two decades. Moreover, the bibliography identified fewer than ten single volumes devoted wholly or even mainly to the Heian period. My own *Insei: Abdicated Sovereigns in the Politics of Late Heian Japan*,

1086–1185, for example, still contains far more political history of the early and mid-Heian period than any other work, although it was published almost thirty years ago, in 1976. For some reason – not only dearth of sources, but also perhaps the difficulty of deciphering them – the Heian period has not attracted the interest of many historians outside Japan. (See the discussion of Western scholarship below.)

The Transition from Nara to Heian, 784–794

The problem with setting a date for the beginning of Heian is related to the complexity of political problems and capital construction in the late eighth century under Emperor Kammu. Kammu, perhaps the strongest emperor in Japanese history, was fortunate ever to have become sovereign. The Nara court had fallen under the influence of the Buddhist priest Dōkyō and his associates during the reign of Empress Shōtoku (764–70), who had previously reigned as Kōken (749–58). Dōkyō was exiled at the empress's death. The courtier responsible for the exile, Fujiwara no Momokawa, was also the primary supporter of Emperor Kōnin (770–81), Kammu's father, who came to the throne at the age of 62. At length, Momokawa was also responsible for Kammu's own accession after the mysterious death of Crown Prince Osabe in 775. Kammu was Kōnin's eldest son, but was not originally seen as the successor due to the low status of his mother (of Paekche descent), but Momokawa eventually swayed the court in Kammu's favor.

Abandoning the capital at Nara after only seventy years was partly a reaction against the deep secular influence of the entrenched Buddhist clergy at Nara, as exemplified by the ascendancy of Dōkyō, as well as by the imposing temple that seem to overwhelm the emperor's own palace. There were political reasons as well (see below), and a fear of the vengeful spirits of the deceased Prince Osabe and his mother. Perhaps more importantly, Emperor Kōnin's accession represented a shift in the imperial line away from the descendants of former Emperor Temmu (r. 668–71) to those of Tenji (r. 672–86), and the move of the capital seems to have represented a choice to move from the seat of the Tenji-based lineage in Yamato province around Nara northeast to Yamashiro, an area in which the Temmu line was dominant.[3]

At any rate, Kammu and his court selected the area in Yamashiro known as Nagaoka for the construction of a new capital and appointed Momokawa's nephew Tanetsugu (whose maternal family was also from the Nagaoka area) to manage the project, which required massive amounts of conscripted peasant labor. Although the city was far from complete, Kammu moved there in the fifth month of 784. Indeed, had things gone according to plan, we might today be studying the "Nagaoka period" of Japanese history, but fate intervened to effect the further transfer to Heian. The proximate cause was the assassination of Fujiwara no Tanetsugu. His death was related to yet another struggle over succession, this time between Kammu's younger brother and Crown Prince Sawara and his eldest son Prince Ate, favored as next sovereign by Tanetsugu. When Tanetsugu was attacked and murdered in the streets of Nagaoka one night in the ninth month of 785, suspicion fell on Prince Sawara and associates in the Otomo family. Exiled to the island of Awaji, Sawara died soon thereafter. Sawara was generally believed to have been the innocent victim of a plot, and his vengeful spirit regarded as the cause of the sudden deaths of Kammu's mother and empress, as well as the source of an epidemic and other unusual occurrences. Haunted by their spirits, Kammu elected to move yet again to Heian.

Thus, the decade from 784 to 794, which saw the move to and abandonment of Nagaoka, falls somewhere between the Nara and the Heian periods. No one has chosen to label this decade the "Nagaoka period," and it is most commonly seen as the tail end of the Nara era. Yet the above discussion suggests that it might just as easily fall within the boundaries of the Heian period as well.

Underlying Assumptions

Two underlying assumptions seem to govern the historiography of Heian Japan. First, there is a sense that the period represents a privatization of the political and economic institutions of the state. The period commences with an attempt to reinvigorate the imported system of administration based upon a Tang Chinese bureaucratic model, largely seen as "public" insofar as land and people were to be nationalized under the public authority of an omnipotent emperor. But slowly, public lands developed into private holdings, specific public offices became the "private" preserves of certain families, and familial and local interest overrode public needs. In slightly different terms, the late John W. Hall, in a path-breaking work, cast the Heian period as a time of "return to familial authority," arguing that the Chinese bureaucratic model was simply laid over an earlier Japan native form of familial authority. It was this "familial authority" that reasserted itself in Heian times, as represented by the *shōen* system, indirect rule by Fujiwara regents and retired sovereigns through familial ties, and incipient feudal warrior bands, bound by patron–client relations to royal and noble houses.[4]

A second and related concept is that Heian Japan represents a return to "native" traditions. This is especially strong in the cultural area, but again is part of the idea that Japan in the Taika and Nara eras had attempted to buttress a weakly organized emergent polity by the wholesale adoption of things Chinese, not only the bureaucratic-legal system, but its language, art and architecture, and Buddhist and Confucian thought as well. By the mid-Heian period, however, with the emergence of the *kana*-based syllabary, a "native" literature blossomed. Moreover, artistic representations became more Japanese, and Shintō–Buddhist religious syncretism resulted in a more "Japanese" form of religious expression. It is in this sense that Heian represents Japan's "classical age," a time when a truly Japanese culture flourished.

Heian Political History

Since the Japanese borrowed the periodization scheme of European history in the Meiji period, and found that it accorded rather well with the Japanese experience, the Heian period has been grouped with the Nara era as constituting "ancient Japan," the establishment of warrior government in Kamakura and the ascendancy of warriors seemingly indicating an easy association with the "medieval" era. This is still the way most texts and sets of volumes devoted to Japanese history present the pageant of

Japanese history; and indeed it works far better than imposing Western historical divisions on China, for example, where the Tang and Song dynasties are assigned the role of "medieval" China with little more justification than that they fall somewhere in the dynastic middle.

But many scholars have not found it so easy to equate "Heian" with "ancient" and "Kamakura" with "medieval," what Wayne Farris has referred to as the "Western analogue" model that once ruled Japanese scholarship and for a long time dominated Western scholarship.[5] On the Japanese side, the dominance of Marxist historical analysis in the decades following World War II sparked a greater concern with social and economic organization and led most scholars to see "medieval" Japan as beginning in the Heian period, connected with the rise of *shōen*. Western scholarship, as well as some Japanese scholars have, in the past several decades, tended instead to narrow the borders of Japan's medieval era by recasting the Kamakura as very early medieval or late ancient, due to the persistence of Heian institutions, wishing to see a more truly medieval, often considered as synonymous with feudal, society commencing with full ascension to political power by the warrior aristocracy in the fourteenth century. Thus the 1997 volume resulting from an Oxford conference in 1994 and edited by the late Jeffrey P. Mass was titled *The Origins of Japan's Medieval World: Courtiers, Cleric, Warriors and Peasants in the Fourteenth Century*.

But if all the Heian period has been normally lumped into the ancient period, tremendous differences in political and economic organization marked off certain centuries of these 400 years, allowing historians to delineate subdivisions of the Heian era. The simplest division is to separate the period into early and late Heian at the mid tenth century. The first period witnesses the survival of the borrowed Tang Chinese *ritsuryō* system, with significant "feudal" tendencies developing in society, and then the latter period represents a greater degree of feudalization in the countryside that undermined the *ritsuryō* state and gave rise to new forms of political control by first the Fujiwara regency, then the retired emperors, and finally yielded to the rule of warriors.

Historians everywhere seem to favor tripartite divisions (a beginning, middle, and end), and so sometimes the early period is seen as followed by a middle period when the Fujiwara dominated the court, and then a late period when retired sovereigns controlled court politics. But a four-part division, an elaboration of the early–late schema with a further elaboration on each end, is perhaps the most common form of Heian periodization. This division is political, following what appears to be somewhat obvious changes in the central administration of the Heian state.

Early Heian, 794–887

The first period, early Heian, is deemed to cover roughly the first 100 years of Heian, the "capital for ten thousand reigns," and focusing on the reigns of Kammu to Uda. It is seen often as an extension of the Nara period, and with good reason since Emperor Kammu lived in the three capitals of the day: enthroned in Nara, he erected a new capital at Nagaoka to which he moved, before once again constructing a larger capital at Heian and moving once again. Kammu, the most vigorous of Heian emperors, had endeavored to breathe life back into the Tang-style administrative system that had developed in Nara times, but he was besieged by problems: the undue

influence of Buddhist clergy in political affairs; recalcitrant and difficult-to-subdue
Ezo in the northeast; the malfunctioning of provincial tax extraction methods, which
resulted in large numbers of absconding peasants; and the murder of Fujiwara no
Tanetsugu and subsequent deaths of several of Kammu's relatives which threw a
decided unease over Nagaoka.

The administrative system, modeled on borrowed Tang Chinese statutes compiled
into the *ritsuryō* code (*ritsu* are the penal laws, *ryō* the administrative statutes), was
designed to recreate on Japanese soil an approximate model of the Tang imperium,
despite the tremendous differences in the levels of development of the two countries.
Primary among the many features of the *ritsuryō*, or statutory, system was a complex
land census system designed to extract taxes for the governing of the state, including
the sizeable incomes of the imperial house and officials who administered the state.
Land was considered national and allotted only to individual families, under a formula
that allocated land differentially to the male, female, and slave members of families on
a regular basis. To make the system work, a national census was to be taken every six
years so that changes in family size would be reflected in each subsequent allocation.
Needless to say, levels of provincial government literacy and talent, not to mention
honesty, hampered the smooth application of such a complex system, with the result
that regularized tax extraction was difficult. Peasants fled in large numbers to escape
harsh taxation – corvée and military service were the most burdensome – and nobles,
temples, and shrines took advantage of loopholes in the system and the fleeing
peasants to form private estate holdings of their own.

Kammu tried various measures, the most important being the appointment of
kageyushi (inspectors), to audit the tax registers and hold accountable the centrally
appointed provincial governors for the proper allocation, accounting, and forwarding
of provincial tax revenues. Attempts to revitalize the statutory system continued under
his next several successors: changes included the stabilization of imperial house finances
through the establishment of the *chokushiden* (edict fields) and a thoroughgoing reform
of state finances. There was also a demonstrated commitment to a court-dominated
Tang cultural style. Noble families established private educational academies; the court
sponsored official national histories; and the new forms of Buddhism introduced from
China, Tendai and Shingon, flourished. Thus, the early Heian period as a whole is
regarded as one in which the Japanese court maintained a dogged adherence to imported
Chinese higher civilization. But changes necessary to shore up the *ritsuryō* system already
presaged significant changes in the second division of the Heian period.

Among those changes was the widespread development of private landholding, the
spread of estates or *shōen*. Furthermore, the rise of what in the next period would
became the full-blown Fujiwara regency style of rule was foreshadowed by the
development of two new regental posts (*sesshō* and *kampaku*) by the father–son duo
of Fujiwara no Yoshifusa and Mototsune. Moreover, the Fujiwara family engineered
several plots that eliminated rivals for power.

The Period 887–967

Against the background of these developments, the second subdivision of Heian
Japan is the eighty-year period in which Emperors Uda and Daigo were able to

exercise considerable power without the influence of Fujiwara regents, which would become dominant by the latter part of the tenth century. This era covers the late ninth to the mid tenth century, was often referred to as the "rule of the Engi and Tenryaku," and was looked back upon fondly by later commentators and modern historians cognizant that the Fujiwara would soon eclipse the imperial house in the exercise of actual power. During the era, the Northern Branch (*Hokke*) of the Fujiwara consolidated power in the clan under Tokihira and Tadahira, although Emperor Uda sponsored Sugawara no Michizane as a counterweight to the Fujiwara. There was an effort to curtail the rising private holdings of nobles and temples and other attempts (notably the ceding of considerable local autonomy to local governors, of which more later) to maintain the emperor-based power structure inherent in the *ritsuryō* system. Moreover, it was an era that saw the addition of amendments (*kyaku* and *shiki*) to make the *ritsuryō* system more appropriate to Japanese social realities, and that also witnessed the compilation of a final national history, the *Sandai jitsuryoku*. Thus, it has often been referred to as a "golden age" of imperial rule.

The Period 967–1068

The third subperiod of Heian times is the era that most Japanese associate with the period as a whole, the roughly 100-year period from the mid tenth through the mid eleventh centuries, which represented the zenith of Fujiwara power and as well as the cultural flourishing of the court. Beginning with the exile of Fujiwara rival Minamoto no Takaakira in the so-called Anna Incident of 969, one lineage within the Northern Branch of the Fujiwara clan came to dominate the positions of regent and chancellor as well as to monopolize many high-ranking posts that constituted the noble (*kugyō*) council where most decisions were made. It was the era in which Fujiwara no Michinaga, widely acknowledged as the most powerful figure at the Heian court, not only in historical retrospect but at the time as well, and his son Yorimichi held power for some seven decades. Besides a few select Fujiwara lineages, only members of the imperial offshoot Murakami branch of the Minamoto held any of the significant posts at court.

The dominant sociopolitical feature of the era was the institution of an essentially permanent regency by one Fujiwara lineage – the so-called Fujiwara regent's house – through the monopolization of the right to provide official consorts to the imperial house. Thus strategic marriages of his many daughters to successive emperors made Michinaga father to three emperors and grandfather to two more. The largely uxorilocal Heian marriage practices guaranteed that emperors were born of Fujiwara mothers and dominated by their maternal kinsmen in Fujiwara mansions from birth. It was this close marital relationship that allowed the exercise of regental power on behalf of increasingly young emperors by their Fujiwara fathers, grandfathers, or uncles.

The era represents the apex of Japanese court life in which the development of Japanese *kana* syllabary led to a burst of literary production, especially by court women. At the top of the list is Lady Murasaki Shikibu's *Genji monogatari* (*The Tale of Genji*), but there were many more works that would later be recognized as Japanese classics, such as *The Pillow Book* (*Makura no sōshi*) of Sei Shōnagon, *Kagerō nikki* (*The Gossamer Diary*) by a court lady known as the Mother of Michitsuna, and the diary of Lady Murasaki (*Murasaki Shikibu nikki*).

The *Insei*, 1068–1185

The final 120 years of the Heian period are normally referred to as the *insei*, characterized by the shift of state power into the hands of three successive retired emperors.
The era is usually regarded as commencing with the accession of Emperor Go-Sanjō in
1068, the first sovereign in 170 years not born to the daughter of a Fujiwara mother.
Consequently, Go-Sanjō exercised an unusual degree of political power, and in abdication directed the succession towards his sons of a Minamoto empress. This paved the
way for a revival of imperial power under Shirakawa, Toba, and Go-Shirakawa, each of
whom served as cloistered (*in*) emperor, directing state affairs from retirement on
behalf of young emperors in much the same way Fujiwara regents had done in the
previous era. Under the *insei* system, the imperial house accumulated estate holdings,
clients, and military supporters in a fashion similar to that of the Fujiwara.

Another key feature of the era was the rise to prominence of the warrior element
in the "peaceful" capital of Heian. Literally *samurai*, or clients in the service of higher
ranking courtiers, warriors provided military and police protection to the state as
mercenary troops, "hired swords," in Karl Friday's term.[6] By the *insei* era, warrior
clientage for the Fujiwara and imperial houses covered several generations, and two
large warrior groupings with widespread provincial holdings, the Taira and
Minamoto, had influence in Heian politics, primarily as provincial governors providing wealth as well as military support for the higher nobility.

The Taira especially, as clients of successive retired emperors, made inroads into
court society, and after two major outbursts of political violence in the capital – the
Hōgen Rebellion of 1156 and the Heiji Rebellion of 1159 – they eclipsed the
Minamoto in military influence. Not only that, but under the leadership of Taira no
Kiyomori, the family was able to break into the heretofore sacrosanct ranks of the
kugyō, thanks to the patronage of former Emperor Go-Shirakawa. By the 1170s,
however, Kiyomori even challenged the power of his patron; and when his own
grandson became emperor (the infant Antoku), he tried to rule in a manner reminiscent of earlier Fujiwara regents. Kiyomori's unprecedented rise to authoritarian power
led to widespread discontent among courtiers both high and low – Kiyomori even
decreed the removal of the capital briefly to Fukuhara (modern Kobe). Responding to a
decree by Prince Mochihito, the Minamoto scion Yoritomo, in exile in Izu Province,
led a movement against the Taira that widened into national civil war, later termed the
Gempei (Minamoto–Taira) War. It pitted various branches of the Minamoto, as well a
considerable numbers of local lords, without respect to clan affiliation, seeking greater
security over land tenure against the Taira-backed court. The resulting defeat of the
Taira forces at the Battle of Dannoura in the third month of 1185 effectively brought
an end not only to the Taira, but to the Heian period as well.

Ōchō Kokka (The "Royal Court State")

What has been described at length above is the standard narrative account of the
unfolding of the Heian period, but it obviously focuses upon slight reconstitutions of
the ruling style or group: from emperor to Fujiwara regent to retired emperor,

leading next to shōgun. It is sketched against a backdrop of the decline and gradual extinction of the *ritsuryō* system (identified as the ancient state) based on the ideal of public lands and public subjects and its replacement by rising provincial warriors in a "feudal" system (identified as medieval Japan) in which private landholding and personal affiliations characteristic of the *shōen*, or manorial, system are paramount. Especially problematic is explaining how the *ritsuryō* state control could decline and provincial administration deteriorate at the same time as the eleventh century witnessed such a brilliant cultural flowering.

Since the 1970s, however, there has arisen a slightly different way of breaking down the Heian period's four centuries that more closely relates the political and cultural developments in the capital with the social and economic changes in the provinces. This is the idea of the so-called *ōchō kokka*, or "royal court state," associated most closely with Sakamoto Shōzō but now widely accepted by historians.[7] Noting that political history is inseparable from state policy-making, Sakamoto argues that there were two substantive changes in the state power structure in Heian times but these did not necessarily result in changes in the holders of power. As Cornelius Kiley once described the manner in which the state gradually lost control over agricultural output and military power: "The government lost a great deal of authority; the nobility, as a class, lost somewhat less."[8] The "royal court state" theory argues that by reorganizing the state the rulers maintained control.

In this now widely accepted division of the Heian period, there are three distinct eras, each marked by a certain reorganization of state power. The first period is relatively similar to that elaborated above, that is, the *ritsuryō* or statutory state structure reinvigorated by Emperor Kammu, which continued until the early tenth century when it was replaced by the "early" royal court state. The early royal court state continued until 1040, when under the regency of Fujiwara no Yorimichi, another major change is instituted, which constitutes the "late" royal court state. That continues until replacement by the "medieval" state represented by the Kamakura bakufu.

Statutory State Period, 784–902

This early period follows that explained in the Heian outline above. It places great emphasis upon the decision to move out of the Temmu-line stronghold of Nara to first Nagaoka, then Heian, both fully located within the Tenji-line of the imperial house represented by Kammu. The move of the capital is coupled with two important political changes. On the one hand, Kammu attempted to administer politics by firm control of the bureaucracy through the operation of the Grand Council of State (*Dajōkan*) within the palace. On the other hand, the noble class underwent something of a structural change, as some important clans of the Nara era fell in the late eighth century, to be replaced by newly risen clans employed by Kammu in the *sangi*, or imperial advisor, rank. For most of the Heian period, no more than ten clans played significant roles.

The primary weakening of the statutory state was, as noted above, the inability of the complex land distribution system based on censuses conducted every six years. The last year it was done on a nation-wide basis was in 800, after which it was conducted only periodically in various of the provinces. In short, the attempt of the state to impose control over the populace through this complex census and tax system failed, although noble attempts were exerted to keep it alive throughout the ninth century, most notably by minister of the left Fujiwara no Tokihira in the early years of Emperor Daigo.

Early Royal Court State, 902–1040

A major change in the state structure occurred with the failure of late ninth-century attempts to reinvigorate the *ritsuryō* system, when Tokihira's brother Fujiwara no Tadahira was minister of the left under Emperor Daigo. This change came in the way in which the state extracted taxes from the provincial populace for support of the court, and was significant enough to cause historians to recognize the existence of the *ōchō kokka*, or royal court state structure, in its early phase. Essentially, the state abandoned a hands-on approach to provincial rule, and instead effectively contracted out local administration to governors, now increasingly known by the term *zuryō* or tax managers. In return for allowing the governors a free hand in the provinces, the state required a fixed amount of tax revenue to be forwarded to the capital. The state did not neglect the provinces, but in actuality the nobles did little more than debate issues submitted to them from the governors for review or decision.

Moreover, the state abandoned the regularized taxation of individuals in favor of taxing the land: it was "real" estate, immobile property, as opposed to unreliable individuals who fled in large numbers to avoid taxation. Lands were now formed into units called *myō*, which became the basic unit for the levying of all manner of taxes. Responsibility for collecting taxes levied on the unit was borne by one of the cultivators termed a *fumyō*, many of whom, through association with the land, later became *myōshu* or "holders of *myō*." Provincial governors were then able to have a free hand in collecting local taxes and allocating corvée labor, as long as they forwarded to the central government the revenues assigned to their provinces. The state did not totally abandon the provinces; and if a major problem arose, central officials would be dispatched to investigate. In times of crisis, a centrally approved expeditionary force might be sent against an uprising.

This scenario alters somewhat our evaluation of the central nobility. Historians had long argued that the Heian nobility, represented by the Fujiwara regent's house, simply surrendered interest in government to concentrate more upon the proper execution of ritual and ceremony in accord with past precedent, which accounted for a decline in politics, which in turn led to the degeneration of local politics. Under the royal court state theory, however, it is argued that the nobility, by contracting out local administration, was able to maintain the state structure by lessening their administrative duties in comparison to the earlier age. But the court nobles, dominated in this age by Michinaga, and then Yorimichi, did not simply occupy themselves with what appears to moderns to be meaningless ritual. In the first place, in Heian society, the distinction between ritual and substance was not recognized, and the proper performance of actions was seen as crucial to successful policies. Second, Michinaga and the other nobles were intensely concerned with politics; and the zeal with which they addressed, for example, the appointment of governors, who guaranteed the flow of income from periphery to the center, was noteworthy.[9]

It was during this period, however, that conditions in the provinces deteriorated, as governors extracted excessive taxes from the peasantry; and powerful local notables, including governors, large-scale farmers, and members of the aristocracy collaborated to expand privately held *shōen* at the expense of publicly held (taxable) land. This was a more important development in the next period, and indeed a close reading of the diary of Fujiwara no Michinaga reveals little information about *shōen*. But the degree of local unrest and discontent was exemplified in this period by the outbreak of two major provincial uprisings in 939, Taira no Masakado in the east and Fujiwara no Sumitomo in the west. Still, the reorganized royal court state was able to subdue them through the appointment of court-appointed commanders leading private forces recruited as mercenaries in the service of the state from among men just like those who rose against the state.[10]

Late Royal Court State, 1040–1185

The royal court theory recognizes Fujiwara no Yorimichi's regency as marking another change in the royal state, especially the numerous changes in administrative structures and systems at the local level. Rising members of the military class were appointed as heads of administrative units such as *gun, gō, ho,* and *mura,* which these local elites gradually turned into private holdings, or *shōen,* over the course of medieval times. The changes in the royal state are seen as commencing with the 1140 *shōen* regulation ordinance (*seiriryō*), the first of a series of ordinances designed to confront the expansion of private estates.

An important step in this effort came during the reign of Go-Sanjō (1068–72), a rare emperor with no Fujiwara family connection, whose unavoidable enthronement (there were simply no male heirs to Fujiwara consorts at the time) caused the resignation of Yorimichi as chancellor in 1067. Among efforts to restore economic health, Go-Sanjō issued an edict in 1069 restricting severely the acquisition of estates by nobles and temple complexes. Moreover, he established the Records Office (*kirokujo*), which provided for the first time a mechanism for adjudicating the legality of holdings. Although it ceased to function shortly after Go-Sanjō's death, the Records Office was revived in 1111, and again in 1156, to serve as an organ of dispute settlement between provincial governors (representing the state) and local landholders. But more importantly, this office, "in its charge to regulate (systematize) the estates, ... established a new syntax of landholding," which really amounted to the possibility of the estate system.[11]

The politics of the late royal court state period involved the three retired sovereigns Shirakawa, Toba, and Go-Shirakawa succeeding in reviving the imperial house as a private competitive source of power, with its own administrative apparatus (*in no chō*), its own retainers and clients, and its own portfolio of estate holdings. While the retired sovereigns did establish new offices and procedures, for the most part they succeeded in dominating the existing organs of state by turning many of the court officials into their clients, including the most powerful warriors house in the land, the Ise Taira. Japanese historians consistently refer to the retired sovereigns as ruling in a "despotic" fashion. In fact, however, they ruled with cooperation with the noble and warrior houses, and with considerable spiritual support from the major temples and shrines in the capital region.

What brought an end to the Heian period in the late royal court state era was a shift in the power structure, as Taira no Kiyomori, long a client in the service of Go-Shirakawa, tried to usurp power from the retired sovereign, most markedly in a major dismissal of anti-Taira courtiers among Go-Shirakawa's followers in 1177, and then in 1179, when he imprisoned Go-Shirakawa and forced the chancellor to resign. After that there was a short-lived Taira regime that dominated the court until anti-Taira elements, led by the forces under Minamoto no Yoritomo, toppled them at the Battle of Dannonura in 1185.

The *Kemmon* Theory of Joint Rulership

Another important development in the way historians regard the Heian period, especially the last century and a half, is the theory of joint rulership espoused by the late Kuroda Toshio.[12] Kuroda's view is broader than just Heian, encompassing the state as organized from the eleventh through the fifteenth centuries. Kuroda regarded the highest authority of the state as shared by three separate but mutually supporting power blocs, or *kemmon*, an abbreviated form of a term that crops up in Heian documents, *kemmon seika*, or "powerful houses and influential families." While historically this referred only to major court families, Kuroda appropriated it and expanded its meaning to include the three power blocs of late ancient and medieval times, the courtiers (*kuge*), the warriors (*buke*), and the major religious institutions (*jisha*).

Earlier, scholars had focused upon the "rise" of the warrior element in the mid- and late Heian period; and although aware of the important linkages, not only spiritual but also in terms of political and economic power, between major religious institutions and both the courtier and warrior orders, they had regarded the great temples separately. Kuroda's work was important because it integrated the religious establishment into the power structure in a more coherent way. There are some problems with Kuroda's analysis, as the religious institutions (primarily Kōfukuji, Enryakuji, and Kōyasan) lacked the same kind of organizing power as the noble families (court) and warriors (bakufu) and did not operate coherently as a single hierarchy, split as they were doctrinally.

Nonetheless, Kuroda argued that the great monasteries had themselves become "*kemmon*-ified" in terms of administrative structure and economic support. All three power blocs shared similar characteristics as elites: private administrative headquarters, edicts for transmitting internal orders, groups of loyal retainers, judicial self-rule within the order, and finally control over private estates. While there was competition among the three elite orders, there was overall a shared rulership, a mutual interdependence that normally overrode competition, as the three elites were "mutually dependent upon each other to maintain their status and wealth: one *kemmon* was never powerful enough to rule without the support of other elites."[13]

Kuroda thus slightly alters the view of Heian political development that had rather mechanically charted the development of courtier power that was then in medieval times replaced by warrior power. While there is no doubt that under the continuing supreme authority of the emperor, ultimate decision-making may have shifted from leading courtiers to warrior hegemons in late ancient and medieval Japan, no *kemmon* was able to rule alone but depended rather upon the support of peers. Thus some scholars now stress the interrelationship between the various *kemmon* in the late Heian–Kamakura period: the Fujiwara family hardly disappeared when the retired sovereigns asserted power during this time, and both continued to share power even after the establishment of the Kamakura bakufu. Meanwhile, the great religious institutions continued to provide religious rituals and comfort for both courtier and warrior elites. It is in fact the continued importance of Heian institutions into the Kamakura era that has led some scholars to push forward the beginning of medieval Japan. Admittedly, few Japanese scholars have adopted outright the terminology of the *kemmon* theory, although their work shows reliance on Kuroda's ideas. In English-language studies, however, it has had an impact, most markedly on the work of Adolphson and Hurst.

Western Scholarship

The study of Japanese history outside Japan has flourished in the past several decades, especially in the United States. (Few have contributed as much as the French scholar Francine Hérail, however.) Doctoral programs at private and public universities have expanded greatly, and few institutions are now without Japanese history courses. Universities and colleges with more than one Japanese historian are no longer uncommon. But the coverage of Japanese history is uneven, as even a quick glance at major bibliographic sources would reveal. There is an obvious imbalance of the modern over the premodern; but even within the premodern period there is likewise unevenness, with the Tokugawa period being the best studied. In fact, there are more English-language books on my shelf devoted to Tokugawa intellectual history than to all of Heian history. This is due to many factors, chief of which is probably the perceived relevance of the later eras to contemporary Japan; and indeed the greater availability of English-language monographs continues to attract more students. Sources likely play a factor: the greater amount of extant historical materials attracts researchers, and the difficulty of deciphering the classical language in the sources discourages would-be scholars of Heian Japan. As a result, there has been little addition to the body of literature in the past three or four decades.

While there is a Further Reading list at the end of this essay, a note about the progress of the study of Heian Japan is in order. There is no one-volume or single-author scholarly book on Heian history in English. There are only a handful that qualify as specifically Heian works: Robert Borgen's work on Sugawara no Michizane, Karl Friday's *Hired Swords*, G. Cameron Hurst's *Insei*, and Ivan Morris's *The World of the Shining Prince*. Several authors devote considerable attention to Heian in works that cover a longer time frame: Asakawa Kan'ichi's pathbreaking *Land and Society in Medieval Japan;* Jeffrey Mass's first and last volumes on the founding of the Kamakura bakufu; two books by William Wayne Farris, one on *Population, Disease, and Land*, the other his *Heavenly Warriors;* Thomas Keirstead's *Geography of Power in Medieval Japan*; another by Friday on *Samurai, Warfare and the State in Early Medieval Japan;* and Michael Adolphson's *Gates of Power*, the first work to deal with the role of the great temples in the Heian era.

Asakawa's collected essays are all pre-World War II, Morris's *Shining Prince* was first published in 1964, Mass's first bakufu volume was published in 1974, Hurst's volume dates to 1976, and Borgen's Michizane book dates back to 1986. The works by Farris and Friday on the Heian military were published in 1992, while Adolphson's volume came out in 2000.

There are of course a number of excellent articles in academic journals devoted to Heian, several of which (Kiley and McCullough) are of such importance that I have included them in the bibliography below. But the point here is to stress just how understudied the Heian period has been in the English-speaking world, indeed anywhere outside of Japan. There are now two indispensable compilations of essays that deal with aspects of Heian history. The old (1974) *Medieval Japan: Essays in Institutional History*, still used as a textbook in many premodern history courses, includes four essays totally devoted to the Heian era and two that touch on it. Currently, the most authoritative coverage of the Heian period is volume 2 in *The Cambridge History of Japan*, whose ten chapters are all devoted to Heian Japan. Although the Cambridge project dates back to the late 1970s – and, as I recall, all those years ago, the Heian conference at which first drafts of chapters were presented was the first to be held – volume 2 was the last to appear, in 1999.

Whereas other eras of Japanese history have been the subject of at least one, if not many conferences, resulting in the publication of excellent collections of essays by Japanese and Western authors in English (Muromachi, Kamakura, Sengoku, etc.), the Heian period was not the subject of a conference for a very long time. Only at length, in 2002, was there a two-day conference at Harvard University on "Centers and Peripheries in Heian Japan," a monumental undertaking originally conceived and planned by a committee consisting of Mikael Adolphson (Harvard), G. Cameron Hurst III (Pennsylvania), Edward Kamens (Yale), Joan Piggott (then Cornell, now University of Southern California), and Mimi Yiengpruksawan (Yale). The conference was composed of five separate panels of three to four papers each, a total of sixteen papers on various aspects of Heian political, institutional, religious, literary, and artistic history. The focus was on the first three centuries of the era, especially the mid-Heian period, or what corresponds to the early royal court state. Each panel, indeed each paper, attempted to wrestle with the interplay between center and periphery in order to provide some balance to the previously overwhelming concentration upon central issues and institutions. Thus issues – such as cross-border traffic in Kyūshū, temple networks in the provinces, provincial rebellion, Chinese traders and their impact on the nobility, the life of commoners in the provinces, and Fujiwara no Michinaga's connection to provincial governors – were for the first time addressed by non-Japanese scholars, or by Japanese scholars in English. The forthcoming publication of this volume will certainly bring the study of the Heian period to a new level and hopefully attract the interest of future researchers.

Despite the importance of the Cambridge History volume and the forthcoming *Centers and Peripheries*, there is a great deal of work to do before English language coverage of the Heian period is fully adequate. Although it would be nonsensical even to suggest that the situation could ever approach the coverage Heian enjoys in Japan, still, non-Japanese works fall woefully behind not only in volume, but also in areas of coverage. Needless to say, interest in Heian political and economic institutions is far less well developed than that in literature and art, and even Heian religion. Thus while we are still looking for adequate historical narratives, there are excellent translations into English of virtually all the major works of Heian literature (indeed, translations of *The Tale of Genji* compete with one another for course adoption!). Moreover there is a growing body of analytical studies of Heian literature, of more broadly textual studies, and of women's language. Scholars of Japanese religion have likewise continued to publish excellent monographs on great Heian religious leaders, the spread of newly introduced Tendai and Shingon, and translations of some of the most important Buddhist texts.

By comparison, there is not a single volume in English devoted, for example, to the Heian land system, despite the fact that it was in mid- and late Heian times that the vast *shōen* system really took shape. Arguably the most important economic institution of premodern Japan, with a history spanning the nine centuries from Nara to Sengoku, the *shōen* is the focus of only one full volume since Asakawa's time, the aforementioned work of Thomas Keirstead. As far as Heian estates are concerned, only the books by Farris, Hall, Hurst, Mass, and more recently Adolphson, have much to say on the subject. Two articles by Elizabeth Sato and Kiley (plus his magisterial, yet unpublished dissertation, on the subject) were all that was available until the two chapters by Kiley and Dana Morris in *The Cambridge History of Japan*. Compare this with the thousands of studies and collections of documents related to *shōen* in Japanese and one can see how limited has been research outside Japan on much other than the political and cultural life of the elite at the Heian court.

The Heian period thus remains a fertile ground for the scholar who wishes to leave his or her mark on Japanese historical studies.

NOTES

1 Shively and McCullough, "Introduction," in Shively and McCullough, eds., *The Cambridge History of Japan*, vol. 2, *Heian Japan*, p. 1.
2 Mesheryakov, "On the Quantity of Written Data Produced by the *Ritsuryō* State," p. 193.
3 Toby, "Why Move Nara? Kammu and the Transfer of the Capital."
4 Hall, *Government and Local Power in Japan, 500–1700*, esp. pp. 99–128.
5 Farris, *Heavenly Warriors*.
6 Friday, *Hired Swords*.
7 Sakamoto's ideas can be found in any number of works. See, for example, *Nihon ōchō kokka taiseiron; Nihon no rekishi, 8, Ōchō kokka; and Shōensei seiritsu to ōchō kokka*.
8 Kiley, "Estate and Property in Late Heian Japan," p. 109.
9 Hurst, "*Kugyō* and *Zuryō*: Center and Periphery in the Age of Fujiwara no Michinaga." Paper presented at "Centers and Peripheries in Heian Japan," Harvard University, June 11, 2002 (to be published in forthcoming volume edited by Mikael Adolphson, *Centers and Peripheries in Heian Japan*).
10 Farris, *Heavenly Warriors*, pp. 131–59; Friday, *Hired Swords*, esp. pp. 144–7.
11 Keirstead, *The Geography of Power in Medieval Japan*, p. 19.
12 Kuroda's formulation of the *kemmon* idea appears in many of his works from the 1960s, but it is perhaps best summarized, in its impact on studies of Heian history, in Adolphson, *The Gates of Power*, pp. 10–18.
13 Ibid., p. 11.

BIBLIOGRAPHY

Adolphson, Mikael. *The Gates of Power: Monks, Courtiers, and Warriors in Premodern Japan.* Honolulu: University of Hawai'i Press, 2000.

Asakawa, Kan'ichi. *Land and Society in Medieval Japan.* Tokyo: Japan Society for the Promotion of Science, 1965.

Borgen, Robert. *Sugawara no Michizane and the Early Heian Court.* Cambridge, Mass.: Council on East Asian Studies, Harvard University, 1986.

Farris, William Wayne. *Population, Disease, and Land in Early Japan, 645–900.* Cambridge, Mass.: Council on East Asian Studies, Harvard University, 1985.

Farris, William Wayne. *Heavenly Warriors: The Evolution of Japan's Military, 500–1300.* Cambridge, Mass.: Council on East Asian Studies, Harvard University, 1992.

Friday, Karl. *Hired Swords: The Rise of Private Warrior Power in Early Japan.* Stanford, Calif.: Stanford University Press, 1992.

Friday, Karl. *Samurai, Warfare and the State in Early Medieval Japan.* New York: Routledge, 2004.

Hall, John W. *Government and Local Power in Japan, 500–1700: A Study based on Bizen Province.* Princeton: Princeton University Press, 1966.

Hall, John W., and Mass, Jeffrey, eds. *Medieval Japan: Essays in Institutional History.* New Haven: Yale University Press, 1974.

Hurst, G. Cameron, III. *Insei: Abdicated Sovereigns in the Politics of Late Heian Japan, 1086–1185.* New York: Columbia University Press, 1976.

Hurst, G. Cameron, III. "Michinaga's Maladies: A Medical Report on Fujiwara no Michinaga." *Monumenta Nipponica* 34 (1979): 101–12.

Keirstead, Thomas. *The Geography of Power in Medieval Japan.* Princeton: Princeton University Press, 1992.

Kiley, Cornelius. "Estate and Property in Late Heian Japan." In John W. Hall and Jeffrey Mass, eds., *Medieval Japan: Essays in Institutional History.* New Haven: Yale University Press, 1974.

Mass, Jeffrey. *Warrior Government in Early Medieval Japan.* New Haven: Yale University Press, 1974.

Mass, Jeffrey. *Minamoto no Yoritomo and the Founding of the First Bakufu.* Stanford, Calif.: Stanford University Press, 2002.

McCullough, William. "Japanese Marriage Institutions in the Heian Period." *Harvard Journal of Asiatic Studies* 27 (1967): 103–67.

Mesheryakov, Alexander. "On the Quantity of Written Data Produced by the *Ritsuryō* State." *Nichibunken Japan Review* 15 (2003).

Morris, Ivan. *The World of the Shining Prince.* New York: Alfred A. Knopf, 1964.

Sakamoto Shōzō. *Nihon ōchō kokka taiseiron.* Tokyo: Tokyo Daigaku Shuppankai, 1972.

Sakamoto Shōzō. *Nihon no rekishi, 8, Ōchō kokka.* Tokyo: Shōgakkan, 1974.

Sakamoto Shōzō. *Shōensei seiritsu to ōchō kokka.* Tokyo: Hanawa Shobō, 1985.

Sato, Elizabeth. "Early Development of the Shoen," in John W. Hall and Jeffrey Mass, eds., *Medieval Japan: Essays in Institutional History,* New Haven: Yale University Press, 1974.

Shinoda, Minoru. *The Founding of the Kamakura Shogunate, 1180–1185.* New York: Columbia University Press, 1960.

Shively, Donald, and McCullough, William, eds. *The Cambridge History of Japan,* vol. 2, *Heian Japan.* Cambridge: Cambridge University Press, 1999.

Toby, Ronald. "Why Move Nara? Kammu and the Transfer of the Capital." *Monumenta Nipponica* 40 (1985): 331–47.

FURTHER READING

There is not a great deal of material in English devoted to Heian history; a far greater amount is available on the literature and culture of the period. Among the books devoted solely or largely to covering Heian history are Mikael Adolphson, *The Gates of Power: Monks, Courtiers, and Warriors in Premodern Japan* (Honolulu: University of Hawai'i Press, 2000); Robert Borgen, *Sugawara no Michizane and the Early Heian Court* (Cambridge, Mass.: Council on East Asian Studies, Harvard University, 1986); William Wayne Farris, *Heavenly Warriors: The Evolution of Japan's Military, 500–1300* (Cambridge, Mass.: Council on East Asian Studies, Harvard University, 1992); Karl Friday, *Hired Swords: The Rise of Private Warrior Power in Early Japan* (Stanford, Calif.: Stanford University Press, 1992); G. Cameron Hurst III, *Insei: Abdicated Sovereigns in the Politics of Late Heian Japan, 1086–1185* (New York: Columbia University Press, 1976); Ivan Morris, *The World of the Shining Prince: Court Life in Ancient Japan* (New York: Alfred A. Knopf, 1964); and Donald Shively and William McCullough, eds., *The Cambridge History of Japan*, vol. 2, *Heian Japan* (Cambridge: Cambridge University Press, 1999). Although dealing with the Kamakura bakufu, two of Jeffrey Mass's works – *Warrior Government in Early Medieval Japan: A Study of the Kamakura Bakufu, Shugo, and Jitō* (New Haven: Yale University Press, 1974) and *Yoritomo and the Founding of the First Bakufu* (Stanford, Calif.: Stanford University Press, 1999) – offer extensive coverage of late Heian history. Forthcoming from University of Hawai'i Press is Mikael Adolphson's edited volume *Centers and Peripheries in Heian Japan*, a book with contributions from American, Japanese, and European scholars that will join the Cambridge History in offering extensive coverage of the Heian period in English.

A number of excellent translations of Heian texts flesh out the offerings: Jennifer Brewster, trans., *Fujiwara no Nagako, the Emperor Horikawa Diary* (Honolulu: University of Hawai'i Press, 1972); Helen Craig McCullough, trans., *Ōkagami, the Great Mirror: Fujiwara no Michinaga and His Times* (Princeton: Princeton University Press, 1980); Helen and William McCullough, trans., *A Tale of Flowering Fortunes: Annals of Japanese Aristocratic Life in the Heian Period*, 2 vols. (Stanford, Calif.: Stanford University Press, 1980); and Judith Rabinovitch, *Shōmonki: The Story of Masakado's Rebellion* (Tokyo: Sophia University Press, 1986). These are only the most historically oriented of the Heian literary genre; much can of course be gleaned from the various translations of *The Tale of Genji*, Sei Shōnagon's *Pillow Book*, *Lady Murasaki's Diary*, and a number of other translations. Translations of several works written after the Heian period are useful in understanding late Heian political history: Helen McCullough, *The Tale of the Heike* (Stanford, Calif.: Stanford University Press, 1988); Minoru Tsunoda, *The Founding of the Kamakura Shogunate, 1180–1185: With Selected Translations from the Azuma Kagami* (New York: Columbia University Press, 1960); and William Wilson, trans., *Hōgen Monogatari: A Tale of the Disorder of Hōgen* (Tokyo: Sophia University Press, 1971).

CHAPTER THREE

Medieval Japan

Andrew Edmund Goble

The medieval era was a fluid one, and the field of medieval history is also one in flux. This paper will take up the topics of: the idea of medieval, the Kamakura and Muromachi bakufu, matters of religion, and overseas contacts.

The Medieval Concept

The term "medieval" is borrowed directly from European history. While the Japanese medieval era begins later and covers a shorter time span than the European case, it retains its utility for two main reasons. First, in contrast to the politically centered and peaceful eras of the classical Heian and early modern Tokugawa eras that precede and follow it, the medieval is distinguished by social flux, significant economic and political change, extensive cultural and commercial contact with other countries, and by warfare. Even though subperiods and longer-term processes are identifiable, the era is distinct within Japanese history. Second, it shares with medieval Europe similarities of economic and social structure, and control of political power by a warrior elite (though an older conceptual approach that utilized feudalism as a medieval marker has been abandoned).[1] While questions have been raised about the applicability of "medieval" as a term, no meaningful alternative either to the term or to the notion of periodization (which creates the need for the term, but which is conceptually ubiquitous) has been offered. Thus the term "medieval" for Japan is not arbitrary or spurious.

"Medieval" is usefully applied to the period from the late twelfth to late sixteenth centuries, a span of approximately 400 years. Several dates or decades for beginning and end points are in common use: 1150s and 1180s; and 1560s and 1570s. Subperiods, based on political change, include Kamakura (named after a city) 1180–1333; Muromachi or Ashikaga (part of a city, and a family) 1336–1573; Kenmu (an era name) 1333–6 or 1333–9; Northern and Southern Courts, 1336–92; Ōnin (year period) 1467–77; and Warring States 1477–1573. Historians also use as references "centuries," Western chronology, and occasionally eras as defined by prominent individuals.

However, there has been debate over the issue of when the medieval era began. Traditionally the founding of the Kamakura bakufu in the 1180s was seen as the beginning of the warrior age and the supplanting of the aristocratic age, and the Muromachi bakufu a continuation of that trend which buried the anomalous remnants of the classical polity. Thus the Kamakura and Muromachi periods constituted the medieval era.

A more recent view is that the Kamakura bakufu was an accretion onto rather than a replacement of the older order, and that the events in the 1330s that brought forth (in quick succession) the Kenmu regime and the Muromachi bakufu denote a repudiation of that older order.[2] A convincing case thus can be made that medieval began with the end of the Kamakura period rather than with its beginning, and that Kamakura is thus a transition era between classical and medieval.[3] The significant qualitative shift in the 1330s, which distinguishes the medieval era, is from a "system" that relied on the force of authority to one that relied on the authority of force; that shift is defined and symbolized by the acceptance of military power as a central element in politics, and by the new phenomenon of endemic warfare in Japanese society.[4] The 1330s, and the fourteenth century more broadly, are thus crucial to any sense of the medieval.

Having said that, one may also adopt the approach that there were two phases of the medieval, an early medieval period that had a bloody and irrefutable end point in 1333, and a high or late medieval period commencing in that same year. The medieval thus may be seen as having two major break points, the 1180s and the 1330s, which revolve around political and military events that lasted for periods of years. We might note that this perception of these decades (and their dominant figures, Minamoto Yoritomo, 1147–99, and Emperor Go-Daigo 1288–1339) as being epochal had already taken root in Japan by 1400. However, scholarly debate has revolved around the significance to be invested in those break points: were they parts of longer-term processes, adjustments to older systems, or significant structural alterations that constituted rupture? In general, the older narrative that charted the rise of the warrior class to prominence has given way to interpretations that acknowledge more nuance regarding the break points and that see the rise of the warriors as more contingent than inevitable (the longer-term historical record wherein that occurred is not itself in question, however). Whether the warriors were the only or the major catalyst for broader changes has also been brought under scrutiny. Finally, lurking in the background is the issue of what may constitute the "Japan" that is under discussion, for it has become apparent that the story of politically and militarily well-documented regions (eastern Japan) or political centers (Kamakura, Kyoto) is not automatically that of "peripheral" areas. Let us comment on the 1180s and the 1330s.

The 1180s

An older view that the emergence of something like a bakufu was merely a matter of time has been replaced by a sense that regional and personal factors, which may have exploited institutional possibilities, explain events better than do imaginary constructs of warrior political ambition or opposition to an aristocratic polity. However, in this decade the traditional aristocratic oligarchy lost the ability to unilaterally sanction or control the activity of part of the warrior class, and it is this that may fairly be acknowledged as a significant historical development.[5]

However, the warrior class was not monolithic. Beyond a possible shared ethos as "warriors," there is no evidence of a nationwide class consciousness or political ideology, and warrior family groups (the core social organization within that class) rarely developed broader regional identifications. One exception to this was the "warrior league" phenomenon – partly a community based on physical proximity, partly an imagined one based upon shared but only occasional military experience – of eastern Japan. Even this did not encompass notions of autonomy, or even region-wide unity. In the 1180s, however, the warrior class of eastern Japan was welded into a social and military interest group under the leadership of an exiled warrior-aristo-crat, Minamoto Yoritomo. Those warriors not partial to his approaches were elimin-ated. His limited goal was to make the east autonomous under his leadership, but the need to respond to military and political efforts to stymie that goal led to nationwide campaigning, the elimination of warrior rivals from other regions of the country, and national hegemony. Yet rather than seek independence or total domination, the Kamakura bakufu elected to legitimize its prerogatives by agreeing – on its terms, and with the content dictated by it – to an autonomy within the existing political and legal framework. The bakufu was not an advocate for the warrior class as a whole, held jurisdiction over only its own followers (except in matters of public order, where it claimed wider policing powers), and worked deliberately to uphold the old order. No effort was made to supplant or eliminate the imperial institution, and expansion of powers was not a policy objective. The result was the creation of a dual polity with overlapping governing hierarchies, and two urban locations, the old imperial city of Kyoto and the new bakufu headquarters in Kamakura (near modern Tokyo).[6]

Nonetheless, the establishment of the bakufu betokened a qualitative shift in the political and social landscape. Its existence made it possible in the following century and a half for the bakufu to become increasingly involved in national issues (defense, imperial succession), issues of legal jurisdiction (property disputes, criminal and peace-keeping activity), and expansion of its authority over a wider number of social groups. This greater presence, inevitably diminishing the latitude of many others, cumulatively engendered a backlash, itself underlain by significant tensions propelled by conflicts (land disputes, inheritance imbroglios) over diminishing resources throughout society.[7]

The 1330s

The 1330s witnessed the bloody extermination of the Kamakura bakufu, the appear-ance of a national regime headed by Emperor Go-Daigo, the establishment of a national warrior government by the Ashikaga family, and the onset of nearly sixty years of civil war. The civil war was propelled by competing ideological visions of two factions of the imperial family and their supporters, and within that dynamic a competition for national pre-eminence between the supporters of Emperor Go-Daigo and those of the Ashikaga warrior family from eastern Japan. There is little debate that the decade of the 1330s was a break point, but much debate ever since over why it was so.

It has not been uncommon to see the conflict as one between an "imperial vision" promoted by Emperor Go-Daigo and a "warrior vision" promoted by the former Kamakura bakufu general Ashikaga Takauji, with the conflict more broadly one between those opposing the ongoing rise of the warrior class and those rising naturally to leadership as a result of that same force of history. The guiding assumption that the warrior class was rising and propelled by the force of history informs the perception that the Kamakura bakufu could only have been followed by another warrior regime, and that the appearance of a unified national regime under a non-warrior (an emperor) was an anomaly.[8] However, these assumptions do not account satisfactorily for the demise of the Kamakura regime, for why an imperial regime would enjoy any success in the first place, and for the many divisions that we find within the warrior class. Moreover, the focus on the imagined Kamakura era warrior class as representative has precluded recognition of the overall militarization of Japanese society from the early fourteenth century.

The Kenmu era was a significant turning point. The aristocratic oligarchy was reshaped by death and by Go-Daigo's repudiation of it as the main support for the imperial system. Militarization of society and endemic warfare were significant and new phenomena. The warriors as a social class did not give automatic preference to warrior political leadership, which thus calls into question the narrative of the inevitable rise of the warrior class. Close examination of the Kenmu administration suggests that it is best interpreted not as one pursuing anachronistic goals, or less administratively adept than earlier regimes, but as one propelling an era of major systemic change whose outcome was uncertain.[9] Close study of a wide range of contemporary writings on politics and society has made it clear that the questioning of inherited ideologies that underlay Go-Daigo's vision was widely shared, and it is thus accordingly apparent that an earlier scholarly focus on texts such as the *Jinnō shōtōki* not only revealed but part of the picture, it also misconstrued the nature of medieval ideological debates on such fundamental issues as the role of the imperial family.[10] Finally, the social fragmentation and endemic warfare of the fourteenth century needs to be regarded as symptomatic of times within which political change was also occurring.

The Kamakura and Muromachi Regimes

These two warrior-led administrations shared much in common as bureaucratic organizations, but existed in very different historical circumstances. Both regimes emerged through warfare, and warfare brought them both to an end. In the Kamakura case, it was destroyed by military forces opposed to it in 1333. In contrast, by the 1570s the Muromachi bakufu was a non-threatening and insignificant military actor in an age of civil war, and passed irrelevantly from the stage. Thus, Kamakura ended with a bang, Muromachi with a whimper. Both regimes shared authority with other institutions, and did not aim for unitary hegemony (though they did not wish to be overshadowed), so should not be regarded as exclusive "national governments." We can delineate institutional evolution for each bakufu, but it is useful to consider the "warrior government" connoted by these institutions as falling into three phases: the Kamakura regime as one chronological unit with national impact; the Muromachi bakufu as having national impact through the late fifteenth century; and from the Ōnin War of the 1470s until its demise the Muromachi bakufu was but one of several elements trying to survive in the chaotic "city-state" of Kyoto.

Kamakura bakufu

The Kamakura bakufu was founded by a warrior. Its constituency was the warrior class of eastern Japan. Its primary administrative activity involved supervising its followers for guard duty, confirming title to and alienations of rights in land of its followers, and providing the legal mechanisms and venues whereby warriors, as plaintiffs or defendants, might defend their interests in civil litigation. The bakufu was staffed by professional and largely hereditary civil bureaucrats only rarely of warrior background. Policy organs, whose duties also included judgment of legal suits, were staffed by a combination of professional bureaucrats and warriors; over time, supporters of the Hōjō family of shogunal regents dominated the warrior group. The "head of state" position, denoted by the title shōgun, was, after the extinction of Yoritomo's direct line in 1219, occupied by young aristocrats or young imperial princes serving their term at the pleasure of the Hōjō. The "head of government" position (shogunal regent) was, after 1221, held by a member of the Hōjō family; initially that figure was concurrently head of the Hōjō family, but later in the period the two were distinct, with supreme power de facto lying in the hands of the house head. The Hōjō represent the first significant instance of social mobility in the warrior class.[11]

Reflecting the goals of its founder, the Kamakura bakufu was devoted to system maintenance and the avoidance of military activity. Its primary public activities became focused on dispute resolution, acting as arbitrator in civil litigation between its warriors and between its warriors and any other third party. The bakufu developed a sophisticated judicial system – laws and regulations, regional branches, detailed procedures, rights of appeal – designed to encourage disputants to reach informal resolution which the bakufu might then acknowledge. Befitting its role as arbitrator, it was not judicially activist, and gave great weight to customary practice.[12]

Muromachi bakufu

The Muromachi bakufu[13] under the Ashikaga family was forced to locate itself in the capital of Kyoto in order to control the imperial family and the political legitimacy that it conferred. The Ashikaga leadership thus removed itself from its traditional landholdings, at a time when income from distant holdings was unreliable and when a devolution of ownership to the local level was eroding the system of absentee landownership upon which Heian era government had been built. Accordingly, as had Go-Daigo, it sought to promote commerce and benefit from taxation of economic activity, mainly within the city of Kyoto. Throughout the fourteenth century the Ashikaga struggled to exercise national hegemony, and overcome regional warrior opponents. While it maintained some strong regional outposts during that time it became dependent for military support on newly emerged regional warrior leaders.[14] However, only the Ashikaga had ambitions at the national level; the result was a central–local consensus that recognized the Ashikaga position in return for acknowledgment of provincial and regional autonomy. Regional figures enhanced their own local claims by harnessing the prestige and legitimacy deriving from "appointments" from the Muromachi bakufu. The Ashikaga in turn derived some of their political legitimacy by a similar mechanism, namely their claimed appointment from the imperial throne. The Muromachi bakufu gained additional legitimacy by its involvement in formal relations with China and Korea: not only did it acquire a monopoly over such matters, but the needs of diplomatic protocol enabled it to acquire (not without some internal controversy) for the shōgun the new title of "King of Japan."

Bureaucratically the Muromachi bakufu closely resembled the Kamakura bakufu, and even inherited a large number of that organ's former bureaucrats. It established a functional administration, with authority over judicial and other bureaucratic matters, and progressively arrogated to itself rights to rule-making and police enforcement within the vicinity of Kyoto.[15] It did not control large numbers of troops, but its retainer corps was always reliable (like its master, it had no real power base outside the city), and it held a preponderance of local power. The growth of commercial activity and increased monetization of the economy introduced new areas of civil contention, and new sources of ready wealth. In an environment where goodwill was scarce and gift-giving an integral part of social life, it is easy to have the impression that the Muromachi bakufu's city administration was akin to a protection racket. However, it was a powerful protector and patron, and it creatively harnessed Zen institutions to provide financial and personnel support for a new area of government activity, foreign relations (see below).

Politically, the Muromachi bakufu differed slightly from the Kamakura bakufu, in that it utilized a number of hereditary retainer families in important organizational positions, including that of deputy shōgun. In time the rivalries between the deputy families and within the Ashikaga family itself were to undercut the political strength of the shogunal institution. Those dynamics were additionally propelled and complicated by the partisan involvement of regional warlords. Thus the family fortunes of actors at several levels, and at the center and in local areas, became increasingly intertwined, and matters of appointments and successions became highly politicized. The destabilizing aspects of this started to become apparent in the 1440s, but it was not until the late 1460s with the outbreak of the decade-long Ōnin civil war[16] – which devastated the city of Kyoto and prompted substantial realignments at the local level – that the structure collapsed.

Post-1470s Kyoto "city-state"

After the Ōnin War the city of Kyoto remained an important center economically, and retained the aura of being the site of ultimate political legitimating power.[17] But it is otherwise helpful, in understanding "bakufu," to regard it as but one population center among many. Indeed, one might see it as an anarchic city-state, and the bakufu as a vestigial city administration occupied primarily with its own survival.[18] However, the Muromachi bakufu was not overtly threatened with elimination and, like the imperial family, remained in the city (albeit there was nowhere else it could go).

The city of Kyoto was a churning urban site, and its morphology altered substantially throughout the medieval era. Its physical shape, and the lives of its inhabitants, were radically affected by the Ōnin War, which basically destroyed its structures. While Kyoto lost its political *raison d'être*, its role as a financial and commercial hub survived and flourished. Kyoto thus made a longer-term transition from being a political city dominated by a hereditary civil elite, to a one with a mixed elite of which one component was warrior, to one in which its neighborhood associations and merchant guilds were the prominent representatives of what we might call local government. Alternately, we might point to a strong sense of local community developed by the urban population that helped it survive the ravages and impositions of both occasional warlords and religious movements such as the Lotus Leagues.

Amid the political chaos Kyoto retained, and even actively expanded, its role at the center of an increasingly monetized economy, as the provider of a wide range of logistical and financial services, and as a center of specialty manufacturing. Kyoto, and its guilds and trade associations, provided new means of creating wealth, generated urban revenues, and gave rise to an entrepreneurial merchant class most visibly symbolized by its moneylenders.[19] A significant by-product of the new wealth was the emergence of a distinct, sophisticated Kyoto urban culture that, working through salons and building upon business networks, nurtured the art of the tea ceremony, kept alive traditions of poetry, and was well known for its connoisseurship of pottery and painting. The urban culture also encouraged experimentation, a certain colorful gaudiness, and big ambitions.

Religion and Culture

Two named religious traditions commingled in medieval Japan. The first was the indigenous animistic faith of Shintō (the way of the gods). The second was the Buddhist tradition which was initially introduced into Japan via the Korean peninsula in the sixth century; additional "waves" of Buddhism that exercised a significant influence on Japanese culture were brought in from China in the ninth century (esoteric schools) and in the thirteenth and fourteenth centuries (Zen). This section will focus on the Buddhist tradition. We will cover three areas: the institutional and monastic traditions, the notions of salvation which underlay a distinctly medieval responses to the human condition, and some developments in the study of medieval religion.

Institutional and monastic traditions

Institutional Buddhism was of two types. That of the esoteric schools and religious establishments that had emerged in the early ninth century, and that of the enlightenment-oriented Zen enterprise which became established in the thirteenth and fourteenth centuries. The religious focus of these enterprises was to comprehend the underlying truths of the cosmos, and both emphasized ritual practice and rigorous training in a monastic environment.

From the classical Heian era and continuing through the medieval period, Buddhist monasteries (and nunneries) and temple complexes were an integral component of the aristocratic and oligarchic polity.[20] Drawing a modernist distinction between "secular" and "religious" is not particularly meaningful for the premodern era as a whole, and can distract from the understanding of the integrated nature of lives individual and institutional, but we may note that religion was consciously and inextricably interwoven into national life. In general terms, one might understand this institutional Buddhism as one of the two wheels of the vehicle of state (as exemplified in the trope ōbō buppō, law of the monarch and law of the Buddha).

That was also the understanding of warrior leaders when they came to power, until in the late sixteenth century the unifier warlord Oda Nobunaga violently repudiated the idea that religious institutions had any business being involved in secular politics (this thus being one of the clear markers of the end of the medieval).[21]

Two religious centers were actively involved in political matters: the Tendai esoteric complex of Mt. Hiei outside Kyoto (destroyed by Nobunaga in 1571), and the religious city of Nara in which Kōfukuji and Tōdaiji were dominant. A third center, the Shingon esoteric center in the mountain fastness of Mt. Kōya, avoided political controversy. There were of course many other temples throughout the country, generally affiliated through a web of hierarchical and patronage relationships to temples located in the capital and its immediate vicinity. Some individual temples, such as Tōji in Kyoto, enjoyed a special position as protectors of the state, with direct links to the imperial family itself.

Most temples enjoyed the support of families, including the imperial, within the oligarchy; aristoctratic offspring not destined for public life were often placed in temples and many of those offspring tended to rise to the top leadership positions within temples. Temples enjoyed a wide array of tax exemptions, and held significant rights in land – in trust or outright – throughout the country, to support their endeavors. While there were a number of sects and teaching traditions represented within Buddhism in Japan, and Buddhism as a whole was central to faith and practice, the esoteric schools of Tendai[22] and Shingon[23] were particularly well represented in ritual practices and observances on behalf of state and aristocracy, and in attending to a wide variety of spiritual and psychological needs. These esoteric schools were understood as having the most powerful understandings of, connections with, and ability to harness the forces which underlay the cosmos. That Mt. Hiei and Mt. Kōya were dynamic centers of learning and interpretation reinforced that perception. It may also be said that they enjoyed unparalleled respect for the depth, range, and creativity of their intellectual output.

The second form of institutionalized Buddhism that focused upon the monastic life was that of Zen Buddhism.[24] Zen stressed meditation and the quest for enlightenment, and was essentially a thirteenth-century import from China – specifically, from coastal south China and from the Yangtze River hinterland as far west as Sichuan province.

Two Zen schools existed in the medieval era. The Sōtō school, founded in Japan by Dōgen after his return from study in China, focused its activities at a provincial headquarters, Eiheiji. The Rinzai school, which began its rise to national prominence subsequent to the patronage extended by the warrior leader Hōjō Tokiyori to the Chinese monk Lanxi Daolong, was both cosmopolitan and metropolitan. It exerted an enormous cultural influence, and the "Zen culture" that is broadly associated with Japanese tradition is a Rinzai product.

Rinzai monks traveled to China for study, Chinese monks emigrated to Japan, and Rinzai monks in general made a concerted effort to imbibe and transmit a wide range of contemporary Chinese culture. They introduced new styles in monastic architecture, poetry, portrait painting, landscape and still-life painting, aesthetic engagement and appreciation of Song-style Chinese pottery, forms of vegetarian cuisine, distinctive dry gardens of pebble and rock, and laid the foundation for the emergence of the art of the tea ceremony. All were considered integral to the religious life, and the arts in particular were considered ways by which religious understanding might be expressed. As a monastic enterprise, Rinzai was able to flourish because it enjoyed widespread support among the political elite of all persuasions. That support was solidified by the adoption of a Gozan or "Five Mountains" system by the Ashikaga bakufu, which gave them official recognition and under which most Zen temples were subsumed.

The focus of Zen training was the quest for enlightenment, and thus the ability to see the true reality of all things. Enlightenment and understanding was the product of individual effort, and it was assumed that all humans were capable of discovering their "Buddha nature." Training stressed a rigorous course of meditation and bodily denial, and was conducted under the (often direct) supervision of teachers who had been recognized as having become enlightened. It was a basic assumption that an individual's enlightenment – an intangible and inexpressible phenomenon – could be recognized only by one already in that state, and this understanding was encapsulated in the notion of "mind to mind" transmission of the truth. One notable technique designed to jolt seekers out of their accustomed mental framework into a perception of the reality underlying all was the mental puzzle known as the *kōan*, which could be a brief "brain teaser" or a seemingly non-sequitur question about a longer story.[25]

Notions of salvation

One of the hallmarks of medieval religion is the appearance of teachings, directed towards the general population, that stressed the notion of salvation.

The basic goal of Buddhism is to end the suffering entailed by the cycle of birth and rebirth (*samsara*) that is conditioned by the workings of karma (the notion that one's present condition is the consequence of prior acts, and that actions in the present will have effects in the future, in this and in successive lives).[26] The monastic tradition of Buddhism which provided the framework for the quest for enlightenment (attainment of which connoted entry into the state of *nirvana*) that would break that cycle of birth and rebirth implicitly assumed that the lay person would not reach enlightenment in this life. However, the development of the notion of the bodhisattva – a being who had attained enlightenment but who chose to remain "in the world" to assist humans – introduced the concept of salvation into Buddhism. Bodhisattvas, and belief in their vows to assist people, thus offered an alternative to enlightenment in the quest to escape *samsara*. In medieval Japan emphasis came to be placed upon two component aspects of salvation: belief that one could be saved, and faith in an object that would do the saving. The most widespread focus of belief was in the saving grace of the Buddha of the Western Pure Land (Amida Buddha),[27] but another influential belief was in the text known as the Lotus Sutra (Hokekyō).[28] Three factors lay behind the growth of salvation-oriented religion.

First, the unattractive (for humans) possibilities of rebirth. The human was only one of several realms of existence into which one could be reborn. Others included that of hungry ghosts (destined to feed off human body products), animals, demons, and a wide variety of hells whose punishments were interminable and graphically explicated. People were enjoined to avoid behavior that might amass karma sufficient to be reborn into such realms; there the suffering was liable to be even greater than that which accompanied an existence as a human being. However, insofar as people remained unenlightened, rebirth was definite; the future life could thus be frightening (even though in that future life one would have no memory of an earlier life).

Second, the development of the eschatological concept of the final ages (*masse*, *mappō*). While this concept became something of a trope in medieval culture, and appears to have been given no credence by pursuers of Zen, it was powerfully grounded. It was held that human ability to understand the truths of Buddhism, and even understand that there were truths in Buddhism, had progressively declined since the age of the historical Buddha Sakyamuni (Gautama). There were three stages to this decline, which would end only when the Future Buddha would appear in the world. People now lived in the final and most dismal stage of decline, and were incapable of achieving their own enlightenment, and escaping the cycle of birth and rebirth. Evidence to support the claim was adduced in such factors as the rise of the warrior class in the form of the Kamakura bakufu, plagues and natural disasters, and (it seems) in such things as the erosion of taxation and property systems, and the increase in numbers of the visibly marginal in society ("lepers," beggars).

Third, powerful articulations of hope – important in a final age when otherwise there was none – for lay people, put forward by a number of charismatic figures (such being fairly unusual in Japanese history), whose messages were sufficiently appealing that they evolved into lasting organized sects. Of these the Amidist sects springing from Hōnen and Shinran,[29] and the Lotus Sect springing from Nichiren,[30] are most well known. Two elements of doctrine are noteworthy.

All three figures stressed that faith in the saving power of their respective focus of belief was essential for salvation, but there was much debate over the extent to which the "quality" of belief played a part in being saved. Hōnen recommended constant expression of belief since it was not known how much was enough to be saved; Shinran argued that since the saving was done by Amida and was granted to all the individual's efforts were not relevant – one utterance of belief should be enough (others suggested that carrying a talisman of belief was sufficient); Nichiren stressed constant and conscious awareness of the power of the Lotus Sutra to save, and so strength of belief was important. The reward for belief was that upon death the believer would be conveyed to a heaven, a place beyond birth and rebirth where there was no suffering and perpetual happiness surrounded by one's loved ones.

Another important aspect of doctrine was the positive confirmation that people of any and every background could be reborn in heaven. That articulation was in contrast to the idea that those in celibate holy orders had best, if not sole, claim to achieving escape from *samsara*. It was also a direct repudiation of the well-entrenched ideology that birth as a female carried its own karmic hindrances (the "five hindrances"; a "deep and heavy evil karma"; as carriers of life, women were more attached to it), and that females needed a further rebirth in male form in order to have best chance of escape. A further point was that people of any social station or karmic background might be saved, and thus the more privileged in life enjoyed no superior claim to salvation. Needless to say, these inclusive standpoints, which addressed the needs of and offered hope to any person, were well received. Though doctrines argued that people would be saved irrespective of their social station, of their existing karma, or even if they had committed acts of a negative karmic nature, the message that "even the wicked will be saved" was not intended as sanction for anti-social behavior. Shinran's analogy was that, just because one has an antidote, that is not a reason to drink poison, and believers were encouraged to strive to act well.

In short, the salvation teachings powerfully addressed existential needs. They emphasized as well the importance of communities of belief – whether generalized or actual physical communities – that would provide positive support in an uncertain world. The social collapse (or ferment) and warfare that marked the medieval era enhanced the appeal of these sects, and indeed in the sixteenth century some religious communities emerged as autonomous and powerful actors on the national political stage. However, they too were dealt with by Nobunaga and his contemporaries.

Some trends in research

The fundamental core of Buddhism is expressed in the Buddha's Four Noble Truths. Beyond that, there is no standard text of the kind that, for example, defines the God-based monotheism of the Abrahamic religions. The Buddhist canon, a body of literature produced in many countries and languages over a period of at least 2,000 years, and comprising well over 70,000 treatises, is immense. It represents a vibrant intellectual engagement of doctrinal issues and doctrinal responses to social and political issues, is emblematic of the decentered nature of "Buddhism," and reflects (notably in Japan) a tendency to eclecticism and fissuring. Scholarship on Buddhism reflects this multiplicity, and so the following is meant as a general guide to three approaches rather than as a comprehensive statement.

One area of research has focused on texts and matters of doctrine emerging from those texts, and is usefully seen as study of Buddhist philosophy. Some texts, such as those produced in India and available in Chinese translation, tended to be regarded as important to the broader Buddhist tradition and not specific to Buddhism in Japan, though by the same token they exercised a profound influence on the development of Buddhism in Japan. Scholarly attention to these types of texts not only facilitated engagement of Buddhist thought and philosophy, but, in an earlier era when the idea of "philosophy" was equated with European traditions, and only the belief that privileged a monotheistic God was considered to be "religion," helped to establish Buddhism as intellectually legitimate. In addition to study of works such as the Lankavatara Sutra, Lotus Sutra, Blue Cliff Record, and the Pure Land Sutras, attention has been given to the works of foundational figures in Japanese schools, such as Kukai, Saichō, and Hōnen. In a different vein, the writings of the Zen thinker Dōgen have come to enjoy greater attention as profound philosophical reflections, even though historically they were available to a comparatively small circle. We also note engagement of broader ideas that were central to debate throughout the medieval era, such as the eschatological notion of the "latter days" (*mappō*), or the idea of original enlightenment (*hongaku*).[31]

Another research approach has been to look at the development of schools, teaching traditions, and at the spread of Buddhist teaching throughout the general population (some of this was noted in the preceding section). Since the Kamakura sects articulated new doctrinal interpretations, particularly relating to the elements of lived religious life, they have often been regarded as the "new" Buddhism in contrast to the "old" Buddhism, and in earlier scholarship their appearance was sometimes seen analogously as a "reformation" movement. Earlier study of the "new"

Buddhism tended to focus on the figures and movements that survived and continued into much later times (including the present). More recent study has expanded to encompass some comparatively "ephemeral" figures (such as Ippen). Other research has come to look at the broader phenomenon of the re-evaluation and rearticulation of teachings that occurred in this same era, and at some of the social ramifications of renewal and revival in older schools, as typified by such figures as Myōe[32] or Eison. This in turn has encouraged a more nuanced understanding of medieval religion that more closely reflects contemporary dynamics.

A third approach engages Buddhism from a more consciously descriptive rather than prescriptive perspective, and embodies what we might regard as an approach found more commonly in the field of religious studies, which examines claims about truth, and inquires into the dynamics of human shaping of doctrine and texts. Topics of research have included Buddhist relics, devotional cults, issues of hospice and medicine, ideological uses of Buddhism for assigning social worth, sexuality and Buddhism, the internal dynamics of monastic institutions, as well as study and translation of private correspondence.[33] These topics individually and collectively convey direct existential concerns, articulations of doctrine, and efforts to reconcile elements of doctrine with the needs of believers. Attention to issues of gender in Buddhist doctrine, and to the manner in which females responded to male-centered discourses that assigned females inferior ability to benefit from the Buddha's message, have greatly expanded our picture of religious activity. Such research has also fruitfully problematized many writings that had been accepted as reflectors rather than shapers of "tradition," and opened up for serious study writings (especially by women) that were traditionally given little attention.[34] For a sense of how research has benefited from these new perspectives, the collection edited by Barbara Ruch, *Engendering Faith: Women and Buddhism in Premodern Japan*, is indispensable.[35]

Overseas Contacts

One of the distinguishing characteristics of the medieval era was extensive, sustained overseas contact. That has been noted for some time, as has the diplomatic structure which provided some of the framework for that contact. More newly noted, and constituting a conceptual leap, is that for the medieval era the idea of "Japanese history" must acknowledge the non-state-centered maritime trading networks, human movements, and cultural exchanges, of the East Asian maritime region of which Japan was a part. That region encompassed south China, the Ryūkyū Islands, southern and western Japan, and the Korean peninsula. In turn, that region constituted one end of, and one of the links in, a trading network comprised of overlapping regions extending on to Southeast Asia, and into the Indian Ocean littoral that included such areas as the Indian subcontinent, much of the non-Mediterranean Islamic world, the east coast of Africa, the Red Sea, and the Persian Gulf. In fact it was by following the trade links in this wider network that Europeans (Portuguese) first encountered Japan in the 1540s, thus initiating a new type of foreign contact that built (largely productively) upon existing links and attitudes to exchange. The essential cessation of active overseas engagement (the *sakoku* or "closed country" policy) that is a hallmark of the post-medieval, early modern Tokugawa era is beyond our scope here. However, it is important to remember that this "closed country" phenomenon ought not be read back into the medieval era. It must be fully appreciated that for the medieval era the low-tide mark around the Japanese archipelago denoted not an end to "Japanese" history, but was another starting point for it.

The overall diplomatic framework

When permanent state-to-state diplomatic relations in East Asia were maintained, they tended to be so within a Sinocentric framework whereby other nations accepted a subordinate vassal status as a tributary state of a Chinese regime. A tribute relationship provided the advantages of external legitimacy, of permission to engage in trade at designated Chinese locations and send missions along specified routes, and in principle the right to ask for Chinese military assistance. However, irrespective of whether such formal relations were maintained, as a matter of practice and necessity, unofficial contacts with China were continuous, and (where geography and transport routes allowed) similarly we find direct relations between non-Chinese states.[36]

Formal Japanese diplomatic cum tributary relationships with China had ceased in the 800s, but were revived in the late 1300s.[37] The late 1300s was a period of regime change and consolidation throughout East Asia: the Ming in China, the Yi in Korea, and the Ashikaga family's Muromachi bakufu in Japan. All appear to have felt that some form of external legitimization was useful. On the Japanese side, the first effort in the fourteenth century to acquire political recognition from the Ming was made by a representative of the Southern Court, Prince Kaneyoshi, who styled himself "King of Japan." While it became apparent that he did not control Japan, the validity of seeking recognition seems not to have been problematic on the Chinese side. It appears that Kaneyoshi's effort provided the model for the Ashikaga, and it was with this title that formal recognition was received by the Muromachi bakufu in 1402. Within Japan the probity of the new title was the subject of some debate, but the Ashikaga position prevailed. The new prominence of a political entity in Japan within the tributary system also influenced Japanese relations with the Korean court, another member of the diplomatic order, and subsequently numerous official missions were exchanged.

Japanese tribute missions were sent on a regular if not predictable basis from the early 1400s into the mid 1500s. Initially the missions were to the direct financial benefit of the Muromachi bakufu and its warrior leadership, and to the Kyoto-based Zen monastic institutions whose monks in effect constituted a foreign service – skilled in Chinese, many had also traveled to China, and they were adept in the forms and protocols of cultural engagement that guided diplomatic negotiation in the East Asian macro-culture. From the 1470s Japan's internal political chaos – and the effective destruction of Kyoto as a political center as a result of the Ōnin War – meant that there was no longer a meaningful counterpart of a Korean or Chinese regime. However, the older framework survived as a useful instrument of trade, and as a practical matter the right to represent Japan in foreign relations was retained by the Muromachi bakufu. Nonetheless, by the 1500s the missions, while requiring possession of documentation from the bakufu, effectively became private endeavors under the sponsorship of and for the benefit of other warrior families (including the powerful Ōuchi family of western Japan) and for merchants based not in Kyoto but in the self-governing port city of Sakai.

Violent aspects of contacts

Warfare or armed conflict between the population of Japan and its East Asian maritime neighbors was rare. However, the instances of such have come to live long in historical memory, essentially because of their occasional political usefulness to later generations. We may note two significant medieval examples: the Mongol invasions of 1274 and 1281, and the "Japanese pirate" phenomenon of the thirteenth through mid sixteenth centuries.

The Mongol invasions of Japan, in Hakata Bay on the island of Kyūshū, were products of the foreign expansionist policy of the Yuan Mongol empire of Qubilai Khan. As in many Mongol military expeditions Mongols were a minority, and so the bulk of the sailors and soldiers in the invading force were Chinese (apparently recruited from the ranks of the defeated southern Song) and Korean (furnished by the subordinate King of Korea). Chinese and Koreans also constituted the bulk of the reported 100,000 or deaths among the invaders. Japanese casualties appear to have been very small. The 1274 invasion may be regarded as a reconnaissance in force. The 1281 invasion was a far larger and more serious effort at conquest, and appears to have been the world's largest sea-borne assault prior to the twentieth century.[38]

The Mongols were defeated in 1281 by a combination of a well-prepared Japanese defense, which prevented the invasion forces from moving off the beaches for a period of about six weeks, and by adverse sea conditions caused by a typhoon that resulted in the destruction of the vast majority of the shipping and invasion personnel. Recent scholarship has suggested that the Japanese warriors would have prevailed in any event, but the cataclysmic impact of the typhoon made the entire matter moot. Any survivors were hunted down, and executed or enslaved. This rare defeat for Mongol arms provided a basis for the claim that Japan had never been successfully invaded; and by interpreting the typhoon as a "divine wind" or *kamikaze* provided grounds for an ideology that Japan enjoyed the special and powerful protection of its indigenous gods, the *kami*. One medieval by-product of the latter was the construction of a discourse, by some proponents of the native religion of Shintō, particularly those in prominent shrines on the island of Kyūshū, of the foreign other.[39]

The short-term invasion impact on northern Kyūshū and its warrior class was of course substantial, in the expenditure of resources and lives, although assessing a specific longer-term impact is more difficult. However, it does seem clear that the invasions added to a range of existing problems. The inability of the Kamakura bakufu to provide appropriate rewards for service or compensation for losses created considerable ill-will, and added further tensions to a warrior society already confronting pressures for better resource allocation and in the midst of altering its inheritance practices in ways that disadvantaged many family members. Family fission generated extensive litigation. The bakufu established new organs to administer Kyūshū, and was in effect forced to place the island under judicial quarantine.[40] Ironically, perhaps, this seems to have enhanced a sense of autonomy on the part of Kyūshū warriors generally, and thereafter the island focused its primary attention on itself and on its maritime links to the East Asian continent.

The phenomenon of the *wakō* or Japanese pirates can be traced for over 300 years, roughly from the 1220s to the 1550s. Japanese pirates were of two types. The first were literally Japanese pirates, drawn from southwestern fishing and coastal warrior communities, who preyed upon the littoral of the Korean peninsula.[41] Their impact was most significant through the early fifteenth century. Tsushima, midway between Japan and Korea, served as a de facto gathering point. While they raided merchant ships, they became notorious for the damage they caused to the finances of the Korean government by seizing tax ships, and for the devastation they inflicted on the Korean population generally. In this latter they raided coastal and hinterland villages and cities, pillaged at will, seized livestock and property, and carried off people to be used as hostages or slaves. Between the 1360s and 1430s raids were large-scale enterprises, and could involve thousands of raiders and hundreds of vessels. This activity, and the uncertain ability of the Muromachi bakufu in Kyoto to control it, strongly influenced the rhythm of Korean–Japanese official relations. The most effective control was exercised by Korean naval activity, as highlighted by a massive Korean punitive expedition in 1419 against Tsushima.

The second type of Japanese pirates is best seen as multinational freebooters, mainly of Chinese and Japanese ethnic origin. This second type of Japanese pirate symbolizes the extensive and continuous non-official maritime activity throughout the East China Sea region.[42] The "Japanese pirate" label, while not inapplicable since people of Japanese birth were among the participants, appears to have served as a convenient fig-leaf that officially disguised the inability of the Ming dynasty to suppress the lucrative coastal piracy, and the unofficial and banned international trade in which Chinese were prohibited to participate, that flourished particularly along the south China coast. "Japanese pirate" activity was a significant drain on Ming government resources, and ultimately became a major domestic political problem. Failure to deal effectively with the issue came to be regarded as one of the signs of the gradual loss of authority, and thus dynastic legitimacy, of the Ming dynasty itself. As it happens, the "Japanese pirate" phenomenon declined along with the Ming. It is unlikely, however, that the disappearance below the political horizon of non-official activity betokened its cessation.

The ubiquity of contacts

The preceding discussion dealt with activities, official and non-official, which occurred on and around the East China Sea. The topics have traditionally been seen as part of foreign or external relations, and because of the relative lack of formal diplomacy and foreign policy have taken a back seat to research on domestic, land-based aspects of Japanese history. In recent years scholars have reconceptualized this approach. Two elements have been key.

First, while Japan is an island nation, this has come to be regarded not as an excuse for limiting study of or understanding of "Japanese history" to the area bounded by the low-tide mark of surrounding waters, but as a reason to incorporate into Japanese history the continuous links made possible by maritime travel. The activities of traders, travelers, and seafarers – which occurred irrespective of formal state relationships – are now seen as an integral part of social and cultural history, rather than separate from it. A natural corollary to this is that the ethnic and national origin of those who are included in "Japanese history" has expanded. Concomitantly, this has facilitated research into the topics of boundaries, borders, and contact zones, which provides new issues and frameworks for writing about Japanese history.[43]

Second, while the notion of center and periphery is a useful one when examining many dynamics and, as John Whitney Hall has articulated so well, the central–local relationship(s) were always symbiotic, scholars have now come to understand that regions and peripheries might be treated as centers in their own rights.[44] Kamakura and eastern Japan during the Kamakura period make that point most obviously, because of the political significance of Kamakura. However, there is significance to regions apart from any role in national-level politics. This is particularly the case with the island of Kyūshū which, rather than being understood as the western (or southern) periphery and far from the center, may be seen as a center of its own.

Thus Kyūshū was anchored by the international trading port of Hakata[45] and the nearby administrative center of Dazaifu, and it had at least two of its own peripheries, namely, the Kyoto region and eastern Japan, and the littoral of the East China Sea (the Ryūkyū Islands, south China, the Korean peninsula). Given that "distance" in medieval Japan was often conceived of as social and temporal rather than as topographical, Kyūshū (here, Hakata) was as closely linked to "other countries" as it was to other parts of Japan. These new understandings of linkage have made it possible to give coherence, and even greater significance, to such things as: the foreign communities that resided in Japan; "mixed-race" unions; trade in pottery and medicines; the journeying and sojourning of Zen monks between China and Japan; that Zen architecture and practices flourished first in Hakata; international art markets; the circulation of manuscripts and books; and the broader phenomenon of an East China Sea macro-culture and trading regime of which Japan was an integral part. All in all, the horizons of Japanese history have literally been extended.[46]

NOTES

1 A nonetheless readable overview of premodern history that takes up the topic is Duus, *Feudalism in Japan*.

2 See Goble, *Kenmu*.

3 See Mass, ed., *The Origins of Japan's Medieval World*.

4 Conlan, *State of War*; Friday, *Samurai, Warfare and the State*; Goble, "War and Injury."

5 See Mass, *Yoritomo and the Founding of the First Bakufu*, and Friday, *Hired Swords*.

6 See Mass, *The Development of Kamakura Rule, 1180–1250*; G. Cameron Hurst, "The Kobu Polity: Court Bakufu Relations in Kamakura Japan," in Mass, ed., *Court and Bakufu in Japan*.

7 See Goble, *Kenmu*, esp. chs. 1–3.

8 Varley, *Imperial Restoration in Medieval Japan*.

9 Goble, *Kenmu*, esp. chs. 5–8.

10 Goble, "Social Change, Knowledge, and History" and "Visions of an Emperor," in Mass, ed., *The Origins of Japan's Medieval World*; Weik, "Kitabatake Chikafusa's Use of the Terms *Dai* and *Sei* in the *Jinnō Shōtōki*."

11 See H. Paul Varley, "The Hōjō Family and Succession to Power," and Andrew Goble, "The Hōjō and Consultative Government," both in Mass, ed., *Court and Bakufu in Japan*. Andrew Edmund Goble, "The Kamakura Bakufu and Its Officials," in Hauser and Mass, eds., *The Bakufu in Japanese History*.

12 See Mass, *The Development of Kamakura Rule, 1180–1250*; Mass, *Lordship and Inheritance in Early Medieval Japan*.

13 See Grossberg, *Japan's Renaissance*, and the various chapters in Hall and Toyoda, eds., *Japan in the Muromachi Age*.

14 See Lorraine Harrington, "The Regional Outposts of the Muromachi Bakufu," in Hauser and Mass, eds., *The Bakufu in Japanese History*; Arnesen, *The Medieval Japanese Daimyō*.

15 Suzanne Gay, "Muromachi Bakufu Rule in Kyoto," in Hauser and Mass, eds., *The Bakufu in Japanese History*.

16 Varley, *The Ōnin War*.

17 Butler, *Emperor and Aristocracy in Japan, 1467–1680*.

18 Berry, *The Culture of Civil War in Kyoto*.

19 Gay, *The Moneylenders of Late Medieval Kyoto*.

20 Adolphson, *The Gates of Power*.

21 Berry, *Hideyoshi*; Lamers, *Japonius Tyrannus*; McMullin, *Buddhism and the State in Sixteenth-Century Japan*.

22 See Groner, *Saichō*; Groner, *Ryōgen and Mt. Hiei*.

23 See Abe, *The Weaving of Mantra*.

24 See Dumoulin, *Zen Buddhism*, and Collcutt, *Five Mountains*.

25 See, for example, Cleary, trans., *The Blue Cliff Record*; Heine and Wright eds., *The Kōan*.

26 See Armstrong, *Buddha*; Rahula, *What the Buddha Taught*.

27 See Inagaki and Stewart, trans., *The Three Pure Land Sutras*. A basic Japanese text in this regard is Genshin's *Teachings Essential for Rebirth* (see Andrews, *The Teachings Essential for Rebirth*).

28 There are several English translations of this. See, for example, Watson, trans., *The Lotus Sutra*.

29 See Bloom, *Shinran's Gospel of Pure Grace*.

30 See Rodd, *Nichiren: A Biography*; Yampolsky, ed., *Selected Writings of Nichiren*.

31 Stone, *Original Enlightenment and the Transformation of Medieval Japanese Buddhism*.

32 See Unno, *Shingon Refractions*; Tanabe, *Myoe the Dreamkeeper*.

33 See, for example, Ruppert, *Jewel in the Ashes*; Faure, *The Red Thread* and *The Power of Denial*; Rogers and Rogers, *Rennyo*. See also the various articles (in English and French) on medieval Japanese religion in the special issue of *Cahiers d'Extrême-Asie*, entitled "Buddhist Priests, Kings and Marginals: Studies on Medieval Japanese Buddhism," 13 (2002–3); Goble, "Truth Contradiction and Harmony in Medieval Japan"; Sharf and Sharf, eds., *Living Images*; LaFleur, "Hungry Ghosts and Hungry People."

34 See Dobbins, *Letters of the Nun Eshinni*; Meeks, "Nuns, Court Ladies, and Female Bodhisattvas."

35 Ruch, ed., *Engendering Faith*.

36 For overseas commerce, see Von Verschuer, *Le Commerce Exterieur du Japon*.

37 Two useful surveys are Tanaka Takeo, "Japan's Relations with Overseas Countries," in Hall and Toyoda, eds., *Japan in the Muromachi Age*, and Kawazoe Shoji, "Japan and East Asia," in Yamamura, ed., *The Cambridge History of Japan*, vol. 3, *Medieval Japan*.

38 Conlan, *In Little Need of Divine Intervention*.

39 For one example, see Haruko Wakabayashi, "The Mongol Invasions and the Making of the Iconography of Foreign Enemies," in Goble, Robinson, and Wakabayashi, eds., *Tools of Culture*.

40 Kyotsu Hori, "The Political and Economic Consequences of the Mongol Invasions," in Hall and Mass, eds., *Medieval Japan*; Mass, *Lordship and Inheritance in Early Medieval Japan*.

41 Hazard, "Japanese Marauding in Medieval Korea."

42 So, *Japanese Piracy in Ming China during the Sixteenth Century*.

43 Batten, *To the Ends of Japan*.

44   Hall, *Government and Local Power in Japan, 500–1700.*
45   Batten, *Gateway to Japan.*
46   See the essays in Goble, Robinson, and Wakabayashi, eds., *Tools of Culture.*

BIBLIOGRAPHY

Abe Ryuichi. *The Weaving of Mantra: Kukai and the Construction of Esoteric Buddhist Discourse.* New York: Columbia University Press, 1999.

Adolphson, Mikael. *The Gates of Power: Monks, Courtiers, and Warriors in Premodern Japan.* Honolulu: University of Hawai'i Press, 2000.

Andrews, Allan. *The Teachings Essential for Rebirth: A Study of Genshin's Ojoyoshu.* Tokyo: Monumenta Nipponica, 1973.

Armstrong, Karen. *Buddha.* New York: Viking, 2001.

Arnesen, Peter. *The Medieval Japanese Daimyō: The Ouchi Family's Rule in Suo and Nagato.* New Haven: Yale University Press, 1979.

Batten, Bruce. *To the Ends of Japan: Premodern Frontiers, Boundaries, and Interactions.* Honolulu: University of Hawai'i Press, 2003.

Batten, Bruce. *Gateway to Japan: Hakata in War and Peace, 500–1300.* Honolulu: University of Hawai'i Press, 2006.

Berry, Mary Elizabeth. *Hideyoshi.* Cambridge, Mass.: Council on East Asian Studies, Harvard University Press, 1982.

Berry, Mary Elizabeth. *The Culture of Civil War in Kyoto.* Berkeley: University of California Press, 1995.

Bloom, Alfred. *Shinran's Gospel of Pure Grace.* Tucson: University of Arizona Press, 1965.

Butler, Lee. *Emperor and Aristocracy in Japan, 1467–1680: Resilience and Renewal.* Cambridge, Mass.: Harvard University Asia Center, 2002.

Cleary, Thomas, trans. *The Blue Cliff Record.* Berkeley, Calif.: Numata Center for Buddhist Translation and Research, 1998.

Collcutt, Martin. *Five Mountains: The Rinzai Zen Monastic Institution in Medieval Japan.* Cambridge: Council on East Asian Studies, Harvard University, 1980.

Conlan, Thomas. *In Little Need of Divine Intervention.* Ithaca, NY: Cornell East Asia Series, 2001.

Conlan, Thomas. *State of War: The Violent Order of Fourteenth Century Japan.* Ann Arbor, Mich.: Center for Japanese Studies, 2004.

Dobbins, James. *Letters of the Nun Eshinni: Images of Pure Land Buddhism in Medieval Japan.* Honolulu: University of Hawai'i Press, 2004.

Dumoulin, Heinrich. *Zen Buddhism: A History,* vol. 2, *Japan.* London: Collier Macmillan, 1990.

Duus, Peter. *Feudalism in Japan,* 2nd edn. New York: Knopf, 1976.

Faure, Bernard. *The Red Thread: Buddhist Approaches to Sexuality.* Princeton: Princeton University Press, 1998.

Faure, Bernard. *The Power of Denial: Buddhism, Purity and Gender.* Princeton: Princeton University Press, 2003.

Friday, Karl. *Hired Swords: The Rise of Private Warrior Power in Early Japan.* Stanford, Calif.: Stanford University Press, 1992.

Friday, Karl. *Samurai, Warfare and the State in Early Medieval Japan.* New York: Routledge, 2004.

Gay, Suzanne. *The Moneylenders of Medieval Kyoto.* Honolulu: University of Hawai'i Press, 2002.

Goble, Andrew Edmund. "Truth Contradiction and Harmony in Medieval Japan: Emperor Hanazono (1297–1348) and Buddhism." *Journal of the International Association of Buddhist Studies*, 12 (1989): 21–63.

Goble, Andrew Edmund. "Social Change, Knowledge, and History: Hanazono's Admonitions to the Crown Prince." *Harvard Journal of Asiatic Studies* 50:1 (1995).

Goble, Andrew Edmund. *Kenmu: Go-Daigo's Revolution*. Cambridge: Council on East Asian Studies, Harvard University, 1997.

Goble, Andrew Edmund. "War and Injury: The Emergence of Wound Medicine in Medieval Japan." *Monumenta Nipponica* 60:3 (Autumn 2005).

Goble, Andrew Edmund, Robinson, Kenneth, and Wakabayashi, Haruko, eds. *Tools of Culture: Japan's Cultural, Intellectual, Medical, and Technological Contacts in East Asia, 1000s–1600s*. Honolulu: University of Hawai'i Press, forthcoming.

Groner, Paul. *Saichō: The Establishment of the Japanese Tendai School*. Berkeley, Calif.: Institute of Buddhist Studies, 1984.

Groner, Paul. *Ryōgen and Mt. Hiei: Japanese Tendai in the Tenth Century*. Honolulu: University of Hawai'i Press, 2002.

Grossberg, Kenneth. *Japan's Renaissance: The Politics of the Muromachi Bakufu*. Cambridge, Mass.: Council on East Asian Studies, Harvard University, 1981.

Hall, John W. *Government and Local Power in Japan, 500–1700: A Study based on Bizen Province*. Princeton: Princeton University Press, 1966.

Hall, John W., and Mass, Jeffrey, eds. *Medieval Japan: Essays in Institutional History*. New Haven: Yale University Press, 1974.

Hall, John W., and Toyoda Takeshi, eds. *Japan in the Muromachi Age*. Berkeley: University of California Press, 1977.

Hauser, William, and Mass, Jeffrey, eds. *The Bakufu in Japanese History*. Stanford, Calif.: Stanford University Press, 1985.

Hazard, Benjamin. "Japanese Marauding in Medieval Korea: The Wakō Impact on Late Koryo." Ph.D. dissertation, University of California, Berkeley, 1967.

Heine, Steven, and Wright, Dale, eds. *The Kōan: Texts and Contexts in Zen Buddhism*. New York: Oxford University Press, 2000.

Inagaki, Hisao, and Stewart, Harold, trans. *The Three Pure Land Sutras*. Berkeley, Calif.: Numata Center for Buddhist Translation and Research, 1995.

LaFleur, William. "Hungry Ghosts and Hungry People: Somaticity and Rationality in Medieval Japan." In Michel Feher, ed., *Fragments for a History of the Human Body*, pt. 1. New York: Zone Publications, 1989, pp. 271–303.

Lamers, Jeroen. *Japonius Tyrannus: The Japanese Warlord Oda Nobunaga Reconsidered*. Leiden: Hotei Publishing, 2000.

Mass, Jeffrey P. *The Development of Kamakura Rule*. Stanford, Calif.: Stanford University Press, 1979.

Mass, Jeffrey P. *Lordship and Inheritance in Early Medieval Japan*. Stanford, Calif.: Stanford University Press, 1989.

Mass, Jeffrey P. *Yoritomo and the Founding of the First Bakufu*. Stanford, Calif.: Stanford University Press, 1999.

Mass, Jeffrey P., ed. *Court and Bakufu in Japan: Essays in Kamakura History*. New Haven: Yale University Press, 1982.

Mass, Jeffrey P., ed. *The Origins of Japan's Medieval World*. Stanford, Calif.: Stanford University Press, 1997.

McMullin, Neil. *Buddhism and the State in Sixteenth-Century Japan*. Princeton: Princeton University Press, 1984.

Meeks, Lori. "Nuns, Court Ladies, and Female Bodhisattvas: The Women of Japan's Medieval Ritsu-School Nuns' Revival Movement." Ph.D. dissertation, Princeton University, 2003.

Rahula, Walpola. *What the Buddha Taught.* New York: Grove Press, 1962.

Rodd, Laurel Rasplica. *Nichiren: A Biography.* Tempe: Arizona State University, 1978.

Rodd, Laurel Rasplica, trans. *Nichiren: Selected Writings.* Honolulu: University of Hawai'i Press, 1980.

Rogers, Minor, and Rogers, Ann. *Rennyo: The Second Founder of Shin Buddhism.* Berkeley, Calif.: Asian Humanities Press, 1991.

Ruch, Barbara, ed. *Engendering Faith: Women and Buddhism in Premodern Japan.* Ann Arbor: Center for Japanese Studies, University of Michigan, 2002.

Ruppert, Brian. *Jewel in the Ashes: Buddha Relics and Power in Early Medieval Japan.* Cambridge, Mass.: Harvard University Asia Center, 2000.

Sharf, Robert H., and Sharf, Elizabeth Horton, eds. *Living Images: Japanese Buddhist Icons in Context.* Stanford, Calif.: Stanford University Press, 2001.

So Kwan-wai. *Japanese Piracy in Ming China during the Sixteenth Century.* East Lansing: Michigan State University Press, 1975.

Stone, Jacqueline. *Original Enlightenment and the Transformation of Medieval Japanese Buddhism.* Honolulu: University of Hawai'i Press, 1999.

Tanabe, George. *Myoe the Dreamkeeper: Fantasy and Knowledge in Early Kamakura Buddhism.* Cambridge, Mass.: Council on East Asian Studies, Harvard University, 1992.

Unno, Mark. *Shingon Refractions.* Boston: Wisdom Publications, 2004.

Varley, H. Paul. *The Ōnin War.* New York: Columbia University Press, 1967.

Varley, H. Paul. *Imperial Restoration in Medieval Japan.* New York: Columbia University Press, 1971.

Von Verschuer, Charlotte. *Le Commerce Exterieur du Japon: Des Origines au XVIe siècle.* Paris: Maisonneuve and Larosse, 1987.

Watson, Burton, trans. *The Lotus Sutra.* New York: Columbia University Press, 1993.

Weik, John F. "Kitabatake Chikafusa's Use of the Terms *Dai* and *Sei* in the *Jinnō Shōtōki*." *Papers on Far Eastern History* 1 (1970): 140–72.

Yamamura, Kozo, ed. *The Cambridge History of Japan*, vol. 3, *Medieval Japan.* Cambridge: Cambridge University Press, 1990.

Yampolsky, Phillip, ed. *Selected Writings of Nichiren.* New York: Columbia University Press, 1990.

Yampolsky, Phillip, ed. *Letters of Nichiren.* New York: Columbia University Press, 1996.

FURTHER READING

Pierre Souyri's *The World Turned Upside Down* (New York: Columbia University Press, 2001) gives good attention to aspects of social history in medieval Japan. *The Cambridge History of Japan*, vol. 3, *Medieval Japan* (Cambridge: Cambridge University Press, 1990), edited by Kozo Yamamura, gives a useful summary of scholarly understandings as of the mid 1980s. The conceptualizations about the relationship between center and regions that inform John Whitney Hall's *Government and Local Power in Japan, 500–1700* (Princeton: Princeton University Press, 1966) continue to be crucial. Relevant sections of William Hauser and Jeffrey Mass's edited volume *The Bakufu in Japanese History* (Stanford, Calif.: Stanford University Press, 1985) are germane. Portions of John Whitney Hall's *Japan from Prehistory to Modern Times* (New York: Dell, 1970), with a focus on institutional history, and H. Paul Varley's *Japanese Culture*, 4th edn. (Honolulu: University of Hawai'i Press, 2000) remain useful.

PART II

Early Modern Japan

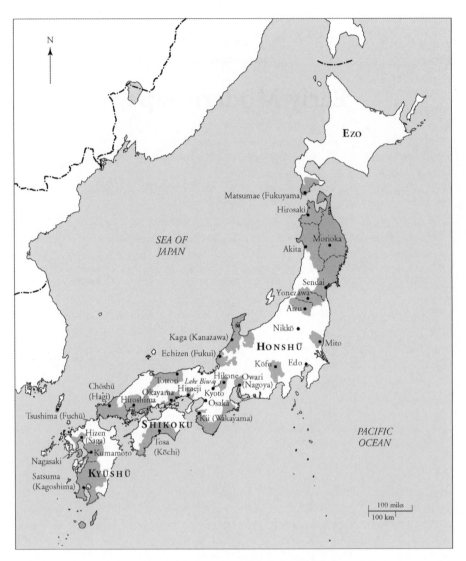

Map 2 Major domains, castle towns, and cities of Tokugawa Japan

CHAPTER FOUR

Unification, Consolidation, and Tokugawa Rule

Philip C. Brown

A major trend in recent scholarship on early modern Japanese politics has been to play the role of the little boy in the crowd who shouted out, "The emperor has no clothes!" In this case, the issue is not the emperor (whom most have generally treated as unimpressively endowed with actual vestments of power), but the shōgun and his attendant authority. The chorus of critical voices is not uniformly harmonious, and there are still defenders of older images of shogunal authority, but the trend is unmistakable. In the case of the starkly honest little boy in the fable, the result was simply to reveal the foolishness of both adult behavior and imperial pretense; the emerging picture of early modern governance and politics is one of considerably greater complexity than such conclusions, however, and not beyond debate. While moving beyond stereotypes of premodern society that dominated images through the mid twentieth century, and while displaying the influence of current trends in Western historiography, the new image of early modern Japan also exhibits some rather remarkable lacunae. Scholars have focused more of their attention on developments at the regional and local level – daimyō domains, cities, towns, and villages – even though we still have significant gaps in our understanding of elite developments, including the shogunate.[1] Simply put, a limited number of workers in the field translates into less comprehensive study than is ideal.

Periodization is fundamental to historical study, but often not directly addressed. It is a slippery subject, made hard to grasp because any scheme is dependent on what subject an author places at the center of her attention. An art historian's periodization will differ from that offered by an economic historian; a demographic historian will note different dividing lines than a student of religion. This essay adopts a political framework for periodization. Broadly speaking, it concerns competition over who has the right to exercise administrative powers and the actual exercise of that authority, including the activities of popular groups to influence policy. Much of the discussion treats the development of political institutions, those formal and informal (that is, customary) structures people create through individual and collective efforts that shape the way in which political authority is exercised and defined as legitimate or illegitimate.

"Early modern" is adopted as a moniker primarily out of convenience; it is the most widely used designation for the period encompassed here. To the degree there are continuities with the "modern" Meiji political and institutional order, those links lie largely in the realm of general attitudes toward authority, government officials, and (semi-)bureaucratic order.[2] The Meiji institutional structure at all levels varied significantly from its predecessor states of the late fifteenth to nineteenth centuries. There is sufficient continuity in political-institutional developments from the late fifteenth to mid nineteenth century, however, to give this period a sense of conceptual integrity.

A Brief Overview of Political Development during the Era

Unlike the rise of new overlords in China or England in which one leading family replaced another in a *coup d'état* or after a short period of civil war, the rise of Tokugawa pre-eminence capped a century of virtually continuous civil wars in Japan from the late fifteenth to late sixteenth centuries. The upshot of the Ōnin War (1467) was fragmentation and devolution of real ruling authority to several hundred territorially limited warlords (*sengoku* or warring states *daimyō*) who fought ceaselessly with each other. That process proved to be highly creative and whatever the cost in blood and treasure, it ultimately created the foundation for the Pax Tokugawa (1600–1867). In broad outline, daimyō (baronial overlords) who survived focused on consolidating power within their domains, increased their direct military power relative to that of enfeoffed retainers, expanded their tax base through investments in expanding arable lands, constructed riparian works to limit flood damage, and extended irrigation works, in addition to demonstrating good political sense and superb generalship. Although ultimately a number of large daimyō re-emerged to take positions of regional or national leadership, relatively small domains of sub-provincial size remained typical until after the Meiji Restoration.

Despite the presence of some 260 daimyō who acted with a high degree of autonomy throughout the era, the new, more stable daimyō domains formed the building blocks for two and a half centuries of peace. Coalitions of such daimyō began to emerge in the mid sixteenth century, increasing the scale of battles to tens and hundreds of thousands of soldiers by 1600.[3] While famous warlords Takeda Shingen (1521–73), Date Masamune (1566–1636), Uesugi Kenshin (1530–78), and others failed to achieve nationwide dominance, the ambitions of Oda Nobunaga (1534–82) and his able general Toyotomi Hideyoshi (1536–98) led to administrative arrangements and controls that finally enabled former Oda ally Tokugawa Ieyasu (1543–1616) to establish a remarkably peaceful reign beginning in 1600 with his victory at Sekigahara. (Foreign threats were minimal, and the last serious disturbance associated with foreign powers was dispatched in 1637 with the suppression of the Shimabara Rebellion in which the Portuguese were implicated.)

The Tokugawa shōguns formally exercised political leadership as the representative of the emperor, but there was no nationwide system of taxation, justice, or military. First and foremost the shōgun was *primus inter pares*, the largest of daimyō (in direct control of about one-eighth of the land). As leader of the victorious coalition of daimyō, Ieyasu's prestige and status was clearly head and shoulders above the other daimyō. By manipulating status symbols, pledges of allegiance, the allocation of domain lands, and certain aspects of daimyō personal behavior (for example, political intermarriage and adoption with key daimyō families), the Tokugawa built an enduring political network with the daimyō. Although seventeenth-century disturbances among daimyō retainers (*oie sōdō*) reflected significant dissatisfaction, daimyō stakes in the emerging order were sufficiently great relative to the costs and risks of taking on the shōgun, and with him, perhaps much of Japan, that they all chose continued, peaceful coexistence under the Tokugawa umbrella.

While administrative powers were limited and never resulted in the establishment of a nationwide, centrally administered bureaucratic government, the prestige and authority of the shōgun had very real political and administrative consequences. Oda Nobunaga, Toyotomi Hideyoshi, and the Tokugawa shōguns could compel military service from daimyō (broadly defined to include items like the rebuilding of shogunal fortifications such as Osaka Castle) and to that end they successfully demanded that daimyō provide estimates of domain value, but they could not compel the implementation of a specific standard on which that value was calculated.[4] The shōgun provided – increasingly – a venue in which diversity issues could be resolved. Through suasion as well as formal court procedures, domains turned to the shōgun to settle border disputes among them, complaints against agents in other territories (including Tokugawa lands), and so on. Later, shogunal officials were active in dealing with popular disturbances that crossed domain boundaries or undertaking regional riparian efforts that likewise transcended the authority of one domain. While weak relative to modern states, this arrangement had sufficient bonds to sustain a stable relationship among daimyō until the mid nineteenth century.

Peace paid extraordinary dividends for Japan. Whether one accepts a figure of 12 million or 18 million souls in 1600, the expansion to some 24 millions by the early eighteenth century, ultimately plateauing at 28 to 30 millions by the early nineteenth century, was extraordinary for a premodern society.[5] Population growth both depended upon and stimulated economic growth (primarily agriculture) and diversification, interregional trade, and regional economic specialization. (While there was historically significant international trade, it was not large enough or sufficiently oriented toward mass consumption goods to make much of a contribution to the expanding economy.)

Urbanization was first dominant in the shogunal headquarters of Edo and daimyō castle towns like Kanazawa or Kōchi that served as domain administrative centers, but later focused on market-oriented towns, and expanded the ranks of the middle classes. Increased trade stimulated the growth of industrial and commercially oriented social strata in the villages too. These groups increasingly participated in a burgeoning national cultural efflorescence identified with the Genroku era (1688–1703) as well as creating political pressures and problems.

By the late seventeenth and early eighteenth centuries the key political issues of the day had shifted from establishing and reinforcing the foundations of a stable polity to issues of resource allocation. Riparian works, urban construction (and reconstruction made necessary by frequent fires and earthquakes), the expansion of arable to its extreme limits given contemporary technological constraints, and similar developments associated with population growth, depleted forest resources, destabilized watersheds, and even exhausted some marine resources. Merchants and parvenu groups in rural areas aroused envy even where their activities did not create suspicion of unfair trading practices and hostility. Daimyō and samurai found themselves strapped. Unable to effectively raise taxes to meet growing expenditures and inflation, daimyō budgets were a sea of red ink. Daimyō resorted to cost-cutting by reducing the salaries paid their samurai and forced loans from well-off merchants and farmers. For samurai, such daimyō-imposed sacrifices came on top of the significantly declining purchasing power of their incomes.

As the eighteenth century ended and the nineteenth began, two major famines and increased popular protests, a number violent, punctuated an emergent sense of malaise. Administrative reforms failed to solve both domain and social problems. Many a commoner and samurai alike felt that proper social order had been turned upside down. Into this environment came increased efforts of Westerners – Russians, British, American – to increase Japanese intercourse with the world. A combination of early seventeenth-century Japanese hostility and a lack of widespread European interest in trade with Japan had resulted in seventeenth-century decline in, and restriction of, foreign contacts. Trade with the Dutch was limited to Nagasaki; Chinese trade was also centered there but was carried out through contacts with the Ryūkyū Islands as well. Contacts with Korea were conducted through the island daimyō of Tsushima (the Sō), initially for the purpose of using diplomatic relations to enhance seventeenth-century shogunal legitimacy, but also for the economic benefits trade brought the daimyō. Porous borders in northern Japan permitted a trade with Japan that expanded in importance for Japanese and Ainu throughout the era.

While the Shimabara Rebellion of 1637 occurred in a context in which Japan was the technological equal of the West and daimyō reaction to the threat largely uniform, nineteenth-century Western efforts to engage Japan took place in a less advantageous technological and domestic political context. Shogunal officials, more than many daimyō, were alert to the changing technological balance between Japan and the West; when Perry arrived in 1853 and 1854, they pursued a pragmatic course and engaged Western nations. Many daimyō, however, reached different conclusions about Western military power and sought to sustain the policy of rejecting Western entreaties that had hardened since the late eighteenth century. In an environment of widely sensed malaise and distrust, the division of opinion and the setting of a new course for resolving mounting domestic problems were ultimately resolved only with the conclusion of the civil war (the Boshin War, 1868–9) that ushered in Japan's first modern government.

Breaking Away from Meiji

Within the broad-brush image just sketched, Western scholars have come to recognize significant positive elements in Japan's early modern, although considerable room for debate remains. This was not always the case. Up through the mid twentieth century, the predominant image of early modern Japan and the preceding Sengoku era was negative. It was characterized as feudal, and the late fifteenth to late sixteenth century especially was seen as something of a Dark Age, filled with disorder and war (in cinema, it serves as the stage for a Japanese equivalent of the Western shoot-'em-up, the *chambara* films of samurai valor). That judgment and a similarly negative image of the Tokugawa owed much to the self-justification of victorious parties in the Meiji Restoration. To legitimate their capture of political power they painted their immediate Tokugawa predecessors as backward and inept. The critical tone was supported by a small army of people like Fukuzawa Yukichi who were ardent supporters of varying degrees of reform along Western lines, the pursuit of "Western Science to preserve Eastern Ethics" (*wakon yōsai*), the creation of a Japan characterized by "Civilization and Enlightenment" (*bunmei kaika*) grounded in a "Rich Country, Strong Army" (*fukoku kyōhei*) capable of preserving Japan's independence and ability to act in the late nineteenth-century world of imperialist state relations.

English-language scholarship, too, tended toward this characterizations, but beginning with the 1968 publication of John Whitney Hall and Marius Jansen's essay collection, *Studies in the Institutional History of Early Modern Japan*, a concerted effort arose to recast Tokugawa (and later, the age preceding it) in a more positive light. The title embodied the effort to throw off the image of feudal society and to highlight the era's positive contributions to the creation of post-Restoration, modern Japan. This approach accompanied the extensive effort to recast late nineteenth- and early twentieth-century Japanese history as a generally positive and successful effort at "modernization," a view that was embodied in the Princeton University Press series, "Studies in the Modernization of Japan," Thomas C. Smith's *The Agrarian Origins of Modern Japan*, and other works.[6]

This liberation of the Tokugawa image from the critical gaze of early Meiji Japan had its own limitations, however; in its own way it made the Tokugawa prisoner to Meiji, encouraging work that looked for positive links between the two eras. The harsh side of Tokugawa life and politics got considerably short shrift. Together with the reconsideration of America's international role during the Vietnam War, Marxist and "progressive" historians not only launched intellectual broadsides at the modernizationist post-Meiji studies, but also at images of Tokugawa Japan implicated in that paradigm. Work appeared on dissenting voices in Japanese history[7] and peasant rebellion.[8] Since that time, several studies have transcended the Meiji Restoration in a further effort to break the constraints of earlier efforts to portray Tokugawa–Meiji links as largely positive, but at the same time present a balanced assessment of the transition.[9]

Both of these broad efforts to break the chains of Meiji must be evaluated in generally positive terms, for they open the possibility of taking the history of the sixteenth to mid nineteenth century much more on its own terms than had been the case previously. The best of recent scholarship on the early modern polity of Japan does precisely that, at least within the bounds of what any historian can do. Without this effort, much of what is described below would not have been possible.

Expanding Interests

Early work on the early modern state and politics devoted substantial attention to the development of shogunal and domain rule. While early studies paid some attention to regional developments, the general thrust was to stress the development of a single pattern of administration, one in which daimyō were clearly in conformity with the emergent national leadership.[10] Recent studies, even of the formative stages of the shogunate offer an alternative to images of extensive hegemonic power.[11] Mark Ravina and Luke Roberts have stressed domain autonomy almost to the point of independence from the shōgun.[12]

The issues generated by such studies are not limited to re-examination of the balance of power between the Tokugawa shōguns and their immediate predecessors (Oda Nobunaga and Toyotomi Hideyoshi) on the one hand, and the daimyō they led on the other; they also provide us with a sense of the diversity of domain administrative structure and the policies as they evolved within domains throughout the era. Ravina presents clear evidence of wavering policy even over such a fundamental issue as the urbanization of samurai (part of the effort to separate warriors from villagers) in Hirosaki domain in the eighteenth century, Brown does so for sixteenth- and seventeenth-century tax structures in Kaga, as does Roberts for eighteenth- and nineteenth-century Tosa economic policy.[13] Within domains a parallel development can be seen as scholars like James McClain explored the degree to which castle town growth could be controlled by daimyō.[14]

The locus of change scholars identify has shifted toward the motivations, incentives, and issues important to daimyō, retainers, townsmen, and villagers. Actors at these levels are now likely to be described as performing with considerable autonomy, and such common directions in policy or the outlines of administrative structure as are still recognized are likely to be explained as the result of a limited array of potential solutions to widespread administrative challenges. Rather than separating warrior from peasant as the result of Hideyoshi's Sword Hunt (1588) and class separation edicts (1591), daimyō are seen as developing a combination of policies over a number of decades that increasingly restricted the number of landholding, rustic samurai and their autonomy to control subordinate villagers.[15] Current scholarship even acknowledges a lesser degree of class separation, though all scholars still treat early modern society as highly stratified and status-conscious. Popular political action (*ikki*) has also drawn recent attention. In addition to Herbert Bix and Stephen Vlastos, case studies were published by William Kelly, Selcuk Esenbel, and Anne Walthall. The most comprehensive treatment, however, has been the political scientist James White's *Ikki: Social Conflict and Political Protest in Early Modern Japan.*[16]

A corollary to increased focus on a wider array of historical actors has been a breakdown of stereotyped images of who participated meaningfully in political activity. While studies of popular protests have particularly dramatic appeal, the most significant evidence comes from those studies that show commoner participation in domain policy formation and the ability of women to act dramatically in both village and national affairs in more ordinary contexts.[17] Extension of scholarly interest into relatively lower levels of society has meant something of a reconceptualization of "Japan." Studies by David Howell, Brett Walker, and Gregory Smits have encompassed Japanese northern and southern borderlands (Hokkaidō and Okinawa) and the political-economic relations between Japanese and local populations.[18] In addition to undermining the image of Japanese isolationism and exploring the subordination of these territories to Japanese overlordship, these authors open the issue of Japanese self-identity. Marcia Yonemoto also takes up the issue of identity and provides useful insights into an emerging sense of domestic connections, at least among the intellectual and ruling elites, despite the awareness of domestic difference.[19] The images she paints of a Japan comprised of provinces as opposed to daimyō domains reveals the expanding proto-national sensitivity that coexisted with strong local domain identities. (The downside of this growing national awareness was development of a stream of thinking that stressed Japan's uniqueness and that was sometimes manifested as blatant anti-foreignism.)[20]

The broadening of scholarly interests extends to consideration of human inter-action with the environment. The political dimensions of such interaction are most clearly seen in the work of Conrad Totman[21] but have also been manifested in Walker's work, among others. In this context, part of the mid-Tokugawa crisis of resource allocation encompassed solving significant ecological problems associated with exhaustion of forest resources (given the levels of technological development at the time).

The Question of Political Early Modernity

Totally apart from the links of Tokugawa Japan to its Meiji successor state, the de-emphasis on the role of a strong political center as a motive force in political history creates an image of the early modern polity that is closer to the more decentralized medieval ruling structure of Ashikaga Japan. Jeroen Lamers's treatment of Oda Nobunaga makes him more of a force in Japan's transition to stability than simply a precursor to Toyotomi Hideyoshi, but the tools Oda employed have an essential continuity with those of Hideyoshi and his successors in their emphasis on controlling the person of subordinate daimyō more than subordinating them in an integrated national administration.[22] Pledges of loyalty, hostage-holding, and visits to a hege-mon's capital, even after they become routinized playscripts in the mid seventeenth century, are fundamentally the cement of a premodern order and gave life to early characterizations of the Tokugawa period as feudal. Recent studies show similar processes at work within domains through at least the mid seventeenth century.

If the growth of centralized political and administrative power, accompanied by the bureaucratic routinization of administration are taken as hallmarks of political early modernity (as Hall did in *Government and Local Power in Japan*), then these occur most clearly within domain administrations (including the house administrative organs of the Tokugawa). Fiefs of subordinate retainers became virtual fictions; even where they remained in form, they were largely gutted of content: typically, enfeoffed retainers could not set their own taxes, compel commoners to serve them, administer justice or undertake many other basic administrative tasks at all. Where such functions remained, retainer autonomy was almost completely restricted by domain ordinance. Daimyō administrative apparatus connected directly to the self-governing institutions of villages, towns, temples, shrines, and even outcaste (*hinin*) communities.

Although less complete at the national level, central authority under Nobunaga, Hideyoshi, Ieyasu, and their successors clearly grew. While based on pledges of loyalty and other medieval techniques, these overlords possessed and used their ability to confirm daimyō overlordship of domains to post them to new lands or to remove them from power. With the major exception of defeat in battles like Sekigahara (1600), Osaka (1614–15), and Shimabara when large enemy daimyō might be destroyed or reduced in size, the daimyō whose domains were reduced, eliminated, or moved were overwhelmingly small and mid-sized, not the large province or multi-province holding lords. Hideyoshi was able to order invasions of Korea in pursuit of subduing China. A semi-bureaucratic structure was established for maintaining con-trol over national networks of temples and shrines; a similar office oversaw the much revived imperial household.[23] Foreign affairs, a very modest issue for much of the period, were the provenance of the shōgun for the most part, and the first late eighteenth- and early nineteenth-century efforts of Russians, Englishmen, and Americans to land at various places throughout Japan and Hokkaidō were met with instructions to go through shogunal channels.

Mid- and late Tokugawa shōguns were able to use their prestige and authority in diversity disputes to chip away at daimyō autonomy or limit the extension of their economic reach, but Japan lacked the substantial and extended external threats that compelled Spain, France, and England (for example) to aggressively compromise baronial autonomy and strengthen the state apparatus. James White notes the degree to which the shōgun monopolized legitimate use of force, and Conrad Totman explores cases of shogunal initiative in public works, but such developments did not result in any integration of domains into a shōgun-directed administrative structure.[24] Indeed, one may read the shōgun's effort to create a consensus through consultation with daimyō after Perry's arrival as an indication of its rather tenuous perch on the top of the Tokugawa political heap. Had it felt in a clearly superior position it is unlikely that this tactic would have been thought useful or necessary.

Yet truth be told, this impression derived from recent scholarship may be a result of the small number of scholars in the field. We have article-length studies of mid-Tokugawa shōguns such as Tsunayoshi (r. 1680–1709 and the so-called "Dog Shōgun," famous for issuing an edict protecting animals from maltreatment), but no extended treatment of their reigns or that of any other shōgun other than Ieyasu.[25] We have an overview of politics in the bakufu, a monographic treatment of one intellectual, Arai Hakuseki, who sought unsuccessfully to extend the authority of the shōgun, and treatments of two other eighteenth-century shogunal advisors (Tanuma Okitsugu and Matsudaira Sadanobu), but little else.

The issue of early modernity extends into the realm of Japan's relationships with and views of non-Japanese. While modern states typically do not conduct economic relations with regions outside their sphere of formally established diplomatic relations, and while such relationships typically specify clearly recognized territorial boundaries, both characteristics were absent in sixteenth- to mid-nineteenth-century Japan. For example, Japan had no formal diplomatic ties with China, yet continued trade with China at Nagasaki. Both China and Japan exercised suzerainty over the Ryūkyū Islands, and the Japanese were clearly aware of the ambiguous status of the archipelago. The international order was seen as rigidly rank-conscious and the idea of equality of states (and peoples) was simply not ascendant. While this situation allowed a significant porous quality to Japan's relationship with its immediate neighbors, it would not survive the modern treaty system that Perry introduced in 1854.[26]

National Integration and the Spread of a Popular National Consciousness

One part of the system of daimyō control, the *sankin kōtai* system compelled daimyō attendance in the shōgun's capital at Edo for alternate years and kept family members hostage when the daimyō was not present. This arrangement not only helped to maintain the peace, it also furthered national integration at multiple social levels. The gathering of powerful families in one place furthered the exchange of ideas among them, including those on how to administer their domains. In Edo, they competed with each other not only for prestige and honor in both the shogunal and imperial ranks, but also as administrators. By the late seventeenth century, for example, it was widely noted that in administrative effectiveness, the domain of Kaga was number one, Tosa number two. Models of land taxation, administrative structure, economic policy, and reform spread through discussions among daimyō and their subordinates while resident in Edo. Daimyō could learn how administrative initiatives were going in other domains and could evaluate what they might learn for use in their own territories.

In order to maintain the system of alternate attendance, a national system of major highways developed under shogunal leadership. Pock-marked with inspection barriers, these served to channel daimyō and other administrators' traffic and permitted inspection of domestic passports (especially for the powerful and their minions). Staffed through special local taxation, these networks attracted opportunists of all stripes, ever ready to earn a few coppers from travelers. Inns, houses of drink and assignation, souvenir shops, and the like increasingly populated the most well-traveled highways. The attraction was clear: a daimyō entourage could consist of hundreds of people, all passing along the same route at one time.

In combination with the costs of maintaining a fully staffed household in Edo, the expenses of *sankin kōtai* cost daimyō approximately a third to one-half of their annual budgets. This meant that taxes raised largely in kind in a domain had to be converted to cash for expenditure in travels to and from Edo as well as for maintenance of the Edo residence. For most domains this meant shipping tax goods (primarily rice) to Osaka for sale, a process that made the city the center of a well-integrated and truly national market.

The markets and roads designed to control and supply daimyō could not be limited to those purposes. They ultimately facilitated the movement of goods, people, ideas, and fashion throughout Japan, increasing commoner awareness of a shared culture vis-à-vis China and the world, even though it was a culture marked by regional variations that were often viewed hierarchically by political, intellectual, and cultural elites.

The Short Arm of the Law

One of the corollaries of rethinking the power of the shōguns has been a general re-evaluation of the reach of the state, whether daimyō or shōgun. While acknowledging the presence of overlord's laws, Herman Ooms has shown in a series of studies that local leaders, commoner leaders, were perfectly capable of marshaling their own interpretation of (for example) laws on outcaste groups to promote their own agendas rather than those of a domain or shōgun.[27] In part this ability is a consequence of the semi-autonomous standing of local commoner governments, but it is equally important to remember that this arrangement made sense because of the limitations of communications technology of the day: in an age of poor (by modern standards) communications, transaction costs of much administration and justice were shifted to local bodies, limiting the need for daimyō and shōgun alike to field larger forces of their own salaried employees into the cities, towns, and villages of the realm. It was this device that permitted the urbanization of most samurai under the watchful eye of the daimyō in his castle town.

Other devices, often designed to limit corruption or prevent samurai from building local alliances with villagers also interfered with effective administrative reach of domain officials; however, these have not yet been explored by English-language scholarship in any depth. For example, samurai officials were rotated frequently. In many parts of Japan, lands administered by the shōgun were exchanged for lands administered by some daimyō, or a daimyō was given villages to oversee on behalf of the shōgun. Similar practices were followed in the commoner organizations that administered groups of villages. There was a great deal of turnover in the composition of these groups of villages. Changes every ten to fifteen years were not uncommon; the size of groups generally increased over time. In combination, such shifting of administrative oversight at both the domain and sub-domain levels made samurai oversight of villages and village groups a huge challenge and increased the autonomy of local authorities. This all left open possibilities for villagers to develop their own distinctive institutions of corporate control of arable land, for example.[28]

At lower levels, a small handful of scholars have treated district and village case studies. In addition to Ooms, Hitomi Tonomura has examined the transition to the early modern era in village and district organization. William Kelly has examined district organization of irrigation networks. Margaret McKean, examining the regulation of common lands (*iriai*), reminds us that villages, too, made and enforced laws, sometimes in very sophisticated fashion.[29] In the urban realm, only McClain has written a monographic study, *Kanazawa*, focused on development of the castle town in the largest independent domain of the time, Kaga.[30]

Law also functioned in a considerably different fashion than what modern people suppose, at least on a day-to-day basis. Earlier work on the legal system stressed the role of conciliation and compromise in the premodern eras, but Constantine Vaporis in particular conveys an impression of flexibility in implementation that one does not expect given the harshness of both the language of the law and the punishments prescribed. Nam-lin Hur's work on the efforts to control activities at a major temple in Edo itself reveal a similarly ineffective effort at enforcement.[31] Much of Tokugawa "law" was hortatory, and followed Chinese patterns of describing an ideal toward which people should strive without regard to the likelihood of enforcement (sumptuary legislation or edicts describing the duties of farmers typically fall into this category). Moral suasion was the primary object, not justicable law in a modern sense. Daniel Botsman's research focuses more on criminal law than other previous studies.[32]

Missing Links

A number of issues of fundamental importance remain virtually or completely untouched by scholars. In addition to the dearth of studies of the shōgun noted above, we find only one significant treatment of samurai.[33] While this treats the very important issue of how this group could simultaneously possess a strong group identification and a strong sense of individual self, issues such as early modern military organization, training, weaponry, and the like have gone unexamined. The peculiarly seventeenth-century phenomenon of house disturbances (*oie sōdō*) has escaped all but passing treatment. Since these latter issues often bear directly on another missing link – study of the process by which daimyō domains negotiated and adapted to new roles under the Tokugawa – these subjects are of particular importance. Of less chronologically restricted import, we have yet to address the nature of "ordinary" samurai interactions with commoners. While mid-century scholars had a clear interest in issues of samurai–commoner intermarriage, the sale of samurai rank, and so on, such subjects remain under-treated on the whole.

Despite Hur's work noted above, only Neil McMullin has devoted substantial attention to the relationship between religious organizations and the state.[34] Study of the changing relationships between religious organizations, the shogunate, daimyō, and village administration remain untouched. We know religious pilgrimage flourished from the eighteenth century, but we have little sense of how authorities dealt with the phenomenon or of the possible links between such policies and the treatment of millenarian movements (*yonaoshi*) of the mid nineteenth century that signaled a broad sense of popular malaise.

Domain administrations' internal workings likewise remain something of a blank, despite the fact that this is where key decisions were made that affected many facets of Tokugawa society. While we have some studies on land taxation, we know little about domain finances, for example. While we have some studies of village and district institutions and politics, and some of upper level domain policy-making, study of the offices that linked the two – even as part of a broader monograph – are rare.

A broad need exists for comparative work in two senses. The first is a need for comparative study of different regions within Japan. This is necessitated by the very deep and widespread regional variation in political practice that characterized much of the era. Such studies might focus on topics such as the following: Why do some domains completely urbanize samurai, while others leave samurai in rural communities or send them back after having moved them into castle towns? In a related vein, how do samurai adapt to peace, including masterless samurai (*rōnin*) in the seventeenth century? Do different structures of domain administration make a difference in degree of daimyō control over (1) domain officials (corruption, abuse of power), (2) commoner populations (for example, taxation effectiveness), and (3) domain finances? It has been relatively easy to identify in skeletal form the links that brought an increased sense of connectedness within Japan, but case studies, especially in the administrative realm, are missing from any current bibliography.

In addition, there is the broad question of the degree to which the history of early modern Japan might be comparable to those of other parts of the world. Such comparisons as there are typically are made to Europe, based on both the apparent similarity of decentralized political organizations ("feudalism") and the influence of Marxist concepts among historians in Japan. While such comparison can be valuable, it may make equal or greater sense to compare Japan with its East Asian neighbors (with which it shares a cultural tradition) or other parts of the world. Such comparisons might suggest new ways for us to understand the unfolding of Japanese history, for example our evaluation of the nature of law in Tokugawa Japan as noted above.

A broader array of comparative cases can help scholars treat the early modern period more on its own terms, further freeing our vision from close links to Meiji.

Simultaneously it would render Japan more comparable to other regional-national histories and likely make its experience more accessible to the English-speaking world. One possible approach might be to employ the concept of the "long eighteenth century," with its failed experiments in centralization, efforts to meet the growing challenge of "new" market forces, and technological developments from experiences broadly shared with a number of regions throughout the world.

The realm of foreign affairs, broadly conceived, has received increased attention in recent years, but a number of interesting possible avenues of investigation remain. As Japan dealt with Perry, it mobilized its coastal defenses, involving villages and towns, but no one has studied this significant development and its implications for the creation of non-samurai armies. This subject suggests the potential for examining the link between foreign affairs and domestic political agendas, a subject that has considerable potential to improve our understanding of the early seventeenth-century settlement between daimyō and shōgun.

As a rule, post-Restoration foreign affairs are treated *de novo*, without connection to Tokugawa ideals, visions, or practice, but a dissertation by Norihito Mizuno suggests that there may be a significant link.[35] Cultural and trade links with other countries remained important, even if those with Europe were not particularly thick. Given Mizuno and Yonemoto's work, we now have clear evidence that such issues deserve more attention. The issues of identity, noted above, might also be effectively approached by examination of the foreign trading communities within Japan (as well as study of outcastes).

Two studies on women have been noted above, but more can be done. While Japanese documentation from village headmen to population registers reveal an awareness of the labor contributions of women, exploration of their political role remains a challenge. This field is growing among Japanese scholars and we can expect their influence to be felt in the English-language scholarship. Since this subject is taken up in another essay in this volume, we simply note the need for work in this field.

In Sum

The preceding discussion reveals an expansion of scholarly interests and shift in the locus of motive forces that scholars are likely to identify, a shift away from the center and toward the regional and local, a shift away from elites toward more ordinary folk. Scholars now present a rather different image of shogunal power than that which encouraged mid-century scholars to characterize the Tokugawa state as a "centralized feudal" order. Shogunal power is now seen as weaker than before. But it has also been painted as growing in some noticeable ways, for example, the monopolization of the legitimate use of force and increased involvement in diversity disputes and problems that crossed domain boundaries. This reappraisal has been furthered by a variety of case studies, the marshaling of methodologies and concepts taken from an array of academic approaches that range from the social sciences to critical cultural studies. Despite growing interest and a burst of studies in the past two decades, much fundamental work clearly remains for us to explore.

NOTES

1 In no small part the reasons for this apparently contradictory image lie in the structure of the field: like most fields of premodern Japanese studies (literature is something of an exception), it is considerably underweighted in the ranks of scholars. The (relatively) small size of the field and the problems in reaching out beyond the community of early modern historians to entice students into the field as well as to convey the significance of the field to other historians is partly grounded in issues of language: prior to the mid nineteenth century, both written and spoken Japanese were considerably more difficult than late nineteenth- and twentieth-century Japanese, and (as some of the developments described below indicate) there was no broad country-wide standardization of terminology for offices, classes, or even biota and fauna. This situation is compounded when people choose topics that virtually demand the use of hand-written manuscript materials. The result is a formidable entry barrier, and even when one is successful in breaching that obstacle, the challenge of translating findings into a language that successfully engages the interest of students and historians in other fields remains great. The result is the use of language and terminology in English that retain Japanese terms rather than translating them and/or the failure to explore English language concepts sufficiently to appropriately adapt their use to analysis of Japan or to convince scholars of European history (for example) that the author understands the concepts they employ.

2 Najita, *Japan*.

3 The first mid-century European contacts introduced hand-held firearms which the Japanese quickly adopted. Their use made it possible to use as soldiers men who had not had a lifetime of training in the use of the sword, bow, or horse. Fusiliers were typically directly dependent on the daimyō which limited their ability to switch sides during a battle – this being a common feature of battle, ideals of samurai loyalty notwithstanding.

4 This was the closest that Oda, Toyotomi, and the Tokugawa came to implementing a nationwide tax, but it never became regularized. The standards domains employed to calculate their value varied significantly and were sometimes manipulated in the most blatant manner (Brown, *Central Authority and Local Autonomy*).

5 This growth is even more remarkable given the emergence of a very large urban population, one that supported a number of seventeenth-century cities of over 100,000 (London, *c.*1600 had a population less than half that figure). Urban areas, even of much smaller size, were population sinkholes. Their natural rate of increase was negative, and they grew only because of immigration from the countryside.

6 Although not explicitly published as an effort to offer Japan as a non-communist model of rapid economic development and social transformation, studies such as these certainly were drawn upon for that purpose by Cold Warriors (Hall and Jansen, eds., *Studies in the Institutional History*; Smith, *The Agrarian Origins of Modern Japan*).

7 Najita and Koschmann, eds., *Conflict in Modern Japanese History*.

8 Bix, *Peasant Protest in Japan*; Vlastos, *Peasant Protests and Uprisings in Tokugawa Japan*.

9 Wigen, *The Making of a Japanese Periphery*; Pratt, *Japan's Proto-Industrial Elite*.

10 Hall, *Government and Local Power in Japan*.

11 Brown, *Central Authority and Local Autonomy*; Berry, *Hideyoshi*.

12 Ravina, *Land and Lordship*; Roberts, *Mercantilism in a Japanese Domain*.

13 Ravina, *Land and Lordship*; Brown, *Central Authority and Local Autonomy*; Roberts, *Mercantilism in a Japanese Domain*. In Japanese, John Morris has developed an analysis parallel to Ravina in *Kinsei Nihon chigyōsei no kenkyū*.

14 McClain, *Kanazawa*.

15 Birt, "Samurai in Passage."

16 Kelly, *Deference and Defiance*; Esenbel, *Even the Gods Rebel*; Walthall, *Social Protest and Popular Culture*; White, *Ikki*.
17 Roberts, *Mercantilism in a Japanese Domain*; Ooms, *Tokugawa Village Practice*; Walthall, *The Weak Body of a Useless Woman*.
18 Howell, *Capitalism from Within*; Walker, *The Conquest of Ainu Lands*; Smits, *Visions of Ryūkyū*.
19 Yonemoto, *Mapping Early Modern Japan*.
20 Wakabayashi, *Anti-Foreignism and Western Learning*.
21 Totman, *The Green Archipelago*; Totman, *The Origins of Japan's Modern Forests*.
22 Lamers, *Japonius Tyrannus*.
23 Butler, *Emperor and Aristocracy in Japan*.
24 White, "State Growth and Popular Protest"; Totman, "Preindustrial River Conservancy."
25 Totman, *Tokugawa Ieyasu*.
26 Norihito Mizuno, in a dissertation recently completed, argues, however, that Meiji Japanese attempted to write into the treaty format a number of their premodern conceptions of their relationships with China and Korea (Mizuno, "Japan and Its East Asian Neighbors").
27 Ooms, *Tokugawa Village Practice*.
28 Brown, *Central Authority and Local Autonomy*.
29 Ooms, *Tokugawa Village Practice*; Tonomura, *Community and Commerce*; Kelly, *Water Control in Tokugawa Japan*; McKean, "Management of Traditional Common Lands."
30 McClain, *Kanazawa*.
31 Henderson, *Conciliation in Japanese Law*; Steenstrup, *A History of Law in Japan*; Vaporis, *Breaking Barriers*; Hur, *Prayer and Play in Late Tokugawa Japan*.
32 Botsman, *Punishment and Power*.
33 Ikegami, *Taming of the Samurai*.
34 McMullin, *Buddhism and the State*.
35 Mizuno, "Japan and Its East Asian Neighbors."

BIBLIOGRAPHY

Berry, Mary Elizabeth. *Hideyoshi*. Cambridge, Mass.: Council on East Asian Studies, Harvard University Press, 1982.
Berry, Mary Elizabeth. "Public Peace and Private Attachment: The Goals and Conduct of Power in Early Modern Japan." *Journal of Japanese Studies* 12:2 (Summer 1986): 237–71.
Birt, Michael P. "Samurai in Passage: The Transformation of the Sixteenth-Century Kantō." *Journal of Japanese Studies* 11:2 (Summer 1985): 369–99.
Bix, Herbert. *Peasant Protest in Japan, 1590–1884*. New Haven: Yale University Press, 1986.
Botsman, Daniel. *Punishment and Power in the Making of Modern Japan*. Princeton: Princeton University Press, 2004.
Brown, Philip C. *Central Authority and Local Autonomy in the Formation of Early Modern Japan: The Case of Kaga Domain*. Stanford, Calif.: Stanford University Press, 1993.
Butler, Lee. *Emperor and Aristocracy in Japan, 1467–1680: Resilience and Renewal*. Cambridge: Harvard University Asia Center, 2002.
Esenbel, Selcuk. *Even the Gods Rebel: The Peasants of Takaino and the 1871 Nakano Uprising in Japan*. Ann Arbor: Association for Asian Studies, 1998.
Hall John W. *Government and Local Power in Japan, 500–1700: A Study based on Bizen Province*. Princeton: Princeton University Press. 1966.
Hall, John W., and Jansen, Marius, eds. *Studies in the Institutional History of Early Modern Japan*. Princeton: Princeton University Press, 1968.

Henderson, Dan. *Conciliation in Japanese Law: Tokugawa and Modern*, vol. 1. Seattle: University of Washington Press, 1965.

Howell, David L. *Capitalism from Within: Economy, Society, and the State in a Japanese Fishery.* Berkeley: University of California Press, 1995.

Hur, Nam-lin. *Prayer and Play in Late Tokugawa Japan: Asakusa Sensōji and Edo Society.* Cambridge, Mass.: Harvard University Asia Center, 2000.

Ikegami, Eiko. *The Taming of the Samurai: Honorific Individualism and the Making of Modern Japan.* Cambridge, Mass.: Harvard University Press, 1995.

Innes, Robert Leroy. "The Door Ajar: Japan's Foreign Trade in the Seventeenth Century." Ph.D. dissertation, University of Michigan, 1980.

Kelly, William. *Water Control in Tokugawa Japan: Irrigation Organization in a Japanese River Basin, 1600–1870.* Ithaca, NY: Cornell China-Japan Program, 1982.

Kelly, William. *Deference and Defiance in Nineteenth-Century Japan.* Princeton: Princeton University Press, 1985.

Lamers, Jeroen. *Japonius Tyrannus: The Japanese Warlord Oda Nobunaga Reconsidered.* Leiden: Hotei Publishing, 2000.

McClain, James. *Kanazawa: A Seventeenth-Century Japanese Castle Town.* New Haven: Yale University Press, 1982.

McKean, Margaret. "Management of Traditional Common Lands (Iriaichi) in Japan." In Daniel Bromley, ed., *Making the Commons Work: Theory, Practice, and Policy.* San Francisco: ICS Press, 1992.

McMullin, Neil. *Buddhism and the State in Sixteenth-Century Japan.* Princeton: Princeton University Press, 1984.

Mizuno, Norihito. "Japan and Its East Asian Neighbors: Japan's Perception of China and Korea and the Making of Foreign Policy from the Seventeenth to the Nineteenth Century." Ph.D. dissertation, Ohio State University, 2004.

Morris, John. *Kinsei Nihon chigyōsei no kenkyū.* Tokyo: Seibundo, 1988.

Najita, Tetsuo. *Japan.* New York: Prentice-Hall, 1974.

Najita, Tetsuo, and Koschmann, J. Victor, eds. *Conflict in Modern Japanese History: The Neglected Tradition.* Princeton: Princeton University Press, 1982.

Nakai, Kate Wildman. *Shogunal Politics: Arai Hakuseki and the Premises of Tokugawa Rule.* Cambridge, Mass.: Council on East Asian Studies, Harvard University, 1988.

Ooms, Herman. *Tokugawa Village Practice: Class, Status, Power, Law.* Berkeley: University of California Press, 1996.

Pratt, Edward E. *Japan's Protoindustrial Elite: The Economic Foundations of the Gōnō.* Cambridge, Mass.: Harvard University Asia Center, 1999.

Ravina, Mark. *Land and Lordship in Early Modern Japan.* Stanford, Calif.: Stanford University Press, 1999.

Roberts, Luke. *Mercantilism in a Japanese Domain: The Merchant Origins of Economic Nationalism in 18th-Century Tosa.* Cambridge: Cambridge University Press, 1998.

Smith, Thomas C. *The Agrarian Origins of Modern Japan.* Stanford, Calif.: Stanford University Press, 1959.

Smits, Gregory. *Visions of Ryūkyū: Identity and Ideology in Early Modern Thought and Politics.* Honolulu: University of Hawai'i Press, 1999.

Steenstrup, Carl. *A History of Law in Japan until 1868.* Leiden: Brill, 1996.

Toby, Ronald. *State and Diplomacy in Early Modern Japan: Asia in the Development of the Tokugawa Bakufu.* Princeton: Princeton University Press, 1984.

Tonomura, Hitomi. *Community and Commerce in Late Medieval Japan: The Corporate Villages of Tokuchin-ho.* Stanford, Calif.: Stanford University Press, 1992.

Totman, Conrad. *Tokugawa Ieyasu: Shōgun.* San Francisco: Heian International, 1983.

Totman, Conrad. *The Origins of Japan's Modern Forests: The Case of Akita*. Honolulu: University of Hawai'i Press, 1984.

Totman, Conrad. *The Green Archipelago: Forestry in Pre-Industrial Japan*. Berkeley: University of California Press, 1989.

Totman, Conrad. "Preindustrial River Conservancy." *Monumenta Nipponica* 47:1 (Spring 1992): 59–76.

Vaporis, Constantine. *Breaking Barriers: Travel and the State in Early Modern Japan*. Cambridge, Mass.: Council on East Asian Studies, Harvard University, 1994.

Vlastos, Stephen. *Peasant Protests and Uprisings in Tokugawa Japan*. Berkeley: University of California Press, 1986.

Wakabayashi, Bob Tadashi. *Anti-Foreignism and Western Learning in Early-Modern Japan: The New Theses of 1825*. Cambridge, Mass.: Council on East Asian Studies, Harvard University, 1986.

Walker, Brett L. *The Conquest of Ainu Lands: Ecology and Culture in Japanese Expansion, 1590–1800*. Berkeley : University of California Press, 2001.

Walthall, Anne. *Social Protest and Popular Culture in Eighteenth-Century Japan*. Tuscon: University of Arizona Press, 1986.

Walthall, Anne. *The Weak Body of a Useless Woman: Matsuo Taseko and the Meiji Restoration*. Chicago: University of Chicago Press, 1998.

White, James W. "State Growth and Popular Protest in Tokugawa Japan." *Journal of Japanese Studies* 14:1 (Winter 1988): 1–25.

White, James W. *Ikki: Social Conflict and Political Protest in Early Modern Japan*. Ithaca, NY: Cornell University Press, 1995.

Wigen, Kären. *The Making of a Japanese Periphery, 1750–1920*. Berkeley: University of California Press, 1995.

Yonemoto, Marcia. *Mapping Early Modern Japan: Space, Place, and Culture in the Tokugawa Period, 1603–1868*. Berkeley: University of California Press, 2003.

FURTHER READING

A number of early works in the field of early modern Japanese studies in the English-speaking world remain essential reading (one consequence of the relative youth of the field and its size). In addition to the small handful of such works noted already, the following are noteworthy: on domains and Tokugawa control mechanisms, Harold Bolitho, *Treasures among Men* (New Haven: Yale University Press, 1974), Toshio Tsukahira, *Feudal Control in Tokugawa Japan: The Sankin Kōtai System* (Cambridge, Mass.: East Asian Research Center, Harvard University, 1966); on foreign relations, C. R. Boxer, *The Christian Century in Japan, 1549–1650* (Cambridge: Cambridge University Press, 1951), Donald Keene, *The Japanese Discovery of Europe* (London: Routledge, 1952), Masao Miyoshi, *As We Saw Them: The First Japanese Embassy to the United States* (Berkeley: University of California Press, 1979); on relations between the state and merchants, William Hauser, *Economic Institutional Change in Tokugawa Japan* (Cambridge: Cambridge University Press, 1974), Charles Sheldon, *The Rise of the Merchant Class in Tokugawa Japan* (Ann Arbor: Association for Asian Studies, 1958); on the role of the emperor, David Earl, *Emperor and Nation in Japan* (Seattle: University of Washington Press, 1964), Herschel Webb, *The Japanese Imperial Institution* (New York: Columbia University Press, 1968); on religion, George Elison, *Deus Destroyed* (Cambridge, Mass.: Harvard University Press, 1973); late eighteenth-century reforms are treated in John W. Hall, *Tanuma Okitsugu* (Cambridge, Mass.: Harvard University Press, 1955), and Herman Ooms, *Charismatic Bureaucrat: A Political Biography of Matsudaira Sadanobu* (Chicago: University of Chicago Press, 1975).

The most comprehensive survey of the era is Conrad Totman, *Early Modern Japan* (Berkeley: University of California Press, 1993). Extended bibliographic reviews of recent work on all aspects of early modern Japan appeared in *Early Modern Japan: An Interdisciplinary Journal*, 10:2 (Fall 2002) to 11:1 (Spring 2003), with extended essays on foreign relations (10:2) and political-institutional history (11:1). More recent work of note includes two essay collections edited by James McClain et al., *Edo and Paris: Urban Life and the State* (Ithaca, NY: Cornell University Press, 1994) and *Osaka: The Merchants' Capital* (Ithaca, NY: Cornell University Press, 1999).

In the realm of foreign relations, Grant Goodman has updated his pioneering work on Dutch relations with Japan in *Japan and the Dutch, 1600–1853* (Richmond, UK: Curzon, 2000). Robert Innes's doctoral dissertation "The Door Ajar" (University of Michigan, 1980) is a very influential study of mid-period relations with China.

CHAPTER FIVE

Social and Economic Change in Tokugawa Japan

Edward E. Pratt

It was the best of times, it was the worst of times. On the one hand, the Tokugawa period witnessed a remarkable economic transformation, perhaps best evidenced in the growth of the three major cities of Edo, Kyoto, and Osaka, not only in terms of population but in the number and scale of commercial and manufacturing enterprises. The transformation was no less pronounced in the countryside, where growing production for the market engendered the rise of a class of wealthy farmers, significant interregional trade, and a mushrooming of local and regional markets. On the other hand, the Tokugawa economy was at times remarkably volatile and unstable. Fortunes were lost as quickly as they were made, famines interrupted periods of growth and devastated the lives of countless farmers, and large numbers of rural dwellers found themselves forced to sell their lands and to earn their livelihoods through the sale of their own and their family labor. The Tokugawa economy defies easy explanation.

The starting point for any examination of the Tokugawa economy is the question of the extent of Japan's commercial contacts with the outside world. Historians on both sides of the Pacific once asserted that the Tokugawa bakufu rigorously pursued a policy of seclusion. From 1639, when only the Dutch of all the European countries were allowed to trade with Japan, until 1853, when Commodore Matthew Perry arrived with his gunboats in Edo Bay, Japan had been cut off from all significant contacts with the outside world. And even the Dutch were restricted in their activities: they could only trade and live on a small man-made island in Nagasaki harbor. This view concerning Japan's isolation reinforced the overall assessment of the Tokugawa economy at the time: that it stagnated under weighty feudal impositions and received no stimulation from commercial contacts with the outside world. It was only with the coerced termination of the seclusion policy in the 1850s that Japan entered the "modern world."

With the 1984 publication of Ronald Toby's *State and Diplomacy in Early Modern Japan*, our thinking on Japan's foreign relations during this period underwent significant change. The bakufu enacted policies restricting contacts with the outside world, not out of anti-foreignism or any desire to cut off trade, but due to concern over legitimacy, especially in terms of not wishing to be a subordinate in the Sino-centric world order. The bakufu was concerned, too, about national security, in particular the very real threat posed by the countries of Western Europe supplying the Catholic missionaries sent to Japan. It had no wish, however, to see a diminution in foreign trade. With the banning of the Portuguese from the Japan trade in 1639, in fact, the bakufu adopted measures to ensure that trade continued as before, even on a greater scale, and it extracted a promise from the Dutch to supply the Japanese with the silk that the Portuguese once handled. The Japanese also continued to trade actively with its Asian neighbors, especially Korea, China, and the Ryūkyū Islands.

Although the bakufu did not initially pursue a policy of seclusion, the situation had radically changed by the end of the eighteenth century, as Bob Wakabayashi contends in his *Anti-Foreignism and Western Learning in Early-Modern Japan*. Bakufu officials began fending off attempts by Western countries for trade and diplomatic contacts by asserting that relations were out of the question, and that this policy was based on hereditary law.

Why the radical shift? Simply put, over the previous century Japan's contacts with other countries had greatly declined. Looking at foreign trade alone, the total volume dropped precipitously beginning around the 1680s. Massive silver exports from Japan, together with the growing depletion of the country's silver mines, led to a domestic shortage and a currency crisis, prompting the bakufu to restrict its outflow. At the same time, the bakufu encouraged the domestic production of silk in order to stem the imports paid for in silver. Silk was particularly important, because it was by far the major import item, and domestic demand seemed to be growing by leaps and bounds. With growing domestic production of silk, total trade volume declined. By the first decades of the eighteenth century Japan's trade with the outside world, including its Asian neighbors, was negligible. In sum, we are forced to argue that, in terms of trade alone, Japan was indeed a closed country, at least from the 1680s. In terms of stimulants to economic growth, Japan was largely left to its own devices.[1] It was only with the opening of the ports in 1859 that foreign trade again had a major impact on the domestic economy.

Another striking feature of the Tokugawa economy is the remarkable degree of urbanization. Much of this urbanization came about, however, not from the gradual or evolutionary concentration of economic powers in the cities but as a result of deliberate political choices. The rise of castle towns, in particular, resulted from a conscious decision on the part of many domain lords to remove the threat posed by samurai with power bases in the countryside. With their forced removal to castle towns, beginning in the late sixteenth and continuing into the seventeenth century, Japan could boast of dozens of towns with populations of 10,000 or more, each with large numbers of merchants and artisans catering to the needs of resident samurai. The metropolis of Edo, too, was a political construct. With the institution of the alternate attendance system, Edo became a bustling urban center with a population of over one million by the early eighteenth century. It relied heavily on imports from Osaka and Kyoto, especially in the first half of the period, but by the mid to late eighteenth century Edo had emerged to become a major manufacturing and commercial center in its own right, taking advantage of increased production for the market in central and eastern Japan.

Kyoto and Osaka, the other two important metropolises, had much deeper historical roots. Whereas Kyoto was the pre-eminent center for the manufacture of luxury goods, especially higher-end silks and other dyed goods, Osaka handled massive quantities of many domains' surplus tax rice. Osaka was also a major center for the sale, not to mention manufacture, of cotton goods, sake, soy sauce, and vegetable oils. William Hauser has described the important position Osaka and the surrounding region occupied in his *Economic Institutional Change in Tokugawa Japan*.

Somewhat surprisingly, English-language scholarship on the economies of these three cities is sparse.[2] The general impression, especially in textbook interpretations, is that the cities and their merchants and manufacturers languished from the mid eighteenth century, unable to compete with upstarts in the countryside. Thomas C. Smith articulated this position most forcefully in his 1973 article "Premodern Economic Growth: Japan and the West." Japan's towns stagnated or lost population, he argues, because of growing competition from residents in rural areas, who increasingly usurped functions once monopolized by urban merchants and manufacturers. The evidence supporting this position is overwhelming: there is an abundance of demographic data showing population decline or stagnation in the major cities and many castle towns and rural towns, and countless documents from the period testify to urban dwellers' growing inability to compete with competitors in the countryside. Hauser, too, has described in some detail the growing power of rural Kinai merchants vis-à-vis the once powerful Osaka wholesalers. Edward E. Pratt touches on the same trend in Edo and Kyoto in his *Japan's Protoindustrial Elite*.

We would be remiss, however, in ignoring Japan's major cities. Simply put, the merchants in the cities were more powerful than merchants elsewhere, and consumer demand was more concentrated in the cities than anywhere else. The textile industry is a case in point. It is true, for example, that established Edo firms saw their textile sales stagnate, beginning in the closing decades of the eighteenth century. Much of this stagnation was due to their growing inability to monopolize the purchase of rural products and to control their prices, but there was also growing competition from newcomers within Edo itself. Many of these new merchants became successful because they adopted innovative business strategies, such as by selling to rural areas, taking advantage of budding rural consumer demand.

The growing literature on samurai life in the cities places us on somewhat firmer ground. We know that the lives of samurai changed in very profound ways as a result of urbanization and the burgeoning consumer culture. Katsu Kokichi's recollections, presented in *Musui's Story*, demolish many of our assumptions about samurai life and the ideals they cherished. Quite unlike the selfless heroes of *Chūshingura*, Katsu's world is populated by thieves, thugs, gamblers, gangs, and prostitutes. Unable and frequently unwilling to seek official appointment, he roamed the country and the streets of Edo in search of self-gratification. *Musui's Story* bespeaks an era in which the lines between samurai and commoner had considerably blurred, though Katsu was not averse to pulling rank when the situation demanded it. Yamakawa Kikue's *Women of the Mito Domain* reinforces the portrayal of hapless samurai, unable to make do on their stipends but, unlike Katsu, finding it necessary to keep up appearances as the domain's elites. Most such families found it necessary to supplement their incomes through outside sources – the men teaching in private schools, for example, and the women sewing garments.

Unlike the pleasure-seeking wealthy commoners traversing the pages of Ihara Saikaku's novels, life was much different for the laborers and underclass in the major cities, as Gary Leupp describes in his *Servants, Shophands, and Laborers*. By the early eighteenth century, large numbers of the cities' commoner populations consisted of day laborers and domestic servants, replacing the hereditary servants of the past. Much of the urban labor force had become proletarianized – owning no land or property and selling its labor power to earn a living. Day laborers oftentimes lived in squalid conditions and were viewed with contempt by their superiors.

The scholarship on the rural economy is extensive and owes a tremendous debt to the works of Thomas C. Smith. In his seminal 1959 book *The Agrarian Origins of Modern Japan*, Smith decisively overturns the view, common at the time in both Japan and the United States, that rural Japan in the Tokugawa period had been resistant to change. Indeed, he argues that rural change was oftentimes dramatic, comparable in many ways with the agricultural revolution in Europe. A central feature of rural change was the growth of the market. By the end of the Tokugawa, farmers grew crops and produced handicrafts not just to meet their subsistence needs but to profit from their sale in the market. Cash crops came to account for a larger and larger portion of the farmers' total product output. Cottage industries also gained in importance, most notably in textiles and cotton spinning.

Perhaps Smith's most important contribution was in documenting the importance of improved technologies and the diffusion of best practices in promoting economic change. The greater use of commercial fertilizers enabled double and triple cropping to be carried out in more areas, for example. Farmers adopted new plant varieties, introduced improved cultivation methods, reclaimed land, and constructed irrigation works. Improvements in such things as reeling, weaving, and sericulture also led to greater productivity in cottage industries.

Equally important, such improvements engendered momentous social changes in rural society. Because improved technology necessitated a more intensive farming of the land, many farmers found that the larger their holding, the more inefficient it became. Largeholders increasingly worked smaller portions of land with the labor of their nuclear family alone and released their hereditary servants, who became independent smallholders, tenants, wage laborers, or some combination thereof. The large cooperative farming units thus gave rise to a system of independent smallholders. Smith never made it clear when this change came about, but most Japanese historians date it from around the last decades of the 1600s, with sometimes significant regional variations.

Smith further advanced our understanding of Tokugawa social and economic history through a number of articles, later reprinted in *Native Sources of Japanese Industrialization*. In "The Land Tax in the Tokugawa Period," Smith contends that political authorities failed to adjust tax rates to take advantage of increased productivity, enabling farmers to retain more of their surplus and providing them with an incentive to invest either in continued agricultural improvements or in commerce and industry. In his study of Kaminoseki country in Chōshū domain, published as "Farm Family By-Employments in Preindustrial Japan," Smith highlights the remarkable extent to which the rural economy had diversified. Although only 18 percent of the county's residents were not classified as farmers, 55 percent of the income of all country residents came from non-agricultural sources. Farmers, in other words,

earned income from sources outside agriculture, especially from such by-employments as salt production and cotton weaving. They also engaged in extensive trade,
both within the county itself and with distant regions.

In "Ōkura Nagatsune and the Technologists," Smith elaborates on the important
role of those responsible for the diffusion of technologies and best practices in both
agriculture and domestic industry. The author of several widely read agricultural
treatises, Ōkura and many others like him devoted much of their lives to learning
these techniques and practices. They then encouraged farmers around the country to
adopt them, arguing that in so doing they could vastly improve their material well-
being. Improving their productivity would come about, they argued, not through
prayers to the gods but as a result of hard work, perseverance, and experimentation.

How have Smith's works withstood the test of time? Recent scholarship has
elaborated on his arguments and provided a more nuanced, indeed more complex,
portrayal of rural change, but his overall contentions concerning growth in the rural
economy have held up remarkably well. Sydney Crawcour, Susan Hanley, and Kozo
Yamamura provided additional support for Smith's contentions. In a 1974 article,
Crawcour argued that the Tokugawa economy was hardly modern in that Japan did
not possess the characteristics of a modern economy, but that the modern economic
growth that started in the Meiji would have been impossible had Japan not been in a
position to make the transition.[3] The bakufu and daimyō increasingly moved away
from the idea of a subsistence economy, sometimes even pursuing policies that
fostered economic growth. Many domains no longer enforced bans on the alienation
of land and restrictions on farmers engaging in non-agricultural pursuits. There was
also an infrastructure in place that facilitated subsequent modern growth: a growing
network of schools led to a remarkably high rate of literacy; commercial and legal
codes were in place that facilitated smooth and impartial business dealings; and a
network of money-changers were already well familiar with the functions of a modern
banking system. Especially important, there was significant growth in both commercial agriculture and cottage industry. Cottage industry laid the foundation for modern economic growth, at the same time providing an important source of capital
accumulation that could be invested in modern industry in the Meiji period.

Hanley and Yamamura argue the case for growth especially forcefully in their
Economic and Demographic Change in Preindustrial Japan. Rejecting the once
dominant view that the Tokugawa economy stagnated from the early eighteenth
century, they contend that the economy grew in all parts of the country. Farmers
reclaimed land, used cash fertilizers, adopted improved agricultural techniques, grew
more cash crops, and engaged in numerous side industries. The profits from productivity gains and increased production largely accrued to the farmers themselves, not
to samurai administration.

In the 1990s, Kären Wigen, David Howell, and Edward E. Pratt used the protoindustrialization rubric to examine economic growth and social change in the late
Tokugawa and Meiji periods. Whereas Smith, Crawcour, and Hanley and Yamamura
emphasized origins, especially those factors enabling Japan to modernize in the Meiji
period, the studies on Japanese protoindustrialization focused more on the local, ties
between center and periphery, the unevenness and social consequences of economic
growth, and its lack of linearity sometimes. Equally important, the protoindustrialization studies crossed the Tokugawa–Meiji divide, thus affording a better

understanding of how much and how little changed after the resumption of foreign trade in 1859. First coined to describe conditions in parts of Western Europe on the eve of industrialization, "protoindustrialization" refers to a process whereby farmers become increasingly involved in the production of handicrafts and other by-employments, and the goods they produced are sold to distant markets. In Japan, proto-industrialization became pronounced from the mid eighteenth century as growing numbers of farmers engaged in new forms of market-related activity. Unlike Western Europe, where many of the goods were exported to other European countries, protoindustrial markets in Tokugawa Japan, at least before the opening of the ports, were entirely internal.

The Shimoina valley in central Japan is the focus of Kären Wigen's *The Making of a Japanese Periphery.* By the mid eighteenth century, Shimoina had become a vibrant entrepot for packhorse transport, having usurped much of the overland trade away from the officially designated post stations to the north. Shimoina's farmers engaged in protoindustrial production, making hardwood wares, textiles, and paper crafts for sale in both local and distant markets. The author's particular strength lies in examining the importance of physical geography in shaping economic and social change. We see this in the role of environmental factors in determining the loci of production. Cocoon production flourished in the milder climate of the valley floor, for example. Because cocoons were perishable, reeling was limited to those areas leading from the castle town, whose merchants handled the cocoon trade. Similarly, paper-making had to take place in regions where there was abundant winter sun and an ample supply of pure water.

Shimoina's experience with protoindustrialization and modern industry reflects how bumpy the trajectory of economic growth could be. With the opening of the ports in 1859 to international commerce, Shimoina's economy began to change radically. As raw silk became the country's most important export item, farmers across the country, including in Shimoina, turned to this more lucrative product. With the growth of the sericulture and reeling industry, many traditional products, such as lacquerware and hairdress ties, lost their markets, while sericulture and reeling came to dominate the regional economy. Shimoina soon became a supply area for distant markets. As other regions dominated in large-scale reeling facilities, residents began to increasingly specialize in cocoon production, which left them particularly vulnerable to price fluctuations, as well as increasingly reliant on outside capital. In Wigen's words, Shimoina became a periphery of a "Tokyo-centered national economy."

David Howell's *Capitalism from Within* rejects in even more forceful terms the linearity of Japan's protoindustrial transformation. Protoindustrialization, he argues, was not necessarily an outgrowth of commercial agriculture, as earlier studies seemed to assume. In regions like the Kinai, where agricultural productivity was high, there were no strong incentives to move toward an industrial system, because local demand for what farmers grew or produced was high. In regions where agricultural productivity was relatively low and where there was not much of a market for the commodities farmers produced, on the other hand, there was a stronger impetus to move toward protoindustrial production. This was the case in Hokkaidō, which had a very weak agricultural base and whose economy was dominated by the fishing industry.

Hokkaidō fishers engaged in a long-distance trade with many regions of Honshū from at least the mid eighteenth century. The most important product was herring-meal fertilizer, which they shipped to regions like the Kinai for use as a commercial fertilizer. Initially, the organization of production was not capitalist in nature, because it was an appendage of Matsumae domain. Matsumae operated a contract fishery system, by which designated merchants controlled the fishing industry. Also, it was not capitalist in that the Ainu labor force so integral to the system was not free.

A confluence of factors came into play in the early decades of the nineteenth century that radically transformed the nature of the Hokkaidō fishing industry. There was a general decline in the Ainu population, on whom the contract fishers relied, together with the appearance of growing numbers of new fishers, many of whom had moved to Hokkaidō from northern Honshū. The adoption of the costly pound net, which enabled larger catches, facilitated the emergence of more capital-intensive enterprises, spurring the decline of the contract fishery system. The organization of production had radically changed. Fishing was now a capitalist enterprise, centered on powerful merchants controlling proletarianized laborers, forced into dependency on their employers as a result of the extension of the credit that they needed to survive.

Pratt's *Japan's Protoindustrial Elite* explores the protoindustrial economy by way of an examination of rural elite families and the world in which they lived. He finds substantial changes taking place, beginning in the mid eighteenth century: rural elites and domains introduced new and improved agricultural and manufacturing techniques to their regions; interregional trade greatly expanded, especially in such products as textiles and their intermediate and raw materials, sake, and tea; and urban merchants established ties with rural elites in important production regions in an attempt to control market share and prices. Many regions saw the rise of a class of very wealthy farmers, known as *gōnō*. Not only did they engage in farming and serve as landlords, but they were also active in interregional trade, operated manufacturing establishments, and served as moneylenders. Many domains borrowed from them when they faced budget crises. The *gōnō* frequently exercised tremendous control over the economic lives of people in their communities and regions. Some of these families owned one-third or more of village arable land, and they controlled access to markets by way of their moneylending activities.

Pratt argues, however, that the protoindustrial economy was extremely fluid and volatile, and that fortunes were lost as easily as they were won. The diffusion of new and improved techniques engendered intense interregional competition; as a result, those production regions dominating production in one period were not always dominant in the next. A few sites of protoindustrial production lost out in the competition and deindustrialized, reverting back to an emphasis on agriculture. Whereas earlier studies emphasized the success stories, looking at the Tokugawa origins of those rural elites rising to positions of economic prominence in the Meiji, Pratt presents a far more complex picture of the transition. The fortunes of many of the country's most powerful rural families, in fact, did not survive intact into the Meiji era. Many families faced headship succession problems, suffered crop failures, fell into debt because of onerous exactions imposed by political authorities, or saw their profits decline as a result of the machinations of city wholesalers seeking to lower the prices of goods they purchased from the countryside.

Recent scholarship has also accorded a far greater role to political authorities in stimulating economic growth, a point Smith well understood but never developed in any systematic way. Domains found themselves besieged by enormous debts, brought on by the excessive service demands of the bakufu, outlays associated with the alternate attendance system, and growing immersion in the consumer economy. In the first century of Tokugawa rule, domains increased income by raising taxes on farmers, but this exacerbated their plight, forcing them to sometimes flee the domain or to rebel. Beginning in the mid-Tokguawa, domain officials had to devise more novel means to address revenue shortfalls.

Luke Roberts describes changes in economic thinking in Tosa domain in his *Mercantilism in a Japanese Domain*. Frustrated by their inability to meet expenditures, domains like Tosa increasingly realized that policies aimed at economic expansion could directly benefit their territories. Equally important, they understood that economic gain derived from sound practices and sound economic policies. It was not simply a product of a world in which the lord acted morally and everyone performed their proper functions based on their position in the social hierarchy, as Confucianists would have it.

The term Tosa officials used – *kokueki*, meaning "the prosperity of the country" but referring more specifically to the domain or province – had its origins in the merchant class, who invoked the term to justify the important role they played in society. By the closing decades of the century, domain officials had appropriated the term to justify policies aimed at encouraging commercial enterprises, so that their profits could be tapped to strengthen domain finances. Tosa encouraged relatively new industries, such as sugar, eggs, and gunpowder, that had export potential or that could reduce the domain's reliance on imports. It also gave support to well-established industries, such as paper, by abolishing existing monopolies and by temporarily suspending taxes.

Mark Ravina describes similar processes at work in Yonezawa, Tokushima, and Hirosaki domains in his *Land and Lordship in Early Modern Japan*. There, too, officials increasingly realized that policies based on the Confucian idea that farmers engaged in agriculture alone and had little contact with markets no longer worked. By the mid-Tokugawa, farmers engaged in numerous forms of side industry and were active market participants and as such their livelihoods were greatly influenced by outside forces. For domain products to gain market share, and for domain cartels to profit from their sale, officials adopted measures to better control prices, acquire the latest techniques and technology, and to ensure the product quality demanded in national markets.

After some disastrous initial missteps, Yonezawa domain adopted several policies, beginning in the 1770s, to encourage greater production. Especially important were the incentives offered to farmers to plant lacquer, mulberry, and paper mulberry trees. With lacquer, although farmers had to sell their product to a domain monopsony, the lacquer itself was exempt from taxes. By the 1790s some officials even questioned the wisdom of monopsonies, because they believed that they served to stifle production rather than promote it. They came to believe that the best remedy for domain finances was to stimulate farmers' "desire for profit" and to reduce their tax burden. When taxes on these products were light, both sides profited: farmers earned extra income, enabling them to pay their taxes to the domain. Yonezawa took particular interest in its sericulture industry. Officials granted mulberry seedlings to farmers free of charge, offered them low-interest loans, and temporarily exempted them from some taxes. Tokushima domain on the island of Shikoku adopted similar policies to promote the growth of its indigo industry, beginning in the 1760s. To ensure that indigo maintained a strong market price, it enacted various quality-control measures and instituted mechanisms to bypass the powerful Osaka merchants who monopolized so much of its sale.

How should we assess the role of political authorities in orchestrating Tokugawa period economic growth? The varied nature of the political landscape forces us to eschew overly simplistic generalizations. While there were many large domains like Tokushima, Tosa, and Yonezawa, as described by Roberts and Ravina, there were far more small domains, non-contiguous parts of domains, bakufu territories, and the lands of bannermen of the Tokugawa house. It proved difficult to institute economic controls in such territories, because political oversight was oftentimes weak and farmers would often move to nearby territories where no such controls existed. Wigen shows that in Shimoina political authorities instituted only weak controls over production, because political jurisdictions there were highly fragmented. Indeed, political fragmentation oftentimes facilitated economic expansion, because authorities found it difficult to regulate commerce or to confine production to castle towns. The same held true on bakufu lands and on the lands of the bannermen of the Tokugawa house.

Also, political authorities could hinder trade as often as foster it. Their incessant requests for loans and contributions, especially in the final two or three decades of the period, contributed to the bankruptcy of many rural elites, as Pratt shows in his case studies of *gōnō* families. Many domains had indeed acquiesced to rural market activity, and even championed it, but their policies toward rural commerce and manufacture oftentimes appear schizophrenic: relaxing controls one decade, reinstituting them the next, and experimenting with new controls in later years. It would be difficult to argue, as well, that officials embraced the concept of free trade. We see this evidenced in domain monopsonies, which appeared in alarming succession, even in the closing decades of the Tokugawa. The bakufu, too, sometimes enacted countrywide price-control policies, much to the detriment of both city and rural merchants, and its periodic restrictions on sake brewing could be disastrous for brewers.[4]

Although there is little debate nowadays that the Tokugawa economy changed in quite remarkable ways, there is far less consensus on the extent to which Japan's population benefited from those changes. One of the more thorny questions for historians has been, if there indeed was growth, why did the population stagnate from the early eighteenth century? Although the population appears to have grown significantly in the first century of rule, it languished at around 26 million people from 1721 until 1846, the last year a nationwide census was conducted. Japanese Marxist historians once attributed this stagnation to the impoverishment of the Japanese population, besieged by periodic famines, pernicious practices such as abortion and infanticide, exploitative domain and bakufu officials, and rapacious rural elites. Beginning in the 1970s, historical demographers in Japan and the United States readdressed the question of stagnation by examining village population records.

In his demographic study *Nakahara*, Thomas Smith contends that one of the major reasons Japan was able to industrialize was because her population consciously pursued a policy of family limitation. In so doing, population growth remained below that of economic growth, thus allowing farmers to increase their economic standing. Nakahara villagers practiced population control primarily by means of late marriage and sex-selective infanticide. Women married late, much later in fact than was the case in Europe at a comparable level of development. They also tended to stop bearing children at an early age, usually after the optimum family size had been reached and the desired proportion of sexes obtained. Thus, infanticide was not a function of poverty or momentary desperation, as Marxist historians once claimed, but rather a conscious form of population control in order to maintain or increase economic well-being.

Hanley and Yamamura make many of the same arguments in *Economic and Demographic Change in Preindustrial Japan*. The rate of economic growth exceeded the rate of population growth, thus raising the living standards of the vast majority of the farmers throughout the period, despite a number of famines and natural disasters. Farmers limited family size through such practices as abortion, infanticide, and delayed marriage in order to realize a rise in their standards of living. Hanley and Yamamura also propose that the country's population figures themselves might be suspect. Although uneven, every region witnessed some population growth over the course of the eighteenth and nineteenth centuries.

More recent scholarship, however, has considerably complicated our understanding of Tokugawa-period demography. Akira Hayami, Japan's leading historical demographer, contends that the term stagnation itself is somewhat elusive. The overall population stagnated, it is true, but some regions witnessed respectable growth, some remained relatively flat, while still others declined. To characterize the lack of any appreciable population increase as stagnation is misleading.[5] Recent scholarship also suggests that the family planning found by Smith and by Hanley and Yamamura was far from universal. Historical demographers in Japan could not find sufficient evidence for the sex-selective infanticide found by Smith, for example, even in a village in close proximity to Nakahara. Saitō Osamu argues that infanticide may not be not such a major factor in explaining low levels of fertility.[6] Explanatory factors that work well for one village, it appears, do not necessarily work well for others.

Akira Hayami[7] and Laurel Cornell[8] have further complicated our understanding of Tokugawa era population dynamics. They contend that greater migration, by which farmers worked for periods away from home, thus reducing coital frequency, accounts for declining fertility rates in some areas, not deliberate family planning. If this is indeed the case, we must question the assumptions of the earlier generation of historical demographers. According to Saitō,

> it is time for us to question the stance taken, explicitly or implicitly, by the second generation of economic and population historians. They were keen to redress the "dark" and dismal image created by their predecessors and wanted to find "brighter" elements in Tokugawa society; as a result, they tended to see every demographic event as a reflection of changing (usually improving) economic situations.[9]

There are equally nagging issues that historical demographers must confront. Even those regions witnessing respectable population increases, for example, grew only modestly, especially from the standpoint of Meiji and later periods, forcing us to question whether economic conditions improved significantly for Tokugawa era farmers. New opportunities created by rural industry and other forms of economic growth would have increased the economic value of surplus family members and eventually stimulated population growth. We have some tantalizing evidence that new side industries led to population growth in some villages,[10] but the nationwide data suggests that such effects were far from universal.

Yet another shortcoming of demographic studies to date is that they largely ignore the broader context in which population changes take place. Most historical demographers of Japan have examined population records alone, without reference to oftentimes extensive other forms of documents. This has been an unfortunate omission, because we can never fully understand population trends without knowledge of other aspects of farmers' lives. What farmers are producing, how production is changing, the village's links to local and national markets, tax rates, farmers' incomes, levels of indebtedness, the distribution of wealth – all of these factors influence how farmers make decisions about family size.

Material culture is another aspect of the broader context of farmers' lives. If indeed the economy grew, we would expect to find substantive changes in such things as what people ate, what they wore, life expectancy, housing and furnishings, sanitation, and consumption patterns in general. Susan Hanley's *Everyday Things in Tokugawa Japan* addresses these topics and offers an abundance of evidence to support her claim that Japanese in the Tokugawa era enjoyed a "relatively high level of physical well-being."[11] House sizes increased and houses were better built, for example. Wooden floors and tatami mats replaced the pounded earthen floors of the past. Japanese ate more nutritious foods, including greater quantities of rice and sweet potatoes. In the cities, mortality rates were lower than might be expected given their size, because residents engaged in beneficial sanitation practices, such as the carting of night soil to the countryside to use as fertilizer. Rural areas became vibrant areas for commerce, with many villages supporting shops selling dozens of consumer goods, including hair ornaments, footwear, oils, pots, and paper. When viewed through the lens of life expectancy, Japanese led surprisingly long lives, even by the standards of Western societies around the same time.

There is no doubt that the lives of Japanese changed in very important ways over the course of the Tokugawa, and that terms like "immiseration" are woefully inadequate in characterizing their lot. We are on somewhat shakier ground, however, in accepting overly rosy assumptions about everyday life. Changing patterns of consumption may indicate that people's material lives are improving but, as we know from our own society, the link between the two is not always so clear. It is not even clear to economic historians of the West that economic growth, especially the process of industrialization, necessarily leads to improvements in people's well-being; in many cases, there is a negative correlation.

We must also guard against generalizations concerning improvements in material well-being that are not rooted in the local, because regional and temporal variations were great. Farmers' fortunes could be highly unstable. The major famines that took place in the 1730s, 1780s, and 1830s devastated the lives of hundreds of thousands of Japanese, but these were not simply punctuations in a seamless flow of economic growth and material improvements. Japanese farmers were constantly at the mercy of nature and economic downturns.[12] A year, even a decade, of plenty might be followed by a crop failure, forcing farmers to sell off much of their land and belong-ings. If we accept the good times, we must also accept that there were some bad times as well, and that the bad years could be very bad indeed.

Equally important, historians cannot ignore the question of who benefits from economic growth. To take a perhaps overly simplistic example, rural commerce and the proliferation of village shops might be an indicator of improved standards of living in the countryside, or they might not. Some farmers made a conscious decision to specialize in particular crops or manufactured items, for example. Whereas in the past they had produced most of what they needed for their own consumption, specializa-tion necessitated that they purchase more of their necessities in markets and shops. Other farmers purchased more because they had lost some of their lands due to indebtedness. They supplemented income from the land with the selling of their labor.

Much of the scholarship on peasant revolts emphasize the extent to which Japanese society became stratified in the second half of the Tokugawa. In reaction to some of the more benign early portrayals of rural society, scholars in the 1980s began to reinsert conflict and contention back into the study of the Tokugawa period. The starting point of the works on rural protest by Anne Walthall, Herbert Bix, Stephen Vlastos, and James White is the acknowledgment that conditions in rural areas had changed. The money economy had permeated much of rural society, but the benefits oftentimes accrued to the few at the expense of the many.[13] While a few families accumulated fortunes through moneylending, commercial activities, and land accumulation, many farmers lost their lands and were unable to subsist through agriculture alone. By the second half of the Tokugawa periods, much of the rural protest was directed against people of wealth in rural society itself, not against political authorities, as had been common in the first half of the period.

How, then, should we evaluate the Tokugawa economy? There is no doubt that the economy changed in fundamental ways, despite the country's lack of significant outside trade from the end of the seventeenth century. The major towns and cities remained as major sites of manufacturing and commercial activity, although they came under increasing assault from rural competitors. The most remarkable trans-formation took place in the countryside. Farmers produced more for the market, and they bought more from the market. Domains and rural elites actively sought out the best agricultural practices and manufacturing techniques, more efficient tools, and higher yielding seed varieties from other parts of the country. There was a remarkable expansion of interregional trade in some goods, and a growing share of this trade was between rural areas, not only between rural and urban areas. Many bakufu and domain officials came to realize that they could benefit from increased rural produc-tion, and adopted policies to encourage it.

While the economy changed in important ways, it is far more difficult to apply generalizations about that growth's linear trajectory. Regions with a weak agricultural base sometimes took the lead in protoindustrialization, but there was no assurance that they would industrialize. Regions constantly jockeyed for competitive advantage, and there were as many losers as winners. The extent to which the population benefited from economic change is also open to continued debate. We are far from certain, as we once were, that farmers engaged in family planning in order to maximize their incomes. It is also clear that some people benefited more from growth than others, and that some people fared very poorly indeed.

NOTES

1 In other ways, Japan continued to be influenced by China, especially through the import of books. See Jansen, *China in the Tokugawa World*.
2 In addition to the work by William Hauser, see Nakai and McClain, "Commercial Change and Urban Growth."
3 Crawcour, "The Tokugawa Period and Japan's Preparation."
4 See Pratt, *Japan's Protoindustrial Elite*, esp. ch. 1.
5 Hayami, *Historical Demography*, pp. 45–9.
6 Saitō, "Infanticide, Fertility and 'Population Stagnation'," pp. 374–5.
7 Hayami, *Historical Demography*, pp. 137–53.
8 Cornell, "Infanticide in Early Modern Japan?", p. 44.
9 Saitō, "Infanticide, Fertility and 'Population Stagnation'," p. 378.
10 See Wigen, *The Making of a Japanese Periphery*, pp. 111–14. Wigen also finds greater parity in sex ratios as a result of the growing importance of women in the burgeoning silk industry. Pratt describes a similar process at work in *Japan's Protoindustrial Elite*, pp. 134–5.
11 Hanley, *Everyday Things*, p. 22.
12 In the Hachiōji area from the 1750s to 1780s, farmers faced a flood or drought every three or four years. See Pratt, *Japan's Protoindustrial Elite*, p. 150.
13 Walthall, *Social Protest and Popular Culture*; Bix, *Peasant Protest in Japan*; Vlastos, *Peasant Protests and Uprisings*; White, *Ikki*.

BIBLIOGRAPHY

Bix, Herbert. *Peasant Protest in Japan, 1590–1884*. New Haven: Yale University Press, 1986.
Cornell, Laurel. "Infanticide in Early Modern Japan? Demography, Culture, and Population Growth." *Journal of Asian Studies* 55:1 (1996): 22–50.
Crawcour, E. Sydney. "The Tokugawa Period and Japan's Preparation for Modern Economic Growth." In John W. Hall and Marius Jansen, eds., *Studies in the Institutional History of Early Modern Japan*. Princeton: Princeton University Press, 1968.
Hanley, Susan B. *Everyday Things in Premodern Japan: The Hidden Legacy of Material Culture*. Berkeley: University of California Press, 1997.
Hanley, Susan B., and Yamamura, Kozo. *Economic and Demographic Change in Preindustrial Japan, 1600–1868*. Princeton: Princeton University Press, 1977.
Hauser, William. *Economic Institutional Change in Tokugawa Japan: Ōsaka and the Kinai Cotton Trade*. Cambridge: Cambridge University Press, 1974.
Hayami Akira. *The Historical Demography of Pre-Modern Japan*. Tokyo: University of Tokyo Press, 1999.
Howell, David. *Capitalism from Within: Economy, Society, and the State in a Japanese Fishery*. Berkeley: University of California Press, 1995.
Jansen, Marius. *China in the Tokugawa World*. Cambridge, Mass.: Harvard University Press, 1992.
Katsu Kokichi. *Musui's Story: The Autobiography of a Tokugawa Samurai*, trans. Teruko Craig. Tucson: University of Arizona Press, 1988.
Leupp, Gary. *Servants, Shophands, and Laborers in the Cities of Tokugawa Japan*. Princeton: Princeton University Press, 1992.
Nakai Nobuhiko, and McClain, James. "Commercial Change and Urban Growth in Early Modern Japan." In John W. Hall, ed., *The Cambridge History of Modern Japan*, vol. 4, *Early Modern Japan*. Cambridge: Cambridge University Press, 1991.

Pratt, Edward E. *Japan's Protoindustrial Elite: The Economic Foundations of the Gōnō.* Cambridge, Mass.: Harvard University Asia Center, 1999.

Ravina, Mark. *Land and Lordship in Early Modern Japan.* Stanford, Calif.: Stanford University Press, 1999.

Roberts, Luke. *Mercantilism in a Japanese Domain: The Merchant Origins of Economic Nationalism in 18th-Century Tosa.* Cambridge: Cambridge University Press, 1998.

Saitō Osamu. "Infanticide, Fertility and 'Population Stagnation': The State of Tokugawa Historical Demography." *Japan Forum* 4:2 (1992): 369–81.

Smith, Thomas C. *The Agrarian Origins of Modern Japan.* Stanford, Calif.: Stanford University Press, 1959.

Smith, Thomas C. *Nakahara: Family Farming and Population in a Japanese Village, 1770–1830.* Stanford, Calif.: Stanford University Press, 1977.

Smith, Thomas C. "Farm Family By-Employments in Preindustrial Japan." In Thomas C. Smith, *Native Sources of Japanese Industrialization, 1750–1920.* Berkeley: University of California Press, 1988.

Smith, Thomas C. "The Land Tax in the Tokugawa Period." In Thomas C. Smith, *Native Sources of Japanese Industrialization, 1750–1920.* Berkeley: University of California Press, 1988.

Smith, Thomas C. "Ōkura Nagatsune and the Technologists" (1973). In Thomas C. Smith, *Native Sources of Japanese Industrialization, 1750–1920.* Berkeley: University of California Press, 1988.

Smith, Thomas C. "Premodern Economic Growth: Japan and the West." In Thomas C. Smith, *Native Sources of Japanese Industrialization, 1750–1920.* Berkeley: University of California Press, 1988.

Toby, Ronald. *State and Diplomacy in Early Modern Japan: Asia in the Development of the Tokugawa Bakufu.* Princeton: Princeton University Press, 1984.

Vlastos, Stephen. *Peasant Protests and Uprisings in Tokugawa Japan.* Berkeley: University of California Press, 1986.

Wakabayashi, Bob Tadashi. *Anti-Foreignism and Western Learning in Early-Modern Japan: The New Theses of 1825.* Cambridge, Mass.: Council on East Asian Studies, Harvard University, 1986.

Walthall, Anne. *Social Protest and Popular Culture in Eighteenth-Century Japan.* Tucson: University of Arizona Press, 1986.

White, James W. *Ikki: Social Conflict and Political Protest in Early Modern Japan.* Ithaca, NY: Cornell University Press, 1995.

Wigen, Kären. *The Making of a Japanese Periphery, 1750–1920.* Berkeley: University of California Press, 1995.

Yamakawa Kikue. *Women of the Mito Domain: Recollections of Samurai Family Life,* trans. Kate Wildman Nakai. Tokyo: University of Tokyo Press, 1992.

FURTHER READING

For the rural economy, see Furushima Toshio's "The Village and Agriculture during the Edo period," in John Whitney Hall, ed., *The Cambridge History of Japan,* vol. 4, *Early Modern Japan* (Cambridge: Cambridge University Press, 1991); Penelope Francks, "Rural Industry, Growth Linkages, and Economic Development in Nineteenth-Century Japan," *Journal of Asian Studies* 61:1 (2002): 33–55; E. Sydney Crawcour, "Economic Change in the Nineteenth Century," in Marius Jansen, ed., *The Cambridge History of Japan,* vol. 5, *The Nineteenth Century* (Cambridge: Cambridge University Press, 1989); and Saitō Osamu, "The Rural Economy: Commercial

Agriculture, By-Employment, and Wage Work," in Marius B. Jansen and Gilbert Rozman, eds., *Japan in Transition: From Tokugawa to Meiji* (Princeton: Princeton University Press, 1986).

Local studies include William Jones Chambliss, *Chiaraijima Village: Land Tenure, Taxation, and Local Trade, 1818–1884* (Tucson: University of Arizona Press, 1965); Mark W. Fruin, *Kikkoman: Company, Clan, and Community* (Cambridge, Mass.: Harvard University Press, 1983); and Arne Kalland, *Fishing Villages in Tokugawa Japan* (Honolulu: University of Hawai'i Press, 1995).

For an overview of merchants and their activities in the major cities, see E. Sydney Crawcour's "Changes in Japanese Commerce in the Tokugawa Period," in John W. Hall and Marius B. Jansen, eds., *Studies in the Institutional History of Early Modern Japan* (Princeton: Princeton University Press, 1968).

On the important role of technology, see Tessa Morris-Suzuki, *The Technological Transformation of Japan: From the Seventeenth to the Twenty-First Century* (Cambridge: Cambridge University Press, 1994), and Penelope Francks, *Technology and Agricultural Development in Pre-war Japan* (New Haven: Yale University Press, 1984).

On the impact of epidemics on mortality, see Ann Bowman Jannetta, *Epidemics and Mortality in Early Modern Japan* (Princeton: Princeton University Press, 1987).

Economic thought is the focus of Tetsuo Najita, *Visions of Virtue in Tokugawa Japan: The Kaitokudō Merchant Academy of Osaka* (Chicago: University of Chicago Press, 1987), and Tessa Morris-Suzuki, *A History of Japanese Economic Thought* (New York: Routledge, 1991).

CHAPTER SIX

Intellectual Change in Tokugawa Japan

Peter Nosco

Introduction

In order to appreciate the changes that occurred among intellectuals and their circles during the Edo period, one would do well to compare what this intellectual world looked like at the outset with its principal features at era's end. At the start of the seventeenth century, Japan's intellectual world was fundamentally Buddhist, though there was remarkably strong interest in Catholic Christianity among some 1–2 percent of the population that included elite circles and commoners alike. Christianity and trade represented Europe, which seemed remote, exotic, and potentially de-stabilizing. Once Christianity was suppressed, as it would be during the Edo period's first decades, even knowledge of Europe itself was forbidden for over a century, and there was not a single place in Japan where one might obtain instruction in European matters. Generally, intellectuals engaged in the production of culture in the early seventeenth century enjoyed either independent wealth or the patronage of a power-ful individual or institution, and there was remarkably little interest in Japan's past history or culture.

Yet two and a half centuries later at the period's end, Japan's intellectual world had become largely Confucian, and as a result more ethnocentric and more historically minded, though Confucianism itself seemed to many passé and demon-strably unable to address the pressing demands of the times. These demands were now military and imperial and came from that same Europe, which had been handled so uncompromisingly within the historical memory and now seemed so intimidating. Christianity, ironically, was on the verge of returning "above ground" after over two centuries underground as a proscribed creed. Intellectuals – along with thoughtful individuals generally – recognized the urgency of the times and sought solutions within the ideas of any number of traditions. And these intellectuals were most often to be found within self-supporting private academies, which operated independently.

These changes all had social and sometimes political contexts. For example, the emergence of a highly commoditized form of popular culture from the 1680s on was facilitated in important ways by the rapid economic expansion, urbanization, improvements to the communications and transportation infrastructure, social de-militarization, and so on that characterized the Edo period's first century. One prominent feature of much of this popular culture was a new realism, which appealed to an urban audience of samurai and commoners and resonated well with efforts elsewhere in intellectual circles to better understand the nature of historical change. Similarly, many intellectuals sought to address the crises of the Tokugawa period's last decades, and their writing cannot be understood well without studying the broader contexts of such thought. The social, political, and even diplomatic developments that form the contexts for these changes are for the most part addressed elsewhere in this volume and will generally not concern us here, and so thoughtful readers will be well advised to see the developments discussed in this chapter alongside developments in other arenas discussed in the immediately preceding and following chapters.

Further, in this chapter we discuss intellectual changes in terms of broad movements such as Confucianism or *kokugaku* (national learning, national studies, or nativism), but the reality was different. Though persons who taught or studied a subject like Confucianism or nativism were certainly aware of their forebearers and contemporaries, they are better understood as a succession of individual schools that usually gathered around a single teacher, than as movements united by common themes and shared goals. Schools like the Confucian academies that emerged after the 1660s actually became a kind of industry: they rivaled each other in the marketplace of ideas, competed for their students, and often spoke quite critically of each other. And of course, by the mid eighteenth century ideas of all sorts circulated in and contributed to a limited public sphere within the otherwise authoritarian environment of the Tokugawa state.[1] Some of these ideas affirmed the status quo, while others unintentionally seemed to destabilize (or at least to harbor the potential to destabilize) it. Unquestionably, these ideas enriched the intellectual world in which they coursed, and it is hoped that this chapter will convey some of that richness and attraction.

Neo-Confucian Orthodoxy and Innovation

Confucianism had of course been known in Japan for over a thousand years before the Edo period, but not in the way that it would come to be known during those years. Originally Confucianism in Japan was identified with the yin–yang and Five Elements cosmology that emerged in China centuries earlier, and included related divinatory practices. This remained the "Confucianism" of the Nara, Heian, and Kamakura periods, and it had little to say on issues of statecraft, the polity, political economy, ethics, citizenship, education, human relationships, or any of the other subjects that figure prominently in Tokugawa Confucianism. During the fifteenth and sixteenth centuries the Ashikaga Gakkō (academy) offered aspiring elites instruction in a "Confucianism" that continued to emphasize divination but expanded to include military science, an obvious accommodation to the needs of those turbulent times.

It was during the twelfth century that Confucianism in China (and then similarly though later in Korea) was refashioned into a new form that represented a sharp challenge to Buddhism. This Neo-Confucianism favored a curriculum centered on the Four Books, that is, *The Analects* of Confucius, the *Mencius*, "The Great Learning," and "Doctrine of the Mean," since these works returned Confucianism to the original ethical and political concerns that figured so prominently in the early canon. Neo-Confucianism likewise taught that the same abstract natural principles that govern the operations of the physical cosmos likewise constitute the moral principles that govern and inform human relations and government. Neo-Confucianism maintained that these principles abide within all humans in the form of an originally good nature or mind, which at times is overwhelmed by the turbulence of an alluring and agitating world. Rein in this turbulence, restore the original balance and calm, and then your original goodness will be restored, or so the Neo-Confucians believed.

During the fourteenth century this same Neo-Confucianism in its so-called Cheng-Zhu form – called this because it was based on the commentaries on the Four Books and other classics by the two Cheng brothers and the brilliant Zhu Xi (Chu Hsi, 1130–1200) – became the authorized curriculum for the Chinese civil service exams, thus acquiring in both China and Korea an unprecedented degree of intellectual orthodoxy, since mastery of these teachings was the key to entrance into the official sphere. Though known in Japan, however, understanding of this orthodox Neo-Confucianism was generally confined during these same centuries to Zen monasteries, where it was represented as a stimulating but still inferior derivative of Zen insights, and knowledge of variant heterodox Neo-Confucian teachings remained limited in Japan.

All this changed when libraries with books on Neo-Confucianism – war booty from Japan's ill-advised invasion of Korea in the 1590s – along with authorities on Neo-Confucianism taken as prisoners began arriving in Japan, attracting fresh attention to the tradition and its richly variegated continental developments. It was owing to these arrivals that one finds the emergence of Fujiwara Seika (1561–1617), a Zen monk who found the newly introduced Neo-Confucian writings sufficiently compelling to break with Zen and to embrace a variety of Neo-Confucian interpretations. So too with Seika's student, Hayashi Razan (1583–1657), who attracted the attention of Tokugawa Ieyasu and served in the governments of the first four Tokugawa shōguns. Razan succeeded in obtaining bakufu assistance for the establishment of the Shōheikō academy in Edo. Headed by Razan's lineal descendants, the Shōheikō served as official interpreters of Neo-Confucianism for successive Tokugawa governments until the period's end.

Hayashi Razan was more narrowly faithful to the orthodox Cheng-Zhu teachings than the more eclectic Fujiwara Seika, and owing to the official attention shown to orthodox Neo-Confucian teachings within bakufu circles, these same teachings rapidly acquired a broad intellectual following. This following was so comprehensive that by the 1650s and 1660s one can begin to discern the contours of an intellectual legacy that included a new humanism, rationalism, ethnocentricity, and historical mindedness in Edo period thought.[2] By then the prestige of these Neo-Confucian teachings was so great, and the interpretations they offered so compelling, that even Shintō theologians, who had in earlier centuries sought to reconcile their teachings to Buddhism, now sought to accommodate belief in *kami* with the most basic assumptions of orthodox Neo-Confucianism. Knowledge of Neo-Confucianism proved so attractive in seventeenth-century Japan that just a few decades later in the 1690s, the popular novelist Ihara Saikaku (1640–93) listed familiarity with Utsunomiya Ton'an's (1634–1710) Neo-Confucian teachings among the accomplishments of a cultured but otherwise wayward urban *chōnin*.[3]

Yamazaki Ansai (1618–82) represents the high-water mark of devotion to the orthodox Cheng-Zhu Neo-Confucian teachings in Tokugawa Japan, though he also espoused a strict moralism that became emblematic of Neo-Confucianism's humorless and dour extremes. This helps to explain Neo-Confucianism's popular decline, since soon after his death in 1682, this moral rigor seemed to many oddly out of step with the more liberal times, and other alternative Confucian voices were now competing to be heard. As noted previously, this competition would now be played out largely within the private academies that hereafter arose around the major Tokugawa intellectuals, since it was the tuition paid by their students that freed these intellectuals from other obligations and enabled them to make a living through their teaching and scholarship.

Despite the prestige of Neo-Confucian teachings and bakufu sponsorship of their study, Neo-Confucians rarely achieved the status of high advisors to different regimes, though individuals familiar with Confucianism often figured prominently as domainal advisors. The most impressive exception to this was Arai Hakuseki (1657–1725), a brilliant and richly gifted scholar, historian, diplomat, and statesman, who eventually rose to the position of personal tutor to the sixth Tokugawa shōgun Ienobu (r. 1709–12) and advisor to both Ienobu and Ienobu's son and shogunal successor Tokugawa Ietsugu.[4]

One alternative Neo-Confucian voice that arose early on was that of Nakae Tōju (1608–48), a follower of Wang Yangming's (1472–1528) heterodox Neo-Confucian teachings that emphasized an intuitive quest for goodness by animating the moral seeds within, obviating the need for rigorous study. Known in Japan as Yōmeigaku (Yangming learning), these teachings were again embraced at the end of the Tokugawa period by activist reformers who found inspiration in Wang Yangming's famous dictum, "Thought initiates action, but action completes thought."

In Japan a more compelling alternative to orthodox Neo-Confucianism was offered by figures like Yamaga Sokō (1622–85) and Itō Jinsai (1627–1705) within the Ancient Learning or Ancient Studies (*kogaku*) movement. It will be recalled that the orthodox Neo-Confucian tradition was grounded in the commentaries by the Cheng brothers and their younger contemporary Zhu Xi on the Confucian Four Books, with these commentaries forming the core curriculum for the civil service examination in China. The commentators themselves maintained that their expositions disclosed in all its fullness the true message of the sage authors of antiquity. What the Ancient Learning scholars shared, by contrast, was the conviction that this true message of the sages might be more effectively accessed by reading these ancient sages' writings themselves, without the distraction of a commentary, and in this way they initiated the systematic study of Chinese historical linguistics in Japan.

This approach was sufficiently radical in 1665 that Yamaga Sokō was exiled for advocating so extreme an alternative to the bakufu's authorized orthodox Neo-Confucianism. By the 1680s, however, the spirit of intellectual pluralism was such that Itō Jinsai's private academy the Kogidō (Hall of Ancient Meanings) flourished in

Kyoto with hundreds of students making it the most successful such venture to date.[5] Emulating the hereditary leadership of the Hayashi School, headship of the private Kogidō passed from father to son, and the school continued to expand after the founder's death. More importantly, Jinsai's success established the private academy as a potential form of livelihood for the private scholar, who soon emerged as a distinctive kind of cultural producer comparable to a popular author or playwright.

Ogyū Sorai (1666–1728) is often thought of as part of this Ancient Learning movement, though he differs in important ways and distinguished himself from these others by styling his movement, the "study of ancient words and phrases" (*kobunji-gaku*). Earlier Confucians and Neo-Confucians in Japan had debated such questions as whether principle was ontologically prior to the material force in which principle ordinarily resides, or whether there were emotional responses appropriate to the circumstances (or whether all emotional responses were essentially suspect). Despite these differences, all of these Confucians and Neo-Confucians regarded the Confucian Way as something that was ontologically linked to Heaven, itself a kind of supreme principle of nature. In this sense, the Confucian Way was understood to be the Way of the Sages, because sages in their nearly supernatural wisdom discerned the outlines of this Way within the world around them, and through observation and insight gleaned many of its particular principles. Confucians and Neo-Confucians alike thus believed that these principles could be found within the sages' canonical writings, and that the principles are both enduring and universal, since they are grounded in the cosmos itself.

Ogyū Sorai challenged this view by asserting that the Way is to be found not in nature or the cosmos but rather in the all too human world of history. He insisted that the "Way" is simply a convenient and comprehensive term inclusive of all those state policies, administrative practices, laws and punishments, rituals, and even music, which have at different times been adopted by ancient rulers in order to alleviate specific problems and to advance civilization and effective government. Sorai thus styled this Way the Way of the Former Kings, and argued that it is there to be found today in ancient texts, which are themselves to be studied, pondered, and have their lessons applied anew, but *only* after taking into account the different circumstances of a different time and place. This novel view of the Way as a dynamic human creation proved immensely attractive and influenced views on everything from literary criticism to the function and responsibilities of samurai in a time of peace.

With such innovations Confucianism by the mid eighteenth century had lost much of its originally foreign character, and only Confucianism's rivals continued to call attention to its continental origins. In fact, some scholars think of Confucianism as a whole as having peaked during the mid eighteenth century, though this may be exaggerated.[6] Confucianism remained the doctrine of first recourse when times seemed troubled and in need of rescue, so that Confucianism was at the heart of the conservative reforms of Matsudaira Sadanobu (1758–1829) in the 1790s, and also during subsequent reform efforts. During the last decades of the Tokugawa, Confucian scholars continued to look within the tradition for solutions to the day's ills, but they had little success in either winning a following or affecting a solution. Some like Ōshio Heihachirō (1798–1837) turned to heterodox Confucianism to justify radical reform, while other more obscure voices hoped that answers might still be found within the Confucian tradition.

Kokugaku

All Confucians and Neo-Confucians in Japan recognized a measure of intellectual indebtedness to China. Some were overtly Sinophilic – none, it was said, more than Ogyū Sorai, who seemed to admire little within his own tradition other than cherry blossoms and Mt. Fuji – but the leading Neo-Confucians all had robust interests in Japanese history and Japan's heritage of *kami* worship. The interest in Japanese history was important because if the Confucian principles were truly universal, then one would expect to find them demonstrated in Japanese history no less than in Chinese. Japanese Confucian historians eventually took this argument of parity a step further by arguing, as Yamaga Sokō and then others did, that Japan's past better represented core Confucian virtues like filial piety and loyalty than did China's. The interest in *kami* worship and native spirituality generally stemmed from the assumption that if Confucian and Neo-Confucian principles are true, and if *kami* are likewise real, then these principles and these deities cannot be in conflict with one another.

Further, these same intellectuals saw their scholarship as representing portions – perhaps the most important portions but still only portions – of a world of scholarship that included a broad range of subjects, encompassing both things Chinese and things Japanese. In this sense, seventeenth-century Sinology and Japanology were simply components of a larger singular world of *gakumon* or scholarship, and thus, the study of Confucianism was able to coexist in an unproblematic manner with such seemingly remote subjects as the study of Japanese history or even Shintō theology.

This changed in the eighteenth century as certain scholars began to assert the study of things Japanese as a field of inquiry distinct from Chinese studies and juxtaposed against it in the marketplace of ideas. This emergence of a new form of Japanese studies is perhaps best understood as a gradual narrowing of Japanese studies in the broadest sense – including the study of Japanese literature, history, customs, language, and religions (particularly Shintō) – to a more ideological and nativist form of Japanese studies that sought to articulate the essence of Japanese culture by looking at its earliest pre-Confucian and pre-Buddhist manifestations in poetry and myth.

This movement came to be known as *kokugaku* (national learning or national studies), and like the Confucians, the *kokugakusha* or nativists were organized by schools, each of which centered on a single leading teacher. Some *kokugakusha* located the genesis of their movement in the writings of the Shingon monk Keichū (1640–1701) whose commentarial work on the *Manyōshū*, Japan's oldest extant poetry anthology, raised scholarship on the anthology to a new level. Others traced their intellectual roots to the efforts of the Shintō theologian Kada no Azumamaro (1669–1736) who sought to establish his own academy in Fushimi wherein Japanese studies were offered as a viable alternative to Chinese studies.

However, it was Kamo no Mabuchi who turned Japanese studies into a philological quest for the very roots of a freshly posited Japaneseness. Mabuchi was enamored of poetry, which he believed represented a more transparent expression of what lay within the individual heart, and whose poetic rhythms he believed replicated the very rhythms of Heaven and Earth. He believed that within Japan's most ancient extant verse, one could find expressions and in some cases echoes of a pre-Confucian, pre-Buddhist arcadia, whose characteristics included august government and a robust polity rooted in such virtues as directness, straightforwardness, and a masculine vigor, of which all were said to partake equally. This, he argued, was in fact the true ancient Way of Heaven and Earth, which had been lost in China owing to the deleterious effects of first Confucianism and then Buddhism. These moral and ethical doctrines, Mabuchi asserted, were originally intended to be a cure for the ills of an earlier age, but instead the antidote proved to be an ironic toxin, as individuals exposed to these doctrines now learned immorality along with morality and indulged in personal scheming.

The good news, according to Mabuchi, was that the original arcadia was recoverable in Japan through the medium of the *Manyōshū*. This was so, he argued, because people now, as then, possess *magokoro*, or true hearts, which enable them to live together successfully and relatively harmoniously without recourse to social, moral, or ethical instruction of any kind. In this way, despite the fact that *magokoro* have been overwhelmed generation after generation by the deleterious effects of Confucian rationalism and Buddhist moralism, through the verses of the *Manyōshū* the effects can be reversed, and persons in Japan can once again enjoy the same blessings as their archaic forebears.[7]

Though he only met Kamo no Mabuchi once, Motoori Norinaga (1730–1801) carried on Mabuchi's teachings and is regarded by many as the greatest of the nativists. Norinaga sought his aesthetic ideals in the less remote past. His theory of *mono no aware* – the sadness or pathos of things in which emotional truth supersedes either literal truth or moral truth – remains perhaps the single most important heuristic principle in literary analysis of Murasaki Shikibu's *Tale of Genji*. In this way, Norinaga decisively overcame the didactic literary criticism that had colored interpretations of the classic novel for centuries, and he applied the same aesthetic principle to his analysis of post-*Manyōshū* Japanese verse.

It was his lifelong project to decipher Japan's oldest extant mytho-history, the *Kojiki* (712), which remains Norinaga's greatest achievement. In his 1771 essay *Naobi no mitama* ("The Rectifying Spirit") Norinaga used his analysis of the earliest myths to conclude that Japan's ancient Way was not the natural Way of Heaven and Earth, as his mentor Mabuchi had argued, but rather the Way of the Kami or Shintō, a Way created neither by humans nor by natural principles but by the deities themselves. A lifelong Buddhist, Norinaga particularly objected to Confucianism's effects on the Japanese heart or mind, but instead of proposing that these effects be overcome through the medium of ancient texts, Norinaga counseled reliance on the rectifying properties of native deities. Only then, he maintained, will one be able to reunite with the deities all around one and to resume one's rightful place in a chain of authority that extends through one's local lords to the divine *tennō* and ultimately as far as the solar deity and imperial ancestress Amaterasu herself.[8]

Norinaga also vilified China and Chinese ways, arguing for Japanese ethnic and cultural superiority largely on religious grounds, and this xenophobic message was later popularized by Hirata Atsutane (1776–1843), who stressed the themes of purity, fecundity, and superiority as he took his appeal beyond the confines of the academy and into the streets and countryside. Less philological than Norinaga but also more spiritual, Atsutane sought verification for his theories in a variety of sources including even proscribed Christian writings imported from China, laying the foundation for a robust Japanism that would re-emerge later with unfortunate consequences.

In the last decades of the Tokugawa period, the antagonism that characterized the relationship between nativism and Confucianism diminished, returning to the comfortable coexistence that prevailed prior to the eighteenth century. Particularly in Mito, where the domain had a tradition of sponsoring pro-imperial historical scholarship, many of the essentialist themes of *kokugaku* were joined to Confucian notions of loyalty and filial piety. This in turn created a powerful emperor-centered essentialist ideology that proved inspirational to many of those who sought to rebuff the nineteenth-century threats from Europe and North America.

Christianity, *Rangaku*, and Worldview

Japan's first contact with Europeans was with those who sought either profit or Catholic converts, and often the two were linked. From the mid sixteenth century on, the Christian presence in Japan expanded rapidly, though always precariously, and at the start of the Tokugawa period and for its first decade there were some 300,000 Christians in Japan, representing just over 1 percent of the population, with significant concentrations in Kyūshū, and all major cities. Even those with little or no spiritual interest in the creed were often attracted to its exotic trappings, such as crosses, rosaries, and other material trappings of the faith.

During the 1620s and 1630s when Christianity was ruthlessly suppressed and the European presence in Japan contracted to the Dutch East India Company factory on the artificial islet of Deshima in Nagasaki harbor, the West as represented by Europe receded from the popular imagination. For nearly a century even non-Christian knowledge of Europe was forbidden and any discussion of it excluded from the public sphere. Knowledge of China was similarly transformed as China began to operate less as a reality during the Tokugawa period – its subjugation by the alien Manchu and their establishment of the Qing dynasty from 1644 having substantially diminished the allure of the Chinese model – and increasingly metaphorically as a symbol of all that was big, grand, rational, dignified, mature, crafty, and so on.[9]

After reaching a peak during the 1650s and 1660s (recall the persecution of Yamaga Sokō for daring to offer an alternative interpretation of Confucianism in 1665), the exaggerated concern with Christianity specifically and Europe generally receded so that by the 1720s during the more enlightened regime of the Shōgun Tokugawa Yoshimune it was possible to enact long overdue calendrical reform, and to relax the proscription on European books, so long as they omitted reference to Christianty. As for the Christians, for nearly a hundred years from the late seventeenth to the late eighteenth centuries, no one in Japan lost her or his life for reasons of personal faith.

Further, with the relaxation of the ban on European books, it became possible to engage in a new field of learning called *rangaku*, short for *Oranda-gaku*, or Dutch (Holland) learning or studies. Though never popular in the way that Confucian or nativist studies became popular, this Dutch or Western learning meant that limited knowledge of European science and mathematics continued to enter the country. Typically, however, this knowledge was pursued not out of some sympathetic predisposition or favor towards Europe but rather so as to obtain vital intelligence about a potential rival.[10] For example, Honda Toshiaki (1744–1821), a leading proponent of this new field, proposed adopting a Western alphabet, expanding Japanese interests to Sakhalin and Kamchatka, and moving Japan's capital to the latter since it would then lie at 51° N Lat., the same as London, and all this not owing to some admiration of things European, but rather as strategies to strengthen Japan's position vis-à-vis an external threat.[11]

Despite the suspicion with which Europe was viewed, Western knowledge contributed to a major shift in attitude in Japan toward China, the West, and even Japan itself. One dramatic example occurred in 1771 when the *rangaku* scholar Sugita Genpaku (1733–1817) witnessed the dissection of a female criminal. Sugita compared what he saw with the anatomical diagrams in a Dutch translation of the German work *Anatomische Tabellen* (1722) by Johann Adam Kulmus. He found that this European work represented human anatomy more accurately than the traditional texts of Chinese medicine, which in turn implied not only that Chinese knowledge might be mistaken and even at least occasionally inferior to European knowledge, but also that Japanese and Europeans might be fundamentally the same on the inside, despite their external differences.[12] Sugita's 1774 translation of the *Anatomische Tabellen* into Japanese made his discoveries more accessible and stimulated the interest of others in learning Dutch and the knowledge that it unlocked.

This exotic Dutch knowledge proved urgently relevant from the 1850s on when the European and now American incursions proved uncontrollable. This explains the interest of a brilliant youngster like Fukuzawa Yukichi (1835–1901) to go to Nagasaki in 1854 to study Western gunnery, and then the next year to Osaka for advanced *rangaku* before being invited to Edo in 1858 to open his own school of Dutch. As he and other *rangaku* authorities learned more about this new world, they discovered to their dismay that Dutch was not the Western lingua franca they had hoped, and so Fukuzawa immersed himself in the study of English prior to joining the first official Japanese mission to the United States as its interpreter in 1860. For Japan and many Japanese a complex world was about to become immeasurably more so.

Ideology, Consensus, and Education

At the start of the Tokugawa period the Shōgun Ieyasu's closest advisors were Buddhist monks like Sūden (1569–1633) and Tenkai (1536–1643), but as we have seen Confucian voices grew more prominent until Confucianism became the most importannt element among the various components of Tokugawa ideology. Still, it is good to remember that throughout almost all of the Tokugawa period all persons in Japan were formally Buddhist, since Buddhist temples served as local registries where births, marriages, deaths, denominational affiliation, and other household records were officially kept. Though the apparent intent of this temple registration (*terauke shōmon*) system was to facilitate enforcement of the bakufu's religious policies, such as those forbidding Christianity, Buddhism's major denominations were the only formal religious options from the state's point of view.[13]

The early decades of the Tokugawa were exceedingly violent, including the siege of Osaka Castle in 1615, and the suppression of the Shimabara Rebellion in 1637–8, but by the mid seventeenth century stability was restored, and the government's authority went largely unchallenged. Tokugawa ideology thus emphasized the Tokugawa accomplishment of restoring peace and order, the prosperity that stemmed as a result, and the gratitude owed by all to the Tokugawa for this. This ideology represented the political order as natural and hence inescapable, effacing its own origins in the violence of Sekigahara, and wrapping the new rulers in a mantle of virtue. It endorsed the status quo, regarding the Tokugawa as the solely legitimate guardians and protectors of the realm, and construing any disruption to their rule as a violation of this natural order. Like nature itself, the political order of the Tokugawa was imagined to extend for 10,000 generations, that is, until the end of time, operating according to principles that extended back into the past no less than to the very end of time. The bakufu found no end of intellectuals eager to endorse these views among the spokesmen of virtually every intellectual tradition except the Christians, but again the largely Confucian contours of this ideology remain unmistakable.[14]

Within Tokugawa intellectual circles there was in fact broad consensus on a number of issues, and even such rivals in the intellectual arena as Confucianism and *kokugaku* shared numerous assumptions. They idealized certain moments in the archaic past, measuring the present against those moments, and holding them up as realizable ideals. They argued that social well-being requires conformity to an ancient Way, and that this Way is encoded within certain canonical ancient texts. They likewise agreed that individuals possess seeds of goodness that, if nurtured, enable one to attain the same degree of spontaneous and unconscious moral perfection once enjoyed by one's forebears.

Similarly if one examines political-economic thought from the Tokugawa period, one finds spokesmen from all major traditions emphasizing the importance of protecting and preserving the peasantry without whom agricultural production would be impossible. Peasants of course constituted some 80 percent of the Tokugawa population and were the sole producers of tax revenue, and so it is understandable that Tokugawa Confucianism saw it as the ruler's highest responsibility to promote policies that support agricultural production and wherever possible to alleviate excessive taxation burdens on agriculturalists.

Of course there were also differences – some quite subtle – among the traditions on political economy, and within the different traditions themselves perspectives changed over time. The Confucian ideal of self-sufficiency moderated somewhat as mercantilist policies proved overall to be more profitable and attractive in many domains. Unlike the Chinese original, Japanese Confucianism eschewed the proposition that a ruler's authority was contingent upon his virtue, and despite the authoritarian government, the Confucian notion of legitimate remonstrance was increasingly accepted during the Tokugawa years until it became the norm.[15] Security concerns, which figured so prominently at the start of the period, receded thereafter only to re-emerge with increasing urgency during the last Tokugawa half-century. And social thought regarding women seemed increasingly out of step with reality in a world where at least some women found ways to initiate divorce and to inherit and manage property, neither of which should have been possible according to law.[16] In this latter regard, note that time and again one encounters biographies of prominent Tokugawa intellectuals who were taught to read by female relatives, though it is not clear how this literacy was shared among women.

This emphasis on literacy was likewise new, as there was little in the way of a doctrine of self-improvement or perfection prior to the Tokugawa years, but from the mid seventeenth century onwards, beginning with the Confucians, virtually all traditions proposed possibilities for individual advancement, justifying this otherwise self-oriented exercise by seeing it as each one doing one's part to support the larger eventual goal of social perfection. Confucianism expressed this perfection in terms of an organic understanding of society, whereby each person had her or his correct place and specific responsibilities in a society that was deemed to go well when each met these responsibilities perfectly, neither exceeding nor falling short of what is appropriate. These responsibilities were fundamentally relational and represent more than a single option, since there are times when one might be a parent, and at others a child, at times a sibling and at other times a ruler (teacher) or subject (student), and so on. One important contribution of this view is that it emphasized the equal importance of each individual to the larger goal of social perfection, even within a highly stratified society that institutionalized inequalities of all sorts.

Kokugaku likewise contributed a similar kind of horizontal leveling in that it proposed an equal degree of Japaneseness – equal possession of distinctively Japanese hearts and minds – for all persons in Japan. This Japaneseness, in turn, carried with it a number of perquisites that derive from Japan's status as the ancestral land such as access to superior rice and the blessing of regular seasonal change and mild climate; equal rights to a cultural patrimony that included classics of prose and poetry, and a shared history and heritage; and so on. Accompanying these nativist boons were the attendant responsibilities to conform oneself to the requirements of either nature (Kamo no Mabuchi) or the deities (Motoori Norinaga). Confucianism and nativism alike thus shared the assumption that even though one's status might be lowly, the correct performance of one's role had significance that extended well beyond the microcosm of the self.

This doctrine of self-improvement embraced initially by the Confucians and then by the nativists, in turn, probably had the most to do with the explosive growth in educational opportunities at all levels. At the start of the Tokugawa period, education was something provided by samurai elites to other samurai. Indeed, many samurai increasingly found such educational opportunities to be of vocational advantage in a highly competitive environment wherein their martial skills were no longer as needed. By the end of the seventeenth century merchants and other non-samurai commoners figured prominently among the student rolls of private academies as they increasingly availed themselves of forms of knowledge to which they or their forebears would have been excluded as recently as a century earlier. In this way knowledge became a socially valuable commodity, conferring prestige no less than possession of a fine brocade. And by the mid eighteenth century, there was nothing unusual for such non-samurai commoners to be themselves the purveyors as well as the consumers of new academic opportunities in classroom environments in which those social distinctions that were so important in the outside world were allowed for the moment to recede. Indeed, one might argue that outside the market, the private academies in Tokugawa Japan provided the single most important opportunity for voluntary association of the sort that characterized the emergence of civil society in Europe and later in North America.[17]

In matters of personal faith, individuals felt less and less bound to uphold the faith of their fathers and increasingly regarded denominational affiliation as something that was theirs to determine, though efforts to change one's parish registration frequently encountered formidable resistance. It is thus noteworthy that many of the major new religious movements of the twentieth century trace their roots to developments in the last Tokugawa decades, as individuals experimented with such variegated forms of praxis as ecstatic dancing and eccentric dietary regimes in order, on the one hand, to find personal solace in troubling times, and on the other hand to do one's part to reverse what many perceived to be the deterioration of the times. Throughout the period the state's policies toward religion and religionists emphasized control and included the well-known proscription of Christianity along with the less well-known persecution of the recalcitrant *fujufuse* movement in Nichiren Buddhism. Nonetheless, there were tens of thousands who chose to defy the *bakuhan* state by continuing their forbidden religious practices underground, and it is clear that for the better part of the eighteenth century the state lost interest in persecuting those who defied its religious policies but were otherwise model taxpayers or townsmen. This reluctance to prosecute allowed a measure of individual autonomy and privacy to emerge in the realm of personal faith, remaining there until the late eighteenth century when for various reasons Confucian reformers like Matsudaira Sadanobu sought to revitalize those policies that were prominent during the early years of the Tokugawa, that is, the years of greatest vigor, even if the original purposes of such policies no longer applied.

Nature, History, and Japanese Identity

When European and North American scholars first studied the Tokugawa period, it was from the perspective that Tokugawa culture supported a feudal state that had to be overcome for Japan to attain modernity, but as these same scholars awakened to the rich diversity of Tokugawa culture and became more appreciative of intellectual change during those years, the period increasingly appeared to have many of the features of modernity. This reappraisal, in turn, prompted a concern with locating a genesis for Japan's modernity, and an effort to situate that genesis on a global scale of modernity(ies).

The political theorist, sociologist, and public intellectual Maruyama Masao (d. 1997) saw the roots of Japan's modern consciousness in Ogyū Sorai's effort to take the Way out of nature and to place it in history, or as Maruyama expressed it, to see an ontological shift from nature (*shizen*) to invention (*sakui*). According to Maruyama, the traditional Confucian belief that the Way was ontologically linked to Heaven and thus nature meant that the assumptions and premises of that Way must necessarily be valid universally. However, by this same logic, once the Way was historicized by seeing it as a human invention or construction, as Ogyū Sorai did, then the state itself was likewise historicized, disclosing its contingent properties and its relentless need to respond to change. Though one can discern traces of this momentous shift in earlier writings, this transition from a naturalist to a historicist ontology was particularly prominent in the mid to late eighteenth century, and Maruyama saw an analog to this in the *kokugaku* shift from Kamo no Mabuchi's natural Way of Heaven and Earth to

Motoori Norinaga's Way of the Gods. Indeed, despite his contempt for Chinese modes of thought, Kamo no Mabuchi had nothing but admiration for ancient Daoists who similarly located an ancient Way in nature, and who condemned Confucian rationalism as a dangerous fallacy. By contrast, Norinaga rejected all ancient Chinese thought including that of the Daoists, extolling instead a native Way created (read "invented") by native deities, that is, a distinctively Japanese Way that operates *in* nature but is not *of* nature.

This represented a transition with a host of implications. For example, when one regards the Way as part of nature, then those canonical texts that are believed to encode the Way necessarily have didactic value, since reading them should literally help to make one a better person. But once one separated the Way from nature and located it in the world of history, then it remained the case that even though one could learn from ancient texts, one could no longer rely on the possibility of being transformed by them. In other words, once those literary or poetic classics that had traditionally been regarded as foundational were separated from moral signifi-cance, one was then free to evaluate these and other works of literature not in terms of their value for teaching moral lessons, but rather for their capacity to amuse or entertain.

This historicized understanding of the Way, according to Maruyama, found its greatest following during the decades following Sorai's death in 1736, and if we take into consideration the coincidence of Norinaga's "Rectifying Spirit" and Sugita Genpaku's autopsy (both in 1771), we see that the Japanese world of ideas as a whole was experiencing a number of dramatic transitions. At every turn one discerns the mixed blessing of liberation from traditional patterns and the emergence of a host of new binaries, such as Confucian rationalism juxtaposed against a nativist appreci-ation of the wondrous, a freshly constructed Japan juxtaposed against an increasingly metaphoric China, and so on.

Other scholars seeking the roots of Japan's modernity have postulated that it is to be found in the condition of early modernity, a stage of historical development said to be distinguished by the state's power to mobilize resources and the construction of collective identity.[18] Building in particular upon the accomplishments of the hege-mon Toyotomi Hideyoshi, the early Tokugawa state did in fact centralize power to a degree that enabled it to mobilize resources to a degree unprecedented in Japanese history, but it is the construction of Japanese identity that concerns us here. The nativists Kamo no Mabuchi and Motoori Norinaga interpreted this identity differently but agreed on the following key points: that Japan, its people, and its culture enjoy a privileged and superior place among the world's countries; that this privileged status is linked to Japan's possession of an ancient and primordial Way, which enables its people to live as their forebears once did in a kind of pre-moral ancient arcadia; and that if not contaminated by foreign learning, Japanese people enjoy characteristics like naivety, straightforwardness, sincerity, respect for authority, and an intuitive propensity for socially constructive behavior, all as prerogatives of simply being Japanese.

It is in this sense that one can begin to speak of nativists like Mabuchi and Norinaga as having constructed a sense of Japaneseness, and this new identity likewise encom-passed a spatial and temporal orientation for which one needed not be nativist or Confucian, but again simply Japanese. For example, a work like Matsuo Bashō's

(1644–94) *Oku no hosomichi* (Narrow Road to Oku), written in 1694, represented a Japan with a new epicenter at Nihonbashi in Edo, and a periphery on the other side of the Shirakawa Barrier, representing a kind of domesticated Other within the boundaries of Japan itself. Bashō's writings provided his readers with vicarious entry into this exoticized nether realm, transporting them out of the quotidian and into a world of natural beauty and historical significance. In various ways this was the "Japan" that came to be represented during the Tokugawa period in countless printed maps of cities, domains, regions, pedestrian highways, scenic routes, holy sites, and pleasure quarters in a spatial taxonomy that became part of the patrimony of one's very Japaneseness. Similarly, both Confucianism, with its emphasis on history, and nativism, with its inward-looking perspective, offered a new temporal orientation whereby all Japanese were now heirs to a patrimony that included both a grand historical narrative and a cultural heritage encompassing a new set of prose classics alongside the traditional poetic canon.

The view most commonly represented in Tokugawa literature of all sorts was that of a Japan juxtaposed against Asia's giants of China and India along metaphorical lines with antecedents that extended into the medieval past. Yet, it was precisely this last spatial orientation, that is, one that presumed to grand scale but still excluded the West, which was on the verge of proving untenable. In 1765 Kamo no Mabuchi brushed one of his most important works titled *Kokuikō* (The Idea of the Nation). In fact, the "idea of the nation" was still in its germinal phase during the Tokugawa period, at least relative to how it would emerge during the subsequent decades. Nonetheless, in arenas that began principally in urban private academies and by the Tokugawa period's end had penetrated impressively into rural environments, one found the building blocks of a new identity that supplemented, but for most had not yet superseded, the traditional identifications of one's household and village locally and one's domain beyond.

NOTES

1   Berry, "Public Life in Authoritarian Japan."
2   De Bary, "Some Common Tendencies."
3   Ihara, *Some Final Words of Advice*, p. 41.
4   Nakai, *Shogunal Politics*.
5   Tucker, *Itō Jinsai's* Gomō Jigi, pp. 1–52.
6   Maruyama, *Studies in the Intellectual History of Tokugawa Japan*, p. 136.
7   Nosco, *Remembering Paradise*, pp. 99–158.
8   Nishimura "Way of the Gods"; Matsumoto, *Motoori Norinaga*.
9   Keene, "Characteristic Responses to Confucianism."
10 Wakabayashi, *Anti-Foreignism and Western Learning*.
11 Keene, *The Japanese Discovery of Europe*.
12 Jansen, *Japan and Its World*.
13 Nosco, "Keeping the Faith."
14 Ooms, *Tokugawa Ideology*.
15 Roberts, *Mercantilism in a Japanese Domain*.
16 Wright, "Severing the Karmic Ties that Bind."
17 Rubinger, *Private Academies in Tokugawa Japan*.
18 Eisenstadt and Schlucter, "Introduction: Paths to Early Modernities."

BIBLIOGRAPHY

Berry, Mary Elizabeth. "Public Life in Authoritarian Japan." *Daedalus* 127:3 (Summer 1998): 133–66.

de Bary, Wm. Theodore. "Some Common Tendencies in Neo-Confucianism." In David S. Nivison and Arthur Wright, eds., *Confucianism in Action*. Stanford, Calif.: Stanford University Press, 1959.

Eisenstadt, Shmuel, and Schlucter, Wolfgang. "Introduction: Paths to Early Modernities – A Comparative View." *Daedalus* 127:3 (Summer 1998): 1–18.

Elison, George. *Deus Destroyed: The Image of Christianity in Early Modern Japan*. Cambridge, Mass.: Harvard University Press, 1988.

Ihara Saikaku. *Some Final Words of Advice*, trans. Peter Nosco. Rutland, Vt.: C. E. Tuttle, 1980.

Jansen, Marius. *Japan and Its World: Two Centuries of Change*. Princeton: Princeton University Press, 1975.

Kasahara, Kazuo, ed. *A History of Japanese Religion*. Tokyo: Kosei Publishing, 2001.

Keene, Donald. *The Japanese Discovery of Europe, 1720–1830*, rev. edn. Stanford, Calif.: Stanford University Press, 1969.

Keene, Donald. "Characteristic Responses to Confucianism in Tokugawa Literature." In Peter Nosco, ed., *Confucianism and Tokugawa Culture*. Princeton: Princeton University Press, 1984.

Maruyama Masao. *Studies in the Intellectual History of Tokugawa Japan*, trans. Mikiso Hane. Tokyo: University of Tokyo Press, 1974.

Matsumoto, Shigeru. *Motoori Norinaga, 1730–1801*. Cambridge, Mass.: Harvard University Press, 1970.

Nakai, Kate Wildman. *Shogunal Politics: Arai Hakuseki and the Premises of Tokugawa Rule*. Cambridge, Mass.: Council on East Asian Studies, Harvard University, 1988.

Nishimura, Sey. "The Way of the Gods: Motoori Norinaga's *Naobi no Mitama*." *Monumenta Nipponica* 46:1 (Spring 1991): 21–41.

Nosco, Peter. *Remembering Paradise: Nativism and Nostalgia in Eighteenth-Century Japan*. Cambridge, Mass.: Council on East Asian Studies, Harvard University, 1990.

Nosco, Peter. "Keeping the Faith: *Bakuhan* Policy towards Religions in Seventeenth-Century Japan." In P. F. Kornicki and I. J. McMullen, eds., *Religion in Japan: Arrows to Heaven and Earth*. Cambridge: Cambridge University Press, 1996.

Ooms, Herman. *Tokugawa Ideology: Early Constructs, 1570–1680*. Princeton: Princeton University Press, 1985.

Roberts, Luke. *Mercantilism in a Japanese Domain: The Merchant Origins of Economic Nationalism in 18th-Century Tosa*. Cambridge: Cambridge University Press, 1998.

Rubinger, Richard. *Private Academies in Tokugawa Japan*. Princeton: Princeton University Press, 1982

Tucker, John Allen. *Itō Jinsai's* Gomō Jigi *and the Philosophical Definition of Early Modern Japan*. Leiden: Brill, 1998.

Wakabayashi, Bob Tadashi. *Anti-Foreignism and Western Learning in Early-Modern Japan: The New Theses of 1825*. Cambridge, Mass.: Council on East Asian Studies, Harvard University, 1986.

Wright, Diana. "Severing the Karmic Ties that Bind: The 'Divorce Temple' Mantokuji." *Monumenta Nipponica* 52:3 (Autumn 1997): 357–80.

FURTHER READING

An excellent collection of translated primary sources along with helpful introductory material can be found in volume 2 of the revised edition of *Sources of Japanese Tradition* (New York: Columbia University Press, 2005), compiled by Wm. Theodore de Bary, Carol Gluck, and Arthur Tiedemann, which is particularly strong in its chapters on Confucianism and *kokugaku*. In addition to Donald Keene's chapter mentioned above, the essays in Peter Nosco's edited volume *Confucianism and Tokugawa Culture* (Princeton: Princeton University Press, 1984) likewise provide helpful further reading. Nishiyama Matsunosuke's *Edo Culture* (Honolulu: University of Hawai'i Press, 1997) offers a wealth of colorful detail regarding the material background of Tokugawa intellectual change. Tetsuo Najita's *Visions of Virtue in Tokugawa Japan: The Kaitokudō Merchant Academy of Osaka* (Chicago: University of Chicago Press, 1987) is a model study of the principal municipally subsidized academy in Osaka. Janine Sawada's *Confucian Values and Popular Zen* (Honolulu: University of Hawai'i Press, 1993) demonstrates the penetration of Confucian assumptions into the spiritual realm of a popular new Tokugawa religious movement.

CHAPTER SEVEN

Cultural Developments in Tokugawa Japan

Lawrence E. Marceau

Introduction

When the first Europeans set foot on Japanese soil in the mid sixteenth century, they encountered a culture that, while vastly different from anything they had experienced, still impressed them with its rich diversity and complexity. Observers report their surprise at the breadth and cleanliness of the avenues of the capital, the beauty of the apartments and gardens at Nijō Castle, and even the sense of personal honor embraced by people high and low.[1] The period of unification after over a century of incessant internal chaos and warfare brought with it patronage of the arts by a new class of warriors, who, reaping the benefits of expanded trade with Asian and European states, projected their wealth and power to a degree never before seen in Japan. Monumental castles, embellished with painted folding screens, sliding doors, and gold-leaf-covered accoutrements, dominated both hills and plains as extensions of the authority of their lords, most notably the hegemons Oda Nobunaga (1534–82) at Azuchi Castle, Toyotomi Hideyoshi (1537–98) at Fushimi and Osaka Castles and the Jurakutei Mansion, and, later, Tokugawa Ieyasu (1542–1616) at Edo and Sunpu Castles. Nobunaga and his successors commissioned the finest artists and artisans in the realm to supply everything from portraits to sculptures, paintings, calligraphy, tea implements and ceramics, lacquerware, fine metalwork, arms and armor, textiles, noh (also spelled "nō") masks, and innumerable other items to embellish their buildings, gardens, and persons.[2] Lesser daimyō (lords) followed suit, each at his own level of wealth, so not only the major urban centers of Kyoto, Osaka, and increasingly Edo, but the seat of each daimyō's castle town came to exhibit the new opulence of the age. Indeed this age of ostentation, conspicuous consumption, and the projection of new martial authority, referred to today as "Momoyama" (after the place upon which Hideyoshi's Fushimi Castle stood), has subsequently been remembered as a particularly prominent era in Japan's cultural history.

This initial burst of cultural efflorescence eventually subsided with the increasing controls over Japanese life following the annihilation of the Toyotomi line and the destruction of Osaka Castle in 1615, which left the Tokugawa, its collateral lines, and its allies as the unrivaled hegemons of state apparatus for the next two and a half centuries. In quick succession the Tokugawa authorities acted to restrict the authority of the warrior class and even the aristocrats and nobles (1615); to close Japan's ports, leaving only Nagasaki open to Dutch and Chinese trade (1616, 1623, 1639, 1641), to limit foreign travel by Japanese and their return from residence abroad (1621, 1633); to restrict the activities of peasants (1625); to establish a system of required residence in Edo for daimyō, thereby hampering their ability to gain power in their provinces (1635); and to ban the practice of Christianity (1639). The opulence of Momoyama culture gradually changed into something reflective of the new age of peace and stability.

Scholars, both in Japan and abroad, have tended to view early modern Japan as consisting of two parts, "early Edo" and "late Edo," the former characterized by the cultural dominance of the Kamigata, or Kyoto–Osaka region to the west, and the latter characterized by the rise of Edo culture in the east. This configuration makes a division around the year 1770, highlighting the Genroku era (1688–1704) as the peak of the earlier Kamigata culture, with the Bunka-Bunsei (or Kasei) eras (1804–30) serving as the apex of the later Edo culture. However, scholars such as Nakano Mitsutoshi have come to reject this periodization, arguing instead for a three-part division, in which the eighteenth century, climaxing with the Tenmei era (1781–9), not only provides a transition and link between the earlier and later periods, but in fact surpasses them in the variety and quality of the literary and other forms of culture produced.[3]

Nakano and others have identified the Japanese terms *ga* and *zoku* as useful poles on an axis for measuring cultural production during this time. *Ga*, written with the character for "courtly" (*miyabiyaka*), refers to the elevated, the refined, the elegant, the aristocratic, the classical, or the Sinified. At the other end of the axis, *zoku*, written with the character for "coarse" (*iyashi*), connotes the base, the common, the popular or plebeian, the vulgar, the contemporary vernacular, or the domestic. Cultural practices in the late sixteenth and early seventeenth centuries tended to be conducted or commissioned by elite individuals and groups, including powerful military houses, large shrine and temple complexes, the imperial court and aristocracy, and wealthy merchants, especially those operating in Kyoto, Osaka, and the port of Sakai. For the most part these classes patronized *ga* activities. Classical waka and linked-verse renga poetry collections continued to be compiled; the Heian court classics and medieval war epics were copied in sumptuous manuscript editions; paintings in the classical Tosa lineage, as well as in the more Sinified Kanō school, were commissioned in ever greater numbers; noh dramas were performed on new stages in castle residences; and the nouveau riche elites came to develop a taste for tea, tea house designs, and the collection of rare and expensive tea utensils, both imported and domestic. While many of these pastimes may have originated from humble, rustic (or *zoku*) origins, by the early seventeenth century they clearly fell within the *ga* rubric.

It is tempting to view early modern Japanese cultural developments as reflecting the triumph of popular (*zoku*) culture over elite (*ga*) culture. Such a view, however, ignores the desire of the new consumers, and increasingly producers, of cultural capital (to apply sociologist Pierre Bourdieu's concept) to emulate the elite classes and their cultural ideals. It might be more helpful to consider the convergence of several factors that led to the rise of popular culture in Japan, while at the same time generating a new network of relationships between the heretofore separate realms of elite and popular culture.

The first of these factors is the "Great Peace" of the Tokugawa sociopolitical system. With peace and social stability, daimyō no longer needed to divert human and material resources to a war effort. While castle construction and fortification continued through the seventeenth century, after the fall of Osaka Castle in 1615, no more castles needed to be attacked or defended from siege. The *bushi*, or samurai class, some 7 percent of the total population, found itself relieved of the task of defending the lord or attacking a rival and, in its place, charged with the job of administering the myriad details involved in ordering the domain. As a result, the warrior–administrative class found itself increasingly encouraged to engage in "civil" (*bun*, encompassing the cultural realm) pursuits, and less encouraged to follow "martial" (*bu*, military) pursuits. With such stimuli, even mid- to lower-ranking samurai began to undergo training in such arts as reading the Chinese classics, singing noh libretti, practicing calligraphy, and preparing powdered tea. Before long they would be engaging in more *zoku* activities as well.

The second factor is the growth of urban areas, and the increased opportunities for the expansion of cultural markets. By the early eighteenth century, the population of Edo had exploded to probably over a million inhabitants, with a samurai population alone of some 500,000; Osaka could boast a population of some 360,000; Kyoto 350,000; Kanazawa 120,000; Nagoya 64,000 (commoners only); and Hiroshima 70,000–80,000.[4] The prominence of urban spaces along the main Tōkaidō thoroughfare linking Edo with Kyoto as well as in each of the provinces provided a fertile environment for increased entertainment, social intercourse, sightseeing, and other possibilities for cultural interaction. Both elite and popular culture could easily cohabit and intermingle within such urban spaces.

Related to the growth of cities is the network that developed to link them. With the system of enforced attendance in Edo over alternate years (*sankin kōtai*) for daimyō, their families (required to remain in Edo as insurance against any possible uprisings from the provinces), and their retinues, the various thoroughfares linking Edo with provinces throughout the country grew in importance. Inns, hostels, fords, bridges, and the roads themselves required constant upkeep, and, of course, not only did daimyō and their retinues utilize them, but people of all classes and backgrounds came to include travel as an option in their lives. Within the restrictions posed by an elaborate system of passes, permits, and checkpoints, people were able to travel to and from various provinces for religious pilgrimages, to hot spring spas for health reasons, for purposes of trade and commerce, on "poetic pilgrimages" to spots made famous in waka and *haikai* poetry, and for purposes of entertainment. The growth of these transportation networks (including river and sea routes) allowed for the exchange of information, news, and stories between the provinces and the urban centers, thus promoting cultural awareness as well.

With the increased complexity of society and the growth of markets and trade networks, it became necessary for samurai, merchants, artisans, and women of all social classes to gain at least basic literacy in the phonetic *kana* syllabaries, to write letters following the conventions of seasonal change, and to make calculations and balance books using a *soroban* or abacus. A literate readership creates a market for reading materials of all types, and publishing houses in Kyoto and Osaka, and later,

Edo, rose to the challenge of providing readers with something to read. Access to education, while by no means universal, allowed for at least some commoners to gain access to elite culture, and for elites to transmit their knowledge to broader groups of students.

The most important cultural development in early modern Japan, made possible by the atmosphere of peace and relative social stability, was the spread of printing and publishing, both official and especially commercial. Henry D. Smith II may actually be understating the power and vitality of Japanese publishing when he writes, "in scale, early modern Japan had a culture of print in every way comparable to that of many European countries of the time, working through the power of reproduction to circulate Edo culture far more broadly than ever before, stimulating a rapid increase in literacy, and moving in the inexorable direction of a mass culture."[5] Since print culture provided the underpinnings for the vast majority of cultural developments in early modern Japan, it is important to focus here on publishing.

Japan was long said to have been the home of the world's oldest printed artifacts, the *Hyakumantō daran*, or "dhāraṇī (Buddhist invocations) in one million pagodas," printed between 764 and 770. However in 1966 a printed dhāranī was discovered in a stone pagoda in Korea, and most likely dates from some time before 751. Given that much of early Japanese technology derives from the Korean peninsula, it is not surprising that printing in Korea should predate that in Japan.[6]

The reproduction and transmission of texts and visual materials in Japan continued in large part through the practice of manuscript copying. With the notable exception of the Gozan-ban, or "Five Mountain (Rinzai sect of Zen Buddhist monasteries) editions" of texts in Chinese published between the thirteenth and the sixteenth centuries, medieval Japanese text and visual culture was nearly exclusively one of manuscripts and drawings. Given the amount of labor and time required to copy a manuscript of a long text, we can assume that only elites enjoyed the resources to function as producers and consumers of manuscript culture.

This changed dramatically in the late-sixteenth-century Momoyama period. Imports of expertise and technology from two overseas sources combined to stimulate the development of domestic printing technology. First, the Jesuit mission press established movable-type printing facilities at its academy in Kyūshū in 1590, printing Christian, Chinese, and Japanese works, as well as dictionaries and grammars, in both romanized Japanese and the Sino-Japanese script, using metal type. Of some 100 titles printed over this period, fewer than forty are extant, many of these in a unique surviving copy. Another "import" was the looting of large numbers of Korean printed books and movable type from the Yi dynasty's Printing Office in Seoul by Hideyoshi's armies during the Bunroku (1592) invasion of the Korean peninsula. It is possible, that, as was the case with Korean ceramic artists, Korean typesetters and printers themselves may have been taken to Japan by force in order to print books and to teach the Japanese techniques of casting bronze type and printing using both bronze and wooden movable type. The existence of Korean movable type in Japan stimulated the production of Japanese type, and native publishers began printing works from both the looted and domestically produced typefaces. The Japanese imperial court as well as the first Tokugawa shōgun, Ieyasu, were actively involved in printing official Confucian and other non-Buddhist Chinese texts (in contrast to the earlier Gozan-ban texts, which had mainly been of Buddhist works), and soon private amateur, commercial, and even religious publishers were publishing their own titles using movable type.

The practice of printing from engraved woodblocks continued as well. João Rodrigues (1561–1633), a Portuguese Jesuit missionary and interpreter who lived in Japan between 1585 and 1610, wrote regarding printing in Japan:

> The Japanese have three methods of printing. ... The first method, and the one most used in China, is done with wooden blocks. The block is made the same size as the desired folio or page and they skilfully carve on its surface the letters of the page, set out and written with all the paragraphs, chapters, commas, full stops, and everything else. ... They are so dextrous in this art that they can cut a block in about the same time as we can compose a page. ... There are as many blocks as there are folios or pages of the book. These blocks belong to the person who ordered the engraving and they last him a long time, so he can print as often as he pleases and any number of copies. When a book is sold out he can print it again because he always keeps the pages made up and ready. And if there should be a mistake on the block, it can be corrected or changed very easily according to his wishes. ... The second method of printing uses movable type, each one made individually of wood or cast from metal. They make up the page just as we do and then print it. ... Afterwards they dismantle the page, wash the letters and put them back in their places so that they can use them again whenever necessary. In this way they can dispense with the large number of blocks, which are made from a certain type of wood not easily obtainable. The third method ... is the opposite of the technique employed in the first method. ... In this third method, the surface of the block stands out and the letters are sunken. ... The letters are left white and the background black. This method is not used for printing books but for printing inscriptions, epitaphs and pictures of men, flowers, plants, trees, animals and other similar things, which are carved on these blocks, sheets (of metal) or stones.[7]

The third method, referred to in Japanese as the *takuhan* or "stone rubbing" technique, is relatively rare, and made little effect on the history of printing in Japan. However, the fact that Rodrigues mentions block printing ahead of the European style of movable-type printing indicates that, prior to 1610 at least, movable-type printing was still a secondary technology. Over the course of the next four decades, though, until about 1650, movable-type printing became the standard in Japan, and for the first time works ranging from the Heian literary classics, such as the *Tales of Ise* and the *Tale of Genji*, to noh libretti, primers on arithmetic, gazetteers, and contemporary fiction appeared in movable-type editions, published by commercial firms in Kyoto and Osaka. These works, while originally expensive, and probably published in small lots as gifts to patrons or clients, became increasingly in high demand, and publishers found it difficult to keep up with the requests for reprints, especially after the first run had been published and the type dismantled and put away for use with the next title. Another reason for the decline of books published in movable-type editions after their initial popularity was that illustrations, especially those combining text and image freely on the same page, were much more easily produced using a block printing technique than they were in combination with movable type. Rodrigues's concern over the difficulty of obtaining the "certain type of wood" (the *yamazakura* variety of cherry, in fact) for engraving seems to have become much less of an issue by the mid seventeenth century, perhaps through the establishment of arrangements with peasants to provide an adequate supply of suitable cherry to publishers.

In short, movable-type printing became a victim of its own success. While ideal for printing small batches of several hundred copies of a particular work in a single edition, this technique proved inadequate for meeting the demand of multiple printings, or works that combined images and text together on the same page. Also, with the continued expansion of basic literacy to broader sectors of the population, including women and children, the need for phonetic glosses next to Chinese characters to serve as reading aids increased. Providing such glosses was cumbersome and time-consuming with movable type, while block printing easily allowed for these modifications to a text. By the second half of the seventeenth century, nearly all printing in Japan had reverted to the earlier woodblock-engraving method.

As Peter Kornicki states, "Print culture in the Tokugawa period matured rapidly into a phenonemon with all the complexity and variety that is customarily associated with only the most advanced Western countries before modern times." At least 3,000 titles appeared annually on average throughout the early modern period, not including reprints of Chinese and Buddhist works, which were also in great demand.[8] Publishing continued to expand, also in the types of materials being published, and in the locations of publishers. Over the course of the early modern period, the number of publishers active at one time or another grew to at least 6,747, according to Inoue Takaaki's compendium of publisher-booksellers.[9] Geographically, publishers spread from the Kamigata region eastward to Edo, and then outward to several other provincial castle seats, such as Nagoya, Sendai, and Kanazawa. Finally, in terms of types of publications produced, the early Buddhist texts, Confucian classics, and Japanese histories came to be joined by noh libretti, jōruri and kabuki playscripts, contemporary fiction, primers for reading and writing letters, gazetteers, poetry collections (both historical and contemporary), painting manuals, sketchbooks, how-to manuals, jokebooks, and a myriad of other subjects. This list does not include single-sheet prints; current events broadsides (*kawaraban*); rankings of sumō wrestlers, actors, and courtesans; calendars; or other more ephemeral materials that were produced in great quantities and on a regular basis. In this manner print media permeated early modern Japanese society, and supported cultural developments from the elite through the populace as a whole.

The Arts: Pluralism in an Urban Environment

Even though the military had controlled Japan for over 400 years, it was not until the establishment of the Tokugawa order and a reduced need for forces on constant ready alert that the notion of "martial arts" (*bugei*) became codified. Such works as the *Gorin no sho* (*Book of Five Rings*, 1645), by the talented if eccentric Miyamoto Musashi (1584–1645), and the *Hagakure* (before 1716), transmitted to a disciple by Yamamoto Tsunetomo (1658–1719), are both relatively well known today, but throughout the early modern period circulated only in manuscript form. Each of the military households kept written codes of conduct for samurai, though, and part of the education of a warrior was to read the Chinese and Japanese classics of strategy, and historical tales of great military exploits. One book, *Budō shoshinshū*, by Daidōji Yūzan (1639–1730) was completed shortly before Yūzan's death, but with its publication in Edo in 1834, became a widely read treatise on samurai attitudes toward life and death. The codification of martial arts helped sustain the samurai when their daily lives had become focused more on paperwork and other clerical duties than on military defense or strategy. Yūzan begins his work with: "One who is supposed to be a warrior considers it his foremost concern to keep death in mind at all times, every day and every night, from the morning of New Year's Day through the night of New Year's Eve."[10] Such statements must have grabbed the attention of samurai whose lives were governed more by concerns about personal debt, drink, and the pleasure quarters than about death. Yūzan doesn't expect warriors to be focused only on martial matters, though; he encourages education and cultural pursuits as well. "If strength is all you have you will seem like a peasant turned samurai, and that will never do. You should acquire education as a matter of course, and it is desirable to learn things such as poetry and the tea ceremony, little by little, in your spare time."[11]

The performing arts exhibited phenomenal development over the course of the early modern period. The medieval noh, patronized by daimyō throughout the country, continued to be performed at felicitous occasions, and schools of noh (and the related *kyōgen*, or animated skits performed between noh acts) performance flourished in Kyoto and, later, Edo. However kabuki and jōruri (the puppet theater tradition known as "bunraku" today) developed from riverbank entertainments in the late sixteenth and early seventeenth centuries. The earliest performers were itinerent dancers and musicians who performed at festivals in one corner of a shrine or temple compound, or other open spaces. Both kabuki and the puppet theater benefitted greatly from the introduction of the shamisen, a three-stringed musical instrument with a clear, high tone, from the Ryūkyū Islands in the second half of the sixteenth century. This new instrument brought with it a revolution in musical performance, and allowed for both the kabuki and the puppet theater to be performed in large theaters, before audiences of hundreds of paying spectators.

Jōruri, or bunraku, became established in Kyoto and Osaka through the seventeenth century. The collaboration between the great early *tayū* (chanter-singer-narrators), Takemoto Gidayū I (1651–1714) and the greatest playwright for the puppet theater, Chikamatsu Monzaemon (1653–1724), led to a great upsurge in jōruri's popularity, and Chikamatsu's playscripts, or *shōhon*, were purchased and read (or chanted) by amateurs for their content and the power of their language. Both historical pieces, or *jidaimono* (which focused on the military class), and contemporary domestic pieces, or *sewamono* (which featured civilian townsfolk, especially rich merchants, their families, and courtesans), gained immense popularity, and, with technical improvements in puppet construction and stage design (the earlier one-handler puppets, manipulated by a single puppeteer, were replaced after 1734 by larger and more expressive three-handler puppets, for which the head and right arm were controlled by the main puppeteer, the legs by a second, and the left arm by a third), jōruri was able to compete successfully with kabuki in the Kamigata area. In fact, with the increasingly prominent dialogue found in jōruri scripts from Chika-matsu's time on, jōruri came to serve as important sources for some of the most successful and popular kabuki plays. Jōruri never gained popularity in the huge Edo market, and even in the Kamigata, kabuki continued to grow in popularity as jōruri declined from the mid eighteenth century on.

Kabuki as we know it today is believed to have been founded by one Izumo no Okuni (fl. 1600), a woman who is said to have performed songs and dances to great acclaim in 1603 at the Kitano Tenjin Shrine and the dry riverbed of the Kamo River at the eastern end of Shijō Avenue, both in Kyoto. The word *kabuku*, used as a verb, connoted behaving or moving about erratically (the base meaning is "to tilt," as in tilting one's head), especially in an irreverent and attention-getting manner. Thus, *kabukimono*, or "those who *kabuku*," were persons who spent their time flaunting the rules, dancing provocatively, dressing in outrageous styles, and otherwise refusing to conform to the status quo of the emerging Tokugawa state. The irreverent and flamboyant dances and skits of these *kabukimono* came to be called kabuki, and at first women performed in various locations. However, because their presence generated social unrest (fights often ensued among male viewers who also vied with one another for sexual favors from the performers), the Tokugawa authorities banned women from performing kabuki, replacing them with adolescent youths (*wakashu*). This led, however, to similar problems, so in 1652 the *wakashu* were in turn replaced by male adults (*yarō*), who continue performing kabuki roles, both male and female, to the present day. Kabuki in the Kamigata was characterized by audience preference for *wagoto*, or realistic, delicate performances, especially as portrayed by such actors as Sakata Tōjūrō I (1647–1709) playing young romantic male roles, and Yoshizawa Ayame I (1673–1729) in the roles of beautiful women. In contrast, the overwhelm-ingly male audiences in the newer, military city of Edo preferred *aragoto*, or "rough business" performances, such as were developed by the great star of Edo kabuki, Ichikawa Danjūrō I (1660–1704).

While attendance at performances held in one of the large theaters in Kyoto, Osaka, or Edo was prohibited for members of the samurai class, they attended in large numbers, usually incognito. In the theaters themselves, men, women, and children of all classes of society occupied seating according to what they could afford, and enjoyed watching the performances, interacting with neighbors, and even eating the box lunches for sale between acts.

In the nineteenth century, the continued growth of kabuki, and the growing interest on the part of the audience in the more problematic "villain" (*aku*, or "evil") characters led to the development of a particular subset of the *sewamono* domestic dramas, called *kizewamono*, or "raw" *sewamono*. These plays focused on impoverished townsfolk or other "down and out" characters, and provided an enhanced sense of realism to a performing art that had developed into a highly stylized form. Tsuruya Nanboku IV (1755–1829) and Kawatake Mokuami (1816–83) perfected the *kizewamono*, and the actors performing these roles enjoyed national fame.

In the visual and graphic arts, again great dynamism is apparent over the course of the early modern period. As the Tokugawa order took shape in the early seventeenth century, most paintings and drawings were commissioned by those in control of Japan's material resources, namely, the bakufu (Tokugawa administration, also referred to as the "shogunate"), and the daimyō of the various domains. These works followed prescribed forms (Chinese sages; images of power including dragons, Chinese lions, and tigers; Chinese recluses; and images from the Japanese classics), and were intended to enhance the interior decor of elite residences and reception halls. The creators of these works hailed from the Kanō school for Chinese-derived images, and from the Tosa school, for images from Heian literary and other Japanese sources. The Chinese-style landscapes, bird and flower images, and biographical portraits that were the province of the Kanō school painters tended to dominate the public areas of a castle or residence, while Tosa school designs tended to be found on sliding doors or folding screens of the more private quarters of a residence, especially the spaces occupied by the women of the household.

While established artists of the Kanō and Tosa schools continued to produce fine works under official patronage, new and highly innovative forms of design were being developed by artists more closely related to merchants in Kyoto society. One such wealthy patron, Suminokura Soan (1571–1632), heir to a shipping fortune, collaborated with Hon'ami Kōetsu (1558–1637), an artist from a line of sword connoisseurs, who in turn collaborated with a commercial fan painter, Tawaraya Sōtatsu (d. 1643). Together these and other artists experimented with printing (the sumptuously decorated books called the "Saga-bon," after the location west of Kyoto where Soan had his atelier, are by Kōetsu and his collaborators), paper design and decoration, lacquerware, and many other media. While such works were probably given to important patrons rather than being sold, Soan, Kōetsu, and Sōtatsu opened the door to new patterns of production and consumption of art works, and served as forerunners to what would later be known as Rinpa (or "Rimpa"), the delicate and highly stylized works designed and produced by Ogata Kōrin (1658–1716), who worked in the medium of painting and design, and his brother, Kenzan (1663–1743), who worked mainly in ceramics and textiles. (The term "Rinpa" comes from the second character of Kōrin's name; hence, "school of Kōrin.")

By the eighteenth century, a number of individualistic painters had appeared, working in a variety of styles. One of the most distinctive of these styles, which began in depictions of genre scenes of contemporary individuals, especially courtesans of the pleasure quarters, actors, sumō wrestlers, and other intriguing figures, came to be known as "ukiyo-e," or "pictures of the floating world." Ukiyo-e artists worked both in painting and also in the medium of print, whereby their works could be reproduced and distributed to a broader audience. These artists are generally associated with urban commoner class known as *chōnin*, which included both merchants and artisans. Working in collaboration with publisher-print-vendors, ukiyo-e artists drew the images that were then transferred to cherry blocks for carving and printing. Images were exclusively monochrome, or hand-tinted, and, from the 1760s onward, were produced in vibrant colors, by which a separate woodblock is engraved and inked for each color used. These polychrome prints became a sensational commodity of Edo, in eastern Japan, and came to be known by consumers from all over the country as *azuma nishiki-e*, or "brocade pictures of the east." Major ukiyo-e artists of Edo include Hishikawa Moronobu (*c*.1618–94), Torii Kiyonobu I (1664–1729), Kaigetsudō Ando (fl. 1704–14), Suzuki Harunobu (1725–70), Katsukawa Shunshō (1726–92), Torii Kiyonaga (1752–1815), Kitagawa Utamaro (*c*.1753–1806), the enigmatic genius Tōshūsai Sharaku (fl. 1794–5), Utagawa Hiroshige (1797–1858), Utagawa Kunisada (1786–1865), Utagawa Kuniyoshi (1797–1861), and the most versatile and productive artist of them all, Katsushika Hokusai (1760–1849). In Kyoto, the most prominent ukiyo-e artist was Nishikawa Sukenobu (1671–1751), while other artists in Osaka focused on actor prints. Not only did ukiyo-e artists work with single-sheet prints, but they also designed print series, such as *Ten Examples of Female Physiognomy* (Utamaro, *c*.1792–3) and *Fifty-Three Stages on the Tōkaidō Highway* (Hiroshige, 1833–4), illustrated works of fiction and poetry, and designed books that consisted almost exclusively of pictures (*ehon*).

With the rise of education and literacy, especially among members of the low to middle echelons of the samurai class who were otherwise restricted from utilizing their abilities for the improvement of society, there arose in the mid eighteenth century a tendency for certain talented individuals to focus on their literary and artistic skills, and to emulate Chinese scholar-poets, called *wenren* in Chinese, about whom they had read. Their Chinese role models were often landed gentry who did not need to earn a living, so they would devote themselves to the "four accomplishments" of playing the *qin*, or koto, playing the game of *go*, enjoying calligraphy, and drawing pictures. The eighteenth-century Japanese, known as *bunjin*, who found this bohemian-like lifestyle desirable, in most cases did not have the financial or material resources to allow for a pure amateur devotion to the arts. In spite of the fact that they were dependent on patrons or sales of their art in order to support themselves, Japanese *bunjin* maintained a state of mind that avoided crass materialism or commercialism, and in their paintings and other works sought a detached, elevated consciousness.

The *bunjin* who are best known today for their achievements in the visual arts include the "pioneers" Yanagisawa Kien (1706–58) and Gion Nankai (1677–1751), the former a high-ranking domainal official, and the latter a Confucian scholar. Another early *bunjin* on the other hand, Sakaki Hyakusen (1697–1752), was born to a family of shopkeepers dealing in Chinese medicines. Ike no Taiga (1723–76) and Yosa Buson (1716–84) are today renowned as the greatest *bunjin* artists, and Buson, especially, is noted for his mastery of *haikai* (the forerunner of today's haiku), and considered second only to the "sage" Matsuo Bashō (1644–94). The *bunjin* distinguished themselves from other artists, writers, and poets by their lofty idealistic nature, and by the freedom and expressiveness they often communicated in their works.

Other artists avoided embracing the ideals of the *bunjin* per se, but still broke away from the established schools of painting, and created highly idiosyncratic works that left them with a reputation as individualists. Itō Jakuchū (1716–1800), Soga Shōhaku (1730–81), and Nagasawa Rosetsu (1754–99) are prime examples of the ability of artists in this period to create works that can be visually eye-catching, emotionally disturbing, and strangely attractive to the viewer at the same time. Also in Kyoto, a new school of painting arose inspired by a combination of Western influences, the *bunjin* phenonemon, and the trend toward greater individual expression prevalent at the time. This school, founded by Maruyama Ōkyo (1733–95) on Shijō (Fourth Avenue), is known today as the Maruyama-Shijō school. Matsumura Goshun (1752–1811), the second great master from this school (after Ōkyo himself), was a protégé of Buson as well, employing the *haikai* poetic sobriquet, Gekkei.

In Edo, artists hailing from the military class were active, such as Sakai Hōitsu (1761–1828), who led a revival of Sōtatsu's earlier Kamigata Rinpa movement, and Tani Bunchō (1763–1840), who was in great demand for his paintings in a *bunjin*-inspired style. The creative activities of other artists active in Osaka, Kyoto, Edo, Nagasaki, and other provincial cities in the nineteenth century attest to the vibrancy and diversity of artistic production in the early modern period.

Space limits us from discussing early modern developments in other important arts, such as ceramics and lacquerware, both of which not only exhibited dramatic expansion and differentiation over the course of the period, but were also important items of export to Korea, China, and Europe. One art that demands our attention, however, is that of tea. The practice of *chanoyu*, in which the preparer adds hot water to powdered green tea in a bowl and then beats the mixture rapidly with a bamboo whisk, continued from the time of tea master Sen no Rikyū (1522–91) throughout the period, especially in the context of Buddhist temples and in teahouses constructed by daimyō lords and other powerful figures. Another form of tea taste, known by the term *sencha*, or steeped tea, grew in popularity with the arrival in Japan of a new sect of Zen Buddhism, known as Ōbaku (Ch., Huangbo) in the 1660s, a development not unrelated to the fall of the Chinese Ming Dynasty and its replacement by the Qing Dynasty ruled by Manchus from the north. The rise of the Qing was seen by many Chinese intellectuals and artists as the defeat of civilization and culture as they knew it, and precipitated the rise among many Ming loyalists of a profound sense of nostalgia for the past, and withdrawal from a harsh sociopolitical environment. This resulted in an exodus of Ming-leaning Buddhist monks, scholars, artists, and merchants from China to neighboring states, including, for some, to Japan. In the Chinese compound in Nagasaki and elsewhere, the existence of a new wave of dissatisfied Chinese promoted the growth of *bunjin* consciousness among many Japanese who also felt the frustrations of dealing with the Tokugawa order, especially with regard to international contacts. The most influential of these Chinese in Japan were immigrant Linji (J., Rinzai) Sect Zen monks from the temple Wanfusi, on Mt. Huangbo in Fujian province. When the abbot of Wanfusi, Yinyuan (J., Ingen, 1592–1673), determined that it was his destiny to spread the Ōbaku faith to the Japanese, and, despite the strong resistance of his disciples, emigrated to Nagasaki in 1654 with a group of some thirty other monks and artisans, Chinese influence on Japanese *bunjin* tastes, not only with regard to tea, but across many artistic genres, increased dramatically. Yinyuan successfully founded a center for the new sect in Uji, just south of Kyoto, and, naming his temple Manpuku-ji (read with the same characters as the original Wanfusi in China), he brought about an opportunity for émigré loyalist notions of critical detachment from the political status quo to gain currency in Japan. As Patricia Graham writes, "During the heyday of Ōbaku in the eighteenth century, there were approximately five hundred Ōbaku temples scattered throughout Japan."[12] Such a spread of contemporary Chinese culture throughout Japan led to new patterns in tea consumption and connoisseurship among intellectually curious Japanese, who emulated the Ōbaku priests and others in their attraction toward things and ideas Chinese.

Literary Production

With the establishment and rapid spread of a printing and publishing art over the course of the early modern period, Japanese literature entered a dynamic phase of development, in which writers and poets for the first time could make a living from their publications, and in which readership expanded with each generation. Men and, to an ever greater degree, women exerted increasing influence on what would be published, as the existence of "bestsellers" came to determine (regardless of the wishes of bureaucratic censors) the market for a particular title or series of titles. As Peter Nosco aptly notes, "popular culture is culture that pays for itself."[13]

The major literary form of the seventeenth century is the *kana-zōshi*, or "books in the phonetic *kana* syllabary." Types of literature covered by this catch-all term include printed versions of the Heian classics, romances, war narratives, ghost story collections, humorous anecdotes, travel guides, literary parodies, ratings of courtesans and actors, and didactic works such as manners guides for young women. Most of the works were published in the Kamigata, but received distribution throughout the country, mainly through the existence of lending libraries, by which readers could borrow books for a small fee from itinerent librarians who would return a few weeks later, collect the borrowed books, and lend out more. What these works provided for the first time in Japanese history were, first, access to knowledge of the past and present and, second, the opportunity for reading entertainment, to anyone who could read basic Japanese. Writers such as Asai Ryōi (*c.*1612–91) wrote collections of ghost stories translated from Chinese sources and adapted to a domestic setting, travel guides to the provinces, especially along the Tōkaidō, or Eastern Coastal Highway, collections of didactic tales and stories for moral edification, and stories of contemporary life and habits. In his *Ukiyo monogatari* ("Tales of the Floating World," Kyoto, 1661) Ryōi's narrator distinguishes between the earlier Warring States era *ukiyo*, written with characters signifying "melancholy world" and the contemporary *ukiyo*, written with the characters for a "floating world." "Cross each bridge as you come to it; gaze at the moon, the snow, the cherry blossoms, and the bright autumn leaves; recite poems; drink saké; and make merry. Not even poverty will be a bother. Floating along with an unsinkable disposition, like a gourd bobbing allong with the current – this is what we call the floating world."[14]

Building upon the now established success of the *kana-zōshi*, the novelist and *haikai* master Ihara Saikaku (1642–93) was able to move the writing of fiction into a sphere of contemporary verisimilitude (this is unlike modern "realism" due in part to the stylized nature of the language employed) that had not been present before. Son of a successful Osaka merchant, Saikaku used his powers of observation, finely honed after years of *haikai* poetic composition, and crafted highly readable and visually compelling stories of longing and lust, martial honor and justice (often from a perspective of homoerotic loyalty between samurai), and the fluid nature of money and its relation to desire in a mercantile society. Such books, beginning with Saikaku's *Kōshoku ichidai otoko* (literally, "An Uninhibited Man of a Single Generation," implying that he left no heir, 1682), offered readers with a contemporary feel, a less than obvious moral (in spite of moralist prefaces to many of the stories), and a source of knowledge about contemporary fashions and mores that spawned imitators and successors, continuing well into the latter half of the eighteenth century. After the demise of these books, known as *ukiyo-zōshi*, or "books of the floating world," early-nineteenth-century authors rediscovered Saikaku, and his writings have since continued to generate interest among scholars and general readers.

In the eighteenth century, the development of the publishing industry in Edo brought with it the appearance of new literary genres, as well as a strengthened sense of cultural autonomy from the traditional center, Kyoto. We have noted the emergence of new, multicolor prints created in Edo workshops, and, in fiction as well, fresh forms arose from the brash and innovative Edo milieu. One such form, developed in the context of a new political atmosphere of cultural flexibility in the wake of Shōgun Tokugawa Yoshimune's (1684–1751, in power 1716–45) Kyōhō Reforms of the 1720s and 30s, was the *dangibon* ("sermon books"), which attracted readers in Edo in the mid eighteenth century. One result of Yoshimune's reforms was the promotion of learning among commoners, which led to the appearance of Buddhist or quasi-Buddhist "preachers" on street corners in Edo and other cities. Some of these preachers recorded and published their sermons for an even broader audience. The distinctive feature of the *dangibon* is their humorous and satirical nature, in which the reader attempts to "unearth" (*ugachi*) the fad or current practice in contemporary Edo society that is being lampooned. The great master of this biting satirical style was Hiraga Gennai (1728–80), a samurai in service to a provincial lord who left his region, relocated to Edo, and involved himself in a variety of scientific and literary projects. Well versed in Dutch Studies (*rangaku*, the term for European scientific studies in Japan), Gennai classified flora and fauna according to principles of *materia medica*, explored the medical uses of electricity, and made the first fire-resistant fabric in Japan using asbestos. While in many ways resembling his contemporary, Benjamin Franklin (1706–90), Gennai lived within a power establishment that was not flexible enough to absorb his ideas. The frustrated Gennai (who wrote under the sobriquet Fūrai Sanjin, or "mountain dweller who comes on the wind") turned to the biting humor of the *dangibon* to give vent to his disaffection with the current state of affairs.

The fictional genre that featured the greatest psychological depth, as well as the greatest capacity for a large-scale epic structure is the *yomihon*, or "reading book," so named because illustrations were limited to a few pages, in contrast to an overwhelming amount of text. Originating in the Kamigata with the works of physician and author Tsuga Teishō (1718–*c*.1794), early *yomihon* were collections of stories, usually of an occult nature, that combined influences from Chinese vernacular collections of the Ming and early Qing dynasties (fourteenth to seventeenth centuries) that were written not in standard literary Chinese of the classics, but in a new hybrid form called *baihua*. Educated Japanese writers and intellectuals who had maintained contact with Chinese in Nagasaki and at Ōbaku temples were intrigued by this new form of Chinese, and were eager to use the works written in *baihua* to enhance their own narratives. Ueda Akinari (1734–1809), adopted son of an Osaka paper and oil merchant and author of the masterful *Ugetsu monogatari* (Tales of Rain and Moon, 1776), wove together nine suspenseful narratives from a rich blend of native and imported sources, endowing them with his heartfelt concern for human frailty, and the seemingly unlimited capacity we have both to help and to hurt one another.

The *yomihon* genre was transferred to the publishing world in Edo in the 1790s through the work of the multi-talented writer Santō Kyōden (1761–1816), son of an Edo pawnbroker. Kyōden took the Kamigata *yomihon* and transformed them into a kabuki-like vehicle for fantastic occurrences, epic struggles, and larger than life heroes and villains. The great master of the Edo *yomihon*, though, was Kyokutei Bakin (1767–1849, also known by his surname of Takizawa), a member of the *bushi* class who left his hereditary status and became a disciple in writing of Kyōden. Bakin extended and expanded Kyōden's style in the *yomihon* and left a prodigious number of bestsellers, including, most notably, his masterpiece *Nansō Satomi Hakkenden* (Lives of the Eight Dog-Heroes of the Nansō Satomi Clan, 1814–42). This massive work, loosely based on the Chinese *baihua* epic, *Shui hu zhuan* ("Water Margin," also "Outlaws of the Marsh," etc., narrated and rewritten by multiple authors over the fourteenth to seventeenth centuries), tells of the virtuous actions of eight heroes, each of whom had been endowed with a magical jewel expressing one of eight fundamental Confucian virtues. Bakin couches his narrative in a didactic framework of "promoting good and chastising evil" (Ch., *quanshan chengwu*; J., *kanzen chōaku*), but the astute reader of his time could sense something latent (*inbi*, one of Bakin's own "Seven Rules Governing the Historical Novel" outlined in a preface to *Hakkenden*) to be found between the lines of his narrative. This latent or hidden message may have to do with the ironic distance between the virtuous heroes and the corrupt world within which they act, or it may deal with the distance between the ideals themselves and how they play through in an imperfect world. For Bakin, the juxtaposition between an overtly didactic framework and a more subtle reading provides a tension that makes his work compelling even today.

Kyōden and Bakin worked in other genres of Edo fiction as well. Including the *yomihon*, these styles and formats of popular, often humorous, narrative are referred to as *gesaku*, or "playful works," and the authors of these works, *gesakusha*. *Gesaku* include the witty and fully illustrated *kibyōshi*, or "yellow covers," in which the text is embedded together as part of the illustration in a manner much like today's comic books. However, the content was clearly not for children, given that *kibyōshi* were parodies of the foibles of adult life. In the early 1790s the government suppressed these works for having gone too far in lampooning official edicts, and for the final decade of their existence, *kibyōshi* steered clear of sensitive issues. Another genre, *sharebon*, or "books of wit," were actually tales of current fashions within the pleasure quarters, and were written in such a manner that in many cases only those fully conversant (*tsū*) with the language and customs of such districts would be able to understand the details. In the early nineteenth century, the *sharebon* yielded to the *ninjōbon* (books of human emotions), which dealt with troubled love affairs between courtesans and customers, both wealthy and humble. Tamenaga Shunsui (1790–1844), son of an Edo publisher-bookseller, was the leading author of this genre, and his works such as *Shunshoku Umegoyomi* (Spring Colors: The Plum Calendar, 1832–3) generated massive followings, especially among female readers. The earlier satirical *dangibon* paved the way for the comic *kokkeibon*, which is best represented by two Edo authors. Jippensha Ikku (1765–1831) made his reputation with the series, *Tōkai-dōchū Hizakurige* (Trotting along the Eastern Coastal Highway, 1802–9). This linear narrative follows a pair of hapless good-for-nothing heroes through episode after episode of slapstick adventures, and proved to be a runaway bestseller, not only due to the strength of the narrative and the attraction/repulsion of the two protagonists, but also for the details provided about the various scenes and sights along the way. The other author to succeed at humorous fiction was Shikitei Sanba (1776–1822), son of a woodblock carver in Edo. Sanba's most memorable works, *Ukiyo-buro* (Bathhouse of the Floating World, 1809–13) and *Ukiyo-doko* (Barber Shop of the Floating World, 1813–14), take the conceit of Ikku's *Hizakurige*, and reverse it, so that, instead of a world in which two characters move through time and space, the reader enjoys a static world (men's bathhouse, women's bathhouse, or hairdresser's) through which various characters enter, exit, and re-enter as the narrative progresses. In both cases the language employed is vernacular to the extreme, and the level of immediacy is such that reading these works today generates a sense of having literally slipped into a world populated by the streetwise townsfolk of Edo and the more rustic inhabitants of the provinces.

The image-oriented *kibyōshi* were in the final decades of the early modern period replaced by longer *gōkan* or *gōkanbon*, which were literally "combined volumes" of short chapbooks that were brought together within paper wrappers to form longer works. In exchange for the more substantial length of the *gōkan*, the effort that had been previously made by the graphic artist to provide an interesting visual image was replaced now by prints of the main characters surrounded completely by text. Thus, while still image–text combinations, clearly at this point the text provides the content and main interest for the reader, while the image merely serves to identify the characters delivering the textual dialogue. The most successful author of *gōkan* was Ryūtei Tanehiko (1783–1842), a low-ranking samurai raised in Edo. His major work, and most likely the bestseller of fiction in the entire early modern period is his *Nise Murasaki inaka Genji* (A False Murasaki's Rustic Genji, 1829–42). With regard to sales, Andrew Markus reports, "*Inaka Genji* was in a class by itself: ... Aeba Kōson insists on sales of 14,000 to 15,000 copies for *Inaka Genji*, even at (an) exorbitant price."[15] As the title implies, this work takes the milieu and many of the characters of the *Genji monogatari* (*The Tale of Genji*, c.1008) and transfers them to the very different world of contemporary Edo. Together with the other works mentioned above, the success of *Nise Murasaki inaka Genji* demonstrates dramatically the complex development of the fiction publishing world in Japan from the seventeenth through the nineteenth centuries.

In poetry, over the course of the early modern period the following developments occurred: the continuation and diffusion of the representative verse form, the thirty-one-syllable waka; a revival among some poets of the archaic extended form, the *chōka*; expansion and increased range of expression in Chinese poetic forms (*kanshi*); the development of humorous verse forms in Japanese and Chinese (*kyōka, kyōshi*), in tandem with the eighteenth-century appearance of satirical narrative forms; and, above all else, the development of a new, less formal verse form in both stand-alone and linked-verse modes, the seventeen-syllable *haikai*, together with its "grass-roots" offshoot, *senryū*.

Waka poetry, the identifying feature of Kyoto court life since before the Heian period, continued unabated throughout the early modern period. Access to secret traditions expanded after warrior general Hosokawa Yūsai (1534–1610) received the transmissions of the *Kokin denju* ("esoteric knowledge concerning the *Kokin waka-shū*") from a member of the court aristocracy. Court poets continued to compose waka following received forms, while, among samurai and commoner poets, new approaches to waka were reflected in their poetry. Scholars such as Keichū (1640–1701), a warrior turned Buddhist priest in Osaka; Kamo no Mabuchi (1697–1769), born into a line of Shintō priests and active in Edo; Kada no Arimaro (1706–51), also hailing from a line of Shintō clergy; Tayasu Munetake (1715–71), son of the eighth shōgun, Yoshimune; Motoori Norinaga (1730–1801), son of a provincial merchant; Ozawa Roan (1723–1801), samurai resident in Kyoto; and Kagawa Kageki (1768–1843), son of a low-ranking domainal vassal, all provided new and innovative ideas, backed by solid scholarship in the classics, which opened up waka composition to all who expressed an interest. By early Meiji, Kageki's school had emerged as the "orthodox school," supported by the imperial court, while the old esoteric transmissions had been abandoned in favor of the new open scholarship into the classics.

As we have seen with narrative fiction, more "serious" forms of poetry became the object of satire and humorous metaphor. For example, in waka, a "deranged" form, called *kyōka*, appeared, and was explosively popular, especially in Edo, during the An'ei and Tenmei heyday of early modern culture (1772–89). Chinese poetry, that most serious and difficult form for the Japanese, also had its "deranged" adversary, called *kyōshi*, which necessarily had a more limited following.

Haikai, *haikai* drawings called *haiga*, and *haikai*-inspired poetic prose called *haibun* all arose during the early modern period. Schools of *haikai* composition competed with one another for pupils, and the results of their gatherings were published and read in great numbers. One poet attempted to rise above the competitive nature of the art as it was developing and work toward *haikai* as a type of "way" or *michi*. This was the "Sage of *Haikai*," Matsuo Bashō (1644–94), born into a family in the provinces at the lowest end of the warrior class. Works such as his *Oku no hosomichi* (Narrow Way to the Depths, 1702) are considered the apex of a *zoku*, or popular, form achieving the heights of a *ga*, or refined, sensibility toward life and the world. The most gifted *haikai* poets after Bashō include Yosa Buson (1716–84) and Kobayashi Issa (1763–1827), both of agrarian backgrounds who each in his own way took *haikai* composition in a new and individualistic direction.

The world of publishing, following the accepted pattern of male inheritance of the proprietor's name from generation to generation, was in effect closed to women. This meant that, with few exceptions, women writers of narrative fiction and female print artists were excluded from the publishing system. Poetic composition, which had, especially in the realm of waka, from earliest times served both as an expressive outlet and as an important form of social interaction, remained open to women as well as to men. Thus we find women as participants in waka and *haikai* poetic gatherings, and their poems published with men's works in poetic compilations and private collections throughout the period. The scholar of nativist studies (*wagaku* or *kokugaku*) Kamo no Mabuchi (1697–1769) was particularly active in admitting women to his school of the Japanese classics and poetics in Edo, and it is reported that "nearly one-third of [Mabuchi's] students at the end of his life were women – a figure among the highest of any major private academy in Tokugawa Japan. ... In fact, there were more women students in Mabuchi's school than merchants and agriculturalists combined, and more than twice as many women as samurai."[16] Important literary women include the following: in the realm of waka composition, the so-called "Three Talented Women of Gion": Kaji (fl. *c.*1700), Yuri (d. 1757), and Machi (1727–84, also known as the artist Tokuyama Gyokuran, spouse of *bunjin* Ike no Taiga); the so-called "Three Poetic Talents of the Mabuchi School": Toki Tsukubako (fl. 1750), Udono Yonoko (1729–88), and Yuya Shizuko (1733–52); also Kada no Tamiko (1722–86), Ōtagaki Rengetsu (1791–1875), and Nomura Bōtō (also Nomura Noto, 1806–67). In the sphere of *wabun*, or composition of prose in archaic styles, we should recognize Arakida Rei (1732–1806) and Tadano Makuzu (1763–1825). Among *kyōka* poets we find Chie no Naishi (1745–1807, spouse of *kyōka* circle leader Moto no Mokuami, 1724–1811), and Fushimatsu no Kaka (1745–1810, another spouse of circle leader Akera Kankō, 1738–99). There are several notable female *haikai* poets, the most well known being Kaga no Chiyo (1703–75). Finally, in the male-dominated world of *kanshi* composition, three names stand out: Ema Saikō (1787–1861), Chō Kōran (1804–79, spouse of *kanshi* poet Yanagawa Seigan, 1789–1858), and Hara Saibin (1798–1859). Of course Yoshiwara and Shimabara courtesans were renowned for their poetic skills as well, especially at the apex of pleasure district culture in the mid to late eighteenth century.

Thus we see that the culture encountered by Europeans in the early seventeenth century developed in highly distinctive ways over the next 265 years. With the spread of literacy and education, publishing became a medium of information, edification, and entertainment that no one could do without. The arts and literature exhibited repeated phases of popularity, decline, and renewed popularity in ever expanding forms, and in the social sphere, the daimyō and other military bureaucrats came to emulate wealthy merchants while merchants lived as though they themselves were daimyō. Urban networks thrived in spite of governmental security concerns, and information spread from the urban centers out to the hinterlands and back again. By the time the next wave of pressure arrived from the West in the middle decades of the nineteenth century, the Japanese had far outgrown their seventeenth-century system of order-based Tokugawa control, and were more than ready to extend, and expand, their cultural development in yet other directions.

NOTES

1   Cooper, comp. and annot., *They Came to Japan*, pp. 277, 280, and 60, respectively.
2   Hickman et al., *Japan's Golden Age*, pp. 19–56.
3   Nakano Mitsutoshi, "The Role of Traditional Aesthetics," pp. 124–5.
4   Totman, *Early Modern Japan*, pp. 152–3.
5   Henry D. Smith II, "The Floating World in Its Edo Locale 1750–1850," in Jenkins, *The Floating World Revisited*, p. 38.
6   Kornicki, *The Book in Japan*, pp. 114–15.
7   Cooper, comp. and annot., *They Came to Japan*, pp. 251–2.
8   Kornicki, *The Book in Japan*, p. 140.
9   Lawrence Marceau, "Hidden Treasures from Japan: Wood-Block-Printed Picture Books and Albums," in Kita, Marceau, Blood, and Farquhar, *The Floating World of Ukiyo-e*, p. 84.
10 Cleary, trans., *The Code of the Samurai*, p. 3.
11 Ibid., p. 95.
12 Graham, *Tea of the Sages*, p. 49.
13 Nosco, *Remembering Paradise*, p. 16.
14 Jack Stoneman, in Shirane, ed., *Early Modern Japanese Literature*, p. 30.
15 Markus, *The Willow in Autumn*, pp. 146–7.
16 Nosco, *Remembering Paradise*, p. 145.

BIBLIOGRAPHY

Cleary, Thomas, trans. *The Code of the Samurai: A Modern Translation of the* Bushidō shoshinshū *of Taira Shigesuke*. Rutland, Vt.: C. E. Tuttle, 1999.

Cooper, Michael, comp. and annot. *They Came to Japan: An Anthology of European Reports on Japan, 1543–1740*. Berkeley: University of California Press, 1965; repr. 1981.

Gerstle, C. Andrew, ed. *Eighteenth Century Japan: Culture and Society*. London: Routledge-Curzon, 2000.

Graham, Patricia. *Tea of the Sages: The Art of Sencha*. Honolulu: University of Hawai'i Press, 1998.

Hickman, Money, et al. *Japan's Golden Age: Momoyama*. New Haven: Yale University Press, 1996.

Jenkins, Donald. *The Floating World Revisited*. Portland, Ore.: Portland Art Museum, 1993.

Kita, Sandy, Marceau, Lawrence E., Blood, Katherine, and Farquhar, James Douglas. *The Floating World of Ukiyo-e: Shadows, Dreams, and Substance*. New York: Harry N. Abrams, 2001.

Kornicki, Peter. *The Book in Japan: A Cultural History from the Beginnings to the Nineteenth Century*. Leiden: Brill, 1998.

Markus, Andrew. *The Willow in Autumn: Ryūtei Tanehiko, 1783–1842*. Cambridge, Mass.: Council on East Asian Studies, Harvard University, 1992.

Nakano Mitsutoshi, "The Role of Traditional Aesthetics." In C. Andrew Gerstle, ed., *Eighteenth Century Japan: Culture and Society*. Richmond, UK: Curzon, 1989.

Nosco, Peter. *Remembering Paradise: Nativism and Nostalgia in Eighteenth-Century Japan*. Cambridge, Mass.: Council on East Asian Studies, Harvard University, 1990.

Shirane, Haruo, ed. *Early Modern Japanese Literature: An Anthology 1600–1900*. New York: Columbia University Press, 2002.

Totman, Conrad. *Early Modern Japan*. Berkeley: University of California Press, 1993.

FURTHER READING

In the field of literature, Haruo Shirane, ed., *Early Modern Japanese Literature: An Anthology 1600–1900* (New York: Columbia University Press, 2002), is required reading. Samuel Leiter's *New Kabuki Encyclopedia* (Westport, Conn.: Greenwood, 1997) provides much detail, not only for kabuki, but for popular culture in general. For art, Robert T. Singer et al., *Edo: Art in Japan 1615–1868* (Washington DC: National Gallery of Art, 1998) provides full-color examples of hundreds of art works encompassing a wide range of types, supplemented by essays written by leading scholars. Christine Guth's *Art of Edo Japan: The Artist and the City* (New York: Harry N. Abrams, 1996) is an excellent survey of painters and printmakers throughout early modern Japan. Richard Lane's *Images from the Floating World: The Japanese Print* (New York: Putnam, 1978) serves both as an interpretive history and as a dictionary of woodblock print artists and their works.

Two fine books and a CD-ROM provide valuable perspectives with regard to the city of Edo, which grew over the course of the period to become the major metropolis of the land. The first, Nishiyama Matsunosuke's *Edo Culture: Daily Life and Diversions in Urban Japan* (Honolulu: University of Hawai'i Press, 1997) is a well-illustrated translation of essays on Edo by the foremost "Edo studies" scholar in Japan. For a visual understanding of Edo, Naito Akira and Hozumi Kazuo's *Edo, the*

City that Became Tokyo: An Illustrated History (Tokyo: Kōdansha International, 2003) provides myriad line drawings of various aspects of life in the metropolis together with informative English-translated text. *Kidai Shōran: Excellent View of Our Prosperous Age* (Berlin: Museum für Ostasiatiche Kunst, 2000) is a multimedia CD-ROM that provides a cross-section of life on the main commercial avenue at Nihonbashi in Edo, *c.*1805, from a beautifully detailed illustrated handscroll, and is meticulously annotated in English and German.

Peter Kornicki's *The Book in Japan: A Cultural History from the Beginnings to the Nineteenth Century* (Leiden: Brill, 1998) explores the impact publishing and print culture made on the Japanese, especially through the early modern period. Chapters 6 through 9 of H. Paul Varley's *Japanese Culture* (Honolulu: University of Hawai'i Press, 2000), now in its fourth revised edition, provide a lucid general background to early modern Japanese cultural history. Likewise, Donald H. Shively's chapter, "Popular Culture," in *The Cambridge History of Japan*, vol. 4, *Early Modern Japan*, ed. John Whitney Hall (Cambridge: Cambridge University Press, 1991), is extremely useful for garnering a sense of the roles played by popular culture in Japan at the time. Finally, four chapters included in Conrad Totman's authoritative *Early Modern Japan* (Berkeley: University of California Press, 1993) focus on cultural developments.

PART III

Modern Japan: From the Meiji Restoration through World War II

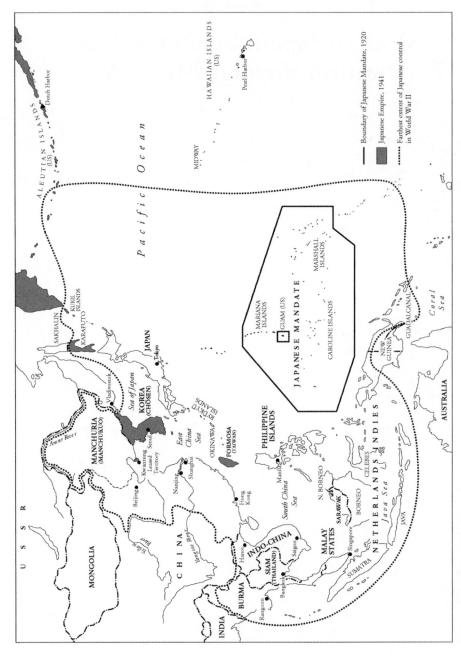

Map 3 The Japanese empire

CHAPTER EIGHT

Restoration and Revolution

James L. Huffman

The nineteenth-century American journalist Edward H. House spent much of his career telling and retelling the story of the 1863–4 Shimonoseki incident, in which ships of four Western nations bombarded Chōshū domain, allegedly in retaliation against earlier Chōshū attacks on the Westerners, then forced Japan to pay a $3 million indemnity. House had two goals: to get the United States to return its share of the indemnity and to correct the standard recollection of the event, which in his view laid unjustified blame on Japan and whitewashed the Western powers' motives. He succeeded in the former goal but failed in the latter.[1] Getting a nation to return loot, he found, was easier than correcting an entrenched historical narrative.

His experience bears striking resemblance to the exigencies of the last century's mainstream tale of Japanese development in the years surrounding the Meiji Restoration. Efforts to change the narrative – both its content and its contours – have been as endless as House's polemics on Shimonoseki. In the 1960s and 1970s, scholars on the left attacked the Western bias of modernization theory; in the 1980s and 1990s, theorists concerned with gender, sexuality, postmodernism, semiotics, deconstruction, cultural studies – and a host of other approaches – argued for the inclusion of new narrative frameworks and ideological transparency. By the beginning of the twenty-first century, the late Tokugawa–Meiji years were being examined from a host of new perspectives; hospital patients, gays and lesbians, factory workers, architectural sites, fishery owners, and local bureaucrats produced more studies than "great men" did, as did discussions on the role of time, place, and power relationships. Harvard University's Helen Hardacre saw this "exercise of breaking down monolithic paradigms of Japan's modern history" as the precursor to a new narrative, "a substitute for a triumphalist interpretation of Japan's modernization."[2]

That these efforts have had great impact cannot be denied, as this essay will argue below. They have complicated our understandings of the early Meiji years. They have given us new languages and concepts for explaining the era, new understandings of power relationships, new information about once ignored actors. But, like House, the heralds of new history are forced to admit that changing the overall understanding of what happened in this era is hard work. The narrative may be richer today, its contours a bit more fuzzy, but the essential story has changed less in fundamental form than in marginal details. This is perhaps most apparent in the harvest of new

English-language surveys of modern Japanese history produced early in the twenty-first century – by members of the newer generation as well as by those more senior. While most of these synthetic works drew on the latest scholarship, they told a story that looked more familiar than radical, suggesting that Carol Gluck was right when she contended that "we remain … conceptual prisoners of Meiji."[3]

The Traditional Account

The conventional story of the Meiji years was captured in a number of works between the 1950s and the 1970s, which drew heavily on establishment scholars in Japan (and all of which gave short shrift to the more Marxist interpretations of E. H. Norman's *Japan's Emergence as a Modern State*): Edwin Reischauer's *Japan, Past and Present*, George Sansom's *The Western World and Japan*, and W. G. Beasley's *The Modern History of Japan* and *The Meiji Restoration*. Their publication coincided with both the emergence of East Asia as a serious part of American university curriculums and a political order dominated by the rhetoric of American-style capitalism and democracy. In this milieu, Japan's story from the 1850s through the 1880s took on an optimistic hue filled with international tension, domestic conflict, strong leadership, and, above all, progress.

In the telling of these writers, the Tokugawa period was peaceful and relatively isolated, yet culturally and economically virile. Its shogunal government had become inefficient and inept by the early 1800s[4] and the *bakuhan* system was buffeted by so many challenges that, barring dramatic reform, eventual collapse seemed inevitable. Into that setting came the foreigners in the 1850s, touching off a decade and a half of intense maneuvering and fighting, both on the battlefield and in the world of politics. A 1868 *coup d'état* by samurai from the southwest put the teenaged Emperor Meiji on the throne and initiated an era of unparalleled change that brought Japan, in little more than a generation, from isolation to the center of world politics. Under the guidance of a small elite, pushed (and pulled) by rich Western nations, the Japanese set about destroying the conservative structures of the past – the samurai class, the domain system, Confucianism's anti-merchant ideas – and creating a modern state replete with compulsory education, a military draft, and, eventually, a constitution. Inhabiting the edges of this narrative were "the people" or *minshū*, whose lives were changed greatly by the decisions and policies of the elite rulers. The people sometimes became engaged in the political process, and they carried out many modernizing projects themselves, but always they remained at the margins of the story.

Within this traditional story, several tropes emerge repeatedly. One is Hirakawa Sukehiro's "turn to the West." In this era, he maintains, "Japan, a non-Western nation, adopted from the West a tremendous amount of what was fundamental and essential to modernization." He sees the adoption process itself as crucial to Japan's survival and self-identity, arguing that without Western "ideas and institutions, the establishment of a national identity would have been impossible, and the existence of an independent Japan … could not have been maintained."[5] Wherever one looks in the late Tokugawa, early Meiji narrative, Western consciousness is close to the surface. Samurai terrorists kill officials because the shōgun agreed to trade with Western nations. Public nudity is banned so as not to scandalize Christians. Currency reform is aimed at making Japan's economy viable internationally. The governor of Kumamoto attempts to modernize by hiring an eccentric Ohioan to create a "Western School." Indeed, an entire scholarly industry – led by Nobutani Noboru in Japan and Ardath Burks in the West – has grown up around the *oyatoi gaikokujin* or foreign employees who instructed the Japanese in railroad construction, constitutional law, and English-speaking. While even the most traditional narrators have come to admit, like Burks, that the foreigners "played only a marginal or an incremental role in the transition ... to modernity in Meiji,"[6] Westerners cast superhuman shadows in all retellings of the traditional narrative.

The "rush to modernity" is the second traditional trope. Whether one looks at government structure, the growth of schools, the advent of transportation systems, or the emergence of political parties, the pace of change in the second half of Japan's nineteenth century was remarkable – and has become a staple of the narrative. John Whitney Hall introduced a set of essays from the 1960 Hakone Conference on Modern Japan with the observation: "The modernization of Japan is a phenomenon which cannot be viewed casually by any serious observer," whether that modernization was seen as "a new 'peril from the East' or, on the contrary, as a miraculous example of progress from out of an Oriental Middle Ages."[7] The Hakone modernization studies evoked enormous controversy because of the ideological way in which they used conditions in the affluent Western democracies to define "modernization," even as they claimed to represent value-free history. But while the term "modernization" largely vanished, it had been replaced by the 1980s with "modernity." And if the two terms differed in definition and connotation, springing as they did from different contexts, both evoked a constant in the narrative: change in the direction of something called "modern" was fundamental. In the words of Kuwabara Takeo of Kyoto University: "Japan succeeded in modernizing, and it did so with a speed unprecedented in world history."[8]

The third trope is the centrality of politics and the state. Until the 1980s, any bibliography of key works on this era was sure to be dominated by studies of Edo or Tokyo government. Biographies told the lives of national political figures such as Sakamoto Ryōma, Yamagata Aritomo, Saigō Takamori, and Ōkubo Toshimichi. Specialized studies focused on domain reform and revolt, the writing of constitutions, the ideas of political thinkers, the diaries of leading officials – or, when a writer looked outside Tokyo, the reaction of local governments to centralizing policies. Not long after the Meiji Restoration, Ōkuma is said to have quipped to the young finance official (and later entrepreneur) Shibusawa Eiichi: "Those who are participating in the planning of the new government are the myriad gods. The gods have gathered together and are now in the midst of discussing how to proceed in building the new Japan."[9] This was the view the establishment passed on to the era's narrators: state-generated politics did not merely lie at the heart of the Meiji story; they were the story.

The fourth trope is Japan's uniqueness – a theme articulated first by the Tokugawa–Meiji thinkers themselves, then repeated by a century of historians. Isolation meant specialness to Tokugawa writers. And during the Meiji years intellectuals commented continually on how different their land was. It was the first Asian nation to write a constitution, the first to modernize the economy, make education compulsory for all citizens, and develop an extensive railway system. That was why

Fukuzawa Yukichi called on his fellow Japanese in 1885 to "leave the ranks of Asian nations and cast our lot with civilized nations of the West," to "simply erase from our minds our bad friends in Asia."[10] Meiji writers also saw themselves as different from Westerners – tardy, perhaps, in adopting modernity but speedier in moving in that direction once they got started. By the 1880s, national uniqueness had become an obsession, as a rising generation grappled with what they saw as both the positive and the negative characteristics that set them apart from other peoples. The cultural geographer Shiga Shigetaka wrote in 1888 that Japan's natural setting had "developed in the Japanese race ... a unique *kokusui*, or national essence."[11] It was an idea that infused nearly every account of Meiji for the following century.

The fifth trope – progress – may be the most telling, and ideological, of all. Certainly not everyone saw the era's changes as good. Teenagers working inhuman hours in the spinning mills did not; neither did Tokugawa samurai who lost their moorings after 1868, nor many women whose lives became more restricted by the mid-Meiji family policies. Yet, despite abundant evidence that most Japanese experienced no uplift in living conditions between the 1850s and 1880s, the traditional stories of Japanese and Western historians alike have focused overwhelmingly on progress: new buildings, more rational political structures, richer literature, spreading newspapers, the growth of capitalism. Sansom set the tone for a generation when he wrote in 1968 that "the most striking feature of the period is not its political clashes, but the alacrity with which the country as a whole seized upon the dogma of perfectibility and threw itself without misgivings into the task of self-improvement."[12]

A major characteristic of the Tokugawa–Meiji studies produced in the 1990s and afterward is the continuing persistence of these old themes, particularly the Western-centrism, the idea of progress, and the preoccupation with politics. This generation of scholars may apply fresh theories to new subjects, but the idea of Western preeminence dominates a surprising number of studies, whether postcolonialists are echoing Tōyama Shigeki's assertion that "there was a real danger that Japan would become a colony" in the 1860s, or traditionalists are agreeing with Andrew Gordon's claim that "connectivity" is the key to modern Japanese history.[13] Indeed, works dedicated to the Westerners' role continue to appear with a frequency that undermines talk about a new narrative: Beasley's writings about Japanese travelers to Europe and America; studies of French–Japanese and British–Japanese relations; depictions of American diplomats and merchants in Yokohama and Edo/Tokyo; work on Western contacts with Okinawa and the Ryūkyūs; continued monographs on *yatoi* as diverse as William Smith Clark, Edward House, and Francis Hall. Many of these works are more nuanced than earlier studies, focusing more on cultural interaction and less on the West-as-model idea. Peter Duus's student-oriented *Japanese Discovery of America*, for example, avoids the earlier assumptions of inequality by concentrating on how Japanese and Americans saw *each other*, spending as much time on Japanese perceptions of American "barbarism" as on American portrayals of the Japanese as "uncivilized." But the volume of discourse on the Western impact reveals how entrenched the idea of Western-centrism has become.

So too the focus on progress. While specialized studies raise complex questions about the darker sides of Japanese life in the nineteenth century, most narratives still resort to "those overarching motives of national independence and future greatness" that prompted Itō Hirobumi to boast that Meiji had brought Japan not only "prosperity, strength, and culture," but "an equal footing in the family of the most powerful and civilized nations of the world."[14] As careful a scholar as David Howell still comments that "*no country* has been so successful at implementing modernity as a matter of public policy as Meiji Japan."[15]

One reason for this continuing obsession with progress lies in the insistence of most historians, even today, on viewing the state as a (often, *the*) central protagonist of the story. Howell may write about capitalism and the Hokkaidō fishery industry, but he looks through a prism of national development. Gregory Pflugfelder may examine male–male relationships, but one of his preoccupations is their treatment in the law. Takashi Fujitani tells us how the state created a "splendid monarchy"; localists such as William Steele and Michael Lewis take the central government as a point of departure, as does Kären Wigen even when she discusses peripheries. Even people's historians like Irokawa Daikichi focus on the interactions between the people and state institutions. Hardacre commented after the influential 1994 Conference on Meiji Studies that most participants, many of them cutting edge scholars who drew "their theoretical inspiration in large part from postmodernist theorists of power," were concerned primarily with "relations of power in some form."[16] Indeed, very few writers find value in looking at farmers, housewives, prostitutes – or even politicians – from the simple perspective of daily affairs. Life, for academic elites, holds little interest if it is not connected to issues of power and politics; so the state stays at the center, and progress continues its grip.

What, Then, is New?

If the broader narratives of Japanese development in the late Tokugawa, early Meiji years remain in the grip of old tropes, many of the era's specialized studies, in both Japan and the West, brim with the kinds of new information and challenging perspectives that are likely, in time, to change even the traditionalists' way of seeing nineteenth-century Japan. Inspiring these studies are two forces: the continuing maturation of Western scholarship on Japan, and the world of theory that has so deeply influenced all of academia in recent decades. The former is driven by the increasing numbers of American and European students working on Japanese history, as well as by their improved training and language skills. Gone are the days when it could justly be said that "Western writing has so far contributed relatively little to our total knowledge of Chinese and Japanese history."[17] Today, as Yoshimi Shun'ya of the University of Tokyo has noted, Western students of this era have as much influence on Japanese historians as the Japanese have long had on the Westerners.[18]

One reason for the maturation of the Western scholarship lies in the second force, the increasingly sophisticated way in which historians of Japan use theory. Inspired by the ideas of Hayden White, Michel Foucault, Eric Hobsbawm, Jacques Derrida, and others, late-Tokugawa–Meiji historians of the last two decades have produced a plethora of theoretically sophisticated, provocative articles and monographs, asking hard questions, utilizing a diversity of sources, interrogating people's motives and ideologies, and applying varied analytical frameworks. The new works have been particularly influenced, it seems to me, by four particular concepts: Eric Hobsbawm's "invention of tradition," Benedict Anderson's "imagined communities," James Scott's "weapons of the weak," and Edward Said's "orientalism." Sometimes using these ideas consciously, sometimes unconsciously; sometimes writing clearly, sometimes obtusely; sometimes applying theory carefully and cogently, sometimes as an add-on to make the work appear up to date, the scholars of this era have turned their attention increasingly to issues of space (site), time, class, and ideology, making us ask questions that once would not even have occurred to us.

The field of cultural studies has had a particularly strong impact, with writers like Naoki Sakai and Harry Harootunian (writing too often in dense, even if provocative, prose) pushing a new generation of researchers to "be alert and sensitive to the political implications of knowledge." Under their influence, the field has begun seriously to look not just at rulers but at subjects, and going further, not just at subjects but at the impact those subjects (and the processes of creating them) have on rulers. The goal, says Sakai, is to seek "a certain reversal of the terms," so that we can understand the politics and ideology that motivate structures and narrators.[19] That process – what Dipesh Chakrabarty calls "unpacking 'ideologies' "[20] – has caused a number of historians to focus on the fact that many "familiar emblems of Japanese culture, including treasured icons, turn out to be modern."[21] And the consequence has been a significant number of studies which have not only changed the specialists' understandings of the late-Tokugawa–early-Meiji years but laid the groundwork for an eventual change in the broader narratives.

One outgrowth of the theoretical turn has been the appearance of new groups and individuals in the pages of history: Edo townsmen aghast or bemused by Matthew Perry's arrival in 1853–4, architects, "leprosy" patients, prostitutes, newspaper readers. In the old rubric, Buddhists remained silent; they were not relevant to the monolithic "modernizing" scheme; in the modernity story, they claim a meaningful place, as evidenced by James Ketelaar's study of how Buddhist leaders adapted to a new age by attempting to create a "modern" faith.[22] Similarly, other religionists, as diverse as travelers on the Iwakura mission, the Christian iconoclast Yamaji Aizan, and religious pilgrims, have been examined in recent studies, as religion comes to be seen not merely as anachronistic – or as part of government efforts to integrate the state – but as an energetic segment of the early Meiji tapestry.

The "people" – that vague category of *minshū* or *heimin* taken by various scholars to connote almost any group outside the ruling elites – constitute one of the more important categories to gain increased attention in recent years. Scholars have long been interested in peasants as rebels, or as participants in the nationalizing scheme; indeed, when Irokawa wrote about mountain political movements in the 1970s, he was expanding on a topic that had interested historians for generations; the same was true of Roger Bowen's studies of popular rights resisters and Mikiso Hane's work on peasants and rebels at the beginning of the 1980s.[23] In recent decades, however, the focus has moved beyond outsiders who merely reacted to (or suffered under) an increasingly centralized system, toward commoners as agents. Oku Takenori discusses the way reportage on scandals spread modern consciousness; Stephen Vlastos shows us the complexity of motives and approaches harbored by peasant activists; Yamamoto Taketoshi shows an expanding populace making possible a profitable urban press in the 1870s and 1880s; Anne Walthall weaves the private and public together – the farming, the poetry, the activism – in the life of the "useless woman" Matsuo

Taseko, arguing that her life calls into question "the distinction between public and private, male roles and females roles and the often hazy margin between conceptual categories that mesh into one another in practice."[24]

An especially insightful study of commoners is Scott Schnell's *The Rousing Drum*, which shows a clash in Hida at the end of the 1860s between mountain culture and the advocates of centralization. His work has not gained as much attention as it merits, possibly because he is an anthropologist rather than a historian, but he represents an expanding – and highly significant – body of work on local histories. M. William Steele, one of those rare Westerners who publishes as much in Japanese as in English, introduced his *Alternative Narratives in Modern Japanese History* with a call for "another look (or looks) at modernity." Local history, he says, "need not be belittled for dealing with the particular; local men and women need not be marginalized for the everyday quality of their deeds. … Just as one can narrate Japanese history from above, one can look from below." In contrast to the center, he argues, there is "a plethora of peripheries," making "the telling of stories from below … open-ended."[25] A consistent theme of those who examine localities is the variety of experiences the Meiji government had in bringing peripheral areas into the new "nation." Michael Lewis tells a story of conflict and regional resistance, showing that even though Tokyo rulers used force and asserted a "cultural homogeneity that probably never existed," it took decades to integrate the Toyama region on the Japan Sea coast. He sees the constant official complaints about "too much drinking, too much gift-giving, too many celebrations of local festivals" as signs that real life differed from the "idealized portraits of proper citizens of model villages."[26] Steele finds a similar situation in Kantō areas. Wigen sees the Shimoina area on the Japan's Pacific side sinking into marginality. And James Baxter tells a different tale, contending that the Ishikawa area north of the Japan Alps came fairly quickly into the spreading national system.[27] People have challenged Baxter's interpretations, but all historians of the peripheries agree that the local leaders tended more to *maneuver* for perks or autonomy than to rebel or resist openly. They also show a much more complex picture, at least into the late 1880s, than the center-dominates-periphery storyline of earlier narratives.

If the demands of theory have forced us to add new groups to our understanding, they have also excavated topics once considered taboo or irrelevant to the story of modernization and progress. Issues of space and temporality have entered the tale; the beginnings of Japanese imperialism are receiving increased attention; Peter Kornicki has done pioneering work on the history of the book;[28] and material culture shows up in ways more varied and interesting than the time-honored depictions of Japanese eating meat (like Westerners), Japanese building Western-style brick buildings, Japanese women wearing Western evening gowns, and Japanese men getting Western-style haircuts.

One of the new topics is the growth of communication, particularly journalism. Despite the crucial role of the printed word in creating imagined communities, in serving as agent and definer of modernity, historians until the late twentieth century largely left study of the press to scholars in journalism schools. That is changing, however, as men like Ariyama Teruo, Yoshimi Shun'ya, and Sasaki Takashi bring communication studies into the mainstream of history, even as they define communication more and more broadly. My own work has attempted to demonstrate that the newspaper press played a pivotal role in Japan's move to modernity by drawing urbanites (and some in rural areas) into the public arena, even as it served as gatekeeper to what the public would debate. Of particular importance is the fact that the papers with the largest circulations, even in the first Meiji decade, were commoner-oriented sheets such as *Yomiuri shimbun*, which specialized in sensation and scandal, demonstrating the existence of a large world (and market!) beyond the respectable circles of the intellectual elites, a world that remains yet to be studied adequately by historians.

The movement into mainstream history has taken press and communications studies in new directions. Giles Richter, for example, has addressed Meiji economic and political history with a study of print capitalism, showing that publishers became influential enough in the Meiji years to force officials to moderate censorship policies and allow publication of popular materials that they would have preferred to ban. The publishers did more than shape their own industries; they changed the state, by forcing it "into a reactive, defensive posture" and demonstrating that "the government could no longer effectively regulate the content of everything that was printed."[29] Taking a different approach to communication history, Joseph Henning represents a growing group of scholars who examine images and representations, both visual and written. His study of how nineteenth-century Americans imposed narrow concepts of race and religion on Japan argues that while several early Meiji visitors treated Japanese culture with respect, the majority made "modernization . . . synonymous with westernization" and, in the process, provided support for demeaning American policies.[30]

Gender and sexuality also have made their way into the late-Tokugawa–early-Meiji narrative, with women becoming ever more visible since the appearance of Sharon Sievers's study of Meiji feminists early in the 1980s. Indeed, gender is one of the few new themes that actually has begun to penetrate even the broad Meiji surveys. The 1990s brought increased complexity to our understandings of women's roles, with Patricia Tsurumi's *Factory Girls* mining rich sources to examine both victimization and the contributions of female textile workers, describing the contrast between the respect afforded early Meiji workers and the abuse those workers received after the 1880s. She concluded with a workers' song that captured the dual nature of their roles: "Who dares to say that / Factory girls are weak? / Factory girls are the / Only ones who create wealth."[31] Particularly influential was *Recreating Japanese Women*, a 1991 collection of essays that challenged stereotypes. One of the articles told the story of the entrepreneur Tatsu'uma Kiyo, who amassed a fortune in brewing; another, by Sharon Nolte and Sally Hastings, made it clear that women's prerogatives actually became narrower in the Meiji era, as state power spread. The essay demonstrated that the state "valued a woman's productive power more than her ability as a mother"[32] – and that the state itself was not a monolithic behemoth but a diverse set of agencies that differed and fought bitterly with each other.

By the late 1990s, works on gender and sexuality represented many, varied segments of Tokugawa–Meiji life. Walthall's study of Matsuo Taseko made "ordinary" women important. Jason Karlin analyzed the role of masculinity in the creation of Meiji nationalism. Jordan Sand looked at how the government created the sphere of the "home as a haven and the housewife as its spiritual center."[33] Pflugfelder showed how male–male sexual engagement moved from respectability in Tokugawa to condemnation in early Meiji, as " 'barbarous,' 'immoral,' or simply 'unspeakable'."[34] And Tsurumi and others used the pages of the *U.S.–Japan Women's Journal* to discuss the gendered nature of Meiji education and politics. One of the most important works, theoretically, was *Women and Class in Japanese History* (1999), with chapters on the nineteenth century showing both the Tokugawa origins of phenomena once thought to have originated with the West and the growing control of the state over hygiene and the female body. The contributions of these gender studies is particularly apparent in the broader, more synthetic works on the era. The nineteenth-century volume of *The Cambridge History of Japan*, which appeared late in the 1980s, does not contain the word "women" in its index, and gender rarely appears in its pages; even discussions of marriage and childbirth use a neutral language that barely suggests gender as a factor. By the end of the decade, such an omission would have been unthinkable. The McClain and Gordon histories, which appeared in 2002 and 2003, weave gender into the story fairly seamlessly. Similarly, a 2002 collection of modern Japanese biographies places women at the center of all three early Meiji chapters.[35]

As should be apparent, the theory-based studies bring more than new subject matter to the nineteenth-century narrative. They are helping us to *conceive* the period differently, to push us to think about motives, about ideology, about power relationships in more complex ways. While one groans occasionally over elitist attempts to use language in clever (and all too often inaccessible) ways, the theorists nonetheless have given us important new ways of understanding what was happening in the years around the Meiji Restoration. Fujitani's study of how the government created old-looking-yet-new structures to foster love of the emperor is a powerful example of how the idea of "invented traditions" has changed the field. Wigen's insistence on the conscious examination of "the interface between history and geography"[36] has influenced not just the study of regional history but the entire language of Meiji studies (witness the title of Pflugfelder's work on sexuality: *Cartographies of Desire*). The interest in differing kinds of spaces (and their relationship to power) leads scholars like Susan Burns of the University of Chicago and Uemori Naoyuki of Waseda University to examine how hospitals and prisons became sites for resistance and subversion. And one can credit both Said's *Orientalism* and Anderson's "imagined communities" with helping to produce Stefan Tanaka's *Japan's Orient*, which shows the changing way in which Meiji scholars conceptualized the relationship between Japan and China while exploring the ideological foundations of Japanese imperialism.

At the heart of these studies lies a preoccupation with power: how it is exerted, how it affects relationships, how it shapes society – with the majority of scholars inclined to look critically at the Meiji state and to find signs of agency and resistance among the populace. Douglas Howland, for example, uses semiotic theory to show both the unevenness of Japanese–Western relationships and the efforts of the Meiji elites to use Western terms such as "rights," "liberty," and "society" to control people. He portrays the progressive Fukuzawa interpreting terms like *ken* (rights) as "state right and sovereignty" rather than as people's rights – because of "the need to maintain Japan's autonomy in an international situation where the Western powers were demonstrating their own willful autonomy in colonial actions against the less civilized."[37] Howell takes a similar tack in his important 2000 essay, "Visions of the Future in Meiji Japan," arguing that while a number of visions competed – the nostalgia of Saigō Takamori's followers, the democratic goals of freedom and popular rights supporters, the moralistic dreams of rural rebels – the statist view of Meiji officials finally won, in part because foreign threats pushed people to defer to national strength, and in part because the state offered the concept of empire to "exponents of the defeated visions."[38]

Indeed, Japan's international role – the country's active grappling with Western definitions of modernity, its efforts to resist yet emulate the West, its changing relationship with Asia – stimulates much of the new thinking about Meiji history. The field continues to produce a few traditional works on international affairs: Michael Auslin's and Louis Perez's work on treaty revision, continuing studies of the *yatoi*, a translation of Kume Kunitake's massive records of the Iwakura mission, and Frederik Schodt's 2003 biography of Ranald MacDonald, a native American who made his way to Hokkaidō in the late 1840s.[39] Akira Iriye also has continued to produce influential works on the cultural underpinnings of Japan's relationships with the West. While these works fill in gaps in our traditional understandings, the narrative is more likely to be stretched by several scholars who have begun asking new questions, some of them drawn from postcolonial studies. In somewhat of a counterpoint to Tanaka, Joshua Fogel's exhaustive study of Japanese travelers to China after the late Tokugawa years shows an "obsession with 'understanding China'," based partly on the archipelago's residents' age-old fascination with China and partly on a propensity to use China as a way to create Japan's own identity.[40] Identity also is a concern of Tessa Morris-Suzuki in several works looking at how Japanese groups saw their country within the world context. And Robert Eskildsen looks at the early stirrings, in the 1870s, of Japan's own imperialism through an examination of press coverage of the Japanese expedition to Taiwan in 1874. He uses woodblock depictions in particular to show Japanese writers exaggerating Taiwanese stereotypes and engaging in what he calls "mimetic imperialism." "The prospect of exporting civilization to Taiwan," he argues, "provided an attractive means of resisting Western imperialism."[41]

There remains, however, a paucity of serious analyses, particularly in English, of *Western* imperialism in these years, works that pay as much attention to the way foreigners forced Japan into semi-colonial status as they do to the Westerners' role as harbingers of civilization. Iriye has discussed the uneven side of the Western incursion, and I have argued elsewhere that Western imperialism made it easy for the Meiji government to rationalize a statist approach to the detriment of its own citizens. Western pressure has always formed an important part of the narrative in Japan, drawn on by scholars and textbooks alike to explain Japan's militarist move. The controversial 2001 middle school text, *Atarashii rekishi kyōkasho* (New History Textbook), for example, is filled with discussions of a "harsh world in which the powerful devour the weak" (*jakuniku shōshoku no kakoku no sekai*). Western historians, by contrast, have been quicker to look at the onset of Japanese aggression than to confront its roots in European and American imperialism in Japan. One hopes that the rising tide of postcolonial studies and the new attention to *Japan's* imperialistic turn will foreshadow fuller critiques of *Western* imperialism in Japan.[42]

The relative silence about Western imperialism is not the only omission in recent studies of the Meiji Restoration years; indeed, several gaps tell as much about Meiji

historiography as the new works do. One of the obvious results of the advance of
theory is a decline in traditional themes; one has to look hard these days for treatments of military history, bakufu (or Meiji) institutions, diplomacy, industrialization,
constitutional thought, or even the Meiji Restoration itself. Studies of Japan's early
incursions into Okinawa are also largely lacking, as are works in comparative history –
a puzzling fact, given the improved language ability of younger scholars and the
broad applicability of theoretical frameworks such as Orientalism and postcolonial-
ism.

Nowhere is the change more obvious than in the decline of institutional political
history. Central political structures and actors are almost as widely ignored in
today's monographs as those on the periphery once were. The continuing focus
on power means that elite voices still are heard, but in muted or harsh tones.
Biographies of "great men" are rare, evoking a yawn from publishers (unless
the writer has the name impact of a Donald Keene, whose massive 2002 biography
of the Emperor Meiji reminds us that the old history still has much to offer
us). While the emperor system inspires theoretical works on the invention of tradition, few write about the ins and outs of Edo/Tokyo government, except as
bureaucrats respond to initiatives in the regions. Indeed, students wanting to examine
the evolution of the Tokugawa–Meiji political system still must rely on classics by
Robert Scalapino, Joseph Pittau, and George Akita – all published half a century
ago.[43] Even the *jiyū minken* movements, which once produced the richest material
about people on the margins, is largely ignored. Julia Thomas looks at *jiyū minken*
thinkers, among others, in her influential consideration of changing concepts of
nature. But aside from side-angle views such as this, the popular rights forces have
lost their voice.

At the same time – and with equal irony – the preoccupation of contemporary
scholars with power relationships means that the narrative still has little to tell us
about everyday life. Harootunian's efforts to get Japan scholars to use the "everyday"
as a rubric for studying Japan's the interwar period notwithstanding, his intellectua-
lization of the word has not resulted in much study of genuine *everyday* life, or what
Susan B. Hanley calls the sociocultural side of life, in the late nineteenth century.
Hanley provides a provocative start, concluding her examination of Tokugawa material culture with a brief look at the Tokugawa–Meiji transition, which concludes that
"it is difficult to see substantial change in the standard of living or the level of physical
well-being during the Meiji period."[44] Changes in Western-inspired European trappings have also provoked some early scholarly forays into daily life: into zoos, travel,
dogs, sports. But the ideologies that underlie most historical narratives have precluded serious examination of those facets of experience that do not have transpar-
ently political meaning.

Whither the Narrative?

Two possibilities emerge, when one attempts to evaluate the state of late-Tokugawa–
early-Meiji studies today. Hardacre articulated the first at the conclusion of
the Conference on Meiji Studies when she described a "rejection of grand theory and
master narrative" in favor of "portrayals of multiple actors, conflicting representations,

and fractured identities, to the point that it becomes impossible to distinguish lasting centers of power and influence."[45] The second argues that there has been no significant change in the overall narrative of the time, that James McClain encapsulated the still dominant storyline when he argued in his 2002 synthesis that "during the 1870s and 1880s new beginnings were to bring to Japan political, economic, and social changes as revolutionary as those experienced by any country in the world during the last three centuries."[46] Which is it: the loss of a grand story, or the persistence of that story in the face of endless challenge?

The truth lies between the two. If one looks at the Meiji story in the sweeping syntheses, the changes seem more like modulations. More women are present; economics matter somewhat more than they once did; the Edo/Tokyo government looks less unified and dominant; the plight of commoners gets a bit more attention. But the themes discussed at the beginning of this essay – the turn to the West, the rush to modernity, the centrality of politics and the state, the uniqueness of the Japanese experience, the focus on progress – remain dominant. If, on the other hand, one looks primarily at the articles, dissertations, and monographs that have appeared since the 1990s, the picture changes significantly. Central politics, the core of traditional Meiji history, has been overshadowed by studies from the periphery. Female voices have been joined by those of farmers, rebels, and same-sex lovers. New sources – architecture, material items, cartoons, photographs, prints – combine with new ways of reading those sources to portray the nineteenth century in fresh ways. Theories regarding modernity, space, time, subjectivity, mimetic imperialism, invented traditions, and imagined communities bring new understandings even when researchers examine old topics. And scholars endlessly question the ideologies of both the narrators and the narrated. If the new themes and interpretations have not yet become central to the synthetic histories, it is hard to imagine that many decades will pass before they do.

If the journalist House had difficulty changing common perceptions about the Shimonoseki affair of 1863–4, he had a different experience with the narrative of modern Japan's first imperialistic excursion, the 1874 expedition to Taiwan when Japanese troops routed Taiwanese mountain warriors and laid the foundation for Japan's absorption of the Ryūkyū Islands. After accompanying the Japanese expedition, House wrote a book-length report, which firmly set the narrative line for this affair. People have questioned its accuracy; Chinese and Taiwanese historians have criticized its assumptions; students of imperialism have attacked his analysis of Japanese intentions. But at the beginning of the twenty-first century, his storyline remained dominant. Not only had his work set the outlines, but his interpretations had coincided with the story that the power elites (this time, including the Japanese) wanted to believe. In time, one suspects, House's narrative will lose its power to dominate our understanding of the Taiwan expedition – but that will happen only gradually, after years' accumulation of new data and fresh interpretations. So too with the story of Japan's Tokugawa–Meiji transition. The old story still holds us in its thrall, as it will continue to do until the new studies and interpretations achieve a mass sufficient to overwhelm it. That, one suspects, will take quite some time.

NOTES

I owe thanks to Dennis Frost for extensive comments and helpful discussions about this chapter.

1 For the story of House's failure at narrative change, see Huffman, "Edward H. House."
2 Hardacre, ed., *New Directions in the Study of Meiji Japan*, p. xxiv.
3 Ibid., p. 11.
4 Indeed, most historians describe the government as inept and inefficient in almost every decade of every era of Japanese history – a fact that ought to provoke inquiry into whether scholars are looking in the right places, or asking the correct questions, in analyzing the sources of energy in Japan's dynamic past.
5 Hirakawa Sukehiro, "Japan's Turn to the West," in Jansen, ed., *The Cambridge History of Japan*, vol. 5, *The Nineteenth Century*, pp. 497–8.
6 Burks, ed., *The Modernizers*, p. 412.
7 John W. Hall, "Changing Conceptions of the Modernization of Japan," in Jansen, ed., *Changing Japanese Attitudes toward Modernization*, p. 7.
8 Kuwabara Takeo, "The Meiji Revolution and Japan's Modernization," in Nagai and Urrutia, eds., *Meiji Ishin*, p. 23.
9 Quoted in Albert Craig, "The Central Government," in Jansen and Rozman, eds., *Japan in Transition*, p. 67.
10 Fukuzawa, "Datsu-a ron" (On Casting Off Asia), in Lu, *Japan: A Documentary History*, p. 353.
11 Shiga, *Nihonjin* (Apr. 18, 1888), in Pyle, *The New Generation in Meiji Japan*, p. 68.
12 Sansom, *The Western World and Japan*, p. 313.
13 Tōyama Shigeki, "Independence and Modernization in the Nineteenth Century," in Nagai and Urrutia, eds., *Meiji Ishin*, p. 29; Gordon, *A Modern History of Japan*, p. xii.
14 McClain, *Japan*, pp. 156–7.
15 Howell, "Visions of the Future," p. 85 (emphasis added).
16 Hardacre, ed., *New Directions in the Study of Meiji Japan*, p. xvii.
17 Beasley and Pulleyblank, *Historians of China and Japan*, p. 19.
18 Interview (June 9, 2003). He noted Carol Gluck, Harry Harootunian, and Takashi Fujitani as historians whose work has exerted influence on Japanese historians.
19 Naoki Sakai, "Translation and Nationalism," in Richter and Schad-Seifert, eds., *Cultural Studies and Japan*, p. 23.
20 Dipesh Chakrabarty, "Afterword: Revisiting the Tradition/Modernity Binary," in Vlastos, ed., *Mirror of Modernity*, p. 288.
21 Ibid., p. 1.
22 Ketelaar, *Of Heretics and Martyrs in Meiji Japan*.
23 Irokawa, *The Culture of the Meiji Period*; Bowen, *Rebellion and Democracy in Meiji Japan*; Hane, *Peasants, Rebels, and Outcastes*.
24 Walthall, *The Weak Body of a Useless Woman*, p. 353.
25 Steele, *Alternative Narratives in Modern Japanese History*, p. 1.
26 Lewis, *Becoming Apart*, pp. 4, 13.
27 Baxter, *The Meiji Unification through the Lens of Ishikawa Prefecture*.
28 Kornicki, *The Book in Japan*.
29 Richter, *Marketing the Word*, pp. 333–4.
30 Henning, *Outposts of Civilization*, p. 171.
31 Tsurumi, *Factory Girls*, p. 197.
32 Sharon Nolte and Sally Ann Hastings, "The Meiji State's Policy toward Women, 1890–1910," in Bernstein, ed., *Recreating Japanese Women*, p. 173.

33 Sand, "At Home in the Meiji Period: Inventing Japanese Domesticity," in Vlastos, ed., *Mirror of Modernity*, p. 205.
34 Pflugfelder, *Cartographies of Desire*, p. 193.
35 Walthall, ed., *The Human Tradition in Modern Japan*, pp. 45–98. There are no biographies from the late Tokugawa years.
36 Wigen, *The Making of a Japanese Periphery*, p. 3.
37 Howland, *Translating the West*, p. 152.
38 Howell, "Visions of the Future," p. 113.
39 Auslin, *Negotiating with Imperialism*; Perez, *Japan Comes of Age*; Kume, *The Iwakura Embassy*; Schodt, *Native American in the Land of the Shōgun*.
40 Fogel, *The Literature of Travel*, p. 302.
41 Eskildsen, "Of Civilization and Savages," p. 389.
42 *Atarashii rekishi kyōkasho* (Tokyo: Fusōsha, 2001), p. 176. See Huffman, *A Yankee in Meiji Japan*, pp. 132–45, 273–7.
43 Scalapino, *Democracy and the Party Movement in Prewar Japan*; Pittau, *Political Thought in Early Meiji Japan*; Akita, *Foundations of Constitutional Government in Modern Japan*.
44 Hanley, *Everyday Things in Premodern Japan*, p. 179.
45 Hardacre, ed., *New Directions in the Study of Meiji Japan*, pp. xxiii–xxiv.
46 McClain, *Japan*, p. 154.

BIBLIOGRAPHY

Akita, George. *Foundations of Constitutional Government in Modern Japan, 1868–1900.* Cambridge, Mass.: Harvard University Press, 1967.

Atarashii rekishi kyōkasho. Tokyo: Fusōsha, 2001.

Auslin, Michael. *Negotiating with Imperialism: The Unequal Treaties and the Culture of Japanese Diplomacy.* Cambridge, Mass.: Harvard University Press, 2004.

Baxter, James. *The Meiji Unification through the Lens of Ishikawa Prefecture.* Cambridge, Mass.: Harvard University Press, 1994.

Beasley, W. G. *The Modern History of Japan.* New York: Praeger, 1963.

Beasley, W. G. *The Meiji Restoration.* Stanford, Calif.: Stanford University Press, 1972.

Beasley, W. G. *Japan Encounters the Barbarian: Japanese Travellers in America and Europe.* New Haven: Yale University Press, 1995.

Beasley, W. G., and Pulleyblank, E. G. *Historians of China and Japan.* London: Oxford University Press, 1961.

Bernstein, Gail Lee, ed. *Recreating Japanese Women, 1600–1945.* Berkeley: University of California Press, 1991.

Bowen, Roger. *Rebellion and Democracy in Meiji Japan.* Berkeley: University of California Press, 1980.

Burks, Ardath W., ed. *The Modernizers: Overseas Students, Foreign Employees and Meiji Japan.* Boulder, Colo.: Westview Press, 1985.

Duus, Peter, ed. with intro. *The Japanese Discovery of America: A Brief History with Documents.* Boston: Bedford Books, 1997.

Ericson, Steven. *The Sound of the Whistle: Railroads and the State in Meiji Japan.* Cambridge, Mass.: Council on East Asian Studies, Harvard University, 1996.

Eskildsen, Robert. "Of Civilization and Savages: The Mimetic Imperialism of Japan's 1874 Expedition to Taiwan." *American Historical Review* 107:2 (Apr. 2002): 388–418.

Fogel, Joshua. *The Literature of Travel and the Japanese Rediscovery of China, 1862–1945.* Stanford, Calif.: Stanford University Press, 1996.

Fu, Charles Wei-Hsun, and Heine, Steven, eds. *Japan in Traditional and Postmodern Perspectives*. Albany: State University of New York Press, 1995.

Fujitani, Takashi. *Splendid Monarchy: Power and Pageantry in Modern Japan*. Berkeley: University of California Press, 1996.

Gordon, Andrew. *A Modern History of Japan: From Tokugawa Times to the Present*. New York: Oxford University Press, 2003.

Hane, Mikiso. *Peasants, Rebels, and Outcastes: The Underside of Modern Japan*. New York: Pantheon, 1982.

Hanley, Susan B. *Everyday Things in Premodern Japan: The Hidden Legacy of Material Culture*. Berkeley: University of California Press, 1997.

Hardacre, Helen, ed. *New Directions in the Study of Meiji Japan*. Leiden: Brill, 1997.

Henning, Joseph. *Outposts of Civilization: Race, Religion, and the Formative Years of American–Japanese Relations*. New York: New York University Press, 2000.

Howell, David L. *Capitalism from Within: Economy, Society, and the State in a Japanese Fishery*. Berkeley: University of California Press, 1995.

Howell, David L. "Visions of the Future in Meiji Japan." In Merle Goldman and Andrew Gordon, eds., *Historical Perspectives on Contemporary East Asia*. Cambridge, Mass.: Harvard University Press, 2000.

Howland, Douglas R. *Translating the West: Language and Political Reason in Nineteenth-Century Japan*. Honolulu: University of Hawai'i Press, 2002.

Huffman, James L. *Creating a Public: People and Press in Meiji Japan*. Honolulu: University of Hawai'i Press, 1997.

Huffman, James L. "Edward H. House: Questions of Meaning and Influence." *Japan Forum* 13:1 (2001): 15–25.

Huffman, James L. *A Yankee in Meiji Japan: The Crusading Journalist Edward H. House*. Lanham, Md.: Rowman and Littlefield, 2003.

Irokawa Daikichi. *The Culture of the Meiji Period*. Princeton: Princeton University Press, 1985.

Jansen, Marius, ed. *Changing Japanese Attitudes toward Modernization*. Princeton: Princeton University Press, 1965.

Jansen, Marius, ed. *The Cambridge History of Japan*, vol. 5, *The Nineteenth Century*. Cambridge: Cambridge University Press, 1989.

Jansen, Marius, and Rozman, Gilbert, eds. *Japan in Transition: From Tokugawa to Meiji*. Princeton: Princeton University Press, 1986.

Karlin, Jason. "The Gender of Nationalism: Competing Masculinities in Meiji Japan." *Journal of Japanese Studies* 28:1 (Winter 2002): 41–78.

Keene, Donald. *Emperor of Japan: Meiji and His World, 1852–1912*. New York: Columbia University Press, 2002.

Ketelaar, James E. *Of Heretics and Martyrs in Meiji Japan: Buddhism and Its Persecution*. Princeton: Princeton University Press, 1990.

Kornicki, Peter. *The Book in Japan: A Cultural History from the Beginnings to the Nineteenth Century*. Leiden: Brill, 1998.

Kume Kunitake. *The Iwakura Embassy, 1871–73: A True Account of the Ambassador Extraordinary & Plenipotentiary's Journeys of Observation through the United States and Europe*, ed. Graham Healey and Chushichi Tsuzuki, 5 vols. Chiba: Japan Documents, 2002.

Lewis, Michael. *Becoming Apart: National Power and Local Politics in Toyama, 1868–1945*. Cambridge, Mass.: Harvard University Press, 2000.

Lu, David J. *Japan: A Documentary History*. Armonk, NY: M. E. Sharpe, 1997.

McClain, James. *Japan: A Modern History*. New York: Norton, 2002.

McClain, James, Merriman, John, and Kaoru, Ugawa, eds. *Edo and Paris: Urban Life and the State in the Early Modern Era*. Ithaca, NY: Cornell University Press, 1994.

Morris-Suzuki, Tessa. *Re-inventing Japan: Time, Space, Nation*. Armonk, NY: M. E. Sharpe, 1998.

Nagai, Michio, and Urrutia, Miguel, eds. *Meiji Ishin: Restoration and Revolution*. Tokyo: United Nations University, 1985.

Norman, E. H. *Japan's Emergence as a Modern State*. New York: Institute of Pacific Relations, 1940.

Oku Takenori. *Sukiyandaru no Meiji: kokumin o tsukuru tame no ressun*. Tokyo: Chikuma Shobō, 1997.

Perez, Louis. *Japan Comes of Age: Mutsu Munemitsu and the Revision of the Unequal Treaties*. Madison, NJ: Fairleigh Dickinson University Press, 1999.

Pflugfelder, Gregory. *Cartographies of Desire: Male–Male Sexuality in Japanese Discourse, 1600–1950*. Berkeley: University of California Press, 1999.

Pittau, Joseph. *Political Thought in Early Meiji Japan, 1868–1889*. Cambridge, Mass.: Harvard University Press, 1967.

Pyle, Kenneth B. *The New Generation in Meiji Japan: Problems of Cultural Identity, 1885–1895*. Stanford, Calif.: Stanford University Press, 1969.

Reischauer, Edwin. *Japan, Past and Present*. New York: Knopf, 1947.

Richter, Giles. *Marketing the Word: Publishing Entrepreneurs in Meiji Japan, 1970–1912*. Ph.D. dissertation, Columbia University, 1999.

Richter, Steffi, and Schad-Seifert, Annette, eds. *Cultural Studies and Japan*. Leipzig: Leipziger Universitätsverlag, 2001.

Sansom, George. *The Western World and Japan: A Study in the Interaction of European and Asiatic Cultures*. New York: Knopf, 1950.

Scalapino, Robert. *Democracy and the Party Movement in Prewar Japan*. Berkeley: University of California Press, 1953.

Schnell, Scott. *The Rousing Drum: Ritual Practice in a Japanese Community*. Honolulu: University of Hawai'i Press, 1999.

Schodt, Frederik. *Native American in the Land of the Shōgun*. Berkeley: Stone Bridge Press, 2003.

Sievers, Sharon L. *Flowers in Salt: The Beginnings of Feminist Consciousness in Modern Japan*. Stanford, Calif.: Stanford University Press, 1983.

Steele, M. William. *Alternative Narratives in Modern Japanese History*. London: Routledge-Curzon, 2003.

Tanaka, Stefan. *Japan's Orient: Rendering Pasts into History*. Berkeley: University of California Press, 1993.

Thomas, Julia. *Reconfiguring Modernity: Concepts of Nature in Japanese Political Ideology*. Berkeley: University of California Press, 2001.

Tonomura, Hitomi, Walthall, Anne, and Wakita Haruko, eds. *Women and Class in Japanese History*. Ann Arbor: Center for Japanese Studies, University of Michigan, 1999.

Tsurumi, E. Patricia. *Factory Girls: Women in the Thread Mills of Meiji Japan*. Princeton: Princeton University Press, 1990.

Vlastos, Stephen, ed. *Mirror of Modernity: Invented Traditions of Modern Japan*. Berkeley: University of California Press, 1998.

Walthall, Anne. *The Weak Body of a Useless Woman: Matsuo Taseko and the Meiji Restoration*. Chicago: University of Chicago Press, 1998.

Walthall, Anne, ed. *The Human Tradition in Modern Japan*. Wilmington, Del.: Scholarly Resources, 2002.

Wigen, Kären. *The Making of a Japanese Periphery, 1750–1920*. Berkeley: University of California Press, 1995.

Yamamoto Taketoshi. *Kindai no shimbun dokusha sō*. Tokyo: Hōsei Daigaku, 1981.

FURTHER READING

A starting point for the Meiji Restoration is Michio Nagai and Miguel Urrutia's *Meiji Ishin: Restoration and Revolution* (Tokyo: United Nations University, 1985), a collection of conference papers that addresses the event from a variety of perspectives that are diverse ideologically and theoretically. William G. Steele's *Alternative Narratives in Modern Japanese History* (London: RoutledgeCurzon, 2003) illustrates the rich lessons that commoners, woodblock prints, foreigners, and the residents of less-known locales have to teach us regarding the Restoration years. Perhaps the most useful work theoretically is Stephen Vlastos's *Mirror of Modernity* (Berkeley: University of California Press, 1998), which includes reflections by leading scholars (Kären Wigen, Dipesh Chakrabarty, H. D. Harootunian, and Carol Gluck, among others) on the implications of Hobsbawm's "invented traditions" for Japanese history.

One of the clearest, most provocative overviews of the Meiji years is David Howell's chapter, "Visions of the Future in Meiji Japan," in Merle Goldman and Andrew Gordon's *Historical Perspectives on Contemporary East Asia* (Cambridge, Mass.: Harvard University Press, 2000), which argues that the Meiji rulers opted for a statist vision that imposed harsh conditions on a majority of the populace. His *Capitalism from Within* (Berkeley: University of California Press, 1995) shows that the growth of capitalism was not dependent solely on Western models and markets. An incisive examination of the negative impact of Western merchants on Meiji development is found in the attacks of journalist Edward H. House, recounted and analyzed in James Huffman's *A Yankee in Meiji Japan* (Boulder, Colo.: Rowman and Littlefield, 2003). For a somewhat idiosyncratic, wonderfully rich example of deep reading and imaginative sources use to create a traditional biography, one should turn to Donald Keene's *Emperor of Japan: Meiji and His World* (New York: Columbia University Press, 2002). The best example of comparative work on this period surely is the volume edited by James McClain, John Merriman, and Ugawa Kaoru, *Edo and Paris* (Ithaca, NY: Cornell University Press, 1994).

CHAPTER NINE

Oligarchy, Democracy, and Fascism

Stephen S. Large

The overthrow of the Tokugawa bakufu necessitated the construction of a new Japanese state capable of commanding the loyalty of the people and mobilizing society in the continuing quest for national wealth and power that had begun before the Meiji Restoration. But the ensuing processes of political centralization, nation-building, industrialization, and integration into the international order created new complexities that tested the ability of the imperial state to govern Japan. As time passed new organized interests had to be accommodated, conflicts between new classes had to be contained, and radical visions of what kind of country Japan should become had to be controlled. What is more, the nature and purposes of the imperial state itself came into question in late nineteenth- and early twentieth-century Japan.

For historians of this period an important issue is how far oligarchic rule (1880–1918), political democracy in the era of party government (1918–32), and fascism (1932–41) constituted successive, albeit overlapping, phases in Japanese attempts to address "the fear and problem of ungovernability" which arises in all modern states, particularly late arrivals on the world stage.[1] Debates about "oligarchy," "democracy," and "fascism" in Japan go back a long way, but in the past fifteen years or so they have been significantly rejuvenated by fresh approaches, interpretations, and discoveries of new evidence. My task here is to convey a general sense of the issues at stake in these debates and their implications for our understanding of modern Japanese political history.

The Question of Oligarchic Rule, 1880–1918

The term "Meiji oligarchy" refers to the group of seven men who took over from Ōkubo Toshimichi, Kido Kōin, and Saigō Takamori, the original leaders of the Meiji regime, and dominated the Japanese government for most of the period from the early 1880s to 1918. They personified to their contemporary critics the tyranny of the "Sat–Chō hanbatsu," or the ruling clique comprised of men from Satsuma and Chōshū, the two domains which, together with Tosa and Hizen, had led the movement to restore the emperor. Their earlier rise to key bureaucratic posts in the regime had enabled them to appoint many of their loyalist comrades from Satsuma and Chōshū to positions of power in local government.

Yet despite their tightening grip on power both in Tokyo and in the provinces, the oligarchs were strongly opposed by loyalists from beyond Satsuma and Chōshū who, like the oligarchs, had come from a middle or lower samurai background and who had likewise fought to restore the emperor. Seeking a share of power these challengers mobilized political parties in the "movement for freedom and popular rights" (*jiyū minken undō*) which advocated representative government on the British model, in the 1870s and 1880s. In 1881 the oligarchs responded by announcing the establishment of constitutional government and an elected assembly within ten years. But such was their loathing for the parties that they would only tolerate "transcendental," non-party, cabinets.

Given their historical significance and the fact that there were seven oligarchs, it is surprising that so far only one, Yamagata Aritomo (1838–1922, from Chōshū), the "father" of the Japanese army, has been the subject of a full-length and thoroughly researched biography in English.[2] Of the other six, Yamagata's main rival among the oligarchs, Itō Hirobumi (1841–1909, also from Chōshū), is the best known, especially for supervising the drafting of the Meiji constitution, promulgated in 1889. By comparison, Inoue Kaoru (1835–1915, Chōshū), Matsukata Masayoshi (1835–1924, Satsuma), Kuroda Kiyotaka (1840–1900, Satsuma), Ōyama Iwao (1842–1916, Satsuma), and Saigō Tsugumichi (1843–1902, Satsuma), remain shadowy figures. What defined the oligarchs as a group – besides their Sat-Chō origins, their contributions to the 1868 Meiji Restoration, and their prior experience in bureaucratic office – was their entirely informal, but nonetheless very significant, responsibility as *genrō* ("elder statesmen") to advise the emperor on the appointment of prime ministers. Later, Yamagata's protégé, General Katsura Tarō (1848–1913, Chōshū) and Prince Saionji Kinmochi (1849–1940) also became *genrō*. Saionji continued to advise the emperor on the appointment of prime ministers after all the other *genrō* had died out, although in the 1930s the "senior statesmen" (*jūshin*, former prime ministers) partly performed this function.

In the 1890s, the first decade of constitutional government, the oligarchs recommended each other as prime minister with the understanding that power would normally rotate between the Satsuma and Chōshū camps. The one exception was a short-lived cabinet (June–November 1898) headed by Ōkuma Shigenobu, which was Japan's first political party cabinet. Ōkuma, from Hizen, had been a member of the ruling circle until his expulsion from the government in 1881 after he had demanded party cabinets within two years. In 1882 he formed the Kaishintō party which evolved into the Kenseitō in 1898 following a merger with the Jiyūtō, a party formed in 1881 by Itagaki Taisuke, from Tosa. Save for the army and navy ministers, the ministers in the Ōkuma cabinet, including Itagaki, were members of the Kenseitō. I will mention this cabinet again shortly but for now, its collapse, chiefly due to clashes between the Ōkuma and Itagaki factions in the Kenseitō, led to Yamagata's third cabinet (November 1898–October 1900) and to Itō Hirobumi's fourth cabinet (October 1900–June 1901). These were the last cabinets with an oligarch serving as prime minister. Subsequently, the oligarchs orchestrated the appointment of prime ministers whom they thought they could manipulate. To begin with, for Yamagata this meant Katsura Tarō and for Itō, Saionji Kinmochi who served as president of the Seiyūkai party, formed in 1900, from 1903 to 1913. Katsura and Saionji alternated as prime minister from 1901 to early 1913.

Now, the oligarchs are generally portrayed by Western historians as enlightened political pragmatists who built the modern Japanese state. The essential features of this interpretation may be summarized very briefly as follows. First, the key point about the oligarchs is that by subordinating their personal and political rivalries to the shared priority of building a "rich country" (*fukoku*) and "strong army" (*kyōhei*), they provided relative political stability and continuity of leadership in a period of rapid change.[3] Second, while the constitutional system they devised was authoritarian and clearly intended to legitimize their informal rule from behind the throne, it provided scope for a loyal opposition in an elected lower House of Representatives that would be balanced by a conservative, appointive upper House of Peers. They opposed party cabinets, but "The measure of the enlightenment of the oligarchs is that they themselves accepted the fact of real participation in the government by the outs as an irreducible minimum for constitutional government."[4] In this, the oligarchs judged, overoptimistically as it turned out, that the parties might help to mobilize popular support for the government's domestic and foreign policies if landed and business interests whose taxes were essential to these policies were consulted through their party representatives in the lower house.

Third, when, beginning with the first Diet in 1890, the parties repeatedly opposed tax increases by using the one significant power afforded them – the power to block supply, which forced the government to revert to the previous year's budget in financing the rising costs of "wealth and power" policies – the oligarchs (at first Itō and later Yamagata) saw the necessity of compromises with the parties in exchange for their cooperation in the Diet. This partly explains the formation of the Ōkuma cabinet in 1898. Itō reasoned that since the strongest parties had blocked the government's proposal to raise the land tax, they should take office and assume the responsibility for "wealth and power" policies. He also sensed, quite rightly, that the Ōkuma government would soon fall apart. Two years later, Itō broke ranks with Yamagata, who was absolutely determined to keep the parties out of power, and became president of the newly formed Seiyūkai, to facilitate the politics of compromise. The parties, in turn, had come to see that working with the oligarchy was the key to attaining power one day in their own right. This readiness of the oligarchy and the parties to make constitutional government viable through the pragmatic politics of compromise led to the alternation of Katsura and Saionji as prime minister and then to a period, from 1914 to 1918, of "covert party government,"[5] reflecting the increasing influence of party leaders. If Yamagata symbolized the past, Hara Kei (1856–1921), who succeeded Saionji as president of the Seiyūkai in 1914, was the face of the future. By 1918, Hara was a very experienced politician, having developed the Seiyūkai as a political force while serving as home minister in three previous cabinets. Thus, the transition from oligarchic rule to party government, which occurred with Hara's appointment as prime minister in September 1918, was the logical outcome of earlier trends.

Fourth, in their prime, the oligarchs had sought "uncontested control of decision-making. In this they were wonderfully successful."[6] By 1900 they had constructed a modern, rational, and highly efficient central bureaucracy, based upon rigorous civil service examinations and an orderly system of promotion, which was deliberately sealed off from the influence of the parties and which the oligarchs could control. A strong state dominated by this bureaucracy was their main legacy to the future, for "over time, with the bureaucracy installed at the center of government and with the passing of the oligarchs, it was the bureaucrats – both military and civilian – who arrogated more and more power to themselves."[7]

This, then, is the prevailing image in Western research of the Meiji oligarchy as a pragmatic, effective, political elite. However, virtually every aspect of this interpretation has been provocatively challenged by Mark Ramseyer and Frances Rosenbluth in their book *The Politics of Oligarchy*, which attests to the increasing influence of rational choice theory in Japanese studies. To summarize their core arguments: first, the key point about the oligarchs is not their far-sighted cooperation for the national good but rather their individual pursuit of power at the expense of each other and their collective unity. Thus, "Instead of establishing an institutional framework that ameliorated their disagreements, the oligarchs institutionalized the suspicion with which they viewed one another."[8]

Second, these rivalries best explain the fatal ambiguity of the Meiji constitution which would seriously undermine the capacity of the state to govern the country effectively. Lest any one of the oligarchs gain too much power, they agreed to disperse it among various elite organs which would check and balance each other: the cabinet and its civilian and military ministries, the House of Representatives, the House of Peers, the Privy Council, the army and navy chiefs of staff offices, and the bureaucracy. Moreover, to prevent the prime minister from becoming too powerful, ministers of state were made responsible not to him but to the emperor. That made it difficult for the prime minister to ensure cabinet unity and it weakened the cabinet as a whole.[9] The chiefs of staff, in charge of military operations, were similarly responsible only to the emperor, who alone had "the supreme command of the army and navy" (article 11). Originally, this was meant to shield the military from possible interference by the political parties. But as another writer points out, in practice "there was no clear definition regarding either the scope of the right of supreme command or the person responsible for exercising it."[10] Consequently the chiefs were in effect responsible only to themselves, with calamitous results for Japan in later years.

Article 1 of the constitution stated, "The Empire of Japan shall be reigned over and governed by a line of Emperors unbroken for ages eternal." Accordingly, the emperor was also invested with a host of other prerogatives, for example the power to convoke, open, close, and prorogue the Diet, to dissolve the lower house, to issue imperial ordinances in place of law, to declare war, make peace, conclude treaties, and to declare martial law. In theory the emperor, who was also the locus of sovereignty and head of state, stood supreme in all civil and military affairs.

In fact, the oligarchs anticipated that the emperor would reign over, but not rule, Japan. His vast prerogatives were to be exercised by other organs and ministers of state who bore responsibility for success or failure and all laws, imperial ordinances, and rescripts had to be countersigned by a minister of state. So, divorced from government by the terms of the Imperial House Law, the emperor's function was to legitimize the government and its policies by formally conferring the "Imperial Will" and publicly to symbolize the national polity (*kokutai*) by virtue of his sacred authority as the lineal descendant of the Sun Goddess. Japan's modern emperors could, and did, strive informally behind the scenes to referee conflicts and promote consensus among their ministers. However, they could not unify the government. This meant that an extra-constitutional mechanism was required to ensure unity. The oligarchy, straddling the civil and military sides of government, provided that mechanism, but it was by no means clear what would happen after the oligarchs had died out.

Third, the oligarchs could have resisted the encroachment of the parties more effectively had they maintained a united front. But Itō destroyed that possibility when he joined the Seiyūkai, hoping to cultivate popular support for his own political ambitions. Yamagata resisted the parties through his protégés but this strategy backfired when in January 1913 Prime Minister Katsura defied him by forming the Dōshikai party which, renamed Kenseikai in 1916 and Minseitō in 1927, would henceforth compete with the Seiyūkai in an emerging two-party system of the "established parties" (*kiseitō*). Katsura could not save his administration, however. One month later he was forced to resign by a vociferous popular "movement to defend constitutional government" and the Seiyūkai's refusal to withdraw a motion of non-confidence. He died soon afterwards.

In 1918 Yamagata ran out of alternatives and finally recommended Hara, whose Seiyūkai was the majority party in the lower house, to be prime minister. However, there were several consolations in this final capitulation to the parties. Yamagata's personal faction, extending across the Peers, the Privy Council, the bureaucracy, the army, and the imperial court, remained intact as a check on the parties. Also still intact was an electoral system which, through various revisions, was devised by the oligarchs to make elections as complicated, internally divisive, and expensive as possible for each of the parties. In addition, although the franchise had been gradually increased from the tiny minority of 450,000 well-off rural and urban male voters who had voted in the first national elections in 1890, at eight million voters (5 percent of the total population) in 1919, it was still far short of popular demands for universal suffrage, which Yamagata opposed. He must have been relieved to find that Hara, having "placed himself firmly on the conservative side of change,"[11] was no less opposed to universal suffrage. Both men had been shaken by the spectacle of spontaneous mass protests against the high price of rice in the nationwide rice riots of 1918. Both feared "the people" as an unruly force.

Fourth, Yamagata had counted on the bureaucracy to counterbalance the parties. But it soon became clear that the oligarchs had not completely insulated the bureaucracy from the parties: the parties found ways to influence the bureaucrats and many bureaucrats, including some who would form party cabinets in the 1920s and early 1930s, joined the parties to work closely with them in framing and expediting public policy. Accordingly, Ramseyer and Rosenbluth conclude that Japan "was not a 'strong state' in the usual sense of the term" (for example, "where the bureaucracy is well-insulated from, if not autonomous of, societal pressures").[12] Instead it was in many ways a "dysfunctional" state.

With some justification, reviewers have criticized *The Politics of Oligarchy* for various theoretical, methodological, and empirical weaknesses.[13] Yet while Ramseyer and Rosenbluth ignore the fact that every historian who has written about the oligarchy has acknowledged the conflicts between the oligarchs, their point that these conflicts are crucial to explaining the ambiguity of the Meiji constitution and the dysfunctional system that arose from that ambiguity is well taken. Similarly, historians have long recognized the inability of the cabinet and indeed the emperor to prevent the military from abusing the emperor's supreme command prerogative. But this point, too, is worth reinforcing, as Ramseyer and Rosenbluth do in their book, for later, the Japanese military ran amok in the name of an emperor (Hirohito) who personally opposed Japan's aggressive wars in the 1930s.[14] Finally, as we shall see, other studies essentially confirm their view concerning the interdependence of the bureaucracy and the political parties.

Wherever historians stand in these debates about oligarchy, most of them would probably agree with Richard Samuels who writes, in his comparative study of leadership in Japan and Italy: "It is obvious that leaders matter." That is, some leaders can "stretch" constraints which they face in choosing the ends and means of policy and thereby produce outcomes that other leaders might not have produced if put into the same historical situation.[15] Viewed from this perspective, Samuels observes succinctly, "Cavour engineered a liberal Italy free of foreign domination and, in the bargain won unification as well. Itō produced a constitutional order that protected imperial prerogative and limited popular influence. Yamagata built authoritarianism into the modern Japanese state."[16]

The Question of Democracy in the Era of Party Government, 1918–1932

However, to reiterate, the state was not so authoritarian as to preclude a shift of power to the political parties. After Hara's assassination by a right-wing fanatic in November 1921, there was a brief hiatus of non-party cabinets that lasted until June 1924, but from then to May 1932, cabinets were formed by either the Kenseikai–Minseitō (June 1924–April 1927 and July 1929–December 1931) or the Seiyūkai (April 1927–July 1929 and December 1931–May 1932). What did party government mean for Japan politically and how far did democracy come to prevail in this period?

The approach of some historians to these questions is to focus on the role of the parties in maintaining the continuity of constitutional government. Not much, if any, attention is paid to the theme of "democracy." Gordon Berger, an authority on the parties, exemplifies this approach. He writes, "By 1918, the parties had already begun to demonstrate their ability to use their ties with nonparty elites to assume the collective *genrō* function of harmonizing political, bureaucratic and economic pressures."[17] They carried out this same function after 1918 with the result that "As molders of elite coalitions, they stabilized the fragile cabinet system created by the Meiji oligarchs."[18]

Then there are those who address the issue of Japanese "democracy," but chiefly with a view to qualifying its significance. To cite just one example, Bernard Silberman asserts: "the period of democratic experimentation, 'Taishō democracy,' was a period of limited pluralism at best. It was a period in which parties and other organizations within a very narrow ideological range were allowed to compete for a share of power and not for control of power."[19] Skeptics on the question of democracy typically make the following points. First, small in membership and tied to influential local interests and big business (especially the zaibatsu), upon which they relied heavily for election campaign funds, the parties in power concentrated on reaching compromises with other, more conservative, political elites to stay in power. This stance prevented any serious challenge to the authoritarian framework of the Meiji constitution. The independence of the supreme command, for example, always remained a bridge too far for the parties, both in and out of government. Second, ideologically, very few party politicians were liberals. The true liberals, such as Yoshino Sakuzō who advocated that government should serve all the people and that policy should always take popular opinion into account, stood outside of and criticized the "established parties" for their conservatism.

Third, to be sure, the victory of democracy over autocracy in the 1917 Russian Revolution and in World War I, the 1918 rice riots, and growing labor unrest amidst the postwar recession, all inspired popular demands for democratic reform in 1920s Japan. Visions of freedom, equality, and justice were variously expressed in terms of liberalism, Marxism, and other varieties of socialism, anarchism, and eventually communism, in the labor and tenant farmer union movements, the student movement, the women's movement, the movement to liberate the *burakumin* (Japan's pariahs), and the new social democratic parties that arose in the late 1920s.

However, for all this popular ferment in the era of "Taishō democracy," Peter Duus states that "Aside from the passage of universal [manhood] suffrage in 1925, the one major landmark of the period, it is difficult to discern any large political or social changes wrought by the parties, even by the reform-minded Kenseikai."[20] The significance of this "one major landmark" is typically overshadowed in narratives which stress that the Peace Preservation Law was also enacted in 1925, primarily to suppress the revolutionary Japanese Communist Party which was established in 1922. By contrast other historians, while conceding the force of some of these arguments, contend that in important respects democracy was stronger in interwar Japan than is usually thought. The case for this view partly rests on the belief that if democratic government is basically government by elected representatives of the people whom the people can hold accountable at the polls, then party government from 1918 to 1932 was democratic government. The case for democracy, as it were, also depends in some measure on depicting a generally favorable context for party government in the 1920s.

Here, the argument goes like something like this. Admittedly, uneven economic growth, manifested in a cycle of recessions and spurts and in a lag between a stagnating agricultural sector and a strengthening industrial sector, contributed to an unstable economic context. Contemporary Japanese criticisms of the zaibatsu for amassing too much wealth inevitably rebounded against the parties when corruption scandals involving party politicians and big business frequently made front-page news. Otherwise, the context in which party government operated was more propitious. The rise of a mass society, the growth of the middle class, the diversity of choice in an expanding consumer culture, the experimentation with new Western lifestyles, and the proliferation of the mass media (including radio, from 1925), all represented and nurtured a greater pluralism in Japanese society, thought, and culture. This pluralist trend, which was most conspicuous in urban Japan, indirectly supported the ascendancy of a "parliamentary ideology" that "situated the practice of parliamentary politics at the center and imperial authority at the legitimating circumference, rather than the reverse" as in the Meiji period.[21] Furthermore, the fact that a relative peace prevailed in East Asia during the 1920s allowed party cabinets to pursue an internationalist policy of "cooperative diplomacy" and free trade while cutting military appropriations, as required of Japan by the Washington Naval Limitation Treaty (1922). Politically, as well, the dropping in 1913 of the provision, introduced by Yamagata in 1900, that army and navy ministers had to be officers on active duty, somewhat strengthened the hand of party government vis-à-vis the military, for that provision had threatened to make it easier for a service minister to bring down a cabinet by resigning. After the provision was restored in 1936, army ministers often did just that.

No historian writing recently has done more to put the theme of Japanese democracy back on the front burner than Andrew Gordon, in his book *Labor and Imperial Democracy in Prewar Japan.* Whereas the term "Taishō democracy" predominates in both Western and Japanese accounts, Gordon proposes the term "imperial democracy," signifying democracy centered on emperor and empire. "Imperial democracy" indeed makes more sense than "Taishō democracy," a term which has always obliged historians to explain that they are referring to democratic ideas and practices that originated before, and continued after, the reign of Emperor Taishō (1912–26). Drawing a distinction between "imperial democracy as a movement" prior to 1918 and "imperial democracy as a structure of rule" from 1918 to 1932, Gordon traces the evolution of a lively "dispute culture" of protest, as found among the workers in the Nankatsu district of Tokyo. He concludes, "the 1920s saw more than a short, superficial fling with a democratic fad. The idioms and ideas of empire, emperor, *and* democracy reached deep into Japanese society."[22] That it ultimately took the combined crises of the Great Depression, right-wing terrorism, and the Manchurian Incident to destroy "imperial democracy as a structure of rule" in the early 1930s attests to the tenacity of "imperial democracy."

It is useful to consider Sheldon Garon's book *The State and Labor in Modern Japan* alongside Gordon's work, for although Garon is less explicitly concerned with the theme of democracy, his discussion of what the parties in power actually did, or tried to do, in the area of public policy bears indirectly on the general issue of Japanese democracy. Here, it matters that at the time, and in retrospect, the Kenseikai and Seiyūkai were quite different in outlook. Before he took office in 1918 Hara had built up the Seiyūkai, for example through patronage to cultivate the local support of prominent rural elites (*meibōka*). But its reliance on these local elites, and the need to compromise with the oligarchs on the road to power, had made the Seiyūkai politically conservative. Hara and his party were instinctively fearful of labor unions and other organizations that championed democratic reform on behalf of "the people."

Not so the Kenseikai which, under the leadership of Hara's rival Katō Takaaki, had followed a more progressive political trajectory: "the Kenseikai and its successor, the Minseitō, took on the trappings of a liberal party intent on attracting the new votes of workers, tenant farmers, and middle-class urbanites."[23] This more pluralist vision informed the Kenseikai's social policies during Katō's tenure as prime minister from June 1924 to January 1926, and those of his Minseitō successors. The result was cooperation with the moderately socialist Japan General Federation of Labor (Nihon Rōdō Sōdōmei) and its political ally, the Social Democratic Party (Shakai Minshūtō), to legislate reforms benefiting the workers. Significantly, progressive "social bureaucrats" in the Social Bureau of the Home Ministry embraced much the same vision and the same strategy. They were neither "liberals" nor "democrats," but rather men who regarded social policies adapted from enlightened Western precedents as the most effective means of containing class conflict and ensuring public order through improved public welfare. Therefore, it was natural that they would work closely with the Kenseikai–Minseitō. Such cooperation was also politically necessary: "meaningful labor legislation would not have emerged from the Home Ministry, much less introduced to the Diet, had it not been for the crucial support by the Kenseikai and Minseitō cabinets."[24] This was true for instance of the Labor Disputes Conciliation Law (enacted in 1926) and even more so of the long campaign to legalize labor unions in the 1920s. This campaign ultimately failed when the House of Peers rejected the union bill put forward in 1931. Nevertheless, that it had been sustained for years against the entrenched resistance of employers and their supporters in the upper house suggests the buoyancy of progressive reform in the era of party government.

Garon's bureaucrats, who contributed much to this drive for reform, reappear in Sally Hastings' more recent study of the working-class ward of Honjo, in Tokyo. She calls them "participation bureaucrats" to highlight their inclusive vision in which "all subjects of the Japanese emperor, without regard for religion, ethnicity, or wealth, would share in both the benefits and the responsibilities of empire."[25] Hastings shows that these bureaucrats indeed encouraged ordinary folk in places like Honjo to participate in all manner of local neighborhood organizations and activities. Of course, this kind of popular participation did not necessarily denote "democracy," and "democracy" was scarcely the dream of the "participation bureaucrats." But by the 1930s voting in elections had become very important to people in Honjo: "For the three-quarters of the electorate in this district who were not enfranchised until 1925, the election politics of the early Shōwa years were more democratic than the Taishō era had been."[26] Hastings concludes that Japan was a "semi-democracy," at least until the eruption of the "China Incident" in July 1937.

The overall picture emerging from these debates on the question of democracy is one of a two-party system in which the conservative Seiyūkai and the reform-minded Kenseikai–Minseitō offered voters a genuine choice at the polls. Another distinctive feature of the era of party government is rising levels of popular participation in Japanese political life. In the 1928 national election, the first since universal manhood suffrage gave the vote to men aged 25 or older, the electorate came to 12.5 million voters or 21 percent of the population. That election was also the first to be contested by social democratic parties appealing to the workers, tenant farmers, and the urban and rural lower middle class. Greater popular participation was likewise apparent both in the growth of organized protest movements demanding a larger share of wealth and power for their members and in the vitality of other organized community activities in places like Honjo.

All of this surely amounts to something more than "limited pluralism." If it also adds up to something less than a well-developed democracy, that is to be expected considering the conservative nature of the Meiji constitutional order and the fact that Japan's experiment in party government had begun so recently, in 1918. Nor is it surprising that loyalty to the imperial house and fidelity to maintaining the empire were the necessary preconditions of democratic discourse and activity in 1920s Japan.

When the radical left pursued the goal of proletarian democracy by aggressively attacking emperor and empire, this course only led to its own destruction.

The Question of Fascism, 1932–1941

Did Japan take a "fascist" turn in the decade prior to the Pearl Harbor attack, which triggered World War II in Asia and the Pacific? Although historians debate this question they do not fundamentally disagree when it comes to narrating what happened politically in 1930s Japan. First, there is a broad consensus that what drove the "established" parties from power in 1932 was a lethal confluence of factors, including the devastating economic and social impact of the Depression on rural and urban Japan, the uproar over the disadvantageous terms for Japan in the 1930 London Naval Treaty, and the crisis of the Manchurian Incident. From these explosive conditions there arose a violent right-wing reaction against party government, the "selfish" zaibatsu and the capitalist system itself.

This extremist movement of militant young officers and civilian terrorists called for a new "Restoration" to redeem Japan from sectarian conflict, social injustice, "decadent" Western influences, and above all a weak, deadlocked government that could be displaced only through a *coup d'état* leading to military rule in the name of the emperor. No coup took place, but the movement claimed the lives of the Minseitō prime minister Hamaguchi Osachi, former finance minister Inoue Junnosuke, the head of the Mitsui zaibatsu Dan Takuma, and in the May 15, 1932 "Incident," the Seiyūkai prime minister Inukai Tsuyoshi, whose assassination brought an end to party government in prewar Japan.

It was not clear, however, that the parties would remain out of power for long. To be sure, the army opposed the continuation of party cabinets and for several years, ironically, the Minseitō and the leading social democratic party in the 1930s, the Shakai Taishūtō, preferred "national unity" cabinets to the alternative of seeing the Seiyūkai back in power. But as late as April 1937, just three months prior to the eruption of war with China, the liberal commentator Baba Tsunego wrote, "I think that in the fairly near future a united parties' [Seiyūkai–Minseitō] cabinet will emerge and the period of party cabinets return again."[27] Unfortunately for the parties, however, Baba was mistaken. They still played an active role in the Diet and "retained considerable power even under extremely adverse conditions in the late 1930s and wartime years."[28] But the parties had to wait until after Japan's defeat in 1945 before they could resume power.

Second, historical narratives commonly emphasize that the eleven prewar cabinets following Inukai's, including five led by a civilian prime minister and six others headed by an admiral or a general, all reflected the gradual political ascendancy of the military.[29] Mounting concerns about national security in the face of perceived foreign threats spurred Japan's other political elites, including the major parties, to defer to the military as their own interests were safeguarded. The political and labor groups comprising the social democratic movement deferred, too, for the same reason.[30] The turning point in the military's rising political fortunes was the swift suppression of the young officers and units under their command in the February 1936 army rebellion, after which the army's Control Faction attained a hegemonic position of power.[31] But the military still had to operate within the framework of the Meiji constitutional system; it still had to cope with the paradox of a highly centralized state in which power was fragmented among competing elites without an effective unifying mechanism. Even during World War II, "Beneath the veneer of national unity, political competition remained intense among and within political elites and the Meiji political order strained to confine conflicts within boundaries permitting stable government."[32]

Third, there is little disagreement among historians that Japan in the 1930s was more authoritarian than it had been in the Meiji period. The communist movement was crushed. Professor Minobe Tatsukichi's longstanding "emperor-organ" theory was denounced in the Diet and disowned by the government in 1935 because it qualified the emperor's prerogatives. Prominent public figures, including members of the Diet, who dared to criticize Japanese aggression overseas were accused of being unpatriotic. The emperor cult, which dated from the Meiji period, now became the focus of a virulent nationalism based on assertions of Japanese racial purity and superiority, affirmations of an authentically Japanese national identity, and visions of Japan as the armed liberator of Asia from Western imperialism and international communism.

Finally, historians agree that the emergency of all-out war with China beginning in 1937 dramatically quickened the process of building an impregnable "national defense state" (*kokubō kokka*). By 1937 this project, which began in the early 1930s, had already led to Japan's recovery from the Depression through industrial rationalization and increased military spending. By the mid 1930s as well, army reformers like General Ishiwara Kanji, "revisionist bureaucrats," and influential intellectuals in the Shōwa Kenkyūkai (Shōwa Research Society) who looked to economic models in Germany and Italy, advocated the urgent need for central economic planning, the rapid development of military-related heavy industries in Japan and elsewhere in the empire, and the further empowerment of the state to mobilize Japan economically for the possibility of total war, as in the 1938 National Mobilization Law.[33]

Mobilization on this scale was also seen to require selected changes of the existing government structure, to concentrate power more efficiently, and to provide greater coordination and unity between ministries. The first steps in this endeavor were the creation of new "superagencies" such as the Manchurian Affairs Bureau in 1934 and the Cabinet Research Bureau in 1935. The next steps, taken in 1940 when Prime Minister Prince Konoe Fumimaro inaugurated the "New Order," were more ambitious: the dissolution of all the political parties into the new Imperial Rule Assistance Association (IRRA), the dissolution of labor organizations into a patriotic labor front, and the organization of other such fronts under government control.

The definition of "fascism" is vigorously contested among historians of both modern Europe and modern Japan.[34] But if one accepts the following definition recently advanced by Robert Paxton, then some aspects of political life in 1930s Japan as I have summarized it would indeed appear to be "fascist":

> Fascism may be defined as a form of political behavior marked by obsessive preoccupation with community decline, humiliation, or victimhood and by compensatory cults of unity, energy, and purity, in which a mass-based party of committed nationalist militants,

working in uneasy collaboration with traditional elites, abandons democratic liberties and pursues with redemptive violence and without ethical or legal restraints goals of internal cleansing and external expansion.[35]

Certainly, Japanese historians down through the years have typically portrayed 1930s Japan as "fascist," using such descriptive terms as "military fascism," "bureaucratic fascism," "emperor-system fascism," "cool fascism," and so forth. In Maruyama Masao's well-known formula, the suppression of the army rebellion in 1936 signified the defeat of terrorist "fascism from below" and the victory of "fascism from above," culminating in the "New Order" of 1940.[36]

The argument that Japan became a "fascist" country in the 1930s crops up now and then in Western historiography too. For instance, in the last chapter of *Labor and Imperial Democracy*, Gordon sees sufficient parallels between Japan, Germany, and Italy to argue that "imperial democracy" yielded to "imperial fascism" in 1930s Japan. In particular, he highlights the priority in Japan of "mobilizing the populace in organized fashion to serve self-proclaimed 'national' goals under the aegis of the state."[37] Since the same priority prevailed in Germany and Italy, he thinks that fascism as a construct has the merit of facilitating comparisons of mobilization in Japan, Germany, and Italy. Yet other studies have demonstrated that useful comparisons can be drawn of mobilization in Japan, Germany, and Italy without insisting that Japan was "fascist,"[38] and in any case it is unlikely that the notion of "imperial fascism" will persuade Western historians who do not accept that Japan took a "fascist" turn.[39] As Peter Duus and Daniel Okimoto argued forcefully some time ago, the concept of "fascism" is widely thought to be too Eurocentric to apply to imperial Japan. It is not clear, though, that their proposed alternative, "corporatism," which theoretically encompasses a wider range of countries (the Soviet Union, the United States, and Great Britain, as well as Japan, Germany, and Italy), is really more useful than the concept of "fascism" for the purposes of historical comparison.[40]

Kato Shūichi's interpretation cuts straight to the heart of the matter: "The history of Japan between the two wars must be understood not as a shift from a democracy (of the British type) to a fascism (of the Nazi type), but as a shift from a phase of liberalization to another phase of bureaucratization and militarization within a political structure which had not basically changed."[41] "Bureaucratization" captures the essence of the "New Order." The IRAA ended up as an amorphous "public body" because the bureaucracy, the "established parties" (which continued to function in the Diet after their formal dissolution), and big business all vehemently opposed the attempt by the army and "revisionist bureaucrats" to make the IRAA a totalitarian mass-based political party such as existed in European fascism.[42] Similarly, militarization produced a leader, General Tōjō Hideki (appointed prime minister in October 1941), who was hardly a führer or a duce. Nothing comparable to the Führerprinzip, or "leadership principle," in European fascism existed in Japan, for that would have compromised the supreme authority of the imperial house.

Doubtless the question of Japanese fascism, like the questions of oligarchy and democracy, will be debated for years to come. But in my opinion the last words, for now at least, on the issue of Japanese "fascism" come from two historians who comment on 1930s Japan after years of studying and writing about fascism in Europe. The first is Stanley Payne:

Japan had evolved a somewhat pluralistic authoritarian system which exhibited some of the characteristics of fascism, but it did not develop fascism's most distinctive and revolutionary aspects. Japan was never subjected to the same degree of radicalization, for imperial Japan on the eve of World War II in many ways approximated the development of Germany's Second Reich more than it did Hitler's nation.[43]

The second is Paxton. He acknowledges some Japanese "structural analogies to Germany and Italy," but stresses that, unlike Germany and Italy, Japan "faced no imminent revolutionary threat." Paxton then concludes, "Though the imperial regime used techniques of mass mobilization, no official party or autonomous grassroots movement competed with the leaders. The Japanese empire of the period 1932–45 is better understood as an expansionist military dictatorship [*sic*] with a high degree of state-sponsored mobilization than as a fascist regime."[44]

NOTES

1   Silberman, "The Bureaucratic State," p. 226.
2   Hackett, *Yamagata Aritomo.*
3   Hackett, "Political Modernization and the Meiji Genrō," pp. 95–6.
4   Akita, *Foundations of Constitutional Government*, p. 66.
5   Duus, *Party Rivalry and Political Change*, p. 86.
6   Silberman, *Cages of Reason*, p. 221.
7   Johnson, *MITI and the Japanese Miracle*, p. 37.
8   Ramseyer and Rosenbluth, *The Politics of Oligarchy*, p. 39.
9   Mitani, "The Establishment of Party Cabinets," pp. 59–64.
10 Masuda, "The Emperor's Right of Supreme Command," p. 79.
11 Dickinson, *War and National Reinvention*, p. 220.
12 Ramseyer and Rosenbluth, *The Politics of Oligarchy*, pp. 161, 198 n. 2.
13 Gownder and Pekkanen, "The End of Political Science?"
14 This theme is documented in Large, *Emperor Hirohito*, chs. 2, 4, and 5.
15 Samuels, *Machiavelli's Children*, pp. 1, 5–6.
16 Ibid., p. 41.
17 Berger, *Parties Out of Power*, pp. 8–9.
18 Berger, "Politics and Mobilization," p. 98.
19 Silberman, "The Bureaucratic State," p. 254 (italics original).
20 Duus, *Party Rivalry*, p. 248.
21 Gluck, *Japan's Modern Myths*, p. 237.
22 Gordon, *Labor and Imperial Democracy*, p. 233 (italics original).
23 Garon, *The State and Labor*, p. 136.
24 Ibid., p. 122.
25 Hastings, *Neighborhood and Nation*, p. 12.
26 Ibid., p. 192.
27 Quoted from Banno, *Democracy in Prewar Japan*, pp. 168–9.
28 Berger, *Parties Out of Power*, p. 358.
29 Note that of the five cabinets headed by a civilian prime minister, three were formed by Prince Konoe Fumimaro (June 1937–Jan. 1939, July 1940–July 1941, and July–Oct. 1941).
30 Large, *Organized Workers*, chs. 6–8.
31 Shillony, *Revolt in Japan.*
32 Berger, "Politics and Mobilization," p. 152.

33 Barnhart, *Japan Prepares for Total War*; Peattie, *Ishiwara Kanji*; and Fletcher, *The Search for a New Order*.
34 McCormack, "Nineteen-Thirties Japan."
35 Paxton, *The Anatomy of Fascism*, p. 218.
36 Maruyama, "The Ideology and Dynamics of Japanese Fascism," pp. 65–80.
37 Gordon, *Labor and Imperial Democracy*, p. 317.
38 Kasza, *The Conscription Society*, and Brooker, *The Faces of Fraternalism*. Brooker found that Japanese efforts to mobilize society using traditionalist methods were more successful than mobilization in Germany and Italy.
39 For example, see Kasza, "Fascism from Above?" and Wilson, *Radical Nationalist in Japan*, which criticizes the idea that Kita Ikki was a "fascist" thinker.
40 Duus and Okimoto, "Fascism and the History of Prewar Japan."
41 Kato, "Taishō Democracy," p. 236.
42 Berger, *Parties Out of Power*, ch. 7.
43 Payne, *A History of Fascism*, p. 336.
44 Paxton, *The Anatomy of Fascism*, p. 200.

BIBLIOGRAPHY

Akita, George. *Foundations of Constitutional Government in Modern Japan, 1868–1900*. Cambridge, Mass.: Harvard University Press, 1967.

Banno Junji. *Democracy in Prewar Japan: Concepts of Government, 1871–1937*, trans. Andrew Fraser. London: Routledge, 2001.

Barnhart, Michael. *Japan Prepares for Total War: The Search for Economic Security, 1919–1941*. Ithaca, NY: Cornell University Press, 1987.

Berger, Gordon. *Parties Out of Power in Japan, 1931–1941*. Princeton: Princeton University Press, 1977.

Berger, Gordon. "Politics and Mobilization in Japan, 1931–1945." In Peter Duus, ed., *The Cambridge History of Japan*, vol. 6, *The Twentieth Century*. Cambridge: Cambridge University Press, 1988.

Brooker, Paul. *The Faces of Fraternalism: Nazi Germany, Fascist Italy, and Imperial Japan*. Oxford: Clarendon Press, 1991.

Dickinson, Frederick. *War and National Reinvention: Japan in the Great War, 1914–1919*. Cambridge, Mass.: Harvard University Asia Center, 1999.

Duus, Peter. *Party Rivalry and Political Change in Taishō Japan*. Cambridge, Mass.: Harvard University Press, 1968.

Duus, Peter, and Okimoto, Daniel. "Fascism and the History of Prewar Japan: The Failure of a Concept." *Journal of Asian Studies* 39:1 (1979): 65–76.

Fletcher, W. Miles. *The Search for a New Order: Intellectuals and Fascism in Prewar Japan*. Chapel Hill: University of North Carolina Press, 1982.

Garon, Sheldon. *The State and Labor in Modern Japan*. Berkeley: University of California Press, 1987.

Gluck, Carol. *Japan's Modern Myths: Ideology in the Late Meiji Period*. Princeton: Princeton University Press, 1985.

Gordon, Andrew. *Labor and Imperial Democracy in Prewar Japan*. Berkeley: University of California Press, 1991.

Gownder, Joseph, and Pekkanen, Robert. "The End of Political Science? Rational Choice Analyses in Studies of Japanese Politics." *Journal of Japanese Studies* 22 (1996): 363–84.

Hackett, Roger. "Political Modernization and the Meiji Genrō." In Robert Ward, ed., *Political Development in Modern Japan*. Princeton: Princeton University Press, 1968.

Hackett, Roger. *Yamagata Aritomo in the Rise of Modern Japan, 1838–1922.* Cambridge, Mass.: Harvard University Press, 1971.

Hastings, Sally A. *Neighborhood and Nation in Tokyo, 1905–1937.* Pittsburgh: University of Pittsburgh Press, 1995.

Johnson, Chalmers. *MITI and the Japanese Miracle: The Growth of Industrial Policy, 1925–1975.* Stanford, Calif.: Stanford University Press, 1982.

Kasza, Gregory. *The Conscription Society: Administered Mass Organizations.* New Haven: Yale University Press, 1995.

Kasza, Gregory. "Fascism from Above? Japan's Kakushin Right in Comparative Perspective." In Stein Ugelvik Larsen, ed., *Fascism Outside Europe: The European Impulse against Domestic Conditions in the Diffusion of Global Fascism.* New York: Columbia University Press, 2001.

Kato, Shūichi. "Taishō Democracy as the Pre-Stage for Japanese Militarism." In Bernard Silberman and H. D. Harootunian, eds., *Japan in Crisis: Essays on Taishō Democracy.* Princeton: Princeton University Press, 1974.

Large, Stephen. *Organized Workers and Socialist Politics in Interwar Japan.* Cambridge: Cambridge University Press, 1981.

Large, Stephen. *Emperor Hirohito and Shōwa Japan: A Political Biography.* London: Routledge, 1992.

Maruyama Masao. "The Ideology and Dynamics of Japanese Fascism." In Maruyama Masao, *Thought and Behavior in Modern Japanese Politics,* ed. Ivan Morris. Oxford: Oxford University Press, 1963.

Masuda, T. "The Emperor's Right of Supreme Command as Exercised up to 1930: A Study based especially on the Takarabe and Kuratomi Diaries." *Acta Asiatica* 59 (1990): 77–100.

McCormack, Gavan. "Nineteen-Thirties Japan: Fascism?" *Bulletin of Concerned Asian Scholars* 14:2 (1982): 15–34.

Mitani Taichirō. "The Establishment of Party Cabinets, 1898–1932." In Peter Duus, ed., *The Cambridge History of Modern Japan,* vol. 6, *The Twentieth Century.* Cambridge: Cambridge University Press, 1988.

Payne, Stanley. *A History of Fascism, 1914–45.* Madison: University of Wisconsin Press, 1995.

Paxton, Robert. *The Anatomy of Fascism.* New York: Knopf, 2004.

Peattie, Mark. *Ishiwara Kanji and Japan's Confrontation with the West.* Princeton: Princeton University Press, 1975.

Ramseyer, J. Mark, and Rosenbluth, Frances M. *The Politics of Oligarchy: Institutional Choice in Imperial Japan.* Cambridge: Cambridge University Press, 1995.

Samuels, Richard. *Machiavelli's Children: Leaders and Their Legacies in Italy and Japan.* Ithaca, NY: Cornell University Press, 2003.

Shillony, Ben-Ami. *Revolt in Japan: The Young Officers and the February 26, 1936 Incident.* Princeton: Princeton University Press, 1973.

Silberman, Bernard. "The Bureaucratic State in Japan: The Problem of Authority and Legitimacy." In Tetsuo Najita and J. Victor Koschmann, eds., *Conflict in Modern Japanese History: The Neglected Tradition.* Princeton: Princeton University Press, 1982.

Silberman, Bernard. *Cages of Reason: The Rise of the Rational State in France, Japan, the United States, and Great Britain.* Chicago: University of Chicago Press, 1993.

Wilson, George. *Radical Nationalist in Japan: Kita Ikki, 1883–1937.* Cambridge, Mass.: Harvard University Press, 1969.

FURTHER READING

For an authoritative survey, see R. L. Sims, *Japanese Political History Since the Meiji Renovation, 1868–2000* (London: Palgrave Macmillan, 2001). Valuable portraits of

Itō Hirobumi, Ōkuma Shigenobu, Hara Takashi (Kei), Inukai Tsuyoshi, and Saionji Kinmochi are presented in Oka Yoshitake, *Five Political Leaders of Modern Japan* (Tokyo: University of Tokyo Press, 1986). Further studies of the oligarchy include Banno Junji, *The Establishment of the Japanese Constitutional System*, trans. J. A. A. Stockwin (London: Routledge, 1992); Stewart Lone, *Army, Empire and Politics in Meiji Japan* (Basingstoke: Macmillan, 2000), which sheds new light on the complex political relationship between Yamagata Aritomo and Katsura Tarō; and Shumpei Okamoto, *The Japanese Oligarchy and the Russo-Japanese War* (New York: Columbia University Press, 1970).

Two excellent studies which bear on the issue of democracy are Tetsuo Najita, *Hara Kei in the Politics of Compromise, 1905–1915* (Cambridge, Mass.: Harvard University Press, 1967), and Sharon Minichiello, *Retreat from Reform: Patterns of Political Behavior in Interwar Japan* (Honolulu: University of Hawai'i Press, 1984). For a nuanced discussion of democracy by a leading Japanese historian, see Matsuo Takayoshi, "The Development of Democracy in Japan – Taishō Democracy: Its Flowering and Breakdown," *Developing Economies* 4:4 (1966): 612–37. Contrasting Japanese perspectives on the question of fascism are Ishida Takeshi, "Elements of Tradition and 'Renovation' in Japan during the 'Era of Fascism' " in his book, *Japanese Political Culture: Change and Continuity* (New Brunswick, NJ: Transaction Books, 1983), and Hayashi Kentarō, "Japan and Germany in the Interwar Period," in James Morley, ed., *Dilemmas of Growth in Prewar Japan* (Princeton: Princeton University Press, 1971). Some intriguing Western perspectives are found in a recent book, E. Bruce Reynolds, ed., *Japan in the Fascist Era* (New York: Palgrave Macmillan, 2004).

CHAPTER TEN

Social and Economic Change in Prewar Japan

Mark Jones and Steven Ericson

How did the big name processes of modernity – political revolution, state formation, industrialization, urbanization, imperialism, wartime mobilization – change the fabric of society and the texture of daily life in prewar Japan? More specifically, how did the peoples of prewar Japan (ranging from unceremoniously disenfranchised samurai of the 1870s to struggling farmers of the 1890s to the brazen modern girl of the 1920s) make sense of, contribute to, take advantage of, resist, or negotiate the dizzying changes occurring around them? As these questions suggest, the social history of prewar Japan cannot be divorced from economic, political, intellectual, and military history. Yet a history of social change must make sense of macro-level change through micro-level analysis. It must above all else be a human story, one that explains and analyzes how individuals affected and were affected by the modern world taking shape around them.

Over the past quarter century (1980–2005), English-language historians of prewar Japan have clarified and complicated our understanding of the transformative processes and human actors at the heart of the major social changes that occurred between the Meiji Restoration (1868) and the beginning of Japan's undeclared war with China (1937). To be sure, they neither speak with one voice nor share a common evaluation of modernity's effect on the individual. Diverse as their works are in topic and viewpoint, these historians nonetheless collectively represent a new generation of interpreters of Japan's modern social transformation. Their scholarship revises older schools of thought and breaks new ground in the study of prewar Japan's social history. To begin with, their stories are full of conflict, for these scholars emphasize that Japan's modernization, once thought to be smooth and successful, was in fact fraught with debate and division, suasion and negotiation, coercion and repression. Furthermore, their stories brim with a panoply of human actors motivated by disparate interests, for these historians try to move beyond older historical paradigms that posited two homogenous groups – the state and the people – as the driving forces of social change in prewar Japan. In addition, their stories are replete with new voices, as these historians turn to the lives of marginalized or underexamined populations (ethnic minorities, female factory workers, members of the middle class) to illuminate significant aspects of Japan's modern social history. Finally, their stories are filled with global comparisons and contrasts, as they try to understand Japan's social transformation as an instance of the modern, one that was not an example of Western influence and Japanese imitation but a story of comparisons and commonalities in modern social experience within and across national borders.

Meanwhile, studies on Japan's prewar economy have shifted over the last half-century from the pioneering though yet to be superseded overviews of G. C. Allen and W. W. Lockwood and subsequent works dealing with such macro issues as the nature of entrepreneurship[1] to detailed analyses of specific modern industries and enterprises.[2] Regardless of their research focus, however, economic historians have continued to grapple with certain broad interpretive questions, including the contribution of agriculture, the timing of Japan's industrial revolution, the role of the state, and the connection between militarism and industrialization. Two recent books by David Howell and Kären Wigen suggest potential new directions, as they challenge conventional views of Japanese economic modernization by addressing issues of uneven development from a regional, trans-Restoration perspective.[3]

State and Society

Hovering over the history and historiography of prewar Japan is the state. After the Meiji Restoration, the Japanese state not only moved to transfigure economic foundations and political institutions but also committed itself to the wholesale restructuring of society and the mobilization of the people, whether through the institution of compulsory elementary education (1872) and military conscription (1873) or through the abolition of status distinctions (1876). In Japan's case, the speed with which this transformation occurred begged for explanation; and, during the 1960s and 1970s, two schools of historians emerged to investigate the respective roles of the state and the people in these rapid social revolutions. The modernization school, largely populated by American and British historians, described Japan's modern metamorphosis in sunny, inspirational tones. "Japan is the first of a class of nations that now occupies a large part of our attention: the underdeveloped, non-Western society determined to modernize herself. So far, she is the only one that has succeeded," wrote one such scholar in 1965.[4] These historians saw the state as a dominant and enlightened force in promoting Japan's modernization and the population as a pliant yet capable mass able to be guided toward modern ways. A second group known as the *minshūshi* ("people's history") school, consisting mostly of Japanese historians, stressed the state's repression of the popular will in the course of enacting its social revolution from above. *Minshūshi* scholars, including Irokawa Daikichi, emphasized how the creative energies of the people were quashed by a government primarily interested in creating a submissive, obedient citizenry.[5]

Now, a newer generation of scholars is challenging the work of these earlier historians and, in the process, complicating our understanding of state–society relations. Nowhere is this trend clearer than in the field of educational history. In the earliest efforts to explain Japan's seemingly speedy and seamless modernization, scholars such as Ronald Dore and Herbert Passin explored what they took to be a significant part of the story: how the Meiji state created a literate, patriotic citizenry through the newly instituted elementary educational system. Their work emphasized the helpful "legacies" (Dore's word) of a late Tokugawa "education boom" and the relative ease with which the Meiji state was able to channel popular enthusiasm for education into participation in the state-sponsored school system.[6] Brian Platt, by contrast, challenges the view of the state's imposition of mandatory schooling as a smooth, uncontested process. By combining a trans-Restoration chronology with local history methodology (a combination employed by an increasing number of historians of nineteenth-century Japan), Platt positions himself to evaluate, in microcosm, the efficacy of the Tokugawa legacy and the ease of Meiji state formation. In a rebuttal to one of the fundamental premises of modernization theory, Platt judges the Tokugawa legacy as obstacle as much as aid. "Rather than ensuring the success of the Meiji government's educational project, this legacy altered the terms of the dialogue through which the new system took shape," he writes.[7] In other words, local schoolteachers and village notables in Nagano prefecture, albeit undeniably enthusiastic about education, also came armed with their own understanding of proper schooling inherited from the pre-Restoration years. Often with great detail and local flavor, Platt makes the important point that the Tokugawa legacy was not black and white, neither entirely help nor entirely hindrance. It was, nonetheless, a legacy that the Meiji government was unable to wantonly ignore or override.

Moreover, Platt's work contributes to an ongoing and important rethinking of the dynamics of state–society relations, especially during the crucial decades of the 1870s and 1880s. In Platt's view, compulsory education and other social transformations were neither simply the work of state officials nor the product of a unitary governmental vision. In Platt's narrative, the local engaged in an ongoing "dialogue" with the national during the 1870s and 1880s, in large part because the views of Nagano villagers were not always consistent with post-Restoration statist visions of an effective educational system. Here, however, Platt's story is not how local communities were overpowered by the Meiji state, as *minshūshi* scholars had it, but, rather, "how local people, brimming with their own ideas about education and their own memories of crisis and restoration, negotiated the formation of the new order in their communities."[8] In the process, they became influential and willing participants in the nation-building project.

Platt's work builds upon the insights Carol Gluck offers in *Japan's Modern Myths*, a seminal contribution to the field of prewar social history. In simplest terms, Gluck chronicles how the Meiji era witnessed not the birth of a singular, state-authored blueprint of social transformation but, rather, the release of a cacophony of voices – some associated with the state, others not; some critical of the state, others not – but each with its own viewpoint. In Gluck's hands, the Meiji era is no longer a time characterized by top-down social change; instead, it becomes a time populated by diverse (and heretofore neglected) individuals and social groups, each striving to play a vocal and active role in the remaking of Japanese society.[9]

Mark Lincicome's book, for example, studies one such group, a collection of early Meiji schoolteachers, normal-school professors, junior-level Ministry of Education bureaucrats, and education journalists who worked to introduce the principles of "developmental education" (*kaihatsu kyōiku*) into the national elementary school curriculum. Echoing Gluck's point, Lincicome shows how these teachers and educators, far from the pawns of the state, were driven by a multiplicity of concerns: a need for professional respectability, a desire for autonomy from state bureaucratic mandates, and an eagerness to integrate the global cutting edge of educational theory into Japan's nascent school system. At the same time, these educators were by no means opponents of the nation-building project, though their views differed markedly from the dominant Ministry of Education view, which saw the educational system as a molder of "little citizens" (shōkokumin). While their often combative efforts to introduce Pestalozzian, child-centered educational theory and practice lost out to the Herbartian, morality-centered version, Lincicome's story highlights the contested nature of social change, the varied motivations of "the people," and the multiple visions of the modern that existed during an era once thought to have been dominated by a monolithic state.[10]

The Middle Classes and Modern Life

Gluck's 1985 book also mirrored and engendered the emergence of another important trend in the historiography of prewar Japan: the decentering of the state as a transformative force and the foregrounding of new social groups and individuals crucial to Japan's modern social revolutions. This trend figures most prominently in the field of urban history. Scholarship by Earl Kinmonth, Donald Roden, Jordan Sand, Barbara Sato, and others examines the making of urban society, in particular the emergence of social icons, institutions, and ideologies that defined prewar Japanese society and, moreover, became enduring features of the twentieth-century Japanese social landscape. Their work centers on the emergence of a social group loosely termed the middle classes, a subject of historical inquiry that, until recently, was largely the province of scholars of postwar Japan. By unearthing the history of this social stratum in the pre-1945 years, these historians not only open up new possibilities for examining continuities between the prewar and the postwar years but also flesh out our understanding of the mediators and mechanisms of prewar social change.

These historians locate the emergence of modern social norms and ideals, whether the twentieth-century incarnations of family and childhood, ideals of masculinity and femininity, or practices of leisure and consumerism, in the urban milieu of so-called prewar middle-class society. Their focus, temporally speaking, is the late Meiji and Taishō years (1890s to 1920s) and, geographically speaking, Tokyo. Their human focus is a new group of academicians and professionals who functioned as modernity's middlemen. Neither representatives of the state nor members of the everyday population, these people were educated elites who became spokespeople for and shapers of a new middle-class society. Whether public intellectuals, university professors, child psychologists, or magazine editors, they investigated topics ranging from domestic architecture to sexology to hygiene, often as discrete fields of study (or gaku); disseminated their opinions to a larger public, often in the pages of mass circulation magazines and books; and saw their views consumed by an emerging middle-class population. In the process, these influential figures shaped the urban imagination and transformed the way people thought, acted, and behaved. Jordan Sand, for instance, details "the public construction of the private sphere," as a cadre of early twentieth-century intellectuals, architects, and reformers worked to redesign domestic interiors and, in the process, reshape the notion of family and home for a new Japan. Similarly, Sabine Frühstück studies the work and words of Taishō and early Shōwa era doctors, eugenicists, and sexologists and recounts their role in the construction of modern Japanese attitudes toward the body, sex, and sexuality.[11]

Crucial to the influence of modernity's middlemen were new urban institutions, sites where communities and hierarchies were (re)produced, modern forms of knowledge disseminated, and modern identities fashioned. The mass media was an institution critical to the building and bounding of a middle-class society, and scholars such as Earl Kinmonth, James Huffman, Barbara Sato, and Jordan Sand have begun to examine the role of the mass media as both mirror and maker of social change.[12] Other urban institutions, from the cafe to the department store to higher schools, also played an important yet underexamined role in stratifying society, creating social groups, and offering individuals new sources of identity. For example, Donald Roden analyzes how the prewar institution of elite higher schools (*kōtō gakkō*) "eased the transition from government by a hereditary feudal social class to government by a new middle-class status group of academic achievers."[13]

This new scholarship on a pre-1945 middle class, while tending to focus on the words of its spokespeople, has nonetheless rendered a picture of prewar society full of heretofore unrecognized opportunities for mobility – geographic, social, economic, educational – among a widening swath of the population. This type of work broadens our understanding of modern social change, for it highlights the new-found prospects that modernity offered to the individual. Take, for example, Earl Kinmonth's book *The Self-Made Man in Meiji Japanese Thought*. By focusing on the emergence of the ideal of *risshin shusse* ("success in life") and the iconic male corporate worker known as the "salaryman," Kinmonth makes the case that prewar Japanese society was a land where meritocratic principles mixed with dreams of social mobility to produce a stratum of individuals committed to getting ahead in the world. For these types, self-centered aspiration, not nationalist fervor, was the primary motivator of individual action. More of this type of work – what Japanese historian Amano Ikuo calls "the social history of education as credential" (*gakureki no sha-kaishi*) – needs to be done, since individualist striving through educational achievement became one of the hallmarks of the twentieth-century Japanese social experience.[14]

The field of women's history has also brought to light women's place as individual opportunists within urban society. While earlier work by Sharon Sievers stressed how Japan's modern social transformation oppressed women, newer work on women's history, such as Gail Bernstein's edited volume *Recreating Japanese Women*, strives to recover women's agency, while still recognizing the economic and social constraints faced by women.[15] For example, Barbara Sato poses the question: "Was there not room within the confines of the nation-state for urban women to find agency – be it in the form of changing fashions; attitudes toward work, love, and sexuality; marriage and the family; communication; or personal self-fulfillment?"[16] Sato examines the varied lives of Taishō era housewives, working women, and modern girls and makes clear how modernity opened new avenues for individual expression and social advancement.

The Underside of Modernity

Furnishing a counterweight to the above scholarship is a group of historians who focus less on the opportunities and more on the costs of Japan's social transformation. These historians attempt to understand how the lives of individuals and social groups were rearranged and ultimately reduced by industrialization, nation-building, imperialism, and other modern forces. The title of Mikiso Hane's book – *Peasants, Rebels, and Outcastes: The Underside of Modern Japan* – makes clear the thematic thrust and the human focus of their works.[17] Yet, even within this group of historians, there is argument and dissent, as they quarrel over the quantitative and qualitative effect of modernity on the lives of farmers, factory workers, and ethnic minorities.

The most vociferous debate has occurred in rural history, a field once dominated by Marxist and Marxist-influenced historians practicing on both sides of the Pacific. The Marxist story was, by and large, straightforward: The reforms of the Meiji government, combined with the takeoff into industrial capitalism and the rise of a parasitic landlord system, shifted the rural economy from a moral economy to a market economy, leaving peasants in materially impoverished, spiritually immiserated circumstances, with little agency to exercise and with no paternal figure willing to minister to their needs in times of distress. Central to the Marxist argument was the rise of tenancy disputes during the 1920s and 1930s, which were interpreted as the boiling over of human rage against an exploitative landlord–tenant system. In his 1986 book, Richard Smethurst challenged this argument, suggesting that tenancy disputes should be seen, instead, as a sign of the "entrepreneurial dynamism" of peasants. According to Smethurst, increased living standards and rising expectations among the peasantry impelled them to behave as rational actors and to ask for more – from rent reductions to improved contract terms – in the hopes that protest would bring an even brighter future. His book was met with reviews vitriolic in tone and thunderous in moral outrage, as a number of scholars accused him of overgeneralizing from a narrow case study, misrepresenting the existing scholarship on the tenancy movement, and neglecting the costs of modernization.[18]

Yet scholarship on rural history that has chosen not to engage directly with this polemical debate reveals a more nuanced, evenhanded picture of social change in the modern rural sector. Edward Pratt's book on the *gōnō*, the wealthy peasants once thought to be the primary engine and beneficiary of socioeconomic change across the nineteenth century, captures the slippery ground that village elites found themselves negotiating in the wake of the Meiji Restoration. In Pratt's view, the late Tokugawa and early Meiji village was not a simple, unchanging world of rich peasants and poor peasants. Even rich peasants had their problems. Increasingly subject to the whims of international trade, the vagaries of a protoindustrial economy, and the intrusions of an aggressive state, the social group known as the *gōnō* ultimately dissolved under the weight of Japan's transition to modernity.[19] Like Pratt, Kerry Smith illuminates another epochal transformation in prewar rural society: the onset of the Great Depression and the rise of the rural revitalization movement during the 1930s. While standard accounts point to state directives and handouts as the primary agents of revitalization, Smith, by grounding his work in a local history of Sekishiba village in Fukushima prefecture, effectively shows how the rural was, in many ways, responsible for its own revitalization and how the ideas and actions of the rural influenced national policy, not the other way around. At the same time, Smith refuses to homogenize the rural population, choosing instead to dissect the village's various populations and to examine their particular methods and motives for revitalization. Such attention to the dynamics of social change and the complexities of human behavior makes for compelling social history.[20]

The rural soil was not the only site where modernity's underside was revealed, negotiated, and resisted. Social and political protest also emerged among city dwellers, factory workers, and ethnic minorities, most noticeably in the years following the Russo-Japanese War of 1904–5. Recent work by Michael Weiner and David Howell, for instance, makes clear how protest against marginalization and discrimination was a constitutive part of the lives of prewar ethnic minorities, including Ainu, Koreans, Chinese, and Okinawans. "A critical aspect of the minority experience in modern Japan has been resistance to racialized exclusions, exploitation and oppression," writes Weiner.[21] For Weiner and other historical investigators of prewar popular protest, questions regarding the protesters' agency and mentality are paramount. What social conditions motivated diverse groups to voice their outrage and demand change? Were protesters able to effect change for themselves and others? Patricia Tsurumi's bleak account of female factory workers in the Meiji cotton and silk-reeling mills details the hostile work environment faced by these women, who often found themselves trapped, harassed, and raped within the confines of the modern factory. Tsurumi, however, does not leave these women powerless. By analyzing the songs they intoned on the factory floor, Tsurumi recovers their discordant words of protest – though, as she herself notes, the only truly effective means of protest for these factory girls was escape, often under the cover of nightfall.[22]

Other works on popular protest by Michael Lewis and Andrew Gordon extend Tsurumi's work, both chronologically and thematically, by emphasizing the budding social and political consciousness of early twentieth-century protesters and the increasing efficacy of their efforts. In the works of Lewis and Gordon, protesters appear not simply as individuals degraded by modernity but as peoples transformed, able to combine a longstanding vocabulary of "Confucian benevolence and the responsibility of social 'superiors' " with new politically aware, socially empowered calls for governmental attention to social welfare. The rice riots of 1918 marked an important moment of transition, Lewis argues, as marginalized populations began to engage in "new forms of political involvement" and to invoke their social right to political citizenship.[23] The nation-building project had now transformed even the unenfranchised into vocal, empowered agents for change. Andrew Gordon makes a related point in his sweeping study *Labor and Imperial Democracy in Prewar Japan*. Gordon probes the inner workings of the factory worker's mentality (what he calls "the intellectual world of factory laborers") and paints this modern figure as able to see modernity's underside yet also unwilling to reject modernity. As Gordon writes, the factory worker was, on the one hand, eager to identify "economic insecurity, epitomized by unemployment, and the indignity of low social status, as the essence of the 'inhumanity of capitalism'." On the other hand, worker protests, whether in the form of strikes or unionization efforts during the 1920s, were "a call less to overthrow or replace existing economic or social systems than to transform them and gain access to them on dramatically improved terms."[24] These factory workers saw no contradiction between demanding, often violently, a minimally humane lifestyle due to a citizen of Japan and, at the same time, remaining loyal to the state and the emperor.

Whereas Weiner, Tsurumi, Lewis, and Gordon focus primarily on the worlds of the protesters, an obvious yet often overlooked part of the story of modernity's underside is the response of the powerful, whether state minister, factory manager, or individual landlord, to the plight of the disaffected. Scholarship by Sheldon Garon, Kathleen Uno, and Jeffrey Hanes has begun to address this lacuna and, in the process, offers important insights into the management of modernity's underside. The most important work is Sheldon Garon's *Molding Japanese Minds*. In an analysis of the prewar regulation of groups ranging from prostitutes to new religions, Garon makes two important points: first, how not just the state but also the middle classes, often in collaboration with the state, worked to monitor and manage society's underclass and, second, how the management of social problems was executed more through morality campaigns than repressive force. Kathleen Uno's work supports and extends Garon's thesis, as she examines the role of female middle-class reformers in the establishment and management of day-care facilities that served to scrutinize and socialize the poor, both parents and children. Jeffrey Hanes's biography of Seki Hajime makes a different yet important point: modernity's social ills were global ones, and urban reformers like Seki both drew upon and contributed to a "transnational progressivism" that attempted to comprehend and cure social sicknesses such as urban poverty and public health problems. This emphasis on the global aspects of Japan's social transformation is a welcome addition to the historiography of prewar Japan, for it steers scholars away from an overemphasis on the exceptionality of Japan's modern development. As Hanes and other historians remind us, Japan's modern social transformation, including the evolution of state–society relations, the rise of the middle classes, and the appearance of modernity's underside, possessed both national peculiarities and global commonalities.[25]

Agriculture and Modern Economic Growth

Several questions concerning Japan's economy before World War II continue to spark lively debate among specialists. One long-running but still unresolved controversy centers on the contribution of agriculture to modern economic growth. A group of economists at Hitotsubashi University who in the 1950s began preparing long-term statistics on Japan's economy from the early Meiji period[26] estimated that between 1880 and 1920 agricultural output in Japan grew at an average annual rate of 2.4 percent. In the mid-1960s James Nakamura disputed their findings: correcting for what he claimed were widespread concealment and underreporting of yields in early Meiji, he arrived at a dramatically lower rate of growth of about 1 percent. The debate has major implications for Japanese economic development. According to the older explanation, agriculture was at a low level of productivity in 1868. Then, with the Meiji unification and the spread of traditional best practice, it took off at a rapid pace concurrently with industry; this agricultural spurt created a substantial surplus, the bulk of which the government through its land tax transferred out of agriculture and into industry. By contrast, in Nakamura's view, agriculture had grown considerably before the Meiji period, so the key to Japan's successful industrialization was not the creation of a surplus during the development process but the redistribution of already existing wealth from non-productive samurai to a modernizing regime and invest-ment-minded landowners. Taking into account Nakamura's caveats, Japanese scholars reworked the data to come up with an average growth rate for agriculture of 1.7 percent a year. The downward revision reflects acknowledgment of a much higher starting point for agriculture in 1868 but still allows for concurrent agricul-tural and industrial expansion, together with the generation of an agrarian surplus, in the period to World War I.

Recent articles by E. Sydney Crawcour, however, suggest that the debate over agriculture's contribution may be far from settled. Citing Nakamura's thesis that the growth rate of the early Meiji economy was "not particularly high," Crawcour states that Japan's economic transition required the government to reallocate "existing resources" as well as "to restrict consumption in the interests of industrial and military investment."[27] He notes that "agricultural progress in the initial phase of Japan's modern economic growth may not have been as fast as was once thought," but that the performance of agriculture was "adequate," as "food production kept up with demand until 1900 and thereafter did not lag far behind."[28] He thus appears to echo Nakamura's contention that during the Meiji era the growth of agricultural output merely coincided with the expansion of population. Like Nakamura, Craw-cour emphasizes the transfer of assets into the hands of landlords with "a high propensity to save and invest in both local and national enterprises."[29] Yet, compli-cating the story, recent research in Japan suggests that scholars have heretofore exaggerated the role of landlords, pointing to the land tax and to noble and merchant wealth as more significant sources of capital for industrial investment than private landowner savings.

Traditional Industry and the Industrial Takeoff

Crawcour downplays the contribution of agriculture to make a more important point about the centrality of traditional industry to Japan's pre-1914 economy. This point relates to another issue concerning the timing and chronology of Japan's industrial takeoff. A standard interpretation is that the breakthrough to modern economic growth represented a transitional period during which the new Meiji government laid the groundwork for industrialization by eliminating obstacles such as the semi-autonomous "feudal" domains and promoting the development of modern financial and communications systems. The transition culminated with the Matsukata financial reform of 1881–5, which, in Henry Rosovsky's words, "cleared the decks" for modern economic growth to begin.[30] After 1885, then, two successive booms in private company formation led by railroads and textiles helped propel the economy into industrial overdrive.

According to an opposing view, in quantitative terms, Japan's industrial revolution did not really begin until after the turn of the century. In fact, a recent trend among Japanese scholars such as Nakamura Takafusa has been to emphasize the continued importance of the traditional sector of the economy, and particularly traditional industry, well into the twentieth century. Granted, industrial production grew sub-stantially before 1900, but the vast majority of that output came not from modern factories but from traditional cottage industries like sake brewing and handweaving. Indeed, it was not until World War I that modern factory production exceeded half of total manufacturing output.[31] Before then, as Crawcour puts it, "the modern sector was still an infant nurtured by the traditional economy rather than the engine of growth that it later became."[32]

Like Japan, the Western followers also witnessed the survival of their traditional sectors into the early decades of the twentieth century, but Japan was somewhat exceptional in the extent to which "traditional industries not only survived but in fact prospered" until the 1920s.[33] Moreover, in some cases, such as the manufacturing of matches and other consumer goods, the Japanese actually transformed modern factory-based industries they had imported from the West in the late nineteenth century into small-scale "traditional" industries relying on labor-intensive, putting-out methods of production. Emphasizing the sustained growth and vitality of the traditional sector through World War I, Saitō Osamu even goes so far as to label the entire century leading up to the 1920s as one long, protoindustrial period, with Japan's industrial revolution breaking out only in the interwar years.[34]

A counterargument advanced by William Wray is that this interpretation underestimates the significance of Japan's modern industrial development prior to World War I. Besides the leading sector of prewar industrialization, cotton spinning, most of the modern growth industries of the interwar period, including steel and chemicals, had started before 1914. Furthermore, the case for delayed industrialization in Japan overlooks various "non-quantifiable engines of growth"[35] – technical and institutional innovations in transportation and communication, finance and trade, and business organization – that appeared in the last three decades of the nineteenth century. These changes, together with the introduction of numerous modern industries, suggest that an industrial revolution may well have gotten under way in Japan in the decades preceding the First World War.

The Role of the State

Another divergence of opinion centers on the contribution of the government to industrial development in Japan. In every follower nation, the state has played a larger role in launching and sustaining industrialization than was the case in Britain, but the question is, how much larger? Depending on one's view of the relative "backwardness" of Japan on the eve of modern economic growth – and, according to one rough estimate, its per capita GNP was little more than a quarter that of the United States and less than half that of Germany at the respective starts of their industrial revolutions[36] – one might expect the government to have played a particularly sizeable role in the Japanese case. Indeed, an older interpretation popularized by Thomas Smith depicted the Japanese state as the grand initiator of industrialization, attaching special importance to the path-breaking enterprises it founded in the 1870s in a wide range of modern industrial fields.

Since the 1970s, however, scholars have tended to minimize the direct contribution of the government to Japan's industrial revolution. Kozo Yamamura has been a leading proponent of this revisionist view. The early state enterprises may have helped introduce modern technology, but in many cases they were managerial and technical failures, and the ones that succeeded usually did so only after the government sold them off to private interests beginning in the 1880s. The most telling evidence comes from the crucial field of textiles. The breakthrough in cotton spinning, when it finally occurred in the 1880s, was almost entirely the result of private initiative: the model for all successful spinning mills came not from the poorly run state plants, which were too small to capture economies of scale, but from a private firm, the larger and more efficient Osaka Spinning Company, established in 1882. In the case of silk reeling, Japan's premier export industry until the 1920s, the problem was just the opposite: the government's celebrated Tomioka Filature was too large and sophisticated to serve as a model for private silk producers, who, even if they mechanized, tended to adopt smaller-scale, simplified versions of Western technology. Admittedly, through the disposal of its industrial works, the Meiji state contributed directly to the rise of big business, as several forerunners of the zaibatsu, the private business combines that dominated the pre-1945 economy, capitalized on their acquisition of state enterprises to expand and diversify their operations.[37] In the case of Mitsui and Mitsubishi, the purchase of government properties, especially mines and shipyards, played a vital role in determining the way in which they developed into combines. But the other two of the "Big Four" zaibatsu – Sumitomo and Yasuda – bought no enterprises from the state and yet grew into giant diversified combines; the sale, therefore, was not indispensable to the emergence of the zaibatsu. Critics of the early state initiatives in the industrial field go on to argue that the main economic function of the government was merely to provide a favorable environment for largely private development of modern industry.

A rebuttal to the revisionist argument is that even this primarily indirect role was extensive and critical. The Japanese state had to resort to a variety of measures to promote industrialization in a setting where, because of the unequal commercial treaties the Western powers had imposed in the late 1850s, Japan was unable to employ protective tariffs until the very end of the Meiji period. Ironically, even as Japan was joining the Western nations as a treaty power in China and creating the bulk of its own colonial empire between 1895 and 1910, it was still technically a semi-colony, for it got rid of the last of the unequal-treaty restrictions, low fixed tariffs, only in 1911. As a result, the Japanese government had some four decades of experience with non-tariff barriers to industrial imports, including preferential buying from domestic producers and manifold financial and technical assistance to them, before it could even begin to use formal tariffs to shelter fledgling industries at home, a course it followed with a vengeance after 1911. In this context, "providing a favorable environment" was no small matter.

One could further argue that the more recent view understates even the direct role of the Japanese government. True, the state privatized most of its industrial enterprises in the 1880s and 1890s, but the ones it retained, especially arsenals and railroad workshops – to which it added when it bought out the major private railroads in 1906–7 – became leading disseminators of advanced technology and management methods to the private sector, proving crucial to the rise of the modern Japanese machinery and machine-tool industries in the early twentieth century. The government also contributed directly to heavy industrialization after the turn of the century by establishing the country's first and largest steel mill, the Yawata Iron and Steel Works, which began operations in 1901. Despite its significant entry into heavy industry, the state in general followed a quasi-laissez-faire policy from the 1890s to the 1920s, as the zaibatsu increasingly took the lead in industrial development. Then, as Japan moved towards a wartime "controlled economy" in the 1930s, the government began to intervene extensively in the private sector, in the process setting precedents for the industrial policies, such as control over foreign exchange, that officials used to promote growth industries in the immediate postwar years.[38]

Militarism and Industrialization

A related issue concerns the role of militarism and empire in Japan's industrial revolution. Did wars and colonies provide the mainspring for industrialization in Japan before 1945, or did they primarily act as a drag on the Japanese economy? The positive view would underscore the centrality for Japan's industrial revolution of military demand, colonial markets, and technological spin-offs from strategic enterprises. In particular, the hothouse created by government military expenditures and captive sources of supply in the empire proved vital to the growth of heavy industries, helping them overtake textiles as the leading sector of Japanese industrialization by the 1930s. That decade also saw the emergence of business combines with close ties to the military, the so-called "new zaibatsu," from which many of the leading high-tech industries of postwar Japan such as Nissan, Hitachi, and Ricoh descended.[39] Other economic benefits of Japanese militarism included the acquisition of the huge China indemnity following the Sino-Japanese War of 1894–5, which largely paid for the pioneering Yawata Iron and Steel Works, as well as the diffusion of advanced technology from state arsenals and naval yards to private manufacturers throughout the pre-1945 era.

In the negative view, both military spending and empire-building proved a net drain on the Japanese economy, taking resources away from more productive uses at home. In addition, although the older explanation of Japan's rapid recovery from the Great Depression stressed expanded armaments budgets, a more recent interpretation places the emphasis squarely on the nation's phenomenal consumer export drive fueled by the drastic devaluation of the yen after 1931. According to Nakamura Takafusa, after exports, the biggest contributor to Japan's rebound was private investment; meanwhile, under the proto-Keynesian "Takahashi finance" of 1932–6, government expenditure on rural relief "may ... have had a stimulating effect on the economy surpassing even that of military spending,"[40] which did not increase significantly until 1937. Moreover, many would contend that, whatever economic benefits Japan may have derived from military and colonial exploits, one must balance these gains against the disastrous consequences of Japanese military expansion into the Pacific War years.

New Directions

This essay has generally observed the conventional "prewar" boundaries of 1868 and the late 1930s. But, just as historians of twentieth-century Japan have increasingly taken up topics cutting across the Pacific War, Howell and Wigen, in their works published in 1995, traverse the usual Restoration divide by treating the nineteenth century as a whole.[41] They offer original critiques of the standard modernization narrative by locating the indigenous origins of industrialization and capitalism in the protoindustrial economies of "peripheral" areas, the Shimoina Valley of present day Nagano prefecture and the west coast of Hokkaidō. Painting a picture of eventual decline and subordination, they underscore the need to study not only growth and industrial progress but also distribution and unequal development among different groups and regions. Finally, both authors suggest the rich possibilities of combining social and economic history to broaden and humanize the story of Japan's modern transformation.

NOTES

1 For the debate on entrepreneurship, see Yamamura, *A Study of Samurai Income and Entrepreneurship*, pp. 137–87, and Nakamura, *Economic Growth in Prewar Japan*, pp. 104–11.
2 Harvard's Council on East Asian Studies spearheaded this movement, with publications such as Wray, *Mitsubishi and the N.Y.K.*; Molony, *Technology and Investment*; and Ericson, *The Sound of the Whistle*.
3 Howell, *Capitalism from Within*; Wigen, *The Making of a Japanese Periphery*.
4 Passin, *Society and Education*, p. xi.
5 On the *minshūshi* school of history, see Gluck, "The People in History." For an example of *minshūshi* scholarship, see Irokawa, *The Culture of the Meiji Period*.
6 Dore, *Education in Tokugawa Japan*; Passin, *Society and Education*.
7 Platt, *Burning and Building*, p. 19.
8 Ibid., p. 2.
9 Gluck, *Japan's Modern Myths*.
10 Lincicome, *Principle, Praxis, and the Politics of Educational Reform*.
11 Frühstück, *Colonizing Sex*.
12 Kinmonth, *The Self-Made Man*; Huffman, *Creating a Public*; Sato, *The New Japanese Woman*; and Sand, *House and Home in Modern Japan*.
13 Roden, *Schooldays in Imperial Japan*, p. 6.
14 Kinmonth, *The Self-Made Man*.
15 Sievers, *Flowers in Salt*; Bernstein, ed., *Recreating Japanese Women*.
16 Sato, *The New Japanese Woman*, p. 9.
17 Hane, *Peasants, Rebels, and Outcastes*.
18 Smethurst, *Agricultural Development and Tenancy Disputes*.
19 Pratt, *Japan's Protoindustrial Elite*.
20 Smith, *A Time of Crisis*.
21 Weiner, ed., *Japan's Minorities*, p. xvii; see also Howell, *Geographies of Identity*.
22 Tsurumi, *Factory Girls*.
23 Lewis, *Rioters and Citizens*, p. xix.
24 Gordon, *Labor and Imperial Democracy*, pp. 206–7.
25 Garon, *Molding Japanese Minds*; Uno, *Passages to Modernity*; Hanes, *The City as Subject*.
26 This "Long-Term Economic Statistics" project provided the raw material for a number of quantitative analyses, including Minami, *The Economic Development of Japan*.
27 Crawcour, "Economic Change in the Nineteenth Century," pp. 615–16.
28 Crawcour, "Industrialization and Technological Change," pp. 411, 413.
29 Ibid., p. 413.
30 Rosovsky, "Japan's Transition to Modern Economic Growth," p. 135.

31 Nakamura, *Economic Growth in Prewar Japan*, p. 80.
32 Crawcour, "Industrialization and Technological Change," p. 390.
33 Nakamura, *Economic Growth in Prewar Japan*, p. 86.
34 See the discussion of Saitō's argument in Wray, "Afterword," pp. 365–8.
35 Ibid., p. 368.
36 Minami, *The Economic Development of Japan*, p. 13.
37 The best source in English on the combines is Morikawa, *Zaibatsu*.
38 For the interwar roots of postwar industrial policy, see Johnson, *MITI and the Japanese Miracle*. For earlier antecedents in the shipping and shipbuilding fields, see Wray, *Mitsubishi and the N.Y.K.*
39 The "new zaibatsu" differed from the old main-line combines in being publicly held rather than family owned and less diversified in non-manufacturing fields like trade and finance. For a case study of a new zaibatsu, see Molony, *Technology and Investment*.
40 Nakamura, "Depression, Recovery, and War," p. 470.
41 Howell, *Capitalism from Within*; Wigen, *The Making of a Japanese Periphery*.

BIBLIOGRAPHY

Allen, G. C. *A Short Economic History of Modern Japan*. New York: St. Martin's Press, 1946; 4th edn., 1981.

Bernstein, Gail Lee, ed. *Recreating Japanese Women, 1600–1945*. Berkeley: University of California Press, 1991.

Crawcour, E. Sydney. "Industrialization and Technological Change, 1885–1920." In Peter Duus, ed., *The Cambridge History of Japan*, vol. 6, *The Twentieth Century*. Cambridge: Cambridge University Press, 1988.

Crawcour, E. Sydney. "Economic Change in the Nineteenth Century." In Marius Jansen, ed., *The Cambridge History of Japan*, vol. 5, *The Nineteenth Century*. Cambridge: Cambridge University Press, 1989.

Dore, Ronald P. *Education in Tokugawa Japan*. Berkeley: University of California Press, 1965.

Ericson, Steven J. *The Sound of the Whistle: Railroads and the State in Meiji Japan*. Cambridge, Mass.: Council on East Asian Studies, Harvard University, 1996.

Frühstück, Sabine. *Colonizing Sex: Sexology and Social Control in Modern Japan*. Berkeley: University of California Press, 2003.

Garon, Sheldon. *Molding Japanese Minds: The State in Everyday Life*. Princeton: Princeton University Press, 1997.

Gluck, Carol. "The People in History: Recent Trends in Japanese Historiography." *Journal of Asian Studies* 38 (1978): 25–50.

Gluck, Carol. *Japan's Modern Myths: Ideology in the Late Meiji Period*. Princeton: Princeton University Press, 1985.

Gordon, Andrew. *Labor and Imperial Democracy in Prewar Japan*. Berkeley: University of California Press, 1991.

Hane, Mikiso. *Peasants, Rebels, and Outcastes: The Underside of Modern Japan*. New York: Pantheon, 1982.

Hanes, Jeffrey. *The City as Subject: Seki Hajime and the Reinvention of Modern Osaka*. Berkeley: University of California Press, 2002.

Howell, David L. *Capitalism from Within: Economy, Society, and the State in a Japanese Fishery*. Berkeley: University of California Press, 1995.

Howell, David L. *Geographies of Identity in Nineteenth-Century Japan*. Berkeley: University of California Press, 2005.

Huffman, James. *Creating a Public: People and Press in Meiji Japan.* Honolulu: University of Hawai'i Press, 1997.

Irokawa Daikichi. *The Culture of the Meiji Period*, ed. Marius Jansen. Princeton: Princeton University Press, 1985.

Johnson, Chalmers. *MITI and the Japanese Miracle: The Growth of Industrial Policy, 1925–1975.* Stanford, Calif.: Stanford University Press, 1982.

Kinmonth, Earl. *The Self-Made Man in Meiji Japanese Thought: From Samurai to Salary Man.* Berkeley: University of California Press, 1981.

Lewis, Michael. *Rioters and Citizens: Mass Protest in Imperial Japan.* Berkeley: University of California Press, 1990.

Lincicome, Mark. *Principle, Praxis, and the Politics of Educational Reform in Meiji Japan.* Honolulu: University of Hawai'i Press, 1995.

Lockwood, W. W. *The Economic Development of Japan: Growth and Structural Change, 1868–1938.* Princeton: Princeton University Press, 1954; expanded edn., 1968.

Minami Ryōshin. *The Economic Development of Japan: A Quantitative Study.* New York: St. Martin's Press, 1986.

Molony, Barbara. *Technology and Investment: The Prewar Japanese Chemical Industry.* Cambridge: Council on East Asian Studies, Harvard University, 1990.

Morikawa Hidemasa. *Zaibatsu: The Rise and Fall of Family Enterprise Groups in Japan.* Tokyo: University of Tokyo Press, 1992.

Nakamura, James. *Agricultural Production and the Economic Development of Japan, 1873–1922.* Princeton: Princeton University Press, 1966.

Nakamura Takafusa. *Economic Growth in Prewar Japan*, trans. Robert A. Feldman. New Haven: Yale University Press, 1983.

Nakamura Takafusa. "Depression, Recovery, and War, 1920–1945." In Peter Duus, ed., *The Cambridge History of Japan*, vol. 6, *The Twentieth Century.* Cambridge: Cambridge University Press, 1988.

Passin, Herbert. *Society and Education in Japan.* New York: Teachers College, Columbia University, 1965.

Platt, Brian. *Burning and Building: Schooling and State Formation in Japan, 1750–1890.* Cambridge, Mass.: Harvard University Asia Center, 2004.

Pratt, Edward E. *Japan's Protoindustrial Elite: The Economic Foundations of the Gōnō.* Cambridge, Mass.: Harvard University Asia Center, 1999.

Roden, Donald. *Schooldays in Imperial Japan: A Study in the Culture of a Student Elite.* Berkeley: University of California Press, 1980.

Rosovsky, Henry. "Japan's Transition to Modern Economic Growth, 1868–1885." In Henry Rosovsky, ed., *Industrialization in Two Systems.* New York: Wiley, 1966.

Sand, Jordan. *House and Home in Modern Japan: Architecture, Domestic Space, and Bourgeois Culture, 1880–1930.* Cambridge, Mass.: Harvard University Asia Center, 2003.

Sato, Barbara. *The New Japanese Woman: Modernity, Media, and Women in Interwar Japan.* Durham, NC: Duke University Press, 2003.

Sievers, Sharon. *Flowers in Salt: The Beginnings of Feminist Consciousness in Modern Japan.* Stanford, Calif.: Stanford University Press, 1983.

Smethurst, Richard. *Agricultural Development and Tenancy Disputes in Japan, 1870–1940.* Princeton: Princeton University Press, 1986.

Smith, Kerry. *A Time of Crisis: Japan, the Great Depression, and Rural Revitalization.* Cambridge, Mass.: Harvard University Asia Center, 2001.

Smith, Thomas C. *Political Change and Industrial Development in Japan: Government Enterprise, 1868–1880.* Stanford, Calif.: Stanford University Press, 1955.

Tsurumi, E. Patricia. *Factory Girls: Women in the Thread Mills of Meiji Japan.* Princeton: Princeton University Press, 1990.

Uno, Kathleen. *Passages to Modernity: Motherhood, Childhood, and Social Reform in Early Twentieth Century Japan.* Honolulu: University of Hawai'i Press, 1999.

Weiner, Michael, ed. *Japan's Minorities: The Illusion of Homogeneity.* London: Routledge, 1997.

Wigen, Kären. *The Making of a Japanese Periphery, 1750–1920.* Berkeley: University of California Press, 1995.

Wray, William. *Mitsubishi and the N.Y.K., 1870–1914: Business Strategy in the Japanese Shipping Industry.* Cambridge, Mass.: Council on East Asian Studies, Harvard University, 1984.

Wray, William. "Afterword." In William Wray, ed., *Managing Industrial Enterprise: Cases from Japan's Prewar Experience.* Cambridge, Mass.: Council on East Asian Studies, Harvard University, 1989.

Yamamura, Kozo. *A Study of Samurai Income and Entrepreneurship: Quantitative Analyses of Economic and Social Aspects of the Samurai in Tokugawa and Meiji Japan.* Cambridge, Mass.: Harvard University Press, 1974.

FURTHER READING

If one goal of social history is to humanize the past by bringing to life its social actors and contexts, then the student of social history is well served to look beyond historians' monographs to novels, memoirs, and biographies. On the life of the *gōnō* during the Restoration era, see the novel by Shimazaki Tōson, *Before the Dawn*, trans. William Naff (Honolulu: University of Hawai'i Press, 1987). Offering a peasant's perspective on social change in the first half of the twentieth century are the novel by Nagatsuka Takashi, *The Soil: A Portrait of Rural Life in Meiji Japan*, trans. Ann Waswo (Berkeley: University of California Press, 1993), and the biography by Simon Partner, *Toshié: A Story of Village Life in Twentieth-Century Japan* (Berkeley: University of California Press, 2004). On the lives of various types of women, from modern girls to political radicals, see the novel by Tanizaki Jun'ichirō, *Naomi*, trans. Anthony Chambers (New York: Vintage, 2001); Ronald P. Loftus, ed., *Telling Lives: Women's Self-Writing in Modern Japan* (Honolulu: University of Hawai'i Press, 2004); Nakano Makiko, *Makiko's Diary: A Merchant Wife in 1910 Kyoto*, trans. Kazuko Smith (Stanford, Calif.: Stanford University Press, 1995); and Mikiso Hane, trans. and ed., *Reflections on the Way to the Gallows: Voices of Japanese Rebel Women* (Berkeley: University of California Press, 1988). Similar works for economic history include Shibusawa Eiichi, *The Autobiography of Shibusawa Eiichi: From Peasant to Entrepreneur*, trans. Teruko Craig (Tokyo: University of Tokyo Press, 1994) – the ubiquitous Shibusawa (1840–1931) helped establish hundreds of private companies during his lifetime – and Haru Matsukata Reischauer, *Samurai and Silk: A Japanese and American Heritage* (Cambridge, Mass.: Harvard University Press, 1986), a dual biography of the author's grandfathers, Finance Minister Matsukata Masayoshi (1835–1924) and silk merchant Arai Ryōichirō (1855–1939).

Several collected works are a boon to students of Japan's modern economic experience. A groundbreaking synthesis of research in Japan, *Nihon keizai shi*, 8 vols. (Tokyo: Iwanami Shoten, 1988–90), is now being published in English in abridged form under the series title *The Economic History of Japan, 1600–1990* (Oxford: Oxford University Press, 2003–). A handy collection is Kozo Yamamura, ed., *The Economic Emergence of Modern Japan* (Cambridge: Cambridge University Press, 1997), which brings together the chapters on Japanese economic history from vols. 5 and 6 of *The Cambridge History of Japan* and from vol. 7, part 2 of Peter Mathias and M. M. Postan, eds., *The Cambridge Economic History of Europe* (Cambridge: Cambridge University Press, 1978). Useful anthologies of journal articles and other previously published essays are W. J. Macpherson, ed., *The Industrialization of Japan* (Oxford: Blackwell, 1994), which also includes an extensive bibliography, and Michael Smitka, ed., *Japanese Economic History, 1600–1960,* 7 vols. (New York: Garland, 1998).

CHAPTER ELEVEN

Intellectual Life, Culture, and the Challenge of Modernity

Elise K. Tipton

The processes of industrialization and urbanization begun in the Meiji period accelerated with expansion of markets for Japanese manufactured goods during World War I, and a rush of democratic, reformist, and radical ideas and ideologies during the 1910s stimulated social and cultural as well as political change. The 1920s, especially after the Kantō earthquake of 1923, was the era when "modern" became the catchword of the times. The "modern life" became the ideal for Japanese, even though most could not yet attain it. While the modern life became the ideal, criticism grew during the 1930s, and a wide variety of intellectuals took up the poet Hagiwara Sakutarō's call for a "return to Japan." Some historians see World War II not only as a war against the economic and military hegemony of the West, but also as a "revolt" against Western cultural imperialism.[1] The "Overcoming Modernity" (*Kindai no chōkoku*) symposium of 1942 has been seen as both symbol and culmination of this anti-Western trend among intellectuals.

But not all intellectuals equated modernity with the West. In fact, intellectuals had great difficulty even defining modernity. However, they all based their evaluations on what they observed and experienced in the everyday life around them. Everyday life, the material, social, and cultural changes of the early decades of the twentieth century, both attracted and repelled them. In H. D. Harootunian's phrase, "the category of everyday life – its performativity in the present – [became] the informing principle of modern life." Everyday life constituted "both a condition of social research and critique and the occasion for looking to a new social and political imaginary in the future."[2]

Here, culture is understood in a broad sense, to include popular culture as well as "high" culture or "pure" literature. This is important because the emergence of the "masses" in modern culture became one of the aspects of modernity that troubled intellectuals, and especially writers. The importance of the masses is evident in the words of the cultural critic Tsuchida Kyōson, writing in 1932: "There has probably been no time in which the 'masses' had such weighty significance as at present. It is possible that it would not be an exaggeration even if one said that the present is the age of the masses."[3]

A wartime cartoon by Sugiura Yukio suggests the extent to which modern values had been disseminated throughout Japanese society. It appeared in the May 1942 issue of the officially sponsored magazine *Manga*.[4] It strikes a Westerner as a little odd and humorous, for it depicts a woman bending over on her knees and combing out dandruff from her hair. The flakes of dandruff are each labelled, and the labels are revealing, for they encapsulate the meaning of modernity for government officials during the prewar and war years: "extravagance," "materialism," and "money worship"; "hedonism," "selfishness," and "individualism"; "liberalism" and "Anglo-American ideas."

In this piece of government propaganda, modernity was explicitly associated with the wartime Anglo-American enemy, but among intellectuals of the 1920s and 1930s modernity was not understood as a mere foreign import. It was no simple and superficial fad. Rather, modernity comprised ideas and values that had spread along with or as a consequence of indigenous processes of industrialization and urbanization. Further, it was not only associated with technological and material changes, but also with cultural values and modes of social relations and behavior. Still, participants in the "Overcoming Modernity" symposium could not in the end find even a common definition of modernity. This was one reason that the debates about modernity were so complicated and full of ambivalence and contradictions.

Yet although definitions abounded and evaluations often clashed, some common themes can be found. Few critics rejected the material improvements brought about by industrialization and modern economic growth. No machines are to be purged in the *Manga* cartoon. Moreover, although well-known writers such as Tanizaki Jun'ichirō lamented the decline of traditional Japanese aesthetic values, they did not want to give up the conveniences of a modern lifestyle. As Tanizaki concluded in 1934, "I am aware of and most grateful for the benefits of the age. No matter what complaints we may have, Japan has chosen to follow the West, and there is nothing for her to do but move bravely ahead and leave us old ones behind."[5] It was the changes in social roles and cultural values that worried critics, and the loss of communal spirit and creativity that they mourned. Modernity was clearly located in the city, but the city was alienating as well as alluring. It meant unceasing and often bewildering change, both the "speed" and fast "tempo" of city life and material changes, and the swirl of new ideas and theories about art, aesthetics and literature as well as science, society and politics.

In addition, it is significant that the *Manga* cartoon depicts a woman in Western dress, rather than a man, needing to get rid of the scurf encrusting her head. The behavior and values associated with the modern life threatened to upset the role for women that not only the government, but also most of society endorsed. The Meiji government had promoted the ideal of "good wife, wise mother" for middle-class women, which situated women's proper place in the home. Nevertheless, by the 1920s higher levels of education, lifestyle aspirations, and financial need in a period of economic stagnation motivated an increasing number of middle-class women to enter the paid workplace and other public places. This growing trend created fears that changed gender roles would undermine the family, which was both the political and social unit at the foundation of the Japanese family-state. The "woman question" was a source of intellectual and social debate from the 1910s onward. Essays on aesthetics and novels of the period reveal a contradictory attraction toward modern women but also a distaste for their independence and public visibility (and especially their bodies) as well as a lament for the disappearance of "traditional" ideals of femininity.

To understand the multiple facets of modernity and the challenge they posed in the view of intellectuals during the 1920s and 1930s, we can begin with the values singled out in Sugiura's cartoon and the diverse responses to them among social critics. Here I shall focus on the cultural and social values, that is, all except for liberalism which represents political ideas and ideologies dealt with elsewhere in this volume. We shall then explore some of the attempts made to meet the challenge, leading to the "Overcoming Modernity" symposium. This will highlight the complexity and ambiguity characterizing responses to modernity and the nature of intellectual life in Japan during these decades.

Materialism and Money Worship

Materialism and money worship were not new values of the interwar years. Concern about them can be traced back to the late Meiji period when the meaning of "success" (*risshin shusse*) began to change. As Earl Kinmonth has demonstrated in his study of youth magazines,[6] wealth rather than government office became the goal of upwardly mobile youths, and individuals increasingly sought success for themselves more than for their families or communities. During the late 1890s the Christian critic Uchimura Kanzō sarcastically criticized the desire for money:

> Get money; get it by all means, for it alone is power in this generation. Wish you to be patriotic? Then get money, for you cannot better serve your country than by getting money for you and it. Be loyal? Then get money, and add wealth to your Master's land. Be filial to your father and mother? You cannot be so without getting money. The strength of your nation, the fear of your name – all come from money. Morality ever for the sake of money.[7]

After the Russo-Japanese War social critics became even more conscious of the changes. In the words of one commentator, "never since the dawn of world history has the growth of the individual been so respected and material happiness so sought after as in present day Japan."[8]

That commentator should have waited another decade or so to make his declaration, for the commercial developments of the 1920s made the getting of money even more desirable. During the early 1920s "culture" (*bunka*) became a catchphrase, and various industries successfully promoted a "cultured life" (*bunka seikatsu*) to the new white collar salaried middle classes in the cities. The economist Morimoto Kōkichi established the Cultured Life Research Association (Bunka Seikatsu Kenkyūkai), which published two periodicals aimed at women's higher school graduates. Morimoto enthusiastically called for the establishment of a cultured life, identifying it with "rational, efficient living."[9] Prominent writers and intellectuals, including Arishima Takeo, contributed to these journals, and the phrase "cultured life" was quickly picked up in more popular media.

Living a "cultured life" consequently became less associated with artistic, literary, or other strictly cultural pursuits than with obtaining its material symbols, namely a "culture house," filled with "culture pots," "culture knives," and other "culture" gadgets and appliances. The burgeoning mass media of national circulation news-papers, popular commercially oriented magazines, and foreign films as well as the transformation of department stores and shopping centers presented images of an affluent "cultured life" and later in the decade a "modern life" (*modan seikatsu* or *modan raifu*) to Japanese people beyond the circles of the elite. As Jordan Sand has shown, displays of Western-style culture houses were more for looking at than buying, however, since most "salarymen" could not yet afford them.[10] Tanizaki's popular novel *Chijin no ai* (A Fool's Love, translated as *Naomi*), serialized in 1922, was largely situated in such a culture house. His description of it as a "fairy-tale house" reflects the extent to which the cultured lifestyle became a widespread ideal and how Japan was becoming a mass consumer society during the 1920s.

Ten years later in his essay *In'ei raisan* (*In Praise of Shadows*), Tanizaki acknow-ledged and lamented the popularity of modern household items over traditional Japanese ones. In particular, he noted that lacquerware was now considered "vulgar and inelegant," blaming this on "the much-vaunted 'brilliance' of modern electric lighting." He much preferred lacquerware to ceramics which "lack the shadows, the depth of lacquerware" and "clatter and clink." Similarly, for aesthetic reasons he preferred Japanese building materials of paper and wood to glass and metal: "unfin-ished wood as it darkens and the grain grows more subtle with the years acquires an inexplicable power to calm and soothe."[11] But in his conclusion Tanizaki had to admit that he did not want to give up the conveniences of modern culture, and according to his wife's recollections, he did not in fact want to live in the kind of house that he described in the essay. Another major writer Nagai Kafū, known even more than Tanizaki for his elegiac novels about the waning of Edo culture, criticized the Westernizing of Japan as superficial but built himself a "truly Western" house with no *tatami* on the floors.[12]

The destruction caused by the Kantō earthquake in 1923 had accelerated these consumer trends. Companies moved their offices out of the old downtown business district of Nihonbashi to Marunouchi, and their managers and workers moved their homes to suburbs south and west of the city. Many did not return to live in the central business area even after reconstruction was complete. Private railway companies re-inforced suburbanization by extending their lines and building culture house devel-opments to attract commuting customers for their new lines. The railway companies also constructed department stores and shopping centers near railway stations, railway terminals, and transfer points, such as Shinjuku. Department stores, especially those in Ginza, had previously sold mainly expensive imported goods and specialty items, but in the aftermath of the earthquake they responded to people's needs for everyday living. They also let in the masses by allowing customers to keep on their shoes and opening dining rooms with Western tables and chairs where diners could keep on their coats. For the first time, middle-class women felt comfortable about eating out in public. Many were now earning incomes in the new occupations open to middle-class women, such as teaching, nursing, clerical and other office work, and retail sales. Most still could not afford to buy many of the fashions and other goods on display in department stores, but browsing and window shopping became a respectable leisure pastime. In fact, it prompted the coining of a new term, *ginbura* ("passing the time in Ginza" or "cruising the Ginza").

Many photographs from this period feature fashionable women window shopping or striding purposefully on the streets of the Ginza. Department stores and consumer product manufacturers targeted women with their advertising and other promotional activities, and the new popular women's magazines and Hollywood movies defined women as consumers. None symbolized the new consumerism more than the "modern girl" (*modan gāru* or *moga*), who grabbed the attention of journalists and intellectuals from the mid-1920s until the early 1930s. The numerous heated debates attempting to define her display the confusion, contradictions, ambivalence, and emotion appropriate to the complicated modernity that she represented. One trait was universally attributed, however: preoccupation with consumption, especially Western clothes, make-up, and hairstyles, and the latest movies and fashion magazines. Wearing a short Western dress and accessories, made up with bright red lipstick and Western cosmetics, and coiffed in a short bob haircut or permanent wave, the modern girl appeared ubiquitously in advertisements for Shiseido cosmetics, Sapporo beer, Suntory wine, and even the Calpis health drink. Matchstick boxes, graphic prints, and even *shinhanga* (new woodblock prints) depicted her, usually with a Western cocktail and a cigarette in hand as well. Intellectuals as well as journalists could not stop writing about her. As Miriam Silverberg has pointed out, members of a round-table discussion in the January 1928 issue of *Shinchō* were supposed to talk about urbanization and various aspects of modern life, but they could not keep away from discussing the modern girl.[13]

Numerous negative evaluations of the modern girl focused on her superficial appearance. When the intellectual women's journal *Fujin kōron*, for example, gathered together opinions in its January 1927 issue, Okada Hachiyo's viewpoint was representative:

> I do not think that *modern girls* are particularly modern in their way of thinking; they just look modern. You see them wearing flashy clothes – a shiny purple and green dress with a big sash tied under the bosom. If that is the criterion for being modern, it is pitiful. It is an insult to the real *modern girl* even to use a word like *modern girl*, which has such derogatory connotations. For me, the word connotes someone who is a total fake, heavily made-up, and who is satisfied with just having something that is new.[14]

Marxist and other socialist intellectuals saw the modern girl's (and modern boy's) preoccupation with consumption as a way for the bourgeoisie to divert her attention from more significant political and economic issues. Gonda Yasunosuke condemned the consumerist trends and the "modern life industry" in an article published in the leftist intellectual journal *Kaizō*, entitled "Modan seikatsu to hentai shikōsei" (Modern Life and Perverse Tastes):

> If I were to define the essence of modern life, I would say that people without ties to labor and production are responsible for creating this society. In terms of class, they are members of the leisure class, or at least those connected to the petty bourgeoisie. Having no direct connection to labor, their lives are rooted solely in consumerism. In terms of age, they are young men and women for whom the name *modern boy* and *modern girl* is appropriate.[15]

The Marxist poet Nakano Shigeharu critiqued the commodification of culture in his 1926 poem "Imperial Hotel" (*Teikoku Hoteru*). During the early twentieth century the nouveau riche in Tokyo frequented the Imperial Hotel, designed by the pre-eminent modernist architect Frank Lloyd Wright. The second part of the poem sarcastically describes the hotel as:

> A large hole
> A large whorehouse
> A large saloon
> A large dampish prison
> A big and seedy sample Japanese marketplace
> Undestroyed even by the earthquake
> In the center of Tokyo
> Over our heads
> Squats, letting loose a stench.[16]

Hedonism

As revealed in Nakano's poem, hedonism often went hand in hand with materialism and consumerism, but hedonism – decadence was another word – referred more specifically to the pursuit of commodified pleasure and to immoral leisure activities and behavior. These were the "perverse tastes" that Gonda Yasunosuke referred to in his 1929 *Kaizō* article, while another leftist intellectual, Kurahara Korehito, used the term "cultural hedonism" to describe the commodification of the everyday. As in the case of consumerism, the modern girl often figured as the central symbol and object of criticism.

Hedonism, like materialism, had been a worry among social critics earlier in the century. Then, as in the 1920s and 1930s, it was applied to the younger generation – "decadent youth." Unlike the materialistic "success youth" who strived for money and their own individual wealth, decadent youth abandoned self-discipline, frugality, and filial piety in pursuit of sensual pleasures, extravagance, and ostentation. Issuance of the Boshin Imperial Rescript in 1908 had attempted to stem the tide and reinstill values of diligence, frugality, and loyalty. Its failure was evident in the recurrence of similar complaints among both intellectuals and government authorities during the interwar decades. Now, however, they blamed the modern entertainments of the cities for spreading ideas of romantic love, free love, and female sexuality and focused their criticisms on young women as well as young men.

These ideas had been entering Japan since the 1910s through translations of Western writers and theorists and through discussions in the feminist literary journal *Seitō* (Bluestocking) as well as other intellectual journals such as *Kaizō* and *Chūō kōron*. Then in 1922 a new magazine with an unconventional word for "woman" as its title, *Josei*, began publication.[17] Its stated purpose was to introduce the modern to educated women. Despite being inaugurated by the Kurabu (Club) cosmetics company, the magazine contained relatively little advertising, and the contributors were well-known writers, literary critics, and intellectuals, representing a wide range of ideological perspectives, such as liberals, feminists of various kinds, and socialists. A 1980s women's magazine described *Josei* as the "bible" of the modern girl, but perhaps because of the high reputations of its contributors, many of its readers were also men.

The most frequently discussed topics in *Josei* proved to be chastity (*teisō*) or the "new chastity" and free love. Writers boldly discussed sexual behavior and relationships and challenged established notions of monogamous marriage. Fujii Kenjirō, for example, introduced the views of English social reformer Henry Sedgwick, who argued that marriage was not only to produce children and that sex in marriage was also for pleasure. Sedgwick's views were similar to those of the influential sexologist Havelock Ellis. Although ultimately conservative in his support for monogamy and the importance of the family, Ellis and other sex researchers were radical in their emphasis on the legitimacy of women fulfilling their sexual needs. Their advocacy of "companionate marriage" and the importance of love in marriage found acceptance among the writers in *Josei*. Some contributors, such as Tsuchida Kyōson, favored free love, taking pains to make clear that it did not mean promiscuity. Others, however, such as Wada Tomiko, criticized the selfish individualistic pursuit of sex, and Fujii Kenjirō argued that personal desires and lust needed to be kept in check for the good of society.

The modern girl and new urban entertainments provoked reactions like Wada's and Fujii's. With her short skirt and bobbed hair, the modern girl literally exhibited her body, moved it confidently as she cruised the Ginza and, in the new leisure spaces of the cafe and dance hall, expressed her sexuality. Intellectuals debated whether or not this represented women's emancipation. Murobuse Kōshin (Takanobu) was one who celebrated the liberating qualities of the cafe where both women and men could mix together freely and seek romantic love (*ren'ai*). He extolled the cafe as *the* symbol of modernity and considered it more significant than even the establishment of the Diet, for, in his view, it represented youth and the future rather than the old bourgeois elite.[18] Others, however, saw only threats of moral depravity and decadence in the erotic service proffered by cafe waitresses. Cafe waitresses appeared frequently as characters in movies and popular fiction of the late 1920s and early 1930s, as women who brazenly flaunted their sexuality and availability. Several years before the heyday of cafes Tanizaki's Naomi had epitomized these traits, leaving the male protagonist Jōji at home to go to dance halls and taking up with one lover after another. The modern girl in this novel is unfaithful and promiscuous, but nevertheless impossible for Jōji to reject.

One might find it unsurprising for a male author to project his fears of losing male domination onto the modern girl, but some prominent feminist theorists also doubted that the modern girl was really free in her pursuit of sexual pleasure. Hiratsuka Raichō, the founder of *Seitō*, questioned the seeming freedom of working women who had the time and money to spend in Ginza department stores and cafes. She saw them instead as fashion slaves and the objects of men's physical desires. A real modern girl would have a social conscience. While she did not see any in Japan of the 1920s, she did have hopes for such women emerging in the future. Marxist feminist Yamakawa Kikue was even more critical of the dissolute lifestyle engaged in by both modern boys and modern girls, but unlike Raichō, was not optimistic about their future. Rather, she saw their obsession with sensual pleasures as signs of the ruling class in decline.[19]

The threat posed by the exposure of women's bodies, their sexuality, and their visibility in public places also underlay Tanizaki's regret for changing ideals of women's beauty. He much preferred women in kimono, especially the way that female bunraku puppets were represented with their bodies, legs, and feet concealed in a long kimono. In his words,

> To me this is the very epitome of reality, for a woman of the past did indeed exist only from the collar up and the sleeves out; the rest of her remained hidden in darkness. A woman of the middle and upper ranks of society seldom left her house, and when she did she shielded herself from the gaze of the public in the dark recesses of her palanquin.[20]

Tanizaki also praised the old customs of blackening the teeth and using a green-black lipstick to hide the red of the mouth and "push everything except the face into the dark." Nostalgically, he recalled his mother going out in a gray kimono with a "small, modest pattern." "Women in those days had almost no flesh. ... Chest flat as a board, breasts paper-thin ... to give the impression not of flesh but of a stick."[21] What a contrast to the modern girl out in public with her bright red lipstick, long exposed legs, and colorful, form-fitting dress!

Tanizaki's regrets for the passing of traditional Japanese ideals of female beauty (and passivity) and aesthetic tastes of darkness and shadows came in the wake of the "erotic, grotesque, nonsense" (*ero-guro-nansensu*) fad that swept literary circles as well as popular entertainments during the early 1930s. This was the height of the Depression, so one can understand why many Marxist as well as right-wing critics interpreted it as a reflection of the last days of decadent bourgeois capitalism. Besides the cafes, *ero-guro* was also represented by the large-scale, glitzy stage revues in Asakusa's Sixth District. These musical productions at theatres such as the Casino Folies featured chorus girls in scanty but elaborate costumes.

The renowned novelist and postwar Nobel laureate Kawabata Yasunari contributed to the fascination with Asakusa's nightlife with his novel *Asakusa kurenai dan* (Asakusa Crimson Gang), which was serialized in the Tokyo *Asahi shinbun* from 1929 to 1930. He had visited Asakusa every day for three years in preparation for writing the novel, which utilized modernist writing techniques to produce kaleidoscopic impressions of the entertainment district. Asakusa had been the place for modern entertainments in Tokyo since the Meiji period, but by the late 1920s had been superseded by Ginza. Consequently, while still extremely popular, especially for the latest movies and the revues, Asakusa had become somewhat tawdry and cheap. Kawabata's descriptions made it a fashionable place for slumming and turned Casino Folies into a household word.[22]

Individualism and Selfishness

As Donald Roden has pointed out, the character Yumiko in *Asakusa kurenai dan* flouts conventional sex roles by alternating between a "masculine" young woman and a "feminine" young man by changing clothes, language, gestures, and even her name. This, Roden argues, reflected fascination with sexual ambivalence in both the popular and high arts of interwar Japan, which, in turn, points to the transition from the Meiji civilization of character to a Taishō culture of personality. According to Roden, "in the culture of personality, the self-actualizing needs of the individual derive from sexual urges as well as philosophic quests."[23]

Contemporary critics of modernity could thus trace both the hedonism and materialism characterizing young modern men and women to individualism and selfishness. Like other Marxists, Ōya Sōichi considered the decadence and perversity as part of the modernist "culture of feeling" in "a society in the last stage of capitalism," but he regarded the modern boys and modern girls who were defying bourgeois notions of respectability and assigned gender roles as the "vanguard" of the next historical stage.[24] In contrast, there were other intellectuals, notably the psychologist and birth control advocate Yasuda Tokutarō, who welcomed the breakdown of sexual barriers and the culture of personality. In a 1935 essay on homosexuality, Yasuda concluded that freer sexuality would lead Japan to a higher level of cultural development.[25]

In the shift to the culture of personality from the civilization of character, instead of self-restraint there was an emphasis on self-expression, and instead of value placed on the normative, there was value placed on the idiosyncratic. Much of the literature of the period exemplified this shift, epitomized in the "I" novel (*shishōsetsu*) which became the distinguishing genre of Japanese fiction during the 1920s. Although literary critics and historians vary as to what constitutes an "I" novel, Donald Keene says that it is confessional, rather than just a recounting of personal events. Authors in the Naturalist tradition especially were "likely to portray [themselves] in the least attractive light, as being shiftless, dissolute, incapable of writing" and often led the dissolute or deviant lives portrayed in their works.[26] Keene points to Kasai Zenzō, who "drank in order to write," as the "emblematic example" of an "I" novelist.[27] Comparing Kasai to another "I" novelist, Makino Shin'ichi, Kawakami Tetsutarō found commonalities in "their doggedness, their intense immersion in their own mental states, the brutal sadism they directed at their own or other people's sentimentality and pride."[28]

Keene distinguishes the "mental attitude" novelists from the "I" novelists. In contrast to the nihilism of the "I" novelists, they found "depth and beauty in incidents of daily lives."[29] The disciples of Shiga Naoya in the Shirakaba (White Birch) group typified the "mental attitude" novelists. Generally regarded as the quintessential Taishō writers, these self-pronounced Tolstoyan humanists often wrote about intergenerational conflict and criticized General Nogi Maresuke's suicide following the death of the Meiji emperor as anachronistic and inhumane.[30]

Despite these differences in attitude, both "I" novelists and "mental attitude" novelists looked inward in their writings. Roy Starrs notes this difference between writers of the interwar years and those of the Meiji period. Even writers, such as Akutagawa Ryūnosuke, Kawabata Yasunari, and Tanizaki Jun'ichirō, who wrote neither "I" novels nor "mental attitude" novels, did not write novels relevant to nation-building or modernization as did Mori Ōgai or Natsume Sōseki of the Meiji period.[31] This again was part of the shift from civilization to culture that distinguishes Taishō culture.[32] Among these, Keene describes Akutagawa as "the most striking literary figure" of the Taishō period. Akutagawa's almost godlike eminence is revealed in the fact that the prize established in his name in 1935 by his friend Kikuchi Kan, the editor of the popular monthly *Bungei shunjū*, was the most sought-after prize among writers. That such a successful writer should commit suicide as he did in 1927 sent a shock wave through not only the literary world, but also the general public. According to Keene, commentators interpreted the suicide as "a symbolic act, an expression of profound anxiety over the state of the times, or of personal inability to resolve the conflicting attraction of Japanese tradition and the wave of the future, represented by proletarian literature."[33]

Modernism versus Marxism

The late 1920s literary world, however, was less marked by an opposition between Japanese tradition and a Western-inspired proletarian literature than by a clash between two modern literary forces – proletarian literature and another Western-inspired movement called New Sensationalism (Shinkankaku). Proletarian literature stood for ideological principles, writing fiction for social purposes, while New Sensationalism stood for literary principles. The New Sensation group, led by Yokomitsu Riichi, were modernists with a capital "M" who experimented with new literary techniques created by European writers after World War I. James Joyce, Marcel Proust, and Paul Valéry influenced them greatly. Along with other modernist groups, including Dadaists, Surrealists, Futurists, and Expressionists, the New Sensation writers deliberately broke with traditional grammatical rules and structures and utilized uncouth expressions. Rather than the self-absorbed confessional writings of "I" novelists, New Sensation novelists wrote in the detached style of an observer, but created often surrealistic images and intense atmospheres through their unconventional sentences and expressions.[34] Yokomitsu's "The Machine" (1930) and Kawabata's *Asakusa kurenai dan* stand out as successful examples of these modernist writings.

Members of the proletarian literature movement decried the New Sensation group and other modernists for their preoccupation with form, which went hand in hand with a denial of moral content. Writers in the Japan Proletarian Literary Federation (Nihon Puroretaria Bungei Renmei) wanted to produce novels with literary quality, but the primary social purpose of advancing the proletarian revolution restricted creativity, especially because of ideological parameters set by the Soviet Union. Most leaders did not come from the proletariat, and when one who did, Tokunaga Sunao, urged creation of popular literature that the proletariat could enjoy, Kobayashi Takiji denounced him for "right-wing, opportunistic tendencies."[35] Tokunaga left the movement the following year in October 1933, protesting against the domination of political over literary concerns.

Tokunaga's withdrawal was part of a wave of conversions or, *tenkō*, from Communism that led to disbandment of the proletarian literature organization in 1934. Proletarian literature had enjoyed a heyday in the last years of the 1920s. Many writers had turned to the left after Akutagawa's suicide, including several from the New Sensation group. However, suppression of the Communist Party and its sympathizers began with mass arrests in March 1928 and April 1929. Kobayashi Takiji's death in jail from police torture suggests the role played by the threat of physical suffering on defections, but it was the apostasy of party leaders Sano Manabu and Nabeyama Sadachika later in 1933 that triggered the torrent of conversions. It is estimated that 95 percent of those imprisoned renounced their Marxism.[36] The degree of sincerity in their renunciations varied considerably, with some converts becoming active supporters of government policies and others lying low and reverting to Marxism after the war ended.

In any case, the process was a traumatic one that spawned a genre of autobiographical writings known as *tenkō* literature. Shimaki Kensaku is the best known among these writers, according to Keene. He wrote stories about the great pressure to convert that he received from family and friends as well as the police. His long *tenkō* novel, *Quest for Life*, received an enthusiastic response from both the general public and government in 1938, but Nakamura Mitsuo was critical of the speed with which *tenkō* writers rushed into print as well as of the lack of discrimination regarding literary quality on the part of readers. As he wrote in 1935,

> One gets used to anything. And one of the cleverest ways of getting along in this dizzy age of ours is to get used to everything, no matter how peculiar, as quickly as possible. Perhaps that is why it does not seem especially strange that there should be a spate of novels these days by so-called tenkō writers who have described their prison experiences. But, when one stops to think about it, this is indeed a truly bizarre phenomenon. In the first place, it is strange that so many authors have been imprisoned. Most of them, moreover, have left prison at almost exactly the same time, and in less than two or three months have published accounts of their prison experiences in the form of autobiographical fiction in the major magazines.[37]

Although Nakamura was scoffing at the *tenkō* writers for commercializing their prison experiences, rejection of their Marxist principles and social purpose was personally devastating and spiritually disorienting. It necessitated finding some other principles and purpose for their literary lives.

The Search for the Lost Home

It was not only *tenkō* converts who sought a new vision of society and culture during the middle and late 1930s. Nakamura's reference to "this dizzy age of ours" points to a more generalized feeling of disorientation and loss of identity. The "speed," "tempo," "jazz," "light," and "brightness" that were equated with the modern city were exciting and stimulating, but at the same time isolating and alienating. The theme of homelessness, both physical and spiritual, arose frequently in writings of the period.

The poet Hagiwara Sakutarō is a particularly good example of a writer who sensed an irretrievable loss and rootlessness in the condition of modernity. His sense of loss is all the more striking because of his role as the leading poet of the modern style during the 1920s, a poet who found inspiration in the writings of Western poets such as Edgar Allan Poe and Charles Baudelaire. Hagiwara's poem "Song of the Wanderer" expresses the poet's inability to find a spiritual home in either past or present, East or West, city or countryside.

You! Wanderer!
You who come from the past and go toward the future
seeking eternal nostalgia
how can you shift your worries back and forth
like a clock's pendulum?[38]

In an earlier poem, "The Homecoming" (*Kikyō*), Hagiwara had expressed a loss of identity with his home in the countryside, but at the same time in "Nogisaka Club" (*Nogisaka Kurabu*) he wrote about the loneliness and emptiness of life in a fashionable district of Tokyo:

Last year I lived in a fifth-floor apartment
in a vast Western-style room
I pushed my bed up against the wall and slept alone.
What is it that troubles me?
Already weary of the emptiness of life
must I now starve like some beast of burden?
I have lost nothing
but I have lost everything.[39]

In 1937 Hagiwara wrote a poem entitled "Return to Japan" (*Nihon e no kaiki*) that seemed to signal an end to his wandering and homelessness, and he joined the Romantic School (Romanha), a group described by Kevin Doak as writers who sought to fulfil their "dreams of difference" from the West. The title of Hagiwara's poem became a slogan taken up by many writers and critics of the late 1930s, and it has served as an umbrella for what were actually quite diverse answers to the problem of "overcoming modernity" that came together in the 1942 symposium by that name. Before examining that discourse, however, we will look at other attempts to solve the problem of homelessness and a sense of discontinuity with the past and tradition.

Marxists were not the only ones who turned away from Western cultural values and ideas. Leading modernist writers, such as Yokomitsu and Kawabata, gradually abandoned modernism. Yokomitsu became absorbed with the meaning of being Japanese, particularly after an extended trip to Europe as a newspaper correspondent in 1936.[40] Kawabata also gave up modernism and wrote novels that have given him a reputation for being a "Japanese" writer. He joined government-sponsored writers' organizations before and during the war and never published political or social views that offended the government. Nevertheless, Kawabata's works do not exhibit a "linear 'return to the East'," but rather a constant move back and forth between East and West.[41] He continued, for example, to use stream-of- consciousness techniques and surrealistic imagery.[42] Moreover, even after 1937 he published articles insisting on freedom of speech and a spirit of rebelliousness against social conventions. He declared that "without a rebellion against conventional morality there can be no 'pure literature'."[43]

Among aesthetics theorists, we have already seen Tanizaki's wistful mourning for the decline of traditional Japanese tastes and standards of female beauty. During the 1930s Tanizaki remained in the Kansai area, away from the modernity of Tokyo, wrote *The Makioka Sisters* (*Sasameyuki*) about an old Osaka family, and rendered the

Heian classic, *The Tale of Genji*, into modern Japanese. This return to traditional Japanese subjects was not deemed sufficiently supportive of the war by government authorities, who banned *The Makioka Sisters*, and certain critics regarded the translation of *The Tale of Genji* into modern Japanese as a contamination of the original work and a pandering to the masses.

Kuki Shūzō is another prominent theoretician of aesthetics who is often presented as an example of the "return to Japan." During the 1920s Kuki spent a long time assimilating European culture and philosophy, which he taught on his return to Japan and appointment at Kyoto University. During the 1930s, however, Kuki became known for his valorization of the Edo taste for *iki*, a difficult-to-translate term that encompasses "chic," "smart," and "refined" all at once. Despite this apparent "return to Japan," Nakano Hajimu argues that Kuki in fact attempted to unify Occidental and Oriental ways of thought. According to Nakano, this distinguishes Kuki from his colleague Watsuji Tetsurō and the thinkers of the Kyoto School of philosophy, who evaluated traditional Japanese culture more highly and had a greater concern with social and political issues.[44]

Yanagita Kunio was also a critic of modernity who turned to the Japanese past for solutions to the problems of modernity, but he went deeper into the past than Kuki. Other thinkers, such as Ōkawa Shūmei, Tachibana Kosaburō, and Gondō Seikei, also developed theories rejecting the modernity of the city, but because their theories were more directly linked to political activism, they are not examined here. Yanagita's concerns were social rather than aesthetic, but his solution ended up being a cultural rather than economic or political one. Travelling to remote villages and the geographical periphery of Okinawa, places that were least touched by modernization, Yanagita collected folk tales and constructed the concept of *jōmin* (abiding folk), an imaginary folk who were complete and unchanging, "everywhere and nowhere." He argued that through folklore studies or ethnology (*minzokugaku*), the religious and spiritual life of the *jōmin* would be reconstituted and counter the disruption of communal life caused by modern technology and the bureaucratic penetration of the countryside.[45]

The "Overcoming Modernity" Symposium

Many intellectuals did not find Yanagita's new nativism able to restore their sense of wholeness and stability, largely because their interests focused on literate culture and the social changes of the city rather than on rural society and oral tradition. Neither did the war provide a common purpose to end the debates over modernity. And, although many intellectuals took up Hagiwara's call to "return to Japan," the results of the 1942 "Overcoming Modernity" symposium reveal an inability to form a consensus on the complex issues of modernity. This is not surprising given the diverse backgrounds of the participants: novelists, poets, literary and film critics, philosophers, composers, scientists, psychologists, and historians. Although they generally represented three groups – the Kyoto School of philosophy, the Romantic School, and the Literary Society (Bungakkai) – none of these groups were unified in their view of modernity. Like the European symposia upon which the Japanese one was modelled,[46] participants failed even to agree on a definition of modernity, much less on ways to overcome it.

Some, such as former Marxists Hayashi Fusao and Kamei Katsuichirō of the Romantic School, blamed the introduction of modernity from the West for the loss of native Japanese spirit. Kamei saw Western egoism and rationality as the "poisons of civilization" and called for a return to belief in the gods (*kami*) and "our classics," although he was still not sure that this would solve the problems of modernity. The leader of the Romantics, Yasuda Yōjūrō, had a stronger belief in the restorative value of the classics, but as Doak points out, members of the Romantic School defined modernity in various ways: "at times it represented a foreign influence – the West; at other times it referred to the Meiji state and its ideology of 'civilization and enlightenment'; and at still others it referred to the reality of Japanese culture in its only existent (if decadent) form."[47] In addition, although Hayashi and others targeted Americanism for the spread of crass, hedonistic materialism among modern girls and boys, the Romantics still "privileged youth and its enthusiasm for imagining a better future, while utilizing the past as a means of negating the present."[48] This was proclaimed in the first issue of their journal: "We have taken up the lofty tune of the youth of our age and, rejecting faddish and vulgar literature, step forward without regret in the declaration of the noble and liberating action of the artist."[49]

Other participants in the symposium disagreed more strongly with Hayashi and Kamei about equating modernity with the West. Nishitani Keiji of the Kyoto School, for example, regarded modernity as a universal problem stemming from the French Revolution, if not earlier. The prominent literary critic Kobayashi Hideo condemned utilitarian bureaucratism, functional specialization, and mass production and consumerism like Hayashi, but rejected the idea that the problems of modernity were the result of Western influence and that reviving the Japanese classics would solve the problems. In 1933 he had written:

> It is a fact that ours is a literature of the lost home, that we are young people who have lost our youthful innocence. Yet we have something to redeem our loss. We have finally become able, without prejudice or distortion, to understand what is at the core of Western writing. With us Western literature has begun to be presented fairly and accurately. At this juncture, it is indeed pointless to call out for the "Japanese spirit" or the "Eastern spirit." Look wherever we might such things will not be found.[50]

Kobayashi was pessimistic in the end about finding a way to overcome modernity. His dilemma characterized the debates during the two days of the "Overcoming Modernity" symposium, and the moderator Kawakami Tetsutarō admitted its failure either to define modernity or to find ways to overcome it.

Conclusion

The lingering contentions and confused outcome of the symposium reflected the nature of debates over modernity among intellectuals and social commentators throughout the interwar decades. Most agreed with the government's critique of modernity, as depicted in the *Manga* cartoon that appeared two months before the symposium, but at the same time none suggested giving up the conveniences of modern science and technology. What they often condemned was the spiritual and cultural consequences of modern technology, efficiency and rationality – the loss of creativity resulting from commodification of culture, the sense of homelessness and loss of communal life resulting from the break with traditional tastes and values, and disorientation in an age of constant change. The modern boy and especially the modern girl epitomized these challenges posed by modernity and, in addition, represented modernity's challenge to accepted gender roles and the centrality of the family.

The critique of modernity intensified during the 1930s, but intellectuals and social critics never resolved their differences over the meaning of modernity and, consequently, could not agree about ways to overcome it. Supporting the war against the Anglo-American powers could not restore a sense of wholeness for many intellectuals because modernity was not a superficial Western import. And, in fact, their sense of alienation and isolation was a condition of modernity shared by their counterparts in Europe and the United States. In one sense, then, they were "overcome by modernity," to use Harootunian's words. But from their reflections on the experience of "modern life," we gain insights into the crucial transformations in Japanese society and culture during the interwar decades. And, from their proposed solutions, we see how sensitive observers everywhere have struggled to confront the challenges of modern social change.

NOTES

1 Najita and Harootunian, "Japanese Revolt against the West."
2 Harootunian, *Overcome by Modernity*, p. 95.
3 Quoted in Soviak, "Tsuchida Kyōson," p. 87.
4 For a reproduction of the cartoon, see Dower, *War without Mercy*, p. 191.
5 Tanizaki, *In Praise of Shadows*, p. 42.
6 Kinmonth, *The Self-Made Man*.
7 Ibid., p. 68.
8 Quoted in Oka, "Generational Conflict," p. 197.
9 Harootunian, *Overcome by Modernity*, p. 98.
10 Sand, "The Cultured Life as Contested Space."
11 Tanizaki, *In Praise of Shadows*, pp. 14, 6.
12 Sand, "The Cultured Life as Contested Space," p. 112.
13 Silverberg, "The Modern Girl as Militant," p. 250.
14 Translated in Sato, *The New Japanese Woman*, p. 55 (italics in translation).
15 Quoted ibid., p. 72 (italics in translation).
16 Translated in Silverberg, "Marxism Addresses the Modern," pp. 139–40.
17 The following section on the magazine is based on Tipton, "Sex in the City."
18 Tipton, "The Café," pp. 119–20.
19 Silverberg, "The Modern Girl as Militant," pp. 248–9.
20 Tanizaki, *In Praise of Shadows*, p. 28.
21 Ibid., pp. 28–9, 33.
22 Keene, *Dawn to the West*, pp. 795–7.
23 Roden, "Taishō Culture and the Problem of Gender Ambivalence," p. 55.
24 Ibid., p. 54.
25 Ibid., pp. 54–5.
26 Keene, *Dawn to the West*, p. 512.
27 Ibid., p. 521.

28 Quoted in Keene, *Dawn to the West*, p. 522.
29 Ibid., p. 513.
30 Starrs, "Writing the National Narrative," p. 216.
31 Ibid., p. 214.
32 For the distinction between "civilization" (*bunmei*) and "culture" (*bunka*), see Harootunian, "Introduction: A Sense of an Ending and the Problem of Taishō."
33 Keene, *Dawn to the West*, pp. 588–9.
34 Ibid., p. 659.
35 Ibid., p. 615.
36 Ibid., p. 847.
37 Quoted ibid., pp. 880–1.
38 "Hyōhakusha no uta," translated in Doak, *Dreams of Difference*, p. 44.
39 Excerpted from the translation in Doak, *Dreams of Difference*, p. 45.
40 Keene, *Dawn to the West*, p. 662.
41 Ibid., p. 810.
42 Starrs, "Writing the National Narrative," p. 223.
43 Quoted in Keene, *Dawn to the West*, p. 803.
44 Nakano, "Kuki Shūzō," pp. 271–2.
45 Harootunian, "Figuring the Folk," pp. 146, 150; Hashimoto, "*Chihō*," pp. 138–42.
46 Doak, *Dreams of Difference*, p. 135. For more detailed analysis on the European symposia and their impact on Japanese writers, see Vidovic-Ferderbar, "In Limine."
47 Doak, *Dreams of Difference*, pp. xvi, 138.
48 Ibid., p. xxxvii.
49 Translated in ibid., p. xxxvii.
50 Translated in Anderer, *Literature of the Lost Home*, p. 54.

BIBLIOGRAPHY

Anderer, Paul. *Literature of the Lost Home: Kobayashi Hideo – Literary Criticism, 1924–1939.* Stanford, Calif.: Stanford University Press, 1995.

Doak, Kevin M. *Dreams of Difference: The Japan Romantic School and the Crisis of Modernity.* Berkeley: University of California Press, 1994.

Dower, John. *War without Mercy: Race and Power in the Pacific War.* London: Faber and Faber, 1986.

Gonda Yasunosuke. "Modan seikatsu to hentai shikōsei." *Kaizō* 11 (1929): 32–6.

Harootunian, H. D. "Introduction: A Sense of an Ending and the Problem of Taishō." In H. D. Harootunian and Bernard Silberman, eds., *Japan in Crisis: Essays on Taishō Democracy.* Princeton: Princeton University Press, 1974.

Harootunian, H. D. "Figuring the Folk: History, Poetics, and Representation." In Stephen Vlastos, ed., *Mirror of Modernity: Invented Traditions of Modern Japan.* Berkeley: University of California Press, 1998.

Harootunian, H. D. *Overcome by Modernity: History, Culture, and Community in Interwar Japan.* Princeton: Princeton University Press, 2000.

Hashimoto Mitsuru. "*Chihō*: Yanagita Kunio's 'Japan'." In Stephen Vlastos, ed., *Mirror of Modernity: Invented Traditions of Modern Japan.* Berkeley: University of California Press, 1998.

Keene, Donald. *Dawn to the West: Japanese Literature of the Modern Era*, vol. 1, *Fiction*. New York: Holt, Rinehart, and Winston, 1984.

Kinmonth, Earl. *The Self-Made Man in Meiji Japanese Thought: From Samurai to Salary Man.* Berkeley: University of California Press, 1981.

Najita, Tetsuo, and Harootunian, H. D. "Japanese Revolt against the West: Political and Cultural Criticism in the Twentieth Century." In Peter Duus, ed., *The Cambridge History of Japan*, vol. 6, *The Twentieth Century*. Cambridge: Cambridge University Press, 1988.

Nakano Hajimu. "Kuki Shūzō and *The Structure of Iki*." In J. Thomas Rimer, ed., *Culture and Identity: Japanese Intellectuals during the Interwar Years*. Princeton: Princeton University Press, 1990, pp. 261–72.

Oka Yoshitake. "Generational Conflict after the Russo-Japanese War." In Tetsuo Najita and Victor Koschmann, eds., *Conflict in Modern Japanese History*. Princeton: Princeton University Press, 1982.

Roden, Donald. "Taishō Culture and the Problem of Gender Ambivalence." In J. Thomas Rimer, ed., *Culture and Identity: Japanese Intellectuals during the Interwar Years*. Princeton: Princeton University Press, 1990.

Sand, Jordan. "The Cultured Life as Contested Space." In Elise K. Tipton and John Clark, eds., *Being Modern in Japan: Culture and Society from the 1910s to the 1930s*. Honolulu: University of Hawai'i Press, 2000.

Sato, Barbara. *The New Japanese Woman: Modernity, Media, and Women in Interwar Japan*. Durham, NC: Duke University Press, 2003.

Silverberg, Miriam. "Marxism Addresses the Modern: Nakano Shigeharu's Reproduction of Taishō Culture." In J. Thomas Rimer, ed., *Culture and Identity: Japanese Intellectuals during the Interwar Years*. Princeton: Princeton University Press, 1990.

Silverberg, Miriam. "The Modern Girl as Militant." In Gail Lee Bernstein, ed., *Recreating Japanese Women, 1600–1945*. Berkeley: University of California Press, 1991.

Soviak, Eugene. "Tsuchida Kyōson and the Sociology of the Masses." In J. Thomas Rimer, ed., *Culture and Identity: Japanese Intellectuals during the Interwar Years*. Princeton: Princeton University Press, 1990.

Starrs, Roy. "Writing the National Narrative: Changing Attitudes toward Nation-Building among Japanese Writers, 1900–1930." In Sharon Minichiello, ed., *Japan's Competing Modernities*. Honolulu: University of Hawai'i Press, 1998.

Tanizaki Jun'ichirō. *In Praise of Shadows*, trans. Thomas J. Harper and Edward Seidensticker. New Haven: Leete's Island Books, 1977.

Tipton, Elise K. "The Café: Contested Space of Modernity in Interwar Japan." In Elise Tipton and John Clark, eds., *Being Modern in Japan: Culture and Society from the 1910s to the 1930s*. Honolulu: University of Hawai'i Press, 2000.

Tipton, Elise K. "Sex in the City: Chastity vs Free Love in Interwar Japan." *Intersections: Gender, History, and Culture in the Asian Context* 11 (Aug. 2005) <http://wwwsshe.murdoch.edu.au/intersections/issue11/tipton.html> accessed Mar. 1, 2006.

Vidovic-Ferderbar, Dragica. "In Limine: Writers, Culture and Modernity in Interwar Japan." Ph.D. dissertation, University of Sydney, 2004.

FURTHER READING

J. Thomas Rimer's collection of essays, *Culture and Identity: Japanese Intellectuals during the Interwar Years* (Princeton: Princeton University Press, 1990), sought to draw attention to the intellectual history of modern Japan as seen in cultural criticism, which had been relatively neglected outside Japan. Among the contributors to that volume, H. D. Harootunian stands out as the most prominent and prolific historian who has focused on intellectuals' concerns with the problems of modernity during the interwar period. His most recent book on the subject, *Overcome by Modernity: History, Culture, and Community in Interwar Japan* (Princeton: Princeton University Press, 2000), examines Japanese intellectuals' reflections on "modern life," focusing on the "mutual imbrication" between politics and culture and between modernism and fascism.

There are numerous studies on individuals and groups in the fields of literature, philosophy, and art. These approach their subjects from their specific disciplinary perspectives, but they often focus on problems of identity and nationalism. Donald Keene's massive *Dawn to the West* (New York: Holt, Rinehart and Winston, 1984) provides a comprehensive introduction to individual writers and literary movements. Works on philosophy include James Heisig and John Maraldo, eds., *Rude Awakenings: Zen, the Kyoto School, and the Question of Nationalism* (Honolulu: University of Hawai'i Press, 1994), and Lesley Pincus, *Authenticating Culture in Imperial Japan: Kuki Shūzō and the Rise of National Aesthetics* (Berkeley: University of California Press, 1996). *Being Modern in Japan: Culture and Society from the 1910s to the 1930s* (Honolulu: University of Hawai'i Press, 2000), edited by Elise K. Tipton and John Clark, includes several chapters on developments in art and design. On *tenkō*, see Patricia Steinhoff, *Tenkō: Ideology and Societal Integration in Prewar Japan* (New York: Garland, 1991).

CHAPTER TWELVE

External Relations

Frederick R. Dickinson

Why have we Japanese, in this way, been driven to war after war over a span of three generations?[1]

Historians of modern Japan confront a host of profound questions. For those writing immediately following World War II, perhaps none was more pivotal than the debate over the causes of Japan's modern wars. Early postwar American specialists of Japanese history devoted their professional careers to analyzing the diplomatic and political causes of war-making in Japan. By contrast, through the mid-1970s, mainstream Japanese scholarship identified internal political and economic "contradictions" as the pre-eminent source of Japanese external aggression. As the momentum for serious analysis of external affairs grew in Japan, American specialists of Japan followed the international migration toward intellectual, social, and cultural history.

Despite the somewhat bumpy road of postwar writing on Japanese external affairs, international historians in both English- and Japanese-speaking academe continue to produce vital work on modern Japan. In many ways, they have adapted their scholarship to reflect trends in the more favored fields of social, cultural, and intellectual history. Although the number of historians trained in international history has declined dramatically in recent years, the best new scholarship continues to demonstrate the profound significance of analyses of external affairs for the understanding of modern Japanese history.

"Kaikoku," "Civilization," and Contingency

The most enduring trend of postwar scholarship on Japanese external affairs remains the refutation of the essential outlines of the "progressive" orthodoxy of the early postwar years. That orthodoxy defined the Tokugawa era as "feudal," the Meiji Restoration as an "incomplete revolution," and the modern era as marked by the steadily expanding power of a military-bureaucratic state, whose antiquated political and economic relationships led Japan invariably to wars of conquest and, ultimately, "fascism."

Integral to the progressive vision of the early modern period was the idea of a "closed country" (*sakoku*), whose insularity from the outside world lay at the heart of the stunted political and economic development considered critical in the ultimate path to war. But in a seminal 1984 study, Ronald Toby epitomized growing scholarly recognition that, despite bans on trade with Spanish and Portuguese merchants and measures to prevent unauthorized Japanese contact with the outside world, Tokugawa Japan maintained an active trade and diplomacy, particularly with its Asian neighbors.[2] Ever since, the principal thrust of Japanese and American scholarship on Tokugawa era external relations has been to document the expansive nature of Japanese contacts with the outer world.[3] Michael Auslin finds shrewd bakufu engagement with the Western powers even in an era typically defined as one of shogunal incompetence, the waning years of the dynasty following Commodore Matthew Perry's arrival in 1853.[4]

Like the story of a "closed" Tokugawa polity, the idea of a Meiji regime steeped more in "feudal" Asian than "modern" Western values long sustained the narrative of political and economic difficulties ultimately leading to unprecedented aggression abroad. But international historians increasingly view Japan's projection of power in the nineteenth century less as the product of aberrant "feudal" impulses than as a bid for inclusion in a modern, universal global system. Recent work on mid-nineteenth-century expansion highlights a meticulous Japanese attention to international norms.[5] On nineteenth- and early twentieth-century relations with Korea, Peter Duus echoes Hilary Conroy's classic emphasis upon national security but also places Japanese expansion squarely within the international vogue of empire-building. Wayne Patterson characterizes Japanese attempts to control recalcitrant Korean nationals in Hawaii as a demonstration of its diplomatic competence and authority. Ishikawa Hiroshi describes Meiji Japan's mid-nineteenth-century overtures toward Korea as attempts to adhere to international law, and both Unno Fukuju and Alexis Dudden detail the path toward annexation in similar terms.[6]

Meiji Japan's wars have also assumed a more benevolent tone compared to the accusatory tenor of early postwar Japanese scholarship. The long maligned foreign minister during the China engagement, Mutsu Munemitsu, emerged as a conscientious professional when his memoirs were republished in Japanese and English in the late 1960s and early 1980s, respectively.[7] Recent biographies of Mutsu accentuate this image.[8]

On Japanese continental policy at the turn of the century, Tsunoda Jun long ago stressed the geopolitical challenges posed by an eastward-expanding Russia. Kitaoka Shin'ichi followed by replacing the story of a military-bureaucratic juggernaut with the tale of nuanced debates within the imperial army. More recently, Stewart Lone has characterized army elder Katsura Tarō as a circumspect soldier, politician and empire-builder.[9]

Among the most measured visions of Japanese diplomacy in the first part of the twentieth century has been the story of Japan's relationship with Great Britain. By subtitling his original study of the Anglo-Japanese alliance "The Diplomacy of Two Island Empires," Ian Nish offered powerful exception to the more prominent association of Japan with aggressive continental expansion.[10] The hundredth anniversary of the alliance spurred a series of new studies by Nish and an impressive roster of British and Japanese specialists, which, by its very scope, underscored the idea of Japan as a "Britain of the East."[11] World War I has become a new arena to showcase a

temperate vision of Japanese diplomacy. Although progressive historians long identified the conflict as the start of Japanese monopoly capitalism, it has not received the
attention among Japan specialists typically lavished in historiographies of modern
Europe and the United States. There is an array of studies on specific aspects of
Japanese wartime diplomacy (Japan's entrance into the war, the "Twenty-one De-
mands," Nishihara Loans, Siberian Intervention, Paris Peace Conference, etc.), and
US–Japan relations specialists have written a handful of classic analyses of wartime
US–Japan negotiations.[12] But only recently have mainstream Japan specialists looked
to the conflict as a transformative event in the twentieth century. Hirama Yōichi finds
Japanese wartime naval operations (ferrying troops to the Indian Ocean, hunting
German U-boats in the Mediterranean) confirmation of Japan's pivotal cooperative
role on the early twentieth-century global stage. Frederick Dickinson highlights the
dramatic political and ideological impact of the Great War on Japan but characterizes
the "Twenty-one Demands" not as an unusually aggressive prelude to conquest in
the 1930s (the orthodox contention), but as an extension of the pattern of great-
power competition in China after 1895.[13]

Since the appearance of the classic multi-volume diplomatic history of the Pacific
War, *Taiheiyō sensō e no michi* in the 1960s, the story of Japan's ultimate road
to conflict in the 1930s has, like the tale of Japanese foreign relations from the
Tokugawa period through the early twentieth century, moved well beyond a discussion of internal turmoil and inevitable strife. By highlighting the intricate details
of military and diplomatic decision-making from 1931 to 1945, the eight-volume
series stressed the highly contingent nature of Japanese relations with the powers
and planning for war.[14] Akira Iriye followed soon after with his classic tale of
the difficulties of great power cooperation in China in the interwar period. For a
more general readership, Iriye described Japanese attempts to adapt to a new
world order only to see the economic foundations of that order collapse.[15] Thomas
Burkman found a genuine "internationalist" bent in interwar Japan in the country's
active participation in the League of Nations. Ian Nish privileged the professionalism
and good intentions of both Japanese and Western diplomats even in a tale of
the ultimate failure of international cooperation over the Manchurian Incident,
and David Lu's study of Japanese foreign minister Matsuoka Yōsuke stressed
the difficult external pressures on Japanese policy-makers in the 1930s, an "agony
of choice."[16]

Recent studies of Japanese policies toward China in the first half of the twentieth
century accentuate the image of a difficult international environment. Usui Katsumi
describes the escalation of Japanese aims in China in the latter 1930s as primarily a
response to the rise of Chinese nationalism. Other studies of China "experts" in both
the Japanese Foreign Ministry and army tell the tale of good intentions ultimately
derailed by more aggressive visions of expansion.[17]

The early 1980s witnessed an influential series of conferences on Japanese colonialism that carried important implications for the study of Japanese external affairs.
The principal contribution of the three conference volumes was to highlight details of
the construction and management of Japan's formal, "informal," and "wartime"
empires from 1895 to 1945.[18] Regarding foreign policy, the series did for English-
speaking audiences what *Taiheiyō sensō e no michi* had done for Japanese debates,
dealing a decisive blow to the idea of a direct line from "feudal" Tokugawa to

"fascist" Shōwa. It not only described Japan's first colonial territories in the wider context of nineteenth-century imperialism: it characterized Japan's presence in China until the formal outbreak of war in 1937 as primarily a commercial venture. And like its Japanese predecessor, coverage of the Sino-Japanese and Pacific Wars stressed the contingent nature of Japanese wartime planning.

Kajima Morinosuke once quipped that Japan had no diplomacy between 1941 and 1945. International historians have since found a silver lining in the most sinister era of modern Japanese history. Just as some political historians have long attempted to downplay the severity of Japanese wartime authoritarianism by rejecting parallels with European "fascism," international historians have found in wartime Japanese relations with Germany encouragement in evidence of only patchy bilateral ties.[19] The most intriguing positive portrayal of wartime Japanese diplomacy shows Tokyo not only not cooperating with Berlin, but directly opposing the most nefarious Nazi policies. Both David Kranzler and Hillel Levine offer a picture of compassionate Japanese diplomats aiding Jewish refugees from Nazi Germany. Although dismissive of the idea of a "pro-Jewish" policy in Tokyo, Pamela Sakamoto exposes the ad hoc nature of Japan's response to Jewish migration, which enabled some Japanese diplomats (most notably, Sugihara Chiune in Kaunus, Lithuania) to provide invaluable assistance to refugees.[20]

Revisiting Aggressive Intent

If, since the 1960s, Anglo-American and Japanese specialists of international history have increasingly stressed the open and "civilized" nature of modern Japan's relationship with the outer world and the contingent character of continental expansion, they have sparked a new debate about the relative degree of aggressive intent in Japan's diplomatic posture. Unhappy with either the accusatory tone of the earlier progressive orthodoxy or the overwhelmingly benign portrait of Japanese external relations promoted by early postwar international historians, a younger group of scholars have constructed a new vision of culpability divorced from the tale of internal political and economic "contradictions." Reiner Hesselink stresses bakufu suspicion, contempt, and torture of Dutch captives in a bid to restore some sense of Tokugawa era "seclusion."[21] And recent coverage of the nineteenth century increasingly pushes back the timetable of Japanese plans for conquest. Whereas Peter Duus dates Japanese aims for empire to the post-Sino-Japanese War years, Ochiai Hiroki reveals active discussions of conquest in the first decade of Meiji, and Robert Eskildsen finds clear Japanese intent to colonize Formosa in 1874. Brett Walker, in his innovative coverage of Tokugawa–Ainu trade, pushes the boundaries of Japanese expansion back to the early modern period.[22]

As for Japan's continental policy and wars of imperialism, Takahashi Hidenao reacted to the new positive spin on the Sino-Japanese War and Foreign Minister Mutsu with a sardonic tale of political intrigue. Although eschewing the class-based narrative of Japanese progressives, Takahashi describes Mutsu as an opportunist, who spurred brinkmanship abroad to overcome a fragile political base at home. Kobayashi Michihiko balks at the nuances in early twentieth-century army policy delineated by Kitaoka Shin'ichi and finds, instead, impressive plans for continental development by army elder Katsura Tarō and protégé Gotō Shinpei. While locating in the diplomacy of Katō Takaaki resonances with actions of the great powers, Frederick Dickinson finds in the worldview of members of the "Yamagata faction" during World War I glimpses of the pan-Asianism of the 1930s. Michael Barnhart similarly finds a link between World Wars I and II in mobilization plans developed within the imperial army in anticipation of another "total war."[23] Erik Esselstrom contests the sharp distinction long made between civil and military interests and developments before and after the Manchurian Incident. Pre-1931 efforts within the Foreign Ministry to expand the jurisdiction of Japanese consular police ultimately led to active civil–military cooperation to apprehend Chinese and Korean "rebels" in Manchuria.[24] Despite the centrality of Anglo-Japanese relations in the two above-mentioned multi-volume series edited by Ian Nish, other studies have begun to downplay both the utility of the pact and its importance relative to developments on the European and Asian continents.[25]

Among the most intriguing "incriminating" coverage of the Pacific War is work on the imperial Japanese navy. Since his 1962 Yale doctoral dissertation on the Washington Conference, Asada Sadao has offered the most influential counterpoint to the notion of a cautious navy hamstrung by aggressive ground forces. In the latest compilation of his work, Asada delineates the critical role played by the Fleet Faction in destroying the legitimacy of the cooperative "Washington system." In a similar vein, John Stephan counters the image of Admiral Yamamoto Isōroku as merely a brilliant strategist doing the bidding of a belligerent government. By the Battle of Midway, Yamamoto had forged a consensus within the armed services to pursue the occupation of Hawaii. More recently, J. Charles Schencking has exposed the impressive scale of Japanese "navalism" long before both world wars.[26].

Domestic Context

As we have seen, younger specialists of Japanese external affairs have begun a slight swing of the pendulum back toward the early postwar progressive orthodoxy by spotting more long-term trends of aggressive intent. Similarly, current scholars are increasingly amenable to linking external relations with domestic developments. Although these specialists reject the dialectic ties between internal politics/economy and foreign policy argued by Japan's progressive historians, they equally object to the overwhelmingly external context of much of the postwar international history. Kitaoka Shin'ichi set the standard in 1978 with his meticulous coverage of debates within the imperial army over early twentieth-century Japanese continental policy. More recently, Komiya Kazuo has highlighted the late nineteenth-century effort to revise Japan's unequal treaties as a pivotal domestic political event. Itō Yukio sees the Russo-Japanese War less as the inevitable result of an expanding Russian empire than as the product of the declining domestic authority of diplomatic "moderate" Itō Hirobumi. Hattori Ryūji describes the Manchurian Incident as a tragedy generated by the loss of conservative politicians of the stature of Hara Takashi.[27]

Some historians have taken the story of domestic factors even further to place foreign policy within the larger context of nation-building. Robert Eskildsen sees Japanese initiatives in Taiwan in 1874 as critical in the formulation of a new modern national identity. Hiyama Yukio highlights the cultural and structural integration spurred by the Sino-Japanese War. And Frederick Dickinson describes Japan's principal political and policy debates during World War I as focused upon the larger effort to redefine the nation.[28]

Part of the new turn toward internal developments is an active debate over the role of the imperial institution in Japanese foreign affairs. Although it was central to the progressive orthodoxy of the early postwar years, the institution became the focus of intense general interest with the passing of the Shōwa emperor in 1989 and the publication of his occupation-era testimonial about the Japanese road to war.[29] Following a vibrant debate in Japan over the implications of the Shōwa emperor's "confessions," several English-language works featured the emperor's wartime role. The most conspicuous of these was Herbert Bix's biography, which won a Pulitzer Prize for describing the emperor's early education as military training and for implicating the emperor in practically all of Japan's wartime activities, including gas warfare in China and the Nanjing Massacre.[30] Meanwhile, a group of Japanese researchers pursued a more modest agenda of precisely locating imperial authority in specific political and policy decisions in the first half of the twentieth century.[31]

As is evident from Bix and others, a salutary effect of the focus on internal developments has been to restore a sense of agency to Japanese foreign policy decision-making. One area of Japanese external affairs where such a restoration has constituted the principal new historiographical development is in the study of the Allied occupation of Japan. Our understanding of the period, traditionally the domain of specialists of American foreign policy, has greatly benefited from growing interest in and creative use of materials that highlight indigenous Japanese efforts at reform. Through extensive coverage of Japanese–American interaction under occupation, Takemae Eiji set an early standard.[32] More recently, Gary Tsuchimochi argues that education reform under US occupation proceeded largely upon Japanese initiative. John Dower won a Pulitzer Prize in 2000 for an exhaustive and absorbing portrayal of everyday Japanese life under occupation, from abject defeat to "Japanizing" democracy.[33]

Economy

Just as they have long promoted contingent external factors in Japanese decisions for war, international historians have rejected the postwar Japanese progressive emphasis upon the internal economic origins of foreign aggression. But, as we have seen with the general attitude toward Japanese expansion and the relationship between external and internal events, current scholarship on Japanese external affairs no longer suffers the same allergy to economic exigencies as it used to. Much of the new work on Tokugawa era external relations highlights Japanese trade in the early modern period.[34] Rejecting his predecessor Conroy's dismissal of commercial considerations, Peter Duus argues that economic underdevelopment in Korea played a key role in luring Japanese involvement on the peninsula in the late nineteenth century.[35]

Economic factors also loom large in recent studies of Anglo-Japanese and Japanese–American relations in the early twentieth century. As noted above, Ian Nish has shepherded a multi-volume project on Anglo-Japanese ties, which includes one volume devoted to economic affairs.[36] On Japanese–American relations, a Japanese study group in 1994 offered powerful refutation of the presumed connection between economic distress and Japanese aggression in the 1930s. Growing bilateral political tensions curbed economic opportunities, not vice versa. The same lesson emerges from Iguchi Haruo's intriguing study of the founder of Nissan, Ayukawa Yoshisuke, and his ties to Detroit and Wall Street.[37]

Perception

If historians of Japanese external affairs have, in recent years, gradually incorporated concerns of early postwar progressive scholarship, they have, similarly, adapted well to the growing popularity of social, cultural, and intellectual history. There is, for example, increasing recognition of the importance of perception in international history. Akira Iriye pioneered the approach in his classic 1967 analysis of American–East Asian relations, *Across the Pacific*. And ever since Marius Jansen identified Tokugawa Japan's intellectual break with China as a critical turning point in the rise of a modern nation, specialists of Japanese diplomacy have attempted to delineate the effect of attitudes vis-à-vis China on policy-making.[38] There is now a cottage industry of studies that chronicle Japanese disparagement of Korea in the ultimate lead-up to annexation, and we know much more today about Japanese perceptions of the enemy during the Sino- and Russo-Japanese Wars.[39] We have numerous anthologies and analyses of observations by some of modern Japan's early sojourners West.[40] And in an interesting biographical approach, Seki Shizuo compares perceptions of the United States, Russia, Germany, and China of seven prominent interwar policy-makers and opinion leaders.[41]

A decade after *Across the Pacific*, Akira Iriye edited the classic work that paved the way for the study of "mutual images" in US–Japan relations. Asada Sadao's analysis of the Japanese navy reveals disparaging views of Wilson's new world order among members of the Fleet Faction in interwar Japan. Kurosawa Fumitaka has found similar discontent within the imperial army regarding "democracy" in interwar Japan. Hasegawa Yūichi et al. locate a complex "ambivalence" in prominent Japanese civilian and military leaders' reactions to perceived American racial exclusionism in the 1910s and 20s. By contrast, Kitaoka Shin'ichi finds favorable views of the United States in an earlier era, during the Russo-Japanese War.[42]

The most celebrated study of mutual perceptions in the last two decades covers the darkest period of bilateral ties, the Pacific War. John Dower's absorbing tale of mutual hatreds and racism at once confirms the virulent anti-Western bias of Japanese wartime propaganda and places it within the context of equally problematic American images of a "subhuman" enemy. Although Dower makes the tenuous argument that American hatred for a fearsome wartime enemy delayed the conclusion of the Pacific War for several months, younger scholars are increasingly able to locate tangible connections between domestic images of the Other and foreign policy decision-making on both sides of the Pacific.[43]

Culture

In tandem with his leadership in the study of perception in external affairs, Akira Iriye pioneered the investigation of culture in foreign policy. Under his editorship, an authoritative group of Japan and China specialists in 1980 produced a rich study of Sino-Japanese political and cultural exchange in the nineteenth and early twentieth centuries. Iriye followed this with a study of the Pacific War that found similar cultural aspirations in the war aims of the United States and Japan.[44]

Iriye's disciples have produced several intriguing studies of the confluence of culture and diplomacy in recent years. Following the movement away from early postwar indictments of Japanese continental aggrandizement, See Heng Teow highlights interwar Foreign Ministry "cultural policy" toward China (aimed at remitting to China funds originally earmarked as an indemnity for the 1900 Boxer Uprising) as a well-meaning effort, parallel with similar efforts by Britain and the United States, to foster Sino-Japanese friendship, not Japanese hegemony. Izumi Hirobe details the complex debate among non-governmental groups on both sides of the Pacific over the 1924 American Immigration Act.[45]

Closely related to the study of culture and diplomacy are analyses of the activities of international cultural and political organizations and of international cultural events. International historians have long highlighted the role of the Hsin-min hui (Peoples's Renovation Society) and the Tōa Dōbunkai (East Asian Culture Society) in both creating a common East Asian cultural sphere and ensuring Japanese hegemony in twentieth-century Sino-Japanese relations.[46] Regarding Japanese relations with the Western world, we now have studies of the International Red Cross in Japan, the Center for International Cultural Relations (Kokusai Bunka Shinkōkai), and the Institute of Pacific Relations.[47] Ayako Hotta-Lister accentuates the image of strong early twentieth-century ties with an analysis of the 1910 Japan-British Exhibition.[48]

Although less tied to investigations of actual policy-making, there are a growing number of titles focusing upon "cultural encounters" across borders. Joshua Fogel has been the most prolific student of Sino-Japanese cultural encounters since his biography of Japanese Sinologist Naitō Konan in 1984.[49] Russo-Japanese cultural contacts have also increasingly attracted Western scholars in recent years.[50]

Memory

Closely related to analyses of both perception and culture is a new fascination among international historians with memory in policy formation. A wave of scholarship on the Russo-Japanese War marked the lead-up to the hundredth anniversary of the conflict. Among those works were a significant number of analyses of the war in Japanese public memory. Nomura Minoru's *Nihonkai kaisen no shinjitsu* describes the interwar exaltation of Admiral Tōgō Heihachirō and his decimation of the Russian Baltic Fleet in the Battle of the Japan Sea. Hara Takeshi speaks of the larger strategic significance of the war and its military application in the 1930s. Tak Matsusaka looks at the Battle of Port Arthur and its refashioning after Portsmouth. And

Frederick Dickinson highlights the role of Russo-Japanese War commemorations in fighting liberal internationalism in interwar Japan.[51]

The political and cultural implications of memories of World War II have been the subject of an increasing number of intriguing studies. Scholars have paid considerable attention to postwar debates over the two most controversial symbols of wartime atrocity, the Nanjing Massacre and Hiroshima.[52] Less well-known is the April 1945 American sinking of the Japanese merchant ship *Awa Maru*, which Roger Dingman highlights as a formidable symbol of American treachery in postwar Japan. Laura Hein and Mark Selden place contemporary Japanese textbook controversies in valuable comparative context. And Takashi Fujitani, Geoffrey White, and Lisa Yoneyama accentuate World War II in Asia as a wide assortment of personal reflections in Japan, the USA, China, Southeast Asia, the Pacific islands, Okinawa, Taiwan, and Korea.[53]

Conclusion

The popularity of international history has declined precipitously over the last two decades, particularly among English-speaking specialists of modern Japan. Interest in related fields, on the other hand, has soared. Spurred by postcolonial discourse, the culture of Japanese imperialism has attracted significant attention in recent years.[54] Many have, likewise, begun to probe the pivotal impact of Japan's modern wars upon Japanese society and culture.[55] There is, finally, an exciting new trend that highlights political, social, cultural, and economic convergences across national borders – "transnational" history.[56]

Although international historians increasingly engage issues of culture, few of those working on the culture of Japanese war and imperialism have much to do with international history. "Transnational" historians, moreover, investigate developments outside of the principal unit of analysis for international historians, the state. In this context, one wonders whether there is a future for specialists of Japanese external affairs.

Since the 1960s, international historians have stood at the vanguard of efforts to refute the early postwar progressive vision of modern Japan. Our current sense of the Tokugawa regime as seriously engaged with the outer world, of imperial Japanese leaders striving to adapt to international norms and of the highly contingent nature of Japanese overseas expansion all come from the painstaking work of international historians. These scholars are uniquely capable of engaging such fundamental issues as the role of politics and economy in Japanese continental expansion. They reposition questions of perception, culture, and memory from the realm of theory to the tangible context of real-world events, and they add to the new vogue of "transnationalism" a substantial factual ballast.[57]

Although one cannot hope that all future specialists of Japanese external affairs, the culture of war and empire, and/or "transnational history" enjoy equal competence in Japanese culture, politics, and foreign affairs, we could feasibly ask for greater synergy across intellectual boundaries. International historians profit by placing Japanese external relations within larger domestic and "transnational" contexts. Students of the culture of war and empire and transnational history in Asia, likewise, could benefit by more attention to the basic outlines of politics and foreign affairs. Collaboration will ensure that our understanding of such fundamental questions as the causes and consequences of war are less obscured than enhanced by the more fashionable investigations into society and culture.

NOTES

1   Rekishigaku Kenkyūkai, ed., *Taiheiyō sensōshi*, vol. 1, p. 1.
2   Toby, *State and Diplomacy.*
3   For a recent study in English, see Laver, "A Strange Isolation."
4   Auslin, *Negotiating with Imperialism.*
5   Eskildsen, "Of Civilization and Savages."
6   Conroy, *The Japanese Seizure of Korea*; Duus, *The Abacus and the Sword*; Patterson, *The Korean Frontier in America*; Ishikawa, "Meiji ishin to Chōsen, taima kankei"; Unno, *Kankoku heigōshi no kenkyū*; Dudden, *Japan's Colonization of Korea.*
7   Hagihara, *Nihon no meicho*; Berger, trans. and ed., *Kenkenroku.*
8   Okazaki, *Mutsu Munemitsu to sono jidai*; Perez, *Japan Comes of Age.*
9   Tsunoda, *Manshū mondai to kokubō hōshin*; Kitaoka, *Nihon rikugun to tairiku seisaku*; Lone, *Army, Empire and Politics in Meiji Japan.*
10 Nish, *The Anglo-Japanese Alliance.* See also Nish, *Alliance in Decline.*
11 The series covers 400 years of history and over 100 Japanese and British personalities who played critical roles in the bilateral relationship. Nish, ed., *Britain and Japan*, and Nish and Kibata, eds., *The History of Anglo-Japanese Relations*, are just two volumes in a five-volume series covering military, economic, and sociocultural relations as well.
12 Two of the most recent of this genre are Kawamura, *Turbulence in the Pacific*, and Shimazu, *Japan, Race and Equality.*
13 Hirama, *Daiichiji sekai taisen to Nihon kaigun*; Dickinson, *War and National Reinvention.*
14 Nihon Kokusai Seiji Gakkai Taiheiyō Sensō Gen'in Kenkyūbu, ed., *Taiheiyō sensō e no michi.*
15 Iriye, *After Imperialism*; Iriye, *Nihon no gaikō* and *Japan and the Wider World.*
16 Burkman, *Japan, the League of Nations, and World Order*; Nish, *Japan's Struggle with Internationalism*. Lu's study, originally published in Japanese in 1981, appeared in English in 2002, entitled *Agony of Choice.*
17 Usui, *Nitchū sensō*, and, more recently, *Nitchū gaikōshi kenkyū*. For the Foreign Ministry, see Brooks, *Japan's Imperial Diplomacy*, and for the Japanese army, see Tobe, *Nihon rikugun to Chūgoku.*
18 Myers and Peattie, eds., *The Japanese Colonial Empire*; Duus, Myers, and Peattie, eds., *The Japanese Informal Empire in China*; Duus, Myers, and Peattie, eds., *The Japanese Wartime Empire.*
19 Meskill, *Hitler and Japan*; Morley, ed., *Deterrent Diplomacy.* More recently, see Martin, *Japan and Germany in the Modern World*; Krug et al., *Reluctant Allies.*
20 Kranzler, *Japanese, Nazis, and Jews*; Levine, *In Search of Sugihara*; Sakamoto, *Japanese Diplomats and Jewish Refugees.*
21 Hesselink, *Prisoners of Nambu.*
22 Duus, *The Abacus and the Sword*; Ochiai, "Meiji shoki no gaiseiron to higashi Ajia"; Eskildsen, "Of Civilization and Savages"; Walker, *The Conquest of Ainu Lands.*
23 Takahashi, *Nisshin sensō e no michi*; Kobayashi, *Nihon no tairiku seisaku*; Dickinson, *War and National Reinvention*; Barnhart, *Japan Prepares for Total War.*
24 Esselstrom, "The Japanese Consular Police in Northeast Asia."
25 O'Brien, ed., *Anglo-Japanese Alliance, 1902–1922.*

26 Asada, *Ryō taisenkan no Nichi-Bei kankei*; Stephan, *Hawaii under the Rising Sun*; Schencking, *Making Waves*.

27 Kitaoka, *Nihon rikugun to tairiku seisaku*; Komiya, *Jōyaku kaisei to kokunai seiji*; Itō, *Rikken kokka to Nichi-Ro sensō*; Hattori, *Higashi Ajia kokusai kankyō no hendō to Nihon gaikō 1918–1931*.

28 Eskildsen, "Of Civilization and Savages"; Lone, *Japan's First Modern War*; Hiyama, ed., *Kindai Nihon no keisei to Nisshin sensō*; Dickinson, *War and National Reinvention*.

29 Terasaki, *Shōwa tennō dokuhakuroku*.

30 Drea, *In the Service of the Emperor*; Wetzler, *Hirohito and War*; Bix, *Hirohito and the Making of Modern Japan*.

31 Itō, *Seitō seiji to tennō*; Itō and Kawada, ed., *Nijū seiki Nihon no tennō to kunshusei*.

32 Takemae's 1983 study was published in English in 2002 as *Inside GHQ*, trans. and adapted by Ricketts and Swann.

33 Tsuchimochi, *Education Reform in Postwar Japan*; Dower, *Embracing Defeat*.

34 See Nagazumi, *Shuinsen*.

35 Duus, *The Abacus and the Sword*.

36 Hunter and Sugiyama, *The History of Anglo-Japanese Relations*, vol. 4.

37 Kamiyama and Iida, eds., *Tairitsu to dakyō*; Iguchi, *Unfinished Business*.

38 Jansen, *Japan and Its World*, later elaborated in more detail in Jansen, *China in the Tokugawa World*. See Toby, "Kara no kanata yori."

39 See Asuka, "Seikanron no zentei." For the Sino-Japanese War, see Lone, *Japan's First Modern War*, and for the Russo-Japanese War, Shimazu, "Love Thy Enemy."

40 See Beasley, *Japan Encounters the Barbarian*; Duus, ed., *The Japanese Discovery of America*; Nish, ed., *The Iwakura Mission in America and Europe*.

41 Seki, *Taishō gaikō*.

42 Iriye, ed., *Mutual Images*; Asada, *Ryō taisenkan no Nichi-Bei kankei*; Kurosawa, *Taisenkanki no Nihon rikugun*; Hasegawa, ed., *Taishōki Nihon no Amerika ninshiki*; Kitaoka, "Shoki Taiyō ni miru Amerika zō."

43 Dower, *War without Mercy*. See Kane, "Hammering Down Nails."

44 Iriye, ed., *The Chinese and the Japanese*; Iriye, *Power and Culture*.

45 Teow, *Japanese Cultural Policy toward China*; Hirobe, *Japanese Pride, American Prejudice*.

46 Iriye, "Toward a New Cultural Order," stresses the genuine bases for Sino-Japanese cooperation, whereas Reynolds, "Training Young China Hands," describes the Tōa Dōbun Shōin as an "enabling arm" of Japanese imperialism. The most recent work stresses both the "civilizing" aims of the Tōa Dōbunkai and its hegemonic activities (see Kubota, "Tōa Dōbunkai no 'shimei' to 'manazashi' ").

47 Checkland, *Humanitarianism and the Emperor's Japan*; Shibasaki, *Kindai Nihon to kokusai bunka kōryū*; and Akami, *Internationalizing the Pacific*, respectively.

48 Hotta-Lister, *Japan-British Exhibition of 1910*.

49 Fogel, *Politics and Sinology*. Other important studies by Fogel on Sino-Japanese cultural encounters include *The Cultural Dimension of Sino-Japanese Relations*, *The Literature of Travel and the Japanese Rediscovery of China*, *Nakae Ushikichi in China*, and his translations of *Life Along the South Manchurian Railway* and of Yosano Akiko, *Travels in Manchuria and Mongolia*.

50 See, for example, Rimer, ed., *A Hidden Fire*, and Wells and Wilson, eds., *The Russo-Japanese War in Cultural Perspective*.

51 Nomura, *Nihonkai kaisen no shinjitsu*; Hara, "Nichi-Ro sensō no keikyō"; Matsusaka, "Human Bullets, General Nogi, and the Myth of Port Arthur"; Dickinson, "Commemorating the War in Post-Versailles Japan."

52 See Fogel, ed., *Nanjing Massacre*; Kasahara, *Nankin jiken to Nihonjin*; Hein and Selden, eds., *Living with the Bomb*; Yoneyama, *Hiroshima Traces*.
53 Dingman, *Ghost of War*; Hein and Selden, eds., *Censoring History*; Fujitani, White, and Yoneyama, eds., *Perilous Memories*.
54 See Ching, *Becoming "Japanese"*; Oguma, *"Nihonjin" no kyōkai*.
55 For the important impact of war on twentieth-century Japanese politics and culture, see Mitani, *Kindai Nihon no sensō to seiji*. For the specific impact of the Sino-Japanese War, see Lone, *Japan's First Modern War*, while for that of the Manchurian Incident, see Young, *Japan's Total Empire*.
56 Watanabe, *Higashi Ajia no ōken to shisō*; Hamashita and Kawakatsu, eds., *Ajia kōekiken to Nihon kōgyōka*.
57 See, for example, Azuma, *Between Two Empires*.

BIBLIOGRAPHY

Akami, Tomoko. *Internationalizing the Pacific: The United States, Japan, and the Institute of Pacific Relations in War and Peace, 1919–45*. London: Routledge, 2002.

Asada Sadao. *Ryō taisenkan no Nichi-Bei kankei: kaigun to seisaku kettei katei*. Tokyo: Tokyo Daigaku Shuppankai, 1993.

Asuka Imasamichi. "Seikanron no zentei." In Furuya Tetsuo and Yamamuro Shin'ichi, eds., *Kindai Nihon ni okeru higashi Ajia mondai*. Tokyo: Yoshikawa Kōbunkan, 2001.

Auslin, Michael. *Negotiating with Imperialism: The Unequal Treaties and the Culture of Japanese Diplomacy*. Cambridge, Mass.: Harvard University Press, 2004.

Azuma, Eiichiro. *Between Two Empires: Race, History, and Transnationalism in Japanese America*. Oxford: Oxford University Press, 2005.

Barnhart, Michael. *Japan Prepares for Total War: The Search for Economic Security, 1919–1941*. Ithaca, NY: Cornell University Press, 1987.

Beasley, W. G. *Japan Encounters the Barbarian: Japanese Travellers in America and Europe*. New Haven: Yale University Press, 1995.

Berger, Gordon, trans. and ed. *Kenkenroku: A Diplomatic Record of the Sino-Japanese War, 1894–95*. Princeton: Princeton University Press, 1982.

Bix, Herbert. *Hirohito and the Making of Modern Japan*. New York: HarperCollins, 2000.

Brooks, Barbara. *Japan's Imperial Diplomacy: Consuls, Treaty Ports, and War in China 1895–1938*. Honolulu: University of Hawai'i Press, 2000.

Burkman, Thomas. *Japan, the League of Nations, and World Order, 1914–1938*. Honolulu: University of Hawai'i Press, 2006.

Checkland, Olive. *Humanitarianism and the Emperor's Japan, 1877–1977*. New York: St. Martin's Press, 1994.

Ching, Leo. *Becoming "Japanese": Colonial Taiwan and the Politics of Identity Formation*. Berkeley: University of California Press, 2001.

Conroy, Hilary. *The Japanese Seizure of Korea, 1868–1910: A Study of Realism and Idealism in International Relations*. Philadelphia: University of Pennsylvania Press, 1960.

Dickinson, Frederick. *War and National Reinvention: Japan in the Great War, 1914–1919*. Cambridge, Mass.: Harvard University Asia Center, 1999.

Dickinson, Frederick. "Commemorating the War in Post-Versailles Japan." In John Steinberg and David Schimmelpenninck, eds., *The Russo-Japanese War Reexamined*. Leiden: Brill, 2005.

Dingman, Roger. *Ghost of War: The Sinking of the Awa Maru and Japanese–American Relations, 1945–1995*. Annapolis, Md.: Naval Institute Press, 1997.

Dower, John. *War without Mercy: Race and Power in the Pacific War.* New York: Pantheon, 1986.

Dower, John. *Embracing Defeat: Japan in the Wake of World War II.* New York: Norton 1999.

Drea, Edward. *In the Service of the Emperor: Essays on the Imperial Japanese Army.* Lincoln: University of Nebraska Press, 1998.

Dudden, Alexis. *Japan's Colonization of Korea: Discourse and Power.* Honolulu: University of Hawai'i Press, 2004.

Duus, Peter. *The Abacus and the Sword: The Japanese Penetration of Korea, 1895–1910.* Berkeley: University of California Press, 1995.

Duus, Peter, ed. with intro. *The Japanese Discovery of America: A Brief History with Documents.* Boston: Bedford Books, 1997.

Duus, Peter, Myers, Ramon, and Peattie, Mark, eds. *The Japanese Informal Empire in China, 1895–1937.* Princeton: Princeton University Press, 1989.

Duus, Peter, Myers, Ramon, and Peattie, Mark, eds. *The Japanese Wartime Empire, 1931–1945.* Princeton: Princeton University Press, 1996.

Eskildsen, Robert. "Of Civilization and Savages: The Mimetic Imperialism of Japan's 1874 Expedition to Taiwan." *American Historical Review* 107:2 (Apr. 2002): 388–418.

Esselstrom, Eric. "The Japanese Consular Police in Northeast Asia, 1880–1942." Ph.D. dissertation, University of California, Santa Barbara, 2004.

Fogel, Joshua. *Politics and Sinology: The Case of Naitō Konan.* Cambridge, Mass.: Harvard University Press, 1984.

Fogel, Joshua. *Nakae Ushikichi in China: The Mourning of Spirit.* Cambridge, Mass.: Harvard University Press, 1989.

Fogel, Joshua. *The Cultural Dimension of Sino-Japanese Relations: Essays on the Nineteenth and Twentieth Centuries.* Armonk, NY: M. E. Sharpe, 1995.

Fogel, Joshua. *The Literature of Travel and the Japanese Rediscovery of China, 1862–1945.* Stanford, Calif.: Stanford University Press, 1996.

Fogel, Joshua, ed. *Nanjing Massacre in History and Historiography.* Berkeley: University of California Press, 2000.

Fogel, Joshua, trans. *Life Along the South Manchurian Railway: The Memoirs of Ito Takeo.* Armonk, NY: M. E. Sharpe, 1988.

Fogel, Joshua, trans. *Travels in Manchuria and Mongolia: A Feminist Poet from Japan Encounters Prewar China*, by Yosano Akiko. New York: Columbia University Press, 2001.

Fujitani, Takashi, White, Geoffrey, and Yoneyama, Lisa, eds. *Perilous Memories: The Asia-Pacific War(s).* Durham, NC: Duke University Press, 2001.

Hagihara Nobutoshi. *Nihon no meicho, 35, Mutsu Munemitsu.* Tokyo: Nihon no Meicho, 1969.

Hamashita Takeshi and Kawakatsu Heita, eds. *Ajia kōekiken to Nihon kōgyōka, 1500–1900.* Tokyo: Riburo Pōto, 1991.

Hara Takeshi. "Nichi-Rō sensō no keikyō." *Gunji shigaku* 36:3/4 (2001).

Hasegawa Yūichi, ed. *Taishōki Nihon no Amerika ninshiki.* Tokyo: Keiō Gijuku Daigaku Shuppankai, 2001.

Hattori Ryūji. *Higashi Ajia kokusai kankyō no hendō to Nihon gaikō 1918–1931.* Tokyo: Yūhikaku, 2001.

Hein, Laura, and Selden, Mark, eds. *Living with the Bomb: American and Japanese Cultural Conflicts in the Nuclear Age.* Armonk, NY: M. E. Sharpe, 1997.

Hein, Laura, and Selden, Mark, eds. *Censoring History: Citizenship and Memory in Japan, Germany, and the United States.* Armonk, NY: M. E. Sharpe, 2000.

Hesselink, Reiner. *Prisoners from Nambu: Reality and Make-Believe in Seventeenth-Century Japanese Diplomacy.* Honolulu: University of Hawai'i Press, 2001.

Hirama Yōichi. *Daiichiji sekai taisen to Nihon kaigun: gaikō to gunji to no rensetsu.* Tokyo: Keiō Gijuku Daigaku Shuppankai, 1998.
Hirobe, Izumi. *Japanese Pride, American Prejudice: Modifying the Exclusion Clause of the 1924 Immigration Act.* Stanford, Calif.: Stanford University Press, 2001.
Hiyama Yukio, ed. *Kindai Nihon no keisei to Nisshin sensō: sensō no shakaishi.* Tokyo: Yūzankaku Shuppan, 2001.
Hotta-Lister, Ayako. *Japan-British Exhibition of 1910: Gateway to the Island Empire of the East.* Richmond, UK: Japan Library, 1999.
Hunter, Janet, and Sugiyama Shinya, eds. *The History of Anglo-Japanese Relations, 1600–2000,* vol. 4, *The Economic-Business Dimension.* New York: St. Martin's Press, 2000.
Iguchi, Haruo. *Unfinished Business: Ayukawa Yoshisuke and U.S.–Japan Relations, 1937–1953.* Cambridge, Mass.: Harvard University Press, 2003.
Iriye, Akira. *After Imperialism: The Search for a New Order in the Far East, 1921–1931.* Cambridge, Mass.: Harvard University Press, 1965.
Iriye, Akira. *Nihon no gaikō: Meiji ishin kara gendai made.* Tokyo: Chūō Kōronsha, 1966.
Iriye, Akira. *Across the Pacific: An Inner History of American–East Asian Relations.* New York: Harcourt, Brace, and World, 1967.
Iriye, Akira. "Toward a New Cultural Order: The Hsin-min Hui." In Akira Iriye, ed., *The Chinese and the Japanese: Essays in Political and Cultural Interactions.* Princeton: Princeton University Press, 1980.
Iriye, Akira. *Power and Culture: The Japanese–American War, 1941–1945* Cambridge, Mass.: Harvard University Press, 1981.
Iriye, Akira. "The Internationalization of History." *American Historical Review* 94 (Feb. 1989).
Iriye, Akira. *Japan and the Wider World: From the Mid-Nineteenth Century to the Present.* London: Longman, 1997.
Iriye, Akira, ed. *Mutual Images: Essays in American–Japanese Relations.* Cambridge, Mass.: Harvard University Press, 1975.
Iriye, Akira, ed. *The Chinese and the Japanese: Essays in Political and Cultural Interactions.* Princeton: Princeton University Press, 1980.
Ishikawa Hiroshi. "Meiji ishin to Chōsen, taima kankei." In Meiji Ishin Shigakukai, ed., *Meiji ishin to Ajia.* Tokyo: Yoshikawa Kōbunkan, 2001.
Itō Yukio. *Rikken kokka to Nichi-Rō sensō: gaikō to naisei, 1898–1905.* Tokyo: Bokutakusha, 2000.
Itō Yukio. *Seitō seiji to tennō.* Tokyo: Kōdansha, 2002.
Itō Yukio and Kawada Minoru, eds. *Nijū seiki Nihon no tennō to kunshusei.* Tokyo: Yoshikawa Kōbunkan, 2004.
Jansen, Marius. *Japan and Its World: Two Centuries of Change.* Princeton: Princeton University Press, 1975.
Jansen, Marius. *China in the Tokugawa World.* Cambridge, Mass.: Harvard University Press, 1992.
Kamiyama Kazuo and Iida Yasuo, eds. *Tairitsu to dakyō: 1930 nendai no Nichi-Bei tsūshō kankei.* Tokyo: Daiichi Hōki Shuppan, 1994.
Kane, Robert. "Hammering Down Nails: Politics, Diplomacy, and the Quest for National Unity in Japan and America, 1912–1919." Ph.D. dissertation, University of Pennsylvania, 2002.
Kasahara Tokushi. *Nankin jiken to Nihonjin: sensō no kioku o meguru nashonarizumu to gurōbarizumu.* Tokyo: Kashiwa Shobō, 2002.
Kawamura, Noriko. *Turbulence in the Pacific: Japanese–U.S. Relations during World War I.* Westport, Conn.: Praeger, 2000.

Kitaoka Shin'ichi. *Nihon rikugun to tairiku seisaku, 1906–1918-nen.* Tokyo: Tokyo Daigaku Shuppankai, 1978.

Kitaoka Shin'ichi. "Shoki Taiyō ni miru Amerika zō." In Suzuki Sadao, ed., *Zasshi Taiyō to kokumin bunka no keisei.* Tokyo: Shibunkaku, 2001.

Kobayashi Michihiko. *Nihon no tairiku seisaku, 1895–1914.* Tokyo: Nansōsha, 1996.

Komiya Kazuo. *Jōyaku kaisei to kokunai seiji.* Tokyo: Yoshikawa Kōbunkan, 2001.

Kranzler, David. *Japanese, Nazis, and Jews: The Jewish Refugee Community in Shanghai.* Hoboken, NJ: KTAV Publishing House, 1976.

Krug, Hans-Joachim, et al. *Reluctant Allies: German–Japanese Naval Relations in World War II.* Annapolis, Md.: Naval Institute Press, 2001.

Kubota Yoshitake. "Tōa Dōbunkai no 'shimei' to 'manazashi'." *Rekishi Hyōron* 614 (2001).

Kurosawa Fumitaka. *Taisenkanki no Nihon rikugun.* Tokyo: Misuzu Shobō, 2000.

Laver, Michael. "A Strange Isolation: The Japanese, the Dutch, and the Asian Economy in the Seventeenth Century." Ph.D. dissertation, University of Pennsylvania, 2005.

Levine, Hillel. *In Search of Sugihara: The Elusive Japanese Diplomat who Risked His Life to Rescue 10,000 Jews from the Holocaust.* New York: Free Press, 1996.

Lone, Stewart. *Japan's First Modern War: Army and Society in the Conflict with China, 1894–95.* New York: St. Martin's Press, 1994.

Lone, Stewart. *Army, Empire and Politics in Meiji Japan: The Three Careers of General Katsura Tarō.* New York: St. Martin's Press, 2000.

Lu, David J. *Agony of Choice: Matsuoka Yōsuke and the Rise and Fall of the Japanese Empire, 1880–1946.* Lanham, Md.: Lexington Books, 2002.

Martin, Bernd. *Japan and Germany in the Modern World.* Providence, RI: Berghahn Books, 1995.

Matsusaka, Y. Tak. "Human Bullets, General Nogi, and the Myth of Port Arthur." In John Steinberg and David Schimmelpenninck, eds., *The Russo-Japanese War Reexamined.* Leiden: Brill, 2005.

Meskill, Johanna Menzel. *Hitler and Japan: The Hollow Alliance.* New York: Atherton, 1966.

Mitani Taichirō. *Kindai Nihon no sensō to seiji.* Tokyo: Iwanami Shoten, 1997.

Morley, James William, ed. *Deterrent Diplomacy: Japan, Germany, and the USSR, 1935–1940.* New York: Columbia University Press, 1975.

Myers, Ramon, and Peattie, Mark, eds. *The Japanese Colonial Empire, 1895–1945.* Princeton: Princeton University Press, 1984.

Nagazumi Yōko. *Shuinsen.* Tokyo: Yoshikawa Kōbunkan, 2001.

Nihon Kokusai Seiji Gakkai Taiheiyō Sensō Gen'in Kenkyūbu, ed. *Taiheiyō sensō e no michi*, 8 vols. Tokyo: Asahi Shinbunsha, 1962–3.

Nish, Ian. *The Anglo-Japanese Alliance: The Diplomacy of Two Island Empires, 1894–1907.* London: Athlone Press, 1966.

Nish, Ian. *Alliance in Decline: A Study in Anglo-Japanese Relations, 1908–23.* London: Athlone Press, 1972.

Nish, Ian. *Japan's Struggle with Internationalism: Japan, China, and the League of Nations, 1931–1933.* London: Kegan Paul, 1993.

Nish, Ian, ed., *Britain and Japan: Biographical Portraits*, 4 vols. Folkestone: Japan Library, 1994.

Nish, Ian, ed. *The Iwakura Mission in America and Europe: A New Assessment.* Richmond, UK: Curzon, 1998.

Nish, Ian, and Kibata, Yoichi, eds., *The History of Anglo-Japanese Relations, 1600–2000: The Political-Diplomatic Dimension*, 2 vols. New York: St. Martin's Press, 2000.

Nomura Minoru. *Nihonkai kaisen no shinjitsu.* Tokyo: Kōdansha, 1999.

O'Brien, Phillips Payson, ed. *Anglo-Japanese Alliance, 1902–1922.* London: Routledge, 2004.

Ochiai Hiroki. "Meiji shoki no gaiseiron to higashi Ajia." In Furuya Tetsuo and Yamamuro Shin'ichi, eds., *Kindai Nihon ni okeru higashi Ajia mondai*. Tokyo: Yoshikawa Kōbunkan, 2001.

Oguma Eiji. *"Nihonjin" no kyōkai: Okinawa, Ainu, Taiwan, Chōsen, shokuminchi shihai kara fukki undō made*. Tokyo: Shinyōsha, 1998.

Okazaki Hisahiko. *Mutsu Munemitsu to sono jidai*. Tokyo: PHP Kenkyūjo, 1999.

Patterson, Wayne. *The Korean Frontier in America: Immigration to Hawai'i, 1896–1910*. Honolulu: University of Hawai'i Press, 1988.

Perez, Louis. *Japan Comes of Age: Mutsu Munemitsu and the Revision of the Unequal Treaties*. Madison, NJ: Fairleigh Dickinson University Press, 1999.

Rekishigaku Kenkyūkai. *Taiheiyō sensōshi*, 5 vols. Tokyo: Tōyō Keizai Shinpōsha, 1953.

Reynolds, Douglas. "Training Young China Hands: Tōa Dōbun Shōin and Its Precursors, 1886–1945." In Duus et al., eds., *The Japanese Informal Empire in China, 1895–1937*. Princeton: Princeton University Press, 1989.

Rimer, J. Thomas, ed. *A Hidden Fire: Russian and Japanese Cultural Encounters, 1868–1926*. Stanford, Calif.: Stanford University Press, 1995.

Sakamoto, Pamela Rotner. *Japanese Diplomats and Jewish Refugees: A World War II Dilemma*. Westport, Conn.: Praeger, 1998.

Schencking, Charles. *Making Waves: Politics, Propaganda, and the Emergence of the Imperial Japanese Navy, 1868–1922*. Stanford, Calif.: Stanford University Press, 2005.

Seki Shizuo. *Taishō gaikō: jinbutsu ni miru gaikō senryakuron*. Tokyo: Minerva, 2001.

Shibasaki Atsushi. *Kindai Nihon to kokusai bunka kōryū – kokusai bunka shinkōkai no sosetsu to tenkai*. Tokyo: Yūshindō Kōbunsha, 1999.

Shimazu, Naoko. *Japan, Race and Equality: The Racial Equality Proposal of 1919*. New York: Routledge, 1998.

Shimazu, Naoko. "Love Thy Enemy: Japanese Perceptions of Russia." In John Steinberg and David Schimmelpenninck, eds., *The Russo-Japanese War Reexamined*. Leiden: Brill, 2005.

Stephan, John. *Hawaii under the Rising Sun: Japan's Plans for Conquest after Pearl Harbor*. Honolulu: University of Hawai'i Press, 1984.

Takahashi Hidenao. *Nisshin sensō e no michi*. Tokyo: Tokyo Sōgensha, 1996.

Takemae Eiji. *Inside GHQ: The Allied Occupation of Japan and Its Legacy*, trans. and adapted by Robert Ricketts and Sebastian Swann. New York: Continuum, 2002.

Teow, See Heng. *Japanese Cultural Policy toward China, 1918–1931*. Cambridge, Mass.: Harvard University Press, 1999.

Terasaki Hidenari. *Shōwa tennō dokuhakuroku: Terasaki Hidenari goyōgakari nikki*. Tokyo: Bungei Shunju, 1991.

Tobe Ryōichi. *Nihon rikugun to Chūgoku "Shina-tsū" ni miru yume to zasetsu*. Tokyo: Kōdansha, 1999.

Toby, Ronald. *State and Diplomacy in Early Modern Japan: Asia in the Development of the Tokugawa Bakufu*. Princeton: Princeton University Press, 1984.

Toby, Ronald. "Kara no kanata yori." In Furuya Tetsuo and Yamamuro Shin'ichi, eds., *Kindai Nihon ni okeru higashi Ajia mondai*. Tokyo: Yoshikawa Kōbunkan, 2001.

Tsuchimochi, Gary. *Education Reform in Postwar Japan: The 1946 U.S. Education Mission*. Tokyo: University of Tokyo Press, 1993.

Tsunoda Jun. *Manshū mondai to kokubō hōshin*. Tokyo: Hara Shobō, 1967.

Unno Fukuju. *Kankoku heigōshi no kenkyū*. Tokyo: Iwanami Shoten, 2000.

Usui Katsumi. *Nitchū sensō: wahei ka sensen kakudai ka*. Tokyo: Chūō Kōronsha, 1967.

Usui Katsumi. *Nitchū gaikōshi kenkyū: Shōwa zenki*. Tokyo: Yoshikawa Kōbunkan, 1998.

Walker, Brett L. *The Conquest of Ainu Lands: Ecology and Culture in Japanese Expansion, 1590–1800*. Berkeley: University of California Press, 2001.

Watanabe Hiroshi. *Higashi Ajia no ōken to shisō*. Tokyo: Tōkyō Daigaku Shuppankai, 1997.

Wells, David, and Wilson, Sandra, eds. *The Russo-Japanese War in Cultural Perspective, 1904–05*. New York: St. Martin's Press, 1999.

Wetzler, Peter. *Hirohito and War: Imperial Tradition and Military Decision Making in Prewar Japan*. Honolulu: University of Hawai'i Press, 1998.

Yoneyama, Lisa. *Hiroshima Traces: Time, Space, and the Dialectics of Memory*. Berkeley: University of California Press, 1999.

Young, Louise. *Japan's Total Empire: Manchuria and the Culture of Wartime Imperialism*. Berkeley: University of California Press, 1997.

FURTHER READING

Several years ago, renowned specialist of US–Japanese relations Akira Iriye defined "international history" as a field that attempts "to go beyond the national level of analysis and to treat the entire world as a framework of study" ("The Internationalization of History," *American Historical Review* 94 (Feb. 1989)). Although this is a tall order, the most compelling recent studies of modern Japanese external affairs do place Japanese ties with the outer world within a very broad setting, encompassing both an expansive domestic and an international comparative context. They recognize that transnational ties have both an official and an unofficial component and that they influence and are affected by a variety of social, cultural, political, military, intellectual, and economic forces within and without Japan.

Given that international historians must, ideally, follow state-to-state ties, gauge internal trends, and highlight comparative international developments at the same time, it is difficult to expect the perfect treatment from any one scholar. But two recent studies stand out for the remarkable breadth of their scope. John Dower's analysis of the Allied occupation of Japan is a model international history in the complex interplay it details between domestic and external forces. Far superseding the parochial focus on American policy-making of earlier histories, *Embracing Defeat* (New York: Norton, 1999) highlights US–Japan relations in the early postwar period as "many occupations," that is, as an intricate negotiation of both public and private actors in the context of the profound political, social, cultural, economic, and intellectual effect of the war upon Japan. Eiichiro Azuma's *Between Two Empires* (Oxford: Oxford University Press, 2005), an analysis of early twentieth-century Japanese immigrants in California, is a model "transnational" history in its rigorous empiricism and novel description of a people with a distinct identity shaped by the complex social, cultural, political, economic, and intellectual forces of two "empires" (Japan and the United States).

CHAPTER THIRTEEN

The Japanese Empire

Y. Tak Matsusaka

Introduction

The modern Japanese nation state took form in the crucible of nineteenth-century imperialism and, narrowly escaping subjugation itself, emerged as one of the more aggressively expansionist powers of the first half of the twentieth century. The opportunities and constraints generated by Japan's imperial project in East Asia channeled the course of its national development, molded its institutions, and fueled the aspirations and anxieties of its people. In ways both intended and unanticipated, Japanese imperialism acted as an agent of transformation in East Asia as a whole. Japan's imperial designs and resistance to them on the part of subject peoples, along with the more nuanced processes of negotiation and mutual adaptation that made the empire work, did much to define the basic contours of East Asian modernity. It was through the agency of imperialism, too, that Japan made its first entrance as a principal actor on the world stage. Consistent with the mimetic pattern that marks much of Japan's early national development, its empire reproduced many of the structures, practices, and even ideologies of its contemporary European counterparts. At the same time, the Japanese forged their Asian dominion in an ultimately unsuccessful bid to challenge the Western-dominated world order. In this respect, the Japanese project might be regarded as the first of many such challenges to the primacy of the West that would mark the twentieth century.

Driven initially by the need for a rigorous post-mortem on the catastrophe of World War II, historians have devoted considerable attention to the record of Japanese imperialism. Early studies tended to treat the empire in light of a Japanese *Sonderweg* that began in the dislocations of the late nineteenth century. The rising thematic pre-eminence of modernization studies during the 1960s and 1970s partly displaced the emphasis on retracing the road to war.[1] The more broadly comparative orientation of such lines of inquiry encouraged historians to regard Japanese imperialism as a derivative of European practice, linked inseparably to the paradigms of modernity adopted by the Japanese in the Meiji era.[2] An important corollary of the trend toward comparison was the growth of Japanese colonial studies. Broader developments in the historiography of modern imperialism, characterized by declining interest in problems of origins and causality, further strengthened this direction.

More recently, the gathering momentum of social and cultural historiography, lea-vened by the influence of postmodern, interdisciplinary, and transnational studies, has eroded the once privileged place of political and economic approaches to the subject. The end of the protracted cold war, along with a reconfiguration of the related but distinct North–South division of the world, have also done much to transform the climate of inquiry. All of these factors have contributed to making Japanese imperi-alism an increasingly diverse and intellectually vibrant field of study more deeply integrated into the history of modern East Asia and offering richer possibilities for comparative investigation.

The Structure and Scope of the Japanese Empire

Any discussion of the Japanese empire must begin with a definition of the geographic and conceptual scope of the subject. Over the course of a relatively short history, Japan exercised dominion over its East Asian neighbors through a variety of means that entailed different degrees of control and that changed significantly over time. The relatively small colonial component of the empire, which Japan ruled directly, consisted of Taiwan (annexed 1895), Karafuto (southern Sakhalin, annexed 1905), Kwantung (the present day Lushun–Dalian metropolitan area, leased 1905), Korea (annexed 1910), and the Nan'yō (Caroline and Marshall Islands, League of Nations Mandate, 1922). Although Japan's imperial architects regarded these colonies as vital, it was the indirect domination of China that, over the long run, drew the lion's share of their attention. Japanese power insinuated itself into the national life of its larger neighbor through a variety of means: the unequal treaty system in which Japan became an increasingly dominant player as the gendarme of East Asia, the control of regional spheres of influence, the management of a network of treaty port enclaves, the establishment of special economic and cultural institutions and, when conditions permitted, the cultivation of client regimes. Northeast China, known to foreigners as Manchuria, was subject to a particularly active form of Japanese control after 1905 that gradually approached the colonial threshold. The armed occupation of this region in 1931 pushed Japanese power across that threshold, but in the place of conventional colonial arrangements, Japan-ese authorities established a nominally independent and purportedly allied state known as Manchukuo. Japan's imperial power in Asia reached its zenith during World War II with the occupation of much of the Chinese heartland and the incorporation of Manchukuo, occupied China, and Western colonial territory in Southeast Asia into a formation known as the Greater East Asia Co-Prosperity Sphere.

Strict constructionists might object to the inclusion within the Japanese empire of areas of East Asia not under direct colonial rule.[3] Although the distinction between formal and informal patterns of control is important, too analytically energetic a separation between the two may exaggerate the differences, a perspective reflected in recent trends in research. There is good reason to believe, indeed, that the heterogeneous, malleable, and loosely organized structure of the Japanese empire was intimately related to the nature of the imperial project. Moreover, as will be discussed subsequently, many of the analytical approaches and concerns of colonial history, which emphasize structures of power and relationships on the ground, are indispensable to an understanding of non-colonial parts of the empire.

Most historians of Japan today would agree that the nation's drive toward expansion stemmed from multiple sources: economic, strategic, geopolitical, and social-imperialist or otherwise domestically political.[4] Moreover, a variety of interested parties, from soldiers and bureaucrats to private individuals pursuing wealth and opportunity, pushed and pulled the project in directions they favored. It is also commonly understood that the impulses driving expansion changed in character and varied in intensity over time. A pattern of expansion that emerged during the Meiji era peaked during World War I and was followed by a trough of moderation during the 1920s that witnessed few new initiatives. Aggressive expansionism resurged in the 1930s, although some would argue that the imperialism of this era represented a new phenomenon linked in some way to radical domestic currents that, at least superficially, resembled fascism.[5]

Within this framework of multiple causality and diversified initiative, however, a strong case may be made for the primacy of national security considerations, championed by an army that also possessed a strong institutional interest in promoting a sustained continental mission.[6] A concept of forward defense, articulated by Yamagata Aritomo in terms of a "line of interest" doctrine in 1890, lay at the core of the logic of the Japanese empire. In Yamagata's view, Japan's survival depended on the establishment of a continental defense perimeter from which all potential adversaries would be excluded, through indirect means if possible, but through occupation and direct control if necessary. Korea and Manchuria thus became vital targets, and as Japan graduated into higher leagues of strategic competition concomitant with its growing power, Yamagata's security cordon came to encompass China as a whole. Threats to national security provided the principal *casus belli* in all of Japan's major wars, and almost all of its expansionist initiatives were ultimately justified in the name of defense. The paramount role of security in Japanese imperialism is consistent with an exclusive emphasis on expansion in the "near abroad," a point Mark Peattie has underscored.[7] Japan's concerns in East Asia bore more similarity to Germany's in Europe than they did to, say, than those of Britain in Asia or Africa. Ronald Robinson has observed that "all the powers, even the French, agreed in the end that it would be absurd to fight a European war for the sake of more colonies in Africa and Asia."[8] The Japanese, operating in their own backyard, however, were playing for different and considerably higher stakes than their European and American counterparts. It is no coincidence, indeed, that the only full-scale war fought between any great powers in East Asia before the 1930s pitted Russia, which had national territory in the region, against Japan.

A forward defense policy, which dovetailed with Japan's long-term economic interests in preventing the domination of East Asia by rival powers, allowed for the occupation of the near abroad if need be but tended to favor pre-emptive action by less costly and risky means. This generally exclusionary as opposed to acquisitive orientation of Japanese imperialism did not preclude the taking of territory if presented with an easy opportunity in which the marginal costs of direct rule as opposed to indirect control were low enough.[9] Members of Japan's imperialist coalition, moreover, were certainly not averse to taking advantage of opportunities created by a pre-emptive defense policy for a range of economic, political, and social goals. Acquisitiveness, nonetheless, played a secondary role. The ideology of Meiji imperialism that set forth Japan's East Asian aims in terms of securing Korea's independence, safeguarding China's territorial integrity, and guaranteeing the peace in East Asia were consistent with this exclusionary approach to exercising power in the region. So too were later formulations of an Asian Monroe Doctrine and a pan-Asian alliance, however hypocritical these prouncements of principle might appear in view of actual Japanese behavior. Japan's relative poverty and weakness also fueled a preference for indirect means, particularly given expansive definitions of the zone of exclusion. Significantly, all but one of Japan's colonies had been acquisitions of opportunity adjunct to wars fought for reasons other than territorial aggrandizement. In the case of Korea, the one exception, it should be noted that more than three decades of informal engagement, including enforced tutelage and various protectorate arrangements, preceded annexation in 1910.[10] Contrary to the claims of older intentionalist arguments about Japan's seizure of Korea, more recent scholarship points to the fact that these indirect forms of control were not conceived by the Japanese as stepping stones to annexation but as normative arrangements in their own right.[11] The instability and ineffectiveness of indirect management ultimately led to direct control. A similar pattern may be seen in Manchuria where the successive breakdown of informal structures, despite efforts to preserve them, gave way to tighter forms of domination. Colonial rule, then, represented only one, and not necessarily the most desirable, of many political options in a polymorphous empire.

Variation in the forms of domination found in the empire was also a reflection of Japanese innovation and adaptation. Creativity became particularly important because Japanese expansion in East Asia found itself confronting an increasingly inimical international environment after the Russo-Japanese War. Rising nationalist challenges and the declining legitimacy of nineteenth-century-style imperialism in the eyes of rival great powers forced the Japanese to modify their approaches repeatedly. Japan's position in the contested and strategically vital region of Manchuria between 1905 and 1931, for example, rested nominally on rights granted the great powers under the unequal treaty system, which governed all foreign activity in China. Direct colonial rule over the region, its possible advantages notwithstanding, would exceed the boundaries of great power tolerance and was not considered by most informed Japanese before 1931 a workable option. In practice, however, through the control of a railway monopoly, the possession of special real estate holdings, and in the 1920s, a relationship with a local client warlord, Japan exercised a degree of power on the ground in Manchuria unparalleled elsewhere in China.[12] The creation of the puppet state of Manchukuo following the Japanese army's invasion and partition of the territory in 1931, too, might be regarded as an adaptive strategy that recast conquest as liberation under the banner of self-determination and pan-Asian cooperation. Given the tight control Japan exercised from within the state apparatus, appointing all high officials and seconding them with Japanese assistants, and from without, through mutual security and trade treaties, Manchukuo might be regarded as a colony disguised as a sovereign state. At the same time, recent scholarship on nationalism would warn against too facile a distinction between "genuine" and "false" nation-states. As Prasenjit Duara observes, authenticity is a contested claim central to the nation-building process.[13] The asymmetry of international power relationships, moreover, renders the notion of "pure" sovereignty entirely free of subordination and dependency illusory.

Taxonomically ambiguous arrangements similar to those governing Manchukuo became the theoretical model for the control of occupied territories during World War II and formed the basis for efforts to reconstruct the Japanese empire as an alliance of Asian states. Commitments to "liberate" Asia ironically accelerated policies of forced assimilation in Korea and Taiwan, reflecting an attempt to eliminate the problematic category of "colony" through the full integration of these territories into the metropole. The reality of Japanese rule over its conquered dominions during the war remained, despite its pan-Asianist and anti-colonial claims, a brutal and expedient military occupation relying on administrative and programmatic makeshifts that offered little in the way of "normal" arrangements, even by the standards set by Manchukuo. What form a Co-Prosperity Sphere at peace might have taken, of course, is something we cannot know, since it collapsed with Japan's defeat in 1945.

Managing the Empire

Where indirect methods employed powerful clients, as in China during World War I, effective control required little penetration beyond the higher levels of the state and could be exercised through military sticks and financial carrots. In most cases, however, Japanese domination, even where indirect, entailed considerable intervention in the life of subject communities in order to deepen control and to extract value, if for no other reason than to offset the costs of rule. The management of empire became an unavoidable problem wherever Japan established a significant measure of control, and, with the long view in mind, the task of management became a project aimed at the transformation of the lands and peoples under Japanese rule.

Much of our understanding of Japan's transformative and social engineering efforts in its subject territories is relatively recent, drawn largely from colonial studies undertaken since the 1970s. This body of work, well represented in the volume *The Japanese Colonial Empire, 1895–1945*, has made a particularly important contribution by placing Japanese colonialism in a comparative context.[14] On the one hand, Japan's wartime practices, including widespread military atrocities, human experimentation, slave labor, and institutions such as the "comfort woman" system, remain uniquely egregious. On the other hand, the management of its peacetime empire, although occupying, in the case of Korea, the brutal end of the spectrum in contemporary colonial practice, was by no means entirely off the comparative scale. Japan drew its models from European colonialism in Africa, inheriting its pseudo-scientific ethos, its notions of development, and its moral claims of a *mission civilatrice*. Japanese colonial policy-makers vacillated between the French idea of integration and assimilation and the British mode of separate rule through modified or reinvented indigenous arrangements. Development policies, broadly similar to colonial practices elsewhere, defined a colony–metropole division of labor that emphasized increasing agricultural productivity, especially in rice, and promoted specialization, such as sugar cultivation in Taiwan. Japan's colonial development policies began to depart from European practice sharply in the 1930s, particularly after the outbreak of the China War in 1937. Under an empire-wide program of military-led industrialization, an unusual concentration of high-technology and heavy industrial ventures emerged in colonial and other subject territories.[15]

Colonial studies of the 1970s and 1980s highlighted the importance of the "Western imprint" on Japanese practices, but they also pointed to the significance of Japan's own experience with transformative upheaval during the Meiji era.[16] Japan began managing an empire and pursuing a "civilizing mission" while itself a relatively poor, developing country whose acquaintance with Western-style "civilization" remained callow. Insofar as colonial social engineering entailed an authoritarian state dragging a reluctant population kicking and screaming into a non-indigenous modernity, such a characterization might also fit Meiji Japan. Indeed, as late as the 1930s, the discourse of "uplifting the benighted natives" could be found in commentaries emanating from urban intellectuals on the crisis in the impoverished villages of Japan's internal rural periphery.[17] In this context, it is not surprising that the Meiji reform program offered, perhaps, an even more important model for colonial management than Western practice. Agricultural policies in Taiwan and Korea drew much from the Meiji pattern, as did education. The role of the policeman as the prime interface between state and civil society, which might be expected in a colonial society, was also the reality in rural Meiji Japan.[18] The Meiji model for social and economic transformation would appear particularly suitable because the societies that the colonial rulers sought to reconstruct were not so different from Japan in the middle of the nineteenth century, and the "level" of civilization to which the Japanese sought to "uplift" their subjects was likewise separated from their own by less than a generation of experience. The potential for a very rapid "catch-up" was a problem inherent in the colonial relationship. In Taiwan, members of the settler community and the colonial bureaucracy lived in fear of the possibility that, given greater educational opportunities, well-educated "natives" would readily close the gap and destroy the hierarchy that defined colonial privilege. Not surprisingly, policies aimed at rapid assimilation and legal integration enjoyed greater support within metropolitan circles than they did among the Japanese elite in the colonies.[19]

Transformative management was most prominent in territories under direct rule where both opportunity and need were greatest, but it was also relevant to other parts of the imperium. Social engineering and economic reconstruction found particularly pronounced expressions in Manchukuo, which Louise Young appropriately dubs "the brave new empire."[20] If the structural arrangements of the "puppet state" represented a revision of traditional colonial forms, then management strategies in Manchukuo reflected a parallel revision of colonial policies devised in Taiwan and Korea. Moreover, in the same manner as the Meiji program informed the transformative project in the older colonies, radical reformist or "renovationist" currents in metropolitan Japan of the 1920s and early 1930s, which favored planned economies and managed societies, influenced policies in Manchukuo. In economic matters, for example, the managers of the Manchurian state challenged the traditional division of labor between colony and metropole and argued in favor of applying the principle of comparative advantage under a system of comprehensive, empire-wide planning. In their efforts at social reconstruction, Manchukuo's designers combined pan-Asianism and corporatist concepts with older paradigms of multicultural empire rooted in Chinese imperial practice. The resulting framework of "racial harmony" displaced the borrowed models of assimilation and separation previously used to structure colonial relations. Transformative initiatives could also be found in Japanese districts in China's treaty ports which were, for most intents and purposes, urban "micro-colonies."[21] In Manchuria before 1931, the Japanese-owned South Manchurian Railway linked a large number of such micro-colonies into an industrial corridor that hosted the first experiments in the making of a "brave new empire."[22] Institutions such as the South Manchurian Railway Company played a vital role in the systematic exercise of Japanese power in non-colonial environments. Telecommunications agencies facilitated the high-speed flow of information throughout the imperium and greatly facilitated its integration.[23] Colonial banks based in Taiwan and Korea as well as the Oriental Development Company extended their operations into China and contributed to building a region-wide financial infrastructure, while trading companies such as Mitsui Bussan made parallel contributions in the field of commerce. Working in concert, these transportation, communication, financial, and commercial networks endowed even the indirectly managed portions of the empire with a significant measure of structural coherence. The Foreign Ministry's consular apparatus, nominally charged with the responsibilities of formal diplomacy, strengthened that coherence through the exercise of extraterritorial administrative and judicial powers. Diplomats thus came to serve essentially colonial functions in the management of power, people, and imperial interest on ground.[24]

Any consideration of the developmental aspects of the imperial project cannot avoid the question of whether these transformative efforts had any positive effects on the lands and peoples toward which they were directed. This is an old and bitterly contested issue inseparable from the polemics of North–South conflict. It may be possible to offer a qualified answer to this question, however, if we were to address it in very narrow economic terms, setting aside the broader problem of the overall effects of imperialism, and, further, if we were to separate from consideration the destructive effects of World War II, an intellectual exercise certainly open to question. Given such qualifications, most Western historians would agree that development under the empire did contribute to improvements in agricultural productivity in the colonies and promoted significant industrialization in some areas, notably northern Korea and northeast China. It also created a cadre, albeit smaller than opportunities and circumstances allowed, of administrators, skilled workers, business managers, teachers, and other professionals that would play an important role after liberation, a factor contributing to the remarkable economic success of some of Japan's former colonies.[25]

State and Civil Society

Given the importance of defense in the imperial project as well as its operative focus on political control, the state was the dominant actor. At the same time, it was by no means the only important player, as expansionist undertakings tended to gather around them a growing constellation of interests in Japanese civil society as well. The emphasis on non-state actors represents one of the most important new trends in the study of Japanese imperialism. Peter Duus explores this dimension of the Korean project in detail, highlighting the activities of business interests, individual entrepreneurs, emigration promoters, and settlers. He also describes the contradictory ways in which Japanese came to imagine Koreans, as alien and inferior on the one hand and, on the other, as a people sharing ancestry and culture with the Japanese and thus susceptible to uplift.[26] One of the distinguishing features of Louise Young's study of Manchukuo lies in her examination of the ways in which the Japanese public was drawn into the Manchurian venture, transforming imperialism into a mass cultural phenomenon. Mobilizing public opinion was, to be sure, a function of the state, but civil society also played an active and independent part as a wide variety of interests found creative ways to appropriate Manchuria for their own purposes.[27]

The high level of popular support enjoyed by the Manchurian venture in the early 1930s, however, had little precedent. Although the problem has received relatively little attention in English-language scholarship, attitudes within the political middle class toward the project of empire before 1931 appear to have been uneven and inconsistent and, averaged over the long term, might be characterized as lukewarm.[28] Expansionist ardor unmistakably spiked during the Sino- and Russo-Japanese Wars, but such enthusiasm proved to be short-lived corollaries of an equally transient war fever. There is no doubt that deep reservoirs of militant nationalism could be found within the Japanese public, but such sentiment, most readily aroused in response to a perceived injury or threat, was not unequivocally expansionist. California no less than China might be a target of popular nationalist demands that the government "show the flag" with the deployment of warships and naval infantry. The fiscal conservatism of the middle class and its parliamentary representatives, moreover, acted as a powerful brake on public support for a potentially costly imperial undertaking. Such a tendency might explain popular enthusiasm for expansion in wartime, when outlays for empire could be subsumed under the costs of waging war in the name of national defense.[29]

A special aspect of the imperial project engaging both state and civil society was emigration. The government encouraged permanent settlement in the colonies and Manchuria first and foremost as a means of securing Japan's position in these territories by creating "facts on the ground" and secondarily as a way of resolving the country's "population problem." Most ordinary Japanese who responded to the call to "go east," however, migrated in pursuit of fortune or "dreams of brocade," as Duus puts it, rather than in conscious service of empire.[30] Not surprisingly, the level and make-up of migration to the imperial periphery fell well short of what the government sought, drawing more sojourners than settlers as well as significant numbers of the more marginal members of Japanese society. Insofar as fortune and opportunity provided the primary incentives to migrate, Hawaii and California, where Japanese immigrants might pursue "dreams of extravagance," represented competing destinations.[31] Significantly, a preponderance of migrants to both continental Asia and North America came from an overlapping group of prefectures in southwestern Japan, a pattern reinforced by chain migration.[32] Ironically, these two sets of émigrés, sharing similar origins and dreams, encountered very different fates upon reaching their destinations. Those who crossed the Pacific to settle in North America became enmeshed in the struggles of an embattled minority on the subaltern side of a color line whose experiences resembled those of colonial subjects. Those who crossed the Straits of Korea or the Yellow Sea became actors in a dramatically different narrative as members of an imperial elite lording it over subject Koreans and Chinese.

The emigration of Japanese to the imperial marches, however, was only one current in the complex patterns of migration generated within the empire. The movement of large numbers of imperial subjects to metropolitan Japan was another and represents one of the many ways in which empire transformed the metropole in ways not entirely anticipated.[33] Whereas the nation-builders of the Meiji era had expended extraordinary effort toward homogenizing Japanese culture and reducing its diversity, immigration from the colonies, and from Korea, in particular, represented a countervailing force. The impact was particularly significant among the working classes who had the most direct interaction with Korean immigrants, which partly helps to explain the explosion of bloody violence against Korean immigrants in Tokyo's working-class neighborhoods in the aftermath of the Kantō earthquake in 1923. The complexity of the relationships generated, however, is highlighted by the election from Tokyo, less than ten years later, of Boku Shunkin, the one and only ethnic Korean member to serve in the lower house of the Imperial Diet.[34]

Subject Societies under Imperial Rule

The shift in emphasis from state to civil society in the study of the Japanese empire has been paralleled by increased attention to subject societies. It has long been recognized that empire cannot be understood from a Japanese vantage point alone but must account for the agency of subject peoples. The development of Korean studies has contributed significantly to illuminating the experience of people under imperial rule as other than passive objects or victims of Japanese policy.[35] At the same time, in the view of a growing number of historians of colonial era Korea, it is important to avoid oversimplifying that agency into the duality of resistance and collaboration favored by nationalist historiography.[36] This new trend in scholarship highlights the contingency of identities generated within the empire. Gender, class, and ethnicity were not subsumed, let alone obviated, by imperial rule into the simple dialectic of colonizer and colonized, nor was contention over the associated issues of civil rights, social equality, and economic opportunity displaced by the reductionist binary of resistance and collaboration.

Subject peoples instead "negotiated" their identities in a colonial framework of relations. The dynamic between Korean workers and Japanese managers at the Onoda Cement factory was, as Soon-won Park argues, a worker–manager as well as a Korean–Japanese issue.[37] To strike against management might be regarded as an act of anti-imperialist resistance, but by extension, did the subsequent settlement of a dispute and the resumption of cooperative relations mean collaboration? The problem of "identity" confronting Korean business magnates such as members of the Kim family studied by Carter Eckert were no less complicated.[38] Business people chafed, on the one hand, against constrained opportunities and discrimination as well as the humiliations faced by all Koreans under Japanese rule, but they also depended on the Japanese authorities for the institutional and legal infrastructure that made modern business possible, for contracts and special opportunities, and, most problematic, for support against labor unrest among fellow Koreans. The expansion of the Kim family enterprises into Manchuria during the 1930s raises yet another dimension of the contingency of colonial identities. Where did Koreans stand as colonial subjects in relation to Japan's imperial project in China? Should they join in solidarity with the

Chinese nationalists against a common foe, or, confronted with repeated acts of anti-Korean violence in Manchuria, seek out the protection of the Japanese authorities and the advantages that came with being treated as a Japanese national? Similar questions confronted Taiwanese who enjoyed Japanese nationality and, in theory, concomitant protection in setting up businesses in mainland China.[39]

There were no simple answers to these kinds of questions, and individuals negotiated their identities in a variety of ways. At the same time, the complex response of subject peoples produced, in aggregate, a dynamic phenomenon described by some scholars as "colonial modernity."[40] Colonialism transformed peasants into Koreans and produced a Korean bourgeoisie. A variant of modern labor relations likewise emerged under enterprises such as the Onoda Cement Company. So too did a modern media, initially driven by politics but, very much like the press in Meiji Japan, increasingly reined in by the demands of the media market.[41] The observation that modernity and colonialism might coexist would seem little different from arguing against the mutual exclusivity of development and imperialism, noted above. What is especially significant about this concept, however, is that it highlights the agency of subject people in constructing that modernity in a colonial setting. Colonial modernity was considerably more than the received outcome of a Japanese "civilizing mission."

Studies of the colonies have led the way in this line of inquiry, but its concerns and approaches are, once again, readily applicable to non-colonial parts of the empire. Prasenjit Duara considers the role of women's organizations that legitimized the state in Manchukuo while, at the same time, asserted a more active role for women in the public sphere than for their counterparts in Japan or China proper. He also identifies a special role for Manchurian redemptive societies in the shaping of an "East Asian modern."[42] Rana Mitter explores Chinese responses to the Manchurian Incident and the creation of Manchukuo and, in doing so, illuminates the messier realities underlying the binary of collaboration and resistance central to the "Manchurian myth" entrenched in the Chinese nationalist narrative.[43] Interactions between the South Manchurian Railway Company and Chinese communities in Manchuria before 1931 offer additional examples of complex and contingent relationships generated under the empire. The officials of the Japanese railway company and local Chinese engaged one another as imperialists and subject peoples on the one hand, and as business managers and clients on the other. Cooperation under these circumstances was not necessarily collaboration, nor confrontation, a reflection of consciously anti-imperialist resistance.[44] Complexity and contingency may be seen in particularly sharp relief in occupied Southeast Asia during World War II. To nationalist leaders who had fought against colonialism, such as Aung San in Burma or Sukarno in Indonesia, the Japanese presented themselves at one and the same time as liberators and as new conquerors. The fact that their responses entailed a shifting mixture of cooperation and resistance, under these circumstances, is hardly surprising.[45]

Future Directions

A concern with colonial modernity and an emphasis on more contingent analyses of imperial relationships represent important trends shaping future scholarship. Consistent with these trends and the emphasis on imperial civil society, the topic of gender and empire will undoubtedly receive greater attention.[46] So, too, will migration and urban development.[47] In addition to new themes and topics, further research on the Japanese empire is likely to place increasing emphasis on interdisciplinary, and in particular, transnational approaches.[48] Of particular interest is the development of transnational interest groups in the empire, which might involve large business organizations, such as Mitsui Bussan or federations of small-scale Chinese, Japanese, Taiwanese, and Korean entrepreneurs.[49]

A new emphasis on the transnational does not diminish the continued importance of studying empire as an aspect of "national" histories. Some of the most important contributions to the field of Japan's imperial history have resulted from the growth of studies in modern Korean history. Much remains to be done on Taiwan, not to mention the Nan'yō.[50] In a similar vein, the study of late Qing and Republican China and its experience under Japanese domination constitutes an expanding field of great relevance to understanding the empire. Imperialism as an integral part of the Japanese experience, moreover, is far from played out. Popular opinion and imperial identity before 1931 remains an area that warrants attention. Japanese settler communities deserve further study as well, along with a framework of investigation for Japanese migration that transcends the traditional divide between a "diaspora" in the Americas and "empire" in East Asia. The cultural impact of the imperial endeavor offers a particularly promising field of inquiry. Kobayashi Hideo hints at the role of Manchuria, for example, in popularizing ice skating in Japan and nurturing some of the nation's early international competitors. Food and empire is another intriguing area of investigation.[51]

One of the most interesting possibilities for future work lies, perhaps, in the historical geography of the empire. Peattie's observation about Japan's expansion exclusively in the near abroad pointed early on to the notion that contiguous, continental models of empire, rather than the European overseas paradigm, might be more appropriate for an analysis of the Japanese case. The pursuit of this idea has been further encouraged by a renewed comparative interest, following the fall of the Soviet Union, in the Russian, Hapsburg, Ottoman, and Qing realms as imperial polities.[52] A conventional framework of inquiry, informed by deeply ingrained definitions of a "new imperialism" linked to modern nationalism and industrial capitalism, would discourage any tendency to think of the Japanese and Qing empires as belonging to comparable categories of polity, yet there are good reasons to breach these conceptual constraints.

Ronald Suny has noted, for example, that contiguous as opposed to overseas empires exhibit a number of distinct features.[53] Among the more intriguing of these differences lies in the fact that expanding contiguous polities present difficulties in any attempt to draw sharp lines between empire-building, in which an expansionist state transforms neighboring territories into a subject periphery, and nation-building, in which a centralizing state integrates and consolidates its borderlands into a unified national polity. When one state engages in both processes simultaneously, the boundaries between internal consolidation and external expansion become blurred. During the second half of the nineteenth century, Japan's nation-builders forged the Meiji nation-state out of an older, heterogeneous Tokugawa realm, integrating semi-autonomous domain states into a unified political community.[54] At the same time, while this nation-state remained a work in progress, a greater Japan, spilling beyond its

Tokugawa confines, began to take form. Hokkaidō, conventionally regarded as one of the four main islands of metropolitan Japan but incorporated and settled only in the modern era, offers a good example of the ambiguity generated by this dual process. In many respects, Hokkaidō was no more or less a settlement colony than Karafuto and provided essential lessons in colonization and the management of newly acquired territories. The Ryūkyū Kingdom, annexed in 1879 following a dispute with China and reorganized as Okinawa prefecture, also lay in a no-man's-land between empire and nation. Much of Okinawa's modern history entailed a process of transforming a peripheral colony into a metropolitan subdivision.[55] The assimilation of Okinawa might be regarded as an outlying case of the integration of elements of Japan's internal periphery into a nation-state. At the same time, it may also be seen as anticipating assimilationist policies in Taiwan and Korea that culminated in the full-scale attempt to absorb these colonies into metropolitan Japan in the late 1930s.[56] The blurring of lines between metropole and periphery and between empire-building and nation-building, as seen in the case of Okinawa, resonates with the application of the Meiji model in early colonial management noted above. This, in turn, suggests the potential value of a broader examination of Japan's domestic social, economic, and political history through the analytical lens of empire.

Conclusion

Broad shifts in historiography have facilitated new trends in the study of the Japanese empire. Such trends are likely to flourish in the immediate future if only because they have broadened the marketplace of ideas and brought the problem of empire to a wider intellectual audience. At same time, it would be unwise to abandon all older themes and topics, bearing in mind that English-language research on the Japanese imperium still lacks the depth and breadth of study devoted to European empires. Much remains to be done, including continued work on institutions of the state. The emergence of a newer historiography has also benefited from the relaxation of the cold war mindset and the gradual removal of some of the political snares that have long constrained this field of scholarship. It would be important, however, not overlook the fact that old polemics are being replaced by new. At least to some degree, a once universally condemned imperialism is undergoing rehabilitation, particularly as applied to the hegemonic role of the United States, which, in turn, is producing a reinvigorated critique. The study of history cannot isolate itself from its political environment, and those who practice this craft must be aware of its many uses and of the context in which they convey their knowledge to a wider public.

NOTES

1 John Dower, "E. H. Norman, Japan, and the Uses of History," in Norman, *Origins of the Modern Japanese State*, pp. 3–101.
2 Marius Jansen, "Japanese Imperialism: Late Meiji Perspectives," in Myers and Peattie, eds., *The Japanese Colonial Empire*, pp. 61–79.
3 Peter Duus, "Introduction," in Duus, Myers, and Peattie, eds., *The Japanese Informal Empire in China*, pp. xi–xxix.

4   Beasley, *Japanese Imperialism*, pp. 1–13.
5   For a discussion of "fascism" in Japan, see Duus and Okimoto, "Fascism and the History of Prewar Japan."
6   Matsusaka, *The Making of Japanese Manchuria*, pp. 92–100.
7   Mark Peattie, "Introduction," in Myers and Peattie, eds., *The Japanese Colonial Empire*, pp. 7–9, 13–15.
8   Ronald Robinson, "The Excentric Idea of Empire," in Mommsen and Osterhammel, eds., *Imperialism and After*, p. 269.
9   Matsusaka, *The Making of Japanese Manchuria*, pp. 22–30.
10 Duus, *The Abacus and the Sword*, esp. pt. 1. On the logic of annexation, see also Dudden, *Japan's Colonization of Korea*.
11 Discussed in Conroy and Wray, eds., *Japan Examined*, pp. 122–40.
12 Matsusaka, *The Making of Japanese Manchuria*, pp. 267–304. See also McCormack, *Chang Tso-lin in Northeast China*.
13 Duara, *Sovereignty and Authenticity*, pp. 9–34.
14 Ramon and Peattie, eds., *The Japanese Colonial Empire*. See also Nahm, ed., *Korea under Japanese Colonial Rule*.
15 On military industrialization, see Peattie, *Ishiwara Kanji*, and Barnhart, *Japan Prepares for Total War*.
16 This is a theme developed in Myers and Peattie, eds., *The Japanese Colonial Empire*.
17 " 'Hyakushō dōjō' kaisetsu an," *Tokyo Asahi shinbun* (Dec. 9, 1933).
18 Westney, *Imitation and Innovation*, pp. 92–9.
19 Tsurumi, *Japanese Colonial Education in Taiwan*, pp. 79–106.
20 Young, *Japan's Total Empire*, pp. 241–303.
21 Mark Peattie, "Japanese Treaty Port Settlements in China," in Duus, Myers, and Peattie, eds., *The Japanese Informal Empire in China*, pp. 166–209.
22 Matsusaka, *The Making of Japanese Manchuria*, pp. 250–8.
23 Yang, *Technology of Empire*.
24 Brooks, *Japan's Imperial Diplomacy*. I am grateful to Anne Reinhardt for her notion of "semicolonial infrastructures" (Reinhardt, "Navigating Imperialism in China").
25 Bruce Cumings, "The Legacy of Japanese Colonialism in Korea," in Myers and Peattie, eds., *The Japanese Colonial Empire*, pp. 478–96.
26 Duus, *The Abacus and the Sword*, pt. 2.
27 Young, *Japan's Total Empire*, pp. 55–114. See also Wilson, *The Manchurian Crisis*.
28 Mark Peattie, "Attitudes toward Colonialism," in Myers and Peattie, eds., *The Japanese Colonial Empire*, pp. 80–127.
29 In Japanese, an informative study on this subject is Miyachi, *Nichi-Ro sengo seiji shi no kenkyū*.
30 Duus, *The Abacus and the Sword*, pp. 289–323.
31 Takaki, *Strangers from a Different Shore*, p. 31.
32 Alan Moriyama, "The Causes of Emigration: The Background of Japanese Emigration to Hawaii, 1885–1894," in Cheng and Bonacich, eds., *Labor Migration under Capitalism*, pp. 248–75.
33 Weiner, *Race and Migration in Imperial Japan*.
34 Shūgi'in, *Gikai seido 70-nen shi*, p. 440.
35 For example, Robinson, *Cultural Nationalism in Colonial Korea*. On Taiwan, see Ka, *Japanese Colonialism in Taiwan*, and Ching, *Becoming "Japanese."*
36 This trend is well represented by the contributors to Shin and Robinson, eds., *Colonial Modernity in Korea*.
37 Park, *Colonial Industrialization and Labor in Korea*.
38 Eckert, *Offspring of Empire*.

39 Barbara Brooks, "Peopling the Empire: The Koreans in Manchuria and the Rhetoric of Inclusion," in Minichiello, ed., *Japan's Competing Modernities*, pp. 25–44; Harold Lamley, "Taiwan under Japanese Rule, 1895–1945: The Vicissitudes of Colonialism," in Rubenstein, ed., *Taiwan: A New History*, pp. 201–60.

40 Michael Robinson and Gi-Wook Shin, "Rethinking Colonial Korea," in Shin and Robinson, eds., *Colonial Modernity in Korea*, pp. 1–18. For more on the concept, see Barlow, ed., *Formations of Colonial Modernity in East Asia*.

41 Michael Robinson, "Broadcasting, Cultural Hegemony, and Colonial Modernity in Korea, 1924–1945," in Shin and Robinson, eds., *Colonial Modernity in Korea*, pp. 54–69.

42 Duara, *Sovereignty and Authenticity*, pp. 103–20, 131–69.

43 Mitter, *The Manchurian Myth*.

44 Matsusaka, *The Making of Japanese Manchuria*, pp. 139–48.

45 Goto Ken'ichi, "Cooperation, Submission, and Resistance of Indigenous Elites of Southeast Asia in the Wartime Empire," in Duus, Myers, and Peattie, eds., *The Japanese Wartime Empire*, pp. 274–301.

46 Wartime sexual slavery has been treated, for example, by Hicks in *The Comfort Women*. Shin and Robinson, eds., *Colonial Modernity in Korea*, contains several articles on women and gender. The broader history of gender dynamics in the Japanese empire awaits further study, a project being undertaken by, among others, Barbara Brooks.

47 For example, William Sewell, "Railway Outpost and Puppet Capital: Urban Expressions of Japanese Imperialism in Changchun, 1905–1945," in Blue, Bunton, and Croizier, eds., *Colonialism and the Modern World*, pp. 283–98.

48 Joshua Fogel is a pioneer in transnational studies of modern East Asia. See for example, Fogel, *The Cultural Dimension of Sino-Japanese Relations*.

49 Uchida Jun is currently working on aspects of this topic as part of her Ph.D. dissertation at Harvard University.

50 Peattie, *Nan'yō*, is one of the few studies of this part of the Japanese empire.

51 Kobayashi, *Mantetsu*, pp. 170–3; Michael Schneider, "Limits of Cultural Rule: Internationalism and Identity in Japanese Responses to Korean Rice," in Shin and Robinson, eds., *Colonial Modernity in Korea*, pp. 97–127.

52 For example, Lieven, *Empire*.

53 Ronald Suny, "The Empire Strikes Out," in Suny and Martin, eds., *A State of Nations*, pp. 23–66.

54 Kären Wigen, in *The Making of a Japanese Periphery*, argues that this process produced a new center and periphery within the Japanese home islands.

55 Koji Taira, "Troubled National Identity: The Ryūkyūans/Okinawans," in Weiner, ed., *Japan's Minorities*, pp. 140–77.

56 Chou Wan-yao, "The Kōminka Movement in Taiwan and Korea: Comparisons and Interpretations," in Duus, Myers, and Peattie, eds., *The Japanese Wartime Empire*, pp. 40–68.

BIBLIOGRAPHY

Barlow, Tani, ed. *Formations of Colonial Modernity in East Asia*. Durham, NC: Duke University Press, 1997.

Barnhart, Michael. *Japan Prepares for Total War: The Search for Economic Security, 1919–1941*. Ithaca, NY: Cornell University Press, 1987.

Beasley, W. G. *Japanese Imperialism, 1894–1945*. Oxford: Clarendon Press, 1991.

Blue, Gregory, Bunton, Martin, and Croizier, Ralph, eds. *Colonialism and the Modern World: Selected Studies*. Armonk, NY: M. E. Sharpe, 2002.

Brooks, Barbara. *Japan's Imperial Diplomacy: Consuls, Treaty Ports, and War in China, 1895–1938.* Honolulu: University of Hawai'i Press, 2000.

Cheng, Lucie, and Bonacich, Edna, eds. *Labor Migration under Capitalism: Asian Workers in the United States before World War II.* Berkeley: University of California Press, 1984.

Ching, Leo. *Becoming "Japanese": Colonial Taiwan and the Politics of Identity Formation.* Berkeley: University of California Press, 2001.

Conroy, Hilary, and Wray, Harry, eds. *Japan Examined.* Honolulu: University of Hawai'i Press, 1983.

Duara, Prasenjit. *Sovereignty and Authenticity: Manchukuo and the East Asian Modern.* Lanham, Md.: Rowman and Littlefield, 2003.

Dudden, Alexis. *Japan's Colonization of Korea: Discourse and Power.* Honolulu: University of Hawai'i Press, 2004.

Duus, Peter. *The Abacus and the Sword: The Japanese Penetration of Korea, 1895–1910.* Berkeley: University of California Press, 1995.

Duus, Peter, and Okimoto, Daniel. "Fascism and the History of Prewar Japan: The Failure of a Concept." *Journal of Asian Studies* 39:1 (1979): 65–76.

Duus, Peter, Myers, Ramon, and Peattie, Mark, eds. *The Japanese Informal Empire in China, 1895–1937.* Princeton: Princeton University Press, 1989.

Duus, Peter, Myers, Ramon, and Peattie, Mark, eds. *The Japanese Wartime Empire, 1931–1945.* Princeton: Princeton University Press, 1996.

Eckert, Carter. *Offspring of Empire: The Koch'ang Kims and the Colonial Origins of Korean Capitalism, 1876–1945.* Seattle: University of Washington Press, 1991.

Fogel, Joshua. *The Cultural Dimension of Sino-Japanese Relations: Essays on the Nineteenth and Twentieth Centuries.* Armonk, NY: M. E. Sharpe, 1995.

Hicks, George. *The Comfort Women: Japan's Brutal Regime of Enforced Prostitution in the Second World War.* New York: Norton, 1997.

Ka, Chih-ming. *Japanese Colonialism in Taiwan: Land Tenure, Development, and Dependency, 1895–1945.* Boulder, Colo.: Westview Press, 1995.

Kobayashi Hideo. *Mantetsu: "Chi no shūdan" no tanjō to shi.* Tokyo: Yoshikawa Kōbunkan, 1996.

Lieven, D. C. B. *Empire: The Russian Empire and Its Rivals.* London: John Murray, 2000.

Matsusaka, Y. Tak. *The Making of Japanese Manchuria, 1904–1932.* Cambridge, Mass.: Harvard University Asia Center, 2001.

McCormack, Gavan. *Chang Tso-lin in Northeast China: China, Japan and the Manchurian Idea.* Stanford, Calif.: Stanford University Press, 1977.

Minichiello, Sharon, ed. *Japan's Competing Modernities: Issues in Culture and Democracy, 1900–1930.* Honolulu: University of Hawai'i Press, 1998.

Mitter, Rana. *The Manchurian Myth: Nationalism, Resistance and Collaboration in Modern China.* Berkeley: University of California Press, 2000.

Miyachi Masato. *Nichi-Ro sengo seiji shi no kenkyū: teikokushugi keisei ki no toshi to nōson.* Tokyo: Tokyo Daigaku Shuppankai, 1973.

Mommsen, Wolfgang, and Osterhammel, Jurgen, eds. *Imperialism and After.* London: Allen and Unwin, 1986.

Myers, Ramon, and Peattie, Mark, eds. *The Japanese Colonial Empire, 1895–1945.* Princeton: Princeton University Press, 1984.

Nahm, Andrew, ed. *Korea under Japanese Colonial Rule: Studies of the Policy and Techniques of Japanese Colonialism.* Kalamazoo, Mich.: Center for Korean Studies, Western Michigan University, 1973.

Norman, E. Herbert. *Origins of the Modern Japanese State: Selected Writings of E. H. Norman,* ed. John Dower. New York: Pantheon, 1975.

Park, Soon-Won. *Colonial Industrialization and Labor in Korea: The Onoda Cement Factory.* Cambridge, Mass.: Harvard University Asia Center, 1999.

Peattie, Mark. *Ishiwara Kanji and Japan's Confrontation with the West.* Princeton: Princeton University Press, 1975.

Peattie, Mark. *Nan'yō: The Rise and Fall of the Japanese in Micronesia.* Honolulu: University of Hawai'i Press, 1988.

Reinhardt, Anne. "Navigating Imperialism in China: Steamship, Semicolony, and Nation, 1860–1937." Ph.D. dissertation, Princeton University, 2002.

Robinson, Michael. *Cultural Nationalism in Colonial Korea, 1921–1925.* Seattle: University of Washington Press, 1988.

Rubenstein, Murray, ed. *Taiwan: A New History.* Armonk, NY: M. E. Sharpe, 1999.

Shin, Gi-Wook, and Robinson, Michael, eds. *Colonial Modernity in Korea.* Cambridge, Mass.: Harvard University Asia Center, 1999.

Shūgi'in. *Gikai seido 70-nen shi: shūgi'in iin meiroku.* Tokyo: Ōkurashō Insatsu Kyoku, 1962.

Suny, Ronald, and Martin, Terry, eds. *A State of Nations: Empire and Nation-Making in the Age of Lenin and Stalin.* New York: Oxford University Press, 2001.

Takaki, Ronald. *Strangers from a Different Shore: A History of Asian Americans.* Boston: Little, Brown, 1998.

Tsurumi, E. Patricia. *Japanese Colonial Education in Taiwan, 1895–1945.* Cambridge, Mass.: Harvard University Press, 1977.

Weiner, Michael. *Race and Migration in Imperial Japan.* New York: Routledge, 1994.

Weiner, Michael, ed. *Japan's Minorities: The Illusion of Homogeneity.* London: Routledge, 1997.

Westney, D. Eleanor. *Imitation and Innovation: The Transfer of Western Organizational Patterns to Meiji Japan.* Cambridge, Mass.: Harvard University Press, 1987.

Wigen, Kären. *The Making of a Japanese Periphery, 1750–1920.* Berkeley: University of California Press, 1995.

Wilson, Sandra. *The Manchurian Crisis and Japanese Society, 1931–1933.* London: Routledge, 2002.

Yang, Daqing. *Technology of Empire: Telecommunications and Japanese Imperialism, 1930–1945.* Cambridge, Mass.: Harvard University Press, 2003.

Young, Louise. *Japan's Total Empire: Manchuria and the Culture of Wartime Imperialism.* Berkeley: University of California Press, 1997.

FURTHER READING

An understanding of the Japanese empire in its larger historical context requires an appreciation of a variety of issues tangential to the construction and management of the imperium, such as the framework of Japan's external relations, postcolonial history, and related developments in the modern histories of Korea, China, and Japan. A few examples of relevant, recent works are offered below.

On Japan's external relations, see Akira Iriye, *China and Japan in the Global Setting* (Cambridge, Mass.: Harvard University Press, 1992) and Ian Nish, *Japanese Foreign Policy in the Interwar Period* (Westport, Conn.: Praeger, 2002). Useful sources on postcolonial history include Bruce Cummings, *The Origins of the Korean War* (Princeton: Princeton University Press, 1981), and by the same author, *Parallax Visions* (Durham, NC: Duke University Press, 1999), and Harald Fuess, ed., *The Japanese Empire in East Asia and Its Postwar Legacy* (Munich: Iudicium, 1998). On modern Korean history, see Andre Schmid, *Korea between Empires* (New York:

Columbia University Press, 2002); on modern Chinese history, Parks Coble, *Facing Japan: Chinese Domestic Politics and Japanese Imperialism, 1931–1937* (Cambridge, Mass.: Harvard University Press, 1991). Comparative perspectives are offered in Robert Bickers and Christian Henriot, eds., *New Frontiers: Imperialism's New Communities in East Asia, 1842–1953* (Manchester: Manchester University Press, 2000), and Caroline Elkins and Susan Pederson, eds., *Settler Colonialism in the Twentieth Century: Projects, Practices, Legacies* (New York: Routledge, 2005). For additional insights into Japanese history, see Stewart Lone, *Japan's First Modern War* (New York: St. Martins Press, 1994), Frederick Dickinson, *War and National Reinvention* (Cambridge, Mass.: Harvard University Asia Center, 1999), and Leonard Humphreys, *The Way of the Heavenly Sword* (Stanford, Calif.: Stanford University Press, 1995).

Chapter Fourteen

The Fifteen-Year War

W. Miles Fletcher III

During the past two decades, Western scholarship on the period of the "Fifteen-Year War," from 1931 to 1945, has emphasized the complexity of the dynamics of Japanese politics and society during this tumultuous era. This period, in fact, encompasses three wars – the Manchurian Incident of 1931–2, the China War (1937–45), and the Pacific War between Japan and the Anglo-American powers, from 1941 to 1945. The passage of time and at least a partial tempering of emotions have enabled scholars to examine the roles of a wider range of sectors of Japanese society in the nation's military expansion abroad and oppression at home. If the debate over blame for the outbreak of the Pacific War in 1941 has become more muted, interest in Japan's strategic errors and atrocities committed by its forces remains high. Also, the perspective of more than half a century has encouraged scholars to place this period in a broader comparative and historical context.

A Fifteen-Year or an Eight-Year War or Neither?

One crucial issue centers on the accuracy of the term, the "Fifteen-Year War." The concept of one extended conflict over a decade and a half takes its cue from the International Military Tribunal of the Far East (1946–8), which accused Japanese leaders of a conspiracy to wage aggressive war from 1928, when the Kwantung Army assassinated Manchurian warlord Zhang Zuolin, through Japan's surrender in 1945. Although Japanese scholars have more frequently used the term,[1] Western scholars have commonly viewed the Manchurian Incident as a turning point in Japanese policies. The Kwantung Army's seizure of Manchuria seemed to signal the rising influence of the military within the Japanese government, an increased emphasis on stifling domestic dissent, and a shift away from the previous priority on cooperative diplomacy with the Western powers to military expansion in Asia.

Recent Western scholarship, though, suggests increasing dissension on the significance of the Manchurian Incident. The essays in *Society and the State in Interwar Japan*, edited by Elise Tipton, question the degree to which basic characteristics of Japanese society changed in the early 1930s. The authors examine a range of topics, such as women primary schoolteachers, policies toward birth control, rural youth associations, the Korean minority, trends in art, coalminers, and a controversy over the preservation of the Okinawan dialect. Tipton concludes that the 1930s "appear as years of social ferment, tension, and conflict ... rather than the beginning of the 'Fifteen Year War' or the 'Road to Pearl Harbor'." The Manchurian Incident did not bring a "sharp discontinuity either in state policies or the concerns and activities of various social groups." It did not, for example, "result in a clear pronatalist policy, in forced assimilation measures for minorities, or in involuntary conscription of labour."[2] Richard Mitchell's analysis of the Teijin Incident – a major trial in the mid-1930s of sixteen business leaders, government officials, and politicians accused of corruption – emphasizes that the verdict of not guilty for all defendants demonstrated the continuing independence of the courts by defying the Ministry of Justice and right-wing opinion that inveighed against greedy and selfish capitalists and party politicians. The criticism that afterwards swirled around the trial suggests that even as censorship expanded during the 1930s, leeway remained for debate on some issues.[3]

Louise Young's major study of the creation of Manchukuo in the 1930s, on the other hand, takes 1931 as a turning point in the development of Japanese imperialism. Confronting the strengthening force of Chinese nationalism, which challenged the Japanese position in Manchuria, the government pursued a new policy of "autonomous imperialism," which claimed the goal of nationalist liberation for the colonized population by creating the nominally independent state of Manchukuo.[4] Sandra Wilson's comprehensive study of the Japanese response to the Manchurian Incident counters by concluding that the crisis in the early 1930s just temporarily boosted Japanese nationalism and militarism. Important sectors of the society expressed ambivalence about Japan's actions in Manchuria, or, after an initial burst of enthusiasm, expressed an indifferent attitude. "For no group in Japanese society or within the establishment, with the exception of some Kwantung Army plotters, did the year 1931 constitute the beginning of a 'fifteen-year war'."[5]

Other scholars have viewed the start of Japan's full-scale war in China in 1937 as a more significant dividing line. Almost immediately the government implemented unprecedented controls on foreign trade and investment, followed by the sweeping National Mobilization Law of 1938. While describing the Manchurian Incident as a "central trigger mechanism" in creating an "atmosphere of war," Gregory Kasza defines the period from 1937 through 1945 as an "administrative revolution" that greatly extended state control into the media and other sectors of the society while reshaping them.[6] Although Andrew Gordon does not stress 1937 as a precise dividing line, he argues that "by the mid-1930s the bureaucratic-military state" had assumed an "unprecedented political role" in mobilizing popular support for military expansion in Asia.[7]

While recognizing an intensification of governmental regulation after 1937, studies of Japan's economic mobilization tend to emphasize the continuity of trends in the 1930s. Chalmers Johnson's influential analysis of the development of Japanese industrial policy, for example, marks the end of the "first phase" of industrial self-control with the passage of the Important Industries Control Law of 1931. Permitting cartels in designated major industries, this act embodied the epitome of self-regulation by enterprises. Concerned about the dominance of the cartels by large firms (zaibatsu), officials then worked to extend their control over the private sector.[8] Okazaki Tetsuji and Okuno-Fujiwara Masahiro posit in their edited volume that a new "Japanese economic system" took form in the 1930s and early 1940s. Not only did the government's control and planning increase, but crucial changes also occurred among corporations. The main source of their financing switched from the stock market to large banks, and long-term employment within large firms became more common. The authors' argument, however, remains ambiguous about the relative significance of changes in the economy after 1931 compared to those after 1937.[9] In general, contributors to the volume acknowledge that important changes began before the China War and accelerated after it had begun.[10] Taking a more abstract approach, Bai Gao emphasizes the rise of the general concept of a "managed economy" and an overall ideology of "developmentalism" between 1931 and 1945.[11] In a case study of a Japanese village in the 1930s, Kerry Smith underlines the similarities between the policies of rural economic revitalization after the Great Depression of 1930 and the mobilization of farmers after 1937. Both campaigns promoted rational planning by families and villages with the goal of enhancing productivity. According to Smith, "the transition from economic recovery to economic mobilization in villages like Sekishiba was, at least initially, more one of degree than an abrupt change in direction."[12] Overall, it seems that the growth of state controls progressed gradually for various reasons in the 1930s. If a single year did not mark an abrupt change, 1937 ushered in an intensification of war mobilization.

Society and the State

Studies of the relationship of various sectors of Japanese society to the wartime state have revamped the general interpretation of the era. The argument that an increasingly powerful military forced its aggressive designs on a resistant, or at least reluctant, civilian populace has lost much of its credibility. Examining the views of a wide spectrum of the society toward the creation of Manchukuo, Louise Young concludes that a "motley crew" built the Japanese empire.[13] The media eagerly competed to glorify the heroic exploits of Japanese forces during the Manchurian Incident in order to increase sales. Although Kwantung Army officers spewed anti-capitalist rhetoric, companies invested in Manchukuo bonds and took advantage of a new market for exports.[14] Convinced with a "remarkable capacity for self-deception" that they were helping to liberate and reform Chinese society, intellectuals carried out research projects for the South Manchurian Railway.[15] Sheldon Garon's broadly gauged study of "moral suasion" in Japan from the prewar to the postwar period illustrates how various interest groups, far from opposing the expanded intervention of the state in society, actively sought the help of government controls to accomplish specific goals. For example, as the government increasingly emphasized an emperor-centered orthodoxy of beliefs, well-established Shintō and Buddhist orders sought official recognition and the suppression of rivals, such as Christian groups and indigenous "new religions." During the 1930s champions of women's rights, such as Ichikawa Fusae, cooperated with the government's mobilization plans in hopes of demonstrating the valuable contribution that women could make to national goals and thus gaining more influence.[16]

A number of case studies of liberal and left-wing intellectuals highlight their support for the government's policies. W. Miles Fletcher's study of intellectuals in the Shōwa Research Association (Shōwa Kenkyūkai), a "brain trust" for Prime Minister Konoe Fumimaro, argues that their plans for a domestic new order and an East Asian Cooperative Body undermined the established constitutional order at home and justified Japanese military expansion abroad. These intellectuals came to see war mobilization as an opportunity to use the power of the state to effect radical political, social, and economic reforms in Japan and to liberate China from Western imperialism.[17] Tomoko Akami's examination of the multinational Institute for Pacific Relations finds that both Western and Japanese "liberals" in that organization were vulnerable to "cooptation" by the state. Even the most idealistic Japanese members who strived in the 1920s to build a peaceful and cooperative Pacific community through mutual international dialogue accepted the nation as their primary locus of loyalty. Accordingly, in the early 1930s they stoutly defended Japan's seizure of Manchuria. Later in the decade, many of these men rationalized Japan's aggression in China as members of the Shōwa Research Association.[18]

Peter High explains the collaboration of Japanese filmmakers with the goals of wartime mobilization by stressing their susceptibility to clever psychological manipulation by "reform bureaucrats," their accommodation of authority, their sincere patriotism, and, as artists, their "desire to keep working and thereby to redeem one's worth from the relentless flood of time."[19] Andrew Barshay's analysis of Nanbara Shigeru, an official and a university professor, and Hasegawa Nyozekan, a prominent journalist, relates how two intellectuals who initially advocated moderate reforms accommodated the nationalistic pressures of the 1930s.[20] Offering only indirect criticism of irrational nationalism centered on the emperor, Nanbara attacked the principle of individual rights. Hasegawa concentrated on studies of Japan's unique national character and mission in Asia. Both men hesitated to offer direct opposition to Japan's policies, because they wanted to remain engaged as "public men" serving the nation.

After 1931, the topic of Japan's cultural distinctiveness became a dominant theme that fit and helped shape the increasing force of nationalism. Leslie Pincus shows how the attempts of philosopher Kuki Shūzō in 1930 to define a distinctive Japanese aesthetic based on the spirit of *iki* (style) from the Tokugawa era (1600–1868) quickly transformed into an avid promotion of the nationalistic ideology of Japan's cultural uniqueness and its mission to protect Asia from the West.[21] H. D. Harootunian examines how prominent intellectuals, such as Kuki, Watsuji Tetsujirō, Yanagita Kunio, and Miki Kiyoshi, increasingly appealed to a "national organic community and its timeless folk" in order to "displace the threat of social dispersion and the agency of historical classes." As the "folkic group" encompassed the "East Asian folk," it "supplied ideological support to a variety of imperial and colonial policies that were demanding regional integration and incorporation."[22]

The role of leaders of Zen Buddhism in Japan and of the prominent Zen-influenced Kyoto School of philosophers has engendered much controversy during the past decade. In 1994, *Rude Awakenings: Zen, the Kyoto School, and the Question of Nationalism*, edited by James Heisig and John Maraldo, probed the extent to which Zen leaders and some of the most famous philosophers of early twentieth-century

Japan supported the rise of militarism and Japan's wars in China and the Pacific. The essays present a variety of perspectives. Kirita Kiyohide, for example, maintains that the well-known propagator of Zen Buddhism overseas, D. T. Suzuki, resisted "movements trying to associate Zen with war and death," while Hirata Seikō admits that "not a few Zen priests joined hands with State Shintō and its imperialist view of history in order to promote the war." In regard to Nishida Kitarō, the famous founder of the Kyoto School, Christopher Ives argues that although Nishida did not intend to promote Japan's aggression, his writings may have "at least validated the main ideological building blocks of militarists" by emphasizing an intense identification with the emperor, loyalty to the state, and the need to liberate Asia from Western domination. Yusa Michiko contends, though, that Nishida consistently criticized growing censorship within Japan, complained about attacks on his writings by right-wing groups, and tried to create an alternative to narrow nationalism.[23] In reply to criticisms of the Kyoto School, David Williams has defended members, such as Nishida and Tanabe Hajime, by arguing that "they concurred with the broad strategy of the Greater East Asia Co-Prosperity Sphere but they dissented forcefully from the military strategy and, even more sharply, from the brutal means by which this strategy was pursued by the Tōjō government."[24] In other words, truly believing in the ideals of the Co-Prosperity Sphere, these men did their best to oppose General and Prime Minister Tōjō Hideki in the early 1940s and to protest military policies in veiled language to the extent possible under tight censorship. Two studies by Brian Victoria, however, severely criticize the ways in which eminent leaders of Zen Buddhism in Japan, including such well-known post-1945 interpreters of Zen to the West as D. T. Suzuki and Yasutani Haku'un, enthusiastically supported Japanese militarism and aggression from 1931 to 1945. According to Victoria, by promoting a total and selfless devotion to the emperor and to the nation, Zen masters "wholeheartedly embraced the role of 'ideological shock troops' for Japanese aggression abroad and thought suppression at home."[25]

Some studies have shown that dissent was possible in the 1930s. Even though Professor Yanaihara Tadao of Tokyo Imperial University defended the creation of Manchukuo as an "economic lifeline" for a stagnating Japanese economy, he consistently cautioned against further challenging the force of Chinese nationalism through territorial expansion. In 1937 he argued that Japanese, who in the late nineteenth century had to mobilize to defend themselves against Western imperialism, should now sympathize with and aid China's attempts to achieve national unity. Reflecting his Christian faith, he posited that nations should aim at "social justice" in protecting the weak instead of seeking material gain. Not long afterwards, the authorities pressed him to resign from his university post and banned his works.[26] The prominent economic journalist Ishibashi Tanzan also accepted Japanese control over Manchuria, but he questioned increased bureaucratic economic controls and argued for more government spending on rural welfare instead of the military. He advocated an accommodation with the Nationalist government of China to promote trade and investment by Japan and the Western powers as the most effective path to prosperity for all sides.[27] The crusty Minseito politician Saitō Takao fearlessly rose in the Diet in 1936 to criticize the military and in 1940 to denounce the China War as costly and pointless.[28] After Saitō's fellow Diet members voted to banish him, he ran for election in 1942 and won.

Clearly, many prominent Japanese intellectuals supported or accepted the government's policies of expansion in Asia and domestic repression. Their main motivations stemmed from a desire to remain engaged as public intellectuals and to maintain influence in guiding reform. The cases of Yanaihara, Ishibashi, and Saitō demonstrate, though, that the government tolerated some dissent. Intellectuals' behavior could also vary between the poles of cooperation and opposition. After studying the lives of six prominent economists active from the prewar era well into the postwar period – including Arisawa Hiromi, Minobe Ryōkichi, and Ōuchi Hyōe – Laura Hein concludes that "neither the concept of collaboration nor of resistance fully captures" the activities and motivations of these men.[29] The experience of being arrested and tried for their criticism of the government's policies did not prevent some of the six from working for the wartime government.

Opportunistic pragmatism prevailed in the business community. Executives wanted both to take advantage of the Japanese seizure of Manchuria and to preserve harmonious trade relations with the Western powers and their colonies. At home, they saw possible benefits from the enactment of national economic controls, as long as businessmen retained influence over them.[30] The industrialist Ayukawa Gisuke evinced a similar type of opportunism.[31] After founding the Nissan Company in 1928, he moved the firm's headquarters to Manchukuo in 1937 and changed its name to the Manchurian Industrial Development Corporation. At the invitation of the Kwantung Army, the company promoted comprehensive industrial development in this latest addition to the Japanese empire. Ayukawa also eagerly sought American trade with Manchukuo and American investment. Within Japan, he tried several times to effect mergers between his firm and the Japanese operations of Ford and General Motors. The failure of both projects resulted from his unwillingness to recognize that by the late 1930s good relations with the United States depended upon Japan slowing the expansion of its Asian empire.

In regard to the labor movement, Andrew Gordon depicts a major change in the 1930s. In the 1920s, new labor unions had created a "dispute culture" while fighting for "improved treatment" of workers; all of the proletarian parties, which had just formed, criticized Japanese expansionism. After 1930, "Japanist" unions began to advocate the "fusion of capital and labor" in service to the nation. Meanwhile, socialist politicians rejected the strategy of class conflict and advocated an alliance "between the proletarian forces and the 'anti-capitalist' and 'reformist' military," because state controls imposed by war mobilization would curb the excesses of capitalism. In essence, like many intellectuals, business leaders, feminists, and religious leaders, the labor movement and left-wing parties adapted to the shift in governmental policies toward authoritarianism and aggression by "riding the tiger."[32] Needless to say, the strategy entailed great risks.

What attitudes did ordinary, non-elite Japanese have toward war mobilization? Two collections of brief oral histories, compiled by Theodore and Haruko Cook and Frank Gibney respectively, provide valuable glimpses of the experiences of people in all walks of life as remembered decades afterwards.[33] The accounts reflect genuine enthusiasm for the war at the time as well as the power of peer pressure and of the authorities; some people explain how they tried to resist. By the end of the war, the privations that it had caused brought a change in popular mood. The first few chapters of John Dower's *Embracing Defeat* depict a general attitude of "exhaustion and despair" and "war-weariness" by 1944 that contradicts the typical image of the Japanese people as fanatically loyal to the bitter end. After the surrender, the rapid appearance of signs of social disintegration – price gouging on the black market, the looting of military supplies, and the quick rejection of militarism – raises doubts about the depth of dedication to nationalistic self-sacrifice among many Japanese.[34]

What Was Wartime Japan?

While the complexity of the interaction between the state and various sectors of the society has become clearer, no consensus has emerged on categorizing Japan from 1931 to 1945. If using the term "militarism" is too narrow and hence misleading, what term is appropriate? The applicability of the concept of "fascism" has sparked the most debate. Some have argued against the use of the concept, because scholars have not been able to agree on a clear definition.[35] Others reject the term for wartime Japan, since it lacked some major institutional features of fascist Italy and Nazi Germany. These include a charismatic leader, a dominant mass party, and the abrupt dismantling of parliamentary institutions.[36] In fact, the Meiji constitution remained intact until 1945.

Scholars have found evidence of specific instances of European fascist influence in Japan. Fletcher argues that members of the Shōwa Research Association based their plans for an East Asian Cooperative Body and a domestic New Order in 1940, which advocated a mass political "national organization" and a state-controlled "new economic order," on the policies of fascist Italy and especially Nazi Germany.[37] The ultimate failure of the fascist New Order Movement, however, meant that the established order remained in place. The plan of officials in the late 1930s to replace labor unions with a "new order" of labor relations took the Nazi "labor front" as its model.[38] While emphasizing the differences in "in structure and ideology between the Japanese regime and the Italian and German regimes," Gregory Kasza argues that fascist ideas and policies strongly influenced various figures, including some prominent government officials, and movements of the "*kakushin* right" (the "renovationist authoritarian right").[39] Using philosopher Kuki Shūzō as an example, Pincus has discerned an ideological similarity between a "fascist turn" in the "discourse on culture" in 1930s Japan and "European fascism," because both expressed a "quest for authenticity" and a "retreat from universal values into the 'community of the nation'."[40]

From another perspective, Andrew Gordon advocates applying the concept of fascism to wartime Japan. Seeking to avoid the "radical nominalism" of those who create a "shopping list" of characteristics of fascism to compare regimes, he contends that Japan, Italy, and Germany in the 1930s had an "impressive realm of shared historical experience." "At some point in the interwar era, critical elements in each nation responded by repudiating parliamentary rule and turning to shrill nationalism, anticommunism, and antidemocratic, yet capitalist, programs to restructure the economy and polity and mobilize for war."[41] As Gordon points out, though, those programs of reform occurred differently in Japan than in its European counterparts. Whereas in the latter cases radical changes resulted from the triumph of mass political parties, in Japan the central bureaucracy initiated reforms, what historian Maruyama Masao decades ago called "fascism from above" as opposed to "fascism from below."[42] Hence, the argument seems to be that Japan was fundamentally fascist, but with significant differences from the European case. A recent collection of essays edited by E. Bruce Reynolds makes a thoughtful case for labeling Japan as fascist, because its policies and structure met a "fascist minimum," and urges more comparative studies of the Axis powers ("Axis Studies").[43] Whatever label one applies to Japan between 1931 and 1945, Reynolds's volume makes clear the prevalence of totalitarian ideas in that era.[44]

Still, rather than continuing the struggle to define fascism as a comparative concept and to pinpoint the start of fascism in Japan, a fresher and more fruitful approach may lie in analyzing developments in Japan in a broader global context. In the 1930s, the Japanese elite had a sharp awareness of contemporary trends in other empires and nations. Careful examination of Japanese perceptions of international trends, such as the growing power of the state and of the force of nationalism, and comparative analyses of Japanese policies and those of other nations, including Italy and Germany, could make a significant contribution to the global history of this era and perhaps suggest new ways of conceptualizing trends in Japan.

Diplomacy and the Road to Pearl Harbor

The general scholarly perspective on the "road to Pearl Harbor" reflects an equanimity perhaps facilitated by the passage of six decades. In some studies, one can detect an undercurrent of criticism of the rigidity of American hostility toward Japan in contrast to the desires of some prominent Japanese for peaceful relations.[45] Many historians, though, have come to emphasize an irreconcilable difference in the worldviews of the two nations as the source of tensions. Walter LaFeber's recent overview of American–Japanese relations contends that "differences in outlooks and objectives led to war," because the goal of a new order in Asia dominated by Japan clashed with the American vision of an open global marketplace. Anthony Best reaches a similar conclusion in regard to Britain and Japan: their disagreements on policy toward China and general trade issues made a war "inevitable" since neither side was ready to make major concessions.[46]

Two studies stress the assumptions that guided American and British policies.[47] Jonathan Marshall argues that from the late 1930s American officials worried most about protecting strategic raw materials, such as rubber and tin, in Southeast Asia. In his view, American support for China aimed not to protect that nation but to prevent the Japanese from moving south. Moreover, in anticipation of a Japanese attack in Southeast Asia in late November 1941, early drafts of a declaration of war by members of Franklin D. Roosevelt's cabinet stressed the importance of strategic resources there. Best reveals that British intelligence on Japan in the late 1930s seriously underestimated the capabilities of the Japanese army and navy while overestimating the debilitating effects of the China War on Japan's economy and the inherent caution of Japanese leaders. The mistaken belief – perhaps rooted in an attitude of racial condescension – that Japanese leaders would not dare to challenge a major Western power created a dangerous complacency in the British government.

The Japanese attack on December 7, 1941 caught British forces in Asia woefully unprepared.

Several works underscore the paucity in Japan of effective advocates of cooperative diplomacy after 1931. Ian Nish's study of the Japanese response to the Manchurian Incident and the subsequent inquiry by the League of Nations exposes the startling weakness of civilian moderates and "internationalists" in the government. Although the emperor himself and senior advisers apparently opposed the army's aggression, they proved powerless to stop it. The emperor even agreed to issue an imperial edict explaining Japan's withdrawal from the League after it voted to recommend the return of Manchuria to Chinese sovereignty.[48] Barbara Brooks's *Japan's Imperial Diplomacy* acknowledges that some officials in the Foreign Ministry sincerely wanted to cooperate with the Western powers and to negotiate a settlement with the Nationalist government in China. Prominent leaders, such as Foreign Minister Shidehara Kijurō, however, failed to offer a determined resistance to the army in 1931. Moreover, many civilian diplomats shortsightedly undermined the authority of their own ministry while attempting to further their careers by supporting the army's demand to create new agencies to handle Japan's relations with Manchukuo and China.[49]

David Lu tackles the ambitious task of rehabilitating the image of the flamboyant diplomat Matsuoka Yōsuke as a moderate. Matsuoka, after all, led the Japanese delegation out of the League of Nations in 1932 and signed the Axis Pact in 1940. Lu posits that Matsuoka, far from wanting to conquer China, really desired a cooperative relationship with the Nationalist government, if it would recognize Manchukuo. Calling Matsuoka a practitioner of realpolitik in the mold of Henry Kissinger,[50] Lu contends that Matsuoka could have reached a pragmatic compromise with the American government on the status of China if American officials had taken a more flexible stance. Similarly, Matsuoka sought an alliance with Germany, not to threaten the United States but to deter it from war with Japan. How, then, does one explain Matsuoka's bellicose statements toward the United States after 1936? Lu speculates that Matsuoka talked tough, because he had learned from his experience of attending high school in Oregon in the 1890s that Americans respected a confrontational style. Matsuoka's unwavering support for the expansion of the Japanese empire can lead one to doubt whether he would have made substantial concessions to reach a compromise with the American government.

The Role of the Emperor

Emperor Hirohito remains the most prominent enigmatic figure of this era. The challenge of assessing his motives and role have inspired several major studies, each with a sharply different perspective. Stephen Large's political biography of Hirohito argues that the emperor opposed Japan's policies of foreign aggression but failed to exert much influence.[51] Large emphasizes Hirohito's verbal reprimand to Prime Minister Tanaka Gi'ichi in 1929 for the army's assassination of the Chinese warlord Zhang Zuolin as well as Hirohito's immediate imposition of martial law to suppress the military rebellion of February 1936, because these actions showed the emperor's resistance to the growing power of the military. The question then arises as to why

Hirohito could not stop the decision for war against the United States in 1941. Here, Large accepts Hirohito's own explanation that as a "constitutional monarch" he had to accept the decision of the cabinet and that his veto of the decision for war might have spurred a military coup by fanatic officers who would have pursued even more aggressive policies.[52]

In contrast, Herbert Bix lays the responsibility for Japan's aggression squarely at Hirohito's feet. Bix views the emperor's reprimand to Prime Minister Tanaka and his quick crushing of the 1936 rebellion as demonstrations of Hirohito's desire to intervene in politics and his considerable power of supreme command over the military. Yet, in 1941 he did little to attempt to derail the cabinet's decision for war with the United States.[53] Both interpretations have vulnerabilities. Large's generous view of the emperor's actions relies on an eight-hour monologue dictated to trusted aides in 1946 in preparation for mounting his defense in a possible trial by the Allies as a war criminal. Bix's analysis leaves little room for ambiguity. Every action taken by Hirohito, even those overtly aimed at constraining the military, become evidence of the emperor's increasing power and hence his responsibility for Japan's aggression.

Peter Wetzler presents an alternative view that accepts and explains contradictory aspects of Hirohito's behavior. The emperor could at times take decisive action, as in 1936, and at others let events drift, as in the three years leading up to the attack on Pearl Harbor.[54] He defied the army's wishes in 1938 by opposing an alliance with Nazi Germany but allowed the Axis Pact in 1940. In 1941 he approved the decision for war against the United States in September, demanded one more attempt to reach a diplomatic compromise in October, and finally approved the start of the war on December 1. Because Hirohito participated actively in discussions of policy behind the scenes, he did not play the role of a passive constitutional monarch, as he claimed after the war; nor did he wield dictatorial power, as Bix argues. Wetzler contends that Hirohito's primary concern centered not on expanding the Japanese empire, preserving peace in the Pacific, or maintaining a constitutional government but on his deeply felt traditional responsibility for preserving the imperial house. Uncertain about the correct course of action, he approved the decision for war with the Anglo-American powers in 1941, because he feared a veto would prompt a rebellion, like the one in 1936, which would threaten the existence of the throne itself. Wetzler's approach suggests that a focus on analyzing the legacy of the imperial institution, Hirohito's education, and his goals as he defined them will help in understanding the motivation for his actions more than imposing external criteria of guilt or innocence for the Pacific War.

The Japanese Military

The fierce determination of the Japanese soldier to fight to the death continues to fascinate observers. Blaming the traditional samurai ethic of *bushidō* (the way of the warrior) and emphasizing the indoctrination of all Japanese in the ideology of absolute loyalty to the emperor are common but incomplete explanations. Specific strategic decisions made by top officers shaped this attitude of self-sacrifice. Alvin Coox's magisterial study of the clash between Japanese and Soviet troops at Nomonhan in 1939 remains an unparalleled gold mine of insights about the strategy, tactics, command structure, and operations of the imperial Japanese army. Particularly salient was officers' stress on compensating for a lack of modern equipment and technology by emphasizing superior fighting spirit.[55] Leonard Humphreys finds that the strategy of stressing "spirit" emerged officially in the 1920s, when the army's leadership realized that it could not afford to equip its troops with the new weapons and equipment introduced in World War I – trench mortars, light machine guns, and tanks – at the same level as the Western powers. In 1928 General Araki Sadao rewrote the army's strategic manual to eliminate the terms "surrender," "retreat," and "defense" and to recognize spirit (*seishin*) as superior to materiel in combat.[56]

At the level of the common soldier, Edward Drea analyzes the various ways in which the army cultivated group loyalty among recruits. The practice of forming regiments out of draftees from a particular region reinforced local ties, while new soldiers came to regard their squad and the barracks as a new family.[57] Emiko Ohnuki-Tierney's study of the kamikaze suicide pilots, whose missions began in late 1944, reveals that they were thoughtful and anguished young men motivated mainly by youthful idealism.[58] Drafted from the student ranks at elite universities, they read widely in Western and Japanese philosophy and literature. Repelled by capitalism and materialistic greed, they sought refuge in the Western doctrines of Marxism, liberalism, and Christianity as they agonized about fundamental issues of human rights, social responsibility, and their commitment to the nation. Significantly, they did not refer to loyalty to the emperor in their diaries and letters but stressed instead the need to defend their homeland and to inspire the building of a new Japan.

Scholarly interest has also concentrated on the strategic and tactical mistakes made by the Japanese military. *Kaigun*, by Mark Peattie and David Evans, and *Sunburst*, by Peattie, provide a wealth of information about the Japanese imperial navy and naval aviation.[59] To be sure, Japanese accomplishments receive their due. At the start of the war against the Anglo-American powers the imperial navy had superior technology in night optics, the I-93 torpedo, and the Mitsubishi "Zero" fighter. In battles in which the opposing naval forces were roughly equivalent, such as the Solomons campaign of 1942–3, the Japanese did well. However, the inability to develop new technologies, such as radar, proved a major problem, as did the decision not to use submarines against civilian shipping. Japan's gravest error, though, was not to plan for a long war.

The belief that a "thunderbolt" attack at the start would stun the Americans into seeking peace or that a "decisive" battle would lead to victory meant that Japanese admirals did not prepare for a war of attrition. Aware that the imperial navy faced a materially superior foe, naval leaders placed a priority on quality over quantity. For example, the decision to produce relatively few pilots but to train them rigorously provided an advantage early in the war but made replacing pilots lost in combat difficult as the war dragged on. Even the famous "Zero" fighter seemed best suited to a short conflict. The plane's light weight gave it a long range and an advantage in maneuverability, but its lack of armor made it vulnerable as the fighting continued.[60] Edward Drea finds the imperial army equally ill prepared for a lengthy struggle. Army strategists planned only a five-month operation in the Southwest Pacific, after which they planned to withdraw fully one-half of their troops for redeployment in Manchuria against the Soviets. The American landing on Guadalcanal in August 1942 caught Japanese generals by surprise, because they thought that a United States counterattack would not occur until late 1943.[61]

At the tactical level and in specific battles, the Japanese made crucial mistakes as well.[62] Lacking construction equipment, they built too few air bases in the Southwest Pacific, which quickly became a major theater of fighting. Although American pilots learned to minimize the advantage of the "Zero" in maneuverability by avoiding individual dogfights and diving at it from a higher altitude, Japanese pilots did not adjust their tactics of attacking in an unstructured "beehive" formation. Poor sea rescue operations caused the needless deaths of many Japanese pilots. Perhaps most seriously, even though the Japanese commanders perceived the defense of Guadalcanal in the Solomon Islands as a decisive battle in 1942, they did not commit sufficient forces to prevail, because they wanted to "win Guadalcanal on the cheap." Moreover, the large Japanese losses of troops and supplies in the Southwest Pacific in 1942 and early 1943 substantially weakened Japan's defenses against the later Allied drive across the Central Pacific.[63]

Atrocities committed by the Japanese military have also received increased attention. While John Dower's *War without Mercy* probes the reasons for the bitterness of the fighting between American and Japanese troops by examining the ways in which the two sides dehumanized each other, subsequent works have focused on the behavior of the Japanese. Using Western and Chinese sources, Iris Chang wrote a widely read account of the Rape of Nanking (Nanjing) in December 1937. The horror of the atrocities that she vividly describes, her contention that Japanese soldiers had slaughtered as many as 300,000 Chinese, her comparison of the event to the Nazi Holocaust in Europe, and her charge of a cover-up, especially by the Japanese, has sparked much debate. Some question the charge of a cover-up, because Japanese scholars have critically examined the Rape of Nanking for several decades.[64] Yamamoto Masahiro's recent study examines Japanese as well as Chinese and Western sources in estimating that in six weeks Japanese forces killed between 45,000 and 65,000 Chinese in Nanking, mostly adult males, "of which 15,000 to 52,000 were killed in unlawful ways." While readily describing what happened at Nanking as a massacre and acknowledging the rape of thousands of Chinese women by Japanese soldiers, Yamamoto insists that there was no set policy to commit a massacre, because the behavior of individual units varied. To Yamamoto, Japanese actions cannot be compared to the "systematic mass pattern of mass killing" that marked the Nazi Holocaust.[65]

Sheldon Harris was among the first Western scholars to report the biological warfare experiments carried out on humans by Unit 731 and Unit 100 of the Japanese army in various locations in Manchuria and China. He also exposes the cynical bargain after Japan's surrender, in which American officials agreed not to place Japanese officers and doctors on trial for war crimes in return for the data from the experiments that they had conducted. Most recently, James Bradley's *Flyboys* presents a gruesome account of Japanese executions of captured American pilots at Chichi Jima in 1945. George Hicks's *The Comfort Women* describes the Japanese military's system of sexual enslavement that began in the late 1930s. The subsequent English translation of Yoshimi Yoshiaki's careful study of relevant government documents demonstrates convincingly the active role of the military in creating and strictly supervising the brothels in which the "comfort women" worked as well as the awareness of Japanese officials that they were violating international law.[66]

The Japanese Empire

The Japanese Wartime Empire, edited by Peter Duus, Ramon Myers, and Mark Peattie, has presented the most comprehensive analysis to date in English of the Greater East Asia Co-Prosperity Sphere. As a whole, the essays emphasize the discrepancy between the ideals of the Co-Prosperity Sphere and its wartime reality, the variety of policies implemented in different regions, and the overreach of Japanese power.[67] In terms of individual case studies, Manchukuo and China have received the most attention. Louise Young's *Japan's Total Empire* explains that from the Japanese perspective the new state of Manchukuo became a "brave new empire" by serving as a laboratory for experimenting with technology, such as high-speed trains, and new ideas of urban planning. Moreover, vast plains promised a better life for poor Japanese farmers, whose emigration would hopefully solve the nation's agrarian crisis.[68] Prasenjit Duara contends that in creating an effective "developmental state" in Manchukuo the Japanese found substantial support there among traditional redemptive and sectarian societies because of their beliefs in pan-Asian ideals and established a useful alliance with local landlords. He perceives an important difference between the state of Manchukuo and Japan's older colonies of Korea and Taiwan, since Manchukuo had at least nominal independence. In this sense, Duara finds Japanese policies in Manchukuo similar to "global imperialism in the interwar years, when direct rule by aliens and sheer exploitation gave way to alternatives, such as indirect rule, collaborative arrangements with local elites, self-government, and quasi-independence, and other means to secure imperialist interests," and views Manchukuo as a precursor to the "client states" of the superpowers after 1945.[69]

To what extent, one might ask, did the Japanese succeed in appealing to the populace in other regions of China? Parks Coble's analysis of Chinese businesses in occupied Shanghai after 1937 reveals a pragmatic attitude by Chinese entrepreneurs. Demonstrating neither heroic resistance nor supine collaboration, they simply wanted to maintain their family enterprises. They avoided collaboration with the Japanese unless it was necessary, because the Japanese offered few material incentives to cooperate until late in the war.[70] Timothy Brook's recent study also presents a strong case for complicating the dominant approach of categorizing Chinese during this period in terms of either heroic resistance or evil collaboration by exploring five case studies of "collaboration" at the local level in Japanese-occupied China. Taking a broad comparative perspective that defines collaboration in terms of responses to an "occupation state," Brook aims to understand the behavior of "collaborators" rather than judge them. He finds that Chinese who offered to help the occupiers tended to be marginal members of local elites who had been denied opportunities to exercise power before, many of whom exhibited ambiguous behavior. "There was collaboration, there was resistance, but there was much else besides. Even what looks like collaboration ends up being far more than resistance's simple opposite."[71]

Japan's Surrender

Skepticism about President Harry S. Truman's decision to use atomic bombs against the Japanese cities of Hiroshima and Nagasaki seemed to peak in 1995, the fiftieth anniversary of Japan's surrender. Afterwards, supporters of the decision gained ground. By the early 1990s, critics of Truman's decision had punctured his claim that use of the atomic bombs had saved between 200,000 and 500,000 American lives that would have been lost in an invasion of Japan, which was scheduled for November. Instead, researchers discovered that American military leaders in June 1945 made predictions of deaths that varied between 25,000 and 46,000 Allied troops.[72] One analysis of American planning for the invasion concludes that Allied casualties would have been high but tolerable, because the Japanese "home-land army was largely untrained, ill-equipped, and pitifully supplied."[73] Since the alternative of invading Japan seemed to be much less costly than previously thought, the question of Truman's motives for using the atomic bomb re-emerged with new intensity. Criticism centered on Truman's reliance on certain advisers, such as Secretary of War Henry L. Stimson and the newly appointed Secretary of State James Byrnes, the President's failure to consider other options, his initial denial that many civilian deaths would result, and his fascination with the weapon's power.[74]

Several more recent studies, on the other hand, have tended either to support Truman's decision or, at least, to shift some blame to the Japanese for not making greater efforts to end the war earlier. Herbert Bix has emphasized, for example, the major responsibility borne by Emperor Hirohito, because in February 1945 he rejected the recommendation of former Prime Minister Prince Konoe Fumimaro and Foreign Minister Shigemitsu Mamoru to open negotiations for peace.[75] Needless to say, a settlement then would have saved many lives all over Asia and would have obviated the need for the American government even to consider using the atomic bomb, which was not tested until July. The Japanese diplomatic historian Asada Sadao has argued that the use of the atomic bombs served a crucial purpose, because the immense power of the weapons gave the Japanese military an excuse to surrender without admitting defeat on the battlefield.[76] Richard Frank points out that Ameri-can intelligence officers learned by July 1945 that Japanese generals had moved many more troops than expected near the projected Allied landing zones on Kyūshū. Thus, American leaders must have known then that Allied deaths in an invasion would far exceed the estimates made in June.[77] Frank dismisses the likelihood for the success of options other than using the atomic bomb, such as offering a conditional surrender with a guarantee for the maintenance of the imperial throne, by noting that the Japanese government had not clarified its terms for surrender.

In seeking a new perspective, other scholars have emphasized the complexity of developments regarding Japan's surrender. Accepting the probability that the use of the atomic bombs saved thousands rather than hundreds of thousands of American lives, J. Samuel Walker nonetheless asserts that Truman acted primarily to end the war as quickly as possible to minimize those losses. He describes as a "myth," however, the belief that Truman faced a stark choice between dropping the atomic bombs and an invasion of Japan. Other options – an offer of a conditional surrender, a demon-stration of the atomic bomb, and a strategy of continuing the naval blockade and conventional bombing – existed and could have induced Japan's surrender in a timely manner, especially if they were used in combination. Walker defines the main chal-lenge facing scholars as "fully considering the situation facing American and Japanese leaders in the summer of 1945."[78]

A recent study by Tsuyoshi Hasegawa uncovers a sobering story that evenhandedly discredits Truman, the Soviet leader Joseph Stalin, and the Japanese government.[79] Taking a multilateral approach that examines Soviet, Japanese, and American archives, Hasegawa analyzes simultaneous diplomatic developments in 1945 between the United States and Japan, the United States and the Soviet Union, and the Soviet Union and Japan. He argues, in brief, that Truman insisted on issuing the Potsdam Declaration in late July with a demand for unconditional surrender after he had already made the decision to use the atomic bomb, because he believed that the highly probable Japanese rejection of the declaration would help justify his decision. Also, after the test of the atomic bomb in July, Truman desperately wanted to end the war to prevent the Soviet Union from entering the conflict and gaining more territory in Asia. This part of his analysis seems to reassert the argument introduced by Gar Alperovitz in the 1960s that cold war politics dominated Truman's decision to use the atomic bombs against Japan.[80] In turn, according to Hasegawa, the Soviet leader, Joseph Stalin, deliberately delayed in responding to Japanese overtures for him to mediate a peace with the Western Allies, because he wanted time to prepare to enter the Pacific War in order to move troops into China and Korea and seize Sakhalin, the Kuril Islands, and even Hokkaidō, if possible. Japanese leaders, meanwhile, failed to form a strong consensus on terminating the war and to define an effective strategy for doing so. Moreover, Hasegawa contends that the Soviet declaration of war on Japan on August 8 had a greater impact on the Japanese decision to surrender than the use of the atomic bombs on August 6 and August 9.

A Broader Context for Interpretation

The perspective of almost six decades has enabled historians to place the significance of the Pacific War in a larger comparative or chronological context. Gregory Kasza's *The Conscription Society*, for instance, cites the organizations created by the Japanese state for wartime mobilization as examples of Administered Mass Organizations (AMOs), which, he argues, have been common and important institutions in many "nondemocratic" regimes in the twentieth century. Other scholars have focused on analyzing the economic links between wartime and postwar Japan. Among Western scholars, Chalmers Johnson was perhaps the first to do so by highlighting continuities in the authority over economic policy gained by the Ministry of Commerce and Industry in wartime and the authority granted to the Ministry of International Trade and Industry after 1949. As noted above, Okazaki Tetsuji has argued that the "Japanese economic system," which achieved a remarkable growth rate from the 1950s to the 1980s, originated in the economic changes of the wartime period. Bai Gao discerns the rise of a general economic ideology of "developmentalism," which promoted state intervention in the economy, as starting in the 1930s and carrying through to the postwar era.[81]

At the level of popular culture, John Dower notes how easily rallying cries for war mobilization transformed into slogans urging the new postwar goals of peace and democracy. "Construct a Greater East Asia Co-Prosperity Sphere" became "Construct a Nation of Peace." As Dower shows with great irony, Emperor Hirohito became the most obvious continuity of all, fully supported by the American occupiers touting the goal of the total reform of Japanese politics and society. Sheldon Garon's *Molding Japanese Minds* explores the continuing preoccupation of the Japanese state with "moral suasion" and "social management" and the continuing willingness of private interest groups to cooperate in this project. Laura Hein's study of six economists shows the consistency of their ideal of improving the lives of the people through a social welfare state but makes clear the vastly increased freedom of action and opportunities for influence that postwar democracy afforded these intellectuals. She remarks in her conclusion that "the link between wartime and postwar Japan cannot be characterized either as a sharp break or a straight line."[82]

Overall, the scholarship of the past two decades or so has raised serious doubts about any particular year as a turning point of complete radical change in Japanese policies – 1931, 1937, or 1945. The Japanese attack on Pearl Harbor in December 1941, of course, marked a momentous expansion of Japan's war in Asia, but this decision built on previous ones. If the passage of time has brought a more dispassionate analysis of the diplomatic tensions leading to the Japanese attack on Pearl Harbor and of the reasons for the fanatic loyalty of Japanese soldiers and of kamikaze pilots, the criticism of strategic and tactical errors by the Japanese military after 1941 has become more pronounced. The main strategic question is: why did Japanese generals and admirals not plan for a long war against the Anglo-American powers? Or, if they were not ready for such a conflict, why did they go to war? Similarly, attention has focused on atrocities committed by Japanese forces. Case studies of the role of various sectors of society in the 1930s have helped to dismantle the view of a dominant military duping or coercing the civilian populace into a reckless war. Defining the special character of wartime Japan, however, remains elusive. Rather than search for a single term that will embody this complicated era, more productive approaches might follow two tracks. One would seek to place developments in Japan from 1931 to 1945 in a global context that would include but go beyond the other Axis Powers. Kasza's *The Conscription Society* is one example. The other would examine Japan in this era as a case study for discerning the complex processes through which modern societies prepare, wittingly or not, for waging war.

NOTES

1 For example, see Ienaga, *The Pacific War*, p. xiii. Ienaga notes the use of the term by Japanese scholars. He prefers not to use it, but defines the Pacific War as lasting from 1931 to 1945.
2 Tipton, ed., *Society and the State in Interwar Japan*, pp. 5–6.
3 Mitchell, *Justice in Japan*.
4 Young, *Japan's Total Empire*, pp. 47–52.
5 Wilson, *The Manchurian Crisis*, p. 219.
6 Kasza, *The State and the Mass Media*, p. 282.
7 Gordon, *Labor and Imperial Democracy*, p. 316.
8 Johnson, *MITI and the Japanese Miracle*, pp. 108–15.
9 Okazaki and Okuno-Fujiwara, eds., *The Japanese Economic System*, pp. 2, 14.
10 For example, see Ueda, "The Financial System and Its Regulations," ibid., pp. 38–43.
11 For example, see Gao, *Economic Ideology*, pp. 22, 67.
12 Smith, *A Time of Crisis*, p. 330.

13 Young, *Japan's Total Empire*, p. 426.

14 Ibid., chs. 3 and 5.

15 Ibid., p. 294.

16 Garon, *Molding Japanese Minds*, chs. 2 and 4.

17 Fletcher, *The Search for a New Order*.

18 Akami, *Internationalizing the Pacific*, pp. 165, 190, 280.

19 High, *The Imperial Screen*, esp. chs. 9 and 14.

20 Barshay, *State and Intellectual in Imperial Japan*.

21 Pincus, *Authenticating Culture*, epilogue.

22 Harootunian, *Overcome by Modernity*, pp. 327–8, 398–9.

23 Heisig and Maraldo, *Rude Awakenings*. The specific essays referred to are Hirata Seitō, "Zen Buddhist Attitudes to War," pp. 3–15 (quotation on p. 11); Kirita Kiyohide, "D. T. Suzuki on Society and the State," pp. 52–76 (p. 61); Christopher Ives, "Ethical Pitfalls in Imperial Zen and Nishida Philosophy: Ichikawa Hakugen's Critique," pp. 16–39 (p. 38); and Yusa Michiko, "Nishida and Totalitarianism: A Philosopher's Resistance," pp. 107–31.

24 Williams, *Defending Japan's Pacific War*, p. 63.

25 Victoria, *Zen at War*, and *Zen War Stories*, chs. 5 and 7 (quotation on p. 83).

26 Townsend, *Yanaihara Tadao*, chs. 6, 8, and 9.

27 Nolte, *Liberalism in Modern Japan*, ch. 7.

28 Kinmonth, "The Mouse that Roared."

29 Hein, *Reasonable Men*, p. 215.

30 Fletcher, *The Japanese Business Community and National Trade Policy*.

31 Iguchi, *Unfinished Business*.

32 Gordon, *Labor and Imperial Democracy*, chs. 8–10, pp. 285, 286–7.

33 Cook and Cook, *Japan at War*; Gibney, *Senso*.

34 Dower, *Embracing Defeat*, chs. 3 and 4.

35 Duus and Okimoto, "Fascism and the History of Prewar Japan," pp. 65–76.

36 For example, see Wilson, "A New Look at the Problem of Japanese Fascism," pp. 401–12.

37 Fletcher, *The Search for a New Order*, pp. 155–8.

38 Garon, *The State and Labor*, pp. 208–18.

39 Kasza, "Fascism from Above?" pp. 224, 232.

40 Pincus, *Authenticating Culture*, epilogue.

41 Gordon, *Labor and Imperial Democracy*, pp. 333–8.

42 Ibid., pp. 338–9; Maruyama, *Thought and Behavior*, pp. 25–83.

43 Reynolds, ed., *Japan in the Fascist Era*. Joseph P. Sotille proposes an emphasis on "Axis Studies" in his essay, "The Fascist Era: Imperial Japan and the Axis Alliance in Historical Perspective," pp. 1–48. Sotille defines a "fascist minimum" on pp. 16–17. Reynolds presents a carefully reasoned case for applying the concept of fascism to Japan, as well as a careful review of the relevant historiography, in his concluding essay, "Peculiar Characteristics: The Japanese Political System in the Fascist Era," pp. 155–97.

44 See, for example, Christopher Szpilman, "Fascist and Quasi-Fascist Ideas in Interwar Japan, 1918–1941," in Reynolds, ed., *Japan in the Fascist Era*, pp. 73–106.

45 For example, Iguchi, *Unfinished Business*, ch. 7, and Lu, *Agony of Choice*.

46 LaFeber, *The Clash*, pp. 214–15; Best, *Britain, Japan, and Pearl Harbor*, ch. 9.

47 Marshall, *To Have and Have Not*; Best, *British Intelligence*.

48 Nish, *Japan's Struggle with Internationalism*, pp. 206–7, 228–9.

49 Brooks, *Japan's Imperial Diplomacy*, pp. 149–50, 157–60, and ch. 5.

50 Lu, *Agony of Choice*, p. 193.

51 Large, *Emperor Hirohito*, chs. 2–4.

52 Ibid., p. 113.

53 Bix, *Hirohito and the Making of Modern Japan*, pp. 208–19, 302–5, and ch. 11.
54 Wetzler, *Hirohito and War*.
55 Coox, *Nomonhan*, pp. 1090–2.
56 Humphreys, *The Way of the Heavenly Sword*, ch. 4.
57 Drea, *In the Service of the Emperor*, ch. 6.
58 Ohnuki-Tierney, *Kamikaze, Cherry Blossoms, and Nationalisms*.
59 Peattie and Evans, *Kaigun*, chs. 7–14; Peattie, *Sunburst*.
60 Peattie and Evans, *Kaigun*; Peattie, *Sunburst*; Bergerud, *Fire in the Sky*.
61 Drea, *In the Service of the Emperor*, ch. 3.
62 Peattie, *Sunburst*; Bergerud, *Fire in the Sky*.
63 Bergerud, *Fire in the Sky*, pp. 660, 663–4.
64 Dower, *War without Mercy*; Chang, *The Rape of Nanking*. For two informative review essays on studies of the Rape of Nanking see Yang, "Convergence or Divergence?", and Wakabayashi, "The Nanking Massacre."
65 Yamamoto, *Nanking*, pp. 115, 145.
66 Harris, *Factories of Death*; Bradley, *Flyboys*; Hicks, *The Comfort Women*; Yoshimi, *The Comfort Women*.
67 Duus, Myers, and Peattie, eds., *The Japanese Wartime Empire*. See Peter Duus, "Introduction: Japan's Wartime Empire: Problems and Issues," pp. xxvii–xxxix, for a summary of these themes.
68 Young, *Japan's Total Empire*, chs. 6–8.
69 Duara, *Sovereignty and Authenticity*, chs. 2 and 3, p. 247.
70 Coble, *Chinese Capitalists*, pp. 111–13, 205–11.
71 Brook, *Collaboration*, pp. 30–1, 233–6.
72 Bernstein, "Understanding the Atomic Bomb and the Japanese Surrender," pp. 232, 263–4.
73 Skates, *The Invasion of Japan*, pp. 254–6.
74 For example, see Lifton, *Hiroshima in America*, pp. 117–42.
75 Bix, *Hirohito and the Making of Modern Japan*, pp. 488–94.
76 Asada, "The Shock of the Atomic Bomb," pp. 505–12.
77 Frank, *Downfall*, pp. 339–43.
78 Walker, *Prompt and Utter Destruction*, p. 110.
79 Hasegawa, *Racing the Enemy*.
80 Alperovitz, *Atomic Diplomacy*.
81 Kasza, *The Conscription Society*; Johnson, *MITI and the Japanese Miracle*; Okazaki, *The Japanese Economic System*; Gao, *Economic Ideology*.
82 Dower, *Embracing Defeat*, ch. 5; Garon, *Molding Japanese Minds*, epilogue; Hein, *Reasonable Men*, p. 216.

BIBLIOGRAPHY

Akami, Tomoko. *Internationalizing the Pacific: The United States, Japan, and the Institute of Pacific Relations in War and Peace, 1919–45*. London: Routledge, 2002.
Alperovitz, Gar. *Atomic Diplomacy: Hiroshima and Potsdam*. New York: Simon and Schuster, 1965.
Asada Sadao. "The Shock of the Atomic Bomb and Japan's Decision to Surrender – A Reconsideration." *Pacific Historical Review* 67 (Nov. 1998): 477–512.
Barshay, Andrew. *State and Intellectual in Imperial Japan: The Public Man in Crisis*. Berkeley: University of California Press, 1988.

Bergerud, Eric. *Fire in the Sky: The Air War in the South Pacific.* Boulder, Colo.: Westview Press, 2000.

Bernstein, Barton. "Understanding the Atomic Bomb and the Japanese Surrender: Missed Opportunities, Little-Known Near Disasters, and Modern Memory." *Diplomatic History* 19:2 (Spring 1995): 227–73.

Best, Anthony. *Britain, Japan, and Pearl Harbor: Avoiding War in East Asia, 1936–1941.* London: Routledge, 1995.

Best, Anthony. *British Intelligence and the Japanese Challenge in Asia, 1914–1941.* New York: Palgrave Macmillan, 2002.

Bix, Herbert. *Hirohito and the Making of Modern Japan.* New York: HarperCollins, 2000.

Bradley, James. *Flyboys: A True Story of Courage.* Boston: Little, Brown, 2003.

Brook, Timothy. *Collaboration: Japanese Agents and Wartime Elites in Wartime China.* Cambridge, Mass.: Harvard University Press, 2005.

Brooks, Barbara. *Japan's Imperial Diplomacy: Consuls, Treaty Ports, and War in China, 1895–1938.* Honolulu: University of Hawai'i Press, 2000.

Chang, Iris. *The Rape of Nanking: The Forgotten Holocaust of World War II.* New York: Basic Books, 1997.

Coble, Parks. *Chinese Capitalists in Japan's New Order: The Occupied Lower Yangtzi, 1937–1945.* Berkeley: University of California Press, 2003.

Cook, Haruko Taya, and Cook, Theodore F. *Japan at War: An Oral History.* New York: Free Press, 1992.

Coox, Alvin D. *Nomonhan: Japan against Russia, 1939,* 2 vols. Stanford, Calif.: Stanford University Press, 1985.

Dower, John. *War without Mercy: Race and Power in the Pacific War.* New York: Pantheon, 1986.

Dower, John. *Embracing Defeat: Japan in the Wake of World War II.* New York: Norton 1999.

Drea, Edward. *In the Service of the Emperor: Essays on the Imperial Japanese Army.* Lincoln: University of Nebraska Press, 1998.

Duara, Prasenjit. *Sovereignty and Authenticity: Manchukuo and the East Asian Modern.* Lanham, Md.: Rowman and Littlefield, 2003.

Duus, Peter, and Okimoto, Daniel. "Fascism and the History of Prewar Japan: The Failure of a Concept." *Journal of Asian Studies* 39:1 (1979): 65–76.

Duus, Peter, Myers, Ramon, and Peattie, Mark, eds. *The Japanese Wartime Empire, 1931–1945.* Princeton: Princeton University Press, 1996.

Fletcher, W. Miles. *The Search for a New Order: Intellectuals and Fascism in Prewar Japan.* Chapel Hill: University of North Carolina Press, 1982.

Fletcher, W. Miles. *The Japanese Business Community and National Trade Policy, 1920–1942.* Chapel Hill: University of North Carolina Press, 1989.

Frank, Richard. *Downfall: The End of the Imperial Japanese Empire.* New York: Random House, 1999.

Gao, Bai. *Economic Ideology and Japanese Industrial Policy: Developmentalism from 1931 to 1965.* New York and Cambridge: Cambridge University Press, 1997.

Garon, Sheldon. *The State and Labor in Modern Japan.* Berkeley: University of California Press, 1987.

Garon, Sheldon. *Molding Japanese Minds: The State in Everyday Life.* Princeton: Princeton University Press, 1997.

Gibney, Frank, ed. *Senso: The Japanese Remember the Pacific War: Letters to the Editor of Asahi Shinbun.* Armonk, NY: M. E. Sharpe, 1995.

Gordon, Andrew. *Labor and Imperial Democracy in Prewar Japan.* Berkeley: University of California Press, 1991.

Harootunian, H. D. *Overcome by Modernity: History, Culture, and Community in Interwar Japan*. Princeton: Princeton University Press, 2000.

Harris, Sheldon. *Factories of Death: Japanese Biological Warfare, 1932–1945 and the American Cover-Up*, rev. edn. New York: Routledge, 2002.

Hasegawa, Tsuyoshi. *Racing the Enemy: Stalin, Truman, and the Surrender of Japan* Cambridge, Mass.: Harvard University Press, 2005.

Hein, Laura. *Reasonable Men, Power Words: Political Culture and Expertise in Twentieth-Century Japan*. Berkeley: University of California Press, 2004.

Heisig, James, and Maraldo, John. *Rude Awakenings: Zen, the Kyoto School, and the Question of Nationalism*. Honolulu: University of Hawai'i Press, 1994.

Hicks, George. *The Comfort Women: Sex Slaves of the Japanese Imperial Forces*. London: Souvenir Press, 1995.

High, Peter. *The Imperial Screen: Japanese Film Culture in the Fifteen Years' War, 1931–1945*. Madison: University of Wisconsin Press, 2003.

Humphreys, Leonard. *The Way of the Heavenly Sword: The Japanese Army in the 1920s*. Stanford, Calif.: Stanford University Press, 1995.

Ienaga Saburo. *The Pacific War: World War II and the Japanese, 1931–1945*, trans. Frank Baldwin. New York: Pantheon, 1978.

Iguchi, Haruo. *Unfinished Business: Ayukawa Yoshisuke and U.S.–Japan Relations, 1937–1953*. Cambridge, Mass.: Harvard University Press, 2003.

Johnson, Chalmers. *MITI and the Japanese Miracle: The Growth of Industrial Policy, 1925–1975*. Stanford, Calif.: Stanford University Press, 1982.

Kasza, Gregory. *The State and the Mass Media in Japan, 1918–1945*. Berkeley: University of California Press, 1988.

Kasza, Gregory. *The Conscription Society: Administered Mass Organizations*. New Haven: Yale University Press, 1995.

Kasza, Gregory. "Fascism from Above? Japan's Kakushin Right in Comparative Perspective." In Stein Ugelvik Larsen, ed., *Fascism Outside Europe: The European Impulse against Domestic Conditions in the Diffusion of Global Fascism*. New York: Columbia University Press, 2001.

Kinmonth, Earl. "The Mouse that Roared: Saitō Takao, Conservative Critic of Japan's 'Holy War' in China." *Journal of Japanese Studies* 25:2 (Summer 1999): 331–60.

LaFeber, Walter. *The Clash: A History of U.S.–Japan Relations*. New York: Norton, 1997.

Large, Stephen. *Emperor Hirohito and Shōwa Japan: A Political Biography*. London: Routledge, 1992.

Lifton, Robert J. *Hiroshima in America: 50 Years of Denial*. New York: Putnam's Sons, 1995.

Lu, David J. *Agony of Choice: Matsuoka Yōsuke and the Rise and Fall of the Japanese Empire, 1880–1946*. Lanham, Md.: Lexington Books, 2002.

Marshall, Jonathan. *To Have and Have Not: Southeast Asian Raw Materials and the Origins of the Pacific War*. Berkeley: University of California Press, 1995.

Maruyama Masao. *Thought and Behavior in Modern Japanese Politics*, ed. Ivan Morris. Oxford: Oxford University Press, 1963.

Mitchell, Richard. *Justice in Japan: The Notorious Teijin Incident*. Honolulu: University of Hawai'i Press, 2002.

Nish, Ian. *Japan's Struggle with Internationalism: Japan, China, and the League of Nations, 1931–1933*. London: Kegan Paul, 1993.

Nolte, Sharon H. *Liberalism in Modern Japan: Ishibashi Tanzan and His Teachers, 1905–1960*. Berkeley: University of California Press, 1987.

Ohnuki-Tierney, Emiko. *Kamikaze, Cherry Blossoms, and Nationalisms: The Militarization of Aesthetics in Japanese History*. Chicago: University of Chicago Press, 2002.

Okazaki, Tetsuji, and Okuno-Fujiwara Masahiro, eds. *The Japanese Economic System and Its Historical Origins.* Oxford: Oxford University Press, 1999.

Peattie, Mark. *Sunburst: The Rise of the Japanese Naval Air Power, 1909–1941.* Annapolis, Md.: Naval Institute Press, 2001.

Peattie, Mark, and Evans, David. *Kaigun: Strategy, Tactics, and Technology in the Imperial Japanese Navy, 1887–1941.* Annapolis, Md.: Naval Institute Press, 1997.

Pincus, Leslie. *Authenticating Culture in Imperial Japan: Kūki Shūzō and the Rise of National Aesthetics.* Berkeley: University of California Press, 1996.

Reynolds, E. Bruce, ed. *Japan in the Fascist Era.* New York: Palgrave Macmillan, 2004.

Skates, John Ray. *The Invasion of Japan: Alternative to the Bomb.* Columbia: University of South Carolina Press, 1994.

Smith, Kerry. *A Time of Crisis: Japan, the Great Depression, and Rural Revitalization.* Cambridge, Mass.: Harvard University Asia Center, 2001.

Tipton, Elise K., ed. *Society and the State in Interwar Japan.* New York: Routledge, 1997.

Townsend, Susan. *Yanaihara Tadao and Japanese Colonial Policy: Redeeming Empire.* Richmond, UK: Curzon, 2000.

Victoria, Brian Daizen. *Zen at War.* New York: Weatherhill, 1997.

Victoria, Brian Daizen. *Zen War Stories.* London: RoutledgeCurzon, 2003.

Wakabayashi, Bob. "The Nanking Massacre: Now You See It . . . " *Monumenta Nipponica* 56:2 (Winter 2001): 521–44.

Walker, J. Samuel. *Prompt and Utter Destruction: Truman and the Use of the Atomic Bombs against Japan.* Chapel Hill: University of North Carolina Press, 1997.

Wetzler, Peter. *Hirohito and War: Imperial Tradition and Military Decision Making in Prewar Japan.* Honolulu: University of Hawai'i Press, 1998.

Williams, David. *Defending Japan's Pacific War: The Kyoto School Philosophers and Post-White Power.* London: Routledge, 2004.

Wilson, George. "A New Look at the Problem of Japanese Fascism." *Comparative Studies in Society and History* 10 (July 1968): 401–12.

Wilson, Sandra. *The Manchurian Crisis and Japanese Society, 1931–1933.* London: Routledge, 2002.

Yamamoto, Masahiro. *Nanking: Anatomy of an Atrocity.* Westport, Conn.: Praeger, 2000.

Yang, Daqing. "Convergence or Divergence? Recent Historical Writings on the Rape of Nanjing." *American Historical Review* 104:3 (June 1999): 842–65.

Yoshimi, Yoshiaki. *The Comfort Women: Sexual Slavery in the Japanese Military during World War II.* New York: Columbia University Press, 2000.

Young, Louise. *Japan's Total Empire: Manchuria and the Culture of Wartime Imperialism.* Berkeley: University of California Press, 1998.

FURTHER READING

Ian Nish's recent book, *Japanese Foreign Policy in the Interwar Period* (Westport, Conn.: Praeger, 2002), provides a concise history of Japanese diplomacy between the two world wars. Akira Iriye's edited volume, *Pearl Harbor and the Coming of the Pacific War: A Brief History with Documents and Essays* (Boston: Bedford, 1999), provides insights into the frantic attempts at negotiations between Japanese and American officials in 1940–1.

Written almost two decades ago, Ronald Spector's *Eagle against the Sun: The American War against Japan* (New York: Vintage Books, 1985) gives a comprehensive account of the Pacific War from 1941 to 1945. Gerhard Weinberg's monumental *A World at Arms: A Global History of World War II* (New York: Cambridge University

Press, 1994; rev. edn., 2005) examines World War II in both the European and Pacific theaters. A recent and concise overview is Mark Roehrs and William Renzi, *World War II in the Pacific* (Armonk, NY: M. E. Sharpe, 2004). H. P. Willmott analyzes, sometimes caustically, the strategy on each side during 1942 and 1943 in *The War with Japan: The Period of Balance, May 1942–October 1943* (Wilmington, Del.: Scholarly Resources Press, 2002). Thomas W. Zeiler, *Unconditional Defeat: Japan, America, and the End of World War II* (Wilmington, Del.: Scholarly Resources Press, 2002), covers the period from 1944 to 1945. E. B. Sledge's memoir, *With the Old Breed at Peleliu and Okinawa* (Annapolis, Md.: Naval Institute Press, 1996), gives a gripping ground-level description of those ferocious battles. Emphasizing the impact of military developments on ordinary soldiers and civilians on all sides, Christopher Bayly and Tim Harper chronicle the Japanese conquest of British colonies in Southeast Asia and the eventual Japanese defeat in *Forgotten Armies: The Fall of British Asia, 1941–1945* (Cambridge, Mass.: Harvard University Press, 2004).

PART IV

Japan since 1945

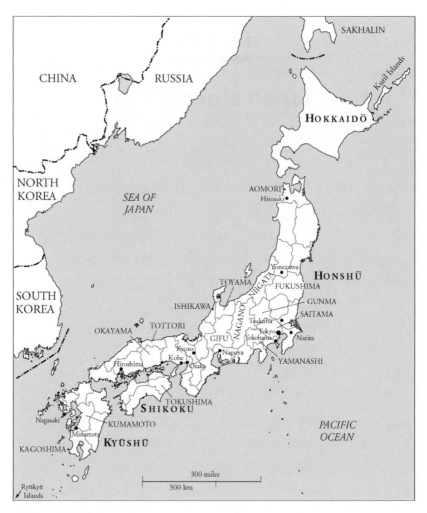

Map 4 Modern Japan

CHAPTER FIFTEEN

The Occupation

Mark Metzler

As history happens, long periods of relative institutional stability are punctuated by brief episodes of revolutionary change, when the events of a few years have structuring effects across wide domains of social practice for many years afterwards. As such a revolutionary, or near-revolutionary moment in modern Japanese history, the occupation is second only to the Meiji Restoration. Like the national reconstruction of the early Meiji period, the occupation was also an induced, top-down revolution, although the "bottom-up" popular movements of the era are a key to understanding it. Unlike the Meiji Reformation, this one was imposed by a Western occupying army. In the words of colonial policy expert Yanaihara Tadao, Japan was "placed on the laboratory table" by the American occupiers,[1] and the experience reveals much about the inner physiology of the Japanese body politic.

Storylines

Like the war, and unlike the seemingly endless social-scientific present of the "postwar" era that followed, the occupation was the stuff of instant history. Participants knew that they were making history, and they wrote about it, abundantly, making the occupation second only to the war itself in the volume of English-language writing devoted to it. Bibliographies and critical reviews of the English-language work on the subject run to over 1,000 pages.[2] To summarize it would take a large book, and the present essay highlights only a few themes prominent in more recent writing and a few aspects of the period that remain less well understood.

Most historical narratives of the occupation are built around a set of more or less standardized storylines. These turn out to be inseparable from an understanding of the chronology of the occupation, usually seen as a two-step movement of revolution followed by conservative stabilization, or "reverse course." The occupation of the Japanese mainland began with the arrival of General Douglas MacArthur and the signing of the surrender agreement on September 2, 1945; Japan's remaking got under way in earnest in October, when MacArthur's General Headquarters, Supreme Commander for the Allied Powers (GHQ/SCAP) was set up to conduct the non-military aspects of the occupation.[3] Japan regained its sovereignty eighty months later, on April 28, 1952. The timing and character of the two-step movement varied across the dozens of policy domains with which the occupation concerned itself. From the standpoint of the Japanese left, the turn from liberation to course reversal began when MacArthur banned the planned general strike of February 1, 1947, although liberal reforms in some policy domains were only then getting under way. From the standpoint of economic policy, the course reversal came fully into effect when Detroit banker Joseph M. Dodge took charge of balancing the Japanese budget in February 1949, by which point most of the reforms were being wound up if not reversed.

The first generation of English-language work, mostly written by former SCAP officials, tended to concentrate on the excitement of the first phase of the occupation. These writers presented a broadly consensual story of successful liberal reform, whereby an aggressive, ultranationalistic, and militaristic polity was converted into a peace-loving, progressive, and pro-American one. And to lose sight of the successes, as some more specialized later work comes close to doing, is to miss the main story. But this is not the only story, nor is it where the story ends. With the recognition of Japan's "economic miracle" after the late 1950s, the sense of success was magnified for many Americans, who now understood "their" reform of Japan as confirmation of the validity of American-style liberal capitalism as a developmental model in the non-Western world.

It was in reaction to the failure of US government policies in this "third" world that the impulse for a new historiography came, undertaken by a new generation of scholars for whom the occupation was no longer personal history and for whom the sources of the American war in Vietnam demanded a re-examination of the lessons of the occupation of Japan. These scholars, most prominently John Dower, Howard Schonberger, and Michael Schaller, investigated the cold war context of American policy and began to understand the occupation as an episode in a larger process of American imperialism (even if they did not necessarily use the word).[4] As leftist Japanese scholars had done since the midpoint of the occupation itself, they emphasized the significance of the anti-communist reverse course, seen as a betrayal of the democratic promise of the early occupation. The first generation of research, including the occupation's own official histories,[5] had been written without access to the relevant US government archives, and the opening of those archives in the 1970s contributed to the work of revision. This new, critical history was denounced in turn as "revisionism" by members of the older generation.[6] Except for Dower's study of the postwar prime minister Yoshida Shigeru, most of this newer work was in the vein of US diplomatic history and, in common with the first generation of work based on American sources, it did not examine the specifically Japanese dynamics of the period. More recently, again with Dower among the leaders of the movement, the occupation has been renaturalized into the stream of Japanese history, and a third generation of scholars, mostly trained as Japan specialists, have turned their interest to the social and cultural interactions between victor and vanquished. The voices of women and bicultural Japanese and American perspectives are prominent in this new work, which is discussed further below. The historiography of the occupation is also at the moment, and likely for some time to come, dominated as are few other fields of Japanese history by a single book, John Dower's *Embracing Defeat* (1999). Much of the following discussion of new tendencies in occupation-era research relates to themes that are reflected and amplified there.

From the Japanese side, the history of occupation was always more personal, all-encompassing, and ambiguous, but some standardized, politically divided storylines were also distilled from the experience. A generally shared national story was of defeat and the long road back. The "burned fields" of Japan's cities – an arresting, iconic image represented again and again in Japanese popular culture – thus became the common postwar starting point. For a broad array of Japanese progressives, the occupation itself began as a liberation – approaching real revolution in the more millenarian visions – that was sacrificed to American cold war interests. In more conservative accounts, arrogant American social engineering and "victor's justice" were succeeded by more sensible policies, once Americans awoke to the communist danger that Japan, allegedly, had been fighting all along. Still, the task of restoring Japan to full sovereignty and "normal" nationhood remains incomplete without revision of the American-imposed constitution. The first phase of the occupation became a vital source of postwar progressive politics, as the reverse course was carried forward as a powerful stream of conservative politics.

Thus, the occupation must be understood in the streams of Japan's history, America's history, and in the history of their interaction. When we approach the reconstruction of Japan as an event in *world* history, still other dynamics come to the foreground.

A Pivot in World Historical Time

The global context of America's occupation of Japan was the radical remaking of the international system as a whole, with the establishment in one sphere of American political-economic hegemony, in another of Soviet socialist hegemony, and the crystallization of the bipolar cold war arrangement. As after World War I, the great postwar movement of peoples and the redrawing of national boundaries was accompanied by a wave of communist-led revolution and anti-communist reaction. Intertwined with, and in many ways more significant than the "first world/second world" story was the dynamic of anti-colonial national liberation – the beginning of the hurried end of Western European global hegemony. This latter movement had its storm center in Asia. The world was also reconstructed ideologically, as the results of the war discredited not only fascism but also colonialism, while validating liberal democracy *and* socialism. (It is often forgotten that liberal, laissez-faire capitalism was not validated by the Allied victory – it was discredited by the Great Depression, which was understood as a cause of the war. War economies had resulted in a great economic extension of the state everywhere, and it was widely assumed that this transformation would be carried forward into a new, "modified capitalism," if not outright socialism.) These changes in the international order were also powerfully reformative dynamics at the domestic level.

At the level of individual national transformations, Japan's remaking was one of many radical reconstructions affecting most of the countries occupied, liberated, or reoccupied as a result of the war – a group of nations that extended from Japan and Korea to China, Southeast Asia, and Eastern, Central, and Western Europe. Beyond the war zones, the list of liberated or reconstructed countries also included a cohort of newly independent countries including India, Pakistan, Syria, Jordan, and Israel. In short, most of Europe and Asia was politically transformed in the late 1940s, yielding a picture of epoch-making efforts at national construction and reconstruction affecting more than half of the world's people. The least radically transformed of these countries were the formerly German-occupied countries of Western Europe (that is, countries of the Western European core), which reverted, more or less, to their prewar state. "Restoration" was impossible in Asia, and the revolutionary remaking of China lay at the other extreme of national reconstructions. Profound as it was, Japan's national reconstruction actually lay somewhere around the middle of this range. Compared to postwar social transformations elsewhere, Japan's postwar reform was also accomplished with little violence and with a complete absence of armed resistance, despite Japanese contingency plans to hide a member of the imperial family and fight a guerrilla war of resistance to the occupation.[7]

The world war and the reconstructions that followed had socially leveling effects almost everywhere, whether along capitalist or communist lines. This was true in the United States as well. Leveling effects were especially strong in Japan, and a sampling of a few of many changes that tended in this direction must serve to suggest the whole process. In the farm villages that were home to almost half of the nation, a "semi-feudal" landlord system, already undermined by wartime food procurement policies, was abolished by the thoroughgoing land reform implemented after October 1946.[8] Nearly as significant were the effects of the postwar food shortages and inflation, which massively redistributed wealth from the formerly privileged urban sector to the formerly exploited farm sector. By the end of the occupation, a new set of social relations was institutionalized. Farmers, no longer divided as landlords and tenants, came to constitute a great, landowning middle class, able to buy and employ new production-enhancing and labor-easing technologies, able to join the new mass market, and supportive of conservative party hegemony.

Factory workers, who had been virtual social outcastes in the first part of the twentieth century, seized the chance to unionize provided by the Labor Union Law of December 1945, and the labor movement quickly outran the goals of most SCAP labor reformers. Unlike farmers, wage workers were the ones who paid for the postwar inflation. At the same time, the inflation further spurred unionization and labor militancy. The end result, after the shock of the Dodge Line price stabilization and the mass layoffs that accompanied it in 1949–50, was to give factory workers too a greater share in national wealth and to bring them into the lower ranks of the new middle-class, mass market Japan. Organized workers also formed a core of support for the leftist opposition that fought to preserve occupation reforms in the face of conservative efforts at rollback during the 1950s, resulting in the institutionalization of a new social settlement.

Legal equality for women, announced as a goal of the occupation in October 1945 and guaranteed in the November 1946 constitution, brought changes in access to education and in laws governing marriage, divorce, property, and inheritance – the legal basis for the new family system discussed further below. Family types were homogenized across social classes, as legal, ideological, and economic forces worked to dissolve the categories of the former class system. At the apex of the social pyramid, the titled aristocracy, the amalgam of hereditary aristocrats and more or less merito-cratically selected members of the governing elite who by official definition dominated prewar Japanese society, was legally abolished. At the base of the extended households of the prewar period was the live-in maid (*jochū*), one of the most common job descriptions into the immediate postwar period, when this form of personal servitude began rapidly to disappear. The experiences of members of disparate social classes were also homogenized by common wartime and postwar travails of the labor and military draft, evacuation to the countryside, and hunger. Accumulated wealth was destroyed by American bombing (although the bombing concentrated, as in Germany, on densely settled working-class districts) and Japanese inflation. The newly ubiquitous rhetoric of "the people," "the masses," and "revolution" was at once normative and descriptive of new realities. War and occupation thus initiated a leveling process that was subsequently carried to its fullest extent by high-speed economic growth. The result was that a society characterized by ferocious social and economic inequality was converted into one of the most socially and economically egalitarian in the capitalist world.

In these ways among others, what Tsuru Shigeto called Japan's "creative defeat" contributed, after a period of conflict, to the creation of a new domestic consensus and a mass domestic market, enabling Japan's conversion into Asia's first mass consumption society in the 1950s and 1960s.[9] Zaibatsu dissolution and economic deconcentration also had an aspect of "creative destruction." Seen by American planners as a way to democratize Japan's economy and to take Japan down a notch industrially, economic deconcentration contributed to the "capital strike" and collapse of industrial production during the early years of the occupation. Accordingly, it was dropped after 1948, when American policy shifted to a pro-business line of rebuilding Japanese industry. The period of disorder also opened the way for the rise of new companies in what amounted to an entrepreneurial revolution, another subject that is awaiting an integrated treatment. Also critical here was the fact that, like the civil bureaucracy (see below), banks were largely undisturbed by the reforms.[10] They were thus in place to serve as the core institutions of the bank-centered *keiretsu* that reconstituted the old zaibatsu groupings in the 1950s.

Like World War I, World War II was followed by a worldwide inflation, which verged into hyperinflation in the defeated countries. Price statistics at the time became arbitrary and chaotic, but even officially controlled prices increased by annual rates in the triple digits during the first half of the occupation. While Japan's inflation did not approach that of Germany after World War I or of contemporary Republican China, it was an overriding fact of daily life and business decisions. Hyperinflations by their nature are moments when economic time is speeded up – to save money and plan in terms of a long-term monetary horizon is meaningless when money loses its value by the day; the only rational response is to make the interval between getting money and spending it as brief as possible, and to deal in goods rather than in money.

The other side of price controls and rationing was the diversion of goods into the black market, a form of illegality to which almost everyone resorted, which has recently gotten attention in studies by John Dower and Owen Griffiths.[11] Inflation and the black market were material foundations of the ephemeral, overheated lifestyles reflected in the work of the "rogue" or "decadent" (*burai-ha*) writers such as Sakaguchi Ango and Tamura Taijirō.[12] Their consciousness and the frantic round-the-clock lifestyles of their milieu also had a pharmacological dimension: black-market amphetamines, not illegal until 1951, were in demand as a means to overcome exhaustion (and to dull hunger); they were also one of few goods in ample supply, owing to the vast amounts produced for the war effort. The crazed character of the final years of the war and the first years of the occupation, for many military and ex-military men especially, can thus be understood as a mass speed psychosis. Nor could the war itself be entirely left behind in the battle zones of Asia and the Pacific – the safety and stability of the long postwar era makes people forget that occupation-era Japan was filled with veteran murderers, rapists, and thieves and could not always find an easy path back. The black markets and the gangs that burgeoned from them drew on these men and on others displaced and orphaned by the war, a development of lasting importance for the underground side of postwar Japan's political economy.

Japan's own liberation from Japanese militarism was simultaneously one of the final episodes of Western colonialism in Asia. Seen from an outer, policy level, a first impression is that America's occupation – whether as the "phase one" reformist exercise in democratization or as the "phase two" rehabilitation of conservative Japan within an American alliance – was utterly different from colonialism. At a close-up, personal level, when the character of the occupation as a racialized hierarchy is brought to the foreground, the look and feel of occupation was much like coloni-alism, a dimension that emerges strongly in recent work by John Dower, Yukiko Koshiro, Michael Molasky, and Mire Koikari.[13] Partially for this reason, the ideas of anti-colonial national liberation fed into a new kind of identification with Asia on the Japanese left.

The Japanese People under Occupation

Policy history has formed the mainstream of English-language occupation historiog-raphy, which has been a history of *America's* occupation of Japan, in which the experiences and thinking of Japanese people have been nearly invisible. Again, Dower's *Embracing Defeat* provided the first comprehensive alternative account.

Amid the desolation and disorder of the early occupation came a burst of cultural creativity, momentarily experienced almost as a cultural revolution, at once enabled by SCAP's lifting of former police-state restrictions and restricted by SCAP's own pervasive censorship of film, radio, and print media. Positively, the occupation's media and cultural policy was expressed in "guidance" applied to drama, literature, and the visual arts (though the latter was of little concern), and efforts were made to root out "feudal" aspects of Japanese culture, ranging from the martial arts to samurai dramas and kabuki. The literature of the occupation era especially opens a vista of subjective experiences and imaginations of the hellish and futile experiences of war and defeat, the nervous collapse that followed, and the bursting forth of the formerly suppressed themes of revolution and love.[14] The outpouring of the erotic, grotesque, and self-consciously decadent added to the widespread feeling – even among those who knew better intellectually – of the loss of "wholesome" state-centered morality. Communist writers offered an alternative "proletarian" morality, and revolutionary allegiances and Communist Party membership were for a time a literary fad, into which J. Victor Koschmann's *Revolution and Subjectivity in Postwar Japan* provides insight. Caught in between were the "victims of a transitional period of morality," in the words of the "decadent" writer Dazai Osamu, who himself flirted with communism but is better known for his depiction of the decaying of the old social elite and for his sensational double love suicide in 1948.

Often suggested in literature, the moral and spiritual transformations of the era are sometimes touched on in historical work but rarely approached as a whole. In 1945, MacArthur saw defeated Japan – as did many Japanese – as "a spiritual vacuum," which he imagined must be filled by either Christianity or by communism.[15] The collapse of the old state-centered official morality was furthered by SCAP's guarantee of freedom of religion and disestablishment of state Shintō. The dismantling of the emperor-centered "*kokutai* cult," which several generations of Japanese had been taught to accept as the moral core of their national being, and the revelation of its hollowness suddenly diminished both state and patriarchal authority. The flurry of interest in Christianity, promoted by MacArthur, was less conspicuous than the interest in communism or the interest in Japanese "new religions," which suddenly proliferated after a period of harsh repression. A bottom-up social-cultural history of religions during the occupation era is still needed, as is a greater understanding of the occupation's total moral and spiritual context, which includes also the influence of Marxism.

"Feudalistic" patriarchal family relations were weakened also by the legal trans-formation of the family system, perhaps the most comprehensive and intimate in its social effects of any of the occupation reforms. The vertically oriented big family (*ie*) system, in which the household head had considerable legal power over family members, was replaced with the small family system centered on the conjugal tie, now established on the legal basis of female equality.[16] The rewritten family code also resulted in a temporary surge of divorces, another aspect of social relations that was "restabilized" during the latter years of the occupation. The deep linkages of the multi-generation *ie* system to the old family-state ideology made the reform of family law a profound political question as well. The connections between legal provisions and actual family relations are complex and non-obvious, and the effects of these changes are in need of deeper research.

The larger subject of women's occupation and the occupation as a phase in gender history is, despite its pivotal importance, only recently opening up as a field of active research. Susan Pharr's brief but significant 1987 study explained the adoption of highly progressive women's rights legislation as the outcome of a policy alliance between Japanese feminist activists and lower-ranking female officials within SCAP.[17] Dower focused attention on both the gender and specifically sexual aspects of the occupation, and Koikari's forthcoming study opens up the subject further by applying ideas adopted from studies of colonialism, gender, and cold war cultural studies.[18] Women's liberation was bound up with the idea that American women were the world's most liberated and that carrying American women's freedom to others was part of a historical mission, a complex of ideas and practices recently deployed to justify the invasion and occupation of Muslim countries. Granting equal rights to Japanese women can also be seen, and was seen by many Japanese men, as American men taking Japanese men down another notch, as an effort "to destabilize existing Japanese male dominance in order to establish their own domin-ance," in the words of Mire Koikari. This impression was strengthened by the way that SCAP ignored requests by Japanese women's groups to reform prostitution, which might have reduced American sexual access to Japanese women, and it

conformed to the racialized and sexualized terms in which many occupiers understood the entire undertaking.

American culture itself suddenly went from being banned to being encouraged
and emulated. American wealth, power, and self-confidence contrasted in the
starkest way with Japanese misery, and the widespread yearning (*akogare*) for America
that is so conspicuous in postwar Japanese popular culture developed in a rush
of American food, big band music, and Hollywood movies. The impression in
Japan of the brightness of the American culture of the era was furthered by SCAP's
banning of American works that depicted the darker sides of American life, such
as *The Grapes of Wrath*. Hunger combined with the availability of American food to
change dietary customs, one facet of what Dower called "horizontal westernization,"
an unprecedented mass encounter between non-elite Americans and non-elite Japanese quite different from a past history of international contacts mainly at the level
of well-educated elites. This encounter was also highly sexualized, as most of the
occupiers were men, and it was Japanese women who often experienced the
most personal interactions. Children who had learned to sing military songs in school
now learned Stephen Foster songs like "Old Black Joe," taught as democratic
American *minka* (people's songs). For Japanese musicians, jamming with American
GIs was another form of horizontal Westernization, and the cultural explosion of
the occupation years also encompassed music, especially jazz.[19] Many American
practices imported then have been naturalized and their exotic origin has
become invisible; many cultural "borrowings" were merely temporary; here and
there, in the bowling alleys or in the watery "Amerikan" coffee and egg salad
sandwiches served in old-fashioned coffee shops, are oddly preserved fragments of
mid-twentieth-century Middle American culture. Despite the fact that this was a
military occupation involving hundreds of thousands of American troops (and
many British Commonwealth personnel as well), historians' focus on policy has
meant that the experiences of ordinary GIs have gotten little study. More neglected
still has been the Japanese side of the encounter. Oral histories are especially needed,
and given the time-consuming nature of oral history research, there is a danger that it
will not get done before the generation who fully experienced the occupation passes
away.

While the cold war context of American policy has now been outlined in convincing detail, the story of the "cold war" *inside* Japan, unfolding amid expectations of
impending world revolution, remains to be grasped as a social, cultural, and political
whole. Dower's *Embracing Defeat* is one of few works to convey the feeling of
revolutionary excitement of the era. Factory seizures and production control by
workers' councils, a high point in the postwar revolutionary surge, have been detailed
by Joe Moore.[20] The radical student movement that absorbed the energies of much
of a generation is part of the experience of the educated elite of the high-speed
growth era that is rarely brought into historical consciousness. And most historical
understandings of the role of the minority but influential Communist Party remain
caught up in cold war categories. The most detailed English-language studies were
themselves part of the anti-communist project, while more sympathetic accounts
often show a reflexive "anti-anticommunism," glossing over the party's Leninist
character and the role of the Cominform, and failing to convey either the grandeur
or the pettiness and pathos of revolutionary politics.

The Japanese State under Occupation

The occupation was above all a political event, and the central focus of occupation historiography, properly, has been on the occupation's political reforms. The most important of these was the new constitution adopted in November 1946. Because these reforms have been so well studied, I pass over them here, and refer the reader again to the works of Dower and Takemae Eiji.[21] Recent studies have clarified the role of Japanese policy input and the role of the Japanese bureaucracy in implementing and partially reshaping the reforms, although the fact that many Japanese government archival materials remain closed continues to keep these processes obscure. These questions are closely connected to the survival and modification of the reforms into the post-occupation period.

Despite so much attention to the reforms initiated by SCAP, the English-language historiography is underdeveloped when it comes to the *Japanese* political history of the period, which is extraordinarily dense and complex. Except for Dower's 1979 study of Yoshida Shigeru, most of the work in English is by Japanese scholars, of which Masumi Junnosuke's translated volume *Postwar Politics in Japan* is the most fundamental.[22] The purge of politicians associated with the wartime regime after January 1946 radically reordered the political parties and brought the "early" appearance of a new generation of political leaders. The partisan politics of the period thus shows the same kind of flux and recrystallization seen in other social domains, although in this case the lasting shape of Japan's postwar party system emerged only three years after the lifting of the purge restrictions and the end of the occupation.

The flux in the political parties contrasted to the relative lack of disturbance in most branches of Japan's civil bureaucracy, purged of its top leaders but essentially continuous across the divide of war and occupation. Thus, under indirect occupation, the Japanese state persisted without administrative rupture. SCAP further enhanced the place of the civil bureaucracy by eliminating the rival claims to power by military and aristocratic circles, and Chalmers Johnson has forcefully argued that the occupation reforms served in the end to provide a democratic facade masking bureaucratic hegemony.[23] The Diet, despite being officially made the highest organ of the state in the 1946 constitution, remained under the occupation what it had been during the prewar period – peripheral. This makes it all the more important to understand the extraordinarily complex intra-bureaucratic politics of the period, during which the Japanese state was overlaid by the occupation superstate to form a double bureaucracy. SCAP itself encompassed left-leaning New Dealers and rightists such as MacArthur's intelligence chief Charles Willoughby, who already in September 1945 was reassuring the Japanese army's vice chief of staff that he too was a "militarist" and that they ought to work together.[24] Thus a set of transnational US–Japanese alliances emerged, as detailed especially by Takemae – whether reformist alliances between SCAP New Dealers and progressive Japanese bureaucrats, politicians, and civil groups; or alliances for course reversal and restoration between SCAP conservatives and Japanese conservatives. The task of understanding is eased by the fact that occupation imposed a brief and unprecedented transparency on the usually opaque Japanese bureaucracy. But foreign occupation also made dissimulation into a principle of organizational survival and forced much of the real politics to become more than ever covert and informal. SCAP's relations with Washington were also complex; MacArthur's jealous protection of the autonomy of "his" occupation ended after 1948–9 when Washington reasserted its authority (and as Wall Street regained influence in Washington).

When conservative leaders were purged in 1946, the Japanese conservative mainstream itself was forced underground. Underground conservative politics were paralleled by and profitably intertwined with the underground economy, suddenly bloated by the organized looting of military stores immediately after the surrender. The tangled web of underground connections that developed between purged members of the governing elite, organized crime, and unrepentant ultranationalists remained in place when the purgees resumed open political activity after the occupation. In a detailed study of the police under occupation, Christopher Aldous argued that, despite being disarmed and temporarily decentralized, the police continued to look to their "traditional masters," an alliance of politicians and bureaucrats who constituted a "shadow government," now connected to organized crime groups and the black market, which itself was "a support for the old regime." In this domain – which like the educational system, was a point at which the state impinged most directly on daily life – the authoritarian, centralized prewar system remained the real essence of the postwar system, Aldous concluded, and the occupation reforms were *tatemae*, a conventional facade.[25]

The picture of occupation politics is incomplete without a full account of the place of leftist–progressive forces, who often had a vital role in realizing occupation reforms and were even more important in maintaining and defending the reforms and ultimately in limiting the scope of the conservative reverse course. Japan's highly centralized education system, for example, like the national police system, was recentralized under the conservative Ministry of Education in the 1950s, but the leftist teachers' unions formed during the occupation continued to resist the reverse course and served as a core of the postwar progressive opposition.[26]

After World War I, postwar economic stabilization as an international project had failed, yielding the Great Depression. After World War II, economic stabilization succeeded, also internationally. In Japan's case, the process of economic stabilization was overlaid on and inseparable from the dynamic of reform and course reversal. During the first phase of the occupation, the chief economic policy initiatives – labor reform, land reform, economic deconcentration – were undertaken to further the political goals of democratization and demilitarization. Otherwise, even as American authorities engaged in active political and social "engineering," they left the economic engineering to the Japanese government, which directed massive subsidies to the vital coal, electrical power, steel, and fertilizer industries. These industrial subsidies were funded by inflationary means (in effect, by taxing Japanese consumers). At the same time, owing in part to MacArthur's determination to keep American companies out, SCAP engaged in no concerted effort to exploit Japan economically (beyond the sheer fact of making the Japanese people pay the costs of the occupation itself). The relatively hands-off American approach to macroeconomic policy changed in February 1949 when SCAP economic advisor Joseph Dodge took direct control over Japanese government budgeting and imposed a deflationary "overbalanced" budget. Dodge's price stabilization succeeded in closing the gap between official and free ("black") market prices; or, to put it another way, brought a return to re-legalized, re-regulated market activity. At the same time, to enable the recovery of Japanese foreign trade, the Japanese yen was fixed at 360 yen to the dollar, placing the yen on a de facto US dollar standard, another foundation of America's postwar international hegemony.[27] In the end, however, full economic stabilization came only with the Korean War, when massive US military procurements in Japan ended Dodge's stabilization depression and – after four and a half years of postwar economic disorder – initiated a robust economic recovery. Korean War spending in Japan was thus the functional equivalent of American Marshall Plan aid in Western Europe. The Korean War also meant Japan's conversion into a kind of giant US military base, bringing Japan into the hardening cold war system, formalized in September 1951 by the San Francisco Peace Treaty and US–Japan Security Treaty. Thus, the period of fluidity from August 1945 to 1947–8 ended with a phase of recrystallization that was equally decisive for establishing the shape of the postwar institutional order and in some ways remains less well understood.

The Ongoing Occupation

The formal occupation of the Japanese mainland ended on April 28, 1952, but the occupation persisted in certain respects through the 1950s, as post-independence Japan continued to be seen by both Japanese and Americans as an informal US protectorate. The US–Japan Security Treaty in its initial form from 1952 until 1960 was an "unequal treaty" that provided for the presence of hundreds of thousands of US troops in Japan and provided for possible US military intervention in Japanese domestic conflict; the pact could be terminated only with American agreement. Outright US military government in Okinawa lasted to 1972, and the ongoing heavy basing of US troops there means that a kind of occupation continues to the present.[28]

The occupation also indisputably opened a new historical era, the "present age" (*gendai*) in Japanese historiography, even if this sense of a new beginning serves also to obscure the substantial continuities of the prewar regime into the present. The remarkably stable institutional framework that was solidified in the early 1950s was the concrete social condition of the peace and prosperity of the "long postwar" era that followed, and this manifestly robust social settlement was established during the occupation and the years immediately after. For the generation who built the postwar "economic miracle," the occupation was a personal departure point, a generationally formative experience of hunger, difficulty, and hope. Politics too, from the advent after 1960 of Prime Ministers Ikeda Hayato and Satō Eisaku until the end of uninterrupted Liberal Democratic Party (LDP) hegemony in 1993, was dominated by the generation who entered politics during the occupation. At the same time, efforts to settle accounts with the occupation – meaning primarily efforts to revise Japan's American-authored constitution – have been a feature of conservative politics since the 1950s and have recently taken on a renewed insistence. Conversely, a central task of leftist–progressive politics has been to preserve intact the constitution and other liberal occupation reforms – a picture of "revisionist" conservatives and of defensive progressives upholding the constitutional status quo. In the United States, the occupation was also an origin point for the new academic field of Japanese studies and for postwar American understandings of Japan. The wider issues at stake in these understandings are revealed in the way that America's remaking of Japan inspired the occupation of Iraq in 2003. The consequences of that occupation will surely color future writing on Japan's own occupation.

It may also be that the occupation's historical place will diminish with time. Pivotal as the occupation was, American accounts sometimes exaggerate its effects, causing a mistaking of surfaces for realities in Japan's postwar politics and economics. The counterpart of such exaggeration is the minimizing of the occupation's effects in many Japanese accounts, which suggest that occupation reforms merely completed efforts that were already under way domestically. The logic of national historiography, national *amour propre*, and the renaturalization of the occupation into the stream of Japanese history all seem likely to further such tendencies toward minimization. Even if minimized and elided, however, the occupation continues to present the historical spectacle that the Meiji Restoration once did – of an incomplete task, whether of incomplete democracy, or of the incomplete reconstruction of a self-respecting Japan that can reclaim its place among the powers.

NOTES

1 Quoted in Barshay, *The Social Sciences in Modern Japan*, p. 61.
2 The volume of English-language writing and the amount of it written during or soon after the occupation itself can be gauged by the 867-page mass of Ward and Shulman's indispensable 1974 annotated bibliography (*The Allied Occupation of Japan, 1945–1952*), which lists 3,167 items (though part of the bulk consists of poorly informed magazine articles whose main value is to illustrate American attitudes at the time). Shulman added a 47-page supplement summarizing more recent scholarly work in 1980 (*Bibliography on the Allied Occupation of Japan*), supplemented further in his 1989 annotated bibliography of Japan (*Japan*, pp. 109–16). A 37-page bibliography that lists more recent work is Dower, with George, *Japanese History and Culture* (pp. 375–414), which also includes a listing of published archival materials. Critical reviews of the literature at various points in its development have been written by John Dower, "Occupied Japan and the Cold War in Asia"; Ray Moore, "The Occupation of Japan as History"; and Carol Gluck, "Entangling Illusions." Key primary sources are located in American archives, above all the massive Records of the U.S. Occupation of Japan, held in the National Archives, College Park, Md. (Microfiche copies are also held in the Kensei Shiryōshitsu of the National Diet Library, Tokyo.)
3 The Allied powers whom SCAP formally represented were excluded from the actual business of government and, unlike the divided occupation of Germany, the occupation of Japan was a nearly unilateral American show. British and British Commonwealth troops also participated, in a mainly unsuccessful effort to retain some influence in the undertaking (see Buckley, *Occupation Diplomacy*).
4 Dower, *Empire and Aftermath*; Schonberger, *Aftermath of War*; Schaller, *The American Occupation of Japan*.
5 The most important of these official histories are in the 55-volume series, *History of the Nonmilitary Activities of the Occupation of Japan*.
6 An exchange on the subject can be found in Williams, "American Democratization Policy for Occupied Japan" and the accompanying replies by John Dower and Howard Schonberger.
7 See Mercado, *The Shadow Warriors*, pp. 174–80, 203–4.

8 The land reform is examined in Dore, *Land Reform in Japan*, a work that seems unlikely to be superseded.

9 Tsuru, *Japan's Capitalism*, pp. 7–65.

10 Tsutsui, *Banking Policy in Japan*.

11 Dower, *Embracing Defeat*; Griffiths, "Need, Greed, and Protest."

12 See Rubin, "From Wholesomeness to Decadence."

13 Dower, *Embracing Defeat*; Koshiro, *Trans-Pacific Racisms*; Molasky, *The American Occupation of Japan and Okinawa*; Koikari, *Pedagogy of Democracy*.

14 Rubin, "From Wholesomeness to Decadence"; Molasky, *The American Occupation of Japan and Okinawa*; and Orbaugh, *The Japanese Fiction of the Allied Occupation*, provide introductions. On the arts in general, see Burkman, ed., *The Occupation of Japan*, which includes an extended discussion of SCAP censorship, and discussions of radio by Marlene Mayo and of satire and political cartoons by Sodei Rinjiro and John Dower. These and related themes are developed further in Sandler, *The Confusion Era*, and in Mayo and Rimer, eds., *War, Occupation, and Creativity*. Best known internationally are the films of the era, a subject explored in the pioneering work of Hirano, *Mr. Smith Goes to Tokyo*, who explicates the movies themselves, occupation censorship and guidance, and the labor struggles in the film industry.

15 Woodard, *The Allied Occupation of Japan*, pp. 243–4. Woodard's 1972 study remains the standard work on Japan's religious reformation.

16 Steiner, "The Occupation and the Reform of the Japanese Civil Code."

17 Pharr, "The Politics of Women's Rights."

18 Dower, *Embracing Defeat*; Koikari, *Pedagogy of Democracy*.

19 Atkins, *Blue Nippon*, pp. 170–84.

20 Moore, *Japanese Workers*.

21 Dower, *Embracing Defeat*; Takemae, *Inside GHQ*.

22 Masumi, *Postwar Politics in Japan*. The essays in Ward and Sakamoto, eds., *Democratizing Japan*, provide briefer introductions.

23 Johnson, *MITI and the Japanese Miracle*.

24 Atkins, *Blue Nippon*, pp. 180–214 (quotation on p. 196).

25 Aldous, *The Police in Occupation Japan*, pp. 216–17. Academic historians have mostly shied away from the subject of organized crime, for which see Whiting, *Tokyo Underworld*, pp. 7–38, and Kaplan and Dubro, *Yakuza*, pp. 31–55.

26 Duke, *Japan's Militant Teachers*.

27 Teranishi and Kosai, eds., *The Japanese Experience of Economic Reforms*, brings together a set of studies of economic reform, stabilization, and deregulation, presented as lessons that Japan's occupation-era experience may provide for the contemporary reform of postsocialist economies. My own present research explores the postwar inflation and deflationary stabilization. Forthcoming work by Scott O'Bryan examines the simultaneous formation of a new economically oriented growthism.

28 See Schaller, *Altered States*; Molasky, *The American Occupation of Japan and Okinawa*.

BIBLIOGRAPHY

Aldous, Christopher. *The Police in Occupation Japan: Control, Corruption and Resistance to Reform*. London: Routledge, 1997.

Atkins, E. Taylor. *Blue Nippon: Authenticating Jazz in Japan*. Durham, NC: Duke University Press, 2001.

Barshay, Andrew. *The Social Sciences in Modern Japan: The Marxian and Modernist Traditions*. Berkeley: University of California Press, 2004.

Buckley, Roger. *Occupation Diplomacy: Britain, the United States, and Japan, 1945–1952.* Cambridge: Cambridge University Press, 1982.

Burkman, Thomas, ed. *The Occupation of Japan: Arts and Culture.* Norfolk, Va.: General Douglas MacArthur Foundation, 1988.

Cohen, Theodore. *Remaking Japan: The American Occupation as New Deal.* New York: Free Press, 1987.

Dore, Ronald. *Land Reform in Japan.* Oxford: Oxford University Press, 1959.

Dower, John. *Empire and Aftermath: Yoshida Shigeru and the Japanese Experience, 1878–1954.* Cambridge, Mass.: Harvard University Press, 1979.

Dower, John. "Occupied Japan and the Cold War in Asia." In John Dower, *Japan in War and Peace: Selected Essays.* New York: New Press, 1993.

Dower, John. *Embracing Defeat: Japan in the Wake of World War II.* New York: Norton, 1999.

Dower, John, with George, Timothy. *Japanese History and Culture from Ancient to Modern Times: Seven Basic Bibliographies,* 2nd edn. Princeton: Markus Wiener, 1995.

Duke, Benjamin. *Japan's Militant Teachers: A History of the Left-Wing Teachers' Movement.* Honolulu: University of Hawai'i Press, 1973.

Gluck, Carol. "Entangling Illusions – Japanese and American Views of the Occupation." In Warren Cohen, ed., *New Frontiers in American–East Asian Relations: Essays Presented to Dorothy Borg.* New York: Columbia University Press, 1983.

Griffiths, Owen. "Need, Greed, and Protest in Japan's Black Market, 1938–1949." *Journal of Social History* 35:4 (Summer 2002): 825–58.

Hirano, Kyoko. *Mr. Smith Goes to Tokyo: Japanese Cinema under the American Occupation, 1945–1952.* Washington DC: Smithsonian Institution Press, 1992.

Johnson, Chalmers. *MITI and the Japanese Miracle: The Growth of Industrial Policy, 1925–1975.* Stanford, Calif.: Stanford University Press, 1982.

Kaplan, David E., and Dubro, Alec. *Yakuza: Japan's Criminal Underworld.* Berkeley: University of California Press, 2003.

Koikari, Mire. *Pedagogy of Democracy: Feminism and the Cold War in the U.S. Occupation of Japan.* Durham, NC: Duke University Press, forthcoming.

Koschmann, J. Victor. *Revolution and Subjectivity in Postwar Japan.* Chicago: University of Chicago Press, 1996.

Koshiro, Yukiko. *Trans-Pacific Racisms and the U.S. Occupation of Japan.* New York: Columbia University Press, 1999.

Masumi Junnosuke. *Postwar Politics in Japan, 1945–1955,* trans. Lonny Carlile. Berkeley: Center for Japanese Studies, University of California, 1985.

Mayo, Marlene, and Rimer, J. Thomas, eds. *War, Occupation, and Creativity: Japan and East Asia, 1926–1960.* Honolulu: University of Hawai'i Press, 2001.

Mercado, Stephen. *The Shadow Warriors of Nakano: A History of the Imperial Japanese Army's Elite Intelligence School.* Washington DC: Brassey's, 2002.

Molasky, Michael. *The American Occupation of Japan and Okinawa: Literature and Memory.* London: Routledge, 1999.

Moore, Joe. *Japanese Workers and the Struggle for Power, 1945–1947.* Madison: University of Wisconsin Press, 1983.

Moore, Ray. "The Occupation of Japan as History: Some Recent Research." *Monumenta Nipponica* 36:3 (Autumn 1981): 317–28.

Orbaugh, Sharalyn. *The Japanese Fiction of the Allied Occupation, 1945–1952.* Stanford, Calif.: Stanford University Press, forthcoming.

Pempel, T. J. "The Tar Baby Target: 'Reform' of the Japanese Bureaucracy." In Robert E. Ward and Sakamoto Yoshikazu, eds., *Democratizing Japan: The Allied Occupation.* Honolulu: University of Hawai'i Press, 1987.

Pharr, Susan J. "The Politics of Women's Rights." In Robert E. Ward and Sakamoto Yoshi-kazu, eds., *Democratizing Japan: The Allied Occupation*. Honolulu: University of Hawai'i Press, 1987.

Rubin, Jay. "From Wholesomeness to Decadence: The Censorship of Literature under the Allied Occupation." *Journal of Japanese Studies* 11:1 (Winter 1985): 71–103.

Sandler, Mark Howard, ed. *The Confusion Era: Art and Culture of Japan during the Allied Occupation, 1945–1952*. Seattle: University of Washington Press, 1997.

Schaller, Michael. *The American Occupation of Japan: The Origins of the Cold War in Asia*. New York: Oxford University Press, 1985.

Schaller, Michael. *Altered States: The U.S. and Japan since the Occupation*. New York: Oxford University Press. 1997.

Schonberger, Howard. *Aftermath of War: Americans and the Remaking of Japan, 1945–1952*. Kent, Ohio: Kent State University Press, 1989.

Shulman, Frank J. *Bibliography on the Allied Occupation of Japan: A Bibliography of Western-Language Publications from the Years 1970–1980*, preliminary edn. College Park: University of Maryland, McKeldin Library, 1980.

Shulman, Frank J. *Japan*. World Bibliography Series. Oxford: Clio Press, 1989.

Steiner, Kurt. "The Occupation and the Reform of the Japanese Civil Code." In Robert E. Ward and Sakamoto Yoshikazu, eds., *Democratizing Japan: The Allied Occupation*. Honolulu: University of Hawai'i Press, 1987.

Supreme Commander for the Allied Powers, General Headquarters. *History of the Nonmilitary Activities of the Occupation of Japan*, 55 vols. Tokyo: Supreme Commander for the Allied Powers, 1952.

Takemae Eiji. *Inside GHQ: The Allied Occupation of Japan and Its Legacy*, trans. and adapted by Robert Ricketts and Sebastian Swann. New York: Continuum, 2002.

Teranishi Juro and Yutaka Kosai, eds. *The Japanese Experience of Economic Reforms*. New York: St. Martin's Press, 1993.

Tsuru Shigeto. *Japan's Capitalism: Creative Defeat and Beyond*. Cambridge: Cambridge University Press, 1993.

Tsutsui, William. *Banking Policy in Japan: American Efforts at Reform during the Occupation*. London: Routledge, 1988.

Ward, Robert E., and Sakamoto Yoshikazu, eds. *Democratizing Japan: The Allied Occupation*. Honolulu: University of Hawai'i Press, 1987.

Ward, Robert E., and Shulman, Frank J., eds. *The Allied Occupation of Japan, 1945–1952: An Annotated Bibliography of Western-Language Materials*. Chicago: American Library Association, 1974.

Whiting, Robert. *Tokyo Underworld: The Fast Times and Hard Life of an American Gangster in Japan*. New York: Vintage Books, 1999.

Williams, Justin. "American Democratization Policy for Occupied Japan: Correcting the Revisionist Version." *Pacific Historical Review* 57:2 (1988): 179–202. Replies by John Dower and Howard Schonberger on pp. 202–18.

Woodard, William. *The Allied Occupation of Japan 1945–1952 and Japanese Religions*. Leiden: Brill, 1972.

FURTHER READING

There are now two books that provide exceptionally full, comprehensive accounts of the occupation. John Dower's *Embracing Defeat: Japan in the Wake of World War II* (New York: Norton, 1999) comes close to the ideal of total history, combining history from the top down and from the bottom up and portraying the broad sweep of events in a committed authorial voice while providing space for numerous individual voices from the most varied sources. A second monumental recent work, Takemae Eiji's encyclopedic *Inside GHQ: The Allied Occupation of Japan and Its Legacy* (New York: Continuum, 2002) is more in the mold of "traditional" policy-oriented occupation history and is likewise a work of admirable scope and balance. These two works also show a kind of Japanese–American convergence, offering broadly similar overall judgments; positive evaluations are combined with criticism and the contradictions of imposed democratization are treated in rich detail.

CHAPTER SIXTEEN

Postwar Politics

Ray Christensen

The study of politics in Japan has been and continues to be eclectic. Some topics have dominated the field, such as the nature or viability of Japanese democracy or the causes and structure of Japan's economic performance. Yet, around these topics have swirled a variety of interesting analyses, ranging from bid rigging practices in the construction industry to support groups for death row inmates. When several scholars take up a specific theme such as the relative power of Japan's economic bureaucracy in creating Japan's economic miracle, they create a sustained dialogue which provides the infrastructure for the study of Japanese politics. Their work, however, important as it is, must be supplemented by other research that, although it can be tied into the larger narrative, deserves its own independent spotlight and analysis.

This eclecticism of topic areas also extends to methodologies or dominant paradigms of how to conduct research in the discipline of political science. Though the dominance of a specific methodology may have waxed or waned across the past sixty years of research on Japanese politics, the practitioners of this research have never lost sight of the ultimate goal of providing the best and most accurate explanations of Japanese politics. The methodological advances of past decades have vastly improved the quality of the data and analyses of Japanese politics available. These advances, however, have come at a cost: a tendency to ignore approaches that lie outside the dominant methodological paradigm. Nevertheless, one of political science's strengths has been its ability to remain eclectic in spite of this dominance. The study of Japanese politics shows this healthy eclecticism in both topic area and methodology despite the growing dominance of the rational choice methodological paradigm across the discipline.

Choice of Topics: The Influence of World Events

Political science is influenced more directly by world events than other disciplines. The research agenda of political scientists is driven, at least in part, by the political issues that are gaining attention in the media and in policy circles. This pattern has also been true for the study of Japanese politics. In the first postwar decades, the immediate concern of both the American government and political scientists studying Japan was the efficacy of the occupation and the transplanted democracy in Japan. These studies contrasted the rise of militarism in the prewar period with the efforts in the first postwar decade to implement functioning democracy in Japan. For example, Robert Scalapino and Masumi Junnosuke's 1962 overview of Japanese politics takes as its central theme the viability of Japanese democracy, citing the US–Japan Security Treaty (Anpo) riots of 1960 as harbingers of future problems.[1]

Beginning in the mid-1960s and carrying over for two decades, additional trends emerged, never, however, supplanting the continuing task of analyzing Japanese democracy. The first of these new trends was an analysis of the Liberal Democratic Party (LDP), spurred by the LDP's tenacious grasp on power and corresponding decline in the leftist electoral threat that peaked in the mid 1950s. Nathaniel Thayer's detailed analysis of the party laid the groundwork for much of the subsequent literature. As opposed to having an identifiable theme, Thayer's work is noteworthy for the light that it shed on relatively unstudied aspects of conservative rule in Japan, including factions, party rules, relations with business, and campaign strategies.[2] The second path-breaking work was even more focused, Gerald Curtis's 1971 analysis of LDP campaign practices which set the research agenda for an entire generation of work on Japanese elections. Curtis highlighted the importance of personal support organizations (*kōenkai*) and documented with detailed examples the extreme intra-party competition fostered by the electoral system within the LDP.[3] Thus, these works shifted the scholarly agenda towards a new goal of explaining LDP organizational and campaign practices that helped the party continue to win elections.

The theme of analyzing the LDP and explaining its dominance has persisted in the three decades that have followed these first works. An important refinement to Thayer's initial observations was Satō Seizaburō and Matsuzaki Tetsuhisa's finding that advancement patterns within the party had become routinized in the 1960s, pointing to an important institutionalization of the personal commitments that were part and parcel of LDP factional politics.[4] Curtis extended his analysis of LDP rule, following the lead of Satō and Matsuzaki in explaining dynamic elements of continuing conservative rule. He expanded his focus to include changes in the other parties and policy questions facing Japan, and he specifically answered the question of why the LDP had been able to stay in power for so long. Curtis found the answer in LDP adaptability as well as the inflexibility of the main opposition party and the over-representation of rural LDP supporters.[5] A final seminal work that explains the LDP and LDP dominance is Kohno Masaru's 1997 critique of both sociocultural and historical explanations of several important events in LDP history: the founding of the party in 1955 by the merger of the Liberal and Democratic Parties and changes in LDP factions. Kohno directly challenges Curtis's explanations as being sociocultural while positing an incentives-based explanation of those same events.[6]

A second theme in the analysis of Japanese democracy emerged in the late 1960s when the opposition began to win control of many of Japan's local governments in urban areas. Scholars flocked to this and related topics about protest movements and citizen participation. The popularity of this line of research is shown by the fact that the two most prominent publications to come out of this line of inquiry are both edited volumes that brought together contributions from a sizeable cross-section of those studying modern Japanese politics and society. Kurt Steiner, Ellis Krauss, and

Scott Flanagan oversaw the first of these surveys, a comprehensive look into the variations of opposition party rule and political activity in the 1970s. Case studies included environmental activism in a specific city and a profile of socialist/communist rule in a specific prefecture. Thematic chapters analyzed such topics as the suburban voter and citizen's movements.[7] Their work was quickly followed by Ellis Krauss, Thomas Rohlen, and Patricia Steinhoff's thematic work on conflict, conflict resolution, and cooperation in Japan's specific cultural milieu. Chapters examined topics like the patterns of conflict and its resolution in gender relations in a municipal office and the transformation of Japanese labor unions from the strike-happy militant organizations that they were in the 1950s to the most docile and cooperative unions in any advanced industrial country. A series of chapters analyzed thematically the role of conflict in LDP policy-making, and conflict and its resolution in LDP relations with the opposition.[8]

Lying at the intersection of LDP rule and the nature and viability of Japanese democracy, analysis of protest, opposition, and conflict had a double appeal for scholars. Tension also existed, however, between these two analytical trends. The explanations of LDP success showed in detail the operation of democracy in Japan, but it was a conservative democracy, considerably different from the democracy envisioned by Japan's occupation reformers and different from the democracy that seemed likely given the vigor of the opposition in the first postwar decade. This new literature on protest movements and opposition parties contrasted with the LDP's version of conservative democracy. The opposition party literature drew support from Western expectations of how democracy should be developing in Japan and lamented the marginalization of these same democratic trends, often citing cultural reasons for that marginalization.

In addition to the rise of the opposition parties, the 1960s also saw an even more significant economic trend that would have a profound impact on the study of Japanese politics. During the 1960s the LDP shifted its policy emphasis from divisive national security issues to rapid economic growth. Interestingly, scholars did not pay attention to this change until the early 1970s when Japan's economic miracle burst onto the public stage. Here again the scholarly response seemed to be following, rather than leading, the public's perceptions of Japan, but the initial delay in attention to Japan's economic miracle was more than compensated for by the subsequent avalanche of publications devoted to this topic. One of the first scholarly studies of Japan's meteoric economic rise was by J. A. A. Stockwin. He focused on the same political issues that Curtis or Thayer addressed in their works but used the question of Japan's economic success as a theme around which to organize the analysis of important components of LDP rule. Stockwin specifically identified investment patterns, savings rates, high labor productivity, an international environment favorable to free trade, and government support as important explanatory factors.[9] This analytical line was picked up in Ezra Vogel's enormously popular 1979 study of Japanese success, *Japan as Number One*. Like Stockwin, Vogel posits a list of contributing factors, but his list is much longer and includes many sociocultural factors not given prominence in Stockwin's study. Vogel also expands his analysis of Japan's success to include not just economic performance but good schools, safe cities, harmonious labor relations, and a relatively egalitarian distribution of wealth.

Subsequent to these more comprehensive works, the study of Japan's economic miracle quickly subdivided into discussions of the impact of specific factors on Japan's stellar economic performance. In this research line is perhaps the most influential of all the books published on Japanese politics, Chalmers Johnson's 1982 analysis of the Japanese bureaucracy and the crucial role that it played in orchestrating the Japanese economic miracle. Johnson's research is noteworthy not just for his careful analysis of MITI (the Ministry of International Trade and Industry) and the role it played in Japan's economic development, but also for the implications of his arguments. Johnson forcefully asserted that Japan was a different type of capitalist state. In fact, the deviations of Japan from the textbook model of a capitalist economy were so significant that Johnson found it necessary to coin the term "developmental state" to describe the role of the Japanese government in the economy.[10] Johnson's model also had implications for the study of politicians as he asserted a strong role for bureaucrats, essentially relegating politicians to the back part of the stage. He castigated those who argued that Japan would become more like Western industrialized countries with the passage of time, and attacked with ferocity the discipline of economics and followers of the economics paradigm in the discipline of political science (rational choice scholars) for their inability to recognize that Japan stood outside of their theoretical models.

Johnson's work, as all important work does, set the stage for the next two decades of debate about Japanese political economy. A first response was Richard Samuels's detailed analysis of the Japanese energy industry and his finding that the government played a smaller role in that sector than governments in comparable advanced industrial countries.[11] Muramatsu Michio and Ellis Krauss continued the response with their claim that political factors and conscious decisions by political leaders helped create a consensus about the priority of economic growth, and this process had been ignored in the more bureaucracy-oriented analyses of Japan's economic miracle. They also found evidence of interest groups having a significant impact in economic policies, even though their input into the process was constrained in ways that caused Muramatsu and Krauss to call this Japanese variant of pluralism "patterned."[12]

Muramatsu and Krauss's line of inquiry was subsequently taken to its extreme in J. Mark Ramseyer and Frances Rosenbluth's direct attack on the fundamental point of Johnson's argument, that the bureaucrats are the dominant political actors in Japan, at least in the realm of political economy. Instead, Ramseyer and Rosenbluth argued from a theoretical perspective that the bureaucrats are simply performing the will of the politicians. The politicians have formal power and authority, and any congruence between bureaucratic actions and the preferences of politicians is the result of the operation (or the fear of the operation) of those levers of power.[13]

While this debate over who actually has power in Japan and what factors are responsible for Japan's economic miracle has raged, concerns about Japanese society and the robustness of Japanese democracy took a back seat. This lack of interest was exacerbated by the decline of the opposition in the late 1970s and 1980s. The LDP and its coalition partners regained control of most of the urban governorships and mayoralties. In addition, the number and intensity of protests movements seemed to wane. As a complement to the rosy depictions of Japan's economic situation, the next wave of work on Japanese democracy and society was more subdued in its criticisms of

Japanese democracy. These authors portrayed Japanese society as a different type of democracy, one with steady conservative rule and special methods of stifling or co-opting dissent. Similar to Johnson's argument that Japan had its own version of capitalism, some of these critics talked about distinctive characteristics of Japanese democracy and society, a society with less dissent and greater stability than comparable advanced industrial democracies.

There are many examples of this analytical trend, but two of the most prominent were Susan Pharr's and Robin LeBlanc's studies of women in politics. Pharr focused on elites and recruitment, LeBlanc on grass roots political participation; both presented Japan not as a unique case, but as a case similar to any other country in which general theories of political participation and feminist interpretation operate. Nevertheless, one cannot escape the conclusion that rules and beliefs that inhibit women's political participation in Japan are not the same rules that operate in other comparable countries.[14] Two journalists contributed to this trend with their analyses of Japanese politics that highlighted the seeming idiosyncrasies of Japanese politics. Karel van Wolferen's analysis of Japanese politics has much in common with Johnson's critique, a claim that Japan is not a "normal" capitalist economy, but van Wolferen added the argument that there is no responsible, central political authority in Japan. A consensus was established during the postwar period for strong economic growth, and there is no leader or consensus among several political leaders that can change that consensus.[15] Jacob Schlesinger argued the opposite with his highly readable account of the bosses that have manipulated Japanese politics from behind the scenes through the decades of the 1970s, 1980s, and 1990s. Although Schlesinger seems to argue that Japan is a democracy run by political machines and corrupt practices much like any other, it is hard to avoid the conclusion that the limitations of Japanese democracy are comparable to limitations existing in other Western democracies only if the comparison point is the most corrupt practices of Western democracies during the worst periods of democratic development.[16]

Once again, in 1989, a real world event changed profoundly the study of Japanese politics. In that year the LDP lost its first national election to the Socialist Party. This event was then followed by a unification of labor union federations, formation of new political parties, and finally the defection of many members of the LDP to new political parties in 1993. This radical transformation of the Japanese political landscape also altered the study of Japanese politics. Suddenly, studies of the opposition, election reform, and bureaucratic reform became essential to our understanding of Japan. Analyses of Japan's economic failure, as opposed to its economic miracle, cropped up as Japan began its decade-long descent into recession and deflation.

A first prominent change in the literature on Japanese politics is the healthy revival of the study of Japanese electoral politics. Spearheading this charge are the several journal articles, many from a rational choice perspective, that have analyzed the incentives and structures of the Japanese electoral system used prior to the watershed events of the early 1990s. One early prominent work was Steven Reed's application of Duverger's Law to the Japanese electoral system and his finding that the number of candidates running in specific districts corresponded with predicted theoretical outcomes. In Japan's three-seat districts, typically four serious candidates would run. Reed found this outcome developing from a process of learning from mistakes by political elites, a position that put his work in direct contradiction with that of rational choice scholars working on the same electoral issues.[17] However, both groups of scholars shared the common enterprise of bringing general theoretical insights to bear on the Japanese case and a renewed focus of attention on Japanese elections and the incentives that color electoral activity. Rational choice scholars made their presence felt in a group of articles that formalized our understanding of electoral incentives and their influence on topics such as the decisions of Diet representatives to choose to defect or not defect from the ruling LDP, the role and electoral success of LDP factions, and the strategic acumen of the LDP in overcoming coordination dilemmas inherent in the Japanese electoral system.[18]

The studies of the economy also quickly shifted perspective from explanations of Japan's economic prowess to explanations of Japan's economic failures or difficulties. Of course, a critical analytical question was how the same characteristics that led Japan to an economic miracle in the 1960s and 1970s could subsequently lead Japan to recession and deflation in the 1990s. One answer was provided by Edward Lincoln in his analysis of the slow pace of economic reform in Japan. He explained how the demands of an increasingly globalized economy and Japan's position at the forefront of that economy make many of the tools that helped Japan leapfrog to the front of the world economic growth engine obsolete. Thus, Lincoln adroitly addressed the question of how the factors that led to Japan's rapid economic growth could in turn become the same factors that contributed to Japan's economic stagnation.[19]

T. J. Pempel addressed the same question but added a comparative perspective and noted the important interplay between political reform and economic changes. Specifically, Pempel found that the economic environment of Japan in the 1990s was sufficiently different from the environment of the 1960s or 1970s as to constitute change in both the economic and the political regime. The bureaucracy that had been the hero of Johnson's work had become tainted with scandals and bad decisions. It had lost the authority and the prestige it once had. The Japanese economy had shifted from an export-driven, mercantilist perspective to the model of Japan as an international investor. Corresponding changes in the political realm also supported these economic changes. The LDP support coalition had shifted to reflect the new prominence of the international investor class.[20]

A final trend to note in the development of Japanese politics in the postwar period is the increase in the volume of scholarship about Japan since the first decades of the postwar period. This increase has allowed a much needed diversification of scholarly literature. Although the major theme of scholarship on Japan in the 1990s has been reform, specialization trends that began in the 1980s have continued unabated, allowing for detailed studies into diverse topics such as minorities, education policy, land use policy, non-government organizations, civil society, and Japan's overseas development assistance. In contrast, in the first twenty or thirty years of postwar scholarship the typical book on Japanese politics was an overview of the entire political system. In the past two decades, such overview books have been completely eclipsed by the now common study of a specialized aspect of Japanese politics.

An example of this earlier pattern is Robert Ward's book, *Japan's Political System*. In many ways his work reflects the topics that would be covered in a university course on Japanese politics. He begins with the history, then discusses society, culture, leaders, after which he turns his focus to specific institutions such as elections, political parties, interest groups, and state structures.[21] With the passage of time, however, the attention paid to Japan has increased so significantly that a chapter-length discussion on Japanese culture or Japanese elections is now no longer suffi-cient. Even Gerald Curtis, who remains one of the few authors attempting such comprehensive works, focused his most recent survey of Japanese politics around the specific theme of reform in Japan in the 1990s.[22]

In the 1970s, specialized topics began to blossom, and this bounty resulted in so many fruitful branches as to make a comprehensive survey of them nearly impos-sible. Nevertheless, one of the most notable of these specialized studies was Thomas Rohlen's classic examination of the Japanese education system through the extremely effective use of case studies of specific types of high schools. Though Rohlen's work is not a study of politics per se, it quickly became noted for its explanation of Japanese education, especially high school education at a time when the Japanese education system was being given partial credit for Japan's strong economic performance and other similar, positive societal trends.[23] Another example of specialized analysis is Susan Pharr's study of conflict in Japan which focused on the role of status in the creation and resolution of conflict. The cases she chose for her study were eclectic, ranging from an analysis of dissenters from the LDP to *burakumin* protests in a specific high school. She employed general theories of conflict and the role that status differentials play in conflict and its resolution, but added specific information as to how this conflict plays out in the Japanese cultural context.[24] A final example of the many facets of specialization is Schwartz and Pharr's 2003 edited volume which addresses the topic of civil society in Japan. One of the themes of their book is the extent to which the state had nurtured or hindered the development of autonomous organizations that are so important for the creation and maintenance of civil society in any country. The essays in this collection also suggest that in many ways the development of civil society and the groups that constitute civil society parallels similar development in other comparable countries.[25]

Schwartz and Pharr's volume (as well as many others previously mentioned) is illustrative of the final point of this overview of the study of politics in Japan. Their study derived from general trends in the discipline of political science. Their work was preceded by prominent analyses of civil society in Europe and the United States which had attracted the attention of political scientists across the discipline. Schwartz and Pharr applied these theoretical insights to the Japanese case, but, oddly enough, the flow of ideas in the opposite direction has rarely occurred. In fact, with few excep-tions, the theoretical contributions of political scientists studying Japan have largely been ignored by the rest of political science. Indeed, the topics addressed by political scientists studying Japan have typically been different from those gaining broad attention across the discipline of political science. This gap in topics occurs because issues that are relevant in Japan may not be relevant to the world at large; similarly issues of international significance may not be relevant to Japan. Just as a presidential election may be fought over the performance of the economy while a senator's race in a specific state in that same election year might be fought over government support of local farmers, so too the issues that are most relevant in the subfield of political science called comparative politics (the study of the politics of other countries) differ from issues that those who study Japanese politics consider to be of the greatest relevance.

The one consistent exception to this trend is the concern of both comparative politics and Japanese politics with democracy and its viability. Democracy was a major issue for both comparativists and Japan specialists from World War II until the mid-1960s. Though studies of democracy and civil society remain relevant in Japanese studies even now, comparative politics has returned to this topic in the past fifteen years with a passion that far eclipses the limited attention this field now receives in the Japanese context. Comparative politics and Japanese politics have also intersected in their shared interest in explaining economic performance. Despite this shared interest, however, the focus of each set of studies has been quite different. In the 1970s, comparativists studying economic performance focused on corporatist structures while the scholars of Japan focused on Japan's bureaucratic structures and company practices. Similarly, the recent turn by Japan specialists to analyze the economic and bureaucratic reforms of the 1990s has also lagged behind by more than a decade the corresponding trend in comparative politics that addressed the earlier reforms of Western Europe and North America.

In other topic areas, the disconnect between Japanese politics and comparative politics runs much deeper. David Laitin mentions the importance of civil wars as one of the prominent topics in comparative politics, but this topic would find little fruit to be picked on the Japanese analytical tree. Similarly, Ronald Rogowski identifies heterogenous states and interest groups as some of the prime topics of comparative politics in the 1980s, and again the Japanese case proved only tangentially relevant for such analysis.[26] Yet even when the attention of both Japan scholars and comparative politics scholars has coincided, there has been a noticeable lack of impact of the Japanese example on the broader, disciplinary debate. This disconnect occurs, in part, because of Japan's status as an advanced industrial democracy located in Asia. For many decades Japan did not fit the stereotypical politics of its Asian and communist neighbors, and it was geographically, linguistically, and historically isolated from its politically similar cousin nations in Western Europe and North America. Some Japanese-speaking scholars have even accentuated these differences, promoting their idea of Japanese uniqueness or *Nihonjinron*, but this viewpoint is largely rejected in most English-language studies of Japan.

Although it is easy to reject arguments of Japanese uniqueness, Japan's special political circumstances are ignored at a researcher's peril. Japan is, after all, the first non-Western state to achieve levels of political and economic development equivalent to those of Western Europe and North America. Japan is also the only democracy with completely free elections to have had one dominant political party over a fifty-year period. Japan has also been an outlier in the low numbers of women involved in politics, and its media is arguably much more docile than the media of any other advanced industrial state. On a variety of indices, whether it is per capita tax burdens or the nature of Japanese capitalism, Japan has arguably been at the far end of the continuum of advanced industrial democracies. Thus, Japan's history and characteristics exacerbate the disconnection between scholarship about Japan and general political science scholarship. If Japan is just an outlier, the work of Japan specialists can be ignored as a bit of oriental obscurity, irrelevant to our understanding of the rest of the world. Although scholars of Japanese politics have fought this trend vigorously, either by specifically denouncing it[27] or going to great pains to include Japan as a case with other Western European nations,[28] the specific characteristics of the Japanese case make bridging the gap between comparative politics and Japanese politics especially difficult.

Choice of Topics: Methodological Biases

A scholar's selection of appropriate topics is affected not only by real world events and their relevance to Japan, but also unconsciously by the dominant methodology for scholarly investigation and the data that fits that dominant methodology. For example, the early postwar period (along with the prewar period) was dominated by what is pejoratively called "constitutionalism" as the methodology of comparative politics at the time. These early studies focused on the formal structures of the state, describing and analyzing in useful detail the formal organizations of state power, including the constitution. This study seemed appropriate for two obvious reasons: First, state structures do matter in understanding politics and especially in assessing the viability of new democracies. Second, the data to study these state structures was readily available. It is always easier to study the formal structures of a state, its constitutions, its legislatures, and its bureaucracies because this information is always made public. It is an obvious starting place in studying the politics of a nation to begin with the structures of the state.

With the 1960s, however, came a rejection of "sterile constitutionalism" and the beginning of the behavioral revolution. The new methodological wave ushered in the use of statistics, especially economic and public opinion data. W. C. Mitchell describes this revolution as "a revolt against what some political scientists viewed as a very sterile, legalistic political science that ignored individuals behaving in political ways."[29] By the mid-1970s, some corrections of the excesses of the behavioralists began to spring up. The importance of the state and its institutions re-emerged in both the comparative politics and the Japanese politics literatures. In addition, rational choice began to make significant headway in establishing itself as the new, dominant methodology in political science. Rational choice argues that individuals maximize their self-interest. Thus, if we know or can posit the preferences of a person, we can then predict their reactions to specific incentives. Because rational choice emphasizes incentive structures, especially those created by institutions, rational choice became a part of the effort to rebalance political analyses to include both individual attitudes and state structures.

Rational choice was well positioned to move into the position of the dominant methodology because it allowed for the analysis of both individual incentives and how institutional structures affect those incentives. In addition, rational choice had a much more powerful methodology than its competitors, specifically borrowing more sophisticated quantitative methodologies and the abstract modeling of game theory into political science. Mitchell goes so far as to claim that this higher sophistication of rational choice methodologies inadvertently led an earlier generation of political scientists to reject rational choice and choose behavioralism as their model for political analysis.[30] Behavioralism gave these young scholars an analytical advantage over their peers with only a modest investment in quantitative methodology. They were less enticed by rational choice because of the higher investment in math necessary for the modeling aspects of rational choice. Yet later, the sophistication of rational choice methods provided the analytical edge for another new generation of political scientists, eager to supplant their predecessors.

Despite these advances, the current dominant methodology, rational choice, is still limited in its choice of topics by methodological assumptions and expectations about data. Just as the behavioralists may have overemphasized cultural attitudes as measured in public opinion surveys in their analyses of democratic viability, the rational choice scholars similarly emphasize explanatory factors that are easily quantified or fit an incentives-based explanation of behavior. Thus, three of the very few articles focusing on Japan published recently in top political science journals all address the question of defections from the LDP in 1993.[31] These defections were an important and crucial event in Japanese politics, but the attention given this one event over other, equally important, events seems misplaced. This overemphasis can be explained, in part, by the fact that a data set of defectors and non-defectors is easily created for analysis. Similarly, the large number of electoral system articles in the same journals also stems, in part, from the easy availability of excellent data on Japanese elections.

The dominance of a particular methodology also appears prominently in publishing patterns. Thus, nearly all of the articles on Japanese politics published in top political science journals in the past decade have used rational choice or quantitative methodologies, as shown in cited examples on the topics of electoral incentives or LDP defections. Other approaches to the study of Japanese politics find outlets as books or in area studies journals. This bias in publishing outlets is so extreme that if an archeologist 1,000 years in the future had access only to our mainstream political science journals, she would be perplexed by our fetish-like fixation on only a few topics of Japanese political science.

Japanese Scholarship on Japanese Politics

Japanese scholars of Japanese politics have moved in the same direction as their American counterparts, but there are still fundamental differences and radically different starting points which help explain differences between the two fields. Although no less a prominent scholar than Inoguchi Takashi can maintain that "it is undeniable that American political science has led political science in the rest of the world,"[32] the Japanese still maintain much of their own indigenous approach to the study of politics. This approach has some obvious deficiencies, but it also has some little recognized strengths, strengths that are prominent in contrast to how political science has developed in the United States.

Traditionally, the study of political science in Japan was about individuals. Whereas political science in the United States has been dominated by approaches or methodologies, in Japan political science has been dominated by specific individuals. Not only was the field dominated by individual scholars – Masumi Junnosuke for example – these scholars also emphasized the role of the individual in their works. To these authors, Japanese politics is best explained by a chronology of events in which a variety of factors play a role, but the decisions, relationships, and proclivities of individuals emerge time and again as decisive explanatory factors. The important source for these analyses of Japanese politics is the memoir of the important political actor. Because so much of Japanese politics occurs behind the scenes, these memoirs provide the only evidence as to the actual factors and discussions that influenced important political events.

This initial bias to the individual in Japanese political science has declined with the importation of American methods of political science analysis and their adoption by some of the most prominent Japanese scholars of political science. These scholars and their colleagues, some educated in the United States and others simply following American trends, have transformed and heightened the levels of methodological sophistication of Japanese political science. There is, however, an important difference in the work of the best political scientists in Japan in contrast to the work of the best American political scientists. These Japanese scholars regularly contribute to nationally relevant policy and political discussions. Even the most methodologically sophisticated Japanese scholar will also write regularly for the general audience in Japan and serve on government commissions. In contrast, while there have always been scholars in the United States that have made these linkages, bridging the chasm between academic scholarship and public debate, their numbers have always been few. In Japan, these scholars are the norm, and this tendency is a strength of Japanese political science scholarship.

Problems of Methodological Biases: Circularity

Methodological advances in political science have brought many advantages to our understanding of Japanese politics. Excellent data, specialization, statistical techniques, and formal modeling allow a researcher to measure separately the influences of different factors, and these methods increase our understanding of a variety of political and societal phenomena in Japan. In addition, the expectations of each methodological wave have opened new doors to collecting data and answering questions about politics. The behavioralists gave us more rigorous scientific inquiry in general and sophisticated public opinion analyses specifically. The rational choice school has advanced our quantitative methodologies and added the beneficial clarity that formal modeling can bring to our understanding of complex causal relationships, producing insights that would not be obvious from other methods. The net result of these advances is better evidence, better methods, and a wider array of questions being asked and answered in the field of Japanese politics.

These advantages are obvious, and perhaps they need not be mentioned. I mention them, however, before I begin my criticism of some of the methodological excesses and blind spots brought about by the dominance of one methodology in order to lay the proper groundwork for these criticisms. Political science is the better for these methodological advances, but the gains they brought do not excuse the problems that accompanied them. The debate in the discipline is not about the worth of the methodological advances; rather it is a debate between an eclecticism in which all methodologies are held to the rigorous standard of the accuracy of explanations they produce, and the dominance of a particular methodology in which that methodology is assumed to produce better results because it uses superior methods. In the dominant methodology paradigm, methodological competitors may exist, but they exist only in subordination to the superior methodology.

Because one methodology dominates political science, there is a tendency to ignore research done under previous and now marginalized paradigms for political research. In contrast to the discipline of history, in which an overview of all previous work on a specific topic is required, it is quite common in political science for entire periods of scholarship to be ignored. Thus, all early work on Japanese politics can be dismissed as "sterile constitutionalism." Rational choice theorists can ignore the work of the behavioralists, in part because the behavioralists conceptualize problems differently than rational choice theorists. Consequently, the literature reviews of political science papers and books have a circular quality. Rational choice theorists cite each other and rarely place their research in the context of what has been done under previous methodological paradigms, even when that research is directly relevant to their topic.

E. B. Keehn, for example, makes the same criticism of Ramseyer and Rosenbluth's rational choice analysis of Japanese politics: "Much of their discussion of LDP electoral and organizational behavior is a rational choice rehashing of classic studies, such as Nathaniel Thayer's *How the Conservatives Rule Japan*, 1969." J. A. A. Stockwin responds similarly, "In fact [Ramseyer and Rosenbluth] also make a good empirical case for marked LDP dominance over the ministries, but the theory adds little (except jargon) to the empirical evidence. It is hardly a new insight that the LDP and the ministries used to work in cahoots with each other for mutual survival."[33] A similar example is Harold Quigley's 1932 book on Japanese politics which is never cited even though it identified and described the issues of electoral coordination that has animated a whole series of political science articles in prominent journals in the 1990s. Not one of the authors in this series of articles (including myself) showed any awareness of Quigley's research on this topic. Our articles in the 1990s could ignore past research because we knew that the analysis of past generations of researchers was inferior to our superior methods. We were wrong. Repackaging the conventional wisdom of a previous era in the jargon of a new methodology is not progress and is not science.

Problems of Methodological Biases: Assumptions

Another potential problem that occurs when one methodology or paradigm dominates a discipline is the tendency for the assumptions of that paradigm to inadvertently limit the field of research inquiry. Theoretical assumptions block the consideration of alternative explanations not recognized or discredited by the orthodox methodology. The work of some researchers seems to reflect an unconscious bias to support the orthodox methodology even when that task seems to conflict with the higher goal of providing the best, unbiased explanations of political events.

Ramseyer and Rosenbluth's 1993 study *Japan's Political Marketplace* provides an example of the uneasy fit between rational choice theorizing and the desire to explain Japanese politics with accuracy. They derive their propositions deductively, based on assumptions that actors behave rationally. They test those assumptions with copious data gathering. In many ways the book is an exceptional and forceful analysis, and it has received widespread attention in the broader political science field. In contrast, its reception in the realm of Japanese politics has been more muted. Negative reactions to the book focus largely on dissatisfaction with the accuracy of the model of Japanese politics that Ramseyer and Rosenbluth describe. For example, Steven Reed argues: "I find much about the rational choice approach irritating, wherever applied. In particular, I am irritated by the tendency to impute intentionality to everything and the propensity to prefer deduction over data." Reed then gives an example of a claim made by Ramseyer and Rosenbluth that he argues is "difficult to reconcile with the historical record."[34]

A similar disquiet shows up in comparing the impact of Ramseyer and Rosenbluth's work to that of Johnson's *MITI and the Japanese Miracle*. Johnson's book was equally unsettling to some of the conventional wisdom of the time, but there was little quibbling about the factual correctness of his work. Rather, critics have contended that his model did not apply as well to different time periods, different issue areas, or different ministries.[35] Johnson's book also sparked a debate about the relative power of politicians and bureaucrats that set the agenda for a decade of academic research. In contrast, Ramseyer and Rosenbluth's work has been largely ignored by most scholars of Japanese politics. In the field of Japanese politics, only rational choice scholars cite Ramseyer and Rosenbluth regularly. Citations by other Japan specialists are typically only an acknowledgment of arguments that Ramseyer and Rosenbluth have made.

Problems of Methodological Biases: Scientific Research

Another bias brought about by methodological paradigms is the discrediting of alternative approaches because they are said to be neither scientific nor theoretical. One of the greatest benefits of methodological advances in political science is the enhancement of the research process in scientific terms. We have rejected anecdotal evidence, biased case selection, and atheoretical studies from our repertoire of research methodologies. However, the fear of weak or unscientific research occasionally manifests itself in unwarranted attacks on perfectly valid and scientific methodologies because they differ from the dominant methodology of the time.

This bias against marginalized methodologies shows up in the pejorative use of the term "area studies" in political science. To some political scientists area studies means the atheoretical, unscientific study of one particular country. Such studies are of marginal worth, they claim, because the studies are not comparative. The studies are said to be atheoretical and unscientific because there is no comparison of cases, allowing for the testing of theoretically derived hypotheses. In addition, a single country case study is unlikely to be generalizable beyond that specific country. Thus, these critics would argue, area studies work does not advance our theoretical knowledge of the world around us; it simply provides idiosyncratic explanations of specific events, precisely the ad hoc analysis and anecdotal evidence that methodological advances in political science had supposedly eliminated.

Chalmers Johnson objects to this critique of area studies, characterizing the detractors of area studies as claiming that "the relationship between area specialists and rational choice theorists is that of a hierarchy, with the area specialist in the role of a gold miner digging away at the cliff face of a foreign culture, while the rational choice theorist is the master goldsmith who can turn this raw ore into beautiful things."[36] Prominent comparativists seem guilty of this charge. Laitin assigns a role to narrative research that essentially supplements the work done in statistical research.[37] David Collier's discussion of case studies similarly gives higher priority to multiple country case studies, though he does cite favorably an extensive and growing literature that recognizes the potential for single country case studies to be both theoretical and scientific.[38]

A subtle bias exists in political science that relegates single country studies to inferior status and automatically elevates multi-country studies to a privileged status, a distinction that is not justified inherently by the rigor or scientific orientation of one approach over the other. This bias is inappropriate. Do we conduct research because it best fits the dominant model of what scientific research should be? Or do we conduct research to better explain the world around us? Under the second goal, a methodologically rigorous and theoretical study that focused on just one country is just as valid and useful as a multi-country study that explicitly separated cases into control groups and test groups for hypothesis testing.

The Future of Political Research on Japan

Though this essay serves as a warning about potential biases that affect political science research, political research on Japan has a bright future of continuing achievement. Though political science has been dominated at times by specific methodological approaches, the discipline has remained open to a variety of external methodologies and approaches, giving hope that an eclectic approach will remain well rooted in the discipline. The current state of political science is a healthy mix of historical (path dependency), sociological (behavioralism), economic (rational choice), and humanities (postmodernism) approaches. Although the rational choice school is ascendant and dominant in some parts of the discipline, a lively debate about rational choice continues in the discipline. The subfield of comparative politics and the specialization of Japanese politics similarly remain healthy with representatives of all approaches making some contributions to our scholarship.

Political science and comparative politics run the danger of slipping into irrelevance if their explanations of events become too subservient to the dominant methodology and its assumptions rather than always serving the ultimate goal of better understanding the world around us. American political science could learn well from its counterpart in Japan where the practical component of the study of politics has remained healthy and respected. Indeed the more prominent a Japanese political scientist is, the more prominent his or her contribution to public discussion is expected to be. In the future, American political scientists must make sure that their research still speaks to a broader audience and still answers relevant questions for that audience.

Despite these concerns, recent political science work has been of exceptional quality and has vastly increased our understanding of Japan specifically and politics generally. The methodological power and rigor brought by behavioralism and rational choice have transformed our study of politics and our understanding of politics for the better. Rational choice modeling has brought new insights and greater clarity of complex causal phenomena. The adherence of political science research to the basic assumptions of the scientific method and expectations of theory building and hypothesis testing have helped steer political science away from unsubstantiated conclusions, and this progress must be continued. Joseph Gownder and Robert Pekkanen's admonition seems especially appropriate given these dangers: "the future of the study of Japanese politics will be best served by accepting works applying a variety of different approaches, as long as these works are done rigorously and stand up to the criteria of good social science. Finally rational choice is one among many competing explanations of political phenomena. It is not the end of political science."[39] What will be studied in the next decades is difficult to predict; it will largely be determined by events, but we can be confident that the study of Japanese politics will remain an eclectic collection of topics and methodologies.

NOTES

1 Scalapino and Masumi, *Parties and Politics.*
2 Thayer, *How the Conservatives Rule Japan.*
3 Curtis, *Election Campaigning Japanese Style.*
4 Satō and Matsuzaki, "Jimintō chōchōki."
5 Curtis, *The Japanese Way of Politics.*
6 Kohno, *Japan's Postwar Party Politics.*
7 Steiner, Krauss, and Flanagan, eds., *Political Opposition and Local Politics.*
8 Krauss, Rohlen, and Steinhoff, eds., *Conflict in Japan.*
9 Stockwin, *Japan: Divided Politics.*
10 Johnson, *MITI and the Japanese Miracle.*
11 Samuels, *The Business of the Japanese State.*
12 Muramatsu and Krauss, "The Conservative Policy Line."
13 Ramseyer and Rosenbluth, *Japan's Political Marketplace.*
14 Pharr, *Political Women in Japan*; LeBlanc, *Bicycle Citizens.*
15 van Wolferen, *The Enigma of Japanese Power.*
16 Schlesinger, *Shadow Shoguns.*
17 Reed, "Structure and Behaviour."
18 For example, Cox and Rosenbluth, "The Anatomy of a Split"; Cox and Rosenbluth, "Factional Competition for Party Endorsement"; Cox, "Is the Single Non-Transferable Vote Superproportional?"
19 Lincoln, *Arthritic Japan.*
20 Pempel, *Regime Shift.*
21 Ward, *Japan's Political System.*
22 Curtis, *The Logic of Japanese Politics.*
23 Rohlen, *Japan's High Schools.*
24 Pharr, *Losing Face.*
25 Schwartz and Pharr, eds., *The State of Civil Society.*
26 Laitin, "Comparative Politics"; Rogowski, "Comparative Politics."
27 Johnson, "Preconception vs. Observation."
28 For example, see Pempel, *Regime Shift*, and Samuels, *Machiavelli's Children.*
29 Mitchell, "Political Science and Public Choice," p. 244.
30 Ibid.

31 Cox and Rosenbluth, "The Anatomy of a Split"; Kato, "When the Party Breaks Up"; Reed and Scheiner, "Electoral Incentives and Policy Preferences."
32 Inoguchi, "Political Science in Three Democracies," p. 1.
33 Keehn, Review of *Japan's Political Marketplace*, p. 250; Stockwin, Review of *Japan's Political Marketplace*, p. 393.
34 Reed, Review of *Japan's Political Marketplace*.
35 Muramatsu and Krauss, "The Conservative Policy Line"; Samuels, *The Business of the Japanese State*.
36 Johnson, "Preconception vs. Observation," p. 172.
37 Laitin, "Comparative Politics," p. 631.
38 Collier, "The Comparative Method."
39 Gownder and Pekkanen, "The End of Political Science?", p. 384.

BIBLIOGRAPHY

Collier, David. "The Comparative Method." In Ada W. Finifter, ed., *Political Science: The State of the Discipline II*. Washington DC: American Political Science Association, 1993.
Cox, Gary. "Is the Single Non-Transferable Vote Superproportional? Evidence from Japan and Taiwan." *American Journal of Political Science* 40 (Aug. 1996): 740–55.
Cox, Gary, and Rosenbluth, Frances. "The Anatomy of a Split: The Liberal Democrats in Japan." *Electoral Studies* 14:2 (1995): 355–76.
Cox, Gary, and Rosenbluth, Frances. "Factional Competition for the Party Endorsement: The Case of Japan's Liberal Democratic Party." *British Journal of Political Science* 26 (1996): 259–69.
Curtis, Gerald. *Election Campaigning Japanese Style*. New York: Columbia University Press, 1971.
Curtis, Gerald. *The Japanese Way of Politics*. New York: Columbia University Press, 1988.
Curtis, Gerald. *The Logic of Japanese Politics*. New York: Columbia University Press, 1999.
Gownder, Joseph, and Pekkanen, Robert. "The End of Political Science? Rational Choice Analyses in Studies of Japanese Politics." *Journal of Japanese Studies* 22 (1996): 363–84.
Inoguchi, Takashi. "Political Science in Three Democracies, Disaffected (Japan), Third-Wave (Korea) and Fledgling (China)." Paper presented at the RC33 Panel Session of the World Congress of the International Political Science Association, Durban, South Africa, June 28–July 4, 2003.
Johnson, Chalmers. *MITI and the Japanese Miracle: The Growth of Industrial Policy, 1925–1975*. Stanford, Calif.: Stanford University Press, 1982.
Johnson, Chalmers. "Preconception vs. Observation, or the Contributions of Rational Choice Theory and Area Studies to Contemporary Political Science." *PS: Political Science and Politics* 30 (1997): 170–4.
Kato, Junko. "When the Party Breaks Up: Exit and Voice among Japanese Legislators." *American Political Science Review* 92 (1998): 857–70.
Keehn, E. B. Review of *Japan's Political Marketplace*, by J. Mark Ramseyer and Frances M. Rosenbluth. *Monumenta Nipponica* 49 (1994): 249–51.
Kohno Masaru. *Japan's Postwar Party Politics*. Princeton: Princeton University Press, 1997.
Krauss, Ellis, Rohlen, Thomas, and Steinhoff, Patricia, eds. *Conflict in Japan*. Honolulu: University of Hawai'i Press, 1984.
Laitin, David. "Comparative Politics: The State of the Subdiscipline." In Ira Katznelson and Helen Milner, eds., *Political Science: The State of the Discipline*. New York: Norton, 2002.
LeBlanc, Robin. *Bicycle Citizens: The Political World of the Japanese Housewife*. Berkeley: University of California Press, 1999.

Lincoln, Edward. *Arthritic Japan: The Slow Pace of Economic Reform*. Washington DC: Brookings Institute Press, 2001.

Masumi Junnosuke. *Contemporary Politics in Japan*. Berkeley: University of California Press, 1985.

Mitchell, W. C. "Political Science and Public Choice: 1950–70." *Public Choice* 98 (1999): 237–49.

Muramatsu Michio and Krauss, Ellis. "The Conservative Policy Line and the Development of Patterned Pluralism." In Kozo Yamamura and Yasuba Yasukichi, eds., *The Political Economy of Japan*, vol. 1, *The Domestic Transformation*. Stanford, Calif.: Stanford University Press, 1987.

Pempel, T. J. *Regime Shift: Comparative Dynamics of the Japanese Political Economy*. Ithaca, NY: Cornell University Press, 1998.

Pharr, Susan. *Political Women in Japan: The Search for a Place in Political Life*. Berkeley: University of California Press, 1981.

Pharr, Susan. *Losing Face: Status Politics in Japan*. Berkeley: University of California Press, 1990.

Quigley, Harold. *Japanese Government and Politics*. New York: Century Co., 1932.

Ramseyer, J. Mark, and Rosenbluth, Frances M. *Japan's Political Marketplace*. Cambridge, Mass.: Harvard University Press, 1993.

Reed, Steven. "Structure and Behaviour: Extending Duverger's Law to the Japanese Case." *British Journal of Political Science* 29 (1991): 335–56.

Reed, Steven. *Making Common Sense of Japan*. Pittsburgh: University of Pittsburgh Press, 1994.

Reed, Steven. Review of *Japan's Political Marketplace*, by J. Mark Ramseyer and Frances M. Rosenbluth. *American Journal of Sociology* 99 (1994): 1654–6.

Reed, Steven, and Scheiner, E. "Electoral Incentives and Policy Preferences: Mixed Motives behind Party Defections In Japan." *British Journal of Political Science* 33 (2003): 469–90.

Rogowski, Ronald. "Comparative Politics." In Ada W. Finifter, ed., *Political Science: The State of the Discipline II*. Washington DC: American Political Science Association, 1993.

Rohlen, Thomas. *Japan's High Schools*. Berkeley: University of California Press, 1983.

Samuels, Richard. *The Business of the Japanese State: Energy Markets in Comparative and Historical Perspective*. Ithaca, NY: Cornell University Press, 1987.

Samuels, Richard. *Machiavelli's Children: Leaders and Their Legacies in Italy and Japan*. Ithaca, NY: Cornell University Press, 2003.

Satō Seizaburō and Matsuzaki Tetsuhisa. "Jimintō chōchōki seiken no kaibō." *Chūō kōron* 99:11 (1984): 66–100.

Scalapino, Robert A., and Masumi Junnosuke. *Parties and Politics in Contemporary Japan*. Berkeley: University of California Press, 1962.

Schlesinger, Jacob. *Shadow Shoguns: The Rise and Fall of Japan's Postwar Political Machine*. New York: Simon and Schuster, 1997.

Schwartz, Frank, and Pharr, Susan, eds. *The State of Civil Society in Japan*. Cambridge: Cambridge University Press, 2003.

Steiner, Kurt, Krauss, Ellis, and Flanagan, Scott, eds. *Political Opposition and Local Politics in Japan*. Princeton: Princeton University Press, 1980.

Stockwin, J. A. A. *Japan: Divided Politics in a Growth Economy*, 2nd edn. New York: Norton, 1982.

Stockwin, J. A. A. Review of *Japan's Political Marketplace*, by J. Mark Ramseyer and Frances M. Rosenbluth. *International Affairs* 70 (1994): 393.

Thayer, Nathaniel. *How the Conservatives Rule Japan*. Princeton: Princeton University Press, 1969.

van Wolferen, Karel. *The Enigma of Japanese Power: People and Politics in a Stateless Nation.* New York: Knopf, 1989.

Vogel, Ezra. *Japan as Number One: Lessons for America.* New York: Harper and Row, 1979.

Ward, Robert E. *Japan's Political System*, 2nd edn. Englewood Cliffs, NJ: Prentice-Hall, 1967.

FURTHER READING

An excellent starting place for understanding Japanese politics is the classics of the subject, those books that laid out the framework of conservative political rule in Japan: two works by Gerald Curtis, *The Japanese Way of Politics* (New York: Columbia University Press, 1988) and *The Logic of Japanese Politics* (New York: Columbia University Press, 1999); Nathaniel Thayer, *How the Conservatives Rule Japan* (Princeton: Princeton University Press, 1969); and J. A. A. Stockwin, *Japan: Divided Politics in a Growth Economy*, 2nd edn. (New York: Norton, 1982). From this foundation it is best to survey the debate over the Japanese economic miracle and the role of the bureaucracy in that miracle: Chalmers Johnson, *MITI and the Japanese Miracle: The Growth of Industrial Policy, 1925–1975* (Stanford, Calif.: Stanford University Press, 1982); Muramatsu Michio and Ellis Krauss, "The Conservative Policy Line and the Development of Patterned Pluralism," in Kozo Yamamura and Yasuba Yasukichi, eds., *The Political Economy of Japan*, vol. 1, *The Domestic Transformation* (Stanford, Calif.: Stanford University Press, 1987); Richard Samuels, *The Business of the Japanese State: Energy Markets in Comparative and Historical Perspective* (Ithaca, NY: Cornell University Press, 1987); and J. Mark Ramseyer and Frances M. Rosenbluth, *Japan's Political Marketplace* (Cambridge, Mass.: Harvard University Press, 1993).

More recent works are much more difficult to group together. T. J. Pempel's study *Regime Shift: Comparative Dynamics of the Japanese Political Economy* (Ithaca, NY: Cornell University Press, 1998) excels in placing Japan in a comparative context, updating the traditional model of Japanese politics both chronologically and comparatively. Edward Lincoln's *Arthritic Japan: The Slow Pace of Economic Reform* (Washington DC: Brookings Institute Press, 2001) provides an excellent analysis of Japan's recent economic woes. Susan Pharr's *Losing Face: Status Politics in Japan* (Berkeley: University of California Press, 1990) and Robin LeBlanc's *Bicycle Citizens: The Political World of the Japanese Housewife* (Berkeley: University of California Press, 1999) open our eyes to the role of women in politics and the consideration of status in political disputes. Kohno Masaru's *Japan's Postwar Party Politics* (Princeton: Princeton University Press, 1997) provides a rational choice interpretation of several political events across the postwar period. This work, while arguing the strength of rational choice explanations of events, also provides an interesting and detailed analysis of several important historical events that are largely ignored in other current analyses of Japanese politics. Steven Reed's charming book *Making Common Sense of Japan* (Pittsburgh: University of Pittsburgh Press, 1994), written largely for an undergraduate audience, is refreshing for its simple yet insightful logic and examples.

CHAPTER SEVENTEEN

The Postwar Japanese Economy

Bai Gao

The postwar Japanese economy has experienced a major swing: from the 1950s to the end of the 1980s, it achieved an astonishing record of economic growth, and then for much of the 1990s it fell into a deep stagnation which lasted into the first decade of the twenty-first century. It has finally shown signs of recovery since the second quarter of 2003. In this essay, I adopt a globalization perspective to explore the causal mechanisms behind the postwar movements of the Japanese economy. This perspective is conceptualized according to the common historical experiences shared by all major industrialized economies. It treats the evolution of the postwar Japanese economy as part of a long-term movement of capitalist economies in the process of globalization. Differing from various structural perspectives that highlight the increasing free flows of capital, commodities, and technology, the globalization perspective adopted in this essay is institutional in nature and emphasizes the interactions between the international economic order and national economic institutions.

According to this perspective, capitalist economies have experienced two major waves of globalization. The first wave started in the 1870s and was sustained by the international gold standard and various international treaties on tariffs under British hegemony. This wave of globalization headed toward a downturn in 1914, triggered by the collapse of the international gold standard and the outbreak of World War I. The decline of the ratio between international trade and world gross domestic product (GDP), the commonly used measurement for the degree of globalization, did not reach its lowest point until 1953, having decreased steadily through the Great Depression and World War II. Sustained by the Bretton Woods system and the General Agreements on Trade and Tariffs, the second wave of globalization began to evolve under American hegemony. It started gaining momentum from the early 1970s as the collapse of the Bretton Woods system brought about two profound structural changes in the long-term movement of capitalist economies: the shift in the cycle of capital accumulation from the expansion of trade and production to the expansion of finance and monetary activity, and the shift in the major policy paradigms in advanced capitalist economies from social protection to the release of market forces.[1]

This globalization perspective holds that the outstanding performance of the Japanese economy before the 1970s can be seen as being sustained by an institutional evolution of the Japanese economic system which started from the early 1930s to cope with the downturn of the first wave of globalization. This evolutionary process progressed further in many ways during World War II, and in the postwar period it reconfigured the Japanese economic system to meet the challenges of a new international environment. The Japanese economic system that resulted from this institutional evolution emphasized coordination and stability. In the postwar period, it was able to stimulate aggressive corporate investments and bank lending through excessive competition and to maintain a high level of employment through a strategy of total employment.[2] There were, however, some deeply rooted dilemmas in this system. Its strong coordination was achieved at the cost of weak control and monitoring. Its high level of stability was maintained at the cost of low capacity within the system to upgrade the economic structure. When the collapse of the Bretton Woods system triggered the globalization of finance and the release of market forces in the 1970s and the 1980s, its weak control and monitoring and its inability to upgrade the economic structure became major challenges to the Japanese economic system. In a series of interactions between international factors and domestic factors, the "bubble economy" rose and fell, leading the Japanese economy into a decade-long stagnation.[3]

This essay is divided into several sections, each of which deals not only with a specific period in postwar Japanese economic history, but also with a specific focus in the current scholarship, such as the postwar recovery, high growth, reversal and stagnation, and reform versus recovery. I use the globalization perspective to drive my analysis of the Japanese economy throughout the postwar era and for each period. In each section, I first briefly discuss the structure of the political economy in a particular period, and then highlight the major issues within that period covered by the current literature. I focus on how Japanese economic institutions evolved in the process of structural change and how scholars have perceived these institutional evolutions. In this sense, this review is as much an institutional history as an intellectual history of the Japanese economy.

The Postwar Recovery

The period 1945–9, that is, between the end of World War II and the implementation of the Dodge Line, was very important to the postwar Japanese economy. Two seemingly conflicting trends can be observed and both of them together have profoundly shaped the postwar Japanese economy. On the one hand, Japan underwent a series of democratic reforms instituted by the occupation authorities. These reforms marked some great departures from Japan's prewar and wartime legacies. On the other hand, however, in a battle for survival amidst severe shortages of materials and the resulting hyperinflation, Japan was also able to preserve many institutions and mechanisms that had developed before and during the war. The coexistence of these two trends has stimulated longstanding continuity–discontinuity debates in academic discussions of the Japanese economy.

To those who emphasize discontinuity, postwar democratic reforms have exerted a profound impact on postwar Japan by bringing about significant changes in the structure of the Japanese economy. The dissolution of zaibatsu changed the organizational structure of the Japanese economy. Despite the fact that former zaibatsu companies were able to reorganize themselves into *keiretsu*, these groupings were never able to control other companies and industries in the same way. The first anti-monopoly law was enacted in 1947. Even though the Fair Trade Commission has been weak and the law was amended twice and often twisted to support Japan's industrial policy, big corporations were restricted in their ability to organize into combines. Labor unions also became more powerful in politics. Although their position was weakened after the implementation of the Dodge Line, they remained a significant political force and their continuing struggle for job security and wages constituted one of the major driving forces for large corporations to institutionalize the lifetime employment system.[4] To those who focus on transwar continuities, the battle for survival in the unprecedented economic crisis in the late 1940s contributed greatly to the institutional inheritance of the prewar and wartime practices.

In the 1945–9 period, underproduction was the major challenge faced by the Japanese economy. As a result of the defeat in World War II, Japan lost all its formal colonies which used to be the major sources of supply of cheap materials and labor, as well as captive markets. Also as a result of the war, much of its infrastructure and production equipment was either destroyed or overused. The production level of the Japanese economy in 1945 was only 37 percent of the 1937 level. It went down to 20 percent in 1946, before going back up to 25 percent in 1947 and 33 percent in 1948. Although production decreased sharply, domestic demand for goods and services increased rapidly as a result of the postwar repatriation of millions of military and civilian Japanese from overseas. This led inevitably to hyperinflation. If the 1937 level is taken as 100, the wholesale price index for major industries was 442 in 1945, 1,210 in 1946, 3,860 in 1947, and 10,508 in 1948.[5]

The Japanese government adopted the famous "priority production program" envisioned by a group of economists headed by Arisawa Hiromi in an effort to promote production with limited resources in the coal, iron and steel, and fertilizer industries. The strategies and philosophies driving the priority production program had a profound impact on the development of the postwar Japanese economy, as a number of the debates on key policy issues during this period laid the intellectual foundation for Japan's postwar economic growth. Production was given the highest priority while consumption was underplayed; class consciousness was suppressed in the interest of national unity to survive the major crisis; economic growth was regarded as more important than sustainability; and national economic independence was considered more important than attracting foreign investments.[6]

The implementation of the priority production program served as an important mechanism of the institutional reproduction of the Japanese economic system through which many practices that had existed before and during the war continued to be used as legitimate means of economic governance. First of all, state intervention was further strengthened and bureaucrats became even more powerful than they had been during the war. The establishment of the Economic Stability Board (ESB), especially its strengthening under the leadership of Wada Hiroo from mid-1947, greatly enhanced the capacity of the Japanese state in policy integration. Both were due partly to strong support from the occupation authorities and partly to the fact that many business leaders who had long opposed efforts to strengthening state intervention in the economy were purged because of their wartime connections to the military.

Two practices that had originated during the war and were subsequently adopted by the ESB greatly influenced postwar Japanese industrial policy. During the war, planning for demand and supply started with annual resource mobilization plans. These remained indispensable in the implementation of the priority production plan as resources were very limited and the state had to ensure the supply of materials. Even after the 1950s, this practice remained useful for the Ministry of International Trade and Industry (MITI) to nurture Japan's strategic industries under the constraints of international payments. Government regulations over the flow of capital, commodities, labor, and materials, which had been another major means of ensuring munitions production during the war, remained important in the priority production program.[7] The easy money policy adopted under the leadership of Ishibashi Tanzan during the priority production program also became a major policy legacy for the postwar Japanese economy. If the impact of government control over resources on the Japanese economy was later reflected in MITI's industrial policy, Ishibashi's expansionary fiscal and monetary policies shaped the policy orientations of the Ministry of Finance and the Bank of Japan through the high growth period.

The main bank system that had originated during wartime mobilization survived the postwar democratic reforms, becoming a major link between banks and corporations. The banking industry as a whole successfully escaped the program of deconcentration of economic power adopted by the Allied occupation. Indirect finance by Japanese corporations through bank loans, and strong links between banks and corporations through *keiretsu* connections, later became the foundation for the Japanese style of aggressive corporate investments and bank lending driven by excessive competition that sustained the high growth.[8]

Because it saw both continuities and discontinuities, the question of how to interpret the nature of the Japanese economy in this period has been a major issue for scholarly debate. An important point of division in the debates is that the continuity arguments always emphasize institutions while the discontinuity arguments focus on economic structures. In the 1950s, the continuity–discontinuity debate focused on comparisons of the prewar and the postwar periods. The prevailing discontinuity arguments at the time highlighted the major departures of the Japanese economy from its prewar structures as a result of the postwar democratic reforms, which were also exemplified by land reform and the structural shift of the economy from textiles to heavy and chemical industries. In the 1960s, however, a continuity argument emerged to reinterpret economic reforms in the postwar period, including land reform and the dissolution of the zaibatsu, as an extension of a long-term trend in state policy that had already started in the early 1930s. From the early 1970s, comparisons of the wartime and postwar economies became more common, as taboos about discussion of the war experience faded and some scholars felt that the omission of the wartime economy in the early postwar debates was less than satisfactory. They contended that many practices during the war, even apparently ad hoc reactions, had profoundly shaped the postwar Japanese economy in many significant ways.[9]

Reflections on the Japanese model of economic development after the collapse of the bubble economy in the early 1990s gave rise to a heated debate on the origins of the Japanese economic system, shedding new light on our understanding of this important period in postwar Japanese economic history. A number of Japanese economic commentators point out that even after half a century, the Japanese economy still operates, both institutionally and ideologically, under the "1940 system," a wartime establishment that had been unknown in prewar Japan. Critics, however, continue to maintain that the postwar changes in Japan's political, economic, and social structures should not be downplayed. To a large extent, the "1940 system" debate in the 1990s inherited the basic characteristics of the earlier continuity–discontinuity debates, being divided by a different focus on either institutions or structural factors.[10]

From the globalization perspective, the "1940 system" debate has limits not only because some changes had started before World War II (or even before the full-scale invasion of China in 1937), but also because the experience of the Japanese economy in the 1945–9 period was part of the long-term movement of Japanese capitalism in the two waves of globalization. Seen through this lens, Japanese efforts to strengthen state intervention and organize the market in the late 1940s were, to a large extent, in line with the general trends of increasing social protection and limiting the negative impact of market forces experienced by all major industrialized countries at the time. In this sense, the "1940 system," which has been assumed to be a product of World War II, may in fact really represent an institutional adaptation aimed at coping with the downturn of the first wave of globalization that started with the collapse of the gold standard in 1914 and accelerated by the Great Depression and World War II. Similarly, much of the democratic reform initiated by the occupation can also be seen as an effort to align Japan with the newly established international economic order characterized by a multilateral free trade regime under the leadership of the United States. Seen in this light, the continuities in Japan's economic institutions and the discontinuities in the structural conditions of the Japanese economy do not, in theory, have to be mutually exclusive in understanding the nature of Japan's early postwar economic history.

The High Growth Era

The Japanese economy grew at an astonishing annual rate of 9.3 percent in the period 1956–73. Between 1955 and 1973, its GDP quadrupled from $3,500 to $13,500 per capita. Even when the first "oil shock" ended such high growth, the Japanese economy still outperformed its counterparts in North America and Western Europe in the ensuing major structural adjustment, achieving an outstanding record of an average annual growth of 4.1 percent in the period 1975–91. Since the 1970s, and especially in the 1980s, the search for the secret of Japanese success in economic development has become a major research preoccupation in the West. A key question in the academic discussions on the Japanese economy has been whether Japanese capitalism is different from the Anglo-Saxon model of liberal capitalism.

Japanese industrial policy has been the most debated issue in studies of the Japanese economy conducted during the 1980s and the 1990s. As opposed to the regulatory state in the United States which only sets the rules of game, the developmental state in Japan was concerned with the economic structure and used its industrial policy to influence the direction of economic change. The Japanese state never left the economy to be driven completely by market forces.[11] The debate over Japanese industrial policy developed along two major lines. The first is whether industrial policy actually made the difference in Japanese economic performance. Some analysts hold that Japan's success was due primarily to the function of market forces, or to the initiatives of the private sector. The second concerns who really formulated Japanese industrial policy. Some analysts contend that the private sector had in fact a great input into Japanese industrial policy.[12] Closely related to the debate on Japanese industrial policy, another controversial issue was the relationship between Japan's banking system and Japanese industrial policy. Some scholars believe that Japan, like France, had a credit-based and price-administered banking system. Because of control by the central bank over private institutions, they argue, private banks have had to respond positively to state requests for cooperation in industrial policy. The critics of this view, in contrast, argue that Japanese banks made their loan decisions independently.[13]

A different approach to the actor-centered debate is to emphasize the type of industrial policy adopted by the Japanese state and what consequences the industrial policy had on the institutional evolution of the Japanese economic system. A premise of this approach is that it is economic institutions that make Japan different from liberal capitalism. This line of investigation shows that there was a distinctive set of economic philosophies and ideologies that constituted the foundation of Japanese developmentalism. It was sustained by nationalism and held a strategic view of the economy. It had a strong orientation toward promotion of exports, which became the backbone of the East Asian model of economic development.[14] Studies on the characteristics of Japanese economic institutions indicate that the Japanese economy was governed by various non-market mechanisms, which clearly distinguish it from liberal market capitalist economies. The *keiretsu* were organized both vertically and horizontally. Major manufacturers relied heavily upon subcontractors and also forged long-term relationships with each other. Cartels were used as an important means to protect sunset industries and weather the downturn in business cycles. Banks not only practiced cross-shareholding with corporations, but were also the major source of industrial capital for Japanese corporations.[15]

Japanese management received a great deal of attention in the 1980s as Western corporations tried to emulate the Japanese practices of lean production and teamwork. The distinctive pattern of Japanese management has been interpreted through two major perspectives. The cultural interpretation links Japanese practice at the company level to the Confucian tradition.[16] By contrast, the economic interpretation applies the framework of corporate governance, and contends that delegated monitoring performed the function of keeping Japanese corporations competitive.[17]

In the globalization debate of the 1990s, the success of the Japanese high growth period was re-examined from new perspectives. New studies have looked beyond the domestic factors that used to dominate the literature by highlighting the importance of international factors which provided an environment conducive to the rapid growth of the Japanese economy. This research shows that the postwar Japanese economy benefited greatly from the international economic order represented by the Bretton Woods system and the General Agreement on Trade and Tariffs (GATT). The fixed exchange rate and restraints on the free flow of capital enabled Japan to apply a combination of expansionary monetary policy to pursue economic growth and deflationary fiscal policy to control inflation simultaneously. The asymmetric cooperation between the United States and its allies in the international trade regime not only enabled Japan to export aggressively while still protecting its own domestic markets; it also provided a great opportunity for Japan to rely upon private institutions for social protection.[18]

Meanwhile, as scholars examined the forces that sustained the performance of the Japanese economic system during the high growth period, unintended factors that may also have supported high growth also began to attract attention. This kind of analysis, which began in Japan as early as the 1960s, questions the assumption that high growth was entirely an outcome of rational action and strategic design. According to this view, strategic design did exist in Japanese industrial policy, but, in the process of implementation, outcomes were often more a product of unexpected than planned consequences.[19] The phenomenon of excessive competition in Japanese industrial finance during this period illustrates well the impact of unanticipated factors on the high growth of the Japanese economy. High saving and high investment have been regarded as critical components in the Japanese high growth model. However, according to this view, while a primary goal of Japanese industrial policy was to control overheated corporate investments and bank lending, excessive competition (resulting from the weak control of shareholders over managers and weak bank monitoring of corporate borrowers) was sustained by the institutional configuration of Japanese corporate governance. In this way, Japan's high economic growth was as much an unexpected consequence of excessive competition as a clear outcome of strategic planning.[20]

Reversal and Stagnation

The growth and the collapse of the bubble represented a major reversal of the Japanese economy. The bubble economy appeared in the second half of the 1980s: the Nikkei index was 12,775 when the Plaza Accord was announced on September 24, 1985. Within two years, the index had doubled. In 1985, 414 million shares on average were traded per day; by 1987 that number had jumped to 946 million per day. At the end of 1987, the market cap of Japanese stocks had reached 346 trillion yen, which was 30 percent higher than the US stock market. At the time, the Tokyo Stock Exchange was the largest stock market in the world.[21] The real estate market also experienced an unprecedented boom. By the end of 1987, the market value of the entire land area in Japan reached 1,673 trillion yen, 2.9 times that of the United States. Between 1980 and 1989, the total loans by Japanese banks to all industries increased by about 120 percent, but loans to the real estate industry increased by more than 300 percent. Moreover, the loans to non-banking industries increased by more than 700 percent and most of the loans in this category went into real estate speculation.[22]

The collapse of the bubble in both stock and real estate markets precipitated a decade-long period of stagnation. According to one estimate, Japan lost 800 trillion yen in these two markets between 1989 and 1992 alone. The annual report on the Japanese economy published in October 2003 indicated that land prices had declined to as little as 55 percent of their bubble-economy peak. Capital losses resulting from declines in both land and stock prices during the period from the end of 1989 to the end of 2001 reached 1,330 trillion yen. Notably, the Japanese economy experienced a liquidity trap in 1997–8. The annual number of corporate bankruptcies before 1996 was 14,000 per year, but increased to 16,365 in 1997 and 19,171 in 1998.[23] In these two years, the Japanese economy also had negative growth rates.

Why did the Japanese economy turn so rapidly from prosperity to stagnation? Various explanations have been offered to explain this reversal of the Japan's economic fortunes. One interpretation pivoted on capital accumulation and the profitability of the system as a whole. Capitalist production, according to this view, is unplanned, uncoordinated, and competitive. Furthermore, competition in manufacturing involves large, fixed-capital investments in facilities and equipment. These facilities, however, tend to become outdated. In the 1950s and 1960s, sustained by a set of institutions that enabled the state, the banks, and the manufacturing industry to coordinate with each other, Japan and Germany enjoyed the advantages of unencumbered modernization through fixed-capital investment. This strong coordination not only protected Japan's domestic markets but also channeled its investments into new technologies. Then, when Japanese and German products penetrated the American market on a massive scale, rival fixed-capital physical plants were locked in confrontation, with no easy escape to alternative lines of production. As a result, profits fell dramatically and in tandem across the entire advanced capitalist world. Even after two decades, they had still not recovered. As lower-cost producers continued to enter global competition, the rate of return on the older capitalist enterprises in advanced industrialized countries was further depressed. As a result, there was intensified, horizontal intercapitalist competition for overbuilt production capacity, and this competition in turn led to the fall of profitability at the aggregate level. The result was the long downturn of capitalism.[24]

Development stage was considered another important factor in the reversal of Japan's economic course. In the 1950s and 1960s, many industries in the Japanese economy were in their infancy. The state's protection of these industries and its promotion of exports helped to sustain a set of catch-up structural processes: the economies of scale increased, the whole economy was shifting toward higher-productivity industries, the country imported technologies aggressively, and productivity increased in the agricultural sector. Meanwhile, the promotion of exports through government subsidies, along with the protection of domestic markets, sustained industrial growth through the rapid development of manufacturing industries. As the Japanese economy matured in the early 1970s, however, exports were no longer able to keep the economy growing. Meanwhile, the system began to resist the transformation of economic structures. Increasingly, state policy was aimed at preserving existing industries in an effort to protect resources unwisely invested in capital-intensive sectors, thereby preventing unemployment and maintaining wage equality. As market-conforming industrial policy was replaced by market-defying industrial policy, the economy was "cartelized" and the dynamics for further growth dampened.[25]

A regime shift, consisting of socioeconomic alliances, political economic institutions, and a public policy profile, was a third interpretation for Japan's economic turn. During Japan's high growth period, conservatives dominated the electoral process. Public policies were adopted that strengthened the regime's socioeconomic base and increased overall public support. The regime also discredited the conservatives' political opponents, enhanced the conservatives' ability to control political offices, and minimized the need for compromise. However, as the economic structure shifted from agriculture to manufacturing industries, family businesses were increasingly replaced by corporations and the tight labor market enhanced the bargaining power of labor unions. At the same time, the electoral pattern switched from two dominant political parties to multiple political parties. That began to threaten the conservatives' electoral hegemony. As a result of these changes, state economic policy-making became politicized, management had to compromise with labor unions, the government had to engage in deficit spending to enhance social infrastructure, and Japanese companies ceased being "embedded mercantilists" and became "international investors." All these factors eventually led to the Liberal Democratic Party's loss of power in the 1993 election.[26]

The cycle of technological innovation is the fourth factor that contributed to the stagnation of the Japanese economy. In the history of capitalism, there have been three identifiable paradigms in technological development. The first in 1760–1870 centered around steam power, which was applied in many types of machines, resulting in the rapid development of the textile, iron and steel, and coal industries, as well as a revolution in transportation. The second in 1880–1975 was organized around the increasing use of human-made materials such as cement, chemical dyes, ammonia, and rubber, and the extensive utilization of electricity. The third, which emphasizes information technology, started in the 1970s. Moreover, the revolution in information technology has taken place in conjunction with the process of globalization. In this kind of structural environment, the non-liberal market economy in Japan does not have the institutional advantage of responding effectively to changes in the relative prices of resources. At the same time, Japan's non-liberal market economy does not tolerate a high level of disparity in income distribution. As a result, the Japanese economy has stagnated.[27]

The profound changes in the international economic order and their impact on national economic systems represent the fifth interpretation. This view emphasizes the importance of understanding the rise and fall of the bubble in the 1980s as the turning point in the reversal of the Japanese economy from prosperity to stagnation. After the Bretton Woods system collapsed, Japan's fixed exchange rate was replaced by floating exchange rates, and process of liberalizing finance also began. With an increasingly free flow of capital, the Japanese economic system, characterized as it was by strong coordination but weak control and monitoring, bore much greater financial risks. After Japan signed the Plaza Accord in 1985, the rapid appreciation of the yen and the policy reversal made by the Bank of Japan contributed to the oversupply of money while domestic pressure for increasing public spending in order to reduce the adjustment pains caused by the high yen created a favorable macroeconomic environment. This kind of macroeconomic environment can spawn a bubble in any economic system. The bubble in the Japanese economy, however, was further inflated by aggressive patterns of corporate investment and bank lending, an outcome of the efforts to strengthen coordination.

From this perspective, the radical reforms in Japan during the 1990s not only dried up the sources of investments; more importantly, they changed the previous institutional logic of the Japanese economic system, creating enormous uncertainties for economic actors in Japan with regard to their future expectations of income and job security. When banks became reluctant to extend loans to corporations after the "Big Bang" (and as the collapse of the stock market and real estate markets seriously damaged corporations), Japanese companies suffered from a shortage of capital for investment. When the government tried to reduce its budget deficit, public spending declined. When discussions of eliminating the practice of permanent employment proliferated, the liquidity trap led to increased corporate bankruptcies, and consumers held onto their money tightly as the unemployment rate rose. In this sense, stagnation has, to some extent, been sustained by the policies and practices dictated by neoliberal reform agendas. This is not to say that Japan should not reform its economic system, but any radical reforms that drastically increase uncertainties in the expectations of economic actors will not fare well in generating immediate improvements in economic performance.[28]

Reform versus Recovery

In struggling with the decade-long stagnation, two questions have dominated the recent discussions and debates on the Japanese economy. First, what caused the decade-long stagnation of the Japanese economy? Second, in the face of the enormous pressures of globalization, will the Japanese economic system be converted to a liberal market economy?

Analysts have identified several major competing views on the factors that led to the stagnation of the Japanese economy in the 1990s. One holds that the stagnation in the 1990s and the early twenty-first century was largely caused by the structural nature of the bubble itself and was macroeconomic in origin. In this view, the collapse of any bubble would create a downward momentum that could potentially last for years. In other words, the stagnation of the Japanese economy was simply an extension of the collapse of the bubble in the early 1990s. Another, more popular, view attributes the stagnation to the slowness or incompleteness of reforms. It points out that, while a number of reforms were made in the 1990s, including the financial "Big Bang," changes in corporate governance, deregulation, and health care and pension reorganization, these reforms were either incomplete or moved Japan in the wrong direction. As a result, vested interests in the establishment have continued to resist and restrain market forces, and the dynamics of economic growth have not been released. Analysts with this view often maintain that a robust economic recovery depends on further systemic reforms.[29]

From the institutional perspective adopted by this essay, the stagnation of the Japanese economy was caused not by the absence of radical reforms, but by the radical reforms themselves which were initiated by the Japanese government in 1996. In that year, the Hashimoto administration simultaneously carried out a deflationary fiscal policy and the "Big Bang" policy for the banking industry. The government limited the combined central and local government budget deficits to 3 percent of GDP until 2003; in addition, it reduced the national debt by 4.3 trillion yen, raised the consumption tax from 3 to 4 percent, introduced local consumption taxes, and withdrew the personal income and property tax relief that had been in effect between 1994 and 1996. Meanwhile, the "Big Bang" program for the banking industry aimed to convert to Article 8 status under the Bank for International Settlements. When a bank's self-capital was between 4 and 8 percent, the bank was required to draft and implement a business improvement plan. When its self-capital stood at less than 4 percent, it was required to: make plans to increase its self-capital; restrain or reduce total assets; refrain from entering new business operations and from opening new branch offices; reduce the number of existing branch offices; downsize the business operations of both domestic and overseas subordinate companies and refrain from establishing new ones; restrain or prohibit payments of dividends; restrain bonuses for senior managers; and restrain or prohibit high-interest deposit services. When banks had no self-capital, they were required to cease their business operations, with a few exceptions. The "Big Bang" was, in its effects, equivalent to or more powerful than a deflationary monetary policy.[30]

Evidence over the past ten years supports this view. Prior to the major actions taken by the Hashimoto administration in 1996, the Japanese economy had in fact already shown signs of recovery. Its growth rate in 1995 reached 2.8 percent. The recent recovery of the Japanese economy, starting from the first half of 2003, provides further support for this view. According to most accounts, Japan has so far not undertaken substantial reforms which would, at least in theory, generate economic recovery. Nevertheless, the recovery of the Japanese economy is a reality: in the fourth quarter of 2003, the Japanese economy grew at a rate of 6.4 percent. There was, of course, an important structural factor, the "China procurement": strong demand from the overheated Chinese economy contributed to 80 percent of Japan's increase in exports in 2003. A conundrum emerges, however, when we compare the impact of Chinese demand on the performance of the Japanese economy in 2003 with the earlier instance of strong demand for Japanese products from the United States in 1997–8. Throughout the second half of the 1990s, the United States, Japan's top trading partner, experienced an unprecedented economic boom (in the form of an internet bubble). In contrast to the situation in 2003, however, strong external demand from the US market in 1997–8 failed to stimulate an economic recovery in Japan. Why?

An important difference between then and now is that in 2003–4, Japanese consumers had regained a sense of certainty about their future. After several years of consideration, and especially after the collapse of the internet bubble and the events of September 11, 2001, the neo-liberalist ideology lost popularity in Japan and the resistance to radical reforms gained more political support. Japanese consumers now feel more confident that radical reforms (that threaten massive layoffs) are unlikely to take place. Under such circumstances, they are responding to favorable structural conditions and willing to increase their spending. This is why, when the "China procurement" factor arose, the Japanese economy was perceived positively by the public, who, as a result, responded with increased spending. For the first time in its history, consumer spending has become the major driving force in a recovery of the Japanese economy.

Throughout the 1990s and the early twenty-first century, Japan has continued to face two conflicting goals in its economic policy: structural reform, and especially the reduction of non-performing loans, versus economic recovery. Radical reforms always create uncertainties in the expectations of economic actors and thus tend to depress investment. Without investment, there can be no economic growth or recovery.

Thus, to promote economic recovery, radical structural reforms have to be delayed. When an economy is in a deep downturn, the government needs to provide fiscal stimulus instead of reducing public spending; banks should provide investment capital for corporations rather than drastically eliminating non-performing loans; corporations should avoid massive layoffs as they would seriously restrain consumers' spending. All these measures could directly delay the structural reforms widely perceived as indispensable in putting the Japanese economy back on the right track for the long term.

The trend of emphasizing economic recovery over reform also suggests that Japan is unlikely to become a liberal market economy, despite the fact that many of its existing economic institutions are experiencing changes. Economic institutions are resilient. Even when changes take place in the Japanese economy, they tend to be path-dependent and incremental. As a result, the national variations between liberal market economies and coordinated market economies will remain.

Specifically, three mechanisms of institutional change shaped by structural factors may keep the Japanese economic system from being converted to a liberal market economy. First, in the institutional changes experienced by the Japanese economy, new forms of functional equivalence have often been created to replace old forms in an effort to cope with a new environment. Thus, while deregulation is widely perceived as one of the major indicators of Japan's convergence, what is actually happening in Japan is frequently not deregulation, but reregulation, with the state establishing new rules for managing the increased economic freedom resulting from freer flows of capital and commodities. Since there were considerable cross-national variations in economic systems prior to deregulation, the outcomes of reregulation, in combination with the liberalization pursued by advanced industrialized countries, including Japan, do not constitute convergence toward a single model of a liberal market economy, but instead suggest continuing distinctive national characteristics.[31]

Second, institutional changes in the Japanese economy often take place at the periphery while the core of the economic system remains resilient. In labor relations, for example, employers and labor unions have continued to cooperate at the plant level to maintain job security for core workers. The changes in the seniority-based wage system are, in fact, not part of a larger process that will inevitably lead to the collapse of the entire Japanese management system and its three pillars of permanent employment, seniority-based wages, and company-based labor unions. Rather, the changes in wage systems are a strategy to reduce labor costs in order to preserve permanent employment. In other words, even if the seniority-based wage system withers away, the practice of permanent employment will continue. One phenomenon, often overlooked in the neo-liberal argument for efficiency that predicts the erosion of the Japanese management system, is the fact that increasing international competition and the development of global production networks have made corporations even more dependent upon predictability on the shop floor.[32]

Third, hybridization, rather than convergence, has often marked the institutional transformation of the Japanese economy amidst globalization. Under the strong structural pressures created by the changing environment of international competition, Japan has adopted many measures to reform its corporate governance, including lifting the ban on holding companies, changing the asset valuation from cost to market value, strengthening banks' monitoring roles over corporations, reducing stable cross-shareholding, and increasing the amount of direct finance through stocks and corporate bonds. Nevertheless, these changes have not established the dominance of shareholders in corporate governance. On the contrary, the shareholders' voice has weakened, partly because institutional investors tend not to attend shareholders' meetings or intervene actively. Instead, such investors tend to use their voice to promote better practices in accounting and board independence. While the labor unions' role in corporate governance is also weakening due to the reform, they still play a significant role in advocating job security for core employees.[33]

Conclusion

The globalization perspective sheds lights on the causal mechanisms behind the movement of the postwar Japanese economy. It shows that the contemporary Japanese economic system has been an outcome of two important periods, the period of coping with the downturn of the last wave of globalization (in which a distinctive set of institutions and mechanisms evolved in Japan to restrain market forces and promote social protection), and the period of adjustment to the upturn of the present wave of globalization under the postwar international economic order represented by the Bretton Woods system and GATT. It also shows that the Japanese economic system, as a product of history, has institutional advantages and disadvantages in different international environments, given its characteristics of strong coordination but weak control and monitoring, and high stability but low capacity within the system to upgrade the economic structure.

Under the postwar order sustained by the Bretton Woods system and GATT, the Japanese economic system positioned itself within an international environment favorable for an export-oriented development strategy. The excessive competition in corporate investment and bank lending resulting from the efforts to strengthen coordination led to high speed economic growth, while the total employment strategy resulting from the efforts to maintain stability provided a solid political foundation for economic expansion. The breakdown of the Bretton Woods system, the oil crises, the liberalization of finance, and the tension in international trade with the United States profoundly changed the international environment of the Japanese economy. Facing increasing investment risks under a floating exchange rate and the free flow of capital, weak control and monitoring began to expose the limits of the Japanese economic system and it experienced serious malfunctions. These eventually gave rise to the bubble economy after the Plaza Accord in 1985.

Despite the apparent problems in Japan's postwar economic system, transforming it through radical reform has proved difficult, especially when economic recovery has been a pressing priority. When radical changes were attempted in 1996, they quickly altered the expectations of economic actors: corporations could no longer expect reliable supplies of industrial capital from banks, and Japanese consumers could no longer count on reliable future income provided by the practice of permanent employment. As government expenditure, corporate investment, and consumer spending declined simultaneously, the Japanese economy suffered two years of negative growth in 1997–8. Only after the Japanese gradually regained confidence in their economic system did the economy began to show signs of recovery.

NOTES

1   For a systematic presentation of this perspective, see Gao, *Japan's Economic Dilemma*, ch.
    2.
2   Total employment is different from full employment in Keynesian economics. Full em-
    ployment means that at the current wage level all those who want to work have a job. In
    contrast, total employment means that all those who want to work have some kind of job,
    but it suggests neither an optimal allocation of human resources nor wage satisfaction. For
    more, see Nomura, *Koyō fuan*.
3   For sources of these data, see Gao, *Japan's Economic Dilemma*, p. 1.
4   For the debate, see Gao, *Economic Ideology*, pp. 121–3.
5   Ibid., p. 129.
6   Gao, "Arisawa Hiromi."
7   Ibid.
8   Gao, *Japan's Economic Dilemma*, ch. 4.
9   Gao, *Economic Ideology*, p. 123.
10 On the "1940 system" debate, see ibid.; Gao, "Globalization and Ideology."
11 Johnson, *MITI and the Japanese Miracle*.
12 Samuels, *The Business of the Japanese State*.
13 Zysman, *Governments, Markets, and Growth*; Calder, *Strategic Capitalism*.
14 Gao, *Economic Ideology*; Murakami, *An Anticlassical Political-Economic Analysis*; Samuels,
    "Rich Nation, Strong Army."
15 Gerlach, *Alliance Capitalism*; Tilton, *Restricted Trade*; Uriu, *Troubled Industries*.
16 Dore, *British Factory Japanese Factory*; Dore, *Taking Japan Seriously*.
17 Aoki, "Monitoring Characteristics of the Main Bank System."
18 Gao, *Japan's Economic Dilemma*.
19 Miyazaki, "Kado kyōsō no kōzai"; Morozumi, "Sangyō taiseiron."
20 Gao, *Japan's Economic Dilemma*.
21 Mitsuhashi and Uchida, *Shōwa keizaishi*, pp. 194–5.
22 Ibid., p. 201.
23 *Facts and Figures of Japan*, p. 46.
24 Brenner, "The Economics of Global Turbulence."
25 Katz, *Japan: The System that Soured*.
26 Pempel, *Regime Shift*.
27 Yamamura, "Germany and Japan in a New Phase of Capitalism."
28 Gao, "Globalization and Ideology"; Gao, *Japan's Economic Dilemma*.
29 Katz, *Japanese Phoenix*; Lincoln, *Arthritic Japan*.
30 For more details, see Gao, *Japan's Economic Dilemma*, ch. 8.
31 Vogel, *Freer Markets, More Rules*.
32 Thelen and Kume, "The Future of National Embedded Capitalism."
33 Jackson, "Corporate Governance in Germany and Japan."

BIBLIOGRAPHY

Aoki, Masahiko. "Monitoring Characteristics of the Main Bank System: An Analytical and
    Developmental View." In Masahiko Aoki and Hugh Patrick, eds., *The Japanese Main Bank
    System*. Oxford: Oxford University Press, 1995.
Aoki, Masahiko, and Patrick, Hugh, eds. *The Japanese Main Bank System: Its Relevance for
    Developing and Transforming Economies*. Oxford: Oxford University Press, 1995.
Arisawa Hiromi, ed. *Shōwa keizaishi*. Tokyo: Nihon Keizai Shinbunsha, 1976.

Brenner, Robert. "The Economics of Global Turbulence." *New Left Review* 229 (1998): 1–265.

Calder, Kent. *Strategic Capitalism: Private Business and Public Purpose in Japanese Industrial Finance.* Princeton: Princeton University Press, 1993.

Calder, Kent. *Crisis and Compensation.* Princeton: Princeton University Press, 1998.

Dore, Ronald P. *British Factory Japanese Factory: The Origins of National Diversity in Industrial Relations.* Berkeley: University of California Press, 1973.

Dore, Ronald P. *Taking Japan Seriously.* London: Athlone Press, 1987.

Facts and Figures of Japan. Tokyo: Foreign Press Center, 1999.

Gao, Bai. "Arisawa Hiromi and His Theory for a Managed Economy." *Journal of Japanese Studies* 20 (1994): 115–53.

Gao, Bai. *Economic Ideology and Japanese Industrial Policy: Developmentalism from 1931 to 1965.* New York and Cambridge: Cambridge University Press, 1997.

Gao, Bai. "Globalization and Ideology: The Competing Images of the Contemporary Japanese Economic System in the 1990s." *International Sociology* 15 (2000): 435–53.

Gao, Bai. *Japan's Economic Dilemma: The Institutional Origins of Prosperity and Stagnation.* New York: Cambridge University Press, 2001.

Gerlarch, Michael. *Alliance Capitalism.* Berkeley: University of California Press, 1992.

Jackson, Gregory. "Corporate Governance in Germany and Japan." In Kozo Yamamura and Wolfgang Streeck, eds., *The End of Diversity? Prospects for German and Japanese Capitalism.* Ithaca, NY: Cornell University Press, 2003.

Johnson, Chalmers. *MITI and the Japanese Miracle: The Growth of Industrial Policy, 1925–1975.* Stanford, Calif.: Stanford University Press, 1982.

Katz, Richard. *Japan: The System that Soured.* Armonk, NY: M. E. Sharpe, 1998.

Katz, Richard. *Japanese Phoenix: The Long Road to Economic Revival.* Armonk, NY: M. E. Sharpe, 2003.

Lincoln, Edward. *Arthritic Japan: The Slow Pace of Economic Reform.* Washington DC: Brookings Institute Press, 2001.

Mitsuhashi Tadahiro and Uchida Shigeo. *Shōwa keizaishi.* Tokyo: Nihon Keizai Shinbunsha, 1994.

Miyazaki Yoshikazu. "Kado kyōsō no kōzai." In Kōsei Torihiki Kyōkai, ed., *Kokusai kyōsō to dokukinhō.* Tokyo: Nihon Keizai Shinbunsha, 1963.

Miyazaki Yoshikazu. *Nihon keizai no kōzō to kōdō.* Tokyo: Chikuma Shobō, 1985.

Miyazaki Yoshikazu. *Fukugō fukyō.* Tokyo: Chūō Kōronsha, 1992.

Morozumi Yoshihiko. "Sangyō taiseiron: tsūsanshōgawa no ichiteian." In Morozumi Yoshihiko, Minosō Hitoshi, Kodō Rikuzō, Masada Tadashi, and Chiyu Yoshihito, eds., *Sangyō taisei no saihensei.* Tokyo: Shunjūsha, 1963.

Murakami Yasusuke. *An Anticlassical Political-Economic Analysis: A Vision for the Next Century,* trans. Kozo Yamamura. Stanford, Calif.: Stanford University Press, 1996.

Nomura Masami. *Koyō fuan.* Tokyo: Iwanami Shoten, 1998.

Okazaki Tetsuji and Okuno Masahiro, eds. *Gendai nihon keizai shisutemu no genryū.* Tokyo: Nihon Keizai Shibunsha, 1993.

Ōkurashō. *Shōwa zaiseishi.* Tokyo: Tōyō Keizai Shinpōsha, 1991.

Pempel, T. J. *Regime Shift: Comparative Dynamics of the Japanese Political Economy.* Ithaca, NY: Cornell University Press, 1998.

Samuels, Richard. *The Business of the Japanese State: Energy Markets in Comparative and Historical Perspective.* Ithaca, NY: Cornell University Press, 1987.

Samuels, Richard. *"Rich Nation, Strong Army": National Security and the Technological Transformation of Japan.* Ithaca, NY: Cornell University Press, 1994.

Thelen, Kathleen, and Kume Ikuo. "The Future of National Embedded Capitalism." In Kozo Yamamura and Wolfgang Streeck, eds., *The End of Diversity? Prospects for German and Japanese Capitalism.* Ithaca, NY: Cornell University Press, 2003.

Tilton, Mark. *Restricted Trade: Cartels in Japan's Basic Materials Industries*. Ithaca, NY: Cornell University Press, 1996.

Uriu, Robert. *Troubled Industries: Confronting Economic Change in Japan*. Ithaca, NY: Cornell University Press, 1996.

Vogel, Steven. *Freer Markets, More Rules*. Ithaca, NY: Cornell University Press, 1996.

Yamamura, Kozo. "Germany and Japan in a New Phase of Capitalism." In Kozo Yamamura and Wolfgang Streeck, eds., *The End of Diversity? Prospects for German and Japanese Capitalism*. Ithaca, NY: Cornell University Press, 2003.

Zysman, John. *Governments, Markets, and Growth*. Ithaca, NY: Cornell University Press, 1983.

FURTHER READING

For an overview of the postwar Japanese economy and the Japanese debates over economic policy issues, see Bai Gao's *Economic Ideology and Japanese Industrial Policy* (New York: Cambridge University Press, 1997). For an overview of the institutional configuration of the Japanese economic system and its postwar evolution up to the end of the 1990s, see Bai Gao's *Japan's Economic Dilemma* (New York: Cambridge University Press, 2001) and T. J. Pempel's *Regime Shift* (Ithaca, NY: Cornell University Press, 1998). Readers can also find useful data in Richard Katz's *Japan: The System that Soured* (Armonk, NY: M. E. Sharpe, 1998). For an overview of the Japanese economy published in Japanese, the two companion volumes of *Shōwa keizaishi*, the first volume edited by Arisawa Hiromi (Tokyo: Nihon Keizai Shinbunsha, 1976), and the second volume coauthored by Mitsuhashi Tadahiro and Uchida Shigeo (Tokyo: Nihon Keizai Shinbunsha, 1994), are highly recommended. Chalmers Johnson's *MITI and the Japanese Miracle* (Stanford, Calif.: Stanford University Press, 1982) is the classic study of Japanese industrial policy. For the debate on Japanese industrial policy, Richard Samuels's *The Business of the Japanese State* (Ithaca, NY: Cornell University Press, 1987) and Kent Calder's *Crisis and Compensation* (Princeton: Princeton University Press, 1998) are important contributions. Murakami Yasusuke's *An Anticlassical Political-Economic Analysis* (Stanford, Calif.: Stanford University Press, 1996) provides a theoretical interpretation of Japanese developmentalism. On the debate over the "1940 system," see Okazaki Tetsuji and Okuno Masahiro, eds., *Gendai nihon keizai shisutemu no genryū* (Tokyo: Nihon Keizai Shinbunsha, 1993).

CHAPTER EIGHTEEN

Postwar Society and Culture

Wesley Sasaki-Uemura

During the postwar period, various segments of Japanese society sought to redefine their culture against constantly shifting political and economic contexts. While the structures and cultural attributes of societies are often described in relatively static terms, this essay focuses on the postwar shifts in demographics, the effects these shifts have had on the composition of communities and social movements, and the changes that migrations and social transformations have had on the Japanese sense of identity.

We should also note that the postwar period has extended till it is now longer than the Meiji and Taishō eras combined and that Japanese society has undergone tremendous transformations during this time. Yet the Japanese still continue to place themselves, perhaps anachronistically, within the postwar framework despite the government's proclamation in its 1955 Economic White Paper that the era had passed. The statement that "it was no longer the postwar" (*mohaya sengo de wa nai*) referred specifically to surpassing the highest levels of production in the prewar–wartime period. But the economic prosperity that followed was linked in the public's memory to the foundational narrative of 1945 in which the country was reborn and inexorably bound to its former enemy, the United States.[1] Concentrating on this bilateral relation has meant that the state offered no final and satisfactory settling of accounts from the war, resolving the issues of Japan's colonization of and aggression toward the rest of Asia in particular, and these ghosts still haunt Japan's postmodern, post-Fordist, globalized consumer society.

Since the narrative threads of postwar social and cultural trends do not conform well to imperial chronologies or neat demarcation according to decades, I suggest an alternate scheme of periodization. To set the broad political and economic contexts for this discussion of society and culture, I have loosely divided the postwar era into three periods, keeping in mind that different topics follow different timelines.

The first period was one of recovery from the war and socioeconomic expansion from 1945 to the early 1970s. Japan had to deal with exhaustion from the war effort[2] and revamp its political and social infrastructure. The official system of value bound up in the body politic or national essence (*kokutai*) was supplanted by the exploration of carnality (*nikutai*) and existentialism. The long American-led occupation both constitutionally empowered previously suppressed social elements and firmly committed Japan to the Western bloc in the developing cold war. The Korean War

(1950–3) spurred industrial retooling with US procurement orders and hastened the end to the occupation in exchange for a mutual security agreement that placed Japan under US military hegemony.

In 1955, significant new political formations set the stage for political confrontation that peaked in 1960. The socialist parties merged and in response the conservative prewar Liberal and Democratic parties joined together to secure a majority of legislative seats and create the one-and-a-half-party system that dominated politics until the 1990s. The Liberal Democratic Party (LDP) made high profile efforts to undo occupation-era reforms and met with enormous resistance in the protests against the renewal of the US–Japan Security Treaty (Anpo) and the labor strike at the Miike coal mines in Kyūshū, both in 1960. As a result, the LDP got rid of its party head and focused its rhetoric on improving the economy through a highly successful "income-doubling" plan. The construction boom around the 1964 Tokyo Olympics, including the Bullet Train (*Shinkansen*), were emblematic of Japan's modernization that was celebrated in Expo '70 in Osaka. At the same time, Japan's involvement in the Vietnam War and the environmental problems that developed from its industrialization again sparked strong opposition and protest.

A new stage of affluence and tighter centralized control began from the early 1970s to the mid-1980s. The first "oil shock" of 1973 and the preceding "Nixon shocks" reinforced a sense of fragility regarding Japan's position in the world. By the early 1970s, US concern about a growing the trade deficit with Japan and other nations prompted President Richard Nixon to unilaterally end fixed currency exchange rates, making Japanese goods more expensive. Politically, he began rapprochement with China without consulting or advising Japan, which the government took as an affront to its political stature. These shocks prompted the government to engage in new contingency planning and administrative restructuring as it pushed major state projects such as the new Tokyo airport at Sanrizuka.[3] The 1973 oil shock, as well as the growing number of residents' movements against environmental pollution, prompted the state and big business to turn towards high-tech and tertiary (service sector) industry and to start moving heavy and chemical industries offshore.[4] The intimate ties between government and big business were evident in the political scandals that forced Prime Minister Tanaka Kakuei from office, although he continued to be the king-maker behind the scenes for the next several administrations.[5] The perception of illegitimate advantages from government–corporate ties and a growing trade deficit exacerbated trade frictions with the United States and Japan-bashing mounted in the 1980s. Japanese conservatives grew more defensive and countered with their own rhetoric of superior cultural traits (*Nihonjinron*, that is, who we are as Japanese), but the Japanese government also accommodated some US demands. When Nakasone Yasuhiro became prime minister in 1982, he began efforts to privatize state-run enterprises and to revise the constitution and remilitarize Japan. It was in this context that plans for a "managed society" (*kanri shakai*) were revised.

A third phase of postwar history started from the latter half of the 1980s in which the "bubble economy" took off and the slogan of "internationalization" (*kokusaika*) was touted. During this period, the Japanese state sought to revise its role on the world stage, both economically and militarily. The call for a general settling of accounts from World War II was to pave the way for Japan's new role, although the second history textbook controversy in 1986 indicated that the thrust of this effort was to erase elements of a "regrettable" past from official memory.[6] When Hirohito, the emperor whose reign spanned wartime and postwar Japan, died in 1989, neither the state nor the emperor had yet uttered a clear public apology to other Asian countries for colonial rule and wartime aggression. Japan's participation in the Gulf War in 1991 was another occasion when the LDP attempted to expand Japan's military. Malfeasance scandals plagued the ruling LDP from 1989, and in 1993 the party finally lost its legislative majority and had to form a coalition government. By this time the bubble had burst and Japan entered a prolonged recession. Compounding those problems, the 1995 Kobe earthquake and the religious cult Aum Shinrikyō's Sarin gas attack on the Tokyo subway system showed the persistence of problems in Japan's infrastructure and the government's inability to respond to emergencies. Japan's energy dependence on the Middle East has compelled it once again to become involved in US military efforts there, but in the 1990s, the slogan of "internationalization" meant that Japan both continued economic expansion abroad and also internalized foreign elements in ways it had not anticipated.

Shifting Population

The demographic profile of Japan's postwar society has changed dramatically. The population has grown by over 50 million since the end of World War II when there were 72 million Japanese.[7] The population is expected to have peaked at around 128 million in 2005 and Japan's population density has exceeded 330 persons per square kilometer for the past decade. This figure is over 100 persons per square kilometer more than in 1950. Moreover, if one considers only the amount of habitable land in these calculations, the concentration of people nearly quintuples.

Demographers were already speaking of Japan's overpopulation crisis in the 1930s, so in the immediate postwar years the government was concerned that the country would be unable to support a baby boom. Therefore, they passed a Eugenics Law in 1949 that allowed for abortion based on economic necessity and engaged in a campaign to reduce fertility. As a result, Japan's fertility rate dropped from 4.5 children per woman in 1947 to 2.0 by 1960. The rate hovered around the replacement level (2.1) during the 1970s, dipping to 1.75 by 1980 and dropping a tenth each decade afterwards. Thus, Japan's population will drop to roughly 100 million by 2050 according to current United Nations projections.

The dramatic rise and fall of the postwar population is accompanied by a major shift in its age composition. Life expectancy has risen by nearly thirty years since the end of World War II. In 1947, it was 50 for men and 54 for women. By 1960 this figure had risen to over 65 for men and over 70 for women and it steadily increased so that by 2000 it was nearly 78 for men and 84.6 for women.[8] One reason for the increase in life expectancy was the precipitous drop in infant mortality from a high of 77 per 1,000 live births in 1945 to 3.3 in 2002, the lowest in the world.[9] Maternal mortality, moreover, is now virtually nil. Public health education, a system of national health insurance, and the dissemination of modern medicine were part of concerted efforts by the government and private organizations to improve pre- and post-natal care. One effect of these efforts has been an amazing reversal in attitudes about where one ought to give birth. In 1950, nearly everyone gave birth at home, but by 1960 only half of Japanese mothers delivered at home and since about 1975 almost everyone has given birth in institutional settings.

The population pyramid at the end of the war in fact looked like a pyramid, but as life expectancy continued to rise and the birth rate dropped, the base of those aged 14 and younger has shrunk, while the percentage of working-aged persons (defined as ages 15–64) has bulged. The number of elderly persons (65 and over) has more than doubled in the last two decades and by the year 2000 was greater than the number of youths. The percentage of the elderly is expected to rise to nearly 27 percent of the total population by 2025 and to over one-third by 2050. This would make Japan the "oldest" industrialized nation within two decades.

The shift in Japan's age composition has generated considerable debate about the problems of its "graying" society, with some experts making dire predictions about the country's ability to take care of its elderly, provide adequate pensions and health care, and maintain the economy as the proportion of younger workers shrinks. In the early 1970s, Ariyoshi Sawako's novel, *The Twilight Years* (*Kōkotsu no hito*), brought to light how the task of caring for the elderly basically fell to the wife given the attitudes about family gender roles, the gendered structure of employment, and the paucity of public care facilities at that time. Improvements, however, have been slow to come.

The aggregate figures for household composition in the postwar period indicate some important trends in Japan's population shifts. The nuclearization of households is an oft-noted trend but the total percentage of nuclear households has held at around 60 percent since 1955, varying by only a few percentage points.[10] Within this category, however, the percentage of households having only a married couple has nearly doubled since 1970 from 11 percent to around 20 percent while that for married couples with children has fallen by slightly more than 10 percent in the same period to 32.8 percent in 2000. The percentage of three-generation households has fallen by a comparable proportion. Meanwhile, single-person households have swelled to roughly one-quarter of the total in 2000. The rise in the percentage of households consisting of only a married couple is one indicator of Japan's aging society. Nearly 14 percent of all households are composed of only elderly people and this points to the problem of depopulation in rural areas, where the number of households has remained relatively constant due to farm landholding but the children have left for urban areas. The rise in longevity means that the elderly continue to occupy these households at least until the death of one spouse.

Households with married persons have also started later than in the early postwar period. From the 1950s into the early 1970s, the mean age at first marriage has held relatively steady at about 27 for men and 24 for women, but by 1980 the respective means had risen to 27.8 and 25.2. In the year 2000 it was 28.8 for men and 27 for women. Since Japan tends toward patterns of an age-grade society, a preponderance of people do the same things at the same stage in life. Thus, the mean age at first marriage is more a typical situation than an average of a broad statistical range. Up to the 1990s, a popular riddle asked why women were like Christmas cakes. The answer was that up until Christmas day, Christmas cakes are highly sought commodities but quickly lose their value afterwards. Similarly, women up to age 25 were highly sought on the marriage market, but after that age had difficulties finding partners.[11] But more and more women have chosen to delay the life-stage of marriage and the joke has now lost its relevance. Women more than men are delaying marriage in part because many more are continuing their education and they have fewer socioeconomic incentives to get married. Also, fewer couples get together via arranged marriages (*miai kekkon*).

The rise in age at first marriage is a key factor in Japan's declining fertility. The average number of childbearing years has become much more constricted since 1950, with the greatest concentration of births by far being between the ages of 25 and 35. A couple's first child is generally born within a few years of marriage and child bearing usually ends another few years hence. The campaigns to reduce fertility and the precipitous drop in infant mortality, together with rising economic prosperity, resulted in families controlling their fertility and investing more of the household income in their children. Initially, control of fertility was achieved primarily through use of induced abortion and abortion prevalence rates shot up from below 15 percent in 1950 to nearly 50 percent by 1955. However, abortions fell back quickly to about half that figure over the next decade, gradually declining to about 10 percent by 1995. On the other hand, contraception practices have risen from below 20 percent in 1950 to over 50 percent by 1965, fluctuating between 50 to 60 percent up to the present.[12] In the case of Japan, the condom has been the primary method of contraception, with 78 percent of those who practice contraception continuing to use this method even in 1998. A combined total of 4 percent used the pill or IUD.[13] The Japanese government in fact approved the sale of the pill only in June 1999. Notions of family gender roles and male dominance of the medical profession have prevented women from controlling their own fertility.[14]

In theory, gender roles are thought of in terms of "complementary incompetencies,"[15] although in practice they are not symmetric and equal. Productive labor is seen as a social, public sphere activity while reproductive work is considered internal, domestic, and private. Men are thought to be competent in the former sphere but incompetent in the latter and vice versa for women. As a consequence, women are expected to manage the home, handle day-to-day finances, and oversee the raising of children and their education. With heavier and heavier investments in children's education in the 1970s and 1980s, the stereotype of the "education mama" (*kyōiku mama*) arose, who devoted herself to providing optimal conditions for their child's educational success. Mothers often had to find part-time work to get the money for supplies, tutors, and cram schools.

On the other hand, businesses continue to follow a gendered structure of employment in which women's labor is considered supplemental to the household income. Companies rarely hire women for full-time permanent positions, despite the passage of the Equal Employment Opportunities Act of 1985. Women are typically hired as "office ladies" whose jobs do not grow or expand over time, or as part-time workers without the various benefits of full-time workers. During the high growth era in particular, companies expected men to give first priority to their jobs rather than their families, assuming that their wives would handle domestic matters. By the late 1970s, salarymen were almost obliged to socialize with co-workers every night, creating the image of the absentee father who returns home after the children have gone to bed and leaves for his morning commute before they wake up, seeing them only on Sunday. Salarymen could also be reassigned to another city for an extended period with the resulting commuter marriage reinforcing the gender separation between residence and work. Since middle-class life often requires more income than the husband alone can provide, his wife is compelled to work, usually re-entering the workforce once the children are older and going to school and *juku* (cram schools). The double burden of taking care of the home and working outside it means that most women look for jobs with flexible hours, often choosing part-time work.[16] Eventually, caring for one's in-laws may force them to exit the labor force once again since over half of the elderly live with their children.

The divorce rate is comparatively low in Japan but it has doubled since 1975 from 1.07 percent to 2.1 percent. Economic factors militate against youthful divorce given the gendered structure of employment. The social stigma one suffers from a court case and the absence of mechanisms to ensure alimony payments also prevent women from divorcing their husbands. Divorced women have difficulty getting mortgages or even credit cards. Despite these problems, in the past few years middle-aged divorce has taken off, when responsibilities for the children have lessened and the economic impact of divorce has been reduced. In the 1990s, retired husbands were likened to *sodai gomi*, the oversized garbage that requires special pick-up, for always sitting around the home without helping out.

Another recent media topic has been "parasite singles," a phrase coined by Tokyo Gakugei University sociologist Yamada Masahiro in 1997. He defined these as men and women in their 20s and early 30s who live off their parents even if they have a job, and he blamed them in part for falling birthrates, the continuing recession, and a general lack of civic concern. The tendency in the press has been to focus more on women, in part because young single women with disposable incomes have been the targets of advertising and consumer products. However, the current recession has meant that companies make fewer new hires and the unemployment rate for young men has risen to about 10 percent. Women for their part realize that few of them will get hired as regular, permanent employees, and that they will be forced out of the labor market when they get married or give birth. Should they re-enter the workforce later on, they will typically make less than they did when they were single.

Shifting Communities

Shifts in the location of Japan's postwar population show its process of urbanization and the centralization of economic structures. Mass migration from the countryside to the cities in the early postwar raised the percentage of Japanese living in urban areas from one-third of the population in 1950 to two-thirds by 1965 and three-quarters by 1975. By far the heaviest in-migration took place in three places – metropolitan Tokyo, the Nagoya region, and the Osaka–Kobe area. Over half of the nation's population lived in these three urban areas by the mid-1980s, and while the rate of in-migration has dropped considerably since 1975, these three areas have more than compensated for any U-turn or J-turn out-migration back to the countryside or the suburbs.

While central Tokyo had been heavily destroyed during the war, it was rebuilt along established patterns because it retained its role as the center of government and business. Its population grew by more than 3 million to over 10 million by 1960. The central wards of the city became saturated by the mid-1960s, and when the ring of surrounding suburbs became saturated in the 1970s, the population of further outlying prefectures grew.[17]

The early postwar urban and suburban growth from migration represented the rise of the middle class in postwar Japan. That is, people who migrated to Tokyo were not primarily factory workers. Postwar heavy industry was built up in more peripheral areas, especially in coastal towns and along waterways to facilitate transportation and waste disposal. Factories were often combined with refineries and related facilities in massive integrated complexes known as *kombinato*. Those with jobs downtown were more typically office workers, those engaged in commerce, and those in light industry related to services such as publishing. The residential outlying suburbs and even more distant bedroom towns were therefore closer to the polluting factories than the central offices downtown. This geographic feature would be important to the composition of residents' movements in the later 1960s and 1970s.

From the mid-1950s, large public housing projects known as *danchi* sprang up in the metropolitan areas, although at the time they were sites of future dreams rather than mature communities, often lacking even grocery stores. They became middle-class enclaves that represented the beginnings of consumer culture and the "bright life" (*akarui seikatsu*) that it was supposed to bring.[18] On the other hand, the *danchi* were also emblematic of the problem of overcrowding in the cities and the difficulty of forging an identity in mass society. Two decades later, a European Economic Community report would still refer to urban Japanese living arrangements as "rabbit hutches."[19] As urban density increased, real estate became overvalued, making it more difficult to afford the closer one got to the city center. People had to choose between longer commutes to work in the city or more expensive housing.

Domestic consumer demand drove Japan's economic growth in the postwar period[20] and the desire for modern labor saving devices for the home and the trappings of middle-class life was crucial. Advertisers in the late 1950s and early 1960s promoted the "Three Imperial Treasures" – not the imperial regalia of sword, mirror, and jewel but rather the refrigerator, washing machine, and TV. Another advertising slogan of the day, the "three Cs," changed from cash, car, and camera to cars, color TV, and coolers (air conditioners) by the late 1960s. The speed with which it became possible for the majority of people actually to purchase such goods rather than just dream about them was breathtaking. The 1960 plan that Prime Minister Ikeda Hayato announced to double people's income within a decade actually succeeded years before its target date (when measured by per capita GDP).

Japan sustained its rapid economic growth by constantly refining and expanding consumer desire. The diffusion rates for TV, for example, rose rapidly in the early 1960s. Only 5 percent of Japanese households had a television set in 1957, but by 1960, a third of them had one and three years later almost 75 percent had a set. By the 1970s, the black-and-white TV market had become saturated, so manufacturers created renewed demand by pushing color television and by 1980 nearly every household had one. This then was followed by video cassette recorder diffusion and more recently by high definition and satellite dish TV.

The diffusion of television in society also shows the transition in key postwar mass media. In the decade after the war, newspapers, radio, and movies were the key media for information, advertising, and mass culture. Newspapers continued to be important, but TV came to supplant radio. In the early 1960s, weekly magazines (*shūūkanshi*) appeared, many of them begun by newspaper companies. Their format covered news items but also presented columns, serialized novels, photo essays, and cultural features to generate broad appeal. Such weeklies continue to the present, but the medium has survived and grown by specializing its content for particular niche markets. In the mid-1970s, FM radio became an important alternative platform for music and tied in with audio cassette players like Sony's Walkman. With the miniaturization of electronic technology and the privatization of the state-run telephone company, cell phones may be the key medium today in Japan, being much more ubiquitous than computers and used far more frequently for text messaging, e-mail, and web access than in the West.

In contrast to these mass forms of communications, citizens' and residents' movements developed their own mini-communications (*mini-komi*) to allow for greater individual expression and debate. Their small-scale publications reflected the movements' emphasis on local autonomy, democratic decision-making, and loose organizational structures in contrast to the 1950s paradigm of Marxist ideology-driven, class-based proletarian movements. As social movements formed in the 1960s and 1970s, especially around issues such as environmental pollution, they used their *mini-komi* to question the direction of Japan's modernization and forge connections with like-minded groups. These movements had specific goals related to their place of residence, whether blocking polluting *kombinato*, seeking redress for the effects of pollution, or protecting and preserving the local environment. Since the movements centered on residential areas, women were more likely to join them due to their association with the domestic sphere. Thus, *mini-komi* often reflected women's concerns and style of writing. At their peak in the 1970s and 1980s, *mini-komi* exchanges linked an extremely diverse network of groups including those concerned with organic food production, alternative lifestyles and communes, arts, women's issues, disabled persons, minority rights, problems in education, peace, and nuclear power generation.

These social movements often gained impetus from the student activism of the late 1960s. The educational system expanded rapidly in the 1950s and university graduates, especially from Japan's top schools, were highly sought by the government bureaucracy and big business. However, students began to question the form of education they were getting and the social costs of Japan's increasing affluence. They were a key element in the Anpo and Miike protests, and students again took the lead when protests broke out in the mid-1960s over Japan's involvement in the Vietnam War. By the late 1960s, campus revolts were ubiquitous, breaking down into two main types. At places like Nihon University, the unrest was sparked by the mass production, assembly line education that students received, while the protests at more elite institutions like Tokyo University were more self-critical about students' possible complicity in the severely flawed social system. Many student activists carried their concerns over to social movements after they graduated.[21]

As society became more affluent in the 1970s, parents invested more income in their children's education and more students advanced to university. Primary and secondary education was organized around the entrance exams to universities and the curriculum tended to standardize knowledge and emphasize rote memorization based on the notion that questions admitted of only one answer. Students who did not display enough potential were guided toward alternate tracks such as vocational-technical schools or junior colleges. In 1975, over 90 percent of Japanese children were gradu-ating from high school; 40 percent of men went on to universities, while 20 percent of women went to junior college and 12.5 percent to universities. Increased competition to gain entrance to good schools and ultimately good universities gave rise to cram schools (*juku* for high school entrance exams, *yobiko* for the universities). By the 1980s, the top-down structure, hierarchic mode of relations, and in-group dynamics of competition led on the one hand to the problem of bullying (*ijime*) in schools, and on the other to children who refused to go to school. The 1983 movie *Family Game* (*Kazoku gēmu*) brilliantly satirized the educational situation by showing the exploits of a private tutor for the child of a middle-class family.

Now, 97 percent of Japanese children graduate from high school. Nearly half of the men go on to universities and a comparable percentage of women go to either junior college (15 percent) or universities (33.8 percent). However, negative population growth has meant that universities have had to restructure themselves to attract dwindling numbers of students. While the top public and private universities still get more applications than their available slots, smaller colleges have had a much more difficult time competing for students to maintain their enrollments and have had to specialize in projected areas of interest and become increasingly production oriented. Universities promote popular courses and teachers and tend toward niche marketing to draw students, including housewife and international tracks.

In survey after survey since the 1970s, the Japanese have overwhelmingly identified themselves as middle class with consistently upwards of 90 percent of those polled claiming this identification. While the gap between rich and poor in Japan is consid-erably smaller than in America, the surveys do not reflect actual income or mean that relationships at work, school, or home are egalitarian. Rather, they show that inter-viewees did not want to be perceived publicly as either rich or poor. The claim of socioeconomic homogeneity in fact masks sharp status competition based sometimes on rather fine distinctions.

Such status competition has helped create consumer demand, and patterns of consumption have been major elements in defining one's identity as reflected in "my car" and "my home"-isms. While the mass production of consumer items means that buyers get essentially the same product, minor variations in features allow consumers to feel that their buying choices exhibit a degree of individuality. Niche marketing has become a key sales strategy and products from electronics to clothes to housewares have a wide range of minor variations so that consumers can find the perfect item to match their lifestyles. The mania for brand-name products also displays the same psychology, as illustrated in Tanaka Yasuo's 1981 "novel" *Nantonaku, kurisutaru* (Somehow, Crystal). Ostensibly a romance, the book became famous for listing a nearly inexhaustible string of brand-name products and trendy shopping areas that defined the characters and their actions. Here it is the choice of particular products that defines one's individuality. Activities as well as goods began to define consumption in the 1970s and the travel and tourism industries boomed. Taking overseas vacations (and buying the appropriate brand-name products) or domestic trips to a villa, hot springs, or ski lodge became elements of status compe-tition and of the definition of one's individual character.

Books and other cultural items are themselves important consumer products. The authors Murakami Haruki and Yoshimoto Banana have sold tens of millions of books and Yoshimoto in fact identifies herself with mass literature and commercial writing rather than "serious" literature. Each of them sells heavily to particular segments of the market. Murakami's works appeal overwhelmingly to men and novels such as *Norwegian Wood* evoke nostalgia for the 1970s generation of college students. Yoshimoto's market is young women in their teens and twenties and her books feature such women in atypical social situations. The rapidity with which writers have to turn out new works, however, means that their novels essentially become disposable products that quickly find their way to used bookstores. The accelerated cycle of disposable cultural consumption applies to television, film, comics, music, fashion, and other artistic ventures.

Production companies and associated businesses are essential to maintaining a constant flow of cultural commodities and culture industries created a further centripetal pull into the metropolitan centers. Stores, designer workshops, and venues for display are concentrated in a few urban spots. Art galleries, the art establishment, and relevant media are also concentrated in metropolitan areas. Musicians come to the city because the recording, radio, and TV studios are headquartered there, as well as print media and production companies.

By the 1980s, a new postwar generation was growing up in affluence without the experience of privation or the sense of political and social fragility that the wartime and early postwar generations felt. Social critics pejoratively applied the term "new humans" (*shinjinrui*) to indicate the social value the younger generation placed on materialism and their spoiled overindulgence that manifested itself in an unwillingness to work at any job that they considered "dirty, dangerous, and dull."[22] However, coming of age at a time when people were acutely aware that the economic bubble would soon burst has also meant that this generation often envisions a dystopic future. From the 1970s, the government promoted a utopian vision of an information society (*jōhō shakai*) in which the management and control of information was the key to actuating a (well-)"managed society." The post-oil-shock transition of the economy and its high-tech emphasis further emphasized the control of information. However, popular science fiction comics (manga) and animation (anime) commonly evoke a near future in which powerful technology and autocratic control of information combine to create the return of a fascistic society, as seen in the famous 1980s manga, *Akira*.

Another effect of the bubble economy was overvalued real estate and speculative investment and these factors led to the problem of landsharking (*jiage*). Urban land prices kept rising to the point that developers for new offices or other projects would employ gangsters to "encourage" small landowners and longstanding tenants (who have residence rights against eviction) to accept buy-out offers and leave. When the housing market fell, those projects were often underutilized and the former urban dwellers now had high payments on inconveniently distant housing.

The 1995 Kobe earthquake revealed more strains to the social infrastructure as the government found it difficult to aid survivors and speed reconstruction. The government's slow response spurred the push for revisions to the law governing NPOs (nonprofit organizations) to ease requirements for registration and enhance tax incentives. With the passage of the new 1998 law, the number of NPOs shot up by 10,000. However, this proliferation does not necessarily signal the growth of civil society and democracy. Given the motivation of tax breaks in exchange for official recognition and regulation, and the non-political character that NPOs are required to maintain, the significance of their proliferation is ambiguous.

While urban sprawl grew steadily in the postwar, rural areas continue to be depopulated and now only 5 percent of the population is engaged in primary industries of farming, fishing, and forestry compared to 48.5 percent in 1950.[23] Farm households often have to rely on non-agricultural income to survive. As young men left the rural areas in the 1950s and 1960s, farmers had to mechanize, increase their use of pesticides and herbicides, and generally standardize their patterns of work to accommodate more capital-intensive modes of farming. Farm households survived and prospered through a combination of farm subsidies, cash cropping, and non-agricultural income. The poorest rural areas such as Tōhoku saw many rural males migrate to urban areas in the off-season to supply the day labor market or to work in factories, getting caught in a vicious cycle of payments that created the urban homeless. Those sons who decided to carry on the family farm found it increasingly difficult to secure wives. Conservative farm life and its hard work have become increasingly less attractive to young women and in the late 1990s some farmers have "imported" Filipino wives.

While rural areas suffered depopulation and were often cast as unsophisticated and backward, a nostalgic "home village boom" (*furosato būmu*) developed in the 1960s and 1970s that idealized the countryside and its traditional values and communal forms.[24] Longing for the *furosato* can be seen in the popularity of the movie series, "It's Tough to be a Man" (*Otoko wa tsurai yo*), which ran from 1969 to 1996. The films feature an itinerant peddler named Tora-san who travels around the countryside trying to get rich quick. His always unrequited love for local women and his eventual return to his sister's home in a traditional urban neighborhood symbolize what Japan left behind in achieving prosperity. Nostalgia for *furosato* values has also been invoked periodically in *Nihonjinron* terms. During the harvest shortfalls in the early 1990s, many in Japan reacted to American pressure to buy its cheaper rice by saying that American rice lacked the particular local conditions and farm community's care that make Japanese rice delicious. The popular comic about cooking *Oishimbo* ran a special series on the "U.S.–Japan Rice Wars" that illustrated these points.

Rural economic problems due to the postwar demographic shift led to various campaigns in the late 1980s and 1990s to revitalize the countryside such as "village revival" (*mura okoshi*) and "hometown creation plans" (*furusato sōseiron*). These initiatives boiled down to finding ways to market rural tradition and social culture, even recreating old-style hamlets as tourist attractions like Shirakawago in Gifu prefecture. The village of Tōno is another example of the attempt to sell the "traditional" culture that ethnologist Yanagita Kunio set down in 1910 in his popular *Tōno monogatari* (Tales of Tōno), fearing that the stories and belief systems they represented would be lost. But in order to market performances of these tales today, Tōno villagers had to be tutored by outside professionals, belying the oral transmission of tradition. The hollowing out of the countryside has contributed to the attenuation of social relations that constituted traditional villages and has led to a drastic graying of that population. Revitalization campaigns have not proven very successful in reviving rural economies or in repopulating those areas. The few who do move from the cities out to the countryside often do not stay there permanently. The "traditional" countryside is not an alternative lifestyle to modern urban life because rural Japan has also had to modernize to survive.

Shifting Identities

Changes in Japan's population and communities have brought significant shifts in thinking about cultural identity in the postwar period. Prewar textbooks presented idealized pictures of village life in which family and community relations were analogies for imperial subjecthood writ small. But with the defeat in World War II, the Japanese were no longer officially defined by their relationship to the emperor, although he survived constitutionally as "the symbol of the State and the unity of the people."[25] The Japanese increasingly saw themselves as thoroughly urban, modern, and by implication international.

Postwar modernity did not, however, translate into cultural convergence with the West despite the influence of the occupation and ties to the Western bloc. Japan's economic success instead led to sharp competition with America and Japan-bashing rhetoric that implied Japan's "unfair practices" derived from premodern remnants in social behavior. One response was to assert that Japan's ethnic homogeneity, essential cultural uniqueness, and group orientation made it better equipped to succeed as a modern nation. The resurgence of this discourse of cultural nationalism, known as *Nihonjinron*, was set in binary opposition to "the West" and served a conservative political agenda that in fact exhibited considerable anxiety over the stability of Japanese identity under rapidly changing social conditions.[26]

Citizen protests and social movements showed that ordinary people did not always share the establishment's idea of what constituted a modern, urban subjectivity. Participants in these movements generally advocated principles of open debate over mass conformity, local autonomy over obedience to the authority, and minority rights over cultural homogeneity. Alternative lifestyle movements questioned the modes of production and consumption that became prevalent during the period of rapid economic growth and they sought to refashion the image of Japanese as economic animals. Middle-class conformity has undoubtedly been overstated as the defining characteristic of Japanese identity today; dissatisfaction with and alienation from society are also widespread.

The postwar proliferation of new religions is one indication of social displacement and alienation. Typically adherents joined these new religions to cope with life's hardships, economic disadvantage, frustrated ambitions, and social discrimination. Some of these religions aim at social reintegration or success through their group, while others try to create alternate economies and self-contained communities. Some view Japan's technological progress as vapid and aimless and seek to give it spirituality and purpose. In the extreme case of the Aum Shinrikyō cult, it recruited those with science backgrounds who were disenchanted with technology to provide it with the means to initiate the apocalypse.[27]

However, the key groups in considering the question of exclusion or alienation from Japanese society are its minorities, such as Ainu, *burakumin*, Okinawans, and Korean and Taiwanese residents. Each come from different historical circumstances and raise different issues with regard to Japanese identity. The Ainu are an indigenous group now largely confined to the northern region of Hokkaidō. The *burakumin* are ethnically Japanese but have a long history of being ostracized from regular society and ghettoized by their associations with ritual "impurity" and irregular occupations. The history and culture of Okinawans place them between China and Japan, but in the Meiji period they were among the first colonials. The Koreans and Taiwanese were victims of Japan's imperialist expansion. While minorities comprise a small percentage of the population in Japan, their status contradicts the equivalences that the postwar state has made between nation, ethnicity, and culture.

Postwar Japanese law strictly defined citizenship according to ethnicity and until the 1990s required cultural conformity, such as adopting Japanese names, in order to naturalize. As Oguma Eiji has pointed out, however, the prewar empire was in principle multi-ethnic and therefore inclusive, so claims of Japan having always been a homogenous society are recent inventions.[28] The vociferousness with which the postwar state has upheld legal and social discrimination against these minorities is due in part to the racial indistinguishability and intermingling of "foreign" and "native."

A crucial legal instrument for excluding people from the postwar nation's closed circle of blood has been the family register system, which until the early 1990s determined citizenship according to paternity. After the defeat, those Korean and Taiwanese who did not repatriate were eventually classified as foreigners by the Japanese government. For second, third, and fourth generation residents, this has meant that they will always be "foreigners" and excluded from the rights and welfare that Japanese citizens receive, while nevertheless being forced to adapt to and adopt Japanese culture. They have been forced to regularly renew their alien registrations, complete with fingerprinting, which creates a sense of being criminalized for their birth, a sense reinforced by the social discrimination they also suffer. The discriminatory treatment of Koreans began to be featured in the media from the mid- to late 1960s as citizens drew analogies to controls they would face in the government's "managed society" and as they questioned Japan's participation in the Vietnam War.[29] By the mid-1980s, many Korean residents whose alien registration cards were coming up for renewal decided to protest this discrimination by refusing to submit to fingerprinting and mounting court challenges to the system.

At the same time, Korean and other non-Japanese entertainers and sports figures were being celebrated in Japanese culture. The quintessential Japanese baseball hero, Sadaharu Oh, was Taiwanese. *Enka*, supposedly the most "Japanese" form of modern popular music, borrowed much from Korea and arguably has Korean origins.[30] Many popular singers and movie stars were ethnic Koreans or Taiwanese "passing" as Japanese. The current popularity of author Yū Miri, a second generation Korean resident in Japan, seems to be due to her in-between state as an internalized "foreign" element and her articulation of alienation and ostracism.[31] This type of internalized foreignness in Japanese cultural identity belies the claims of cultural homogeneity and uniqueness in *Nihonjinron*.

As Japanese economic expansion overseas took managers and salarymen's families overseas, the obverse case of "foreign" residents was created, that of "returnees" (*kikokushijo*), or children with extended living experience and education overseas. Although born and raised partly in Japan, the government still considered returnees insufficiently Japanese in culture and education and in need of remedial training. Returnees also suffered some discrimination for being "strange" but were also sometimes envied for being more international. From the late 1980s several of these returnees became radio and TV media figures, acting as a bridge between their Japanese audience and foreign experiences.

Japan's investment in Asia, its dependence on international trade, and the recent import of foreign labor have forced the Japanese to acknowledge that their economic survival increasingly depends on understanding their nation as multi-ethnic. This was not how the government envisioned "internationalization" in the 1980s when it was more concerned with fostering acceptance of Japanese business and culture overseas than with making the Japanese people more cosmopolitan. While *kokusaika* highlighted relations with the West, dealings with Asia and the non-West have arguably had a more significant impact, although the specter of World War II looms behind Japan's attempts to assert hegemony in its relationships with other Asian peoples.[32]

Economic penetration of East and Southeast Asia in the 1970s and 1980s raised fears that Japan was trying to revive the wartime Greater East Asia Co-Prosperity Sphere. Japanese businessmen on sex tours to the Philippines, Thailand, and other countries symbolized renewed aggression, this time in business suits rather than military uniforms. A subtext to the problem of Japanese sex tours was the issue of wartime "comfort women." These women, some 80 percent of whom were Korean, were held in a system of military slavery that Japan instituted during the China and Pacific Wars. While women's groups began raising the issue in the late 1980s, the Japanese government has consistently refused to admit the existence of this system. Postwar sex tourism also required complex collaboration between Japanese corporations, travel companies, airlines, hotels at Asian sites, and local bars and procurers, in a regularized system. But as Asian protests mounted against sex tourism in the late 1980s, the flow of traffic reversed. Rather than Japanese businessmen traveling to Asia, Asian women dubbed *Japa-yuki-san* ("bound for Japan") were increasingly brought to Japan on entertainment visas to service the existing sex industries.

This signaled the trend of foreign workers coming to Japan to fill the "dirty, dangerous, and dull" jobs that young Japanese workers were unwilling to perform. Brazilian Japanese workers (who received special visa status as returning *Japanese*) and significant numbers of people from Southeast Asia have replaced the rural day laborers who migrated to the cities during Japan's high growth era. Workers from South Asia, the Middle East, and even Africa have found it worth their while to come to Japan to earn money. Often these workers have been "invisible" to society because they work in remote areas or at jobs where they do not directly interface with the public (such as construction work).

However, the awareness of foreign workers in Japan has resulted in consumer demand for non-Western cultural products. Since Japan's consumer economy is constantly driven by the demand for new products and images to sell, foreignness itself has become a marketable commodity. The "Exotic Japan" campaign that the Japan Railways conducted in the 1980s foreshadowed the approach of selling something foreign, and hence exotic, as something that could be safely domesticated and consumed. Playing off the popularity of the NHK television documentary series on the Silk Road, the campaign showed exotic, seemingly continental, locales that were actually in Japan and could be reached by train.[33] This approach foreshadowed the "ethnic boom" of the 1990s typified by the consumption of a smorgasbord of food and cultures without the discomforts or dangers of actual foreign travel. (Here, "ethnic" denotes something non-Western.)

The consumer ethnic boom could also substitute for the lack of direct substantive contact with foreign communities within Japan. It was not mere coincidence that Latin music and Japanese groups such Orquesta de la Luz (who performed solely in Spanish) gained popularity as South American Japanese begin to migrate to Japan to look for work. Okinawan culture and music from pop singers to more traditional musicians gained acceptance in the wake of campaigns to sell Okinawan tourism as a domestic substitute for Hawaii or Southeast Asia which were still foreign and exotic. The vogue for ethnic culture might seem to recapitulate the rather shallow form of brand-name consumption. Indeed, one claim of *Nihonjinron* is that Japanese culture is unique in its ability to absorb foreign influences while maintaining an essential, homogeneous core. However, as the old adage "you are what you eat" implies, the consumption and internalization of foreign cultures can also give the Japanese a new perspective on their own society, one that celebrates the diversity of its elements.

NOTES

1   Gluck, "The Past in the Present," p. 93; Igarashi, *Bodies of Memory,* pp. 14, 19–46.
2   Dower emphasizes the aspects of exhaustion, despair, and their cultural effects in the early postwar years in chs. 3 and 4 of *Embracing Defeat.*
3   The airport is more commonly known as Narita, a nearby town, but Sanrizuka is the hamlet where the airport is located. For a description of the farmers' struggle against the airport, see Apter and Sawa, *Against the State.*
4   Ishinomori presents a succinct summation of structural changes to the economy following the first oil shock in his comic *Japan, Inc.*, p. 159. Residents' movements proliferated in the 1970s as the price of Japan's affluence became clear. The last of the "big four" pollution cases (Minamata, Niigata, Toyama, and Yokkaichi City) was decided in 1973, building on the strict environmental pollution laws that were passed in 1970.
5   Tanaka Kakuei was forced from office in 1974, and then in 1976 the US Senate investigation into the Lockheed scandal revealed that Tanaka had taken $2 million in bribes from the company in a deal brokered by President Nixon in exchange for purchasing Lockheed airplanes for All Nippon Airways.
6   The first major textbook controversy occurred in 1982. The issue resurfaced in the early and late 1990s with the descriptions of the Rape of Nanking, the colonial administration of Korea and Taiwan, biochemical warfare experiments, and the "comfort women" issues being the focal points. International protests in these cases have tempered revisions that would minimize negative portrayals of Japan's actions, but the Ministry of Education continues to encourage such changes.
7   All demographic figures are from the 2003 English edition of "Latest Demographic Statistics" compiled by the National Institute of Population and Social Security Research (affiliated with the Ministry of Health and Welfare), except where noted. The full report can be viewed on-line and downloaded at <http://www.ipss.go.jp/p-info/e/psj2003/PSJ2003.pdf> accessed Mar. 18, 2006.
8   By 1970, life expectancy had climbed four years to 69 for men and 74 for women, and by 1980 those figures had risen another four years for each. In 1990, men's life expectancy was nearly 76 and women's nearly 82.
9   By 1950, infant mortality had dipped to slightly over 60 per 1,000 live births, by 1961 the figure had fallen to 30, by 1965 it had dropped below 20, and by 1975 it was slightly over 10.

10   The figures vary according to which source one uses. The population census puts the figure at 59.6 percent for 1955, rising to a high of 63.9 percent in 1975, and then falling back to 60.1 percent in the year 2000.

11   Brinton, "Christmas Cakes and Weddings Cakes," p. 80.

12   Abortion and contraception prevalence rates come from the Mainichi Shinbun Population Problems Research Council, *The Population and Society of Postwar Japan based on Half a Century of Family Planning* (Tokyo: Mainichi Shinbun Population Problems Research Council, 2000).

13   Norgen, *Abortion before Birth Control*, p. 10.

14   Coleman, *Family Planning in Japanese Society*, pp. 204–19.

15   Edwards, *Modern Japan through Its Weddings*, pp. 116–26.

16   Brinton, *Women and the Economic Miracle*, pp. 176–88.

17   White, *Migration in Metropolitan Japan*, pp. 20–1.

18   Vogel, *Japan's New Middle Class*, pp. 71–85, 271–81.

19   "Europe Toughens Stand against Japan's Exports," *New York Times* (Apr. 2, 1979).

20   Hein, "Defining Growth," pp. 112–15.

21   Igarashi, "Zenkyōtō sedai," pp. 208–26.

22   The English "three Ds" does not quite match the Japanese "three Ks" of *kitanai, kiken, kitsui*, literally dirty, dangerous, and severe.

23   This fell to 32.7 percent in 1960, 19.3 percent in 1970, 10.9 percent in 1980, and 7.1 percent in 1990.

24   Kelly, "Finding a Place in Metropolitan Japan," p. 194. The hick image of rural areas was partly due to the sizeable gap with urban areas in the diffusion of household consumer goods in the 1960s and 1970s.

25   Article 1 of the constitution of Japan.

26   According to Yoshino, *nihonjinron* has in actual practice resonated more with business-men trying to organize their thoughts on social organization, especially in cross-cultural encounters, than with educators and intellectual elites. This rhetoric subsided once the recession hit Japan and Western criticism of Japan's economic position faded (Yoshino, *Cultural Nationalism in Contemporary Japan*, pp. 158–84).

27   See the English translation of Murakami's *Underground* for his interviews with Aum members.

28   Oguma, *Tan'itsu minzoku shinwa no kigen*, pp. 3–15. This book has been translated into English by David Askew as *A Genealogy of "Japanese" Self-Images*.

29   One incident in particular brought the problem of discrimination against Korean residents to the fore, the case of Kim Hee Roh in 1968, who killed some gangsters and then took hostages in order to stave off his capture. He used the occasion to demand that the media broadcast his descriptions of the situation of Korean residents.

30   This is a controversial point, as Yano points out, made all the more ironic by the number of "foreign" resident singers and the popularity of overseas Korean and Taiwanese *enka* singers in Japan (Yano, *Tears of Longing*, pp. 9, 30).

31   Wender, *Lamentation as History*, pp. 188–233.

32   See Pollack's article on the comic *World Apartment Horror*, which links the landsharking problem with foreign immigration (especially from Asia) and the legacy of Japan's colonial past (Pollack, "Revenge of the Illegal Asians," pp. 677–714).

33   The campaign was an extension of the highly successful "Discover Japan" campaign that the advertising giant, Dentsū, mounted for the Japan National Railways in the 1970s. That campaign featured modern urban youth – especially women – discovering through rail travel the traditional, hence rural, culture with which they had lost touch (Ivy, "Formations of Mass Culture," pp. 251–6; see also Ivy, *Discourses of the Vanishing*, pp. 29–65).

BIBLIOGRAPHY

Apter, David, and Sawa Nagayo. *Against the State: Politics and Social Protest in Japan.* Cambridge, Mass.: Harvard University Press, 1984.

Brinton, Mary. "Christmas Cakes and Weddings Cakes: The Social Organization of Japanese Women's Life Course." In Takie Lebra, ed., *Japanese Social Organization.* Honolulu: University of Hawai'i Press, 1992.

Brinton, Mary. *Women and the Economic Miracle: Gender and Work in Postwar Japan.* Berkeley: University of California Press, 1993.

Coleman, Samuel. *Family Planning in Japanese Society: Traditional Birth Control in a Modern Urban Culture.* Princeton: Princeton University Press, 1983.

Dower, John. *Embracing Defeat: Japan in the Wake of World War II.* New York: Norton 1999.

Edwards, Walter. *Modern Japan through Its Weddings: Gender, Person, and Society in Ritual Portrayal.* Stanford, Calif.: Stanford University Press, 1989.

Gluck, Carol. "The Past in the Present." In Andrew Gordon, ed., *Postwar Japan as History.* Berkeley: University of California Press, 1993.

Hein, Laura. "Defining Growth: Debates on Economic Strategies." In Andrew Gordon, ed., *Postwar Japan as History.* Berkeley: University of California Press, 1993.

Igarashi Akio. "Zenkyōtō sedai." In Uchiyama Hideo and Kurihara Akira, eds., *Shōwa dōjidai o ikiru: sorezore no sengo.* Tokyo: Yūhikaku, 1986.

Igarashi, Yoshikuni. *Bodies of Memory: Narratives of War in Postwar Japanese Culture, 1945–1970.* Princeton: Princeton University Press, 2000.

Ishikawa Hiroyoshi. *Yokubō no sengoshi: shakai shinrigaku kara no apurōchi.* Tokyo: Taihei Shuppansha, 1981.

Ishinomori Shotarō. *Japan, Inc.: An Introduction to Japanese Economics,* trans. Betsey Scheiner. Berkeley: University of California Press, 1988.

Ivy, Marilyn. "Formations of Mass Culture." In Andrew Gordon, ed., *Postwar Japan as History.* Berkeley: University of California Press, 1993.

Ivy, Marilyn. *Discourses of the Vanishing: Modernity, Phantasm, Japan.* Chicago: University of Chicago Press, 1995.

Kariya Tetsu and Hanasaki Akira. *Oishinbo, 36, Nichi-Bei kome sensō.* Tokyo: Shogakkan, 1992.

Kelly, William. "Finding a Place in Metropolitan Japan: Ideologies, Institutions, and Everyday Life." In Andrew Gordon, ed., *Postwar Japan as History.* Berkeley: University of California Press, 1993.

Murakami Haruki. *Underground: The Tokyo Gas Attack and the Japanese Psyche,* trans. Alfred Birnbaum and J. Philip Gabriel. New York: Vintage International, 2000.

Murayama Hisashi. *Mini-komi sengoshi: jānarizumu no genten o motomete.* Tokyo: San'ichi Shobō, 1985.

Norgren, Tiana. *Abortion before Birth Control: The Politics of Reproduction in Postwar Japan.* Princeton: Princeton University Press, 2001.

Oguma Eiji. *Tan'itsu minzoku shinwa no kigen: "Nihonjin" no jigazō no keifu.* Tokyo: Shinyōsha, 1995.

Oguma Eiji. *A Genealogy of "Japanese" Self-Images,* trans. David Askew. Melbourne: Trans Pacific Press, 2002.

Pollack, David. "Revenge of the Illegal Asians: Aliens, Gangsters, and Myth in Kon Satoshi's *World Apartment Horror." positions: east asia cultures critique* 1:3 (Winter 1993): 677–714.

Rohlen, Thomas. *Japan's High Schools.* Berkeley: University of California Press, 1983.

Steiner, Kurt, Krauss, Ellis, and Flanagan, Scott, eds. *Political Opposition and Local Politics in Japan.* Princeton: Princeton University Press, 1980.

Traphagan, John, and Knight, John, eds. *Demographic Change and the Family in Japan's Aging Society.* Albany: State University of New York Press, 2003.

Vogel, Ezra. *Japan's New Middle Class: The Salary Man and His Family in a Tokyo Suburb,* 2nd edn. Berkeley: University of California Press, 1963.

Wender, Melissa. "Lamentation as History: Literature of Koreans in Japan, 1965–1999." Ph.D. dissertation, University of Chicago, 1999.

White, James W. *Migration in Metropolitan Japan.* Berkeley: Institute of East Asian Studies, University of California, 1982.

Wilkinson, Thomas. *The Urbanization of Japanese Labor, 1868–1955.* Amherst: University of Massachusetts Press, 1986.

Yamada Masahiro. *Parasite Single no jidai.* Tokyo: Chikuma Shobō, 1999.

Yano, Christine. *Tears of Longing: Nostalgia and the Nation in Japanese Popular Song.* Cambridge, Mass.: Harvard University Asia Center, 2002.

Yoshino, Kosaku. *Cultural Nationalism in Contemporary Japan: A Sociological Inquiry.* London: Routledge, 1992.

FURTHER READING

Many topics have not been covered in this article, perhaps most notably a discussion of the workplace environment and its structures. Numerous works cover both factory and office settings, but for a structured introduction to this topic, see Kumazawa Makoto, *Portraits of the Japanese Workplace: Labor Movements, Workers, and Managers,* ed. Andrew Gordon, trans. Andrew Gordon and Mikiso Hane (Boulder, Colo.: Westview Press, 1996). For an analysis of after hours socializing and its function, see Anne Allison, *Nightwork: Sexuality, Pleasure, and Corporate Masculinity in a Tokyo Hostess Club* (Chicago: University of Chicago Press, 1994). Several works have appeared recently on foreign workers in Japan, such as John Lie, *Multiethnic Japan* (Cambridge, Mass.: Harvard University Press, 2001). With regard to foreigners in Japan in general, see Komai Hiroshi, *Foreign Migrants in Contemporary Japan,* trans. Jens Wilkinson (Melbourne: Trans Pacific Press, 2001).

Although many excellent works have appeared on consumption in Japan, fewer books have explored the exportation of Japanese culture as a regional process of globalization, the topic of Iwabuchi Kōichi, *Recentering Globalization: Popular Culture and Japanese Transnationalism* (Durham, NC: Duke University Press, 2002). Several good books have also been published recently on specialized topics concerning women, such as Glenda Roberts, *Staying on the Line: Blue-Collar Women in Contemporary Japan* (Honolulu: University of Hawai'i Press, 1994). One book on women's political behavior that should be mentioned is Robin LeBlanc, *Bicycle Citizens: The Political World of the Japanese Housewife* (Berkeley: University of California Press, 1999).

Histories of the postwar are beginning to appear, ranging from intellectual histories such as J. Victor Koschmann, *Revolution and Subjectivity in Postwar Japan* (Chicago: University of Chicago Press, 1996) to social histories such as Timothy George, *Minamata: Pollution and the Struggle for Democracy in Postwar Japan* (Cambridge, Mass.: Harvard University Asia Center, 2001), and E. Taylor Atkins, *Blue Nippon: Authenticating Jazz in Japan* (Durham, NC: Duke University Press, 2001).

CHAPTER NINETEEN

Japan in the World

Glenn D. Hook

Debates on Japan in the world in the period following the end of World War II have been shaped profoundly by the rise of Japan in the international system, the scholarly approaches dominant in the field of international studies, and the sociopolitical context in which the scholarship on Japan has been produced. Japanese researchers, particularly during the Allied occupation of Japan (1945–52), often have been concerned with producing scholarship aimed at influencing government policy and public opinion in regard to Japan's role in the world, particularly in respect of securing peace for the nation. The specific theoretical approach adopted in this endeavor has been of less concern in comparison with the overwhelming interest in charting the path of the postwar Japanese state. In contrast, American scholars have often been more interested in applying a particular theoretical approach to the case of Japan, be that realism, liberalism, or more recently constructivism, or their variant forms; or in producing scholarship with policy relevance for the US government. Clearly, therefore, synthesizing the scholarship on Japan in the world calls for sensitivity to the global and national as well as the academic environments in which it is produced.

Indeed, unlike in the case of the United Kingdom, which established the first chair of international politics in the world in 1919 at the University of Wales in Aberystwyth, the scholars who took part in the debate on the future course of Japan in the early postwar years were not necessarily scholars of international relations in the narrow sense, but rather public intellectuals from mainly the social science disciplines, set on using their analytical skills to promote the peace of the Japanese nation. The first course by a specialist in international politics was not taught at a Japanese university until the late 1950s. Similarly, unlike in the United States and the United Kingdom, which even in the early postwar years already maintained a tradition of peer-reviewed articles in specialist journals of political science and international relations, scholars in Japan frequently publish their research as books and articles in university journals or in leading current affairs journals, such as *Sekai*, a journal similar to *Foreign Affairs*, except for being left-of-center in political orientation. Thus, what needs to be noted about the emergence of the scholarly debate on Japan in the world in the early postwar years is that it did not take place in an ivory tower atmosphere – nor in terms of the application of a particular theoretical approach to the topic – but rather in the context of how the knowledge and insights generated by social scientific analysis could be employed in order to try to influence government policy on the postwar role of Japan in the world.

With the above perspectives as background, the purpose of this chapter is to focus on the key debates on Japan in the world, with a particular emphasis on those that emerged during the post-1945 period in Japan and the United States. This is where most of the scholarship on Japan's international relations has been produced, reflecting the central role of the United States in defeating the Japanese empire and shaping the postwar politics and global role of the newly emerging economic superpower, and the interest of Japanese scholars in influencing the international relations of the postwar Japanese state. A bird's eye view of the postwar period highlights a range of themes of concern in this scholarly debate. Two have remained central throughout. First is the question of how to ensure the security of Japan in the world, which during the early cold war era pitted supporters of the security treaty with the United States against those in favor of unarmed neutralism. The first section addresses this topic and the changes that have taken place in Japanese security policy in the later cold war and post-cold-war years. The second theme relates to the nature of Japan's role in the world, and whether it can be considered as "proactive" or "reactive." The second section deals with this question by investigating the nature of Japanese leadership, or lack of leadership, in the region and the world. By addressing these two key themes, this chapter aims to show that, irrespective of characterizations of Japan as an anomalous, if not aberrant or abnormal, actor in the world, it is in fact normal.

The Postwar Choice: The US–Japan Security Treaty

The debate on national security to emerge in Japan following the empire's defeat was carried out not only in the scholarly world, but also more broadly on the political and mass levels. A key reason for this was the desire of academics to influence the future role of Japan in the world by proposing the future options available to ensure peace was secured after the end of the occupation. It was a position born of their failure to mount a forceful opposition to Japan's military aggression and path to war in the 1930s and early 1940s. Thus, rather than the specific theoretical approach adopted, although the main trends of scholarship were influenced by either Marxism or modernism (*kindaishugi*),[1] their works' *relevance* to the contemporary world was of central concern.

The debate over the final shape of the postwar settlement and the future course of Japan set a group of scholars known collectively as the Peace Issues Discussion Group (PIDG) against the government of Prime Minister Yoshida Shigeru and its intellectual allies. Members of the PIDG such as Maruyama Masao, regarded as perhaps the most important political thinker of the postwar era, and Shimizu Ikutarō, soon to emerge as one of the nation's leading sociologists and political commentators, were thus at loggerheads with historian Hayashi Kentarō and other academic supporters of Prime Minister Yoshida's proposal to sign a "one-sided" peace treaty (basically a treaty excluding the communist states) as well as a security treaty with the United States.[2]

This policy choice by the Prime Minister, which over time became known as the "Yoshida Doctrine," tied Japanese security to the United States, including the so-called "nuclear umbrella," and enabled the government to place priority on economic recovery, growth, and catching up with the industrially developed West. The choice implied a build-up of Japanese military forces and was thus a challenge to Article 9 of the 1947 constitution, which states in part that "land, sea, and air forces, as well as other war potential, will never be maintained." Japan was as a result integrated into US strategy, but the pressure on respective Japanese governments to build up the military was nevertheless not met with the abandonment of Article 9 of the constitution, but rather with the flexible reinterpretation of its meaning.[3] For instance, instead of a regular military the government in 1954 established the Self-Defense Forces (SDF), whose role has been restricted. The revision of the security treaty in 1960, which took place in spite of mass opposition, and the extension of the security treaty in 1970, ensured that Japan remained tied to the United States. Over the years, though, the SDF have gradually grown more robust and active, as seen in the decision to start US–Japan combined exercises at the end of the 1970s, patrol the sea lines of communication in the early 1980s, and play a more proactive military role in the post-cold-war world.

This more proactive role is illustrated by the dispatch of minesweepers after the end of the Gulf War in 1991, participation in United Nations Peace Keeping Operations (PKO) from 1992, the refueling of US and other naval vessels in the war against Afghanistan in 2001, and the deployment for the first time of SDF ground troops involved in humanitarian work in the warlike situation in Iraq in early 2004. In comparison with the 1950s and 1960s, in particular, this represented a far greater military role for Japan in the world. The debate now centres on *how*, rather than whether, Japan should play a role in the world using the SDF. Article 9 has served to limit the military role played by Japan, although over time its interpretation has been expanded by the government and its academic supporters.

What is often lacking in the debate on the Yoshida Doctrine and the increasingly wider interpretation of Article 9, though, is the costs. The human costs are most vividly evidenced in the deployment of US troops in Okinawa. While certain voices of concern have been raised in the United States, Japan, and elsewhere,[4] the inhabitants of Okinawa have borne the major domestic costs of the security treaty, as seen in the environmental destruction caused by the bases and military activities on Okinawa; the crimes of military personnel, including murder, rape, and robbery; and the generally debilitating effects the location of nearly 75 percent of US bases on only 0.6 percent of Japanese land has exerted on the economic, social, and political life of Okinawans. Yet in the context of the overall US–Japan security relationship, the costs borne by the people of Okinawa are usually excluded from the debate on Japan's role in the world. What alternatives have been suggested?

The Alternatives

The alternative to the Yoshida Doctrine put forward by the PIDG was a policy of unarmed neutralism, not allowing any foreign power to establish bases in Japan, whether US or Soviet. The Group was keenly aware of the ability of a state not simply to be shaped by international relations, but to shape them: the fact that the world was not one but two worlds, capitalist and communist, meant that Yoshida's policy to side with the capitalist world and permit the deployment of US troops would only exacerbate international tensions. Indeed, the PIDG feared that, as a result of signing a one-sided treaty and allowing US troops to be based in Japan as part of the nation's security treaty obligations, the possibility of war between the "two worlds" would become more likely. The alternative policy the Group proposed was rooted in an analysis of the destructive power of nuclear weapons, which drew on Japan's singular experience of being atom-bombed, as well as the provisions of Article 9 of the constitution. In short, the PIDG proposed that Japan's role in the world should be to promote peaceful coexistence between the East and West, not to risk increasing the possibility of war by signing a security treaty with either of the two sides, and, by pursuing such a policy, to ensure the nation's peace. Indeed, from the perspective of the PIDG, the signing of the US–Japan Security Treaty, and the provision of bases for US forces in Japan, served not only to tie Japan into the Western side of the cold war divide, but also to preclude the pursuit of the sort of independent foreign policy possible for a neutral state. For these reasons, the Group remained opposed to the US–Japan Security Treaty.

While the scholarly debate on Japan in the world was pushed forward by members of the PIDG, the Japan Socialist Party (JSP) aimed to give concrete form to the policy by making Japan a "peace state" – a call which tapped into anti-militarist norms at the mass level. Although the party was never able to garner enough votes to form a government, its opposition to the security treaty and the legitimacy of the SDF and its proposal to pursue a policy of unarmed neutralism provided a concrete alternative to the government's policy of building up the military and strengthening security ties with the United States. The combination of this alternative to the security treaty existing in both the academic and political worlds helped to keep the issue alive, although the end of the cold war soon saw the JSP abandon not only the policy of unarmed neutralism, but also opposition to the security treaty and the SDF.

On the other hand, the US scholarship on Japan that emerged in the early postwar period was similarly concerned with the role of Japan in the world, but with the focus placed squarely on a security relationship with the United States, or the practical outcome of the foreign policy decisions made by the Yoshida government, rather than the debates within Japan about the course the nation should chart in the cold war world in order to ensure peace. The view of US academics was of a bifurcated world, divided between capitalism and communism, with the alternative to American alignment being seen not as neutralism but as communism. Thereafter, the US debate has been frequently concerned with the lack of balance in the security relationship and the need for Japan to take on a greater burden, although the general consensus seems to be that the treaty is in Japan's interest. Indeed, what is striking about the American debate on the security policy pursued by Japan is the high degree of consensus on the benefit of the security treaty to Japan and the need to deploy troops in Okinawa and elsewhere, whereas this remains a point of contention in Japan. Thus, even though the security treaty was revised in 1960, leading to a greater emphasis on mutuality, criticism has continued to be leveled against Japan for not doing enough.

More concretely, as mainstream US scholarship has been dominated by realism, Article 9 appears as an encumbrance, the ideas of the PIDG as "idealistic," and both as a hindrance to Japan playing a full role in support of the United States. Those US scholars more interested in policy-making than realism, of course, often arrived at the same conclusions simply by placing priority on the national interest. Or, as Cox has said, "theory is always *for* some one, and *for* some purpose."[5] In the 1960s, for instance, the security policy pursued by Japan was seen as a restriction on cooperation with the US war in Vietnam: unlike Australia and South Korea, Japan did not dispatch troops to support the US war effort. In the 1970s and 1980s, US concern was manifest in the idea of Japan as a "free rider" which was seen to be benefiting from the global order kept in place through US power rather than contributing to the maintenance of that order. It was not until the post-cold-war period that major academic voices in the United States were raised in favor of pulling the troops out of Japan.[6]

Nuclear Weapons

While a policy of unarmed neutrality was put forward by academics and taken up by the JSP as an alternative to the US–Japan Security Treaty signed by Yoshida, as seen above, another alternative emerged as part of the Japanese academic debate in the 1980s: nuclear weapons. It is certainly true that, as far back as the late 1950s, Prime Minister Kishi Nobusuke stated that nuclear weapons were constitutional, stirring debate on the issue. It seems there was some investigation of the issue in later years, too. At the time of Satō Eisaku's premiership, for instance, two reports issued in 1968 and 1970 and drafted by an unofficial study group headed by Rōyama Michio concluded that, although Japan had the potential to develop nuclear weapons, this was not the recommended course of action.[7]

The academic debate on Japan going nuclear, however, did not emerge into the spotlight until the publication of Shimizu Ikutarō's *Japan yo, kokka tare* (Japan, Be a State) in 1980, which called for the possession of nuclear weapons in order to make Japan a state in the fullest sense of the word.[8] This created quite a stir, as the overwhelming majority of academic specialists in international relations were opposed to Japan's possession of nuclear weapons. One strand of opposition, represented by scholars such as Sakamoto Yoshikazu, was rooted in the same sort of opposition as the PIDG: the threat of nuclear war and constitutional provisions.[9] The other strand, however, saw Japan's security as best guaranteed by maintaining a close security relationship with the nuclear superpower, the United States, not by a Gaullist-type policy of greater independence based on Japan's own nuclear capability. As with Nagai Yonosuke, most agreed that the Yoshida Doctrine served Japan well.[10]

But the question of Japan going nuclear remains, and politicians have made periodic calls for the debate to be revived. For instance, in October 1999 Nishimura Shingo, defense vice minister, was fired by then prime minister Obuchi Keizō for calling for an airing of the issue in the weekly magazine *Shukan Playboy*. Again, comments made in May 2002 by political leaders, Chief Cabinet Secretary Fukuda Yasuo and Deputy Chief Cabinet Secretary Abe Shinzō, suggesting that there might be public support for Japan to develop nuclear weapons, again stirred controversy. As in the past, however, little academic support for Japan taking the nuclear option exists. As seen from the position of a specialist at the National Defense Academy, no real support exists for the nuclear option, not least because of strong public antipathy towards nuclear weapons.[11]

As far as the American debate on the nuclear issue is concerned, opinion has been split among those who have sought to explain Japan in the world by reference to the structure of the international system, the rising economic power of Japan, and other elements of a realist view of the world; those who see Japan as preferring not to shoulder the economic and political costs of the nuclear option, preferring to rely instead on the United States, which some see in the context of "burden-sharing" or Japan as a "free rider"; and, finally, those, often adopting a constructivist approach, who see the war, the atomic bombings, and the occupation of Japan has having changed the body politic and political norms, such that developing or possessing nuclear weapons is anathema.

The realist approach, which sees Japan as the "next in line" to be a great power, including the possession of nuclear weapons, is represented by Kenneth Waltz. For Waltz, it would be a "structural anomaly" for Japan not to opt for such great power status.[12] The "free rider" argument became particularly salient in the 1980s, when the United States faced a series of challenges from key Japanese industries, although the concern for burden-sharing continued into the 1990s and early twenty-first century. Here it was often thought that the best path for Japan to follow was to rely on the US nuclear umbrella and to share the burden, not to develop an independent nuclear capability.[13] Finally, in the 1990s a number of mainly American works drew attention to the role of anti-military norms and culture in limiting the possibility of Japan pursuing the nuclear option.[14] In short, the debate on Japan's nuclear option has been significantly influenced by the type of approach adopted.

Japan as a Normal State

Given the resistance to the possession of nuclear weapons, then, the major debate to emerge in the 1990s and early 2000s, stimulated by the then leader of the Liberal Party Ozawa Ichirō's 1994 book *Blueprint for a New Japan* has been the idea of Japan as a "normal state."[15] Here "normal state" functions as a euphemism for Japan as a state willing to use its full range of power resources – including the military – in order to realize its regional and global interests. More specifically, while the question of what is "normal" has been subject to scrutiny,[16] the idea of Japan as a normal state served to stimulate a debate in the academic community and wider political world over exactly what role Japan should play in the post-cold-war world, and to what extent this would involve the use of the SDF.

Thus, the question of how to ensure the peace of the nation in the cold war world, which pitted supporters of the security treaty against those in favor of unarmed neutralism, has been replaced in the post-cold-war world with a debate over the extent of Japan's military cooperation with the United States and more broadly the international community. In this sense, the end of the cold war shattered the basis at the heart of the earlier debate on Japan in the world: on the one hand, if the cold war no longer exists, what justification can the supporters of the security treaty offer in the face of the collapse of the very enemy the treaty was forged to protect Japan against;

on the other hand, if the Soviet Union has collapsed, how can the opponents of the treaty gain support for neutrality between a division which no longer exists?

The 1991 Gulf War brought the question of Japan's role in the world to the forefront of scholarly and popular debate. At the time, the type of contribution Japan was to make was debated in the context of the constitution and the restraint this placed on the government in making a military contribution. At one end of the spectrum were those who argued that, due to Article 9, Japan could make only a financial or other non-military contribution, whereas others argued that, in order to make a visible contribution, Japan should make some sort of "human contribution," whether by the creation of new special forces to carry out peace-keeping and hu-manitarian work or by the deployment of the SDF. In the end, the government's contribution to the Gulf War was financial assistance to the tune of $13 billion and the dispatch of the Maritime Self-Defense Forces for mine-clearing after the end of the war.

Indeed, the Gulf War can be regarded as a watershed in the debate on Japan in the world. For the large payment made towards the costs of the war did not lead to widespread recognition of Japan's contribution, but rather to criticism of Japanese "check book diplomacy," and the government did not even receive thanks for its efforts. The academic debate in the wake of the 1991 Gulf War now includes more frequent calls to revise the constitution: the aim is to enable Japan to make a full international contribution, particularly a contribution in support of US strategy. What some have in mind, as suggested by the call for Japan to become the "Britain of the Far East," is a strengthening of the military relationship with the United States and the creation of the same sort of "special (military) relationship" Britain and the United States enjoy.[17]

It is certainly true that, in comparison with the 1980s, Japan's military role today is far greater, with PKO forces dispatched to Cambodia and elsewhere, support for the war in Afghanistan, and the deployment of ground troops in Iraq. With the pressure on Japan to do more, however, the academic debate has taken up the question of why Japan does not do more. As indicated above, one interpretation is that, as a result of the constitution and the anti-militarist or, more loosely, "pacifist" orientation of the public, Japan is unable to play a full military role in support of the United States. In other words, anti-militarist norms are at the heart of the problem. The second interpretation places emphasis more on how, with the widely accepted decline of these anti-militarist norms, Japan will become a "normal state" along the lines of a Britain of the Far East. In other words, Japan should begin to use its military resources in the same way as Britain. At the least, this is the desire of some academics seeking to influence the debate on the Japanese role in the world. The third inter-pretation is that, in the end, Japanese leaders are pragmatists for whom not only military but also economic security is essential.[18] In this latter case, the idea is of US forces as a "military shield" and economic links with countries essential to Japanese prosperity as a "mercantile sword." The point here is that, as in the case of Japan's participation in the war against Afghanistan, policy-makers will do only the minimum necessary to satisfy US demands,[19] and not fully develop Japan into a "normal state." Indeed, for Japanese policy-makers, security is seen in a much wider context than simply military security, taking into account economic as well as other non-military factors.[20]

Japan as Leader? The Debate on Reactivity and Proactivity

One of the key points in the broader scholarly debate on Japan in the world has been whether the role played can be accounted for by internal or external pressures, *gaiatsu*, especially those from the United States, and more generally whether changes in the Japanese role have occurred due to one, the other, or a combination of the two. A number of variables can help to answer this question fully. To start with, the specific issue area can influence the range of actors involved in the policy-making process. For instance, Japanese farmers are much more likely to act as an interest group in trying to influence policy regarding the wider opening of the Japanese market to foreign rice than they are in the case of the SDF being dispatched on PKO. Similarly, depending on whether a policy is implemented in response to a crisis, or is short-, medium-, or long-term, the actors involved in the decision-making process are likely to differ. For instance, the Koizumi Jun'ichirō government's response to the crisis created by the kidnapping of Japanese citizens in Iraq in April 2004 engaged a different range of actors to those promoting the much longer-term policy goal of gaining a seat on the United Nations Security Council. Again, the geographical focus of a policy will often be of concern to different actors, as Japan's interests differ considerably depending on the policy's scope. For instance, Japan has historically maintained much stronger ties with East Asia than with Africa, suggesting the former is likely to enjoy a higher profile in the policy-making process than the latter. We can also expect the actors to differ depending on whether the issue is consensual or controversial in nature. For instance, even though the United States may exert pressure on the government to play a greater military role in support of American regional or global strategy, as this is a controversial issue domestically the efficacy of such external pressure is likely to be weaker than in the case of an issue enjoying wider consensus among domestic actors, such as Japan offering humanitarian aid under United Nations auspices. Finally, whether Japanese and US interests are shared, different, or in conflict with each other could influence Japan's role in the world, with American pressure likely to be more effective when interests are shared than when they are in conflict. In short, in seeking to explain Japan's more proactive role in the world, whether through an examination of external pressures, internal pressures, or both, a full account of their respective roles would need to take into consideration these types of variables.

Although space precludes an examination of the impact these variables may exert, we can nevertheless point to a tendency in the debate on Japan in the world for some commentators to try to explain Japan's role by placing greater emphasis on external pressures and for others to pay greater attention to internal pressures on the policy-making process. It was Kent Calder who, in a 1988 article, first put forward a conceptual way to understand Japan's susceptibility to foreign (US) pressure with the idea of Japan as a reactive state. By focusing on foreign economic policy, he demonstrated how Japan reacts to rather than shapes international relations.[21] More specifically, the argument is that, due to domestic constraints, particularly those imposed by the bureaucracy and interest groups, Japan is constrained in any attempt to play a leadership role in the world, and instead simply reacts to US pressures in determining policy.

Other research has shown that, even though *gaiatsu* may be an important variable, the extent to which this external pressure is successful or not is less than clear-cut. In the case of the US–Japan trade talks in the 1980s, for instance, Leonard Schoppa found US pressure was most efficacious when a domestic constituency in support of the policy existed in Japan. Satō Yōichirō, in turn, demonstrated how US pressure has been used by the Ministry of International Trade and Industry (MITI, now Ministry of Economy, Trade and Industry, METI) to bolster its monitoring of key sectors of the economy, on the one hand, whereas supermarkets like Toys "R" Us were able to escape MITI's clutches by the use of US pressure, on the other.[22] Other participants in the debate such as T. J. Pempel have shown how the change in Japanese foreign economic policy, characterized as a move from an exporter to an overseas investor, resulted from internal, rather than external, factors, especially the changing power relationship between politicians and bureaucrats.[23] All in all, as shown by the application of Putnam's "two level game" approach to US–Japanese economic negotiations in the 1980s,[24] both internal and external pressures can help us to understand more fully the changing role of Japan in the world.

For Japanese academics such as Kamo Takehiko, however, the asymmetrical nature of the relationship between Japan and the United States, with Japan naturally in the weaker position, is viewed as crucial for understanding Japan in the world.[25] For this makes Japanese policymakers especially vulnerable to pressures exerted by the United States, and this in turn constrains their development of an independent Japanese role. It is such asymmetric interdependence that makes policy-makers vulnerable to US pressure even in the area of Official Development Assistance (ODA), where Japan is widely accepted to play a key global role. Building on previous work on ODA policy, such as that by Robert Orr, who gives weight to external factors, and Dennis Yasutomo, who emphasizes internal factors, Miyashita Akitoshi demonstrates how Japan's response to US pressure is not due in any sense to a dearth of intelligible policy, but rather results from a calculated decision.[26] The question of the degree to which the nation can pursue an independent role in the world, given the asymmetric relationship with the United States and the different role of US pressure, remains a point of debate in Japan's ODA and other policies. It is certainly a challenge to the idea of Japan as a reactive state.

Regional Leadership: A Proactive Role in East Asia?

Whether external or internal pressures influence the increasingly proactive role of Japan, what does seem to gain a certain degree of consensus in the debate on Japan's role in the world is in terms of Japanese engagement with a specific geographic region, East Asia. The identity of this region has been controversial, though: on the one hand, the strong security, political and economic ties with the United States has given "Asia-Pacific" a particular salience, neatly co-joining the United States (Pacific) and Japan (Asia) in a common identity. On the other hand, the moves to develop new regional organizations focused on East Asia, the 1997 East Asian financial and wider crises, and the increasing domestic salience of Asianist norms, have strengthened the East Asian identity in recent years. Whether in terms of a Japanese role in Asia Pacific or in East Asia, however, an issue Japanese policymakers have had to face is how to rebuild relations with former colonies and neighbors. In particular, a major task for Japan during the postwar era has been to overcome the historical legacy of imperial expansion, the war, and the more recent cold war divisions in order to carve out a new role in the region. In this process, policymakers have used ODA and promoted trade and investment as a way to contribute to economic development and the longer term goal of integrating the East Asian political economy.[27]

Thus, even during the cold war period Japan played a leading role in the economic development of the Newly Industrializing Economics of Hong Kong, Singapore, South Korea, and Taiwan, as well as the developing economies of Southeast Asia, together with the integration of the regional political economy. The change in the structural features of the international system, as symbolized by the end of the cold war, however, opened up new opportunities for Japan to play an even greater regional role. Indeed, Japan's leadership role in the region has been more pronounced in the wake of the ending of the cold war, with Japanese governmental and non-governmental actors taking a leading role in promoting new multilateral forums for holding dialogue on economic, political and security issues. This is illustrated by Japanese efforts to promote the Asia-Pacific Economic Cooperation Forum, the Association for Southeast Asian Nations (ASEAN) Regional Forum (ARF), and the ASEAN plus Three (China, Japan, and South Korea).

As Funabashi Yōichi makes clear, Japan worked with Australia in pushing forward the creation of APEC at the end of the 1980s.[28] Although the degree to which Japan played a supporter role to Australia, or was more proactive when a range of governmental and non-governmental actors are taken into account, has been a point of debate,[29] Japan clearly seems to have played a part in promoting this multilateral institution. Despite a greater role played by the United States in setting the APEC agenda, as seen in the greater emphasis on security issues in the wake of the September 11, 2001 terrorist attacks, the Japanese government still remains a key member of this forum.

In the case of the proposal to establish the first multilateral forum for security dialogue in the region, the ARF, in 1991, Japan more clearly played an independent leadership role. The Minister of Foreign Affairs at the time, Nakayama Tarō, put the proposal forward, reflecting the increasing recognition of the need for Japan to play a security role in the post-cold-war period, on the one hand, and to overcome the historical obstacles to strengthening links with its East Asian neighbors, on the other.[30] This promotion of security multilateralism in East Asia was not, though, a rejection of bilateralism centring on the US-Japan Security Treaty, but rather a supplement to that relationship. In other words, Japan was playing a greater leadership role in East Asia, but this was not a challenge to the hegemonic role played by the United States.

The leadership role played by Japan in East Asia was again demonstrated at the time of the 1997 East Asian financial crisis. In response to the crisis, Japan proposed the creation of an Asian Monetary Fund (AMF). True, due to US and other objections, the Japanese withdrew their proposal and instead offered to support the Manila Framework, as proposed at a meeting of the Asia-Pacific Economic Cooperation forum in Manila in November 1997. From the short-term perspective of the AMF proposal, therefore, the leadership role taken by Japan in seeking to assist the affected economies of East Asia was squashed by foreign pressures. While over the short-term, this may appear as a failure of Japanese policy, over the longer term the government has played a proactive role in promoting the further integration of the region, especially financial integration, as illustrated by the New Miyazawa Initiative, the Chiang Mai Initiative, and the creation of the ASEAN plus Three.[31] In short, as noted above, over the longer term Japan has been playing a proactive role in promoting the integration of the East Asian regional political economy.

What Kind of Leadership?

The debate about whether Japan is a reactive or proactive state goes hand in hand with one about the nature of Japanese leadership. The main impetus for the salience of this debate was the economic rise of Japan to economic superpower status, and the perceived challenge this posed to the United States during the 1980s. The large trade surpluses Japan chalked up with the United States, on the one hand, and the protection of domestic industries and barriers to foreign direct investment, on the other, meant intense pressure was exerted on Japan to reduce the trade surplus and open up the domestic market. The debate to emerge over the trade surplus was in terms of the trade-off between Japan pursuing a mercantilist policy, while relying on the United States for its security, and the need for it to make a military contribution to the maintenance of the global order. While focus was at the time placed on Japan's mercantilist role in the world,[32] the longer term interest has been on how this increased economic power has fed into the Japanese role in the post-cold-war world. Certainly, during the heyday of the "bubble economy," when the nation's economic might led to Japan being touted as a possible challenger to the United States, the rise of Japan to economic superpower status caught the imagination of especially US academics, who were concerned about Japan's apparent unwillingness to provide "public goods" and carry out the responsibilities associated with its new status.[33]

A 1986 article by Erza Vogel, in particular, stimulated the debate on the question of Japan's leadership role.[34] It saw the rise in Japanese economic might as embodying the potential to be transformed into political and perhaps even military leadership in the world – the provocative possibility of a "Pax Nipponica." To be fair, Vogel was in essence suggesting a limited form of hegemony, but the potential for Japan was clearly not as a "reactive" state, but as a "great power" playing a leadership role in the world. While criticism was raised of the idea of a hegemonic Japan in terms of whether the nation actually sought to play such a role, the fraught question of whether converting economic power into its political and military equivalent was possible, given domestic constraints and other potential challengers to the United States, such as China and India, the future role of Japan in the world was clearly a major point of concern for scholars at the time. What, indeed, would be Japan's future role in the world?

The scenarios painted by Inoguchi Takashi are suggestive of the wider possibilities. He saw four: pax Americana, phase II, with the United States as the hegemon continuing to play the key military role and Japan continuing a mainly economic role in the world; bigemony, with Japan and the United States cooperating together and Japan's economic power being translated into military power; pax consortis, with coalitions built internationally and Japan playing an economic role and promoting non-military solutions to human problems; and pax Nipponica, with Japan taking on a hegemonic role in the world, although for Japan to play such a role in the security field would require de-nuclearization. Writing before the end of the cold war, Inoguchi envisioned pax Americana phase II and bigemony as the most likely scenarios until 2015.[35] After the end of the cold war, much of the debate has focused on Japan emerging to play a supplementary role in support of the United States, but there remains the question of what type of leadership role Japan is actually playing.

Michael Green, for instance, points to the increasingly proactive role of Japan, and suggests this results from a new "realism."[36] Others have argued instead that Japanese leadership represents a different type of leadership, certainly different to that practiced by the United States. Alan Rix, for instance, has suggested the idea of Japan "leading from behind," as seen in the type of long-term leadership demonstrated by Japan in shaping the Asia Pacific order through trade, investment, and aid, not dominant behavior.[37] Reinhard Drifte sees Japanese leadership is practiced by "stealth"; Terada Takashi talks about "directional leadership"; and Glenn Hook *et al* speak in terms of "quiet diplomacy."[38] What all of these authors are seeking to add to the debate is a view of a Japan as a state that practices leadership, but in ways that do not fit easily with a model of US-style leadership. It is, in other words, a state that seeks to shape, not simply respond to, the world.

Conclusion

The role of Japan in the world has been elucidated by focusing on a range of issues related to security and leadership, as these two themes have continued to be of central concern in both the cold war and post-cold-war periods, despite the radical transformation in the structure of the international system symbolized by the ending of the cold war. While the choice between unarmed neutralism and a security treaty with the United States no longer informs the debate about the role of Japan in the post-cold-war world, the highlighting of the potential to choose one or the other has been fundamental to the way the debate on the nation's peace has developed in Japan. In this sense, the debate is linked to the question of Japan as a proactive or reactive state, as choice implies the potential for policymakers to shape, not simply be shaped by, the world. The American debate, in contrast, took a more Hobbesian view of the world as a state of war of "all against all," and saw the only option for Japan as to join one camp or the other in the divided world of the cold war years. While those Japanese scholars supportive of the Yoshida line were sympathetic to this view of the world, seeing the members of the PIDG as hopelessly idealistic, the absence of any meaningful debate on Japan joining the socialist, rather than capitalist camp, highlights a major difference with the debate in the United States. The existence of unarmed neutralism as an option, even if in the scholarly debate rather than in government policy, contributed to the indiginization of the constitution and the inculcation of anti-militarist norms in Japanese society. Whether the constitution will continue as a constraint or be revised, and whether these norms will continue to influence the debate on the appropriate military role for Japan in the post-cold-war world, is still to be seen, but both will remain important in determining the role of Japan in the world.

The debate on Japan's leadership role has become intricately linked with the deployment of military means, and how these will be employed in East Asia and the wider world. While Japan has practiced leadership in the East Asian region, albeit not in the same style as the United States and the United Kingdom, the focus has been placed overwhelmingly on economic development and regional integration, reflecting a wider view of security than simply military security. If Japan's dispatch of the SDF to Iraq is illustrative of a move to exploit the full range of power resources, including the military, whether in support of the United States or in pursuit of Japanese interests, then Japan's East Asian neighbors will no doubt continue to monitor its leadership role. While nuclear weapons can be expected to remain a marginal issue in the debate over Japan's future role in the world, how policymakers decide to utilize the nation's military forces will be central to both the region and the world. Whatever type of leadership role Japan plays, though, the constitution and antimilitarist norms will prove crucial in its determination.

NOTES

1 Barshay, *The Social Sciences in Modern Japan*.
2 Hook, *Militarization and Demilitarization*; Igarashi, "Peace-Making and Party Politics."
3 Hook and McCormack, *Japan's Contested Constitution*.
4 Johnson, *Okinawa*.
5 Cox, "Social Forces, States, and World Order," p. 87.
6 Johnson and Keehn, "East Asian Security."
7 *Asahi shinbun* (Nov. 13, 1994).
8 Shimizu, *Japan yo, kokka tare*.
9 Sakamoto, *Kakujidai no kokusai seiji*.
10 Nagai, "Moratoriamu kokka no bōeiron."
11 Kamiya, "Nuclear Japan."
12 Waltz, "The Emerging Structure," pp. 55, 66.
13 Pharr, "Japan's Defense Foreign Policy," pp. 255–6.
14 Katzenstein, *Cultural Norms and National Security*; Hook, *Militarization and Demilitarization*.
15 Ozawa, *Blueprint for a New Japan*.
16 Hook, Gilson, Hughes and Dobson, *Japan's International Relations*.
17 Armitage and Nye, "The United States and Japan."
18 Heginbotham and Samuels, "Japan's Dual Hedge."
19 Ibid., p. 115.
20 Hughes, *Japan's Security Agenda*.
21 Calder, "Japanese Foreign Economic Policy Formation."
22 Schoppa, *Bargaining with Japan*; Satō, "Modeling Japan's Foreign Economic Policy."
23 Pempel, "From Exporter to Investor."
24 Schoppa, "Two Level Games and Bargaining Outcomes."
25 Kamo, "The Internationalization of the State."
26 Orr, *The Emergence of Japan's Foreign Aid Power*; Yasutomo, *The New Multilateralism*; Miyashita, "*Gaiatsu* and Japan's Foreign Aid."
27 Hook, Gilson, Hughes, and Dobson, *Japan's International Relations*.
28 Funabashi, *Asia Pacific Fusion*.
29 Krauss, "Japan, the U.S., and the Emergence of Multilateralism."
30 Midford, "Japan's Leadership Role."

31 Hook, Gilson, Hughes, and Dobson, "Japan and the East Asian Financial Crisis."
32 Prestowitz, *Trading Places.*
33 Gilpin, *The Political Economy of International Relations.*
34 Vogel, "Pax Nipponica."
35 Inoguchi, "Four Japanese Scenarios," p. 222.
36 Green, *Japan's Reluctant Realism.*
37 Rix, "Japan and the Region," p. 65.
38 Drifte, *Japan's Foreign Policy*, Terada, "Directional Leadership in Institution-Building";
    Hook, Gilson, Hughes, and Dobson, *Japan's International Relations.*

BIBLIOGRAPHY

Armitage, Richard, and Nye, Joseph. "The United States and Japan: Advancing toward a Mature Partnership." Washington DC: Institute for National Strategic Studies, 2000. Available at <http://www.ndu.edu/inss/strforum/SR_01/SR_Japan.htm> accessed Feb. 28, 2006.

Barshay, Andrew. *The Social Sciences in Modern Japan: The Marxian and Modernist Traditions.* Berkeley: University of California Press, 2004.

Calder, Kent. "Japanese Foreign Economic Policy Formation: Explaining the Reactive State." *World Politics* 40:4 (1988): 517–41.

Cox, Robert. "Social Forces, States, and World Order" (1981). In Robert Cox, with T. J. Sinclair, *Approaches to World Order.* Cambridge: Cambridge University Press, 1996.

Drifte, Reinhard. *Japan's Foreign Policy for the Twenty-First Century: From Economic Superpower to What Power?*, 2nd edn. London: Macmillan, 1998.

Funabashi Yōichi. *Asia Pacific Fusion: Japan's Role in APEC.* Washington DC: Institute for International Economics, 1995.

Gilpin, Robert. *The Political Economy of International Relations.* Princeton: Princeton University Press, 1987.

Green, Michael. *Japan's Reluctant Realism: Foreign Policy Challenge in an Era of Uncertain Power.* New York: Palgrave Macmillan, 2001.

Heginbotham, Eric, and Samuels, Richard. "Japan's Dual Hedge." *Foreign Affairs* 81:5 (2002): 110–21.

Hook, Glenn D. *Militarization and Demilitarization in Contemporary Japan.* London: Routledge, 1996.

Hook, Glenn D., and McCormack, Gavan. *Japan's Contested Constitution: Documents and Analysis.* London: Routledge, 2001.

Hook, Glenn D., Gilson, Julie, Hughes, Christopher, and Dobson, Hugo. *Japan's International Relations: Politics, Economics and Security.* London: Routledge, 2001.

Hook, Glenn D., Gilson, Julie, Hughes, Christopher, and Dobson, Hugo. "Japan and the East Asian Financial Crisis: Patterns, Motivations, and Instrumentalisation of Japanese Regional Economic Diplomacy." *European Journal of East Asian Studies* 1:2 (2002): 177–98.

Hughes, Christopher. *Japan's Security Agenda: Military, Economic, and Environmental Dimensions.* Boulder, Colo.: Lynne Rienner, 2004.

Igarashi Takeshi. "Peace-Making and Party Politics: The Formation of the Domestic Foreign-Policy System in Postwar Japan." *Journal of Japanese Studies* 11:2 (Summer 1985): 323–56.

Inoguchi Takashi. "Four Japanese Scenarios for the Future." In Kathleen Newland, ed., *The International Relations of Japan.* Basingstoke: Macmillan, 1990.

Johnson, Chalmers, ed. *Okinawa: Cold War Island.* Cardiff, Calif.: Japan Policy Research Institute, 1999.

Johnson, Chalmers, and Keehn, E. G. "East Asian Security: The Pentagon's Ossified Strategy." *Foreign Affairs* 74:4 (1995): 103–15.

Kamiya Matake. "Nuclear Japan: Oxymoron or Coming Soon?" *Washington Quarterly* 26:1 (Winter 2002–3): 63–75.

Kamo Takehiko. "The Internationalization of the State: The Case of Japan." In Yoshikazu Sakamoto, ed., *Global Transformation: Challenges to the State System*. Tokyo: United Nations University Press, 1994.

Katzenstein, Peter. *Cultural Norms and National Security: Police and Military in Postwar Japan*. Ithaca: Cornell University Press, 1996.

Krauss, Ellis. "Japan, the U.S., and the Emergence of Multilateralism in Asia." *Pacific Review* 13:3 (2000): 473–94.

Midford, Paul. "Japan's Leadership Role in East Asian Security Multilateralism: The Nakayama Proposal and the Logic of Assurance." *Pacific Review* 13:3 (2000): 367–98.

Miyashita Akitoshi. "*Gaiatsu* and Japan's Foreign Aid: Rethinking the Reactive–Proactive Debate." *International Studies Quarterly* 43:4 (Dec. 1999): 695–731.

Nagai Yonosuke. "Moratoriamu kokka no bōeiron." *Chūō Kōron* (Jan. 1981): 74–108.

Orr, Robert. *The Emergence of Japan's Foreign Aid Power*. New York: Columbia University Press, 1990.

Ozawa Ichirō. *Blueprint for a New Japan*. New York: Kodansha, 1994.

Pempel. T. J. "From Exporter to Investor: Japanese Foreign Economic Policy." In Gerald Curtis and Michael Blaker, eds., *Japan's Foreign Policy after the Cold War: Coping with Change*. Armonk, NY: M. E. Sharpe, 1993.

Pharr, Susan. "Japan's Defense Foreign Policy and the Politics of Burden Sharing." In Gerald Curtis and Michael Blaker, eds., *Japan's Foreign Policy after the Cold War: Coping with Change*. Armonk, NY: M. E. Sharpe, 1993.

Prestowitz, Clyde, Jr. *Trading Places: How We Allowed Japan to Take the Lead*. New York: Basic Books, 1988.

Rix, Alan. "Japan and the Region: Leading from Behind." In Richard Higgott, Richard Leaver, and John Ravenhill, eds., *Pacific Economic Relations in the 1990s: Cooperation or Conflict?* St. Leonards, Australia: Allen and Unwin, 1993.

Sakamoto Yoshikazu. *Kakujidai no kokusai seiji*. Tokyo: Iwanami Shoten, 1982.

Satō Yōichirō. "Modeling Japan's Foreign Economic Policy with the United States." In Miyashita Akitoshi and Satō Yōichirō, eds., *Japanese Foreign Policy in Asia and the Pacific: Domestic Interests, American Pressure, and Regional Integration*. New York: Palgrave Macmillan, 2001.

Schoppa, Leonard. "Two Level Games and Bargaining Outcomes: Why *Gaiatsu* Succeeds in Japan in Some Cases and Not Others." *International Organization* 47:3 (Summer 1993): 353–86.

Schoppa, Leonard. *Bargaining with Japan: What American Pressure Can and Cannot Do*. New York: Columbia University Press, 1997.

Shimizu Ikutarō. *Japan yo, kokka tare*. Tokyo: Bungei Shunju, 1980.

Terada, Takashi. "Directional Leadership in Institution-Building: Japan's Approaches to ASEAN in the Establishment of PECC and APEC." *Pacific Review* 14:2 (2001): 195–220.

Vogel, Ezra. "Pax Nipponica." *Foreign Affairs* (Spring 1986): 752–67.

Waltz, Kenneth. "The Emerging Structure of International Politics." *International Security* 18:2 (Autumn 1993): 44–79.

Yasutomo, Dennis. *The New Multilateralism in Japan's Foreign Policy*. New York: St. Martin's, 1995.

FURTHER READING

Kent Calder's essay, "Japanese Foreign Economic Policy Formation: Explaining the Reactive State" (*World Politics* 40:4 (1988): 517–41) proposes the idea of Japan as a "reactive state" by examining foreign economic policy. It suggests Japan is susceptible to US pressure and lacks leadership potential due to domestic factors. Michael Green's *Japan's Reluctant Realism: Foreign Policy Challenge in an Era of Uncertain Power* (New York: Palgrave Macmillan, 2001) focuses on Japanese foreign policy in the post-cold-war period and discusses how the government has become more assertive. He concludes the US–Japan alliance can survive despite the international and domestic changes taking place. Glenn D. Hook, Julie Gilson, Christopher Hughes and Hugo Dobson, in their book *Japan's International Relations: Politics, Economics and Security* (London: Routledge, 2001), seek to treat Japan as a normal state by using structure, agency, and norms to explain the nation's international behavior in the three dimensions of politics, economics, and security in relations with the United States, Europe, East Asia, and global institutions. Christopher Hughes's *Japan's Security Agenda: Military, Economic, and Environmental Dimensions* (Boulder, Colo.: Lynne Rienner, 2004) offers an analysis of the security policies pursued by Japan and examines the way policy-makers take a much broader view of security than just military security. It shows how security is viewed comprehensively and includes economic and environmental security. Peter Katzenstein in *Cultural Norms and National Security: Police and Military in Postwar Japan* (Ithaca, NY: Cornell University Press, 1996) explains Japanese security policy by examining the role of norms, showing why the government has been reluctant to abandon non-violent policy responses, despite international pressure. Miyashita Akitoshi and Satō Yōichirō's edited volume *Japanese Foreign Policy in Asia and the Pacific: Domestic Interests, American Pressure, and Regional Integration* (New York: Palgrave Macmillan, 2001) examines Japanese foreign policy taking into account both domestic interests and US pressure. Through a range of case studies it moves the debate on the reactive state forward.

PART V

Themes in Japanese History

CHAPTER TWENTY

Women and Sexuality in Premodern Japan

Hitomi Tonomura

Changing gender relations shaped the contours of a millennium and a half of premodern Japanese history. The pattern of transformation was more gradual than sudden, and was defined more by sustained processes than by notable events. For organizational purposes, we nonetheless divide this history into three "moments," each with its own thematic problems of long-lasting consequences. The first moment is the so-called *ritsuryō* period, the seventh and eighth centuries, during which the centralizing elites adopted the Tang Chinese institutional model and adjusted it to create Japan's first bureaucratic government, headed by an emperor, with the full force of *ritsu* (penal) and *ryō* (civil) codes. The growth of military organizations and values supporting the spread of raw violence in the mid fourteenth through sixteenth centuries marks the second, albeit long, moment. Especially among warrior families, gender differentiation sharpened in the areas of production, property-holding, and family relations, as well as in the social perception of cultural and sexual authority. The third focus is the seventeenth century, the time of the establishment of the centralized regime supported by the status-specific, morally imbued discursive agenda of the new warrior government that instituted undisputed peace and order. In this regime, gender considerations overrode the status-based prescriptions as often as they were subsumed by them.

The Impact of the *Ritsuryō* Code

Japan's first set of codes (*ritsuryō*) introduced what Sekiguchi Hiroko calls a "patriarchal family paradigm" upon existing gender relations.[1] The codes imposed Confucian-style institutional perquisites and responsibilities but their application also highlighted the incongruence between the language of the law and the persistent features of Japanese society that differed from China's androcentric ideals.

Bureaucracy and the throne

The new bureaucracy at its center was fundamentally gendered male. Female officials mostly belonged to the twelve offices in the inner palace that supported imperial business. The men's offices, titles, and ranks granted highly coveted perquisites and concretely manifested the ideal paternalistic matrix of Confucian-style loyalty to the emperor. Female officials, whose promotional track differed from that of men's, nonetheless performed significant functions, such as dispatching imperial announcements (*naishi sen*) from within the inner palace, and personally assisting the emperor in ceremonial matters, for example by distributing special ceremonial compensations to male officials. However, by the end of the eighth century, the term *nyokan* ("female officials") had replaced the term "officials" (or, "kingly service persons") (*kunin, miyahito*) in the case of women. A century later, powerful male aristocrats (*kurōdo*) who, according to Yoshikawa, had been eyeing the political weight of the inner palace, began assuming certain duties of the female officials. By the end of the tenth century, female officials commanded mostly household responsibilities, such as cleaning and lamp-lighting, while the new category of "ladies-in-waiting" (*nyōbō*) emerged. Exemplified by Murasaki Shikibu and Sei Shōnagon, authors of *The Tale of Genji* and *The Pillowbook of Sei Shōnagon* respectively, they exercised tremendous cultural authority and power.[2]

Above the bureaucratic offices presided the emperor whose gender was legally unspecified. This condition lasted until 1889 when male reign and direct patrilineal succession became legally prescribed in the Meiji Imperial Law. Thus six women, all imperial daughters, assumed eight out of the sixteen reigns beginning with Suiko (r. 592–628), believed to be the first to use the term *tennō* (emperor), followed by Kōgyoku (642–45); Saimei (655–61, also known as Kōgyoku); Jitō (690–97); Gemmei (707–15); Genshō (715–24); Kōken (749–58); and Shōtoku (764–70, also known as Kōken). Recent scholarship holds the eight female reigns as a logical extension of Japan's prehistoric pattern of frequent female rule. It argues against the previously dominant views that deny female emperors full political authority by characterizing them as either "shamans" or "intermediaries" situated between legitimate male rulers.[3]

Himiko, a queen whose rule over the third-century kingdom of Yamatai is described in the Chinese chronicle *Wei zhi*, exemplifies the prehistoric female rule. Assisted by her brother, Himiko conducted diplomacy with China, in addition to communicating with deities and forces of nature; a large mound, a sign of power, was built upon her death. Succession by a male king brought chaos until Himiko's 13-year-old female relative Iyo (or Toyo) replaced him and restored order.[4] The examples of Himiko and Iyo question the widely held co-rule paradigm that posits gender-specific sharing of spiritual/shamanistic (female) and administrative/diplomatic (male) authority by a pair of female and male chiefs.[5] Himiko and Iyo administered both spiritual and secular matters. In diplomacy, they communicated with China's Wei dynasty in AD 239 and Western Jin dynasty in AD 266. The Wei dynasty emperor bestowed upon Himiko a golden seal and the title of "King of Wa, Friendly to Wei." A gender-conscious reading of other sources also reveals the participation of male rulers in spiritual endeavors as well as the involvement of female chiefs in administrative and military capacities.[6]

Evidence of female rule includes skeletal burial remains with a pattern of regional differentiation that favors females in the west and males in the northeast.[7] Entries in Japan's own earliest "histories" (*Kojiki*, comp. AD 712, and *Nihon shoki*, comp. AD 720) also depict powerful semi-legendary female figures among heroic male rulers. Jingū, after the death of her husband-emperor, Chūai (r. AD 192–200), is recorded to have ruled for seventy years, during which she led expeditions against Korea while pregnant. Female regional chiefs also appear in the *Nihon shoki* entries.[8] The legendary Emperor Keikō (r. AD 71–130), for example, encountered in Suwo "a woman, by the name of Kamu-natsu-so-hime, whose followers were exceedingly numerous. She was the chieftain of that whole country."[9] Finally, the assignment in the origin myth of Amaterasu (the Sun Goddess) as the ancestral deity of the imperial line forcefully upholds the early significance of female authority.[10]

If female rule had been unquestioned, why did it "end" in 770? A standard explanation points to Shōtoku's love affair with a priest, Dōkyō, whom she sought to elevate to the highest administrative position, a move that so threatened the aristocrats that they moved the capital out of the Buddhist-entrenched city of Nara and terminated the morally dangerous female rule. The revised view first of all complicates the question by pointing to the ongoing institutional possibility of female rule throughout the premodern period, indeed until 1889, as illustrated by the proposed enthronement of Hachijō-in, a daughter of Emperor Toba, in the late twelfth century and the actual reigns of two female emperors in the Tokugawa period.[11] The definitive institutional "end" of female rule came only with modernity.

Rather than dwelling on Shōtoku's putative feminine moral flaw, more recent scholarship considers the pattern of broader social transformation that elevated male authority. Evidence shows that women of the imperial line who had earlier lived in an independent residential quarter with an equally independent economic base began to assume the role of "wife," as illustrated by the move into her husband's residential palace of the wife of Emperor Kōnin, who succeeded Shōtoku.[12] Yoshie Akiko asserts that this change signaled the loss of women's independent political identity that had sustained the title of the head of the state.[13] This development, as it turns out, created a combination of factors used by the non-imperial Fujiwara family to optimally control the throne: the established practice of raising children at the maternal parent's home, the male gender of the emperor, and the flexibility in the ranking and number of imperial wives. The Fujiwara women produced crown princes who were then raised in the Fujiwara home where they acquired an appropriate sense of lineage loyalty. The so-called *ritsuryō* society initially endorsed women's established political authority as chiefs and emperors, especially royal daughters. But in time, wives and mothers of emperors, who were mostly of the Fujiwara lineage, gained the historical spotlight, as imperial daughters receded into the shadow of political insignificance.

Household, family, and taxation

In the area of broad social organization that involved all commoners, the code's normative language and its principle were extensive but far removed from Japan's native conditions.[14] The Law of Households in the *Yōrō ritsuryō* advanced provisions for a comprehensive taxation and landowning system.[15] The country's arable land theoretically was the throne's and was redistributed to the people according to the composition of each residence unit (*ko*) that was recorded in the newly compiled registry (*koseki*). For creating an orderly registry, the code assumed a

Chinese-style family system organized by patrilineal descent and patrilocal marriage practices within a definable "household" that was headed by a "household head." In this Chinese system, specific ceremonies (*li*) formalized marriage; all sexual relations unsanctioned by *li* were regarded as adultery; premarital sex was disallowed for women; the statuses of wife and mistress were clearly distinguished; surname endogamy was prohibited; and a woman's natal family was insignificant after her marriage.

The application of the code highlighted the incongruity between the legal provisions and the social organization under the emergent state that attached no established definition for descent, marriage, or household. Japan's ancient marriage and sexual practices generally required no formal, official, or contractual agreements. No prescribed ceremony or ritual defined marriage which often was preceded by sex, probably continuing the pre-*ritsuryō* practices illustrated in Japan's oldest extant writings such as local gazetteers, *fudoki*, and the *Kojiki*. *Fudoki* illustrate youthful engagement in songfests, which occasioned a festive exchange of poems between girls and boys for the purpose of community-based sexual unions.[16] The creation stories featured in the *Kojiki* show no moral censure toward sex per se, which is fundamental to cosmic "becoming," and there was no vocabulary for virginity. The process of "household registration" found "family units" typically composed of the mother and her children, with a husband whose attachment to the household likely was determined through sexual relations that began and ended flexibly. Consequently, registration created on paper a large number of single-parent households which put daughters with the mother and sons with the father.[17] The fluidity of "family" contradicted the codal goal predicated on the stability of self-perpetuating "households."[18]

Land came to be allotted based on the newly created registry. Unlike the Tang Chinese law which allotted land to no women except widows, Japanese *ritsuryō* reflected the custom and provided: "man: two tan [of paddy]; for woman, reduce this by one-third." This was unequal to be sure, but for receiving two-thirds of the men's portion, women had fewer obligations. Able-bodied men were levied with a labor service (*yō*, *zōyō*), including a military and a head tax (*chō*), which was usually paid in kind, that is, cloth typically woven by women. Wakita Haruko explains that the apparent tax advantage given to females prompted many men to register as women.[19] Conversely, the law that exempted women from military service officially barred them from it. The military, the profession that, in historical hindsight, would evolve into the most powerful and influential occupation, was codified as male, both in conscription and official posts, whether or not women were in combat. Other gender-based dispensations included different forms of punishment for the same crime, and a delay in execution of a pregnant convict till twenty days after the birth of the child who "should be taken care of by close relatives, neighbors, or others who desire him/her despite differences in name (*sei*)."[20] These provisions reflected the law's paternalistic principle that likened the state to a family headed by a benevolent emperor.

The founding law's affirmation of an individual woman's rights to land both reflected and perpetuated the existing social and economic structure. As the allotment system deteriorated, in 723 and 743 the government permitted private possession of newly reclaimed land. Such laws were gender-neutral; documents and wooden tablets (*mokkan*) of the sale and commendation of private land show, in addition to male names, female names in the format that proves separation of ownership from their husbands.[21]

The *ritsuryō* code had a limited impact on the ways of sex and marriage despite the principle of androcentric heterosexual union upon which the imperial bureaucratic institution had been built. Some provisions, such as the one for naming adultery, "had no actual function" according to Inoue Mitsusada, who wonders if the codifiers "sought to educate the people in the ways of Chinese family morality and propriety in order to bring order."[22] The code also includes the Confucian notion of women's "Seven Outs and Three Not-Outs": a husband may divorce a wife for being childless, adulterous, disobedient to her parents-in-law, and talkative, as well as for stealing, being jealous, and suffering from an incurable disease; he may not divorce her if she kept the household during mourning for her parents-in-law, if the household has risen in status, and if she has nobody to whom to return. As Inoue states, "It is questionable how these provisions actually functioned in Japan where divorce was relatively freely practiced."[23] Indeed, the letter of the law would be ignored and the gap between it and social practices would remain wide for many centuries to come. Writings from the Heian period (710–1185), long after the demise of the household registration system, confirm the ongoing absence of official, social, or religious concerns over the flexible mating arrangements. In reality, among aristocrats, pragmatic concerns, such as the lineage, rank, and title of partners' parents, probably guided the direction of most long-term relationships, possibly more than the desires and passions depicted in *The Tale of Genji* that so exquisitely colored the court.[24] Sexual relationships which received no official or moral censure included male–male bonding, especially among aristocrats and monks. Fujiwara Yorinaga's (1120–56) journal, *Taiki*, famously describes his escapades and satisfaction with men he courts, not to the exclusion of relationships with women, whom he omits from his writing as his object of courting.[25]

The combination of the clearly ranked system of prestige embedded in the imperial bureaucracy, the prevailing mode of sexuality, the absence of external foes and major wars, and the income that flowed into the capital from the provinces, all contributed to the making of the Heian aristocratic culture and the emergence of now world renowned classic female authors. The pattern of heterosexual union, that is, "marriage," would be transformed during the medieval period and attain a form somewhat closer to the *ritsuryō* ideal.

Gender Relations in Times of Raw Violence

At the end of the Genpei War (1180–85), Minamoto Yoritomo established the first warrior government (bakufu, 1190–1333) alongside the imperial government. Yoritomo was supported by provincial warriors whose land rights he guaranteed or augmented through *jitō-shiki* (stewardship), a title he dispensed to a large portion of the country's estates (*shōen*). Estates had evolved gradually, paralleling the disintegration of the *ritsuryō* allotment system. Each represented nested land interests (*shiki*) held at once by people and institutions of different social statuses, such as princesses, monks, warriors, peasants, and temples and shrines. Importantly, these interests were gender-neutral and also inheritable, divisible, and transferable. *Jitō-shiki* was a new layer in the existing hierarchy of rights initially granted most often for meritorious service in the Genpei War. Women were among its recipients, especially as war widows, and later as beneficiaries of inheritance.

Property with rights and obligations

Warrior society was more "advanced" in gender relations than was the aristocratic society, at least in practicing patrilocal marriage and patrilineal descent. "Marriage" and "divorce," however, were equally unceremonial, with no contractual agreement or official registration. Women in the warrior class held firm economic rights deriving from inheritance, most frequently as a daughter and less often as a wife. Upon marriage women maintained their natal family name and their property independent of their husbands. The bakufu law (*Jōei Shikimoku*, 1232) and its active judicial system upheld legitimate property rights, including those of women. Despite the prevalence of patrilineal descent, the law ensured the customary rights of a woman to adopt a daughter or son, regardless of her marital status.[26]

Land rights pertaining to *jitō-shiki* were unique in Japan's gender history: for women or men, the rights entailed the bakufu-generated guard and other military duties in proportion to the size of the *shiki* portion. Guaranteed by the prevailing custom of divided inheritance, daughters, along with sons, frequently received a *jitō-shiki* portion and thus were a link in the bakufu's lord–vassal (*gokenin*) structure, even without the formal and coveted designation of *gokenin*. Women maintained the associated rights and obligations independent of their husbands upon marriage, who occasionally also willed a portion to their wives. Female and male holders of land rights left copious documentation not only of their rights but also of trial records produced as defendants or plaintiffs. However, by the end of the thirteenth century, a combination of factors began to threaten women's land rights.

First, repeated land division negatively affected the economic foundation of the family. In this context, women's property rights in particular became an issue. The inevitable consequence of the combination of patrilineal descent and the daughter's inheritance rights was that a daughter's holdings typically went to her children, who carried her husband's lineage. Unless the daughter was married endogamously, or she bequeathed the land to members of her natal family (probably causing conflict with her children), her portion would be lost to her natal family in the subsequent generation.

Second, the ability of women to fulfill military duties became suspect during the Mongol invasions of 1274 and 1281. These unprecedented attacks from outside required actual combat, for the first time in Kamakura history. Although many men also dispatched proxy fighters, the absence of women in particular led to the bakufu's injunction against "daughters' portions." The legal provision itself had little immediate impact on the direction of land division in each family, but it foreshadowed the demise of property rights for warrior-class women, a trend that was clear by the mid fourteenth century.

Third, the increasing financial insolvency among the warriors and escalation of intra-class violence caused each family to invest all resources in one "primary" son (*chakushi*) by consolidating previously divided land as a way to strengthen its economic and military base. Daughters and widows began receiving a lifetime portion that "returned" to the heir upon their death, or simply received sustenance land. Secondary sons also became dependants or else vassals of other warrior groups. Devoid of *jitō-shiki*, "feudal" rights that demanded service, women as a gender lost the government-sanctioned "public" role. The erosion in formal property rights significantly diminished women's presence in the historical records. Changing property-holding patterns signaled the evolution in the structure of the military that prepared itself for the thoroughly decentralized *sengoku* (country-at-war) age of the late fifteenth to sixteenth centuries.[27]

Women of fame

Two women of exceptional political influence, situated three centuries apart, marked the pages of governance that are otherwise dominated by male activities. Hōjō Masako (1157–1225), the wife of the first Kamakura shōgun, Minamoto Yoritomo (1147–99), supervised their sons, Yoriie and Sanetomo, who succeeded Yoritomo as the second and third shōgun, respectively. As a woman, Masako could not hold the official title of shōgun (more fully, Sei'i taishōgun or "Barbarian-Conquering Generalissimo"), which the emperor conferred as a military post within the male-gendered imperial bureaucracy. In reality, Masako partook in actual governance along with the male members of the Hōjō, her natal family, that controlled Kamakura politics as regents to the shōgun who, subsequent to Masako's "rule," were defenseless aristocrats and imperial princes. The youthful Masako's midnight escapade in the rain to see Yoritomo, whom she chose as her lover-husband against parental wishes, and her outrage at his affair during her pregnancy are well-known incidents that attest to her willfulness and an environment that allowed such public expressions of what would later be considered female moral failure.[28]

Hino Tomiko (1440–96), the wife of the eighth Ashikaga shōgun, Yoshimasa (1436–90), was also involved in practical details of administration. Tomiko comes down in history as the archetypal female villain. She gave birth to a son after Yoshimasa's younger brother, Yoshimi, had already been selected to be the next shōgun. She sought the support of vassals to elevate her son, Yoshihisa (1465–89), instead, and caused a division among those who sided with one or other candidate. This led in part to the Ōnin War (1467–77), premodern Japan's biggest civil war, which devastated Kyoto and precipitated Japan's descent into the period of perpetual wars. Tomiko's son succeeded her husband in 1473 at the age of 8, but later died in battle. Tomiko then took charge of determining his successors. Typically, it is as a widow that a woman in a patrilocal and patrilineal marriage structure gains authority as a representative of the deceased husband's family. But Tomiko had been actively engaged in politics first as the wife of one and then as the mother of another shōgun while they were still alive. Tomiko also exerted influence in the commercialized world of Kyoto by amassing enormous personal profits, especially through loan house operations. Less well known is her treatment of the defeated troops in the aftermath of that war. She arranged to have land awarded to the Ōuchi, on the losing side, to remove the stain of shame, and to have the daughter of the defeated Yoshimi (Tomiko's niece) appropriately placed in a nunnery.[29]

Violence and women

In the Muromachi period (1336–1572), the centripetal force of allegiance that tied the country's warriors to the bakufu weakened significantly. The estate system which had accommodated the landed interests of all classes was breaking down as warriors seized the income allotted to aristocrats by legal and illegal means. Provincial warriors, without formal attachment to the bakufu, advanced independent power based on full control of land, resources, transportation, and inhabitants. Rivalry over resources led to actual and potential armed conflicts. Battles damaged both the natural and human-built environment. Non-combatants, perhaps the fighters' relatives and friends, were often victimized. Some were simply killed, some were maimed, some were raped, and some were abducted as slaves. The victims were not just women, although young women and young boys were particularly vulnerable.[30]

For warrior-class women, the reality of violence negatively affected their social standing in a number of ways, as it sharpened the gendered division of labor and created a hierarchy of values that tended to constrain them. Although the Kamakura bakufu cited women's failure actually to fight the Mongol forces as a reason for sanctions against their property rights, women in fact participated in some war efforts. Hangaku was praised for her superior shooting skills in the *Azuma kagami*. Shot in her thigh by a bakufu man, she was captured and taken as a wife by one of the bakufu vassals who wanted a brave son.[31] The story of Tomoe, a legendary beauty and a superb fighter featured in the *Tale of the Heike*, which describes the Genpei War, also suggests female participation in battles. Tomoe became an icon in later art forms, such as literature, noh, and pictorial scrolls.[32] During the *sengoku* period, some women are said to have formed a cavalry force and others fought near their fortresses.[33] The wives of Nikaidō Moriyoshi, Narita Ujinaga, and Okumura Eifuku are known for having refused to surrender but instead defended their castles while their husbands were away or negotiated a settlement with the opponent.[34] But overall, Japan's medieval battlefields were a masculine space. Men's injured bodies abound in war tales, paralleling the practice of recording the actual injuries for submission to their lord as a proof of their loyal service that, ideally, led to rewards. The lord promoted the concept and vocabulary of loyalty in order to solicit service, and injuries became equated with glory and rewards. This mutually reinforcing ideology of loyalty and reward, whether or not it was acted upon, boosted the masculine values that dominated late medieval Japan. Women were excluded from the structure of reward, and thus what bravery and loyalty they exhibited necessarily had a different shape.

The condition of perpetual war in *sengoku* Japan reshaped the meanings of conjugal relationships. As before, no restrictions were articulated for forms of sexual acts per se. Sodomy and masturbation were unnamed and entirely uncensured. Virginity also remained unnamed and unobserved. However, in order to pre-empt internal conflicts among vassals, adulterous relationships between a man and a married (or engaged) woman were now punished with severity. While in the Kamakura period, both the woman and the man each lost half of their property, in the *sengoku* period, the wronged man was to cut down the adulterous male. *Jinkaishū*, the Date House Laws from 1536, demanded killing the woman as well, unless the husband caught the man in the bedroom. If the killing of the interloper took place outside, the wife also had to be killed, in order to prove to society that this was execution for adultery, not common revenge, an act strictly forbidden by the House Laws. These laws also saw no distinction between adultery and rape.[35] At the same time, the independent warlords sometimes exercised pragmatic flexibility in property transmission by including a provision in the Law: "As for the daughter's portions, leave it up to the parents," and even designated a daughter as the main heir in the absence of a son born to the main wife.[36]

In *sengoku* Japan, both women and men were sent to other houses to serve as a "security" link, producing more heroes and heroines than in any previous time in Japanese history. A niece of Mōri Motonari, daimyō of Aki province, was married four times, first to Yamanouchi, next to Kobayakawa, then to Sugihara, and finally to another Sugihara. These were all powerful warrior houses of Aki province and she must have played a crucial role in connecting their interests. Tragic and sometimes self-sacrificing female paragons were forced to choose their path when their husband's house was destroyed. The daughter of Hōjō Ujimasa was married to Takeda Katsuyori (1546–82) and committed suicide at the age of 19 when the Takeda were destroyed by Oda Nobunaga. Oichi no kata (1548–83), Oda Nobunaga's younger sister, was first married by Nobunaga to Azai Nagamasa. After Nobunaga destroyed Azai, he married Oichi to another warrior, Shibata Katsuie. When Nobunaga destroyed Shibata, Oichi allowed her three daughters from her first marriage to escape and committed suicide with Shibata.[37]

These famous examples tend to overshadow the work of other women who lived and died less dramatically. The condition of war demanded a gendered division of labor that charged wives with crucial domestic tasks. They oversaw the calendar of complicated and frequent ceremonial matters, supervised weapons storage, and, of course, created offspring. The education of children and organization of visits by relatives, vassals, traveling salesmen, religious personnel, and entertainers all were highly important tasks that demanded precision in speech, manners, and movements, so as to pre-empt any potential for interpersonal conflict or suspicion-arousing inappropriate gesture. Even the incorrect placement of a ceremonial item could be read as treason. Because the wife was an outsider serving as a fragile link between two houses, she needed to take extreme care in observing the proprieties, including differentiated forms of address for her husband's relatives and her own family members. Breach of ceremonial etiquette would not only be bad manners but might even start a war.[38]

Economy and society

This period of war saw a rise in the production of goods and the creation of a money economy. Commoners began to write and actively to preserve documents. These records, kept in villages, indicate that a not insignificant portion of the peasants' land was held in the name of women. In contrast to their productive role, however, women had little formal authority in community administration, which was typically based in the area's shrine and its organization. Quite contrary to the female spiritual authority of ancient times, formal authority in the medieval shrine organization (*za*) was predominantly male.[39] The body of documents left by commoners contain little information on women's daily life and activities. Visual materials, such as pictorial scrolls, help to suggest how men and women may have participated in a flourishing economy with a variety of mercantile and productive enterprises, as well as forms of entertainment.[40]

A Moment of Peace and Order

The articulation of the *ie* (the androcentric corporate and continuing "household"), diminution of women's property rights, and proliferation of moralistic discourses, combined with an expanding economy, the rising education rate, and greater employment opportunities, characterized the rapidly changing gender relations in the early modern times of peace and order. When Hideyoshi definitively ended the period of the "country-at-war" by implementing the first national land survey in the 1590s, he swept away the legacy of the medieval estate system with layered landed interests, including those of women, and instituted a new system of land registry that listed mostly men. Building on Hideyoshi's measures, which separated the samurai from the peasants, Tokugawa Ieyasu further enumerated and classified the population into clearly defined status categories (*mibun*: samurai, peasants, and artisan-merchants or townspeople). The idealized Neo-Confucian vision of hierarchy defined each group's own social and economic functions (*yaku*) and status-appropriate behavior, environment, housing, and even tools. Differences between statuses within the imagined organic whole defined and supported the ideal realm, but gender as a category often superseded the significance invested in the status-based differences. "Women" (*onna*) were named as a naturalized category and often received special attention, separate from men, who usually were the ungendered, universal "humans" (*hito*).

Practice

Samurai, the ruling group for which the well-being of the *ie* mattered most, derived income, representing benefice, from their position in the bureaucracy headed by the shōgun or daimyō. The bakufu bureaucracy was a male preserve, except for the female-exclusive inner quarter. The income-benefice and associated duties of each samurai house at all levels descended patrilineally to the male heir. In early Tokugawa times, *sengoku*-period exceptionality sometimes guided the samurai's ways, even granting women an award. Chizuru received a fief worth 2,000 *koku* from her older brother, Shimazu Iehisa, a *tozama* (or "outer") daimyō, for serving, with her daughter, as the voluntary "hostages" to the Tokugawa from 1613 to 1619.[41] But as the seventeenth century ended, land grants to women disappeared, save as trousseaux given to the daughters of shōgun and daimyō, who maintained this land independent of their husbands. The centralized regime produced many laws that formally dictated how property was to be transmitted. The law of primogeniture was set in the Kyōhō era (1716–35),[42] and a house without a biological son adopted a boy following elaborate requirements, such as the adoption of a relative before a non-relative.

Reflecting patrilineal authority, a widow could not officially adopt a son, but a husband without a wife could.[43]

As an exception to the masculinist bureaucracy, the ōoku (Great Interior), or the inner quarter of the shogunal household that biologically reproduced the shogunal heir, maintained women on its official payroll.[44] Usually numbering around 300, but 900 under Ienari (eleventh shōgun, r. 1787–1837), these women had their entire existence rationalized to perpetuate the shogunal ie.[45] Each ōoku woman's job description (shoku) determined her pay, which came in gold and/or silver, rice, and other forms.[46] Eight junior-level assistants (chūrō) had sex with the shōgun. The most senior woman slept near the shōgun and his night's mate and reported on the night's activities to the elder (toshiyori) the next day. These women's path to promotion and the possibility of their demise depended on their own or their master's reproductive performance and sexual expression. Ejima (1681–1741) began receiving a 400 koku stipend five years into her job (1709) when her mistress Okiyo successfully gave birth to the son of the sixth shōgun, Ienobu. Ejima's stipend increased to 600 koku when the 4-year-old child was appointed as the seventh shōgun, Ietsugu (1709–16).[47] Ejima occupied the highest post, Ōdoshiryori, but she was exiled for her reputed sexual involvement with a kabuki actor. Meanwhile, in the imperial bureaucracy in Kyoto, nyōbō, women with a similar function as ōoku, also received incomes ranging from 100 to 200 koku and exerted tremendous influence as middlewomen between ministers and the emperor.[48]

Peasant women, too, gradually lost property rights around the end of the seventeenth century. The government may have been ahead of the family in invalidating female property rights. Seizaemon in 1700 wrote a bequest assigning his land and wealth jointly to his wife and their adopted son. Seizaemon died a year later, prompting the widow to officially document the transfer of the rights. The office disallowed this transaction; the adopted son was to be the sole holder of the estate who would provide some income as a "widow's portion."[49] Women's actual rights were also sometimes hidden behind the facade of androcentric documentation. In 1637 Sōemon, a well-to-do peasant, granted his paddies and fields to one son and allocated the harvest from these lands in an equal division to him and his three sisters, while dispensing silver cash in the ratio of four to six between the son and daughters. Although the daughters thus received income, if not gender parity, the government's record shows only the son's name as the designated taxpayer.

Women in the merchant class, especially in large cities, had the greatest freedom to possess and manage wealth. The numerous acknowledgments of debt from Kyoto residents with female names, which were signed singly or jointly, are evidence of the pattern of female property rights in both household goods and land. Seventeenth- and eighteenth-century publications depict a large number of shop and job types that were oriented toward women, from the making of cloth and fans to the selling of sake, vinegar, and vegetables, and even the matchmaking of a lactating woman with a nursing baby.[50] The Mitsui, the grand merchant house that rose in the seventeenth century, owed its initial success to the work of the founder's mother, according to Mitsui records.[51] Regulations to restrict "female names" from household headships were passed in Osaka in 1730 and in Kyoto in 1751, apparently to no avail. According to Yasukuni, these regulations in fact were intended less to restrict female headships than to legislate the burgeoning sex-related shops.[52]

Owing to peace, stability, and prosperity, the magnificent and thriving urban culture, equated with the Buddhist notion of the "floating world" of suspended time and space, developed around prostitution, which in turn provided material and fed the imagination for art forms such as kabuki, books, painting, and sumō. The erotic pursuits that dominated the literary and visual spaces showed flexibility in love-object choices. In all combinations depicted in art – an adult male and a younger male, an adult male and a female, women and women, or women and young men – however, the primary gaze was that of the adult male. Continuing the pattern from pre-Tokugawa times, there was no official censure of sexuality per se, but adultery was severely punished, differing according to the status of those involved and the circumstances. It would also be a mistake to imagine that female sexuality in general went unscathed. Sone Hiromi has depicted the Tokugawa sex industry's grim hierarchy and the vulnerability of women engaged in it. Instances of sexual assault and the harassment of employed servant women in both urban and village settings, often by a group of young men, appear in official records and journals of village headmen.[53]

Discourse

As moralists proffered opinions, boosting the philosophical foundation of the new Tokugawa order, the economy boomed, publication houses multiplied, and discourses abounded. Amidst this abundance, men and women of all status groups bore the burden of moral education.[54] Among all texts aimed at exhorting womanly virtues, none is equal in notoriety to *The Greater Learning for Women* (*Onna daigaku*, published in the early eighteenth century), probably incorrectly attributed to the Confucian scholar, Kaibara Ekiken (1630–1714).[55] In standard scholarship, *The Greater Learning* stands as an archetypal representation of the oppressive feudal system; it epitomizes the inferiority of women by "encapsulat[ing] the discourse that subordinates women to their husbands (and /or their houses) and entrap[ping] them within the home, based on a gendered division of labor for housework, reproduction, and child rearing."[56] The text indeed spells out the classic Neo-Confucian principles of "seven reasons" for divorcing a wife and the essential moral "illnesses" (*yamai*) from which "at least seven or eight out of ten" women suffer, including disobedience, anger, slander, jealousy, and stupidity. Women have no master but the husband who is lord and Heaven.[57] Similar Confucian language had appeared in the *Yōrō ritsuryō* code of the eighth century and other moralistic texts in the medieval age,[58] but, unlike the earlier writings with their limited audience and influence, *The Greater Learning* was widely circulated and reached all classes of people, down to ordinary farm women, and thus by logic had an enormous impact on how society and women themselves viewed the female gender.[59]

A closer reading of *The Greater Learning* and a better understanding of its discursive position, writing structure, and the social context in which it came to be written and disseminated, can offer alternative ways to appreciate its message and significance. The popularity of the text must attest to its usefulness, rather than oppressive quality, for it served as a practical parental manual for raising daughters and a girls' instructional booklet for acquiring winning manners in situations that occur beyond the home. The text's subtext is concern for a daughter's life in marriage. Girls require a stricter upbringing than do boys because they will leave one home to go to another to serve their in-laws, with the possibility of shameful eviction should relations suffer. It is a mistake for a wife to blame her husband and his family; the blame is on the parents who failed to raise her properly. The text includes precise instructions, for example, on how to manage a husband's debauchery: admonish him in a gentle voice without being jealous and, if unheeded, repeat the admonition after his heart has calmed. It recommends that the woman not be lured into divination or pray indiscriminately; before reaching the age of 40, she should avoid crowded places such as temples and shrines, and should not see such lewd acts as kabuki and jōruri; she should be modest in drinking tea and sake.[60]

As Martha Tocco has elucidated, the structure of writing in *The Greater Learning* also served as a textbook for the ABCs in writing and reading, both in Japanese and in "male letters," that is, Chinese, in a society that was deeply committed to the reading and writing of complex written forms.[61] Yokota Fuyuhiko evaluates *The Greater Learning* as a text situated in a multidimensional discourse that emerged from the context of increasing commercialization and opportunities for outside work. He notes that *The Greater Learning* was one chapter in *Onna daigaku takarabako* (A Treasure Chest of Greater Learning for Women, first published 1716), which contained a variety of moralistic, educational, and practical materials, such as descriptions of occupations performed by women, poems in *The Tale of Genji*, biographies of filial children in China, and instructive tips on raising children and administering emergency medical treatment. The *Treasure Chest* itself was also one of many writings on female occupations that flooded the market. Yokota contends that the value of *The Greater Learning* is its relationship to the realistic Tokugawa context, in which most women's work situations involved potentially sexualized service work. *The Greater Learning* helped women to understand how to cultivate the exemplary behavior necessary for "protect[ing] themselves from the accusation of being sexually corruptible" in the workplace.[62]

To what extent, then, did the ideals presented in *The Greater Learning for Women* correspond to the reality? We probe this question by focusing on divorce which, the text states, can result from "seven leaves" and represents women's "life's shame."[63] No divorce or marriage was formally registered, but Laurel Cornell used household registration (*shūmon aratamechō*) and deduced a ratio of one divorce in five to nine marriages, depending on the rate of marrying in or out of the village.[64] "Divorce was a common feature of life in the Edo period," which cut across status and regional differences, declares Harald Fuess.[65] Does this finding mean that many women apparently were subjected to "seven leaves" and lived "a life of shame"? The prevalence of the "three-and-a-half line" divorce announcement of the husband, which gave no specific reason, seems to attest to the vulnerable position of women. Recent studies provide a more complex picture, however. Despite the husband's signature on the "three-and-a-half line," many divorces were initiated by the woman or her parents, who demanded this statement in order to facilitate the woman's remarriage, which was also frequent, contrary to the Confucian dictum that "a virtuous woman takes not two husbands."[66]

The ideals embodied in *The Greater Learning for Women* also contradict the specific provisions set forth in the bakufu's laws. Upon marriage, *The Greater Learning* states, a woman was to serve her parents-in-law "more dutifully than she does her own" because she "succeeds not to her own parents but to her father- and mother-in-law."[67] The bakufu's mourning rules (*bukkiryō*), issued in 1684 and revised five times by 1734, define one's proximity to family relations in terms of the number of avoidance and mourning days after death and other taboos. Accordingly, for her own parents, a wife is to observe 50 days of avoidance and 13 months of mourning, but for her parents-in-law, only 30 days and 150 days respectively. A wife had no obligations toward her husband's family members, except for her husband and parents-in-law. A wife's mourning duties for her natal family members did not change upon marriage. For a wife's death, no one other than her husband on his side of family had obligations.[68] Therefore, laws did not elevate in-laws above a woman's own parents.[69] The gap between the language in *The Greater Learning* and social customs and bakufu laws illustrates the danger of the historiographical tendency to mistake a discursive formulation for actual gender relations.

This is not to say that Confucian virtues were ignored by the authorities or the people. As the founding ideals of stability confronted growing signs of social and economic transformation, the political authorities campaigned for Confucian moral virtues, for example, by establishing a reward system and publishing its news throughout the country in such documents as the *Kankoku kōgiroku* (Official Records of Filial Piety, *c.*1790s). The eleven types of virtues were mostly awarded to men, loyalty leading the list for the samurai and filial piety for the peasant men. For women, unsurprisingly, chastity topped all.[70]

The variety of discourses that abounded in Tokugawa society included "national learning" (*kokugaku*) and "Dutch learning" (*rangaku*). Kamo no Mabuchi (1697–1769), a national learning scholar, for example, emphasized the maternal origin of Japan's antiquity.[71] In her "Solitary Thoughts" ("Hitori kangae"), Tadano Makuzu (1763–1825) criticized Confucianism's male-centered views which she deemed poorly suited to the Japanese heart. Makuzu's writing suggests her exposure to various intellectual influences and in turn reminds us of the deeply complex and transformative social dynamic that underlies the more obvious Neo-Confucian dictum. It is unfortunate that Takizawa Bakin, an author and publisher, to whom she submitted her work, only circulated it privately.[72]

Conclusion

This chapter has sought to present dimensions of the gendered histories of Japan from ancient through early modern times with a focus on women. Women's real life situations varied tremendously, as did men's, depending on factors such as class, status, natal region, economic resources, and family composition. A history of women should show this variety from the perspective of the women themselves, if possible, to avoid complicit engagement with the views of the authorities that often took women as one, and even more often, as an essential category. Our task is difficult, however, for what we can know about each group at any time depends on the availability of sources. The imbalance in the quantity and quality of sources has pushed me to focus, unevenly and inconsistently, on the ancient aristocrats and the medieval warriors. The Tokugawa period posed a different problem of information overload, which made any act of generalization dangerously simplistic. This modest chapter hardly is a summary of premodern Japanese women's history. Such a summary would be as impossible to produce as one of men's history for the same millennium and a quarter.

NOTES

1 Sekiguchi, "The Patriarchal Family Paradigm," p. 27.
2 Wakita, Hayashi, and Nagahara, eds., *Nihon joseishi*, pp. 28–9; Yoshikawa, "Ritsuryō kokka," pp. 106–40; Nomura, *Kōkyū to jokan*, pp. 18–27.
3 Embedded in the modern norm of masculine imperial rule, the old views position female emperors first as wives and mothers and code their abdication as forfeiture – an aspect of their "fill-in" role, in contrast to the purpose and power assigned to male emperors' abdications. If women indeed served as intermediaries, why more such "intermediaries" were not installed to avoid the crisis that occurred between 770 and 1630 is a question that these views do not address. Yoshie, "Kodai joteiron," p. 23, and Tsurumi, "The Male Present," also addresses this historiographical bias.
4 Lu, *Japan*, pp. 11–14.
5 Naitō Torajirō and Shiratori Kurakichi presented and established this view in 1910 (Yoshie, *Tsukurareta Himiko*, p. 191; see Piggott, "Chieftain Pairs," for more on co-rule).
6 Sōgō Joseishi Kenkyūkai, ed., *Nihon josei no rekishi*, pp. 28–9; Wakita, Hayashi, and Nagahara, eds., *Nihon joseishi*, pp. 16–17.
7 Sōgō Joseishi Kenkyūkai, ed., *Nihon josei no rekishi*, p. 25; Makabe, who organized burial site data according to the size of mound, sex, and region, has found that larger tombs in Kyūshū tended to have more females than males, while in the northeast larger tombs had more males. As for smaller mounds, she found those in Kyūshū contained more males than females, and those in the northeast about the same number of each (Makabe, "Kofun to josei," pp. 12–13).
8 Aston, trans., *Nihongi*, pp. 224–53.
9 An entry for the twelfth year, ninth month, fifth day, of Emperor Keikō. Aston romanizes her name Kamu-nashi-hime. The entry continues: "When she heard that the Emperor's messengers had arrived, she … addressed them, saying: 'I beseech you, do not have recourse to arms. None of my people, I assure you, are rebellious. They will presently submit themselves to virtue. But there are mischievous brigands. The name of one is Hanatari' " (Aston, trans., *Nihongi*, pp. 192–3; Sōgō Joseishi Kenkyūkai, ed., *Shiryō ni miru Nihon josei*, p. 2).
10 For references to Amaterasu see Philippi, trans., *Kojiki*, glossary, p. 454; for references to the Sun Goddess see Aston, trans., *Nihongi*, index, p. 441.
11 The Meiji Imperial House Law made female succession illegal but recognized the accession of sons born from a non-primary wife, thereby insuring the availability of sons. After the Pacific War, the Imperial Household Act of 1947 reconfirmed exclusion of females from the imperial succession, but without the provision for multiple wives, thus setting the stage for the current problem of there being no male issue to succeed to the throne (Yoshie, "Kodai joteiron," pp. 45–6).
12 Suiko, Kyōgoku, Jitō, and Gemmei had husbands and produced children. Genshō and Kōken/Shōtoku, as well as the two Tokugawa female emperors, had no husbands.
13 Yoshie, "Kodai joteiron," pp. 38–40; Piggott, "The Last Classical Female Sovereign." On female emperors as imperial daughters, see Fukutō, *Rekishi no naka no kōjotachi*; Nishino, "Kodai."
14 Sekiguchi, "The Patriarchal Family Paradigm," p. 28; Yoshie, "Gender," pp. 439–48.
15 For translation of some of the codes, see Lu, *Japan*, pp. 33–6.

16 See Philippi, trans., *Kojiki*; Aoki, *Izumo no kuni fudoki*, and Aoki, trans., *Records of Wind and Earth* for translation of *Fudoki*; Aoki, *Ancient Myths*, pp. 143–55, for songfest.

17 Yoshie, "Kodai no kazoku," pp. 220–1.

18 Wakita, Hayashi, and Nagahara, eds., *Nihon joseishi*, pp. 31–2; Inoue et al., eds., *Nihon shisō taikei*, 3, pp. 225–61, 548–72.

19 Wakita, Hayashi, and Nagahara, eds., *Nihon joseishi*, p. 26.

20 Inoue et al., eds., *Nihon shisō taikei*, 3, pp. 456, 461, 462.

21 Yoshie, "Kodai no mura," p. 144.

22 Articles 26 and 27 on marriage formalities and adultery.

23 Inoue et al., eds., *Nihon shisō taikei*, 3, p. 564; Lu, *Japan*, pp. 35–6.

24 See Murasaki, *The Tale of Genji*. One's mother and father transmitted the lineage-based prestige. The bloodline resulting from sexual activities was significant, but parenthood without them, that is adoption, also served the purpose. The highest ranking example of adoption is the previously mentioned Hachijō-in, who was a daughter of Emperor Toba and also a younger sister of Emperor Goshirakawa by a different mother. Though single, she adopted Goshirakawa's second son, Prince Mochihito (1151–80), and his daughter. She supported Mochihito in the Genpei War against the Taira. After his demise, she continued her protection of Mochihito's daughter. She created ties with both the defeated Taira and the victorious Minamoto, and amassed the largest block of estates in the country. Mochihito's real mother was a Fujiwara but not of the regency line, a negative factor against his becoming a crown prince (Sōgō Joseishi Kenkyūkai, ed., *Shiryō ni miru Nihon josei*, pp. 69–70). On sexuality, see Tonomura, "Black Hair and Red Trousers."

25 Tōno, "Nikki ni miru Fujiwara Yorinaga"; Gomi, *Inseiki shakai*, pp. 416–41; Fukutō, *Heianchō no onna*, pp. 150–64.

26 Tonomura, "Women and Inheritance," pp. 595–608.

27 Ibid., pp. 608–33.

28 *Azuma kagami* addresses Masako as "Niidono," Madame Junior Second Rank, an honorable aristocratic rank conferred upon her by the imperial government, and identifies the six years of her quasi-shogunal rule as "the time of Niidono." Jealousy was one of the seven Confucian female obstructions but Masako had a vassal destroy the house where the mistress was kept; Yoritomo cut off the poor vassal's topknot (Tabata, *Hōjō Masako*, pp. 18–19).

29 Nomura, "Chūsei josei," p. 179; Wakita, *Chūsei ni ikiru onnatachi*; Tabata, *Hōjō Masako*.

30 Fujiki, *Zōhyōtachi no senjō*, and Fujiki, *Sengoku no mura*, esp. ch. 3.

31 *Azuma kagami*, vol. 17, entries for 1201.6.28 and 29, in Kishi, *Zenyaku Azuma kagami*, vol. 3, pp. 55–6. In the final analysis, it was her reproductive capacity that was ultimately valued (by men).

32 McCullough, *The Tale of the Heike*, pp. 291–3.

33 Ebisawa, "15 seiki no sensō," pp. 90–5.

34 Wakita, Hayashi, and Nagahara, eds., *Nihon joseishi*, p. 106.

35 Tonomura, "Sexual Violence against Women," pp. 138–45.

36 The Date, the Mōri, and the Rokkaku had similar provisions for daughters and widows (*Jinkaishū*, no. 104, in Ishii et al., eds., *Chūsei seiji shakai shisō*, p. 228; *Rokkakushi shikimoku*, no. 48, in Ishii et al., eds., *Chūsei seiji shakai shisō*, p. 295; Wakita, Hayashi, and Nagahara, eds., *Nihon joseishi*, p. 115; Nagano, "Bakuhanhō to josei," p. 167).

37 Wakita, Hayashi, and Nagahara, eds., *Nihon joseishi*, p. 102.

38 See, for example, the prescription written by Hōjō Gen'an, in Hōjō, "Hōjō Gen'an oboegaki."

39 Tonomura, *Community and Commerce*, pp. 57–61.

40 See, for example, the late sixth-century version of *Rakuchū rakugai zu*, "scenes from in and out of the capital city" (Okami and Satake, *Hyōchū rakuchū rakugai byōbu*).

41 Note that the "hostage" practice was an extension of a daimyō-initiated *sengoku* practice. Chizuru was then a widow. Her brother had killed her father-in-law, and the brothers and mother of her husband had also been executed. In 1619 her daughter married a nephew of Tokugawa Ieyasu, and Chizuru went home to marry Shimazu Hisamoto for the second time. Note also that remarriage continued to be practiced uncensored, and was often encouraged (Sōgō Joseishi Kenkyūkai, ed., *Shiryō ni miru Nihon josei*, pp. 90–2).

42 Wakita, Hayashi, and Nagahara, eds., *Nihon joseishi*, p. 119.

43 Nagano, "Bakuhanhō to josei," pp. 166–9.

44 Totman, *Politics in the Tokugawa Bakufu*, p. 97, describes the women's quarter in Chiyoda Castle.

45 Yanagi, "Josei no seikatsu kūkan," p. 390. The only primary wife of a Tokugawa shōgun who bore a surviving child was the wife of the second shōgun Hidetada (r. 1605–23).

46 Sōgō Joseishi Kenkyūkai, ed., *Nihon josei no rekishi*, p. 149.

47 Yanagi, "Josei no seikatsu kūkan," p. 388.

48 Sōgō Joseishi Kenkyūkai, ed., *Nihon josei no rekishi*, p. 151.

49 Miyashita, "Kinsei zenki ni okeru *ie*," pp. 11–19.

50 Yasukuni, "Kinsei Kyōto," p. 88.

51 "The origin of the Mitsui business is this Juhō (mother)," states "Shōbaiki," written by Takaharu, third son of Takatoshi, the founder (Hayashi, "Machiya josei," pp. 96–9).

52 Sōgō Joseishi Kenkyūkai, ed., *Nihon josei no rekishi*, p. 152; Yasukuni, "Kinsei Kyōto," p. 75.

53 See Pflugfelder, *Cartographies of Desire*, on male–male sex; Sone, Terashima, and Walthall, trans., "Prostitution and Public Authority," on prostitution; Nagano, "Nōson in okeru josei," pp. 60–4, on assault.

54 Sugano, "State Indoctrination of Filial Piety," pp. 170–1.

55 Sakai, "Kaibara Ekken," pp. 43–56. One must be careful in reading the introduction to this translation, which reflects the 1930s essentialized view of Japanese women (Araki and Inoue, *Nihon shisō taikei*, 34, pp. 202–5).

56 Yokota, "Imagining Working Women," p. 153.

57 Sakai, "Kaibara Ekken," pp. 51–2; Araki and Inoue, *Nihon shisō taikei*, 34, pp. 202–3.

58 Yōrō code, for example, no. 28 in "koryō," in Inoue et al., eds., *Nihon shisō taikei*, 3, p. 234. See Morrell, "Mirror for Women," for a medieval example.

59 Yokota, "Imagining Working Women," p. 154.

60 Araki and Inoue, *Nihon shisō taikei*, 34, pp. 203–4.

61 Tocco, "Women's Education," pp. 195, 200. *The Greater Learning* included both the Japanese phonetic *kana* syllabary and Chinese characters, as well as the *kana* readings of the Chinese characters. As with boys, girls' education involved reading an abundance of poems and Confucian classics such as *The Book of Filial Duty* and *The Analects*. Gender differentiation developed after the age of 10, when the acquisition of sewing and weaving skills redirected girls' efforts (Kuwabara, "Kinseiteki kyōyō bunka," pp. 173–4).

62 Yokota, "Imagining Working Women," pp. 155–65.

63 Sakai, "Kaibara Ekken," p. 51.

64 Cornell, "Peasant Women and Divorce," p. 718.

65 Fuess, *Divorce in Japan*, pp. 18–46, esp. p. 24.

66 Cornell, "Peasant Women and Divorce," p. 724; Smith and Wiswell, *The Women of Suye Mura*; Takagi, *Naite waratte mikudarihan*. The existence of "divorce temples," namely Mantokuji and Tōkeiji, has been misunderstood as evidence that women's recourse to divorce was to literally run into these temples. See Wright, "Severing the Karmic Ties that Bind."

67 Sakai, "Kaibara Ekken," pp. 52, 54. Other moralistic writings also elevated duties to in-laws above those to the woman's own parents (Miyashita, "Kinsei zenki ni okeru ie," pp. 34–5).

68 Hayashi, "Hōteki hōmen kara mita Edo jidai no yome," pp. 159–60.

69 Earlier moralistic texts enjoined the wife to give the same degree of mourning to both sets of parents, but later the language changed to give greater weight to the in-laws, as seen in *The Greater Learning* (ibid., p. 179).

70 Sugano, "State Indoctrination of Filial Piety," pp. 170–1.

71 Kamo no Mabuchi, "Nihimanabi," quoted in Wakita, Hayashi, and Nagahara, eds., *Nihon joseishi*, p. 174.

72 Kuwabara, "Kinseiteki kyōyō bunka," pp. 188–91. In English, see the translation and commentary in Goodwin et al., trans., "Solitary Thoughts."

BIBLIOGRAPHY

Aoki, Michiko Yamaguchi. *Ancient Myths and Early History of Japan: A Cultural Foundation.* New York: Exposition Press, 1974.

Aoki, Michiko Yamaguchi, trans. *Izumo no kuni fudoki.* Tokyo: Sophia University, 1971.

Aoki, Michiko Yamaguchi, trans. *Records of Wind and Earth: A Translation of Fudoki, with Introduction and Commentaries.* Ann Arbor, Mich.: Association for Asian Studies, 1997.

Araki Kengo and Inoue Tadashi, comp. *Nihon shisō taikei*, 34, *Kaibara Ekiken, Muro Kyūso.* Tokyo: Iwanami Shoten, 1970.

Aston, W. G., trans. *Nihongi: Chronicles of Japan from the Earliest Times to A.D. 697.* Rutland, Vt.: Charles E. Tuttle, 1980.

Cornell, Laurel. "Peasant Women and Divorce in Preindustrial Japan." *Signs* 15:4 (1990): 710–32.

Ebisawa Miki. "15 seiki no sensō to josei." In Nishimura Hiroko, ed., *Sensō, bōryoku to josei*, 1, *Ikusa no naka no onnatachi.* Tokyo: Yoshikawa Kōbunkan, 2004.

Fuess, Harald. *Divorce in Japan: Family, Gender, and the State 1600–2000.* Stanford, Calif.: Stanford University Press, 2004.

Fujiki Hisashi. *Zōhyōtachi no senjō: chūsei no yōhei to doreigari.* Tokyo: Asahi Shinbunsha, 1995.

Fujiki Hisashi. *Sengoku no mura o yuku.* Tokyo: Asahi Shinbunsha, 1997.

Fukutō Sanae. *Heianchō no onna to otoko.* Tokyo: Chūō Kōronsha, 1995.

Fukutō Sanae, ed. *Rekishi no naka no kōjotachi.* Tokyo: Shōgakkan, 2002.

Gomi Fumihiko. *Inseiki shakai no kenkyū.* Tokyo: Yamakawa Shuppan, 1984.

Goodwin, Janet, Gramlich-Oka, B., Leicester, E., Terazawa, Y., and Walthall, A., trans. "Solitary Thoughts: A Translation of Tadano Makuzu's *Hitori Kangae.*" *Monumenta Nipponica* 56:1 (2001): 21–38; 56:2 (2001): 173–95.

Hayashi Reiko. "Machiya josei no sonzai keitai." In Joseishi Sōgō Kenkyūkai, ed., *Nihon joseishi*, 3. Tokyo: Tokyo Daigaku Shuppankai, 1982.

Hayashi Yukiko. "Hōteki hōmen kara mita Edo jidai no yome to shūto shūtome: bukkiryō to jokunsho o megutte." In Tanaka Masako, Ōguchi Yūjirō, and Okuyama Kyōko, eds., *Engumi to josei: ie to ie no hazamade.* Tokyo: Waseda Daigaku Shuppanbu, 1994.

Hōjō Gen'an. "Hōjō Gen'an oboegaki." In Setagaya-ku, comp., *Setagaya-ku shiryō*, 2. Tokyo: Tokyo-to Setagaya-ku, 1959.

Inoue Mitsusada, Seki Akira, Tsuchida Naoshige, and Aoki Kazuo, eds. *Nihon shisō taikei*, 3, *Ritsuryō.* Tokyo: Iwanami Shoten, 1976.

Ishii Susumu. "Foreword by the Editor." *Acta Asiatica* 81 (2001): pp. iii–vii.

Ishii Susumu, Ishimoda Shō, Kasamatsu Hiroshi, Katsumata Shizuo, and Satō Shin'ichi, eds. *Chūsei seiji shakai shisō*, 1. Tokyo: Iwanami Shoten, 1976.

Kishi Shōzō, comp. *Zenyaku Azuma kagami*, ed. Nagahara Keiji, 5 vols. Tokyo: Shinjinbutsu Ōraisha, 1977.

Kuwabara Megumi. "Kinseiteki kyōyō bunka to josei." In Joseishi Sōgō Kenkyūkai, ed., *Nihon josei seikatsushi*, 3. Tokyo: Tokyo Daigaku Shuppankai, 1990.

Lu, David J. *Japan: A Documentary History.* Armonk, NY: M. E. Sharpe, 1997.

Makabe Yoshiko. "Kofun to josei." *Rekishi hyōron* 493 (1991): 9–16.

McCullough, Helen Craig, trans. *The Tale of the Heike*. Stanford, Calif.: Stanford University Press, 1988.

Miyashita Michiko. "Kinsei zenki ni okeru *ie* to josei no seikatsu." In Joseishi Sōgō Kenkyūkai, ed., *Nihon josei seikatsushi*, 3. Tokyo: Tokyo Daigaku Shuppankai, 1990.

Morrell, Robert. "Mirror for Women: Mujū Ichien's *Tsuma Kagami*." *Monumenta Nipponica* 35:1 (1980): 45–50.

Murasaki Shikibu. *The Tale of Genji*, trans. Royall Tyler. New York: Viking, 2001.

Nagano Hiroko. "Bakuhanhō to josei." In Joseishi Sōgō Kenkyūkai, ed., *Nihon joseishi*, 3. Tokyo: Tokyo Daigaku Shuppankai, 1989.

Nagano Hiroko. "Nōson in okeru josei no yakuwari to shosō." In Joseishi Sōgō Kenkyūkai, ed., *Nihon josei seikatsushi*, 3. Tokyo: Tokyo Daigaku Shuppankai, 1990.

Nishino Yukiko. "Kodai: kōjo ga tennō ni natta jidai." In Fukutō Sanae, ed., *Rekishi no naka no kōjotachi*. Tokyo: Shōgakkan, 2002.

Nomura Ikuyo. "Chūsei josei no funsō kaihi doryoku." In Nishimura Hiroko, ed., *Ikusa no naka no onnatachi*. Tokyo: Yoshikawa Kōbunkan, 2004.

Nomura Tadao. *Kōkyū to jokan*. Tokyo: Kyōikusha, 1978.

Okami Masao and Satake Akihiro. *Hyōchū rakuchū rakugai byōbu: Uesugibon*. Tokyo: Iwanami Shoten, 1983.

Pflugfelder, Gregory. *Cartographies of Desire: Male–Male Sexuality in Japanese Discourse*. Berkeley: University of California Press, 1999.

Philippi, Donald, trans. *Kojiki*. Tokyo: University of Tokyo Press, 1983.

Piggott, Joan R. "Chieftain Pairs and Corulers: Female Sovereignty and Early Japan." In Hitomi Tonomura, Anne Walthall, and Wakita Haruko, eds., *Women and Class in Japanese History.* Ann Arbor: Center for Japanese Studies Publications, University of Michigan, 1999.

Piggott, Joan R. "The Last Classical Female Sovereign: Kōken-Shōtoku tennō." In Dorothy Ko, J. Haboush, and J. R. Piggott, eds., *Women and Confucian Cultures in Premodern China, Korea, and Japan*. Berkeley: University of California Press, 2003.

Sakai Atsuharu. "Kaibara Ekken and *Onna-daigaku*." *Cultural Nippon* 7:4 (1939): 43–56.

Sei Shōnagon. *The Pillow Book of Sei Shōnagon*, trans. Ivan Morris. New York: Penguin, 1967.

Sekiguchi Hiroko. *Nihon kodai kon'inshi no kenkyū*, 2 vols. Tokyo: Hanawa Shobō, 1993.

Sekiguchi Hiroko. "The Patriarchal Family Paradigm in Eighth-Century Japan." In Dorothy Ko, J. Haboush, and J. Piggott, eds., *Women and Confucian Cultures in Premodern China, Korea, and Japan*. Berkeley: University of California Press, 2003.

Smith, Robert J., and Wiswell, E. L. *The Women of Suye Mura*. Chicago: University of Chicago Press, 1982.

Sōgō Joseishi Kenkyūkai, ed. *Nihon josei no rekishi: onna no hataraki*. Tokyo: Kadokawa Shoten, 1993.

Sōgō Joseishi Kenkyūkai, ed. *Shiryō ni miru Nihon josei no ayumi*. Tokyo: Yoshikawa Kōbunkan, 2000.

Sone Hiromi, Terashima Akiko, and Anne Walthall, trans. "Prostitution and Public Authority in Early Modern Japan." In Hitomi Tonomura, Anne Walthall, and Wakita Haruko, eds., *Women and Class in Japanese History.* Ann Arbor: Center for Japanese Studies Publications, University of Michigan, 1999.

Sugano Noriko. "State Indoctrination of Filial Piety in Tokugawa Japan: Sons and Daughters in the Official Records of Filial Piety." In Dorothy Ko, J. Haboush, and J. Piggott, eds.,

Women and Confucian Cultures in Premodern China, Korea, and Japan. Berkeley: University of California Press, 2003.

Tabata Yasuko. *Hōjō Masako to Hino Tomiko.* Tokyo: Kōdansha, 1996.

Takagi Tadashi. *Mikudarihan to enkiridera.* Tokyo: Kōdansha, 1992.

Takagi Tadashi. *Naite waratte mikudarihan: onna to otoko no enkiri sahō.* Tokyo: Kyōiku Shuppan, 2001.

Tocco, Martha. "Women's Education in Tokugawa Japan." In Dorothy Ko, J. Haboush, and J. Piggott, eds., *Women and Confucian Cultures in Premodern China, Korea, and Japan.* Berkeley: University of California Press, 2003.

Tōno Haruyuki. "Nikki ni miru Fujiwara Yorinaga no nanshoku kankei: ōchō kizoku no vita sekusuarisu." *Hisutoria* 84 (1979): 15–29.

Tonomura, Hitomi. "Women and Inheritance in Japan's Early Warrior Society." *Comparative Studies in Society and History* 32:3 (1990): 592–623.

Tonomura, Hitomi. *Community and Commerce in Late Medieval Japan: The Corporate Villages of Tokuchin-ho.* Stanford, Calif.: Stanford University Press, 1992.

Tonomura, Hitomi. "Black Hair and Red Trousers: Gendering the Flesh in Medieval Japan." *American Historical Review* 99:1 (1994): 129–54.

Tonomura, Hitomi. "Sexual Violence against Women: Legal and Extralegal Treatment in Premodern Warrior Societies." In Hitomi Tonomura, Anne Walthall, and Wakita Haruko, eds., *Women and Class in Japanese History.* Ann Arbor: Center for Japanese Studies Publications, University of Michigan, 1999.

Totman, Conrad. *Politics in the Tokugawa Bakufu, 1600–1843.* Berkeley: University of California Press, 1967.

Tsurumi, E. Patricia. "The Male Present versus the Female Past: Historians and Japan's Ancient Female Emperors." *Bulletin of Concerned Asian Scholars* 14:4 (1992): 71–5.

Wakita Haruko. *Chūsei ni ikiru onnatachi.* Tokyo: Iwanami Shoten, 1995.

Wakita Haruko, Hayashi Reiko, and Nagahara Kazuko, eds. *Nihon joseishi.* Tokyo: Yoshikawa Kōbunkan, 1987.

Wright, Diana. "Severing the Karmic Ties that Bind: The 'Divorce Temple' Mantokuji." *Monumenta Nipponica* 52:3 (Autumn 1997): 357–80.

Yanagi Miyoko. "Josei no seikatsu kūkan: kaku kaisō o megutte." In Fukuda Mitsuko, ed., *Onna to otoko no jikū, Nihon joseishi saikō,* 4, *Ranjuku suru onna to otoko.* Tokyo: Fujiwara Shoten, 1995.

Yasukuni Ryōichi. "Kinsei Kyōto no shomin josei." In Joseishi Sōgō Kenkyūkai, ed., *Nihon joseishi,* 3. Tokyo: Tokyo Daigaku Shuppankai, 1982–3.

Yokota Fuyuhiko. "Imagining Working Women in Early Modern Japan," trans. Mariko Tamanoi. In Hitomi Tonomura, Anne Walthall, and Wakita Haruko, eds., *Women and Class in Japanese History.* Ann Arbor: Center for Japanese Studies Publications, University of Michigan, 1999.

Yoshie Akiko. "Gender in Early Classical Japan: Marriage, Leadershi, and Political Status in Village and Palace," trans. Janet R. Goodwin. Monumenta Nipponica 60: 4 (winter 2005): pp. 437–79.

Yoshie Akiko. "Kodai no mura no seikatsu to josei." In Joseishi Sōgō Kenkyūkai, ed., *Nihon josei seikatsushi,* 1. Tokyo: Tokyo Daigaku Shuppankai, 1990.

Yoshie Akiko. "Kodai no kazoku to josei." In Asao Naohiro et al., eds., *Iwanami kōza Nihon tsūshi,* 6, *kodai 5.* Tokyo: Iwanami Shoten, 1995.

Yoshie Akiko. "Kodai joteiron no kako to genzai." In Amino Yoshihiko et al., eds., *Tennō to ōken o kangaeru,* 7, *jendā to sabetsu.* Tokyo: Iwanami Shoten, 2002.

Yoshie Akiko. "Gender in Early Classical Japan: Marriage, Leadership, and Political Status in Village and Palace," trans. Janet R. Goodwin. Monumenta Nipponica 60:4 (Winter 2005): pp. 437–79.

Yoshie Akiko. *Tsukurareta Himiko: "onna" no sōshutsu to kokka*. Tokyo: Chikuma Shobō, 2005.

Yoshikawa Shinji. "Ritsuryō kokka no nyokan." In Joseishi Sōgō Kenkyūkai, ed., *Nihon josei seikatsushi*, 1. Tokyo: Tokyo Daigaku Shuppankai, 1990.

FURTHER READING

Additional useful collections of essays include Gail Bernstein, ed., *Recreating Japanese Women, 1600–1945* (Berkeley: University of California Press, 1991), which covers the Tokugawa and modern periods, and Barbara Ruch, ed., *Engendering Faith: Women and Buddhism in Premodern Japan* (Ann Arbor: Center for Japanese Studies Publications, University of Michigan, 2002), which contains twenty essays, ten of which are translations of Japanese works. *U.S.–Japan Women's Journal* regularly offers an "English Supplement" with both translations of the Japanese articles and English-language works. The Japanese-language field of women's history has advanced exponentially since the publication in the 1980s and early 1990s of the multivolume collections Joseishi Sōgō Kenkyūkai, ed., *Nihon joseishi*, 5 vols. (Tokyo: Tokyo Daigaku Shuppankai, 1982–3); Joseishi Sōgō Kenkyūkai, ed., *Nihon josei seikatsushi*, 5 vols. (Tokyo: Tokyo Daigaku Shuppankai, 1990); and Wakita Haruko, *Bosei o tou*, 2 vols. (Kyoto: Jinbun Shoin, 1985). A full list of relevant titles, including English-language works, is in *Nihon joseishi kenkyū bunken mokuroku*, 1–4 (Tokyo: Tokyo Daigaku Shuppankai, 1983–), with volume 5 forthcoming.

CHAPTER TWENTY-ONE

Gender and Sexuality in Modern Japan

Sally A. Hastings

In the modern Japanese nation-state, as elsewhere, the official positions of the state have until quite recently been filled by men and the state has been conceptualized as a family, with women in supporting roles. The Meiji Restoration of 1868 represented a sharp break with the hereditary social order of the past. As men donned Western style military uniforms and suits and left the house to carry out the functions of modernity in military barracks, schools, and government offices, it might seem that men were constructing modernity while women continued to live traditional lives. In point of fact, the modern state required the productive as well as the reproductive labor of women. As men left home to work in factories, government offices, and far-flung corners of the empire, women bore different but equally critical responsibilities for reproducing culture. Their duties were by no means confined to the home. More-over, the experience of women living under the modern Japanese state was influenced for decades by the variety of regional and class cultures that existed in Tokugawa (1600–1868) Japan.

Although historical change occurs incrementally, it is easier to conceptualize it in broad periods. For the purposes of this essay, the periodization provided by the imperial reigns works rather well to divide the modern era into three parts. The first broad period of the modern era coincides with the reign of the Meiji Emperor (1868–1912), when the basic institutions of modern Japan took shape. Gender was essential to national identity and ordinary people experienced change as the government and the capitalist economy intruded into local life. The death of the Meiji Emperor in 1912 and the succession of his son, the Taishō Emperor, provides a somewhat artificial demarcation for an era that lasted until 1945, one characterized by a more mature industrial economy, enhanced communication and transportation, mass participation, highly contested politics, and, last but by no means least, war and defeat. The postwar era marked a new beginning not only because of the legal reforms under the American occupation that enfranchised women and gave them other legal rights but also because of economic changes that shaped women's roles in the home and in the labor force.

The Tokugawa Heritage

In conventional accounts of women's history, the Tokugawa era was a valley of darkness, the culmination of centuries of military rule that had deprived women of the cultural privileges and property rights they had enjoyed in the Heian era. In such narratives, passages from the prescriptive text *Onna daigaku* provide the proof of women's lowly estate. The only redeeming feature of the era is the class hierarchy that allowed women of the merchant or peasant classes relatively more freedom in comparison to their upper-class sisters.[1]

Recent scholarship allows us a much more nuanced understanding of the society from which the modern Japanese state emerged. One important contribution is Martha Tocco's deconstruction of the iconic status of the *Onna daigaku*; she provides an understanding of the context in which the prescriptive literature was read.[2] Moreover, literary scholars and art historians have drawn attention to the fact that under warrior government women were not entirely excluded from cultural and intellectual life. Arakida Reijo, one of the most prolific female authors in Japanese history, wrote during the Tokugawa era. Ema Saikō (1787–1861), a physician's daughter who became an outstanding Chinese-style painter and poet, was exceptional but by no means unique. She compiled a scroll that included the work of twenty-two other women. In an illuminating essay, Atsuko Sakaki reflects on how and why such writers have been selectively remembered.[3] Anne Walthall brings a historian's insight to the question of how a peasant woman could use the conventions of classical poetry to reduce the differences that separated samurai from commoner, man from woman. In her biography of Matsuo Taseko, a peasant woman active in poetry circles, Walthall draws attention to the several women who were political actors in the events leading up to the Meiji Restoration.[4] The musical talents of courtesans and geisha were, of course, an essential component of the culture of the licensed prostitution quarter of the era.[5]

Any study of women's work must take into account the fact that the vast majority of women in the Tokugawa era lived in peasant households. Young women from poor families might be sent out as indentured servants to wealthier households. To contribute to the economy of their families, married women in ordinary farm families planted, cultivated, weeded, and harvested both paddy field and vegetable plots. Farm women at all levels of the village hierarchy engaged in spinning, weaving, and sewing.[6] Women of other classes were far from idle. The wives of merchants or artisans were often directly engaged in the family business. Even women of high samurai rank worked as ladies-in-waiting, wet nurses, or governesses in the households of feudal lords. In ordinary samurai households, women prepared food, wove cloth, sewed clothing, and entertained guests. From Kate Wildman Nakai's translation of Yamakawa Kikue's record of her mother's life, we see that samurai women also laundered the bedding and even gardened.[7]

Whatever class a woman was born into, her relationship to the larger society was determined by her position within the household (*ie*) system, a construct that has attracted considerable scholarly attention. Customs with respect to premarital sexuality, divorce, and remarriage varied considerably with class. A number of scholars have drawn attention to the fact that, in the Tokugawa era, women were not defined primarily as mothers. Because of their considerable responsibilities for productive labor, women often spent little time caring for the children to whom they had given birth. Instead, childcare responsibilities were widely shared among grandparents, older siblings, and maids. Fathers, rather than mothers, had ultimate responsibility for raising children.[8]

Because the Tokugawa rulers and their feudal retainers cared about maintaining the productive labor of their territories, they cared about women's bodies. Beginning in the late seventeenth century, domainal authorities condemned abortion and infanticide as unnatural. At the same time, the boundary between wives and prostitutes became more fixed. As Susan Burns has noted, "the reproducing female body had become implicated in the authority of the household and the state."[9] Although some critics blamed failed political policy for infanticide, the dominant discourse shifted the onus to immoral parents. In this moral framework the Kagawa school of obstetrics, which prided itself on saving women's lives by using instruments to extract a fetus, became subject to accusations that their practitioners were performing abortions.[10]

Reproductive sex is, of course, implicit in studies of demography, political economy, and Confucian morality of government and household. Until the late 1980s, however, academic study of sexual desire has been relatively rare, especially with respect to same-sex relationships. Paul Schalow broke this silence with a number of literary studies.[11] In *Cartographies of Desire*, Gregory Pflugfelder provides a constructionist analysis of male–male erotic desires and practices. His investigation of the popular and legal discourses on male–male love in the Tokugawa era illuminate the woodblock prints and popular fiction (particularly that of Ihara Saikaku, 1642–93) already known to Anglophone students of Japanese culture through many fine translations. Pflugfelder articulates clearly that in the Edo period male–male erotic behavior was widely acknowledged to be part of Japanese history.

Meiji

The new Japanese government established in 1868 in the name of the emperor was instrumental in defining new roles for women. As the young leaders set out to transform Japan into a strong and wealthy nation, they abolished the feudal domains and asserted the authority of the central government to appoint officials and collect taxes. The new government proclaimed an end to the feudal distinctions of the past and with the establishment of a conscript military it defined the modern Japanese subject as male.[12] The Meiji state, like its Tokugawa predecessor, relied upon bureaucrats to carry out its functions. By the end of the Meiji era, the higher schools and imperial university established to produce bureaucratic leaders deliberately inculcated an anti-female masculinity that eschewed anything effeminate. The rough, spiritual masculinity of the monastic higher schools stood in contrast to a more refined masculinity, that of the dandified Western gentleman, whose characteristics were acquired through travel abroad and mastery of etiquette books. The spiritual masculinity won recognition as an authentic, indigenous national identity in contrast to the degenerate material culture of the West.[13]

Women's history reflected the dominance of political themes in national history in that some of the first scholarly works on women in the Meiji period were accounts of the women such as Kishida Toshiko (1863–1901) and Fukuda Hideko (1865–1927), who joined the Freedom and People's Rights Movement (*jiyū minken undō*) to assert that women, too, deserved political rights.[14] Recent work by Mara Patessio affords us a glimpse of how a broader range of women joined this movement.[15] There has also been considerable interest in the participation of women such as Kanno Suga in the early socialist and anarchist movements.[16] It was not until the late Meiji period that the Japanese state formally excluded women from even attending political meetings and articulated the notion that women should contribute to society as productive "good wives and wise mothers."[17] This formulation emerged only after Japan's quest to establish its proper place in the community of nations generated considerable anxiety about gender relations. How should women dress? What social events should they attend? Women's bodies, whether those of mothers or of prostitutes, were contested sites of national identity.[18]

For women, one of the most important aspects of state formation was the establishment of a modern educational system that mandated elementary education for both boys and girls. The Meiji leaders recognized that in the eyes of the Western powers the accomplishments of women were a measure of the level of civilization. In 1871, the government sent five girls to the United States for education. Two returned to Japan after a short time, but three spent ten years in the United States. Once back in Japan the American-educated women provided leadership in education and in feminine activities such as charity bazaars and women's associations. The youngest of the three, Tsuda Umeko, founded what is now Tsuda College in 1900. The short-lived Takebashi Girls' School in Tokyo was another government experiment of the 1870s.[19]

By the end of the Meiji era the required number of years of education for all children had been set at six and there was fairly high compliance with the law. To be sure, for much of the era parents were quicker to send their sons than their daughters to school, and the illiterate mother, dependent upon her children to read simple communications, remained a familiar figure. For the girls whose parents encouraged education, it was exhilarating to succeed in a predominantly male environment. Moreover, there developed jobs for women with academic skills. Recognizing that women who were teachers of children in the home could serve the state as educators in state-sponsored schools, the leaders of the central state established the Women's Normal School in 1874. Because of its interest in women's bodies, the state asserted its right to license midwives and nurses and fostered education for those careers.[20]

With the exception of the Women's Normal School, in the early Meiji era, most educational opportunities for women's education beyond the elementary school level were in private hands. Christian missionaries made women's education one of their goals, and some schools that continue in existence today claim origins in the 1870s and 1880s.[21] In parallel to these institutions funded and staffed from overseas, the daughters, wives, and widows of Confucian scholars founded schools for girls that emphasized study of the Chinese classics. These schools, too, claim origins in the early Meiji era. By the end of the nineteenth century the government had mandated girls' higher schools in every prefecture. Two institutions founded at the turn of the century by Japanese Christians, Tsuda English Academy and Japan Women's College, emerged as important sites for women's education in the liberal tradition.[22]

The vast majority of Japanese women were integrated into the economic production of the nation through their households, and most of those households were, of course, engaged in agriculture. Scholarly interest in women's work, however, has focused primarily on the young women who left their villages to work in spinning and textile factories, where they constituted a significant portion of the industrial labor force. In her classic study, Patricia Tsurumi drew on contemporary government reports and the songs of the factory girls themselves to recover their work experiences.[23] A recent essay by Anne Walthall illustrates how a woman with cultural capital could leverage it into income in the new Meiji society.[24] One site for scholarly analysis of women's domestic duties has been the "home" (*katei*), a word newly coined in the Meiji era. A phenomenon occurring among urban professional households in the late nineteenth century, the home centered on the nuclear rather than the extended family. Kathleen Uno shows how the separation of work and home came to define mothers as the primary caretakers of children.[25] All aspects of women's lives were reflected in the works of important women writers. Robert Danly's translations of Higuchi Ichiyo first opened Meiji women's writings to Western readers. Rebecca Copeland has ably contextualized Higuchi's work within the broader array of women who wrote in this era such as Miyake Kaho, Wakamatsu Shizuko, and Shimizu Shikin.[26]

By the end of the Meiji era, there had taken shape a number of organizations that allowed women to work in public for the good of society without impinging on the male monopoly on political rights. The Red Cross incorporated the wives of peers and bureaucrats into its ranks. Elite women were also recruited into organizations to promote education, hygiene, and support for the military. The Patriotic Women's Association, founded in 1901, soon had local branches throughout Japan.[27] Although most of these women's organizations mobilized women to act on behalf of the state, there were some instances of organized women criticizing the existing order. In 1886 Yajima Kajiko founded the Tokyo Women's Reform Society, which eventually affiliated with the International Women's Christian Temperance Union. The Women's Reform Society petitioned the government regarding social problems such as concubinage and licensed prostitution, both at home and overseas. The members likewise demanded that the government institute monogamy. Women also agitated on behalf of women's political rights. Yajima Kajiko, the writer Shimizu Shikin, and others expressed their outrage in 1890 when women were barred as even observers to the newly instituted Diet proceedings, a decision that was soon rescinded.[28]

Men and women who did not fit within the state construction of the male national subject and his home graced by a legal wife were increasingly subsumed under a medicalized discourse. The state stigmatized female prostitutes as sources of venereal disease that threatened the health of men, and this taint extended to women such as waitresses and factory workers who ventured outside the home to earn money. Under the influence of Western discourse, there developed a concept of "same-sex love," which was categorized as abnormal. In popular culture, male–male sexuality was relegated to the margins of civilization, to the feudal past, to the southwest periphery of the archipelago, and to adolescence.[29]

Taishō and Early Shōwa

The first prominent feminist literary organization coincides roughly with the dawn of the Taishō era. The women of the Bluestocking Society, which began publication of its literary magazine in September 1911, aspired to give expression to their literary creativity. In contrast to the women of the People's Rights and socialist movements, they demanded the recognition not only of human rights but also of female sexuality. Hiratsuka Raichō provided the leadership for the endeavor and well-known writers such as Yosano Akiko and Tamura Toshiko contributed their work.[30] The prominent writers who participated in the Bluestocking Society differed among themselves on the centrality of motherhood to self-fulfillment and they aired their disagreements in the pages of newspapers and general circulation magazines as well as in women's periodicals. These debates have attracted considerable scholarly attention. Scholars from the disciplines of both history and literature have written about Hiratsuka Raichō, Itō Noe, and Yamakawa Kikue.[31] The members of the Bluestocking Society challenged prescribed gender roles not only in their rhetoric but also in their lives. Several members were involved in sexual scandals, some with men and some with women.[32]

The efforts of the Bluestockings to organize women on behalf of women's self-realization were soon followed by women's organizations dedicated to obtaining women's political rights. The victory of the democratic powers in World War I and mass demonstrations at home in 1918 against rising rice prices prompted demands for universal manhood suffrage. Whereas in the Freedom and People's Rights Movement women had joined in demands for rights not yet enjoyed by any Japanese subjects, in the Taishō period, women were joining a chorus of Japanese subjects such as workers and petty bourgeoisie who demanded a voice in the polity to which they were contributing their wealth as well as their sons. The cause of women's suffrage met with modest success in 1931 when the cabinet of Prime Minister Hamaguchi Osachi sponsored a bill supporting limited voting rights for women. To be sure, the bill would not have bestowed upon women rights equal to those of men. The women's suffrage movement in fact opposed the bill, which was in any case rejected by the upper house. As Sharon Nolte noted, however, "the bill signified the achievement of legitimacy for women's rights."[33]

The outbreak of the Manchurian Incident on September 18, 1931 marked the beginning of an era when a sense of crisis in Japan delegitimized reformist efforts such as the extension of suffrage to women. The All-Japan Women's Suffrage Congress continued to meet, but by 1935, it had retreated from its earlier emphasis on peace and suffrage. The outbreak of full-scale war in China in 1937 prompted mobilization of all national resources and women's organizations, too, cooperated with the war regime. By 1937, large numbers of women had already been recruited into the older Patriotic Women's Association and the newly formed Women's National Defense Association. In February 1942, all women's groups were amalgamated into the

Greater Japan Women's Association. The mobilization of the nation for war included the incorporation of women's expertise into national commissions; the suffragist Ichikawa Fusae was among those who accepted an appointment to an official committee.[34]

In the economic and social realm, scholars have devoted considerable attention to the varieties of women's work in early twentieth-century Japan. In the Taishō and early Shōwa eras, the growth of the national economy created a greater variety of jobs for women. Whereas women constituted only 6.5 percent of white collar employees in 1930, by 1940 they occupied 15 percent of such jobs.[35] Margit Nagy and Barbara Sato have explored the experience of women working in newly created urban positions such as telephone operator, bus girl, and office worker. Mariko Tamanoi has drawn our attention to the *komori*, the caretakers of poor rural children. Regine Mathias has illuminated the lives of women coalminers in the early twentieth century.[36] Historians of women have also been attentive to the fact that women continued well into the twentieth century to constitute more than half of the industrial workforce.[37] Women who worked outside the home became objects of fascination to the mass media. Barbara Sato and Miriam Silverberg have investigated the imagined construct of the "modern girl" that flourished in the 1920s, while Silverberg and Elise Tipton have written about the relationship of the modern to the invention of the cafe waitress.[38] At a more elite level, women activists, actors, and writers were well-known figures whose pictures and opinions appeared in the mass media. Such public figures were particularly prominent in the pages of women's magazines.

In the early twentieth century, sexuality was conceptualized as either normal or perverted. Same-sex love, whether between men or between women, was classified as perverted. Same-sex relationships between women came to public notice through schoolgirl crushes and double suicides. The idea of perversion quickly became part of popular discourse where, in contrast to its condemnation in medical literature, it was consumed and celebrated.[39] The Takarazuka all-female revue, founded in 1913, was one of the forms in which perversion was consumed. The glamor of the revue provided a respite from the domesticity prescribed for women by society.[40]

When Japan became engaged in full-scale war on the Asian continent in 1937, the state took greater interest in the reproductive functions of women than in the contributions they could make to industrial production. Only unmarried women were recruited as factory labor. In keeping with that policy, the generation of women who attended higher schools during the war spent considerable time in the production of munitions. The emphasis in government policy on women was, however, on motherhood in the service of the state. Mothers were expected to have large families and to sacrifice their sons.[41] The state was interested not only in how many children women had but also in the genetic quality of Japan's population. In the 1930s the fledgling field of sexology was overshadowed by the emergence of the concept of "racial hygiene." Socialist feminists, who argued that birth control was preferable to continental expansion as a solution to Japan's population problem, had contributed to the development of a eugenic discourse that denied the right of reproduction to victims of certain diseases such as mental illness, syphilis, and tuberculosis and recommended sterilization for some. Eugenic thinking was codified in the National Eugenics Law of 1940.[42]

Because of its desire to manage the sexuality of soldiers, the state also facilitated non-reproductive sex. The right to regulate prostitution, which the state enjoyed in the home islands, expanded in wartime to direct management of military brothels. A high percentage of the women lured into this system of sexual slavery were Korean. As some of these women have come forward in the 1980s and 1990s to make claims against the Japanese government, Japanese feminists have been active in exposing wrongdoing and fighting for compensation.[43]

Postwar

Under the shadow of military defeat and foreign occupation, the women of Japan acquired legal rights equal to those of men. In December 1946 the Japanese parliament, admittedly under some pressure from the occupation authorities, passed legislation that gave women the right to vote and run for office. Significant numbers of women availed themselves of these rights. On April 10, 1946, in the first election in which women could participate, seventy-nine women stood as candidates and thirty-nine won seats. At a time when there were only ten women in the US Congress, these were dramatic results, and there has been a modest degree of scholarly attention to these events.[44] In fact, this success rate could not be sustained. Although a considerable number of women were willing to take their places in politics, the political world was not prepared to incorporate them. All but four of the thirty-nine ran for re-election, but only fourteen of them ever again held a national legislative seat. (The number of votes per voter and the boundaries of the election districts were changed between 1946 and 1947 in ways that worked against independent candidates.) Seven of the fourteen, however, continued in office at least until 1968. The national constituency of the newly formed upper house provided access to office to women of national renown. Although it was not easy for women to win political office, the total number of women in the Japanese legislature never fell below twenty.[45]

Elected women were conspicuous in debates about legislation affecting the lives of women, including the revision of the eugenics law and the passage of the anti-prostitution law in 1956. Their roles varied from impassioned advocacy to decorous representation of their parties. Although a few women were elected as independents representing feminist interests (most notably Ichikawa Fusae), the majority of elected women functioned as members of the party to which they belonged. As advocates of peace and members of student organizations, women participated in civic movements such as the anti-government agitation surrounding the revision of the security treaty with the United States in 1960. Women were also active in new citizen movements addressing consumer and environmental issues. The citizen movements, which developed beginning in the mid-1950s, maintained independence from the political parties.

The 1947 constitution guaranteed women legal equality with men.[46] The document explicitly states that marriage should be based on the equal rights of husband and wife. Policies on the choice of spouse, property rights, inheritance, place of residence, and divorce should all conform with "the essential equality of the sexes."

Society, of course, does not change as rapidly as laws do, and many women did not exercise their newly acquired rights. Siblings often signed their inheritance rights away to the oldest son, and parents continued to arrange marriages. Harald Fuess notes that because of the continued legality of consensual divorces, the actual practice of divorce remained largely unchanged.[47]

The aspect of Japanese women's experience under the American occupation that has attracted the most scholarly attention is their relationship with the men of the occupying military force. Yuki Tanaka documents sexual violence inflicted by the occupying forces, the establishment of official brothels, and the increase in the number of prostitutes during the period of occupation.[48] In her book on racism during the occupation, Yukiko Koshiro touches on both war brides and mixed blood children.[49] Although Koshiro's emphasis is on the racism of both US and Japanese government policies, her work draws attention to non-commercial, long-term relationships between Japanese women and American men.

For a variety of reasons, the research that has shaped our understanding about women in Japan since 1952 has been done primarily by anthropologists, sociologists, and political scientists. "Woman" did not emerge as a subject of scholarly research in Japan until the 1970s. Historians, for their part, have been slow to acknowledge Japan's long postwar era as their disciplinary territory. In the 1970s, when American social scientists undertook the study of Japanese women, their field of vision was dominated by the Japanese housewife. The high visibility of wives was due in large measure to the economic transformations of the immediate postwar era. Large-scale migration from farms to urban areas divided work from home along gendered lines. Male adults spent their days in factories and offices and companies encouraged workers to have full-time wives to maintain the home. At the other end of the social scale, the wages of maids rose to the point where they became beyond the reach of all but the very wealthy. Suzanne Vogel was one of the first to articulate the concept of the "professional housewife." Sociologist Anne Imamura and anthropologists Anne Allison and Joy Hendry are just a few of the many scholars who have added to our knowledge of middle-class housewifery and motherhood. Dorinne Kondo's participant-observer study in a working-class neighborhood of Tokyo is an important corrective to the class bias inherent in the essentialization of the Japanese woman as housewife.[50] The strong pressures on postwar women to succeed as wives and mothers inform our best studies of women's political participation, Susan Pharr's inquiry into the self-conceptualization of women political activists of the 1970s and Robin LeBlanc's analysis of the relationship of housewives to politics in the 1990s.[51]

The constitution guaranteed women equal pay for equal work, but a number of factors contributed to a pattern in which women earned much less than men. Until the mid-1950s, over half of employed women worked in agriculture. The rapid decline in the 1950s in the percentage of the population engaged in agriculture contributed to a decline between 1955 and the mid-1970s in the rate of women's participation in the labor force.[52] The lifetime employment system that developed in Japan to meet the needs of male workers kept female wages low. A number of talented historians have combined their archival skills with ethnography to extend our understanding of women's work. Gail Bernstein's participant-observer research in Iwate in the mid-1970s provides us with insights into the lives of farm women. Simon Partner reconstructed the life of Toshié, a woman born into a farm household in Niigata in

1926 to examine changes in the social and economic life of the Japanese countryside during the Shōwa era. Drawing insights from her extensive research on New Hampshire mill workers, Tamara Hareven conducted interviews over a number of years with the weavers of the Nishijin district of Kyoto. She interviewed both men and women and set her findings in the context of the intersection of family and work.[53]

The postwar reform of the educational system gave women access to the same educational opportunities enjoyed by male students. Mary Brinton has shown, however, that at least until the 1980s, mothers were considerably more interested in university education for sons than for their daughters. For women, the chief incentive for higher education has been to make a better marriage match or to be a better mother.[54] Some of the relatively few women who availed themselves of the new access to higher education have achieved prominence as politicians, bureaucrats, and scholars.

Organized women have continued to be a factor in the public sphere even after the attainment of suffrage and legal equality in the postwar reforms. Large numbers of women have been members of regional women's associations and the Housewives' Federation (Shufuren). The Housewives' Federation, founded by Oku Mumeo in 1948, has brought numerous consumer issues to government attention, beginning with the defective matches that occasioned the founding of the organization.[55] Affiliates of international organizations such as the Women's Christian Temperance Union (WCTU), the Young Men's Christian Association (YMCA), and the Women's International League for Peace and Freedom (WILPF) have joined forces to protest on issues such as the revival of prewar holidays and sex tours to Korea.[56] Ichikawa Fusae's suffrage movement was institutionalized in the postwar era as the League of Women Voters. Ichikawa built up around her organization a center that issues a journal on women's political activities and has been influential in the publication of materials on the history of the women's movement. In the 1970s, Japanese women participated in a liberation movement. Tanaka Mitsui's "Fighting Women," for instance, denounced the prevailing conventions that divided women into mothers or whores.[57] The demands of the Japanese movement were somewhat different from those of its American counterpart. Reproductive rights were not central, for from the late 1940s Japanese women had easy access to birth control and abortion. Most of the rights that American women sought in the Equal Rights Amendment had been inscribed in the 1947 Japanese constitution. To be sure, the Japanese women's movement has had to fight off sporadic efforts to curtail access to abortion. The fact that the Japanese government did not approve the birth control pill for general use until 1999 (after Viagra had won approval) is certainly indicative of the low priority government policy-makers place on women's control over their own bodies, but the issue was not a major one for women's organizations. Some of the legal issues for which women have fought are the right to retain their own names after marriage and an end to discrimination against illegitimate children.

One important concern of the postwar women's movement has been the sexual exploitation of women. Japanese and Korean women joined forces in the 1970s to protest against sex tours of Japanese businessmen to Korea. Feminist organizations have been active in recent years in meeting the needs of women brought from Southeast Asia to work as "entertainers." As noted above, Japanese feminists have fought for compensation for the wartime "comfort women."

In terms of achieving legal equality for women, always one of the benchmarks for determining women's position in a society, the Equal Employment Opportunity Act (EEOA) that the Diet passed in 1985 as part of a broader effort to bring Japan into conformity with the United Nations (UN) Convention on the Elimination of All Forms of Discrimination against Women (CEDAW) stands as a major landmark. The EEOA prohibited gender discrimination in recruitment, hiring, transfer, and promotion. Several factors limited the degree of social change that resulted from the new legal provisions, however. The opening of management positions in large companies to women affected only the small number of women with the academic credentials eligible for such jobs. Moreover, the EEOA went into effect just as the economy sank into a long-lasting recession, making new positions more difficult for anyone to obtain, regardless of gender. Other changes that were made to bring Japan into conformity with the UN convention have had greater effects on the lives of women. Under the revised Nationality Law, both men and women could transmit Japanese citizenship, which was defined by blood rather than place of birth, to their children. Up to that time, only the children of Japanese fathers were recognized as Japanese citizens. On a more mundane level, in 1994 home economics became a compulsory subject for both boys and girls.[58]

In every era of modern Japanese history, women who sought personal, political, and financial autonomy have faced both the weight of tradition (sometimes invented) and the power of the state. The effects of the EEOA have played out in what demographers characterize as "Japan's aging population." Demographers have been concerned since the 1970s with the implications for government finances of Japan's high life expectancy and its low birth rate. In the new millennium, the average age of first marriage has risen while the birth rate has continued to fall. Policy-makers alternate between castigating young women and offering concessions to make marriage more attractive. It seems likely that the next set of struggles between feminists and policy-makers will center around these demographic concerns.

NOTES

1 See, for instance, Hane, *Reflections on the Way to the Gallows*, pp. 5–7.
2 Tocco, "Norms and Texts."
3 Fister, "Female Bunjin"; Sakaki, "Sliding Doors."
4 Walthall, *The Weak Body* and "The Cult of Sensibility."
5 Seigle, *Yoshiwara*.
6 Uno, "Women and Changes in the Household Division of Labor"; Walthall, "The Life Cycle of Farm Women."
7 Uno, "Women and Changes in the Household Division of Labor"; Yamakawa, *Women of the Mito Domain*.
8 Uno, "Women and Changes in the Household Division of Labor"; Walthall, "The Life Cycle of Farm Women"; Niwa, "The Formation of the Myth of Motherhood." For an exploration of literary images of the family system, see Nagata, "Images of the Family on Stage."
9 Burns, "The Body as Text," p. 193.
10 Ibid., pp. 203–5.

11 See, for instance, Schalow, "Male Love in Early Modern Japan."

12 Drawing on the work of Linda Kerber, Ueno Chizuko has been attentive to the correlation between military conscription and first-class citizenship in modern nation-states (Ueno, *Nationalism and Gender*, p. 166).

13 Karlin, "The Gender of Nationalism." On the higher schools, see Roden, *Schooldays in Imperial Japan.*

14 Sievers, *Flowers in Salt*; Mackie, *Creating Socialist Women in Japan*, pp. 2–12, 28, 60–6; Hane, *Reflections on the Way to the Gallows*, pp. 29–50.

15 Patessio, "Women's Participation in the Popular Rights Movement."

16 See, for instance, Hane, *Reflections on the Way to the Gallows*, pp. 51–74.

17 Nolte and Hastings, "The Meiji State's Policy toward Women."

18 See, for instance, Hastings, "The Empress' New Clothes" and "A Dinner Party Is Not a Revolution"; Frühstück, *Colonizing Sex.*

19 On Yamakawa Sutematsu, Nagai Shigeko, and Tsuda Umeko, the three girls educated in America, see Furuki, *White Plum*, and Rose, *Tsuda Umeko and Women's Education.*

20 Nurses and midwives have generally not been incorporated into histories of Japanese feminists, but a number of recent studies provide insight into these professions. See for instance Terazawa, "The State, Midwives, and Reproductive Surveillance."

21 On Kobe College, see Ishii, *American Women Missionaries at Kobe College.*

22 On the life of Tsuda Umeko, founder of Tsuda English Academy, see Furuki, *White Plum*, and Rose, *Tsuda Umeko and Women's Education.*

23 Mary Brinton points out that in the 1909 factory census, the first done in Japan, women made up 62 percent of the manufacturing sector. Of those women, 84 percent were in the textile industry (Brinton, *Women and the Economic Miracle*, p. 118; see also Tsurumi, *Factory Girls*).

24 Walthall, "Nishimiya Hide."

25 See Nishikawa, "The Changing Form of Dwellings"; Sand, "At Home in the Meiji Period"; Uno, *Passages to Modernity*, pp. 38–46.

26 Danly, *In the Shade of Green Leaves*; Copeland, *Lost Leaves.*

27 On the Patriotic Women's Association, see Sievers, *Flowers in Salt*, pp. 114–15. For the life of a woman active in pro-state organizations, see Hastings, "Hatoyama Haruko."

28 On the Tokyo Women's Reform Society, see Sievers, *Flowers in Salt*, pp. 87–113, and Garon, *Molding Japanese Minds*, pp. 98–100.

29 Frühstück, *Colonizing Sex*; Pflugfelder, *Cartographies of Desire.*

30 A good account of the Bluestocking Society (Seitōsha) is provided by Sievers, *Flowers in Salt*, pp. 163–88.

31 Rodd, "Yosano Akiko and the Taishō Debate"; Molony, "Equality versus Difference." On Yamakawa Kikue, see Tsurumi, "Visions of Women and the New Society in Conflict."

32 Wu, "Performing Gender."

33 Nolte, "Women's Rights and Society's Needs," p. 690.

34 Nishikawa, "Japan's Entry into War."

35 Brinton, *Women and the Economic Miracle*, p. 118.

36 Sato, *The New Japanese Woman*; Nagy, "Middle-Class Working Women"; Tamanoi, *Under the Shadow of Nationalism*, pp. 55–83; and Mathias, "Female Labour in the Japanese Coal-Mining Industry."

37 See for instance Molony, "Activism among Women," and Hunter, "Textile Factories, Tuberculosis, and the Quality of Life."

38 Sato, *The New Japanese Woman*; Silverberg, "The Modern Girl as Militant"; Silverberg, "The Café Waitress Serving Modern Japan." See also Tipton, "The Café."

39 Pflugfelder, *Cartographies of Desire*, pp. 286–8.

40 Robertson, *Takarazuka.*

41   Miyake, "Doubling Expectations."
42   Frühstück, *Colonizing Sex*.
43   Mackie, *Feminism in Modern Japan*, pp. 110–11; Tanaka, *Japan's Comfort Women*.
44   On the 1946 election, see Ōgai, "The Stars of Democracy." Helen Hopper has written a
     biography of Katō Shizue, one of the first thirty-nine elected, in *A New Woman of Japan*.
45   For an overview of women in the national legislature, see Hastings, "Women Legislators
     in the Postwar Diet."
46   Susan Pharr has documented how women's rights came to be included in the constitution
     (Pharr, "The Politics of Women's Rights").
47   Fuess, *Divorce in Japan*, p. 147.
48   Tanaka, *Japan's Comfort Women*, pp. 110–66.
49   Koshiro, *Trans-Pacific Racisms*.
50   Vogel, "Professional Housewife"; Imamura, *Urban Japanese Housewives*; Allison, "Pro-
     ducing Mothers"; Hendry, "The Role of the Professional Housewife"; Kondo, *Crafting
     Selves*.
51   Pharr, *Political Women in Japan*; LeBlanc, *Bicycle Citizens*.
52   Brinton, *Women and the Economic Miracle*, p. 27.
53   Bernstein, *Haruko's World*; Partner, *Toshié*; Hareven, *The Silk Weavers of Kyoto*.
54   Brinton, *Women and the Economic Miracle*, pp. 42, 199.
55   On the Housewives' Federation, see Narita, "Women in the Motherland."
56   See, for instance, Mackie, *Feminism in Modern Japan*, 205.
57   Ibid., pp. 144–5.
58   Ibid., pp. 191–2.

BIBLIOGRAPHY

Allison, Anne. "Producing Mothers." In Anne Imamura, ed., *Reimaging Japanese Women*.
     Berkeley: University of California Press, 1996.
Bernstein, Gail. *Haruko's World: A Japanese Farm Woman and Her Community*. Stanford,
     Calif.: Stanford University Press, 1983.
Brinton, Mary. *Women and the Economic Miracle: Gender and Work in Postwar Japan*. Berkeley:
     University of California Press, 1993.
Burns, Susan. "The Body as Text: Confucianism, Reproduction, and Gender in Tokugawa
     Japan." In Benjamin Elman, John Duncan, and Herman Ooms, eds., *Rethinking Confu-
     cianism: Past and Present in China, Japan, Korea, and Vietnam*. UCLA Asian Pacific
     Monograph Series. Los Angeles: UCLA, 2002.
Copeland, Rebecca. *Lost Leaves: Women Writers of Meiji Japan*. Honolulu: University of
     Hawai'i Press, 2000.
Danly, Robert Lyons. *In the Shade of Spring Leaves: The Life and Writings of Higuchi Ichiyō, a
     Woman of Letters in Meiji Japan*. New Haven: Yale University Press, 1981.
Fister, Patricia. "Female Bunjin: The Life of Poet-Painter Ema Saikō." In Gail Bernstein,
     ed., *Recreating Japanese Women, 1600–1945*. Berkeley: University of California Press, 1991.
Frühstück, Sabine. *Colonizing Sex: Sexology and Social Control in Modern Japan*. Berkeley:
     University of California Press, 2003.
Fuess, Harald. *Divorce in Japan: Family, Gender, and the State, 1600–2000*. Stanford, Calif.:
     Stanford University Press, 2004.
Furuki, Yoshiko. *The White Plum: A Biography of Ume Tsuda, Pioneer in the Higher Education
     of Japanese Women*. New York: Weatherhill, 1991.
Garon, Sheldon. *Molding Japanese Minds: The State in Everyday Life*. Princeton: Princeton
     University Press, 1997.

Hane, Mikiso. *Reflections on the Way to the Gallows: Voices of Japanese Rebel Women*. Berkeley: University of California Press, 1988.

Hareven, Tamara. *The Silk Weavers of Kyoto: Family and Work in a Changing Traditional Industry*. Berkeley: University of California Press, 2002.

Hastings, Sally Ann. "The Empress' New Clothes and Japanese Women, 1868–1912." *Historian* 55:4 (Summer 1993): 677–92.

Hastings, Sally Ann. "Women Legislators in the Postwar Diet." In Anne Imamura, ed., *Reimaging Japanese Women*. Berkeley: University of California Press, 1996.

Hastings, Sally Ann. "A Dinner Party Is Not a Revolution: Space, Gender, and Hierarchy in Meiji Japan" *U.S.–Japan Women's Journal*, English Supplement 18 (2000): 107–32.

Hastings, Sally Ann. "Hatoyama Haruko: Ambitious Woman." In Anne Walthall, ed., *The Human Tradition in Modern Japan*. Wilmington, Del.: Scholarly Resources, 2002.

Hendry, Joy. "The Role of the Professional Housewife." In Janet Hunter, ed., *Japanese Women Working*. London: Routledge, 1993.

Hopper, Helen. *A New Woman of Japan: A Political Biography of Kato Shidzue*. Boulder, Colo.: Westview Press, 1996.

Hunter, Janet. "Textile Factories, Tuberculosis, and the Quality of Life in Industrializing Japan." In Janet Hunter, ed., *Japanese Women Working*. London: Routledge, 1993.

Imamura, Anne. *Urban Japanese Housewives: At Home and in the Community*. Honolulu: University of Hawai'i Press, 1987.

Ishii, Noriko Kawamura. *American Women Missionaries at Kobe College, 1873–1909: New Dimensions in Gender*. London: Routledge, 2004.

Karlin, Jason. "The Gender of Nationalism: Competing Masculinities in Meiji Japan." *Journal of Japanese Studies* 28:1 (2002): 41–77.

Kondo, Dorinne. *Crafting Selves: Power, Gender and Discourses of Identity in a Japanese Work Place*. Chicago: University of Chicago Press, 1990.

Koshiro, Yukiko. *Trans-Pacific Racisms and the U.S. Occupation of Japan*. New York: Columbia University Press, 1999.

LeBlanc, Robin. *Bicycle Citizens: The Political World of the Japanese Housewife*. Berkeley: University of California Press, 1999.

Mackie, Vera. *Creating Socialist Women in Japan: Gender, Labour and Activism, 1900–1937*. Cambridge: Cambridge University Press, 1997.

Mackie, Vera. *Feminism in Modern Japan: Citizenship, Embodiment, and Sexuality*. Cambridge: Cambridge University Press, 2003.

Mathias, Regine. "Female Labour in the Japanese Coal-Mining Industry." In Janet Hunter, ed., *Japanese Women Working*. London: Routledge, 1993.

Miyake, Yoshiko. "Doubling Expectations: Motherhood and Women's Factory Work under State Management in Japan in the 1930s and 1940s." In Gail Bernstein, ed., *Recreating Japanese Women, 1600–1945*. Berkeley: University of California Press, 1991.

Molony, Barbara. "Activism among Women in the Taishō Cotton Textile Industry." In Gail Bernstein, ed., *Recreating Japanese Women, 1600–1945*. Berkeley: University of California Press, 1991.

Molony, Barbara. "Equality versus Difference: The Japanese Debate over 'Motherhood Protection,' 1915–1950." In Janet Hunter, ed., *Japanese Women Working*. London: Routledge, 1993.

Nagata, Mary Louise. "Images of the Family on Stage in Early Modern Japan." *Japan Review* 13 (2001): 93–105.

Nagy, Margit. "Middle-Class Working Women during the Interwar Years." In Gail Bernstein, ed., *Recreating Japanese Women, 1600–1945*. Berkeley: University of California Press, 1991.

Narita Ryūichi. "Women in the Motherland: Oku Mumeo through Wartime and Postwar." In Yamanouchi Yasushi, J. Victor Koschmann, and Narita Ryūichi, eds., *Total War and "Modernization."* Ithaca, NY: East Asia Program, Cornell University, 1998.

Nishikawa Yūko. "The Changing Form of Dwellings and the Establishment of the Katei (Home) in Modern Japan." *U.S.–Japan Women's Journal*, English Supplement 8 (1995): 3–36.

Nishikawa Yūko. "Japan's Entry into War and the Support of Women." *U.S.–Japan Women's Journal*, English Supplement 12 (1997): 48–83.

Niwa Akiko. "The Formation of the Myth of Motherhood in Japan." *U.S.–Japan Women's Journal*, English Supplement 4 (1993): 70–82.

Nolte, Sharon H. "Women's Rights and Society's Needs: Japan's 1931 Suffrage Bill." *Comparative Studies in Society and History* 28:4 (1986): 690–714.

Nolte, Sharon H., and Hastings, Sally Ann. "The Meiji State's Policy toward Women, 1890–1910." In Gail Bernstein, ed., *Recreating Japanese Women, 1600–1945*. Berkeley: University of California Press, 1991.

Ōgai Tokuko. "The Stars of Democracy: The First Thirty-Nine Female Members of the Japanese Diet." *U.S.–Japan Women's Journal*, English Supplement 11 (1996): 81–117.

Partner, Simon. *Toshié: A Story of Village Life in Twentieth Century Japan*. Berkeley: University of California Press, 2004.

Patessio, Mara. "Women's Participation in the Popular Rights Movement (Jiyū Minken Undō) during the Early Meiji Period." *U.S.–Japan Women's Journal* 27 (2004): 3–26.

Pflugfelder, Gregory. *Cartographies of Desire: Male–Male Sexuality in Japanese Discourse*. Berkeley: University of California Press, 1999.

Pharr, Susan. *Political Women in Japan: The Search for a Place in Political Life*. Berkeley: University of California Press, 1981.

Pharr, Susan J. "The Politics of Women's Rights." In Robert E. Ward and Sakamoto Yoshikazu, eds., *Democratizing Japan: The Allied Occupation*. Honolulu: University of Hawai'i Press, 1987.

Robertson, Jennifer. *Takarazuka: Sexual Politics and Popular Culture in Modern Japan*. Berkeley: University of California Press, 1998.

Rodd, Laurel Rasplica. "Yosano Akiko and the Taishō Debate over the 'New Woman'." In Gail Bernstein, ed., *Recreating Japanese Women, 1600–1945*. Berkeley: University of California Press, 1991.

Roden, Donald. *Schooldays in Imperial Japan: A Study in the Culture of a Student Elite*. Berkeley: University of California Press, 1980.

Rose, Barbara. *Tsuda Umeko and Women's Education in Japan*. New Haven: Yale University Press, 1992.

Sakaki, Atsuko. "Sliding Doors: Women in the Heterosocial Literary Field of Early Modern Japan." *U.S.–Japan Women's Journal*, English Supplement 17 (1999): 3–38.

Sand, Jordan. "At Home in the Meiji Period: Inventing Japanese Domesticity." In Stephen Vlastos, ed., *Mirror of Modernity: Invented Traditions of Modern Japan*. Berkeley: University of California Press, 1998.

Sato, Barbara. *The New Japanese Woman: Modernity, Media, and Women in Interwar Japan*. Durham, NC: Duke University Press, 2003.

Schalow, Paul Gordon. "Male Love in Early Modern Japan: A Literary Depiction of the 'Youth'." In Martin Bauml Duberman et al., eds., *Hidden from History: Reclaiming the Gay and Lesbian Past*. New York: NAL, 1989.

Seigle, Cecilia Segawa. *Yoshiwara: The Glittering World of the Japanese Courtesan*. Honolulu: University of Hawai'i Press, 1993.

Sievers, Sharon. *Flowers in Salt: The Beginnings of Feminist Consciousness in Modern Japan.* Stanford, Calif.: Stanford University Press, 1983.

Silverberg, Miriam. "The Modern Girl as Militant." In Gail Bernstein, ed., *Recreating Japanese Women, 1600–1945.* Berkeley: University of California Press, 1991.

Silverberg, Miriam. "The Café Waitress Serving Modern Japan." In Stephen Vlastos, ed., *Mirror of Modernity: Invented Traditions of Modern Japan.* Berkeley: University of California Press, 1998.

Tamanoi, Mariko Asano. *Under the Shadow of Nationalism: Politics and Poetics of Rural Japanese Women.* Honolulu: University of Hawai'i Press, 1998.

Tanaka, Yuki. *Japan's Comfort Women: Sexual Slavery and Prostitution during World War II and the U.S. Occupation.* London: Routledge, 2002.

Terazawa, Yuki. "The State, Midwives, and Reproductive Surveillance in Late Nineteenth and Early Twentieth Century Japan." *U.S.–Japan Women's Journal,* English Supplement 24 (2003): 59–81.

Tipton, Elise K. "The Café: Contested Space of Modernity in Interwar Japan." In Elise K. Tipton and John Clark, eds., *Being Modern in Japan: Culture and Society from the 1910s to the 1930s.* Honolulu: University of Hawai'i Press, 2000.

Tocco, Martha. "Norms and Texts for Women's Education in Tokugawa Japan." In Dorothy Ko, JaHyun Kim Haboush, and Joan R. Piggott, eds., *Women and Confucian Cultures in Premodern China, Korea, and Japan.* Berkeley: University of California Press, 2003.

Tsurumi, E. Patricia. *Factory Girls: Women in the Thread Mills of Meiji Japan.* Princeton: Princeton University Press, 1990.

Tsurumi, E. Patricia. "Visions of Women and the New Society in Conflict: Yamakawa Kikue versus Takamure Itsue." In Sharon Minichiello, ed., *Japan's Competing Modernities: Issues in Culture and Democracy 1900–1930.* Honolulu: University of Hawai'i Press, 1998.

Ueno Chizuko. *Nationalism and Gender,* trans. Beverly Yamamoto. Melbourne: Trans Pacific Press, 2004.

Uno, Kathleen. "Women and Changes in the Household Division of Labor." In Gail Bernstein, ed., *Recreating Japanese Women, 1600–1945.* Berkeley: University of California Press, 1991.

Uno, Kathleen. *Passages to Modernity: Motherhood, Childhood, and Social Reform in Early Twentieth Century Japan.* Honolulu: University of Hawai'i Press, 1999.

Vogel, Suzanne. "Professional Housewife: The Career of Urban Middle Class Japanese Women." *Japan Interpreter* 12:1 (1978): 16–36.

Walthall, Anne. "The Life Cycle of Farm Women in Tokugawa Japan." In Gail Bernstein, ed., *Recreating Japanese Women, 1600–1945.* Berkeley: University of California Press, 1991.

Walthall, Anne. "The Cult of Sensibility in Rural Tokugawa Japan: Love Poetry by Matsuo Taseko." *Journal of the American Oriental Society* 117:1 (1997): 70–86.

Walthall, Anne. *The Weak Body of a Useless Woman: Matsuo Taseko and the Meiji Restoration.* Chicago: University of Chicago Press, 1998.

Walthall, Anne. "Nishimiya Hide: Turning Palace Arts into Marketable Skills." In Anne Walthall, ed., *The Human Tradition in Modern Japan.* Wilmington, Del.: Scholarly Resources, 2002.

Wu, Peichen. "Performing Gender along the Lesbian Continuum: The Politics of Sexual Identity in the Seitō Society." *U.S.–Japan Women's Journal,* English Supplement 22 (2002): 64–86.

Yamakawa Kikue. *Women of the Mito Domain: Recollections of Samurai Family Life,* trans. Kate Wildman Nakai. Tokyo: University of Tokyo Press, 1992; repr. Stanford, Calif.: Stanford University Press, 2001.

FURTHER READING

The two-volume set, *Gender and Japanese History*, edited by Wakita Haruko, Anne Bouchy, and Ueno Chizuko (Osaka: Osaka University Press, 1999), provides access to recent work by Japanese scholars. The single best account of the women's movement in modern Japan is Vera Mackie, *Feminism in Modern Japan* (Cambridge: Cambridge University Press, 2003). The articles collected in Gail Bernstein, ed., *Recreating Japanese Women, 1600–1945* (Berkeley: University of California Press, 1991) and Janet Hunter, ed., *Japanese Women Working* (London: Routledge, 1993) are highly readable and invaluable sources of information on the lives of ordinary women. *Flowers in Salt* by Sharon Sievers (Stanford, Calif.: Stanford University Press, 1983) provides an excellent account of feminism in the Meiji era. In *The New Japanese Woman* (Durham, NC: Duke University Press, 2003), Barbara Sato has used cultural history to illuminate the lives of urban middle-class women in the interwar years. Translations and ethnographic studies allow insights into particular times and places in Japanese society. The selections in Mikiso Hane, *Reflections on the Way to the Gallows* (Berkeley: University of California Press, 1988) give voice to women across several decades who opposed the Japanese state. Nakano Makiko, *Makiko's Diary: A Merchant Wife in 1910 Kyoto* (Stanford, Calif.: Stanford University Press, 1995), provides an extraordinary window into an urban merchant household. Karen Colligan-Taylor has performed an extraordinary service in translating Yamazaki Tomoko's *Sandakan No. 8: An Episode in the History of Lower-Class Japanese Women* (Armonk, NY: M. E. Sharpe, 1999), Yamazaki's investigative report on the Japanese women who worked overseas as prostitutes in the prewar era. In *Women of Okinawa: Nine Voices from a Garrison Island* (Ithaca, NY: Cornell University Press, 2000), Ruth Ann Keyso records the experience of women on the margins of Japanese society. Jackie Kim, in her book *Hidden Treasures: Lives of First-Generation Korean Women in Japan* (Lanham, Md.: Rowman and Littlefield, 2005), tells the stories of women whose long sojourns in Japan began during the colonial era. The best historical overview of sexual knowledge in modern Japan is Sabine Frühstück, *Colonizing Sex* (Berkeley: University of California Press, 2003). Gregory Pflugfelder, *Cartographies of Desire* (Berkeley: University of California Press, 1999) is an essential source on male–male desire and practice.

CHAPTER TWENTY-TWO

Class and Social Stratification

Ian Neary

Social stratification is usually associated with classes, people who share similar life chances as a result of their position within the labor market. However societies may also be structured around ascriptions of status or ability to command. Thus, John Scott explains, class situations

> arise from the property and market relations that establish patterns of domination by virtue of constellations of interests and that result from the rational calculative alignment of economic interests. Status situations ... result from communal relations through which domination on the basis of prestige is established ... command situations are a consequence of the relations of command that are built into structures of legitimate domination.[1]

Rarely will a society be organized around either class or status or command; more usually there will be a complex interplay between the three and over time it will be possible to observe changes in their relative significance. This chapter will provide an overview of the main themes relating to social stratification in Japan in the early modern period and postwar, and review the situation of outcaste groups.

The Early Modern Period

The *shi-nō-kō-shō* (samurai, peasant, artisan, merchant) system is one of the defining features of Tokugawa Japan. It apparently set the parameters for political, social, and economic interaction and yet it has received relatively little specialist attention in the English-language literature. Here I want to explore some of the writing on the topic beginning with two introductory texts before moving on to the more specialist literature.

Jon Halliday starts his *Political History of Japanese Capitalism* with a review of the class structure of Tokugawa Japan. He notes that the formalization of the class system amounted to an attempt to "re-feudalize" Japan and was intimately connected to the seclusion policy (*sakoku*). Prior to the 1630s, Japan's emergent merchant class had been developing trade links with Asia, extending their economic and social influence and supporting the political ambitions of their local lords. This posed a real threat to the centralizing Tokugawa rulers and for that reason after 1638 Japan's merchant class was forced to direct their attention inside the country. Moreover, the Neo-Confucian orthodoxy adopted by the Tokugawa family suggested that merchants were unproductive members of society who deserved their place on the lowest rung of the social structure. Nevertheless, the rapid development of urban areas from the late seventeenth century and the commercialization of the economy led to an alliance between "the urban bourgeoisie, almost wholly dependent on domestic trade and finance and … a parasitic aristocracy split from the land."[2] Rural industry was unable to develop independent of the "urban bourgeois aristocracy bloc,"[3] and this for Halliday provides an explanation of the disposition of class forces on the eve of the Meiji Restoration which set the parameters for the development of capitalism in the later nineteenth century.

As a Marxist, Halliday begins with a class analysis but he succeeds in demonstrating how the ruling class, the "samurai aristocracy" as he calls them, had only an indirect relationship to the means of production, land. Conrad Totman, in a more recent history of Japan, begins his discussion of the social structure of the Tokugawa period by noting that the *shi-nō-kō-shō* model "creates a misleading sense of hierarchical relationships, implies clear division where only vague ones exist, obscures economic disparities, and omits important segments of society."[4] Instead he identifies an elite, the official others, and the unofficial others. The elite he regards as having been composed of the imperial aristocracy, the higher status samurai and affiliated merchants and literati. This alliance was different to previous ruling coalitions only in that the samurai elite was more firmly entrenched than before and based in Edo or their castle towns, while the imperial aristocracy was reconstituted in Kyoto and bound by rules of conduct imposed by Edo. This elite cut across the four major classes but was composed of no more than a few thousand people. Among the samurai there were a few who performed well-paid and important administrative jobs, but the overwhelming majority were engaged in ill-paid, inconsequential, and routine tasks.[5]

Merchants and artisans formed the basis of the urban economy. As the boundaries of the status system were strengthened in the late seventeenth century, merchants were excluded from privileged society but were nevertheless able to retain a de facto position as dominant within the urban economy. Less prominent socially but equally important economically were the artisans. The new Tokugawa government destroyed their craft guilds and so they were forced to work as independent professionals. Some found themselves elite patrons but the majority sold their goods and services to fellow urban residents as the opportunities arose. The biggest group, the peasantry, was both large – 80 percent of the entire population – and diverse. A few were literate wealthy landowners, some were unschooled small-scale cultivators but most were subordinate members of large households or indentured farm laborers. They lived in villages controlled by officials who represented the village to higher authority, usually the local lord who collected taxes, organized forced labor, and enforced peace.

Outside the four-class structure in rural areas there were thousands of lesser clerics who officiated at shrines and temples, and in urban areas there were a vast number of shop assistants and household servants; 10 percent of the population of Edo were servants of samurai households. Part of the urban population was made up of day laborers, some of whom were poor villagers who were working away from home during the quiet season, but some of them settled in the cities. Another element was the outcaste population – *eta*, *kawata*, or *hinin* – about which more later, and on the edge of the traditional outcaste communities were groups of entertainers, singers, dancers, and actors who gathered within or on the edges of the licensed quarters.

Thus Totman sketches a social structure within which stratification was much more complex than the simple model advocated by contemporary Confucian theorists and projected in many histories. Irrespective of their formal status some well-to-do samurai, merchants, and village leaders lived comfortable lives with servants, schooling, and luxury. Those who earned middling incomes had lives of modest comfort "while the poor, whether samurai, shopkeeper, craftsman or villager, struggled to get by with wretched housing, poor nutrition, scraps of well worn possessions, and chronic uncertainty about the future."[6] Neither class nor status position by themselves could tell us much about an individual's life chances.

The essays in *The Cambridge History of Japan* provide more nuanced discussions of the status structure from its formation to the period of its disintegration and transformation. Wakita Osamu argues for example, that there was little the *chūsei* (medieval) and *kinsei* (early modern) periods had in common. Whereas previously there was the idea that land belonged in some sense to the local lord, Hideyoshi insisted that land was only ever held in trust for the present and that it was open to the overlord to reallocate it as appropriate. During the early 1590s a village census was carried out as a way to prevent peasants from absconding from the land at the same time as edicts were introduced that prevented changes of status from samurai to merchant or farmer to merchant. "Sword hunts" disarmed the peasantry, which both tightened Hideyoshi's military control and established clear distinctions between the peasants and samurai classes. Moreover, Hideyoshi was ruthless in carrying out a survey of tilled land so that the agricultural wealth of each region could be calculated. Taxes on land were calculated on the basis of productivity and paid in rice, whether or not the land was used to grow rice.

Implementing his ideas about the tenant nature of lordship, Hideyoshi forced several daimyō to relocate, taking all their followers with them. Moreover he and the Tokugawa rulers who followed him reserved the right to relocate others. After 1651 very few fief transfers took place, although the threat still remained. By 1690 the enforced residence system (*sankin kōtai*) meant that five out of six daimyō had been born in Edo and could expect to spend at least half their lives there. Their *han* (domains) remained their sources of wealth and prestige but they were not home. Meanwhile many samurai were decisively separated from the land and forced to move into castle towns. It is reported that 50,000 samurai plus their families moved into Kanazawa city from the surrounding area between the 1580s and the 1650s.[7] Thus not only were daimyō separated from their domains but the samurai were separated from the landholding peasantry. In Tosa, Satsuma, and a few other regions, samurai remained based in the villages. Where samurai were rarely, if ever, present, villagers were free to engage in cash cropping, tax evasion, unreported land reclamations, and land sale and purchase.[8] Villages where they remained rarely developed economically. The populations of big cities grew rapidly as tax concessions were used to attract merchants and artisans from the villages and market towns. A secondary migration of rural villagers took place as peasants went to work in construction or as servants.

Confucian officials aimed to prevent the development of commercial commodity production and rulers from Hideyoshi onwards sought to tax the peasantry so as "to keep them at the far edge of existence."[9] But especially where the samurai had been withdrawn, elites emerged within peasant villages who were able to accumulate surpluses. By 1770 all peasants in Kinki were growing commercial crops, and fifty years later they were being widely raised in the Kantō area too. A vast web developed to distribute agricultural and craft products to and between the urban centers; by the mid eighteenth century there were 5,000 wholesalers in 400 different kinds of business in Osaka alone.[10] Urban merchant wealth was inconsistent with their lowly social status and worried the political elite. By the 1830s there were complaints about their business ethics and scorn for their social behavior.[11] By the nineteenth century, social class may have determined occupation, but it said little about income.

Essays by Donald Shively and John Whitney Hall from the 1960s and 1970s respectively focus explicitly on the nature of status and how this affected everyday life. Shively describes aspects of the vast hierarchy of sumptuary regulations that sought to prescribe in detail the clothing to be worn by members of each class from daimyō's wives to the peasantry. The fundamental principle was that "there must be orderly classification of the population by function on an hierarchical scale."[12] First rounds of these regulations were produced in the 1630s but they became increasingly elaborate from the early eighteenth century, extending even to underclothes. There were some subtle differences of purpose of these sumptuary regulations. The rules for the samurai were intended to insist on the need for a balance between extravagance and parsimony, while the regulations for the merchants and peasants were used as a way to reinforce status inferiority, "rule by status," as Hall puts it.

Very little in the English-language scholarship explores what it was like to live in such a society. Herman Ooms's *Tokugawa Village Practice* is possibly the only exception. He focuses on the experiences of a few people in a village in what is now Nagano prefecture. Using a class framework not dissimilar to Scott's, he describes the formation of the village from the start of the Tokugawa period. His central point is that villages were not stable entities that existed at the start of the period and were subject to economic and social pressures that caused change thereafter. The surveys of the 1590s and thereafter did not simply record pre-existing communities; rather the process often created them or at least designated them for particular purposes: to farm newly developed land, to serve as way stations on highways, or simply for administrative convenience.[13] Within these communities, some – mainly those with a claim to a warrior background – were accountable for the tribute, others not. He characterizes the control system as "colonial": the military authority based in towns used coercive force to exact tribute from the villages through a co-opted elite. Moreover, because the military authorities in the towns also had obligations to the Tokugawa government in Edo, the whole country was a latent garrison which in theory could be mobilized by the shōgun. It never happened, but the existence of this notional power provided additional "symbolic capital" to the local elite.

A ladder of prestige stretched down from the titled peasants to lesser peasants to lifelong servants to bonded servants, with movement along this spectrum being linked to economic and political power. Broadly speaking, at this level social status was linked to economic well-being: do well and people would respect you. Status regulations were issued from the towns but there were also village codes on dress, greetings, and behavior. Regulations, which did not go unchallenged, were period-ically reimposed as commercialization of the economy improved the circumstances of some and worsened those of others.[14]

Status was the ostensible principle of social stratification and there is no doubt that status regulation was intensified over the 250 years of Tokugawa rule in efforts to enhance status awareness. However, in parallel with this, the development of a commodity economy was undermining the foundations of the status structure, not only in the villages but also in the towns. Complex distribution systems and accom-panying financial institutions created an economic structure that the military rulers in Edo and the castle towns could neither understand nor control. Ooms describes the Tokugawa government as holding this in place by a regime of conquest. The samurai class was able to use command power to extract the agricultural surplus out of the peasantry and maintain itself in control. Insistence on strict status distinctions at macro and micro social levels was one way it sought to keep its social bloc in control and disguise the military base of its power.

Although a skeletal structure of the four-caste hierarchy was maintained into the nineteenth century, it was clear that one's life chances depended much less on which of them one belonged to than what economic power one had access to within the local community. The more economic power subverted the significance of com-mand power the more difficult it was for the samurai to maintain itself as the dominant social bloc. In this sense we can regard the Meiji Restoration as a "readjustment" (as economists sometimes describe collapses of stock market prices) in which there was a drastic reduction in the power of the samurai social bloc while that of the merchant class significantly increased. The next eighty years – which separate early Meiji from the end of the war in the Pacific – were a period of transition during which the stratification system based on command power grad-ually dwindled and economic power became the most salient element in social stratification. We will return to the mainstream class structure shortly, but will first look at the groups that lay outside the class system in early modern and twentieth-century Japan.

Outcaste Japan

Status was clearly one element of the stratification system of Tokugawa Japan, even if it was not the only criterion applied. An extreme version of a status society would be a caste society composed of "closed social groups based on ascribed status character-istics from which systematic advantages and disadvantages flow."[15] As we have seen, the four-class description of Tokugawa society did not encompass everyone and, in additional to those of indeterminate status, in town and countryside there were those who were defined as beyond the realm of accepted society to the extent of being regarded as barely human at all.

Apart from passing references to *eta* or *chori* in the works of such writers as Basil Hall Chamberlain and Lafcadio Hearn, the first serious writing about *burakumin* in English was a master's thesis by Ninomiya Shigeaki published in 1933. Ninomiya eloquently summarizes the meager amount of research that existed in Japan at that time.[16] Occupation authorities knew little about the issue; their only sources apart from Ninomiya were a couple of briefing papers. Serious historical and sociological research by Japanese scholars did not begin until the late 1940s and the few Americans who took an interest in the problem were anthropologists. John Cornell and John Donoghue published ethnographical accounts of *buraku* in Okayama and Aomori following visits during the 1950s. However, the work which placed *burakumin* firmly on the academic agenda was *Japan's Invisible Race*, edited by George DeVos and Wagatsuma Hiroshi, published first in 1966 and revised in 1972. This brought together historical studies, six ethnographies including chapters by Cornell and Donoghue, plus chapters on the social and psychological dimensions of caste. The key questions for both Japanese and American scholars at the time, although they approached it from quite different perspectives, were those of origins and character. Was *buraku* discrimination a feature deeply embedded within Japan's social structure or was it a relatively recent social phenomenon? What was the most constructive way to understand it: as a question of class, caste, or race? While in Japan most analysts sought to locate the *buraku* issue within a Marxist class frame of reference, DeVos and Wagatsuma adopted a socio-psychological perspective in which "racism and caste attitudes are one and the same phenomenon."[17] The book is sometimes as much about race in the United States as it is about *buraku mondai* (the "*buraku* problem").

There was dispute among historians about the extent to which the class structure of the Tokugawa period was similar to that of earlier periods. This debate had much greater significance for researchers on the *buraku mondai*. On the one hand there are scholars such as Nagahara Keiji who argue that the problem originated in the ancient and medieval periods, "sustained basically because of beliefs held regarding pollution caused by death."[18] Nevertheless he makes clear that the social function of the outcaste groups changed to better serve the contemporary social structure. Under the *shōen* system some functional specialization developed and this was reinforced by daimyō in the sixteenth century who organized outcaste communities "for the purpose of obtaining military necessities."[19] The 1965 Dōwa Commission unequivocally stated that *burakumin* are ethnically identical to mainstream Japanese, and not descendants of a different racial group that had somehow found its way to the islands of Japan at some time in the past. The Buraku Liberation League (BLL) emerged as a mass movement in the mid-1950s and was probably at the peak of its influence in the 1960s. Its preferred account of the origins and nature of the problem focused on the way many outcaste communities had come into existence in the Tokugawa period, even if there were some who were formed before 1600. Put crudely, if discrimination could be shown to be the outcome of policies imposed by the Tokugawa regime, then firstly there was someone who could be blamed, and secondly it was possible that a policy designed to reverse the cycle of decline could improve *buraku* conditions and even liberate them from discrimination and prejudice.

Gerald Groemer, while acknowledging the significance of the medieval legacy, focuses on the administrative control of outcastes, particularly the position of Danzaemon, hereditary leader of the Kantō outcaste communities, both the *kawata/eta* (mainly leatherworkers) and the *hinin* (mostly beggars and street performers). In addition members of both of these groups undertook a variety of dirty, marginal, and polluting tasks such as disposing of dead animals, keeping the streets clean, and working in prisons and as executioners.[20] He demonstrates that what at the end of the sixteenth century was merely customary prejudice which could be mobilized to serve the interests of local lords, had by the later eighteenth century produced a rigid, systematic, and state-sanctioned order of discrimination in the capital where certain people were relegated to a position deemed outside and below commoner society.[21]

Ooms shows that this evolution of discriminatory practice was not confined to the capital. In Shinshū before the 1690s, marriages between *kawata* and majority Japanese were not unknown and usually unproblematic. However, a hundred years later administrative pressure "led to severe sanctions against mixed marriages, now categorized with adultery."[22] The gradual build-up in status restrictions and institutionalized discriminatory practice occurred alongside the emergence of theories of different racial origins, with some writers denying that outcastes were human at all.[23] However, the Tokugawa intelligentsia was by no means unanimous about this and few, if any, of the outcastes themselves bought into these ideas. Senshū Fujiatsu (1815–64) produced a brief tract which concluded that *kawata* were not a separate race, but a product of the status system which should be abolished. Ooms quotes several examples from the final decades of the Tokugawa era of *hinin* or *kawata* protesting about unjust, discriminatory treatment on the basis of their common humanity, even if the state did not recognize their "citizenship."[24]

The transition from their position as outcastes in a highly regulated feudal society to marginal communities within a developing capitalist society has not received much attention. Ian Neary focused on their political involvement with the liberal political movement of the 1870s and beyond as the background to understanding the emergence of the Suiheisha (Leveling Society) which sought between 1922 and 1942 to inspire *burakumin* to defend themselves against prejudice and demand state aid to remove discrimination. N. McCormack focuses more narrowly on how prejudice and discrimination were recreated in the Meiji period in a way that kept *kawata* and *hinin* groups marginal despite their formal restrictions having been removed in 1871. He notes, for example, the development of the notion of an "*eta*" bloodline, despite the fact that outcaste communities in different parts of the country had had little in common before the 1870s. Psuedo-scientific explanations of *buraku* inferiority emerged which confirmed that marriage with them was undesirable. This encouraged the practice of arranged marriage and the need for detective agencies to investigate bloodlines before marriage.[25] McCormack's central argument is that the construction of a sense of nationhood required, or at least encouraged, the continued existence of marginal groups as Others against whom the identity of "We Japanese" could be defined.

There was something of a hiatus in the development of what we might call *burakumin* studies following the publication of *Japan's Invisible Race*. Significant work was produced in the 1970s and 1980s by established scholars who "branched out" to work on *buraku* issues. Thus in 1976 Thomas Rohlen, who had previously worked on high school education, produced an article on the serious confrontation that broke out between supporters of the Japan Communist Party and the BLL following an incident of alleged discrimination in Yoka High School. In 1980 Frank Upham, a legal scholar, published the first of what would develop into a series of analyses of the implementation of Dōwa projects which were financed by the Special Measures Legislation which was the main outcome of the Dōwa Commission, whose report had been published in 1965. And, in 1990, Susan Pharr re-examined the Yoka High School case as an example of a Japanese approach to handling social conflict.

The quality and quantity of Japanese studies in North America and Australasia expanded after the 1980s and began to embrace the study of *buraku*. We may be able to identify a new generation working in the area. Already we have noted the work of McCormack on the role played by *buraku* in the transition from a politically frag-mented and socially divided state structure to a modern unitary state in the early twentieth century. Alastair McLauchlan in New Zealand has not only translated one of the most widely distributed introductions to *buraku mondai*[26] but has also started to publish his own work on the impact of the Dōwa programs on living standards in *buraku* communities. He concludes that, although there has sometimes been spec-tacular progress in reducing discrimination, there is evidence that these gains are not secure and, after ten years of national economic stagnation, *buraku* living standards may be falling and significant differentials re-emerging. Emily Reber produced an ambitious synoptic overview of the position of *burakumin* in the 1990s. Illustrating her generalities with examples from the Asaka *buraku* in Osaka, her essay concludes with a series of policy recommendations for the Japanese government to prohibit discriminatory practices and to create a central agency to provide redress for all kinds of discrimination. On a completely different theme, William Bodiford analyzes the role played by Sōtō Zen Buddhism in sustaining some of the prejudices that are held by mainstream Japanese about *burakumin*. It was only in the 1980s that Sōtō leaders started to do anything to eliminate discriminatory practices, a process still incomplete in the 1990s.[27]

Important issues remain unaddressed. Firstly, in emphasizing the sameness of *burakumin*, in attempts to overcome their image as Other, there is a danger of perpetuating notions of Japan as a homogeneous society. It is important to demon-strate the ambiguity of the boundaries believed to separate *burakumin* from other Japanese in a way that does not create or reinforce boundaries which further separate them from either the well-established Korean community or the newly arrived migrant workers from Asia or Latin America.[28] Secondly, Western critics especially need to be sensitive to the fact that solutions to the *buraku* problem may turn out not to be the same as apparently similar problems elsewhere. We need to look beyond the policy prescriptions based on ideas of race, ethnicity, or caste which derive from North American or Western European analyses.[29] Finally, it is important to combine our knowledge of class with our analysis of caste to gain a rounded understanding of what is happening. John Davis, for example, suggests that the fact that only 24.3 percent of children from *buraku* communities go into higher education compared to 36 percent nationally is prima facie evidence of continued discrimination.[30] However, this assumes that the class structure of *buraku* communities mirrors that of the nation as a whole when it probably does not. Meanwhile, we know that class background is closely related to access to higher education, particularly for children of lower ability.[31] It is therefore not obvious that the figures quoted by Davis are evidence of discrimination (which I do not deny still exists) rather than evidence that these children, or their parents, share the same lack of ability or desire to go to university as others who occupy similar positions within the labor market. While there is ample and welcome evidence that the caste elements of social stratification are weakening, evidence of the existence of class structures remains strong.

From Restoration to Defeat

Between the late 1860s and mid 1930s the status system was transformed even though elements of the elite retained political and economic power. Restrictions on dress, occupations, and intercourse between members of the main status groups were abolished and, probably because they were only poorly supported by the economic structures, they soon ceased to have much relevance for daily life. However, the core people who had orchestrated the Meiji Restoration were keen to consolidate their hold on power, and when a *kazoku* (peerage) was created in 1884 it included most of them.

The merchant class divided into two. Some worked in close cooperation with the government to develop manufacturing industry and infrastructural services such as railways and shipping lines. They formed the core of the capitalist class and their importance was formally recognized when the most successful entrepreneurs were ennobled from the 1890s onwards. Not all merchants and artisans prospered in the new era, and some were unable to compete in the more open markets and fell into the working class. Others continued to trade through their shops and survived into the twentieth century as the "old middle class."

The government created a bureaucracy at the same time as assisting with the creation of large companies. Both required a new kind of white collar worker. At first they came from the old elite but, as the university system developed, a more meritocratic system emerged. Office workers in the public and private bureaucracies formed a new middle class and, once again, the most successful of these had their achievement recognized by the grant of a peerage.

A landowning class had developed within the villages despite Tokugawa regulations, and the land settlement of the 1870s confirmed its position and forced the large majority of rural residents into the role of tenant farmers. Meanwhile, economic policies successfully promoted the development of modern industry. By 1900 there were half a million employed in factories, although over half of them were women working on short contracts in small textile factories. Even in 1935, when there were 5.9 million industrial workers, most of them, about 95 percent, were employed in enterprises of fewer than thirty workers.[32]

This is not the place to discuss the prewar class structure in any detail. What is significant for our purposes is to point out firstly that a new class structure evolved between the 1870s and the 1940s whose contours were evident in daily life. People were strongly aware of the differences in mores and life chances that related to class origin: landlord/tenant, capitalist/worker, new/old middle class. Secondly, this new class structure was integrated at the higher level into a status hierarchy, at the pinnacle of which was the emperor. Finally, although the command elite had been reduced in power in society as a whole, the reconstructed military system reserved a special role for the members of the elite group who had engineered the Meiji Restoration and who served in the armed forces. Their special right of access to the emperor was written into the Meiji constitution which gave them a degree of command power not available to the new elites, for example those created within representative institutions. Thus command power, though apparently eclipsed by the events of the 1920s, was to re-emerge in the later 1930s and dominated Japan at war.

Class and Social Stratification in Postwar Japan

Much of the writing about class and social status in postwar Japan has been descriptive, often written by anthropologists using some form of participant observation. For example in the 1960s Ezra Vogel and Robert Cole produced studies of the new middle class and blue collar workers. Since the 1990s, Edward Fowler, Carolyn Stevens, and Tom Gill have written accounts of the "underclass" in Tokyo, Yokohama, and Osaka, and there have been more studies of working-class lives in the work of James Roberson, Christena Turner, and Glenda Roberts. In complete contrast, Takie Lebra wrote a study of the surviving though dispossessed aristocracy. However important these are in extending our knowledge of the texture of the lives of Japanese people and in challenging stereotypes of Japanese behavior, it seems to me that in the end they do not have much to say about the central theme of class and social stratification in late twentieth-century Japan. Or, to the extent that they do, it would take much more than a few thousand words to encompass their contribution. For this reason I will maintain a fairly narrow focus on the sociological debate about class as it has developed since the early 1960s.

The occupation disrupted the prewar class system. It was meant to. Land reform eliminated the basis of the landlord–tenant relationship. The rapid postwar inflation destroyed much of the wealth of the old middle class. The new constitution committed the government to the abolition of the aristocracy, caste discrimination, and the command power of the military. Within academia Marxism became the orthodoxy and for a time few disputed that class struggle provided the best explanation of social phenomena. Given the extent of strikes and other forms of working-class struggle at the time, it was hard to deny that class was one, perhaps the only, explanator of social action and life chances. However, by the 1960s, after a period of sustained economic growth, strikes became less frequent and the voices of those who had doubts about the appropriateness of class analyses of Japanese society started to be heard.

Not all social scientists were Marxist and there were some in the early 1950s who, influenced by American social science, began to organize the collection of data about social stratification. In 1955 the first Social Stratification and Social Mobility Survey (SSM) was conducted and it has been repeated every ten years since.[33] Analysis of the SSM generated the first debate about the nature of class in Japan, particularly its "middle class." Odaka Kunio argued that the survey showed that the external differences between different classes were no longer as obvious as in the 1930s, whether judged in terms of external appearances or views, judgments, and values.[34] His model of social class was one based on a combination of occupation, status, and income, but he was well aware of the great confusion, even then, in the use of the term "middle." Secondly, he noted the high proportion of the (male) sample who regard themselves as "working class": 74 percent in the 1955 SSM, 57–62 percent in a similar survey carried out in Tokyo in 1960. There is, he comments, "no other economically advanced country in which so many people regard themselves in this light."[35] Finally, he predicted for the near future "a widening of the gaps between different classes [and] an increase in social tensions and insecurity."[36]

However, contrary to Odaka's fears, economic growth resulted in a decrease in social tension. By the end of the 1960s one prominent anthropologist, Nakane Chie, was arguing that class was not a concept appropriate for describing Japanese society, "even if social classes like those in Europe can be detected in Japan ... the point is that in actual society this stratification is unlikely to function and that it does not really reflect the social structure."[37] More important than horizontal stratification by class was the vertical structuration by institution or group of institutions. As we have seen earlier, the historical record is ambivalent about this. Society in Tokugawa Japan is at least as amenable to analysis by vertical structures within groups as horizontal ones outside them. Odaka's solution to the problem had been to propose that the Japanese worker had a "double identity," one within the company to its vertical structures, and one to the union with its commitment to "horizontal solidarity."[38]

The end of the 1970s saw a "second dispute about the middle class" which was triggered by a series of three articles that appeared in the *Asahi shinbun* in 1977. Murakami Yasusuke noted that for the previous ten years a poll conducted by the Prime Minister's Office showed that 90 percent of Japanese regarded themselves as "middle class," compared to only 72 percent in 1957. He suggested that this showed the emergence of a new middle class "whose members are highly homogeneous in style of life and attitudes" and that was "expanding in size and relentlessly encroaching on the strata above and below it."[39] The rapid postwar economic growth blurred distinctions between white and blue collar, uniform patterns of consumption brought "urbanization" even to rural areas, and the rise of the mass media and expansion of higher education contributed to the standardization of information and attitudes. This, he suggested, created a situation very different from even the recent past, a situation "unmatched in any other industrial nation."[40] He was later to expand his ideas and differentiate between the middle class and the "new middle mass" (*shin chūkan taishū*), arguing that conditions in advanced industrial societies work against consistent stratification. They become "destructurated" and a "new middle mass emerges." Japan, Murakami argued, was different from other industrial nations only in that it happened sooner and more completely.[41]

Kishimoto Shigenobu responded to this by pointing out the lack of clarity in the term "middle." Even if we accept that there is more homogeneity in wealth distribution, this does not prove the disappearance of the structural principle of bipolarity, that is, that the working population remains split between the capitalist employer and the wage laborers employed by them. He proposed as a definition of "middle class" those who, while unlikely to become rich, did not face the prospect of desperate poverty because they possessed sufficient assets to be able to maintain themselves should they cease to be employed.[42] However, Kishimoto noted, there was no evidence that this group was large or that their number was increasing. In fact,

Murakami in his later statement did argue that the state provision of social security provides sufficient income security to enable most people to make lifetime plans "equivalent to having a certain level of 'wealth'." Thus he concluded that his "middle mass" was quasi-propertied.[43]

Tominaga Kenichi, the third contributor to the discussion, was the key organizer of the third SSM of 1975. He maintained that the "underlying structural principle" put forward by Kishimoto was inadequate as a conceptual tool for sociological theory. However, he also rejected as unsustainable Murakami's view that because 75 or 90 percent of Japanese people regard themselves as "middle class," the blue and white collar, self-employed, and non-self-employed constitute a homogeneous group. Rather, he picked up on the evidence of status inconsistencies. Applying the technique called cluster analysis to data collected by the 1975 SSM, he argued that, "using six status variables," only 41 percent of the sample show status consistency – 11 percent consistently high and 30 percent consistently low – thus about 60 percent fall in the middle. According to Tominaga, this was not evidence of the homogeneity claimed by Murakami, but rather of a "diverse middle class."[44]

Thus far the controversy had remained mainly within Japan or the realm of Japanese studies. Two studies undertaken at the end of the 1980s sought to use data generated by the 1975 SSM to test hypotheses about the nature of the class structure and status hierarchies in Japan. Thus the debate about the nature of class in Japan was brought into the sociological mainstream. Ishida Hiroshi sought to test four hypotheses: First, the *homogeneity hypothesis* put forward by Murakami that there are no longer any fundamental differences in lifestyle between classes in contemporary Japan; second, the *bipolarity hypothesis* that the distribution of various status characteristics is polarized along the lines of the ownership of the means of production, as argued by Kishimoto and in a more sophisticated form by Rob Steven;[45] third, the *status inconsistency hypothesis* of Tominaga which suggests that classes will not be characterized by either consistently high or consistently low status attributes; and fourth, the *dual structure hypothesis* which suggests that employees should be differentiated not only by class position but also by firm size.[46] Ishida's method was to assess the distribution of status characteristics – occupation, education, income, home ownership, and stock investment – among classes and to compare the results for Japan with a similar analysis performed on an American data set. Six classes were identified – employers, petty bourgeoisie, professional/managerial, non-manual working class, skilled and non-skilled working class – on the basis of control over the means of production and control over labor, one's own and that of others.

There is room here only to summarize Ishida's conclusions. Firstly, he finds no evidence to support the hypothesis either of homogeneity of status characteristics in Japan or that Japanese classes are more status-homogeneous than American classes. Secondly, Japanese class structure was found to be characterized by bipolarity at the extremes: "the employer class occupies the most advantageous positions in the distribution of most status attributes, while the manual working class are at the bottom of all status hierarchies." But he also found strong status inconsistency among "classes which occupy partially dominant and contradictory locations in the social relations of production," that is, the professional management class and the petty bourgeoisie. However, this same set of tendencies was also identified in the American class structure, which does not support the claims of people like Tominaga that status inconsistency is a generalized feature of Japanese social structure or that it is more pronounced in Japan than in other societies. Finally, the dual structure hypothesis – that employees in large firms have more favorable character-istics than those in small and medium sized enterprises – was supported in the Japanese data whereas in the United States firm size makes no difference in the status composition of the manual working classes.[47]

Ishida also took part in a study on intergenerational class mobility with John Goldthorpe and Robert Erikson. In a highly technical paper they sought to explore whether the hypothesis that industrial societies share similar rates of inter-generational mobility could be applied to Japan. They pointed out that, on the one hand, Nakane argued that within Japanese society the dominant structural feature was "not that of horizontal stratification by class or caste but of vertical stratification by institution or group of institutions." If she was correct that basic forms of traditional social structure have persisted through the course of industrial-ization, "western concepts of social stratification and hypotheses from them are unlikely to be applied with much success to the Japanese case."[48] Ishida, Gold-thorpe, and Erikson also wanted to test their hypothesis against the position taken by Tominaga who argued, contra to Nakane, that traditional institutional forms have been undermined and that in their place an open form of stratification had developed, based not on family kinship or place of origin, but achieved attributes of education, occupation, and income. If Japan were to be the "land of opportunity" described by Tominaga, the authors expected to find fluidity levels consistently higher than the "core" levels found in their other studies and also that the essential features of the mobility regime would be difficult to represent in a fixed model. Moreover, although the authors do not mention this, Tominaga's view that contem-porary Japan was characterized by a high degree of "status inconsistency" generated by "democratisation of the distribution criteria for social resources and rewards"[49] would also lead one to expect rather different results in Japan from those generated by the authors' previous studies of seven western and two eastern Euro-pean societies.

Again to go straight to the conclusions: Ishida, Goldthorpe, and Erikson found that the Japanese case did not create special problems for their hypothesis and they found no support for any claim that Japan is either *sui generis* or possesses a quite different form of social stratification to European societies. Contrary to what Nakane might have led us to expect, class structure did indeed function "to generate a pattern of unequal mobility chances." However, they did not want to challenge the view that class awareness was weakly developed. For their analysis this was not an issue. For them class was less about how people viewed their world than what actually happened to them in it. While the data suggested a degree of social fluidity above their "core" model and greater than some European societies, Japan could not be regarded as radically different. Moreover they found no evidence of a steadily rising trend in social mobility of the kind proposed by Tominaga. Finally, to the extent that they found any exceptionalism it was within particular sets of class recruitment. For example, to focus on the working class, the proportion of industrial workers who were sons of industrial workers was only 21 percent, compared to the European range of 39–78 percent. Meanwhile only 56 percent of the sons of working-class fathers were themselves working class, unlike the 61–73 percent in Europe. With low self-recruitment and low stability, both of which were quite easily explained by Japan's late development, the authors suggested it is no wonder that the Japanese working class has such a poorly developed "demographic identity." Having relatively few "hereditary" or "lifetime" proletarians may well be an important factor in explaining the relatively weak working-class consciousness, although this conflicts with the findings of Odaka in the early 1960s.[50]

Class and Social Stratification in Contemporary Japan

So far we have dealt mainly with the class controversy of the 1970s. I want finally to turn briefly to more recent contributions on class and social stratification. First of all let us deal with the characterization of Japan as a middle-class or classless society. There is nothing uniquely Japanese about this. Table 22.1 demonstrates similar results can be obtained from surveys in several other industrial countries and Kōsaka Kenji quotes evidence that shows that approximately 90 percent of people also described themselves as "middle class" in Brazil, India, South Korea, and the Philippines.[51]

Using data from the 1995 SSM survey, Hashimoto Kenji constructed a four-class structure for Japan as follows:

- *Capitalist class* (9.2 percent of working population)   Executives and directors of enterprises of 5+ employees, independent proprietors and family workers in business enterprises of the same scale. Economically privileged, rich in both assets and consumer durables, satisfied with life and politically conservative.
- *New middle class* (23.5 percent of working population)   Employees engaged in professional, administrative, and clerical work (except female clerical workers). Intermediate in income and assets owned, but high level of education. Corporate fringe benefits give them relatively high standards of living but they are not automatically conservative, and if anything are somewhat disaffected.

Table 22.1   International comparisons of "middle class" consciousness

Country	Upper	Upper middle	Middle middle	Lower middle	Lower	Total middle
Italy	2.2	12.5	70.5	10.8	3.0	93.8
France	1.8	10.8	61.2	18.9	6.3	90.9
Germany	0.9	15.9	53.7	21.5	3.4	91.1
Holland	11.2	32.5	44.4	6.5	3.8	83.4
UK	0.4	7.2	53.6	28.1	8.1	88.9
USA	1.5	16.7	54.4	21.6	5.2	92.7
Japan	1.1	10.9	53.6	26.9	5.4	91.4

Source: Hashimoto Kenji, *Class Structure in Contemporary Japan* (Melbourne: Trans Pacific Press, 2003), p. 31.

- *Working class* (45.2 percent of working population)   Employees other than the new middle class (but including female clerical workers). Economically underprivileged with a low standard of living; 75 percent of them identified themselves as working class but, despite dissatisfactions with life, they do not seek change through political action or involvement.
- *Old middle class* (21.9 percent of working population)   Owners of enterprises with fewer than 5 workers, self-employed proprietors, and family workers in small-scale enterprises. The farming sector of this group is gradually giving way to self-employed traders. Comparatively asset-rich, although individual income not large; politically conservative.

Overall, Hashimoto concludes that, although these four classes overlap somewhat, each inhabits a quite different world. He is in no doubt that Japan is a class society.[52] However, the existence of classes might not be as significant if there were mobility between them. Up to the early 1990s there was no clear evidence to support a "decreasing mobility hypothesis" but Hashimoto suggests that analysis of the 1995 data give it credibility. He concludes that each class remains separated by barriers that, while not insurmountable, continue to present significant difficulties for intergenerational mobility.[53]

Class and social structure in the first part of the twenty-first century are likely to be influenced by two factors: globalization and the related changes in the Japanese employment system. Global forces have persuaded transnational corporations to relocate their production facilities overseas. Those employees who remain based in Japan are either the well-educated new middle class involved in high technology and/or in company headquarters, or those engaged in sales, services, and transportation, working-class employment that cannot be "exported" as it needs to be located close to consumers. These trends are likely to increase disparities between classes.

The postwar constitution decisively eliminated the influence of command power within Japanese society but it was not as easy to remove the status and class elements of social stratification. Despite claims to the contrary, Japan, just like any other capitalist society, has recreated a stratification structure based on class and to a lesser extent on status. While older forms of status stratification seem to be fading, new ones based on nationality or ethnicity may be taking their place. Demographic change poses challenges for Japan and the number of foreign workers has increased. What impact has this had on the class and social stratification system? What impact will the decade of economic recession have had on people's assessment of their status and class position? What will future SSM surveys reveal?

NOTES

1   Scott, *Stratification and Power*, p. 192.
2   Halliday, *A Political History*, p. 10.
3   Ibid., p. 11.
4   Totman, *A History of Japan*, p. 223.
5   Ibid., p. 226.
6   Ibid., p. 228.

7   Nakai and McClain, "Commercial Change and Urban Growth," p. 526.
8   Bolitho, "The Han," pp. 189–90.
9   Wakita, "The Social and Economic Consequences," p. 125.
10 Nakai and McClain, "Commercial Change and Urban Growth," p. 573.
11 Ibid., p. 594.
12 Shively, "Sumptuary Regulation and Status Regulation," p. 156.
13 Ooms, *Tokugawa Village Practice*, p. 78.
14 Ibid., pp. 200–6.
15 W. Lloyd Warner, *Social Class in America* (1949), quoted in Scott, *Stratification and Power*, p. 115.
16 Ninomiya, "An Enquiry."
17 DeVos and Wagatsuma, eds., *Japan's Invisible Race*, p. xx.
18 Nagahara, "The Medieval Origins," p. 401.
19 Ibid., p. 400.
20 Groemer, "The Creation of the Edo Outcaste Order," p. 288.
21 Ibid., p. 292.
22 Ooms, *Tokugawa Village Practice*, p. 278.
23 Ibid., pp. 292, 304.
24 Ibid., p. 267.
25 McCormack, "Prejudice and Nationalisation," pp. 72–7.
26 Kitaguchi, *An Introduction to the Buraku Issue*.
27 Bodiford, "Zen and the Art of Religious Prejudice," p. 18.
28 Davis, "Blurring the Boundaries," p. 111.
29 Ibid., p. 120.
30 Ibid., p. 118.
31 See, for example, Hashimoto, *Class Structure*, p. 133.
32 Halliday, *A Political History*, pp. 57, 62–3.
33 For more detail, see Kōsaka, *Social Stratification*, pp. 12–16; Hashimoto, *Class Structure*, pp. 86–8.
34 Odaka, "Middle Classes in Japan," p. 542.
35 Ibid., p. 544.
36 Ibid., p. 551.
37 Nakane, *Japanese Society*, p. 90.
38 Kōsaka, *Social Stratification*, p. 14.
39 Murakami, "The Reality of the New Middle Class," p. 1.
40 Ibid., p. 3.
41 Murakami, "The Age of New Middle Mass Politics," pp. 33–4.
42 Kishimoto, "Can the New Middle Class Theory be Sustained?," p. 6.
43 Murakami, "The Age of New Middle Mass Politics," pp. 38–9.
44 Tominaga, "An Empirical View," p. 11; see also Kōsaka, *Social Stratification*, pp. 49–52.
45 Steven, *Classes in Contemporary Japan*.
46 Ishida, "Class Structure and Status Hierarchies," pp. 65–6.
47 Ibid., pp. 71–8.
48 Ishida, Goldthorpe, and Erikson, "Intergenerational Class Mobility," p. 958.
49 Tominaga, "An Empirical View," p. 1.
50 Ishida, Goldthorpe, and Erikson, "Intergenerational Class Mobility," p. 984.
51 Kōsaka, *Social Stratification*, p. 110.
52 Hashimoto, *Class Structure*, pp. 88–95, 111.
53 Ibid., p. 134.

BIBLIOGRAPHY

Bodiford, William. "Zen and the Art of Religious Prejudice." *Japanese Journal of Religious Studies* 23:1/2 (1996): 1–27.

Bolitho, Harold. "The Han." In John W. Hall, ed., *The Cambridge History of Modern Japan*, vol. 4, *Early Modern Japan*. Cambridge: Cambridge University Press, 1991.

Cole, Robert. *Japanese Blue Collar*. Berkeley: University of California Press, 1971.

Davis, John. "Blurring the Boundaries of the Buraku(min)." In J. Eades, Tom Gill, and Harumi Befu, eds., *Globalization and Social Change in Contemporary Japan*. Melbourne: Trans Pacific Press, 2000.

DeVos, George, and Wagatsuma Hiroshi, eds. *Japan's Invisible Race: Caste in Culture and Personality*, rev. edn. Berkeley: University of California Press, 1972.

Fowler, Edward. *Sanya Blues*. Ithaca, NY: Cornell University Press, 1996.

Gill, Tom. *Men of Uncertainty*. Albany: State University of New York Press, 2001.

Groemer, Gerald. "The Creation of the Edo Outcaste Order." *Journal of Japanese Studies* 27:2 (2001): 263–93.

Hall, John W. "Rule by Status in Tokugawa Japan." *Journal of Japanese Studies* 1:1 (1974): 39–49.

Halliday, Jon. *A Political History of Japanese Capitalism*. New York: Monthly Review, 1975.

Hashimoto Kenji. *Class Structure in Contemporary Japan*. Melbourne: Trans Pacific Press, 2003.

Ishida Hiroshi. "Class Structure and Status Hierarchies in Contemporary Japan." *European Sociological Review* 5:1 (1989): 65–80.

Ishida Hiroshi, Goldthorpe, John, and Erikson, Robert. "Intergenerational Class Mobility in Postwar Japan." *American Journal of Sociology* 96:4 (1991): 954–92.

Kishimoto Shigenobu. "Can the New Middle Class Theory be Sustained?" *Japan Interpreter* 12:1 (1978): 5–8.

Kitaguchi Suehiro. *An Introduction to the Buraku Issue*, trans. Alastair McLauchlan. Richmond, UK: Japan Library, 1999.

Kōsaka Kenji. *Social Stratification in Contemporary Japan*. London: Kegan Paul, 1994.

Lebra, Takie. *Above the Clouds: Status Culture of the Modern Japanese Nobility*. Berkeley: University of California Press, 1993.

McCormack, N. "Prejudice and Nationalisation: On the Buraku Problem." Ph.D. dissertation, Australian National University, 2002.

McLauchlan, Alastair. "The Current Circumstances of Japan's Burakumin." *New Zealand Journal of Asian Studies* 2:1 (2000): 20–144.

Murakami Yasusuke. "The Reality of the New Middle Class." *Japan Interpreter* 12:1 (1978): 1–5.

Murakami Yasusuke. "The Age of New Middle Mass Politics: The Case of Japan." *Journal of Japanese Studies* 8:1 (1982): 29–72.

Nagahara Keiji. "The Medieval Origins of the Eta/Hinin." *Journal of Japanese Studies* 5:2 (1979): 385–403.

Nakai Nobuhiko and McClain, James. "Commercial Change and Urban Growth in Early Modern Japan." In John W. Hall, ed., *The Cambridge History of Modern Japan*, vol. 4, *Early Modern Japan*. Cambridge: Cambridge University Press, 1991.

Nakane Chie. *Japanese Society*. Berkeley: University of California Press, 1970.

Neary, Ian. *Political Protest and Social Control in Pre-war Japan: The Origins of Buraku Liberation*. Manchester: Manchester University Press, 1989.

Ninomiya Shigeaki. "An Enquiry concerning the Origin, Development, and Present Situation of the Eta in Relation to the History of Social Classes in Japan." *Transactions of the Asiatic Society of Japan* 10 (1933): 47–154.

Odaka Kunio. "Middle Classes in Japan." In Reinhard Bendix and Seymour Martin Lipset, eds., *Class, Status, and Power: A Reader in Social Stratification*. New York: Free Press, 1963.

Ooms, Herman. *Tokugawa Village Practice: Class, Status, Power, Law*. Berkeley: University of California Press, 1996.

Pharr, Susan. *Losing Face: Status Politics in Japan*. Berkeley: University of California Press, 1990.

Reber, Emily A. Su-lan. "*Buraku Mondai* in Japan." *Harvard Human Rights Journal* 12 (1999): 297–359.

Roberson, James. *Japanese Working Class Lives*. London: Routledge, 1998.

Roberts, Glenda. *Staying on the Line: Blue-Collar Women in Contemporary Japan*. Honolulu: University of Hawai'i Press, 1994.

Rohlen, Thomas. "Violence at Yoka High School." *Asian Survey* 16:7 (1976): 682–99.

Scott, John. *Stratification and Power*. Cambridge: Polity, 1996.

Shively, Donald. "Sumptuary Regulation and Status Regulation in Early Tokugawa Japan." *Harvard Journal of Asiatic Studies* 25 (1965): 123–64.

Steven, Rob. *Classes in Contemporary Japan*. Cambridge: Cambridge University Press, 1983.

Stevens, Carolyn. *On the Margins of Japanese Society: Volunteers and the Welfare of the Urban Underclass*. London: Routledge, 1997.

Tominaga, K. "An Empirical View of Social Stratification." *Japan Interpreter* 12:1 (1978): 8–12.

Totman, Conrad. *A History of Japan*. Oxford: Blackwell, 2000.

Turner, Christena. *Japanese Workers in Protest*. Berkeley: University of California Press, 1995.

Upham, Frank. "Ten Years of Affirmative Action for Japan's Burakumin." *Law in Japan* 13:39 (1980): 39–73.

Upham, Frank. *Law and Social Change in Postwar Japan*. Cambridge, Mass.: Harvard University Press, 1987.

Upham, Frank. "Unplaced Persons and Movements for Place." In Andrew Gordon, ed., *Postwar Japan as History*. Berkeley: University of California Press, 1993.

Vogel, Ezra. *Japan's New Middle Class: The Salary Man and His Family in a Tokyo Suburb*, 2nd edn. Berkeley: University of California Press, 1971.

Wakita Osamu. "The Social and Economic Consequences of Unification." In John W. Hall, ed., *The Cambridge History of Modern Japan*, vol. 4, *Early Modern Japan*. Cambridge: Cambridge University Press, 1991.

FURTHER READING

A different perspective on Japan's elite structures can be found in Albrecht Rothacher's *The Japanese Power Elite* (New York: St. Martin's, 1993), and Karel van Wolferen's *The Enigma of Japanese Power* (New York: Knopf, 1989) provides a stimulating if rather less academic analysis of Japan's ruling elite and social structure. Ian Neary gives a now slightly dated account of the situation and challenges faced by *burakumin* but in a volume which contains chapters about the key minority groups in Japan, Michael Weiner, ed., *Japan's Minorities* (London: Routledge 1997). Perhaps the biggest challenge facing the Japanese social structure in the twenty-first century is posed by the arrival of migrant workers from Southeast Asia and South America. Discussion of related issues can be found in such works as Mike Douglass and Glenda Roberts, eds., *Japan and Global Migration* (London: Routledge, 2000).

CHAPTER TWENTY-THREE

Japan in Asia

Leo Ching

Introduction

"Japan in Asia" is not a fact but a geopolitical proposition. It is an enunciation and qualification that signals a desire to inscribe the putative unity of Japan into an equally putative unity of Asia. That we don't often hear the phrases "China in Asia" or "Korea in Asia" – for those stipulations seem unnecessary, if not oxymoronic – only accentuates the particular relationship not only of Japan *in* Asia, but also between Japan *and* Asia. The proposition itself speaks to the aporia of Japan's historical positionality vis-à-vis Asia: it is simultaneously a part of, and apart from, Asia. Hence, the proposition is less about physical geography than it is concerned with what Edward Said has called an "imaginative geography" and discursive ideology. It is a series of modern colonial spatializations that serve to demarcate and calibrate difference and sameness between Japan and Asia, East and West through various discourses of culturalism, racialism, and nationalism. Is Japan an Asian nation? What political claims are being made when Japan is positioned either within Asia or without? The self-knowledge of Japan is predicated on the complex and contradictory processes of differentiation, identification, and subjugation of Asia. The question of Asia therefore is a question of Japan's self-identification. The totality of Japan's relation to Asia (whether *in* or *and*), however, is intelligible only in contradistinction to another putative unity, that is, the West. The impulse and exigency to construct Asia as an epistemological category – in social, cultural, economic, and political terms – and Japan's real and imagined relation to it, is both a reaction and a compensation to Western colonial design and Japan's own imperialist endeavor. Despite centuries of intra-regional trafficking and exchange in the Sinocentric imperium, the question of Japan in/and Asia is a decidedly modern one, dating only to the late nineteenth century. It is also a specifically Japanese problematic and preoccupation as Asia constituted the referential point and coordinates to which Japan's role as the only non-Western, non-white colonial power is to be defined and articulated. "Japan in/ and Asia" thus has its historical condition of possibility in the interstices of modernity/coloniality.

As the sole non-Western imperialist power with a contiguous empire in Asia, modern Japanese identity is continuously and constitutively constructed in the vacillating imaginative geographies between Asia and the West. It is an internalization of a Eurocentric model of the world where the West is represented as modern, progressive, and therefore superior whereas Asia is represented as premodern, stagnant, and therefore inferior. The superior–inferior hierarchy can be reversed, however, by asserting the non-modern or trans-modern qualities of Asian culturalism and spirituality vis-à-vis the West's militarism and materialism, predicated on Japan's unique and superior position-ality within Asia. This Japan-led Asianist identity remains trapped in Eurocentric thinking because the overturning of the qualitative values does not refute the binary construction of East and West and tacitly accepts the essentialization of the incommensurability between East and West that made value judgments possible in the first place. Whereas Japan may attempt to relocate its identity between Asia and the West, Eurocentrism continues to allocate meanings and undergird the process of Japan's self-identification.

The shifting relationship of Japan to Asia in the Western dominant world system can be heuristically organized into three paradigmatic moments: the modern/colo-nial, postwar/cold war and post-cold-war/globalization. The modern/colonial mo-ment marks the initial reflection on the question of Japan in Asia in the context of Western encroachment and emerging Japanese imperialist desire. The postwar/cold war moment is characterized by the subordination of Japan under the US hegemony in Asia where questions of decolonization and war responsibilities over Asia are repressed in the interest of political conservatism and economic development. The post-cold-war/globalization moment signals the beginning of a new regional eco-nomic and cultural configuration where the relationship between Japan and Asia is rekindled by the rapid economic development in East Asia and the recurring questions of Japanese colonialism and war responsibilities at the end of the East–West conflict. The three moments outlined below are not intended to be static and self-contained. They are not meant to convey an evolutionary narrative towards some kind of resolution or progress. They represent dominant tendencies characterizing Japan's relationship to Asia and the West in the modern era. Like any historical characterizations, they are necessarily incomplete, selective, and partial. Japan's mod-ern identity and self-definition has been predicated on the inferior position of Asia in relation to the West in the world system. The East–West configuration is under-going some systemic shift with the unprecedented economic development in Asia, especially in East and Southeast Asia, in the last two decades. The emergence of China as both a political and an economic power in the region has potential ramifications for Japan's self-prescribed superiority in the region. (There have never been two super-powers in the history of modern Asia.) While Japan continues to ally itself to the West, especially with the United States, an increasingly multilateral Asia will undoubt-edly change the relationship between Japan and Asia: a new historical horizon where the proposition "Japan in Asia" might cease to be the dominant paradigm in Japan's self-definition.

The Modern/Colonial Moment

Fukuzawa Yukichi and Okakura Kakuzō constitute the two paradigmatic approaches to Japan and Asia in the modern/colonial moment. Fukuzawa's "Datsu-a ron" ("On Leaving Asia") (1885) and Okakura's *The Ideals of the East* (1903), with their seemingly opposite methods of envisioning Japan's relation to Asia, emerged as two pivotal points of departure for thinking about Japan/Asia that all subsequent theorization must invariably attend to. Fukuzawa's text warns of the inevitable coming of Western civilization to the East and the prudent decision Japan needs to make in this time of crisis: "For those of us who live in the Orient, unless we want to prevent the coming of Western civilization with a firm resolve, it is best that we cast our lot with them. If one observes carefully what is going on in today's world, one knows the futility of trying to prevent the onslaught of Western civilization. Why not float with them in the same ocean of civilization, sail the same waves, and enjoy the fruits and endeavors of civilization?" Fukuzawa, however, is not uncritical of the West as he likens the movement of Western civilization to the spread of measles. While the communicable disease could be damaging and fatal, the spread of civilization is accompanied by benefits that outweigh its disadvantages. Without confronting the incoming wave of Western civilization and pursuing the necessary sociopolitical changes, Fukuzawa argues, Japan may lose its national independence.

The desire to join the ranks of the Western civilization necessitates a radical shift in Japan's attitude towards Asia, specifically China and Korea. Fukuzawa puts it succinctly: "Our basic assumptions could be summarized in two words: 'Leave Asia' (*datsu-a*)." To take leave of Asia also meant to shed any resemblance to China and Korea in the eyes of "civilized Westerners." Despite similarity "nurtured by Asiatic political thoughts and mores," there are significant differences (race, heredity, education, etc.) marking the Japanese from the other two peoples who have much more in common. More importantly, both China and Korea are stubbornly holding on to their ancient and stagnant ways. The spread of Westernization has a force akin to that of measles and China and Korea continue to "violate the natural law of its spread." Therefore, in Fukuzawa's view, they cannot survive as independent nations. Despite the noticeable difference between Japan's and China and Korea's reactions to Western civilization, their geographical promixity might lead Westerners to misperceive and therefore misjudge Japan accordingly. Fukuzawa compares Japan's place in Asia to "the case of a righteous man living in a neighborhood of a town known for foolishness, lawlessness, atrocity, and heartlessness. His action is so rare that it is always buried under the ugliness of his neighbors' activities." The only reasonable path for Japan to follow is to "leave the ranks of Asian nations and cast our lot with civilized nations of the West," and to treat China and Korea in the same manner as the Westerners do. Japan must "simply erase from our minds our bad friends in Asia."[1]

If Fukuzawa advocates that Japan take leave of Asia amidst the onslaught of Western civilization, Okakura seems to take a diametrically opposed approach. Written in English and intended for a Western readership, *The Ideals of the East* begins with the following famous dictum:

> Asia is one. The Himalayas divide, only to accentuate, two mighty civilizations, the Chinese with its communism of Confucius, and the Indian with its individualism of the Vedas. But not even the snowy barriers can interrupt for one moment that broad expanse of love for the Ultimate and the Universal, which is the common thought-inheritance of every Asiatic race, enabling them to produce all the great religions of the

world, and distinguishing them from those maritime peoples of the Mediterranean and
the Baltic, who love to dwell on the Particular, and to search out the means, not the
end, of life.[2]

Unlike Fukuzawa's call for Japan to abandon its neighbors and his recognition of
the inevitability of Westernization, Okakura constructs an organic Asianness that
attempts to overturn the material superiority of the West by an imagined culturalism
of the East. Okakura is not oblivious to the diversity and difference that exist within
Asia. The unity of Asia, despite periodic intertribal upheavals and numerous
ethnic conquests, lies in the "old energy of communication" embodied by Chinese
humanism and Indian spirituality so that the Asiatic races form a single mighty
web. In spite of the irreducible historical contingencies and differences in particular
regions or locales, there exists a perceivable unitary structure: "Arab chivalry,
Persian poetry, Chinese ethics, and Indian thought, all speak of a single ancient
Asiatic peace, in which there grew up a common life, bearing in different regions
different characteristic blossoms, but nowhere capable of a hard and fast dividing
line."[3]

Whereas Fukuzawa sees modern civilization and the old conventions of Asia as
mutually exclusive, Okakura advocates the superiority of Asia's spirituality over the
scientific progress of the West: "The simple life of Asia need fear no shaming from
that sharp contrast with Europe in which steam and electricity have placed it today."
Whereas Fukuzawa sees the futility of resisting the West and urges Japan to delink
from China and Korea, Okakura envisions the past as a way to create new paths for
the future and contends that Asia, not the West, should be the agent of historical
change. He ends the book with the following:

> We await the flashing sword of the lightning which shall cleave the darkness. For the
> terrible hush must be broken, and the raindrops of a new vigor must refresh the earth
> before new flowers can spring up to cover it with their bloom. But it must be from Asia
> herself, along the ancient roadways of the race, that the great voice shall be heard.
> Victory from within, or a mighty death without.[4]

Although Okakura's Asianism and Fukuzawa's de-Asianism appear to be articulating two opposing positions of Japan in relation to its Asian neighbors, it would be
wrong to view them as incommensurable and irreconcilable. The two approaches
converge on a Japan-centrism that, regardless of their respective symbolizations of
Asia, bestows upon Japan a privileged position within the region in the emerging
imperialist-colonial world system. First and foremost, the opposition between Fukuzawa and Okakura derived from the same sense of crisis: the confronting of Western
civilization.[5] It was this imminent threat that necessitated the rearticulation of the
Japan–Asia relationship as a modern problem that constituted a rupture from the
China-centered worldview. Fukuzawa sees Western civilization as a kind of epidemic,
although with greater benefits than measles. Okakura sees it as inferior, as totally
absorbed in the consideration of means rather than ends. Both were confronted with
the opposing relation of East and West, and an existing Asia. More importantly, they
also subjected Asia to symbolization away from geographical or environmental de-
terminism.

In these tumultuous times, Fukuzawa and Okakura ascribe to Japan a unique role in between East and West which ultimately gives rise to a hierarchical relation of nations that affords Japan a special status within Asia, but does not fundamentally challenge the Eurocentric mapping of the world's peoples in terms of race and development. The archipelago therefore becomes an apt metaphor for both Fukuzawa and Okakura in their imagining of Japan in its new role in the sea of empire. For Fukuzawa, although "Japan is located in the eastern extremities of Asia, … the spirit of her people has already moved away from the old conventions of Asia to the Western civilization." This location and disposition will allow Japan to float in the "same ocean of civilization, sail the same waves, and enjoy the fruits and endeavors of civilization." The eastern extremities of Japan's location also, in Okakura's view, bestowed upon Japan "the unique blessing of unbroken sovereignty, the proud ancestral ideas and instincts at the cost of expansion [and] made Japan the real repository of the trust of Asiatic thought and culture." Japan is therefore the living museum of Asiatic civilization where the historic wealth of Asiatic culture can be studied through its treasured specimens. However, Japan is more than a museum "because the singular genius of the race leads it to dwell on all phases of the ideals of the past, in that spirit of living Advaitism which welcomes the new without losing the old." The history of Japanese art therefore becomes the history of Asiatic ideals: "the beach where each successive wave of Eastern thought has left its sand-ripple as it beat against the national consciousness."[6]

Prior to the publication of Fukuzawa's "On Leaving Asia" and Okakura's *The Ideals of the East*, Japan had already claimed sole sovereignty over the Ryūkyū Islands and established Hokkaidō as a settlement colony. Between the time of their publications, Japan defeated China in the Sino-Japanese War which was fought on the soil of the Korean peninsula and as a result acquired its first overseas colony in Taiwan (1895) while preparing for the formal annexation of Korea in 1910. In short, by the early twentieth century, Japan had emerged as an imperialist power, albeit not in content, but certainly in form. Asia, as part of the Japanese empire, could no longer exist only at the levels of symbolization and discourse; it had become the object of Japanese colonization and subjugation with formal policies, informal practices, and ideologies.

Asia remained an integral site of articulation for the Japanese empire's self-identification and in its differentiation from the West. The specific historical conditions of the Japanese empire elicited different strategies of positionality vis-à-vis its Asian colonized and Western imperialist counterparts. Unlike the expansive imperialist outreach of the British and French empires, Japanese expansionism was limited to peoples in close physical proximity to the Japanese islands in East Asia, in what could be called a contiguous empire. Japan was also a latecomer in the great game. By the late nineteenth century, over 80 percent of the world's surface was occupied by European powers. More importantly, Japan was the only non-Western and non-white modern imperialist power. Japan's entry into the geopolitical arena of global imperialism is already upheld by the coloniality of power. One constitution of the coloniality of power is the classification and reclassification of the world population wherein the concept of "race" becomes crucial in delineating and discriminating peoples in their relative positionalities to the omnipresent and omnipotent "West" through the dichotomous schemata of underdevelopment/development, premodern/modern, incivility/civility, etc. This ambivalence – "not white, not quite, yet alike" – colored Japanese colonial discourse in Asia and its relationship to the white imperialist powers throughout the modern colonial period.[7] For it is in part to justify Japanese rule and to differentiate it from the Western powers as benign and liberating for the "colored" peoples of Asia that notions such as "common script, common race," and "universal brotherhood" were propagated as the endowed mission of the Japanese nation to assimilate all its subjects under the benevolent rule of the emperor.

Like the various colonial rules and discourses of Western imperialisms, the Japanese empire was neither homogeneous nor without contradictions. There was substantial difference between rhetoric and policy not only between the earlier colonies of Taiwan and Korea but also between the formal colonies and the puppet state of Manchukuo. Unlike other colonies, Manchukuo was officially designated as an independent state based on the idea of harmony between the five nations of Japan, Korea, Manchuria, China, and Mongolia. Setting aside such differences for the moment, we may devise a general contour of Japanese rule under the gradual shifts from incorporation to assimilation to integration as the three dominant moments of Japanese colonial practice and discourse in Asia. What can be observed here is how, as Asia became incorporated into the Japanese empire, Japan's imperial imaginary gradually abandoned the Western model of modernity for an Asia-centric counter-modernity that attempted to justify and legitimize Japan's colonial rule and imperialist expansionism until the defeat of Japan in World War II.

There was no clear colonial policy based on the supposed racial and cultural similarity between the Japanese and its colonized peoples in the early period of incorporation. There were arguments that the Taiwanese were too underdeveloped and the Koreans too ethnocentric to ensue the policy of assimilation. In the early phase of Japanese colonialism, there was neither consistency nor consensus in imperial Japan's association with its supposedly culturally and racially similar subjects. In the 1920s, assimilation emerged as the dominant ideology of the Japanese empire. The shift in colonial policy, from incorporation to assimilation, was a response of Japanese imperialism to the changing conditions between Japan and China and the world situation at large. It was a response to the expansion of Japanese imperialism onto the continent and to contain and accommodate the growing demands of the colonial elite. Furthermore, with growing tension among the imperialist nations and mounting unease about Japanese expansionism, Japanese colonialism had to legitimize itself based on its difference from European colonialism through a precarious discourse of identity with its colonized peoples. It is significant that Okakura's proclamation that "Asia is one" was appropriated and rearticulated by the Japanese only during the height of the Pacific War. With increased imperialist competition and regionalist conflict, the Japanese sought to further integrate its colonies and possessions into the empire, accelerating its assimilationist policies into what has come to be known as "imperialization" (kōminka) where colonial subjects are encouraged and coerced into becoming Japanese subjects under imperial benevolence. The Greater East Asia Co-Prosperity Sphere is but the most visible manifestation of this wartime mobilization and integration.

Postwar/Cold War

On August 15, 1945, through a static-filled radio broadcast, Emperor Hirohito, in a highly formalized language, spoke to his subjects for the first time in his reign, announcing that the war did not bode well for Japan and asking the people to endure the unendurable and to bear the unbearable. Although few could make out the meaning of the message from the emperor, soon after the rescript was summarized in everyday language, the profound reality and immediacy of the emperor's words became clear: that the great Japanese empire had come to an end.

The dissolution of the Japanese empire and the insertion of Japan into the postwar order dominated by US hegemony in the region ensured a disengagement of Japan from Asia that was radically different from that of the modern/colonial moment. A new postwar national identity based on singularity and exclusivity dominated the discussion. A postwar Japanese identity was constructed by the effacement of the memories of war and empire. Instead of an outstretched and vast imperial landscape, Japan, as both a geographical and a cultural signifier, was now enclosed and delimited within the borders of an "island country." The militaristic imperialist nation was replaced by the self-absorbed and timeless "snow country." The multi-ethnic composition of the "Japanese," as necessitated by the incorporating logic of the empire, was readily discarded and disavowed in the immediate postwar years. Instead, a singular national/racial identity, or what Oguma Eiji has called "the myth of the homogeneous nation," was inaugurated and consolidated in conjunction with Japan's refusal to confront its war crimes and colonial past. The new understanding was that Japan had been a natural community integral to the Japanese archipelago since antiquity. In the postwar construction of Japanese national history, Japan's modern past and its relation to Asia was never properly grasped as a history of empire-building and where former subjects of the Japanese empire had been totally obliterated from its discourse. It was by effacing and denying the traces of coloniality that the postwar cultural identity of the Japanese as a homogeneous people was established as Japan's self-image. Even the occasional interrogation of and response to the issues of war responsibility more often than not deflected and bypassed the questions of Japanese colonialism in Asia.

Dissociation from the empire, and the delinking from Asia, was due to the peculiar way in which the Japanese empire liquidated itself without going through the process of decolonization. The Potsdam Declaration stripped Japan of its colonial and occupying territories, with Japanese sovereignty limited to Honshū, Hokkaidō, Kyūshū, and Shikoku. Unlike the French and the British, the Japanese did not have to concern themselves with prolonged, and at times violent, procedures of decolonization. There was no debate within Japan regarding the fate of its possessions; it was as obvious as defeat itself. The Japanese empire simply vanished. As a result, decolonization was never a domestic concern; it was the problem of other peoples. What has been precluded from intellectual and popular discourses alike in postwar Japan is the question: what exactly constituted the decolonization of the Japanese empire? It is a question that will re-emerge in the postcolonial/globalization moment, as we shall see later. In this way Japan was deprived of, or rather conveniently relinquished, a sustained discussion and debate over its responsibilities not only for the Pacific War but also for its overall colonial legacy. The abrupt withdrawal of the Japanese colon-izer, however, had dire consequences for many who found themselves thrust into an era of postcoloniality only to be mired in another neo-colonial struggle under the American-led postwar regional order. The lack of decolonization and the dominance of American political and economic activities in the postwar era played a pivotal role in severing Japan's historical and colonial relationship with Asia and moving Japan towards a new sub-imperialist relationship with the United States.

The end of World War II, the dissolution of the Japanese empire, and the ensuing cold war structure were followed by a number of hot wars in Asia. The Korean War, the Vietnam War, and the civil wars were largely fought under the premises of the superpowers. As a consequence, Northeast and Southeast Asia (not to mention South Asia) were characterized primarily by fragmentation and high levels of mutual hostil-ity. The alliances forged out of the cold war further militated against any serious regional cohesion in Asia. The United States sought to create a "grand crescent" of anti-communist regimes housing US military bases from the Aleutian Islands through Japan, South Korea, and Taiwan, and extending further south through the Philip-pines and South Vietnam. As the leader of this alliance structure, the United States worked assiduously to maintain bilateral relations with its various alliance partners and to resist more than perfunctory efforts at closer intra-Asian ties, which it saw as a potential challenge to American dominance in the region.[8] The political orientation towards the United States was instrumental in preventing and obstructing much intra-regional dialogue and interaction among the intellectuals and cultural workers.

Political and cultural fragmentation under US geopolitical interest divided not only Asia, but also affected Japan's relationship with Asia. For obvious reasons, Japan had been quite heavily linked with Asia through trade during the prewar years, with nearly 52 percent of Japanese exports going to Asia and 36 percent of Japan's imports coming from Asia. Western trade played a far less substantial role as the war ap-proached. This balance was rather quickly reversed for Japan following the loss of the country's colonies and its domestic economic prowess in World War II. As a conse-quence, during the 1940s and 1950s, Asia receded in economic and strategic signifi-cance, and the West, particularly the United States, became much more dominant.[9] For Japan, it was a period focused on domestic economic revitalization under the nuclear and security umbrella of the United States, combined with virtually unre-stricted access to the rich US market for Japanese goods.

During this time, trade and aid became the principal mechanisms for Japan's postwar developing involvement with its Asian neighbors. This took the form of Japanese wartime reparations. Between 1955 and 1965, Japan negotiated agreements with a total of ten East and Southeast Asian countries, transferring about $1.5 billion in reparations and economic and technical assistance. The bulk of this money was tied to the purchase of Japanese goods and services, thereby opening up these markets to Japanese companies and creating ever more important bilateral economic links be-tween these countries and Japan. This was congruent with postwar Japan's broader economic strategy which relied primarily on importing raw materials, largely from Asia and the Middle East, and using them to produce manufactured goods in a host of ever more sophisticated plants within Japan. These products were then sold within the Japanese domestic market and also exported, primarily to the United States and only secondarily to the rest of Asia.[10] Although 70 percent of Japanese government aid went to Asia, it was almost invariably linked to the development and expansion of markets for Japanese companies.

Most Asian states traded heavily with Japan as well as with the United States. At the time Asian "regionalism" meant largely that a number of countries in the Asian region had similar bilateral economic links with Japan and the United States; there was little complex economic activity within the region as a whole.[11] In short, for most of the first three decades following World War II, Japan was linked primarily to the United States and only secondarily to Asia. Relations between Japan and the rest of Asia were highly asymmetrical. Asia was principally a source of raw materials for Japan as well as an outlet for Japan's manufactured goods. In this context, Asia continued to exist as underdeveloped Other to the fast developing and modernizing Japan. In the "triangle of growth" between the pivotal United States and the peripheral Asian Newly Industrialized Economies (NIEs), Japan acted as an important mediating economic agent. To summarize the process: as the United States played the important role of providing an immense market and basic technology development, Japan imported the basic know-how and applied it to practical use; subsequently, Japan was able to sell or dispose of previously used "secondhand" technology (machinery and equipment) to the peripheral NIEs; the NIEs, in turn, used this "secondhand" technology and equipment to launch their export-oriented industries.[12]

The dominant intellectual discourse that justified the development-centric model of the postwar/cold war system was modernization theories propagated by American social scientists in the 1950s. At their core, modernization theories argued that factors internal to an enclosed nation-state and culture, such as a traditional agrarian structure, the traditional attitude of the population, the low division of labor, etc., are responsible for underdevelopment. Differences in structure and historical origin are considered of little importance; international dependencies are not taken into account. As a result, a change in these endogenous factors is the only strategy for development. The industrialized countries are the model for economy and society; this model is universal and will be reached sooner or later. There is a continuum between the least and the most developed countries on which each country has its position, with the less developed nations separated from the industrialized countries by the degree of backwardness that has to be made up for. Suitable measures are the modernization of the production apparatus, capital aid, and transfer of know-how, so that the developing countries can reach the stage of industrialized countries as soon as possible. Development is seen as an increase in production and efficiency and is measured primarily by comparing per capita incomes.

Firmly ensconced in theories of evolution and functionalism, modernization theories sought to promote the core economic interests of the United States as a developmental imperative. Japan was hoisted up during the cold war years as an inspiring exemplar of evolutionary modernization and a model for developing nations to follow. Within the specific context of Asia, Japan was represented as a westernized Asian nation, an example of development that any non-Western (read non-white) people could emulate. Japan was the ideal model because it had become an American colony and client state, complete with a permanent army of occupation. There are two mutually related factors that went into making Japan the showcase of modernization in the cold war era: the active involvement of an American military occupation between 1945 and 1952 and its continuation since that time under the provisions of the US–Japan Security Treaty, and the recoding of Japan's modern history into an instance of modernization in scholarly social science writing in the 1960s, 1970s, and early 1980s.[13] The Japanese, of course, reconstructed their own regionalized modernization theory in the 1970s as the changes in global economic circumstances made re-Asianization an imperative for the Japanese economic machine. In the so-called "flying geese" model, initially advanced in the 1930s and revived in the 1970s, Japan was the lead goose heading a flying-V pattern of Asian economic geese. The other Asian countries, maintaining their respective and relative positions in the formation, were to follow and replicate the developmental experience of the Japanese and other "geese" in front of them. Over time, the Asian nations would proceed collectively toward mutually beneficial advances in industrialization and manufacturing, and eventually achieve prosperity, with Japan remaining the undisputed development leader in the region.[14] American modernization theories and its Japanese variant are simply a mutation of an imperialism and colonialism discredited by World War II.[15]

Postwar stability reached a crisis in the 1970s which forced Japan to alter and redefine its economic relationship with Asia. The breakdown of the Bretton Woods monetary system (1971), the quadrupling of world oil prices (1973), and the growing trade surpluses with the United States led to a shift in Japanese foreign economic policy. First, foreign direct investment by Japanese firms gradually became more important than simple trade. Second, Asia became more important to Japan's overall economic strategies. Japan's refocus on markets in Asia begun in 1970s, but accelerated vigorously following the Plaza Accord of 1985 and the consequent 40 percent appreciation in the value of the Japanese yen by 1987.[16] As a consequence, Japanese foreign direct investment (FDI) in 1986 was nearly double that of 1985. By 1988 the figure had doubled once again and it peaked in 1989 at $67.5 billion. While the bulk of this investment went to North America, principally the United States, roughly one-quarter was targeted at the rest of Asia, making a profound impact on economics throughout the region. Furthermore, between 50 and 60 percent of Japan's Asian investment was in manufacturing, especially in consumer electronics and automobile industries, moving and expanding towards a intra-regional and intra-industrial division of labor. For the single year 1993, Asian FDI by Japan accounted for a much higher proportion of total Japanese FDI (33 percent).[17]

One of the consequences of growing Japanese FDI and expanding manufacturing facilities in Asia and the fast developing consumerist economies in Asia is the proliferation of Japanese mass culture in the region, especially in Thailand, Hong Kong, Taiwan, and other Chinese-speaking communities in Southeast Asia. Largely because of Japanese colonialism and war crimes, Japanese cultural products were until recently officially banned in some of its former colonies such as Taiwan and South Korea. Although limited products, mostly TV animation, were broadcast in Taiwan and South Korea from the 1970s, any associations with Japanese culture were erased or modified. The systematic proliferation and transnationalization of Japanese mass image, sound, and commodity in Asia took place only in the 1990s, a period that coincided with the heightened process of globalization in the region in the wake of the thawing of the cold war.

Post-Cold War/Globalization

The end of the cold war and the inherent contradictions of postwar Japanese economic development which culminated in the decade-long recession of the 1990s have significantly altered hitherto repressed and neglected postwar Asia–Japan relations. Furthermore, the process of economic globalization has greatly facilitated intra-Asia circulation of peoples, commodities, and images to an extent unseen since the Japanese empire. The end of the purported East–West, capitalist–communist confrontation in East Asia hastened the various democratic and people's movements in Northeast Asia, especially in high economic growth countries and Japan's former colonies of South Korea and Taiwan. The coming out of the former Korean "comfort women" and the localization of Taiwanese cultural politics contributed to the re-examination and reassessment of Japanese colonial rule and its legacy. The long recession in Japan rekindled latent neo-nationalist sentiment regarding not just Japan's defeat and its subsequent submission under US hegemony, but the entire modern history of Japan. In short, the end of the cold war opened up, as if by whim, all the repressed contradictions of postwar Japan. The discussions, although motivated by the bursting of the "bubble economy" and the fallacy of social equity and economic benefit, have been linked to historical issues relating to Asia. As these issues re-emerge, we have also witnessed an unprecedented integration within Asia, especially in popular and youth culture under the process of globalization. In this stage of geohistorical development, we are perhaps witnessing the waning of a bipolar "Japan and Asia" and the emerging of a multi-polar configuration and power balance, with China taking a major role in defining the questions of Asia.

The redefining of Japan's relation to Asia, once again, has been intimately linked to Japan's self-definition during the uncertainty of its long economic downturn, especially by the neo-nationalists. The economic crisis and Japan's embarrassing role as financial lackey to the United States in the first Gulf War culminated in a deep reflection on the identity of Japan and its relation to the outside world. A representative of this rearticulation of Japanese identity and its relationship to Asia is the literary critic Katō Norihiro. Reflecting on the modes of postwar Japanese epistemological and existential subjectification in *Haisengoron* (On Defeat, 1995), Katō employs the notion of *nejire*, or "twistedness," as the core of the Japanese being. Since the Pacific War has been condemned as a war of aggression, Katō argues, those Japanese who died believing in the cause of the state died meaningless deaths. For those who survived, they could not maintain the continuity of their wartime identity, nor could they deny it and break from it by their own choice. This "suspended identity" is the culmination of a repressed "twistedness" in the Japanese psyche that includes both the Japanese state and society.[18] The postwar Japanese state would, on occasion, apologize to its Asian neighbors for "acts of aggression," but in other instances, glorify Japan's "acts of liberation" and justify what Japan did to its neighbors. This schizophrenic duality and subject position is the consequence of the reluctance of the Japanese state and society to confront this repressed "twistedness" in its postwar history.

Given this externally inflicted but internalized condition, it is important for the Japanese to first acknowledge the presence of the "twistedness," and overcome the split personality through the constitution of a singular "we" as a nation which can then qualify as a body able to apologize to others. And here is Katō's own "twist": he proposes that the Japanese adopt a particular national procedure – the mourning of the three million Japanese war dead and the constituting of a "we" that have collectively paid tribute to our war dead. Then, and only then, can the Japanese apologize to their Asian neighbors for having killed twenty million of them.[19] Simply put, Katō argues that in order to offer an authentic apology for the twenty million Asian victims of Japan's war aggression, it is first necessary to form a national subject (*kokumin shutai*) though the process of mourning for the three million Japanese war dead. Katō's position suggests that in an era of recession, the perceived need to apologize to other Asians for Japanese aggression and atrocities can be appropriated as a pretext for national mobilization. It also reveals deep-seated anxiety over a perceived decline in national power and prestige. It can also be understood as an effort to settle accounts with Asia on the issue of war guilt as a necessary step toward cultivating a more "ordinary" military as well as political and economic role for Japan in international affairs, whether it is to join the United Nations Security Council or mobilize military actions abroad. The emergence of neo-nationalism in the 1990s is best represented by the collective campaign by intellectuals around 1996 against the "postwar view of history." These intellectuals and elites argued that the "postwar view of history," which they claimed dominates school textbooks, is a "masochistic view of history," which sees only the vices and not the virtues of the Japanese nation.[20]

The neo-nationalists' attempt to redefine Japan's postwar history and its role in Asia is only a symptom of the larger process of incomplete decolonization in the postwar era. The continuous wrangling over the Northern Territories with Russia, the Diaoyu/Senkaku Islands with China/Taiwan, and the more recent Tokto/Take-shima controversy are unresolved territorial disputes stemming from the legacy of Japanese imperialism. The lingering effects of the Japanese empire and its war responsibilities are paradoxically intersected and interspersed by the growing Japanese cultural hegemony and intra-Asian popular cultural flows. It is important, however, to note that the emerging Japanese soft power does not constitute an alternative or opposition to other forms of cultural power such as Americanization. Instead, the rise of Japanese cultural exports can be read as a symptom of the shifting nature of transnational cultural power in a context in which intensified global cultural flows has decentered the power structure and vitalized local practices of appropriation and consumption of foreign cultural products and meanings.[21] In the circuitry of glob-alizing the regional, Japan has arguably, for the first time, encountered other Asian nations as "modern" cultural and economic neighbors. The binary opposition be-tween "traditional" and "underdeveloped" Asia and the "developed" West, which was instrumental in modern Japan's construction of its national identity in a West-dominated world, is no longer feasible. The denial of the role of Japan as a mediator-translator between Asia and the West does not signal the end of Japan-centric thinking in the consumption of intra-regional cultural flows. This is evident in the fantasy and nostalgia for a supposedly bygone or lost Japan in the identification and consumption of Asia.

A partial explanation of the popularity of Japanese mass culture amongst youth in Taiwan and other Asian countries is founded on the emerging sense of a coeval temporality with Japan. This sense of contemporaneousness, however, is not shared by the Japanese, thus underscoring the persisting uneven and asymmetrical relationship between Japan and other Asian countries.[22] Instead of coevality, Japan sees a lag between developing Asia and itself and tends to view Asia nostalgically as a kind of bygone Japan. This kind of nostalgia and longing is predicated on the familiar scheme of modernization, development, and even colonialism. The neo-nationalist and manga artist Kobayashi Yoshinori has discovered the lost "Japanese spirit" in Taiwan, especially among Taiwanese over the age of 60 who speak Japanese and experienced Japanese rule. He also contrasts the vibrancy and energy of the Taiwanese youth with the disillusioned and insecure young Japanese.[23] The presence of "Japan" in Taiwan represents the era of high growth filled with "innocent" hope and vitality of modernization, a bygone era in Japan which most Japanese youth can no longer experience. Japanese reception of Hong Kong popular culture, although driven by the former British colony's economic strength and advanced cultural production, may also remind Japanese women (who make up its largest fan base) of Japanese music and idols of the 1980s.[24] The recent popularity of the "Korean Wave," especially the television melodrama series "Winter Sonata," has most of its middle-aged female fans longing for a simpler and purer love that supposedly reminds them of their younger days.

This sentiment of nostalgia is really not about the past, but about the present predicament of Japan's place in the world and in Asia. It reflects anxiety over the Japanese nation and society and what Japan itself has lost or is about to lose in contradistinction to the present vigor and dynamism of a promising Asia. The lack of mooring deeply felt by the neo-nationalists and consumers has to do with the breakdown of the postwar Japanese system under the auspices of the American military and economic umbrella, and the secondary status of the Asian economies. The growing importance of trade and economics has made the regional relationship more multilateral and interdependent. With Taiwan, Hong Kong, and South Korea moving into subsidiary, but nonetheless important, roles in the march toward Asian integration, the result is a much more complicated criss-crossing and interpenetration of economic forces than the earlier pattern, in which Japan was the center and the other countries of Asia were at the periphery, connected to one another primarily through Tokyo.[25]

Conclusion: A Withering Japan in Asia

Nihon Keizai Shinbun (Japan's equivalent of the *Wall Street Journal*), in its annual 2001 ranking of "the bestselling products" in the format of a sumō tournament, listed the baseball player "Ichirō" and the phrase "Made in China" as the west and east grand champions respectively. Sukuki Ichirō, with his unprecedented success as the first Japanese position player to star in the US major leagues, has become the symbol of Japan's "soft exports" (*sofuto yushutsu*). The proliferation of China-produced consumer goods has profoundly affected the commodity prices and manufacturing structures of Japan. It is estimated, for example, that three-quarters of all imported clothing and over half of all imported vegetables in Japan in 2000 came from China. The juxtaposition of "Ichirō" and "Made in China," with its corresponding though unintended "West" and "East" orientations, points to the double structure of Japan's role in the current world system. One the one hand, the choices speak to the contemporaneousness of the changing economic activities from inside the political and cultural boundaries of the nation-state to the new de-territorialized and disengaged flow of globalization. With its major manufacturing sectors moving overseas and the gradual opening of its heretofore protected domestic market, "Made in China" is only a symptom of a larger structural transformation of Japanese capitalism since the 1970s. On the other hand, the juxtaposition also symbolizes the shift from manufacturing of "hard" goods to the exporting of "soft" entertainment, of which Suzuki Ichirō is only the latest example.

What this radical shift conceals, however, is the persistent ambivalence of Japan in-between East and West, an irreducible characteristic of Japanese modernity since the late nineteenth century. Ichirō is a "real deal" (*honmono*) only after his proven success in the West despite his numerous achievements in Japan. It is only through the recognition and approval of the West that the worth of a Japanese identity can be realized. The narrative of Japan's move from being a producer of hardware to an exporter of software and China's emergence as a global factory reinforces the developmentalist rhetoric of modernization discourse that gives rise to a hierarchy of national development (advanced, developed, developing, underdeveloped) that ignores the highly uneven development within these economic units. We should recall that the emergence of Japan as a modern nation-state required not only the recognition of the West through its own version of imperialism and colonialism, but also the overturning and inverting of the historical superior–inferior relationship between China and Japan, and its disengagement from the Sinocentric subsystem into the world of global colonialism.

US hegemony notwithstanding, it has been argued that capitalism, divorced for the first time from its historically specific origins in Europe, has become an authentically global abstraction.[26] This de-territorialization is accompanied by a spatial displacement of capitalist epicenters, from Western Europe since the sixteenth century to North America in the twentieth century, to East Asia in the new millennium. Each change of command in the capitalist world economy reflects the "victory" of a "new" region over an "old" region. Whether a fresh change of command and a new stage of capitalist development are imminent remain unclear, especially in the wake of post-9/11 US "new imperialism." The displacement of an "old" region (North America) by a "new" region (East Asia) as the most dynamic concentration of processes of capital accumulation is already a reality.

China, of course, plays a significant role in the reconfiguration of this "new" hegemony and will continue to do so. Predictably, there are growing alarmist and opportunist readings of Japan's relation to the re-emergence of China. While some see China as a threat to Japan, both economically and militarily, others see China as presenting an unprecedented business opportunity for the sagging Japanese economy. The resurgence of China bears an uncanny similarity to the "tributary system" of the Sinocentric imperium where Japan existed as a subordinate unit.[27] If we recall that Japan's ascendance to the status of a modern power was through its disassociation from the Sinocentric world order, what would a seeming return to a China-centered regionality mean for Japan and its relationship with Asia? What would "Japan in Asia" mean in the region where Japan is no longer an Asian exception, but simply an Asian nation without qualification?

NOTES

1 Fukuzawa, "On Leaving Asia," pp. 351–2.
2 Okakura, *The Ideals of the East*, p. 1.
3 Ibid., pp. 3–4.
4 Ibid., p. 244.
5 Sun, "How Does Asia Mean? (Part 1)," p. 21.
6 Okakura, *The Ideals of the East*, pp. 8–9.
7 Ching, *Becoming "Japanese," p.* 26.
8 Pempel, "Trans-Pacific Torii," p. 49.
9 Ibid., p. 53.
10 Ibid., p. 56.
11 Ibid., p. 57.
12 Twu, *Tōyō shihonshugi*, pp. 169–71.
13 Harootunian, *The Empire's New Clothes*, p. 78.
14 Ching, "Globalizing the Regional," p. 251.
15 Harootunian, *The Empire's New Clothes*, p. 80.
16 Pempel, "Trans-Pacific Torii," p. 57.
17 Ibid., p. 60.
18 Hanasaki, "Decolonialization," p. 71.
19 Ibid., pp. 71–2.
20 Fujioka, *"Jigyaku shikan" no byōri*.
21 Iwabuchi, *Recentering Globalization*, p. 35.
22 Ibid., p. 155.
23 Kobayashi, *Shin gomanizumu sengen special Taiwanron*, p. 8.
24 Iwabuchi, *Recentering Globalization*, p. 176.
25 Pempel, "Trans-Pacific Torii," p. 51.
26 Dirlik, *After the Revolution*, p. 51.
27 Arrighi, Hamashita, and Selden, eds., *The Resurgence of East Asia*, p. 269.

BIBLIOGRAPHY

Arrighi, Giovanni, Hamashita Takeshi, and Selden, Mark, eds. *The Resurgence of East Asia: 500, 150, and 50 Year Perspectives*. London: Routledge, 2003.

Ching, Leo. "Globalizing the Regional, Regionalizing the Global: Mass Culture and Asianism in the Age of Late Capital." *Public Culture* 12:1 (2000): 233–57.

Ching, Leo. *Becoming "Japanese": Colonial Taiwan and the Politics of Identity Formation*. Berkeley: University of California Press, 2001.

Dirlik, Arif. *After the Revolution: Waking to Global Capitalism*. Hanover, NH: Wesleyan University Press, pub. by University Press of New England, 1994.

Dower, John. *Embracing Defeat: Japan in the Wake Of World War II*. New York: Norton, 1999.

Fujioka Nobukatsu. *"Jigyaku shikan" no byōri*. Tokyo: Bungei Shunjū, 1997.

Fukuzawa Yukichi. "On Leaving Asia" (1885). In David Lu, ed., *Japan: A Documentary History*. Armonk, NY: M. E. Sharpe, 1996.

Hanasaki Kōhei. "Decolonialization and Assumption of War Responsibility." *Inter-Asia Cultural Studies* 1:1 (2000): 71–84.

Harootunian, Harry D. *The Empire's New Clothes: Paradigm Lost, and Regained*. Chicago: Prickly Paradigm Press, 2004.

Higashi Ajia Bunshitetsu Nettowaku, ed. *Kobayashi Yoshinori "Taiwanron" o koete*. Tokyo: Sakuhinsha, 2001.

Iwabuchi Kōichi. *Recentering Globalization: Popular Culture and Japanese Transnationalism*. Durham, NC: Duke University Press, 2002.

Katō Norihiro. *Haisengoron*. Tokyo: Kodansha, 1997.

Katzenstein, Peter, and Shiraishi, Takashi, eds. *Network Power: Japan and Asia*. Ithaca, NY: Cornell University Press, 1997.

Kobayashi Yoshinori. *Shin gomanizumu sengen special Taiwanron*. Tokyo: Shogakkan, 2000.

Koschmann, J. Victor. "Asianism's Ambivalent Legacy." In Peter Katzenstein and Takashi Shiraishi, eds., *Network Power: Japan and Asia*. Ithaca, NY: Cornell University Press, 1997.

McCormack, Gavan. *The Emptiness of Japanese Affluence*, 2nd rev. edn. Armonk, NY: M. E. Sharpe, 2001.

Oguma Eiji. *A Genealogy of "Japanese" Self-Images*, trans. David Askew. Melbourne: Trans Pacific Press, 2002.

Okakura Kakuzō. *The Ideals of the East with Special Reference to the Art of Japan* (1903). New York: ICG Muse, 2002.

Pempel, T. J. "Trans-Pacific Torii: Japan and the Emerging Asian Regionalism." In Peter Katzenstein and Takashi Shiraishi, eds., *Network Power: Japan and Asia*. Ithaca, NY: Cornell University Press, 1997.

Sun Ge. "How Does Asia Mean? (Part 1)." *Inter-Asia Cultural Studies* 1:1 (2000): 13–47.

Sun Ge. "How Does Asia Mean? (Part 2)." *Inter-Asia Cultural Studies* 1:2 (2000): 319–41.

Tanaka, Stefan. *Japan's Orient: Rendering Pasts into History*. Berkeley: University of California Press, 1993.

Twu, Jaw-Yann. *Tōyō shihonshugi*. Tokyo: Kōdansha, 1990.

FURTHER READING

The most comprehensive and concise assessment of the concept of "Asia" in Japanese intellectual history is Sun Ge's two-part essay "How Does Asia Mean?" which was published in the inaugural and second issue of *Inter-Asia Cultural Studies* (1:1 (2000): 13–47; 1:2 (2000): 319–41). David Askew's translation of Oguma Eiji's *A Genealogy of "Japanese" Self-Images* (Melbourne: Trans Pacific Press, 2002) provides a historical account of various contested discourses on Japan's self-identity through the construction of its modern empire and argues that the myth of Japanese ethnic homogeneity was a postwar derivation that effaced the traces of Japanese imperialism and colonization in Asia. Stefan Tanaka's *Japan's Orient* (Berkeley: University of California Press, 1993) is a powerful and lucid study of how the concept of *tōyōshi* (Oriental Studies) authorized a particularistic view of Japan's place in the modern world system that not only posited Japan's equivalence to the West, but also reversed the historical subordinate position of Japan to imperial China. For postwar and recent discussions on Japan and Asia, Peter Katzenstein and Takashi Shiraishi's coedited *Network Power: Japan and Asia* (Ithaca, NY: Cornell University Press, 1997) is indispensable; T. J. Pempel and J. Victor Koschmann's contributions to the volume are especially useful in delineating the postwar re-emergence of Asian regionalism and the legacy of colonial Asianism respectively. For a critique of the resurgence of neo-nationalism in 1990s Japan, the special issue of the *South Atlantic Quarterly*, "Millennial Japan: Rethinking the Nation in the Age of

Recession,'' edited by Tomiko Yoda and Harry Harootunian, offers many insights. Iwabuchi Kōichi's *Recentering Globalization* (Durham, NC: Duke University Press, 2002) examines the circulation of Japanese popular culture in Asia and the increasing albeit asymmetrical intra-regional flows between Japan and its neighbors. For a historical perspective on the return to a Sinocentric hegemony, see Giovanni Arrighi, Hamashita Takeshi, and Mark Selden, eds., *The Resurgence of East Asia* (London: Routledge, 2003).

CHAPTER TWENTY-FOUR

Center and Periphery in Japanese Historical Studies

Michael Lewis

Introduction

Historians have widely, if at times casually and implicitly, used the idea of center and periphery to interpret Japanese history. Their work has explored the political, economic, military, and cultural centers – Yamatai, Yamato, the imperial court, Kyoto, the shogunate, Kantō, Edo, Osaka, Tokyo, Tokyo University, the Ministry of Finance – that abound on both material and mental maps. Studies have also described the dependent places, people, and institutions locked in orbit, however wobbly, around these "cores." In general, the common approach has conformed to a basic definition of the center–periphery bond as "geographical, economic, social, cultural, and political structures that exist in space in order to indicate some kind of hierarchical and polarized organization of this space."[1]

The center–periphery model originated in the social sciences, where its elasticity allowed for a wide variety of applications. Writing in the 1960s, the sociologist Edward Shils was among the first to use it to explain a "consensualist" society in which the metropolitan center is the site for creating and propagating cultural values. According to Shils, people on the margins not only defer to these values, but in their mental maps also identify their particular social and cultural place in relation to the metropolitan pole star.[2] In contrast to Shils, Immanuel Wallerstein, who developed "world-system theory," employs "core and periphery" to explain conflict instead of consensus. Drawing on Marx, Lenin, and dependency theories of imperialism, Wallerstein and his followers treat not single societies but transnational cores and peripheries, along with intermediate "semi-peripheries," to explain the origins and contradictions of the modern capitalist world. As an antidote to the optimistic metanarrative of modernization theory, world system theory delineates how first-world industrialized states (cores) dominate and exploit the third world through manipulation of semi-peripheral developing states. The dominance of core states expands as they benefit from the inequalities inherent in the system while insuring dependency and underdevelopment everywhere else. As a theory of change grounded in a Leninist dialectic, however, cores are not immortal. The system's contradictions can ultimately end in revolution.[3]

Historians of Japan have adopted and adapted the idea of center and periphery as a tool for exploring the past within Japan's historical and modern borders as well as through its regional and international ties. In a manner paralleling the idea's flexible use in other disciplines, the model has been used to explain the cooperative working of social, political, and economic hierarchies across time and space and the creation of consensus among rulers and ruled. It has also been used to demonstrate exploit-ation and dependence in explorations of dominant political, economic, and cultural hegemonies. Although not as often, it has occasionally been applied to determining Japan's place in a world economic and political system. This position has ranged from the periphery, semi-periphery, and at the core depending on the historical moment.

The concept of reflexivity, that the periphery can influence the core and that central values and institutions can be reshaped by ideas and actions at the margins, has worn away any kind of definitional rigidity in the center–periphery approach. In the practice of Japanese history, as was the case early on in work done in other histories and social science disciplines, it was also recognized that people exist in a relativistic world of multiple centers and peripheries and that these change over time. Furthermore, the creation of this plural order is not just a modern phenomenon or one linked to capitalist development, but something that has occurred over long premodern his-torical periods within a constellation of changing regional relations. These consider-ations have softened any kind of binary or economically determined use of the center–periphery model.

The narrower use of cores and peripheries in Wallersteinian theory has also been re-evaluated. In part, this has resulted from the collapse of the Soviet state and its periphery and the realization that Wallerstein's theoretical model insufficiently matches observable reality. The recognition that non-economic factors, particularly cultural factors, significantly shape political and social linkages has also called forth more expansive uses of center–periphery approaches applied to the world before the emergence of modern capitalism. Recently, historians and archaeologists of Japan have used the world system theory to describe Japan's place in a premodern, indeed even prehistoric, regional order in Asia.[4]

Variable Centers, Porous Peripheries: Amino Yoshihiko and Premodern Japanese History's Modern Implications

Few if any serious historians or geographers accept the notion that Japan emerged in a single location inhabited by one ethnically homogeneous people. Nevertheless, the idea that Japan was settled by several groups coming from the Asian mainland and Southeast Asia, which ultimately created a highly centralized and uniform culture that was distinctly "Japanese" continues in *Nihonjinron* discourse. The geographical and temporal cradle for this centering is the Yamato "state" near present day Nara during the fifth and sixth centuries. The creators of the Yamato order are said to have been strongly influenced by Chinese models of statecraft that shaped the practices of the *ritsuryō* system of criminal and civil laws. The order also adapted notions of political mapping that established units of governance, some more nom-inal than substantial, over wide areas of the main islands of Honshū, Shikoku, and Kyūshū.

In past historical and geographical accounts, this Kinai state, literally the region "within the boundaries," established an essential core that within a few centuries developed into an imperial institution. By the time it came to be based at a new capital, Heian-kyō, this center had become a political, economic, and cultural metropolis within a network of secondary cities and peripheral regions demarcated as subordinate political units. Trunk roads (*dō*) connected the Kinai center with the major peripheral regions (also called *dō* but meaning areal units), which contained "provinces" (*kuni*) and were subdivided into still smaller administrative units including post and temple towns, districts, and *go* or *ri* (loosely translatable as "villages").[5] According to traditional accounts – and still present in versions of the *Nihonjinron* discourse – this orderly landscape was peopled by groups distinguished by membership in sacred and secular occupational estates (inherited in some cases) and dependent on an agrarian economy supported by rice-growing peasant farmers. The essential characteristics of this original "Japan" were ethnic unity, control of contiguous territory, and integrated political rule based on shared recognition of centralized secular and sacred authority. Although this capsule description is necessarily a caricature, it nonetheless captures the essence of a static and agreeably neat model that has enjoyed wide currency.

Amino Yoshihiko has demolished this unified image. Through essays and books written since the 1970s, notable for their popularity among the Japanese reading public as well as professional historians in and outside Japan, Amino has steadily hammered away at both the general and specific arguments supportive of Japan's early ethnic and political unity. Instead of a single core, he posits a multiplicity of centers and peripheries and accordingly downplays the supposedly superior political potency of Kinai ruling groups. Overall, the revision constitutes a kind of reversal of a Copernican-like Yamato-centered explanation in favor of historical depiction based on far broader and less concise considerations. Among the most important are the varying influences of the natural environment, the diversity of the premodern economy and occupational groups, and the varieties of trade and diplomatic ties within Asia.

Although Amino has been known primarily as a scholar of medieval history, his work questions Japan's earliest origins and has implications for the contemporary understanding of Japanese ethnic identity. In iconoclastic arguments that are as blunt as they are powerful, he dismisses notions of any sort of original "Japanese" people or place concluding that "the argument that from Jōmon times there has been in Japan a 'single race' and a 'single state' is a baseless fabrication."[6] He also calls into question the association of the imperial house as ruling over a uniform agrarian society in which those of the periphery were in absolute thrall to those at the center. On this issue he concludes that "the proposition that the society has been agricultural from ancient times until now is dubious. Consequently, the notion that the emperor, as one of the kings born into this society, might be described as exclusively connected with paddy fields is completely wrong."[7] Taking the emperor out of the sacred rice fields may appear to be a minor point. But Amino's argument is a powerful revision that breaks the imperial institution's monopoly on secular and sacred symbolism by demonstrating that people joined together to pursue plural "medieval utopias."[8] His questioning even extends to raising doubts about the historical applicability of the word "Japan"

(*Nihon*), which he contends at best enjoyed limited and contested use during the premodern period.[9]

Overall, Amino's scholarship works to decenter our understanding of the origins of what eventually became the modern Japanese nation-state. In searching for new origins and elevating the importance of diverse historical actors, his arguments necessarily raise doubts about the legitimacy of the *modern* imperial institution and the necessity of sacrifices made in the name of sanctity which he finds entirely specious. While demoting the historical significance of a single central imperial order, Amino endorses the importance of Japan as being composed of various autonomous or semi-autonomous zones in coastal regions and mountain settlements. Within these zones, some of them frontiers, people worked in a variety of callings, not just as peasant farmers, but also as fisherfolk, traders, potters, and silk weavers.

One of the most important arguments Amino makes on the basis of lively pre-modern non-farming economic activity is that capitalism developed far earlier in this decentralized order than has been previously understood. He demonstrates its appearance in studies of medieval temple moneylenders, the use of monetary instruments in financial transactions, and payment of taxes in commodities other than grain. He concludes that as early as the fourteenth century regions within Japan had already experienced "growth in commerce, industry, finance, and shipping, the close-knit development of a distribution system necessary for supporting a stable credit economy, and thriving trade and other contacts ranging from northern East Asia all the way down to Southeast Asia."[10] Amino's work on contentious regional relations between different groups within Japan, which he associates with the existence of a basic east–west divide, argues for variable political and economic centers with their own or shared peripheries. As he makes plain in his discussion of the rise and decline of the Nara–Kyoto-based imperial order, Japan's history has not been a unidirectional march toward ever greater political and economic centralization, but one of twists and turns and even backtracking as regional fortunes changed over time.

Amino has been joined by other historians in Japan who, if less absolute in their revision of premodern center–periphery relations, endorse his doubts about the state's unified origins. They also tend to view Japan's heterogeneous past as a construct repeatedly contested and remade before it became "Japanese history" in relatively modern times. Murai Shōsuke is representative in viewing the borders of medieval Japan as existing less as hard and fast lines than as zones which, accordion-like, expanded and contracted. Following Amino, he de-emphasizes the agrarian basis of premodern Japan in highlighting the importance of trade relations at frontier zones. These ties involved economic exchange and indicated places where ethnically identical people engaged in "foreign" trade within the space now known as Japan. At the same time, other groups in coastal ports and harbors participated in exchanges that were almost "domestic" even though they engaged ethnically different partners from across the China Sea, the Sea of Japan, and from the Ryūkyūs and Hokkaidō.[11]

Bruce Batten has expanded on the decentering work of Amino, Murai, and others by applying various social science theories across far wider time frames. In *To the Ends of Japan: Premodern Frontiers, Boundaries, and Interactions* he explicitly poses "big questions" such as "What is 'Japan'?" "When did it come to be?" "How did it change over time?" and "How does it fit into the larger world?" His attempts to answer these queries aim at creating nothing less than "a new synthesis on Japanese history."[12] Batten's wide-ranging study uses center and periphery both as a generic concept and as world system theory to describe the creation of ethnic difference within Japan. The approach distinguishes his work from Amino's. But when it comes to cases, many of their conclusions are mutually supporting. Both emphasize flexible borders and frontiers, not as "places" but as "margins or interfaces" in economic, political, and cultural contact with a Japan that was multi-centered until it emerged as a "nation-state" in the nineteenth century.[13] Until that time, Batten depicts Japan as both a world system in its own right and a subsystem within Asia. Thereafter, its economic, political, and military networks merged with those of the wider capitalist world and "Japan lost all claims to systemic integrity."[14]

By questioning popularly accepted notions of national unity and singular origins, erasing any distinct borderlines separating historical Japan from non-Japan, and reassessing the process that forged Japanese ethnic identity, Amino and kindred historians have gone beyond rearranging the conceptual furniture to knocking down walls and opening new doorways. Although much of the work of what might be loosely called the "Amino school" has been done to explain the premodern past, it has been, like all good history, indubitably present-minded. Rereading the premodern has forced reconsiderations of both what it means to be "Japanese," and the basis for any pretensions of cultural or ethnic uniqueness based on *Nihonjinron* notions.

As might be expected, historical revision so sweeping has called forth criticism. Some of this has come from citizens offended by new interpretations that fail to support an unambiguous national identity based on unique blood and soil origins. Less easy to discount is criticism by serious historians who question the revisionists' methods and conclusions. One noticeable drawback to Amino's work is that it tends to be more convincing when it explains what was not than what was. When moving from puncturing received explanations to creating new interpretations, extrapolation at times outruns empirically thin evidence. Although the Amino school's composite portrait of premodern Japan is far more colorful, lively, and diverse than the monochromatic uniformity of an emperor-centered, rice-based agrarian society, aspects of the newer image are nonetheless impressionistic. Likewise, pushing back the advent of capitalism to the thirteenth century (or earlier), while an exciting transformation of how we have considered the past, risks anachronistically confusing premodern methods of exchange with more modern economic systems. These reservations notwithstanding, Amino and kindred researchers have contributed greatly to a fresh understanding of Japan's past.

Medieval Japan: Bringing the Warriors Back In, Village Views, and New Discourses on Spatiality and Power

In the essays in *The Cambridge History of Japan*, volume 3, *Medieval Japan*, identifiable centers continue to exert a good deal of autonomous authority.[15] Although power sharing mediates their political influence, the Heian court, Kamakura and Muromachi shogunates, and Buddhist establishments nevertheless maintain familiar institutional identities. Chapters on economic changes generally, and on the *shōen* in particular, impart a sense that the story is following a sturdy and familiar plotline that will culminate at a new starting point of recentralization.

Since the appearance of the Cambridge volume, new studies have appeared that shift the focus from central institutions to take a closer look at changes on the periphery as they develop in their own right. Pierre Francois Souryi's appropriately titled work, *The World Turned Upside Down: Medieval Japanese Society,* does this by suggesting the entire medieval period from 1180 to 1600 was one of "those below overturning those above" (*gekokujō*). His emphasis on the key role of warrior politics and social relations gives the samurai and commoner groups pivotal roles in reshaping the history of the medieval period. His interest in groups on the peripheries accordingly leads him to give less attention to the longevity and adaptability of central institutions. Souryi focuses instead on the dispersal of political power and increases in local autonomy, which he contends began about two centuries before the usually accepted date in the fourteenth century. According to his interpretation, changes from the twelfth century brought forth a full-scale social transformation by the Muromachi period. Although some standard histories have viewed the age as one of "decline," Souryi argues that it was in fact a time of social dynamism, artistic creativity, and economic growth.[16] The influence of Amino Yoshihiko is reflected in this decentered vision. In place of an overriding concern with the fate of once stable central institutions, he pays more attention to the lively social conditions that were transforming Japan from the margins inward. Here he finds populations who did not live their lives as somehow peripheral to either court or shogunate. This emphasis is particularly evident in his discussion of the Muromachi and *sengoku* periods. In chapters titled "Emancipation of the Serfs," "The People of the Sea," "Dancers and Courtesans," and "The Pariah," Souryi makes clear that the actions of groups of commoners at the "margins" played an important role in shaping the social and economic history of the medieval order.

Historians have not universally accepted Souryi's depiction of medieval Japan as a world overturned. In criticisms resembling those leveled at Amino's work, Souryi has been taken to task for being stronger on enthusiasm than empirical evidence. His interpretation has also been challenged as too eager to discard previous explanations, particularly those that stress the continuing importance of the court and shogunate throughout most of the medieval period. His pushing back the *gekokujō* age to 1180 also gives only passing consideration to that hoary institution of the *shōen* and the evolution of medieval land relations. The criticisms tend to recenter what Souryi has attempted to decenter. Yet, his work to shift the focus from central institutions and a center-outward perspective is a contribution that has undeniably enlivened medieval studies.

Hitomi Tonomura's work demonstrates that redirecting attention from the center to the margins need not require turning the world upside down, but simply shifting the level of analysis to the village. Her *Community and Commerce in Late Medieval Japan: The Corporate Villagers of Tokuchin-ho* scrutinizes the *sō*, "a village-based corporate group marked by various forms of collective ownership and administration."[17] In a study that is reminiscent of historical ethnography, Tonomura considers how local farmers, merchants, and others interacted and coped with demands imposed by major central institutions. This latter group includes the emperor, court, religious orders, and bakufu, a collection historians commonly refer to as the *kenmon*, or the "gates of power and authority."[18]

Tonomura's contextualization of the *sō* in networks of local and central political and economic relationships demonstrates how villagers manipulated "vertical alliances" with the *kenmon* to defend local interests. This symbiotic relationship served both center and periphery in slowing expansion of local samurai control of land and commerce as well as mediating intra-village conflicts. On balance, however, it may have been more helpful to the central institutions by prolonging their capacity to regulate land relations and thereby forestalling a decline in their local authority.

Thomas Keirstead's work is also concerned with medieval local history, but differs from Tonomura's in considering the fate of the central institutions as largely irrelevant. In fact, his work tends to reject the conclusions of scholars such as Nagahara Keiji and Araki Moriaki, who differ in their specific interpretations, but are united in their overall explanation of the "decline" of the *shōen* system.[19] Keirstead's stated aim in studying the medieval *myō*, the fundamental field unit for collecting levies and rents and a subcomponent of the *shōen* system, is to get beyond "endpoints" and the conventional categorization of medieval Japan and local systems as economic or political history. In his view, "to comprehend the estate system one must shift registers and approach it not on an economic or political level, but more broadly as a cultural system."[20] This approach is another way of turning the world of medieval historiography upside down through the use of critical theory. In creating new interpretations of a medieval "geography of power," Keirstead relies on discourse analysis and methods influenced by Raymond Williams, Michel Foucault, and Michel de Certeau to apprehend but not necessarily explain or generalize. In discourse analysis, basic assumptions are themselves objects for interrogation, and in adhering to this methodology Keirstead seems unconcerned with quantitatively or qualitatively "proving" anything. But he is intent on providing "a different model of how cultural formations change." According to him, the necessity to do so arises because other models have removed the historian from history in conforming to processes where outcomes are all but foreordained.[21]

The difficulty is determining if this approach, heavily dependent on a reading of the documents (in the deconstructivist sense of "reading"), is any better than any other. The question is not the historian's ability to see the signs, but in selecting which signs to interpret. No matter how sensitive Keirstead's reading, the difficulty of accurately apprehending meaning from the scant documents and other "artifacts" available seems an insurmountable task. It is all the more formidable considering that the inhabitants of the Japanese medieval world, as the Amino school demonstrates, were obviously a mixed and fluid lot, distant from us not only temporally but perhaps in unwritten (unsigned?) cultural assumptions. Keirstead's theoretical approach raises more questions than it resolves. But this may be the precise point of his chosen methodology.

While Keirstead is explicitly concerned with critical theory, major sections of his study of the *myō* also show the influence of Amino's social history approach. This is particularly evident in chapters titled "A Wandering State" and "Inventing the Hyakushō." Although his general approach rejects the drawing of conclusions, these chapters, the most accessible in the study, do generalize about the period in depicting a decentered medieval world in flux. In general form, it is a place not unlike that described by Amino and others.

Early Modern Japan: The Centralizing State and States on the Periphery

Historians generally agree that the reforms of Oda Nobunaga, Toyotomi Hideyoshi, and Tokugawa Ieyasu culminated in a political, social, and religious order more peaceful, united, and stable than that of the preceding century. Beyond this easy agreement on the comparative peace and order after the Warring States period, interpretations differ over the nature of center–peripheral ties.

Views that emphasize the new strength of the Edo center contend that the early modern period (*c*.1570–1868) was one of increasing political centralization that brought Japan to the verge of nationhood. Advocates of this position, building on the earlier work of John Whitney Hall, point out the newly created or expanded powers of the Edo shogunate to enforce national standards at home and to represent Japan abroad. The emergence of a powerful new political center also compelled acceptance of uniform social, economic, and religious systems that shaped individual identities even at the very fringes of the periphery. The centralizing changes are said to be evident locally in tangible things such as commonly accepted measurements for commodities and land, standard currency, and definite borders. These borders, eventually printed in maps and described in texts, recognized internal divisions, not as frontiers, but increasingly as firm divisions between discrete political units sanctioned by Edo's central political authority. In addition to concrete manifestations like measures and boundary lines, historians who emphasize growing centralization also point to the transformation of social hierarchies and diplomatic practices. The former included the imposition and acceptance of fixed statuses or "estates" for all ranks of society (the *mibun* system) which divided samurai from commoners. These became instituted through the mandating of countrywide regulations for land assessment and taxation. Centrally created and enforced laws and sumptuary regulations that carried specific sanctions for different estates helped cement and maintain a widely recognized division of society between ruling samurai and subject commoners.

Foreign relations also went through a similar unifying transformation. The bakufu usually spoke for an entire "country" in conducting diplomacy in Asia and later with Western nations. Although a few domains at times engaged in "foreign" contacts (including ties with Ezo and the Ryūkyūs), mainly for trading purposes, this was usually done with bakufu permission, or at least its sufferance. The fact that regional Asian and Western states recognized that the bakufu represented "Japan," and that domain governments acceded, however passively, to Edo's right to set "foreign policy," further attests to the emergence of a new center of unprecedented political authority. This view of growing centralization during the early modern period does not deny that domains still possessed significant autonomy within their own borders, so much so that they have been characterized as shogunates writ small. Yet domain autonomy was local and could be trumped by demands from the center when, for example, the bakufu required additional levies for public works or when local violation of central laws called forth intervention. In short, the overarching laws, social practices, religious beliefs, and cultural production and consumption (endorsed or enforced) from the Edo center imparted to individuals on the periphery an identity and membership in an entity that went far beyond the local.

This view modifies the once prevailing idea of "centralized feudalism" by placing greater emphasis on the central side of the equation. Yet, historians and social scientists who share this interpretation are careful not to revive earlier notions of "Tokugawa absolutism." They recognize that the newly centralized system was also subject to change over time and space. Conformity to status hierarchies obviously loosened from one generation to the next and in accord with changing economic realities evident, for example, in the appearance of impoverished samurai and wealthy commoners. Likewise, the enforcement of bakufu authority had to adjust to regional variations among the domains, a problem that at times proved particularly difficult in dealing with powerful *tozama* regimes. The shift from personal-martial to more impersonal-bureaucratic ties between the shōgun and his subordinates may have also contributed to diminished central authority, especially during the final decades of the Edo period. Yet, as Eiko Ikegami points out, if the period was not "absolutist," it was clearly "centrally integrated."[22] Widespread acceptance of the legitimacy of central institutions, ideas, and practices helped anchor the system and supported an enduring symbiotic relationship between bakufu and domains. Over time, centrally sited integration transformed the once uneasy balance of power inherent in an incongruent warrior-dominated society into a stable, increasingly uniform, and largely demilitarized bureaucratic order that possessed remarkable staying power.[23]

In contrast to the Edo-centered interpretation of integration and uniformity, two monographs from the late 1990s present alternative views that emphasize the independence and autonomy of domains and their state-like existence. Mark Ravina's *Land and Lordship in Early Modern Japan* locates a budding nationalism focused not on the Edo center or an abstract idea of Japan, but within the "countries" he views as internally complex parts of a "compound state." His analysis of the history of three separate domains demonstrates that local rulers and ruled were preoccupied with pursuing their own particular internal economic and political interests. In Ravina's treatment, the domains of Yonezawa, Hirosaki, and Tokushima emerge as richly diverse "states." Yet, although they differed one from another in their local industries and commerce, economic problems, and relations between samurai and commoners, they were united in the local use of various "ideologies" that defended their independence in negotiating economic and political ties with the Tokugawa regime. Ravina also sees an emergent nationalism resulting from domain leaders' efforts to downplay samurai versus commoner status distinctions to increase economic productivity. This leveling process helped foster a new common identity as a member of the "state," albeit not the one located in distant Edo.

Luke Roberts's *Mercantilism in a Japanese Domain: The Merchant Origins of Economic Nationalism in 18th-Century Tosa* also finds a major source of local nationalism in the domain's independent economic activities and new bonds between samurai and merchants. In his careful analysis of the domain government's attempt to deal with a fiscal crisis that worsened throughout the eighteenth century, he shows that commoners urged mercantilist measures (in one instance recommended through petition boxes) to achieve *kokueki* or "national" benefit, in this case meaning an outcome beneficial to the domain. Roberts attaches much significance to *kokueki* as an indication of the independent identity of Tosa people engaged in "international" ties, economic and political, with other domains. In teasing out the implications of local nationalism, Roberts suggests that the idea was one that could be expanded to embrace the idea of membership in the nation-state, and this transference in fact helps explain the strong nationalism evident in Japan after the Meiji Restoration.

It bears noting that neither of these studies of what might be called "centers on the peripheries" claims to represent conditions in domains generally during the early modern period. Nevertheless, they are part of a growing body of similar works that explicitly emphasize political, economic, and ideological developments on the margins. Conrad Totman generalizes this approach in *Early Modern Japan*. Although his subject is not just one domain but also a general survey of the entire period, his approach is one that treads lightly on the development of central political and economic institutions in favor of exploring the intersection of human and environmental history. He also devotes attention to the problems of local domains, such as coping with fiscal crisis, to demonstrate that the provincial leaders confronted difficulties not so different from those faced by the shōgun's officials.

Herman Ooms's work on village practice and Philip Brown's study of the domain further demonstrate both the autonomy of local political practice and rich diversity in solving particular problems. Brown's study of Kaga and the local regulation of land assessment and taxation emphasizes the independence and initiative that might be taken in regulating the domain's own affairs.[24] In Ooms's work, the villages are shown to possess a similar independence in being highly self-regulated sites for contesting outside authority, even though not every contest resulted in a victory for local villagers. They are also places where local people attempted to borrow the domain's thunder to struggle against village authorities and putative social betters.[25] In these studies, the shogunal regime comes off less as a centralizing core than as an authority that is at times more pretense than real power. The limits of its reach suggest that integration was never as complete as bakufu officials might have intended. In some instances, the same can be said for domains. Although magistrates nominally controlled villages within their boundaries, in many areas of local life, villagers in fact quite effectively managed affairs on their own.

The Nation-State and Mediated Peripheries

Rather than restore an ancient (and probably imaginary) center–periphery order, the Meiji Restoration hastened the creation of a new and unambiguously centralized and modern nation-state. Within a few short decades of the official beginning of the nation-building project, Tokyo had become the political and economic capital of a state that replaced semi-autonomous domains with newly created prefectures subordinate to central laws and centrally appointed administrators. Even pre-Restoration village and shrine boundaries were redrawn according to Tokyo's fiat. New transportation and communication systems, subsidized directly and indirectly by the national treasury, served as centralizing sinews connecting outlying regions to the Tokyo center.

Parallel to the centering of power and authority inside Japan, leaders of this new nation-state struggled to secure a definite place for Japan within a global order. Their efforts culminated in heretofore ambiguous borders and frontier zones being remade as clearly drawn boundary lines determined by negotiations, wars, and sometimes both. By the end of World War I, the premodern emperor had not really been restored, but Japan had certainly been recreated as a thoroughly modern empire, one replete with colonies and a population forged into a national "citizenry."

A comparison of Japan's domestic and international circumstances before 1868 and after 1918 provides a stunning contrast. Accordingly, historians (as well as geographers, economists, anthropologists, and literary theorists) generally recognize the centralizing results of a forced march toward national modernity. Studies concerned with center–periphery relations are accordingly less concerned with the obvious outcome than the multiple processes that yielded this result. They also engage questions about the nature of the new order and how people at both center and periphery dealt with new demands that profoundly changed their lives. Studies have taken up the remaking of social organizations and transformation of individual values and identities necessary to conform to new laws, calendars, educational regimes, and a flood of imported ideas compelled by forces ranging from specific regulations, general models of worldly success, and the irresistible force of fashion.

Carol Gluck in her study of prewar national ideology in Japan provides one of the most comprehensive and convincing accounts of how these myriad changes came to be popularly accepted. Dispensing with the notion of a single all-powerful "emperor system" (*tennōsei*) suddenly imposed from the top-down (or center-outward), she has demonstrated the "congeries of ideologies" created in late Meiji society and widely shared throughout the prewar years. These collectively gave individuals identity as subjects of Japan but also "depoliticized" politics.[26] Takashi Fujitani describes how new incorporating rituals were refashioned or created from whole cloth to make the refurbished emperor the symbolic and ritual center of a new national ethos.[27]

Alongside these careful studies of ideology, emperorship, and state-making, other scholars have investigated the role of enlightened central bureaucrats. Their work emphasizes the role of Tokyo's political elites, especially Home Ministry bureaucrats and party leaders, cooperating with local officials and members of an emerging middle class in fostering beliefs supportive of national programs and goals. In this respect, Sheldon Garon's work stands out in its depiction of the leadership that moved the public to embrace the nation or, less positively, enabled the idea of nation to overcome its subjects.[28] James Huffman views the process of national integration as proceeding in a far more diffuse way through the development of popular culture, specifically the emergence of a modern commodified and centrally dominated media. His work demonstrates how the press fostered attitudes that soon enabled Japanese subjects to embrace a new identity as proud citizens of a powerful state. Modern newspaper journalism, produced for a national audience, intersected with post-Restoration mass education, mass politics, mass culture, mass production, and the mass market in creating a national public.[29]

Yet, once formed, this modern national hegemony still rested uneasily in the minds of many. Historians working on events at the periphery find it easy to agree with Gluck's observation that "it is fair to say that the dominant ideology in imperial Japan imagined a nation that was more unified and society that was more stable than those who lived within them knew to be the case."[30] In my study of the breakdown in civil order in 1918, a conflict that resulted in martial law and Japanese soldiers shooting Japanese citizens, I argue that state-making was still a work in progress. The centralizing policies undertaken since 1868 clearly made Tokyo the dog that wagged the regional tail. Nevertheless, direct and indirect challenges to the state evident in popular protests, labor disputes, and tenant strikes repeatedly raised questions about the relationship between central authority and local rights. Despite official rhetoric about the unity inherent in the family state, open defiance, a vote of no confidence expressed through protests of varying severity, implied doubts about the rulers' right to rule.[31]

Explorations of Japanese margins, either peripheries that existed at the time of Meiji state-building or others created commensurate with the process, tend to support Gluck's observation about continuing ideological diversity and disunity beneath the appearance of unity. They often focus on local protests that belie notions of nation-building as a simple process achieved with great unanimity. But as Neil Waters and William Steele have demonstrated in their careful studies of pragmatic local leaders, it would also be a mistake to construe the process of folding the local into the national as simply central subjugation of the periphery. Their work delineates how local interests often found common ground with imperial ambitions and how local people embraced the nation while continuing to believe in the sanctity of home districts and the importance of genuine local betterment.[32]

Various local studies take a similar tack in demonstrating a mix of motives that changed over time and could be seen in the repertoire of local strategies used to respond to centrally mandated programs. In studying nation-building in Toyama, I found a gamut of responses among villagers and townspeople targeted to implement centralizing programs. These ran from passive sabotage and negotiated compliance, to enthusiastic acceptance, the response depending heavily on perceptions of how newly mandated policies and programs would help or hurt at the local level. Of course, the responses were not always uniform even at the periphery. Furthermore, they were also open to change as interests shifted at the local level or when finally pressed to implement what had previously been supported as an attractive abstraction. Initial local support for expansion of the overseas empire in Manchuria is a case in point. Although patriotic rallies and donations for monuments suggest that imperialism was popularly supported in Toyama, local people strongly resisted official appeals that they become pioneers in Manchukuo.[33]

Much of the new attention on the periphery is possible only because of the wealth of historical materials made available through local archives and history compilation projects in Japan. Studies written outside Japan have also benefited enormously from studies by Japanese historians. Works by Ariizumi Sadao, Abe Tsunehisa, and Furumaya Tadao on Niigata and Yamanashi demonstrate the contested process of Japanese state-making in reconsidering local identity as emerging or being revived through attempts to keep the state at bay or mediate its locally disruptive policies. Their perspective on how Japan's modern history was shaped by center–periphery conflict and mediation focuses primarily on events during and after the onset of the Meiji transformation and demonstrates the importance of local political awareness and agency in shaping outcomes.[34]

Other studies take a longer view in explaining the creation of regional marginal-ization, both economic and political, and how populations were acted upon in processes that led to the creation of a modern nation-state. Kären Wigen's work on the Shimoina valley in Nagano from 1750 to 1920 demonstrates how a once vital region could be transformed into a kind of internal colony subservient to Tokyo. In using approaches influenced by the Annales school and social geography, she inter-prets the way center–periphery ties were reforged from the mid nineteenth century as strongly influenced by political, environmental, and economic relations that had prevailed earlier. Wigen also shows that newly created peripheries in Japan had a bearing on Japan's role in the world economy. She observes that "the development of the silk industry played a highly contradictory role in regard to Shimoina's space-economy: while it turned the valley into a clearly subordinate periphery of the Japanese state, that very subordination was critical to the contemporary Japanese state's ability to escape becoming a periphery of the global capitalist system."[35] As a sophisticated critique of modernization theory, Wigen's work calls attention to the complicated and inadvertent creation of losers and winners resulting from centrally dominated economic development.

New Visions of Hokkaidō and the Ryūkyūs

Discussing histories of Hokkaidō and the Ryūkyūs toward the end of this essay is not to suggest that they are a coda to what has preceded them. In fact, the place of these "peripheries" is central in the works of many of the historians discussed above. Studies of Ezo/Hokkaidō and the Ryūkyūs, along with other parts of expanding and contracting "frontiers," have provided new interpretations of the nature of the early Japanese state, the formation of ethnic identities, and the effects of centrally directed industrialization. If anything, the large number of books and essays that push the geographical margins to the forefront indicates a lively boom in histories of so-called Japanese peripheries. These studies are many and vary widely in their use of theory, specific subjects, and historical coverage. What unites them is their depiction of Japanese history as a decentered process involving diverse peoples and social systems.

   Multicultural Japan: Palaeolithic to Postmodern provides a representative sampling of essays by anthropologists and archaeologists as well as historians that depict the shifting place of Hokkaidō and the Ryūkyūs in their historical relations with Japan. One thing that stands out in the relationships, regardless of historical period, is that they were highly malleable and susceptible to reshaping to meet Japanese ends. Chapters by Tessa Morris-Suzuki, Richard Pearson, and Hanazaki Kōhei on "Centre and Periphery" directly address the place of frontiers and generalizations about Ainu and Okinawan ethnic differences in creating nationalizing notions of Japanese iden-tity.[36] Demonstrating an intellectual debt to Amino Yoshihiko and others who emphasize the use of frontiers in creating notions of nationhood, Morris-Suzuki depicts the manipulation of Ainu and Okinawan communities for domestic and international ends. She points out that before the nineteenth century, the frontier zones proved useful for demarcating "Japanese-ness" from the otherness of peoples at the northern and southern frontier margins. After Japan's engagement in the international system, however, these peoples and their territories had to be folded into the nation as a means of securing borders and making clear the new nation-state's area of autonomous political control.[37] Morris-Suzuki elaborates on these themes in her *Re-inventing Japan: Time, Space, Nation* and in journal articles. Although her focus is not on Japan's modern colonial empire, her depiction of attempts to turn Okinawans and Ainu into Japanese subjects suggests elements of the colonial system used in Taiwan, Korea, and elsewhere in Asia.

Other studies of the Ryūkyūs and Hokkaidō are less concerned about creating narratives to explain a Japanese center than they are with describing each place in its own terms. Gregory Smits's *Visions of Ryūkyū: Identity and Ideology in Early-Modern Thought and Politics* is a representative work of this type. He observes that although early modern Ryūkyū was obviously not a nation-state, indigenous thinkers "advanced visions of Ryūkyū in which the kingdom became an imagined political and cultural community with the potential to subsume all Ryūkyūans within its totalizing ideology."[38] For Smits, early modern Ryūkyūans could never be completely free from ties to their more powerful Japanese and Chinese neighbors, but they did manage to exercise a good deal of "autonomy and agency" in negotiating these relationships.[39]

Brett Walker demonstrates that the same was not the case for the Ainu. In his analysis of the *longue durée* in Ezo/Hokkaidō, from 1590 to 1800, he depicts the creation of Ainu dependence through the imposition of a system of Japanese trading posts during the seventeenth century. This not only upset the basis of the pre-existing local economy but also disrupted the Ainu's direct and indirect trade ties with Russia and China. In a manner reminiscent of world system theory in microcosm, Ainu integration into the dominant trading system introduced by the Japanese led to ever greater dependence which left the Ainu deracinated and unable to resist ultimate subjugation.[40]

Works by Morris-Suzuki, Smits, and Walker are just a few of the major studies on Hokkaidō and Ryūkyūan peripheries that demonstrate both autonomy and the consequences of relations with more powerful regional centers. Together with studies such as David Howell's *Capitalism from Within: Economy, Society, and the State in a Japanese Fishery* and Michael Weiner's edited work, *Japan's Minorities: The Illusion of Homogeneity*, they create an image of Japanese history that is more a rough mosaic than something smoothly uniform, seamless, and flat.

Whither the Model?

The simple definition of the center–periphery bond introduced earlier as "geographical, economic, social, cultural, and political structures that exist in space in order to indicate some kind of hierarchical and polarized organization of this space" accurately describes aspects of Japan's historical and contemporary political and economic relations. It can help delineate the political and economic ties between the central government and the prefectures and help locate the place of Japanese capitalism in a global economic system. Used in these ways, it is a valuable tool for depicting hegemonic structures and relationships that benefit centralized hierarchies or considering the subtle ways that people on the peripheries manipulate ostensibly subordinate positions for local benefit.

Yet, the model can also be criticized for leading to conclusions that are overly general and obvious. This is abetted by a lack of precision resulting from the existence of entities and structures in temporal and spatial webs that make them *both* central and peripheral depending on context. One recent study of an outer island in the Ryūkyū chain, for example, describes the place as "a periphery on the periphery," which means, of course, that it exists in a subordinate relationship with an oxymoronic "local center." The multiplicity and variability of center–peripheral ties leads to questions about which links in the nexus are most significant or representative. A somewhat different problem is the essential binary quality inherent in the center–periphery approach. Using the model makes it easy to slip into a narrative that suggests a uniform "we" versus an equally uniform "them." In so doing, conflicts and cooperation arising from complex relationships based on class, gender, and ethnicity *within* centers and peripheries tend to be minimized. The preoccupation with differences based on spatial location can obscure alliances based on class interests or gender that might unite groups regardless of their geographical location. The best use of the center–periphery approach takes care to show that local interests are not uniform or unchanging. It also works toward a dry-eyed appreciation of the historical dynamics of local politics and avoids the airbrushed presentation of local life that is always virtuous at the grassroots level.

The studies by historians and social scientists described in this essay generally recognize and avoid the pitfalls that can arise from the loose use of the center–periphery model. In carefully qualified studies, they have accomplished a decentering of Japan that breaks free from preordained narratives, whether based on the march of capitalism or the rise and fall of institutions. Their work also challenges past depictions of Japanese ethnicity and culture as overly homogenous. These achievements demonstrate that the study of center–periphery relationships, particularly the view from the margins looking inward, can provide new and imaginative ways to understand the past.

NOTES

1   Guarini, "Center and Periphery," p. 75.
2   Shils, *Center and Periphery.*
3   Wallerstein, *The Capitalist World Economy* and *The Modern World System.*
4   Batten, *To the Ends of Japan*, pp. 128–30; Hudson, *Ruins of Identity*, p. 193.
5   Senda, "Territorial Possession in Ancient Japan," pp. 109–15.
6   Amino, "Deconstructing 'Japan'," p. 138.
7   Amino, "Emperor, Race, and Commoners," p. 236.
8   Ishii, "Foreword," p. iv.
9   Amino, "Deconstructing 'Japan'," pp. 125–7.
10 Amino, "Commerce and Finance in the Middle Ages," p. 181.
11 Murai, "The Boundaries of Medieval Japan," pp. 72–87.
12 Batten, *To the Ends of Japan*, pp. 6–7.
13 Ibid., pp. 11, 121.
14 Ibid., p. 232.
15 Yamamura, ed., *The Cambridge History of Japan*, vol. 3.
16 Souryi, *The World Turned Upside Down.*
17 Tonomura, *Community and Commerce*, p. 3.

18 Ibid., pp. 191–2.
19 Keirstead, *The Geography of Power*, pp. 100–2 .
20 Ibid., p. 105.
21 Ibid., pp. 111–12.
22 Ikegami, *The Taming of the Samurai*, pp. 164–86.
23 For a summary of these arguments see Toby, "Three Realms/Myriad Countries," pp. 15–45, and Toby, "Rescuing the Nation," pp. 197–237.
24 Brown, *Central Authority and Local Autonomy.*
25 Ooms, *Tokugawa Village Practice.*
26 Gluck, *Japan's Modern Myths*, pp. 5, 16.
27 Fujitani, *Splendid Monarchy.*
28 Garon, *Molding Japanese Minds.*
29 Huffman, *Creating a Public.*
30 Gluck, *Japan's Modern Myths*, p. 39.
31 Lewis, *Rioters and Citizens.*
32 Steele, *Alternative Narratives*; Waters, *Japan's Local Pragmatists.*
33 Lewis, *Becoming Apart*, pp. 188–243.
34 Abe, *Kindai Nihon chihō seito-shi ron*; Ariizumi, *Meiji seiji shi no kiso katei*; Furumaya, "'Ura Nihon' no seiritsu to tenkai," pp. 349–64.
35 Wigen, *The Making of a Japanese Periphery*, p. 266.
36 Morris-Suzuki, "A Descent into the Past," pp. 81–94; Pearson, "The Place of Okinawa," pp. 95–116; Hanazaki, "Ainu Moshir and Yaponesia," pp. 117–31.
37 Morris-Suzuki, "A Descent into the Past," pp. 81–92.
38 Smits, *Visions of Ryūkyū*, p. 161.
39 Ibid., p. 155.
40 Walker, *The Conquest of Ainu Lands.*

BIBLIOGRAPHY

Abe Tsunehisa. *Kindai Nihon chihō seitō-shi ron: "Ura Nihon"-ka no naka no Niigata-ken seitō undō.* Tokyo: Hasuyo Shobō Shuppan, 1996.

Amino Yoshihiko. "Deconstructing 'Japan'," trans. Gavan McCormack. *East Asian History* 3 (June 1992): 121–42.

Amino Yoshihiko. "Emperor, Race, and Commoners." In Donald Denoon, Mark Hudson, Gavan McCormack, and Tessa Morris-Suzuki, eds., *Multicultural Japan: Palaeolithic to Postmodern.* Cambridge: Cambridge University Press, 1996.

Amino Yoshihiko. "Commerce and Finance in the Middle Ages: The Beginnings of 'Capitalism'." *Acta Asiatica* 81 (2001): 1–19.

Ariizumi Sadao. *Meiji seiji shi no kiso katei.* Tokyo: Yoshikawa Kan, 1979.

Batten, Bruce. *To the Ends of Japan: Premodern Frontiers, Boundaries, and Interactions.* Honolulu: University of Hawai'i Press, 2003.

Brown, Philip C. *Central Authority and Local Autonomy in the Formation of Early Modern Japan: The Case of Kaga Domain.* Stanford, Calif.: Stanford University Press, 1993.

Chow, Kai-wing, Doak, Kevin, and Fu, Poshek, eds. *Constructing Nationhood in Modern East Asia.* Ann Arbor: University of Michigan Press, 2001.

Fujitani, Takashi. *Splendid Monarchy: Power and Pageantry in Modern Japan.* Berkeley: University of California Press, 1996.

Furumaya Tadao. " 'Ura Nihon' no seiritsu to tenkai." In Iwanami Kōza, ed., *Iwanami kōza Nihon tsūshi*, 17, *kindai 2.* Tokyo: Iwanami Shoten, 1994.

Garon, Sheldon. *Molding Japanese Minds: The State in Everyday Life.* Princeton: Princeton University Press, 1997.

Gluck, Carol. *Japan's Modern Myths: Ideology in the Late Meiji Period.* Princeton: Princeton University Press, 1985.

Guarini, Elena Fasano. "Center and Periphery." *Journal of Modern History* 67 supplement (Dec. 1995): 74–96.

Hanazaki Kōhei. "Ainu Moshir and Yaponesia: Ainu and Okinawan Identities in Contemporary Japan." In Donald Denoon, Mark Hudson, Gavan McCormack, and Tessa Morris-Suzuki, eds., *Multicultural Japan: Palaeolithic to Postmodern.* Cambridge: Cambridge University Press, 1996.

Howell, David. *Capitalism from Within: Economy, Society, and the State in a Japanese Fishery.* Berkeley: University of California Press, 1996.

Hudson, Mark J. *Ruins of Identity: Ethnogenesis in the Japanese Islands.* Honolulu: University of Hawai'i Press, 1999.

Huffman, James. *Creating a Public: People and Press in Meiji Japan.* Honolulu: University of Hawai'i Press, 1997.

Ikegami, Eiko. *The Taming of the Samurai: Honorific Individualism and the Making of Modern Japan.* Cambridge, Mass.: Harvard University Press, 1995.

Ishii Susumu. "Foreword by the Editor." *Acta Asiatica* 81 (2001): pp. iii–vii.

Keirstead, Thomas. *The Geography of Power in Medieval Japan.* Princeton: Princeton University Press, 1992.

Lewis, Michael. *Rioters and Citizens: Mass Protest in Imperial Japan.* Berkeley: University of California Press, 1990.

Lewis, Michael. *Becoming Apart: National Power and Local Politics in Toyama, 1868–1945.* Cambridge, Mass.: Harvard University Press, 2000.

Morris-Suzuki, Tessa. "A Descent into the Past: The Frontier in the Construction of Japanese History." In Donald Denoon, Mark Hudson, Gavan McCormack, and Tessa Morris-Suzuki, eds., *Multicultural Japan: Palaeolithic to Postmodern.* Cambridge: Cambridge University Press, 1996.

Morris-Suzuki, Tessa. *Re-inventing Japan: Time, Space, Nation.* Armonk, NY: M. E. Sharpe, 1998.

Murai, Shōsuke. "The Boundaries of Medieval Japan." *Acta Asiatica* 81 (2001): 72–91.

Ooms, Herman. *Tokugawa Village Practice: Class, Status, Power, Law.* Berkeley: University of California Press, 1996.

Pearson, Richard J. "The Place of Okinawa in Japanese Historical Identity." In Donald Denoon, Mark Hudson, Gavan McCormack, and Tessa Morris-Suzuki, eds., *Multicultural Japan: Palaeolithic to Postmodern.* Cambridge: Cambridge University Press, 1996.

Ravina, Mark. *Land and Lordship in Early Modern Japan.* Stanford, Calif.: Stanford University Press, 1999.

Roberts, Luke. *Mercantilism in a Japanese Domain: The Merchant Origins of Economic Nationalism in 18th-Century Tosa.* Cambridge: Cambridge University Press, 1998.

Senda, Minoru. "Territorial Possession in Ancient Japan." In *Geography of Japan,* ed. Association of Japanese Geographers. Tokyo: Teikoku Shoin, 1980.

Shils, Edward. *Center and Periphery: Essays in Macro Sociology.* Chicago: University of Chicago Press, 1975.

Smits, Gregory. *Visions of Ryūkyū: Identity and Ideology in Early-Modern Thought and Politics.* Honolulu: University of Hawai'i Press, 1999.

Souryi, Pierre Francois. *The World Turned Upside Down: Medieval Japanese Society,* trans. Käthe Roth. New York: Columbia University Press, 2001.

Steele, M. William. *Alternative Narratives in Modern Japanese History.* London: Routledge-Curzon, 2003.

Toby, Ronald. "Rescuing the Nation from History: The State of the State in Early Modern Japan." *Monumenta Nipponica* 56:2 (Summer 2001): 197–237.

Toby, Ronald. "Three Realms/Myriad Countries: An 'Ethnography' of Other and the Rebounding of Japan, 1550–1750." In Kai-wing Chow, Kevin Doak, and Poshek Fu, eds., *Constructing Nationhood in Modern East Asia*. Ann Arbor: University of Michigan Press, 2001.

Tonomura, Hitomi. *Community and Commerce in Late Medieval Japan: The Corporate Villages of Tokuchin-ho*. Stanford, Calif.: Stanford University Press, 1992.

Totman, Conrad. *Early Modern Japan*. Berkeley: University of California Press, 1993.

Walker, Brett L. *The Conquest of Ainu Lands: Ecology and Culture in Japanese Expansion, 1590–1800*. Berkeley: University of California Press, 2001.

Wallerstein, I. M. *The Modern World System*. New York: Academic Press, 1974.

Wallerstein, I. M. *The Capitalist World Economy: Essays*. Cambridge: Cambridge University Press, 1979.

Waters, Neil. *Japan's Local Pragmatists: The Transition from Bakumatsu to Meiji in the Kawasaki Region*. Cambridge, Mass.: Harvard University Press, 1983.

Weiner, Michael, ed. *Japan's Minorities: The Illusion of Homogeneity*. London: Routledge, 1997.

Wigen, Kären. *The Making of a Japanese Periphery, 1750–1920*. Berkeley: University of California Press, 1995.

Yamamura, Kozo, ed. *The Cambridge History of Japan*, vol. 3, *Medieval Japan*. Cambridge: Cambridge University Press, 1990.

FURTHER READING

An essay limited primarily to English-language works necessarily neglects the rich and varied scholarship on Japanese history written in Japanese. Primary materials, interpretive monographs, and journals abound. These merit use, not just for mining empirical data, but also to better understand new theoretical approaches in Japanese scholarship (aka the old "problem consciousness"). A case in point is Amino Yoshihiko's works, of which only a small fraction have appeared in English or other non-Japanese languages. Going to Japanese sources imparts a sense of the political context for contemporary research on the lively issue of center–periphery relations and broadens the frog-in-the-well perspective that results from relying exclusively on English-language sources.

In English, additional insight into the center–periphery model in Japanese history is provided through archaeology, geography, anthropology, political science, and other social sciences. The Fujimura scandal has rocked the world of Japanese archaeology, causing a complete reconsideration of Japan's earliest origins and authentic original "centers." Recent works, such as Mark Hudson's *Ruins of Identity: Ethnogenesis in the Japanese Islands* (Honolulu: University of Hawai'i Press, 1999), are instructive as to possible new directions. The English-language works of the geographer Takeuchi Keiichi – "The Japanese Imperial Tradition, Western Imperialism and Modern Japanese Geography," in Anne Godlewska and Neil Smith, eds., *Geography and Empire* (Oxford: Blackwell, 1994) and "Nationalism and Geography in Modern Japan, 1880s to 1920s," in David Hooson, ed., *Geography and National Identity* (Oxford: Blackwell, 1994) – provide insights into the political implications of place, space, and empire in discussing the development of geographical science in Japan. Anthropologists have produced multiple works employing the center and periphery model in Japan in which they consider created communities and manufactured local traditions. Jennifer Robertson's *Native and Newcomer: Making and Remaking a Japanese City* (Berkeley: University of California Press, 1991) and Theodore Bestor's *Neighborhood Tokyo* (Stanford, Calif.: Stanford University Press, 1989) are among the works that have contributed to this literature. The impact of local politics on central policies since 1945 has been analyzed in detail in many works, including Muramatsu Michio, *Local Power in the Japanese State* (Berkeley: University of California Press, 1988). Among studies that touch on center–regional relations and modern interest-based politics, see Gilbert Rozman's essay "Backdoor Japan: The Search for a Way Out via Regionalism and Decentralization," *Journal of Japanese Studies* 25:1 (Winter 1999): 3–31.

To return to history, recent works on the idea of the nation in Japan and the development of mass educational institutions devoted to propagating national identity bear directly on center–periphery relations. Brian Platt's *Burning and Building: Schooling and State Formation in Japan, 1750–1890* (Cambridge, Mass.: Harvard University Press, 2004) and Mark Lincicome's *Principle, Praxis, and the Politics of Educational Reform in Meiji Japan* (Honolulu: University of Hawai'i Press, 1995) consider these issues in works that are theoretically innovative and carefully researched. These recent works, of course, stand on the shoulders of earlier scholarship. Historiographical essays surveying the history of recent history – such as Carol Gluck's "House of Mirrors: American History-Writing on Japan," in Anthony Molho and Gordon Wood, eds., *Imagined Histories: American Historians Interpret the Past* (Princeton: Princeton University Press, 1998), and Christopher Hill's "National Histories and World Systems: Writing Japan, France, and the United States," in Q. Edward Wang and Georg Iggers, eds., *Turning Points in Historiography: A Cross Cultural Perspective* (Rochester, NY: University of Rochester Press, 2002) – provide a sense of what has come before while suggesting new fields for exploration. Works critical of the area studies approach, such as Masao Miyoshi and H. D. Harootunian, eds., *Learning Places: The Afterlives of Area Studies* (Durham, NC: Duke University Press, 2002), provide thought-provoking counterpoint.

CHAPTER TWENTY-FIVE

Modernity, Water, and the Environment in Japan

Gavan McCormack

Civilization and Water

The quest for a mode of industrial civilization that would be "sustainable" and symbiotic with the natural world rather than exploitative becomes in the twenty-first century a matter of life and death. Humanity cannot, except in the short term, live beyond the limits of its resources. It cannot for long continue "future eating," or consuming its stock, but must learn to live off the flow, the continuing or renewable surplus.[1]

Seventeenth- and eighteenth-century Japan deserves attention because it may constitute a model of such a society. It is sometimes described as "an eco-society without peer"[2] by contrast with the societies of Europe or North America where the relationship with nature has tended to be antagonistic and exploitative.[3] One major study suggests the traditional heritage lives on today, referring to Japan as "a highly industrialized society living in a luxuriantly green realm," adding: "the people of Japan have done less to ravage their land and bring ruin upon it than many other societies past and present that have been favored by a less dense population and more benign terrain."[4] Some go even further, referring to a "contest between the aesthetic sense of Japan and the material power of the West."[5] Japan's environmental endowment is both natural and social. Because it escaped the direct onslaught of the quaternary ice age, it possesses an unusual ecological richness, with more than 5,000 varieties of higher plant life including 500 species of indigenous trees (as against 250 for North America and 80 for Western Europe).[6] Among industrial counties, it is second only to Finland in terms of forest cover (67 percent).

However, it is not so much the mountainous terrain, heavy monsoonal rainfall (average annual precipitation of 1,720 mm), or wide temperature variation as the social adaptation to the environment that truly distinguishes Japan. Over the centuries, an intricate network of latticed channels was constructed to filter the humus-rich waters from the mountains that cover most of the country through terraced hillsides to the elaborate patchwork of paddy fields on the alluvial flood plains and to the sea.[7] Underground water bubbled readily to the surface around most human settlements and was treated with care so as not to pollute or waste it. Irrigation, navigation, and waterworks steadily extended the area of cultivation and the density and variety of crops. The forest cover broadened and deepened as its essential role in the agricultural cycle was appreciated.

The work of farming – tending forests, irrigation channels, and paddies – enriched and replenished the environment. Where other cultures cleared their forests for fuel or building materials or land to plough, and were forced to steadily expand their ecological footprint, Japan thrived on the maintenance and cultivation of its forests.[8] Environmental impoverishment occurred in proportion to the degree that the land was *not* farmed. Each hectare of well-tended paddy retains 1,000 cubic meters of water.[9] The paddies and their water canals constituted in sum a gigantic premodern dam structure, holding a staggering 8 billion tons of water[10] and constituting a multifunctional resource serving not only for rice cultivation but also water conservation ("green dam"), flood prevention, landslide prevention, soil erosion prevention, biodegrading of organic wastes, and improvement of air quality.[11] The land and environmental functions of rice paddies remain of incalculable importance and value, worth something like 12 trillion yen per year, or up to three times the value of the rice produced.[12]

Few, if any civilizations did what traditional Japan did: flourish while nourishing, rather than depleting, its resource base. Productivity for rice grew about fivefold in the approximately 1,300 years since rice agriculture was established.[13] The regular, monsoonal rainfall, and occasional flooding, enriched and flushed the paddies, and fertilizer, in the form of "grass, scrub brush, and leaf fall," was applied intensively.[14] Repeated cropping was therefore possible. In modern times, the machine and fossil fuel input introduced a non-sustainable element, but the process remained essentially cyclical and eco-sustainable. In contrast to Japan's virtuous and sustainable agricultural cycle, European and American ploughed and/or irrigated field agriculture tended to progressively impoverish the soil, which unless artificially replenished soon depleted. "Western" agriculture may be described as "an agro-industrial system for the conversion of fossil fuel into food. ... [F]or each calorie of food the system harvests, it burns about 2.5 calories of fossil fuel."[15]

Japan's agricultural society slowly evolved its basic precepts and values, but codified them only during the turbulent seventeenth century. Between approximately 1580 to 1640 resources were drawn down at an unsustainable rate. Countless trees were felled to construct castle towns, land was reclaimed for agricultural or town building, and many canals and other large-scale engineering works were undertaken; the outcome was deforestation, flood, and famine.[16] To meet that crisis, and to recover sustainability in a "closed-circuit," or "eco-cyclic," system, the water problem was recognized as paramount.[17] *Chisui* (regulation of water) became central to the science, technology, and philosophy of Edo Japan. In policy terms, it meant attention to the whole of the water cycle: to the forests and paddies, which served as dams and dykes by absorbing and holding large volumes of water and releasing it slowly; to the holding ponds (*yūsuichi*), areas deliberately left for retention of flood waters in order to protect downstream agriculture areas; to the mid-river forest belts (*bōbirin* or *kahanrin*), designed to block and absorb the immediate force of rising flood waters; and to the levees, usually of stone or earth, constructed in downstream flood-prone areas. Occasional floods were seen as an acceptable price to pay for the nutriment they brought to the paddies. Forests were divided into closed, open, and temporarily reserved, the cutting of certain trees was forbidden, and in some areas infringement of the regulations was punished under the uncompromising rule of *ki ippon, kubi hitotsu* (chop one tree, forfeit one head). The society practiced what in today's terminology would be called zero-emission and total recycling.

Such in broad outline was the design by which Japan's "green archipelago" was created and sustained for around two and a half centuries. During the Edo period (1600–1868) the cultivated area grew by more than two and a half times.[18] By the year 1700, with around 29 million people, Japan was more populous than either France (22 million) or Russia (20 million), and in global terms inferior only to the land empires of China and India.[19] It flourished at a relatively high level of equilibrium, balancing population and productivity within a framework of sustainability.

By the early nineteenth century, the grain productivity of Japanese paddy was fifteen times greater than that of European farmland.[20] Faced with the nineteenth-century crisis of European imperialism, however, "green archipelago" Japan chose to adopt not only Western science and technology but Western views of nature and practices of environmental engineering, particularly hydro-engineering. The Shintō or Daoist elements in Japanese culture were steam-rolled under a wave of Confucian abhorrence for nature combined with Western positivism and modernism. The outcome is that the "green archipelago" is now no more. Modern Japan became supremely, perhaps even uniquely, careless of its environment, obsessed with the achievement of economic growth at all costs, and in the second half of the twentieth century turned its back on its own history, resolute almost to the point of obsession in the concreting of its coast and rivers.[21] The ecological problem it faces now is both common to contemporary industrial civilization and yet also distinctive because of Japan's unique eco-historical circumstances. Though greenness steadily diminished through what might be called the "long twentieth century," that cannot continue indefinitely. Sooner or later, as in the "premodern" future-eating "short seventeenth century," profligacy will run its course and a new "green archipelago" (and indeed a green and sustainable world) will have to be created. Consumption will again have to be balanced against nurture and replenishment.

Modernizing Water

When the city of Edo/Tokyo became the capital of the bakufu government at the beginning of the seventeenth century, the Tone River crossed the Kantō plain and debouched into the sea by in the vicinity of present day Edo and Ara Rivers, frequently turning the whole area into a morass of swamp and bog. The present river, a modest 322 kilometers long, is in fact Japan's greatest. Especially in its lower reaches, it is the creation of hundreds of years of intensive civil engineering, digging of channels, draining of swamps and wetlands, and the building of dykes, directing the river eastwards away from the capital. Only when thus secured did the region begin to flourish.

In the turmoil of political and social change that accompanied the "opening" of the country in the mid nineteenth century, the traditional eco-system fell into disrepair and floods began to recur, of considerable severity especially in 1882 and then again through the 1890s. In 1896, exceptionally severe floods sent a mass of poisonous copper effluent from the slag dumps left by the Ashio copper mines pouring over the embankments of the Watarase River (a tributary of the Tone) to the east of Tokyo. The "Ashio Copper Mine Incident," which actually extended over more than a decade, attested to the national priority given to copper, symbol of the modern and source of national strength, wealth and power, over water and agriculture. The floods happened because the surrounding mountains had lost much of their water retention capacity when the trees were killed by sulfur-laden winds and rain. So great was the devastation that recovery after more than 100 years is only partial.[22] Attention therefore concentrated on "fixing," then on exploiting, these Tokyo rivers.

From 1872 the Japanese government had employed a group of Western specialists, most of them from Holland. Despite the contrasting topography, Dutch irrigation technology was thought the world's best. Having studied Japan's premodern "low dyke" technology, and been immensely impressed by it, the Dutch expert advice was that no major change was needed.[23] However, a "modernizing" faction in the new Japanese bureaucracy, led by the newly appointed Tokyo Imperial University professor of civil engineering, argued instead for a "modern," technological solution. For Furuichi Kimitake (1854–1934), recently returned from five years' study in France, river policy meant flood control, and modern "high dyke" technology was the answer.[24] In adopting the Western way, the Western experts were overruled.

Three "modern" laws for nature control were adopted in 1896: the Rivers Law, the Forest Law, and the Dyke Law. The emphasis in water administration shifted from a balance of accommodation and usage, in which flood prevention, transport, irrigation, and forestry were considered as a whole, to a primary, almost exclusive, concern with flood prevention and control (as *chisui* came to be redefined). Modernizing rivers henceforth meant straightening them, containing them within high, continuous dyke walls, and cutting them off from the surrounding countryside, so that their waters would be channelled as directly as possible from the mountains to the sea. The flood ponding areas, riverbank woods, and flood plains, rich with the alluvial deposits of thousands of years, gradually gave way to towns and settlements built closer and closer to the dykes. Where the "premodern" paradigm had been organic, symbiotic, and adaptive, the modern one was divisive, dominating, and controlling. The river and lake came to be seen as a bundle of functions – flood control, town water, irrigation for agriculture, and (in the twentieth century) electrical power generation – requiring an appropriate mix of economic, engineering, and agricultural policies. The "modern" changes in the relationship between humanity and nature, overturning the wisdom of 2,000 years, constituted a revolution no less far-reaching than the political changes attendant upon the transition from feudalism to capitalism.[25]

For a time, continuous "high dyking" seemed almost magically effective in stopping the disasters that had occasionally befallen riverine and coastal Japan. Towns and cities, industry and agriculture, grew adjacent to the dykes and in the river estuaries.[26] Determined to overcome the floods that wrought havoc on the Tone River, a "once in 100–200 year" flood level was calculated at a maximum flow of 3,750 cubic meters per second at Awabashi (in Saitama prefecture), and work on the "Great Wall" of the Tone River continuous dyke was launched in 1900. In the early decades of the twentieth century, this project was the biggest engineering works in the world. Not completed till 1930, it required the moving of 220 million cubic meters of earth, compared to 180 million in the construction of the Panama Canal.[27] However, as reliance for flood control shifted to modern technology and the high dyke, the Edo wisdom of comprehensive care for the environment was gradually forgotten. The modern calculus of water failed to take account of the effects of deforestation in the headwaters or the loss of traditional devices designed to slow and absorb the flow. Ten years into the Tone project, floods saw the Awabashi flow rise to double the estimates on which the "Great Wall" had been based (that is, to 7,000 cubic meters per second) and banks and levees were ruptured in many places. Then in 1935, five years after completion, further, unexpected floods swept over them. The "flood contingency" level was reset at 10,000 cubic meters. When typhoon Kathryn struck in 1947, however, the Awabashi flow reached 17,000 cubic meters, which was unprecedented in the history of Japanese rivers and nearly five times the maximum that had been calculated half a century earlier.[28]

During the 1930s and 1940s Japan concentrated on war. Not only along the Tone River, but throughout Japan, the forests and the defenses against natural disaster were neglected or recklessly exploited, with the result that for fifteen years after the war's end around 1,000 people died each year in floods and disasters.[29] From the 1950s, priority shifted back to high dyking and intensive *seibi* (fixing) of the environment. A second, much more intensive, wave of modernization rolled over Japan's rivers and lakes, powered by earth-moving equipment (especially the bulldozer), cheap oil, and concrete, and driven by growing prosperity and an unquenchable techno-optimism. Despite the embrace of liberal and then neo-liberal principles by conservative Japanese governments, centralized planning, as originally adopted from communist (Soviet) and fascist (Nazi) examples in 1930s Manchukuo, continued to play a key role. The Comprehensive National Development Plans (*Zensō*) of 1962, 1969, 1977, 1985, and 1998 outlined the design for the national infrastructure, and the necessary resource application was conducted under the *Zaitō*, or Fiscal Investment and Loan Program. Under *Zaitō*, the Ministry of Finance's Trust Fund Bureau administered the vast pool of national savings in post office accounts and state pension and insurance schemes,[30] investing them as required to pursue their grand design for the rationalization and industrialization of the archipelago. Capital, technology, and people were concentrated along the Pacific coast and especially around the conurbations headed by Tokyo, while the resources of nature were mobilized and exploited. High growth industrialization was accompanied in particular by plans for managing the storage, transmission, and purification of water for industry, urbanization, hydropower, flood control, and irrigation.

Already in the late 1950s the first concrete dams were built, and celebrated as triumphant symbols of Japan's recovery. Under the 1961 Water Resources Development Promotion Law, comprehensive plans were developed for damming all the major river systems. One thousand dams (defined as held back by a retaining wall of higher than 15 meters) were built in the dam heyday between 1956 and 1990.[31] Japan became the most intensively dammed of countries. Through the high, medium, and low growth phases of its economy, water policy continued to rest on the assumption that production and consumption of water would and should increase steadily, as if it were a simple commodity, and that dam construction should be pursued to the utmost.

The plans drawn up in the 1960s were predicted on steady population growth. Water supply (industrial, town, agricultural) would likewise have to grow. In the "Long-Term Water Supply and Demand Plan" of 1978 and the "National Comprehensive Water Resource Plan" ("Water Plan 2000") of 1983, estimates of demand were based on the assumption of 4 and 2 percent annual growth in demand respectively.[32] Projections beyond that date pointed to a further increase of 80 percent.[33] The gap between projected and actual demand began to widen from the early 1970s. Industrial water demand declined from 1973 while town water demand continued to grow until the end of the 1980s, but at rates well below those estimated.[34] Despite the spread of an affluent lifestyle and an accompanying extravagance with water, overall water demand peaked in 1991 and 1992 at 89.4 billion cubic tons, before falling by 2000 to 87 billion.[35] In the city of Tokyo and its surrounds, planners insisted demand would triple during the fifteen-year period from 1985 to 2000. Actually it peaked in the early 1990s and began to decline as water efficiency and shifts in industrial structure took effect. In gross terms, over that period consumption rose from a 10 million cubic meters per day maximum in 1985 to approximately 14 million in 1992 and 1994, but declined to 13 million by 2002. Per capita consumption likewise leveled out at 322 litres per day.[36] Tokyo came to enjoy a surplus of around 1.5 million cubic meters of water per day.[37]

Expenditure on rivers as a proportion of public works, and expenditure on public works as a proportion of the general budget, altered only slightly between 1975 and 1996, but in an expanding economy this meant that in absolute terms expenditure on rivers tripled. For the period from 1983 to 2000 the target for expansion of water supply was fixed at 37 percent,[38] to provide an additional 60 million cubic meters of water per day.[39] After 1989, everything in the economy slowed down: agriculture continued its steady decline, manufacture accelerated its shift offshore, the population began to age rapidly, and the prospect of absolute decline in the coming century loomed ahead. The predictions of the water men in Tokyo strained credibility. Though proved wildly inaccurate, they were never revised.

However, the dam development imperative was national policy. As such, it was beyond the scope of political intervention. The bureaucratic development designs, once adopted, held absolute sway. Accustomed only to graphs of increase, expansion, and growth, bureaucrats, having completed works to "proof" rivers against the risk of once-in-30-years flooding, raised their sights to once in 50, once in 100, and once in 200 years. By the early 1990s, they still had hundreds more dams at the planning stage or under construction, which were likely to cost many trillions of yen eventually.[40]

In 1987, when most rivers had been engineered to withstand nominal once-in-100-years force flooding and the major river systems to once-in-200-years level, works began on a whole new generation of "super-dykes" (or "super-levees" as the Construction Ministry preferred to call them in English) designed to withstand floods of even greater, what might be called biblical, force. In the following decade, 7.8 of a planned 800 kilometers were built, mostly in strips of a few hundred meters here and there. The cost ran to about 50 billion yen per kilometer. Progress, at about one kilometer a year, seemed slow, but was on schedule.[41] It was, however, an unusual schedule, even by Japanese bureaucratic standards, for it was to continue for 1,000 years, with completion anticipated around the year 2987. Not only would it "flood-proof" much of Japan, but it would "quake-proof" it too. In the late 1990s a fresh justification was adopted – as a stimulus for the stagnant national economy. Hōsei University's river specialist, Igarashi Takayoshi, however, commented that the Ministry was simply prioritizing bureaucratic privilege. These were, as he put it, "works for the sake of works."[42]

The public works and water policy was riddled with contradictions. While on the one hand the state insisted on the need for massive and continuing dam construction, on the other it instructed farmers to take their fields out of production. The 700,000 hectares of paddy field removed from agricultural production under this *gentan* policy between 1966 and 2001 amounted to the demolition of a "dam" of 700 million cubic meter capacity, more than twice the capacity of all the concrete dams together. The official estimates also tended to belittle the difficulties associated with the mass application of concrete to Japan's mountainous landscape, especially the fact that the dams silt up twice as quickly as in the United States. The possibility of addressing water needs and flood control by alternative means – including reinforcement of the natural capacities of the forests – was neglected.

Kawarayu (Yanba Dam)

In the Kantō plains, with Tokyo at their center, industrialization and urbanization during the high growth decades from around 1960 were intense. Much river, coastal, and lakefront land was designated as sites for industrial or other development. Dykes and flood control systems, hydro-power generation, sewerage, and water supply issues became prime policy concerns. Under the 1969 "new" *Zensō*, the Kantō region was transformed by huge projects, among them the New Tokyo International Airport at Narita, the Tsukuba Research Complex at Tsukuba, and the Kashima Coastal Industrial Zone. Dams were designed and built up into the headwaters of the Tone River system. From 1974, Lake Kasumigaura was sealed off from the sea as the Hitachi River Locks, completed in 1963 as a flood prevention measure, were permanently closed, and the lake, together with the Tone River, was assigned the role of "town water" supply for Tokyo. Banks and channels of the lake were reinforced by concrete, sections of the adjacent wetlands reclaimed, and parts of the forest cleared for housing and urban development, and the waters were drawn off through giant pipes for long distance transportation and application to industrial, agricultural, and town water purposes, in effect turning Japan's second largest lake into a dam.

The cry of future need served to justify major plans. Following a series of unusually dry summers and occasional water restrictions in the late 1980s and 1990s, the question of water supply in the Tokyo area became very sensitive. However, although the shortages were bureaucratically manipulated to legitimize dam construction, and the bureaucrats insisted that dams would have to be constructed at more than thirty sites deep into tributary rivers of the Tone and Arakawa River systems,[43] the connection was forced. Such summer shortages could be addressed without great difficulty by temporary diversion of water from agriculture (which took over 60 percent of the total available water resource) and the steady decline of agriculture meant a natural reduction in agricultural extractions anyway.[44]

Kawarayu, an ancient hot springs resort on the upper reaches of the Tone River in Gunma prefecture, was designated as a central site in the bureaucratic plan. Yanba Dam would submerge the village and the Agatsuma Gorge, serving purposes of town water supply, flood control, and water for irrigation. Issued with a bureaucratic notification of its demise back in 1952, however, Kawarayu village fought back, eventually yielding only four decades later, in 1992, as the strain of prolonged resistance wore down its aging population.[45]

Post-1947 flood control planning for the Tone River system assumed a repetition of something like the 1947 disaster and postulated a theoretical, maximum, once-in-200-years peak flow of 22,000 cubic meters per second, more than one-fifth above the level at the time of typhoon Kathryn.[46] To cope, they insisted, Yanba (and other dams) would be necessary. However, it seems clear in retrospect that the 1947 disaster was largely caused by the degradation of the forests due to wartime neglect and uncontrolled clearing. As the renowned river engineer Takahashi Yutaka put it, it was due to *structural*, not natural, causes, that is, to policy mistakes.[47] The bureaucrats' confidence in their "modern" high dykes was therefore both bad science and bad policy. Once the forests began to recover and the dykes were repaired, in the half century to 2004 the river's peak flow did not once rise rose above 10,000 cubic meters per second level. The contradiction between the ends of flood control, requiring low levels during the summer months of potential storms and typhoons on the one hand, and water supply, requiring maximum capacity during precisely that same period, also remained unresolved.[48] In short, the basic logic of reduced rainfall necessitating dam construction was faulty, the justification in terms of steadily rising town water demand was proven mistaken by events, and the flood prevention argument likewise was unconvincing. The experts insisted that even if Yanba had existed in 1947 it would have done little to mitigate the damage and might actually have intensified it.[49] As for cost, the original (1986) estimate of 211 billion yen blew out in November 2003 to 460 billion, and with ancillary costs (resettlement of the villagers, etc.), was expected to rise further to a total of 880 billion, of which residents of Tokyo and its adjacent districts would bear 420 billion and the national treasury the remaining 460 billion.[50] By 2004, only related works, roads, and replacement village facilities had been built, and work on the main dam itself had yet to commence; the official completion date of 2010 seemed improbable, an additional decade quite likely. Already in water surplus, its population by then falling, Tokyo had no need of Yanba.[51] By the time it became available, its water might claim to be both the most expensive and the least needed in the world.

Hagiwara Yoshio, the village inn-keeper who had struggled for more than forty years against the plan to inundate his village, wrote of the struggle as one which pitted local democracy against central bureaucratic despotism, and of modern Japanese civilization as being based on lowland and downstream (urban) Japan's exploitation of mountain and upstream Japan, the sacrifice of the weak for the benefit of the strong.[52] He wrote of a village that had lost its will to live. As of 2004, a last-ditch effort to block the dam was being mounted by more than 5,000 residents of Tokyo metropolis and the five prefectures who were expected to bear about half of the overall dam cost. Petitions were separately filed with the audit authorities of each of the six local authorities to have the expenditure declared illegal on grounds that the water was unnecessary.[53] Opponents of the project also protest that the soft and porous limestone karst of the Agatsuma Gorge is dangerous ground on which to construct an enormous dam. The region is tracered with earthquake fault lines, renowned for sulfurous hot springs, and is just 20 kilometers from the active volcano of Mount Asama, which in 2004 was erupting spectacularly, if still on a relatively gentle scale. Rather than assuring downstream of safe water and flooding control, a dam in such a site might rather threaten it with catastrophe.[54]

Itsuki Village (Kawabe River Dam)

At the other end of Japan, in Kumamoto prefecture in Kyūshū, Itsuki is a "typical" Japanese mountain village, of the kind celebrated in nostalgic memory even as it disappears from present consciousness.[55] The Kawabe River, flowing through the village, is short (61 kilometers) but fast-flowing, and is renowned for having the purest waters in the country (as of 1997),[56] and very high levels of bio-diversity.[57] In 1965, an estimated 1,600 millimeters of rain fell between July 18 and August 6, including 400 millimeters on the night of July 18.[58] In the floods that ensued, six people were killed and over 1,000 houses destroyed. The maximum flow, by the official estimate (although that estimate has been questioned, on which see below), reached 7,000 cubic meters per second and 9,000 cubic meters per second at Hitoyoshi and Yatsushiro respectively; the idea of damming the river, thereby reducing the maximum flow at the above two points to 4,000 and 7,000 meters per second, was adopted as the remedy to prevent future flooding. In 1976, with the goals of irrigation water supply and hydro-power generation added, the design was officially adopted under the "Special Multi-Purpose Dam Law." The dam waters would rise behind a 107.5-meter-high wall. The center of the village, including the school, village office, shops, and some 528 households, would be swallowed up.[59]

The village was stunned to learn of the plan.[60] The village assembly protested, and then local farmers and fishermen launched a series of actions in the courts against the national and provincial bureaucracy. Over time, however, as in Kawarayu, the villagers grew old and tired, divided into groups of unconditional opponents and those who fought just to get the best possible terms of settlement, yielded to the pressure of promised cash payments, or simply sank into despair under the pressure. In 1982, the mayor and village assembly withdrew their opposition, followed, two years later, by the first group of landowners, and eight years after that by the last of them. Thereafter opposition centered on the fishermen, who fought against the loss of their fishing rights; farmers, who fought against the imposition of an unwanted irrigation plan; downstream residents, who feared an expensive and dangerous imposition on their environment; and the slowly awakening national ecological movement.

All of the dam's supposed functions – flood prevention, hydro-power generation, irrigation – were disputed. Opponents of the dam argued that it was the degradation of the forest, not the quantity of the rain, that had caused the 1960s floods. Subsequent years had seen a gradual recovery of the "green dam" of the forest, whose capacity to hold water correspondingly reduced the need for a "white" or concrete dam.[61] In July 1995, rain substantially above the Ministry of Construction's worst case scenario fell, yet no significant flooding damage ensued.[62]

So far as the generation of hydro-electric power was concerned, the post-dam output from the Kawabe River would be 16,500 kilowatts per second. Since the four small existing plants in current use, destined to be submerged by the dam, were generating 18,900 kilowatts per second, construction would therefore achieve a net *reduction* in electric power generation.[63] So far as irrigation was concerned, the Land Improvement Law stipulates that state resources be allocated only to projects where the land area is greater than 3,000 hectares and at least two-thirds of the farmers to benefit from the project are united in petitioning for it. In this case, an official survey in 1983 did indeed find 98 percent (of 4,000 designated beneficiaries) in favor of the plan, but in June 1996, 870 of them launched a court action to have it cancelled, complaining that they did not want the water and that their original consent had been extracted by deception, pressure, or bribery.[64] Others subsequently joined them, raising the numbers to over 2,000, more than half of the supposed beneficiaries.[65] Most were dry field farmers, cultivating crops that can cope with occasional dry spells, and worried about the prospective cost of the irrigation waters. They noted that even in the "100 year drought" of 1994, when the rainfall was a full 200 millimeters less than ever previously recorded, they had coped, with little inconvenience, while the farmers on neighboring Kuma River, who had had the supposed advantage of the protection of the Ichifusa Dam, had suffered substantial losses.

Fishermen protested at what they saw as the destruction of a major regional and national resource. The *shaku-ayu* of Kawabe are highly prized throughout the country, and constitute a substantial industry.[66] Despite the blandishments and inducements of the Tokyo bureaucrats, the Kawabe River fishing cooperative's 1,500 members decided at special general meetings in February and November 2001 to reject the government's buy-out offer for their fishing rights. In an unprecedented move, the government then resorted to the procedure for *compulsory* purchase under the Compulsory Purchase of Land Law, insisting that the dam was necessary "to protect the lives and property of residents along the river."[67] The dam is widely seen in Kyūshū as a bureaucratic project, foisted on the village and accepted with extreme reluctance as something determined by "the authorities" against which until very recent times there would never have been any appeal. Money was spent lavishly to ensure the bureaucratic will would be implemented, both in the form of the strictly "legal" payments, usually in the order of three times the estimated annual income, for the land acquired, and of the much more dubious sums by which the negotiating process was facilitated whenever necessary.[68]

The cost, originally estimated (in 1976) at 35 billion yen, blew out in 1998 to 265 billion, and in 2004 to 330 billion. By 2004, work on the actual dam site itself had still not commenced, although the project was said to be 70 percent complete. As other economic activities in and around the village gradually shrank or ceased, the Ministry of Construction became the major employer in the village. However, support for the dam steadily shrank. By 2001, only one in five voters supported, while between two and three opposed, the project.[69] Throughout the long struggle, Tokyo officials would countenance no future for the village other than that based on the dam. In May 2003, the Fukuoka district court issued a dramatic judgment, reversing a previous decision three years earlier and holding that the government had indeed acted illegally in pursuing the project without the necessary two-thirds consent.[70] However, though initially shaken, the government persisted in its commitment, simply redoubling its efforts at persuasion.[71] A second front was opened, under the title of a "new irrigation plan" and with the slogan of "farmers as masters," to ensure the project would go ahead.

Super Dykes and Neo-Nature

In the late twentieth century, Japan's rivers, lakes, and forests were all under pressure. The struggles over development issues grew from relatively small and local to large events that captured national attention. Japan's civil society began to realize that the twenty-first century was opening to the inundation of the mountain villages of Kawarayu and Itsuki, just as the twentieth had opened with the inundation of the mountain village of Yanaka. Yet the climate of opinion was changing. Sakakibara Eisuke, Vice-Minister for International Finance (known in the 1990s as "Mr Yen" in recognition of his position at the center of Japan's financial policy-making), spoke of "the progressivist domination of nature, or anthropocentrism," and called for harmony and cohabitation to be substituted for conquest and development.[72] Criticizing the "public works state," he called for Japan to be turned instead into a "pastoral urban state."[73] Bureaucratic plans and statements, shifting slowly from "growth-at-all-costs-ism," began to express concern for nature, conservation, and the need for a new philosophy of water. The Fifth Comprehensive National Plan, adopted by the Obuchi government in 1997, entitled "Grand Design for the Twenty-First Century" had the subtitle "The Creation of Beautiful National Land." It was rich in expressions about the preservation and restoration of nature and the creation of a pleasant lifestyle.[74] The Ministry of Construction began to represent itself as environmentally sensitive. Nature itself might be profoundly, perhaps even irrevocably modified or damaged, but with the right techniques something closely resembling it could be put back in its place. "Neo-nature" engineering (literally, "multi-nature-mode," or *tashizengata*) became a key part of the prescription for Japan's rivers, lakes, and sea coast.

By 1993 there were 1,600 pilot works on Japanese rivers.[75] "Neonatural river reconstruction" would create "a new ecosystem which protects the surviving inhabitants, restores ecological balance and improves the living situation of animal and plant life."[76] The beds and banks of the rivers and lakes would be treated with a range of materials, including pebbles, stones, logs, lattice brushwood, turf, shrubs, and flowers, and the furnishing of fish paths and fish hides, in such a way that concrete is hidden from view "and a harmonious relationship between nature and man" would flourish.[77] Nature would be contained, but in a neat and tidy "neo-nature," or "bonsai," way. Large budgets would be required for many years to come, as this process costs at least 10 to 20 percent more than for "standard" river engineering. At best, however, neo-naturing amounted to an attempt to construct artificially by extremely complex human-engineered interventions a kind of virtual reality in place of the nature that has gone.

While even Construction White Papers began to refer to the "spiritual affluence that exists not only in human-centred activities but also in symbiosis with nature,"[78] nevertheless the possibility that there might have been a flaw in the blueprint of development was ruled out.[79] The Rivers Law, revised in May 1997, gave legislative recognition to the principle of consultation and declared for the first time a "river environment" value, to be adjusted and preserved in tandem with the traditional river policy ends of flood control and irrigation/power generation. As the advisory committees were set up, however, grass roots, local, and environmental movements were given minimal voice or influence.

Conclusion

In all the advanced capitalist counties a significant paradigm shift in attitudes to water is under way, but in no country has the political and economic system been so deeply embedded in a public works or "construction state" as Japan, and consequently none experiences such entrenched bureaucratic and corporate resistance to change. Rivers, lakes, and wetlands in late nineteenth- and twentieth-century Japan were transformed into components of an elaborate plumbing system. The human capacity, or right, to control and subjugate nature was rarely doubted.

The once water-rich Edo realm became during the twentieth century the world's greatest water importer, in the sense of being an importer of foods which concentrated the water of other countries, such as the United States, Australia, Canada, Brazil, and China. It imports in this way the equivalent of 74.4 billion tons of water, as against a total Japanese domestic water use in 2002 of 87.8 billion tons (agriculture 57.9, household 16.4, and industrial 13.5).[80] The once green archipelago ranks with semi-desert Algeria, frozen Iceland, and jungle Congo in its inability to feed itself.[81]

Counter-intuitively, modern Japan in the twentieth century accomplished a steady, policy-driven attrition in its agriculture and forestry and a diminution of its water resource, since the white dams of the twentieth century were never able to match the water retention, flood prevention, and environmental amenity qualities of the green dams of the eighteenth century. While all Japan's dams together have a capacity of 320 million cubic meters, that pales into insignificance before the forests' capacity to retain 4,270 million.[82] In the twenty-first century, the modern network of dams, the nation's pride just two generations ago, approaches the end of its utility because of the accumulation of silt and muck and the degradation of the concrete. Demolition is destined in the years ahead to become for Japan a huge, continuing, and unplanned expense, a problem akin to that of demolishing worn-out nuclear reactors. The elaborate modern system of flood prevention by dyke and dam, whether designed to resist once-in-30-, 50-, 100-, or 200-year probability flood levels, could not match that of 200 years ago, since properly tended forest, nature's "green dam," absorbs percolating water at 100 to 150 millimeters per hour while a forest which has degenerated, due to fire, grazing, and deforestation, can cope, at best, with only up to 1 millimeter.[83] "Modern" waters therefore, straightened and reinforced with concrete and less and less regulated by the forests, pour in a torrent down the concrete reinforced floodways to the sea. They tend to alternate between drying up and flooding, and thus to *require* damming. The modern triumph over the environment was at best ambiguous.

By the dawn of the twenty-first century, the hubris, fiscal irresponsibility, and collusive structural corruption of the public works state, and its social, economic, and political costs, were plain, but the bureaucratic response to mounting criticism, and to the demand for decentralization, bureaucratic accountability, and fiscal restraint, was to consolidate public works power under a giant "super-ministry," the 70,000 strong Ministry of Land, Infrastructure, and Transport.[84] The entrenched, centralized, bureaucratic systems of water supply, sewerage, and flood control, with their complex of huge dams, aqueducts, and tunnels, remained unscathed.[85] National plans lacked long-term (century and beyond) perspective and ignored fiscal principles or environmental impact.

The prevalent philosophical assumption in Japan for over a century has been that nature subjected to control, *seibi*, is preferable to nature in the raw. Many, perhaps most, Japanese, feeling deep in their bones the insecurity of life in an archipelago subject to typhoon, earthquake, and volcano, came to believe uncritically in *seibi*, in technology, for the regulation and control of nature rather than in adaptation to it. Rivers, mountains, and sea were therefore straightened and "fixed" without limit. Japan's construction state thrived on that mentality, with devastating fiscal and ecological consequences.[86] For all the talk about sensitivity to nature and "farmers as masters," early twenty-first-century society was increasingly structured around massive centralized institutions of water, power, and defense, with its population concentrated in standardized, mass-consuming, and mass-waste-generating megalopolises.

NOTES

1   Flannery, *The Future Eaters.*
2   Takahashi, *Kasen ni motto jiyū o*, p. 217.
3   For a comprehensive discussion, see Kalland and Asquith, "Japanese Perceptions of Nature."
4   Totman, *The Green Archipelago*, p. 1.
5   Kawakatsu, "Toward a Country of Wealth and Virtue."
6   Kawano, "Nihon no shinrin ni nani ga okite iru ka," p. 136.
7   Tomiyama, *Nihon no kome,* p. 184.
8   This point is central to the writings of Tomiyama.
9   Tomiyama, *Mizu to midori*, p. 27.
10   Watabe, *Nihon kara suiden ga kieru hi*, p. 48.
11   Udagawa, "Development and Transfer of Environment-Friendly Agriculture," p. 92.
12   Mitsubishi Research Institute survey, quoted in Tashiro, "An Environmental Mandate," p. 43.
13   See table reproduced in McCormack, *The Emptiness of Japanese Affluence*, p. 140.
14   Totman, *The Green Archipelago*, p. 173.
15   Goodman, Sorj, and Wilkinson, *From Farming to Biotechnology*, p. 101.
16   Totman, *The Green Archipelago*, pp. 4–5; Fukuoka, *Mori to mizu no keizaigaku*, pp. 2–3; Tanaka, "The Cyclical Sensibility of Edo-Period Japan."
17   Mutō, "Ecological Perspectives on Alternative Development," p. 5.
18   Tomiyama, *Mizu to midori*, p. 92.
19   Tomiyama, *Nihon no kome*, pp. 164, 184.
20   Tomiyama, "Nō wa bunka to kankyō o sodamu."

21 McCormack, *The Emptiness of Japanese Affluence*; Kerr, *Dogs and Demons*.
22 Details in Ui, *Industrial Pollution in Japan*, pp. 27, 41, 46, 61.
23 Here I am following the analysis of Tomiyama, *Nihon no kome*.
24 Tomiyama, *Mizu to midori*, pp. 93–6, 99–100.
25 Ibid., p. 14.
26 Takahashi, *Kasen ni motto jiyū o*, p. 205.
27 Tomiyama, *Mizu to midori*, pp. 17–18.
28 Ministry of Construction estimate.
29 Takahashi, *Kasen ni motto jiyū o*, p. 205.
30 McCormack, "Breaking the Iron Triangle," pp. 11–12.
31 Kuwahara, "Kawa kaihatsu no shisō," pp. 33–45.
32 Ui, *Nihon no mizu wa yomigaeru ka*, pp. 278–9.
33 Shimazu, "Damu kensetsu kono sōdai na muda," p. 56.
34 Shimazu, *Mizu mondai genron*. Tables at pp. 16, 18, 100.
35 "Ministry Rules Out New Dam Drojects," *Asahi shinbun* (Apr. 7, 2004).
36 Takahashi, *Kasen ni motto jiyū o*, p. 167.
37 Shimazu, "Shutoken no jumin ni totte."
38 Shimazu, *Mizu mondai genron*, p. 111 (citing National Land Agency's 1987 estimates).
39 Ibid., p. 130.
40 Thirteen trillion according to Ueno, "Damu ni mirai wa nai," and 20 trillion according to Fukuoka, *Kuni ga kawa o kowasu wake*.
41 Igarashi, " 'Mayaku no ronri'," p. 63.
42 "Kansei made 1000-nen nan te – Kensetsushō 'supā teibō' suishin chū," *Asahi shinbun*, evening edn. (Dec. 15, 1998).
43 Shimazu, *Mizu mondai genron*, p. 55.
44 Shimazu, "Damu kensetsu kono sōdai na muda," p. 56.
45 Shimazu, *Mizu mondai genron*, p. 21.
46 Okuma, "Datsu damu o habamu," p. 125.
47 Takahashi, *Kasen ni motto jiyū o*, p. 205.
48 Shimazu, "Damu kensetsu kono sōdai na muda," p. 56.
49 Details in Shimazu, "Shutokuken no jumin."
50 Ibid.
51 Ibid.
52 Hagiwara, *Yanba damu no arasoi*.
53 "Petitions Submitted against Yanba Dam," *Japan Times* (Sept. 11, 2004).
54 Kuji, *Anata wa Yanba damu no mizu o nomenmasu ka*.
55 For general details of the village, see Itsuki-Mura Minzoku, *Itsuki no minzoku*.
56 Environment Agency, Dec. 8, 1998, quoted in Seiryū Kawabegawa o mirai ni tewatasu kai, *Kawauso* 22 (Kumamoto-ken: Hitoyoshi, n.d.).
57 Fukuoka, *Kuni ga kawa o*, pp. 20 ff.
58 Takasugi, *Nihon no damu*, p. 65.
59 Momoi Kazuma, "Mokushiroku," *Sapio* (Mar. 24, 1999), pp. 60–3.
60 The village assembly adopted a resolution on July 23, 1966, nine days after the announcement.
61 Takasugi, *Nihon no damu*, p. 194.
62 447.1 millimeters in two days, leading to a flow of 3,800 cubic meters per second at Hitoyoshi and 5,700 at Yatsushiro, well below the figures used by the Ministry to justify the dam (Fukuoka, *Kuni ga kawa o*, p. 231).
63 Fukuoka, "Meibun naki kensetsu," pp. 44–7.
64 Fukuoka, *Kuni ga kawa o*, pp. 168–76.

65 Takashi Nakayama, "Stop Kawabe River Dam Before It's Too Late," *Asahi shinbun* (July 30, 1999).
66 Takahashi, "Kawabegawa damu," p. 51.
67 "Ministry Hardens Stance on Dam," asahi.com (Dec. 12, 2001) <http://www.asahi.com>
68 Fukuoka, *Kuni ga kawa o*, pp. 185–6, 182–214.
69 Kawabegawa Damu Mondai Shuzaihan, "Kawabegawa damu hontai chakkō e no seinenba," *Asahi shinbun* (Nov. 14, 2001). In November 2001, a *Kumamoto nichinichi shinbun* survey found 17.4 percent for and 54 percent against the dam (Takahashi, "Fukaikan o hyōmei shita," pp. 52–3).
70 "Hantai nōka gyakuten shōso," *Kumamoto nichinichi shinbun* (May 17, 2003).
71 Mori Norikazu, "Gyakuten shōso hanketsu kara shin risui keikaku sakutei e," Kawabegawa mondai shiryōshū, no. 68, *Kawabegawa* (Aug. 2004): 8–13.
72 Sakakibara, "The End of Progressivism," p. 13.
73 Yasumasa Inoue, "Nurturing 'Pastoral Urban State'," Daily Yomiuri Online (Sept. 2, 1998) <http://www.yomiuri.co.jp/dy/>
74 Kawakatsu, "Towards a Country of Wealth and Virtue."
75 Kensetsushō, *Tashizengata kawazukuri.*
76 Aso, "Bio-diversity Reconstruction."
77 Ibid.
78 Kensetsushō, *Kensetsu hakusho.*
79 Ui, *Nihon no mizu*, p. 202.
80 Takahashi, *Chikyū no mizu*, pp. 108–9.
81 In global terms, Japan ranks approximately at number 150 in grain self-sufficiency (Tomiyama, *Kankyō mondai*, p. 149).
82 "Nihon chizan chisui kyōkai shiryō" materials quoted in Tomiyama, *Mizu to midori*, p. 47.
83 Tomiyama, *Mizu to midori*, p. 30.
84 Hobo Takehiko, "Go zensō rosen no tenkan to chihō no bunken," *Kankyō to kōgai* 29:1 (Summer 1999): 5–10.
85 Murota, *Genpatsu no keizaigaku*, pp. 196–7.
86 McCormack, *The Emptiness of Japanese Affluence*, pp. 93–113, and "Breaking the Iron Triangle."

BIBLIOGRAPHY

Aso Yuya. "Bio-diversity Reconstruction: Restoring Japan's Rivers to Ecological Vibrance." Ministry of Land, Infrastructure and Transport homepage <http://www.mlit.go.jp/river/english/bio-d1.html> accessed Feb. 28, 2006.
Flannery, Tim. *The Future Eaters.* Chatswood, Australia: Reed Books, 1994.
Fukuoka Kensei. *Kuni ga kawa o kowasu wake.* Fukuoka: Ashi Shobō, 1994.
Fukuoka Kensei. "Meibun naki kensetsu mokuteki." *Shūkan kinyōbi* (Dec. 8, 1995): 44–7.
Fukuoka Tetsuya. *Mori to mizu no keizaigaku.* Tokyo: Tōyō Keizai Shimpōsha, 1987.
Goodman, David, Sorj, Bernardo, and Wilkinson, John. *From Farming to Biotechnology.* Oxford: Blackwell, 1987.
Hagiwara Yoshio. *Yanba damu no arasoi.* Tokyo: Iwanami Shoten, 1996.
Igarashi Takayoshi. " 'Mayaku no ronri' ga makaritōru kensetsugyō kuwaseru dake no kōkyō jigyō ga kuni o horobosu." *Ekonomisuto* (Jan. 18, 2000): 63.
Itsuki-Mura Minzoku Chōsadan (Murata Hiroshi), ed. *Itsuki no minzoku.* Itsuki: Itsuki Village Office, 1994.

Kalland, Arne, and Asquith, Pamela. "Japanese Perceptions of Nature – Ideals and Illusions." In Pamela Asquith and Arne Kalland, eds., *Japanese Images of Nature: Cultural Perspectives.* Richmond, UK: Curzon, 1997.

Kawakatsu Heita. "Toward a Country of Wealth and Virtue." *Japan Echo* 26:2 (Apr. 1999).

Kawano Shōichi. "Nihon no shinrin ni nani ga okite iru ka." *Sekai* (Nov. 1996): 136–40.

Kensetsushō, Kasenkyoku Chisuika. *Tashizengata kawazukuri.* Tokyo: Kensetsushō, n.d. (?1995).

Kensetsushō, Kasenkyoku Chisuika. *Kensetsu hakusho.* Tokyo: Kensetsushō, 1998.

Kerr, Alex. *Dogs and Demons: Tales from the Dark Side of Modern Japan.* New York: Hill and Wang, 2001.

Kuji Tsutomu. *Anata wa Yanba damu no mizu o nomemasu ka.* Tokyo: Marujusha, 2001.

Kuwahara Minoru. "Kawa kaihatsu no shisō." *Oruta* 3 (Winter 1992): 33–45.

McCormack, Gavan. *The Emptiness of Japanese Affluence,* 2nd rev. edn. Armonk, NY: M. E. Sharpe, 2001.

McCormack, Gavan. "Breaking the Iron Triangle." *New Left Review* 13 (Jan.–Feb. 2002): 5–23.

Murota Takeshi. *Genpatsu no keizaigaku.* Tokyo: Asahi Shinbunsha, 1993.

Mutō Ichiyō. "Ecological Perspectives on Alternative Development: The Rainbow Plan." *Capitalism Nature Socialism* 9:1 (Mar. 1998): 3–23.

Okuma Takashi. "Datsu damu o habamu 'kihon kōsui'." *Sekai* (Oct. 2004): 121–31.

Sakakibara Eisuke. "The End of Progressivism." *Foreign Affairs* (Sept.–Oct. 1995): 8–14.

Shimazu Teruyuki. *Mizu mondai genron.* Tokyo: Hokuto Shuppan, 1991.

Shimazu Teruyuki. "Damu kensetsu kono sōdai na muda." *Ekonomisuto* (Feb. 18, 1997): 54–7.

Shimazu Teruyuki. "Shutoken no jumin ni totte no Yanba damu to wa?" Paper presented to "Jūmin kansa seikyū hōkoku daishūkai." Shinjuku Sumitomo Hall, Sept. 12, 2004.

Takahashi Yurika. "Kawabegawa damu yami no gyogyō hoshō gōi kokudo kōtsū fukudaijin ga chōsa o meigen." *Shūkan kinyōbi* (Oct. 26, 2001): 51.

Takahashi Yurika. "Fukaikan o hyōmei shita Shiotani Kumamoto kenchiji." *Shūkan kinyōbi* (Dec. 21, 2001): 52–3.

Takahashi Yutaka. *Kasen ni motto jiyū o.* Tokyo: Sankaidō, 1998.

Takahashi Yutaka. *Chikyū no mizu wa abunai.* Tokyo: Iwanami Shinsho, 2003.

Takasugi Shingo. *Nihon no damu.* Tokyo: Sanseidō Sensho, 1980.

Tanaka Yūko. "The Cyclical Sensibility of Edo-Period Japan." *Japan Echo* 25:2 (Apr. 1998).

Tashiro Yōichi. "An Environmental Mandate for Rice Self-Sufficiency." *Japan Quarterly* (Jan.–Mar. 1992): 34–44.

Tomiyama Kazuko. *Mizu no bunkashi.* Tokyo: Bungei Shunjusha, 1980.

Tomiyama Kazuko. *Mizu to midori to tsuchi.* Tokyo: Chūkō Shinsho, 1974, 1986.

Tomiyama Kazuko. *Nihon no kome.* Tokyo: Chūkō Shinsho, 1993.

Tomiyama Kazuko. *Kankyō mondai to wa nanika.* Tokyo: PHP Shinsho, 2001.

Tomiyama Kazuko. "Nō wa bunka to kankyō o sodamu." *Asahi shinbun* (Aug. 29, 2004).

Totman, Conrad. *The Green Archipelago: Forestry in Pre-industrial Japan.* Berkeley: University of California Press, 1989.

Udagawa, Taketoshi. "Development and Transfer of Environment-Friendly Agriculture." In *Sustainable Agricultural Development in Asia,* ed. Asian Productivity Organization. Tokyo: APO, 1994.

Ueno Hideo. "Damu ni mirai wa nai." *Sekai* (Aug. 1995).

Ui Jun. *Industrial Pollution in Japan.* Tokyo: United Nations University Press, 1992.

Ui Jun. *Nihon no mizu wa yomigaeru ka.* Tokyo: NHK Raiburari, 1996.

Watabe Tadayo. *Nihon kara suiden ga kieru hi.* Tokyo: Iwanami, 1993.

FURTHER READING

This chapter is part of a larger study on water in the modernization of East Asia. Previously published chapters include, on China, Gavan McCormack, "Water Margins: Competing Paradigms in China," *Critical Asian Studies* 33:1 (Mar. 2001): 5–30; on Korea, Gavan McCormack, "Water, Development, and Nature in Korea," *Asian Cultural Studies* 30 (2004): 111–26; on the Ogasawara Islands, Gavan McCormack and Nanyan Guo, "Coming to Terms with Nature: Development Dilemmas on the Ogasawara Islands," *Japan Forum* 13:2 (2001): 177–93; and on Okinawa, Gavan McCormack, "Okinawa and the Structure of Dependence," in Glenn Hook and Richard Siddle, eds., *Japan and Okinawa: Structure and Subjectivity* (London: RoutledgeCurzon, 2003).

For profound reflections on the history of modernity and the concept of "nature" in Japan, there could be no better starting point than the work of Julia Adeney Thomas: see her essay, "The Cage of Nature: Modernity's History in Japan," *History and Theory* 40 (Feb. 2001): 16–36, and her book, *Reconfiguring Modernity: Concepts of Nature in Japanese Political Ideology* (Berkeley: University of California Press, 2001). On pollution incidents, see Timothy George's *Minamata: Pollution and the Struggle for Democracy in Postwar Japan* (Cambridge, Mass.: Harvard University Asia Center, 2001); on the history of forests and forestry in Japan, see Conrad Totman's books *The Green Archipelago: Forestry in Pre-industrial Japan* (Berkeley: University of California Press, 1989) and *The Lumber Industry in Early Modern Japan* (Honolulu: University of Hawai'i Press, 1985); on contemporary environmental policy issues, see Miranda Schreurs's *Environmental Politics in Japan, Germany, and the United States* (Cambridge: Cambridge University Press, 2002). Conrad Totman's textbook *A History of Japan* (Oxford: Blackwell, 2000) is an ambitious attempt to rethink the contours of Japanese history from an environmental perspective.

CHAPTER TWENTY-SIX

Popular Culture

E. Taylor Atkins

Popular culture has been a high growth field in Japanese studies since the 1990s. This is due to the general scholarly acceptance of popular culture as a legitimate object of inquiry, but also to the increasing visibility of Japanese cultural products – ranging from comics to sumō wrestling, popular music to animated films – in the global marketplace. At the end of the twentieth century, Pokémon, Nomo Hideo, Miyazaki Hayao, sushi, and Godzilla were household names and words of global prominence. Whereas a scant decade earlier Japan was more renowned for its mimetic appropriation of Western cultural products, now many are convinced of Japanese creative genius as expressed in popular culture. The study of Japanese popular culture has evolved significantly. Previously the realm of connoisseurs and antiquarians, who were entranced by the aesthetic peculiarities of Edo period artifacts, popular culture has captivated the scholarly interests of historians and social scientists, who use it to address broader issues pertaining to gender relations, national identity, social demography, political economy, and colonialism. At the dawn of the twenty-first century, few question the scholarly legitimacy of popular culture for understanding Japan.

The English term *popular culture* possesses several meanings and connotations that deserve clarification, for these definitions are complex and often contradictory. Japanese terms generally translated as *popular culture* offer slightly more explicit ideological undertones. It is important to note at the outset that popular culture originated as a *relational* concept within a stratified social milieu: that is, the *popular* has meaning only in contrast to the *high culture* or *fine art* of social elites. As such, *popular culture* has both aesthetic and social connotations. The aesthetic connotation is that popular culture possesses less artistic value than high or elite culture because it is purportedly less sophisticated and profound and requires less cultivation to appreciate. The social connotation is that popular culture (*minshū bunka* or *chōnin bunka* in Japanese) is by and for non-elites, the status-disadvantaged, or undereducated groups, who by virtue of their station have neither the means nor the capacity to produce culture comparable in aesthetic value to that of their social betters. The status or ideological orientation of the observer determines whether the "lowborn" pedigree and artistic simplicity of popular culture are considered positive or negative. Scholars with populist sympathies envisage popular culture as *folk culture* (*minzoku bunka*): participatory rather than passively consumed, produced by a community for itself, rather than for a paying audience. Moreover, it is (or can be) a vehicle for resistance against social oppression. Practitioners of so-called "people's history" (*minshūshi*) romanticize popular culture as *counterculture*: an inherently subversive and irreverent inversion of elite values, a space where non-elites and oppressed populations can define and valorize themselves, even making a virtue of their low station.[1] Since the *populus* (*minshū*) itself is implicitly responsible for cultural production, popular culture is thus an authentic expression of non-elite sensibilities, anxieties, and aspirations, woven into the very fabric of social life.

By contrast, other observers regard popular culture as synonymous with *mass culture* (*taishū bunka*), the product of industrial techniques of manufacture and dissemination. Popular culture thus conceived is not actually produced by the *populus* but rather by a culture industry motivated only by profit and the preservation of elite privilege. It is thus the very antithesis of folk culture: even if a cultural form originates among the *populus*, the culture industry appropriates, repackages, and mass markets it, thereby neutralizing or trivializing its subversive potential. Cultural commodities are consumed passively by hapless masses who have essentially surrendered to this industry both the prerogative and the means to initiate cultural production. Moreover, since cultural commodities are produced for profit and therefore must appeal to the broadest possible audience, there is a concomitant homogenization of cultural products, an unwarranted exaltation of the trivial, and aesthetic degradation. Art and iconoclasm can no longer thrive, for "the mass crushes beneath it everything that is different, everything that is excellent, individual, qualified and select."[2] More ominously, popular culture as envisaged by Antonio Gramsci becomes a means whereby dominant elites exert hegemony over subordinate groups, not through force or coercion but via a negotiated "ideological consensus" to which mass media and culture can contribute. While this entails concessions to the tastes and interests of the subordinate masses, it "cannot touch the essential ... the decisive function exercised by the leading group in the decisive nucleus of economic activity."[3]

Already complex and fluid, definitions of popular culture have become even more so under the influence of postmodern theory. In an age in which so-called highbrow or elite culture is as readily available via the same media as so-called popular forms, and in which purportedly "inaccessible" avant-garde techniques are widely used in popular music, television ads, and action movies, the social and aesthetic distinctions between elite, popular, and folk expressions seem increasingly porous and less analytically useful. "There are no longer any agreed and inviolable criteria which can serve to differentiate art from popular culture," Dominic Strinati asserts. "Art becomes increasingly integrated into the economy both because it is used to encourage people to consume through the expanded role it plays in advertising, and because it becomes a commercial good in its own right."[4] Moreover, postmodernists have exposed the ways in which artistic canons serve the interests of those in power. This is not to say that social and aesthetic distinctions have completely lost operational power in social life (for instance, ghetto pedigree or "street cred" are deemed essential for legitimate participation in the self-defined "counterculture" of hip hop). But it is worth pondering whether such distinctions have only recently (in the era of late capitalism) ceased to conform with the reality of cultural production and consumption, or if they ever did. As explained below, as early as the seventeenth century Japanese popular culture pillaged from and signified on elite culture, while elites found the diversions of the rabble so intoxicating that they risked censure to join the party.[5]

As durable definitions of popular culture have become more elusive, the object of cultural analysis has shifted as well from production to consumption. A key question is who dictates the terms and content of popular culture, the producers or the audience? Who is responsive to whom? Early twentieth-century mass culture theorists, Marxists, and the Frankfurt School insisted that the industrial manufacture of culture served the interests of the corporate elite, manipulated popular taste, and induced apathy among the supine masses, whose interests would be better served making revolution.[6] Subsequent scholarship – generically dubbed "reception studies" – restored agency to consumers, arguing that cultural texts are open to multiple, even seditious, readings and uses. For instance, Lawrence Levine has argued that methods of industrial production and dissemination do not necessarily invalidate cultural products as "authentic" expressions of popular sentiment. Since mass cultural products are read in diverse ways and put to different uses by consumers, they constitute the "folklore of industrial society," which can even be deployed to contest the dominance of those who produced them. "Modernity dealt a blow to artisanship in culture as well as in material commodities," Levine concedes. "But to say this is not to say that, as a result, people have been rendered passive, hopeless consumers. What people *can* do and *do* do is to refashion the objects created for them to fit their own values, needs, and expectations."[7] But Jackson Lears questions Levine's assertions of the consumer's sovereignty:

> Levine remains oblivious to the fundamental fact of cultural power: not its capacity to manipulate consciousness but its existence as a set of givens that form the boundaries of what the less powerful can do or can even (sometimes) imagine doing ... Each human subject is born into a world filled with chains of signifiers: the expressive forms in which social and cultural power is constituted. ... The chains are not unbreakable: they can be constructed and reconstructed to meet the needs and desires of the individual subject. But they *are* chains.[8]

Nowadays, mass-manufactured cultural products with anti-establishment messages are abundant and lucrative, allowing the culture industry to endure and profit through self-excoriation. This is clearly a concession to popular taste for the risqué and rebellious, but one that admittedly does nothing to endanger corporate control of cultural production. Thus chastened, we hereby proceed with a notion of popular culture less beholden to rigid, ideologically loaded social and aesthetic categories, and which embraces its paradoxical nature as its defining trait. Popular culture is a "compromise equilibrium," a continual struggle for "sovereignty" between consumers and producers.[9] It simultaneously provokes new, sometimes revolutionary thoughts and behaviors as it encourages frivolity and indifference. It is also the arena in which competing constituencies debate matters of great material and spiritual import. Popular culture initiates and sustains discussions on gender norms, inequities of wealth and status, tolerance, national identity, sexual morality, political and civil rights, and social violence, matters that are not or cannot be addressed via formal political processes, legal channels, or grievance procedures.

Japan has had mass-produced, commodified, urban popular culture since the seventeenth century and its influence has been dramatic. One need only glance at the Tokugawa government's copious sumptuary edicts, censorship regulations, and field surveys to realize how pervasive popular culture was and how staggering its impact. Many contemporaneous observers (and not a few subsequent scholars) detected the warrior elite's ruin in its insatiable appetite for slumming with the common folk in their theaters, teahouses, and bordellos. Popular culture – the "impulse to create, to enrich leisure time with cultural pursuits, to imitate the life-style of the upper-class" – made a joke of the Tokugawa social hierarchy, by creating social spaces and imaginary realms in which assigned status (*mibun*) was irrelevant.[10]

An exhaustive chronological account of various media and forms of Japanese popular culture is impossible in this chapter, so the following discussion is organized around four themes – commerce, aesthetics, appropriation, and contestation – and draws on examples from early modern, modern, and contemporary popular culture. This approach enables us to identify conjunctures between recent studies and to envision new approaches for future scholarship.

Commerce

Walter Benjamin dated the revolution in "technical reproduction" that enabled mass cultural manufacturing to the early 1900s. This revolution made it possible to produce and disseminate works of art on an unprecedented scale and "to cause the most profound change in their impact upon the public." "Quantity has been trans-muted into quality," he added. "The greatly increased mass of participants has produced a change in the mode of participation."[11] These transformations were no less profound in early twentieth-century Japan than in the rest of the industrialized world, but neither were they entirely unprecedented. The commodification and mass production and distribution of cultural products in Japan dates from the early modern era. Premodern forms of popular culture were rooted in rural religious observances, finding most vibrant expression in *matsuri* (festivals) to pacify spirits, promote fertility, commemorate seasonal changes, or celebrate harvests. There were itinerant professional entertainers (bards, shrine dancers, theatrical troupes), but their performances did not supplant the more participatory cultural practices of villagers, who performed their own dances, songs, and dramas in conjunction with *matsuri*.

With the advent of castle towns in the sixteenth century, increasingly large numbers of merchants and craftspeople settled permanently in incipient urban centers, thereby creating conditions favorable to the development of urban popular culture. *Matsuri* continued even in the cities of Edo, Osaka, and Kyoto, but the variety of diversions and entertainments increased exponentially, as a vibrant culture industry developed in the seventeenth century. But, while many of its cultural products and methods of dissemination presaged the manufacture and marketing of modern mass culture, conventional mass culture theories fail to explain the culture industry of the Edo period. Tokugawa society was nightmarishly complex, a nascent capitalist system under a feudal facade, in which wealth rarely corresponded with status. How could the culture industry serve the interests of the ruling elite when it was essentially in the hands of a despised caste? It rather undermined samurai privilege by making cultural products (teeming with sexual, violent, and scatological content) widely available to commoners, who were thereby distracted from performing their assigned economic and normative roles, and by sanctioning spaces where the castes could mingle, in the most intimate ways.[12] Burgeoning commercial networks even enabled theatrical troupes, entertainers, and printed matter to infiltrate isolated rural communities. By the early nineteenth century, rural folk had erected their own kabuki and puppet theaters (in blatant disregard of bakufu prohibitions limiting theaters to urban licensed districts) and mounted their own amateur productions. "They acted in plays not because traveling troupes were unavailable," Walthall maintains, "but because they wanted to act."[13]

Technological innovation and capital accumulation stimulated the growth of the culture industry in the mid seventeenth century, and again in the early twentieth. Woodblock printing (which replaced movable type adopted from Korea) enabled cheaply reproducible calligraphic and technicolor flights of fancy in print media, and foreshadowed the media revolution (for example, sound recording, moving pictures, newspapers, mass magazines) of the early 1900s. Innovations in stage effects and puppetry heightened Edo era audience expectations for spectacle, just as the use of miniatures in war films (for example, *The War at Sea from Hawaii to Malaya*, 1942) and 1960s monster movies (*kaijū eiga*) set new industry standards for special effects. Edo period publishing houses and theater companies likewise prefigured modern record companies, movie studios, and production companies, establishing the practice of contracting major talent to crank out increasingly formulaic products. Through organized fan clubs, cross-promotions, and celebrity endorsements of products and fashions, early modern practices presaged modern marketing strategies that exploited reverence for celebrity. Some have argued that Japanese culture was ravaged by the modern capitalism of "ruthless European and American entrepreneurs,"[14] but cultural commodification was in fact a wholly indigenous development, making the modern mass culture revolution merely a continuation and intensification of processes set in motion during the Edo period.[15]

Political conditions favored concentrating the means of cultural production in a handful of companies and discouraging the rampant proliferation of independent voices. In the Edo period, theater proprietors vied for a limited number of official licenses to operate within the walled pleasure districts of Osaka, Kyoto, and Edo, a system that facilitated surveillance.[16] Censorship regimes established by the Tokugawa and modern imperial governments found it easier to monitor smaller numbers of producers, a proclivity most visible during World War II, when massive consolidation sharply reduced the number of recording companies, publishers, and movie studios. Censorship of political and sexual content was random and arbitrary, but its effect on cultural producers could be chilling if they did not exercise restraint. On the other hand, failure to deliver titillating goods to insatiable consumers could just as easily put them out of business.

Key to the development of commercial popular culture was the rise of consumer classes, newly empowered by literacy, surplus cash, and leisure time to partake of the blossoming market in cultural goods.[17] Literacy was encouraged among Edo period *chōnin* (urban commoners) as necessary for conducting business, and later among all Japanese as fundamental to the Meiji state's modernization project. Mass literacy enabled commoners to breach status barriers, gain access to elite culture, and prosper economically to the extent that a night at a teahouse, dance hall, or movie palace would not break the bank. Denied real political rights by the Tokugawa and modern imperial regimes, consumers nonetheless wielded some authority as customers of the culture industry. Decided in their likes and dislikes, consumers made clear what they found entertaining by doling out or withholding their cash. *Chōnin* were the "new arbiters of taste," who realized that "stories of their own antics and aberrations were as entertaining as any of the tales imported from China, or handed down in their own country."[18] Regarding kabuki, Shively contends, it was "good box office to electrify an audience with bold passages and parodies that spoke to the experience of the commoner."[19]

The introduction of profit motives, of course, fundamentally transformed artistic production and cultural behavior. Luminaries such as Ihara Saikaku and Chikamatsu Monzaemon were very prolific because much of their work was formulaic, heeding conventions for subject matter (that is, dissolute rakes and harlots, love suicides) that had already proven profitable. Commodification also clarified distinct relations of production and consumption, a trend perhaps most visible in *matsuri*. Although a participatory ethos remains strong within many communities, *matsuri* have become increasingly commercialized, secularized, truncated, and packaged for tourists and spectators. Not only *matsuri*, but "Japan" itself – "generically imagined and presented" – has become a consumable object, the consumption of which promises a (re)discovery of cultural "self."[20]

Commerce and culture remain inextricably entwined in contemporary Japanese life, and not merely in the sense of art's utility for advertising. Anne Allison, writing about comics, remarks on the productive utility of recreation: "*manga* are utilized as a diversionary and escapist 'play' that 'works' to relieve everyday tensions and thereby replenish a person's energy so that he or she can, for example, return to work."[21] By providing respites from the grinding work and study routines that characterize modern life, play and pop thus keep Japan's economic engines running. Interestingly, this logic, too, has precedent in the Edo period, when official sanction of pleasure quarters was based on the assumption that commoners required temporary release from the pressures of a tightly wound social structure. Only a prescient few imagined that such diversions would contribute to that structure's very doom: as Confucian scholar Dazai Shundai lamented in 1729, "our kabuki plays of today put on licentious and unrestrained matters which ... cater to vulgar sentiment. ... There is nothing worse than this in breaking down public morals."[22]

Aesthetics

In Japan, no less than in other traditionally stratified societies, theoretically clear aesthetic distinctions corresponded to social status. The dichotomy between *ga* (elegant) and *zoku* (vulgar) cultural forms not only reinforced distinctions between hereditary elites (courtiers and prominent warrior clans) and common people, but also denied the possibility of the comparable aesthetic worth of their respective expressive forms. Moreover, in premodern times elite culture required mastery of written language, whereas commoner culture was transmitted orally, an important contrast in East Asian societies in which literacy signified status. Although elite and non-elite forms alike often shared a religious basis, commoner culture was assumed to lack the refinement, restraint, and moral value of elite cultural forms such as *gagaku* (court music and dance), Chinese and vernacular poetry, or Buddhist iconography. Intent on instilling Confucian virtues or Buddhist spiritual truths, elite culture was further distinguished by its unabashed didacticism as well as its elegant simplicity, stylized melancholy (*sabi*), and affected rusticism (*wabi*).

Yet the distinction between *ga* and *zoku* began to cloud as early as medieval times, when shōgun Ashikaga Yoshimitsu patronized a *sarugaku* ("monkey music") theatrical troupe. Yoshimitsu's protégé Zeami refined *sarugaku*'s coarser attributes and in the process created the noh (*nō*), which would remain the exclusive province of warrior elites for the next four centuries. By purging *sarugaku* of its more "vulgar" tendencies, and seeking profundity (*yūgen*) in each movement and scripted line, Zeami aspired no less than to communicate esoteric truths and provoke Zen epiphanies. Nonetheless, here was an elite art with clear plebeian pedigree.

Further complicating matters was the penchant of Edo period playwrights, artists, musicians, and writers for plundering and inverting elite aesthetics. The ability to make allusions to classical literature, poetry, historical events, and myths (many of Chinese origin) had traditionally been the exclusive province of courtiers and warrior elites. But the producers of early modern pop ostentatiously dropped references to *The Tale of Genji* and continental culture into their plays, novels, and prints, a tendency that would have mattered little had there not been an increasingly literate and savvy audience to appreciate such erudite displays. Wealthy *chōnin* indeed prided themselves on their intertextual literacy, their ability to recognize or brandish allusions to the classical Sino-Japanese literary canon. Commoner and elite cultures also shared a preference for "commingled media,"[23] that is, adding poems to paintings, or setting literature to music.

However, within the pleasure quarters commoners developed their own aesthetic terminology – for example, *tsū* (connoisseurship), *sui* (elegance), or *iki* (refinement) – or shunned elite culture's esoterica, cultivated restraint, and elegiac sorrow in favor of the quotidian, lewd, obnoxious, and over-the-top. No less an authority than master playwright Chikamatsu, for whom common people in uncommon plights were favored subjects, insisted that "Art is something which lies in the slender margin between the real and the unreal."[24] Some artists, to whom Chikamatsu must have seemed priggish, positively venerated *zoku*, finding elegance in vulgarity. This was, in essence, what *iki* represented: the rendering of (unconsummated) erotic desire into aesthetic experience.[25] Most kabuki and jōruri dramas emphasized spectacle, acrobatics, swordplay, and virtuoso manipulation of puppets at the expense of literary quality. The "culture of play" of the late Edo period disregarded morality and the "Heavenly Way" (*tendō*) in favor of the "gargantuan joys of the flesh." "Bodily imagery in both verbal and illustrated texts signified a different kind of social reality with an inverted scale of priorities for the Edo townsmen. It was an order that had as its head the genitalia or anus and as its heart the stomach."[26]

The Meiji era importation of Western aesthetics was revolutionary, though its influence was uneven. Scholars have typically celebrated the arrival of naturalism in Japanese theater, visual art, and literature as indicative of "progress" toward more "realistic" renderings of the natural world. Donald Richie's work on film, for instance, assumes a dichotomy between traditional Japanese "mediation" or "presentation" (art is "rendered a particular reality by way of an authoritative voice") and Western "representation" ("in which one assumed the reality of what was being shown").[27] Meiji reformers did in fact disparage kabuki specifically for its fantastic scenarios and its stylized, deliberately unrealistic acting techniques,[28] and crafted new theatrical genres (*shinpa* and *shingeki*) to address these "defects." The confessional fiction genre known as the "I-novel" (*shishōsetsu*), too, was partially a concession to naturalist tastes. But newer work points out realist strains in pre-Meiji art – early experiments with linear perspective and ocular technologies, an obsession with material, social, and psychological detail – that make it difficult to argue that Japanese culture developed naturalist tendencies only under Western influence.[29]

Notwithstanding the undeniable aesthetic impact of the West, modern Japanese popular culture has clearly – and self-consciously – retained time-honored, native aesthetic principles. A fascinating example is the silent film narrator (*katsuben* or *benshi*), whose performances captivated movie audiences for the first three decades of the twentieth century. Genealogically linked to medieval bards, *etoki* and *gidayū* narrators, and *rakugo* storytellers, *katsuben* provided an authoritative mediating presence and a link to earlier narrative conventions at a time when Japanese film showings were hardly "autonomous" but rather "commingled" with live stage performances.[30] In later years, filmmakers as stylistically distinct as Ozu Yasujirō and Kurosawa Akira drew on native aesthetics, Ozu in his modest framings and elegiac moods, and Kurosawa in his adaptation of noh music and acting techniques in films such as *Throne of Blood* (1958). Ties to the past likewise remain a central aspect of contemporary sumō, which, in spite of many modern innovations that "genesis amnesia" has rendered invisible, exudes an aura of indisputably native traditionalism.[31]

Still, the aesthetics of modern Japanese popular culture suggest how globalized (or, some would say, homogenized) standards of popular taste have become. Most Japanese today are thoroughly desensitized to the charms of *wabi/sabi*, *iki*, or *yūgen*. Anyone approaching Godzilla or television programs such as, say, *Iron Chef* or *Crayon Shin-chan*, with the cardinal principles of classical Japanese aesthetics (suggestion, asymmetry, perishability, and simplicity) in mind risks disillusion.[32] Since the early twentieth century, imported entertainment (*hakurai geinō*) has largely dictated standards of popular taste, particularly in music and cinema. Surprisingly few Japanese have ever seen cinematic masterpieces by Kurosawa or Ozu, voicing a clear preference for the Hollywood product. Those with niche interests in jazz, reggae, hip hop, or so-called "ethnic" musics cherish the aura of exoticism and authenticity enshrined in imported records and fanzines straight from "the source" (*honba*). In the 1990s it was *tres chic* to purchase vintage Levi's jeans worn by "real Americans," suggesting that imported cultural goods still enjoy aesthetic cachet at the turn of the millennium.

Appropriation

Japan is often described as a "hybrid" culture: a memorable line from the 1991 documentary *The Japanese Version* asserts that borrowing from other cultures "is as Japanese as eating rice." A corollary cliche is that once Japanese appropriate a foreign cultural artifact, they domesticate it, or "make it Japanese" (whatever that means), without compromising their "national/cultural core." Iwabuchi Kōichi maintains that this sponge-like "Japanese capacity for cultural borrowing and appropriation does not simply articulate a process of hybridization in practice, but it is strategically represented as a key feature of Japanese national identity itself."[33]

Such depictions of nonchalant, "strategic" appropriation underestimate the tensions aroused in the process. Since the foreign origins of so much of what is known as "Japanese culture" are indisputable, two issues are always at stake: the "authenticity" of the appropriated artifact or cultural form;[34] and the integrity and clarity of Japanese cultural identity. Such trepidation may have been more acute in the modern era: the adoption of Portuguese pantaloons and the Okinawan *shamisen* seems to have generated considerably less controversy over national identity or authenticity in the sixteenth century than the importation of sleeveless dresses and the "lascivious" saxophone did in the twentieth. Nonetheless, the Confucian revival of the seventeenth and eighteenth centuries was essentially a quest for a more authentic Confucianism, to be procured through the study of original ancient texts rather than later commentaries, just as the "national learning" (*kokugaku*) movement was in part a reaction to this renewed influx of Chinese thought and culture, an attempt to identify and recover an indigenous cultural, spiritual, and moral heritage uncontaminated by foreign influence.

Kokugaku foreshadowed the modern *Nihonjinron* (theories of Japaneseness), which sought to recoup a national character allegedly menaced by Western modernity. In the realm of popular entertainment, perhaps no single medium better expresses discontent over Japanese hybridity than the *enka* song genre, whose principal message, in Yano's estimation, is "We long for our past Japanese selves." Indeed, among *enka* fans, flirtation with imported culture is depicted as a life stage, a youthful indiscretion: "Fans explain their turning to enka in terms of a musical taste that lay dormant, waiting only for their life experiences and, for some, a sense of their innate Japaneseness, to catch up to its lyrics and music."[35] Paradoxically, cultural appropriation had served Japan well as a strategy for *preserving* national sovereignty and integrity. Sinification of politics, music, religion, and art from the sixth through the eighth centuries was intended to earn the esteem of Tang China and thereby stave off a possible invasion. And the study and implementation of Mongol military tactics after the 1274 invasion helped repulse the second attempt in 1281. So, when the Western imperial powers came knocking in the mid nineteenth century, the new Meiji state had historical precedent for believing that a determined effort to study and replicate what they called "international standards" might achieve similar objectives. Popular diversions were not exempted from such attention.[36]

The effects of Meiji cultural reforms – which emphasized emulation of Western models in music, theater, literature, visual art, and architecture – were rapid and dramatic in some quarters, less so in others. Commoners not so well integrated into the modern age continued to enjoy their *yose* (variety shows), *rakugo*, and *misemono* (peep show) entertainments. And when the government tampered too much with their beloved kabuki, they simply created new variants (*taishū engeki*, popular theater) that retained the bawdy irreverence of old and still allowed cheering, jeering, and spontaneous disruptions of stage action. If "enlightenment" meant sitting quietly in one's seat, then enlightenment be damned.

The longstanding official contempt for popular entertainment now enjoyed a new rationale, based on "scientific" notions of progress, pragmatism, and "enlightenment," not to mention the prudery of Victorian era Western culture. Ury Eppstein argues that the practical utility of Western music, rather than its "artistic merits," intrigued Meiji leaders, some of whom apparently were within earshot of the military music emanating from British warships when they shelled Kagoshima in 1863. Besides its military applications, they believed that Western music could also have educational value for "character building, maintaining good order, and promoting clear enunciation and good reading ability."[37] The government also encouraged the proliferation of school *undōkai* (sports days) and the adoption of "manly" American and European sports such as baseball, rugby, fencing, gymnastics, and swimming, hoping to promote moral education, military efficacy, and modern lifestyles, and to offset the presumed physical inferiority of the Japanese.[38] The leaders were less enchanted, however, with Western-style political cartooning, with which dissenters ridiculed officials and their programs. Cartoonist Honda Kinkichirō satirized the Meiji milieu (and circumvented libel laws) with a "hybrid cartoon vocabulary" that "drew both on the cultural knowledge from the world into which he had been born and from the outside world that had impinged on it."[39]

In virtually all respects, including cultural policy, the Meiji transformation was a "revolution from above," no less than the ancient Taika Reforms had been. But with the technological revolution that produced modern mass media – sound recording, radio broadcasting, moving pictures, and print media – and the increasing integration of the world economy during the era of colonialism and World War I, cultural products from abroad literally poured into Japan, more or less directly into the laps of consumers, unfiltered and undiluted by elite intervention as in previous times. To be sure, censors prevented Japanese movie audiences from ever seeing Rudolph Valentino's lips touch those of his leading lady ("kissing movies" were not permitted until the American occupation, during which there was a veritable deluge), but nativists fretted over the direct influence he and other Hollywood screen idols exerted on the mating rituals of so-called "modern girls and boys" (*moga* and *mobo*). By the early 1900s, Japanese partook of a cosmopolitan smorgasbord of foreign literature and plays in translation, popular songs, sports, and films. After World War I, American entertainment and lifestyle eclipsed those from Europe, but opera (Italian or Beijing), French *chanson*, Argentine tango, American jazz, Hawaiian hula, Russian ballads, and Cuban rumba were all available for musical entertainment. Even "Arirang" – a folk song which for Koreans expressed indignation toward Japanese colonial rule – was a hit record in interwar Japan, in several recorded versions.

By the 1920s, then, Japan was fully integrated into a new globalized "community of taste": cultural appropriation was thoroughly routinized, an everyday occurrence, in which mass media empowered practically anyone to participate.[40] So firmly rooted were such voracious habits that wartime measures to cleanse Japan of foreign influences and "overcome modernity" (*kindai no chōkoku*) seem laughably naive in hindsight. Defeat, occupation, and close cold war ties with the United States only intensified the flow of cultural goods into Japan, creating a cultural "trade deficit" that only in very recent times is becoming more balanced due to the global popularity of Japanese anime (animation) and video games. Flows of cultural goods are indeed more complex today, as are Japanese reactions to them. Regarding film, Richie remarks, somewhat hyperbolically, "Whether something is traditionally Japanese or not is no longer a concern – no one can tell and no one cares. Tradition is not to be guarded. It is to be augmented as the riches of the rest of the world are assimilated."[41]

It is astounding to contemplate the reversals of the turn of the millennium: as Japan's economic influence has waned (a model of capitalist development to avoid rather than emulate), its prominence as an exporter of play has soared. Of course, Japanese culture has enjoyed global prominence for some time – consider late nineteenth-century *japonisme* and its influence on French Impressionism, karate and jūdō, or monster films from the 1950s and 1960s. But who could have predicted the current dominance of Japanese animated cartoons on American children's television, the Major League Baseball success of Nomo Hideo and Suzuki Ichirō, the prominence of Japanese "idol singers" and soap operas in Taiwan, Malaysia, and Thailand, the astounding reception of *Iron Chef* (*Ryōri no tetsujin*) and sumō wrestling on the Food Network and ESPN, respectively, or the popularity of manga cartooning styles and "character goods" (for example, Hello Kitty, Pokémon) among children in much of the developed world?

Iwabuchi argues that Japanese corporations, with tacit government support, export cultural products to "improve international understanding of Japan, particularly in Asian countries," hoping to "soothe – even suppress" bitter memories of Japanese colonial aggression.[42] Whether "pop culture diplomacy" can achieve Japanese objectives in Asia remains to be seen, but one result of Japan's export of cultural products is undeniable: an upsurge of general interest in Japan – including Japanese language – among American consumers of such products. My own classes, and those of my colleagues, overflow with anime, martial arts, and video game enthusiasts, for whom Japan represents not mimetic but creative genius. They favor anime's "thematic complexity" and disdain the "psychological comfort" and "satisfying resolutions" they find endemic in American popular culture.[43] Anime director Miyazaki Hayao thus deposes George Lucas in their pantheon of master storytellers.

Contestation

Popular culture discredits conventional notions of Japanese society as homogeneous and harmonious. In Japan popular culture provided a forum in which the state, the culture industry, and various constituent actors, representing every conceivable demographic, ideological, or regional affiliation, discoursed on weighty issues regarding citizenship, gender roles, identities, sexuality, social inequities, tradition, and modernity. Recent studies have moved away from notions of popular culture either as simply an imposition of hegemony from above (the Marxist/Frankfurt School take), or as a vehicle for resistance from below (the *minshūshi* take), and rather have embraced a more complex and flexible concept of popular culture as a public space in which a plethora of agendas, interests, and values compete.[44]

It goes without saying that the state, working through the culture industry, did attempt to exert hegemony via popular culture. This is evident in the Tokugawa government's designation of pleasure quarters as "evil places" (*akusho*), assigned to remote, swampy districts; in the modern imperial state's heavy-handed pre-production censorship regime, its severe taboos regarding media depictions of the imperial family, and its ubiquitous prescriptions for proper Japaneseness; even in the American occupation's doublespeak encouraging "free speech" while handing down "recommended" and "forbidden" subjects for film and press. Neither can we deny that popular culture functioned as the "hidden transcript" by which recalcitrant non-elites shrewdly articulated desires for personal liberation, social justice, and control of their own destinies.[45] This was certainly the case during the Freedom and People's Rights Movement (*jiyū minken undō*) of the late 1800s, when oratorical singers (*enkashi*) belted out protest songs on the streets, thereby circumventing censorship of publications and earning reputations as "singing street guerillas."[46]

But a simplistic domination–resistance polarity does no justice to popular culture's historical and sociological role. One complicating factor is the fact that, contrary to Marxist schematics, the respective interests of the state and the culture industry rarely coincided neatly, in part because of the very marketability of counter-hegemonic cultural practices and art forms. Moreover, to assume that people consumed cultural products under duress is to deny them rationality and agency, not to mention accountability, for their choices, tastes, and habits. This plays right into the hands of those who insist that ordinary Japanese were victims of their own government, bearing no responsibility whatsoever for aggressive militarism and colonial expansion. Lastly, there are numerous examples of a synergy of interests, in which the culture industry manufactured products that simultaneously satisfied popular tastes and served agendas of the state. Jennifer Robertson identifies one such confluence in the all-female Takarazuka troupe's staging of "colonialist revues" set in exotic Asian locales targeted for Japanese intervention. Another example is the proactive role jazz musicians took to create a new form of nationalistic popular music, rather than docilely mothball their horns under threat of a wartime ban.[47]

Chikamatsu's melodramatic *giri-ninjō* (duty versus emotion) tragedies illustrate that contestation need not entail direct confrontation: rather than explicitly assaulting Tokugawa social structures and moral codes, his stories circuitously address them by depicting the consequences for human happiness of living by such precepts. *Giri*'s inevitable triumph may have reinforced samurai hegemony, but its devastating effects were laid bare on stage for audiences to ponder. Likewise, it is difficult to imagine even hardcore technophiles leaving a screening of the animated film *Akira* unaffected by its dystopic imagery. Many acclaimed anime express ambivalent attitudes toward technology,[48] forcing the audience to reflect on the spiritual, social, and moral costs of the very technological overdevelopment that makes such sophisticated animation possible.

Popular culture raises disturbing questions about personal and group identities in a society many still consider sublimely homogeneous. For instance, the prevalence of Osaka dialect in *manzai* (comic dialogues) is a defiant assertion of localism in the face of Tokyo hegemony. Michael Ashkenazi argues that *matsuri*, too, as "one of the last culturally legitimate bastions of localism left," constitute a "local counterattack" against the capital's "tyranny." In the 1990s residents of Kyoto's low-rent Higashi-kujō district – including Korean-Japanese, disabled, and working-class folk – held a *madang* (Korean-style festival) exploiting their "neighborhood's notoriety to make a political point: democracy means difference."[49] "Against a state that celebrates genetic and cultural homogeneity," Caron writes, "and where democracy is conflated with a desire for uniform equality, this neighborhood festival celebrates difference as a form of democracy and espouses an open, inclusive public sphere."[50]

Gendered identities have been a durable fixation of Japanese popular culture. Canonical icons such as *onnagata* (female impersonators), which emerged as a necessary response to a government ban on female kabuki performers, and the Takarazuka Revue's *otokoyaku* (male impersonator) performed idealized representations of femininity and masculinity, respectively, but also made it possible to envisage gendered identities as fluid rather than tied to biological sex.[51] For women, Barbara Sato suggests, popular culture "created a new set of images by which they could better understand who they were, or at least who they might be." When Matsui Sumako took the stage as Nora in the 1911 production of Henrik Ibsen's *A Doll's House*, her electrifying performance stirred ongoing debates on women's roles as homemakers, mothers, autonomous economic actors, and public figures, a discussion that continued in the pages of *Seitō* (Bluestocking), a product of the print media explosion of the early 1900s.[52]

Indeed, popular culture empowers people to don or shed identities at will, even to contest the very boundaries of Japaneseness itself. John Russell's ethnography of the commodification and consumption of "blackness" concludes that many Japanese get dark tans, listen to African diasporic music, choose hip hop fashions, or pursue sexual encounters with people of African descent as acts of "resistance, self-discovery, and empowerment." As evident in an entire subgenre of explicit sexual fiction, in black-face burlesque, and club nightlife, indulgence in black culture and mingling in the most intimate ways with black people become ways of transcending the limits of the "homogeneous nation" (*tan'itsu minzoku*): "Consumption of the black body and its essence liberates one's full potential, one's 'true self'."[53] Russell's study indicates that a "consuming passion" for blackness reflects profound discontent about Japanese national, ethnic, and gendered identities, an insight that might elude us in the absence of sophisticated scholarship on popular culture.

Conclusion

Scholarship on Japanese popular culture is growing in quality and quantity. The historiography of the Edo period demi-monde is more voluminous than that of modern pop, but until recently has lagged behind in theoretical development, as it has traditionally been concerned more with artistic techniques and aesthetics than with social issues or political economy. Most early work on Edo period pop delighted in pointing out aspects that indicated a peculiarly Japanese genius, rather than situating it within a more comparative theoretical framework of popular (or mass) culture. However, in preparing lessons on early modern popular culture, I am continually struck by how Edo period patterns of cultural commodification, production, and consumption portend what happens in the twentieth century. Future studies may indeed highlight continuities transcending the chronological boundary between early modern and modern, as I have attempted to do here. In recent decades historians of Japan have increasingly emphasized continuities that transcend the "watershed" moments or "turning points" usually used to make sense of Japanese history, such as the unification of the country, the Meiji Restoration, or the American occupation. Such conceptions have been instructive regarding Japan's political, social, and economic orders, but we may be similarly enlightened by a view of popular culture in the *longue durée*. Moreover, from a global perspective, we may be surprised how prescient the purveyors of pop in early modern Japan were regarding the development and marketing of mass popular culture.

The most promising trend in the study of Japanese popular culture has been the increased willingness to take it seriously as an object of historical investigation, to go beyond the connoisseur's fixation with aesthetics, and to integrate it into broader areas of social and ideological inquiry. Specifically, recent studies highlight the engagement of interwar and wartime popular entertainment with colonial, fascist, nationalist, and gendered ideologies, challenging previous notions of pop culture as a vehicle for escape from the earth-shattering events of Japan's mid twentieth century. We are developing an appreciation for the ways that popular culture helped shape Japan's modern history and the behavior and consciousness of the Japanese people, how it facilitated exchange on contentious issues within Japanese society, and the role it has played in Japan's interactions with the outside world. Popular culture is ignored now only at great peril to the historian's comprehensive understanding of the Japanese experience

NOTES

1 Gluck, "The People in History," pp. 34, 38–40; Walthall, "Peripheries," p. 372.
2 Dwight MacDonald, "A Theory of Mass Culture," in Rosenberg and White, eds., *Mass Culture*, p. 62. Quotation from José Ortega y Gasset, "The Coming of the Masses," in Rosenberg and White, eds., *Mass Culture*, p. 45.
3 Gramsci, *Selections from the Prison Notebooks*, p. 161. See also Strinati, *An Introduction to Theories of Popular Culture*, pp. 165–71
4 Strinati, *An Introduction to Theories of Popular Culture*, p. 226.
5 Nakano, "The Role of Traditional Aesthetics," pp. 130–1; Shively, "Popular Culture," p. 708.
6 Strinati, *An Introduction to Theories of Popular Culture*, p. 80.
7 Levine, "The Folklore of Industrial Society," p. 1373.
8 Lears, "Making Fun," pp. 1422–3 (emphasis added).
9 Gramsci, *Selections from the Prison Notebooks*. See also Storey, *Cultural Studies*, pp. 4–5.
10 Walthall, "Peripheries," p. 386.
11 Benjamin, "The Work of Art," pp. 221–2, 241.
12 Thompson and Harootunian, *Undercurrents*, p. 10; Donald Shively, "The Social Environment of Tokugawa Kabuki," in Hume, ed., *Japanese Aesthetics*, p. 218.
13 Walthall, "Peripheries," p. 382. See also Nishiyama, *Edo Culture*, pp. 95–112.
14 Nishiyama, *Edo Culture*, p. 247.
15 Weisenfeld, *Mavo*, p. 167.
16 Seigle, *Yoshiwara*, p. 22.
17 Shively, "Popular Culture," pp. 706–8, 715–33.
18 Hibbett, *The Floating World*, pp. 36, 35.
19 Shively, "The Social Environment of Tokugawa Kabuki," p. 194.
20 Ashkenazi, *Matsuri*, p. 140. Quotation from Ivy, *Discourses of the Vanishing*, pp. 35, 41.
21 Allison, *Permitted and Prohibited Desires*, p. 74. On the engagement between avant-garde art and commercial culture in the early 1900s, see Weisenfeld, *Mavo*, pp. 165–215.

22 Shively, "The Social Environment of Tokugawa Kabuki," pp. 195–6, 197.
23 Anderson, "Spoken Silents," pp. 262–5. Quotation from Hibbett, *The Floating World*, p. 65.
24 Chikamatsu quoted in Wm. Theodore de Bary, ed., "The Vocabulary of Japanese Aesthetics I, II, III," in Hume, ed., *Japanese Aesthetics*, p. 74.
25 Nakano, "The Role of Traditional Aesthetics," p. 129; Nishiyama, *Edo Culture*, p. 56.
26 Thompson and Harootunian, *Undercurrents*, p. 27.
27 Richie, *A Hundred Years of Japanese Film*, pp. 25–6.
28 See Yuichirō Takahashi, "*Kabuki* Goes Official: The 1878 Opening of the Shintomi-za," in Leiter, ed., *A Kabuki Reader*, pp. 140–2.
29 See Screech, *The Lens within the Heart*; Thompson and Harootunian, *Undercurrents*, pp. 27–8.
30 Anderson, "Spoken Silents," p. 270.
31 Guttman and Thompson, *Japanese Sports*, pp. 142–5.
32 See Donald Keene, "Japanese Aesthetics," in Hume, ed., *Japanese Aesthetics*, pp. 27–41.
33 Iwabuchi, *Recentering Globalization*, p. 53. See also Russell, "Consuming Passions," p. 144.
34 See, for instance, Atkins, *Blue Nippon*, pp. 19–43.
35 Yano, *Tears of Longing*, pp. 178, 6.
36 Takahashi, "*Kabuki* Goes Official," pp. 140–2.
37 Eppstein, "Musical Instruction," pp. 1, 4.
38 Guttman and Thompson, *Japanese Sports*, pp. 68–95.
39 Duus, "The *Marumaru Chinbun*," pp. 50–4.
40 Atkins, *Blue Nippon*, pp. 90–1.
41 Richie, *A Hundred Years of Japanese Film*, p. 217.
42 Iwabuchi, *Recentering Globalization*, p. 75.
43 Napier, *Anime*, pp. 256, 251.
44 See Silverberg, "Constructing a New Cultural History," p. 116; and Robertson, *Takarazuka*, p. 37.
45 Scott, *Domination*, pp. 2–4.
46 Yano, *Tears of Longing*, p. 31.
47 Robertson, *Takarazuka*, pp. 89–138; Atkins, *Blue Nippon*, pp. 132–9, 152–9.
48 Napier, *Anime*, pp. 86–9.
49 Ashkenazi, *Matsuri*, p. 133.
50 Caron, "On the Downside," pp. 433–4.
51 Donald Shively, "*Bakufu* versus *Kabuki*," in Leiter, ed., *A Kabuki Reader*, pp. 36–7; Samuel Leiter, "From Gay to *Gei*: The *Onnagata* and the Creation of *Kabuki*'s Female Characters," in Leiter, ed., *A Kabuki Reader*, pp. 211–29; Robertson, *Takarazuka*, p. 40.
52 Sato, *The New Japanese Woman*, pp. 19, 14–15.
53 Russell, "Consuming Passions," p. 135.

BIBLIOGRAPHY

Allison, Anne. *Permitted and Prohibited Desires: Mothers, Comics, and Censorship in Japan.* Berkeley: University of California Press, 2000.
Anderson, J. L. "Spoken Silents in the Japanese Cinema; or, Talking to Pictures: Essaying the *Katsuben*, Contexturalizing the Texts." In Arthur Noletti, Jr. and David Desser, eds., *Reframing Japanese Cinema.* Bloomington: Indiana University Press, 1992.
Ashkenazi, Michael. *Matsuri: Festivals of a Japanese Town.* Honolulu: University of Hawai'i Press, 1993.

Atkins, E. Taylor. *Blue Nippon: Authenticating Jazz in Japan*. Durham, NC: Duke University Press, 2001.

Benjamin, Walter. "The Work of Art in the Age of Mechanical Reproduction." In Hannah Arendt, ed., *Illuminations*. New York: Harcourt, Brace, and World, 1968.

Caron, Bruce. "On the Downside of Japan's Old Capital: Higashi-kujo." *Public Culture* 11:3 (Fall 1999): 433–40.

Duus, Peter. "The *Marumaru Chinbun* and the Origins of the Japanese Political Cartoon." *International Journal of Comic Art* 1:1 (1999): 42–56.

Eppstein, Ury. "Musical Instruction in Meiji Japan: A Study of Adaptation and Assimilation." *Monumenta Nipponica* 40:1 (Spring 1985): 1–37.

Gluck, Carol. "The People in History: Recent Trends in Japanese Historiography." *Journal of Asian Studies* 38 (Nov. 1978): 25–50.

Gramsci, Antonio. *Selections from the Prison Notebooks*. London: Lawrence and Wishart, 1971.

Guttmann, Allen, and Thompson, Lee. *Japanese Sports: A History*. Honolulu: University of Hawai'i Press, 2001.

Hibbett, Howard. *The Floating World in Japanese Fiction*. Rutland, Vt.: C. E. Tuttle, 1959.

Hume, Nancy, ed. *Japanese Aesthetics and Culture: A Reader*. Albany: State University of New York Press, 1995.

Ivy, Marilyn. *Discourses of the Vanishing: Modernity, Phantasm, Japan*. Chicago: University of Chicago Press, 1995.

Iwabuchi Kōichi. *Recentering Globalization: Popular Culture and Japanese Transnationalism*. Durham, NC: Duke University Press, 2002.

Kasza, Gregory. *The State and the Mass Media in Japan, 1918–1945*. Berkeley: University of California Press, 1988.

Lears, T. J. Jackson. "Making Fun of Popular Culture." *American Historical Review* (Dec. 1992): 1417–30.

Leiter, Samuel, ed. *A Kabuki Reader*. Armonk, NY: M. E. Sharpe, 2002.

Levine, Lawrence. "The Folklore of Industrial Society: Popular Culture and Its Audiences." *American Historical Review* (Dec. 1992): 1369–99.

Nakano Mitsutoshi, "The Role of Traditional Aesthetics." In C. Andrew Gerstle, ed., *Eighteenth Century Japan: Culture and Society*. Richmond, UK: Curzon, 1989.

Napier, Susan. *Anime from* Akira *to* Princess Mononoke. New York: Palgrave Macmillan, 2000.

Nishiyama Matsunosuke. *Edo Culture: Daily Life and Diversions in Urban Japan*. Honolulu: University of Hawai'i Press, 1997.

Richie, Donald. *A Hundred Years of Japanese Film*. Tokyo: Kōdansha, 2001.

Robertson, Jennifer. *Takarazuka: Sexual Politics and Popular Culture in Modern Japan*. Berkeley: University of California Press, 1998.

Rosenberg, Bernard, and White, David Manning, eds. *Mass Culture: The Popular Arts in America*. New York: Free Press, 1957.

Russell, John. "Consuming Passions: Spectacle, Self-Transformation, and the Commodification of Blackness in Japan." *positions* 6:1 (1998): 113–77.

Sato, Barbara. *The New Japanese Woman: Modernity, Media, and Women in Interwar Japan*. Durham, NC: Duke University Press, 2003.

Scott, James. *Domination and the Arts of Resistance*. New Haven: Yale University Press, 1990.

Screech, Timon. *The Lens within the Heart: The Western Scientific Gaze and Popular Imagery in Later Edo Japan*. Honolulu: University of Hawai'i Press, 2002.

Seigle, Cecilia Segawa. *Yoshiwara: The Glittering World of the Japanese Courtesan*. Honolulu: University of Hawai'i Press, 1993.

Shively, Donald. "Popular Culture." In John Whitney Hall, ed., *The Cambridge History of Japan*, vol. 4, *Early Modern Japan*. Cambridge: Cambridge University Press, 1991.

Silverberg, Miriam. "Constructing a New Cultural History of Prewar Japan." In Masao Miyoshi and H. D. Harootunian, eds., *Japan in the World*. Durham, NC: Duke University Press, 1993.

Storey, John. *Cultural Studies and the Study of Popular Culture*, 2nd edn. Athens: University of Georgia Press, 2003.

Strinati, Dominic. *An Introduction to Theories of Popular Culture*. London: Routledge, 1995.

Thompson, Sarah, and Harootunian, H. D. *Undercurrents in the Floating World: Censorship and Japanese Prints*. New York: Asia Society Galleries, 1991.

Walthall, Anne. "Peripheries: Rural Culture in Tokugawa Japan." *Monumenta Nipponica* 39:4 (Winter 1984): 371–92.

Weisenfeld, Gennifer. *Mavo: Japanese Artists and the Avant-Garde 1905–1931*. Berkeley: University of California Press, 2002.

Yano, Christine. *Tears of Longing: Nostalgia and the Nation in Japanese Popular Song*. Cambridge, Mass.: Harvard University Asia Center, 2002.

FURTHER READING

Paul Varley's *Japanese Culture*, 4th edn. (Honolulu: University of Hawai'i Press, 2000), provides an overview emphasizing arts and culture. Numerous recent collections focus on modern and contemporary pop: Richard Powers and Hidetoshi Katō's *Handbook of Japanese Popular Culture* (New York: Greenwood, 1989); Joseph Tobin's *Re-made in Japan* (New Haven: Yale University Press, 1992); Lise Skov and Brian Moeran's *Women, Media and Consumption in Japan* (Honolulu: University of Hawai'i Press, 1995); John Treat's *Contemporary Japan and Popular Culture* (Honolulu: University of Hawai'i Press, 1996); Mark Schilling's *Encyclopedia of Japanese Pop Culture* (New York: Weatherhill, 1997); Sepp Linhart and Sabine Frühstück's *The Culture of Japan as Seen through Its Leisure* (Albany: State University of New York Press, 1998); D. P. Martinez's *The Worlds of Japanese Popular Culture* (Cambridge: Cambridge University Press, 1998); Timothy Craig's *Japan Pop!* (Armonk, NY: M. E. Sharpe, 2000); and Douglas Slaymaker's *A Century of Popular Culture in Japan* (Lewiston, Me.: Edwin Mellen, 2000). Recent studies emphasizing gender and sexuality include: Timon Screech, *Sex and the Floating World: Erotic Images in Japan, 1700–1820* (Honolulu: University of Hawai'i Press, 1999); Joshua Mostow et al., eds., *Gender and Power in the Japanese Visual Field* (Honolulu: University of Hawai'i Press, 2003); and Phyllis Birnbaum's *Modern Girls, Shining Stars, the Skies of Tokyo* (New York: Columbia University Press, 1999).

CHAPTER TWENTY-SEVEN

Rural Japan and Agriculture

Eric C. Rath

A Functionalist Definition of Rural Japan

The "rural" regions of Japan can be defined as those areas that are less populated and developed, where the chief occupations are in agriculture or forestry, and where these livelihoods and the environment encourage the inhabitants to live cohesively with one another and with nature.[1] This definition of the rural can be called "functionalist" for its focus on land use, settlement patterns, and employment.[2] The city, with its denser populations, more intensive economic and industrial development, blue and white collar workforces, and landscape of buildings and pavement, is the point of comparison for defining the rural according to a functionalist definition. This difference can be viewed spatially, as when one travels out of the city and into the countryside. It can also be thought of as a historical progression in which the characteristics of cities are viewed as advanced while the underdeveloped countryside lags behind. Viewed from the perspective of population density, Japan can be said to have transformed from a rural to an urban country within the last seventy years. By 1990, 70 percent of the population lived in cities inhabited by at least 50,000 people.[3]

A functionalist definition of the rural has been employed to conjecture about the thinking of people living in the countryside. The historians Edwin Reischauer and Albert Craig once called this the "cake of custom," meaning the cluster of "premodern" social, political, and ethical practices that fostered harmonious behavior in Japanese villages.[4] A Japanese rural sociologist wrote in a similar vein that "the typical farmer was a man capable of being content with his lot and of integrating himself harmoniously in the group."[5] These scholars share the view that agrarian values have faded over the course of the twentieth century, especially after World War II. Historians such as Nagahara Keiji and Nagakura Tamotsu have looked back to the late nineteenth century as marking the beginning of the decline in the "organic quality of village life" with the rise of commercial farming and an increased discrepancy in wealth, landownership, and access to resources within the agrarian class.[6]

One could go much further back in history to find observations of a difference between the city and countryside. Poems in the eighth-century *Manyōshū* (Collection of Myriad Leaves), which date from shortly after cities first appeared in Japan, mention the "countryside" (*inaka*), a term meaning "rural area" in modern Japanese. In the eighth century, however, the word *inaka* referred to the five provinces of Yamato, Settsu, Kawachi, Yamashiro, and Izumi, the areas outlying the capitals of Nara and Kyoto. These five provinces were literally "within the capital [region]" (Kinai), forming a buffer against the remote "hinterlands" (*hina*) inhabited by the "uncivilized barbarians of the East" (*Kantō no ebisu*). In later centuries, as the culture and power of the capital region spread, the areas considered native *inaka* widened while the borders of the hinterlands were pushed further away. Thirteenth-century commentaries on the *Manyōshū* gloss the term *inaka* to mean not just the provinces around Kyoto, but also former "hinterlands" of the east.[7]

The word *inaka* became a more general term for rural area by the early modern period, reflecting the growth of cities such as Edo and Osaka and the urbanization of castle towns like Kanazawa. Before 1600, only Kyoto could be rightly called a city with its population around 100,000 without rival in Japan. However, by late 1700 as much as 7 percent of Japan's population lived in a city, compared to only 2 percent of Europe.[8] Kyoto and Osaka surpassed a population of 300,000 and 500,000 respectively, while the population of Edo grew to one million, making it the largest city in the world. Urbanization in Japan from the seventeenth century occurred at a more rapid rate than elsewhere in the world, a trend that continued in the twentieth century.[9]

In the early modern period, cities gave rise to businesses, industries, and a vibrant urban culture described elsewhere in this volume, but further differences between the city and countryside were the result of government policies. Cities were under the direct administration of the Tokugawa warrior government (bakufu). In both the bakufu's territories and the daimyō's domains, rule was delegated to commoners at the local level in both urban and rural areas but urban magistrates (*machi bugyō*) oversaw the affairs of merchants and craftsmen in cities, and rural magistrates (*kōri bugyō*) did the same for villages and peasants. Sumptuary laws (*ken'yakurei*) characterized the bakufu's efforts to maintain the differences between these two populations and the most onerous of these were borne by the rural farmers. As a legacy of Toyotomi Hideyoshi's "sword hunt" of 1588, peasants were deprived of the ownership of weapons. They were also denied the use of surnames and silk clothing which were the prerogative of the samurai. In 1642 a bakufu edict stated that peasants should not eat polished rice as their staple food. Peasants grew rice for tribute payments (*nengu*) to the bakufu or daimyō, but were supposed to eat other grains like barley, millet, and barnyard millet (*hie*) instead of white rice. The same edict stated that peasants could not make or purchase foodstuffs that were readily available in cities, like wheat noodles and tofu. Finally, peasants could not use the rice they grew to brew alcohol, nor could they travel to towns and cities to buy sake.[10] Though sumptuary laws were often ignored and wealthier peasants did consume more elite fare, the distinction between city-dwellers eating polished white rice, which lacked vitamin B1, and peasants eating healthier brown rice mixed with other grains seems to have been reflected in the term for beriberi, a disease caused by B1 deficiency: beriberi earned the name "Edo sickness" (*Edo yamai*), a disease that could be "cured" by a trip to the countryside, where highly polished rice was not consumed. City-dwellers who could afford it ate rice three times daily, as was the custom in Kyoto by the sixteenth century, but two meals remained the custom in rural areas until the end of the seventeenth century.[11] By the eighteenth century, most city-dwellers flavored their foods with soy sauce, while people in rural areas used miso for seasoning until the twentieth century.[12]

Notwithstanding these differences in lifestyle, the rift between the countryside and city became most acutely perceived in the early twentieth century as a result of Japan's rapid urbanization which occurred at a rate unrivaled in other parts of the world. The population of Tokyo, for instance, grew from 1.48 million in 1905 to over two million by 1930, while the urbanization of the areas surrounding the capital was more remarkable with the eighty-two villages and towns near Tokyo growing in population from 420,000 to 2.9 million in the same period. Nationwide, the number of settlements with over 10,000 people grew from 18 to 32 percent between 1898 and 1920, while the population in Japan's six largest cities doubled. Most of this urbanization was privately undertaken without the benefit of close government control, leading to problems associated with urban sprawl.[13]

Given these circumstances, it is understandable that the worst effects of urbanization would have been on the minds of contemporary observers who formulated a functionalist definition of rural Japan. Rural Japan became a topic of scholarly inquiry in the 1920s and 1930s when Japanese academics witnessed the rapid disappearance of agricultural communities and rural patterns of living in the wake of rapid urbanization in areas surrounding Tokyo and other major cities. The rural became a site where geographers, historians, economists, agricultural specialists, and folklorists sought to map the impact of cities on "suburban villages" (*kōson*), a neologism coined in 1915.[14] Scholars measured this impact in terms of the disappearance of "rural" characteristics due to urbanization. By transposing the teleology of modernization onto geography and then conflating places with certain attributes, scholars created a definition of rural Japan as backward, traditional, and the antithesis of the modern city. This view was later confirmed with references to Marx and Max Weber.

One step in the crystallization of the Japanese concept of the rural was the formation of the Society for Rural Studies (Kyōdokai) in 1910 by Nitobe Inazo, famous for introducing the word "bushidō" to the West, and Yanagita Kunio, the father of Japanese folklore studies. Yanagita received his higher education in agropolitics from Tokyo Imperial University in 1900 and worked briefly for the Ministry of Agriculture and Commerce before quitting to become a reporter and to pursue research on folklore. The aim of their society was to understand the problems facing rural Japan, such as the impoverishment of the rural economy, conflicts between tenant farmers and landowners, and the disappearance of farmlands. According to these scholars, such problems were most acute in villages near cities, where, "land prices were high, independent cultivators sold their land to tenant farmers, labor supplies were inadequate and paddy fields were being converted to dry fields."[15]

Yanagita expressed great concern for the plight of farmers in his 1929 study *Toshi to nōson* (City and Countryside). As he implied by the title, Yanagita affirmed that the rural and the urban needed to be defined in relationship to one another. This paradigm has remained a pivot point in both urban and rural studies in Japan.[16] For Yanagita, the life of rural areas might be less developed in material ways, but it was rich in moral content. The cities, in contrast, lacked the ethos of the "traditional" village and were a "desert of human emotions," as he stated in *Toshi to nōson*. He warned that the one-sided, extractive economic linkage between cities that consumed and the rural areas that produced was akin to a master–slave relationship. He feared that the attraction to the luxuries of urban life would not only lead to a decline in the moral character of the countryside, but also produce a society where people forget how to produce and can only consume. According to Minoru Kawada, Yanagita's subsequent ethnographic research on Japanese folkways grew from his "need to solve . . . the growing social and economic tension in the urban–rural relationship."[17]

The perceived loss of rural space and ways of life in the wake of urbanization became a political agenda in the bureaucratic and popular agrarianism (*nōhonshugi*) which emerged in the 1870s and reached a culmination by the 1930s. Agrarianism has been defined by Thomas Havens as a "conviction that agriculture was crucial for creating a stable, harmonious Japan." One of the most vociferous advocates for agrarianism was Yokoi Tokiyoshi (d. 1927), professor of agriculture at Tokyo Nōka Daigaku, who coined the term. Yokoi viewed farmers as the gatekeepers of moral values who were exploited by a government which sought to promote industry at the expense of agriculture.[18] Yokoi advocated government intervention to raise rice prices and to protect agriculture and the domestic situation for farmers. Though many agrarianists took issue with government farm policies, the agrarian movement eagerly supported ultranationalism in the 1930s, and as a result of this close association it disappeared after World War II.

Reconsidering "Rural Japan"

While the view of rural Japan considered thus far seems natural and corresponds with both governmental and scholarly conceptualizations of the landscape and populations outside of cities, the functionalist definition has recently been criticized by scholars within and outside of the field of Japanese studies. Noting the surprising prevalence of farming in major cities including Tokyo, the geographer Gil Latz has written that the terms "rural" and "urban" need reassessment when used to refer to population density, employment, and land use in Japan.[19] The economist Kawamura Yoshio has criticized the simplistic bifurcation of the modern, economically advanced city and the more socially organic but backward village.[20] Moreover, prominent Japanese historians such as Amino Yoshihiko have recently emphasized the role of non-agricultural populations and of regional differences in medieval Japanese history in an effort to challenge the idea that life outside of Japan's urban centers was homogeneous. Others have criticized folklorists and ethnologists, including Yanagita Kunio, for their efforts to locate the heart of Japanese culture in the rural hinterland.[21] Indeed, it is the attempt to draw conclusions about the mentality of farmers, who until recently constituted 80 percent of the population, that is perhaps most troubling about the functionalist approach. In a critique of several studies of peasant and tenant movements in early modern and modern Japan, Roger Bowen noted: "Japanologists . . . make the Japanese agrarian narrow and hence comprehensible." Bowen concludes that such "generalizations about nationwide peasant behavior lead to over reliance either on ideological formations or on anecdotal material."[22]

Consequently, it seems that the word "rural" needs to be used with discretion by historians, and requires qualification. Marc Mormont's observations about the history of rural sociology in Belgium seem applicable to Japan. He writes, "in preindustrial society there is no rural identity" in the modern sense of the term, that is, as an alternative to modern city life where harmonious ethical values endured for a people whose livelihood kept them closely tied to the land.[23] Rather than taking the rural as a given, historians of Japan might consider how people in "rural" areas themselves distinguish between the rural and the urban in their personal lives and economic, social, religious, and political relations. This approach would show how fluid and politically charged terms such as "rural" and "urban" are while determining what these concepts meant for people in different settings historically.

Agricultural Technology and Village Life in the Early Modern Period

In the early modern period, rice served as a unit of currency, tribute payment (*nengu*), and the salary for officials. This made paddy agriculture an income-generating device for the bakufu and daimyō, and they invested in its development by promoting land reclamation and by sponsoring the creation of canals and waterways for irrigation. The geographer Gil Latz estimated that over 70 percent of irrigation facilities used in 1960s were established in the Tokugawa period.[24] This contributed to the doubling in the size of the arable land from 1550 to 1650. To determine the amount of tribute they could collect, domainal or bakufu officials surveyed village lands and calculated the level of productivity measured in *koku* (44.8 gallons). Tribute payments were often as high as 50 percent of the yield. However, mistakes in tribute assessment usually favored the cultivator.[25] Officials also taxed peasants with duties such as on the handicraft goods they produced and required that they perform corvée labor. While these duties may not have amounted to much for most peasants, corvée was particularly onerous for peasants who lived along the major roads and provided bearers and horses.

The government's unit for tribute collection was the village (*mura*) although only the "titled peasants" (*honbyakushō*), the wealthiest landowners who claimed descent from the village's founders, were registered in the cadastral surveys as taxpayers. Among these *honbyakushō* were the village headman (*shōdai*) and other officials who decided how the tribute payment would be divided among all of the village's members. Payment was the joint responsibility of "five member groups" (*goningumi*) who were also mutually liable for one another's legal behavior. Other groups such as the young men's association (*wakamonogumi*) took charge of policing duties, fire protection, and village celebrations. In this manner, villages were self-administering. Villagers wrote legal codes, tried and punished wrongdoers, sometimes imposing the most severe penalty of ostracism (*mura hachibu*).

Not all of the members of the village were titled, but they were linked to the *honbyakushō* as servants or as recipients of their patronage. Since peasants practiced unigeniture, only one person might inherit a household, but second sons might create a branch household (*kadoya*) or they might continue to farm the lands of the main household while living in a separate building. Titled peasants might augment their household labor force by purchasing lifelong servants (*fudai*) or by employing bond servants (*genin*) who came from the ranks of the village's landless and poor.

Having to pay half of their assumed yield as tribute made for desperate situations in lean years when villagers did not produce the predetermined amount. Famines, of which there were twenty major ones, poor harvests, and other catastrophes

occasionally prompted peasants to resort to petition to domainal and bakufu authorities for relief. If their pleas for justice were unheeded, they could turn to illegal forms of
protest, running riot, absconding, or striking out against authority. In some instances,
for example one in Chōshū domain in 1831, the size of these protests reached
100,000. However, peasants never considered attempting to overthrow the Tokugawa
regime and took little part in the Meiji Restoration. Though the authorities occasionally capitulated to peasants' demands, in the aftermath of these protests the ringleaders
were invariably rounded up and put to death, usually in cruel ways. Nevertheless, there
is considerable debate among historians over how peasants fared in bad and good years.
Taking a long view of their situation, we can say that peasants probably did better in the
latter part of the period than at the beginning if only because levels of production
increased and the warrior hegemons did not usually raise tribute rates to reflect this,
allowing villagers to keep the surplus.

Production increased through the use of fertilizers such as ash, pond mud, and
sardines. Improvements in farming techniques and plant species contributed to
increased yields and double cropping became widely practiced if these conditions
were met. Only 10 percent of peasants could afford to own draft animals like oxen to
plow their fields.[26] The laborious work of preparing the earth for planting was done
by hand using a hoe with a long blade. Farmers could learn about new strains of rice
and farming techniques from agricultural manuals (nōsho), the first of which was
Miyazaki Antei's Nōgyō zensho (The Complete Text on Agriculture), published in
1697.[27] Farm manuals described methods for pest control such as the application of
ash from persimmon trees against aphids infesting daikon.[28] Land reclamation continued but at a slower pace from the late seventeenth century. Nonetheless, when the
new Meiji government first surveyed the country, it discovered large tracts of lands
not on the tax rolls.

The peasants best able to reap benefits from advances in agriculture were ones near
the large cities of Kyoto, Osaka, and Edo who had access to and could afford to buy
commercial fertilizers like sardines and night soil. In addition to paddy which was
dedicated to rice for tribute, peasants maintained upland fields for vegetables and
grains like wheat and barley for personal consumption. However, farmers near cities
could concentrate on raising vegetables for cash crops since they could readily sell
these to townspeople and had easy access to night soil for fertilizer. These conditions
allowed "urban" farmers living in and near cities to grow a wide variety of vegetables
in two or three croppings yearly. Farmers in Kyoto and other cities used night soil
which provided an excellent fertilizer for growing large amounts of vegetables,
enabling them to raise produce for commercial sale, something their rural counterparts could not emulate. By the mid seventeenth century, farmers near Osaka and
Kyoto were growing other goods commercially including cotton, rape seed for lamp
oil, tea, indigo, hemp, and safflower. Commercial farming spread to the other
provinces in the Kinai area by 1770 and to the Kantō region by the second decade
of the nineteenth century. Due to local conditions, certain regions could specialize in
particular cash crops such as mulberry for silk larvae in central Honshū, cotton in the
Kinai, and sugar cane in southern Kyūshū.[29] In select villages in western Japan, 70
percent of farm acreage was dedicated to cotton production.[30]

Historians can know details of peasant life such as economic status and demographic trends from registers (shūmon ninbetsu aratamechō) that were prepared

annually by villagers. These provide names, ages, household, and information about property such as animals and landholdings. Interpreting such data has allowed historians to conclude that peasants limited the number of children they had to stem population growth and maintain a more stable existence. They limited family size by allowing only the successor to the household to marry, having other children adopted out, permitting only farmers with sufficient income to marry, regulating the age of marriage, and practicing abortion and sometimes even infanticide.[31] Yet, divorces occurred, and childless widows remarried, although widows with children usually did not remarry except into the husband's family.[32] Life expectancy for peasants was about 40 for men and women, which was comparable to the West in the nineteenth century.[33]

The unit for agricultural production in the Tokugawa period was the family, but the size and form of the family unit evolved during the period. Thomas Smith's study *The Agrarian Origins of Modern Japan* delineates this shift from extended family households of approximately twenty members to the smaller nuclear family of five to eight members. Smith's reasoning for this change was that nuclear families adapted better to technological changes and commercial farming which required intensive cultivation. Small farms fared better due to the development of technical expertise which facilitated increases in production on smaller plots of land. This pattern began in the southwest areas, which were engaged in commercial farming operations, before spreading to the rest of Japan in the eighteenth century.

Commercialization of the farm economy was accompanied by the spread of tenant farming as titled peasants divested themselves of parts of their large holdings. Despite the fact that the bakufu prohibited the buying and selling of land in 1643, farmers skirted this law by leasing land for life. Tenant farmers, the so-called "water-drinking peasants" (*mizunomibyakushō*) who rented lands from titled peasants, usually depended on their landlords for tools, housing, and access to the commons. In return, tenants paid their rent in labor or in kind. Wealthy landlords might invest in rural industries like soy sauce brewing or enjoy polite pursuits and entertaining, but these were out of reach of the poorer members of the village who engaged in by-employments in order to survive. An increase in intra-village conflicts between poor and wealthy peasants in the second half of the Edo period has gained the attention of historians.

Agriculture, Farmers, and Modernization

In the Meiji period, the technology of agriculture did not see a dramatic break from that of the early modern period. Instead, pre-existing methods associated with commercial farming spread more widely. New varieties of rice were developed which had higher yields but at the cost of the need for greater application of fertilizer and deeper plowing which necessitated the use of draft animals. Japan began to import chemical fertilizers and then manufactured its own from the 1880s. The government established a Ministry of Agriculture and Commerce in 1881, which founded agricultural research stations throughout the country. However, as Penelope Francks notes, most of the innovations in Meiji agriculture occurred in piecemeal fashion and many, such as the creation in 1877 of the *shinriki* strain of rice, came from farmers themselves.[34] From the 1880s, farmers created their own local agricultural societies for the study and dissemination of new information about cultivation techniques. Collectively, these changes, which began in the southwest, allowed more areas gradually to practice double cropping and to produce goods like silk commercially for the overseas market. This enabled agricultural output to keep pace with population growth, allowing Japan to escape the need for food imports until the 1920s.

Historians once asserted that land taxes from the agricultural sector financed Japan's modernization at the expense of the farmers themselves. The land tax did provide for 80 to 85 percent of the government's income in the first two decades of the Meiji period.[35] However, this so-called "Japanese model" of development no longer seems tenable. In the first place, statistical information about agricultural yields for the Meiji years, especially 1880–1920, is unreliable, so it is hard to have a clear view of productivity. Additionally, instead of seeing the non-agricultural side of the economy as exploiting agriculture, the view adopted by Francks and others is that the agricultural and industrial sectors evolved symbiotically with farmers providing part-time labor in factories in the off season and industry creating commercial fertilizers to help boost agricultural productivity.[36]

In contrast to early modern practices, the Meiji government collected its taxes in cash assessed at 3 percent of land value. Landowners received title deeds to their property which authorized their right to it. The size of typical farm holdings, however, remained relatively unchanged from the Tokugawa period of approximately one *chō* (2.45 acres), though some farmers worked less than 1.1 acres. Wealthier families owned several times this amount, but fewer than 10 percent of them held more than five *chō* (12.25 acres).[37] The wealthy usually farmed a portion themselves, and rented out the remainder. Landless peasants continued to pay their rents in kind at roughly half of the yield, depending on the region.[38] Their number increased in the Meiji period from 27 percent in 1868 to as much as 45 percent in 1908.[39] While the burden of taxation and a recession made life difficult for many farmers, the impact of Finance Minister Matsukata Masayoshi's deflationary policy beginning in 1881 appears to have had a greater effect on the increase in tenant farming and rural poverty. Deflation caused the price of rice to plummet in 1884 to 50 percent of its value in 1880, and the price of other agricultural commodities also fell. To cover their losses, poorer farmers took out loans against their property at exorbitant rates which they ultimately could not repay. Poorer farmers reacted to these problems with demonstrations, voicing their demands for reduction in usurious interest rates and rents. Tenant movements, calling for similar demands, grew in the twentieth century. Several thousand protests occurred annually in the 1920s and 1930s, and many of these were led by tenant unions which formed to support grievances against landlords.[40]

While tensions emerged in the vertical relations between wealthy landowners and tenant farmers, rural communities remained constituted through lateral bonds which the government fostered for its wartime mobilization during the 1930s and 1940s. The government co-opted the village youth organizations (*wakamonogumi*) and transformed them into "youth corps" (*seinendan*) which promoted ethics and physical training.[41] According to Richard Smethurst, similar groups such as the Imperial Military Reserve and the Women's Association allowed Japan's military to be totally integrated into village life by the 1930s.[42] These organizations were disbanded after the war, but the 1942 Food Control Law which mandated government purchase, storing, and distribution of rice, as well as price controls over rice and other commodities, set the basis for the postwar government's support of rice farmers and control over the price of Japan's most basic foodstuff. Price controls did more than any other government reform in the 1920s and 1930s to stem tenant agitation by paying more for rice from tenant farmers than from their landlords.

Postwar Reforms, Prosperity, and the Decline of the Agricultural Sector

The revolution in the Japanese countryside occurred in the era of the occupation, and resulted from land reform legislation in 1945 and 1946 and from the modernization of Japanese agriculture. Landlords were limited to one *chō* of land to rent out, and absentee landlordism was abolished completely. Farmers could not hold more than four *chō* (9.8 acres) of land in most parts of Japan. The remainder had to be sold. The occupation established land commissions comprised of tenants, landlords, and owner farmers to oversee the sale of land, allowing tenants to purchase land at 1945 prices. Though some aspects of these reforms, such as the provisions against absentee landlords and the size limits on the ownership of agricultural land, were later overturned, the number of tenant farmers fell to below 10 percent. Rents now have to be paid in cash, cannot exceed 25 percent of that year's crop value, and tenancy contracts must be in writing.[43]

The mechanization of agriculture which began in the 1930s took firm hold in the postwar years with the introduction and widespread use of machines such as the rototiller in the 1950s and rice transplanters and harvesters in the 1960s. Postwar agriculture was also marked by the introduction of improved varieties of rice tolerant to the application of chemical fertilizers and pesticides. The extent of these changes can be best understood when viewed in terms of the labor needed to grow rice. In 1955, it took 155 hours to grow ten acres of rice, but by 1983 it took only 56.5 hours of work on the same size of land to yield 30 percent more rice.[44] Thanks to these developments, Japan was faced with a surplus of rice in excess of 2.5 million tons by 1969.[45] Since the government continued to buy half of all the farmers' yields directly from farmers at a fixed price, prices remained high. On the positive side, by the 1970s farmers reached a level of income and standard of living that rivaled those of urban workers. But on the negative side, for consumers the price of rice in Japan reached eight times world levels in the 1980s.[46] The government employed rice and other agricultural subsidies to keep the cost of rice high, which pleased farmers and thereby ensured the political support of agricultural areas which are historically over-represented in the Diet. This relationship gave farmers considerable political clout, on the one hand, while helping maintain the legislative control of the Liberal Democratic Party (LDP), on the other. It also helps explain why Japan is a leader among industrialized countries in price supports for agriculture.[47]

The government purchases rice from farmers, but the Farmers' Cooperative (Nōkyō), also called the JA Group, an organization with over 400,000 employees, is responsible for marketing it. As Richard Moore describes, rice farmers receive a down payment from the government in April and the remainder after the harvest at the end of the year. This down payment is negotiated through a contract with the JA, and usually deposited directly into a cooperative bank. The JA is structured like a *keiretsu*, one or more companies tied to a trading company or bank, and, in fact, it has both a bank (Nōrinchūkin) and a trading company (Zennō). Since a higher price of rice brings more money to its bank, the JA has been a staunch supporter in pushing for government agricultural subsidies, and is another reason for the political clout farmers have.[48]

Government subsidies of agriculture have come at a high cost for consumers, as noted above, and for the government itself, which by 1986 was spending one trillion yen annually on farm subsidies. To lower these costs, the government tried from the 1970s to encourage farmers to convert to other crops instead of rice. Since the late 1980s, it has taken a more aggressive stance, lowering subsidies in 1987 to 560 billion yen, forcing some farmers to convert to other crops, and taking steps to reduce barriers for imported foods.[49] In 1999 the government passed a new Basic Law on Food, Agriculture, and Rural Areas, which promises further retrenchment of farm subsidies while setting a goal for greater agricultural self-sufficiency. However, in the fiscal year 2003 the government still spent 687.5 billion yen on agricultural subsidies. Another reason for a reduction in government support for agriculture is a marked decline in the number of farm households. From the Meiji period to World War II there were roughly 5.5 million farm families, a number which climbed to 6.2 million in 1950. However, the total declined in the subsequent decades from 5.4 million in 1970 to 3.3 million in 1998. Over the same time period, there has been a corresponding fall in the population of farmers from 37.7 million in 1950 to 14.8 million in 1998.[50] In 2001 the agricultural population fell to 10.1 million and consisted of 2.29 million households. Hence, the rural voting block that the LDP has depended on for so long has been slowly disappearing.

Advances in technology allow most farmers in Japan to work only part-time in agriculture and earn most of their living elsewhere. As of 2001, only 19 percent of farmers worked exclusively in agriculture. Of the 80 percent of farmers who take on work outside of agriculture, 83 percent of them derive most of the income from non-agricultural employment.[51] The prevalence of part-time employment has been prominent in Japanese agriculture since before World War II, if not earlier. Mikiso Hane cites one survey in 1939 which showed that 24 percent of farm families relied on jobs outside of agriculture for income.[52] In 1960 two-thirds of farmers worked part-time in agriculture.[53] The small size of farm holdings allows farmers to work in other sectors of the economy. Today, the average farm holding is around one hectare (2.47 acres), which is not much different from the size of land worked by most Tokugawa and Meiji period farmers.[54]

Alternatives to Modern Agriculture

The decline in the number of farmers has sparked a sense of crisis among some observers of Japan's agricultural sector, and some farmers are turning to alternative methods to reconsider the direction of agricultural development. Recently, organic agriculture has been the most prominent alternative to the chemical fertilizers and pesticides that are the hallmark of conventional farming. Japanese agriculture before World War II could be called "organic" by some definitions. In this regard, Franklin

King's glowing, but overly romantic, description of the achievements of farmers in Japan, China, and Korea in the 1920s bears recounting:

> in their systems of multiple cropping; in their extensive and persistent use of legumes; in their rotations of green manure to maintain the humus of the soils and for composting; and in the almost religious fidelity with which they have returned to their fields every form of waste which can replace plant food removed by the crops, these nations have demonstrated a grasp of essentials and of fundamental principles which may well cause western nations to pause and reflect.[55]

However, the trend toward organic farming does not mean a return to traditional methods, and organic agriculture in Japan did not take off until the 1970s, when fears of pollution and contamination by agricultural chemicals were heightened by the publication of books like Rachel Carson's *Silent Spring* (1960), translated as *Chinmoku no haru* by Aoki Ryōichi in 1974, and novelist Ariyoshi Sawako's *Fukugō osen* (Multiple Contamination, 1975).[56] Consumers seeking safer food sources formed groups such as "The society to have safe vegetables grown" (Anzen na Tabemono o Tsukute Taberu Kai), established in 1974 in Tokyo.[57] Such groups allow consumers to purchase directly from farmers who in turn enjoy a lucrative market for their produce. Organic produce is also available in supermarkets labeled with the JAS Organic Certification Seal which indicates that it has been produced in compliance with the Japan Agricultural Standards Association (JAS).

Critics warn that labeling produce as "organic" might transform healthy food into "brand goods" which only the wealthy can afford. There are already some select fruits and vegetables that command high prices. In the last decade, highly priced "heirloom vegetables" (*dentō yasai*) grown in Kyoto and marketed under the "Kyoto Brand Name" have been sold in higher class department stores throughout Japan.[58] But if there is ever a prize awarded for expensive Japanese produce, it would have to go to the beautifully packaged fruit sold as gifts. In May 2002 the branch of Mitsukoshi department store in Sapporo paid over $3,000 for two locally grown melons which were the first of the season, an astronomical price given that ordinary melons sell for about $4 to $6 each in Japan.[59]

One of the most vociferous advocates for a revolution in food production and consumption is the farmer Fukuoka Masanobu who has been advocating "natural farming" (*shizen nōhō*) for the last forty years. Fukuoka's method "renounces all human knowledge and intervention" in its principle of no tillage, no fertilizer, no pesticides, no weeding, and no pruning. His philosophical roots can be found in Daoism and Buddhism, but his conviction that tampering less with nature yields more than other methods is based on his observations on his farm and orchards where vegetables grow wild on mountain slopes and rice seedlings are pushed by hand into the unploughed earth. Perhaps he is the best embodiment of the modern functionalist definition of the rural farmer as one who attempts to live in harmony with the earth. He writes: "people brought up eating unnatural food develop into artificial, anti-natural human beings with an unnatural body prone to disease and an unnatural way of thinking."[60] For Fukuoka at least, a more "rural" lifestyle – the type historians and social scientists once tried to document before it disappeared completely – is the only answer for Japanese agriculture and civilization.

NOTES

1   The Japanese government designates rural areas by the term "county" (*gun*) and urban
    areas by the word "city" (*shi*). Reflecting the fact that the densely inhabited areas of cities
    frequently extend beyond the city itself, the 1960 census introduced the term "densely
    inhabited district" (DID) to refer to developing areas near cities "with a gross population
    of forty or more people per hectare and a total population of 5,000" (Nakai, "Commer-
    cial Change and Urban Growth," p. 198). The term DID attempted to distinguish areas
    undergoing intensive urbanization from less populated and less developed "rural" regions
    (Kornhauser, "Coefficients of Urban Intensification," p. 141).
2   Cloke and Thrift, "Introduction," p. 2.
3   Sorensen, *The Making of Urban Japan*, p. 173.
4   Reischauer and Craig, *Japan*, p. 203.
5   Fukutake, *Japanese Rural Society*, p. 213.
6   Howell, "Hard Times in the Kantō," p. 351.
7   Tsukamoto, *Tokai to inaka*, pp. 37–40.
8   Nakai, "Commercial Change and Urban Growth," p. 519.
9   Bodart-Bailey, "Urbanization and the Nature of the Tokugawa Hegemony," p. 101.
10 Ishii, ed., *Tokugawa kinreikō*, law no. 2784, pp. 153–4.
11 Kuriki, "Kyōyasai no rekishi to shokuseikatsu," p. 17.
12 Ishige, *The History and Culture of Japanese Food*, pp. 102, 112–15.
13 Sorensen, *The Making of Urban Japan*, p. 92.
14 Miyata, "Toshi to minzoku bunka," p. 22.
15 Morse, *Yanagita Kunio and the Folklore Movement*, p. 84.
16 Miyata, "Toshi to minzoku bunka," pp. 8, 15.
17 Kawada, *The Origin of Ethnography*, pp. 52–65.
18 Havens, *Farm and Nation*, pp. 7, 98–108.
19 Latz, "The Persistence of Agriculture," pp. 232–3.
20 Kawamura, "Toshi kakudai to nōgyō no imi," p. 31.
21 Morris-Suzuki, "The Invention and Reinvention of 'Japanese Culture'," p. 772.
22 Bowen, "Japanese Peasants," pp. 823, 830.
23 Mormont, "Who is Rural?", pp. 28, 24.
24 Latz, *Agricultural Development in Japan*, p. 14.
25 Brown, "The Mismeasure of Land."
26 Satō, "Tokugawa Villages and Agriculture," p. 67.
27 For a discussion of these writing, see Robertson, "Japanese Farm Manuals."
28 Sugiyama, *Edo jidai no yasai*, p. 41.
29 Furushima, "The Village and Agriculture," p. 510.
30 Satō, "Tokugawa Villages and Agriculture," p. 73.
31 Laurel Cornell contests the degree to which infanticide was practiced and argues that most
    childhood deaths were due to natural causes (Cornell, "Infanticide in Early Modern
    Japan?").
32 Smith, *Nakahara*, p. 101.
33 Hanley and Yamamura, *Economic and Demographic Change*, p. 295.
34 Francks, *Technology and Agricultural Development*, pp. 56–9.
35 Hane, *Peasants, Rebels, Women, and Outcastes*, p. 17.
36 Francks, *Technology and Agricultural Development*, p. 279.
37 Hane, *Peasants, Rebels, Women, and Outcastes*, pp. 29, 104.
38 Ibid., pp. 104–5.
39 Waswo, "The Transformation of Rural Society," pp. 542–3.
40 For an analysis of tenant unions in the 1920s, see Waswo, "In Search of Equity."

41 Waswo, "The Transformation of Rural Society," p. 573.
42 Smethurst, *A Social Basis for Japanese Militarism*, p. xvi.
43 Moore, *Japanese Agriculture*, pp. 85–7, 288.
44 Ibid., p. 108.
45 Latz, *Agricultural Development in Japan*, p. 32.
46 Sorensen, *The Making of Urban Japan*, p. 235.
47 Mulgan, *The Politics of Agriculture in Japan*, pp. 1–4.
48 Moore, *Japanese Agriculture*, pp. 149–51, 154.
49 Ohnuki-Tierney, *Rice as Self*, p. 17.
50 Mulgan, *The Politics of Agriculture in Japan*, p. 3.
51 *Japan in Figures 2003*, p. 21.
52 Hane, *Peasants, Rebels, Women, and Outcastes*, p. 31.
53 Kumagai, "Concept of 'Sustainable and Regional Agriculture'," p. 36.
54 Mulgan, *The Politics of Agriculture in Japan*, p. 2.
55 King, *Farmers of Forty Centuries*, p. 241.
56 One dictionary of fertilizer terms did not include the term "organic fertilizer" in 1969, but added it when it was revised in 1978 (Masayoshi, "The Use of Organic and Chemical Fertilizers in Japan," p. 7).
57 Honda, "Yūki nōgyō to sanshō teiki," pp. 194–5, 198.
58 Rath, "New Meanings for Old Vegetables in Kyoto."
59 Reuters wire service report, "Department Store Displays $1,000 Melons."
60 Fukuoka, *The Natural Way of Farming*, pp. 5, 39–40.

BIBLIOGRAPHY

Bodart-Bailey, Beatrice. "Urbanization and the Nature of the Tokugawa Hegemony." In Nicolas Fiévé and Paul Waley, eds., *Japanese Capitals in Historical Perspective: Place, Power, and Memory in Kyoto, Edo, and Tokyo*. London: RoutledgeCurzon, 2003.

Bowen, Roger. "Japanese Peasants: Moral? Rational? Revolutionary? Duped? A Review Article." *Journal of Asian Studies* 47:4 (1988): 821–32.

Brown, Philip. "The Mismeasure of Land: Land Surveying in the Tokugawa Period." *Monumenta Nipponica* 42:2 (1987): 115–55.

Cloke, Paul, and Thrift, Nigel. "Introduction: Reconfiguring the Rural." In Paul Cloke et al., eds., *Writing the Rural: Five Cultural Geographies*. London: Paul Chapman, 1994.

Cornell, Laurel. "Infanticide in Early Modern Japan? Demography, Culture, and Population Growth." *Journal of Asian Studies* 55:1 (1996): 22–50.

Francks, Penelope. *Technology and Agricultural Development in Pre-war Japan*. New Haven: Yale University Press, 1984.

Fukuoka Masanobu. *The Natural Way of Farming: The Theory and Practice of Green Philosophy*, trans. Frederic Metreaud. Madras: Book Venture, 1985.

Fukutake Tadashi. *Japanese Rural Society*, trans. Ronald Dore. Ithaca, NY: Cornell University Press, 1967.

Furushima Toshio. "The Village and Agriculture during the Edo Period." In John Whitney Hall, ed., *The Cambridge History of Japan*, vol. 4, *Early Modern Japan*. Cambridge: Cambridge University Press, 1991.

Hane, Mikiso. *Peasants, Rebels, Women, and Outcastes: The Underside of Modern Japan*, 2nd edn. Lanham, Md.: Rowman and Littlefield, 2003.

Hanley, Susan B., and Yamamura, Kozo. *Economic and Demographic Change in Preindustrial Japan, 1600–1868*. Princeton: Princeton University Press, 1977.

Havens, Thomas. *Farm and Nation in Modern Japan: Agrarian Nationalism, 1870–1940*. Princeton: Princeton University Press, 1974.

Honda Shigeru. "Yūki nōgyō to sanshō teiki." In Takayama Toshihiro, ed., *Toshi to nōson o musubu*. Tokyo: Fumin Books, 1991.

Howell, David. "Hard Times in the Kantō: Economic Change and Village Life in Late Tokugawa Japan." *Modern Asian Studies* 23:2 (1989): 349–71.

Ishige Naomichi. *The History and Culture of Japanese Food*. London: Kegan Paul, 2001.

Ishii Ryōsuke, ed. *Tokugawa kinreikō*, 5. Tokyo: Kōbunsha, 1959.

Japan in Figures 2003. Tokyo: Ministry of Public Management, Home Affairs, Posts and Telecommunications, 2002.

Kawada Minoru. *The Origin of Ethnography in Japan: Yanagita Kunio and His Times*, trans. Toshiko Kishida-Ellis. London: Kegan Paul, 1993.

Kawamura Yoshio. "Toshi kakudai to nōgyō no imi." In Takayama Toshihiro, ed., *Toshi to nōson o musubu*. Tokyo: Fumin Books, 1991.

King, Franklin. *Farmers of Forty Centuries; or, Permanent Agriculture in China, Korea, and Japan*, ed. J. P. Bruce. Erasmus, Penn.: Organic Gardening Press, 1927.

Kornhauser, David. "Coefficients of Urban Intensification for Japanese Cities." In Frank J. Costa et al., eds., *Urbanization in Asia: Spatial Dimensions of Policy Issues*. Honolulu: University of Hawai'i Press, 1989.

Kumagai Hiroshi. "Concept of 'Sustainable and Regional Agriculture' in Japan." In Hiroshi Sasaki et al., eds., *Geographical Perspectives on Sustainable Rural Systems: Proceedings of the Tsukuba International Conference on the Sustainability of Rural Systems*. Tokyo: Kaisei Publications, 1996.

Kuriki Fumio. "Kyōyasai no rekishi to shokuseikatsu." In Kyōyasai Kenkyūkai, ed., *Kyōyasai no seisan, ryūtsū, kyōhi to chiiki seikatsu seika ni kan suru kenkyū*. Kyoto: Kyoto Sangyō Daigaku Kokudo Riyō Kaihatsu Kenkyūjo, 1998.

Latz, Gil. *Agricultural Development in Japan: The Land Improvement District in Concept and Practice*. Chicago: University of Chicago Geography Research Paper no. 225, 1989.

Latz, Gil. "The Persistence of Agriculture in Urban Japan: An Analysis of the Tokyo Metropolitan Area." In Norton Ginsburg et al., eds., *The Extended Metropolis: Settlement Transition in Asia*. Honolulu: University of Hawai'i Press, 1991.

Masayoshi Koshiro. "The Use of Organic and Chemical Fertilizers in Japan." *Food and Fertilizer Technology Extension Bulletin* 312 (1990): 4–15.

Miyata Noboru, "Toshi to minzoku bunka." In Miyata Noboru et al., eds., *Nihon minzoku bunka taikei*, 11, *Toshi to inaka*. Tokyo: Shogakkan, 1985.

Moore, Richard. *Japanese Agriculture: Patterns of Rural Development*. Boulder, Colo.: Westview Press, 1990.

Mormont, Marc. "Who is Rural? or, How to be Rural: Towards a Sociology of the Rural." In Terry Marsden et al., eds., *Rural Restructuring: Global Processes and Their Responses*. London: David Fulton, 1990.

Morris-Suzuki, Tessa. "The Invention and Reinvention of 'Japanese Culture'." *Journal of Asian Studies* 54:3 (1995): 759–80.

Morse, Ronald. *Yanagita Kunio and the Folklore Movement: The Search for Japan's National Character and Distinctiveness*. New York: Garland, 1990.

Mulgan, Aurelia George. *The Politics of Agriculture in Japan*. London: Routledge, 2000.

Nakai Nobuhiko. "Commercial Change and Urban Growth in Early Modern Japan," trans. James McClain. In John Whitney Hall, ed., *The Cambridge History of Japan*, vol. 4, *Early Modern Japan*. Cambridge: Cambridge University Press, 1991.

Ohnuki-Tierney, Emiko. *Rice as Self: Japanese Identities through Time*. Princeton: Princeton University Press, 1993.

Rath, Eric. "New Meanings for Old Vegetables in Kyoto." In Theodore and Victoria Bestor, eds., *Cuisine, Consumption, and Culture: Food in Contemporary Japan*. Berkeley: University of California Press, forthcoming.

Reischauer, Edwin, and Craig, Albert. *Japan: Tradition and Transformation*, rev. edn. Boston: Houghton Mifflin, 1989.

Robertson, Jennifer. "Japanese Farm Manuals: A Literature of Discovery." *Peasant Studies* 11:3 (1984): 169–94.

Satō Tsuneo. "Tokugawa Villages and Agriculture." In Nakane Chie and Ōishi Shinzaburō, eds., *Tokugawa Japan: The Social and Economic Antecedents of Modern Japan*, trans. Conrad Totman. Tokyo: University of Tokyo Press, 1990.

Smethurst, Richard. *A Social Basis for Japanese Militarism: The Army and the Rural Community.* Berkeley: University of California Press, 1974.

Smith, Thomas C. *The Agrarian Origins of Modern Japan.* Stanford, Calif.: Stanford University Press, 1959.

Smith, Thomas C. *Nakahara: Family Farming and Population in a Japanese Village, 1770–1830.* Stanford, Calif.: Stanford University Press, 1977.

Sorensen, Andre. *The Making of Urban Japan: Cities and Planning from Edo to the Twenty-First Century.* London: Routledge, 2002.

Sugiyama Tadayoshi. *Edo jidai no yasai no saibai to riyō.* Tokyo: Hōyashi, 1998.

Tsukamoto Manabu. *Tokai to inaka.* Tokyo: Heibonsha, 1991.

Waswo, Ann. "The Transformation of Rural Society, 1900–1950." In Peter Duus, ed., *The Cambridge History of Japan*, vol. 6, *The Twentieth Century.* Cambridge: Cambridge University Press, 1988.

Waswo, Ann. "In Search of Equity: Japanese Tenant Unions in the 1920s." In Ann Waswo and Nishida Yoshiaki, eds., *Farmers and Village Life in Twentieth-Century Japan.* London: Routledge, 2003.

FURTHER READING

For medieval villages, see Hitomi Tonomura's *Community and Commerce in Late Medieval Japan: The Corporate Villages of Tokuchin-ho* (Stanford, Calif.: Stanford University Press, 1992), and for medieval agriculture, see Kristina Troost's "Peasants, Elites, and Villages in the Fourteenth Century," in Jeffrey Mass, ed., *The Origins of Japan's Medieval World* (Stanford, Calif.: Stanford University Press, 1997). Thomas Smith's *The Agrarian Origins of Modern Japan* (Stanford, Calif.: Stanford University Press, 1959) remains a classic introduction to farming and farm families in the early modern period. Herman Ooms's *Tokugawa Village Practice: Class, Status, Power, Law* (Berkeley: University of California Press, 1996) illuminates the legal and status consciousness of peasants.

There has been considerable scholarship in English on peasant uprisings in the early modern period; recent works include Herbert Bix's *Peasant Protest in Japan, 1590–1884* (New Haven: Yale University Press, 1986); William Kelly's *Deference and Defiance in Nineteenth-Century Japan* (Princeton: Princeton University Press, 1985); Stephen Vlastos's *Peasant Protests and Uprisings in Tokugawa Japan* (Berkeley: University of California Press, 1986); Anne Walthall's *Social Protest and Popular Culture in Eighteenth-Century Japan* (Tucson: University of Arizona Press, 1986); and James W. White's *Ikki: Social Conflict and Political Protest in Early Modern Japan* (Ithaca, NY: Cornell University Press, 1995). For narratives of a few rebellions from the peasants' perspective, see Anne Walthall's *Peasant Uprisings in Japan: A Critical Anthology of Peasant Histories* (Chicago: University of Chicago Press, 1991).

On conflicts between tenants and landowners in the modern period see Richard Smethurst's *Agricultural Development and Tenancy Disputes in Japan 1870–1940*

(Princeton: Princeton University Press, 1986) and Ann Waswo's *Japanese Landlords: The Decline of a Rural Elite* (Berkeley: University of California Press, 1977). For details about the hardship of life in the prewar countryside, see Mikiso Hane's *Peasants, Rebels, Women, and Outcastes: The Underside of Modern Japan* (Lanham, Md.: Rowman and Littlefield, 2003) and Nagatsuka Takashi's 1910 novel *The Soil*, trans. Ann Waswo (Berkeley: University of California Press, 1989). For a few happier recollections of country life see Jun'ichi Saga, *Memories of Silk and Straw: A Self-Portrait of Small-Town Japan*, trans. Garry Evans (New York: Kōdansha International, 1987).

Richard Moore's *Japanese Agriculture: Patterns of Rural Development* (Boulder, Colo.: Westview Press, 1990) is essential reading for understanding rural development in the twentieth century, as is Penelope Francks's volume *Technology and Agricultural Development in Pre-war Japan* (New Haven: Yale University Press, 1984). Aurelia George Mulgan's extensive study *The Politics of Agriculture in Japan* (London: Routledge, 2000) analyzes the political fortunes of Japanese farmers in the postwar period.

CHAPTER TWENTY-EIGHT

Business and Labor

Charles Weathers

The non-technical labor relations literature on Japan is dominated by three themes: historical evolution, interpretation of labor–management relations, and the role of the firm. The main historical issue concerns the evolution of a cooperative, enterprise-based employment system. Tension persisted for decades between manual workers seeking respect and factory managers seeking to inculcate tight workplace discipline, usually with greater moral or patriotic exhortation than provision of tangible benefits. A complex mix of policies, practices, and demands ultimately evolved after 1950 into a more or less mutually desirable accommodation in which the "core" blue collar workers were incorporated into enterprises as full members, though a stiff price was paid in the marginalization of laborers, small-firm workers, and women. Easily the dominant figure is Andrew Gordon whose three books, assorted articles, and translated works define the historical industrial relations field.

The historical theme does not generate great controversy (at least in the English literature), but the interpretation of Japan's postwar (post-1945) or contemporary labor–management relations system is strongly contested. Clearly, Japan's labor and employment practices have contributed greatly to the country's impressive postwar economic performance, but there is fierce disagreement about whether workers and the general population have benefited proportionately. This debate is closely tied to the issue of whether Japanese unions are independent of management. Advocates of Japanese labor–management relations believe that unions have served worker interests and responded to their desires by cooperating pragmatically in efforts to raise productivity, thereby raising living standards and bolstering job security. Critics believe that cooperation was nearly unconditional, leading to neglect of work conditions and the interests of marginal workers. The leading English-language critic is, again, Gordon, while a leading advocate is the prolific Ronald Dore.[1] Among Japanese scholars, advocates are well represented by the contributors to Shirai Taishiro's 1983 edited volume and critics by Kumazawa Makoto.[2]

The third theme regards the nature of work, particularly the central role of the firm (and work) in society as well as the economy. The employment/industrial relations system is strongly enterprise-centered, as famously manifested in the "three treasures" of lifetime (more accurately, long-term) employment, strong seniority weighting in wages and promotions (the *nenkō* system), and enterprise unions, which include the members of only one firm. Although the distinctiveness of the system's features (notably lifetime employment) is frequently exaggerated, Japan boasts probably the closest labor–management cooperation achieved in any industrial democracy.

An emergent theme, so far covered only sketchily in English, regards major changes in employment practice that have occurred since the collapse of the "bubble economy" around 1991. Prolonged economic stagnation has created strong pressure to make labor more flexible and to reduce costs, as well as to better incorporate women into the workforce. Needless to say, the efforts of firms to reduce commitments to employees (or to extend them to fewer employees) has entailed great change in employment practices and altered the meaning of work in people's lives. One major subfield, inspired by Japan's unusually pronounced and persistent gendered division of labor, has been a large volume of work on women workers.[3] Research on changing employment practices, non-regular employees, and female workers should become increasingly intermeshed in future as equal opportunity (along with family-friendly) policy-making and cost-cutting management strategies advance in uneasy tandem.

Because Japanese employment practices differ significantly from Western practices, because work occupies a central role in people's lives and identities, and (more arguably) because industrial relations tend to be "informal," participant-observer and ethnographic research is central to the labor research agenda.[4] Much of the best research on Japan has sought to demystify or demythologize employment practices while attacking the tendency (all too conveniently) to attribute cooperation and other behavior to Japanese culture.

Some characteristics of Japan's postwar industrial relations system render it difficult to understand. First, some institutions function quite differently from foreign counterparts even when they are not inherently complex – the classic example is the enterprise union. Second, negotiations and decision-making often lack transparency. The ascent of cooperative unionism has entailed a decline in collective bargaining in favor of informal, secretive labor–management discussion at the enterprise level. The unions' failure to conduct assertive collective bargaining has elevated the importance of formal policy-making, in which representatives of unions, business, and the government bureaucracy participate. Though not necessarily secretive, the policy-making processes and outcomes hardly lend themselves to easy interpretation. Finally, employment practices are predominantly informally institutionalized, that is, they are not strongly or clearly embedded in laws. This is an important source of economic flexibility, but worsening job and income insecurity since around 1991 has strengthened the case for establishing more explicit rules and a stronger social safety net.

The historical evolution of the employment system can be summarized as follows. The precursors of modern employment practices emerged as early as the 1870s, and were first established on a significant scale in the 1920s. Employment practices were modified and in many important respects reinforced by governmental wartime labor policies in the wartime era (1930s–45). They assumed their contemporary form in the 1950s and 1960s (high growth era), and thereafter reached maturation while contributing importantly to Japan's impressive economic performance in the 1970s and 1980s (years of slow or, more optimistically, steady growth). Buoyed by powerful export industries, the employment system was remarkably stable through the early 1990s, but the combination of stagnant growth, technological advances, and intensifying foreign competition in strategic industries such as electronics have reduced the benefits, including strong job and income security, once seemingly assured by the nation's manufacturing prowess, impressive though it still is. Consequently, employment practices have undergone major changes.

The Labor Force

Japan was heavily urbanized by the 1700s, and many of the city residents became wage workers, including numerous servants and day laborers, and a few production workers. Some scholars believe that the Tokugawa era bequeathed a large supply of skilled labor to Meiji Japan. Others see little continuity, but the technology gap between Japan and the West in the latter half of the nineteenth century was small enough that artisans could be readily retrained in modern production practices. The agricultural sector served as an important source of labor for industry from the 1880s to the 1960s, and to some extent as an absorber of surplus workers as well when economic activity slowed (family businesses long served a similar function). The proportion of working persons employed in agriculture fell from 81 percent in 1872 to 42 percent in 1936. After rising in the difficult post-1945 era, it plunged rapidly from around 40 percent in 1955 to 10 percent in 1980. In the Meiji era, primogeniture laws and smallish plots meant that a steady stream of men unable to support themselves in farming moved to cities, often becoming industrial workers. Yet until the early 1930s, a majority of factory workers were female. From the late nineteenth century tens of thousands of women from impoverished, mostly peasant, families spent several years working in textile mills. Many, perhaps most, were brutally exploited.[5] The early industrial workforce was concentrated in light industry, which employed 94 percent of the approximately 450,000 factory workers in 1900, but the leading role in industrial relations formation was played by large firms, many of them government-operated. These emerged quickly in Meiji Japan, notably in "modern" industries such as machinery, shipbuilding, mining, and armaments. Large firms became the primary sites of skill formation and (reflecting the weakness of the traditional guilds) the development of nascent worker consciousness as well.

Political oppression and hostility from social elites, along with the early establishment of large firms (that is, strong employers), created a difficult environment for Meiji era labor. Blue collar workers were disrespected, if not despised, both within factories and in general society throughout the pre-1945 era. The large status differences separating factory workers (and the rest of the underclass) from supervisors and white collar workers long poisoned labor relations, and implicitly encouraged the exploitation of marginal workers, particularly unskilled laborers, mine workers, and female factory operators. Although treatment improved over time, poverty and dangerous working conditions remained the norm for factory workers and laborers. In retrospect, the oppression and discrimination seem paradoxical since many workers fervently sought self-improvement in terms of occupation, education, and social status. Early labor leaders and workers' associations or unions emphasized worker dignity while campaigning for social respect, and advocated moderation and non-confrontation in dealing with management. Many female textile workers were lured into the mills in part through promises (mostly false) of educational opportunity.

Pre-1945 Labor–Management Relations

Although widespread poverty and rapid population growth ensured an abundant supply of cheap unskilled labor, employers were long vexed about training and retaining skilled workers. The high mobility of Meiji era workers, heirs to the Tokugawa tradition of independent artisans, helped to disseminate skills throughout the country, but frustrated the efforts of individual managers to hold down turnover and impose modern factory discipline. Pioneering efforts, from as early as the early 1870s, focused largely on developing wage and promotion systems that would reward ability and create incentives for valuable workers to stay with employers. Regular increases of the day wage were "the most distinctive" personnel innovation of nineteenth-century Japanese managers, and a precursor of postwar seniority pay systems.[6]

During the early twentieth century, companies began offering a variety of retirement or severance pay packages, incentive bonuses, and welfare programs. Many firms, notably government-run factories and shipyards, instituted training programs. Nevertheless, retention rates remained very low during the early 1900s, largely because numerous workers prior to the 1910s found job-switching an effective means of developing skills and raising pay. Others wished to remain independent, or to found their own firms. Firms steadily began to treat white collar workers as firm members, and sometimes extended similar treatment to factory supervisors as well, but production workers invariably received inferior benefits or were excluded altogether. Other common causes of worker resentment included output pay, favoritism and arbitrary behavior by supervisors, and sudden curtailments of benefits when economic conditions soured. Supervision presented another challenge. Until around 1900, managers relied heavily on *oyakata* (independent labor bosses), a Tokugawa legacy, not only to supervise, but often even to train, hire, and pay production workers. By the early years of the century, most large firms, aided by the steady mechanization of production, had established direct supervision of workers. However, the quality of shop-floor supervision tended to be poor until the 1950s, leaving managers heavily dependent on skilled workers.

A significant labor movement emerged in the late 1890s, but Meiji era unions and mutual aid societies consistently folded in short order because of lack of worker solidarity and government pressure. The Public Order and Police Law of 1900 proscribed strikes, and activists risked imprisonment along with dismissal. In contrast to the West, artisans had little impact on Japan's labor movement, partly because Tokugawa era industries were undermined by modernization. Workers in large factories became the main players in forging new forms of worker organization, negotiation, and protest, and the earliest worker protests or actions were primarily non-union. Gordon emphasizes that prewar workers displayed greater activism and exerted more influence on labor policies than previously believed.[7] They sometimes forced managers, for instance, to raise pay or curtail discriminatory practices.

Some important general patterns from the dawn of Japan's labor movement have persisted to the present. Workers have been predominantly organized within workplaces, a situation that has undermined efforts to coordinate union activities, or to unify the union movement. Workers and unions have usually emphasized protection of jobs within firms (or their affiliates), and rarely resisted the introduction of new technology. Foremen and skilled workers tended to form the core of prewar labor organizations, while managers, well aware of their crucial leadership role, worked to integrate them into company hierarchies. The influence of this template – labor organization centered on workplaces, focused on job protection, and guided by supervisors – remains quite strong, although major postwar unions generally evolved from workplace-centered to enterprise-centered entities.

By the 1910s, rising education levels had begun to stimulate worker consciousness; that, along with better labor organization and the demand for labor generated by rapid industrial growth, strengthened protest capabilities. In addition, government pressure eased somewhat. In this slightly more favorable environment appeared Japan's first durable major union, the Friendly Society (Yūaikai). It was renamed the General Federation of Labor (Sōdōmei) in 1921. Labor grew increasingly militant in the late 1910s as a result of persistent discrimination, economic recession, and heady international influences, notably the Russian Revolution. Consequently, the 1918–21 period witnessed a wave of major strikes. However, these disputes marked the peak of labor power, as a prolonged economic slump brought drastic cutbacks in employment in heavy industry.

Labor was also weakened by ideological factionalism. Sōdōmei's left wing exited the federation in 1925, and the union movement has remained divided between right (cooperative) and left wings ever since. In addition, ultra-cooperative unionists advocating the fusion of labor and management interests appeared in the early 1920s. Simplistically schematized, the cooperative wing has been divided between factions preferring close cooperation with, or independence from, managers, while the left has been similarly divided between moderate (often socialist-oriented) and more radical (left socialist and/or communist-influenced) factions. In many cases, a three-sided schematization of closely cooperative, moderate, and radical is also appropriate.

The labor unrest in the late 1910s and early 1920s led government and business to revise their labor policy approaches. The government softened its labor stance somewhat, and consented to join the International Labor Organization (ILO). Some national bureaucrats had for years feared the effects of harsh management practices on the working population, and on political order.[8] Labor bureaucrats sought to establish progressive policies and regulations, notably the 1912 Factory Law, which protected women and children in factories, although the powerful business community diluted the law and delayed its implementation. Some liberal national bureaucrats sought in the 1920s to establish stronger labor rights, but an ambitious Home Ministry bill to recognize labor unions met defeat in the Diet in 1931.

Large-firm managers began to respond to worker demands for equality, partly by intensifying the use of paternalism, and by (slightly) better grounding it in benefits such as job and wage protection. Recent historians have attacked claims that these represented altruistic practices, viewing them more as variations of corporate welfare policies. Certainly, the benefits hardly matched the rhetoric. Probably more effective were factory councils, which provided workers with a voice but minimal influence. Despite their limitations, factory councils proved useful in displacing unions. In 1931, the organization rate reached its prewar peak of 7.9 percent, though in reality organized labor was already in decline, with employers having virtually eliminated unions and activists from the strategic modern industries.

The 1920s slump helped shift management attention from turnover to rationalization. Large (especially government-owned) firms enthusiastically applied scientific management and other American-style management practices, notably by linking wages to productivity, though the gains from such efforts were limited until the 1950s.[9] The slide into war after 1930 brought a massive military build-up and consequent rapid growth of the industrial workforce, and ushered in a highly nationalistic phase in industrial relations. From the late 1930s, all unions, and eventually business associations as well, were forced to dissolve themselves into the corporatist Greater Japan Industrial Patriotic Association (Sanpō). The government also mandated livelihood (that is, based on family need) wage systems and other measures intended to stabilize workforces during the war. These policies were generally unsuccessful. However, many business or governmental initiatives – notably scientific management and livelihood-based wage systems – which had done little to instill harmony or raise productivity before 1945 served as precursors of the vastly more successful practices of the postwar era. Even the fascistic and notoriously ineffective Sanpō promoted egalitarian consciousness and organizational practices; these are believed to have strongly encouraged the postwar emergence of enterprise unionism.

The Early Postwar Era

The United States played contradictory roles in shaping postwar labor practices. During the early phase of the occupation, American officials forced the government to enact progressive labor laws and include strong labor rights in the constitution, and encouraged workers to organize unions. As the policy-making priority shifted from democratization to economic revival, however, they began helping managers and the government to roll back union influence. Union membership exploded from zero at war's end to nearly five million by December 1946. The enterprise union quickly became the predominant form of labor organization in Japan. This reflected, in addition to the historic tendency to form workplace-based units, the influence of the government's wartime labor policies and desperate postwar economic conditions that left employees little chance of finding work in other companies. The rise of enterprise unions also reflected a desire to expunge hated status differentials, and indeed they contributed enormously to democratization and, in the longer term, labor–management cooperation by promoting egalitarianism, albeit primarily within firms and among men. There were limits to such change, of course. Despite considerable social leveling and a rapid improvement of educational and other opportunities, status consciousness remained strong.[10] Another uncertain legacy was the role played by white collar workers, who generally led enterprise unions but reclaimed some of their earlier prerogatives as the rollback of union influence gathered force in the late 1940s. Blue collar workers, though aware of such potential dangers, had often judged that the benefits of more inclusive unionism outweighed the risks. For better or worse, one result was that the typical Japanese union is not just an enterprise union but a combination (kongō) union combining all workers (especially blue and white collar) in a firm.

The first postwar labor protests were conducted largely by Koreans and Chinese (many essentially slave laborers) whose example encouraged Japanese workers to become more aggressive. Unions soon played important roles in preventing layoffs. Workers in some firms seized control of production from managers in production control strikes; these are now widely viewed as having been driven largely by employee distrust of management rather than revolutionary Marxist consciousness. In 1946, cooperative labor leaders re-established Sōdōmei, and left-wing leaders founded the Japan Council of Industrial Labor Unions (Sanbetsu), reconstituting the prewar left/right division. Sanbetsu initially boasted twice the membership of Sōdōmei and held the labor leadership initiative. Public sector unions were major forces in Sanbetsu (despite significant weakening and steady privatization, these same unions still anchor labor's left wing). Sanbetsu led preparations for a politically oriented general strike on February 1, 1947, but American authorities forced a last moment cancellation, dealing a severe blow to the labor left.

Fearing that labor activists were undermining economic recovery, American officials began encouraging government and employer efforts to combat left-wing unions. Consequently, the government rescinded the right to strike for public sector workers in July 1948 and revised the Trade Union Law in 1949, clearing the way for companies to reject no-dismissal clauses and rationalize workforces. The Tōshiba strike (1949) served as a crucial test showdown. The company encouraged the emergence of a cooperative "second union," undermining the first union. Managers were then able to revise the labor contract and rationalize the workforce through large-scale dismissals. In addition, the government conducted the Red Purge (a purge of communist or allegedly communist labor leaders) in 1950. Probably the American policy most damaging to organized labor was the 1949 Dodge Line, a set of harsh anti-inflationary policies. In 1948, hardline business leaders founded the employers' association Nikkeiren to reassert strong management authority. The federation played an important role in assisting firms in rolling back union prerogatives in 1949–51. Nikkeiren's influence on labor affairs declined thereafter, though it continues to coordinate policy-making for employers.

The union organization rate peaked at 55.8 percent in 1949, then fell nearly 10 points in a year, while Sanbetsu collapsed. A more inclusive federation, Sōhyō, was established in 1950. Unfortunately, unity was short-lived as the cold war and ideological tensions soon induced Sōhyō to turn leftward. Cooperative unions promptly began seceding, eventually forming the rival federation Dōmei in 1964.

Shaping Industrial Relations in the High Growth Era

The 1950s were a period of political tension, but workplaces calmed as managers and cooperative labor leaders steadily strengthened their authority and established the foundations of the contemporary employment system. Workers generally consented to a close-cooperation-based system. One reason was that most preferred cooperation with employers, especially those hired from the countryside where the tradition of respect for authority remained strong. In addition, employers greatly improved their personnel and labor management practices (as outlined below), responding to the blue collar workers' demands for equal status and security as well as raising

productivity. Finally, high growth helped resolve socioeconomic tensions by stimulating job creation and forcing up wages. Long-term job security was institutionalized
from the early 1950s. By then, many workplaces had forced left-wing activists out,
and labor shortages during the high growth era induced managers to make further
accommodations, notably wage increases for young workers. Considerable activism
by the courts was also crucial.[11] Labor law itself provides little protection for jobs, but
court decisions (*hanrei*) in the early 1950s essentially mandated job protection.
Consequently, job security for regular workers is strong, yet remains informal and
conditional (depending especially on a firm's stability). In theory firms must justify
lay-offs, especially if they are large and resource-rich, but many smaller firms bend
such rules. Furthermore, women and activists have often been denied equal protection. In the early postwar years, laborers and other marginal workers often lacked job
and income security since benefits were largely firm-based. Rapid economic growth
and labor shortages enabled nearly all men to land good jobs by the 1960s, greatly
easing social tensions.

When disputes occurred, they often followed the earlier Tōshiba pattern in which
cooperative second unions emerged. One of the most important disputes was the
1953 Nissan strike, in which managers helped white collar workers to establish a new
union that displaced the original, left-wing, union. The dispute severely damaged
prospects for establishing strong industrial unionism in Japan. Today's industrial
unions serve primarily to coordinate the activities of affiliates under the guidance of
their most prestigious members (for example, Toyota Union plays the lead role in the
Auto Workers' Federation).

Large firms, influenced by enterprise union-driven egalitarian principles as well as
the desire to raise productivity, drastically redesigned labor management practices in
the 1950s and 1960s. They ultimately created personnel systems that formally unified
blue and white collar personnel systems (though in reality, education level still tends
to determine promotion possibilities). The rationalization (and standardization) of
promotion, pay, and other personnel practices often helped strengthen the sense of
fairness, but also facilitated the efficient deployment of workers – making it easier, for
instance, to transfer people between jobs or factories as massive investment quickly
transformed workplaces. An important step in this reorganization was the great
strengthening of shop-floor supervision. Not only did companies improve training
for supervisors (notably the "new" foremen of the steel industry), but they clarified
the criteria for promotion, thereby encouraging their most talented and ambitious
workers to channel their energies toward seeking promotion (and away from, say,
unionism). The well-trained supervisors put an end to the old problems of favoritism
and inept shop-floor supervision. In addition, they were integrated into centralized
managerial structures, enabling top managers to tighten their control over decision-
making, and partially displaced unions as worker representatives. Japanese manufacturing workplaces utilize large numbers of supervisors, creating opportunities for
promotion, and strengthening monitoring capabilities as well.

Rapid technological upgrading and fast rising education levels supported the
efforts of employers to rapidly transform workplaces and employment practices.
Massive investment quickly raised the level of automation in production, and increased the need for education-based skill while reducing the importance of experi-
ence-based skill. Many firms achieved the decades-long goal of controlling the skill

development process as they replaced experienced skilled workers with newly trained foremen and systematized on-the-job training (OJT). Prewar firms frequently faced the dilemma of whether to provide greater rewards to skill or loyalty; postwar firms resolved the dilemma in part by refining enterprise-based training, thereby making skills relatively non-portable.

While steel and shipbuilding firms tended to take the lead in introducing major labor personnel innovations, the auto industry was a leader in developing production technology and rationalizing assembly line work. Toyota, for example, redesigned production to enable workers to perform multiple tasks simultaneously. Academics have accordingly debated whether Japanese practices promote upskilling or simply multi-tasking (performing numerous unskilled or semi-skilled jobs). Certainly, automation eliminated many of the most physical and dangerous manufacturing tasks, but worsened work conditions in other ways, notably by making it easier for managers to speed the pace of work and squeeze rest times. Productivity-raising activities increased the fear among many workers that their jobs would be eliminated, though these concerns receded considerably as economic growth accelerated. The rapid transformation of production workplaces occurred in large part because Japanese managers pursued productivity-raising more intensively than their Western counterparts. They were driven by the desire to reassert managerial legitimacy following the shocking loss of authority to unions immediately after the war, and to assert Japan's status as a major industrial nation. Further, they received important assistance from the government, and enjoyed the support of numerous labor leaders, including many in Sōhyō.

Contributing greatly to productivity-raising was a network of non-profit scientific management-related organizations, such as the Japanese Union of Scientists and Engineers (JUSE).[12] JUSE led the development of quality control circles (QCCs),[13] the most important of the "small group activities" that encouraged ordinary production workers to participate actively in planning and designing production. Participation was not always voluntary, as managers insisted, but it helped to bolster morale against the increasingly routinized tedium of factory work. Small group activities epitomized Japan's capacity for applying extensive redesign and innovation to techniques originally borrowed from the West to create distinctive Japanese practices. Their effectiveness also indicated one way in which scientific management has exerted a stronger impact in Japan than in any country bar, possibly, the United States. The Japan Productivity Center (JPC) led a high profile productivity campaign after its founding in 1955, but its importance has been exaggerated.

While Japan's large firms function as de facto economic leaders in many respects (by setting labor standards, and in economic policy-making), most salaried workers are still employed in smaller firms. In the late 1980s, about 70 percent of all employees (and about 75 percent of manufacturing sector workers) were in firms of fewer than 100 workers. Many smaller firms are subcontractors, notably in manufacturing and construction, but functions and capabilities vary greatly, from fronting low-cost labor operations for large firms to conducting technologically advanced production. Compensation, job security, social status, and safety standards are generally inferior to those at larger firms. Managers can behave arbitrarily, and some sources allege that problems like illegal dismissals and sexual harassment are common in small firms. The differentials are partly justified as reflecting merit (for example, people who perform better in school get the better jobs in large firms), though in reality lifestyle choices or entrepreneurial ambitions are important to many small-firm workers. They are much more job-mobile (voluntarily or otherwise) than their large-firm counterparts. Many small-firm workers perceive advantages such as relative informality and flexibility in socialization and work. Small firms thus present a "combination of enablement and restraint."[14]

In contrast to the private sector, labor relations in the public sector remained contentious into the 1980s, partly because of constant political interference. The tension led to an unusual intervention from the ILO, which admonished both sides in the late 1960s, though to little effect. The disputes were especially bitter in the National Railways, where postwar management suffered perhaps its one major defeat when a campaign to bust the left-wing unions backfired disastrously around 1970. Japan's shift from coal-based to oil-based energy brought severe dislocation in the mining sector, culminating in the 1960 strike at Mitsui's Miike coal mine. The union responded to the company's plan to slash the workforce with a tenacious 313-day strike in which large-scale bloodshed was barely averted. Nonetheless, managers won a total victory in what was Japan's last truly major private sector strike, and dealt a severe setback to Sōhyō.

The Firm-Based Accord

High growth, massive investment, and the well-executed redesign of labor management created a virtuous circle for manufacturing firms. Companies could hire new graduates very cheaply under the age-based wage system, and expect to recover the cost of their training through long years of service since turnover was relatively low. Worker loyalty (or commitment) was strong because skills were non-portable between large firms, and small firms paid less. The system encouraged teamwork and acceptance of new technology since older workers could accept new technology and train younger workers at no risk (in theory) to their own job security. Certainly, Japanese managers faced rigidities, notably providing job security and automatic *nenkō* wage increases even for the less productive, but in return they enjoyed very high flexibility in deploying workers, deciding work hours, hiring non-regular workers, and adjusting pay levels (for example, reducing overtime and bonuses in response to business slumps). While the uniqueness of Japanese practices is often exaggerated, average tenure is long by OECD standards, and the age-based wage curve is very steep.

The company enjoys high prestige in Japan, and on this foundation an impressively seamless interaction developed amongst job, family, education, and gender.[15] Employment prospects for men depended primarily on educational attainment, creating an enviably effective school-to-workplace linkage; the implicit linkage of security (job, income, and family) reinforced managers' espousal of cooperation and loyalty to the company; and housewives provided support for hard-working husbands while pushing male children to study in order to land good jobs. Housewives, whose role was extolled, were expected to "supplement" family incomes by accepting low-paid part-time jobs, if they worked at all. Even individuals' social lives (regular socializing with fellow employees) and marriage patterns (strong propensity to marry co-workers) reflected the central role of company and work in society. The mutual dependence of employees and managers within the firm was expressed in the phrase "community of fate."

The employment system functioned impressively from the mid 1950s until relatively recently, although critics emphasized problems, including the overdependence of workers on firms, and personnel practices such as long work hours and sudden transfers to new locations. In addition, numerous welfare and tax policies were designed to strengthen ties of employees to employers, but the government's subsidization of enterprise-based benefits (like health insurance and recreational facilities) disproportionately benefited large-firm employees, and indirectly entailed neglect of public services.

The Union Movement and Wage-Setting

After plunging from its 1949 peak of 55.8 percent, the organization rate soon leveled off at around 35 percent until the mid 1970s. Although Sōhyō was the largest labor federation throughout its existence (1950–89), it began losing influence practically from the moment of its inception. By the mid 1960s it was a primarily public-sector-based federation. Sōhyō and the cooperative Dōmei were less important than commonly assumed; more influential than the conventional labor centers was the International Metalworkers Federation – Japan Council (IMF-JC). Though established in 1964 as a Japanese affiliate of the International Metalworkers Federation, the IMF-JC's real concern has been domestic labor affairs. As with Nikkeiren, the nature of the IMF-JC's activities and its degree of influence defy easy understanding. Its tangible activities have been limited to matters such as coordinating union policy-making, but the federation has functioned more importantly as a platform for promoting close enterprise-centered cooperation. The leading IMF-JC unions and many other cooperative unions scorn strikes, though that is the belief that dares not speak its name.

In 1955, eight left-leaning private sector industrial unions launched *shuntō* (the spring offensive). Sōhyō leaders intended to use wage struggles to stimulate the workers' class consciousness and create a stronger labor movement (as well as a foundation for future political and class struggle). The majority of workers were too moderate to fulfill their Marxist-tinged aspirations, but as a means of coordinating wage-setting *shuntō* proved useful to companies and unions alike. The *shuntō* settlements of leading enterprises soon came to serve as authoritative guidelines for wage raises nationwide. The so-called *shuntō* average raises reached double digits every year but one from 1961 to 1974, although it was high growth, a shortage of young workers, and high inflation that accounted for nearly all the wage increases. There were *shuntō* strikes, to be sure, but they were largely for show.

The victory of managers in the 1957 and 1959 steel industry wage disputes ended organized labor's last good chance to establish meaningful industrial unionism. The workers enjoyed a potentially strong position in 1957, but were too moderate to conduct an assertive strike. They accordingly lost, undermining the left-wing leadership and allowing cooperative leaders to take control of the steel unions. (Unlike most other major unions, the steelworker unions are mostly original unions, not second unions created with management support.) The cooperative unionists were led by

Miyata Yoshiji, who was probably Japan's most influential labor leader. He was certainly the most important advocate of close labor–management cooperation on the labor side.

Japan's cooperative unions are easy targets for criticism, but it should be noted that there is rather little social support for greater activism. As demonstrated in the 1957 and 1959 steel strikes, workers probably desired somewhat stronger unions, but enterprise consciousness consistently trumped efforts to instill worker solidarity across enterprises. Further, the government and the legal system seek to promote cooperative relations by emphasizing compromise and administrative guidance (inducements or pressures toward voluntary compliance) rather than compulsory laws and authoritative rulings. There are no authoritative European-style labor courts, and the regular courts are slow and conservatively inclined. Few but committed activists or the morally outraged bother to pursue lawsuits. Finally, culture or social values seem to discourage activism. The point should not be overstated, since Japan certainly has a tradition of protest, and lawsuits are crucial to establishing or expanding employee rights such as job security and greater gender equality. Nonetheless, many individuals are ambivalent about demanding rights, and those who file complaints often find themselves censured by co-workers, even when they seemingly have just cause.

The Steady Growth Era

The 1973 "oil shock" brought an abrupt end to high economic growth, but also stimulated new efforts to increase productivity and reduce costs; these initiatives helped turn Japan into the world's pre-eminent manufacturing-exporting nation by the early 1980s. Leading manufacturers and cooperative unions quickly transformed *shuntō* into probably the tightest instrument of wage restraint among industrial democracies, though it also continued to help raise the pay of low-end earners and maintain a sense of economic fairness. The most prestigious metalworking firms (notably Toyota, Hitachi, Tōshiba, Nippon Steel, and Mitsubishi Heavy Industries) and their unions systematized their leadership over labor affairs, especially wage-setting. This prestige-based leadership continues today, though in less clear-cut fashion, thanks to the continued pre-eminence of the auto and electronics industries.

After the oil shock, cooperative unions elected to emphasize participation in labor-related policy-making rather than demand high wage increases. They reasoned that improving real living standards required continued shop-floor cooperation plus support for appropriate public policies (for example, tax reductions, employment support programs) instead of high wage increases, which risked undermining international economic competitiveness. The outcome is controversial. The unions have exerted influence, but it is hard to say how much, and the aims of left and right are still frequently opposed. Further, national labor bureaucrats rather than unions have often taken the lead in reformist policy-making.[16]

Cooperative unions became more closely intertwined with management from the 1960s.[17] Officials in mainstream cooperative unions tend to rotate into supervisors or managerial positions after serving terms of two to six years. Justified or not, close cooperation has undoubtedly contributed to the decline of organized labor by feeding the perception that unions have little influence, especially on wages. The organization rate has fallen steadily since 1975, sinking below 20 percent by 2003. The widespread perception of union ineffectiveness has aggravated the problem of "distancing from unions" (*kumiai-banare*), the loss of interest in union activities even among union members. Many firms make effective use of informal employee associations (perhaps reprising the prewar factory councils) to provide employees with a voice but limited influence.

Despite those problems, cooperative unions steadily strengthened their influence in organized labor as the left declined. This decline was hastened by the public sector unions' 1975 "strike for the right to strike," in which they sought to restore their strike rights, but succeeded mainly in angering the public. In the 1980s, Sōhyō was further weakened by the government's restructuring of the public sector. In 1987 the cooperative unions formed a new national labor federation, Rengō, which Sōhyō's public sector unions reluctantly entered in 1989. The consolidation of Rengō, which then accounted for nearly eight million workers, some 60 percent of the organized workforce, represented a victory for the vision of cooperative unionism. However, the longstanding ideological division, though greatly attenuated, continues to weaken the union movement. Seeking to revitalize unionism, Rengō has sought to better represent women and non-regular workers, and to work with other social organizations, especially the small (and invariably left-leaning) "community" unions. Such initiatives, however, are hindered by the apathy or opposition of many enterprise unions.

Contemporary Employment Issues

Following the oil crisis, employers intensified the rationalization of workplaces, partly by increasing automation and reducing the numbers of full-time workers. Although Japan has had enviably low levels of both unemployment and inflation, firms have sometimes reduced core workforces, notably following the 1973 oil shock and the 1986 "high yen" recession, and during the extended post-bubble slump. In the 1970s, transfers to affiliates were the core means of reduction, but more important recently has been so-called "voluntary early retirement," aimed primarily at older workers. Japan maintained high levels of manufacturing employment into the early 1990s, and avoided making fundamental changes in employment practices for longer than its Western counterparts, partly because of the manufacturing sector's strong competitiveness.

Nevertheless, new forces began to undermine "traditional" practices and to erode job security, especially after 1991. Japanese manufacturing firms, which once sought to keep jobs and core technologies at home, began to expand foreign direct investment significantly from the mid 1980s. Steady rationalization in the face of low-cost Asian competitors is now eliminating or devaluing many of the remaining production jobs. Japan's large enterprises were once highly stable, but since the late 1990s even prestigious firms, notably in finance and manufacturing, have faced retrenchment. Construction and public works functioned as Japan's Keynesian policy equivalent during the postwar era, accounting for proportionately two to three times more jobs than in other industrialized countries, and protectionist policies shielded jobs in many non-competitive sectors, like food processing. However, such costly policies have become unsustainable, leading to painful shakeouts.

The pressure to reduce labor costs has brought about a steady erosion of many practices that were never formally institutionalized, notably seniority-based pay increases and job security. The intensification of competitive pressures has turned labor cost-cutting into normal practice, rendering existing legal restraints on dismissal less effective. The "wage raise *shuntō*" appears dead, and many or most regular employees, civil servants included, have suffered pay cuts since 1999. Certainly, long-term employment remains important in principle and practice. Employers continue to recruit school-leavers and expect them to dedicate themselves to the firm. However, they have steadily reduced the number of regular workers in favor of lower-paid non-regular workers. Employers have also reduced the importance of *nenkō*-based raises and other leveling practices in favor of merit- or performance-oriented promotion and pay schemes.

The increased emphasis on merit has created better opportunities for the most talented and ambitious, women included, but working conditions and pressures appear to be worsening. This situation has strengthened the reform position in the longstanding debate about whether quality of life has been sacrificed to economic growth. Poor work conditions, especially long hours, are now regarded one of the major barriers to equal opportunity for women and a source of serious health problems. Death by overwork (*karōshi*) became a major issue in the 1990s, and activist pressure has brought a gradual easing of standards for proving it. In addition, long work hours are believed to hold down new job creation.

Labor market conditions have deteriorated since the late 1990s. The peak unemployment rate, 5.4 percent in 2002, remained well below European levels, but non-regular employment has grown rapidly (academics sometimes debate whether non-regular jobs are "replacing" regular jobs, though most other observers certainly assume they do). School-leavers could until recently be relatively sure of finding decent work, but the previously tight school-to-work link has been severed[18] and youth unemployment has reached double figures. Considerable attention has focused on "freeters," youths who live with their parents and work at marginal jobs rather than pursuing careers and raising families. Elder unemployment was a labor policy priority for years, but Japan has quickly joined other OECD countries in shifting resources toward alleviating youth unemployment. However, employment-support-related expenditures remain very low by OECD levels.

The changed socioeconomic environment has altered the dynamics of labor policy-making. Like other industrialized countries, Japan now seeks to utilize market principles to encourage the creation of new (and better) jobs rather than protect old ones, and to better incorporate women into the workforce. In the mid 1990s, the Cabinet began more closely to support business demands for increased labor flexibility through direct intervention in labor policy-making. The white collar and service sectors (which, in contrast to manufacturing, were long notorious for low labor productivity) have been an important target of liberalization (or deregulation). By 2004, the main obstacles to hiring contract and agency temporary workers were mostly eliminated.

Japan has enjoyed great success in channeling women into economically useful roles, especially dedicated housewives and low-wage workers,[19] but this legacy means that the country now lags badly in instituting equal opportunity. The deterioration of economic conditions in the early 1970s prompted managers to intensify the use of women as non-regular employees, a strategy that clashed with the simultaneous emergence of gender equality (or equal opportunity) as a global norm. Consequently, the 1985 Equal Employment Opportunity Law (EEOL) was enacted largely to placate international opinion, and did not actually prohibit discrimination.[20] Equal opportunity was further undermined by government policies encouraging women to emphasize their roles as homemakers.

Nonetheless, women continued to advance in the working world, while new concerns – especially the falling birthrate and the desire to raise workforce quality – led policy-makers to view equal opportunity more seriously from around 1990. Childcare support has been steadily upgraded, and the Revised EEOL (1997) prohibited discrimination, though it has few teeth. The greatest obstacle to equal opportunity now is less overt discrimination than strong economic incentives to utilize low-cost non-regular workers (primarily part-timers, but also contract workers, agency temporaries, and *arubaito*, people doing low-status jobs like restaurant work).[21] Non-regulars earn less than regular workers and are much easier to dismiss, though many perform the same tasks as regular (full-time) workers, so the incentives to hire them grow ever stronger as competitive pressures intensify. Non-regular employees now account for 30 percent of the workforce, and more than half of female employees. The belief (of government bureaucrats especially) that poor work conditions dissuade couples from having more children is an important force presently driving much labor-related policy-making. Japan continues to emphasize market-oriented policies (which hold down spending) and incremental reforms (which do not challenge managerial prerogative), but many observers believe that the real priorities should be improving work conditions and strengthening the social safety net.

The 700,000-plus foreign workers in Japan pose another vexing problem. Although they are already essential to some industries, many are illegal aliens who work in hazardous jobs and lack basic rights. The steady decline of the working-age population means that Japan probably faces a choice between accepting far more foreign workers and accepting much lower economic growth or even economic decline.

Conclusion

The period since the burst of the bubble has seen great change in employment policies and practices, yet labor–management cooperation remains strong, as does the work ethic. Nonetheless, Japan, once seemingly impervious to the problems of poverty and youth unemployment troubling other societies, is now also being forced to consider how to prevent the socioeconomic marginalization of growing numbers of citizens. While close labor–management cooperation generated major controversy in past decades, the next great theme in labor-related studies may center on employment policy. Many observers believe that Japanese labor and welfare institutions resemble those of Europe's social democratically oriented societies, others that they are closer to American-style market-driven practices. Research on new labor practices and the relatively neglected policy-making arena should play a leading role in the next stage of the ongoing controversy about the relative benefits of Japan's employment and industrial relations practices.

NOTES

1   Gordon, *The Wages of Affluence*; Dore, *British Factory Japanese Factory*. Clear-cut advocates seem to be much more common among Japanese than non-Japanese scholars.
2   Shirai, ed., *Contemporary Industrial Relations in Japan*; Kumazawa, *Portraits of the Japanese Workplace*.
3   See Hunter, ed., *Japanese Women Working*; Roberts, *Staying on the Line*.
4   For example, Cole, *Japanese Blue Collar*.
5   Tsurumi, *Factory Girls*.
6   Gordon, *The Evolution of Labor Relations*, p. 45.
7   Gordon, *The Evolution of Labor Relations* and *Labor and Imperial Democracy*; similarly Tsurumi, *Factory Girls*.
8   Garon, *The State and Labor*.
9   Tsutsui, *Manufacturing Ideology*.
10 For example, Rohlen, *For Harmony and Strength*; Clark, *The Japanese Company*.
11 Foote, "Judicial Creation of Norms."
12 Tsutsui, *Manufacturing Ideology*.
13 Cole, *Strategies for Learning*.
14 Roberson, *Japanese Working Class Lives*, p. 94.
15 Rohlen, *For Harmony and Strength*; Clark, *The Japanese Company*.
16 Foote, "Law as an Agent of Change?"
17 Suzuki, "The Death of Unions' Associational Life?"
18 Honda, "Formation and Transformation."
19 Female factory operators made crucial contributions to the textile and consumer electronics industries. Thanks to the public sector unions, women have enjoyed relatively equal treatment in public teaching and the local civil service.
20 Lam, *Women and Japanese Management*.
21 The proportion of male non-regular workers is rising, but three-quarters or more are still women.

BIBLIOGRAPHY

Clark, Rodney. *The Japanese Company*. New Haven: Yale University Press, 1979.
Cole, Robert. *Japanese Blue Collar*. Berkeley: University of California Press, 1971.
Cole, Robert. *Strategies for Learning: Small-Group Activities in American, Japanese, and Swedish Industry*. Berkeley: University of California Press, 1989.
Dore, Ronald P. *British Factory Japanese Factory: The Origins of National Diversity in Industrial Relations*. Berkeley: University of California Press, 1973.
Foote, Daniel. "Judicial Creation of Norms in Japanese Labor Law: Activism in the Service of Stability?" *UCLA Law Review* 43:3 (Feb. 1996): 635–709.
Foote, Daniel. "Law as an Agent of Change? Governmental Efforts to Reduce Working Hours in Japan." In Harald Baum, ed., *Japan: Economic Success and Legal System*. Berlin and New York: Walter de Gruyter, 1997.
Garon, Sheldon. *The State and Labor in Modern Japan*. Berkeley: University of California Press, 1987.

Gordon, Andrew. *The Evolution of Labor Relations in Japan, Heavy Industry, 1853–1955*. Cambridge, Mass.: Council on East Asian Studies, Harvard University, 1985.

Gordon, Andrew. *Labor and Imperial Democracy in Prewar Japan*. Berkeley: University of California Press, 1991.

Gordon, Andrew. *The Wages of Affluence: Labor and Management in Postwar Japan*. Cambridge, Mass.: Harvard University Press, 1998.

Honda, Yuki. "The Formation and Transformation of the Japanese System of Transition from School to Work." *Social Science Japan Journal* 7:1 (Apr. 2004): 103–15.

Hunter, Janet, ed. *Japanese Women Working*. London: Routledge, 1993.

Industrial Relations, special issue: "Japanese Industrial Relations in the New Millennium" (Oct. 2002).

Kumazawa Makoto. *Portraits of the Japanese Workplace: Labor Movements, Workers, and Managers*, ed. Andrew Gordon, trans. Andrew Gordon and Mikiso Hane. Boulder, Colo.: Westview Press, 1996.

Lam, Alice. *Women and Japanese Management: Discrimination and Reform*. London: Routledge, 1992.

Roberson, James. *Japanese Working Class Lives*. London: Routledge, 1998.

Roberts, Glenda. *Staying on the Line: Blue-Collar Women in Contemporary Japan*. Honolulu: University of Hawai'i Press, 1994.

Rohlen, Thomas. *For Harmony and Strength: Japanese White-Collar Organization in Anthropological Perspective*. Berkeley: University of California Press, 1974.

Shirai Taishiro, ed. *Contemporary Industrial Relations in Japan*. Madison: University of Wisconsin Press, 1983.

Suzuki Akira. "The Death of Unions' Associational Life? Political and Cultural Aspects of Enterprise Unions." In Frank Schwartz and Susan Pharr, eds., *The State of Civil Society in Japan*. Cambridge: Cambridge University Press, 2003.

Tsurumi, E. Patricia. *Factory Girls: Women in the Thread Mills of Meiji Japan*. Princeton: Princeton University Press, 1990.

Tsutsui, William. *Manufacturing Ideology: Scientific Management in Twentieth-Century Japan*. Princeton: Princeton University Press, 1998.

FURTHER READING

This article admittedly neglects technical studies, but perhaps the most prominent economic analyst is Koike Kazuo. While arguing that most Japanese practices are not unique, Koike's *The Economics of Work in Japan* (Tokyo: LTCB International Library Foundation, 1995) does emphasize the importance of continuous, long-term skill formation leading to the "white-collarization" of blue collar workers, who enjoy benefits and career ladders resembling those of white collar workers. Edward Lincoln and Arne Kalleberg's *Culture, Control and Commitment: A Study of Work Organization Work Attitudes in the U.S. and Japan* (Cambridge: Cambridge University Press, 1990) utilizes extensive comparative surveys of Japanese and US workers to argue for the success of Japanese corporate welfare practices. The surge in Japanese overseas investment from the 1980s enabled researchers to conduct in-depth research on Japanese work practices without Japanese language skills, giving rise to the "Japanization" literature. One excellent example is Laurie Graham's *On the Line at Subaru-Isuzu* (Ithaca, NY: ILR Press, 1995). Like a number of other works in this genre, it alleges poor work conditions and other problems. Two useful sources on recent changes are Suzuki Akira's essay "The Rise and Fall of Interunion Wage

Coordination and Tripartite Wage Coordination and Tripartite Dialogue in Japan,'' in Harry Katz, Wonduck Lee, and Joohee Lee, eds., *The New Structure of Labor Relations: Tripartism and Decentralization* (Ithaca, NY: Cornell University Press, 2004), and the October 2002 special issue of the journal *Industrial Relations* on "Japanese Industrial Relations in the New Millennium.''

For readers wishing to glimpse Japanese perspectives, Nimura Kazuo's study of mine workers, *The Ashio Riot of 1907: A Social History of Mining in Japan*, ed. and trans. Andrew Gordon (Durham, NC: Duke University Press, 1997), does double duty as an extended critique of Japanese-language studies of Meiji era labor. Important contributions have been made by scholars in works ranging well beyond labor affairs. They include Thomas Smith on economic history, Frank Upham on litigation, Michael Cusumano on the auto industry, Frank Schwartz on policy-making, and Hugh Whittaker on small firms.

CHAPTER TWENTY-NINE

Authority and the Individual

J. Victor Koschmann

In 1995, a flurry of news articles announced that a "volunteer revolution" was under way in Japan. Ironically, the occasion was provided by the massive earthquake that struck the Kobe–Osaka area early in the morning on January 17, 1995, killing over 6,400 people and rendering more than 300,000 homeless. In the wake of the disaster, as government agencies fumbled in red tape, over a million volunteers from all over Japan mobilized to provide emergency relief to the victims. This outpouring of civic-spirited initiative was hailed in the press, and some scholars soon concluded that, when added to other trends, the volunteer boom signified the advent at long last of a modern "civil society" in Japan.[1] Of course, civil society is defined variously, but the broadest contemporary usage draws from Alexis de Tocqueville to locate civil society in "the social relations and structures that lie between the state and the market."[2] Some emphasize the proliferation of organizations and associations while others, especially in Japan, think primarily of the qualities and activities of "citizens." Political scientist Iokibe Makoto explains that, "When Japanese political scientists use the term 'civil society,' it is usually as the abstract concept of the society of citizens in contrast to the apparatus of the state. The same term may remind Americans of more specific, nongovernmental private organizations. The society of citizens and private organizations are not conflicting concepts."[3]

The recent excitement in Japan over volunteering and civil society is of immediate interest in relation to the problematic of authority and the individual in part because in post-World War II Japan, civil society and the ideal of the citizen have been debated primarily with reference to political activism and protest. For example, political scientist Matsushita Keiichi was one who paid special attention to the "citizens' movements" (*shimin undō*) that sprang up in the 1960s and early 1970s in opposition to war, environmental pollution, and political corruption. Writing in 1971, he characterized the emerging Japanese citizen as "free, a self-respecting human being, capable of effectively organizing and initiating political policy. He is active in politics because he is concerned with the problems of daily life rather than with an abstract sense of duty to the nation." Such citizens were beginning to resist what Matsushita called the "control model" of political integration that centered on "an elitist, bureaucratic mentality." In its place they sought to institute a "citizen participation model" of political integration and policy formation from the grass roots.[4] Like other left-leaning scholars who believed that Japan's modern revolution had been only partial and that the project of modernity was therefore woefully incomplete, especially in the realm of political culture and values, Matsushita expected that these new citizens would finally build a progressive civil society.

However, in the discourse on civil society and volunteering that has emerged since 1995, these concepts have often been divested of their former association with political dissent. Of course, this does not mean that they have no political implications, but merely that those implications now tend to be subtle and implicit. In order to perceive them it is often necessary to depart from the usual assumptions regarding historical agency, power, and resistance.

Civil Society and the State

The viewpoint that genuine civil society has only recently emerged in Japan is supported by a particular way of looking at Japanese history. For example, Iokibe proposes three prerequisites for a healthy civil society – pluralism, appreciation for the intrinsic value of the "people" and the private realm, and awareness of the public interest – and offers an historical analysis to show how these failed to develop fully in Japan. He finds that in the early modern era (1600–1868), the regional decentralization of the Tokugawa regime and the hierarchical division of society into separate castes of samurai, merchant, artisan, and farmer created the basis for forms of cultural diversity that could be expressed as pluralism. In regard to the dignity of the people, however, he finds that the spiritual concept of respect for each individual as a manifestation of the Buddha, and comparable ideas in the Confucian tradition, were never allowed to "evolve into a theory of democratic principles" or to "come into play in the realities of politics and government" because of the separation of the "private," as partial and unworthy, from the all-powerful "public" authority of power structures. The emergence of a general notion of the public interest was prevented by the same social differentiation and compartmentation that gave rise to diversity.[5]

In the modern era, following the Meiji Restoration of 1868, Japan's potential for civil society is seen as having been retarded by a new set of circumstances. These included the Meiji state's drive to centralize and develop Japan economically from the top down in the manner typical of "late-developing societies," the bureaucracy's increasing authority and dominance, and the predatory environment of imperialism in which Japanese leaders strove both to defend Japan and to launch their own imperial and colonial ventures. Nevertheless, the 1920s brought an "associational revolution" in the proliferation of a wide variety of private organizations of the sort that suggest an active civil society. These included businessmen's groups, labor unions, welfare societies, and academic, cultural, and international groupings of all kinds. Nevertheless, Iokibe concludes that: "The privately initiated endeavors of this period were troubled by the inherent vulnerability of greenhouse-cultivated plants. They had not put down the sturdy roots that were needed to endure the cruel assault of ultranationalism and militarism that swept the country following the Manchurian Incident."[6]

The post-World War II American occupation "liberated" individuals and the private realm in some ways, but at the same time preserved the central bureaucracy and, implicitly, its ethos of monopolistic domination. Moreover, the postwar government's extreme emphasis on economic recovery and growth not only reinforced bureaucratic dominance and the values of "productionism," but encouraged the hierarchical loyalism that during the war had focused on the state to be redirected toward corporations, labor unions, and other economic entities, thus continuing to impede the formation of multiple, cross-cutting affiliations and associations. Only in the 1980s did the private realm gain sufficient independence and freedom to allow a true civil society to emerge.

The American historian of modern Japan, Sheldon Garon, takes a different approach. He begins his historical reflections by expressing doubts about the wisdom of importing the concept of civil society to Japan, where it did not originate. He also attempts to avoid preconceptions regarding the degree of "success" civil society might have had in the Japanese historical context. As a result, he provides a nuanced and sober argument, looking not at the overall orientation of state policy, like Matsushita, but rather at how representatives of the state actually interacted with a variety of components of civil society in the prewar, wartime, and postwar eras. For him, civil society includes "the groups and public discourses that exist in spaces between the state and the people" as well as "various forms of media." He adds that, "These associations and media are usually established independently of the state, but not always." Using this definition, he finds that although government intervention and domination, as well as voluntary cooperation on the part of private entities, wax and wane in modern Japan, the net result is a civil society subject to varying degrees of dependence on the state. Garon recognizes the many limits the Tokugawa shogunate imposed on developments conducive to civil society. Nevertheless, he also notes that eventually, even in the early modern period, "significant space opened up for public discussion and associational life." Noting the spread of literacy, he mentions especially the proliferation of publications, private and domainal academies, merchant societies, and intellectual and cultural associations among rich peasants. However, rather than threatening the existing order, these activities "generally served to manage the populace and stabilize the rule of higher authorities."[7] Garon is also impressed by the relative "autonomy" and "spirited resistance to the government" that are evident in the late nineteenth century, following the Meiji Restoration, when newspapers mushroomed, a new middle class began to be active in the cities, wealthy peasants as well as urban intellectuals formed study groups, the Freedom and People's Rights Movement (*jiyū minken undō*) spread, and Christians inspired by the social gospel "founded private charities, orphanages and reformatories."[8]

From the turn of the twentieth century, however, the state intervened with increasing vigor, passing a variety of laws that gradually reorganized and regulated a variety of rural agricultural, trade, and social organizations under the state: "In each case, the regime provided associations and cooperatives with subsidies and other benefits. In exchange, the associations surrendered their autonomy, becoming part of hierarchical organizations intended to further official policies."[9] This pattern would be repeated frequently in the decades to come. Although Garon notes the strong resurgence in the 1920s of civil society in the form of associations, mass media, women's groups, and religious sects, he cautions against exaggeration: "Despite its vitality, civil society did not develop as autonomously from the state as historians commonly portray in their accounts of interwar Japan." Private organizations often eagerly cooperated with state bureaucracies, trading autonomy for varying combinations of legitimacy, power, and financial support. The result is ambiguous:

> On balance, the interwar alliances between societal activists and bureaucrats served to enmesh popular groups, making it difficult for civil society to challenge the state. At the same time, these associations could be quite assertive, and the state was forced eventually to include many societal actors in the apparatus of governance. In this sense, the interwar expansion of civil society altered and, ironically, "popularized" the state's management of society.[10]

Garon's account is especially persuasive in relation to the wartime and postwar periods, from the early 1930s down to the 1990s. In the case of wartime, he finds that the state did, indeed, attempt to "obliterate civil society." Nevertheless, it either could not, or decided not to, transform entirely the patterns of interaction among state institutions, private organizations, and individuals that had developed in the preceding decades. Many private media were allowed to continue because of their potential usefulness in mobilizing the populace. Moreover, many local and other associations were left more or less intact but incorporated into newly established, hierarchical frameworks. The new "totalitarian designs" for society had paradoxical effect, in that "authoritarian incorporation often had the unintended effect of relocating civil society's spirited debates and competition within the state itself." Thus, "officials were compelled to 'democratize' their managerial apparatus, deputizing previously powerless elements."[11]

Garon's organizational analysis can be supplemented with an intellectual history of the 1930s and early 1940s, and such a history would likely suggest that the devolution of a certain amount of autonomy to organizations and individuals, even within an explicitly "totalistic" framework, was not entirely unintended. For example, in a 1940 report prepared under the auspices of a think tank that advised the prime minister, philosopher Miki Kiyoshi and economist Ryū Shintarō rationalized the controlled economy through an ideology of "cooperativism" that emphasized "the individuality, spontaneity, and creativity of each person, thereby encouraging free competition to secure a higher level of functionality." People had to be persuaded of the practicality of the economic plan so they could "participate in it spontaneously and actively."[12] Similarly, in June 1942 social policy expert Ōkōchi Kazuo hailed the appearance of a new worker who had "the knowledge and insight necessary to grasp the objective facts of wartime economic controls, and an active, spontaneous desire to size up the situation and determine what kind of economic activity is required"; and in 1944, the famous economic historian Ōtsuka Hisao promoted a new economic ethic that would combine intense "inner originality" with "instrumental rationality."[13] In other words, a number of wartime intellectuals who advised government agencies recognized that if economic and social mobilization for total war were to succeed, it would require not just passive obedience but active, constructive participation by all segments of the population. They also believed that such high motivation would emerge only as the counterpart to a modicum of freedom and autonomy. In other words, certain elements of civil society had to be enhanced, even in the context of a highly integrated, controlled system.

Following Japan's surrender, the occupation forces set about dismantling social structures that had supported Japan's version of fascism, and had a great deal of success. However, as Garon points out, especially at the level of organizational networks and dynamics, significant continuity survived the transition from wartime to postwar: "A more assertive civil society unquestionably emerged during the early postwar years. At the same time, many seemingly autonomous groups remained intertwined with the state."[14] At the local level, organizations reconstituted themselves along wartime lines, and at the regional and national level organizations of women, youth, unionists, and businessmen again showed their willingness to cooperate with, and to some extent be dominated by, state bureaucracies. For its part, the postwar state continued its practice of subsidizing, and thereby both strengthening and sapping the independence of, a wide range of associations. Garon admits that the rise of oppositional citizens' movements in the 1960s and 1970s "strained" relations between civil society and the state, but "officials soon found ways of harnessing popular energy to achieve national goals." Apropos of the volunteer boom, he observes that:

> To address the problem of Japan's rapidly aging society, the Ministry of Health and Welfare spearheaded efforts to muster ever-increasing numbers of community "volunteers" to assist the elderly and others during the 1980s and 1990s. ... Of course, many of these people have decided on their own to help out. Still, we should not forget that the core of these so-called volunteers are members of existing local associations that have long cooperated with the authorities.[15]

As Garon suggests, the "volunteer revolution" post-1995 combined spontaneous activism by individuals with vigorous encouragement from government and the media.

Volunteer Boom

Partly in response to the public discourse on volunteering and civil society that expanded so rapidly in the 1990s, in 1998 the National Diet passed the so-called Nonprofit Organization (NPO) Law, or Law to Promote Specified Nonprofit Activities. The law, which was intended to facilitate citizen participation in activities that "benefit society" and "contribute to the advancement of public welfare," led to significant increases in the number of officially recognized NPOs. By one reckoning the number of authorized NPOs reached about 5,000 by mid-2002, 10,000 by 2003, and over 15,000 by 2004. Most are in health and social welfare, adult education, community development, youth affairs, and international cooperation. The volunteers who staff them are from various walks of life, and identify themselves as housewives (31 percent), retirees (18 percent), businesspeople (14 percent), or self-employed persons (10 percent). Overall, substantially more women than men volunteer, although executives of NPOs tend to be male.[16]

Even such a rough breakdown of participants raises the question of motivation. The fact that women and retirees tend to be the most numerous suggests that a depressed labor market that discriminates against women and recently generates increased numbers of relatively young retirees might be a factor in the volunteer boom. According to Lynne Nakano,

> Statistics show that the rates of volunteering peak among women in the thirties and men in the sixties, ages when workforce participation rates for men and women are at their lowest. In this way, volunteering is partly a product of institutional structures that privilege young women's and middle-aged and younger men's participation in the workforce, and leave the lowest paying and the least desirable jobs to middle-aged and older women and older men.[17]

In 2002, over 60 percent of female Japanese workers were part-time and/or held "permanently temporary status" in the workforce. Moreover, so-called part-time workers often have to work virtually the same hours as full-time workers.[18] When these working conditions are combined with tax laws that penalize wives who make more than one million yen per year, it is not surprising that many married women volunteer instead, especially since many volunteers in NPOs are actually paid a small amount.

However, several studies suggest that material conditions alone provide an inadequate account of volunteers' motivation. Apparently, it is necessary to take into account values and, more broadly, issues related to personal identity and meaning. In her study of "housewife" volunteers, for example, Robin LeBlanc observed that they were motivated in part by the values of "openness, equality, flexibility, and respect for individual difference with a general emphasis on 'humanity' in relations (as opposed to rank, custom, or prestige)." Even more interestingly, she finds that local volunteering – in a neighborhood center for the handicapped, in this case – reinforces and overlaps with the encompassing identity of "housewife." That is, volunteering not only requires many of the same skills as homemaking but it functions as a counterpart to, and even a means to realizing, the fundamental identity of a housewife.[19] At the same time, it generates the knowledge and power that put housewives in contact with local bureaucrats and power-brokers, thereby in some cases complicating and even threatening the egalitarian, humanitarian values they espouse. To be sure, according to LeBlanc, the housewife-volunteer identity is inherently political because it provides a way of situating oneself in relation to public expectations.[20] It is a public persona that is recognized and provides a locus for self-expression and a certain authority. Yet it is also subjectively "anti-political" in that the women consider neighborly, housewifely values to be fundamentally opposed to those informing the political world.[21]

Identity, in the sense of a personal life strategy that provides meaning, satisfaction, and public respect, was also important in the cases investigated by Lynne Nakano. In Japan's affluent society, individuals are conscious of making choices among alternative lifestyles and identities, and volunteering is one choice.[22] Similarly, in commenting on a publication by a group of young people volunteering in the day-laborer slums of Tokyo, Carolyn Stevens reports that, for the authors, volunteering has to do primarily with "one's own will and desire." Their approach to volunteering "does not necessarily focus on the cause or the object of the work, but focuses on the actors themselves. In other words, volunteering has just as much to do with the volunteers themselves as the services they perform."[23] Such observations are borne out in Akihiro Ogawa's ethnographic study of an educational NPO in which the volunteers "were just looking for 'something' to satisfy their own individual needs." As one volunteer remarked, "We primarily try to enhance ourselves through volunteering."[24] Apparently, many contemporary Japanese are attracted to volunteering for personal reasons involving identity and lifestyle quite apart from any sense of duty or desire to contribute to society and the world. At the same time, by its very nature, volunteering through the media of NGOs, NPOs, or local, unofficial groups and associations is tightly imbricated in the sociopolitical world.

To what degree is the recent increase in volunteer-type civil association and activism actually new and unprecedented? Some, including Iokibe and Matsushita, mention the "citizens' movements" of 1960 and after as manifestations of a postwar ethos of activism in civil society. It is true that recent manifestations of volunteerism seem to differ from the 1960s in their relatively low level of overt politicality. On the other hand, the various forms of social organization that fed into the political demonstrations of the 1960s and fueled the environmental and other movements of the early 1970s were not necessarily political from the beginning. In his eye-opening study of the origins of citizen participation in the massive movement against the US–Japan Security Treaty in 1960, Wesley Sasaki-Uemura shows that "the groundwork for grassroots activism had already been laid by various circle movements that had formed in the 1950s. These were small, informal, voluntary organizations whose face-to-face contact may be have been their most salient characteristic." In the 1950s, such groups were usually focused on cultural activities such as singing, dancing, poetry, hiking, or nature appreciation. Members were very often women, and "what distinguished circles from other social relations was that people created and maintained them on the basis of common personal interests" rather than in response to government or other organizations' mobilization efforts. Even those initiated by the Communist Party retained considerable independence and spurned party directives.[25]

For example, the women who comprised the Grass Seeds (Kusa no Mi Kai) circle "had come together to study and discuss problems that women faced in everyday life." Accordingly, they sought to remain non-partisan, even though many members eventually participated in the 1960 anti-Treaty demonstrations. According to Sasaki-Uemura, "The model of informal, egalitarian gatherings that also had a public character suited the Grass Seeds and other such citizen movements that organized themselves on the principles of local autonomy and voluntary, individual participation."[26] In other words, groups such as the Grass Seeds should be considered typical elements of modern civil society. While oriented primarily to civil rather than political matters, they are quite aware of the political relevance of their concerns and are ready to act politically if it serves their purposes. In this regard, such associations are not unlike the contemporary volunteer groups studied by LeBlanc.

On the other hand, some argue convincingly that contemporary Japanese volunteerism depends heavily on technological and cultural conditions specific to the cybernetic age. The explanation offered by historian of social thought Nakano Toshio emphasizes the choices among the wide range of alternative identities made available to young people via the Internet. He postulates that, "the weakening of social bonds as a result of the hyper-informationalization of society leads to expansion and diversification of information impacting on individuals, and exposes them to the influence of pluralistic social forces." By hyper-informationalization he refers primarily to individuals' constant access to electronic media:

Children who once learned established customs and skills … through "helping" their parents are now seated in front of television and computer screens and, through animation and role-playing games as well as e-mail and telephone interactions with others, learn multiple "realities" and "lifestyles" in abstraction from both temporal frame and national and class connections; as a result, they absorb a wide range of emotional expressions and ways of communicating. …[T]hese individuals are like terminals in which multifarious knowledges (powers) intersect, or like nodes of information processing and selection.

The various identities they encounter are "abstract," in that they are not embedded in real life contexts; nevertheless they provide an unprecedented degree of what Alberto Melucci calls "potential for individualization." That is, individuals are confronted with many alternatives, and from them can eclectically piece together their own identity. However, this set of possibilities – in other words, "freedom" – is always ambivalent:

On the one hand, individuals at the intersection of plural social forces are confronted with many behavioral alternatives, and to that extent their ability to reflect and adapt is heightened …; on the other hand, in order to gain access to objects of desire and the codes through which they can be obtained and understood, the individual must depend on various interventionist social forces that manipulate symbols, and these forces are capable in some cases of thoroughly subjecting the individual to control.[27]

Therefore, the "potential for individualization" is ambivalently situated as the precondition both for freedom and unfreedom.

Forces for national solidarity and social order respond in different ways to the individual's potential for freedom. On the one hand, they can negate that potential by coercing or cajoling the individual into established roles and responsibilities; on the other, they may seek to guide the individual's "free" and "spontaneous" search for self-identity in such a way that it supports and merges with the established social system. When successful, either response can narrow the individual's range of choice and reduce his experience of difference, but it is the latter response that is consistent with "glorification of 'volunteering as a way of life'," and mobilization of "abstract volunteer subjects." By abstract, here Nakano means they are committed for personal reasons to volunteering as such rather than merely employing it as a means. Moreover, precisely because this spontaneous subject is abstract, it has a "built-in affinity for the dominant discursive mode in the contemporary 'public' realm (and, therefore, an affinity for nationalism in the broad sense, which incorporates us as a 'we')."[28] In other words, so long as people seek opportunities to volunteer merely in pursuit of personal goals, such as identity formation, meaning in life, self-respect, etc., while making minimal value judgments in selecting one opportunity over another, they are likely to end up in volunteer programs that ratify the status quo. This tendency toward "abstract" volunteering is likely to be intensified by recent publications extolling volunteerism, which dwell not on the social usefulness or significance to the state of volunteer activity but rather on its intrinsic value to the volunteer, that is, the supposedly salutary effect of the "volunteer lifestyle."[29]

Civil Society and Neo-Liberal Governance

Among the recent developments often mentioned as preconditions for the volunteer boom are Japan's trade surpluses of the 1980s, which created the conditions for remarkable increases in foreign aid, including the Japan Overseas Cooperation Volunteer program which sent young people abroad for people-to-people aid. Such programs contributed to the attractiveness of volunteering as at least a temporary alternative to corporate life. The same surpluses also generated pressure for an expansion of corporate philanthropy, exemplified in the One Percent Club formed in Keidanren (Japan Federation of Economic Organizations) in 1989 to urge member corporations to donate 1 percent of their pre-tax revenues to charity. Environmental pollution and the expansion of research regarding such issues as global warming raised consciousness regarding international environmental issues and the uses of activism. Moreover, the cold war ended, which lowered barriers among nations and created a more pluralistic global environment for transnational civil society.[30] Popular consciousness of and interest in non-profit organizations was stimulated by the national press. According to one study, articles on NGOs and NPOs in the three major dailies numbered 178 in 1990, 850 in 1992, and 1,455 in 1994. After the quake they jumped to 2,151 in 1995 and 2,868 in 1997.[31]

The most important factor mentioned, however, was the turn in the 1980s toward the "politics of Ronald Reagan, Margaret Thatcher, and [Japanese Prime Minister] Nakasone Yasuhiro," who "advocated private-sector participation in public projects and privatization of public enterprises, stressing the market economy and small government." According to Iokibe, "the determination in the 1980s to invigorate the private sector without relying on the government provided important conditions for the development of civil society."[32] This "determination" was manifested in part in the Ad Hoc Commission on Administrative Reform, an advisory organ to the prime minister. Among the results was the establishment of "government-private burden-sharing" as the guiding principle of reform. Government policy, therefore, is centrally involved in the "volunteer boom." This is evident from a number of angles. The Central Council for Education, which advises the Ministry of Education, Culture, Sports, Science, and Technology, recently issued a draft revision of the Fundamental Law of Education that promoted the principle of "civic responsibility for proactively participating in public affairs." Ogawa quotes the draft revision:

> It is the responsibility of people living in a democratic country to be proactively involved in matters of the state and society. ... However, so far we Japanese are liable to depend on somebody else's action regarding these issues. We believe it is someone else's responsibility. That is not acceptable. Instead, we need to cultivate a sense of public awareness.

It is striking that here the conservative Education Ministry is criticizing political and social passivity and promoting participatory activism by appealing to the same developmental model of Japanese backwardness that has been a staple of left-wing discourse. More specifically, the Ministry has begun promoting volunteerism as a way of life:

> Volunteering should be considered a key for solving and answering social problems we are now facing. Volunteering provides an opportunity for social participation as independent, autonomous individuals. Such individuals are expected to contribute to generating and supporting the new "public." [Their participation] will become crucial in the drive to support a rich, civil society.[33]

Note the emphasis here on public service and solving social problems rather than personal growth. The phrasing echoes wartime injunctions to "serve the public and suppress the self" (*messhi hōkō*).

It is important to note, however, that, as evidenced in the wording of the NPO Law, the government encourages only certain kinds of volunteer activities. The law explicitly excludes any organization or activity that is "for the purpose of recommending, supporting, or opposing a political principle" or "candidate ... for public office." Such exclusions are clearly intended to distinguish the new NPOs from the partisan, oppositionally oriented citizens' movements that Matsushita sought to promote in 1971.

The government also promotes selected NPOs by providing them with financing. The two major income sources for NPOs are membership fees and government support. Welfare NPOs, which are the most numerous, get over 82 percent of their income from government sources.[34] More importantly, since passage of the NPO Law, governments (especially municipal governments) have not only verbally encouraged volunteering but become actively involved in recruiting volunteers and/or forming NPOs under the rubric of "cooperation" and "collaboration" (*kyōdō*). Through such relationships, government officials "entrust" certain tasks to NPOs while retaining a level of control. This often allows governments to reduce their own staff and budgets in line with efforts to streamline government operations through "privatization."[35] As one scholar noted, "To maximize utility ..., it is essential that the nonprofit sector participate in the market along with government and business and that each of the three function to the fullest. NPOs in Japan, however, are still in their infancy, making it necessary to facilitate their development in tandem with administrative reform."[36]

The perceived need to "facilitate" the development of NPOs leads government officials to try to motivate and mobilize "volunteers," who inevitably have their own desires and agendas, while at the same time maintaining substantial control. The tortuous verbiage of an informal government paper conveys vividly the contradictions involved:

> Speaking of the continuing education policy, the basic principle should be self-learning by residents themselves. The learning activities should be operated by the residents' spontaneous will. However, such opportunity for learning should be strategically arranged and intentionally organized by the municipal government. ... The residents are expected to not only acquire some new knowledge and skills but also to enhance themselves and improve the quality of their lives through involvement in this project. Thus, the proposed project of continuing education would be "hand-made" by the volunteer-residents.[37]

In one case investigated by Ogawa, government officials felt they had to recruit volunteers openly, so they hung posters calling for people to contribute their time and talents to the project. At the same time, they were unwilling to leave the recruitment process entirely to chance, so they personally invited some favored individuals to "volunteer." By the time the education center opened, there were 47 resident volunteers, of whom 34 had been recruited by the officials themselves. They then maneuvered these hand-picked "volunteers" into leadership positions in the newly formed NPO.[38]

The interventionist role that government officials assume in order to carry out neo-liberal administrative reform brings to mind Michel Foucault's discussion of govern-mentality. For Foucault, "neo-liberalism" refers not merely to the early modern realization that state rationality is incapable of knowing and controlling everything within the space of governance and that therefore solidarities and processes within civil society itself, including market mechanisms, must to some extent be allowed to participate in governing. The result of that initial realization was *liberalism*. On the other hand, *neo-liberalism* responded to the fully modern realization that markets and other phenomena of civil society are not always already there, as quasi-natural phenomena, but must be constructed and maintained by the state.[39] When a gov-ernment seeks to privatize various functions in the spirit of neo-liberal reform, it cannot just hand those functions over to pre-existing private institutions or leave them to be determined by pre-existing markets, but must invent and construct institutions and markets for that purpose. In the case of volunteers, the government must construct volunteers to do its bidding. The government would prefer these volunteers to be motivated by a spirit of service to the state, but they are more likely to volunteer for their own purposes.

System Society

How persuasive, then, is the "civil society" interpretation of the contemporary volunteer boom? The first problem, of course, has already been alluded to, and that is that it perpetuates an image of Japan and Japanese history as developmentally retarded. In other words, it implies that, as Iokibe tends to argue, Japan's develop-ment of a "normal" civil society was stunted at a stage of incomplete modernization. Such a view has become increasingly difficult to sustain in light of research suggest-ing, for example, a high degree of modernization precisely during World War II when, it was thought, the country tended to revert to a premodern value system.[40] Rather, some critics argue, Japan's wartime leaders put in place a system of institu-tions and relationships that survived in most respects right down to the 1970s and 1980s. Economist Noguchi Yukio has called this the "1940 system" (*1940-nen taisei*).[41]

Others, including the historian of social thought Yamanouchi Yasushi, have argued convincingly that the postwar era saw the formation of a "system society," in which state and civil society, and the public and private realms, were increasingly merged. In such a society, citizens tend to share a single, internalized value system that helps maintain system integration based on homeostatic equilibrium among a variety of mutually dependent subsystems, including politics, business, family, and others. Economically, the system society was characterized by large-scale industrial produc-tion and centralization of institutions. People were often mobilized in such a system, but usually in groups rather than as individuals, and typically in ways that mirrored their institutional position in the system.[42] Most of those who argue for the system society analysis also contend that that society began to crumble in the 1980s, precisely when the government began to move toward neo-liberal deregulation. Since then, the system society has gradually eroded in favor of less tightly integrated and increasingly globalized forms of neo-liberal governance.

The viewpoint that between the 1940s and the 1980s Japan had a system society that distinguished it not only from the 1930s and before, but also from the period of the 1990s to the present, may help us understand some of the changes that, as we have seen, distinguish 1960s notions of civil society from those employed in the past several years. It also might make us more fully aware that the assumptions of a decade or two ago regarding the state's interaction with civil society and the nature of domination and resistance cannot always be applied without modification to the contemporary situation. Under the disintegration that characterizes neo-liberalism – which, of course, is by no means total but always in process – power relations are indirect and mediated. Therefore, domination of individuals and private associations must often employ a kind of "remote control." The state must be capable of motivating and controlling not only hand-picked agents but relatively autonomous subjects, such as those who volunteer on their own initiative primarily to reform their own identities and to fashion lives for themselves. How and why do such volunteers become active subjects (*shutai*) devoted to public objectives and ideals? Traditional conceptions of power make this difficult to visualize, but Foucault goes farther than most in attempting to elaborate a new understanding of power for that purpose.

Especially useful is the Foucauldian insight that government "is a 'contact point' where techniques of domination – or power – and *techniques of the self* 'interact' "; in other words, government is where "technologies of domination of individuals over one another have recourse to processes by which the individual acts upon himself and, conversely, ... where techniques of the self are integrated into structures of coercion."[43] Governing takes place when the government's efforts to mobilize and direct the population come into contact with and work through the "techniques" individuals develop, not only to manage their daily lives and interact with institutions and each other, but also to secure and enhance meaning and identity.

Some of the ways in which volunteering, as a technique of the self, connects with domination in the contemporary Japanese context might be illustrated by analogy with an American example, the "self-esteem movement." Initiated by the California Task Force to Promote Self-Esteem and Personal Responsibility in 1983, this movement seeks to build "citizenship" and social responsibility. Movement advocates claim that self-esteem "empowers" people – especially "poor urban people of colour" – and at the same time imbues them with a sense of responsibility to "exercise responsible citizenship." Individuals are called upon to "act, to participate." They "join programs, volunteer, but most importantly, work on and improve their self-image." In the ideology of the movement, self-esteem motivates people to engage in new forms of social action, for example, volunteering; conversely social action generates further self-esteem. As a Task Force publication urges, "Government and experts cannot fix these problems for us. It is only when each of us recognizes our individual personal and social responsibility to be part of the solution that we also realize higher 'self-esteem'." As Cruikshank sums it up, "self-esteem is a technology of citizenship and self-government for evaluating and acting upon our selves so that the police, the guards and the doctors do not have to."[44]

The analogy with the Japanese case is not perfect, but in Japan as well, government and other authorities have established a normative link between personality development (techniques of the self) and the social responsibility expressed in volunteering. It seems clear that most people initially volunteer out of personal motives having to do mostly with identity and meaning in life. Often, that is also how volunteering is discussed in the media. At the same time, as we have seen, the government is very concerned to instill in its citizens a strong sense of responsibility to contribute to society and its governance. A further example might be found in the ruling Liberal Democratic Party (LDP)'s anxious belief that Japanese citizens should feel increased responsibility for national defense. On June 15, 2004, the party's Project Team for Constitutional Revision proposed that the constitution be revised so as to establish explicitly the citizens' duty to cooperate with authorities in cases of national defense. Yasuoka Okiharu, chairman of the LDP's Constitutional Problems Research Council, recently explained: "It seems doubtful that today's young people have any consciousness of national defense. ... Why shouldn't they think a bit more about contributing to peace in their own country and the world, and about enhancing national security?"[45] Some speculate that if the LDP prevails, the result will be Japan's first conscription system since World War II.

Conclusion

It has recently been contended that a modern civil society, along with all the individual freedom and public participation that ideal implies, has developed in Japan only very recently, perhaps only since the "volunteer boom" of the mid-1990s. However, that contention is based in part on assumptions and habits of mind typical of the view that Japan continues to trail the West in modernization, and that view has recently been subjected to searching criticism. It is increasingly clear that Japan's social change has been more or less commensurate with that of other heavily industrialized societies in America and Europe. An alternative explanation for the "volunteer boom" would emphasize the gradual turn since the 1980s toward neo-liberal efforts to disaggregate the system society and rely more heavily on private institutions and individuals to provide social services and augment governance.

Under neo-liberalism, the government not only strives to shift a range of social responsibilities and risks to private citizens but intensifies its efforts to affect the values and behavior of the citizenry through a variety of means, including education and advertising as well as legislation. By such means, government agencies seek to channel people's aspirations, life choices, values, and behavior toward activities that are conducive to self-reliance, stable governance, productivity, and security. Because directly coercive means would be inconsistent with neo-liberal principles that emphasize privatization, decentralization, and personal freedom, authorities must stimulate individuals to govern themselves, and take responsibility for their own and others' welfare. In other words, neo-liberalism governs "through the regulated choices of individual citizens, now construed as subjects of choices and aspirations to self-actualization and self-fulfillment. Individuals are to be governed through their freedom."[46]

At the same time, in contemporary Japan a variety of conditions, including not only global neo-liberalism but affluence, the highly "informationalized" society, and the long recession that began in the early 1990s, have created an environment for individuals in which questions of meaning, identity, and "lifestyle" arise with new intensity, and imaginable alternatives proliferate, especially for young people. It is under such conditions that volunteer activity has become a popular vehicle for forming and enhancing identity, personal satisfaction, social prestige, and self-esteem. However, under neo-liberalism volunteering also becomes a crucial means of social mobilization. From the government's viewpoint, therefore, volunteering – whether to improve the environment, provide social services, or contribute to the national defense – should be a social obligation rather than merely a lifestyle choice. It is for these reasons that volunteerism, the discourse on civil society, and the proliferation of NPOs constitute primary sites for the emergence of new patterns of interaction between authority and the individual in the contemporary milieu.

NOTES

1 Yamamoto, "Emergence of Japan's Civil Society," p. 98; Iokibe, "Japan's Civil Society," pp. 88–96.
2 Ehrenberg, *Civil Society*, p. 235.
3 Iokibe, "Japan's Civil Society," p. 91.
4 Matsushita, "Citizen Participation in Historical Perspective," pp. 172–5.
5 Iokibe, "Japan's Civil Society," pp. 52–61.
6 Ibid., p. 75.
7 Garon, "From Meiji to Heisei," p. 44–6.
8 Ibid., p. 48.
9 Ibid., p. 50.
10 Ibid., pp. 55–6.
11 Ibid.
12 Shōwa Kenkyūkai, "Kyōdōshugi no keizai rinri," pp. 349, 355.
13 Ōkōchi, " 'Keizaijin' no shūen," pp. 421–2; Ōtsuka, "Saikōdo 'jihatsusei' no hatsuyō," p. 343.
14 Garon, "From Meiji to Heisei," p. 58.
15 Ibid., p. 61.
16 Ogawa, "The Failure of Civil Society?", pp. 43–4.
17 Nakano, "Volunteering as a Lifestyle Choice," p. 96.
18 Lee, "Taking Gender Seriously," p. 2.
19 LeBlanc, *Bicycle Citizens*, pp. 103–4.
20 Ibid., p. 59.
21 Ibid., pp. 96–7.
22 Nakano, "Volunteering as a Lifestyle Choice," pp. 94, 104.
23 Stevens, *On the Margins of Japanese Society*, p. 229.
24 Ogawa, "The Failure of Civil Society?", pp. 102, 112.
25 Sasaki-Uemura, *Organizing the Spontaneous*, pp. 26–8.
26 Ibid., pp. 39–40.
27 Nakano, *Ōtsuka Hisao to Maruyama Masao*, pp. 274–5.
28 Ibid., p. 281.

29 Ibid., p. 272.
30 Iokibe, "Japan's Civil Society," p. 87.
31 Yamamoto, "Emergence of Japan's Civil Society," pp. 101–2.
32 Iokibe, "Japan's Civil Society," pp. 85–6.
33 Ogawa, "The Failure of Civil Society?", pp. 108–10.
34 Ibid., p. 46.
35 Ibid., p. 105.
36 Ota, "Sharing Governance," p. 126.
37 Ogawa, "The Failure of Civil Society?", p. 99.
38 Ibid., pp. 98–100.
39 Burchell, "Liberal Government," pp. 23–4.
40 Evidence is presented in Yamanouchi, Koschmann, and Narita, eds., *Total War and "Modernization."*
41 Noguchi, *1940-nen taisei.*
42 Yamanouchi, "Total War and System Integration," pp. 14–23.
43 Burchell, "Liberal Government," p. 20. Also see Foucault, "Technologies of the Self," pp. 16–19.
44 Cruikshank, "Revolutions Within," pp. 232–5.
45 "Senkyo chokuzen kenpō gekiron," pp. 16–17.
46 Rose, "Governing 'Advanced' Liberal Democracies," p. 41.

BIBLIOGRAPHY

Burchell, Graham. "Liberal Government and Techniques of the Self." In Andrew Barry, Thomas Osborne, and Nikolas Rose, eds., *Foucault and Political Reason: Liberalism, Neo-Liberalism and Rationalities of Government.* Chicago: University of Chicago Press, 1996.

Cruikshank, Barbara. "Revolutions Within: Self-Government and Self-Esteem." In Andrew Barry, Thomas Osborne, and Nikolas Rose, eds., *Foucault and Political Reason: Liberalism, Neo-Liberalism and Rationalities of Government.* Chicago: University of Chicago Press, 1996.

Cruikshank, Barbara. *The Will to Empower: Democratic Citizens and Other Subjects.* Ithaca, NY: Cornell University Press, 1999.

Ehrenberg, John. *Civil Society: The Critical History of an Idea.* New York: New York University Press, 1999.

Foucault, Michel. "Technologies of the Self." In L. Martin, H. Gutman, and P. Hutton, eds., *Technologies of the Self: A Seminar with Michel Foucault.* Amherst: University of Massachusetts Press, 1988.

Garon, Sheldon. "From Meiji to Heisei: The State and Civil Society in Japan." In Frank Schwartz and Susan Pharr, eds., *The State of Civil Society in Japan.* Cambridge: Cambridge University Press, 2003.

Iokibe Makoto. "Japan's Civil Society: An Historical Overview." In Yamamoto Tadashi, ed., *Deciding the Public Good: Governance and Civil Society in Japan.* Tokyo: Japan Center for International Exchange, 1999.

LeBlanc, Robin. *Bicycle Citizens: The Political World of the Japanese Housewife.* Berkeley: University of California Press, 1999.

Lee, Joohee. "Taking Gender Seriously: Feminization of Nonstandard Work in Korea and Japan." *Asian Journal of Women's Studies* 10:1 (2004): 25–48.

Matsushita Keiichi. "Citizen Participation in Historical Perspective." In J. Victor Koschmann, ed., *Authority and the Individual in Japan: Citizen Protest in Historical Perspective.* Tokyo: University of Tokyo Press, 1978.

Nakano, Lynne. "Volunteering as a Lifestyle Choice: Negotiating Self-Identities in Japan." *Ethnology* 39 (2000): 93–105.

Nakano Toshio. *Ōtsuka Hisao to Maruyama Masao: Dōin, shutai, sensō sekinin.* Tokyo: Seidosha, 2001.

Noguchi Yukio. *1940-nen taisei.* Tokyo: Tōyō Keizai Shinpōsha, 1995.

Ogawa, Akihiro. "The Failure of Civil Society? An Ethnography of NPOs and the State in Contemporary Japan." Ph.D. dissertation, Cornell University, 2004.

Ōkōchi Kazuo. " 'Keizaijin' no shūen: atarashii keizai rinri no tame ni." Reprinted in *Ōkōchi Kazuo chosakushū.* Tokyo: Seirin Shoin Shinsha, 1942.

Ota Hiroko. "Sharing Governance: Changing Functions of Government, Business, and NPOs." In Yamamoto Tadashi, ed., *Deciding the Public Good: Governance and Civil Society in Japan.* Tokyo: Japan Center for International Exchange, 1999.

Ōtsuka Hisao. "Saikōdo 'jihatsusei' no hatsuyō: keizai rinri to shite no seisan sekinin ni tsuite." Reprinted in *Ōtsuka Hisao chosakushū,* 8. Tokyo: Iwanami Shoten, Tokyo, 1969–86.

Rose, Nikolas. "Governing 'Advanced' Liberal Democracies." In Andrew Barry, Thomas Osborne, and Nikolas Rose, eds., *Foucault and Political Reason: Liberalism, Neo-Liberalism and Rationalities of Government.* Chicago: University of Chicago Press, 1996.

Sasaki-Uemura, Wesley. *Organizing the Spontaneous: Citizen Protest in Postwar Japan.* Honolulu: University of Hawai'i Press, 2001.

"Senkyo chokuzen kenpō gekiron: shiriizu 1 Jimintō." *Shūkan kinyōbi* 513 (2004): 14–17.

Shōwa Kenkyūkai. "Kyōdōshugi no keizai rinri" (?1940). Reprinted in Sakai Saburō, *Shōwa kenkyūkai: aru chishikijin shūdan no kiseki.* Tokyo: TBS Buritanika, 1979.

Stevens, Carolyn. *On the Margins of Japanese Society: Volunteers and the Welfare of the Urban Underclass.* London: Routledge, 1997.

Yamamoto Tadashi. "Emergence of Japan's Civil Society and Its Future Challenges." In Yamamoto Tadashi, ed., *Deciding the Public Good: Governance and Civil Society in Japan.* Tokyo: Japan Center for International Exchange, 1999.

Yamanouchi Yasushi. "Total War and System Integration: A Methodological Introduction." In Yamanouchi Yasushi, J. Victor Koschmann, and Narita Ryūichi, eds., *Total War and "Modernization."* Ithaca, NY: East Asia Program, Cornell University, 1998.

Yamanouchi Yasushi, Koschmann, J. Victor, and Narita Ryūichi, eds. *Total War and "Modernization."* Ithaca, NY: East Asia Program, Cornell University, 1998.

FURTHER READING

No one has written a comprehensive history of power and authority from the early modern period to the present. I can list here only a few publications in English which, when added to those listed above, barely suggest what such a work would have to include. For early modern Japan, David Howell's *Geographies of Identity in Nineteenth-Century Japan* (Berkeley: University of California Press, 2005) explores shifting criteria of status and power in the Tokugawa and Meiji periods. Intricate relations of duty and authority among urban commoners are evoked in the Tokugawa era puppet dramas collected in Donald Keene, trans., *Four Major Plays of Chikamatsu* (New York: Columbia University Press, 1964). For the post-Restoration period, it is necessary to include Irokawa Daikichi's *The Culture of the Meiji Period* (Princeton: Princeton University Press, 1985), on rising political consciousness among rural elites, and Andrew Gordon's *Labor and Imperial Democracy in Prewar Japan* (Berkeley: University of California Press, 1991), which provides a broad perspective on urban crowds and workers down to World War II. The "rice riots" of 1918 are analyzed in Michael Lewis's *Rioters and Citizens: Mass Protest in Imperial Japan* (Berkeley: University of California Press, 1990). On the politics of the private realm, see Sharon Nolte and Sally Hastings, "The Meiji State's Policy toward Women, 1890–1910," in Gail Bernstein, ed., *Recreating Japanese Women, 1600–1945* (Berkeley: University of California Press, 1991). A provocative analysis of race, culture, and power in the colonial context is Komagome Takeshi's essay "Japanese Colonial Rule and Modernity: Successive Layers of Violence," in Meaghan Morris and Brett de Bary, eds., *"Race" Panic and the Memory of Migration* (Hong Kong: Hong Kong University Press, 2001). For a candid account of rural life largely insulated from rising militarism in the 1930s, see Robert J. Smith and Ella Wiswell, *The Women of Suye Mura* (Chicago: University of Chicago Press, 1982). The limits of dissent among wartime intellectuals are suggested in Hashikawa Bunsō, "The 'Civil Society' Ideal and Wartime Resistance," in J. Victor Koschmann, ed., *Authority and the Individual in Japan: Citizen Protest in Historical Perspective* (Tokyo: University of Tokyo Press, 1978). On power and authority at the individual level in recent decades, see Susan Pharr's *Political Women in Japan: The Search for a Place in Political Life* (Berkeley: University of California Press, 1981) and Dorinne Kondo's *Crafting Selves: Power, Gender and Discourses of Identity in a Japanese Workplace* (Chicago: University of Chicago Press, 1990). Jeffrey Broadbent dissects the politics and social dynamics of rural protest in *Environmental Politics in Japan: Networks of Power and Protest* (Cambridge: Cambridge University Press, 1998).

CHAPTER THIRTY

National Identity and Nationalism

Kevin M. Doak

Japanese nationalist rhetoric developed from premodern foundations in Neo-Confucian political thought, yet it eventually incorporated both Shintō and even Christian elements as this rhetoric developed into full-fledged nationalism. Nationalism moved Japanese conceptions of identity outside the Neo-Confucian geo-cultural order toward a principle of cultural distinctiveness, and introduced a concept of the people as the agency of that distinctiveness. This concept was a product of modernity, as represented by the ideals and achievements of the Meiji Restoration (*Meiji ishin*). Yet, nationalism in Japan has always carried with it a certain ambivalence toward modernity. And, as in other non-Western societies, this ambivalence toward modernity has also often taken the form of a rebellion against the West. In the case of Japanese nationalism, this dual structure of ambivalence toward the West and modernity stemmed from the formative paradox of Japanese nationalism: nationalism was the agent that liberated Japanese from the traditional hegemony of Chinese culture, yet by its very nature nationalism also called for a new tradition that would secure the image of an independent and particular cultural identity derived from Western ideas. At its very inception in the late nineteenth century, then, Japanese nationalism was born with an oedipal complex: in order to thrive, it must kill its source (whether conceived as traditional China or the modern West); by rejecting its source, it could neither sustain itself as an independent cultural identity nor accept modern political forms as legitimate containers of this traditional identity. In vivid – and at times, violent – ways, this tension made itself known through various efforts, never entirely successful, to wed concepts of national identity (*kokumin, minzoku*) to the new political entity of the state (*kokka*). The story of Japanese nationalism is largely the narrative of efforts to seek a unification of national identity with the state: the goal, for all nationalists, was to effect the image and reality of a nation-state (*kokumin-kokka, minzoku-kokka*).

The Premodern Order and the Question of a Japanese National Identity

Any study of nationalism must come to terms with the problem of anachronism that plagues much of the writing about nationalism. For nationalism to be effective, it must locate its origins in a remote past, an originary moment whose remoteness is its very guarantee of authenticity. Yet, scholars of nationalism have come to recognize that the nation is "an imagined community," a product of modern industrialization, or even of modernity itself. Consequently the first step toward a study of nationalism, whose conclusions are not determined by nationalism itself, is to locate a time prior to the emergence of nationalism, a moment that can be usefully contrasted with the moment that follows the onset of nationalism. This need is particularly acute in the case of Japan, as primordial nationalism is quite strong among Japanese nationalists, and this primordialism leads to arguments about the origins of Japanese national identity in such early moments as 660 BC (the legendary origins of the imperial lineage), the rise of the Yamato "state" in the fourth century, the first use of the name "Japan" in diplomatic exchanges with China in the middle of the seventh century, or even in ethnological studies of the origins of the Japanese people that assert the beginnings of the ethno-nation several thousand years ago. Of course, each of these arguments elides several important points. The first confused monarchy and nationalism, the second and third rely on a loose definition of "state" and beg the question of whether the "state" also comprises the nation, and the last is mired in both confusion between ethnic identity and nationalism and the methods and lessons of modern ethnology. In the final analysis, these and other primordialist arguments for the origins of Japanese nationalism will not be silenced by careful scholarship: they are expressions of a nationalist faith and a reminder that Japanese nationalism, alive and well today, often informs scholarship on nationalism.

A more useful beginning may be found, not in the ancient past, but in the middle of things. Contrasting the socio-politico-cultural world prior to the Meiji Restoration with the nationalist ideals that followed gives a clearer sense of the historical origins and implications of nationalism in Japan. Before the reforms that followed the Meiji Restoration in 1867, Japan was neither a nation nor a state, and thus the historian Kano Masanao refers to the "discovery of Japan" only after the "discovery of the West" in the middle of the nineteenth century. And this "discovery of Japan" refers to only the beginnings of a consciousness of Japanese identity: the concept of *kokka* still referred mainly to the local domains, not to a nation-state.[1] The territory that comprised most of what we now call Japan was still divided into roughly 250 semi-autonomous hereditary domains (*han*), as it had been for about 800 years. This horizontal fracturing of the political landscape was echoed in the vertically differentiated sociocultural order. The people living in the archipelago had very little consciousness of themselves as a single community. Rather, they were more likely to see themselves in terms of their membership in relatively fixed socioeconomic orders (merchants, artisans, peasants, and samurai, in ascending order). These hereditary orders prevented most social mobility and developed their own "cultural" identities, including their own mores and language patterns. Yet, even these orders did not provide a universal "class" consciousness across the land, as they were intersected by domainal allegiances. To some degree, samurai could conceive of themselves as a universal order and identify with other samurai outside their domains, but they could never forget their primary allegiance to their domainal overlord and their enmity, potential or historical, with samurai from other domains. Where this trans-domainal identity was most significant was at the theoretical level, particular through Neo-Confucian political ideas that elevated the samurai to the level of a servant of political culture like his counterparts in China and Korea. Unifying such a fractured socio-politico-cultural world was not only complicated by internal divisions, but also by the parallels, forced or real, across Northeast Asian societies during the eighteenth and nineteenth centuries.

It was this tradition of the potential transcendence of the samurai class that provided the matrix for the sociocultural changes and that led to the Meiji Restoration, the birth moment of Japanese nationalism. Its origins may be found in the samurai scholars of Mito domain, a collateral house of the ruling Tokugawa shogunate, but one that nursed a long simmering sense of status inconsistency: Mito was close to power, but allowed to write only history, not policy. Nonetheless, one Mito samurai, Aizawa Seishisai, offered his *New Thesis* in 1825 in an effort to propose a definition of Japan's "national polity" (*kokutai*) on the basis of troubling encounters with Russians off Japan's northern coasts. Aizawa called for the samurai to unite in protecting Japan's *kokutai*. But what was this *kokutai*? Was it an early form of nationality? The term was open to all sorts of interpretations, and Aizawa's contribution was to shift its meaning from the shogunal governing structure to a sense of cultural continuity located in the monarchy that would mark Japan as distinctive from all other places. This return to the monarchy as the cultural core of Japan's distinctiveness joined with the cultural exceptionalism of Motoori Norinaga and those who shaped the "nativist" (*kokugaku*) movement against Chinese and foreign cultures. Ultimately, this cultural distinctiveness became tied to calls to restore the monarch to power, as "overthrowing the bakufu and restoring the monarchy" became the rallying cry for disaffected samurai who, armed with swords, would upset the political order in the name of loyalty to the monarch. This they did in 1867.

The Meiji State and the Challenge of Nationalism

The movement that overthrew the shogunate effected a revolution, but it cannot be called nationalist in its political inspiration or objectives. While anti-foreignism and loyalty to the monarch were conjoined to a sense of nativism, those who participated in the war for Restoration were largely samurai and the key players came from a handful of western domains (chiefly, Satsuma and Chōshū). Few if any envisioned a new society in which samurai privileges would be abolished and peasants elevated to equal status with themselves. Even fewer could imagine the collective people of Japan as sovereign, and cultural differences and domainal loyalties remained pronounced among them. Nor was it immediately clear that political reform would lead to a new, nationally centralized state. Rather, even before the fighting was over, tensions broke out among leading participants as to whether the monarchical court (the Meiji monarch was only 14 years old at the time of the Restoration), or whether the samurai from Satsuma, Chōshū, Tosa, or other domains would take over leadership of the realm. It was only in the immediate years after the Meiji Restoration of 1867 that the new direction towards centralization and a constitutional state became clear, a direction that was not entirely the expectation of those who had fought to overthrow the shogunate.

Centralization of the political realm can be explained as a combination of two pressures, internal and external, both of which were largely beyond the control of the new leadership of Japan. First, and most pressing, was the need to have a legitimate government with authority over the entire territory in order to negotiate with the Western powers that had forced unequal treaties on Japan in 1854. Ōkubo Toshimichi was a key player in forcing through centralization of Japan's political structure during the 1870s and in elevating the monarch as an absolute ruler in line with Prussian advice. Ōkubo was the leading statist of the early post-Restoration years, but he was no nationalist. His death in 1878 at the hands of a disgruntled samurai angry at Ōkubo's centralizing policies is a stark reminder that the Meiji state was not the result of nationalism. The second force promoting centralization of the government was the need to find a new principle to unite the disparate political forces within the domestic realm. The Restoration had displaced the old *bakuhan* order, its reliance on Neo-Confucianism, and its social hierarchy based on the caste system. Yet, in the immediate aftermath of revolution, there was a real risk that Satsuma and Chōshū might simply replace the Tokugawa in a new shogunal government. Pressure from other domains and the court ensured that this would not happen. Instead, some leaders in the new government, especially Inoue Kowashi, considered a variety of Western models of a centralized, monarchical nation-state along with new concepts of the Japanese people as a single national community.

Evidence of this growing nationalism is available from the outset of the new Meiji government. Even before the new governmental structure was determined, social reform policies registered aspirations for creating a new national body. In 1870, commoners were allowed the dignity (previously reserved for samurai) of using a surname and the following year they were allowed the privilege of marrying into aristocratic families. If one sign of nationalism is the effort to extend the dignity of aristocrats to all members of the national community, then the Japanese people were well on the way to becoming a nation. By 1872, this process of abolishing the social estates of the *ancien régime* was well under way, with additional laws opening education to all people and permitting freedom of occupation and travel within the country. At the same time, some samurai, sensing their declining privileges, introduced republican theories of nationalism and sought to assert their voices in the development of the new nation. Key actors were affiliated with the old Tosa domain, an ally of Restoration but a relatively small domain and thus easily marginalized by Satsuma and Chōshū. Former samurai from this domain, such as Itagaki Taisuke and Gotō Shōjirō, submitted a petition in 1874 for the establishment of a popularly elected legislature. This act dramatized and intensified the belief of many samurai activists that their aspirations for a "new world" that would arise from the Restoration were being undermined by the evolving "despotism" of the new government.

Those anti-government activists associated with this petition formed the core of what would later be known as the Freedom and People's Rights Movement (*jiyū minken undō*). Initially composed of samurai and some urban intellectuals, the movement soon encompassed rural people as well and claimed a membership of 200,000 by 1881. That year it forced a promise from the government to establish a legislature within ten years, but the movement declined after 1882, when members grew increasingly violent and the government began to suppress it through force. Yet, throughout the first two decades of the Meiji period, when government and society were in formative stages, the Freedom and People's Rights Movement voiced a range of political theories that contested the right of the state to determine political affairs without the sanction of the nation. At the same time, it was theorists within the movement who played key roles in articulating what the nation was and how it might function in the new Japan. It was these political theorists who began to identify with the position of *kokumin*, and they made a sharp distinction between this emerging sense of nation and what they often called the "despotic" government.

The response by the government was to focus on state-building in the belief that the state would create the nation. In its earliest days, the provisional government (the Dajōkan) included senior councilors like Etō Shimpei and Inoue Kowashi, who were influenced by nationalism and sought to build a true nation-state. As minister of justice, Etō had tried to introduce a French republican legal system with an emphasis on civil rights. But when that failed, he left the government and joined the Freedom and People's Rights Movement, ultimately dying in an armed revolt against the government in 1874. For Etō, the state no longer held out promise of forming a republican nation (*kokumin*), so he abandoned it. His choice contrasts nicely with that of Inoue. Inoue adopted a more gradualist approach, continuing to believe that legal reforms would transform the state into a nation-state. But even he abandoned this position after the 1881 political crisis. The political crisis of that year was a result of a rift in the government between the national (*kokumin*) faction in the government and the statist (*kokka*) faction. The former was represented by Ōkuma Shigenobu, who supported the People's Rights petition for a popularly elected assembly, and the latter by Itō Hirobumi who· advocated a Prussian-style constitutional monarchy. Itō's faction prevailed, and Ōkuma and many of his supporters left the government. Inoue stayed in the government with Itō, however, since he believed it was important to establish the legal structure of the new government, a government of laws rather than of mystical monarchical privilege. Inoue believed that the nation (*kokumin*) could be incorporated into the new monarchical state, even without popular sovereignty or an elected assembly, as the nation was the particular position of the people as defined by the scope of law in the new state.[2] By remaining within the government, Inoue provided an example of the priority of law and structure in the shaping of the new state. But the ultimate settlement of the legal system of the state, in the form of the Meiji constitution of 1889, made it clear that sovereignty rested with the monarch and the people were reduced to his "subjects" (*shinmin*), not codified as a nation (*kokumin*) with national rights.[3] The imperial constitution was aptly named: it rejected the concept of a nation-state for a monarchical empire in which territory was more important than the sovereignty of the nation (*kokumin*). Karatani Kōjin has summed up this achievement succinctly: "the Meiji Restoration created a state, but it was not able to form a nation."[4]

The Meiji constitution then did not resolve the nationalist longings of the Japanese people. Instead, it exacerbated the gap between the elitist monarchical state and those who had hoped that, in the aftermath of the Meiji Restoration, Japan would become a true nation-state (*kokumin-kokka*). Even as the nature of the impending constitution became clear, leading nationalist intellectuals organized groups and publications to contest "the superficial Westernization" of the constitution and to promote what they felt was the cultural essence of the nation (*kokusuishugi*). Tokutomi Sohō was the prime mover behind the formation of the Society of Friends of the Nation (Min'yūsha) in 1887, and Miyake Setsurei and Shiga Shigetaka were key players in the formation of the Society for Political Education (Seikyōsha) the following year.

The Society of Friends of the Nation published its views in its journal *Kokumin no tomo* (Friends of the Nation) – the name was directed inspired by the American radical journal *The Nation*) – and in its newspaper, the *Kokumin shimbun* (National News). The Society for Political Education made its views known in its journal *The Japanese*, and members of the Society were on close terms with Kuga Katsunan who founded his journal *Japan* in 1889. Although one can find some differences among these Societies and their journals (especially after Tokutomi lent his support to the state around the Russo-Japanese War), in general they intoned a nationalism that was critical of the pro-Western cultural policies of the Meiji state, its apparent weak diplomacy vis-à-vis the Western powers, and its indifference to the cultural, social, political, and economic rights of the nation. The overall thrust of this populist nationalism was toward a greater incorporation of the people into the state: not as subjects of the emperor, as the Meiji constitution defined them, but as the true cultural core of the Japanese nation.

Empire and Nationalism: An Uneasy Relationship

If the Meiji constitution was not designed to create a nation (*kokumin*) but to suppress nationalism (*kokuminshugi*) in favor of loyalty to the monarchical state, this new state nonetheless remained concerned with methods of incorporating the people's hearts and minds as loyal subjects. The state had powerful tools at its disposal: the bureaucracy, compulsory education, and the draft. By the end of the nineteenth century, the education system and the civil service hierarchy had largely been formalized, and "the civil bureaucracy had emerged by 1900 as the primary instrument of decision making and the primary structure of political leadership selection."[5] This step effectively insulated the government from the pressures of nationalism that often came from the political parties as they promoted the legacies of Ōkuma Shigenobu and the Freedom and People's Rights Movement. Under the Meiji constitution, conscription became a universal duty of men and the right to service by proxy was abolished. These mechanisms for incorporating the people into the state were tested in 1894 when Japan went to war with Qing China over hegemony in Korea. In some respects, the Sino-Japanese War was an ideal opportunity for the state to absorb and control the forces of nationalism. It was a war propelled by nationalism, insofar as it represented the application of the principle of nationalism to a region that had been organized by the Sinocentric claims of dynastic hegemony. And this sense that Japan was fighting to liberate Koreans (and by extension, all Asians) from Sinocentric hegemony to their own nationalism was a heady intoxicant for many Japanese. As the influential Christian intellectual Uchimura Kanzō wrote in *Friends of the Nation*, "Our goal is to wake up China and show her what her calling is, to set her to work cooperating with us in the reformation of the Orient. We are fighting for the realization of eternal peace."[6] This sense that national unity and purpose could best be realized through the state's actions in the region changed the dynamics of Japanese nationalism, as now the state could be idealized as the agent for social justice in the region, and not merely seen as oppressing the Japanese people at home.

A new state-centered nationalism was on the horizon. In May 1897, after the victory in the Sino-Japanese War and the Triple Intervention by Russia, Germany, and France which forced Japan to return many of its war spoils to China, Inoue Tetsujirō and Kimura Takatarō formed the Great Japan Society and published their journal *Nipponshugi*. In this journal, they outlined a new nationalism called "Japanism" (*Nipponshugi*). As Oguma Eiji has pointed out, this "Japanism" was directed against Christian nationalists like Uchimura who were still uneasy with a monarch that was increasingly laden with Shintō religious significance.[7] In this social Darwinist climate, it was easy to believe that a nation had to either expand or be colonized, and expansion required the power and legitimacy of a state. No longer was the state seen as the embodiment of a foreign culture; rather, the state seemed the only hope for the protection of the Japanese people against the encroachments of Western imperialism. Takayama Chogyū was the most influential advocate of this nationalist reconciliation with the monarchical state. He returned to the concept of *kokutai* and reinterpreted it as the core of modern Japanese nationalism, a nationalism that found its full expression in the monarchical state. Thus Takayama argued it was time "to return to a correct statism (*kokkashugi*) ... that is fully mindful of the special qualities of our national popular sentiment and its development."[8] This statist "Japanism" abandoned the empathy for the weak and the plight of the people that had informed the earlier cultural nationalism and its protest of environmental pollution and labor exploitation (for example, the Ashio copper mine incident, the Takashima coal mine incident). Instead, "Japanism" increasingly connected nationalism with the pride of the strong and unleashed this arrogance in Japan's relations with others in East Asia.[9]

Along with this return to the concept of a "national polity" (*kokutai*) located in the monarchy in order to shore up domestic support for the state's wars in Asia, Japanism also advocated ethnic assimilation as a method of supporting the state's colonial ventures, especially in Korea and Taiwan. This inevitable concern with assimilation of different ethnic peoples under the jurisdiction of the Japanese empire raised the question of the relationship of ethnicity to national identity, both for non-Japanese in the region and for the Japanese themselves. The issue of ethnicity and national identity was complicated, however, by the strong arguments put up by Christians like Watase Jōkichi, who accepted ethnic nationality (*minzoku*) as a distinctive social identity but argued that it should be subordinated to a higher religious principle, not to a political institution like the state. Watase's main concern was the state's effort to redefine the monarch as a national ethical figurehead after the 1890 Imperial Rescript on Education. Inoue Tetsujirō, a founding member of the Japanist group, used the Rescript for his attacks on Christians as "un-Japanese." Japanist ideologues found themselves in the awkward position of upholding the monarch as both a tribal chieftain for the ethnic Japanese and a principle of unity for colonized ethnic groups. This position was most clearly expressed by ethicist Yumoto Takehiko, who argued that "our state is composed exclusively of the Yamato nation (*minzoku*), and even if one maintains that it gradually came to include other ethnic nations (*i-minzoku*), these all became Japanized and did not retain their own ethics or morality as distinctive ethnic nations." This contradiction (between empire as the space of ethnic assimilation and empire as rooted in the monarch as the ethnic chieftain of the Yamato nation) was never resolved during the imperial period, but efforts to address it continually brought anthropological and ethnological theories to the center of debates over national identity.[10]

An unintended consequence of Japanism's effort to find a more solid foundation for national identity in the ethnic nation-state and the greater attention given to the concept of ethnic identity in nationalist debates was the unleashing of this concept of ethnicity from the state. *Minzoku* became the preferred lens through which to understand nationalism among those who drew from the Freedom and People's Rights Movement and its effort to address the concerns of the weak and the dispossessed. Nationality, in this ethnic sense, went precisely in the opposite direction from that in which the Japanists had tried to direct it: it became dislodged from the political state, a kind of free-floating national identity whose unfixity was precisely a measure of its radical possibilities, both domestically and throughout the emerging empire.

The best example of agents of this ethnic nationalism in the empire is that loosely affiliated group of activists, frustrated politicians, thugs and ne'er-do-wells known as the "continental adventurers" (*tairiku rōnin*). A rather amorphous group, it included members of right-wing organizations such as the Gen'yōsha and the Amur River Society, the Christian liberationist Miyazaki Tōten and the socialist Kita Ikki. Many traced their intellectual and political lineage back to the Freedom and People's Rights Movement. Miyazaki's older brother Hachirō, for example, was a leader of the People's Rights Party in Kumamoto and the Gen'yōsha was formed in 1881, during the height of that movement, by Hiraoka Kōtarō, a survivor of the Satsuma Rebellion. He was joined by Tōyama Mitsuru who had spent time in jail for his participation in the Hagi Uprising of 1876. Hiraoka was elected to the lower house of the Diet just as the Sino-Japanese War broke out, and he is a good reminder that party politicians, especially those who traced their lingeage to the Freedom and People's Rights Movement, often were quick to work independently of the state in their pan-Asianist agendas. But it was the formation of the Amur River Society in 1901, drawing on many members of the Gen'yōsha, that marked a significant shift towards intervention in Asia in the name of ethnic nationalism. Founded in 1901 by Uchida Ryōhei, the Society announced, as one of its guiding principles, the encouragement of "the Asian ethnic nations (*Ajia minzoku*) and their resistance to legalism, which they felt had restricted the people's freedom."[11] While the Amur River Society was not opposed to the annexation of Korea (largely due to their opposition to growing Russian influence in the region), they strongly championed pan-Asianism and ethnic nationalism in China and the Philippines. Needless to say, their pan-Asianism was deeply influenced by their anti-Western culturalism, and their support for ethnic nationalism often was combined with a belief that constitutions and states were unwelcome impositions of Western political ideas on traditional Asian cultures.

Anti-imperialist nationalism also had a domestic face, and it did not always look to the right. Socialists led the charge against imperialism at home, and it should be noted that almost all the leaders of Japan's first socialist party were Christian.[12] Socialism and Christianity often were conjoined in the Meiji period – both in their anti-imperialism and in their support for a nationalism of the dispossessed, a nationalism that often turned to ethnic nationality rather than the state for its ideal community. The Russo-Japanese War, particularly the arguments leading up to it, served as a catalyst for bringing socialists and Christians together and changing the context of Japanese nationalism. In August 1903, pan-Asianists Konoe Atsumaro and Tōyama Mitsuru criticized the government for not moving quickly enough to demand that Russia withdraw its troops from the region and for neglecting Japan's divine mission to bring peace to East Asia by liberating Manchuria from Qing China. Forming the Anti-Russia Society, they sparked a nationalist movement around the country. They were joined by Tokutomi's *National News* and Miyake's *The Japanese* in advocating war with Russia. Opponents of the war included the Christian Uchimura Kanzō, socialist Kōtoku Shūsui, and anarchist Sakai Toshihiko, all journalists for the *Yorozu chōhō*. When the editor of *Yorozu chōhō*, Kuroiwa Ruikō, came out in favor of the war, this anti-war group broke off and started their own newspaper, the *Commoner's News*. This newspaper, and the Society of Commoners behind it, gave rise to a new form of populist nationalism which invoked the concept of the nation that had appeared first in the 1870s in conjunction with the dissolution of the Edo period caste system. Whether socialist or Christian, its supporters envisioned the nation in terms of an egalitarian social body and not in terms of the glories of the military or the imperialist state. As Sakai noted, "our reverence and attachment to Tokutomi and the Min'yūsha was almost complete."[13] By this, Sakai meant their attraction to Tokutomi's earlier nationalism (*kokuminshugi*), not his later advocacy of the war and support for the imperialist state.

The Russo-Japanese War forced a deeper divide in Japanese nationalism. Some populist nationalists like Tokutomi felt that it was time to unite nation with state in the pursuit of international power and recognition. Others were pulled into populist nationalism by their opposition to the state's militarist expansion. As we have seen, this new emphasis on the people as the true nation, along with the sustained inter-ethnic social relations that empire created, had introduced the concept of *minzoku* into early twentieth-century nationalist rhetoric. But this concept of the people as an ethnic group had ambivalent uses. In the hands of statists, it was used as a tool for cultural integration into the state and its projects, as we have seen with Takayama. But after 1905, it was increasingly used by domestic critics of the state: by defining the people as neither imperial subjects (*shinmin*) nor members of the state (*kokumin*), they used ethnic nationality to situate the Japanese as a cultural national body independent of the constitutional state. This form of ethnic nationalism often added an element of pan-Asian, or at least anti-Western, sentiment to its cache. Shirayanagi Shūko illustrates well the subsequent adventures of this ethnic nationalism.[14] Shirayanagi began as an activist working with the Commoners Society, along with Kōtoku and Sakai. He turned to historical studies to identify the essence of the Japanese nation, suggesting that its origins well predated the recently constructed Meiji state and its Western constitutional form. Most importantly, he identified the subject of his national history as that of the *minzoku*, not the state. This advocacy of ethnic nationalism, while it would seem to have its origins on the political left, actually took Shirayanagi (and quite of few other post-Marxists) to national socialism in the 1930s.

While the origins of the national socialist and "ultra-nationalist" movements of the 1930s can be traced back to the rise of this populist nationalism in the early twentieth century (or in some senses, even back to the Freedom and People's Rights Movement of the late nineteenth century), the most immediate historical factor in shaping ethnic nationalism was World War I. Until recently, historians have neglected the impact of World War I on Japan, deeming it a "European war."[15] Unlike the Russo-Japanese War, it was not the fighting, nor the enhanced prestige gained through the war, that was most influential on Japanese nationalism. In fact, Japan played a minor role in the hostilities. Rather it was the broader influence of the concept of ethnic nationalism, both as a cause of the Serbian uprising and as conceived by Woodrow Wilson as the solution to a lasting peace. Kamei Kan'ichirō, a personification of this shift towards national socialism, put it best when he reflected at the height of World War II, "the word *minzoku* (ethnic nation) first appeared in print in actual world politics after the Versailles Treaty."[16] Kamei's point needs to be qualified: there were discussions on *minzoku* and *minzokushugi* in publications on world politics and political theory in Japanese journals prior to 1919.[17] Yet, he has a point, as the tremendous flood of articles and books on ethnic nationalism that appeared in Japanese after 1920 is underscored by later historians who do not share Kamei's political biases.[18]

The effects of World War I on Japanese domestic politics were not limited to ideological ones. Just as the aftermath of the war spawned Mussolini's Fascist movement and the early forms of Hitler's national socialism, in Japan too populist, right-wing nationalist groups began to spring up, often with fatal consequences for the political elite. One example is the Society of Those Left Behind (Yūzonsha). Formed in 1919 by Ōkawa Shumei and Mitsukawa Kametarō, the Yūzonsha drew on this new concept of nationality to advocate Asian liberation abroad and reform of the state at home. The Society published Kita Ikki's *Outline Plan for the Reorganization of Japan* in 1923, the book that inspired the 1936 military coup attempt by radical officers in the imperial army. Soon after, the Society dissolved due to differences between Kita and Ōkawa. But it would be a mistake to conclude that the influence of these men and their revolutionary nationalism died out with the dissolution of the Society. Such groups were legion in the interwar period, and individuals moved in and out of them, frequently belonging to several different groups at the same time.

Defenders of the imperial state did not sit idly by and watch this gathering threat. They organized to defend the state, most notably in the National Foundation Society (Kokuhonsha), which Baron Hiranuma Kiichirō sponsored in 1924 after an assassination attempt on Emperor Hirohito. The Society amassed 200,000 members from the bureaucracy, military, and business worlds and sought, as its name indicates, to reassert the true foundations of the Japanese state. It identified this foundation in the spirit of the *kokutai*, which did not clarify much, except to signal a repudiation of more novel concepts of national identity and an identification with those who had turned to "*kokutai*" in earlier moments of national crisis. From Aizawa to Takayama, the concept of "*kokutai*" had established a tradition of nationalism associated with the political body rather than with the people as the nation, and it was mobilized in this service again. By the middle of the 1920s, there was more than a theoretical concern over the potential dangers from those who would act in the name of "the people," now often conceived and mobilized as "a mob." Socialism was growing strong (and had influenced Namba Daisuke, the would-be assassin of Emperor Hirohito), and the power of the mob had made itself felt in the widespread attacks on Koreans and Chinese following the 1923 Kantō earthquake. With the death of Matsukata Masayoshi in 1924, Saionji Kinmochi was the last surviving *genrō* (elder statesman), the parties were at the height of their power and, after universal manhood suffrage went into effect in 1928, the Minseitō (People's Government) party replaced the Seiyūkai (Friends of Constitutional Government) party in office. By the end of the decade, the effects of the Great Depression were ravaging Japan's already weak economy, Marxist movements were strengthening their hold over Japan's laborers, and fears of another revolution were running high.

The imperial state was far more successful in suppressing leftist movements than it was in suppressing radical nationalism. An important turning point was 1933. In that year, two members of the central committee of Japan's Communist Party, Sano Manabu and Nabeyama Sadachika, announced from prison their abandonment of Marxism in favor of national socialism and support of the state. Their declaration was heavily couched in the language of ethnic nationalism: what made the difference was their belief that the Japanese state was now willing to support nationalism premised on ethnic identity. This idea reverberated through leftist circles, and many Japanese leftists followed Sano and Nabeyama. Two of them, Hayashi Fusao and Kamei Katsuichirō, joined with the cultural conservative Yasuda Yojūrō in celebrating the Japanese ethnic nation as an eternal ideal. Calling themselves the "Japan Romantic School," these intellectuals, writers, and poets did more than anyone to garner popular support for Japan's role in World War II, not because they had found respect for the constitutional monarchical state, but because they idealized the war as the expression of the will of the ethnic Japanese people as resisting imperialism.[19] For these romantics, it was a war against modernity: both the modernity represented by the external enemy (the West) and the modernity which they felt had seeped into their souls, corrupting the essence of their primordial ethnic culture. Once again, the imperial state did not just sit idly by and watch. In 1937, while the Japan Romantic School was at the height of its influence, it counterattacked with the release of *Kokutai no hongi* (The True Meaning of Kokutai). This volume adopted the primordialism of the romantics' nationalism, only to substitute the imperial lineage as the core of Japanese national identity and loyalty to the monarch as "the way of the subject." This was a concerted ideological effort to influence understandings of national identity: the first 300,000 copies were disseminated to teachers in Japan, from elementary to university levels. By 1943, the Cabinet Printing Bureau had sold nearly two million copies of the book. Yet, because of its difficult literary style, *Kokutai no hongi* did not put an end to the tensions between state and nation in modern Japanese nationalism. At best, it represented an intensive effort by the state, at one of its strongest moments, to achieve national unity around itself through mobilization and indoctrination. But with the defeat in the war and the destruction of the imperial state, whatever unity Japanese nationalism had achieved under its aegis was quickly dissolved.

Redefining National Identity in Postwar Japan

Japan's defeat in World War II and its subsequent occupation was a major watershed in Japanese nationalism, second only to the events surrounding the Meiji Restoration. To call this moment a watershed in Japanese nationalism is not to underestimate the force of prewar nationalist ideas and actors who moved almost seamlessly into the postwar years. Continuity, especially in ideas and actors, was significant. But the context of Japanese nationalism had changed in fundamentally important ways. In the first place, the terms of surrender meant that the Meiji imperial state ceased to exist. After September 2, 1945, when General Umezu Yoshirō and Shigemitsu

Mamoru signed the surrender documents on the USS *Missouri* in Tokyo Bay, the Japanese state no longer existed as an independent polity. This is not to say that the bureaucracy ceased to function: it played a key role in maintaining certain governmental services under the US occupation. But until the occupation ended in 1952, the previous discourse that sought to invest national identity in the state (*kokka*) or to codify the people as imperial subjects (*shinmin*) was seriously compromised by the lack of an independent Japanese state. Moreover, until the postwar constitution went into effect in 1947, the Japanese people still were unable to claim the formal status of nationals (*kokumin*). What was left was the notion that they were members of an ethnic group (*minzoku*) and that this ethnicity was the core of their national identity, a national identity that could not be affected by political events like military defeat or foreign occupation and which did not require codification in laws and constitutions. Ironically, the chronological order in which these three key concepts of Japanese nationalism were established (*kokka, kokumin, minzoku*) was reversed from the order in which they had been introduced in the Meiji years. Now, a consciousness of ethnic identity (*minzoku*) came first, then in 1947 the legal codification of being members of a constitutionally defined sovereign nation (*kokumin*), and finally in 1952, a nation with its own independent state (*kokka*).

Events and ideologies converged in augmenting this sense of ethnic nationalism in the early postwar years. The end of the imperial state meant the end of the multi-ethnic empire. Korean subjects were now "liberated" to their own ethnic nationalism, although the implications this ethnic nationalism posed for where they should reside were not always attractive. Many chose to remain in Japan, where they had now lost their rights as Japanese subjects and became in many ways "stateless" people. Similarly, Taiwanese were liberated from Japanese colonialism, only to turn to their own nationalist wars between Mao Zedong and Jiang Jieshi. Japan was being recreated as a mono-ethnic nation-state, and this ideal was represented in the Nationality Act of 1950, which relied heavily on the principle of *ius sanguinis* in determining Japanese nationality.[20]

At the same time, Marxist intellectuals were enjoying unparalleled prestige, as the only consistent critics of the war. Released from prison and protected by the occupation, they led the way in criticizing the emperor as bearing the brunt of responsibility for the war, and many demanded not merely his abdication but his execution. Yet, as Oguma Eiji has noted, "the pursuit of the emperor's war responsibility in the immediate postwar was not a rejection of nationalism but a searching for a new national identity."[21] This new national identity was one which equated the Japanese people with ethnic identity and which called for the removal of the emperor (along with the military and financial "cliques" and all "reactionary" politicians and organizations) as a traitor to the ethnic nation. For Marxists like Nosaka Sanzō, Tōyama Shigeki, Ishimoda Shō, and others, ethnic nationalism was an attractive means of aligning the Japanese with the rest of Asia in the global war of Marxism against the capitalist imperialism of the West. An influential non-Marxist intellectual who joined this discourse was Takeuchi Yoshimi. Takeuchi was a cultural conservative and Sinologist who after the war outlined a national identity for the Japanese that would draw from the tradition of ethnic nationalism and find its expression not in the political form of the state but in culture, especially through what Takeuchi called "national literature." He was not alone among conservatives who turned to pan-Asianism and ethnic nationalism in the early postwar years. Yasuda Yojūrō, Takeuchi's high school classmate and leader of the wartime Japan Romantic School, added his voice (under a pseudonym, since he was purged by the occupation officials) through the journal *Sokoku* (The Fatherland) during the years 1949–55. Like Takeuchi and their erstwhile opponents, the Marxist historians, Yasuda tried to resituate Japanese nationality on an Asian foundation. Unlike the Marxists, however, he defined Asia in a thoroughly romantic way, envisioning "Asia" as the symbol of an absolute ethical pacifism. This ethnic nationalist renaissance gained important support from ethnologists and anthropologists such as Yanagita Kunio, Ishida Eiichirō, Egami Namio, and others, many of whom had participated in the wartime effort to legitimate the Greater East Asia Co-Prosperity Sphere by propagating ethnic ideology. For all these ethnic nationalists, whether anthropologists, romantics, or Marxists, the lessons of the war were to avoid the political state: they said nothing about the dangers of ethnic nationalism.

Even those in charge of the postwar state shared this wariness of a nationalism predicated on the state. Only three years after Japan regained political independence in 1952, a convergence of political parties yielded the structure that has governed Japan ever since. The "1955 System" consolidated political power in the hands of the meta-party, the Liberal Democratic Party (LDP), while relegating its opponents mainly to the new Socialist Party (which combined right- and left-wing factions). The Liberal faction of the LDP, led by Yoshida Shigeru, never trusted political nationalism and was able to retain control within the LDP for most of the postwar years by substituting economic growth for political nationalism. Their greatest moment came in December 1960, when Prime Minister Ikeda Hayato regained popular support after the disastrous US–Japan Security Treaty revision riots by announcing a policy to double incomes within ten years. So long as economic growth continued, pan-Asian and ethnic nationalism was sublimated to the LDP's close relations with the United States and its support for economic growth.

Nationalism during the 1960s and even into the 1970s was largely a matter of cultural identity, especially evident in theories about Japanese identity that purported to explain the harmonious nature of Japanese labor and social relations. After the "Nixon shock" of floating the dollar in 1971 and the "oil shock" of a fourfold increase in the petroleum price in 1973, the LDP promise of everlasting economic growth became increasingly difficult to sell. During the 1970s, ethnic nationalism began to reassert the gap between cultural identity and the state. In the middle of the 1980s, Prime Minister Nakasone tried to intervene in this emerging gap between ethnic national identity and a nationalism centered on the state, while simultaneously trying to strengthen the office of prime minister to empower himself as a neo-nationalist leader. His "grand design" for Japan sought to reconcile the state, internationalism, and ethnic nationalism into a new form of nationalism that he called "liberal nationalism."[22] Yet, most liberals harshly criticized Nakasone's nationalism for its ethnic and racial biases, as well as for his effort to reconcile ethnic nationalism with the state, an effort that seemed redolent of the wartime Japanese state, which in fact Nakasone had served as an official in the Home Ministry. Since Nakasone, nationalism and debates over national identity in Japan have become highly conscious of the moral and political differences between a nationalism couched in ethnic terms (*minzoku*) and one conceived in political terms (*kokumin*). And an appreciation of the value of multi-ethnic society has grown during the same period. Moreover, outright opposition to the state has tempered somewhat, both as the wartime generation passes on and with the maturation of a younger generation, to whom the state has been more an agent of economic growth and technological pride than of militarist expansion.

Three characteristics stand out in contemporary discourse on nationalism in Japan. One is that, amidst a flurry of books on the nation-state (*kokumin-kokka*), there is little open advocacy of ethnic nationalism. The second is the central role of history in these debates, a role that came to the fore in 1995 when Fujioka Nobukatsu established the "Liberal School of History" and announced plans to revise Japanese history textbooks. Fujioka (who was influenced in his youth by *minzoku* Marxist historians like Tōyama Shigeki) insists his concern is with restoring pride in the state in the aftermath of Japan's humiliating "checkbook diplomacy" during the first Gulf War. Yet, his critics often question whether he really is just sublimating ethnic nationalism into his reappraisal of the state. Nonetheless, as Rikki Kersten has pointed out, the fact that Fujioka and his group feel compelled to wrap themselves in the mantle of liberalism (whether sincerely or not) "tells us that liberalism retains its value as a legitimizing idea in contemporary Japan."[23] And finally, the new nationalism, often described as "healthy nationalism," has spilled out beyond the bounds of academia, and is often espoused by journalists, politicians, and others who appeal less to intellectuals than to ordinary citizens. The passage by the National Diet in August 1999 of a law that finally established the *hinomaru* as the national flag and the "Kimigayo" as the national anthem may be seen as the most recent evidence of this continued effort to bring together a democratic legal system with a long tradition of an ethnic nationalism that distrusts the state. Whether, and how, the nation and the state will be fully reconciled in Japan remains to be seen. But we can be confident that, however these issues are addressed in the future, the weight of this past history of contestation between nation and state will need to be taken into account in any explanation of politics, nationalism, or identity in modern Japan.

NOTES

1. Kano, *Kindai nihon shisō annai*, pp. 30–4.
2. Yamamuro, *Kindai nihon no chi to seiji*, pp. 109–17.
3. Satō, *Meiji nashonarizumu no kenkyū*, pp. 43–4.
4. Karatani, *"Senzen" no shikō*, p. 25.
5. Silberman, *Cages of Reason*, p. 222.
6. Uchimura Kanzō, "Nisshin sensō no ki," cited in Harada, "Nisshin sensō no keika to kokunai no ugoki," p. 145.
7. Oguma, *Tan'itsu minzoku shinwa no kigen*, p. 57.
8. Takayama Chogyū, "Jidai seishin no tōitsu wo ronzu," cited in Satō, *Meiji nashonarizumu no kenkyū*, p. 63.
9. Satō, *Meiji nashonarizumu no kenkyū*, p. 63.
10. Oguma, *Tan'itsu minzoku shinwa no kigen*, pp. 57–64; Yumoto, *Nihonshugi*, 1, cited ibid., p. 62.
11. Ino Kenji, cited in Doak, "Ethnic Nationalism and Romanticism," p. 82.
12. On the leading role played by Christians like Abe Isō and Katayama Sen in early Japanese socialism, see Scheiner, *Christian Converts and Social Protest*, pp. 243–7.

13 Sakai Toshihiko, quoted in Hirabayashi Hajime, "Ukita Kazutami to Tokutomi Sohō,"
     Kumamoto bandō kenkyū (Tokyo, 1965), cited in Scheiner, *Christian Converts and Social
     Protest*, pp. 218–19.
14 See Shirayanagi, *Nihon minzoku ron*. In English, see Doak, "What is a Nation and Who
     Belongs?", pp. 289–99.
15 Dickinson, *War and National Reinvention*, pp. 34, 177.
16 Kamei, *Dai tōa minzoku no michi*, p. 301.
17 Doak, "Culture, Ethnicity, and the State," pp. 186–92.
18 Habu and Kawai, "Minzokushugi shisō," pp. 330–3.
19 Hashikawa, *Nihon rōmanha hihan josetsu*, p. 33.
20 Morris-Suzuki, *Re-inventing Japan*, p. 190.
21 Oguma, *"Minshu" to "aikoku,"* p. 122.
22 Pyle, *The Japanese Question*, pp. 100–1.
23 Kersten, "Neo-nationalism and the 'Liberal School of History'," p. 202.

BIBLIOGRAPHY

Dickinson, Frederick. *War and National Reinvention: Japan in the Great War, 1914–1919.*
    Cambridge, Mass.: Harvard University Asia Center, 1999.
Doak, Kevin M. "Ethnic Nationalism and Romanticism in Early Twentieth-Century Japan."
    Journal of Japanese Studies 22:1 (1996): 77–103.
Doak, Kevin M. "What is a Nation and Who Belongs? National Narratives and the Ethnic
    Imagination in Twentieth Century Japan." *American Historical Review* 102:2 (Apr. 1997):
    283–309.
Doak, Kevin M. "Culture, Ethnicity, and the State in Early Twentieth-Century Japan." In
    Sharon Minichiello, ed., *Japan's Competing Modernities: Issues in Culture and Democracy,
    1900–1930.* Honolulu: University of Hawai'i Press, 1998.
Habu Nagaho and Kawai Tsuneo. "Minzokushugi shisō." In Tamura Hideo and Tanaka
    Hiroshi, eds., *Shakai shisō jiten.* Tokyo: Chūō Daigaku Shuppanbu, 1982.
Harada Katsumasa. "Nisshin sensō no keika to kokunai no ugoki." In Fujiwara Akira, Imai
    Seiichi, and Ōe Shinobu, eds., *Kindai Nihonshi no kiso chishiki.* Tokyo: Yūhikaku, 1979.
Hashikawa Bunzō. *Nihon rōmanha hihan josetsu.* Tokyo: Miraisha, 1965.
Kamei Kan'ichirō. *Dai tōa minzoku no michi.* Tokyo: Seiki Shobō, 1941.
Kano Masanao. *Kindai nihon shisō annai.* Tokyo: Iwanami Shoten, 1999.
Karatani Kōjin. *"Senzen" no shikō.* Kōdansha gakujutsu bunko 1477. Tokyo: Kōdansha, 2001.
Kersten, Rikki. "Neo-Nationalism and the 'Liberal School of History'." *Japan Forum* 11:2
    (1999): 191–203.
Morris-Suzuki, Tessa. *Re-inventing Japan: Time, Space, Nation.* Armonk, NY: M. E. Sharpe,
    1998.
Oguma Eiji. *Tan'itsu minzoku shinwa no kigen: "Nihonjin" no jigazō no keifu.* Tokyo:
    Shin'yōsha, 1995.
Oguma Eiji. *"Minshu" to "aikoku": sengo Nihon no nashonarizumu to kōkyōsei.* Tokyo:
    Shin'yōsha, 2002.
Pyle, Kenneth B. *The Japanese Question: Power and Purpose in a New Era.* Washington DC:
    AEI Press, 1992.
Satō Yoshimaru. *Meiji nashonarizumu no kenkyū: seikyōsha no seiritsu to sono shūhen.* Tokyo:
    Fuyō Shobō, 1998.
Scheiner, Irwin. *Christian Converts and Social Protest in Meiji Japan.* Berkeley: University of
    California Press, 1970.
Shirayanagi Shūko. *Nihon minzoku ron.* Tokyo: Chikura Shobō, 1942.

Silberman, Bernard. *Cages of Reason: The Rise of the Rational State in France, Japan, the United States, and Great Britain.* Chicago: University of Chicago Press, 1993.
Yamamuro Shin'ichi. *Kindai nihon no chi to seiji Inoue Kowashi kara taishū engei made.* Tokyo: Bokutakusha, 1985.

FURTHER READING

There have in recent years been a good many published works on Japanese nationalism written in Japanese that pay close attention to the particular forms of nationalism in Japan (especially *minzokushugi* and *kokuminshugi*). However, I will limit myself below to some key works on Japanese nationalism that have appeared in English. Oguma Eiji's *Tan'itsu minzoku shinwa no kigen* (The Origin of the Myth of a Mono-Ethnic Nation) has been translated by David Askew and published as *A Genealogy of "Japanese" Self-Images* (Melbourne: Trans Pacific Press. 2002). Askew made an unfortunate choice to emphasize literary smoothness of style over meaning, and thus the central concept of *minzoku* (ethnic nationality) gets rendered in a variety of ways, leaving the book's central thesis difficult to follow at times. Nonetheless, this is a valuable sourcebook on the depth and breadth of ethnic nationalism in modern Japan. For more on the Japan Romantic School and its ethnic nationalism, see Kevin M. Doak's *Dreams of Difference: The Japan Romantic School and the Crisis of Modernity* (Berkeley: University of California Press, 1994). Curtis Gayle's *Marxist History and Postwar Japanese Nationalism* (London: RoutledgeCurzon, 2003) picks up where Oguma and Doak left off, tracing the influence of prewar concepts of ethnic nationality on postwar Marxist historiography. His study shows how ethnic nationalism survived the war to become the basis of a postwar cultural nationalism that appealed to nationalists on both sides of the political spectrum. His view of postwar nationalism is complemented by Brian McVeigh's *Nationalisms of Japan: Managing and Mystifying Identity* (Lanham, Md.: Rowman and Littlefield, 2004). McVeigh's concise study is a very important contribution insofar as he recognizes and even presents a typology of the plurality of nationalisms in contemporary Japan. Yumiko Iida's *Rethinking Identity in Modern Japan: Nationalism as Aesthetics* (London: Routledge, 2002) is a challenging Marxist-inspired interpretation of postwar Japanese nationalism as an "aesthetic" displacement of class consciousness, and thus an ideology that merely supports the capitalist state. It should be read together with James Orr's *The Victim as Hero: Ideologies of Peace and National Identity in Postwar Japan* (Honolulu: University of Hawai'i Press, 2001) and Kosaku Yoshino's *Cultural Nationalism in Contemporary Japan: A Sociological Enquiry* (London: Routledge, 1992). On gender and nationalism (Ueno Chizuko is the leader in this subfield in Japanese), see Jason Karlin, "The Gender of Nationalism: Competing Masculinities in Meiji Japan," *Journal of Japanese Studies* 28:1 (Winter 2002): 41–77. Rather than simply applying nationalism to gender (as, for example, the oppression of women by the patriarchal state), Karlin's essay demonstrates the constructed and contested nature of both gender and the nation in Meiji Japan. For a more traditional approach to gender and nationalism, see Mariko Tamanoi, *Under the Shadow of Nationalism: Politics and Poetics of Rural Japanese Women* (Honolulu: University of Hawai'i Press, 1998). On literary representations of identity, see the various chapters in Haruo

Shirane and Tomi Suzuki, eds., *Inventing the Classics: Modernity, National Identity, and Japanese Literature* (Stanford, Calif.: Stanford University Press, 2000).

One important volume that introduces how several influential scholars understand the problem of Japanese nationalism is Sandra Wilson's edited collection *Nation and Nationalism in Japan* (London: RoutledgeCurzon, 2002). An emerging approach to Japanese nationalism has been to emphasize metaphors of space and region, especially by placing Japanese nationalism in relationship to other identities and nationalisms in East Asia. See the chapters on Japan by Kevin Doak, Stefan Tanaka, and Ronald Toby in Kai-wing Chow, Kevin Doak, and Poshek Fu, eds., *Constructing Nationhood in Modern East Asia* (Ann Arbor: University of Michigan Press, 2001). The various essays in Dick Stegewerns, ed., *Nationalism and Internationalism in Imperial Japan* (London: RoutledgeCurzon, 2003) explore the various strategies through which nationalism was intertwined with internationalism in the imperial period. Also, Prasenjit Duara's *Sovereignty and Authenticity: Manchukuo and the East Asian Modern* (Lanham, Md.: Rowman and Littlefield, 2003) is a good reminder that prewar Japanese national identity and nationalism encompassed many people whom today we would not necessarily think of as "Japanese."

Consolidated Bibliography

Abe Ryuichi. *The Weaving of Mantra: Kukai and the Construction of Esoteric Buddhist Discourse*. New York: Columbia University Press, 1999.

Abe Tsunehisa. *Kindai Nihon chihō seitō-shi ron: "Ura Nihon"-ka no naka no Niigata-ken seitō undō*. Tokyo: Hasuyo Shobō Shuppan, 1996.

Adolphson, Mikael. *The Gates of Power: Monks, Courtiers, and Warriors in Premodern Japan*. Honolulu: University of Hawai'i Press, 2000.

Adolphson, Mikael, ed. *Centers and Peripheries in Heian Japan*. Honolulu: University of Hawai'i Press, forthcoming.

Akami, Tomoko. *Internationalizing the Pacific: The United States, Japan, and the Institute of Pacific Relations in War and Peace, 1919–45*. London: Routledge, 2002.

Akita, George. *Foundations of Constitutional Government in Modern Japan, 1868–1900*. Cambridge, Mass.: Harvard University Press, 1967.

Aldous, Christopher. *The Police in Occupation Japan: Control, Corruption and Resistance to Reform*. London: Routledge, 1997.

Allen, G. C. *A Short Economic History of Modern Japan*. New York: St. Martin's Press, 1946; 4th edn., 1981.

Allison, Anne. "Producing Mothers." In Anne Imamura, ed., *Reimaging Japanese Women*. Berkeley: University of California Press, 1996.

Allison, Anne. *Permitted and Prohibited Desires: Mothers, Comics, and Censorship in Japan*. Berkeley: University of California Press, 2000.

Alperovitz, Gar. *Atomic Diplomacy: Hiroshima and Potsdam*. New York: Simon and Schuster, 1965.

Amino Yoshihiko. "Deconstructing 'Japan'," trans. Gavan McCormack. *East Asian History* 3 (June 1992): 121–42.

Amino Yoshihiko. "Emperor, Race, and Commoners." In Donald Denoon, Mark Hudson, Gavan McCormack, and Tessa Morris-Suzuki, eds., *Multicultural Japan: Palaeolithic to Postmodern*. Cambridge: Cambridge University Press, 1996.

Amino Yoshihiko. "Commerce and Finance in the Middle Ages: The Beginnings of 'Capitalism'." *Acta Asiatica* 81 (2001): 1–19.

Anderer, Paul. *Literature of the Lost Home: Kobayashi Hideo – Literary Criticism, 1924–1939*. Stanford, Calif.: Stanford University Press, 1995.

Anderson, J. L. "Spoken Silents in the Japanese Cinema; or, Talking to Pictures: Essaying the *Katsuben*, Contexturalizing the Texts." In Arthur Noletti, Jr. and David Desser, eds., *Reframing Japanese Cinema*. Bloomington: Indiana University Press, 1992.

Andrews, Allan. *The Teachings Essential for Rebirth: A Study of Genshin's Ojoyoshu*. Tokyo: Monumenta Nipponica, 1973.

Aoki, Kenichi, and Tuljapurkar, Shripad. "Hanihara's Conundrum Revisited: Theoretical Estimates of the Immigration into Japan during the 1000 Year Period from 300 BC to AD 700." *Anthropological Science* 108 (2000): 305–19.

Aoki, Masahiko. "Monitoring Characteristics of the Main Bank System: An Analytical and Developmental View." In Masahiko Aoki and Hugh Patrick, eds., *The Japanese Main Bank System*. Oxford: Oxford University Press, 1995.

Aoki, Masahiko, and Patrick, Hugh, eds. *The Japanese Main Bank System: Its Relevance for Developing and Transforming Economies*. Oxford: Oxford University Press, 1995.

Aoki, Michiko Yamaguchi. *Ancient Myths and Early History of Japan: A Cultural Foundation*. New York: Exposition Press, 1974.

Aoki, Michiko Yamaguchi, trans. *Izumo no kuni fudoki*. Tokyo: Sophia University, 1971.

Aoki, Michiko Yamaguchi, trans. *Records of Wind and Earth: A Translation of Fudoki, with Introduction and Commentaries*. Ann Arbor, Mich.: Association for Asian Studies, 1997.

Apter, David, and Sawa Nagayo. *Against the State: Politics and Social Protest in Japan*. Cambridge, Mass.: Harvard University Press, 1984.

Araki Kengo and Inoue Tadashi, comp. *Nihon shisō taikei, 34, Kaibara Ekiken, Muro Kyūso*. Tokyo: Iwanami Shoten, 1970.

Ariizumi Sadao. *Meiji seiji shi no kiso katei*. Tokyo: Yoshikawa Kan, 1979.

Arisawa Hiromi, ed. *Shōwa keizaishi*. Tokyo: Nihon Keizai Shinbunsha, 1976.

Armitage, Richard, and Nye, Joseph. "The United States and Japan: Advancing toward a Mature Partnership." Washington DC: Institute for National Strategic Studies, 2000. Available at <http://www.ndu.edu/inss/strforum/SR_01/SR_Japan.htm> accessed Feb. 28, 2006.

Armstrong, Karen. *Buddha*. New York: Viking, 2001.

Arnesen, Peter. *The Medieval Japanese Daimyō: The Ouchi Family's Rule in Suo and Nagato*. New Haven: Yale University Press, 1979.

Arnold, Jeanne. E. "The Archaeology of Complex Hunter-Gatherers." *Journal of Archaeological Method and Theory* 3 (1996): 77–126.

Arrighi, Giovanni, Hamashita Takeshi, and Selden, Mark, eds. *The Resurgence of East Asia: 500, 150, and 50 Year Perspectives*. London: Routledge, 2003.

Asada Sadao. *Ryō taisenkan no Nichi-Bei kankei: kaigun to seisaku kettei katei*. Tokyo: Tokyo Daigaku Shuppankai, 1993.

Asada Sadao. "The Shock of the Atomic Bomb and Japan's Decision to Surrender – A Reconsideration." *Pacific Historical Review* 67 (Nov. 1998): 477–512.

Asakawa, Kan'ichi. *Land and Society in Medieval Japan*. Tokyo: Japan Society for the Promotion of Science, 1965.

Ashkenazi, Michael. *Matsuri: Festivals of a Japanese Town*. Honolulu: University of Hawai'i Press, 1993.

Aso Yuya. "Bio-diversity Reconstruction: Restoring Japan's Rivers to Ecological Vibrance." Ministry of Land, Infrastructure and Transport homepage <http://www.mlit.go.jp/river/english/bio-d1.html> accessed Feb. 28, 2006.

Aston, W. G., trans. *Nihongi: Chronicles of Japan from the Earliest Times to A.D. 697*. Rutland, Vt.: Charles E. Tuttle, 1972, repr. 1980.

Asuka Imasamichi. "Seikanron no zentei." In Furuya Tetsuo and Yamamuro Shin'ichi, eds., *Kindai Nihon ni okeru higashi Ajia mondai*. Tokyo: Yoshikawa Kōbunkan, 2001.

Atarashii rekishi kyōkasho. Tokyo: Fusōsha, 2001.

Atkins, E. Taylor. *Blue Nippon: Authenticating Jazz in Japan*. Durham, NC: Duke University Press, 2001.

Auslin, Michael. *Negotiating with Imperialism: The Unequal Treaties and the Culture of Japanese Diplomacy*. Cambridge, Mass.: Harvard University Press, 2004.

Azuma, Eiichiro. *Between Two Empires: Race, History, and Transnationalism in Japanese America*. Oxford: Oxford University Press, 2005.

Banno Junji. *Democracy in Prewar Japan: Concepts of Government, 1871–1937*, trans. Andrew Fraser. London: Routledge, 2001.

Barlow, Tani, ed. *Formations of Colonial Modernity in East Asia*. Durham, NC: Duke University Press, 1997.

Barnes, Gina L. "Origins of the Japanese Islands: The New 'Big Picture'." *Japan Review* 15 (2003): 3–50.

Barnhart, Michael. *Japan Prepares for Total War: The Search for Economic Security, 1919–1941*. Ithaca, NY: Cornell University Press, 1987.

Barshay, Andrew. *State and Intellectual in Imperial Japan: The Public Man in Crisis*. Berkeley: University of California Press, 1988.

Barshay, Andrew. *The Social Sciences in Modern Japan: The Marxian and Modernist Traditions*. Berkeley: University of California Press, 2004.

Batten, Bruce. *To the Ends of Japan: Premodern Frontiers, Boundaries, and Interactions*. Honolulu: University of Hawai'i Press, 2003.

Batten, Bruce. *Gateway to Japan: Hakata in War and Peace, 500–1300*. Honolulu: University of Hawai'i Press, 2006.

Baxter, James. *The Meiji Unification through the Lens of Ishikawa Prefecture*. Cambridge, Mass.: Harvard University Press, 1994.

Beasley, W. G. *Rise of Modern Japan*. New York: Praeger, 1963.

Beasley, W. G. *Meiji Restoration*. Stanford, Calif.: Stanford University Press, 1972.

Beasley, W. G. *Japanese Imperialism, 1894–1945*. Oxford: Clarendon Press, 1991.

Beasley, W. G. *Japan Encounters the Barbarian: Japanese Travellers in America and Europe*. New Haven: Yale University Press, 1995.

Beasley, W. G., and Pulleyblank, E. G. *Historians of China and Japan*. London: Oxford University Press, 1961.

Benjamin, Walter. "The Work of Art in the Age of Mechanical Reproduction." In Hannah Arendt, ed., *Illuminations*. New York: Harcourt, Brace, and World, 1968.

Berger, Gordon. *Parties Out of Power in Japan, 1931–1941*. Princeton: Princeton University Press, 1977.

Berger, Gordon. "Politics and Mobilization in Japan, 1931–1945." In Peter Duus, ed., *The Cambridge History of Japan*, vol. 6, *The Twentieth Century*. Cambridge: Cambridge University Press, 1988.

Berger, Gordon, trans. and ed. *Kenkenroku: A Diplomatic Record of the Sino-Japanese War, 1894–95*. Princeton: Princeton University Press, 1982.

Bergerud, Eric. *Fire in the Sky: The Air War in the South Pacific*. Boulder, Colo.: Westview Press, 2000.

Bernstein, Barton. "Understanding the Atomic Bomb and the Japanese Surrender: Missed Opportunities, Little-Known Near Disasters, and Modern Memory." *Diplomatic History* 19:2 (Spring 1995): 227–73.

Bernstein, Gail. *Haruko's World: A Japanese Farm Woman and Her Community*. Stanford, Calif.: Stanford University Press, 1983.

Bernstein, Gail Lee, ed. *Recreating Japanese Women, 1600–1945*. Berkeley: University of California Press, 1991.

Berry, Mary Elizabeth. *Hideyoshi*. Cambridge, Mass.: Council on East Asian Studies, Harvard University Press, 1982.

Berry, Mary Elizabeth. "Public Peace and Private Attachment: The Goals and Conduct of Power in Early Modern Japan." *Journal of Japanese Studies* 12:2 (Summer 1986): 237–71.

Berry, Mary Elizabeth. *The Culture of Civil War in Kyoto*. Berkeley: University of California Press, 1995.

Berry, Mary Elizabeth. "Public Life in Authoritarian Japan." *Daedalus* 127:3 (Summer 1998): 133–66.

Best, Anthony. *Britain, Japan, and Pearl Harbor: Avoiding War in East Asia, 1936–1941*. London: Routledge, 1995.

Best, Anthony. *British Intelligence and the Japanese Challenge in Asia, 1914–1941*. New York: Palgrave Macmillan, 2002.

Birt, Michael. "Samurai in Passage: The Transformation of the Sixteenth-Century Kantō." *Journal of Japanese Studies* 11:2 (Summer 1985): 369–99.

Bix, Herbert. *Peasant Protest in Japan, 1590–1884*. New Haven: Yale University Press, 1986.

Bix, Herbert. *Hirohito and the Making of Modern Japan*. New York: HarperCollins, 2000.

Bleed, Peter. "Almost Archaeology: Early Archaeological Interest in Japan." In R. J. Pearson, G. L. Barnes, and K. L. Hutterer, eds., *Windows on the Japanese Past: Studies in Archaeology and Prehistory*. Ann Arbor: Center for Japanese Studies, University of Michigan, 1986.

Bleed, Peter. "Cheap, Regular, and Reliable: Implications of Design Variation in Late Pleistocene Japanese Microblade Technology." In R. G. Elston and S. L. Kuhn, eds., *Thinking Small: Global Perspectives on Microlithization*. Archeological Papers of the American Anthropological Association 12. Arlington, Va.: American Anthropological Association, 2002.

Bloom, Alfred. *Shinran's Gospel of Pure Grace*. Tucson: University of Arizona Press, 1965.

Blue, Gregory, Bunton, Martin, and Croizier, Ralph, eds. *Colonialism and the Modern World: Selected Studies*. Armonk, NY: M. E. Sharpe, 2002.

Bodart-Bailey, Beatrice. "Urbanization and the Nature of the Tokugawa Hegemony." In Nicolas Fiévé and Paul Waley, eds., *Japanese Capitals in Historical Perspective: Place, Power, and Memory in Kyoto, Edo, and Tokyo*. London: RoutledgeCurzon, 2003.

Bodiford, William. "Zen and the Art of Religious Prejudice." *Japanese Journal of Religious Studies* 23:1/2 (1996): 1–27.

Bolitho, Harold. "The Han." In John W. Hall, ed., *The Cambridge History of Modern Japan*, vol. 4, *Early Modern Japan*. Cambridge: Cambridge University Press, 1991.

Borgen, Robert. *Sugawara no Michizane and the Early Heian Court*. Cambridge, Mass.: Council on East Asian Studies, Harvard University, 1986.

Botsman, Daniel. *Punishment and Power in the Making of Modern Japan*. Princeton: Princeton University Press, 2004.

Bowen, Roger. *Rebellion and Democracy in Meiji Japan*. Berkeley: University of California Press, 1980.

Bowen, Roger. "Japanese Peasants: Moral? Rational? Revolutionary? Duped? A Review Article." *Journal of Asian Studies* 47:4 (1988): 821–32.

Bradley, James. *Flyboys: A True Story of Courage*. Boston: Little, Brown, 2003.

Brenner, Robert. "The Economics of Global Turbulence." *New Left Review* 229 (1998): 1–265.

Brewster Jennifer, trans. *Fujiwara no Nagako, the Emperor Horikawa Diary*. Honolulu: University of Hawai'i Press, 1972.

Brinton, Mary. "Christmas Cakes and Weddings Cakes: The Social Organization of Japanese Women's Life Course." In Takie Lebra, ed., *Japanese Social Organization*. Honolulu: University of Hawai'i Press, 1992.

Brinton, Mary. *Women and the Economic Miracle: Gender and Work in Postwar Japan*. Berkeley: University of California Press, 1993.

Brook, Timothy. *Collaboration: Japanese Agents and Wartime Elites in Wartime China*. Cambridge, Mass.: Harvard University Press, 2005.

Brooker, Paul. *The Faces of Fraternalism: Nazi Germany, Fascist Italy, and Imperial Japan*. Oxford: Clarendon Press, 1991.

Brooks, Barbara. *Japan's Imperial Diplomacy: Consuls, Treaty Ports, and War in China, 1895–1938*. Honolulu: University of Hawai'i Press, 2000.

Brown, Delmer M., ed. *The Cambridge History of Japan*, vol. 1, *Ancient Japan*. Cambridge: Cambridge University Press, 1993.

Brown, Philip. "The Mismeasure of Land: Land Surveying in the Tokugawa Period." *Monumenta Nipponica* 42:2 (1987): 115–55.

Brown, Philip C. *Central Authority and Local Autonomy in the Formation of Early Modern Japan: The Case of Kaga Domain.* Stanford, Calif.: Stanford University Press, 1993.

Brownlee, John. *Japanese Historians and the National Myths, 1600–1945.* Vancouver: UBC Press, 1997.

Brownlee, John., ed. *History in the Service of the Japanese Nation.* Toronto: University of Toronto–York University Joint Centre on Modern East Asia, 1983.

Buckley, Roger. *Occupation Diplomacy: Britain, the United States, and Japan, 1945–1952.* Cambridge: Cambridge University Press, 1982.

Burchell, Graham. "Liberal Government and Techniques of the Self." In Andrew Barry, Thomas Osborne, and Nikolas Rose, eds., *Foucault and Political Reason: Liberalism, Neo-Liberalism and Rationalities of Government.* Chicago: University of Chicago Press, 1996.

Burkman, Thomas. *Japan, the League of Nations, and World Order, 1914–1938.* Honolulu: University of Hawai'i Press, 2006.

Burkman, Thomas, ed. *The Occupation of Japan: Arts and Culture.* Norfolk, Va.: General Douglas MacArthur Foundation, 1988.

Burks, Ardath W., ed. *The Modernizers: Overseas Students, Foreign Employees and Meiji Japan.* Boulder, Colo.: Westview Press, 1985.

Burns, Susan. "The Body as Text: Confucianism, Reproduction, and Gender in Tokugawa Japan." In Benjamin Elman, John Duncan, and Herman Ooms, eds., *Rethinking Confucianism: Past and Present in China, Japan, Korea, and Vietnam.* UCLA Asian Pacific Monograph Series. Los Angeles: UCLA, 2002.

Butler, Lee. *Emperor and Aristocracy in Japan, 1467–1680: Resilience and Renewal.* Cambridge, Mass.: Harvard University Asia Center, 2002.

Calder, Kent. "Japanese Foreign Economic Policy Formation: Explaining the Reactive State." *World Politics* 40:4 (1988): 517–41.

Calder, Kent. *Strategic Capitalism: Private Business and Public Purpose in Japanese Industrial Finance.* Princeton: Princeton University Press, 1993.

Calder, Kent. *Crisis and Compensation.* Princeton: Princeton University Press, 1998.

Caporaso, S. A. "Comparative Politics: Diversity and Coherence." *Comparative Political Studies,* 33 (2000): 6–7, 699–702.

Caron, Bruce. "On the Downside of Japan's Old Capital: Higashi-kujo." *Public Culture* 11:3 (Fall 1999): 433–40.

Chang, Iris. *The Rape of Nanking: The Forgotten Holocaust of World War II.* New York: Basic Books, 1997.

Checkland, Olive. *Humanitarianism and the Emperor's Japan, 1877–1977.* New York: St. Martin's Press, 1994.

Cheng, Lucie, and Bonacich, Edna, eds. *Labor Migration under Capitalism: Asian Workers in the United States before World War II.* Berkeley: University of California Press, 1984.

Ching, Leo. "Globalizing the Regional, Regionalizing the Global: Mass Culture and Asianism in the Age of Late Capital." *Public Culture* 12:1 (2000): 233–57.

Ching, Leo. *Becoming "Japanese": Colonial Taiwan and the Politics of Identity Formation.* Berkeley: University of California Press, 2001.

Chow, Kai-wing, Doak, Kevin, and Fu, Poshek, eds. *Constructing Nationhood in Modern East Asia.* Ann Arbor: University of Michigan Press, 2001.

Clark, Rodney. *The Japanese Company.* New Haven: Yale University Press, 1979.

Cleary, Thomas, trans. *The Blue Cliff Record.* Berkeley, Calif.: Numata Center for Buddhist Translation and Research, 1998.

Cleary, Thomas, trans. *The Code of the Samurai: A Modern Translation of the* Bushidō shoshinshū *of Taira Shigesuke.* Rutland, Vt.: C. E. Tuttle, 1999.

Cloke, Paul, and Thrift, Nigel. "Introduction: Reconfiguring the Rural." In Paul Cloke et al., eds., *Writing the Rural: Five Cultural Geographies*. London: Paul Chapman, 1994.

Coble, Parks. *Chinese Capitalists in Japan's New Order: The Occupied Lower Yangtzi, 1937–1945*. Berkeley: University of California Press, 2003.

Cohen, Theodore. *Remaking Japan: The American Occupation as New Deal*. New York: Free Press, 1987.

Cole, Robert. *Japanese Blue Collar*. Berkeley: University of California Press, 1971.

Cole, Robert. *Strategies for Learning: Small-Group Activities in American, Japanese, and Swedish Industry*. Berkeley: University of California Press, 1989.

Coleman, Samuel. *Family Planning in Japanese Society: Traditional Birth Control in a Modern Urban Culture*. Princeton: Princeton University Press, 1983.

Collcutt, Martin. *Five Mountains: The Rinzai Zen Monastic Institution in Medieval Japan*. Cambridge: Council on East Asian Studies, Harvard University, 1980.

Collier, David. "The Comparative Method." In Ada W. Finifter, ed., *Political Science: The State of the Discipline II*. Washington DC: American Political Science Association, 1993.

Conlan, Thomas. *In Little Need of Divine Intervention*. Ithaca, N.Y.: Cornell East Asia Series, 2001.

Conlan, Thomas. *State of War: The Violent Order of Fourteenth Century Japan*. Ann Arbor, Mich.: Center for Japanese Studies, 2004.

Conroy, Hilary. *The Japanese Seizure of Korea, 1868–1910: A Study of Realism and Idealism in International Relations*. Philadelphia: University of Pennsylvania Press, 1960.

Conroy, Hilary, and Wray, Harry, eds. *Japan Examined*. Honolulu: University of Hawai'i Press, 1983.

Cook, Haruko Taya, and Cook, Theodore F. *Japan at War: An Oral History*. New York: Free Press, 1992.

Cooper, Michael, comp. and annot. *They Came to Japan: An Anthology of European Reports on Japan, 1543–1740*. Berkeley: University of California Press, 1965, repr. 1981.

Coox, Alvin D. *Nomonhan: Japan against Russia, 1939*, 2 vols. Stanford, Calif.: Stanford University Press, 1985.

Copeland, Rebecca. *Lost Leaves: Women Writers of Meiji Japan*. Honolulu: University of Hawai'i Press, 2000.

Cornell, Laurel. "Peasant Women and Divorce in Preindustrial Japan." *Signs* 15:4 (1990): 710–32.

Cornell, Laurel. "Infanticide in Early Modern Japan? Demography, Culture, and Population Growth." *Journal of Asian Studies* 55:1 (1996): 22–50.

Cox, G., and Niou, E. "Seat Bonuses under the Single Nontransferable Vote System: Evidence from Japan and Taiwan." *Comparative Politics* 26 (1994): 221–36.

Cox, Gary. "Is the Single Non-Transferable Vote Superproportional? Evidence from Japan and Taiwan." *American Journal of Political Science* 40 (Aug. 1996): 740–55.

Cox, Gary, and Rosenbluth, Frances. "The Anatomy of a Split: The Liberal Democrats in Japan." *Electoral Studies* 14:2 (1995): 355–76.

Cox, Gary, and Rosenbluth, Frances. "Factional Competition for the Party Endorsement: The Case of Japan's Liberal Democratic Party." *British Journal of Political Science* 26 (1996): 259–69.

Cox, Robert. "Social Forces, States, and World Order" (1981). In Robert Cox, with T. J. Sinclair, *Approaches to World Order*. Cambridge: Cambridge University Press, 1996.

Crawcour, E. Sydney. "The Tokugawa Period and Japan's Preparation for Modern Economic Growth." In John W. Hall and Marius Jansen, eds., *Studies in the Institutional History of Early Modern Japan*. Princeton: Princeton University Press, 1968.

Crawcour, E. Sydney. "Industrialization and Technological Change, 1885–1920." In Peter Duus, ed., *The Cambridge History of Japan*, vol. 6, *The Twentieth Century*. Cambridge: Cambridge University Press, 1988.

Crawcour, E. Sydney. "Economic Change in the Nineteenth Century." In Marius Jansen, ed., *The Cambridge History of Japan*, vol. 5, *The Nineteenth Century*. Cambridge: Cambridge University Press, 1989.

Crawford, Gary W. "Prehistoric Plant Domestication in East Asia." In C. W. Cowan and P. J. Watson, eds., *The Origins of Agriculture: An International Perspective*. Washington DC: Smithsonian Institution Press, 1992.

Cruikshank, Barbara. "Revolutions Within: Self-Government and Self-Esteem." In Andrew Barry, Thomas Osborne, and Nikolas Rose, eds., *Foucault and Political Reason: Liberalism, Neo-Liberalism and Rationalities of Government*. Chicago: University of Chicago Press, 1996.

Cruikshank, Barbara. *The Will to Empower: Democratic Citizens and Other Subjects*. Ithaca, NY: Cornell University Press, 1999.

Curtis, Gerald. *Election Campaigning Japanese Style*. New York: Columbia University Press, 1971.

Curtis, Gerald. *The Japanese Way of Politics*. New York: Columbia University Press, 1988.

Curtis, Gerald. *The Logic of Japanese Politics*. New York: Columbia University Press, 1999.

Danly, Robert Lyons. *In the Shade of Spring Leaves: The Life and Writings of Higuchi Ichiyō, a Woman of Letters in Meiji Japan*. New Haven: Yale University Press, 1981.

Davis, John. "Blurring the Boundaries of the Buraku(min)." In J. Eades, Tom Gill, and Harumi Befu, eds., *Globalization and Social Change in Contemporary Japan*. Melbourne: Trans Pacific Press, 2000.

de Bary, Wm. Theodore. "Some Common Tendencies in Neo-Confucianism." In David S. Nivison and Arthur Wright, eds., *Confucianism in Action*. Stanford, Calif.: Stanford University Press, 1959.

DeVos, George, and Wagatsuma Hiroshi, eds. *Japan's Invisible Race: Caste in Culture and Personality*, rev. edn. Berkeley: University of California Press, 1972.

Dickinson, Frederick. *War and National Reinvention: Japan in the Great War, 1914–1919*. Cambridge, Mass.: Harvard University Asia Center, 1999.

Dickinson, Frederick. "Commemorating the War in Post-Versailles Japan." In John Steinberg and David Schimmelpenninck, eds., *The Russo-Japanese War Reexamined*. Leiden: Brill, 2005.

Dingman, Roger. *Ghost of War: The Sinking of the Awa Maru and Japanese–American Relations, 1945–1995*. Annapolis, Md.: Naval Institute Press, 1997.

Dirlik, Arif. *After the Revolution: Waking to Global Capitalism*. Hanover, NH: Wesleyan University Press, pub. by University Press of New England, 1994.

Dixon, Robert M. W. *The Rise and Fall of Languages*. Cambridge: Cambridge University Press, 1997.

Doak, Kevin M. *Dreams of Difference: The Japan Romantic School and the Crisis of Modernity*. Berkeley: University of California Press, 1994.

Doak, Kevin M. "Ethnic Nationalism and Romanticism in Early Twentieth-Century Japan." *Journal of Japanese Studies* 22:1 (1996): 77–103.

Doak, Kevin M. "What is a Nation and Who Belongs? National Narratives and the Ethnic Imagination in Twentieth Century Japan." *American Historical Review* 102:2 (Apr. 1997): 283–309.

Doak, Kevin M. "Culture, Ethnicity, and the State in Early Twentieth-Century Japan." In Sharon Minichiello, ed., *Japan's Competing Modernities: Issues in Culture and Democracy, 1900–1930*. Honolulu: University of Hawai'i Press, 1998.

Dobbins, James. *Letters of the Nun Eshinni: Images of Pure Land Buddhism in Medieval Japan.* Honolulu: University of Hawai'i Press, 2004.

Dodo Yukio, Doi Naomi, and Kondo Osamu. "Ainu and Ryūkyūan Cranial Nonmetric Variation: Evidence which Disputes the Ainu–Ryūkyū Common Origin Theory." *Anthropological Science* 106 (1998): 99–120.

Dore, Ronald P. *Land Reform in Japan.* Oxford: Oxford University Press, 1959.

Dore, Ronald P. *Education in Tokugawa Japan.* Berkeley: University of California Press, 1965.

Dore, Ronald P. *British Factory Japanese Factory: The Origins of National Diversity in Industrial Relations.* Berkeley: University of California Press, 1973.

Dore, Ronald P. *Taking Japan Seriously.* London: Athlone Press, 1987.

Dore, Ronald P., ed. *Aspects of Social Change in Modern Japan.* Princeton: Princeton University Press, 1967.

Dower, John. *Empire and Aftermath: Yoshida Shigeru and the Japanese Experience, 1878–1954.* Cambridge, Mass.: Harvard University Press, 1979.

Dower, John. *War without Mercy: Race and Power in the Pacific War.* New York: Pantheon, 1986.

Dower, John. "Occupied Japan and the Cold War in Asia." In John Dower, *Japan in War and Peace: Selected Essays.* New York: New Press, 1993.

Dower, John. *Embracing Defeat: Japan in the Wake of World War II.* New York: Norton 1999.

Dower, John, ed. *Origins of the Modern Japanese State: Selected Writings of E. H. Norman.* New York: Pantheon, 1975; London: Faber and Faber, 1986.

Dower, John, with George, Timothy. *Japanese History and Culture from Ancient to Modern Times: Seven Basic Bibliographies*, 2nd edn. Princeton: Markus Wiener, 1995.

Drea, Edward. *In the Service of the Emperor: Essays on the Imperial Japanese Army.* Lincoln: University of Nebraska Press, 1998.

Drifte, Reinhard. *Japan's Foreign Policy for the Twenty-First Century: From Economic Superpower to What Power?*, 2nd edn. London: Macmillan, 1998.

Duara, Prasenjit. *Sovereignty and Authenticity: Manchukuo and the East Asian Modern.* Lanham, Md.: Rowman and Littlefield, 2003.

Dudden, Alexis. *Japan's Colonization of Korea: Discourse and Power.* Honolulu: University of Hawai'i Press, 2004.

Duke, Benjamin. *Japan's Militant Teachers: A History of the Left-Wing Teachers' Movement.* Honolulu: University of Hawai'i Press, 1973.

Dumoulin, Heinrich. *Zen Buddhism: A History*, vol. 2, *Japan.* London: Collier Macmillan, 1990.

Duus, Peter. *Feudalism in Japan*, 2nd edn. New York: Knopf, 1976.

Duus, Peter. *Party Rivalry and Political Change in Taishō Japan.* Cambridge, Mass.: Harvard University Press, 1968.

Duus, Peter, ed. *The Cambridge History of Japan*, vol. 6, *The Twentieth Century.* Cambridge: Cambridge University Press, 1988.

Duus, Peter. *The Abacus and the Sword: The Japanese Penetration of Korea, 1895–1910.* Berkeley: University of California Press, 1995.

Duus, Peter. "The *Marumaru Chinbun* and the Origins of the Japanese Political Cartoon." *International Journal of Comic Art* 1:1 (1999): 42–56.

Duus, Peter, ed. with intro. *The Japanese Discovery of America: A Brief History with Documents.* Boston: Bedford Books, 1997.

Duus, Peter, and Okimoto, Daniel. "Fascism and the History of Prewar Japan: The Failure of a Concept." *Journal of Asian Studies* 39:1 (1979): 65–76.

Duus, Peter, Myers, Ramon, and Peattie, Mark, eds. *The Japanese Informal Empire in China, 1895–1937.* Princeton: Princeton University Press, 1989.

Duus, Peter, Myers, Ramon, and Peattie, Mark, eds. *The Japanese Wartime Empire, 1931–1945.* Princeton: Princeton University Press, 1996.

Earle, Timothy. *How Chiefs Come to Power: The Political Economy in Prehistory.* Cambridge: Cambridge University Press, 1997.

Ebisawa Miki. "15 seiki no sensō to josei." In Nishimura Hiroko, ed., *Sensō, bōryoku to josei,* 1, *Ikusa no naka no onnatachi.* Tokyo: Yoshikawa Kōbunkan, 2004.

Eckert, Carter. *Offspring of Empire: The Koch'ang Kims and the Colonial Origins of Korean Capitalism, 1876–1945.* Seattle: University of Washington Press, 1991.

Edwards, Walter. *Modern Japan through Its Weddings: Gender, Person, and Society in Ritual Portrayal.* Stanford, Calif.: Stanford University Press, 1989.

Ehrenberg, John. *Civil Society: The Critical History of an Idea.* New York: New York University Press, 1999.

Eisenstadt, Shmuel, and Schlucter, Wolfgang. "Introduction: Paths to Early Modernities – A Comparative View." *Daedalus* 127:3 (Summer 1998): 1–18.

Elison, George. *Deus Destroyed: The Image of Christianity in Early Modern Japan.* Cambridge, Mass.: Harvard University Press, 1988.

Eppstein, Ury. "Musical Instruction in Meiji Japan: A Study of Adaptation and Assimilation." *Monumenta Nipponica* 40:1 (Spring 1985): 1–37.

Ericson, Steven. *The Sound of the Whistle: Railroads and the State in Meiji Japan.* Cambridge, Mass.: Council on East Asian Studies, Harvard University, 1996.

Esenbel, Selcuk. *Even the Gods Rebel: The Peasants of Takaino and the 1871 Nakano Uprising in Japan.* Ann Arbor: Association for Asian Studies, 1998.

Eskildsen, Robert. "Of Civilization and Savages: The Mimetic Imperialism of Japan's 1874 Expedition to Taiwan." *American Historical Review* 107:2 (Apr. 2002): 388–418.

Esselstrom, Eric. "The Japanese Consular Police in Northeast Asia, 1880–1942." Ph.D. dissertation, University of California, Santa Barbara, 2004.

Facts and Figures of Japan. Tokyo: Foreign Press Center, 1999.

Farris, William Wayne. *Population, Disease, and Land in Early Japan, 645–900.* Cambridge, Mass.: Council on East Asian Studies, Harvard University, 1985.

Farris, William Wayne. *Heavenly Warriors: The Evolution of Japan's Military, 500–1300.* Cambridge, Mass.: Council on East Asian Studies, Harvard University, 1992.

Farris, William Wayne. *Sacred Texts and Buried Treasures: Issues in the Historical Archaeology of Ancient Japan.* Honolulu: University of Hawai'i Press, 1998.

Faure, Bernard. *The Red Thread: Buddhist Approaches to Sexuality.* Princeton: Princeton University Press, 1998.

Faure, Bernard. *The Power of Denial: Buddhism, Purity and Gender.* Princeton: Princeton University Press, 2003.

Fister, Patricia. "Female Bunjin: The Life of Poet-Painter Ema Saikō." In Gail Bernstein, ed., *Recreating Japanese Women, 1600–1945.* Berkeley: University of California Press, 1991.

Flannery, K. V. "The Ground Plans of Archaic States." In G. M. Feinman and J. Marcus, eds., *Archaic States.* Santa Fe, NM: School of American Research Press, 1998.

Flannery, Tim. *The Future Eaters.* Chatswood, Australia: Reed Books, 1994.

Fletcher, W. Miles. *The Search for a New Order: Intellectuals and Fascism in Prewar Japan.* Chapel Hill: University of North Carolina Press, 1982.

Fletcher, W. Miles. *The Japanese Business Community and National Trade Policy, 1920–1942.* Chapel Hill: University of North Carolina Press, 1989.

Fogel, Joshua. *Politics and Sinology: The Case of Naitō Konan.* Cambridge, Mass.: Harvard University Press, 1984.

Fogel, Joshua. *Nakae Ushikichi in China: The Mourning of Spirit.* Cambridge, Mass.: Harvard University Press, 1989.

Fogel, Joshua. *The Cultural Dimension of Sino-Japanese Relations: Essays on the Nineteenth and Twentieth Centuries.* Armonk, NY: M. E. Sharpe, 1995.

Fogel, Joshua. *The Literature of Travel and the Japanese Rediscovery of China, 1862–1945.* Stanford, Calif.: Stanford University Press, 1996.

Fogel, Joshua, ed. *Nanjing Massacre in History and Historiography.* Berkeley: University of California Press, 2000.

Fogel, Joshua, trans. *Life Along the South Manchurian Railway: The Memoirs of Ito Takeo.* Armonk, NY: M. E. Sharpe, 1988.

Fogel, Joshua, trans. *Travels in Manchuria and Mongolia: A Feminist Poet from Japan Encounters Prewar China,* by Yosano Akiko. New York: Columbia University Press, 2001.

Foote, Daniel. "Judicial Creation of Norms in Japanese Labor Law: Activism in the Service of Stability?" *UCLA Law Review* 43:3 (Feb. 1996): 635–709.

Foote, Daniel. "Law as an Agent of Change? Governmental Efforts to Reduce Working Hours in Japan." In Harald Baum, ed., *Japan: Economic Success and Legal System.* Berlin and New York: Walter de Gruyter, 1997.

Foucault, Michel. "Technologies of the Self." In L. Martin, H. Gutman, and P. Hutton, eds., *Technologies of the Self: A Seminar with Michel Foucault.* Amherst: University of Massachusetts Press, 1988.

Fowler, Edward. *Sanya Blues.* Ithaca, NY: Cornell University Press, 1996.

Francks, Penelope. *Technology and Agricultural Development in Pre-war Japan.* New Haven: Yale University Press, 1984.

Frank, Richard. *Downfall: The End of the Imperial Japanese Empire.* New York: Random House, 1999.

Friday, Karl. *Hired Swords: The Rise of Private Warrior Power in Early Japan.* Stanford, Calif.: Stanford University Press, 1992.

Friday, Karl. *Samurai, Warfare and the State in Early Medieval Japan.* New York: Routledge, 2004.

Frühstück, Sabine. *Colonizing Sex: Sexology and Social Control in Modern Japan.* Berkeley: University of California Press, 2003.

Fu, Charles Wei-Hsun, and Heine, Steven, eds. *Japan in Traditional and Postmodern Perspectives.* Albany: State University of New York Press, 1995.

Fuess, Harald. *Divorce in Japan: Family, Gender, and the State, 1600–2000.* Stanford, Calif.: Stanford University Press, 2004.

Fujiki Hisashi. *Zōhyōtachi no senjō: chūsei no yōhei to doreigari.* Tokyo: Asahi Shinbunsha, 1995.

Fujiki Hisashi. *Sengoku no mura o yuku.* Tokyo: Asahi Shinbunsha, 1997.

Fujioka Nobukatsu. *"Jigyaku shikan" no byōri.* Tokyo: Bungei Shunjū, 1997.

Fujitani, Takashi. *Splendid Monarchy: Power and Pageantry in Modern Japan.* Berkeley: University of California Press, 1996.

Fujitani, Takashi, White, Geoffrey, and Yoneyama, Lisa, eds. *Perilous Memories: The Asia-Pacific War(s).* Durham, NC: Duke University Press, 2001.

Fukunaga, S. "Social Changes from the Yayoi to the Kofun Periods." In *Cultural Diversity and the Archaeology of the 21st Century,* ed. Society of Archaeological Studies. Okayama: Kōkogaku Kenkyūkai, 2004.

Fukuoka Kensei. *Kuni ga kawa o kowasu wake.* Fukuoka: Ashi Shobō, 1994.

Fukuoka Kensei. "Meibun naki kensetsu mokuteki." *Shūkan kinyōbi* (Dec. 8, 1995): 44–7.

Fukuoka Masanobu. *The Natural Way of Farming: The Theory and Practice of Green Philosophy,* trans. Frederic Metreaud. Madras: Book Venture, 1985.

Fukuoka Tetsuya. *Mori to mizu no keizaigaku.* Tokyo: Tōyō Keizai Shimpōsha, 1987.

Fukutake Tadashi. *Japanese Rural Society,* trans. Ronald Dore. Ithaca, NY: Cornell University Press, 1967.

Fukutō Sanae. *Heianchō no onna to otoko*. Tokyo: Chūō Kōronsha, 1995.

Fukutō Sanae, ed. *Rekishi no naka no kōjotachi*. Tokyo: Shōgakkan, 2002.

Fukuzawa Yukichi. "On Leaving Asia" (1885). In David Lu, ed., *Japan: A Documentary History*. Armonk, NY: M. E. Sharpe, 1996.

Funabashi Yōichi. *Asia Pacific Fusion: Japan's Role in APEC*. Washington DC: Institute for International Economics, 1995.

Furuki, Yoshiko. *The White Plum: A Biography of Ume Tsuda, Pioneer in the Higher Education of Japanese Women*. New York: Weatherhill, 1991.

Furumaya Tadao. " 'Ura Nihon' no seiritsu to tenkai." In Iwanami Kōza, ed., *Iwanami kōza Nihon tsūshi*, 17, *kindai 2*. Tokyo: Iwanami Shoten, 1994.

Furushima Toshio. "The Village and Agriculture during the Edo Period." In John Whitney Hall, ed., *The Cambridge History of Japan*, vol. 4, *Early Modern Japan*. Cambridge: Cambridge University Press, 1991.

Gao, Bai. "Arisawa Hiromi and His Theory for a Managed Economy." *Journal of Japanese Studies* 20 (1994): 115–53.

Gao, Bai. *Economic Ideology and Japanese Industrial Policy: Developmentalism from 1931 to 1965*. New York and Cambridge: Cambridge University Press, 1997.

Gao, Bai. "Globalization and Ideology: The Competing Images of the Contemporary Japanese Economic System in the 1990s." *International Sociology* 15 (2000): 435–53.

Gao, Bai. *Japan's Economic Dilemma: The Institutional Origins of Prosperity and Stagnation*. New York: Cambridge University Press, 2001.

Garon, Sheldon. *The State and Labor in Modern Japan*. Berkeley: University of California Press, 1987.

Garon, Sheldon. *Molding Japanese Minds: The State in Everyday Life*. Princeton: Princeton University Press, 1997.

Garon, Sheldon. "From Meiji to Heisei: The State and Civil Society in Japan." In Frank Schwartz and Susan Pharr, eds., *The State of Civil Society in Japan*. Cambridge: Cambridge University Press, 2003.

Gay, Suzanne. *The Moneylenders of Medieval Kyoto*. Honolulu: University of Hawai'i Press, 2002.

Gerlarch, Michael. *Alliance Capitalism*. Berkeley: University of California Press, 1992.

Gerstle, C. Andrew, ed. *Eighteenth Century Japan: Culture and Society*. London: Routledge-Curzon, 2000.

Gibney, Frank, ed. *Senso: The Japanese Remember the Pacific War: Letters to the Editor of Asahi Shinbun*. Armonk, NY: M. E. Sharpe, 1995.

Gill, Tom. *Men of Uncertainty*. Albany: State University of New York Press, 2001.

Gilpin, Robert. *The Political Economy of International Relations*. Princeton: Princeton University Press, 1987.

Gluck, Carol. "The People in History: Recent Trends in Japanese Historiography." *Journal of Asian Studies* 38 (Nov. 1978): 25–50.

Gluck, Carol. "Entangling Illusions – Japanese and American Views of the Occupation." In Warren Cohen, ed., *New Frontiers in American–East Asian Relations: Essays Presented to Dorothy Borg*. New York: Columbia University Press, 1983.

Gluck, Carol. *Japan's Modern Myths: Ideology in the Late Meiji Period*. Princeton: Princeton University Press, 1985.

Gluck, Carol. "The Past in the Present." In Andrew Gordon, ed., *Postwar Japan as History*. Berkeley: University of California Press, 1993.

Goble, Andrew Edmund. "Truth Contradiction and Harmony in Medieval Japan: Emperor Hanazono (1297–1348) and Buddhism." *Journal of the International Association of Buddhist Studies*, 12 (1989): 21–63.

Goble, Andrew Edmund. "Social Change, Knowledge, and History: Hanazono's Admonitions to the Crown Prince." *Harvard Journal of Asiatic Studies* 50:1 (1995).

Goble, Andrew Edmund. *Kenmu: Go-Daigo's Revolution*. Cambridge, Mass.: Council on East Asian Studies, Harvard University, 1997.

Goble, Andrew Edmund. "War and Injury: The Emergence of Wound Medicine in Medieval Japan." *Monumenta Nipponica* 60:3 (Autumn 2005).

Goble, Andrew Edmund, Robinson, Kenneth, and Wakabayashi, Haruko, eds. *Tools of Culture: Japan's Cultural, Intellectual, Medical, and Technological Contacts in East Asia, 1000s–1600s*. Honololu: University of Hawai'i Press, forthcoming.

Gomi Fumihiko. *Inseiki shakai no kenkyū*. Tokyo: Yamakawa Shuppan, 1984.

Gonda Yasunosuke. "Modan seikatsu to hentai shikōsei." *Kaizō* 11 (1929): 32–6.

Goodman, David, Sorj, Bernardo, and Wilkinson, John. *From Farming to Biotechnology*. Oxford: Blackwell, 1987.

Goodwin, Janet, Gramlich-Oka, B., Leicester, E., Terazawa, Y., and Walthall, A., trans. "Solitary Thoughts: A Translation of Tadano Makuzu's *Hitori Kangae*." *Monumenta Nipponica* 56:1 (2001): 21–38; 56:2 (2001): 173–95.

Gordon, Andrew. *The Evolution of Labor Relations in Japan, Heavy Industry, 1853–1955*. Cambridge, Mass.: Council on East Asian Studies, Harvard University, 1985.

Gordon, Andrew. *Labor and Imperial Democracy in Prewar Japan*. Berkeley: University of California Press, 1991.

Gordon, Andrew. *The Wages of Affluence: Labor and Management in Postwar Japan*. Cambridge, Mass.: Harvard University Press, 1998.

Gordon, Andrew. *A Modern History of Japan: From Tokugawa Times to the Present*. New York: Oxford University Press, 2003.

Gownder, Joseph, and Pekkanen, Robert. "The End of Political Science? Rational Choice Analyses in Studies of Japanese Politics." *Journal of Japanese Studies* 22 (1996): 363–84.

Graham, Patricia. *Tea of the Sages: The Art of Sencha*. Honolulu: University of Hawai'i Press, 1998.

Gramsci, Antonio. *Selections from the Prison Notebooks*. London: Lawrence and Wishart, 1971.

Green, Michael. *Japan's Reluctant Realism: Foreign Policy Challenge in an Era of Uncertain Power*. New York: Palgrave Macmillan, 2001.

Griffiths, Owen. "Need, Greed, and Protest in Japan's Black Market, 1938–1949." *Journal of Social History* 35:4 (Summer 2002): 825–58.

Groemer, Gerald. "The Creation of the Edo Outcaste Order." *Journal of Japanese Studies* 27:2 (2001): 263–93.

Groner, Paul. *Saichō: The Establishment of the Japanese Tendai School*. Berkeley, Calif.: Institute of Buddhist Studies, 1984.

Groner, Paul. *Ryōgen and Mt. Hiei: Japanese Tendai in the Tenth Century*. Honolulu: University of Hawai'i Press, 2002.

Grossberg, Kenneth. *Japan's Renaissance: The Politics of the Muromachi Bakufu*. Cambridge, Mass.: Council on East Asian Studies, Harvard University, 1981.

Guarini, Elena Fasano. "Center and Periphery." *Journal of Modern History* 67 supplement (Dec. 1995): 74–96.

Guttmann, Allen, and Thompson, Lee. *Japanese Sports: A History*. Honolulu: University of Hawai'i Press, 2001.

Habu, Junko. *Ancient Jōmon of Japan*. Cambridge: Cambridge University Press, 2004.

Habu Nagaho and Kawai Tsuneo. "Minzokushugi shisō." In Tamura Hideo and Tanaka Hiroshi, eds., *Shakai shisō jiten*. Tokyo: Chūō Daigaku Shuppanbu, 1982.

Hackett, Roger. "Political Modernization and the Meiji Genrō." In Robert Ward, ed., *Political Development in Modern Japan*. Princeton: Princeton University Press, 1968.

Hackett, Roger. *Yamagata Aritomo in the Rise of Modern Japan, 1838–1922*. Cambridge, Mass.: Harvard University Press, 1971.

Hagihara Nobutoshi. *Nihon no meicho*, 35, *Mutsu Munemitsu*. Tokyo: Nihon No Meicho, 1969.

Hagiwara Yoshio. *Yanba damu no arasoi*. Tokyo: Iwanami Shoten, 1996.

Hall, John W. *Government and Local Power in Japan, 500–1700: A Study based on Bizen Province*. Princeton: Princeton University Press, 1966.

Hall, John W. *Japanese History: New Dimensions of Approach and Understanding*, 2nd edn. Washington DC: Service Center for Teachers of History, publication no. 24, 1966.

Hall, John W. "Rule by Status in Tokugawa Japan." *Journal of Japanese Studies* 1:1 (1974): 39–49.

Hall, John W., ed. *The Cambridge History of Japan*, vol. 4, *Early Modern Japan*. Cambridge: Cambridge University Press, 1991.

Hall, John W., and Jansen, Marius, eds. *Studies in the Institutional History of Early Modern Japan*. Princeton: Princeton University Press, 1968.

Hall, John W., and Mass, Jeffrey, eds. *Medieval Japan: Essays in Institutional History*. New Haven: Yale University Press, 1974.

Hall, John W., and Toyoda Takeshi, eds. *Japan in the Muromachi Age*. Berkeley: University of California Press, 1977.

Halliday, Jon. *A Political History of Japanese Capitalism*. New York: Monthly Review, 1975.

Hamashita Takeshi and Kawakatsu Heita, eds. *Ajia kōekiken to Nihon kōgyōka, 1500–1900*. Tokyo: Riburo Pōto, 1991.

Hanasaki Kōhei. "Decolonialization and Assumption of War Responsibility." *Inter-Asia Cultural Studies* 1:1 (2000): 71–84.

Hanazaki Kōhei. "Ainu Moshir and Yaponesia: Ainu and Okinawan Identities in Contemporary Japan." In Donald Denoon, Mark Hudson, Gavan McCormack, and Tessa Morris-Suzuki, eds., *Multicultural Japan: Palaeolithic to Postmodern*. Cambridge: Cambridge University Press, 1996.

Hane, Mikiso. *Peasants, Rebels, and Outcastes: The Underside of Modern Japan*. New York: Pantheon, 1982.

Hane, Mikiso. *Modern Japan: A Historical Survey*. Boulder, Colo.: Westview Press, 1986.

Hane, Mikiso. *Reflections on the Way to the Gallows: Voices of Japanese Rebel Women*. Berkeley: University of California Press, 1988.

Hane, Mikiso. *Peasants, Rebels, Women, and Outcastes: The Underside of Modern Japan*, 2nd edn. Lanham, Md.: Rowman and Littlefield, 2003.

Hanes, Jeffrey. *The City as Subject: Seki Hajime and the Reinvention of Modern Osaka*. Berkeley: University of California Press, 2002.

Hanihara, K. "Dual Structure Model for the Population History of the Japanese." *Japan Review* 2 (1991): 1–33.

Hanley, Susan B. *Everyday Things in Premodern Japan: The Hidden Legacy of Material Culture*. Berkeley: University of California Press, 1997.

Hanley, Susan B., and Yamamura, Kozo. *Economic and Demographic Change in Preindustrial Japan, 1600–1868*. Princeton: Princeton University Press, 1977.

Hara Takeshi. "Nichi-Rō sensō no keikyō." *Gunji shigaku* 36:3/4 (2001).

Harada Katsumasa. "Nisshin sensō no keika to kokunai no ugoki." In Fujiwara Akira, Imai Seiichi, and Ōe Shinobu, eds., *Kindai Nihonshi no kiso chishiki*. Tokyo: Yūhikaku, 1979.

Hardacre, Helen, ed. *New Directions in the Study of Meiji Japan*. Leiden: Brill, 1997.

Hardacre, Helen, ed. *The Postwar Development of Japanese Studies in the United States*. Leiden: Brill, 1998.

Hareven, Tamara. *The Silk Weavers of Kyoto: Family and Work in a Changing Traditional Industry*. Berkeley: University of California Press, 2002.

Harootunian, H. D. "Introduction: A Sense of an Ending and the Problem of Taishō." In H. D. Harootunian and Bernard Silberman, eds., *Japan in Crisis: Essays on Taishō Democracy*. Princeton: Princeton University Press, 1974.

Harootunian, H. D. "Figuring the Folk: History, Poetics, and Representation." In Stephen Vlastos, ed., *Mirror of Modernity: Invented Traditions of Modern Japan*. Berkeley: University of California Press, 1998.

Harootunian, H. D. *Overcome by Modernity: History, Culture, and Community in Interwar Japan*. Princeton: Princeton University Press, 2000.

Harootunian, H. D. *The Empire's New Clothes: Paradigm Lost, and Regained*. Chicago: Prickly Paradigm Press, 2004.

Harris, Sheldon. *Factories of Death: Japanese Biological Warfare, 1932–1945 and the American Cover-Up*, rev. edn. New York: Routledge, 2002.

Harunari Hideji and Imamura Mineo, eds. *Yayoi jidai no jitsunendai: tanso 14 nendai o megutte*. Tokyo: Gakuseisha, 2004.

Hasegawa, Tsuyoshi. *Racing the Enemy: Stalin, Truman, and the Surrender of Japan* Cambridge, Mass.: Harvard University Press, 2005.

Hasegawa Yūichi, ed. *Taishōki Nihon no Amerika ninshiki*. Tokyo: Keiō Gijuku Daigaku Shuppankai, 2001.

Hashikawa Bunzō. *Nihon rōmanha hihan josetsu*. Tokyo: Miraisha, 1965.

Hashimoto Kenji. *Class Structure in Contemporary Japan*. Melbourne: Trans Pacific Press, 2003.

Hashimoto Mitsuru. "*Chihō*: Yanagita Kunio's 'Japan'." In Stephen Vlastos, ed., *Mirror of Modernity: Invented Traditions of Modern Japan*. Berkeley: University of California Press, 1998.

Hastings, Sally Ann. "The Empress' New Clothes and Japanese Women, 1868–1912." *Historian* 55:4 (Summer 1993): 677–92.

Hastings, Sally A. *Neighborhood and Nation in Tokyo, 1905–1937*. Pittsburgh: University of Pittsburgh Press, 1995.

Hastings, Sally Ann. "Women Legislators in the Postwar Diet." In Anne Imamura, ed., *Reimaging Japanese Women*. Berkeley: University of California Press, 1996.

Hastings, Sally Ann. "A Dinner Party Is Not a Revolution: Space, Gender, and Hierarchy in Meiji Japan" *U.S.–Japan Women's Journal*, English Supplement 18 (2000): 107–32.

Hastings, Sally Ann. "Hatoyama Haruko: Ambitious Woman." In Anne Walthall, ed., *The Human Tradition in Modern Japan*. Wilmington, Del.: Scholarly Resources, 2002.

Hatta, Y., et al. "HLA Genes and Haplotypes Suggest Recent Gene Flow to the Okinawa Islands." *Human Biology* 71 (1999): 353–65.

Hattori Ryūji. *Higashi Ajia kokusai kankyō no hendō to Nihon gaikō 1918–1931*. Tokyo: Yūhikaku, 2001.

Hauser, William. *Economic Institutional Change in Tokugawa Japan: Ōsaka and the Kinai Cotton Trade*. Cambridge: Cambridge University Press, 1974.

Hauser, William, and Mass, Jeffrey, eds. *The Bakufu in Japanese History*. Stanford: Stanford University Press, 1985.

Havens, Thomas. *Farm and Nation in Modern Japan: Agrarian Nationalism, 1870–1940*. Princeton: Princeton University Press, 1974.

Hayami Akira. *The Historical Demography of Pre-Modern Japan*. Tokyo: University of Tokyo Press, 1999.

Hayashi Reiko. "Machiya josei no sonzai keitai." In Joseishi Sōgō Kenkyūkai, ed., *Nihon joseishi*, 3. Tokyo: Tokyo Daigaku Shuppankai, 1982.

Hayashi Yukiko. "Hōteki hōmen kara mita Edo jidai no yome to shūto shūtome: bukkiryō to jokunsho o megutte." In Tanaka Masako, Ōguchi Yūjirō, and Okuyama Kyōko, eds., *Engumi to josei: ie to ie no hazamade*. Tokyo: Waseda Daigaku Shuppanbu, 1994.

Hazard, Benjamin. "Japanese Marauding in Medieval Korea: The Wakō Impact on Late Koryo." Ph.D. dissertation, University of California, Berkeley, 1967.

Heginbotham, Eric, and Samuels, Richard. "Japan's Dual Hedge." *Foreign Affairs* 81:5 (2002): 110–21.

Hein, Laura. "Defining Growth: Debates on Economic Strategies." In Andrew Gordon, ed., *Postwar Japan as History*. Berkeley: University of California Press, 1993.

Hein, Laura. *Reasonable Men, Power Words: Political Culture and Expertise in Twentieth-Century Japan*. Berkeley: University of California Press, 2004.

Hein, Laura, and Selden, Mark, eds. *Living with the Bomb: American and Japanese Cultural Conflicts in the Nuclear Age*. Armonk, NY: M. E. Sharpe, 1997.

Hein, Laura, and Selden, Mark, eds. *Censoring History: Citizenship and Memory in Japan, Germany, and the United States*. Armonk, NY: M. E. Sharpe, 2000.

Heine, Steven, and Wright, Dale, eds. *The Kōan: Texts and Contexts in Zen Buddhism*. New York: Oxford University Press, 2000.

Heisig, James, and Maraldo, John. *Rude Awakenings: Zen, the Kyoto School, and the Question of Nationalism*. Honolulu: University of Hawai'i Press, 1994.

Henderson, Dan. *Conciliation in Japanese Law: Tokugawa and Modern*, vol. 1. Seattle: University of Washington Press, 1965.

Hendry, Joy. "The Role of the Professional Housewife." In Janet Hunter, ed., *Japanese Women Working*. London: Routledge, 1993.

Henning, Joseph. *Outposts of Civilization: Race, Religion, and the Formative Years of American–Japanese Relations*. New York: New York University Press, 2000.

Hesselink, Reiner. *Prisoners from Nambu: Reality and Make-Believe in Seventeenth-Century Japanese Diplomacy*. Honolulu: University of Hawai'i Press, 2001.

Hibbett, Howard. *The Floating World in Japanese Fiction*. Rutland, Vt.: C. E. Tuttle, 1959.

Hickman, Money, et al. *Japan's Golden Age: Momoyama*. New Haven: Yale University Press, 1996.

Hicks, George. *The Comfort Women: Sex Slaves of the Japanese Imperial Forces*. London: Souvenir Press, 1995.

Hicks, George. *The Comfort Women: Japan's Brutal Regime of Enforced Prostitution in the Second World War*. New York: Norton, 1997.

Higashi Ajia Bunshitetsu Nettowaku, ed. *Kobayashi Yoshinori "Taiwanron" o koete*. Tokyo: Sakuhinsha, 2001.

High, Peter. *The Imperial Screen: Japanese Film Culture in the Fifteen Years' War, 1931–1945*. Madison: University of Wisconsin Press, 2003.

Hirama Yōichi. *Daiichiji sekai taisen to Nihon kaigun: gaikō to gunji to no rensetsu*. Tokyo: Keiō Gijuku Daigaku Shuppankai, 1998.

Hirano, Kyoko. *Mr. Smith Goes to Tokyo: Japanese Cinema under the American Occupation, 1945–1952*. Washington DC: Smithsonian Institution Press, 1992.

Hirobe, Izumi. *Japanese Pride, American Prejudice: Modifying the Exclusion Clause of the 1924 Immigration Act*. Stanford, Calif.: Stanford University Press, 2001.

Hiyama Yukio, ed. *Kindai Nihon no keisei to Nisshin sensō: sensō no shakaishi*. Tokyo: Yūzankaku Shuppan, 2001.

Hōjō Gen'an. "Hōjō Gen'an oboegaki." In Setagaya-ku, comp., *Setagaya-ku shiryō*, 2. Tokyo: Tokyo-to Setagaya-ku, 1959.

Honda Shigeru. "Yūki nōgyō to sanshō teiki." In Takayama Toshihiro, ed., *Toshi to nōson o musubu*. Tokyo: Fumin Books, 1991.

Honda, Yuki. "The Formation and Transformation of the Japanese System of Transition from School to Work." *Social Science Japan Journal* 7:1 (Apr. 2004): 103–15.

Hook, Glenn D. *Militarization and Demilitarization in Contemporary Japan*. London: Routledge, 1996.

Hook, Glenn D., and McCormack, Gavan. *Japan's Contested Constitution: Documents and Analysis*. London: Routledge, 2001.

Hook, Glenn D., Gilson, Julie, Hughes, Christopher, and Dobson, Hugo. *Japan's International Relations: Politics, Economics and Security*. London: Routledge, 2001.

Hook, Glenn D., Gilson, Julie, Hughes, Christopher, and Dobson, Hugo. "Japan and the East Asian Financial Crisis: Patterns, Motivations, and Instrumentalisation of Japanese Regional Economic Diplomacy." *European Journal of East Asian Studies* 1:2 (2002): 177–98.

Hopper, Helen. *A New Woman of Japan: A Political Biography of Kato Shidzue*. Boulder, Colo.: Westview Press, 1996.

Hoston, Germaine. *Marxism and the Crisis of Development in Prewar Japan*. Princeton: Princeton University Press, 1986.

Hotta-Lister, Ayako. *Japan-British Exhibition of 1910: Gateway to the Island Empire of the East*. Richmond, UK: Japan Library, 1999.

Howell, David. "Hard Times in the Kantō: Economic Change and Village Life in Late Tokugawa Japan." *Modern Asian Studies* 23:2 (1989): 349–71.

Howell, David L. *Capitalism from Within: Economy, Society, and the State in a Japanese Fishery*. Berkeley: University of California Press, 1995.

Howell, David. "Visions of the Future in Meiji Japan." In Merle Goldman and Andrew Gordon, eds., *Historical Perspectives on Contemporary East Asia*. Cambridge, Mass.: Harvard University Press, 2000.

Howell, David L. *Geographies of Identity in Nineteenth-Century Japan*. Berkeley: University of California Press, 2005.

Howland, Douglas R. *Translating the West: Language and Political Reason in Nineteenth-Century Japan*. Honolulu: University of Hawai'i Press, 2002.

Hudson, Mark J. "Japanese and Austronesian: An Archeological Perspective on the Proposed Linguistic Links." In K. Omoto, ed., *Interdisciplinary Perspectives on the Origins of the Japanese*. Kyoto: International Research Center for Japanese Studies, 1999.

Hudson, Mark J. *Ruins of Identity: Ethnogenesis in the Japanese Islands*. Honolulu: University of Hawai'i Press, 1999.

Hudson, Mark J. "For the People, By the People: Postwar Japanese Archaeology and the Early Paleolithic Hoax." *Anthropological Science* 113:2 (Aug. 2005): 131–9.

Huffman, James. *Creating a Public: People and Press in Meiji Japan*. Honolulu: University of Hawai'i Press, 1997.

Huffman, James L. "Edward H. House: Questions of Meaning and Influence." *Japan Forum* 13:1 (2001): 15–25.

Huffman, James L. *A Yankee in Meiji Japan: The Crusading Journalist Edward H. House*. Lanham, Md.: Rowman and Littlefield, 2003.

Hughes, Christopher. *Japan's Security Agenda: Military, Economic, and Environmental Dimensions*. Boulder, Colo.: Lynne Rienner, 2004.

Hume, Nancy, ed. *Japanese Aesthetics and Culture: A Reader*. Albany: State University of New York Press, 1995.

Humphreys, Leonard. *The Way of the Heavenly Sword: The Japanese Army in the 1920s*. Stanford, Calif.: Stanford University Press, 1995.

Hunter, Janet. "Textile Factories, Tuberculosis, and the Quality of Life in Industrializing Japan." In Janet Hunter, ed., *Japanese Women Working*. London: Routledge, 1993.

Hunter, Janet, ed. *Japanese Women Working*. London: Routledge, 1993.

Hunter, Janet, and Sugiyama Shinya, eds. *The History of Anglo-Japanese Relations, 1600–2000*, vol. 4, *The Economic-Business Dimension*. New York: St. Martin's Press, 2000.

Hur, Nam-lin. *Prayer and Play in Late Tokugawa Japan: Asakusa Sensōji and Edo Society*. Cambridge, Mass.: Harvard University Asia Center, 2000.

Hurst, G. Cameron, III. *Insei: Abdicated Sovereigns in the Politics of Late Heian Japan, 1086–1185*. New York: Columbia University Press, 1976.

Hurst, G. Cameron, III. "Michinaga's Maladies: A Medical Report on Fujiwara no Michinaga." *Monumenta Nipponica* 34 (1979): 101–12.

Ienaga Saburo. *The Pacific War: World War II and the Japanese, 1931–1945*, trans. Frank Baldwin. New York: Pantheon, 1978.

Igarashi Akio. "Zenkyōtō sedai." In Uchiyama Hideo and Kurihara Akira, eds., *Shōwa dōjidai o ikiru: sorezore no sengo*. Tokyo: Yūhikaku, 1986.

Igarashi Takayoshi. " 'Mayaku no ronri' ga makaritōru kensetsugyō kuwaseru dake no kōkyō jigyō ga kuni o horobosu." *Ekonomisuto* (Jan. 18, 2000): 63.

Igarashi Takeshi. "Peace-Making and Party Politics: The Formation of the Domestic Foreign-Policy System in Postwar Japan." *Journal of Japanese Studies* 11:2 (Summer 1985): 323–56.

Igarashi, Yoshikuni. *Bodies of Memory: Narratives of War in Postwar Japanese Culture, 1945–1970*. Princeton: Princeton University Press, 2000.

Iguchi, Haruo. *Unfinished Business: Ayukawa Yoshisuke and U.S.–Japan Relations, 1937–1953*. Cambridge, Mass.: Harvard University Press, 2003.

Ihara Saikaku. *Some Final Words of Advice*, trans. Peter Nosco. Rutland, Vt.: C. E. Tuttle, 1980.

Ikawa-Smith, Fumiko. "Late Pleistocene and Early Holocene Technologies." In R. J. Pearson, G. L. Barnes, and K. L. Hutterer, eds., *Windows on the Japanese Past: Studies in Archaeology and Prehistory*. Ann Arbor: Center for Japanese Studies, University of Michigan, 1986.

Ikawa-Smith, Fumiko, ed. *Early Paleolithic in South and East Asia*. The Hague: Mouton, 1978.

Ike, Nobutaka. *A Theory of Japanese Democracy*. Boulder, Colo.: Westview Press, 1980.

Ikegami, Eiko. *The Taming of the Samurai: Honorific Individualism and the Making of Modern Japan*. Cambridge, Mass.: Harvard University Press, 1995.

Imamura, Anne. *Urban Japanese Housewives: At Home and in the Community*. Honolulu: University of Hawai'i Press, 1987.

Imamura, Keiji. *Prehistoric Japan: New Perspectives on Insular East Asia*. Honolulu: University of Hawai'i Press, 1996.

Inada, Takashi. "Subsistence and the Beginnings of Settled Life in Japan." In *Cultural Diversity and the Archaeology of the 21st Century*, ed. Society of Archaeological Studies. Okayama: Kōkogaku Kenkyūkai, 2004.

Inagaki, Hisao, and Stewart, Harold, trans. *The Three Pure Land Sutras*. Berkeley, Calif.: Numata Center for Buddhist Translation and Research, 1995.

Industrial Relations, special issue: "Japanese Industrial Relations in the New Millennium" (Oct. 2002).

Ingold, Tim. "On the Social Relations of the Hunter-Gatherer Band." In R. B. Lee and R. Daly, eds., *The Cambridge Encyclopedia of Hunters and Gatherers*. Cambridge: Cambridge University Press, 1999.

Innes, Robert Leroy. "The Door Ajar: Japan's Foreign Trade in the Seventeenth Century." Ph.D. dissertation, University of Michigan, 1980.

Inoguchi, Takashi. "Four Japanese Scenarios for the Future." In Kathleen Newland, ed., *The International Relations of Japan*. Basingstoke: Macmillan, 1990.

Inoguchi, Takashi. "Political Science in Three Democracies, Disaffected (Japan), Third-Wave (Korea) and Fledgling (China)." Paper presented at the RC33 Panel Session of the World Congress of the International Political Science Association, Durban, South Africa, June 28–July 4, 2003.

Inoue Mitsusada, Seki Akira, Tsuchida Naoshige, and Aoki Kazuo, eds. *Nihon shisō taikei*, 3, *Ritsuryō*. Tokyo: Iwanami Shoten, 1976.

Iokibe Makoto. "Japan's Civil Society: An Historical Overview." In Yamamoto Tadashi, ed., *Deciding the Public Good: Governance and Civil Society in Japan*. Tokyo: Japan Center for International Exchange, 1999.

Iriye, Akira. *After Imperialism: The Search for a New Order in the Far East, 1921–1931*. Cambridge, Mass.: Harvard University Press, 1965.

Iriye, Akira. *Nihon no gaikō: Meiji ishin kara gendai made.* Tokyo: Chūō Kōronsha, 1966.

Iriye, Akira. *Across the Pacific: An Inner History of American–East Asian Relations.* New York: Harcourt, Brace, and World, 1967.

Iriye, Akira. "Toward a New Cultural Order: The Hsin-min Hui." In Akira Iriye, ed., *The Chinese and the Japanese: Essays in Political and Cultural Interactions.* Princeton: Princeton University Press, 1980.

Iriye, Akira. *Power and Culture: The Japanese–American War, 1941–1945* Cambridge, Mass.: Harvard University Press, 1981.

Iriye, Akira. "The Internationalization of History." *American Historical Review* 94 (Feb. 1989).

Iriye, Akira. *Japan and the Wider World: From the Mid-Nineteenth Century to the Present.* London: Longman, 1997.

Iriye, Akira, ed. *Mutual Images: Essays in American–Japanese Relations.* Cambridge, Mass.: Harvard University Press, 1975.

Iriye, Akira, ed. *The Chinese and the Japanese: Essays in Political and Cultural Interactions.* Princeton: Princeton University Press, 1980.

Irokawa Daikichi. *The Culture of the Meiji Period,* ed. Marius Jansen. Princeton: Princeton University Press, 1985.

Ishida Hiroshi. "Class Structure and Status Hierarchies in Contemporary Japan." *European Sociological Review* 5:1 (1989): 65–80.

Ishida Hiroshi, Goldthorpe, John, and Erikson, Robert. "Intergenerational Class Mobility in Postwar Japan." *American Journal of Sociology* 96:4 (1991): 954–92.

Ishige Naomichi. *The History and Culture of Japanese Food.* London: Kegan Paul, 2001.

Ishii, Noriko Kawamura. *American Women Missionaries at Kobe College, 1873–1909: New Dimensions in Gender.* London: Routledge, 2004.

Ishii Ryōsuke, ed. *Tokugawa kinreikō,* 5. Tokyo: Kōbunsha, 1959.

Ishii Susumu. "Foreword by the Editor." *Acta Asiatica* 81 (2001): pp. iii–vii.

Ishii Susumu, Ishimoda Shō, Kasamatsu Hiroshi, Katsumata Shizuo, and Satō Shin'ichi, eds. *Chūsei seiji shakai shisō,* 1. Tokyo: Iwanami Shoten, 1976.

Ishikawa Hiroshi. "Meiji ishin to Chōsen, taima kankei." In Meiji Ishin Shigakukai, ed., *Meiji ishin to Ajia.* Tokyo: Yoshikawa Kōbunkan, 2001.

Ishikawa Hiroyoshi. *Yokubō no sengoshi: shakai shinrigaku kara no apurōchi.* Tokyo: Taihei Shuppansha, 1981.

Ishinomori Shotarō. *Japan, Inc.: An Introduction to Japanese Economics,* trans. Betsey Scheiner. Berkeley: University of California Press, 1988.

Ito Takeo. *Life Along the South Manchurian Railway: The Memoirs of Ito Takeo,* trans. Joshua Fogel. Armonk, NY: M. E. Sharpe, 1988.

Itō Yukio. *Rikken kokka to Nichi-Rō sensō: gaikō to naisei, 1898–1905.* Tokyo: Bokutakusha, 2000.

Itō Yukio. *Seitō seiji to tennō.* Tokyo: Kōdansha, 2002.

Itō Yukio and Kawada Minoru, eds. *Nijū seiki Nihon no tennō to kunshusei.* Tokyo: Yoshikawa Kōbunkan, 2004.

Itsuki-Mura Minzoku Chōsadan (Murata Hiroshi), ed. *Itsuki no minzoku.* Itsuki: Itsuki Village Office, 1994.

Ivy, Marilyn. "Formations of Mass Culture." In Andrew Gordon, ed., *Postwar Japan as History.* Berkeley: University of California Press, 1993.

Ivy, Marilyn. *Discourses of the Vanishing: Modernity, Phantasm, Japan.* Chicago: University of Chicago Press, 1995.

Iwabuchi Kōichi. *Recentering Globalization: Popular Culture and Japanese Transnationalism.* Durham, NC: Duke University Press, 2002.

Jackson, Gregory. "Corporate Governance in Germany and Japan." In Kozo Yamamura and Wolfgang Streeck, eds., *The End of Diversity? Prospects for German and Japanese Capitalism.* Ithaca, NY: Cornell University Press, 2003.

Janhunen, Juha. "A Framework for the Study of Japanese Language Origins." In T. Osada and A. Vovin, eds., *Perspectives on the Origins of the Japanese Language*. Kyoto: International Research Center for Japanese Studies, 2003.

Jansen, Marius. *Japan and Its World: Two Centuries of Change*. Princeton: Princeton University Press, 1975.

Jansen, Marius. *China in the Tokugawa World*. Cambridge, Mass.: Harvard University Press, 1992.

Jansen, Marius, ed. *Changing Japanese Attitudes toward Modernization*. Princeton: Princeton University Press, 1965.

Jansen, Marius, ed. *The Cambridge History of Japan*, vol. 5, *The Nineteenth Century*. Cambridge: Cambridge University Press, 1989.

Jansen, Marius, and Rozman, Gilbert, eds. *Japan in Transition: From Tokugawa to Meiji*. Princeton: Princeton University Press, 1986.

Janssens, Rudolph, and Gordon, Andrew. "A Short History of the Joint Committee on Japanese Studies," available online at <http://www.ssrc.org/programs/publications_editors/publications/jcjs.pdf> accessed Mar. 1, 2006.

Japan in Figures 2003. Tokyo: Ministry of Public Management, Home Affairs, Posts and Telecommunications, 2002.

Japan in the World, the World in Japan. Ann Arbor: University of Michigan Center for Japanese Studies, 2001.

Japanese Archaeological Association, ed. *Zen, chūki kyūsekki mondai no kensho*. Tokyo: Nihon Kōkogaku Kyōkai, 2003.

Jenkins, Donald. *The Floating World Revisited*. Portland, Oreg.: Portland Art Museum, 1993.

Johnson, Chalmers. *MITI and the Japanese Miracle: The Growth of Industrial Policy, 1925–1975*. Stanford, Calif.: Stanford University Press, 1982.

Johnson, Chalmers. "Preconception vs. Observation, or the Contributions of Rational Choice Theory and Area Studies to Contemporary Political Science." *PS: Political Science and Politics* 30 (1997): 170–4.

Johnson, Chalmers, ed. *Okinawa: Cold War Island*. Cardiff, Calif.: Japan Policy Research Institute, 1999.

Johnson, Chalmers, and Keehn, E. G. "East Asian Security: The Pentagon's Ossified Strategy." *Foreign Affairs* 74:4 (1995): 103–15.

Ka, Chih-ming. *Japanese Colonialism in Taiwan: Land Tenure, Development, and Dependency, 1895–1945*. Boulder, Colo.: Westview Press, 1995.

Kalland, Arne, and Asquith, Pamela. "Japanese Perceptions of Nature – Ideals and Illusions." In Pamela Asquith and Arne Kalland, eds., *Japanese Images of Nature: Cultural Perspectives*. Richmond, UK: Curzon, 1997.

Kamei Kan'ichirō. *Dai tōa minzoku no michi*. Tokyo: Seiki Shobō, 1941.

Kamiya Matake. "Nuclear Japan: Oxymoron or Coming Soon?" *Washington Quarterly* 26:1 (Winter 2002–3): 63–75.

Kamiyama Kazuo and Iida Yasuo, eds. *Tairitsu to dakyō: 1930 nendai no Nichi-Bei tsūshō kankei*. Tokyo: Daiichi Hōki Shuppan, 1994.

Kamo Takehiko. "The Internationalization of the State: The Case of Japan." In Yoshikazu Sakamoto, ed., *Global Transformation: Challenges to the State System*. Tokyo: United Nations University Press, 1994.

Kane, Robert. "Hammering Down Nails: Politics, Diplomacy, and the Quest for National Unity in Japan and America, 1912–1919." Ph.D. dissertation, University of Pennsylvania, 2002.

Kano Masanao. *Kindai nihon shisō annai*. Tokyo: Iwanami Shoten, 1999.

Kaplan, David E., and Dubro, Alec. *Yakuza: Japan's Criminal Underworld*. Berkeley: University of California Press, 2003.

Karatani Kōjin. *"Senzen" no shikō.* Kōdansha gakujutsu bunko 1477. Tokyo: Kōdansha, 2001.

Kariya Tetsu and Hanasaki Akira. *Oishinbo,* 36, *Nichi-Bei kome sensō.* Tokyo: Shogakkan, 1992.

Karlin, Jason. "The Gender of Nationalism: Competing Masculinities in Meiji Japan." *Journal of Japanese Studies* 28:1 (Winter 2002): 41–77.

Kasahara, Kazuo, ed. *A History of Japanese Religion.* Tokyo: Kosei Publishing, 2001.

Kasahara Tokushi. *Nankin jiken to Nihonjin: sensō no kioku o meguru nashonarizumu to gurōbarizumu.* Tokyo: Kashiwa Shobō, 2002.

Kasza, Gregory. *The State and the Mass Media in Japan, 1918–1945.* Berkeley: University of California Press, 1988.

Kasza, Gregory. *The Conscription Society: Administered Mass Organizations.* New Haven: Yale University Press, 1995.

Kasza, Gregory. "Fascism from Above? Japan's Kakushin Right in Comparative Perspective." In Stein Ugelvik Larsen, ed., *Fascism Outside Europe: The European Impulse against Domestic Conditions in the Diffusion of Global Fascism.* New York: Columbia University Press, 2001.

Kato, Junko. "When the Party Breaks Up: Exit and Voice among Japanese Legislators." *American Political Science Review* 92 (1998): 857–70.

Katō Norihiro. *Haisengoron.* Tokyo: Kōdansha, 1997.

Kato, Shūichi. "Taishō Democracy as the Pre-Stage for Japanese Militarism." In Bernard Silberman and H. D. Harootunian, eds., *Japan in Crisis: Essays on Taishō Democracy.* Princeton: Princeton University Press, 1974.

Katsu Kokichi. *Musui's Story: The Autobiography of a Tokugawa Samurai,* trans. Teruko Craig. Tucson: University of Arizona Press, 1988.

Katz, Richard. *Japan: The System that Soured.* Armonk, NY: M. E. Sharpe, 1998.

Katz, Richard. *Japanese Phoenix: The Long Road to Economic Revival.* Armonk, NY: M. E. Sharpe, 2003.

Katzenstein, Peter. *Cultural Norms and National Security: Police and Military in Postwar Japan.* Ithaca, NY: Cornell University Press, 1996.

Katzenstein, Peter, and Shiraishi, Takashi, eds. *Network Power: Japan and Asia.* Ithaca, N.Y.: Cornell University Press, 1997.

Kawada Minoru. *The Origin of Ethnography in Japan: Yanagita Kunio and His Times,* trans. Toshiko Kishida-Ellis. London: Kegan Paul, 1993.

Kawakatsu Heita. "Toward a Country of Wealth and Virtue." *Japan Echo* 26:2 (Apr. 1999).

Kawamura, Noriko. *Turbulence in the Pacific: Japanese–U.S. Relations during World War I.* Westport, Conn.: Praeger, 2000.

Kawamura Yoshio. "Toshi kakudai to nōgyō no imi." In Takayama Toshihiro, ed., *Toshi to nōson o musubu.* Tokyo: Fumin Books, 1991.

Kawano Shōichi. "Nihon no shinrin ni nani ga okite iru ka." *Sekai* (Nov. 1996): 136–40.

Keally, C. T. "Environment and the Distribution of Sites in the Japanese Palaeolithic: Environmental Zones and Cultural Areas." *Bulletin of the Indo-Pacific Prehistory Association* 10 (1991): 23–39.

Keehn, E. B. Review of *Japan's Political Marketplace,* by J. Mark Ramseyer and Frances M. Rosenbluth. *Monumenta Nipponica* 49 (1994): 249–51.

Keene, Donald. *The Japanese Discovery of Europe, 1720–1830,* rev. edn. Stanford, Calif.: Stanford University Press, 1969.

Keene, Donald. *Dawn to the West: Japanese Literature of the Modern Era,* vol. 1, *Fiction.* New York: Holt, Rinehart and Winston, 1984.

Keene, Donald. "Characteristic Responses to Confucianism in Tokugawa Literature." In Peter Nosco, ed., *Confucianism and Tokugawa Culture.* Princeton: Princeton University Press, 1984.

Keene, Donald. *Emperor of Japan: Meiji and His World, 1852–1912.* New York: Columbia University Press, 2002.

Keirstead, Thomas. *The Geography of Power in Medieval Japan*. Princeton: Princeton University Press, 1992.

Kelly, William. *Water Control in Tokugawa Japan: Irrigation Organization in a Japanese River Basin, 1600–1870*. Ithaca, N. Y.: Cornell China-Japan Program, 1982.

Kelly, William. *Deference and Defiance in Nineteenth-Century Japan*. Princeton: Princeton University Press, 1985.

Kelly, William. "Finding a Place in Metropolitan Japan: Ideologies, Institutions, and Everyday Life." In Andrew Gordon, ed., *Postwar Japan as History*. Berkeley: University of California Press, 1993.

Kensetsushō, Kasenkyoku Chisuika. *Tashizengata kawazukuri*. Tokyo: Kensetsushō, n.d. (?1995).

Kensetsushō, Kasenkyoku Chisuika. *Kensetsu hakusho*. Tokyo: Kensetsushō, 1998.

Kerr, Alex. *Dogs and Demons: Tales from the Dark Side of Modern Japan*. New York: Hill and Wang, 2001.

Kersten, Rikki. "Neo-Nationalism and the 'Liberal School of History'." *Japan Forum* 11:2 (1999): 191–203.

Ketelaar, James E. *Of Heretics and Martyrs in Meiji Japan: Buddhism and Its Persecution*. Princeton: Princeton University Press, 1990.

Kilby, E. Stuart. *Russian Studies of Japan*. London: Macmillan, 1981.

Kiley, Cornelius. "Estate and Property in Late Heian Japan." In John W. Hall and Jeffrey Mass, eds., *Medieval Japan: Essays in Institutional History*. New Haven: Yale University Press, 1974.

King, Frank. *The Development of Japanese Studies in Southeast Asia*. Hong Kong: Centre of Asian Studies, University of Hong Kong, 1969.

King, Franklin. *Farmers of Forty Centuries; or, Permanent Agriculture in China, Korea, and Japan*, ed. J. P. Bruce. Erasmus, Penn.: Organic Gardening Press, 1927.

Kinmonth, Earl. *The Self-Made Man in Meiji Japanese Thought: From Samurai to Salary Man*. Berkeley: University of California Press, 1981.

Kinmonth, Earl. "The Mouse that Roared: Saitō Takao, Conservative Critic of Japan's 'Holy War' in China." *Journal of Japanese Studies* 25:2 (Summer 1999): 331–60.

Kishi Shōzō, comp. *Zenyaku Azuma kagami*, ed. Nagahara Keiji, 5 vols. Tokyo: Shinjinbutsu Ōraisha, 1977.

Kishimoto Shigenobu. "Can the New Middle Class Theory be Sustained?" *Japan Interpreter* 12:1 (1978): 5–8.

Kita, Sandy, Marceau, Lawrence E., Blood, Katherine, and Farquhar, James Douglas. *The Floating World of Ukiyo-e: Shadows, Dreams, and Substance*. New York: Harry N. Abrams, 2001.

Kitaguchi Suehiro. *An Introduction to the Buraku Issue*, trans. Alastair McLauchlan. Richmond, UK: Japan Library, 1999.

Kitaoka Shin'ichi. *Nihon rikugun to tairiku seisaku, 1906–1918-nen*. Tokyo: Tokyo Daigaku Shuppankai, 1978.

Kitaoka Shin'ichi. "Shoki Taiyō ni miru Amerika zō." In Suzuki Sadao, ed., *Zasshi Taiyō to kokumin bunka no keisei*. Tokyo: Shibunkaku, 2001.

Kobayashi Hideo. *Mantetsu: "Chi no shūdan" no tanjō to shi*. Tokyo: Yoshikawa Kōbunkan, 1996.

Kobayashi Michihiko. *Nihon no tairiku seisaku, 1895–1914*. Tokyo: Nansōsha, 1996.

Kobayashi Yoshinori. *Shin gomanizumu sengen special Taiwanron*. Tokyo: Shogakkan, 2000.

Kohno Masaru. *Japan's Postwar Party Politics*. Princeton: Princeton University Press, 1997.

Koikari, Mire. *Pedagogy of Democracy: Feminism and the Cold War in the U.S. Occupation of Japan*. Durham, NC: Duke University Press, forthcoming.

Komiya Kazuo. *Jōyaku kaisei to kokunai seiji*. Tokyo: Yoshikawa Kōbunkan, 2001.

Kondo, Dorinne. *Crafting Selves: Power, Gender and Discourses of Identity in a Japanese Workplace*. Chicago: University of Chicago Press, 1990.

Kondō Yoshirō. *Zenpōkōenfun no jidai*. Tokyo: Iwanami, 1983.

Kornhauser, David. "Coefficients of Urban Intensification for Japanese Cities." In Frank J. Costa et al., eds., *Urbanization in Asia: Spatial Dimensions of Policy Issues*. Honolulu: University of Hawai'i Press, 1989.

Kornicki, Peter. *The Book in Japan: A Cultural History from the Beginnings to the Nineteenth Century*. Leiden: Brill, 1998.

Kōsaka Kenji. *Social Stratification in Contemporary Japan*. London: Kegan Paul, 1994.

Koschmann, J. Victor. *Revolution and Subjectivity in Postwar Japan*. Chicago: University of Chicago Press, 1996.

Koschmann, J. Victor. "Asianism's Ambivalent Legacy." In Peter Katzenstein and Takashi Shiraishi, eds., *Network Power: Japan and Asia*. Ithaca, NY: Cornell University Press, 1997.

Koshiro, Yukiko. *Trans-Pacific Racisms and the U.S. Occupation of Japan*. New York: Columbia University Press, 1999.

Kosugi, Y. "Jōmon bunka ni sensō wa sonzai shita no ka?" In *Bunka no tayōsei to hikaku kōkogaku*, ed. Society of Archaeological Studies. Okayama: Kōkogaku Kenkyūkai, 2004.

Koyama Shūzō and Thomas, D. H., eds. *Affluent Foragers: Pacific Coasts East and West*. Osaka: National Museum of Ethnology, 1981.

Kranzler, David. *Japanese, Nazis, and Jews: The Jewish Refugee Community in Shanghai*. Hoboken, NJ: KTAV Publishing House, 1976.

Krauss, Ellis. "Japan, the U.S., and the Emergence of Multilateralism in Asia." *Pacific Review* 13:3 (2000): 473–94.

Krauss, Ellis, Rohlen, Thomas, and Steinhoff, Patricia, eds. *Conflict in Japan*. Honolulu: University of Hawai'i Press, 1984.

Krug, Hans-Joachim, et al. *Reluctant Allies: German–Japanese Naval Relations in World War II*. Annapolis, Md.: Naval Institute Press, 2001.

Kubota Yoshitake. "Tōa Dōbunkai no 'shimei' to 'manazashi'." *Rekishi Hyōron* 614 (2001).

Kuji Tsutomu. *Anata wa Yanba damu no mizu o nomemasu ka*. Tokyo: Marujusha, 2001.

Kumagai Hiroshi. "Concept of 'Sustainable and Regional Agriculture' in Japan." In Hiroshi Sasaki et al., eds., *Geographical Perspectives on Sustainable Rural Systems: Proceedings of the Tsukuba International Conference on the Sustainability of Rural Systems*. Tokyo: Kaisei Publications, 1996.

Kumazawa Makoto. *Portraits of the Japanese Workplace: Labor Movements, Workers, and Managers*, ed. Andrew Gordon, trans. Andrew Gordon and Mikiso Hane. Boulder, Colo.: Westview Press, 1996.

Kume Kunitake. *The Iwakura Embassy, 1871–73: A True Account of the Ambassador Extraordinary & Plenipotentiary's Journeys of Observation through the United States and Europe*, ed. Graham Healey and Chushichi Tsuzuki, 5 vols. Chiba: Japan Documents, 2002.

Kuriki Fumio. "Kyōyasai no rekishi to shokuseikatsu." In Kyōyasai Kenkyūkai, ed., *Kyōyasai no seisan, ryūtsū, kyōhi to chiiki seikatsu seika ni kan suru kenkyū*. Kyoto: Kyoto Sangyō Daigaku Kokudo Riyō Kaihatsu Kenkyūjo, 1998.

Kurosawa Fumitaka. *Taisenkanki no Nihon rikugun*. Tokyo: Misuzu Shobō, 2000.

Kuwabara Megumi. "Kinseiteki kyōyō bunka to josei." In Joseishi Sōgō Kenkyūkai, ed., *Nihon josei seikatsushi*, 3. Tokyo: Tokyo Daigaku Shuppankai, 1990.

Kuwahara Minoru. "Kawa kaihatsu no shisō." *Oruta* 3 (Winter 1992): 33–45.

LaFeber, Walter. *The Clash: A History of U.S.–Japan Relations*. New York: Norton, 1997.

LaFleur, William. "Hungry Ghosts and Hungry People: Somaticity and Rationality in Medieval Japan." In Michel Feher, ed., *Fragments for a History of the Human Body*, pt. 1. New York: Zone Publications, 1989, pp. 271–303.

Laitin, David. "Comparative Politics: The State of the Subdiscipline." In Ira Katznelson and Helen Milner, eds., *Political Science: The State of the Discipline*. New York: Norton, 2002.

Lam, Alice. *Women and Japanese Management: Discrimination and Reform*. London: Routledge, 1992.

Lamers, Jeroen. *Japonius Tyrannus: The Japanese Warlord Oda Nobunaga Reconsidered*. Leiden: Hotei Publishing, 2000.

Large, Stephen. *Organized Workers and Socialist Politics in Interwar Japan*. Cambridge: Cambridge University Press, 1981.

Large, Stephen. *Emperor Hirohito and Shōwa Japan: A Political Biography*. London: Routledge, 1992.

Latz, Gil. *Agricultural Development in Japan: The Land Improvement District in Concept and Practice*. Chicago: University of Chicago Geography Research Paper no. 225, 1989.

Latz, Gil. "The Persistence of Agriculture in Urban Japan: An Analysis of the Tokyo Metropolitan Area." In Norton Ginsburg et al., eds., *The Extended Metropolis: Settlement Transition in Asia*. Honolulu: University of Hawai'i Press, 1991.

Laver, Michael. "A Strange Isolation: The Japanese, the Dutch, and the Asian Economy in the Seventeenth Century." Ph.D. dissertation, University of Pennsylvania, 2005.

Lears, T. J. Jackson. "Making Fun of Popular Culture." *American Historical Review* (Dec. 1992): 1417–30.

LeBlanc, Robin. *Bicycle Citizens: The Political World of the Japanese Housewife*. Berkeley: University of California Press, 1999.

Lebra, Takie. *Above the Clouds: Status Culture of the Modern Japanese Nobility*. Berkeley: University of California Press, 1993.

Lee, Joohee. "Taking Gender Seriously: Feminization of Nonstandard Work in Korea and Japan." *Asian Journal of Women's Studies* 10:1 (2004): 25–48.

Lee, R. B., and DeVore, I. "Problems in the Study of Hunters and Gatherers." In R. B. Lee and I. DeVore, eds., *Man the Hunter*. Chicago: Aldine, 1968.

Leiter, Samuel, ed. *A Kabuki Reader*. Armonk, NY: M. E. Sharpe, 2002.

Leupp, Gary. *Servants, Shophands, and Laborers in the Cities of Tokugawa Japan*. Princeton: Princeton University Press, 1992.

Levine, Hillel. *In Search of Sugihara: The Elusive Japanese Diplomat who Risked His Life to Rescue 10,000 Jews from the Holocaust*. New York: Free Press, 1996.

Levine, Lawrence. "The Folklore of Industrial Society: Popular Culture and Its Audiences." *American Historical Review* (Dec. 1992): 1369–99.

Lewis, Michael. *Rioters and Citizens: Mass Protest in Imperial Japan*. Berkeley: University of California Press, 1990.

Lewis, Michael. *Becoming Apart: National Power and Local Politics in Toyama, 1868–1945*. Cambridge, Mass.: Harvard University Press, 2000.

Lieven, D. C. B. *Empire: The Russian Empire and Its Rivals*. London: John Murray, 2000.

Lifton, Robert J. *Hiroshima in America: 50 Years of Denial*. New York: Putnam's Sons, 1995.

Lincicome, Mark. *Principle, Praxis, and the Politics of Educational Reform in Meiji Japan*. Honolulu: University of Hawai'i Press, 1995.

Lincoln, Edward. *Arthritic Japan: The Slow Pace of Economic Reform*. Washington DC: Brookings Institute Press, 2001.

Lockwood, W. W. *The Economic Development of Japan: Growth and Structural Change, 1868–1938*. Princeton: Princeton University Press, 1954; expanded edn., 1968.

Lockwood, William, ed. *The State and Economic Enterprise in Japan*. Princeton: Princeton University Press, 1965.

Lone, Stewart. *Japan's First Modern War: Army and Society in the Conflict with China, 1894–95*. New York: St. Martin's Press, 1994.

Lone, Stewart. *Army, Empire and Politics in Meiji Japan: The Three Careers of General Katsura Tarō*. New York: St. Martin's Press, 2000.

Lu, David J. *Japan: A Documentary History*. Armonk, NY: M. E. Sharpe, 1997.

Lu, David J. *Agony of Choice: Matsuoka Yōsuke and the Rise and Fall of the Japanese Empire, 1880–1946*. Lanham, Md.: Lexington Books, 2002.

Machida, H. "The Impact of the Kikai Eruptions on Prehistoric Japan." In M. J. Hudson, ed., *Interdisciplinary Study on the Origins of Japanese Peoples and Cultures*. Kyoto: International Research Center for Japanese Studies, 2000.

Mackie, Vera. *Creating Socialist Women in Japan: Gender, Labour and Activism, 1900–1937*. Cambridge: Cambridge University Press, 1997.

Mackie, Vera. *Feminism in Modern Japan: Citizenship, Embodiment, and Sexuality*. Cambridge: Cambridge University Press, 2003.

Makabe Yoshiko. "Kofun to josei." *Rekishi hyōron* 493 (1991): 9–16.

Marcus, Joyce. "The Peaks and Valleys of Ancient States: An Extension of the Dynamic Model." In G. M. Feinman and J. Marcus, eds., *Archaic States*. Santa Fe, NM: School of American Research Press, 1998.

Markus, Andrew. *The Willow in Autumn: Ryūtei Tanehiko, 1783–1842*. Cambridge, Mass.: Council on East Asian Studies, Harvard University, 1992.

Marshall, Jonathan. *To Have and Have Not: Southeast Asian Raw Materials and the Origins of the Pacific War*. Berkeley: University of California Press, 1995.

Martin, Bernd. *Japan and Germany in the Modern World*. Providence, RI: Berghahn Books, 1995.

Maruyama Masao. "The Ideology and Dynamics of Japanese Fascism." In Maruyama Masao, *Thought and Behavior in Modern Japanese Politics*, ed. Ivan Morris. Oxford: Oxford University Press, 1963.

Maruyama Masao. *Thought and Behavior in Modern Japanese Politics*, ed. Ivan Morris. Oxford: Oxford University Press, 1963.

Maruyama Masao. *Studies in the Intellectual History of Tokugawa Japan*, trans. Mikiso Hane. Tokyo: University of Tokyo Press, 1974.

Masayoshi Koshiro. "The Use of Organic and Chemical Fertilizers in Japan." *Food and Fertilizer Technology Extension Bulletin* 312 (1990): 4–15.

Mass, Jeffrey P. *Warrior Government in Early Medieval Japan: A Study of the Kamakura Bakufu, Shugo, and Jitō*. New Haven: Yale University Press, 1974.

Mass, Jeffrey P. *The Development of Kamakura Rule Rule, 1180–1250*. Stanford, Calif.: Stanford University Press, 1979.

Mass, Jeffrey P. *Lordship and Inheritance in Early Medieval Japan*. Stanford, Calif.: Stanford University Press, 1989.

Mass, Jeffrey P. *Yoritomo and the Founding of the First Bakufu*. Stanford, Calif.: Stanford University Press, 1999.

Mass, Jeffrey P., ed. *Court and Bakufu in Japan: Essays in Kamakura History*. New Haven: Yale University Press, 1982.

Mass, Jeffrey P., ed. *The Origins of Japan's Medieval World*. Stanford, Calif.: Stanford University Press, 1997.

Masuda, T. "The Emperor's Right of Supreme Command as Exercised up to 1930: A Study based especially on the Takarabe and Kuratomi Diaries." *Acta Asiatica* 59 (1990): 77–100.

Masumi Junnosuke. *Contemporary Politics in Japan*. Berkeley: University of California Press, 1985.

Masumi Junnosuke. *Postwar Politics in Japan, 1945–1955*, trans. Lonny Carlile. Berkeley: Center for Japanese Studies, University of California, 1985.

Mathias, Regine. "Female Labour in the Japanese Coal-Mining Industry." In Janet Hunter, ed., *Japanese Women Working*. London: Routledge, 1993.

Matsumoto, Shigeru. *Motoori Norinaga, 1730–1801.* Cambridge, Mass.: Harvard University Press, 1970.

Matsusaka, Y. Tak. *The Making of Japanese Manchuria, 1904–1932.* Cambridge, Mass.: Harvard University Asia Center, 2001.

Matsusaka, Y. Tak. "Human Bullets, General Nogi, and the Myth of Port Arthur." In John Steinberg and David Schimmelpenninck, eds., *The Russo-Japanese War Reexamined.* Leiden: Brill, 2005.

Matsushita Keiichi. "Citizen Participation in Historical Perspective." In J. Victor Koschmann, ed., *Authority and the Individual in Japan: Citizen Protest in Historical Perspective.* Tokyo: University of Tokyo Press, 1978.

Matsu'ura, S. "A Chronological Review of Pleistocene Human Remains from the Japanese Archipelago." In K. Omoto, ed., *Interdisciplinary Perspectives on the Origins of the Japanese.* Kyoto: International Research Center for Japanese Studies, 1999.

Mayo, Marlene, and Rimer, J. Thomas, eds. *War, Occupation, and Creativity: Japan and East Asia, 1926–1960.* Honolulu: University of Hawai'i Press, 2001.

McClain, James. *Kanazawa: A Seventeenth-Century Japanese Castle Town.* New Haven: Yale University Press, 1982.

McClain, James. *Japan: A Modern History.* New York: Norton, 2002.

McClain, James, Merriman, John, and Kaoru, Ugawa, eds. *Edo and Paris: Urban Life and the State in the Early Modern Era.* Ithaca, NY: Cornell University Press, 1994.

McCormack, Gavan. *Chang Tso-lin in Northeast China: China, Japan and the Manchurian Idea.* Stanford, Calif.: Stanford University Press, 1977.

McCormack, Gavan. "Nineteen-Thirties Japan: Fascism?" *Bulletin of Concerned Asian Scholars* 14:2 (1982): 15–34.

McCormack, Gavan. *The Emptiness of Japanese Affluence,* 2nd rev. edn. Armonk, NY: M. E. Sharpe, 2001.

McCormack, Gavan. "Breaking the Iron Triangle." *New Left Review* 13 (Jan.–Feb. 2002): 5–23.

McCormack, N. "Prejudice and Nationalisation: On the Buraku Problem." Ph.D. dissertation, Australian National University, 2002.

McCullough, Helen Craig, trans. *Ōkagami, the Great Mirror: Fujiwara no Michinaga and His Times.* Princeton: Princeton University Press, 1980.

McCullough, Helen Craig, trans. *The Tale of the Heike.* Stanford, Calif.: Stanford University Press, 1988.

McCullough, Helen Craig, and McCullough, William, trans. *A Tale of Flowering Fortunes: Annals of Japanese Aristocratic Life in the Heian Period,* 2 vols. Stanford, Calif.: Stanford University Press, 1980.

McCullough, William. "Japanese Marriage Institutions in the Heian Period." *Harvard Journal of Asiatic Studies* 27 (1967): 103–67.

McKean, Margaret. "Management of Traditional Common Lands (Iriaichi) in Japan." In Daniel Bromley, ed., *Making the Commons Work: Theory, Practice, and Policy.* San Francisco: ICS Press, 1992.

McLauchlan, Alastair. "The Current Circumstances of Japan's Burakumin." *New Zealand Journal of Asian Studies* 2:1 (2000): 20–144.

McMullin, Neil. *Buddhism and the State in Sixteenth-Century Japan.* Princeton: Princeton University Press, 1984.

Meeks, Lori. "Nuns, Court Ladies, and Female Bodhisattvas: The Women of Japan's Medieval Ritsu-School Nuns' Revival Movement." Ph.D. dissertation, Princeton University, 2003.

Mehl, Margaret. *History and the State in Nineteenth-Century Japan.* Basingstoke, UK: Macmillan, 1998.

Mercado, Stephen. *The Shadow Warriors of Nakano: A History of the Imperial Japanese Army's Elite Intelligence School.* Washington DC: Brassey's, 2002.

Mesheryakov, Alexander. "On the Quantity of Written Data Produced by the *Ritsuryō* State." *Nichibunken Japan Review* 15 (2003).

Meskill, Johanna Menzel. *Hitler and Japan: The Hollow Alliance.* New York: Atherton, 1966.

Midford, Paul. "Japan's Leadership Role in East Asian Security Multilateralism: The Nakayama Proposal and the Logic of Assurance." *Pacific Review* 13:3 (2000): 367–98.

Mills, B. J. "The Establishment and Defeat of Hierarchy: Inalienable Possessions and the History of Collective Prestige Structures in the Pueblo Southwest." *American Anthropologist* 106 (2004): 238–51.

Minami Ryōshin. *The Economic Development of Japan: A Quantitative Study.* New York: St. Martin's Press, 1986.

Minichiello, Sharon, ed. *Japan's Competing Modernities: Issues in Culture and Democracy, 1900–1930.* Honolulu: University of Hawai'i Press, 1998.

Mitani Taichirō. "The Establishment of Party Cabinets, 1898–1932." In Peter Duus, ed., *The Cambridge History of Modern Japan*, vol. 6, *The Twentieth Century.* Cambridge: Cambridge University Press, 1988.

Mitani Taichirō. *Kindai Nihon no sensō to seiji.* Tokyo: Iwanami Shoten, 1997.

Mitchell, Richard. *Justice in Japan: The Notorious Teijin Incident.* Honolulu: University of Hawai'i Press, 2002.

Mitchell, W. C. "Political Science and Public Choice: 1950–70." *Public Choice* 98 (1999): 237–49.

Mitsuhashi Tadahiro and Uchida Shigeo. *Shōwa keizaishi.* Tokyo: Nihon Keizai Shinbunsha, 1994.

Mitter, Rana. *The Manchurian Myth: Nationalism, Resistance and Collaboration in Modern China.* Berkeley: University of California Press, 2000.

Miyachi Masato. *Nichi-Ro sengo seiji shi no kenkyū: teikokushugi keisei ki no toshi to nōson.* Tokyo: Tokyo Daigaku Shuppankai, 1973.

Miyake, Yoshiko. "Doubling Expectations: Motherhood and Women's Factory Work under State Management in Japan in the 1930s and 1940s." In Gail Bernstein, ed., *Recreating Japanese Women, 1600–1945.* Berkeley: University of California Press, 1991.

Miyashita Akitoshi. "*Gaiatsu* and Japan's Foreign Aid: Rethinking the Reactive–Proactive Debate." *International Studies Quarterly* 43:4 (Dec. 1999): 695–731.

Miyashita Michiko. "Kinsei zenki ni okeru *ie* to josei no seikatsu." In Joseishi Sōgō Kenkyūkai, ed., *Nihon josei seikatsushi*, 3. Tokyo: Tokyo Daigaku Shuppankai, 1990.

Miyata Noboru, "Toshi to minzoku bunka." In Miyata Noboru et al., eds., *Nihon minzoku bunka taikei*, 11, *Toshi to inaka.* Tokyo: Shogakkan, 1985.

Miyazaki Yoshikazu. "Kado kyōsō no kōzai." In Kōsei Torihiki Kyōkai, ed., *Kokusai kyōsō to dokukinhō.* Tokyo: Nihon Keizai Shinbunsha, 1963.

Miyazaki Yoshikazu. *Nihon keizai no kōzō to kōdō.* Tokyo: Chikuma Shobō, 1985.

Miyazaki Yoshikazu. *Fukugō fukyō.* Tokyo: Chūō Kōronsha, 1992.

Miyoshi, Masao, and Harootunian, H. D., eds. *Learning Places: The Afterlives of Area Studies.* Durham, NC: Duke University Press, 2002.

Mizoguchi, Koji. "The Reproduction of Archaeological Discourse: The Case of Japan." *Journal of European Archaeology* 5 (1997): 149–65.

Mizoguchi, K. *An Archaeological History of Japan, 30,000 B.C. to A.D. 700.* Philadelphia: University of Pennsylvania Press, 2002.

Mizuno, Norihito. "Japan and Its East Asian Neighbors: Japan's Perception of China and Korea and the Making of Foreign Policy from the Seventeenth to the Nineteenth Century." Ph.D. dissertation, Ohio State University, 2004.

Molasky, Michael. *The American Occupation of Japan and Okinawa: Literature and Memory.* London: Routledge, 1999.

Molony, Barbara. *Technology and Investment: The Prewar Japanese Chemical Industry.* Cambridge, Mass.: Council on East Asian Studies, Harvard University, 1990.

Molony, Barbara. "Activism among Women in the Taishō Cotton Textile Industry." In Gail Bernstein, ed., *Recreating Japanese Women, 1600–1945.* Berkeley: University of California Press, 1991.

Molony, Barbara. "Equality versus Difference: The Japanese Debate over 'Motherhood Protection,' 1915–1950." In Janet Hunter, ed., *Japanese Women Working.* London: Routledge, 1993.

Mommsen, Wolfgang, and Osterhammel, Jurgen, eds. *Imperialism and After.* London: Allen and Unwin, 1986.

Moore, Joe. *Japanese Workers and the Struggle for Power, 1945–1947.* Madison: University of Wisconsin Press, 1983.

Moore, Ray. "The Occupation of Japan as History: Some Recent Research." *Monumenta Nipponica* 36:3 (Autumn 1981): 317–28.

Moore, Richard. *Japanese Agriculture: Patterns of Rural Development.* Boulder, Colo.: Westview Press, 1990.

Morikawa Hidemasa. *Zaibatsu: The Rise and Fall of Family Enterprise Groups in Japan.* Tokyo: University of Tokyo Press, 1992.

Morley, James, ed. *Dilemmas of Growth in Prewar Japan.* Princeton: Princeton University Press, 1971.

Morley, James William, ed. *Deterrent Diplomacy: Japan, Germany, and the USSR, 1935–1940.* New York: Columbia University Press, 1975.

Mormont, Marc. "Who is Rural? or, How to be Rural: Towards a Sociology of the Rural." In Terry Marsden et al., eds., *Rural Restructuring: Global Processes and Their Responses.* London: David Fulton, 1990.

Morozumi Yoshihiko. "Sangyō taiseiron: tsūsanshōgawa no ichiteian." In Morozumi Yoshihiko, Minosō Hitoshi, Kodō Rikuzō, Masada Tadashi, and Chiyu Yoshihito, eds., *Sangyō taisei no saihensei.* Tokyo: Shunjūsha, 1963.

Morrell, Robert. "Mirror for Women: Mujū Ichien's *Tsuma Kagami.*" *Monumenta Nipponica* 35:1 (1980): 45–50.

Morris, Ivan. *The World of the Shining Prince: Court Life in Ancient Japan.* New York: Alfred A. Knopf, 1964.

Morris, John. *Kinsei Nihon chigyōsei no kenkyū.* Tokyo: Seibundo, 1988.

Morris-Suzuki, Tessa. "The Invention and Reinvention of 'Japanese Culture'." *Journal of Asian Studies* 54:3 (1995): 759–80.

Morris-Suzuki, Tessa. "A Descent into the Past: The Frontier in the Construction of Japanese History." In Donald Denoon, Mark Hudson, Gavan McCormack, and Tessa Morris-Suzuki, eds., *Multicultural Japan: Palaeolithic to Postmodern.* Cambridge: Cambridge University Press, 1996.

Morris-Suzuki, Tessa. *Re-inventing Japan: Time, Space, Nation.* Armonk, NY: M. E. Sharpe, 1998.

Morse, Ronald. *Yanagita Kunio and the Folklore Movement: The Search for Japan's National Character and Distinctiveness.* New York: Garland, 1990.

Mulgan, Aurelia George. *The Politics of Agriculture in Japan.* London: Routledge, 2000.

Murai, Shōsuke. "The Boundaries of Medieval Japan." *Acta Asiatica* 81 (2001): 72–91.

Murakami Haruki. *Underground: The Tokyo Gas Attack and the Japanese Psyche,* trans. Alfred Birnbaum and J. Philip Gabriel. New York: Vintage International, 2000.

Murakami Yasusuke. "The Reality of the New Middle Class." *Japan Interpreter* 12:1 (1978): 1–5.

Murakami Yasusuke. "The Age of New Middle Mass Politics: The Case of Japan." *Journal of Japanese Studies* 8:1 (1982): 29–72.

Murakami Yasusuke. *An Anticlassical Political-Economic Analysis: A Vision for the Next Century,* trans. Kozo Yamamura. Stanford, Calif.: Stanford University Press, 1996.

Muramatsu Michio and Krauss, Ellis. "The Conservative Policy Line and the Development of Patterned Pluralism." In Kozo Yamamura and Yasuba Yasukichi, eds., *The Political Economy of Japan,* vol. 1, *The Domestic Transformation.* Stanford, Calif.: Stanford University Press, 1987.

Murasaki Shikibu. *The Tale of Genji,* trans. Royall Tyler. New York: Viking, 2001.

Murayama Hisashi. *Mini-komi sengoshi: jānarizumu no genten o motomete.* Tokyo: San'ichi Shobō, 1985.

Murota Takeshi. *Genpatsu no keizaigaku.* Tokyo: Asahi Shinbunsha, 1993.

Mutō Ichiyō. "Ecological Perspectives on Alternative Development: The Rainbow Plan." *Capitalism Nature Socialism* 9:1 (Mar. 1998): 3–23.

Myers, Ramon, and Peattie, Mark, eds. *The Japanese Colonial Empire, 1895–1945.* Princeton: Princeton University Press, 1984.

Nagahara Keiji. "The Medieval Origins of the Eta/Hinin." *Journal of Japanese Studies* 5:2 (1979): 385–403.

Nagai, Michio, and Urrutia, Miguel, eds. *Meiji Ishin: Restoration and Revolution.* Tokyo: United Nations University, 1985.

Nagai Yonosuke. "Moratoriamu kokka no bōeiron." *Chūō kōron* (Jan. 1981): 74–108.

Nagano Hiroko. "Bakuhanhō to josei." In Joseishi Sōgō Kenkyūkai, ed., *Nihon joseishi,* 3. Tokyo: Tokyo Daigaku Shuppankai, 1989.

Nagano Hiroko. "Nōson in okeru josei no yakuwari to shosō." In Joseishi Sōgō Kenkyūkai, ed., *Nihon josei seikatsushi,* 3. Tokyo: Tokyo Daigaku Shuppankai, 1990.

Nagata, Mary Louise. "Images of the Family on Stage in Early Modern Japan." *Japan Review* 13 (2001): 93–105.

Nagazumi Yōko. *Shuinsen.* Tokyo: Yoshikawa Kōbunkan, 2001.

Nagy, Margit. "Middle-Class Working Women during the Interwar Years." In Gail Bernstein, ed., *Recreating Japanese Women, 1600–1945.* Berkeley: University of California Press, 1991.

Nahm, Andrew, ed. *Korea under Japanese Colonial Rule: Studies of the Policy and Techniques of Japanese Colonialism.* Kalamazoo, Mich.: Center for Korean Studies, Western Michigan University, 1973.

Najita, Tetsuo. *Japan.* New York: Prentice-Hall, 1974.

Najita, Tetsuo, and Harootunian, H. D. "Japanese Revolt against the West: Political and Cultural Criticism in the Twentieth Century." In Peter Duus, ed., *The Cambridge History of Japan,* vol. 6, *The Twentieth Century.* Cambridge: Cambridge University Press, 1988.

Najita, Tetsuo, and Koschmann, J. Victor, eds. *Conflict in Modern Japanese History: The Neglected Tradition.* Princeton: Princeton University Press, 1982.

Nakahashi Takahiro and Iizuka Masaru. "Anthropological Study of the Transition from the Jōmon to the Yayoi Periods in Northern Kyūshū Using Morphological and Paleodemographic Features." *Anthropological Science,* Jap. ser. 106 (1998): 31–53.

Nakai, Kate Wildman. *Shogunal Politics: Arai Hakuseki and the Premises of Tokugawa Rule.* Cambridge, Mass.: Council on East Asian Studies, Harvard University, 1988.

Nakai Nobuhiko. "Commercial Change and Urban Growth in Early Modern Japan," trans. James McClain. In John Whitney Hall, ed., *The Cambridge History of Japan,* vol. 4, *Early Modern Japan.* Cambridge: Cambridge University Press, 1991.

Nakai Nobuhiko and McClain, James. "Commercial Change and Urban Growth in Early Modern Japan." In John W. Hall, ed., *The Cambridge History of Modern Japan,* vol. 4, *Early Modern Japan.* Cambridge: Cambridge University Press, 1991.

Nakamura, James. *Agricultural Production and the Economic Development of Japan, 1873–1922*. Princeton: Princeton University Press, 1966.

Nakamura Takafusa. *Economic Growth in Prewar Japan*, trans. Robert A. Feldman. New Haven: Yale University Press, 1983.

Nakamura Takafusa. "Depression, Recovery, and War, 1920–1945." In Peter Duus, ed., *The Cambridge History of Japan*, vol. 6, *The Twentieth Century*. Cambridge: Cambridge University Press, 1988.

Nakane Chie. *Japanese Society*. Berkeley: University of California Press, 1970.

Nakano Hajimu. "Kuki Shūzō and *The Structure of Iki*." In J. Thomas Rimer, ed., *Culture and Identity: Japanese Intellectuals during the Interwar Years*. Princeton: Princeton University Press, 1990, pp. 261–72.

Nakano, Lynne. "Volunteering as a Lifestyle Choice: Negotiating Self-Identities in Japan." *Ethnology* 39 (2000): 93–105.

Nakano Mitsutoshi, "The Role of Traditional Aesthetics." In C. Andrew Gerstle, ed., *Eighteenth Century Japan: Culture and Society*. Richmond, UK: Curzon, 1989.

Nakano Toshio. *Ōtsuka Hisao to Maruyama Masao: dōin, shutai, sensō sekinin*. Tokyo: Seidosha, 2001.

Napier, Susan. *Anime from* Akira *to* Princess Mononoke. New York: Palgrave Macmillan, 2000.

Narita Ryūichi. "Women in the Motherland: Oku Mumeo through Wartime and Postwar." In Yamanouchi Yasushi, J. Victor Koschmann, and Narita Ryūichi, eds., *Total War and "Modernization."* Ithaca, NY: East Asia Program, Cornell University, 1998.

Neary, Ian. *Political Protest and Social Control in Pre-war Japan: The Origins of Buraku Liberation*. Manchester: Manchester University Press, 1989.

Nihon Kokusai Seiji Gakkai Taiheiyō Sensō Gen'in Kenkyūbu, ed. *Taiheiyō sensō e no michi*, 8 vols. Tokyo: Asahi Shinbunsha, 1962–3.

Ninomiya Shigeaki. "An Enquiry concerning the Origin, Development, and Present Situation of the Eta in Relation to the History of Social Classes in Japan." *Transactions of the Asiatic Society of Japan* 10 (1933): 47–154.

Nish, Ian. *The Anglo-Japanese Alliance: The Diplomacy of Two Island Empires, 1894–1907*. London: Athlone Press, 1966.

Nish, Ian. *Alliance in Decline: A Study in Anglo-Japanese Relations, 1908–23*. London: Athlone Press, 1972.

Nish, Ian. *Japan's Struggle with Internationalism: Japan, China, and the League of Nations, 1931–1933*. London: Kegan Paul, 1993.

Nish, Ian, ed. *Britain and Japan: Biographical Portraits*, 4 vols. Folkestone: Japan Library, 1994.

Nish, Ian, ed. *The Iwakura Mission in America and Europe: A New Assessment*. Richmond, UK: Curzon, 1998.

Nish, Ian, and Kibata, Yoichi, eds., *The History of Anglo-Japanese Relations, 1600–2000: The Political-Diplomatic Dimension*, 2 vols. New York: St. Martin's Press, 2000.

Nishida, Masaki. "The Emergence of Food Production in Neolithic Japan." *Journal of Anthropological Archaeology* 2 (1983): 305–22.

Nishikawa Yūko. "The Changing Form of Dwellings and the Establishment of the Katei (Home) in Modern Japan." *U.S.–Japan Women's Journal*, English Supplement 8 (1995): 3–36.

Nishikawa Yūko. "Japan's Entry into War and the Support of Women." *U.S.–Japan Women's Journal*, English Supplement 12 (1997): 48–83.

Nishimura, Sey. "The Way of the Gods: Motoori Norinaga's *Naobi no Mitama*." *Monumenta Nipponica* 46:1 (Spring 1991): 21–41.

Nishino Yukiko. "Kodai: kōjo ga tennō ni natta jidai." In Fukutō Sanae, ed., *Rekishi no naka no kōjotachi*. Tokyo: Shōgakkan, 2002.

Nishiyama Matsunosuke. *Edo Culture: Daily Life and Diversions in Urban Japan*. Honolulu: University of Hawai'i Press, 1997.

Niwa Akiko. "The Formation of the Myth of Motherhood in Japan." *U.S.–Japan Women's Journal*, English Supplement 4 (1993): 70–82.

Noguchi Yukio. *1940-nen taisei*. Tokyo: Tōyō Keizai Shinpōsha, 1995.

Nolte, Sharon H. "Women's Rights and Society's Needs: Japan's 1931 Suffrage Bill." *Comparative Studies in Society and History* 28:4 (1986): 690–714.

Nolte, Sharon H. *Liberalism in Modern Japan: Ishibashi Tanzan and His Teachers, 1905–1960*. Berkeley: University of California Press, 1987.

Nolte, Sharon H., and Hastings, Sally Ann. "The Meiji State's Policy toward Women, 1890–1910." In Gail Bernstein, ed., *Recreating Japanese Women, 1600–1945*. Berkeley: University of California Press, 1991.

Nomura Ikuyo. "Chūsei josei no funsō kaihi doryoku." In Nishimura Hiroko, ed., *Ikusa no naka no onnatachi*. Tokyo: Yoshikawa Kōbunkan, 2004.

Nomura Masami. *Koyō fuan*. Tokyo: Iwanami Shoten, 1998.

Nomura Minoru. *Nihonkai kaisen no shinjitsu*. Tokyo: Kōdansha, 1999.

Nomura Tadao. *Kōkyū to jokan*. Tokyo: Kyōikusha, 1978.

Norgren, Tiana. *Abortion before Birth Control: The Politics of Reproduction in Postwar Japan*. Princeton: Princeton University Press, 2001.

Norman, E. Herbert. *Origins of the Modern Japanese State: Selected Writings of E. H. Norman*, ed. John Dower. New York: Pantheon, 1975.

Norton, Mary Beth, ed. *The American Historical Association's Guide to Historical Literature*, 3rd edn. New York: Oxford University Press, 1995.

Nosco, Peter. *Remembering Paradise: Nativism and Nostalgia in Eighteenth-Century Japan*. Cambridge, Mass.: Council on East Asian Studies, Harvard University, 1990.

Nosco, Peter. "Keeping the Faith: *Bakuhan* Policy towards Religions in Seventeenth-Century Japan." In P. F. Kornicki and I. J. McMullen, eds., *Religion in Japan: Arrows to Heaven and Earth*. Cambridge: Cambridge University Press, 1996.

O'Brien, Phillips Payson, ed. *Anglo-Japanese Alliance, 1902–1922*. London: Routledge, 2004.

Ochiai Hiroki. "Meiji shoki no gaiseiron to higashi Ajia." In Furuya Tetsuo and Yamamuro Shin'ichi, eds., *Kindai Nihon ni okeru higashi Ajia mondai*. Tokyo: Yoshikawa Kōbunkan, 2001.

Odaka Kunio. "Middle Classes in Japan." In Reinhard Bendix and Seymour Martin Lipset, eds., *Class, Status, and Power: A Reader in Social Stratification*. New York: Free Press, 1963.

Ōgai Tokuko. "The Stars of Democracy: The First Thirty-Nine Female Members of the Japanese Diet." *U.S.–Japan Women's Journal*, English Supplement 11 (1996): 81–117.

Ogawa, Akihiro. "The Failure of Civil Society? An Ethnography of NPOs and the State in Contemporary Japan." Ph.D. dissertation, Cornell University, 2004.

Oguma Eiji. *Tan'itsu minzoku shinwa no kigen: "Nihonjin" no jigazō no keifu*. Tokyo: Shinyōsha, 1995.

Oguma Eiji. *"Nihonjin" no kyōkai: Okinawa, Ainu, Taiwan, Chōsen, shokuminchi shihai kara fukki undō made*. Tokyo: Shinyōsha, 1998.

Oguma Eiji. *"Minshu" to "aikoku": sengo Nihon no nashonarizumu to kōkyōsei*. Tokyo: Shinyōsha, 2002.

Oguma Eiji. *A Genealogy of "Japanese" Self-Images*, trans. David Askew. Melbourne: Trans Pacific Press, 2002.

Ōhama Eikan. *Yaeyama no kōkogaku*. Ishigaki: Sakishima Bunka Kenkyūjo, 1999.

Ohnuki-Tierney, Emiko. *Rice as Self: Japanese Identities through Time*. Princeton: Princeton University Press, 1993.

Ohnuki-Tierney, Emiko. *Kamikaze, Cherry Blossoms, and Nationalisms: The Militarization of Aesthetics in Japanese History.* Chicago: University of Chicago Press, 2002.

Oka Yoshitake. "Generational Conflict after the Russo-Japanese War." In Tetsuo Najita and Victor Koschmann, eds., *Conflict in Modern Japanese History.* Princeton: Princeton University Press, 1982.

Okakura Kakuzō. *The Ideals of the East with Special Reference to the Art of Japan* (1903). New York: ICG Muse, 2002.

Okami Masao and Satake Akihiro. *Hyōchū rakuchū rakugai byōbu: Uesugibon.* Tokyo: Iwanami Shoten, 1983.

Okazaki Hisahiko. *Mutsu Munemitsu to sono jidai.* Tokyo: PHP Kenkyūjo, 1999.

Okazaki Tetsuji and Okuno Masahiro, eds. *Gendai nihon keizai shisutemu no genryū.* Tokyo: Nihon Keizai Shibunsha, 1993.

Okazaki, Tetsuji, and Okuno-Fujiwara Masahiro, eds. *The Japanese Economic System and Its Historical Origins.* Oxford: Oxford University Press, 1999.

Ōkōchi Kazuo. " 'Keizaijin' no shūen: atarashii keizai rinri no tame ni." Reprinted in *Ōkōchi Kazuo chosakushū.* Tokyo: Seirin Shoin Shinsha, 1942.

Oku Takenori. *Sukiyandaru no Meiji: kokumin o tsukuru tame no ressun.* Tokyo: Chikuma Shobō, 1997.

Okuma Takashi. "Datsu damu o habamu 'kihon kōsui'." *Sekai* (Oct. 2004): 121–31.

Ōkurashō, ed. *Shōwa zaiseishi.* Tokyo: Tōyō Keizai Shinpōsha, 1991.

Olsen, John W. "China's Earliest Inhabitants." *Journal of East Asian Archaeology* 2 (2000): 1–7.

Ooms, Herman. *Tokugawa Ideology: Early Constructs, 1570–1680.* Princeton: Princeton University Press, 1985.

Ooms, Herman. *Tokugawa Village Practice: Class, Status, Power, Law.* Berkeley: University of California Press, 1996.

Orbaugh, Sharalyn. *The Japanese Fiction of the Allied Occupation, 1945–1952.* Stanford, Calif.: Stanford University Press, forthcoming.

Orr, Robert. *The Emergence of Japan's Foreign Aid Power.* New York: Columbia University Press, 1990.

Osada Toshiki and Vovin, Alexander, eds. *Perspectives on the Origins of the Japanese Language.* Kyoto: International Research Center for Japanese Studies, 2003.

Ota Hiroko. "Sharing Governance: Changing Functions of Government, Business, and NPOs." In Yamamoto Tadashi, ed., *Deciding the Public Good: Governance and Civil Society in Japan.* Tokyo: Japan Center for International Exchange, 1999.

Ōtsuka Hisao. "Saikōdo 'jihatsusei' no hatsuyō: keizai rinri to shite no seisan sekinin ni tsuite." Reprinted in *Ōtsuka Hisao chosakushū,* 8. Tokyo: Iwanami Shoten, Tokyo, 1969–86.

Ozawa Ichirō. *Blueprint for a New Japan.* New York: Kōdansha, 1994.

Park, Soon-Won. *Colonial Industrialization and Labor in Korea: The Onoda Cement Factory.* Cambridge, Mass.: Harvard University Asia Center, 1999.

Partner, Simon. *Toshié: A Story of Village Life in Twentieth Century Japan.* Berkeley: University of California Press, 2004.

Passin, Herbert. *Society and Education in Japan.* New York: Teachers College, Columbia University, 1965.

Patessio, Mara. "Women's Participation in the Popular Rights Movement (Jiyū Minken Undō) during the Early Meiji Period." *U.S.–Japan Women's Journal* 27 (2004): 3–26.

Patterson, Wayne. *The Korean Frontier in America: Immigration to Hawai'i, 1896–1910.* Honolulu: University of Hawai'i Press, 1988.

Paxton, Robert. *The Anatomy of Fascism.* New York: Knopf, 2004.

Payne, Stanley. *A History of Fascism, 1914–45.* Madison: University of Wisconsin Press, 1995.

Pearson, Richard J. "The Nature of Japanese Archaeology." *Asian Perspectives* 31 (1992): 115–27.

Pearson, Richard J. "The Place of Okinawa in Japanese Historical Identity." In Donald Denoon, Mark Hudson, Gavan McCormack, and Tessa Morris-Suzuki, eds., *Multicultural Japan: Palaeolithic to Postmodern*. Cambridge: Cambridge University Press, 1996; rev. edn., 2001.

Pearson, Richard J. "Excavations at Sumiya and Other Sakishima Sites: Variations in Okinawan Leadership around AD 1500." *Bulletin of the Indo-Pacific Prehistory Association* 23 (2003): 95–111.

Peattie, Mark. *Ishiwara Kanji and Japan's Confrontation with the West*. Princeton: Princeton University Press, 1975.

Peattie, Mark. *Nan'yō: The Rise and Fall of the Japanese in Micronesia*. Honolulu: University of Hawai'i Press, 1988.

Peattie, Mark. *Sunburst: The Rise of the Japanese Naval Air Power, 1909–1941*. Annapolis, Md.: Naval Institute Press, 2001.

Peattie, Mark, and Evans, David. *Kaigun: Strategy, Tactics, and Technology in the Imperial Japanese Navy, 1887–1941*. Annapolis, Md.: Naval Institute Press, 1997.

Pempel, T. J. "The Tar Baby Target: 'Reform' of the Japanese Bureaucracy." In Robert E. Ward and Sakamoto Yoshikazu, eds., *Democratizing Japan: The Allied Occupation*. Honolulu: University of Hawai'i Press, 1987.

Pempel. T. J. "From Exporter to Investor: Japanese Foreign Economic Policy." In Gerald Curtis and Michael Blaker, eds., *Japan's Foreign Policy after the Cold War: Coping with Change*. Armonk, NY: M. E. Sharpe, 1993.

Pempel, T. J. "Trans-Pacific Torii: Japan and the Emerging Asian Regionalism." In Peter Katzenstein and Takashi Shiraishi, eds., *Network Power: Japan and Asia*. Ithaca, NY: Cornell University Press, 1997.

Pempel, T. J. *Regime Shift: Comparative Dynamics of the Japanese Political Economy*. Ithaca, NY: Cornell University Press, 1998.

Perez, Louis. *Japan Comes of Age: Mutsu Munemitsu and the Revision of the Unequal Treaties*. Madison, NJ: Fairleigh Dickinson University Press, 1999.

Pflugfelder, Gregory. *Cartographies of Desire: Male–Male Sexuality in Japanese Discourse*. Berkeley: University of California Press, 1999.

Pharr, Susan. *Political Women in Japan: The Search for a Place in Political Life*. Berkeley: University of California Press, 1981.

Pharr, Susan J. "The Politics of Women's Rights." In Robert E. Ward and Sakamoto Yoshikazu, eds., *Democratizing Japan: The Allied Occupation*. Honolulu: University of Hawai'i Press, 1987.

Pharr, Susan. *Losing Face: Status Politics in Japan*. Berkeley: University of California Press, 1990.

Pharr, Susan. "Japan's Defense Foreign Policy and the Politics of Burden Sharing." In Gerald Curtis and Michael Blaker, eds., *Japan's Foreign Policy after the Cold War: Coping with Change*. Armonk, NY: M. E. Sharpe, 1993.

Philippi, Donald, trans. *Kojiki*. Tokyo: University of Tokyo Press, 1968; repr. 1983.

Pietrusewsky, Michael. "A Multivariate Craniometric Study of the Inhabitants of the Ryūkyū Islands and Comparisons with Cranial Series from Japan, Asia, and the Pacific." *Anthropological Science* 107 (1999): 255–81.

Piggott, Joan R. *The Emergence of Japanese Kingship*. Stanford, Calif.: Stanford University Press, 1997.

Piggott, Joan R. "Chieftain Pairs and Corulers: Female Sovereignty and Early Japan." In Hitomi Tonomura, Anne Walthall, and Wakita Haruko, eds., *Women and Class in Japanese History*. Ann Arbor: Center for Japanese Studies Publications, University of Michigan, 1999.

Piggott, Joan R. "The Last Classical Female Sovereign: Kōken-Shōtoku tennō." In Dorothy Ko, J. Haboush, and J. R. Piggott, eds., *Women and Confucian Cultures in Premodern China, Korea, and Japan*. Berkeley: University of California Press, 2003.

Pincus, Leslie. *Authenticating Culture in Imperial Japan: Kūki Shūzō and the Rise of National Aesthetics*. Berkeley: University of California Press, 1996.

Pittau, Joseph. *Political Thought in Early Meiji Japan, 1868–1889*. Cambridge, Mass.: Harvard University Press, 1967.

Platt, Brian. *Burning and Building: Schooling and State Formation in Japan, 1750–1890*. Cambridge, Mass.: Harvard University Asia Center, 2004.

Pollack, David. "Revenge of the Illegal Asians: Aliens, Gangsters, and Myth in Kon Satoshi's *World Apartment Horror*." *positions: east asia cultures critique* 1:3 (Winter 1993): 677–714.

Pratt, Edward E. *Japan's Protoindustrial Elite: The Economic Foundations of the Gōnō*. Cambridge, Mass.: Harvard University Asia Center, 1999.

Prestowitz, Clyde, Jr. *Trading Places: How We Allowed Japan to Take the Lead*. New York: Basic Books, 1988.

Pyle, Kenneth B. *The New Generation in Meiji Japan: Problems of Cultural Identity, 1885–1895*. Stanford, Calif.: Stanford University Press, 1969.

Pyle, Kenneth B. *The Japanese Question: Power and Purpose in a New Era*. Washington DC: AEI Press, 1992.

Quigley, Harold. *Japanese Government and Politics*. New York: Century Co., 1932.

Rabinovitch, Judith, trans. *Shōmonki: The Story of Masakado's Rebellion*. Tokyo: Sophia University Press, 1986.

Rahula, Walpola. *What the Buddha Taught*. New York: Grove Press, 1962.

Ramseyer, J. Mark, and Rosenbluth, Frances M. *Japan's Political Marketplace*. Cambridge, Mass.: Harvard University Press, 1993.

Ramseyer, J. Mark, and Rosenbluth, Frances M. *The Politics of Oligarchy: Institutional Choice in Imperial Japan*. Cambridge: Cambridge University Press, 1995.

Rath, Eric. "New Meanings for Old Vegetables in Kyoto." In Theodore and Victoria Bestor, eds., *Cuisine, Consumption, and Culture: Food in Contemporary Japan*. Berkeley: University of California Press, forthcoming.

Ravina, Mark. *Land and Lordship in Early Modern Japan*. Stanford, Calif.: Stanford University Press, 1999.

Reber, Emily A. Su-lan. "*Buraku Mondai* in Japan." *Harvard Human Rights Journal* 12 (1999): 297–359.

Reed, Steven. "Structure and Behaviour: Extending Duverger's Law to the Japanese Case." *British Journal of Political Science* 29 (1991): 335–56.

Reed, Steven. *Making Common Sense of Japan*. Pittsburgh: University of Pittsburgh Press, 1994.

Reed, Steven. Review of *Japan's Political Marketplace*, by J. Mark Ramseyer and Frances M. Rosenbluth. *American Journal of Sociology* 99 (1994): 1654–6.

Reed, Steven, and Scheiner, E. "Electoral Incentives and Policy Preferences: Mixed Motives behind Party Defections In Japan." *British Journal of Political Science* 33 (2003): 469–90.

Reinhardt, Anne. "Navigating Imperialism in China: Steamship, Semicolony, and Nation, 1860–1937." Ph.D. dissertation, Princeton University, 2002.

Reischauer, Edwin. *Japan, Past and Present*. New York: Knopf, 1947.

Reischauer, Edwin, and Craig, Albert. *Japan: Tradition and Transformation*, rev. edn. Boston: Houghton Mifflin, 1989.

Rekishigaku Kenkyūkai. *Taiheiyō sensōshi*, 5 vols. Tokyo: Tōyō Keizai Shinpōsha, 1953.

Reynolds, Douglas. "Training Young China Hands: Tōa Dōbun Shōin and Its Precursors, 1886–1945." In Duus et al., eds., *The Japanese Informal Empire in China, 1895–1937*. Princeton: Princeton University Press, 1989.

Reynolds, E. Bruce, ed. *Japan in the Fascist Era*. New York: Palgrave Macmillan, 2004.

Rice, P. M. "On the Origins of Pottery." *Journal of Archaeological Method and Theory* 6 (1999): 1–54.

Richie, Donald. *A Hundred Years of Japanese Film*. Tokyo: Kōdansha, 2001.

Richter, Giles. *Marketing the Word: Publishing Entrepreneurs in Meiji Japan, 1970–1912*. Ph.D. dissertation, Columbia University, 1999.

Richter, Steffi, and Schad-Seifert, Annette, eds. *Cultural Studies and Japan*. Leipzig: Leipziger Universitätsverlag, 2001.

Rimer, J. Thomas, ed. *A Hidden Fire: Russian and Japanese Cultural Encounters, 1868–1926*. Stanford, Calif.: Stanford University Press, 1995.

Rix, Alan. "Japan and the Region: Leading from Behind." In Richard Higgott, Richard Leaver, and John Ravenhill, eds., *Pacific Economic Relations in the 1990s: Cooperation or Conflict?* St. Leonards, Australia: Allen and Unwin, 1993.

Roberson, James. *Japanese Working Class Lives*. London: Routledge, 1998.

Roberts, Glenda. *Staying on the Line: Blue-Collar Women in Contemporary Japan*. Honolulu: University of Hawai'i Press, 1994.

Roberts, Luke. *Mercantilism in a Japanese Domain: The Merchant Origins of Economic Nationalism in 18th-Century Tosa*. Cambridge: Cambridge University Press, 1998.

Robertson, Jennifer. "Japanese Farm Manuals: A Literature of Discovery." *Peasant Studies* 11:3 (1984): 169–94.

Robertson, Jennifer. *Takarazuka: Sexual Politics and Popular Culture in Modern Japan*. Berkeley: University of California Press, 1998.

Robinson, Michael. *Cultural Nationalism in Colonial Korea, 1921–1925*. Seattle: University of Washington Press, 1988.

Rodd, Laurel Rasplica. *Nichiren: A Biography*. Tempe: Arizona State University, 1978.

Rodd, Laurel Rasplica, trans. *Nichiren: Selected Writings*. Honolulu: University of Hawai'i Press, 1980.

Rodd, Laurel Rasplica. "Yosano Akiko and the Taishō Debate over the 'New Woman'." In Gail Bernstein, ed., *Recreating Japanese Women, 1600–1945*. Berkeley: University of California Press, 1991.

Roden, Donald. *Schooldays in Imperial Japan: A Study in the Culture of a Student Elite*. Berkeley: University of California Press, 1980.

Roden, Donald. "Taishō Culture and the Problem of Gender Ambivalence." In J. Thomas Rimer, ed., *Culture and Identity: Japanese Intellectuals during the Interwar Years*. Princeton: Princeton University Press, 1990.

Rogers, Minor, and Rogers, Ann. *Rennyo: The Second Founder of Shin Buddhism*. Berkeley, Calif.: Asian Humanities Press, 1991.

Rogowski, Ronald. "Comparative Politics." In Ada W. Finifter, ed., *Political Science: The State of the Discipline II*. Washington DC: American Political Science Association, 1993.

Rohlen, Thomas. *For Harmony and Strength: Japanese White-Collar Organization in Anthropological Perspective*. Berkeley: University of California Press, 1974.

Rohlen, Thomas. "Violence at Yoka High School." *Asian Survey* 16:7 (1976): 682–99.

Rohlen, Thomas. *Japan's High Schools*. Berkeley: University of California Press, 1983.

Rose, Barbara. *Tsuda Umeko and Women's Education in Japan*. New Haven: Yale University Press, 1992.

Rose, Nikolas. "Governing 'Advanced' Liberal Democracies." In Andrew Barry, Thomas Osborne, and Nikolas Rose, eds., *Foucault and Political Reason: Liberalism, Neo-Liberalism and Rationalities of Government*. Chicago: University of Chicago Press, 1996.

Rosenberg, Bernard, and White, David Manning, eds. *Mass Culture: The Popular Arts in America*. New York: Free Press, 1957.

Rosovsky, Henry. "Japan's Transition to Modern Economic Growth, 1868–1885." In Henry Rosovsky, ed., *Industrialization in Two Systems*. New York: Wiley, 1966.

Rowley-Conwy, P., and Zvelebil, M.. "Saving It for Later: Storage by Prehistoric Hunter-Gatherers in Europe." In P. Halstead and J. O'Shea, eds., *Bad Year Economics: Cultural Responses to Risk and Uncertainty.* Cambridge: Cambridge University Press, 1989.

Rubenstein, Murray, ed. *Taiwan: A New History.* Armonk, NY: M. E. Sharpe, 1999.

Rubin, Jay. "From Wholesomeness to Decadence: The Censorship of Literature under the Allied Occupation." *Journal of Japanese Studies* 11:1 (Winter 1985): 71–103.

Rubinger, Richard. *Private Academies in Tokugawa Japan.* Princeton: Princeton University Press, 1982.

Ruch, Barbara, ed. *Engendering Faith: Women and Buddhism in Premodern Japan.* Ann Arbor: Center for Japanese Studies, University of Michigan, 2002.

Ruppert, Brian. *Jewel in the Ashes: Buddha Relics and Power in Early Medieval Japan.* Cambridge, Mass.: Harvard University Asia Center, 2000.

Russell, John. "Consuming Passions: Spectacle, Self-Transformation, and the Commodification of Blackness in Japan." *positions* 6:1 (1998): 113–77.

Saitō Osamu. "Infanticide, Fertility and 'Population Stagnation': The State of Tokugawa Historical Demography." *Japan Forum* 4:2 (1992): 369–81.

Sakai Atsuharu. "Kaibara Ekken and *Onna-daigaku.*" *Cultural Nippon* 7:4 (1939): 43–56.

Sakaki, Atsuko. "Sliding Doors: Women in the Heterosocial Literary Field of Early Modern Japan." *U.S.–Japan Women's Journal,* English Supplement 17 (1999): 3–38.

Sakakibara Eisuke. "The End of Progressivism." *Foreign Affairs* (Sept.–Oct. 1995): 8–14.

Sakamoto, Pamela Rotner. *Japanese Diplomats and Jewish Refugees: A World War II Dilemma.* Westport, Conn.: Praeger, 1998.

Sakamoto Shōzō. *Nihon ōchō kokka taiseiron.* Tokyo: Tokyo Daigaku Shuppankai, 1972.

Sakamoto Shōzō. *Nihon no rekishi,* 8, *Ōchō kokka.* Tokyo: Shōgakkan, 1974.

Sakamoto Shōzō. *Shōensei seiritsu to ōchō kokka.* Tokyo: Hanawa Shobō, 1985.

Sakamoto Yoshikazu. *Kakujidai no kokusai seiji.* Tokyo: Iwanami Shoten, 1982.

Samuels, Richard. *The Business of the Japanese State: Energy Markets in Comparative and Historical Perspective.* Ithaca, NY: Cornell University Press, 1987.

Samuels, Richard. *"Rich Nation, Strong Army": National Security and the Technological Transformation of Japan.* Ithaca, NY: Cornell University Press, 1994.

Samuels, Richard. *Machiavelli's Children: Leaders and Their Legacies in Italy and Japan.* Ithaca, NY: Cornell University Press, 2003.

Sand, Jordan. "At Home in the Meiji Period: Inventing Japanese Domesticity." In Stephen Vlastos, ed., *Mirror of Modernity: Invented Traditions of Modern Japan.* Berkeley: University of California Press, 1998.

Sand, Jordan. "The Cultured Life as Contested Space." In Elise K. Tipton and John Clark, eds., *Being Modern in Japan: Culture and Society from the 1910s to the 1930s.* Honolulu: University of Hawai'i Press, 2000.

Sand, Jordan. *House and Home in Modern Japan: Architecture, Domestic Space, and Bourgeois Culture, 1880–1930.* Cambridge, Mass.: Harvard University Asia Center, 2003.

Sandler, Mark Howard, ed. *The Confusion Era: Art and Culture of Japan during the Allied Occupation, 1945–1952.* Seattle: University of Washington Press, 1997.

Sansom, George. *The Western World and Japan: A Study in the Interaction of European and Asiatic Cultures.* New York: Knopf, 1950.

Sasaki Ryōsaku and Kunimasa Takeshige. *Ippyōsa no jinsei, Sasaki Ryōsaku no shōgen.* Tokyo: Asahi Shinbunsha, 1989.

Sasaki-Uemura, Wesley. *Organizing the Spontaneous: Citizen Protest in Postwar Japan.* Honolulu: University of Hawai'i Press, 2001.

Sato, Barbara. *The New Japanese Woman: Modernity, Media, and Women in Interwar Japan.* Durham, NC: Duke University Press, 2003.

Sato, Elizabeth. "Early Development of the Shoen." In John W. Hall and Jeffrey Mass, eds., *Medieval Japan: Essays in Institutional History.* New Haven: Yale University Press, 1974.

Sato Hiroyuki. *Nihon kyūsekki bunka no kōzō to shinka.* Tokyo: Kashiwa Shobō, 1992.

Satō Seizaburō and Matsuzaki Tetsuhisa. "Jimintō chōchōki seiken no kaibō." *Chūō kōron* 99:11 (1984): 66–100.

Satō Tsuneo. "Tokugawa Villages and Agriculture." In Nakane Chie and Ōishi Shinzaburō, eds., *Tokugawa Japan: The Social and Economic Antecedents of Modern Japan,* trans. Conrad Totman. Tokyo: University of Tokyo Press, 1990.

Sato, Y., Yamanaka, S., and Takahashi, M. "Evidence for Jōmon Plant Cultivation Based on DNA Analysis of Chestnut Remains." In J. Habu, J. M. Savelle, S. Koyama, and H. Hongo, eds., *Hunter-Gatherers of the North Pacific Rim.* Osaka: National Museum of Ethnology, 2003.

Satō Yōichirō. "Modeling Japan's Foreign Economic Policy with the United States." In Miyashita Akitoshi and Satō Yōichirō, eds., *Japanese Foreign Policy in Asia and the Pacific: Domestic Interests, American Pressure, and Regional Integration.* New York: Palgrave Macmillan, 2001.

Satō Yoshimaru. *Meiji nashonarizumu no kenkyū: seikyōsha no seiritsu to sono shūhen.* Tokyo: Fuyō Shobō, 1998.

Scalapino, Robert A. *Democracy and the Party Movement in Prewar Japan.* Berkeley: University of California Press, 1953.

Scalapino, Robert A., and Masumi Junnosuke. *Parties and Politics in Contemporary Japan.* Berkeley: University of California Press, 1962.

Schaller, Michael. *The American Occupation of Japan: The Origins of the Cold War in Asia.* New York: Oxford University Press, 1985.

Schaller, Michael. *Altered States: The U.S. and Japan since the Occupation.* New York: Oxford University Press. 1997.

Schalow, Paul Gordon. "Male Love in Early Modern Japan: A Literary Depiction of the 'Youth'." In Martin Bauml Duberman et al., eds., *Hidden from History: Reclaiming the Gay and Lesbian Past.* New York: NAL, 1989.

Scheiner, Irwin. *Christian Converts and Social Protest in Meiji Japan.* Berkeley: University of California Press, 1970.

Schencking, Charles. *Making Waves: Politics, Propaganda, and the Emergence of the Imperial Japanese Navy, 1868–1922.* Stanford, Calif.: Stanford University Press, 2005.

Schlesinger, Jacob. *Shadow Shoguns: The Rise and Fall of Japan's Postwar Political Machine.* New York: Simon and Schuster, 1997.

Schnell, Scott. *Rousing Drum: Ritual Practice in a Japanese Community.* Honolulu: University of Hawai'i Press, 1999.

Schodt, Frederik. *Native American in the Land of the Shōgun.* Berkeley: Stone Bridge Press, 2003.

Schonberger, Howard. *Aftermath of War: Americans and the Remaking of Japan, 1945–1952.* Kent, Ohio: Kent State University Press, 1989.

Schoppa, Leonard. "Two Level Games and Bargaining Outcomes: Why *Gaiatsu* Succeeds in Japan in Some Cases and Not Others." *International Organization* 47:3 (Summer 1993): 353–86.

Schoppa, Leonard. *Bargaining with Japan: What American Pressure Can and Cannot Do.* New York: Columbia University Press, 1997.

Schwartz, Frank, and Pharr, Susan, eds. *The State of Civil Society in Japan.* Cambridge: Cambridge University Press, 2003.

Scott, James. *Domination and the Arts of Resistance.* New Haven: Yale University Press, 1990.

Scott, John. *Stratification and Power.* Cambridge: Polity Press, 1996.

Screech, Timon. *The Lens within the Heart: The Western Scientific Gaze and Popular Imagery in Later Edo Japan*. Honolulu: University of Hawai'i Press, 2002.

Sei Shōnagon. *The Pillow Book of Sei Shōnagon*, trans. Ivan Morris. New York: Penguin, 1967.

Seigle, Cecilia Segawa. *Yoshiwara: The Glittering World of the Japanese Courtesan*. Honolulu: University of Hawai'i Press, 1993.

Seki Shizuo. *Taishō gaikō: jinbutsu ni miru gaikō senryakuron*. Tokyo: Minerva, 2001.

Sekiguchi Hiroko. *Nihon kodai kon'inshi no kenkyū*, 2 vols. Tokyo: Hanawa Shobō, 1993.

Sekiguchi Hiroko. "The Patriarchal Family Paradigm in Eighth-Century Japan." In Dorothy Ko, J. Haboush, and J. Piggott, eds., *Women and Confucian Cultures in Premodern China, Korea, and Japan*. Berkeley: University of California Press, 2003.

Senda, Minoru. "Territorial Possession in Ancient Japan." In *Geography of Japan*, ed. Association of Japanese Geographers. Tokyo: Teikoku Shoin, 1980.

"Senkyo chokuzen kenpō gekiron: shiriizu 1 Jimintō." *Shūkan kinyōbi* 513 (2004): 14–17.

Serafim, Leon A. "When and from Where Did the Japonic Language Enter the Ryūkyūs?" In T. Osada and A. Vovin, eds., *Perspectives on the Origins of the Japanese Language*. Kyoto: International Research Center for Japanese Studies, 2003.

Seyock, Barbara. *Auf den Spuren der Ostbarbaren: Zur Archäologie protohistorischer Kuturen in Südkorea und Westjapan*. Münster: LIT Verlag, 2004.

Sharf, Robert H., and Sharf, Elizabeth Horton, eds. *Living Images: Japanese Buddhist Icons in Context*. Stanford, Calif.: Stanford University Press, 2001.

Shibasaki Atsushi. *Kindai Nihon to kokusai bunka kōryū – kokusai bunka shinkōkai no sosetsu to tenkai*. Tokyo: Yūshindō Kōbunsha, 1999.

Shillony, Ben-Ami. *Revolt in Japan: The Young Officers and the February 26, 1936 Incident*. Princeton: Princeton University Press, 1973.

Shils, Edward. *Center and Periphery: Essays in Macro Sociology*. Chicago: University of Chicago Press, 1975.

Shimazu, Naoko. *Japan, Race and Equality: The Racial Equality Proposal of 1919*. New York: Routledge, 1998.

Shimazu, Naoko. "Love Thy Enemy: Japanese Perceptions of Russia." In John Steinberg and David Schimmelpenninck, eds., *The Russo-Japanese War Reexamined*. Leiden: Brill, 2005.

Shimazu Teruyuki. *Mizu mondai genron*. Tokyo: Hokuto Shuppan, 1991.

Shimazu Teruyuki. "Damu kensetsu kono sōdai na muda." *Ekonomisuto* (Feb. 18, 1997): 54–7.

Shimazu Teruyuki. "Shutoken no jumin ni totte no Yanba damu to wa?" Paper presented to "Jūmin kansa seikyū hōkoku daishūkai," Shinjuku Sumitomo Hall, Sept. 12, 2004.

Shimizu Ikutarō. *Japan yo, kokka tare*. Tokyo: Bungei Shunju, 1980.

Shin, Gi-Wook, and Robinson, Michael, eds. *Colonial Modernity in Korea*. Cambridge, Mass.: Harvard University Asia Center, 1999.

Shinoda, Minoru. *The Founding of the Kamakura Shogunate, 1180–1185*. New York: Columbia University Press, 1960.

Shirai Taishiro, ed. *Contemporary Industrial Relations in Japan*. Madison: University of Wisconsin Press, 1983.

Shirane, Haruo, ed. *Early Modern Japanese Literature: An Anthology 1600–1900*. New York: Columbia University Press, 2002.

Shirayanagi Shūko. *Nihon minzoku ron*. Tokyo: Chikura Shobō, 1942.

Shively, Donald. "Sumptuary Regulation and Status Regulation in Early Tokugawa Japan." *Harvard Journal of Asiatic Studies* 25 (1965): 123–64.

Shively, Donald. "Popular Culture." In John Whitney Hall, ed., *The Cambridge History of Japan*, vol. 4, *Early Modern Japan*. Cambridge: Cambridge University Press, 1991.

Shively, Donald, ed. *Tradition and Modernization in Japanese Culture*. Princeton: Princeton University Press, 1971.

Shively, Donald, and McCullough, William, eds. *The Cambridge History of Japan*, vol. 2, *Heian Japan*. Cambridge: Cambridge University Press, 1999.

Shōwa Kenkyūkai. "Kyōdōshugi no keizai rinri" (?1940). Reprinted in Sakai Saburō, *Shōwa kenkyūkai: aru chishikijin shūdan no kiseki*. Tokyo: TBS Buritanika, 1979.

Shūgi'in. *Gikai seido 70-nen shi: shūgi'in iin meiroku*. Tokyo: Ōkurashō Insatsu Kyoku, 1962.

Shulman, Frank J. *Bibliography on the Allied Occupation of Japan: A Bibliography of Western-Language Publications from the Years 1970–1980*, preliminary edn. College Park: University of Maryland, McKeldin Library, 1980.

Shulman, Frank J. *Japan*. World Bibliography Series. Oxford: Clio Press, 1989.

Sievers, Sharon. *Flowers in Salt: The Beginnings of Feminist Consciousness in Modern Japan*. Stanford, Calif.: Stanford University Press, 1983.

Silberman, Bernard. "The Bureaucratic State in Japan: The Problem of Authority and Legitimacy." In Tetsuo Najita and J. Victor Koschmann, eds., *Conflict in Modern Japanese History: The Neglected Tradition*. Princeton: Princeton University Press, 1982.

Silberman, Bernard. *Cages of Reason: The Rise of the Rational State in France, Japan, the United States, and Great Britain*. Chicago: University of Chicago Press, 1993.

Silverberg, Miriam. "Marxism Addresses the Modern: Nakano Shigeharu's Reproduction of Taishō Culture." In J. Thomas Rimer, ed., *Culture and Identity: Japanese Intellectuals during the Interwar Years*. Princeton: Princeton University Press, 1990.

Silverberg, Miriam. "The Modern Girl as Militant." In Gail Lee Bernstein, ed., *Recreating Japanese Women, 1600–1945*. Berkeley: University of California Press, 1991.

Silverberg, Miriam. "Constructing a New Cultural History of Prewar Japan." In Masao Miyoshi and H. D. Harootunian, eds., *Japan in the World*. Durham, NC: Duke University Press, 1993.

Silverberg, Miriam. "The Café Waitress Serving Modern Japan." In Stephen Vlastos, ed., *Mirror of Modernity: Invented Traditions of Modern Japan*. Berkeley: University of California Press, 1998.

Skates, John Ray. *The Invasion of Japan: Alternative to the Bomb*. Columbia: University of South Carolina Press, 1994.

Smethurst, Richard. *A Social Basis for Japanese Militarism: The Army and the Rural Community*. Berkeley: University of California Press, 1974.

Smethurst, Richard. *Agricultural Development and Tenancy Disputes in Japan, 1870–1940*. Princeton: Princeton University Press, 1986.

Smith, Kerry. *A Time of Crisis: Japan, the Great Depression, and Rural Revitalization*. Cambridge, Mass.: Harvard University Asia Center, 2001.

Smith, Robert J., and Wiswell, E. L. *The Women of Suye Mura*. Chicago: University of Chicago Press, 1982.

Smith, Thomas C. *Political Change and Industrial Development in Japan: Government Enterprise, 1868–1880*. Stanford, Calif.: Stanford University Press, 1955.

Smith, Thomas C. *The Agrarian Origins of Modern Japan*. Stanford, Calif.: Stanford University Press, 1959.

Smith, Thomas C. *Nakahara: Family Farming and Population in a Japanese Village, 1770–1830*. Stanford, Calif.: Stanford University Press, 1977.

Smith, Thomas C. "Farm Family By-Employments in Preindustrial Japan." In Thomas C. Smith, *Native Sources of Japanese Industrialization, 1750–1920*. Berkeley: University of California Press, 1988.

Smith, Thomas C. "The Land Tax in the Tokugawa Period." In Thomas C. Smith, *Native Sources of Japanese Industrialization, 1750–1920*. Berkeley: University of California Press, 1988.

Smith, Thomas C. "Ōkura Nagatsune and the Technologists" (1973). In Thomas C. Smith, *Native Sources of Japanese Industrialization, 1750–1920*. Berkeley: University of California Press, 1988.

Smith, Thomas C. "Premodern Economic Growth: Japan and the West." In Thomas C. Smith, *Native Sources of Japanese Industrialization, 1750–1920*. Berkeley: University of California Press, 1988.

Smits, Gregory. *Visions of Ryūkyū: Identity and Ideology in Early-Modern Thought and Politics*. Honolulu: University of Hawai'i Press, 1999.

So Kwan-wai. *Japanese Piracy in Ming China during the Sixteenth Century*. East Lansing: Michigan State University Press, 1975.

Sōgō Joseishi Kenkyūkai, ed. *Nihon josei no rekishi: onna no hataraki*. Tokyo: Kadokawa Shoten, 1993.

Sōgō Joseishi Kenkyūkai, ed. *Shiryō ni miru Nihon josei no ayumi*. Tokyo: Yoshikawa Kōbunkan, 2000.

Sone Hiromi, Terashima Akiko, and Walthall, Anne, trans. "Prostitution and Public Authority in Early Modern Japan." In Hitomi Tonomura, Anne Walthall, and Wakita Haruko, eds., *Women and Class in Japanese History*. Ann Arbor: Center for Japanese Studies Publications, University of Michigan, 1999.

Sorensen, Andre. *The Making of Urban Japan: Cities and Planning from Edo to the Twenty-First Century*. London: Routledge, 2002.

Souryi, Pierre Francois. *The World Turned Upside Down: Medieval Japanese Society*, trans. Käthe Roth. New York: Columbia University Press, 2001.

Soviak, Eugene. "Tsuchida Kyōson and the Sociology of the Masses." In J. Thomas Rimer, ed., *Culture and Identity: Japanese Intellectuals during the Interwar Years*. Princeton: Princeton University Press, 1990.

Spriggs, M. "Early Agriculture and What Went Before in Island Melanesia: Continuity or Intrusion?" In D. R. Harris, ed., *The Origins and Spread of Agriculture and Pastoralism in Eurasia*. London: UCL Press, 1996.

Starrs, Roy. "Writing the National Narrative: Changing Attitudes toward Nation-Building among Japanese Writers, 1900–1930." In Sharon Minichiello, ed., *Japan's Competing Modernities*. Honolulu: University of Hawai'i Press, 1998.

Steele, M. William. *Alternative Narratives in Modern Japanese History*. London: Routledge-Curzon, 2003.

Steenstrup, Carl. *A History of Law in Japan until 1868*. Leiden: Brill, 1996.

Steiner, Kurt. "The Occupation and the Reform of the Japanese Civil Code." In Robert E. Ward and Sakamoto Yoshikazu, eds., *Democratizing Japan: The Allied Occupation*. Honolulu: University of Hawai'i Press, 1987.

Steiner, Kurt, Krauss, Ellis, and Flanagan, Scott, eds. *Political Opposition and Local Politics in Japan*. Princeton: Princeton University Press, 1980.

Stephan, John. *Hawaii under the Rising Sun: Japan's Plans for Conquest after Pearl Harbor*. Honolulu: University of Hawai'i Press, 1984.

Steven, Rob. *Classes in Contemporary Japan*. Cambridge: Cambridge University Press, 1983.

Stevens, Carolyn. *On the Margins of Japanese Society: Volunteers and the Welfare of the Urban Underclass*. London: Routledge, 1997.

Stockwin, J. A. A. *Japan: Divided Politics in a Growth Economy*, 2nd edn. New York: Norton, 1982.

Stockwin, J. A. A. Review of *Japan's Political Marketplace*, by J. Mark Ramseyer and Frances M. Rosenbluth. *International Affairs* 70 (1994): 393.

Stone, Jacqueline. *Original Enlightenment and the Transformation of Medieval Japanese Buddhism*. Honolulu: University of Hawai'i Press, 1999.

Storey, John. *Cultural Studies and the Study of Popular Culture*, 2nd edn. Athens: University of Georgia Press, 2003.

Strinati, Dominic. *An Introduction to Theories of Popular Culture*. London: Routledge, 1995.

Sugano Noriko. "State Indoctrination of Filial Piety in Tokugawa Japan: Sons and Daughters in the Official Records of Filial Piety." In Dorothy Ko, J. Haboush, and J. Piggott, eds., *Women and Confucian Cultures in Premodern China, Korea, and Japan*. Berkeley: University of California Press, 2003.

Sugiyama Tadayoshi. *Edo jidai no yasai no saibai to riyō*. Tokyo: Hōyashi, 1998.

Sun Ge. "How Does Asia Mean? (Part 1)." *Inter-Asia Cultural Studies* 1:1 (2000): 13–47.

Sun Ge. "How Does Asia Mean? (Part 2)." *Inter-Asia Cultural Studies* 1:2 (2000): 319–41.

Suny, Ronald, and Martin, Terry, eds. *State of Nations: Empire and Nation-Making in the Age of Lenin and Stalin*. New York: Oxford University Press, 2001.

Supreme Commander for the Allied Powers, General Headquarters. *History of the Nonmilitary Activities of the Occupation of Japan*, 55 vols. Tokyo: Supreme Commander for the Allied Powers, 1952.

Suzuki Akira. "The Death of Unions' Associational Life? Political and Cultural Aspects of Enterprise Unions." In Frank Schwartz and Susan Pharr, eds., *The State of Civil Society in Japan*. Cambridge: Cambridge University Press, 2003.

Tabata Yasuko. *Hōjō Masako to Hino Tomiko*. Tokyo: Kōdansha, 1996.

Takagi Tadashi. *Mikudarihan to enkiridera*. Tokyo: Kōdansha, 1992.

Takagi Tadashi. *Naite waratte mikudarihan: onna to otoko no enkiri sahō*. Tokyo: Kyōiku Shuppan, 2001.

Takahashi Hidenao. *Nisshin sensō e no michi*. Tokyo: Sōgensha, 1996.

Takahashi Yurika. "Kawabegawa damu yami no gyogyō hoshō gōi kokudo kōtsū fukudaijin ga chōsa o meigen." *Shūkan kinyōbi* (Oct. 26, 2001): 51.

Takahashi Yurika. "Fukaikan o hyōmei shita Shiotani Kumamoto kenchiji." *Shūkan kinyōbi* (Dec. 21, 2001): 52–3.

Takahashi Yutaka. *Kasen ni motto jiyū o*. Tokyo: Sankaidō, 1998.

Takahashi Yutaka. *Chikyū no mizu wa abunai*. Tokyo: Iwanami Shinsho, 2003.

Takaki, Ronald. *Strangers from a Different Shore: A History of Asian Americans*. Boston: Little, Brown, 1998.

Takasugi Shingo. *Nihon no damu*. Tokyo: Sanseidō Sensho, 1980.

Takemae Eiji. *Inside GHQ: The Allied Occupation of Japan and Its Legacy*, trans. and adapted by Robert Ricketts and Sebastian Swann. New York: Continuum, 2002.

Tamanoi, Mariko Asano. *Under the Shadow of Nationalism: Politics and Poetics of Rural Japanese Women*. Honolulu: University of Hawai'i Press, 1998.

Tanabe, George. *Myoe the Dreamkeeper: Fantasy and Knowledge in Early Kamakura Buddhism*. Cambridge, Mass.: Council on East Asian Studies, Harvard University, 1992.

Tanaka, Stefan. *Japan's Orient: Rendering Pasts into History*. Berkeley: University of California Press, 1993.

Tanaka, Yuki. *Japan's Comfort Women: Sexual Slavery and Prostitution during World War II and the U.S. Occupation*. London: Routledge, 2002.

Tanaka Yūko. "The Cyclical Sensibility of Edo-Period Japan." *Japan Echo* 25:2 (Apr. 1998).

Tanizaki Jun'ichirō. *In Praise of Shadows*, trans. Thomas J. Harper and Edward Seidensticker. New Haven: Leete's Island Books, 1977.

Tashiro Yōichi. "An Environmental Mandate for Rice Self-Sufficiency." *Japan Quarterly* (Jan.–Mar. 1992): 34–44.

Teow, See Heng. *Japanese Cultural Policy toward China, 1918–1931*. Cambridge, Mass.: Harvard University Press, 1999.

Terada, Takashi. "Directional Leadership in Institution-Building: Japan's Approaches to ASEAN in the Establishment of PECC and APEC." *Pacific Review* 14:2 (2001): 195–220.

Teranishi Juro and Kosai Yutaka, eds. *The Japanese Experience of Economic Reforms*. New York: St. Martin's Press, 1993.

Terasaki Hidenari. *Shōwa tennō dokuhakuroku: Terasaki Hidenari goyōgakari nikki.* Tokyo: Bungei Shunju, 1991.

Terasawa Kaoru. "Commentary on the Productive Capacity of Early Japanese Rice Farming." In Yasuda Yoshinori, ed., *The Origins of Pottery and Agriculture.* New Delhi: Lustre Press, 2002.

Terazawa, Yuki. "The State, Midwives, and Reproductive Surveillance in Late Nineteenth and Early Twentieth Century Japan." *U.S.–Japan Women's Journal,* English Supplement 24 (2003): 59–81.

Teshigawara Akira. *Jōmon bunka.* Tokyo: Shin Nihon, 1998.

Thayer, Nathaniel. *How the Conservatives Rule Japan.* Princeton: Princeton University Press, 1969.

Thelen, Kathleen, and Kume Ikuo. "The Future of National Embedded Capitalism." In Kozo Yamamura and Wolfgang Streeck, eds., *The End of Diversity? Prospects for German and Japanese Capitalism.* Ithaca, NY: Cornell University Press, 2003.

Thomas, Julia. *Reconfiguring Modernity: Concepts of Nature in Japanese Political Ideology.* Berkeley: University of California Press, 2001.

Thompson, Sarah, and Harootunian, H. D. *Undercurrents in the Floating World: Censorship and Japanese Prints.* New York: Asia Society Galleries, 1991.

Tilton, Mark. *Restricted Trade: Cartels in Japan's Basic Materials Industries.* Ithaca, N.Y.: Cornell University Press, 1996.

Tipton, Elise K. "The Café: Contested Space of Modernity in Interwar Japan." In Elise K. Tipton and John Clark, eds., *Being Modern in Japan: Culture and Society from the 1910s to the 1930s.* Honolulu: University of Hawai'i Press, 2000.

Tipton, Elise K. "Sex in the City: Chastity vs Free Love in Interwar Japan." *Intersections: Gender, History, and Culture in the Asian Context* 11 (Aug. 2005) <http://wwwsshe.murdoch.edu.au/intersections/issue11/tipton.html> accessed Mar. 1, 2006.

Tipton, Elise K., ed. *Society and the State in Interwar Japan.* New York: Routledge, 1997.

Tobe Ryōichi. *Nihon rikugun to Chūgoku "Shina-tsū" ni miru yume to zasetsu.* Tokyo: Kōdansha, 1999.

Toby, Ronald. *State and Diplomacy in Early Modern Japan: Asia in the Development of the Tokugawa Bakufu.* Princeton: Princeton University Press, 1984.

Toby, Ronald. "Why Move Nara? Kammu and the Transfer of the Capital." *Monumenta Nipponica* 40 (1985): 331–47.

Toby, Ronald. "Kara no kanata yori." In Furuya Tetsuo and Yamamuro Shin'ichi, eds., *Kindai Nihon ni okeru higashi Ajia mondai.* Tokyo: Yoshikawa Kōbunkan, 2001.

Toby, Ronald. "Rescuing the Nation from History: The State of the State in Early Modern Japan." *Monumenta Nipponica* 56:2 (Summer 2001): 197–237.

Toby, Ronald. "Three Realms/Myriad Countries: An 'Ethnography' of Other and the Rebounding of Japan, 1550–1750." In Kai-wing Chow, Kevin Doak, and Poshek Fu, eds., *Constructing Nationhood in Modern East Asia.* Ann Arbor: University of Michigan Press, 2001.

Tocco, Martha. "Women's Education in Tokugawa Japan." In Dorothy Ko, J. Haboush, and J. Piggott, eds., *Women and Confucian Cultures in Premodern China, Korea, and Japan.* Berkeley: University of California Press, 2003.

Tocco, Martha. "Norms and Texts for Women's Education in Tokugawa Japan." In Dorothy Ko, JaHyun Kim Haboush, and Joan R. Piggott, eds., *Women and Confucian Cultures in Premodern China, Korea, and Japan.* Berkeley: University of California Press, 2003.

Tominaga, K. "An Empirical View of Social Stratification." *Japan Interpreter* 12:1 (1978): 8–12.

Tomiyama Kazuko. *Mizu no bunkashi.* Tokyo: Bungei Shunjusha, 1980.

Tomiyama Kazuko. *Mizu to midori to tsuchi.* Tokyo: Chūkō Shinsho, 1974, 1986.

Tomiyama Kazuko. *Nihon no kome*. Tokyo: Chūkō Shinsho, 1993.

Tomiyama Kazuko. *Kankyō mondai to wa nanika*. Tokyo: PHP Shinsho, 2001.

Tomiyama Kazuko. "Nō wa bunka to kankyō o sodamu." *Asahi shinbun* (Aug. 29, 2004).

Tōno Haruyuki. "Nikki ni miru Fujiwara Yorinaga no nanshoku kankei: ōchō kizoku no vita sekusuarisu." *Hisutoria* 84 (1979): 15–29.

Tonomura, Hitomi. "Women and Inheritance in Japan's Early Warrior Society." *Comparative Studies in Society and History* 32:3 (1990): 592–623.

Tonomura, Hitomi. *Community and Commerce in Late Medieval Japan: The Corporate Villages of Tokuchin-ho*. Stanford, Calif.: Stanford University Press, 1992.

Tonomura, Hitomi. "Black Hair and Red Trousers: Gendering the Flesh in Medieval Japan." *American Historical Review* 99:1 (1994): 129–54.

Tonomura, Hitomi. "Sexual Violence against Women: Legal and Extralegal Treatment in Premodern Warrior Societies." In Hitomi Tonomura, Anne Walthall, and Wakita Haruko, eds., *Women and Class in Japanese History*. Ann Arbor: Center for Japanese Studies Publications, University of Michigan, 1999.

Tonomura, Hitomi, Walthall, Anne, and Haruko, Wakita, eds. *Women and Class in Japanese History*. Ann Arbor: Center for Japanese Studies, University of Michigan, 1999.

Torrence, R. "Hunter-Gatherer Technology: Macro- and Microscale Approaches." In C. Panter-Brick, R. H. Layton, and P. Rowley-Conwy, eds., *Hunter-Gatherers: An Interdisciplinary Perspective*. Cambridge: Cambridge University Press, 2001.

Totman, Conrad. *Politics in the Tokugawa Bakufu, 1600–1843*. Berkeley: University of California Press, 1967.

Totman, Conrad. *Tokugawa Ieyasu: Shōgun*. San Francisco: Heian International, 1983.

Totman, Conrad. *The Origins of Japan's Modern Forests: The Case of Akita*. Honolulu: University of Hawai'i Press, 1984.

Totman, Conrad. *The Green Archipelago: Forestry in Pre-industrial Japan*. Berkeley: University of California Press, 1989.

Totman, Conrad. "Preindustrial River Conservancy." *Monumenta Nipponica* 47:1 (Spring 1992): 59–76.

Totman, Conrad. *Early Modern Japan*. Berkeley: University of California Press, 1993.

Totman, Conrad. *A History of Japan*. Oxford: Blackwell, 2000.

Totman, Conrad. *Early Modern Japan*. Berkeley: University of California Press, 1993.

Townsend, Susan. *Yanaihara Tadao and Japanese Colonial Policy: Redeeming Empire*. Richmond, UK: Curzon, 2000.

Traphagan, John, and Knight, John, eds. *Demographic Change and the Family in Japan's Aging Society*. Albany: State University of New York Press, 2003.

Trigger, Bruce G. *A History of Archaeological Thought*. Cambridge: Cambridge University Press, 1989.

Tsuboi Kiyotari and Tanaka Migaku. *The Historic City of Nara: An Archaeological Approach*. Paris and Tokyo: UNESCO and Centre for East Asian Cultural Studies, 1991.

Tsuchimochi, Gary. *Education Reform in Postwar Japan: The 1946 U.S. Education Mission*. Tokyo: University of Tokyo Press, 1993.

Tsude, H. "The Kofun Period and State Formation." *Acta Asiatica* 63 (1992): 64–86.

Tsukada, M. "Vegetation in Prehistoric Japan: The Last 20,000 Years." In R. J. Pearson, G. L. Barnes, and K. L. Hutterer, eds., *Windows on the Japanese Past: Studies in Archaeology and Prehistory*. Ann Arbor: Center for Japanese Studies, University of Michigan, 1986.

Tsukamoto Manabu. *Tokai to inaka*. Tokyo: Heibonsha, 1991.

Tsunoda Jun. *Manshū mondai to kokubō hōshin*. Tokyo: Hara Shobō, 1967.

Tsunoda, Minoru. *The Founding of the Kamakura Shogunate, 1180–1185: With Selected Translations from the Azuma Kagami*. New York: Columbia University Press, 1960.

Tsunoda, Ryusaku., and Goodrich, L. Carrington. *Japan in the Chinese Dynastic Histories.* South Pasadena, Calif.: P. D. and Ione Perkins, 1951.

Tsuru Shigeto. *Japan's Capitalism: Creative Defeat and Beyond.* Cambridge: Cambridge University Press, 1993.

Tsurumi, E. Patricia. *Japanese Colonial Education in Taiwan, 1895–1945.* Cambridge, Mass.: Harvard University Press, 1977.

Tsurumi, E. Patricia. *Factory Girls: Women in the Thread Mills of Meiji Japan.* Princeton: Princeton University Press, 1990.

Tsurumi, E. Patricia. "The Male Present versus the Female Past: Historians and Japan's Ancient Female Emperors." *Bulletin of Concerned Asian Scholars* 14:4 (1992): 71–5.

Tsurumi, E. Patricia. "Visions of Women and the New Society in Conflict: Yamakawa Kikue versus Takamure Itsue." In Sharon Minichiello, ed., *Japan's Competing Modernities: Issues in Culture and Democracy 1900–1930.* Honolulu: University of Hawai'i Press, 1998.

Tsutsui, William. *Banking Policy in Japan: American Efforts at Reform during the Occupation.* London: Routledge, 1988.

Tsutsui, William. *Manufacturing Ideology: Scientific Management in Twentieth-Century Japan.* Princeton: Princeton University Press, 1998.

Tucker, John Allen. *Itō Jinsai's* Gomō Jigi *and the Philosophical Definition of Early Modern Japan.* Leiden: Brill, 1998.

Turner, Christena. *Japanese Workers in Protest.* Berkeley: University of California Press, 1995.

Twu, Jaw-Yann. *Tōyō shihonshugi.* Tokyo: Kōdansha, 1990.

Uchiyama, J. "San'ei-cho and Meat-Eating in Buddhist Edo." *Japanese Journal of Religious Studies* 19 (1992): 299–303.

Udagawa, Taketoshi. "Development and Transfer of Environment-Friendly Agriculture." In *Sustainable Agricultural Development in Asia*, ed. Asian Productivity Organization. Tokyo: APO, 1994.

Ueno Chizuko. *Nationalism and Gender*, trans. Beverly Yamamoto. Melbourne: Trans Pacific Press, 2004.

Ueno Hideo. "Damu ni mirai wa nai." *Sekai* (Aug. 1995).

Ui Jun. *Industrial Pollution in Japan.* Tokyo: United Nations University Press, 1992.

Ui Jun. *Nihon no mizu wa yomigaeru ka.* Tokyo: NHK Raiburari, 1996.

Unno Fukuju. *Kankoku heigōshi no kenkyū.* Tokyo: Iwanami Shoten, 2000.

Unno, Mark. *Shingon Refractions.* Boston: Wisdom Publications, 2004.

Uno, Kathleen. "Women and Changes in the Household Division of Labor." In Gail Bernstein, ed., *Recreating Japanese Women, 1600–1945.* Berkeley: University of California Press, 1991.

Uno, Kathleen. *Passages to Modernity: Motherhood, Childhood, and Social Reform in Early Twentieth Century Japan.* Honolulu: University of Hawai'i Press, 1999.

Uno Takao. *Ritsuryō shakai no kōkogakuteki kenkyū.* Toyama: Kashiwa Shobō, 1991.

Upham, Frank. "Ten Years of Affirmative Action for Japan's Burakumin." *Law in Japan* 13:39 (1980): 39–73.

Upham, Frank. *Law and Social Change in Postwar Japan.* Cambridge, Mass.: Harvard University Press, 1987.

Upham, Frank. "Unplaced Persons and Movements for Place." In Andrew Gordon, ed., *Postwar Japan as History.* Berkeley: University of California Press, 1993.

Uriu, Robert. *Troubled Industries: Confronting Economic Change in Japan.* Ithaca, NY: Cornell University Press, 1996.

Usui Katsumi. *Nitchū sensō: wahei ka sensen kakudai ka.* Tokyo: Chūō Kōronsha, 1967.

Usui Katsumi. *Nitchū gaikōshi kenkyū: Shōwa zenki.* Tokyo: Yoshikawa Kōbunkan, 1998.

van Wolferen, Karel. *The Enigma of Japanese Power: People and Politics in a Stateless Nation.* New York: Knopf, 1989.

Vaporis, Constantine. *Breaking Barriers: Travel and the State in Early Modern Japan*. Cambridge, Mass.: Council on East Asian Studies, Harvard University, 1994.

Varley, H. Paul. *The Ōnin War*. New York: Columbia University Press, 1967.

Varley, H. Paul. *Imperial Restoration in Medieval Japan*. New York: Columbia University Press, 1971.

Victoria, Brian Daizen. *Zen at War*. New York: Weatherhill, 1997.

Victoria, Brian Daizen. *Zen War Stories*. London: RoutledgeCurzon, 2003.

Vidovic-Ferderbar, Dragica. "In Limine: Writers, Culture and Modernity in Interwar Japan." Ph.D. dissertation, University of Sydney, 2004.

Vlastos, Stephen. *Peasant Protests and Uprisings in Tokugawa Japan*. Berkeley: University of California Press, 1986.

Vlastos, Stephen, ed. *Mirror of Modernity: Invented Traditions of Modern Japan*. Berkeley: University of California Press, 1998.

Vogel, Ezra. *Japan's New Middle Class: The Salary Man and His Family in a Tokyo Suburb*. Berkeley: University of California Press, 1963; 2nd edn., 1971.

Vogel, Ezra. *Japan as Number One: Lessons for America*. New York: Harper and Row, 1979.

Vogel, Ezra. "Pax Nipponica." *Foreign Affairs* (Spring 1986): 752–67.

Vogel, Steven. *Freer Markets, More Rules*. Ithaca, NY: Cornell University Press, 1996.

Vogel, Suzanne. "Professional Housewife: The Career of Urban Middle Class Japanese Women." *Japan Interpreter* 12:1 (1978): 16–36.

Von Verschuer, Charlotte. *Le Commerce Exterieur du Japon: Des Origines au XVIe siècle*. Paris: Maisonneuve and Larosse, 1987.

Wakabayashi, Bob Tadashi. *Anti-Foreignism and Western Learning in Early-Modern Japan: The New Theses of 1825*. Cambridge, Mass.: Council on East Asian Studies, Harvard University, 1986.

Wakabayashi, Bob. "The Nanking Massacre: Now You See It . . . " *Monumenta Nipponica* 56:2 (Winter 2001): 521–44.

Wakasa, T. "Water Rights, Water Rituals, Chiefly Compounds, and *Haniwa*: Ritual and Regional Development in the Kofun Period." In *Cultural Diversity and the Archaeology of the 21st Century*, ed. Society of Archaeological Studies. Okayama: Kōkogaku Kenkyūkai, 2004.

Wakita Haruko. *Chūsei ni ikiru onnatachi*. Tokyo: Iwanami Shoten, 1995.

Wakita Haruko, Hayashi Reiko, and Nagahara Kazuko, eds. *Nihon joseishi*. Tokyo: Yoshikawa Kōbunkan, 1987.

Wakita Osamu. "The Social and Economic Consequences of Unification." In John W. Hall, ed., *The Cambridge History of Modern Japan*, vol. 4, *Early Modern Japan*. Cambridge: Cambridge University Press, 1991.

Walker, Brett L. *The Conquest of Ainu Lands: Ecology and Culture in Japanese Expansion, 1590–1800*. Berkeley: University of California Press, 2001.

Walker, J. Samuel. *Prompt and Utter Destruction: Truman and the Use of the Atomic Bombs against Japan*. Chapel Hill: University of North Carolina Press, 1997.

Wallerstein, I. M. *The Modern World System*. New York: Academic Press, 1974.

Wallerstein, I. M. *The Capitalist World Economy: Essays*. Cambridge: Cambridge University Press, 1979.

Walthall, Anne. "Peripheries: Rural Culture in Tokugawa Japan." *Monumenta Nipponica* 39:4 (Winter 1984): 371–92.

Walthall, Anne. *Social Protest and Popular Culture in Eighteenth-Century Japan*. Tucson: University of Arizona Press, 1986.

Walthall, Anne. "The Life Cycle of Farm Women in Tokugawa Japan." In Gail Bernstein, ed., *Recreating Japanese Women, 1600–1945*. Berkeley: University of California Press, 1991.

Walthall, Anne. "The Cult of Sensibility in Rural Tokugawa Japan: Love Poetry by Matsuo Taseko." *Journal of the American Oriental Society* 117:1 (1997): 70–86.

Walthall, Anne. *The Weak Body of a Useless Woman: Matsuo Taseko and the Meiji Restoration.* Chicago: University of Chicago Press, 1998.

Walthall, Anne. "Nishimiya Hide: Turning Palace Arts into Marketable Skills." In Anne Walthall, ed., *The Human Tradition in Modern Japan.* Wilmington, Del.: Scholarly Resources, 2002.

Walthall, Anne. *Japan: A Cultural, Social, and Political History.* Boston: Houghton Mifflin, 2006.

Walthall, Anne, ed. *The Human Tradition in Modern Japan.* Wilmington, Del.: Scholarly Resources, 2002.

Waltz, Kenneth. "The Emerging Structure of International Politics." *International Security* 18:2 (Autumn 1993): 44–79.

Ward, Robert E, ed. *Political Development in Modern Japan.* Princeton: Princeton University Press, 1968.

Ward, Robert E., and Sakamoto Yoshikazu, eds. *Democratizing Japan: The Allied Occupation.* Honolulu: University of Hawai'i Press, 1987.

Ward, Robert E., and Shulman, Frank J., eds. *The Allied Occupation of Japan, 1945–1952: An Annotated Bibliography of Western-Language Materials.* Chicago: American Library Association, 1974.

Waswo, Ann. "The Transformation of Rural Society, 1900–1950." In Peter Duus, ed., *The Cambridge History of Japan,* vol. 6, *The Twentieth Century.* Cambridge: Cambridge University Press, 1988.

Waswo, Ann. "In Search of Equity: Japanese Tenant Unions in the 1920s." In Ann Waswo and Nishida Yoshiaki, eds., *Farmers and Village Life in Twentieth-Century Japan.* London: Routledge, 2003.

Watabe Tadayo. *Nihon kara suiden ga kieru hi.* Tokyo: Iwanami, 1993.

Watanabe Hiroshi. *Higashi Ajia no ōken to shisō.* Tokyo: Tōkyō Daigaku Shuppankai, 1997.

Waters, Neil. *Japan's Local Pragmatists: The Transition from Bakumatsu to Meiji in the Kawasaki Region.* Cambridge, Mass.: Harvard University Press, 1983.

Weik, John F. "Kitabatake Chikafusa's Use of the Terms *Dai* and *Sei* in the *Jinnō Shōtōki.*" *Papers on Far Eastern History* 1 (1970): 140–72.

Weiner, Michael. *Race and Migration in Imperial Japan.* New York: Routledge, 1994.

Weiner, Michael, ed. *Japan's Minorities: The Illusion of Homogeneity.* London: Routledge, 1997.

Weisenfeld, Gennifer. *Mavo: Japanese Artists and the Avant-Garde 1905–1931.* Berkeley: University of California Press, 2002.

Wells, David, and Wilson, Sandra, eds. *The Russo-Japanese War in Cultural Perspective, 1904–05.* New York: St. Martin's Press, 1999.

Wender, Melissa. "Lamentation as History: Literature of Koreans in Japan, 1965–1999." Ph.D. dissertation, University of Chicago, 1999.

Westney, D. Eleanor. *Imitation and Innovation: The Transfer of Western Organizational Patterns to Meiji Japan.* Cambridge, Mass.: Harvard University Press, 1987.

Wetzler, Peter. *Hirohito and War: Imperial Tradition and Military Decision Making in Prewar Japan.* Honolulu: University of Hawai'i Press, 1998.

White, James W. *Migration in Metropolitan Japan.* Berkeley: Institute of East Asian Studies, University of California, 1982.

White, James W. "State Growth and Popular Protest in Tokugawa Japan." *Journal of Japanese Studies* 14:1 (Winter 1988): 1–25.

White, James W. *Ikki: Social Conflict and Political Protest in Early Modern Japan*. Ithaca, NY: Cornell University Press, 1995.

Whiting, Robert. *Tokyo Underworld: The Fast Times and Hard Life of an American Gangster in Japan*. New York: Vintage Books, 1999.

Wigen, Kären. *The Making of a Japanese Periphery, 1750–1920*. Berkeley: University of California Press, 1995.

Wilkinson, Thomas. *The Urbanization of Japanese Labor, 1868–1955*. Amherst: University of Massachusetts Press, 1986.

Williams, David. *Defending Japan's Pacific War: The Kyoto School Philosophers and Post-White Power*. London: Routledge, 2004.

Williams, Justin. "American Democratization Policy for Occupied Japan: Correcting the Revisionist Version." *Pacific Historical Review* 57:2 (1988): 179–202. Replies by John Dower and Howard Schonberger on pp. 202–18.

Wilson, George. "A New Look at the Problem of Japanese Fascism." *Comparative Studies in Society and History* 10 (July 1968): 401–12.

Wilson, George. *Radical Nationalist in Japan: Kita Ikki, 1883–1937*. Cambridge, Mass.: Harvard University Press, 1969.

Wilson, Sandra. *The Manchurian Crisis and Japanese Society, 1931–1933*. London: Routledge, 2002.

Wilson, William, trans. *Hōgen Monogatari: A Tale of the Disorder of Hōgen*. Tokyo: Sophia University Press, 1971.

Woodard, William. *The Allied Occupation of Japan 1945–1952 and Japanese Religions*. Leiden: Brill, 1972.

Wray, William. *Mitsubishi and the N.Y.K., 1870–1914: Business Strategy in the Japanese Shipping Industry*. Cambridge, Mass.: Council on East Asian Studies, Harvard University, 1984.

Wray, William. "Afterword." In William Wray, ed., *Managing Industrial Enterprise: Cases from Japan's Prewar Experience*. Cambridge, Mass.: Council on East Asian Studies, Harvard University, 1989.

Wray, William. *Japan's Economy: A Bibliography of Its Past and Present*. New York: Marcus Wiener, 1989.

Wright, Diana. "Severing the Karmic Ties that Bind: The 'Divorce Temple' Mantokuji." *Monumenta Nipponica* 52:3 (Autumn 1997): 357–80.

Wu, Peichen. "Performing Gender along the Lesbian Continuum: The Politics of Sexual Identity in the Seitō Society." *U.S.–Japan Women's Journal*, English Supplement 22 (2002): 64–86.

Yamada Masahiro. *Parasite Single no jidai*. Tokyo: Chikuma Shobō, 1999.

Yamakawa Kikue. *Women of the Mito Domain: Recollections of Samurai Family Life*, trans. Kate Wildman Nakai. Tokyo: University of Tokyo Press, 1992; repr. Stanford, Calif.: Stanford University Press, 2001.

Yamamoto, Masahiro. *Nanking: Anatomy of an Atrocity*. Westport, Conn.: Praeger, 2000.

Yamamoto Tadashi. "Emergence of Japan's Civil Society and Its Future Challenges." In Yamamoto Tadashi, ed., *Deciding the Public Good: Governance and Civil Society in Japan*. Tokyo: Japan Center for International Exchange, 1999.

Yamamoto Taketoshi. *Kindai no shimbun dokusha sō*. Tokyo: Hōsei Daigaku, 1981.

Yamamura, Kozo. *A Study of Samurai Income and Entrepreneurship: Quantitative Analyses of Economic and Social Aspects of the Samurai in Tokugawa and Meiji Japan*. Cambridge, Mass.: Harvard University Press, 1974.

Yamamura, Kozo. "Germany and Japan in a New Phase of Capitalism." In Kozo Yamamura and Wolfgang Streeck, eds., *The End of Diversity? Prospects for German and Japanese Capitalism*. Ithaca, NY: Cornell University Press, 2003.

Yamamura, Kozo, ed. *The Cambridge History of Japan*, vol. 3, *Medieval Japan*. Cambridge: Cambridge University Press, 1990.

Yamamura, Kozo, and Yasuba Yasukichi, eds. *The Political Economy of Japan*, vol. 1, *The Domestic Transformation*. Stanford, Calif.: Stanford University Press, 1987.

Yamamuro Shin'ichi. *Kindai nihon no chi to seiji Inoue Kowashi kara taishū engei made*. Tokyo: Bokutakusha, 1985.

Yamanouchi Yasushi. "Total War and System Integration: A Methodological Introduction." In Yamanouchi Yasushi, J. Victor Koschmann, and Narita Ryūichi, eds., *Total War and "Modernization."* Ithaca, NY: East Asia Program, Cornell University, 1998.

Yamanouchi Yasushi, Koschmann, J. Victor, and Narita Ryūichi, eds. *Total War and "Modernization."* Ithaca, NY: East Asia Program, Cornell University, 1998.

Yampolsky, Phillip, ed. *Selected Writings of Nichiren*. New York: Columbia University Press, 1990.

Yampolsky, Phillip, ed. *Letters of Nichiren*. New York: Columbia University Press, 1996.

Yanagi Miyoko. "Josei no seikatsu kūkan: kaku kaisō o megutte." In Fukuda Mitsuko, ed., *Onna to otoko no jikū, Nihon joseishi saikō*, 4, *Ranjuku suru onna to otoko*. Tokyo: Fujiwara Shoten, 1995.

Yang, Daqing. "Convergence or Divergence? Recent Historical Writings on the Rape of Nanjing." *American Historical Review* 104:3 (June 1999): 842–65.

Yang, Daqing. *Technology of Empire: Telecommunications and Japanese Imperialism, 1930–1945*. Cambridge, Mass.: Harvard University Press, 2003.

Yano, Christine. *Tears of Longing: Nostalgia and the Nation in Japanese Popular Song*. Cambridge, Mass.: Harvard University Asia Center, 2002.

Yasuda Yoshinori. *Prehistoric Environment in Japan: Palynological Approach*. Sendai: Institute of Geography, Tōhoku University, 1978.

Yasukuni Ryōichi. "Kinsei Kyōto no shomin josei." In Joseishi Sōgō Kenkyūkai, ed., *Nihon joseishi*, 3. Tokyo: Tokyo Daigaku Shuppankai, 1982–3.

Yasutomo, Dennis. *The New Multilateralism in Japan's Foreign Policy*. New York: St. Martin's Press, 1995.

Yokota Fuyuhiko. "Imagining Working Women in Early Modern Japan," trans. Mariko Tamanoi. In Hitomi Tonomura, Anne Walthall, and Wakita Haruko, eds., *Women and Class in Japanese History*. Ann Arbor: Center for Japanese Studies Publications, University of Michigan, 1999.

Yonemoto, Marcia. *Mapping Early Modern Japan: Space, Place, and Culture in the Tokugawa Period, 1603–1868*. Berkeley: University of California Press, 2003.

Yoneyama, Lisa. *Hiroshima Traces: Time, Space, and the Dialectics of Memory*. Berkeley: University of California Press, 1999.

Yosano Akiko. *Travels in Manchuria and Mongolia: A Feminist Poet from Japan Encounters Prewar China*, trans. Joshua Fogel. New York: Columbia University Press, 2001.

Yoshie Akiko. "Kodai no mura no seikatsu to josei." In Joseishi Sōgō Kenkyūkai, ed., *Nihon josei seikatsushi*, 1. Tokyo: Tokyo Daigaku Shuppankai, 1990.

Yoshie Akiko. "Kodai no kazoku to josei." In Asao Naohiro et al., eds., *Iwanami kōza Nihon tsūshi*, 6, *kodai* 5. Tokyo: Iwanami Shoten, 1995.

Yoshie Akiko. "Kodai joteiron no kako to genzai." In Amino Yoshihiko et al., eds., *Tennō to ōken o kangaeru*, 7, *jendā to sabetsu*. Tokyo: Iwanami Shoten, 2002.

Yoshie Akiko. *Tsukurareta Himiko: "Onna" no sōshutsu to kokka*. Tokyo: Chikuma Shobō, 2005.

Yoshikawa Shinji. "Ritsuryō kokka no nyokan." In Joseishi Sōgō Kenkyūkai, ed., *Nihon josei seikatsushi*, 1. Tokyo: Tokyo Daigaku Shuppankai, 1990.

Yoshimi, Yoshiaki. *The Comfort Women: Sexual Slavery in the Japanese Military during World War II*. New York: Columbia University Press, 2000.

Yoshino, Kosaku. *Cultural Nationalism in Contemporary Japan: A Sociological Inquiry.* London: Routledge, 1992.

Young, Louise. *Japan's Total Empire: Manchuria and the Culture of Wartime Imperialism.* Berkeley: University of California Press, 1997.

Zysman, John. *Governments, Markets, and Growth.* Ithaca, NY: Cornell University Press, 1983.

Index